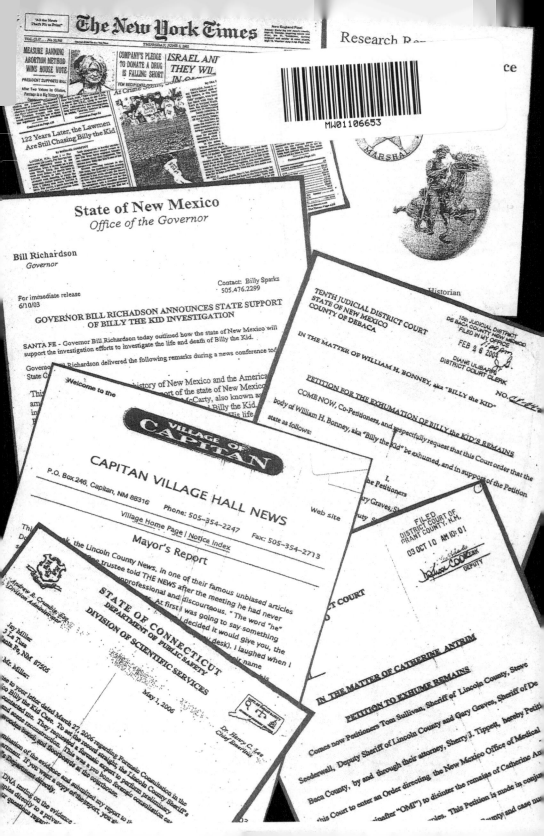

# CRACKING
# THE BILLY THE KID
# CASE HOAX

## THE STRANGE PLOT TO
## EXHUME BILLY THE KID,
## CONVICT SHERIFF PAT GARRETT
## OF MURDER, AND BECOME
## PRESIDENT OF THE UNITED STATES

### BY
### GALE COOPER, M.D.

GELCOUR
BOOKS

COVER AND BOOK DESIGN BY GALE COOPER

**THIRD EDITION**
ISBN: 978-0-9860226-7-8
LCCN: 2013935317

GELCOUR BOOKS
13170 Central Avenue SE # 289
Albuquerque, NM, 87123-5588

ORDERING
Amazon.com, BarnesandNoble.com, bookstores

*Printed in the United States of America on acid free paper*

---

**OTHER BILLY THE KID BOOKS BY AUTHOR:**

*JOY OF THE BIRDS: A NOVEL*

*BILLY AND PAULITA: A NOVEL*

*MEGAHOAX: THE STRANGE PLOT TO EXHUME BILLY THE KID
AND BECOME PRESIDENT*

*BILLY THE KID'S PRETENDERS: "BRUSHY BILL & JOHN MILLER*

*BILLY THE KID'S WRITINGS, WORDS, AND WIT*

*PARDON FOR BILLY THE KID: AN ANALYSIS*

---

## FOR WILLIAM HUDSPETH,
## BILLY THE KID'S NEW DEAD PAL

I have never made but one prayer to God, a very short one: "O Lord, make my enemies ridiculous." And God granted it.

*Voltaire*
*(May 16, 1767 Letter to M. Damiliville)*

What's the use of looking on the gloomy side of everything. The laugh's on me this time.

*William H. Bonney aka Billy the Kid*
(December 28, 1880. *Las Vegas Gazette*)

I understand that I will be made to suffer for my actions but I will be satisfied if the federation of secret law, unequal pardon and irresistible executive powers that rule the world that I love are revealed even for an instant.

*Edward Snowden*
(June 9, 2013. *The Guardian*)

Lincoln County is a moral proving ground. Evil here's so powerful it breaks people where they're weakest.

*Fred Waite to Billy Bonney*
(Excerpt from Gale Cooper's docufiction novel,
*Billy and Paulita*)

# TABLE OF CONTENTS

## CHAPTER 4:
## LAUNCHING THE BILLY THE KID CASE HOAX

## CHAPTER 5:
## FIGHTING HOAXER EXHUMATIONS OF
## BILLY THE KID AND HIS MOTHER

## CHAPTER 6:
## BILLY THE KID CASE HOAX PLAYERS

## CHAPTER 7:
## BILLY THE KID CASE HOAX TAKE-OFF
## AND CRASH LANDING

# CHAPTER 8:
## DEBUNKING BILLY THE KID'S PRETENDERS

# CHAPTER 9:
## DIGGING UP MORE THAN JOHN MILLER

# CHAPTER 10:
## IDEALISTICALLY I INVESTIGATE INJUSTICE

# CHAPTER 11:
## HOAX RESURECTION AND
## THE DOOMSDAY DOCUMENT

## CHAPTER 17:
## PRO SE MEANS ALL ALONE

## CHAPTER 18:
## HOAX LAWYERS, JUDGE, AND ME

## CHAPTER 19:
## SHOVELGATE: HOAX TO SCANDAL

# FIGURES LIST

# APPENDIX

## SOURCES
### ANNOTATED BIBLIOGRAPHY

# Forward

This here book's basically about this here author taking on trouble again by fighting for Billy the Kid's repatation. And I'm here jawing, cause I'm the old-timer jump-starting all her books. And, being fictional, I'm right perfect, cause this book's about the Billy the Kid Case, which is fiction too: it being a fake, meaning a hoax, done by a pack of lawman fraudsters and lying politicians.

Leastways, me being fictional means ain't nothing nobody can do to me - unlike to the author here. I told her it was foolhardy to go up against nowadays varmint pack called the Santa Fe Ring; cause that's what fighting that Billy the Kid Case hoax took.

What the heck. She knew that better then anybody after writing her books on Billy. Who won the Lincoln County War in Billy's day? Course it was the Santa Fe Ring; being politicians, lawmen, judges, and moneybags playing dirty tricks. And them same crooks is just recycled now. And they's just as rough as in Billy's day. And this Billy the Kid Case hoax was their game.

You could say the author eased into trouble, first figering she was taking on some two-bit, Lincoln County lawmen hijacking Billy's history to pocket bucks from TV programs and such.

But I says to her, "Missy, didn't you notice in your own books about Billy, that every damn fool - excuse the French - that backed Billy was killed. Then he escaped? For starters, John Tunstall, Alexander McSween, Charlie Bowdre, and Tom O'Folliard got put to bed with a pick and shovel. Billy's being all heart atop and all guts below attracts trouble." Course, Billy's luck ended on July 14, 1881 when Garrett plugged him - but that was just one bad break.

When Missy finally wised-up about the fact that the biggest politico honchos was behind them Billy the Kid Case hoaxer lawmen, I says to her, "Ain't nobody broken that Santa Fe Ring from Billy's day to this minute. And Ring means ring, Missy - like links of a chain. Try to pull down one New Mexico official - and add their lawyers - and you're hauling the whole passel. They's thick as thieves; cause that's what they is."

But I couldn't stop her. She's pigheaded and high-minded - like Billy - about one person making a difference and such.

Funniest part is that she had to smoke the peace-pipe, so to speak, with Pat Garrett. Like me - being on Billy's side and knowing that Billy's Lincoln County War was a freedom fight by the little people - she never cottoned to Garrett, cause of him killing Billy. But there she was, sweating blood for years to save Garrett's lawman repatation, cause this hoax was basically a plot kicking mud on Garrett's name. So Missy was protecting the guy topping her least-liked list. I got a laugh out of that.

Course, it was loco of Governor Bill Richardson to think up the scam: to have his cronies say Pat never shot Billy, but plugged some innocent cowpoke as filler for that Fort Sumner grave.

That fella, Bill Richardson, knew he was a big fish in ol' New Mexico; but he figered that, being a little fish in the U.S. of A., he needed to catch some attention from back-East papers for his running for president in 2008. So he come up with this stunt to dig up Billy and check out his bones with some faked DNA science. Then he'd pardon them bones for some faked reason. Ain't that the most loco plan for getting to be president you ever heard?

To stop the tomfoolery, poor Missy, Billy's loyal author, ended up fighting the same bunch of Santa Fe Ring varmints as the good people did in Billy's day - except, back then, the good people was fighting over being cheated out of money; which makes more sense. This here author was fighting for truth, which left her pretty much on her own. Anyways, just like Billy, she ended up tangled in court cases with judges who was political tools and with two-faced lawyers having water-shy consciences.

But I did get me a kick out of watching her. She wouldn't let go, even if it meant just her teeth was left hanging on. Leastways, she followed one piece of my advice: don't lose your sense of humor, or it'll really get to you. I figer, the sillier your enemies, the easier it is to prove they is silly. And the Billy the Kid Case hoax was rolled out by the biggest passel of high-up people ever to make fools of theirselves in public whiles keeping a straight face.

Vern Blanton Johnson, Jr.
Lincoln, Lincoln County,
New Mexico
July 14, 2014

# AUTHOR'S METHODOLOGY

This book's length and bibliography prove labor-intensity of exposing the corrupt and colluding public officials in the Billy the Kid Case hoax. Many documents cited are from open records requests, court filings, or newspapers. All are intended to create a virtual reality so the reader can experience my ongoing fight to stop that hoax's damage to the Old West history. [Summary of the Billy the Kid Case hoax and its litigation is in APPENDIX: 1.]

## ANNOTATION OF PRIMARY DOCUMENTS IN TEXT:

In copied primary documents, simple errors of grammar and punctuation are retained; with "sic" for more serious errors of fact. For space constraints, legal documents are compressed by single spacing. Author's comments are added by bracketed inserts.

## FIGURES AND APPENDIX:

More, or more complete, primary documents are given in numbered Figures (if scanned originals) or in Appendices (if retyped). All are referenced by number in the text.

## BIBLIOGRAPHY:

### IN LIEU OF FOOTNOTES:

- Because thousands of references were used - some multiple times, for background or for verifications - it was decided not to use footnotes, but to divide the Bibliography into two parts: 1) sources for the Billy the Kid Case hoax, litigation against it, and Billy the Kid pretenders' exposé; and 2) sources for the 19th century history of Billy the Kid and the Lincoln County War.

- Within each of the Bibliography's two sections, are topics with their sources listed in chronological order; and, where applicable, also by geographic location of their production.

### ANNOTATION:

- Some bibliographic sources are annotated to highlight their significance.

# CHAPTER 1:

# BILLY THE KID, ME, AND TROUBLE

Joy of the Birds

A Novel
By
Gale Cooper

BILLY AND PAULITA

A NOVEL
GALE COOPER

# BACKGROUND AND FOREGROUND

On December 18, 2012, I waited in my car with restrained terror in a parking lot on flatlands north of Albuquerque, New Mexico, for the 8 AM opening of the Sandoval County District Courthouse. A multi-day trial-like hearing would pit me, representing myself, against seasoned attorneys defending corrupt lawmen I had fought for the past decade. Four of my past attorneys had to be fired for apparent attempts to throw my case. My last lawyer had quit suspiciously, leaving me no time to get a replacement before facing these tigers who scorn sheep.

By then, I knew these beasts ranged through New Mexico, Arizona and Texas; up to Washington, D.C. By my half-decade litigation, I had stumbled on political corruption's key: friendship. Holding hands, my crooks played ring-around-the-rosie from Lincoln County's Sheriff's Department to Washington, D.C.'s U.S. Marshall's Service, the Department of Justice, and the President.

And I learned corrupt politicians' dirtiest secret - and it was not betraying Constitutional and democratic ideals by the Patriots' Act, by Guantanamo Bay, by warrantless arrests, by NSA spying, and by torture in the name of public safety. In a decade, I learned learn first hand that our leaders' construction of totalitarian's machinery created a power elite of public officials, insulated by cronyism, who were free to pursue self-aggrandizing crimes of their own, confident of immunity to legal redress. Public official thugs reigned. A citizen's redress was near hopeless.

I learned my lessons as a reluctant whistleblower. But as my personal danger increased, I persisted. When democracy is imperiled, it is a privilege to protect it. And, in my case, there was an ironic twist. The crime I cracked was so absurd that it made its perpetrators' arrogance of power ridiculous; turned their conspiratorial malevolence comic; and exposed them publicly by inflating their cover-ups into a million dollar taxpayer debacle.

# WHISTLEBLOWER'S LAMENT

New Mexico calls itself the "Land of Enchantment." This is true if "enchantment" includes the ghostly miasma of wickedness hanging over the populace since the days of Billy the Kid. My shining light on its public officials, grimly conspiring - like their antique predecessors - to subvert law and hide their crimes, may finally break that spell by laughter's purification. Their motive was ludicrous: hijacking Billy the Kid's history. They called their fake investigation "the Billy the Kid Case." I blew the whistle on them. They fought back as if it was 1878's Lincoln County War.

Battling an absurd crime still takes courage. Unfortunately, I am a coward - bad for a whistleblower. Cowards worry about danger. Whistleblowers live it. But I got no threats. Threats mean the crooks think you would back down. They knew I would not. If anything happens to me, it will be in New Mexico's Old West tradition; just like Billy the Kid got his - ambush.

New Mexico's governor from 2003 to 2008, Bill Richardson, the man behind the Billy the Kid Case, hated me. Cunning, but not smart, he called me "that woman who wrote that book about me." Its 2010 title was *MegaHoax*. Someone must have told him the contents. Richardson could not even write his autobiography. This current book continues my exposé of him and his fellows.

An ambush can be clean like a bullet; or messy like running you in your car off a road into a deep canyon - still called an arroyo from when the land was Old Mexico's - to fly before you die.

Big drop-offs occur in New Mexico's Sandia Mountains. Sandia is Spanish for "watermelon." That range's stony west face glows pulp-red at sunset. I live on the eastern side, in pine forest, off road, with few neighbors. But if they want to get you, you can be in a town full of friends, as was Billy Bonney aka Billy the Kid on July 14th of 1881. Pat Garrett got him anyway. But my bad guys did not know about me for the first four dangerous years; and, when getting my name, only recently considered me a risk.

The "Land of Enchantment" motto is for tourists. For residents, it is a big, poor, rural state with a small multi-generational population oppressed by corruption. The patronage system took hold when the place was still northern Mexico. After the U.S. won another a war for "manifest destiny" in 1848, and gobbled up northern Mexico, that patronage system continued in New Mexico Territory as an Anglo political Ring for land-grabbing from the remaining Hispanics. When modernized after statehood in 1912, that Santa Fe Ring included any ethnicity of crook. The state motto could be "Might Makes Right."

I moved there in 1999, a New Yorker via Massachusetts and Los Angeles. It was culture shock; but I came for that to write a novel about Billy the Kid. New Mexico was no stretch as the Old West. First of all, it had limited development. Billy could come back and show you around. On the road, you saw old pick-ups whose drivers wore Stetsons. People drawled and said words like "supposably." Irish, English, and German settlers, and post-Civil War southerners drifting westward, had joined the Hispanic and native American base; and, with one of the country's lowest levels of education, melded a language and culture. Grandparents - you were commonly and implausibly told - had known Billy the Kid; or once had a gun of his which they lost. Scrubby flat-land still had cattle; though not old-time longhorns. Mainly, there was physicality; not city-style brash, but self-sufficient. And guns were everywhere; even if you couldn't see them. Artsy Santa Fe was considered Californian by "real" New Mexicans; but Billy the Kid could come back and still recognize its political corruption. And statewide, uppity women were disliked. Uppity meant smart, with an aggressive mouth. That was unchanged too. In Billy's day, Susan McSween, widowed in the lost 1878 Lincoln County War, but continuing its fight in courts, was hated and maligned.

My first year in New Mexico, I wore a Stetson. That was a mistake. People would ask, "Where's the fair, ma'am?" Men wore Stetsons. So I stuck with cowboy boots and jeans. I was deep in Old West enchantment, where old West meeting new West was real - though when it came to Billy it got weird. I am in my second decade there, and things get stranger. This is how it all began.

On a July day in 1998 - possibly the 14th - my life was heading in a logical direction for a liberally idealistic, Harvard-educated, M.D. psychiatrist. I was doing forensic murder case consultation for the defense, and treated patients so desperate that they were turned away as legal hot potatoes; as in: "What brings you to a psychiatrist?" "I'm going to kill myself today."

My office was in Beverly Hills. My big house, with stables, was in a gated, San Fernando Valley community. I bred miniature horses. That year, one got National Grand Champion. And I had ridden horses since childhood. Horsemanship and forensics would come in handy in New Mexico.

As a student in the northeast, I was valedictorian in high school and summa cum laude and Phi Beta Kappa in college. That just meant I got good grades by hard work. A college psychology class film on "conscience" summarized me. A boy toddler is put in room with toys plus an open box with a hamster. The male experimenter gives him a stick, tells him to keep the hamster in, then leaves. Immediately the child heads for the toys. A trick-bottom drops. The hamster disappears. The man returns. The boy's reaction is checked for conscience. Next is a little girl. When alone, she delicately pushes back the climbing hamster. Time passes. She keeps pushing. Time passes. The experimenter gives up, returns, and thanks her. I realized I was a Hamster Girl. Being a Hamster Girl would come in handy in New Mexico.

Before that July 1998 day, I had done just one impulsive thing in my life. Right after medical school, in a pet shop, I met a tall, animal loving man, who looked like Tom Selleck. I am an animal lover. He was a rebel. I married him in a few months, without being sure what he did for a living. His mother called my parents after we eloped to give them her sympathy. I divorced him in a few years. He was too wild. But I had caught up a bit on life.

My second impulsive thing began on that July day, which could have been the 14th, with an aimless visit to a Barnes and Noble bookstore in the San Fernando Valley. All I knew about Billy the Kid was that he was an outlaw killed young by a Sheriff Pat Garrett; certainly not that July 14th was key to his life. On my way out, I stopped at a sale table. There was a short reprinted book from 1882 titled *The Authentic Life of Billy the Kid: The Noted Desperado*. (As an aside, during my New York City childhood, I played with plastic cowboys and horses, never dolls. And my going-to-sleep fantasy was being chased by a posse until safe in my secret cave.) I bought the book for about five dollars.

Another aside is that I read fast. At home, the book was done in under an hour. It had been ghostwritten by Pat Garrett's journalist boarder, Ashmun "Ash" Upson. Upson wrote in the lurid dime-novel style of 1882 - the year after Garrett killed the Kid.

Using my psychiatric background, I read between-the-lines. Two things struck me. First was that 21 year old Billy, his day's most famous outlaw, after a jailbreak just before hanging, headed north to New Mexico Territory's town of Fort Sumner, where everyone knew him and death was almost certain; instead of south to Old Mexico and safety. Secondly, lawman Garrett seemed guilty about killing him. Garrett was quoted: "It will never be known whether the Kid recognized me or not." Did Garrett feel morally trumped? Why? What more had he known about Billy? And what made Billy risk death? I guessed a true-love.

An Internet search immediately yielded the "Billy the Kid Outlaw Gang." Its past president, Carolyn Allen, listed her phone number. I called. "Was there a girl involved?" I asked. She said it was young Paulita Maxwell, the richest heiress in New Mexico Territory. "Why might Garrett feel guilt?" She said Billy was a bi-cultural, freedom fighter in the Lincoln County War against the corrupt Santa Fe Ring. Carolyn did not tell me that her take on Billy was not in history books. I was impressed. This homeless drifter and high-born Paulita were an American Romeo and Juliet.

By late July, I flew to New Mexico to meet with Carolyn Allen, big-haired, bawdy, and a poker lover. We toured Lincoln, site of the war, site of Billy's near-impossible jailbreak three years later from its courthouse-jail. Then we went to Billy's Fort Sumner gravesite a hundred-fifty miles away. There I met pudgy shy Marlyn Bowlin, founder of that Billy the Kid Outlaw Gang with her then dead, flamboyant husband, Joe. Marlyn had a souvenir shop cum little museum beside the cemetery. Born in Fort Sumner, she told me she had been drawn to Billy's grave since she was six years old. She now tended it daily, removing tourists' leavings: a mélange of bullets, fresh cans of beer, and love notes.

Because generations of visitors also wanted a piece of that grave, some chipped from its tombstone saying "Pals" (because contiguous graves held Billy's two friends, shot also by Pat Garrett when tracking him down). And the small footstone saying Billy had killed a man for each year of his life was even stolen in the 1950's, but was recovered. So the site is slabbed in concrete and within a barred cage, whose door Marlyn fastened with a bulky chain and padlock. She opened that door to let me in. I had brought wildflowers that I picked in Lincoln town. Marlyn told me that a Deluvina Maxwell, the unemancipated Navajo slave of Paulita Maxwell's family, had placed wildflowers on Billy's grave for 40 years after his death. Deluvina had been sent into the ambush room first to see if Billy was dead. Deluvina loved him. Carolyn Allen and Marlyn Bowlin saw the coincidence of my bringing those flowers without knowing that story.

They told me a secret. The site was marked for tourists. Billy was probably a distance away, where the red earth of the walled-in half acre had weeds. Marlyn also said that the day before tourists from Croatia had come to honor Billy as a freedom fighter.

Back in Lincoln County, Carolyn Allan's house had her extensive library on Billy. I replicated it for myself; as well as getting copies of almost all archival documents - like 15,000 pages by the Secret Service agent sent to New Mexico to kill Billy in arguably one of that agency's first political murders.

And I was changing. Shy, bookish, and reclusive, never having danced, I bought CD's of old-style, Mexican, ranch music: music to which bi-cultural Billy would have danced. I danced to it for hours into nights. And I started my novel on Billy - freedom fighting Billy, wildly romantic Billy, a Billy who had seen the same New Mexico I was seeing - as I studied his history and amassed ultimately 40,000 pages of books and archival documents.

By October of 1998, I returned to New Mexico to see more historical sites. With Carolyn Allen and a tracker guide, we trailed Billy, about 120 years later, even crossing 40 miles of the Guadalupe Mountains, which Billy, in 1877, had crossed on foot after losing his horse in Apache ambush and nearly dying; and going to the murder site of Billy's beloved boss, John Henry Tunstall, where we located where Tunstall's body had likely been hidden. And the guide fired a single action revolver so I could hear it in the clearing where Billy and Tunstall's other men halted after fleeing his ambush, and would have heard its same echoing.

A digression is needed. Strange things were happening more often. After learning that New Mexico had caves, I described to the tracker my childhood's "dream cave" - without its back-story. To my surprise, he took me to it, near Lincoln town.

There was more. My novel's New Mexico mining town of Silver City was to be bleak and trauma-filled for young adolescent Billy. Carolyn, the tracker, and I arrived there at night. I got us rooms in a run-down motel. Mine had a broken clock radio, so I asked for a wake-up call. Before that call, in sunlit morning, from that dead radio came Mexican ranch music. I awoke and danced. And I knew that Silver City would start my story of Billy with dancing and with joy - the joie de vivre with which he lived all his days.

There was more. I researched while writing. For literary impact, I had overlapped Billy's birth in 1859 with Pat Garrett's being 9½ and at his family's Louisiana plantation. Beginning Garrett's killing trajectory, I had him shout to a companion: "Let's shoot squirrels." Months later, I read Garrett's biography by a Leon Metz. It stated that Garrett's childhood hobby was shooting squirrels. By coincidence, I wrote before I knew.

Of course, coincidence started with my impulse buying of Garrett's *Authentic Life of Billy the Kid* on or about July 14th: Billy Bonney's death day, at a little before midnight.

Others had Billy the Kid coincidences too. Years later, after I had written many books on Billy, major Old West collectors, Jim and Theresa Earle told me how they got the gun that killed Billy: Garrett's single action, Colt .44 revolver, nick-named by its serial number: "the fifty-five-O-ninety-three." It went from Garrett's youngest son, Jarvis, to a dealer; then to a Texas man living a few hours from the Earles. They visited that man and his wife, but left at a price impasse, and at night. On the road, Theresa said to Jim, "This is a once-in-a-lifetime chance." They turned back. A deal was struck with the seller couple in bathrobes. Writing the check, the Earles realized it was July 14th, a little before midnight.

Billy Bonney himself lived and died in coincidences. His boss, John Tunstall, who turned Billy from dangerous delinquent to rebel with a cause, was murdered February 18, 1878. On February 18, 1879, Billy and some of Tunstall's Santa Fe Ring murderers had a peace meeting in Lincoln. But after it, two of those Ringmen shot down an Attorney Huston Chapman (in town to file charges for the Lincoln County War murder of Billy's other boss, Alexander McSween). Billy was an eyewitness. He used his potential testimony against Chapman's murderers to bargain for a pardon for his Lincoln County War murders from Territorial Governor Lew Wallace. Billy did testify. But Lew Wallace issued no pardon. Billy's death as an "outlaw" became inevitable.

Even Billy's death day was coincidental. The Lincoln County War, in which he was the most famous fighter, started on July 14, 1878. Billy got his fatal Garrett bullet on July 14, 1881.

Back in California after my October 1998 New Mexico trip, my passion for Billy and his lost cause became a migratory drive. By early 1999, I moved to New Mexico. For the next ten years, I wrote my docufiction novel, *Joy of the Birds* (later titled *Billy and Paulita*), and became Billy Bonney's revisionist historian.

But by 2003, and at the completion of my novel's first draft, an interruption sliced through my dancing and writing routine, ending life as I knew it. On June 5, 2003, strangeness hit again. A friend back east, knowing my Billy the Kid interest, faxed me that day's *New York Times*. On its front page was: "122 Years Later, The Lawmen Are Still Chasing Billy the Kid." Announced by Governor Bill Richardson was a murder investigation of

Pat Garrett *for killing an innocent victim - not Billy the Kid*! "High-tech DNA forensics" would prove that Billy was not in his Fort Sumner grave. A Texan named "Brushy Bill" Roberts, who died in 1950 claiming he was Billy the Kid, was cited for the Kid's survival proof. And Richardson planned to use his investigation to decide about granting Billy the Kid a posthumous pardon.

The perpetrators named it the Billy the Kid Case. Lined up for that media gravy train were sheriffs, lawyers, a history professor, complicit press, and hopeful believers in "Brushy Bill" as Billy.

"The governor's been tricked," I thought. "Garrett killed Billy. And there's no provable Kid DNA on the planet. And "Brushy" was an imposter, under 2 years old at Billy's death. And what governor would ruin his state's history and tourism for a hoax?"

I called a friend and past New Mexico Secretary of Economic Development, who had known Richardson for years. He laughed. (New Mexicans laugh about corruption - like they are in on the joke.) He said, "Richardson cares about Richardson. He's planning to run for president. To him, any publicity is good publicity."

My reaction was white-out panic. The magnificent history would be destroyed for no reason. Then I decided that New Mexicans and historians would rally. No one did. Panic punctuated my next 10 years. As a coward, I phobicly avoided first the hoax's articles, then its legal documents in my fight; proving desensitization fails if your phobia is correct. Snake phobics build up to a cuddly pet boa. Getting only rattlesnakes fails. So I stayed phobic, fighting the hoaxers like a machine that kept jamming.

There was irony too. I detest Pat Garrett for slaying Billy. But to protect Billy's true history, I had to protect Garrett's reputation as Billy's true killer.

And there was strangeness. One could not miss that the hoaxers were a rerun of the same antique, corrupt, Santa Fe Ring characters that made up Billy the Kid history: the governor and Lincoln County Sheriff. Soon, more old-time slots were filled by modern judges, lawyers, and big money. And still making the fight newsworthy was Billy the Kid himself.

There was more. Cracking the hoax needed forensic DNA background, world-class knowledge of Billy the Kid history, and willingness to endure risk to protect it. On the planet, that left: Gale Cooper. As the period's most famous historian, Frederick Nolan, told me poetically when I exclaimed to him that the coincidence seemed statistically impossible: "You got caught in a current of history." That translated into: "Better you than me."

# MORE BOOKS ABOUT BILLY THE KID

Whistleblowers who obsess about assassination exaggerate. Political crooks avoid publicity. Look what one bullet did for Billy the Kid. He is still around. Calling you crazy is a better obliteration tactic. Thomas Benton Catron, head of the first Santa Fe Ring, wrote to President Rutherford B. Hayes about a woman named Mary McPherson, who was exposing him: "She is crazy."

It took years for the hoaxers to call me crazy, because I stayed incognito. Once they did call me crazy, I realized they had a point. Not that I am crazy, but it that it looked crazy to fight for a kid sub-titled in Pat Garrett's 1882 book as *The Noted Desperado of the Southwest, Whose Deeds of Daring and Blood Made His Name a Terror in New Mexico, Arizona, and Northern Mexico.*

Billy's image problem was contagious. Even Billy knew he had an image problem. He read his own press. His Santa Fe Ring enemies made up his catchy nick-name, "Billy the Kid" to go with his fake outlawry they concocted to cover their own crimes. It worked. Today, books, movies, and documentaries still repeat Billy's defamation. Even his gravesite's footstone fabricates that he killed a man for each year of his life - that makes 21.

So I was forced to publish revisionist non-fiction books to prove Billy was a freedom fighter; and to expose the Richardson hoax. I wrote *MegaHoax: The Strange Plot to Exhume Billy the Kid and Become President.* I wrote *Billy the Kid's Pretenders: Brushy Bill and John Miller* to address that hoax's use of fake identity claimants. Then came my *Billy the Kid's Writings, Words, and Wit,* which let Billy speak for himself; and had a new letter of his that I authenticated, further proving his anti-Ring agenda.

The revisionist reality is that Billy's life is a grand hero journey precisely because he had to die - and he accepted that without the morbid self-pity that burdened me in my own fight. Billy was the last fighter in the lost, multi-cultural Lincoln County War against the Santa Fe Ring. If the British had won the Revolutionary War, Georgie Washington and Tommy Jefferson would have been outlaws too. The victor writes the history. The Santa Fe Ring's cover-up - with a claim that it never existed – had failed because of Billy. The Lincoln County War period left too many documents to expurgate. And many were Billy's own.

Later, Richardson's hoax crumbled on its own lies. But making people care about its defeat required real Billy's inspiration.

# From Start to Finish

It took me years to crack the Billy the Kid Case hoax. "Cracking" meant uncovering its secret goal and obtaining enough of its forensic, DNA records to prove its fakery. But its motive was obvious from day one: publicity-seeking ambitious greed.

The hoax was also hard to expose because it was brilliant. The brilliance was accidental. Every time I foiled its scheme, the hoaxers blithely re-wrote the hoax. So their contradictory product, though gibberish, read like Einstein's Theory of Relativity - which almost no one can follow; but everyone assumes is pure genius.

Next, was public trust in titles. The hoaxers were a seated governor, sheriffs and deputies, lawyers, judges, a forensic expert, an editor of an Old West magazine, a university professor, and an historian for the U.S. Marshals Service. Secret compatriots, one would vouch for another to mimic expert consensus.

Also, laymen could not conceive that the hoax's' historical-sounding, forensic-sounding, and legal-sounding pronouncements were purposeful double-talk. Laymen assumed the blather must be beyond them, and went into brain-freeze adulation.

As to cracking the hoax, there were more problems. First, I wrongly assumed it was just for publicity. Second, the hoaxers, bad at keeping most secrets, were top-flight in keeping their second objective secret. Third, that objective was unthinkable. Years passed before I got their obscure document revealing it.

In retrospect, the clues and hints for cracking the hoax were everywhere. But the hoaxer's goal was more audacious and more disastrous than I could conceive. Unconsciously, I had assumed that the hoaxers had inhibitions. I was wrong.

# Billy the Kid Madness

Billy Bonney aka Billy the Kid has a strange effect on some people. That was why, in 2003, Bill Richardson, New Mexico's 30th governor, decided that Billy's history, if hijacked for a headline-grabbing publicity stunt, could help him win the presidency of the United States by 2008. On the surface this was daft; and to its depths, this scheme was daft too.

Billy the Kid-madness had also manifested by the second quarter of the 1900's as more than two dozen old-timers claimed to be Billy by having not been killed on July 14, 1881 by Sheriff Pat Garrett. They were considered crazy when alive. Dead, they still are considered crazy (except by their believers). And they were.

And, in the late 19th century days, when Billy Bonney himself frenetically shot and galloped and danced and made love in New Mexico Territory, he over-stimulated compatriots to comparably unrealistic extremes. It is no coincidence that his gravesite is crammed with two other, Pat Garrett killed corpses, listed on their group tombstone with Billy as his "pals." Not everyone gets their pals into that much trouble.

Before that stuffed gravesite, was the 1878 Lincoln County War. Bi-cultural Billy was its zealot spark for a mostly Hispanic freedom fight of just 60 people against Territorial robber barons and the U.S. military. Billy made the impossible seem possible.

So, in Bill Richardson's New Mexico of 2003, the Billy the Kid Case historical/forensic hoax seemed possible to its hatchers. They would learn the hard way that their plot's problem was not just that it was fakery, but that it involved Billy the Kid.

Cracking the Billy the Kid Case hoax is not intended to imply more grandiose quashing of Billy the Kid madness itself. Billy Bonney loved to joke. He would have enjoyed all the absurdity.

# FOLLOWING FAMOUS HOAXES

Hoaxes are inherently pathetic products of wannabes and wannabelieves, conartists and dupes: failures craving celebrity or the amazing, but achieving only the pretend. Hoax magnitude varies, often in proportion to budget.

If Mark Twain had commented on the Billy the Kid Case hoax, he might have quoted from his *Life on the Mississippi*: "It was without compeer among swindles. It was perfect, it was rounded, symmetrical, complete, colossal." Also, the Billy the Kid Case hoax dwarfed past hoaxes. But, after all, their perpetrators were not aiming for the presidency of the United States.

Most hoaxes are pranks - like crop circles made by flattening high-stalked corn or wheat with compass rigs to feign alien invaders for an audience longing for the paranormal.

Or one can take the Loch Ness Monster Photo Hoax. Also called the "Surgeon's Photograph" Hoax from its 1934 blurry picture of that rare beast's skinny-necked head rising from water, and taken by a doctor, Robert Kenneth Wilson. That Scottish

Nessie picture swam on in publications until 1994, when a Christian Spurling confessed it was faked for Wilson by his stepfather, Marmaduke Wetherall, by putting an upright rod on a toy submarine. Since hoaxes come with believers, Spurling's apologia had no effect. To this day, Loch Ness Monster articles use the Wilson-Wetherall faked photo as "Nessie evidence." But by October 4, 2013 there was a re-run. *Dailymail Online* reporter Lizzie Edmonds published the confession of Loch Ness cruise boat skipper, George Edwards, as: " 'My Nessie picture IS a hoax!': His 'most convincing Loch Ness Monster photo ever' was faked with a realistic fibre-glass hump." And skipper Edwards offered a quote echoing Governor Richardson's amoral hoaxers: "Why should I feel guilty for having a bit of fun?"

More effort went into the Piltdown Man Hoax, since its motive was an academic plum: possible fellowship in the British Royal Society. Its scam was "finding" Charles Darwin's predicted, but elusive, "missing link" in evolution between apes and men.

This "missing link" was planted piecemeal, between 1908 and 1912, in and near Piltdown gravel quarry in East Sussex, England; and "discovered" piecemeal by an amateur anthropologist named Charles Dawson. He accumulated parts of a human-like skull, an ape-like jawbone, a hominid-seeming canine tooth; plus an ivory tool and Stone Age animal teeth - for a Stone Age touch. "Museum experts" assembled the skull and jawbone into a creature they named *Eanthropus dawsoni*, to honor Charles Dawson. Popularly called "Piltdown Man," it kept its spot in human beings' evolutionary family tree for over 40 years.

And Charles Dawson was rewarded. In 1938, at a Piltdown memorial consecration, a Sir Arthur Keith enthused about him: "So long as man is interested in his long history, in the vicissitudes which our early forerunners passed through, and the varying fare which overtook them, the name of Charles Dawson is certain of remembrance." That sentiment failed.

By 1953, Sir Kenneth Oakley, using a new fluorine absorption test, proved Piltdown Man was a composite of medieval human skull bones and an antique orangutan's jawbone - all stained to match. And the jawbone's teeth were filed to fit the skull.

Prime hoaxer suspect was Charles Dawson, incriminated further by his other "archeological finds," also manufactured.

Suspicious others were Dawson's publicizers: Arthur Smith Woodward of the British Museum and eulogizer Arthur Keith.

Also, Dawson's contemporary curator of zoology, Martin Hinton, had a trunk, found in 1975, with bones stained like Piltdown Man's. All suspects preempted confrontation by earlier deaths.

Oddly, Piltdown Man got life-extension for being a hoax. Creationists cite "him" as evidence that evolutionists are fakers. The moral, however, is that a good hoax never dies. And, as will be seen, the Billy the Kid Case hoaxers eventually pulled a similar stunt of skeletal assembly when the going got rough.

DNA provides new opportunity for hoaxing with its awesome power to of science - like: "DNA solved the crime!" - making its mere mention imply truth. But in 2004, by waving DNA's magic wand, a hoax paralleled the Billy the Kid Case's own forensic chicanery. It was the "Cloning of the First Human Stem Cells Hoax." South Korean scientist, Hwang Woo-suk, faked his laboratory data to claim that Nobel-prize-worthy cloning result - if it had been real. So Hwang Woo-suk ended up a dog cloner - redeeming since he helped grieving pet owners get back dead Fido; and nice, since there is usually nothing good to say about hoaxers. The Hwang Woo-suk moral, however, is that forensic results, forensic scientists, and forensic labs can hoax as well as anyone else - a point relied upon by the Billy the Kid Case hoaxers.

Billy the Kid himself has towed his dozens of hoaxing pretenders since his death, proving that fame is a hoaxer magnet. As to dead Billy Bonney's weird coterie, two of his old-timer imposters - Oliver "Brushy Bill" Roberts and John Miller - landed hoaxing authors and consequent duped audiences. "Brushy Bill" was the more successful literary product, and got followers as fervent as others convinced that Elvis Presley and Princess Diana are still among us on this side of the great veil. And, as corpses with potential for exhumation, "Brushy Bill" and John Miller joined Governor Bill Richardson's Billy the Kid Case hoax; bringing along their own believers, with hopes and dreams that their man would be declared "Billy the Kid."

But when it comes to historic and forensic hoaxes, I predict that the Billy the Kid Case will be the greatest of them all.

# CHAPTER 2:

# BILLY POSSUM, BILL RICHARDSON, MORE BILLS, AND DOLLAR BILLS

This cartoon published in the Atlanta Constitution was the origin of "Billy Possum."

If "Teddy Bear" why not "Billy Possum"

Bill Richardson tarnished by scandal

By Andy Barr
February 9, 2009

http://ww...

THE SUN

GOVZILLA 24

HIGH AMBITION: RICHARDSON EYES THE WHITE HOUSE

AS GOVERNOR, BILL RICHARDSON HAS PUSHED AN AGGRESSIVE A...
AND IS WILDLY POPULAR — BUT CRITICS GRUMBLE
THAT HE'S A POWER-HUNGRY, SELF-AGGRANDIZING BULLY

# Richardson withdraws name

**'Pay-to-play' probe won't be completed by Cabinet hearings**

Nedra Pickler
The Associated Press

WASHINGTON — New Mexico Gov. Bill Richardson abandoned his nomination to become commerce secretary under pressure of a grand jury investigation into a state contract awarded to his political donors — an investigation that threatened to embarrass President-elect Barack Obama.

Richardson insisted he would be cleared in the investigation and Obama stood by the governor as an "outstanding public servant." But both men said it has become clear that a grand jury probe would not be finished in time for

Richardson's confirmation hearings and could keep him from filling the post in a timely matter.

Richardson's withdrawal was the first disruption of Obama's Cabinet process and the second "pay-to-play" investigation that has touched Obama's transition to the presidency. The president-elect has remained above the fray in both the case of arrested Illinois Gov. Rod Blagojevich and the New Mexico case.

A federal grand jury is investigating how a California company that contributed to Richardson's political activities won a New Mexico transportation contract worth nearly $1.5 million. Richardson said in a statement issued by the Obama transition office that the investigation could take weeks or months but expressed confidence it will show he and his administration acted properly.

File photo/The Associated Press

New Mexico Gov. Bill Richardson, left, speaks last month at a news conference in Chicago with President-elect Barack Obama.

Obama spokesman Robert Gibbs said he expected a new commerce secretary to be nominated soon but didn't have a

timetable. Gibbs said the problem with Richardson's nomination wasn't a matter that those tasked to look into his background missed something.

"I think the totality of our Cabinet picks is impressive and I think our vetters have done a good job," Gibbs told reporters traveling with Obama as he moved to Washington last night.

A senior Obama adviser said Richardson gave assurances before he was nominated last month that he would come out fine in the investigation and the president-elect had no reason to doubt it. But as the grand jury continued to pursue the case, it became clear that confirmation hearings would have to be delayed for six weeks or even longer until the investigation was complete, said the adviser.

Aides to both men insisted that Richardson made the decision to

withdraw and was not pushed out by Obama. But one Democrat involved in discussions over the matter said transition officials became increasingly nervous during the last couple of weeks that the investigation was a bigger problem than Richardson had originally indicated.

Richardson spokesman Gilbert Gallegos said the governor believed the grand jury matter would be cleared up by this time, but decided to withdraw when it became clear it wouldn't. "It was the governor's idea, and his decision," Gallegos said.

Obama said he has accepted Richardson's withdrawal, first reported by NBC News, "with deep regret." Richardson said in his statement that he will remain as governor and told Obama, "I am eager to serve in the future in any way he deems useful."

...than $400,000.

...ondence with the D...

...rutions from UBS d...

# BILLY POSSUM RETURNS

Backing the Billy the Kid Case hoax took corruption and dimwittedness. In 2003, New Mexico had the man: Governor Bill Richardson. To build media interest for his presidential bid in 2008, he announced that Billy the Kid's history never happened.

Hijacking the Kid's history was as dimwitted as presidential candidate William Howard Taft's 1908 choice of an opossum as his mascot - aiming for Teddy Roosevelt's 1904 Teddy Bears. Taft's mascot, named "Billy Possum," looked like a rat - a bad image for any politician. Ultimately, Billy Possum got no farther than opossum campaign pins and slogans: "Good bye, Teddy Bear. Hello, Billy Possum." And, in Taft's dismal first year as president, cartoonists drew him as lost child looking for his Teddy Bear.

Richardson's comparable folly with Billy the Kid yielded unmatched political farce by forcing his power-monger New Mexico cronies into back-room conniving and thug-drenched threats growling about Billy the Kid and calling themselves historians. To that absurdity, Richardson added his humorless monarchial streak, which scorned retreat; while his public official and lawmen compatriots, with increasing hollowness, announced for years that they were having fun; as they scrambled to cover-up their faked forensics; until they were left whining in courtroom litigation that they had somehow lost all records of their Billy the Kid Case's touted DNA of Billy the Kid.

Not surprisingly, Bill Richardson's Billy the Kid gambit failed. He lost in the 2008 presidential primaries and as a pick for vice-president. And publicity he did get in 2008 was not for the Kid; it was for the rest of his corruption. That taint lost him yet another national post and any Washington, D.C. foothold. But Richardson still refused to give up his Billy Possum-like Billy the Kid Case. To keep it alive, he used his crooked cronies - which meant, for me, getting to know many moral monstrosities.

# ABOUT "DOLLAR BILL" RICHARDSON

*HOAXBUST: The Billy the Kid Case was just the rotten cherry topping Richardson's confection of career corruption; though it is probably unique as a pay-to-play scheme with a governor trying to barter his state's iconic history and tourism. As surprising, was that Richardson and his fellow schemers happened to fill all the antique slots left by real Billy the Kid history's 19th century, dishonest, Santa Fe Ring characters: the governor, the Lincoln County Sheriff, judges, lawyers, and big money. And to stop Richardson's hoax, I needed to confront that entire corrupt bunch.*

One cannot comprehend the near invincibility of the Billy the Kid Case hoax without comprehending the depth of Bill Richardson's corruption and amorality - because corruption and lack of morals were all that kept it going.

For example, in 2008, when it was certain that the U.S. presidency would not be his, Richardson betrayed his long-term backers - Bill and Hillary Clinton - and threw his super-delegate card in the presidential ring of Barak Obama, not Hillary's. For that, James Carville slammed him as "Judas Iscariot."

After winning, Obama, not realizing or not caring that Richardson's presence was a litmus test for corruption, offered him rewards. Secretary of State was floated. Then Commerce Secretary. So this new Judas seemed about to get a place at another banquet table: the President's Cabinet.

But by January 4, 2009, newspapers announced that Richardson had bowed out. A quirk of fate forced him to. Another crooked man's headlines resounded with catchy alliteration: "Selling Senate Seat." An FBI wiretap had nabbed, eventually-indicted, Illinois Governor Rod Blagojevich in that pay-to-play - the two P's making a reporter's dream headline.

Right then, Governor Richardson was facing the same two P's in an Albuquerque grand jury. His alleged pay-to-play involved CDR Financial Products Inc., a company whose political contributions to him allegedly got them a big state contract. Soporific fiscal complexities, plus public virginity about pay-to-play, might have left only simmering scandal; but Blagojevich's S's sizzled, and made Richardson's two P's flare hot.

So kissing Obama did not work out as planned; and got worse as Obama started looking bad enough to return the taint. In that same 2009 year, conservative journalist, Michelle Malkin, featured Richardson in her book, *Culture of Corruption: Obama and his Team of Tax Cheats, Crooks, and Cronies.*" By then, my own six years of tracking of the Billy the Kid Case, and getting secret informers, had revealed more than Michelle Malkin knew about Richardson's CDR Financial Products litigation.

Later, Obama with Attorney General Eric Holder easily trumped Richardson by continuing Bush-Cheney era torture of prisoners; and adding warrantless arrests, IRS harassment of opponents, cover-ups of Fast and Furious firearms trafficking, drone killings of U.S. citizens, NSA spying on all Americans, and 2013 shutdown of the whole government in a partisan budget squabble. In July 26, 2013, a *Dailymail Online* headline was: "Revealed: Eric Holder told the Russian's that Edward Snowden [whistleblower on NSA's spying] will NOT face the death penalty or torture if he's returned to the U.S." When America's highest judicial officer glibly mouths "torture," this is no longer the America of our founders. It is the land where "Richardsons" roam free in both parties; and an eccentric peccadillo like the Billy the Kid Case hoax heralds a government careening out-of-control.

## CAREER OF CORRUPTION

Besides exposed corruption, two things can ruin a politician: sex and silliness. Sex gossip stuck poorly to married Richardson; but David Letterman went for silliness. Letterman's January 15, 2009 monologue said: "[Richardson] announced: 'I've been doin' some stuff maybe too illegal to be in the Cabinet, but just about right to keep me as governor of New Mexico.'"

Richardson had a reverse Dorian Gray problem: bloated, he looked like the painting in the attic. Beard-fuzzed fat circled his neck like a ferret suffocating under his jowls. Letterman hit that lard, saying Richardson "was chubby; and everybody said but he was the best guy for the gig [of Commerce Secretary] ... and he said yes; and he got a little fatter; and he said, 'Sign me up.'" On screen came Richardson - flaunter of his Hispanic ethnicity - as a Taco Bell fan, captioned: "Bill Richardson: mmmm hungry."

Notwithstanding racism, that picture harked to another era: the 1870's, when Thomas Nast's newspaper cartoons exposed robber baron, "Boss" Tweed, in *his* gluttonous adiposity. Richardson made an artist unnecessary. Each photo caricatured his greed - augmented by his dead eyes of a soul on vacation.

The Billy the Kid Case hoax was about dishonest self-promotion. So was Bill Richardson. He was 55 in 2003 when he started it in his first term as governor. By then, he had already manufactured fake aggrandizement by calling himself a "major-league baseball draft for the Kansas City Athletics," when only a pitcher in college. For the Billy the Kid hoax, he became an "historian." This near-delusional sociopathic narcissism made Richardson trust that his fake CSI forensics would yield a "media circus" making him a household name and presidential shoe-in. All he had to do was dig up Billy the Kid, and hide that his investigation was a hoax - until he had to hide its scandal, stretching over three states - with me in pursuit.

In 2006, I sought out Richardson's gubernatorial opponent, John Dendahl, hoping for an ally in stopping the Billy the Kid Case hoax. However, Dendahl not only lost the election, but I was told that Dendahl's sister's unsolved beating was by Richardson's thugs. Not surprisingly, Dendahl had left New Mexico. He told me: "Richardson is the most corrupt politician in America."

Richardson's résumé distracted from that: New Mexico's governor, its congressman from 1983 to 1997; an Ambassador to the United Nations from 1997 to 1998, and Secretary of Energy under President Bill Clinton from 1998 to 2001.

Rumor was that he had returned to New Mexico to "clean up his image" for his presidential bid. That backfired. As Greg Palast, investigative author, wrote in his 2007 *Armed Madhouse*: New Mexico is "the second-most corrupt state in the USA." Opportunities from its Santa Fe Ring-style patronage system of pay-to-play would prove too tempting for Mr. "Mmmm Hungry."

Nevertheless, on December 3, 2008, President-Elect Obama, in a Chicago news conference, had announced his nomination of Richardson as Commerce Secretary, stating: "Bill Richardson is a man who shares my values." As to those shared "values," Michele Malkin, in *Culture of Corruption*, wrote:

> Richardson's heavy-handed cronyism had been documented for years by both the Right and the Left in his home state. His political horse-trading with private businesses – campaign donations for infrastructure projects, patronage jobs, and board appointments – was so notorious it earned him the moniker "Dollar Bill." [by *San Diego Reader* reporter Don Bauder]

Richardson's "Black Sunday" of January 4, 2009, started on December 15, 2008, when Martin Braun and William Selway of *bloombergnews.com* broke his pay-to-play CDR Financial Products scandal as "Grand Jury Probes Richardson Donor's New Mexico Financing Fee." That story got media sharks swarming.

The same day, James Ridgeway of *Mother Jones News*, under "Why Did Obama's Transition Team Ignore Bill Richardson's Long History of Dubious Dealings?" recounted Richardson's serving on oil company boards; and, among the presidential candidates, being a leading recipient of political donations from them.

Ridgeway also linked him to the 2001 to 2002 Peregrine Systems software company scandal - "a financial scam in the Enron style" - which had phony accounting to mask losses. Its CEO, Stephen Gardner - Richardson's wife's brother-in-law - was charged with obstruction of justice and securities fraud. According to reporter Ridgeway, Richardson claimed "ignorance;" though he had been at board meetings about "cooking the books."

Also that January 4, 2009, Geoffrey Dunn of *Huffington Post*, headlined: "Richardson's Lies Have Finally Caught Up to Him." After rolling out the baseball draft lie, Dunn gave others. Presidentially-campaigning Richardson had reported poignant talks with the mother of a killed, New Mexico, Iraq vet - except she denied any conversations. Also Richardson lied about opposing his state's Yucca Mountain as a nuclear waste repository. And in 1999, when Secretary of Energy, he had framed New Mexico's Los Alamos National Laboratory's scientist, Wen Ho Lee, as a nuclear spy. In August 22, 2005, Margot Roosevelt, for *Time* magazine, under "Bill Richardson: The Presidential Contender," emphasized that Wen Ho Lee was absolved in 2000.

Geoffrey Dunn's article also reminded that as U.N. Ambassador Richardson had helped President Clinton by offering Monica Lewinsky a United Nations job to get rid of her. Michele Malkin, in *Culture of Corruption*, called Lewinsky Richardson's only achievement as U.N. Ambassador. In fact, if Bill Clinton owed him for Monica, Richardson emptied that bank account by backing Obama. It was rumored that Bill Clinton instigated the CDR Financial Products grand jury investigations.

Another January 4, 2009 blow came from *abcnews.com's* George Stephanopoulos, in "Impossible for Obama to Keep Richardson." Stephanopoulos stated: "That the Obama transition team didn't know about these allegations against Gov. Bill Richardson is shocking." It also may be untrue. Through a connection, I had provided Richardson pay-to-play evidence to Campaign Manager David Axelrod, Michelle Obama, and initial vice-presidential vetter, Jim Johnson - though my angle of "Billy the Kid" (as in "Billy the Kid Case") may have strained credulity.

John Dendahl, in a January 13, 2009 *RuidosoNews.com* editorial, slammed his hated adversary in "Leaving Emperor Bill's Realm - and the corruption of New Mexico." Dendahl wrote: "Under the 'leadership' of Gov. Bill Richardson, political corruption had grown from several pockets to envelop the entire state." Attributing his "exile" to Colorado for that reason, Dendahl listed "Emperor Bill's" alleged pay-to-play schemes. There was a railroad "boondoggle" of buying, with $75 million taxpayer dollars, Burlington Northern Santa Fe Railroad track; and getting "tens of thousands" for his campaign from them and affiliates. In 2006, highway access for real estate development was granted the family of Pete Daskalos; and given in return was "something like $130,000" to Richardson's campaign coffers. Dendahl peppered his prose with "disgusting," "a pandering liar," "bad character," "a dictator" with "hubris," and user of "brute intimidation."

Applicable to Richardson's scandal list is one bigger than the others: the New York Retirement Fund $100 million investment in the Wall Street Quadrangle Group, whose money manager was a Steven Rattner. In *Culture of Corruption*, Michele Malkin writes:

In 2005, Quadrangle won a $20 million contract from the New Mexico State Investment Council, headed by New Mexico Governor Bill Richardson ... [Steven] Rattner donated a total of $20,000 to Richardson's 2002 and 2006 gubernatorial campaigns.

Malkin does not tell that ultimately $93 million dollars were lost in these fake New Mexico investments, which seemed to be a feeding trough for Richardson's cronies' by "finders fees." An example is a Mark Correra, who pocketed $22 million dollars in "finders fees;" and happened to be the son of Richardson's good friend, Anthony Correra - whose murky employment history involved a brief tenure on the State Investment Council. By May 6, 2011, Rob Nikolewski of New Mexico's *watchdog.org* wrote "The shoe finally drops: New Mexico files lawsuits in federal and state courts in 'pay to play' scandal." Included were father and son Correras for "ill gotten gains." Ongoing, that litigation involves over 70 of the "finders;" though Richardson himself is not named. Reporter Nikolewski, however, quoted the lawsuits' saying that Anthony Correra "often purporting to speak on behalf of Governor Richardson ... instructed, requested and/or suggested ... alternative investments that would benefit politically connected individuals, many of whom made and solicited contributions ... to or for the benefit of Governor Richardson's election campaigns."

But was "Dollar Bill" himself gorging from generous spills at the monetary feeding troughs? That is concealed. But upon ending his two terms of gubernatorial plunder, he bought a $1.67 million dollar Cape Cod, Massachusetts "vacation home" - after having gotten an annual governor's salary of $100,000.

Howling rage at Bill Richardson's corruption characterizes a 2006 book called *Frozen Lightning* by a Bill Althouse. Its back cover, with yellow fan for radioactivity, declares:

> *Frozen Lightning* takes you into the radioactive wasteland of New Mexico's political landscape, exposing Bill Richardson's insatiable thirst for power and his methods of destroying political opponents. Amidst the carnage lie the ruins of the State's once-proud institutions: the press, the justice system, and the political process itself. In exploring the theme of Richardson's political genius, an epic portrait of a megalomaniac emerges, rendered in the unflattering light cast by a politician driven to evil by his presidential aspirations.

John Dendahl's "Leaving Emperor Bill's Realm" article had added: "No New Mexico news organization has a sustained effort to ... critique, Richardson's pay-to-play, his profligate spending or his ruthlessness." That meant "press cover-up."

Richardson's pocket newspaper, the *Albuquerque Journal*, the state's biggest, had Editor-in-Chief Kent Walz (later one of my Billy the Kid Case cover-up nemeses) with a brother who was a Richardson backer. The *Albuquerque Journal* buried Richardson's cabinet withdrawal in its second section on January 5, 2008 as "Richardson withdraws name." Reporter, Nedra Pickler's damage control soothed: "Richardson insisted he would be cleared."

A February 11, 2007, an *Albuquerque Journal*, front section promo was: "Govzilla 24/7: As Governor, Bill Richardson Has Pushed an Aggressive Agenda and is Wildly Popular - But Critics Grumble That He's a Power-hungry, Self-aggrandizing Bully." The fawning subtitle was "Political heavyweight comes home."

Reporter Steve Terrell, in his October 15, 2006 *Free New Mexican* article in the: "Richardson: Raw ambition guides all career moves." Terrell wrote: "His critics call him self-aggrandizing and mock him as 'King Bill,' portraying him as a pampered elitist grown accustomed to living a flashy lifestyle on the taxpayer's dime and an opportunist whose national ambitions outweigh his commitment to his adopted state." Terrell had his limits. He refused to cover the Billy the Kid Case hoax - even when its taxpayer bill approached a million dollars. But that distinguished Terrell from no other major reporter in the state.

## THE INDICTED OR NOT INDICTED QUESTION

The Billy the Kid Case hoax would have vaporized if the CDR Financial Products Inc. pay-to-play scheme had put Richardson out of commission (meaning jail). By 2009, my attempts to stop the Billy the Kid Case hoax had the unexpected side-effect of positioning me to hear political gossip. I was told that Richardson's first grand jury on CDR Financial Products was thrown by corrupt, and (surprisingly) Republican, U.S. Attorney David Iglesias, by keeping out needed evidence. (Iglesias was later removed by President Bush.) So after Richardson backed away from Commerce Secretary, was he eventually declared innocent? Well, it depends on what you mean by "declared," and "innocent."

Protecting Billy the Kid history had led me from presidential hopeful Richardson, to actual president, Barack Obama; because it appears that, by 2009, Obama may have kissed Judas back. And for a moment in history - June to August of 2009 - the burden of preventing Richardson's and Obama's apparent cover-up about CDR Financial Products Inc. was on my shoulders.

This is what transpired. On August 29, 2008, *nmpolitics.net*, under Heath Haussamen and Trip Jennings of the *New Mexico Independent*, reported:

> The New Mexico Finance Authority says it's "cooperating fully" with federal investigators who are looking into the dealings between the state and a California firm that was paid almost $1 million under a state contract related to a $1.6 billion transportation program.
> Investigators are looking into at least two financial contributions the company involved, CDR Financial Products, made to political committees formed by Gov. Bill Richardson

around the time it won the state contract related to Governor
Richardson's Investment Partnership (GRIP) in 2004.

That Richardson investigation was being conducted by the
FBI. The prosecutor was Iglesias's replacement: U.S. Attorney
Greg Fouratt. Fouratt had the stomach to take on Richardson.
By May of 2009, I got leaks from my sources about an ensuing
grand jury indictment. The problem was that my confiders, not
me, were positioned to break that story. They refused.

By December of 2008, I had contacted *Bloomberg News's*
Bill Selway and Martin Braun, who broke Richardson's CDR
Financial Products story. I passed my information to them.
Somewhat pathetically, I seemed to be their best source.
By February, 2009, the rumor circulated in New Mexico that
President Obama would intervene to prevent Richardson's
indictment. By May 22, 2009, I was told - and passed it to Bill
Selway - that grand jury indictments were imminent. But no one
involved would call Bill Selway. By June 30, I passed along to
Martin Braun that a Richardson indictment announcement would
be in two weeks. But my source refused to be interviewed. By
July 16, 2009, I learned from a connection to a Santa Fe legislator
that "something bad would happen in a month." Also, word was
out that Richardson's Lieutenant Governor, Diane Denish, was
disassociating from him in case he stepped down.

By early August, high level, New Mexican Republicans were
spilling specifics to my sources. On August 10th, I passed along to
*Bloomberg New*s what I received: the Republicans knew that:
1) Richardson *had been indicted* in a *second* grand jury;
2) that U.S. Attorney General Eric Holder was retaining the
indictments in his Washington, D.C. Justice Department with a
possible plan to secretly quash them; 3) that President Obama
was possibly behind it; 4) that Richardson had been desperately
"calling in his chips;" 5) that "Obama's people" were trying to get
Republican, New Mexico U.S. Attorney Greg Fouratt removed
(for conducting the grand jury); and 6) that the sticking point in
Fouratt's removal was President Bush's own embarrassment from
his David Iglesias removal in which Democrats had squawked
about "lack of Bush's authority" and his "playing politics." So it
was awkward for Democrats to do the same thing!

Supposedly, those high level, New Mexico Republicans
in-the-know about the potential indictment scandal of Richardson
would be meeting with their party head, Harvey Yates, to decide
about breaking that news.

Meanwhile, through a contact, I had gotten the first edition of my *MegaHoax* book exposé to a Mike Rivero, a supposedly "fearless" radio announcer and blogger broadcasting under the title "What Really Happened?" I was to be on his program (with an audience of "millions") on August 12th. On August 11th, I called Mike Rivero asking if I could break the Richardson-Holder-Obama-indictment story, hoping that exposure would block cover-up. Rivero said yes.

My possible breaking of the story seemed to hearten my source's source, whose name I was not told; so I uncreatively called him Republican X. He was to listen to the Mike Rivero program; then meet the next day, a Thursday, with his Party Chairman Harvey Yates, to decide what to tell Bill Selway to break the story from the inside. I prepared Selway for that.

But something scared "fearless" Mike Rivero by my interview the next day. He barely let me say *"MegaHoax"* and "Santa Fe Ring," before blocking me with hectic babble about the Old West, Chisum, Tunstall, cattle and sheep wars, even Wyatt Earp. When I finally interrupted that I had breaking news about Governor Richardson, Rivero said we were out of time, and clicked me off. And Republican X, the next day, did not call Bill Selway.

This scenario was a rerun of "Larry King Live." Through another contact I had presented the Billy the Kid Case hoax to program producer Rosy Stephanatos; and my appearance on the show was being considered. By July of 2009, Stephanatos had *MegaHoax* in hand. By month's end, she said they were not interested because Bill Richardson was no longer news.

Strangely, on August 4th, none other than no-longer-news Bill Richardson was on their program, in an interview with fawning Larry King about Richardson's getting North Korean hostages released. I wondered if that interview was part of Richardson's ploy of "calling in his chips."

By August 21, I told Bill Selway of *Bloomberg News* that Republican X refused to talk, but had told my source that the Republicans had devised a strategy. Since public announcement was soon made that Richardson's past Secretary of State Rebecca Vigil-Giron had been indicted for millions of dollars in money laundering, it did seem possible that the Republicans would act.

Then actual Richardson news broke. It had nothing to do with *Bloomberg News* reporters. It came from Richardson himself. On August 27, 2009, *The Wall Street Journal Digital Network*

*Online* proclaimed: "Gov. Richardson Says Feds Won't File Charges in Corruption Probe." The reporter, Leslie Eaton, gave what seemed Richardson's self-serving "leak." She stated:

New Mexico Gov. Bill Richardson's office said federal prosecutors won't bring charges in a corruption probe that forced him to withdraw his nomination to a cabinet position in the Obama administration.

"While the U.S. Attorney's Office has not notified Governor Richardson about the completion of its investigation, it appears that no action will be taken as a result of the year-long inquiry," Deputy Chief of Staff Gilbert Gallegos said in a statement released late Thursday ...

**[AUTHOR'S NOTE: Do not miss that "federal prosecutors" will not be taking action, even though Richardson has not been informed that the investigation is completed!]**

A federal grand jury was looking into whether his administration steered a financial-advisory contract to CDR Financial Products of Beverly Hills, Calif., in 2004 after an executive with that company made large contributions to Mr. Richardson's political action committees.

Both the governor and the company denied that the contributions were linked to the contract, under which CDR made about $1.5 million.

The Associated Press reported earlier Thursday, citing an unnamed source, that the Justice Department in Washington had decided not to press charges in the case.

**[AUTHOR'S NOTE: Observe that the Justice Department appears to be over-riding the New Mexico grand jury which did the indicting.]**

In a statement, Harvey Yates Jr., chairman of the New Mexico Republican Party, raised questions about possible political influences in the decision to drop the case.

**[AUTHOR'S NOTE: Though holier-than-thou here, Yates appeared to have been instrumental in preventing the leaks that could have prevented cover-up of indictments.]**

Last month, Mr. Richardson made headlines by meeting with diplomats from North Korea, in one of a series of steps North Korea has taken recently that suggest it wants to improve relations with the United States and its allies.

**[AUTHOR'S NOTE: Since this is Richardson's own leak, he put in a plug for himself!]**

The same day, *NYTimes.com,* had "No Charges for Governor after Inquiry Into Contract." Reporter James C. McKinney Jr. and Michael Haederle wrote:

Federal prosecutors have decided not to pursue criminal charges against Gov. Bill Richardson and other New Mexico officials after a yearlong inquiry into accusations that his administration steered a lucrative contract to a high-profile political donor, according to an official letter sent to witnesses before the grand jury ...

Mr. Richardson's aides have long maintained that the acting United States attorney, Gregory J. Fouratt, a Republican, went after Mr. Richardson for political reasons, effectively sabotaging his chance to serve in the cabinet. Mr. Fouratt has denied that.

Mr. Fouratt took the unusual steps of bringing in a new prosecutor to present evidence last fall and then empanelling a new grand jury in January, after it became clear that the first grand jury was not ready to indict, lawyers for several of the witnesses before the grand jury said.

In the letter, Mr. Fouratt's office said he would not pursue criminal charges, but it added that "pressure from the governor's office resulted in the corruption of the procurement process" and said that the letter "should not be interpreted as exoneration of any party's conduct in that matter."

But government officials informed of the decision said top Justice Department officials concurred with Mr. Fouratt's decision to drop the inquiry. And some witnesses before the grand jury noted that the agreement to extend the statute of limitations on the accusations was set to expire on Friday, and that no one from the Justice Department had asked them to sign another one.

"We were waiting for the other shoe to drop," said William C. Sisneros, chief executive of the New Mexico Finance Authority, who testified before the grand jury ...

Mr. Richardson was traveling on a trade mission to Cuba. His spokesman, Gilbert Gallegos, issued a statement saying that while the United States attorney's office had yet to notify Mr. Richardson officially, the investigation appeared to be over.

"Governor Richardson is gratified that this yearlong investigation has ended with the vindication of his administration," Mr. Gallegos said.

For nearly a year, federal investigators have been scrutinizing how CDR Financial Products Inc. of Beverly Hills, Calif., got two consulting contracts in 2004 worth about

$1.4 million to advise the state on a large bond issue for building infrastructure. The president of the company, David Rubin, a major Democratic contributor, had given more than $110,000 to two political action committees controlled by the governor from 2003 to 2005.

The largest of those donation, $75,000, was made less than a week before CDR was chosen by the Finance Authority to handle the investment of bond proceeds. The investigation focused on whether the governor's former chief of staff, David Contarino, played a role in hiring CDR.

Prosecutors also subpoenaed records of another former Richardson aide, David Harris, who was executive director of the Finance Authority, and one of the governor's closest political advisers, Michael Stratton, a political consultant in Denver who also worked as a lobbyist for CDR.

Lawyers for Mr. Harris and Mr. Contarino did not return calls seeking comment.

The charges and the countercharges that the prosecution was influenced by politics started immediately. Allies of Mr. Richardson said the investigation took too long to complete and crippled him politically.

On the other side, the state Republican Party chairman, Harvey Yates Jr., was quick to raise suspicions that the Obama administration had dropped the inquiry for political reasons.

"Was this decision made contrary to the advice of experienced, nonpolitical, career prosecutors and the F.B.I.?" Mr. Yates asked in a statement.

On August 28, 2009, the *Albuquerque Journal* shouted in a three inch, front page-topping headline: "IN THE CLEAR: Feds Criticize Gov.'s Office But Skip Indictments." [APPENDIX: 2] For it, an old 2008 photo of Richardson with Obama and American flags, had the bloated-faced dead-eyed governor with his brutal down-twisted mouth, and begged for the caption: "Could this man be innocent?" But the actual caption said: "President Barack Obama announced at a news conference with Gov. Bill Richardson on Dec. 3 that he was appointing Richardson to be secretary of commerce. Richardson withdrew from consideration for the post on Jan. 4." Reporters Mike Gallagher and Dan Boyd appeared hopeful that their readers would stop at the boldface headline; because the article itself did not prove "in the clear." It oozed potential cover-up between the lines. Gallagher and Boyd wrote:

Gov. Bill Richardson and two top advisors can breathe a sigh of relief over the Justice Department's decision not to pursue indictments in connection with a 1.6 billion highway bond deal, but if they were looking for clear vindication from prosecutors, they didn't get it.

A letter to defense lawyers from U.S. Attorney Greg Fouratt sent late Thursday said the United States "will not seek to bring charges against your clients" arising out of the New Mexico Finance Authority's award of financial work to California-based CDR Financial products.

Fouratt went on to say, however, that the investigation revealed that CDR and its officers made substantial contributions to Richardson's political organizations while the company was seeking the work and the "pressure from the governor's office resulted in corruption of the procurement process so that CDR would be awarded such work."

The three paragraph letter - obtained by the Journal from private attorneys in the case - said the notification "shall not preclude the United States or the grand jury from reinstituting such an investigation without notification ... if circumstances warrant ..." Fouratt would not comment and would not provide a copy of the letter.

**The letter said," It is not to be interpreted as an exoneration of any party's conduct."** [author's boldface]

Richardson's spokesman Gilbert Gallegos responded late Thursday, saying, "The prosecutor's letter is wrong on the facts and appears to be nothing more than sour grapes."

The investigation cost Richardson a spot in President Barack Obama's Cabinet as commerce secretary. The governor withdrew his name in January when it became clear the probe would not end soon.

**The decision not to pursue indictments was made by the Department of Justice in Washington, D.C., according to attorneys familiar with the case - a development that prompted questions by Republicans in New Mexico about possible political tampering.** [author's boldface]

Richardson's office earlier Thursday issued a statement saying he had been vindicated - although it was before his lawyers received any formal notification and before the Journal informed Gallegos about Fouratt's letter ...

### Contributions

The investigation dealt with whether more than $100,000 in political contributions made by CDR and its principals influenced the company's selection as an adviser to the New Mexico Finance Authority for the GRIP bond program.

It focused on Richardson, his former chief of staff and confidant, Dave Contarino, and UNM Executive Vice President David Harris, who was in charge of the Finance Authority in 2004 when the bond program was initiated ...

Attorneys for Richardson, Harris and Contarino in April signed 90-day waivers of the statute of limitations to have the case reviewed by top prosecutors in Washington, according to attorneys familiar with the case ...

Under "Explanation sought" the article says, "State Republican Party Chairman Harvey Yates Jr. said Attorney General Eric Holder owed an explanation on how the decisions were made." (This obviously omits that Yates had told Republican X to conceal the indictment.) Yates, with his photo, got a quote:

Was this decision made contrary to the advice of experienced, nonpolitical, career prosecutors and the FBI? If so, what was the justification for ignoring the advice of experienced, nonpolitical prosecutors and FBI investigators?

Richardson's Lieutenant Governor Diane Denish, also with a photo, got in her doubletalk (hoping to be the next governor):

Assuming news reports are accurate, this is good news for the people of New Mexico. But the fact remains that public confidence has been eroded by the numerous investigations into possible wrongdoings by other government officials. We need strong ethics reform to make state government more open and accountable, and I will continue to lead that fight.

Then came the man who could have made history, the man who knew the truth, a Republican theoretically not bound to Democratic party cronyism, the man who could have broken 239 years of Santa Fe Ring dominance: U.S. Attorney Greg Fouratt. Along with his young face was his capitulation:

The investigation further revealed that pressure from the governor's office resulted in corruption of the procurement process ... At this time, however, the United States will not seek to bring charges against your clients.

With the papers now talking, I checked with my sources. From one, I learned that shortly before these public announcements, Richardson had allegedly met with high-ranking Republicans to make "a deal": Grumble but don't spill the beans. The beans were that Richardson had been indicted for pay-to-play in the Fouratt's grand jury. Indictment specifics were that Richardson had accepted campaign contributions from CDR Financial Products in

October of 2003. Seven months later, in April of 2004, CDR Financial Products got their big state contract.

And who made that non-bean spilling deal? The names I was given - along with Harvey Yates and past party Chairman Allen Weh - were Pat Rogers, Mickey Barnett, and Rod Adair. Those last three ended up also playing a major role in Billy the Kid Case cover-up and in my life. And I heard that my silent Republican X had some regrets - but his lips remained sealed.

Possibly all these bean-retaining people knew the great truth: "There is no two party system in New Mexico; only the single Favor and Fear Party." Or as a bumper sticker I saw on a car with New Mexico plates and the state's Native American Zia symbol stated: "This is not a Democracy. It is an auction."

But to return to "how Billy the Kid got me up to Washington": this is what I learned. My source told me that Attorney General Eric Holder simply held Richardson's indictment - whose statute of limitations started ticking in 2003 - till its time ran out. Then Richardson was declared "cleared." So Obama, through Holder, may have turned Richardson's crime to a "non-occurrence." Thus, cover-up of that indictment by Attorney General Holder may have been Obama's real pay-back to his Judas Iscariot.

How is that done? Is it legal? It depends on what you mean by "done" and "legal." My contacted experts on constitutional law told me that the Washington Attorney General - Eric Holder here - is the "boss" of the state U.S. Attorneys. Pursuing indictments is at his "prosecutorial discretion." That means he can hand you a "get out of jail free card." Does that sound like a set-up for political quid pro quo? How about it sounding like a variation of pay (support me for president) to play (stay out of jail and have fun)? Do you think it is illegal for Obama and Eric Holder to do that?

If you thought yes, you are wrong. According to the expert consults, if you are high on the totem pole - like Richardson - you really are above the law. When one gets to morality, however, the answer is different. Holder had a moral responsibility not to perform in a manner unbecoming to an attorney. Most importantly, there exists no federal law requiring any of this to be made public: the indictments or their cover-up. The necessary congressional act as to the public's right to know about indictments, and actions taken on them, has never been created.

Why? Can you visualize any American politician - like the participants in Richardson's cover-up, or the people you will meet in this Billy the Kid hoax story, for example - pursuing that legislation? The magic of the Land of Enchantment, thus, extends to Washington, D.C., along with its Santa Fe Ring- style cronyism.

So was Richardson really indicted? On May 25, 2010, I did an open records request to the Department of Justice. The answer returned was that the case was sealed until his demise.

Bill Richardson, however, did win a special contest in 2010. It was for the country's most "unethical and incompetent" governor. Chosen as one out of 50, Richardson's distinction was the result of a poll taken by Citizens for Responsibility and Ethics in Washington.

## BETWEEN WORLDS AND AGAINST INTELLECT

Bill Richardson's life is an openable book, as a ghost-written (by a Michael Ruby) autobiography titled *Between Worlds* - like one written for Richard Nixon and omitting Watergate. In it, Los Angeles born, Richardson proclaims, citing his "American father and Mexican mother": "I am representative of ... multicultural future." One hopes not.

*Between Worlds* sets the stage for Bill Richardson's brawny anti-intellectualism. According to the book, Bill was forced by his father to attend the man's alma mater, Tufts University; and though a mediocre student, was admitted to its Fletcher School of Law and Diplomacy by intervention of its dean - his father's friend. Richardson admits, "I was out of my league." Apparently, that left him vindictive, rather than humbled by academia.

John Dendahl's 2009, *RuidosoNews.com*, "Emperor Bill" article says that, upon assuming governorship, Richardson soon removed constitutionally appointed, university regents; their replacements being forced to provide undated letters of resignation for his potential use.

That was 2003: the year the Billy the Kid Case hoax began. Was it coincidental that a compliant professor was picked from the University of New Mexico to be its "official" historian? Richardson had also appointed that university's President, David Harris - who immediately tried to stop blocking of Billy the Kid Case's fake exhumations by the state's Office of the Medical Investigator by removing their lawyer. (Is the name "David Harris" familiar? Recall that the CDR Financial Products investigation showed that its largest donation, $75,000, was made less than a week before

CDR was chosen by the Finance Authority to handle investment of bond proceeds. And David Harris was that Finance Authority executive director, and Bill Richardson's close political adviser.)

Of course, the Billy the Kid Case hoax itself epitomizes Richardson's virulent anti-intellectualism, by empowering two-bit lawmen and a bottom-of-the-barrel historian to push it through.

Richardson's academia-hating reached its Everest by his appointment of political hack, Manny Aragon, as president of New Mexico Highlands University - until the frantic school paid Aragon $200,000 to leave. Later, Aragon was indicted for an Albuquerque, court house construction, kick-back scheme of millions of dollars; and sentenced, in 2009, to prison. Greg Palast, in *The Best Democracy Money Can Buy*, had already fingered Manny Aragon as both lobbyist and concrete supplier for a prison-building company called Wackenhut. When Palast asked a state senator about illegality of that combination, the man responded, "Welcome to New Mexico." So did Aragon take Richardson's rap?

Also rewarded was Richardson's gubernatorial spokesman, Billy Sparks (active in the Billy the Kid Case hoax by handing out "bribery checks" at Richardson's Santa Fe office to the first, participating, Lincoln County Sheriff). Billy Sparks got the lucrative Directorship of Communications for the University of New Mexico Hospital. But he had no required college degree. No problem. The university's board of regents, appointed by Richardson, and university President, David Harris, appointed by Richardson, re-wrote job specs low enough to fit Sparks.

All these shenanigans may cast doubt on Richardson's morals. As intriguing is his self-image. Does he feel invisible? Fuzzing hair to hide his dead ferret neck roll of fat, may be a clue.

Take his *Between Worlds* list of "Richardson's Rules," twenty-five treacley maxims that are the equivalent of his neck-ferret: embarrassing and revealing denial - because that simple-minded 2005 book, like the Billy the Kid Case hoax, was intended to advertise his presidential-level acumen. The third "Richardson's Rule" is: "Be discreet and don't volunteer too much information."

That tactic was known to Mark Twain, who said: "It is better to keep your mouth shut and appear stupid, than to open it and remove all doubt."

And, if anything, the Billy the Kid Case epitomizes Richardson's stupidity and oblivion as to its obviousness.

Marlyn Bowlin, now deceased, and the previously mentioned founder of the Billy the Kid Outlaw Gang and Fort Sumner resident, told me she was sitting at a restaurant table adjoining Richardson's during his 2002 gubernatorial campaign there. She heard Richardson ask an aid: "Who killed Billy the Kid?" So much for him as an "historian" in the Billy the Kid Case investigation.

Some "Richardson's Rules" he did not follow - like his eighteenth, which had: "Never lie ... lies catch up with you."

"Richardson's Rules" tempted me to add "Richardson's Implied Rules." Central is: "The public are suckers."

For example, in his 2002 gubernatorial campaign, he set the Guinness Book of World's Records for handshakes in 8 hours. It was 13,392 - at a state fair. It was his "man of the people" ploy. Once elected governor, Richardson ended marathon handshaking, it being impossible from his speeding cadre of black SUV's, while entertaining Hollywood film celebrities lured to the state with his film production incentives and for his fun. Next, he used taxpayer money to buy himself a $5 million dollar jet, and abandoned entirely the ground - and "suckers" and their hands below.

The magnitude of Richardson's rampages may cause one to miss the point: Richardson is just a well-connected thug. His true colors are better seen in his hit-and-runs than his pay-to-plays.

On November 26, 2008, he was involved (if you believe those who claim to know) or not involved (if you believe him) in an horrific, night-time, hit-and-run vehicular homicide of a pedestrian in Santa Fe. The claim-to-know version placed drunken Richardson in the headlights-off, speeding, black BMW's back seat. The driver (all agree) was a Richardson's lawyer named Carlos William Fierro - and drunk. In the car's passenger seat was State Police Sergeant Alfred Lovato (all agree), a member of Richardson's security team. The pedestrian victim (hit by the 50 mph vehicle, which kept on going) was as good a man as can be conceived (all agree): a Pueblo native American, William Tenorio, 46, described in reporter Gale Courey Toensing's January 2, 2009 *KRQE-TV.com's* "Politically-connected lawyer charged in hit-and-run death of Pueblo man" as "a local disc jockey, a volunteer kid's soccer coach, a catechism teacher ... and a leadership facilitator who ran a youth group." Tenorio's daughter pleaded: "I ask that the laws of New Mexico be applied regardless of prestige, power, and influence." (Fierro got a 7 year sentence, but served about 4.)

In the claim-to-know scenario, Richardson had fled the murder car and the scene. By January 9, 2009, the *Santa Fe New Mexican's* Jason Auslander reported on Richardson's fleeing the crime scene as "Police work to dispel hit-run rumors." By January 10, 2009, *KRQE News 13* reported: "Richardson cleared in hit-and-run crash." Quoted was Santa Fe Police Chief Eric Johnson:"[T]here is nothing to indicate the governor had any connection to the case." As to Attorney Carlos William Fierro, he did not even get disbarred for drunken hit-and-run killing of a man, plus jail-time.

Then Richardson hit-and-ran again; except in the water and without a doubt. He was in a boat allegedly operated by his chief of staff, Brian Condit, and with his budget secretary, Katherine Miller. A September 10, 2009 *wonkette.com* article by Jim Newell was titled "Bill Richardson & Pals Smash into Docket Boat, Flee." Newell wrote: "[Richardson's] life has very little purpose now [after the Obama Commerce Secretary fiasco]. That's a good thing. The man deserves a break from his prison of Ambition, a passion that has kept him busy in hundreds of semi-important government jobs over the years. Now he has time to dance! He also has time to flee boat crashes - you know, like when the boat he's on demolishes another boat, and destroys a marina [in New Mexico's Elephant Butte State Park] in general, and then he and his buddies just pop off and never tell anyone" [for two days]. Heath Haussamen's article of the same day in his *nmpolitics.net* was titled "Wonkett skewers gov over weekend boat crash," and added that Richardson took no responsibility, saying that "[H]e was napping when it happened."

The Billy the Kid Case hoax unfolded in similar high aether of private jetting hubris, immunity to prosecution, and secret power elites, placing Bill Richardson in a continuum from hit-and-runs, to pay-to-plays, to torture-for-truth; as our government, from bottom to top, veered into the sewer.

The point is that when accountability of public officials ends, their violations are not just unconstitutional, but personal. Without accountability of law, public offices and positions are converted to private gain - and private revenge. As Richardson wrote in his *Between Worlds*, but left off his list of "Richardson's Rules": "One of my political axioms is that when you're hit, you always need to hit back - harder if possible." Savvy New Mexicans, under the Santa Fe Ring's yoke for generations, would have heard a "Richardson's Implied Rule": "If you don't play, you'll pay."

# More Bills and Billy the Kid

If in doubt naming major players in the Billy the Kid Case hoax, guess "Bill."

There were Governor Bill Richardson; his official spokesman, Billy Sparks; his major political donor, Attorney Bill Robins III; and Bill Kurtis of a self-named TV production company poised to film the Billy the Kid Case hoax's TV documentaries.

And there was a random man - dead 72 years - who could wreak vengeance on the bunch of Bills. He was secretly and accidentally exhumed in Prescott, Arizona, in the Billy the Kid Case hoax. His name is William Hudspeth.

Of course, real Billy made it all possible. Born William Henry McCarty, becoming William Henry Antrim after gaining a step-father named William Henry Harrison Antrim, later self-named William H. Bonney, he was finally dubbed by his murderous Santa Fe Ring enemies: Billy the Kid.

Of all these Bills, the oddest was "Brushy Bill," the best known Billy the Kid pretender. Born Oliver P. Roberts, living from 1879 to 1950, he probably believed he was the Kid (as well as a dozen other old West characters), and achieved ridicule and a hoodwinking author - another Bill, William V. Morrison - during his life. And in death, "Brushy Bill" became the surprise winner of the Billy the Kid Case hoax.

# Santa Fe Ring-Style Friends

"Dollar Bill" Richardson and his Billy the Kid Case hoax could not have existed without two, long-dead, brilliant, ruthlessly corrupt, robber baron, law partner attorneys: Thomas Benton Catron and Stephen Benton Elkins, the 1870 founders of the Santa Fe Ring. To make New Mexico Territory their fiefdom, they instituted cronyism politics of "loyalty to friends." So when Richardson's hoax began in 2003, Ring "friends" had oppressed New Mexicans for 133 years. Originally, the citizens fought back.

First occurred the 1876 Grant County Rebellion in New Mexico Territory's southwest. Beginning a few years earlier, it had centered in Silver City - coincidentally when young Billy Bonney (as Henry Antrim) lived there. Increasingly enraged at Ring corruption and suppression of rights, the locals, by 1876, drew up the "Grant County Declaration of Independence;" and published it in the main newspaper: the *Grant County Herald*. Proposed was seceding from New Mexico Territory and joining Arizona Territory; whose border they shared. They were quashed by a combination of political oppression and placation.

More violent was the 1877 Colfax County War in northern New Mexico Territory. There, a year after Grant County's rebellion, Ringmen and settlers fought. Over 200 died. Citizens, through their newspaper, and by letter writing to President Rutherford B. Hayes, demanded removal of the Ring-partisan governor, Samuel Beech Axtell. The Colfax County War ended by the Ring's murder of the leaders and by military intervention.

The next year, 1878, was the anti-Ring Lincoln County War, made famous by Billy Bonney himself; and lost by murders, arson, and illegal military intervention backed by corrupt Territorial politicians and law enforcement.

Modern historian, D.W. Meinig, in his book, *The Shaping of America, A Geographical Perspective on 500 Years of History, Volume. 3, Transcontinental America 1850 - 1915* portrayed the Santa Fe Ring as an economic phenomenon engulfing America and imperiling its freedom and democracy. Meinig stated:

> In the 1870's anticipation of railroad connections to the East began to alter the prospects [in New Mexico] for profits and position. Slowly forming over the years, the "Santa Fe Ring" now emerged into full notoriety: "it was essentially a set of lawyers, politicians, and businessmen who united to run the territory and to make money of this particular region. Although located on the frontier, the ring reflected the corporative, monopolistic, and multiple enterprise tendencies of all American business after the Civil War. Its uniqueness lay in the fact that, rather than dealing with some manufactured item, they regarded land as their first medium of currency." "Land" meant litigation, and "down the trail from the states came ... an amazing number of lawyers" who, "still stumbling over their Spanish, would build their own political and economic empire out of the tangled heritage of land grants." And so, somewhat belatedly, a general repetition of the California situation got under way, and with the same general results: "eventually over 80 per cent of the Spanish grants went to American lawyers and settlers." Important differences were the presence in New Mexico of a much greater number of Hispanic peasants and

communities well rooted on the land, the considerable resistance and violence generated by this American assault, and the sullen resentment created in an increasingly constricted and impoverished people who felt they had been cheated out of much of their lands. In contrast to common representations it was not a case of vigorous, expanding society moving upon "a static culture," for "the Hispanos were still settling and conquering New Mexico, ever-extending their control" when the Anglos arrived. Here even more starkly than in California the conflict arose not just out of simple imperial position and crass chicanery but out of the clash of two fundamentally different sets of values, perceptions, and motivations. For ordinary Hispanos land was simply basic to a comfortable existence: "enough land to farm, enough pasture for stock, enough game to hunt, enough wood to burn, and enough material to build," all "to help one live as one ought to live" - including the continuity of such life generation after generation. Although operating to a great extent on tradition and custom, this was not the simple, "primitive" society most Anglos took it to be; it had its own laws relating to land and water, its own complexities of status, politics, and factions. To the Anglos land was a commodity to buy and sell, to exploit as quickly as possible, a means of profit and propellant of one's personal progress. Furthermore, "American land policy featured precise measurement and documentation, assumed individual ownership, and came out of a tradition that expected western land to be open for settlement." And it came out of eastern lands - out of the humid woodlands of Europe and America - and its assumptions about settlement and family farms, its rigid uniform rectangular survey system, its laws relating to water, cultivation, and seasonal use were incongruous with the needs and practices of Hispano farming and stock raising in the arid southwest. The most vulnerable parts of the Hispano system were the common lands, essential to the grazing economy, but often used without title, or held by a patrón who ultimately sold or lost his title, or by a community grant that was readily challenged under American law and likely to be declared by the courts to be public land subject to routine survey and sale. This process of Anglo encroachment went through several phases over several decades but reached an important victory in an early court approval of the Maxwell Grant, an infamous case wherein the original 97,000 acres was inflated to nearly

2 million covering a huge county-sized area of prime piedmont lands. Well before the owner had certain title to this baronial tract he sold it to London speculators, and once the country that had "seemed worthless to Kearny's soldiers" became "an item in the stock exchange and a topic of interest in a dozen investment houses in Europe," the invasion of New Mexico had taken on a new momentum.

D.W. Meinig did not specify the land-grab that started the Santa Fe Ring. In 1870, Attorneys Thomas Benton Catron and his law partner, Steven Benton Elkins, cheated their client and grant owner, Lucien Bonaparte Maxwell, out of his two million acres. Maxwell got only $600,000 from the sale. Catron and Elkins immediately resold it for more than double that price; and their enrichment led to their founding the Santa Fe Ring. (Billy Bonney also intersected Maxwell family history, with his young lover being Lucien Maxwell's daughter, Paulita; and with his killing by Sheriff Pat Garrett being in their Fort Sumner mansion.)

Thomas Benton Catron brought the Santa Fe Ring into the 20th century. When, in 1912, he spent a million dollars to become New Mexico's first senator, he needed only the legislature's appointment. So who got that million? To help you guess, living New Mexicans recall leaving an attaché case with $10,000 in bills when they met with a legislator to present a project.

History recycles characters like Richardson. Take William March "Boss" Tweed (rotund as Catron and Richardson), head of New York City's Democratic party machine, Tammany Hall, and object of Thomas Nast's glutton cartoons. "Boss" Tweed finally got convicted, in the 1870's, for pocketing up to $200 million taxpayer dollars. Before his fall, Tweed had growled: "Stop them damned pictures." Tweed lived by two connected rules: Keep your shenanigans secret; and you can always dupe the public.

My modern Santa Fe Ring adversaries added nothing more. So their bloated Billy the Kid Case hoax - like their bloated "Boss" Richardson - eventually became their own "Thomas Nast" cartoon. Fighting to prevail, these friends circled wagons for over a decade, merely ensuring their place in history as buffoons. And I definitely kept "them damned pictures" going.

# CHAPTER 3:

# BILLY THE KID'S REAL HISTORY

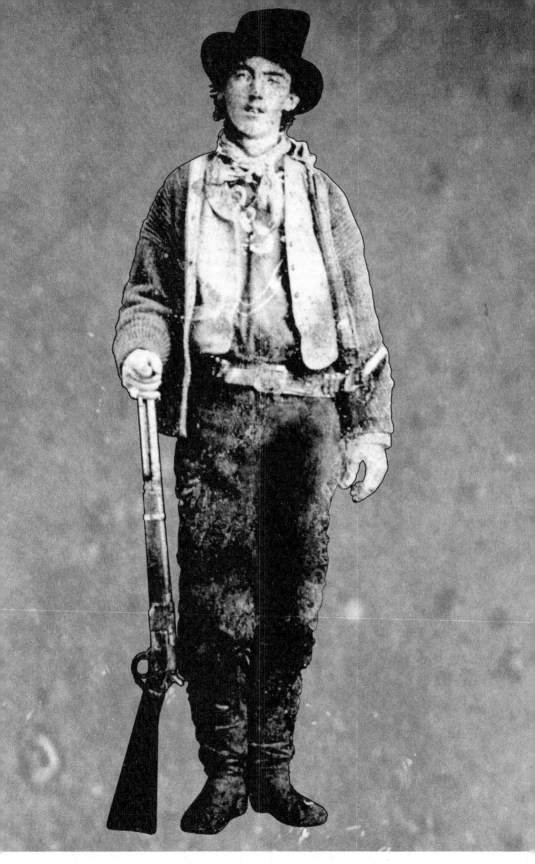

# BILLY THE KID AND PAT GARRETT HISTORY

*HOAXBUST: The foolhardiness of the Billy the Kid Case hoax is demonstrated by profuse proof of the true history - as this book's bibliography demonstrates. There is no doubt that on July 14, 1881, Pat Garrett, Lincoln County Sheriff and a Deputy U.S. Marshal, shot dead Billy the Kid. He had reason to. After Billy - sentenced to hang for murdering an earlier Lincoln County Sheriff - escaped from Garrett's jail by killing his two deputy guards, Garrett's job was getting Billy dead or alive. Not being Billy's friend, dead was likely. Garrett's 1880 posse pursuits had already killed Billy's pals, Tom O'Folliard and Charlie Bowdre; and had missed Billy only by accident. After Garrett did kill Billy in Fort Sumner, the corpse was identified by about 200 townspeople and a Coroner's Jury inquest, which closed the case as justified homicide. The hoaxers ignored or denied all those facts, while fabricating their tall tales without any supporting evidence.*

Billy the Kid Case hoaxers audaciously ignored mountainous information backing the true history. In 1997, Billy the Kid publications were listed by a Kathleen Chamberlain for the University of New Mexico's Center for the American West. Leaving out archival documents and fictions, she found 14 documentaries and 394 non-fiction books. Those non-fiction books include top-notch historian authors starting with Robert N. Mullin, Maurice Garland Fulton, Walter Noble Burns, and Philip Rasch. Frederick Nolan's *The Lincoln County War: A Documentary History*, uses his decades of research. Leon Metz wrote *Pat Garrett: The Story of a Western Lawman*. And Jerry Weddle's *Antrim is My Stepfather's Name*, detailed Billy's adolescence.

Archival documents for that period of history number in the thousands of pages. The portion of the Secret Service reports, which I own, is 15,000.

A 1878 report for the Departments of Justice and the Interior, with depositions about John Henry Tunstall's murder - including Billy Bonney's own - was done for President Rutherford B. Hayes by an attorney named Frank Warner Angel. I own that. An 1879 military Court of Inquiry for potential Court Martial of the fort commander who had intervened in the Lincoln County War has a transcript of testimony of over a hundred war participants - including Billy Bonney. I own that too.

And there are Billy Bonney's letters to Governor Lew Wallace, his deposition for Attorney Frank Warner Angel, and his military court testimony. I have all these.

Billy Bonney's 19th century old-timer pretenders required this history to fake being Billy. But the sources were not assembled until long after the imposters' deaths. So real history undid them.

The Billy the Kid Case hoaxers, with the modern sources available, relied on audience ignorance. And in their years of posturing on the world stage, these hoaxers presented not a single piece of evidence contradicting that Pat Garrett killed Billy the Kid. That was their biggest secret.

## BILLY THE KID'S REAL HISTORY

*HOAXBUST: What follows is history omitted by the hoaxers and the pretenders, either by ignorance or intent; and replaced by their concoctions. Both groups of fraudsters relied on public ignorance of erudite history tomes, or public reliance on Hollywood's film mythology of Billy the Kid.*

Ground zero for debunking all the historical fakers, is Billy Bonney's real history. That history is complex, colorful, traumatic, and amazing, since one boy fit so much into his 21 years. Besides historical names and a few main events, this information was unknown territory to Billy's old-timer pretenders. All of it was a problem to the modern Billy the Kid Case hoaxers.

This is what actually happened in the life and death of William Henry McCarty Antrim Bonney aka The Kid and Billy the Kid.

*******

In a hot, full-mooned, New Mexico Territory night as bright as day, the 21 year old, homeless youth, Billy Bonney, with trusting stockinged feet, approached the porticoed, two story, Fort Sumner mansion of the Maxwell family, at about a quarter to mid-night.

That day, July 14, 1881, was the third anniversary of the Lincoln County War's start, which had left Billy the most hunted outlaw in the country; though, to himself, he was a freedom fighter: the last Regulator and only War participant, out of 200, to be tried. His sentence on April 9, 1881 had been death by hanging. Now, only his enemies called him "Billy the Kid."

That July night, Billy intended to cut a free, dinner steak from the side of beef hanging - at the patrón's generosity - on the mansion's north porch. But first he would go to the south porch's corner bedroom of that patron: the town's owner, Peter Maxwell.

Asleep in that mansion was Billy's secret lover, Maxwell's sister, Paulita, seventeen, and just pregnant with Billy's child.

Also in the mansion, was a never-emancipated Navajo slave, Deluvina; purchased, as a child, by Peter's and Paulita's fabulously wealthy, deceased father, Lucien Bonaparte Maxwell. Then, the family lived in Cimarron, the town Lucien built on his and his wife's almost two million acre land grant, encompassing northern New Mexico Territory and southern Colorado Territory.

That was before Lucien was cheated out of the Maxwell Land Grant by Santa Fe law partners, Thomas Benton Catron and Stephen Benton Elkins, the founders of the Santa Fe Ring.

As Billy knew, that corrupt collusion of politicians, attorneys, lawmen, and big money still held New Mexico Territory in a stranglehold. Billy's failed Lincoln County War of 1878 had been a grass roots fight against that Santa Fe Ring; as had been the Colfax County War, a year before, and in the northern part of the Territory. And in 1876, Grant County, to the west, had threatened secession from the Territory to escape that Ring's clutches.

That July day was 2½ months since Billy's jailbreak escape from his scheduled hanging on May 13th. Billy knew that relentless Lincoln County Sheriff Pat Garrett would be in pursuit. Garrett had captured him on December 22, 1880, at Stinking Springs, for his hanging trial; and in his jailbreak on April 28, 1881, Billy had shot dead Garrett's two deputy guards: James Bell and Robert Olinger. Garrett would kill him on sight.

When first tracking Billy in late 1880, Pat Garrett had even killed his closest friends, Tom O'Folliard and Charlie Bowdre - missing Billy only by chance in consecutive ambushes. In fact, at the Stinking Springs capture of Billy and his companions, Garrett fatally shot Bowdre because he mistook him for Billy: the prize.

To be near his beloved Paulita, Billy had made his reckless choice to return to Fort Sumner, instead of fleeing to Old Mexico. But he trusted in the Maxwell family's protection; as well affection of the townspeople, who knew him since late 1877.

Billy's whole life had been traumatic. Illegitimate, he was a second son, born on November 23, 1859, in New York City, as William Henry McCarty. Raised with his older brother, Josie, by his mother, Catherine, in Indiana; Billy became "Henry Antrim" after she married an Indiana local, William Henry Harrison Antrim, in 1873 in New Mexico Territory; the family having arrived there after a stint in Kansas. Antrim became a miner, and the family resided in the mining town of Silver City.

In his young adolescence in Silver City, Billy, exceptionally smart, probably learned the Spencerian-style script he would use for the literate letters that would later seal his fame. He also probably became bi-lingual then; and thereafter amicably bridged Anglo and Hispanic sub-cultures in those racist times.

After only a year and a half in Silver City, Billy was orphaned by his mother's tuberculosis death in 1874, and was left a homeless victim of his stepfather's avarice. In 1975, his last year in Silver City, he supported himself by petty thievery and butcher shop and hotel work. That year he was arrested for laundry and revolver theft by Silver City's Sheriff, Harvey Whitehill. Facing ten years hard labor - the law having no provision for juveniles - Billy made his first desperate and dramatic escape, through the jail chimney; and fled to Bonita, in Arizona Territory.

In Arizona, as Henry Antrim, Billy again combined work - cooking at a small hotel - with crime: stealing blankets, saddles, and horses. In 1876, jailed with his accomplice, John Mackie, Billy escaped the local Fort Grant's guardhouse by wriggling through a ventilation space under the roof. But he stayed in Bonita, the rustling charges having been dropped through a technicality.

In Bonita, on August 17, 1877, Billy's life changed again. His argument at Atkin's Cantina with a bullying blacksmith, Frank "Windy" Cahill, escalated to Billy's fatally shooting that unarmed man. Billy escaped on a stolen race horse. The Coroner's Jury, biased to Cahill, declared Billy - as Henry Antrim - guilty of homicide, though in absentia and by ignoring self-defense.

So at 17½, Billy escaped hanging in Arizona Territory by returning to New Mexico Territory with an alias: William Henry Bonney - Billy Bonney. By September of 1877, Billy had joined the murderous, Santa Fe Ring-affiliated gang of outlaw, Jessie Evans.

But within weeks, by October, Billy changed course, hiring on as a Lincoln County ranch hand for wealthy Englishmen, John Henry Tunstall, a Santa Fe Ring competitor. Soon Tunstall's older workers had affectionately nick-named him "Kid."

Billy's fortunes seemed changed as his charismatic combination of high spirits, intelligence, sharp shooting, singing, and dancing made him popular. John Tunstall, under the Homestead Act, even gave Billy a ranch on the Peñasco River in partnership with another employee, half-Chickasaw Fred Waite. That was likely Billy's proudest and most optimistic moment.

After only 4½ months of stability, Billy's life was again cataclysmically changed by the February 18, 1878, Santa Fe Ring murder/mutilation of John Tunstall. And the slide began into that July's Lincoln County War.

By the July 1878 Lincoln County War, the Civil War had already ruined the life of Patrick "Pat" Floyd Garrett. Born to an Alabama plantation family; relocated to Claiborne Parrish, Louisiana, when 9½ - and Billy was just born - young Garrett was even willed a slave by his maternal grandfather. His family lost everything in the Civil War. Garrett wandered westward, ending up in Texas. There, he may have abandoned a common-law wife and child, as well as possibly murdering a black man, before becoming a buffalo hunter from 1876 to 1878 with two partners, and, initially, with a kid named Joe Briscoe. One irritable day in camp, Garrett shot that kid point-blank, but successfully claimed self-defense. In those days, Garrett never met fellow buffalo hunter, John William Poe. Later Garrett's, Poe's, and Billy's histories would merge on the fateful night of July 14, 1881.

By 1878, 6'4" Pat Garrett settled in New Mexico Territory's Fort Sumner, where he saw the transient, Billy Bonney, at Hargrove's or Beaver Smith's Saloons. Of different generations, they were given townspeople's nicknames, "Big Casino" and "Little Casino," for their poker playing and height discrepancies.

The original Fort Sumner, yielding the town's name, was built in 1865 by the U.S. government on desert flatlands east of the Pecos River for soldiers guarding Bosque Redondo: a concentration camp holding 3,500 Navajos and 400 Apaches. Their starvation became an embarrassment; and, in 1868, the Navajos were sent back to their homeland, the Apaches already having escaped.

In 1870, that military property, with fort and surrounding thousands of acres, was purchased by Lucien Bonaparte Maxwell, by then one of the Territory's richest men. There he moved his family - wife, Luz Beaubien; daughters, including Paulita; and only son, Peter; having refurbished the military buildings around the original parade ground into residences and businesses; and having rebuilt the officers' quarters as his mansion.

Retained was the half acre military cemetery for his family. It eventually received Billy's body, to lie beside Pat Garrett's earlier shooting victims: Billy's Lincoln County War Regulator pals, Tom O'Folliard and Charlie Bowdre.

Lucien Maxwell also planted a peach orchard and crops; and ranched primarily sheep. He died in 1875, leaving his town to the care of his wife and his son, Peter, who would be the family's ruin through financial mismanagement. But when Pat Garrett and Billy Bonney gambled there, Fort Sumner was still thriving.

Before buying Fort Sumner, Lucien Maxwell's wealth came first from his almost 2 million acre Maxwell Land Grant with its rich gold mine, then by his selling that Grant; though he was cheated by his negotiating attorneys, Thomas Benton Catron and Steven Elkins, who soon resold the Grant for twice the amount.

That Catron-Elkins profit and technique was used to start the Santa Fe Ring, an ongoing land grab scheme to disenfranchise Hispanic land grant owners. Recruited, by favor or fear, were the Territorial Governor, Samuel Beach Axtell; other public officials and law enforcement officers; and the local military.

Those robber barons, Catron and Elkins, profited immensely, in land, railroads, banks, and mines. Catron would eventually own six million acres - more than any man in United States history. And, during the Lincoln County War period, Thomas Benton Catron held the Territory's highest legal position: U.S. Attorney.

By 1878, Pat Garrett and Billy Bonney had separate lives, though connected to Fort Sumner's Gutierrez sisters: Juanita, Apolinaria, and Celsa. Billy befriended Celsa, married to her cousin, Saval Gutierrez, a Maxwell sheep herder. Garrett married Juanita, who died shortly of a possible miscarriage. Two years later, Garrett married Apolinaria, with whom he would father eight children. It was a double marriage with his Fort Sumner, best friend, Maxwell's foreman, Barney Mason, later a spy assisting Garrett's capture of Billy.

In 1878, Pat Garrett still lacked financial security. Initially, he drove a wagon for Peter Maxwell. Then Garrett worked with a local hog raiser, Thomas "Kip" McKinney. A bartending job in Hargrove's Saloon was little improvement.

Then came 1880 and the opportunity of Pat Garrett's life. Lincoln County - the largest county in America; almost a quarter of New Mexico Territory, and big enough to fit Massachusetts, Connecticut, Vermont, Rhode Island, and Delaware - needed a new sheriff for its November election, one compatible with Santa Fe Ring interests. To qualify, Garrett moved with his wife, Apolinaria, to that county's town of Roswell; adding, as a boarder, an unemployed journalist named Ashmun "Ash" Upson.

By 1880, Lincoln County was finally emerging from its 1878 war, about which Garrett knew little. Its town of Lincoln, epicenter of that Lincoln County War, had also been the epicenter of Santa Fe Ring abuses. There, "the House," a giant two-story all-purpose store run by local Ring bosses, Lawrence Murphy and James Dolan, bled cash-poor Mexicans and white homesteaders with exorbitant credit on goods and farm supplies.

Redress was impossible, since the Ring controlled law enforcement and the courts. In 1875, when a rancher, named Robert Casey, won an election against Lawrence Murphy, he was assassinated the same day. And the anti-Ring Mexican community leader, Juan Patrón, was likewise shot by James Dolan's partner, John Riley; though Patrón survived as a cripple.

The future Lincoln County uprising began in late 1876 with the Lincoln town arrival of sweet-tempered, wealthy, English merchant, John Henry Tunstall; persuaded to settle there by a resident attorney, Alexander McSween, a Ring opponent, but once legal counsel to Murphy and Dolan and "the House."

By 1877, John Tunstall built, just a quarter mile northeast of "the House," his own large store with a bank; and he purchased land for two cattle ranches - all constituting direct competition with the Santa Fe Ring. Tunstall also hoped to wrest from "the

House" its beef and flour traderships to local Fort Stanton and to the Mescalaro Indian Reservation; and he even aggressively exposed, in a local newspaper, corrupt Lincoln County Sheriff William Brady's abuse of taxpayer money to pay for Ring cattle.

So John Tunstall was next for elimination on the Santa Fe Ring's hit list. Attorney Alexander McSween was a close second.

Ringmen preferred to kill with guise of legality. So they entangled John Tunstall in a web of fabricated criminality. Its thread began with Tunstall's friend, Attorney Alexander McSween, who was representing the estate of "the House's" founding partner, Emil Fritz, who had died intestate in 1874, and had two siblings in the Territory and a life insurance policy.

The Ring focused on that Fritz, life insurance policy. McSween had litigated to get its $10,000 proceeds from its dishonestly evasive, New York City, insurance company. When collection was achieved, the New York law firm used by McSween subtracted fees of $3,000.

Alexander McSween dug in strategically, knowing that the Murphy-Dolan House - on the verge of bankruptcy from Tunstall competition - would wrangle that Fritz money from the local heirs. He did not turn over the remaining $7,000; justifying that by claiming additional possible heirs in Germany.

Then McSween left on business to St. Louis with his wife and with John Tunstall's business associate, the cattle king, John Chisum, then also president of the bank in Tunstall's store.

The Ring pounced, declaring McSween an embezzler of the Fritz insurance money. Ring head, U.S. Attorney Thomas Benton Catron, issued arrest warrants for McSween before he left the Territory. McSween was captured and brought to Mesilla to be indicted by Ring judge, Warren Bristol (later Billy's hanging judge). By luck, McSween avoided near-certain assassination if incarcerated under Ringman Lincoln County Sheriff William Brady in Lincoln's underground pit jail. Honest Deputy Sheriff Adolph Barrier, from McSween's arrest site in Las Vegas, New Mexico, volunteered to keep McSween in his personal custody.

But Ringman Judge Warren Bristol had set traps for McSween. When Bristol indicted McSween, he did two things. First, Bristol set McSween's bail at $8,000; but granted bail approval only to Ringman, District Attorney William Rynerson, who refused all bondsmen. That left McSween vulnerable to being taken into possibly fatal custody at any time by Sheriff Brady.

Bristol's second stipulation was the clincher. He attached McSween's personal property to the sum of $10,000 - falsely deemed as the amount of embezzled money - to satisfy any judgment against McSween at that April's Grand Jury trial. The catch was that Bristol also falsely declared that *Tunstall was in partnership with McSween, and attached Tunstall's property also.* And Sheriff Brady and his deputies would do the attaching.

Hoped for was a violent response from Tunstall and his men to achieve Tunstall's "justifiable" killing. But Tunstall refused confrontation, saying any man's life was worth more than all he owned. But he protectively transferred his fine horses, which were immune to the attachment.

On February 18, 1878, that stock movement by Tunstall, from his ranch back to Lincoln, was, nevertheless, used by Sheriff Brady to send his posse (illegally including outlaw, Jessie Evans, and his boys) to pursue Tunstall and his ranch hands, including Billy, for alleged absconding with property. In the pursuit, Tunstall became separated from his fleeing men and was murdered; and his body and slain horse were mutilated.

This martyrdom, and its aftermath, triggered the Lincoln County War through escalating Santa Fe Ring outrages.

The first outrage was Sheriff Brady's blocking of murder warrants' service on Tunstall killers - who included James Dolan, Jessie Evans, and other possemen. Those warrants, legally issued by Justice of the Peace John "Squire" Wilson, had been given, for service, to Tunstall employees, Billy and Fred Waite, whom Wilson had appointed as deputy constables under Town Constable Atanacio Martinez. So, illegally, Sheriff Brady briefly jailed Billy, Waite, and Martinez in Lincoln's pit jail to prevent their arresting James Dolan and others. Brady also confiscated Billy's beloved Winchester '73 carbine - likely a gift from Tunstall.

But persistent Justice of the Peace "Squire" Wilson next deputized Tunstall's foreman, Dick Brewer, who made Tunstall's men, including Billy, his posse to serve those murder warrants.

Meanwhile, recognizing his extreme risk from the Ring, Attorney McSween, with Deputy Sheriff Barrier, went into hiding.

By March of 1878, Brewer's posse had captured Tunstall murder possemen, William "Buck" Morton and Frank Baker, who were shot attempting escape. Billy was in the firing group.

**At that point, including "Windy" Cahill, Billy Bonney was now involved in three murders.**

McSween-side successes elicited more Ring outrages. Governor Samuel Beach Axtell, by official posted proclamation, illegally removed John Wilson's Justice of the Peace title, outlawed Dick Brewer's posse, and declared Sheriff William Brady Lincoln County's only law enforcer.

Enraged, Tunstall's men named themselves "Regulators" after pre-Revolutionary War vigilantes. The Regulators included Billy; Fred Waite; John Middleton; Jim "Frenchie" French; cousins, George and Frank Coe; Charlie Bowdre; and a John Chisum cattle detective, Frank MacNab. Dick Brewer was chosen as leader.

April 1, 1878 was the next crisis: the return of Alexander McSween for his Lincoln, Grand Jury embezzlement trial. To prevent his murder by Sheriff William Brady, five Regulators - four with carbines, and Billy with only a revolver - ambushed him and his three deputies from behind an adobe corral wall at the southeast side of the Tunstall store.

Brady and his Deputy, George Hindman, died on Lincoln's street. Recklessly, Billy, with Jim "Frenchie" French, ran out to retrieve his confiscated, Winchester '73 carbine from Brady's body. And both youths got leg wounds from firing, surviving deputy, Jacob Basil "Billy" Matthews.

Three days later, April 4th, was a Regulator debacle as Deputy Dick Brewer, in search of stolen Tunstall horses, led Billy, Tom Middleton, Fred Waite, Frank Coe, George Coe, and Charlie Bowdre to Blazer's Mill - a privately owned, way station, surrounded by the Mescalaro Indian Reservation. Instead, they encountered bounty-hunter and Tunstall murder posseman, Andrew "Buckshot" Roberts, for whom they had a warrant.

Charlie Bowdre shot "Buckshot" Roberts in the belly; but Roberts pumped his Winchester carbine, hitting Bowdre's belt buckle. That ricocheting bullet struck and wrenched George Coe's extended revolver, mutilating his trigger finger. Middleton, though shot in the chest by Roberts, survived. Roberts next killed Brewer; and later died himself. Billy had not fired a shot.

**Billy's murder involvement now totaled six men; though only "Windy" Cahill was demonstrably by his own hand.**

The April, 1878, Grand Jury exonerated McSween. That energized his attacks on the Ring. Knowing that murder of a foreign citizen could elicit a Washington D.C. investigation, McSween informed the British ambassador and President Rutherford B. Hayes about Tunstall's murder by public officials.

In response, investigating attorney, Frank Warner Angel, was sent by the Departments of the Interior and Justice. Once in New Mexico Territory, Attorney Angel took over a hundred depositions, among them Billy's.

Public optimism of Santa Fe Ring exposure and defeat grew further when the Lincoln County Commissioners' appointed John Copeland, a McSween-sympathizing sheriff to replace dead Brady.

Optimism was short-lived. New Regulator leader, Frank MacNab, was killed by James Dolan and Seven Rivers men on April 28th. By May 28th, because new Sheriff John Copeland had forgotten a technicality of posting a tax collecting bond, Governor Samuel Beach Axtell, by another proclamation, removed him and appointed, as replacement, George Peppin, a Ring partisan and past Brady deputy - present at Brady's killing.

Alexander McSween was unaware that Santa Fe Ring influence extended to Washington, D.C.; but Attorney Frank Warner Angel, after documenting the illegalities of Governor Axtell, U.S. Attorney Catron, and Sheriff Brady's posse, concluded in his formal report - likely under duress - that no U.S. officials had been involved in John Tunstall's murder.

But Thomas Benton Catron did resign as U.S. Attorney. And Governor Axtell was removed by President Hayes; and was replaced by Civil War General Lew Wallace on October 1, 1878.

Alexander McSween did not live to see those achievements. War fervor had built, with Tunstall men and local Mexicans calling themselves "McSweens." Billy's affiliation with local, firebrand youth, Yginio Salazar, and Billy's closeness to Hispanic residents of nearby San Patricio and Picacho, arguably forged the bond that brought the Mexicans into the McSween alliance.

By April 30th, McSweens were skirmishing with Ring partisans, known as "Murphy-Dolans;" though Lawrence Murphy was by then dying of alcoholism. Of necessity, McSween hid, often in San Patricio. With John Kinney's rustler gang from Mesilla, Sheriff George Peppin retaliated, leading a July 8th, massacre there of men, women, children, and farm animals.

The Lincoln County War began six days later, on July 14th. McSween, with sixty men - Regulators and Hispanic residents of San Patricio and Picacho - rode into Lincoln to take a stand.

Reflecting McSween's optimism at peaceful victory was the fact that in his big double-winged house had remained his wife; her sister, with her five young children; and that sister's attorney husband's law intern, Harvey Morris.

McSween's men took strategic positions in houses throughout the mile-long town, most of whose inhabitants had fled.

When Seven Rivers and John Kinney men joined James Dolan and Sheriff George Peppin, Billy; his friends, Yginio Salazar and Tom O'Folliard; and San Patricio men - José Chávez y Chávez, Ignacio Gonzales, Florencio Chávez, Francisco Zamora, and Vincente Romero - rushed to McSween's house, where Jim French had been alone as guard.

Though the Dolan men attained the foothills south of the town, they were kept at bay for five days by McSweens. It seemed that the McSweens would win by unassailable stand-off.

But Attorney McSween was unaware that nearby Fort Stanton's new commander, Colonel Nathan Augustus Monroe Dudley, was a Ring partisan. Further reassuring McSween, was that, the month before, the Posse Comitatus Act was enacted in Washington D.C., baring military intervention in civilian disputes.

On July 16th, following the days of mutual gunfire, a fort soldier, cavalryman - Private Berry Robinson, sent to Lincoln by Commander Dudley for fact-finding - had almost been hit. Without basis, McSween was blamed. To further set-up military intervention, on July 18th, James Dolan informed Commander Dudley that women and children were at risk at the Lincoln home of Ring-partisan resident, Saturnino Baca.

The next day, July 19th, risking Posse Comitatus Act violation, Commander N.A.M. Dudley marched on Lincoln with 60 troops - white infantry, black 9th Cavalry, and white officers - two ambulances; a mountain howitzer cannon; and a Gatling gun: that period's most awesome weapon of war.

Panicked by the military might, the McSweens - except for those in his besieged house - fled north across the nearby Bonito River. Dudley personally informed McSween that, if any of his soldiers was shot, he would raze his house with his cannon and Gatling gun. Furthermore, Dudley left three soldiers at the McSween property, and provided three more to accompany Sheriff Peppin - though these soldiers did no shooting themselves.

In addition, Dudley forced Justice of the Peace "Squire" Wilson to write out arrest warrants for Alexander McSween and his men as alleged assailants of Private Berry Robinson.

With those inhibitory advantages, that July 19th, Sheriff George Peppin's men soon took strategic positions around McSween's house, setting fire to its west wing; while Commander Dudley kept his non-participating soldiers encamped at the east side of town. Evacuated were only McSween's wife, Susan, her sister, and her sister's children. Trapped inside the burning building were McSween, Billy, and the other fighters.

By nightfall, the McSween house conflagration - worsened by an exploding gunpowder keg inside - left the desperate men marooned in the remaining east wing. At about 9 PM, escape was made into the fire-lit shooting adversaries. In Billy's group was law intern, Harvey Morris, whom Billy saw fatally shot.

And, before Billy and others escaped across the Bonito River to rescue by fellow Regulators, he witnessed Commander Dudley's secret and treasonously illegal intervention: three of Dudley's white soldiers had been with the burning building's assailants, and had fired at least one volley at Billy and his escaping fellows from the rear corner of Tunstall's adjacent property.

Shot dead at the house were Alexander McSween, Francisco Zamora, and Vincente Romero. Yginio Salazar survived, but with two bullets permanently in his back. The war was lost.

Symbolizing Billy's trauma and horror, that night the starving, yard chickens ate the eyeballs of McSween's corpse. Again was murder and mutilation in Lincoln County.

Though most Regulators fled the Territory, Billy stayed. With Tom O'Folliard and Charlie Bowdre, who had relocated to Fort Sumner with his wife Manuela, Billy made guerilla attacks of cattle rustling on Catron's brother-in-law, Edgar Walz, and the man he most blamed: John Chisum, who had refused make-or-break aid of his 80 cowboys to Tunstall or McSween; and had reneged on his promise to pay Tunstall's men for their services.

For his stolen stock, Billy used non-Ring outlets: Pat Coghlan in the western part of the Territory; and Dan Dedrick. Dedrick was a counterfeiter and rustler owner of Bosque Grande, a ranch 12 miles south of Fort Sumner, who, with his two brothers, also owned a livery stable in White Oaks, a town about 45 miles northwest of Lincoln. Billy also sold rustled horses in Tascosa, Texas, where he wrote a subsequently famous, bill of sale to a

Dr. Henry Hoyt for an expensive sorrel. With his rustling being petty, Billy also sought money by gambling a circuit from Fort Sumner to Las Vegas, New Mexico.

October 1, 1878 brought hope for Lincoln County citizens with new Governor, Lew Wallace: son of an Indiana governor; a Civil War Major General; the Abraham Lincoln murder trial's prosecutor; author of best selling novel, *The Fair God*; and then writing the novel, *Ben-Hur*. Talented Wallace had desired an ambassadorship to exotic Turkey, not this backwater.

To address the "Lincoln County troubles," blasé elitist Lew Wallace merely posted, a month after his arrival, an Amnesty Proclamation. It excluded those already indicted. Billy had been indicted for the murders of Sheriff William Brady, Deputy George Hindman, and Andrew "Buckshot" Roberts.

Also yielding local hope was an attorney, Huston Chapman, brought to Lincoln by Alexander McSween's intrepid widow, Susan, to charge Commander Nathan Augustus Monroe Dudley with murder of her husband and the arson of her home.

In that atmosphere of legal scrutiny, James Dolan made peace overtures, first to McSween's widow; then to Billy - thereby acknowledging that teenager's threat to the Ring. Bi-lingual Billy's bond to Hispanic people had arguably contributed to their joining the war - and could do so again in another uprising.

The Billy-Dolan peace meeting was fatefully scheduled on February 18, 1879, the anniversary of Tunstall's murder. It ended in calamity. As James Dolan; Billy; Jessie Evans and Jessie's new gang member, Billy Campbell; and Billy's friends, Tom O'Folliard and Josiah "Doc" Scurlock, walked Lincoln's dark street after the meeting, they encountered Attorney Huston Chapman.

Dolan and Campbell fired at point-blank range, killing Chapman, and igniting his clothing. Billy was an eye-witness. And again there was murder and mutilation in Lincoln County.

Huston Chapman's murder forced Governor Lew Wallace to go to Lincoln at last. Once there, however, Wallace revealed only an ignorant and quixotic plan for quelling unrest by eliminating outlaws and rustlers. A probable Ring partisan accused Billy as an outlaw.

Informed about Governor Wallace's astronomical reward of $1000 on his head, Billy wrote his subsequently famous letter of

March 13, 1879 to him, offering him his eye-witness testimony against Huston Chapman's murderers in exchange for a pardon for his own Lincoln County War indictments. This was Billy's bold and calculated risk for negating Ring power over himself.

That masterfully articulate letter, in fine Spencerian cursive handwriting, led to the March 17, 1879, nighttime meeting of Billy and Lew Wallace in Justice of the Peace "Squire" Wilson's Lincoln house. There Billy was led to believe by Wallace that a pardon-for-testimony deal was reached; though he was likely tricked.

Next, from Wallace, Billy requested arrest as a blind to prevent his assassination before his April Grand Jury testimony. For that, he was kept in the home of Juan Patrón, the town jailer and a McSween sympathizer. Billy wore shackles for that sham.

By then, Alexander McSween's widow, Susan, had retained Attorney Huston Chapman's associate, Attorney Ira Leonard, to continue her case against Commander N.A.M. Dudley. But aware of his legal risks, Dudley had already obtained defamatory affidavits from Ring partisans, stating that she was a woman of low repute, thus, lacking courtroom credibility.

Dudley also requested a Court of Inquiry into his Lincoln County War conduct, knowing that being cleared by a military court would almost guarantee acquittal in the civilian court. And his military court vindication was inevitable, though he had two prior Court Martials. For one, a year before the Lincoln County War, he had been represented by Thomas Benton Catron himself.

For the Court of Inquiry, Catron's friend, past Chief Justice Henry Waldo, represented Dudley. And the Presiding Judge of three was Dudley's best friend: Colonel Galusha Pennypacker.

But, annoyingly, Governor Wallace planned to testify against Dudley, ignoring - or unaware of - Ring machinations.

Though testifying in that Dudley Court of Inquiry was not part of Billy's Wallace pardon deal, Billy volunteered, doing so on May 28th and 29th of 1879, during his Patrón house incarceration. In his precise and articulate way, unfazed by Attorney Henry Waldo's bullying, Billy devastatingly stated that he had seen three white soldiers fire a volley - that meant officers; that meant under orders; that meant Dudley was guilty of treason (firing on American citizens in violation of the Posse Comitatus Act). And, had the Dudley Court of Inquiry been fair, Dudley would have progressed to Court Martial for Posse Comitatus Act violations.

The month before, Billy fulfilled his Wallace pardon deal by testifying for the prosecution in the Lincoln County Grand Jury. He achieved indictments of James Dolan and Billy Campbell for the murder of Huston Chapman, and indictment of Jessie Evans as accessory to Chapman's murder.

Then Ringmen acted to protect their fellows. With Billy still held in Juan Patrón's house, District Attorney William Rynerson and Judge Warren Bristol changed Billy's own trial venue from Lincoln to Mesilla for the murders of Andrew "Buckshot" Roberts, Sheriff William Brady, and Deputy George Hindman. Their plan was to transport then hang Billy quickly, before he could testify in future murder trials of indicted Dolan, Campbell, and Evans. But no pardon came from Wallace, further indicating his trickery.

Billy, at that point, had achieved two things: Ring enmity at the highest level; and friendship with Susan McSween's attorney, Ira Leonard, who, for the next two years, pressed Lew Wallace for Billy's pardon; and then represented Billy initially in his 1881 hanging trial in Mesilla.

Also, on April 25, 1879, while Billy was still in Patrón's house-jail, he would have heard that an assassination attempt had been made in Lincoln on Ira Leonard to stop his legal pursuit of Commander Dudley - just as Huston Chapman had been stopped.

So, without a pardon, and with imminent transport to Mesilla for a hanging trial, Billy simply walked out of his fake house arrest in July; though it was called an "escape" to conceal the original scheme. But that exit spawned a myth of Billy's "slipping" wrist shackles by having double-jointed thumbs or small hands.

When Billy was loose, he would have heard that N.A.M. Dudley was exonerated at the Court of Inquiry on July 5, 1879. But Billy stayed in the Territory. The Ring had to kill that gadfly.

Billy's gunman reputation also stimulated bounty hunters and competitors. It almost got him killed on January 3, 1880, when he was leaving Hargrove's Saloon in Fort Sumner. A Texan stranger named Joe Grant tried to shoot him in the back. Saved only by Grant's gun's misfiring, Billy retaliated fatally. Obvious self-defense, that killing was not legally pursued.

**Billy was now linked to murders of seven men: Cahill, Brady, Hindman, Roberts, Morton, Baker, and Grant.**

In this period, Billy may have heard first mythological whispers of his having killed a man for each year of his life. The Santa Fe Ring was setting its legal trap for capturing and eliminating him. In addition to murderer and rustler, Billy would be declared a counterfeiter to bring in the Secret Service, a branch of the Treasury Department with the funding to track him down. Ringman, James Dolan, himself initiated that process by reporting receipt of a counterfeit $100 bill in his Lincoln store.

By September 11, 1880, Secret Service Special Operative Azariah Wild was on his way to Lincoln. Dolan's counterfeit bill was falsely linked to Billy. It actually came from two youths who worked with the real counterfeiter, Dan Dedrick; but who also occasionally rustled with Billy and his regulars: Tom O'Folliard, Charlie Bowdre, and a "Dirty Dave" Rudabaugh.

Special Operative Azariah Wild was led to believe by James Dolan and other Ringmen, that Billy was in the country's biggest counterfeiting and rustling gang. In December of 1880, the *New York Sun* featured Billy as: "Outlaws of New Mexico. The Exploits of a band headed by a New York Youth ... War Against a Gang of Cattle Thieves, Murderers, and Counterfeiters." Billy was alias "the Kid." His national fame had begun.

That defamatory Ring plan almost backfired when Azariah Wild was assured by Attorney Ira Leonard that Billy would testify against the actual counterfeiters. Wild wrote in his daily report to his Chief, James Brooks, on October 8, 1880, that he would arrange Billy's pardon in exchange for that testimony. But Wild told James Dolan about that pardon plan, resulting in Dolan's convincing Wild that Billy was the gang's leader!

In his October 14, 1880 report, Azariah Wild wrote that he would arrest Billy in their upcoming meeting with Attorney Leonard about Billy's testimony. By then, Billy was cautious. He held up the stagecoach with Operative Wild's mail, read that report, and avoided apprehension by avoiding that meeting.

The Ring had another problem. They needed a Lincoln County sheriff willing to arrest Billy. George Peppin, having quit, had been replaced by a McSween-side sympathizer, George Kimbrell.

The Ring chose Pat Garrett. Secretly, Wild worked with Garrett and Dolan to create a dragnet to capture Billy and his "rustler-counterfeiter gang;" while, for the upcoming sheriff's election, Garrett was advertised as a law-and-order man to new gold-rush settlers in White Oaks; unaware of Lincoln County War issues, but a third of Lincoln County's population.

In the November 2, 1880 sheriff's election, Pat Garrett got 358 votes to George Kimbrell's 141. Azariah Wild, convinced that Kimbrell was shielding the "Kid gang," granted Garrett Territorial power for capture by making him a Deputy U.S. Marshall.

Billy, unaware, would have believed Garrett's Lincoln County authority could not extend to Fort Sumner's San Miguel County.

Also, unaware of his locally publicized "outlawry," Billy still brought stolen horses to the Dedrick brothers' White Oaks livery.

On November 22, 1880, a White Oaks posse ambushed Billy, Tom O'Folliard, Billy Wilson, Tom Pickett, and "Dirty" Dave Rudabaugh at nearby Coyote Spring, killing two of their horses before they escaped.

Five days later, that posse surrounded them at the way station ranch of "Whiskey" Jim Greathouse, 45 miles northeast of White Oaks; killing one of their own men, Jim Carlyle, in friendly fire; but blaming Carlyle's death on Billy.

That accusation prompted another of Billy's ultimately famous letters to Lew Wallace. On December 12, 1880, Billy wrote to deny his outlawry and the Carlyle murder. Wallace never responded.

On December 22nd, Governor Wallace placed a notice in the *Las Vegas Daily Gazette* saying, "Billy the Kid: $500 Reward."

Lew Wallace would repeat that reward notice in the *Daily New Mexican* on May 3, 1881, after Billy's jailbreak. Wallace's betrayal of the implied pardon deal was complete.

Dreadful days were about to begin for Billy, unaware that Pat Garrett had assembled posses to ride after him, using mostly Texans, since New Mexicans refused.

The first Garrett ambush was on December 19, 1880, when Billy, Tom O'Folliard, Charlie Bowdre, Billy Wilson, Tom Pickett, and Dave Rudabaugh rode into Fort Sumner on its snowy night. O'Folliard was shot dead by Garrett. The rest escaped.

Billy and the others, trying to flee the Territory in another massive snowstorm, stopped, on December 21, 1880, at a shepherds', rock-walled, line cabin at Stinking Springs. There Garrett ambushed them the next morning, killing Bowdre, mistaken for Billy by wearing his sombrero. The rest surrendered.

Stinking Springs was Pat Garrett's greatest moment - before slaying Billy seven months later.

Garrett transported his prisoners by train, via Las Vegas, New Mexico, to the Santa Fe jail. Billy remained in the Santa Fe jail from December 27, 1880 to March 28, 1881, awaiting completion of the railroad to Mesilla - so fearful was the Ring of his rescue by partisans - a measure of Billy's following as a freedom fighter.

In fact, Billy nearly escaped the Santa Fe jail by an intercepted tunneling out with fellow prisoners.

And from his cell, Billy wrote four unanswered letters to Governor Lew Wallace, pleading and cajoling for his pardon; on March 4, 1881, saying, "I have done everything that I promised you I would, and you have done nothing that you promised me."

Billy's Mesilla murder trial, under Ringman judge, Warren Bristol, began on March 30, 1881. That changed venue from Lincoln County guaranteed jurors unaware of the War's issues.

Billy was represented by Attorney Ira Leonard for Case Number 411, the United States versus Charles Bowdre, Josiah Scurlock, Henry Brown, William Bonney alias Henry Antrim alias the Kid, John Middleton, Frederick Waite, Jim French, and George Coe for the murder of Andrew Roberts.

Surprising everyone, Ira Leonard got that indictment quashed based on a technicality that the federal government, listed as the plaintiff, had no jurisdiction over Blazer's Mill, the murder site; since private property, like it, was under *Territorial jurisdiction*. The fact that the property was surrounded by the federally controlled Mescalaro Reservation was irrelevant. The argument was correct. Judge Bristol was forced to quash to indictment.

It seemed possible that Billy could win. Left only were the Brady and Hindman indictments; and, not only had Billy been firing in a group, he had only a revolver, arguably lacking accurate range. But, suddenly, Ira Leonard withdrew, possibly after a Ring threat. That was a disastrous set-back for Billy.

Billy received a court appointed attorney, Albert Jennings Fountain, who, though not a Ringman, considered Billy an outlaw.

On April 8th and 9th of 1881, was Billy's Brady murder trial. His Spanish-speaking jury, given no translator, heard only prosecution witnesses - including James Dolan. After Judge Bristol's instructions (with translator) required Billy's mere presence to be the same as killing, the jury found Billy guilty of first degree murder; its sole punishment being hanging. On April 13th, triumphant Judge Bristol set Billy's hanging date for May 13th, insuring insufficient time for an appeal. And Billy was to be hanged in Lincoln town by its Sheriff, Pat Garrett.

Ironically, the new Lincoln jail, where Billy was incarcerated under Garrett to await hanging, was in the past House. James Dolan, cleared of his Huston Chapman murder indictment by October of 1880 by Judge Bristol, had repositioned himself financially, first mortgaging "the House" to Thomas Benton Catron, then buying the vacated Tunstall store for himself. Catron, in turn, had sold the building to Lincoln County; which converted it into the new courthouse with a second floor jail.

On April 21, 1881, Billy arrived to Sheriff Garrett's custody. For Billy's 24 hour guard, Garrett had deputized a White Oaks man, James Bell, and a Seven Rivers man, Robert Olinger. Garrett's further precaution against escape was shackling Billy at wrists and ankles, and securing him to a ring in the plank floor - all to guarantee Billy's hanging death.

But on April 27th, Garrett left for three days to collect White Oaks's taxes. On April 28th, Billy escaped. An unknown accomplice either left Billy a revolver in the outdoor privy, or Billy wrested away Deputy James Bell's revolver while being guarded.

Likely for providing an outhouse gun was the building's caretaker: Gottfried Gauss. Gauss had been John Tunstall's loyal cook and was present when Tunstall and his men rode from the ranch to their murderous ambush three years earlier.

So, with a revolver, Billy shot Deputy James Bell as the man fled down the jail's stairway. That weapon was never found.

Deputy Robert Olinger, across the street at the Wortley Hotel, taking lunch with other jail prisoners, either heard the shot, or was told. Olinger ran back. Billy awaited him at the second-floor jail's eastward-facing window, and shot him with his own Whitney double-barrel shotgun.

Billy then broke his leg chain with a miner's pick. Taking more weapons from the building's armory, he escaped on a stolen pony.

**As of that April 28, 1881, Billy had been involved in the murder of nine men, James Bell and Robert Olinger adding to Frank "Windy" Cahill and Joe Grant as Billy's only provable killings. Of the dead, Billy would have said he was a posseman at the deaths of William "Buck" Morton**

and Frank Baker, would have denied shooting at Andrew "Buckshot" Roberts, would have called Cahill and Grant self-defense, and would have seen Deputy Bell's death as necessary to save himself from unjust hanging.

Only Ring-partisan Robert Olinger, hated as present in each confrontation - from the Tunstall murder posse to the Frank MacNab ambush murder, to the war in Lincoln - would have been killed purposefully. Billy's rage was so great, that after the shooting, he smashed apart Olinger's shotgun to throw it down on him, delaying his own escape.

That count of nine killed men - with only four certain - remained as Billy's final tally.

Billy's escape route was across the east to west, Capitan Mountains, en route to the Las Tablas home of his friend, Yginio Salazar. From there, he returned to Fort Sumner and Paulita, where he hid in the Maxwell's outlying sheep camps.

Though speculation, the elopement of Billy and Paulita was possible. Paulita's oldest sister, Virginia, had chosen that option in Cimarron, leaving for New York with the local Indian Agent, Captain A.S.B. Keyes, in 1870, the year their father sold the Maxwell Land Grant.

By July 14, 1881, though he was unaware, Billy had traitors among Fort Sumner's trusted townspeople. Barney Mason, Garrett's friend and Secret Service Operative Azariah Wild's informant - though no longer Peter Maxwell's foreman - still had spies, evidenced by Mason's claiming that Billy was in the town.

Garrett's two deputies for the pursuit to Fort Sumner, John William Poe and Thomas "Kip" McKinney, did not know Billy. Poe, a buffalo hunter, a past Deputy U.S. Marshall in Texas, a cattle detective, and a recent White Oaks settler, had met Garrett during the Azariah Wild-assisted, tracking of the "Kid gang." McKinney knew Garrett from their 1878, hog farming days.

Once in Fort Sumner, Garrett was pessimistic about Billy's presence. Poe urged staying and, as a stranger, did recognizance in town on July 14, 1881, while Garrett and McKinney stayed hidden a few miles away. Poe also checked, seven miles to the north, with the Sunnyside postmaster, Milnor Rudolph.

That night of July 14th, when Poe joined Garrett and McKinney, he was convinced that Billy was near; and the ambush was planned for Peter Maxwell's bedroom. While Poe and McKinney went to the vicinity of the Maxwell mansion, Garrett checked the peach orchard. There he saw distant shadowed figures - possibly Billy with Paulita - before he went to Maxwell's bedroom to await Billy's arrival. Poe and McKinney remained outside, presumably to prevent Billy's escape.

Near midnight, Billy exited the converted barracks house of Celsa and Saval Gutierrez, carrying their butcher knife to cut his dinner steak, and wearing only sox. He crossed Fort Sumner's 300 yard, square, parade ground, with buildings as its perimeter.

The almost full moon was special. Rising southeast at about 10 PM, it never rose high that night, and only skimmed the horizon in gigantic moon illusion while mimicking daylight.

Approaching the mansion, occupying much of the parade ground's west side, Billy went first to Maxwell's curtained darkened bedroom, a task likely assigned to Billy by an additional, and never revealed, Fort Sumner traitor.

Peter Maxwell was in bed as a decoy. Beside the bed, Pat Garrett waited with his blued, Colt .44, single action revolver, with a 7½ inch barrel and serial number 55093.

Though strangers in town would have been common, Billy, as the most hunted man in the country, reacted with caution to John William Poe on the mansion's south porch, drawing his revolver and asking in Spanish - presumably as a disguise - who he was. Poe guessed Billy was merely a Maxwell worker or guest.

Then Billy entered Peter Maxwell's purposefully darkened bedroom (or the moonlight would have revealed Garrett).

But almost immediately, sensing someone in shadows, Billy asked, in Spanish, who it was. Garrett recognized his voice.

In seconds, Poe, McKinney, and townspeople heard Garrett's shot. Garrett then fired another wild. But Billy was already dead.

As Peter Maxwell ran out to the porch, Poe, thinking Maxwell was Billy escaping, almost shot him. Then Garrett exited.

Uncertainty that Billy was dead, made Peter Maxwell send in family servant, Deluvina with a candle. She would have been the first to see the deceased boy, 21 years old. Then Garrett checked.

Townspeople were permitted to take Billy's body across the parade ground to the town's carpenter's shop for a candlelit vigil. Billy was laid out on its sheet-covered workbench.

In the morning of July 15th, the Coroner's Jury of six men met. Their foreman was Sunnyside postmaster Milnor Rudolph. Rudolph, a Ringman politician and father of Charlie Rudolph, who had ridden on one of Garrett's pre-Stinking Springs posses, was no backer of Billy. The jurymen identified the body as Billy's; interviewed the  eye-witness, Peter Maxwell; and declared the killing by Pat Garrett to be justifiable homicide. The case was, thus, legally closed.

Billy was buried in the northwest corner of the Maxwell family's cemetery, beside Charlie Bowdre and Tom O'Folliard. One gravedigger was Billy's local friend, Paco Anaya; who later wrote a memoir: *I Buried Billy.*

Modern old-timers and old photographs confirm Billy's gravesite as a weed-strewn plot, not at the current, more central location in the cemetery's half acre.

That memorial for tourists, dating to the 1930's, is now protected against souvenir-seekers by covering of red-brown concrete (with three mounds - for Billy, and his murdered friends), inside a protective barred cage; within which is a big granite headstone, proclaiming "Pals" and their names. A small foot-stone, at Billy's place, declares that he killed a man for each of his 21 years. Mythology was, thus, Billy's marker.

By 1882, a year after killing Billy, Pat Garrett sought fame and fortune by his book, *The Authentic Life of Billy the Kid*, ghostwritten by his Roswell boarder, journalist "Ash" Upson. Though its sales were disappointing, Garrett got a life of acclaim for killing Billy. He died in 1908, shot in ambush by his goat herder, tenant, Wayne Brazel, (declared innocent by a jury); or by political intriguers unrelated to his killing of Billy Bonney.

By 1937, Garrett's *Authentic Life of Billy the Kid* was reprinted because of "Billy the Kid's" expanding fame, as glory-seekers and profit-seekers emerged with sufficient "Billy firearms" for an arsenal, enough Garrett possemen for an army, and even nubile relatives claiming motherhood of Billy's alleged children.

The Maxwell family lost ownership of Fort Sumner by 1884 in a continued downward economic slide. But 45 years after Billy's death, one local Maxwell descendant claimed to have Billy's corpse's carpenter's bench for a little museum she created to profit from first waves of Billy the Kid tourists and historians.

And Billy was sighted alive for years after his demise - as he had been seen sighted around America, when really in Fort Sumner after his great escape. When early movies added to Billy's fame, crazy, 20th century, old-timers called themselves him.

Billy's mother, Catherine Antrim, also rode his popularity in the mid-1900's. Two hundred sixty miles southwest of Billy's Fort Sumner grave, in Silver City's Memory Lane Cemetery, her granite gravestone was arbitrarily placed for tourists, in 1947 - seventy-three years after her demise, and in that cemetery's new section! Catherine Antrim had first and truly been buried, in September of 1874, in a downtown, Silver City cemetery. But that cemetery was purchased in 1881 by a wealthy local to build his residence. He agreed to rebury all remains outside the town. But there was no scrutiny. And Catherine Antrim's bones may have been gone by then, since her cemetery's land had been subject to extreme flooding for years. Rumor is that Catherine Antrim's marker was once at Memory Lane's entrance - in the old section. That makes three graves, all impossible to verify, for Billy Bonney's mother.

# UPSHOT OF SHOT BILLY

New Mexico has demonstrated a bad record of maintaining or keeping track of its Billy the Kid and Catherine Antrim graves.

But the Billy the Kid Case hoaxers' first hoaxing was to declare as certain the gravesites of Billy and his mother. They had to. They were after any bones they could get their hands on; but those bones needed to seem like Billy the Kid's and his mother's.

# CHAPTER 4:

# LAUNCHING THE BILLY THE KID CASE HOAX

"All the News That's Fit to Print"

# The New York Times

New England Final
Benson: Early fog and mostly cloudy, high 63. Tonight, lingering clouds and drier, low 57. Tomorrow, turning brighter and milder in most places, high 72. Weather map is on Page A23.

VOL. CLII . . . No. 52,505    Copyright © 2003 The New York Times    THURSDAY, JUNE 5, 2003    ONE DOLLAR

## MEASURE BANNING ABORTION METHOD WINS HOUSE VOTE

## COMPANY'S PLEDGE TO ...

## ...ESTINIANS SAY ...E FIRST STEPS ...IDEAST PEACE

PRESIDENT ...

---

## State of New Mexico
### Office of the Governor

Bill Richardson
*Governor*

For immediate rel...
6/10/03

GOVER...

SANTA FE - G...
support the in...

Governor Bi...
State Capito...

This is a...
am ann...
investig...
Bonne...
captur...
nearer, Morto...
at the...
uniqu...

My...

I a...
M...
A...
...

---

## LINCOLN COUNTY SHERIFF'S DEPARTMENT
### Case #2003-274
### Probable Cause Statement

In the struggle dubbed the "Lincoln County War", investigators soon learned that nothing was as it seemed. As they poured through the volumes of information, documents, paperwork, reports, county records, books and examine newly discovered evidence, it became apparent no clear lines could be drawn as to who was working with or for whom. What first appeared to be clear quickly became clouded as new information was uncovered, it's diffic... ...be the "good guys" and the "bad guys" were. One would think that the ... ...epartment would be on the side of the law. However, it w... ...Deputies that shot and killed John Tunstall, in w... ...ize as an unprovoked murde...

Evidence shows ...
him (Tunstall) ...
Morton threw ...
nearer, Morto...
Tunstall thro...
law they wer...
War and inv...
facts and pr...

No one fr...
beyond s...
scen...
fact...
clea...

---

## Forensic Research & Training Center
### Forensic Examination Report

| | |
|---|---|
| Date of Request: | May 22, 2004 |
| Requested By: | Lincoln County Sheriff's Office, New Mexico |
| | Investigation History Program, Kurtis Production |
| Local Case No. | 2003-274 |
| Date of Report: | February 25, 2005 |
| Report to: | Steve Sederwell |
| | Lincoln County Sheriff's Office, New Mexico |

### Introduction

FOR YOUR INFORMATION.
THIS MUSEUM IS OWNED BY THE NIECE AND NEPHEW OF PETE MAXWELL—IT WAS IN THIS HOME WHERE BILLY THE KID WAS KILLED BY SHERIFF PAT GARRETT. WE WILL ASSURE AND NOT MISREPRESENT ANY ONE WHO IS INTERESTED IN THE SOUTH-WEST AND ITS NOTORIOUS OUTLAW BILLY THE KID. THERES NOT JUST ONE OR TWO ANTIQUES BUT SEVERAL THINGS OF INTEREST. DATED BACK 18-81 AND TERRITORIAL DAYS.

# THE SHIP OF FOOLS SETS SAIL

*HOAXBUST: The Billy the Kid Case hoax had spectacular promulgators: a governor, sheriffs, a forensic expert, a history professor, and attorneys. All brought in laudatory national press.*

## *THE BELL TOLLS FOR ME*

June 5, 2003 changed my life. The day began happily, because the first draft of my docufiction novel on Billy Bonney, was completed. Then the bell tolled for me. It was a fax ring. The Billy the Kid Case hoax had officially begun.

From a back east friend, aware that I was interested in Billy the Kid, came a *New York Times* front page blaring, "122 Years Later, The Lawmen Are Still Chasing Billy the Kid." [Appendix: 3] That news shared the front page with: "Israel and Palestinians Say They Will Take First Steps in Quest For Mideast Peace," and "Martha Stewart Indicted by U.S. On Obstruction."

The article's writer, Michael Janofsky, reporting from New Mexico, announced that Sheriff Pat Garrett had *not shot* Billy the Kid! Janofsky was parroting Governor Bill Richardson's own press release for the Lincoln County Sheriff's Department case, which he identified as No. 2003-274 [Appendix: 4]: his starting self-promotion for his 2008 presidential bid. The public got this:

> LINCOLN, N.M. – For more than 120 years, Pat Garrett has enjoyed legendary status in the American West, a lawman on a par with Wyatt Earp, Bat Masterson, even Matt Dillon. As sheriff here in Lincoln County in 1881, Garrett is credited with shooting to death the notorious outlaw known as Billy the Kid, a killing that made Garrett a hero .... But now, modern science is about to interrupt Garrett's fame in a way that some would say could expose him as a liar who covered up a murder to save his own skin and reputation.

Officials in New Mexico and Texas are working out plans to exhume and conduct genetic tests on the bodies of a woman buried in New Mexico who was believed to be the Kid's mother and a Texas man known as Brushy Bill Roberts, who claimed to be the Kid and died in 1950 at the age of 90. If test results suggest that the two were related, it would add new evidence to a long-held alternative theory that Garrett shot someone other than the Kid and led a conspiracy to cover up his crime ...

Beyond renewing interest in the Kid saga, the possibility that testing could enlarge Garrett's reputation or destroy it has even caught the fancy of Gov. Bill Richardson of New Mexico, who has offered state aid for the investigation and a possible pardon that an earlier New Mexico governor had once promised to the Kid for a murder he committed.

"The problem is, there's so much fairy tale with this story that it's hard to nail down the facts," said Steve Sederwall, Mayor of Capitan, N.M., who is working with Lincoln County's current sheriff, Tom Sullivan, to resolve the matter. "All we want is the truth."

From a Pat Garrett great-nephew was granted only a token: Garrett was "a law abider, not a law breaker."

Jannay Valdez, owner of "The Billy the Kid Museum" of Canton, Texas - *his* museum for pretender, "Brushy Bill" Roberts; and author of a 1995 book, *Billy the Kid: "Killed" in New Mexico - Died in Texas*, countered: "I'm absolutely convinced that Garrett killed someone else and that Brushy Bill was the Kid."

That suspicion given, Capitan Mayor and Deputy Steve Sederwall introduced their scheme. They were opening a real murder case in the Lincoln County Sheriff's Department against Pat Garrett for killing an innocent victim to let Billy get away! Sederwall boasted that "a Dallas law firm was helping; and a Governor Richardson spokesman said the state would assist by clearing any legal hurdles to gain access to the mother's body."

Billy's mother's DNA would be compared with his grave's DNA to decide if a stranger lay there. Then there were pretenders to check and validate. With CSI glamour, the Janofsky article ended:

And even if tests disqualify Brushy Bill as the Kid, other "Kids" have emerged over the years, including a man named John Miller, who died in 1937 and is buried in Prescott Ariz. Mr. Sederwall said efforts would be made to exhume his body as well. The investigators conceded that much is riding on their quest. Sheriff Sullivan, a tall, strapping man who carries a turquoise-handled .357 magnum on his right hip, said he, like so many others in the West, revered Garrett for gunning down the Kid. The uniform patch with Garrett's likeness was his design. Now the legend is threatened.

"I just want to get to the bottom of it," said Sheriff Sullivan, who is retiring next year. "My integrity's at stake. So's my department's. So's what we believe in and even New Mexico history. If Garrett shot someone other than the Kid, that makes him a murderer and then he covered it up. He wouldn't be such a role model then, and we'd have to take the patches off the uniforms."

To quote cowboy slang, I knew the article "was as shy of the truth as a goat is of feathers." Janofsky had not bothered to contact any reputable historian. So Janofsky, having "scooped" the Billy the Kid Case - without realizing it was a con job - became its first dupe. Years later, I got the hoaxers' "Contact List" for their Case 2003-274. Michael Janofsky is listed under "Media."

I was shocked. How could they call Garrett a murderer when his killing of the Kid was so well documented? How could they talk about DNA from the Kid's and mother's graves when their uncertain locations were just tourist markers? Why was long-discredited pretender "Brushy Bill" Roberts given any credence? And what did any Garrett "murder investigation" have to do with Governor Richardson pardoning Billy the Kid posthumously? And who were those other people: Richardson's fellow hoaxers?

## LAYING THE HOAX FOUNDATION

The hoaxers had been excitedly preparing for the world stage. Lincoln County Deputy and Mayor Steve Sederwall, who would emerge as the hoaxers' most glib promoter, pre-empted Michael Janofsky's *New York Times* announcement by a month. To locals, Sederwall's nick-name - behind his back - was "snake;" and he was seen as a con-artist. In his May 2003 Capitan "Mayor's Report" [Appendix: 5], a chatty taxpayer-funded creation he enclosed with his constituents' monthly water bills, he had boasted about opening the Garrett investigation with Sheriff Sullivan, claiming no statute of limitations for a murder case.

Sederwall knew the ambitious plans. He wrote that the DNA matchings would be done by the lab used for World Trade Center remains; also a TV program was in the works. And he added the first hoax mantra: "It is a crazy idea but won't it be fun." And Sederwall's "Mayor's Report" focused on "Brushy Bill":

This investigation came about after Sheriff Sullivan and I talked about a man by the name of Brushy Bill Roberts. In 1950 Roberts came to the Governor of New Mexico with his attorney; saying he was Billy the Kid. He said that Pat Garrett shot a man by the name of Billy Barlow and buried his body claiming to be that of Billy the Kid. Roberts said he lived out a life within the bounds of the law under an assumed name and wanted a pardon that was promised to him by Governor Wallace.

On the surface of this story you would say "so what?" But if you look at this man's claim he is saying our Sheriff Pat Garrett is a murderer. Garrett knew the Kid and killed someone else. What this says also is that Pete Maxwell who said the body is of The Kid is a co-conspirator in a murder. There is no statute of limitations on Murder, so the Lincoln County Sheriff''s Office has opened a case to pursue the investigation. If Brushy Bill Roberts is Billy the Kid then history changes.

Tom Sullivan, the Lincoln County Sheriff who deputized Sederwall, was considered by locals as a lazy poseur, who brandished his turquoise-gripped revolver and had not solved a murder in his multiple terms as sheriff - giving rise to their joke: "If you want to commit murder, come to Lincoln County." In fact, Sullivan had declared a beaten corpse in a dumpster, "a suicide."

On April 30, 2003, Sullivan, on departmental letterhead, wrote to Charles Ryan, Director of the Arizona Department of Corrections. Sullivan was setting the stage for exhumations in Arizona (John Miller) and Texas ("Brushy Bill"). Sullivan wrote:

On April 28th, 2003, I, along with Deputy Steve Sederwall, pulled case 2003-278 [sic- 274] in the investigation of the murder of the two law officers that Bonney killed in his escape. Our investigation shall look at, among other things, where William H. Bonney was buried. If Bonney is buried anywhere other than Fort Sumner, and either Miller or Roberts turns out to be William H. Bonney, history changes, and Sheriff Pat Garrett committed a murder . Our investigation has led us out of our county and into other New Mexico counties, as well as Texas and Arizona."

On June 11, 2003, Richardson's mouthpiece, the *Albuquerque Journal*, joined in with front page, "State Not Kidding Around: Governor won't mind if probe of the notorious 19th century N.M. outlaw boosts tourism." [APPENDIX: 6] It reflected Richardson's

"Implied Rule": "The public are suckers," since it touted tourism benefits in a case designed to destroy that history and its sites by destroying their credibility - for no reason.

According to the reporter, Anthony DellaFlora, Richardson's press conference with Lincoln County Sheriff Tom Sullivan and his deputy, Steve Sederwall, had occurred in Richardson's capitol building's Cabinet room. And Richardson was "throwing the weight of the state behind an investigation."

Theatrically, next to a blow-up photo of Billy, were the two lawmen in Old West garb. "Around the world" would be publicity, the Governor said. He said he was separating "fact from fantasy" in addressing whether Garrett shot the right man, or had been complicit in The Kid's escape "as some history buffs have alleged."

Those alleged "history buffs," happened to be right in that Cabinet room. With lawmen, Sullivan and Sederwall, also sat Richardson's appointed, state salaried, "official" historian and lackey: Professor Paul Hutton of the University of New Mexico.

DellaFlora did not mention that an attorney from Silver City was there too. Her hoax role would emerge in four months.

Taxpayer costs were called "minimal." Actually, taxpayers would be bled. Richardson claimed police would supervise ... "crime scene analysis." What crime scene? The Maxwell house in Fort Sumner, where Billy was shot, had been torn down in 1887. And DellaFlora quoted Richardson that "Los Alamos ... would volunteer ... ground penetrating radar to locate remains."

As may be recalled, Richardson "has a thing" with Los Alamos (like framing its scientist Wen Ho Lee). And under Richardson's governorship, security there was like a sieve. The facility's board members were allegedly e-mailing classified information about the composition of America's nuclear arsenal, according to a June 25, 2007 newsweek.com article by a John Barry titled "Lax and Lazy at Los Alamos." And break-ins and computer theft there became so common, that spies must have quit for lack of challenge, as indicated by a Joan Lowy in a *Newsweek* Internet article titled "69 computers missing from nuclear weapons lab."

DellaFlora's article lastly re-introduced the non sequitor from the June 5, 2003 *New York Times* article: "Richardson said the investigation could result in the pardon of Billy the Kid."

That *New York Times* article had also mentioned that a "Dallas" law firm was helping. A partner in that mega-rich firm would emerge as a key to cracking the Billy the Kid Case hoax - and the firm was in Houston, with branches in New Mexico.

# THE BILLY THE KID CASE HOAX

*HOAXBUST: The genius of the Billy the Kid Case was to file its hoaxed contention - Pat Garrett did not kill Billy the Kid - as a real Lincoln County Sheriff's Department murder investigation against Garrett for killing an innocent victim. That got taxpayers to foot the bills; and got law enforcement's privilege to exhume bodies for forensic DNA - starting with the Kid and his mother. After that, it would be clear sailing: fake a new Kid history backed by faked DNA results; then do an "exhumation industry" with pretenders - or become an "historian" President named Richardson. Lacking any real evidence, smoke and mirrors was the hoaxers' only m.o.*

## *HOAXING HALLMARKS*

The Billy the Kid Case is willful deception. A hoax, according to thefreedictionary.com is: "1. An act intended to deceive or trick; 2. Something that has been established ... by fraudulent means."

Even its name, made up by its promulgators, was misleading. It was about Pat Garrett. Billy's fame brought the "media circus."

As a murder investigation, it could be filed by a sheriff; but it was also a fake investigation by having a dead suspect.

As a CSI forensic DNA investigation by exhumations, it lacked any verifiable DNA of Billy or his mother; and there was no crime scene. And later use of an old carpenter's bench was bogus.

As to claimants to the Kid's identity, their histories alone debunked them as pretenders; removing need for exhumations.

Also, the Billy the Kid Case crossed into criminality. Using a sheriff's department for it, was law enforcement fraud. And there were no legal justifications to exhume Billy and his mother. Later exhumations in Arizona were felonious, since DNA matching was intended; but the hoaxers had no Kid DNA for matching - and one body exhumed was of a random man. The hoaxers' hope had been to conceal all their improprieties by concealing all their records.

Probably the biggest mistake of the hoaxers was discounting that they did the Billy the Kid Case as public officials. So the warehouse worth of public records - like their Case 2003-274 file and their DNA documents - were subject to open records requests. They added to their paper trail by profuse newspaper articles; and they generated a movie and TV programs (one, never shown, even filmed their illegal Arizona exhumation).

So when I did years of open records requests, the hoaxers were left only with concealments, cover-ups, and then costly litigation.

Throughout, as a strange non sequitor, the hoaxers linked exhumation and pardon. My guess was double publicity: first an exhuming "media circus," then a pardon "media circus." I was wrong. And discovering the link would finally crack the hoax.

## HOAXER TRICKS

Lacking truth or proof, the hoaxers used hucksters' tricks of smoke and mirrors and lies; hoping no one noticed.

### COMPLEXITY

A good cover was that the hoax was confusing, being really four hoaxes in one: 1) **Legal** - filing a murder case against suspect Garrett; 2) **Historic** - claiming Garrett did not kill the Kid; 3) **Forensic** - alleging DNA matching to prove suspect Garrett's guilt; and 4) **Pretender-based** - using old-timer, Garrett shooting survival claims for substantiating Garrett's "innocent victim."

### "WHAT IF" ILLOGIC

Without any supporting evidence, the hoaxers were left with fabricating false suspicion and creating straw-man conclusions or fake ones. Suspicion was on the order of: "How do you know *for sure?*" It ignored all historical, legal, scientific, and logical evidence. But making things up, does not make them true.

Suspicion was followed by "what ifs." The "what if" statement was then used as if proven. I called it "alien invasion illogic;" as in: "What if aliens landed in Fort Sumner and by mind-control made 200 townspeople think they saw the body of Billy the Kid - but it was not him? Therefore, since it was not the Kid's body ..." Etc.

### USELESS HEARSAY

The few documents cited by the hoaxers are useless hearsay: statements by parties removed from events or obviously lying - the kind of information real historians dismiss. Thus, after-death sightings of Billy - anywhere in the country - were used as hoaxer "proof" that he was not killed. Omitted, was that Billy's *pre-death* sightings all over the country were as profuse after his jail escape (when he was alive and hiding-out in Fort Sumner)!

## CONFABULATION

Confabulation is a mental disorder yielding made-up stories. Not purposeful lying, it usually arises from mental illness or chronic alcoholism's brain damage. As defined by Harold Kaplan's and Benjamin Sadock's *Synopsis of Psychiatry*, it is "unconscious filling of gaps in memory by imagined or untrue experiences that a person believes but have no basis in fact."

Confabulation was used in the hoaxers' old-timer affidavits and pretenders' claims. Give-aways are over-embellished details mimicking real experience, though provably false and fantasized.

## RICOCHET VALIDATION

Since most of the hoaxers had official titles - and were not publicly known to be in cahoots - for newspapers and legal documents they would vouch for each other. More pernicious, was use of the same technique to denigrate or defame hoax opposition.

## SHAPE-SHIFTING AND SWITCHEROOS

Lack of conscience made the hoaxers, if cornered, shape-shift by lies. So, for example, to hide DNA records, they would say Case 2003-274 was not a Garrett murder investigation, but an investigation of the Kid's jail-break murders of his deputy guards. Or, having difficulty getting into the graves of Billy the Kid and his mother, they claimed to have found the bench on which the Kid was laid out - thus, blithely switching from "Kid not shot" to "Kid shot." And when finally subject to my open records act litigation, they all shape-shifted from "we're cops" to we were "amateur historian hobbyists" generating private records.

## LYING AND CRIMINALITY

Obviously, when all else failed, and with participants being sociopaths, lying was a frequent option. After all, the entire Billy the Kid Case is just lies. And the judges for the New Mexico exhumations were beholden, recent Richardson appointees making preposterous rulings to get them done. And finally, when legally cornered by my litigation, the hoaxers tampered evidence, lied under oath, drained taxpayer coffers up to a potential million dollars, and attempted to influence my own attorneys. And their creative whine for the press was that their murder case against Pat Garrett had been done "to protect his reputation."

# FAKING LAW IN THE BILLY THE KID CASE

*HOAXBUST: The Probable Cause Statement for Case # 2003-274, justification for the Billy the Kid Case and murder accusation of Pat Garrett, is a brilliant fake, with misstated history and illogic, providing no evidence at all that Garrett did not kill Billy. It is presented below, in entirely, with interpolated debunking (with its footnotes placed in the text instead of at page bottoms like in the original; and the original's italics maintained).*

The Billy the Kid Case hoax rested on one legal document to support its claims and exhumations: "Lincoln County Sheriff's Department Case # 2003-274 Probable Cause Statement." It cemented the hoax as a real criminal investigation, and Pat Garrett as its criminal suspect. And, though making no sense and containing no evidence, it appeared scholarly and official. It was the Billy the Kid Case's crown jewel. Its counterpart was filed in the De Baca County Sheriff's Department as Case # 03-06-136-01 for access to that county's Billy the Kid grave.

A probable cause statement in a murder investigation is crucial, since it justifies law enforcement's conduct of a case by: 1) establishing with probability that the alleged crime occurred; and 2) the reasons - probable cause - to accuse the suspect.

As can be imagined, the hoaxers did not want it seen by outsiders. So they refused my open records requests for it by claiming an exception for ongoing criminal investigations.

That statute's Section 14-2-1, Subparagraph A(4) blocks public access to "records that reveal confidential sources, methods, information or individuals accused but not charged with a crime." The real-world purpose of that exception is to prevent escape of suspects or destruction of evidence. With Pat Garrett dead since 1908, and his alleged "crime scene" in the Maxwell mansion long gone - to say nothing of lacking a murder at all - the hoaxers were just hoaxing an excuse to hide the document. But I was stymied.

There was, however, hope. The hoaxers soon filed that "Probable Cause Statement" as their "Plaintiffs' Exhibits 1 and 2" in a brief, dated January 5, 2004, for their Silver City petition to exhume Billy the Kid's mother. It was then publicly available; so I got it. And it came with a bonus: an affidavit to then-Sheriff Tom Sullivan by a confabulating old-timer named Homer Overton.

The Probable Cause Statement should be required reading for conartists. Dense as concrete, it was camouflaged as historical research; replete with obscure footnotes, and abstruse archival, historical information that no one was expected to have (but I did).

Entirely hoaxing, it used misinformation, sly innuendo, lies, and gullible trust in law enforcement and forensics. And it is a poster child for "alien invasion illogic" of "what ifs." Filed on December 31, 2003, it was signed by then-Sheriff of Lincoln County, Tom Sullivan, and by Steve Sederwall, as his Deputy Sheriff. And its Overton Affidavit was dated September 22, 2003.

Dissecting the "Probable Cause Statement's" tangled double-talk, reveals no probable cause at all to doubt that Pat Garrett's victim on July 14, 1881 was Billy Bonney.

Historical experts Frederick Nolan, Robert Utley, and Leon Metz, with whom I discussed it, agreed. Frederick Nolan said it was so enragingly duplicitous, that he could not read it sitting down, but had to pace.

## *DISSECTING THE PROBABLE CAUSE STATEMENT*

### MURDER INVESTIGATION

The "Probable Cause Statement for Case # 2003-274" claims to establish Pat Garrett as a murder suspect. It has eleven pages of single-spaced footnoted text, combining double-talk with mock erudition. Lacking any real evidence, and with constant misinformation, it groundlessly concludes that Garrett was likely a murderer of someone other than Billy the Kid; thus, justifying a murder case against him as the killer of an innocent victim who died by his hand on July 14, 1881. Garrett's crime would be proven by DNA comparisons of remains of Billy the Kid's mother, Catherine Antrim, and of Billy the Kid (to determine if Billy, or Garrett's unknown victim, lay in his grave).

An additional two pages were the Overton Affidavit, addressed to Sheriff Sullivan, swearing that Pat Garrett had not shot the Kid; but crumbling under confabulation and contradictory dates.

The upshot is that the Probable Cause Statement presents no reason to assume that Garrett did not kill the Kid. But its audacity and labor in production take one's breath away. One can guess that expecting no opposition, the hoaxers had written it for their complicit judges who were expected to rubber-stamp their exhumations, but might want backing to bearing scrutiny.

## SUB-INVESTIGATION

A sub-investigation in the Probable Cause Statement is the Kid's jailbreak murder of his deputy guards, James Bell and Robert Olinger. Its purpose is to fabricate a murder motive for Garrett - since there is none. Used is "alien invasion illogic": *If* Garrett gave Billy the revolver used for the jailbreak, he and Billy *might* have been friends. And *if* they were friends, Garrett *might* again have helped Billy escape in Fort Sumner by killing an innocent victim.

Of course, there is no evidence for the "ifs." And there exists no historical friendship between Garrett and Billy the Kid. Also, no evidence is provided in the sub-investigation, except old-timers' useless hearsay tales of post-death sightings. Also, no escape "weapon" was ever substantiated; Garrett has never been linked to the jailbreak escape, being out-of-town at the time; and Garrett had no motive to assist that jailbreak.

Subsequently, however, this sub-investigation was called the *total* Case 2003-274 by the hoaxers to hide their criticized accusation of Garrett, or to hide their acquisition of DNA for that murder investigation. That switcheroo required "Richardson's Implied Rule" that the public are suckers, since it removed any reason to dig up Billy and his mother - or anyone else - to "solve" those "deputy killings." Nevertheless, the sub-investigation had its own fake CSI forensics; and a one-time firing of a gun.

## UNDERLYING MYSTERIES

Authorship of the Probable Cause Statement was later claimed, under oath, by Steve Sederwall. But the mystery thickens with likely contributions by his fellow hoaxer, U.S. Marshals Service Historian David Turk, who also contributed to it his pamphlet titled "U.S. Marshals Service and Billy the Kid." Also, in 2008, I discovered the Probable Cause Statement's unsigned progenitor, titled: "Lincoln County Sheriff's Office, Lincoln County New Mexico, Case: William H. Bonney, a.k.a. William Antrim, a.k.a. The Kid, a.k.a. Billy the Kid: An Investigation into the events of April 28, 1881 through July 14, 1881 - seventy-seven days of doubt." The latter would ultimately help to crack the Billy the Kid Case hoax. And its author may have been not only a contributor, but the case's mastermind.

\* \* \* \* \* \* \*

# LINCOLN COUNTY SHERIFF'S DEPARTMENT
## CASE # 2003-274
## Probable Cause Statement

In the struggle dubbed the "Lincoln County War" investigators

[AUTHOR'S COMMENT: Taken to mean the Probable Cause Statement's signers: Tom Sullivan and Steve Sederwall.]

soon learned that nothing was as seemed.

[AUTHOR'S COMMENT: This is "alien invasion illogic suspicion."]

As they poured through the volumes of information, documents, paperwork, reports, county records, books and examined newly discovered evidence, it became apparent no clear lines could be drawn as to who was working with or for whom. What first appeared to be clear quickly became clouded as new information was uncovered,

[AUTHOR'S COMMENT: More "alien invasion illogic" with unsubstantiated and irrelevant "suspicion." And the "newly discovered evidence" is never presented.]

it's difficult to judge who the "good guys" and the "bad guys" were. One would think that the Lincoln County Sheriff's Department would be on the side of the law. However, it was a duly sworn posse of Lincoln County Deputies that shot and killed John Tunstall, in what investigators in clean conscience can only cauterize [sic] as an unprovoked murder.

[AUTHOR'S COMMENT: Tunstall's murder is irrelevant. It occurred when William Brady was Sheriff of Lincoln County; and was 3½ years before Garrett killed the Kid. And this feigned "research" is used for "alien invasion illogic suspicion." But Brady's dishonesty is irrelevant to Garrett as a murderer.]

Evidence shows that posse-men, Hill and Morton

[AUTHOR'S COMMENT: Error: Tom Hill was not Brady's official posseman; he was in Jessie Evans's criminal gang. Brady, in writing, swore he used no known outlaws on that posse.]

committed murder when *"Hill called to him* (Tunstall) *to come up and that he would not be hurt; at the same time both Hill and Morton threw up their guns, resting their stocks on their knees; that after Tunstall came nearer, Morton fired and shot Tunstall through the breast, and then Hill fired and shot Tunstall through the head ..."* [1]([1]Deposition of Albert Howe, Angel Report) Although these deputies were acting under the color off the law they were not acting within the law. This behavior permeates the Lincoln County War and investigators will not make judgments on that behavior but rather uncover the facts and present the facts without varnish.

[AUTHOR'S COMMENT: Repeating that lawman are not always honest, is irrelevant to proving Garrett a murderer.]

No one from the Governor to the District Attorney to the Sheriff of Lincoln County is beyond suspicion of deception and covering up the true facts in this case.

[AUTHOR'S COMMENT: Again, "alien invasion illogic suspiciousness" is irrelevant to Garrett.]

This can be seen in a number of examples. In a letter to Riley and Dolan of the Murphy-Dolan faction from District Attorney W. L. Rynerson of the 3rd Judicial District, the attorney clearly demonstrates he himself plays a part in the hostile actions when he writes, *"Shake that McSween outfit up until it shells out and squares up and then shake it out of Lincoln. I will aid to punish the scoundrels all I can."*[2] ([2]Rynerson letter to Riley and Dolan, Feb. 7, 1878, University of Arizona Special Collection)

[AUTHOR'S COMMENT: Error: The letter is dated February 14, 1878; and it is irrelevant to Garrett.]

When investigators began to look at the murder of Deputy Sheriff J.W. Bell and Deputy Robert Olinger on April 28, 1881, it was found that much of the information we now know as "history" came from Pat F. Garrett's book, "The Authentic Life of Billy the Kid" published in 1882.

[AUTHOR'S COMMENT: Error: Bell/Olinger murder information was not from Garrett, who was away at White Oaks; but was from eyewitness, Gottfried Gauss, the building's caretaker, and from the jail's Tularosa Ditch War prisoners.]

Investigators learned that much of this history is flawed for the reason historian Robert Utley writes: *"Although not many copies of the Authentic Life were sold, it nevertheless had a decisive impact on the Kid's image. More than any other single influence, the Garrett-Upson book fed the legend of Billy the Kid. As the legend blossomed, writers turned to the Authentic Life for details. Ash Upson's fictions became implanted in hundreds of " histories" that followed. For more than a century, only a few students thought to question the wild fantasies that flowed from Ash's imagination. In the evolution of the Kid's image, the Authentic Life is a book of enormous consequence."*[3] ([3]Robert M. Utley. Billy the Kid a short and violent life. University of Nebraska Press, 1989.)

[AUTHOR'S COMMENT: Utley is merely describing evolution of the Billy the Kid legend. And Garrett's ghostwritten book, though in dime novel style, states his shooting of Billy. True historical research was done by Robert Mullin, Walter Noble Burns, and Maurice Garland Fulton in the 1920's, and later by Frederick Nolan, Leon Metz, and Robert Utley himself. They all confirm that Garrett fatally shot Billy the Kid.]

On March 23, 1879, Governor Lew Wallace met with William Bonney (Kid) in Lincoln.

[AUTHOR'S COMMENT: Error: Meeting was on March 17, 1879]

In this meeting it is demonstrated that Wallace convinced the Kid that it would be to his advantage to work for the government.

[AUTHOR'S COMMENT: False. Billy proposed to Wallace, by a letter of about March 13, 1879, to give eye-witness court testimony against the murderers of Huston Chapman in exchange for Wallace's annulling his Lincoln County War indictments. The hoaxers, however, are setting up their straw man argument below.]

The Kid becomes, what would be referred to in today's terminology as a "Confidential Informant." In Governor Wallace's hand we read "Statements made by Kid, Made Sunday night March 23, 1879."[4] ([4]Statements by Kid, Lew Wallace Collection, Indiana Historical Society Library) It was through this meeting Wallace devised a plan and attempted to deceive when he and the Kid entered into an agreement where by the Kid would appear to have been arrested.

[AUTHOR'S COMMENT: Saying there was an attempt "to deceive" is a misleading switcheroo. The hoaxers have admitted to Billy's confidential informant status. The arrest plan was devised by both Wallace and Billy to prevent Billy's being killed before his giving grand jury testimony against Chapman's murderers: James Dolan and Billy Campbell. The hoaxers, however, are still pumping the irrelevant claim that everyone was deceptive. Of course, that claim is irrelevant to their Garrett as murderer contention.]

The Kid later talks of this and says he was allowed to wear his guns and he left when he wanted to leave.

David S. Turk, Historian for the United States Marshals Service has discovered other such deceptions in his study of official records.

[AUTHOR'S COMMENT: Referring to "other such deceptions" is a hoaxer "what if" technique: Falsehoods are given and later used as a "proven facts" to build more falsehoods. Turk's "other deceptions" are never given. And Turk, as an active hoaxer, is presented later in this book.]

It is commonly believed

[AUTHOR'S COMMENT: Misstatement: It is a known historic fact, confirmed by Garrett's possemen and the Maxwell family.]

that Lincoln County Sheriff Pat F. Garrett arrested the Kid in December of 1880 in Stinking Springs near Fort Sumner. But the records show that Garrett was elected in November of 1880 and

did not take office until January of 1881.[5] ([5]Lincoln County Commissioners Records, November 8, 1880).

[AUTHOR'S COMMENT: So what?]

He went to Fort Sumner as a Deputy United States Marshall, but even that Commission and authority are now questioned.

[AUTHOR'S COMMENT: By whom? Garrett was made a U.S. Deputy Marshall in November or December of 1880 by Secret Service Operative Azariah Wild, sent to New Mexico Territory as a counterfeiting investigator for the U.S. Treasury Department. Wild appointed Garrett to capture Billy and his alleged counterfeiter gang. Wild believed that Lincoln County Sheriff, George Kimbrell, was partisan to Billy; and, with Garrett just elected as Sheriff on November 2, 1880, he would not have assumed duties until January 1, 1881 without Wild's intervention. Also, Wild's appointment of Garrett - fully accepted in his day, and reported to his Secret Service Chief James Brooks, - gave Garrett Territory-wide jurisdiction to arrest Billy when and where he actually did: San Miguel County's Stinking Springs. Also, this misinformation and sly innuendo is irrelevant to whether Garrett was a murderer. If anything, it proves that Operative Wild believed Garrett's fitness for a marshal's title.]

Secret Service Special Operative Azariah F. Wild of New Orleans writes in his daily logs *"I this day went to Lincoln to meet Capt. Lea & Garrett who are to organize the Posse Comatatus (sic) to make a raid on Fort Sumner to arrest counterfeiters."*[6] ([6]Report of Azariah F. Wild, November 11, 1880, Record Group 87, National Archives) Garrett shot and killed Charles Bowdre and Tom O'Folliard during the chase and arrested the Kid. Later, Secret Service Special Operative Azariah F. Wild writes to his superior and admits he was deceptive in his commission of Garrett. *"I will respectfully state that I applied to Marshall Sherman to appoint P.F. Garrett as a Deputy Marshall to which he paid no attention. I was in great need of Mr. Garrett*

**[AUTHOR'S COMMENT: Error: Quote reads "Mr. Garrett's <u>aid</u>."]**

*at that time and took one of the Commissions Sherman sent to John Hurley (he having sent two) and substituted P.F. Garrett the very man who has rendered the Government such a valuable service in killing and arresting these men who I was in pursuit."*[7] ([7]Report of Azariah F. Wild, January 4, 1881, Record Group 87, National Archives)

**[AUTHOR'S COMMENT: Error: Report is dated January 3, 1881. And though this paragraph is irrelevant to whether Garrett was a murderer, it implies, falsely, that Wild was deceptive. In fact, there was no deception. Wild was following proper procedure. One of only 40 Special Operatives in America, he was answerable only to Secret Service Chief, James Brooks. The Secret Service's powers were flexible, and extended beyond counterfeiting. In Billy's case, Wild's pursuit of him included alleged large-scale rustling. For that - as Wild reported to his Chief - he needed Garrett's services. Note also the mention of Charles Bowdre, killed by Garrett on December 22, 1880. Billy's gravesite is contiguous with Bowdre's. This mingled gravesite was later an issue in the hoaxers' exhumation attempts.]**

No one in 122 years has been able to speak with clear certainty where the gun came from that William Bonney used to kill Deputy J.W. Bell.

[AUTHOR'S COMMENT: Hold your hat for this whip-lash subject change. It starts the fake accusation of Garrett as Billy's accomplice in the jailbreak's deputy murders.]

With the information investigators have seen they question Garrett's involvement in the Kid obtaining a weapon.

[AUTHOR'S COMMENT: Why? You will not find out later, though it is needed to accuse Garrett of "involvement" in getting Billy the jailbreak "weapon." Instead, what follows is just "alien invasion illogic" to fake a "friendship" motive for Garrett's alleged "innocent victim" murder in Fort Sumner.]

It would go to reason that if the body in Fort Sumner is anyone other than William Bonney then Garrett no doubt had a hand in allowing the Kid to escape on July 14, 1881.

[AUTHOR'S COMMENT: Catch your breath here for the genius switcheroo. No legitimate historian says the body in Billy's grave is "anyone other than William Bonney." But the hoaxers need that for a murder claim; so they slip it in here – by "ifs" of "alien invasion illogic": "*If* the body in Fort Sumner is not Billy's, Garrett *might* have given the Kid a gun for an escape."]

If the body at Fort Sumner is anyone other than William Bonney, then Garrett, whether by accident or design, is responsible for homicide of the person resting in that grave.

[AUTHOR'S COMMENT: Another leap of "what ifs." But no credible source says the body is not Bonney's; and the hoaxers' double-talk provides nothing contrary.]

If it is not Bonney in the grave at Fort Sumner it would also go to reason that Garrett would be looked at as a suspect in furthering the escape of the Kid on April 28, 1881 when the two Lincoln County Sheriffs were murdered.

[AUTHOR'S COMMENT: Here is the switcheroo. Now the fake "if" is used as fact: "if it is not Bonney" – but not proven. THIS IS THE HOAXERS' FAKED PROBLE CAUSE FOR GARRETT AS A MURDERER: only "alien invasion illogic ifs" to fake a friendship motive: *If* Garrett gave Billy the escape gun, he was a friend. *If* he was a friend, he would later murder someone else to protect Billy again. But the giving of the gun and the friendship are just fabrications. No evidence been given; and none exists. And Pat and Billy were not friends.

[AUTHOR'S COMMENT: What follows next is built on the hoaxers' false claims that (1) they established Garrett's murder motive, and that (2) they established need to check Billy's grave for Garrett's unidentified "innocent victim."]

Although the investigation will deal with what happened in the Lincoln County court house on April 28, 1881, this writing will deal with the alleged shooting of William Bonney at Fort Sumner on the night of July 14, 1881.

[AUTHOR'S COMMENT: Do not let this fast-one slip by. The deputy murders "sub-investigation" at the courthouse consisted merely of: (1) firing a gun inside to test if it could be heard across the street; and (2) bringing in a forensic consultant (Dr. Henry Lee) whose finding of blood on the upstairs hallway floorboards was a hoaxer lie. Lying more, the hoaxers said the "blood" was Bell's. Olinger is left out. Also left out is that this "investigation" has nothing to do with the gun used to shoot Bell. And, even if it did, that would have nothing to do with whether Garrett gave it to Billy, or whether Garrett shot an innocent victim 2 ½ months later, making him a murderer. The "upstairs blood," though irrelevant, will be discussed later in this book, along with the rest of the fake forensic findings. Most important to note now, however, is that this "deputy murder investigation" was periodically shape-shifted as *the entire Billy the Kid case*. The only facts are that no escape gun was ever found, and there is no way to know where Billy got it. And the hoaxers have never given contrary evidence. What is known is that Garrett was not present at the murder day of Deputies Bell and Olinger. He left Lincoln to collect taxes in White Oaks on April 27, 1881. Billy's escape, after murdering the deputies, occurred the next day, the 28th. Garrett did not return to Lincoln until April 30th.]

[AUTHOR'S COMMENT: At this point, the hoaxers abandon the deputy murders and the Garrett murder motive. But they pretend that they (1) established Garrett's Billy friendship, (2) Garrett's escape weapon involvement, (3) Garrett's murder motive, and (4) Garrett's murder of the innocent victim.]

This writing will set forth probable cause as to why investigators question who is in the grave in Fort Sumner and seek DNA from Catherine Antrim.

[AUTHOR'S COMMENT: Probable cause of Garrett as a murderer has not been established. But this double exhumation is the hoaxers' hoped-for publicity coup.]

[AUTHOR'S COMMENT: What follows is the hoaxers' attempt to fake that someone other than William Bonney was shot by Garrett. It is back to "alien invasion illogic": *If* there was any inconsistency in reporting of events around the murder, something is "suspicious;" ergo, Garrett killed someone else. But inconsistencies can be merely reporting errors. Also, the hoaxers fail to prove a single inconsistency; and give only their own fabricated ones!]

The detractors of this investigation hold up the statements of Lincoln County Sheriff Pat F. Garrett, Deputy Sheriff John W. Poe, and the Coroner's Jury report as proof it is William H. Bonney that Sheriff Garrett shot and killed on July 14, 1881 and that the Kid is buried in Ft. Sumner.

[AUTHOR'S COMMENT: Using straw man arguing, the hoaxers give this truncated list, omitting both witnesses and historical information proving Garrett shot Billy. Later, in this document, in slip-ups, the hoaxers accidentally present that proof!]

Historian Philip J. Rash [sic - Rasch] tells the story history puts forth about the shooting of the Kid in the following manner:

*Garrett led them to the mouth of Taiban Arroyo, arriving after dark on 13 July. When Brazil failed to appear, Poe, who was unknown in the area, agreed to ride into fort Sumner the next morning to see what he could learn. Finding the inhabitants suspicious and uncommunicative, he proceeded to Sunnyside, about seven miles north, to visit Milnor Rudolph, the postmaster and an old friend of Garrett's. Rudolph was nervous and evasive. He denied all knowledge of the Kid's whereabouts, but Poe was sure he was concealing something.[8] ([8] Poe, John W. The Death of Billy the Kid. New York: Houghton Mifflin Company, 1933) There is a curious story that while the officer was on the way to Sunnyside, John Collins (Abraham Gordon Graham), a former member of Billy's gang, headed to Lobato's camp to warn the outlaw that officers were in the vicinity. On the way he met the Kid, bound for Fort Sumner. "Billy," he warned, "don't go down there. I just saw Poe, and no doubt Pat Garrett and a posse are around town looking for you."*

[AUTHOR'S COMMENT: Recall that Poe was unknown to the locals; so this irrelevant hearsay further lacks credibility.]

*The Kid merely laughed and answered, "Oh, that's O.K. I'll be alright," and rode on, leaving Collins badly puzzled."*[9] ([9]Ben Kemp. *Dead Men, Who Rode Across the Border.* Unpublished. No date.)

*That night Poe rendezvoused with Garrett and McKinney at La Punta de la Glorietta [sic], four miles north of Fort Sumner. Poe's report of both his failure to learn anything definite and his suspicions that there was so much smoke there must be some fire only increased the sheriff's skepticism. After some discussion he commented that the Kid was a frequent visitor to the house of Celsa Gutierrez (sister of Pat's wife Polineria [sic] Gutierrez) and suggested that they watch her home. Their vigil proved fruitless. As midnight approached Garrett and Poe decided that there was only one other possible source of information - Peter Maxwell, the town's most prominent citizen.*

*The officers arrived at his home about 12:30 AM on Friday, the 15th [sic]. Pat instructed Poe and McKinney to wait outside while he went in to talk to Maxwell. Sitting down on the edge of the bed, he asked in a low voice whether the Kid was on the premises. Maxwell became very agitated, but answered that he was not. At that point a bare headed, bare footed man in his shirt sleeves, carrying a butcher's knife in his left hand and a revolver in his right sprang through the door and asked Maxwell who the two men outside were.*

*Maxwell whispered, "That's him."*

[AUTHOR'S COMMENT: Note the hoaxer slip-ups in presenting this source: (1) *Their* Garrett cannot recognize Billy, though they claimed he and Billy are such good friends that Garrett killed for Billy; and (2) Maxwell identifies the victim as Billy!]

*Sensing a third person in the room, the intruder backed toward the door, at the same time demanding, "Quien es? Quien es?"*

*Pat jerked his gun and fired twice.*[10] [11] ([10]*Las Vegas Daily Optic, July 18, 1881.* [11]*Santa Fe Daily New Mexican, July 21, 1881) As the man fell Maxwell plunged over the foot of the bed and out the door, closely followed by the sheriff. Maxwell would surely have been shot by Poe if Garrett had not struck the latter's gun down saying, "Don't shoot Maxwell." He added, "That was the Kid that came in there onto me, and I think I have got him."*

[AUTHOR'S COMMENT: This is Peter Maxwell's second Billy identification; and not contradicting Garrett's statement.]

*Poe was not so sanguine. "Pat," he answered, "the Kid would not come to this place, you shot the wrong man." All was quiet inside. After some persuasion Maxwell brought a tallow candle and placed it on the outside of the window sill. By its light the body of a man could be seen. Deluvina Maxwell, a Navajo servant, entered the room, examined the body, and found that it was indeed the Kid's.*

[AUTHOR'S COMMENT: Here is another hoaxer slip-up: a third victim identification as being Billy! And Billy was well known to Deluvina, which the hoaxers later confirm themselves. And the Poe quote, from his wife's posthumous biography of him, merely states *he* could not identify Billy, by not knowing him. But Poe's surprise is used here to fake a non-Billy victim.]

*Garrett's first shot had struck him in the left breast just above the heart; the second had gone wild. Later it was learned that Billy had been staying at the house of Juan Chavez.*

[AUTHOR'S COMMENT: A fourth Billy identification!]

*Becoming hungry, he had gone to Maxwell's to slice a steak from a yearling Pete had killed that morning.*
*The corpse was taken to a carpenter's shop and laid on the work bench.*

[AUTHOR'S COMMENT: This bench became the hoax's key.]

*Fearing an assault from Billy's friends, the officers remained awake and on guard the rest of the night. However, it passed without incident.*

[AUTHOR'S COMMENT: A hoaxer slip-up by the quote proving the body's viewing by townspeople, already called "Billy's friends." Note also that Garrett does not try to conceal the body of the supposed innocent victim of his heinous crime.]

*When morning came, Justice of the Peace Alejandro Segura convened a jury, with Rudolph as president.*

[AUTHOR'S COMMENT: The Justice of the Peace convenes the Coroners Jury. Later the hoaxers will switcheroo this fact.]

*They rendered a verdict that William Bonney, Alias "Kid," had been killed by Garrett and were "unanimous in the opinion that the gratitude of the whole community is due the said Garrett for his act and that he deserves to be rewarded".*

**[AUTHOR'S COMMENT: Note that the job of a Coroners' Jury was to identify the body. They did. Billy was known to them. The hoaxers already quoted historian Rasch saying Rudolph was nervous when interviewed by Poe - indicating he knew Billy, and knew he was in the area. Crucial also is the fact that the Coroner's Jury declared the killing justifiable homicide. That closed the case legally. Re-opening it would be double jeopardy: precisely what the hoaxers are doing.]**

*That afternoon Jesus Silva and Vincente Otero dug a grave for the outlaw in the old military cemetery.*[12] ([12]Philip Rasch. *Trailing Billy the Kid* by Philip J. [sic] Outlaw-lawman research series Volume 1, University of Wyoming, Laramie, Wyoming, 1993.)

On face value this looks to be the truth. However, if you study the statements of the eye witness [sic] and the documents they do not match up and both can not be true.

**[AUTHOR'S COMMENT: This unsubstantiated claim is followed by faked "inconsistencies." Later it will be used in their conclusion as if proved.]**

Deputy John Poe says the following:

*It was understood when I left my companions in the morning that in case of my being unable to learn any definite information in Fort Sumner, I was to go to the ranch of Mr. Rudolph (an acquaintance and supposed friend of Garrett's) whose ranch was located some seven miles north of Fort Sumner at a place called "Sunnyside," with the purpose of securing from him, if possible, some information as to the whereabouts of the man we were after. Accordingly I started from Fort Sumner about the middle of the afternoon for Rudolph's ranch,*

**[AUTHOR'S COMMENT: Remember "in the middle of the afternoon," because it will later be a switcheroo, with Poe leaving for Rudolph's <u>at night</u>.]**

*arriving there sometime before night. I found Mr. Rudolph at home, presented the letter of Introduction which Garrett had given me, and told him that I wished to stop overnight with him.*[13] ([13]Poe, John W. Billy the Kid. Privately published by E.A. Brininstool. Los Angeles, CA.)

[AUTHOR'S COMMENT: With this unpublished, Brininstool source - and reasonable assumption of its unavailability to any reader - the hoaxers are about to construct another straw man.]

In this part of Deputy Poe's statement he tells us he was sent to Rudolph's ranch by Garrett because Rudolph was *"an acquaintance and supposed friend of Garrett's,"* that the ranch was located seven miles north of Ft. Sumner, at Sunnyside. Poe also tells Rudolph he is going to spend the night at the ranch.

[AUTHOR'S COMMENT: The fakery here is omission of part of the historical quote. Brininstool information is as follows: There was no "Brininstool book." Poe wrote his account, including the Rudolph episode, for Charles Goodnight in 1917. In 1919, an Edward Seymour in New York contacted Goodnight for information on the Kid. Goodnight referred him to Poe. Poe sent his account of Billy's death to Seymour, who sent it to Brininstool, who published it in British *Wild World Magazine*, in December of 1919, later making it a brochure. It was also used in in Poe's book, *The Death of Billy the Kid*, which the hoaxers earlier cited as possessing. In its page 22, Poe states he declined the invitation to spend the night. But the hoaxers omitted its pages 25-26. There, Poe states: "Darkness was now approaching, and I said to Mr. Rudolph that inasmuch as myself and my horse were by this time pretty well rested, having had a good meal, I had changed my mind, and instead of stopping with him, would saddle up and ride during the cool of the evening to meet my companions. This I accordingly did, much, I thought, to the relief of Rudolph."]

In Sheriff Garrett's statement he gives about the same facts of where he was headed and how far it was from Ft. Sumner. Garrett differs with Poe in one area when he says he "arranged with Poe to meet us that night at moonrise" rather then spend the night with Rudolph, as can be seen below:

[AUTHOR'S COMMENT: This fakery is intended to indicate that Garrett presented contradictions. But Poe *did not* spend the night. The hoaxers merely omitted Poe's quote saying that - as shown above. So they are faking "contradictions."]

*I advised him* (Poe) *also, to go to Sunnyside, seven miles above Sumner, and interview M. Rudolph Esq. In whose judgment and discretion I had great confidence. I arranged with Poe to meet us that night at moonrise, at La Puenta de la Glorietta, four miles north of Fort Sumner.*[14] ([14]Garrett, Pat F. The Authentic Life of Billy the Kid. University of Oklahoma Press, Norman. Oklahoma. 2000)

> [AUTHOR'S COMMENT: That was it: the hoaxers' alleged inconsistency: whether Poe did or did not spend the night at Milnor Rudolph's. But both Poe and Garrett agree that Poe did not. There is no inconsistency. Nevertheless, this hoaxer double-talk is later repeated on the same subject.]

Deputy Poe then gives his account of when he says he first saw the Kid when he writes:

*I observed that he was only partly dressed, and was both bare-headed and bare-footed - or rather, had only socks on his feet, and it seemed to me that he was fastening his trousers as he came toward me art a very brisk walk.*

*As Maxwell's was the one place in Fort Sumner that I considered above suspicion of harboring "The Kid," I was entirely off my guard, that thought coming into my mind that the man approaching was either Maxwell*

> [AUTHOR'S COMMENT: This quote dovetails with Poe's question about the correct man, since he could not identify Billy. Also note Poe's lack of alarm. It will be misstated by the hoaxers.]

*or some guest of his who might have been staying there. He came on until he was almost within arm's length of where I sat before he saw me, as I was partly concealed from his view by the post of the gate. Upon his seeing me he covered me with his six-shooter as quick as lightening, sprang onto the porch, calling out in Spanish, "Quien es?" (Who is it?), at the same time backing away from me toward the door through which Garrett only a few seconds before had passed, repeating his query, "Quien es?" in Spanish several times. At this I stood up and advanced toward him, telling him not to be alarmed: that he should not be hurt, and still without the least suspicion that this was the very man we were looking for.*

This statement raises many questions with investigators. Poe says he sees a man *"partially dressed, and was bare-headed and bare-footed - or rather, had only socks on his feet, and it seemed to me that he was fastening his trousers as he came toward me art a very brisk walk."* Then the man covers him with his six shooter. Where did the man put the *"six-shooter"* when he was *"fastening his trousers"*?

[AUTHOR'S COMMENT: This is an accidentally hilarious hoaxer contrivance of the impossibility of doing two things at once! Actually, one can hold a revolver and button your pants. And Billy was a gunman and ambidextrous, so even more able!]

He did not stop and lay it down because Poe says he *"he came toward me art a very brisk walk."*

[AUTHOR'S COMMENT: Triple tasking!]

Another question that investigators struggle with is would it not go without saying Poe would have had a description of the Kid as he ventured into Ft. Sumner to scout around and gather information. It is beyond reason that he would go searching for a man without at least having a description of the man for whom he was searching?

[AUTHOR'S COMMENT: It is not beyond reason. Garrett was not an experienced lawman. And Poe's task was not to search for Billy, but to find out from locals about Billy's whereabouts.]

In a town of about 200 people, many of which were Hispanic would Poe be unable to recognize the Kid from this description as he claims?

[AUTHOR'S COMMENT: What description? It seems Poe had none. Also, this is racist. Many people of Hispanic background are Spanish, and could be as fair as Billy was.]

Deputy Poe continues his statement with these words:

*As I moved toward him trying to reassure him, he backed up into the doorway of Maxwell's room, where he halted for a moment, his body concealed by the thick adobe wall at the side of the doorway, from whence he put his head out and asking in Spanish for the fourth or fifth time who I was. I was within a few feet of him when he disappeared into the room.*

When the Kid asks Poe who he is in Spanish and has his pistol pointed at the deputy, what is Deputy McKinney doing at this time? Why is he not shouldering his rifle, and at least deploying to the side to cover his partner Deputy Poe from this very real threat? Today the shooting policy for police officers is tight and narrow: in 1881 a shooting policy was non-existent. Investigators believe the deputies had to have a description for whom they were searching. With a threat such as Poe describes, a man with a gun, added to the description of the most wanted man in New Mexico, there would have been cause for both deputies to have fired on the suspect.

> [AUTHOR'S COMMENT: Here comes a straw man. Who says Poe had the description, or thought the gun was a threat? Back then, most men were armed. Poe even shows lack of alarm by reassuring the stranger. And McKinney, for whatever reason, was unavailable for the hoaxers' fantasized shoot-out!]

Even if the deputies chose not to fire, would they have allowed the man who was threatening their lives with a gun

> [AUTHOR'S COMMENT: Note this switcheroo from faking alarm of "threatening their lives," to making it a fact.]

to walk in on the unaware Sheriff in the dark? If they chose to allow the man with a gun to walk in on the Sheriff would these seasoned lawmen

> [AUTHOR'S COMMENT: "Kip" Kinney was just a hog farmer friend of Garrett's, no "seasoned lawman."]

not at least have warned the Sheriff of the danger?

> [AUTHOR'S COMMENT: No danger is established.]

In Garrett's statement he relates the following:

*From his step I could perceive he was either barefooted or in his stocking feet and held a revolver in his right hand and butcher knife in his left.*

*He came directly towards me. Before he reached the bed, I whispered, "Who is it Pete?"*

[AUTHOR'S COMMENT: If Garrett is unsure of Billy, there goes the hoaxers' best buddies murder plot! Note also that Maxwell identifies Billy. Again the hoaxers undo their own fakery.]

*But I received no response for a moment. It struck me that it might be Pete's brother-in-law. Manuel Abrea, who had seen Poe and McKinney and wanted to know their business. The intruder came close to me, leaned both hands on the bed, his right and almost touching my knee, and asked in a low tone: "Who are they, Pete?" At the same moment Maxwell whispered to me, "That's him!" Simultaneously the Kid must have seen, or felt, the presence of a third person at the head of the bed. He raised quickly his pistol, a self cocker, within a foot of my breast. Retreating rapidly across the room he cried: "Quien es? Quien es? (Who's that? Who's that?) All this occurred in a moment. Quickly as possible I drew my revolver and fired, threw my body aside, and fired again. The second shot was useless: The Kid fell dead ..."*

Investigators find it hard to believe that Garrett could see a 6 inch knife in the Kid's hand.

[AUTHOR'S COMMENT: That night had an unusual full moon that stayed close to the horizon. It would have been almost as light as day. When Billy opened the door, he and a held weapon would have been visible. Also July is hot in Fort Sumner. It is unlikely that draperies would have been fully closed. Garrett's real problem was staying unseen himself.]

Yet the Kid could not see a six foot, five inch man.

[AUTHOR'S COMMENT: This confirms only that the big man was hiding. Note that this is a half-way point, the killing is done, and nothing indicates that the victim was not Billy.]

Deputy    talks about what happened after the shooting of the Kid. He writes:

[AUTHOR'S COMMENT: Quote source has no footnote.]

*Within a very short time after the shooting, quite a number of the native people had gathered around, some of them bewailing the death of their friend,*

98

[AUTHOR'S COMMENT: Another hoaxer slip-up: These people, who can recognize Billy, will later be given his body to lay out.]

*while several women pleaded for permission to take charge of the body, which we allowed them to do. They carried it to the yard to a carpenter's shop, where it was laid on a workbench, the women placing candles lightened around it, according to their ideas of properly conducting a "wake" for the dead.*

[AUTHOR'S COMMENT: By this point, there are profuse eye-witness identifications of Billy!]

Investigators keep Deputy Poe's statement in mind as they studied the Coroner's Jury Report:

*Greetings:*

*On this 15th day of July, A.D. 1881, I, the undersigned, Justice of the Peace of the adobe named precinct, received information that a murder had taken place in Fort Sumner, in said precinct, and immediately upon receiving said information I proceeded to the said place and named Milnor Rudolph, Jose Silva, Antonio Sevedra, Pedro Antonio Lucero, Lorenzo Jaramillo and Sabal Gutierres a jury to investigate the case and the above jury convened in the home of Luz B. Maxwell and proceeded to a room in the said house where they found the body of William Bonney alias "Kid" with a shot in the left breast and having examined the body they examined the evidence of Pedro Maxwell, which evidence is as follows: "I being in my bed in my room, at about midnight on the 14th day of July, Pat F. Garrett came into my room and sat down. William Bonney came in and got close to my bed with a gun in his hand and asked me "who is it" and then Pat F. Garrett fired two shots at the said William Bonney and the said William Bonney fell near my fire place and I went out of the room and when I came in again about three or four minutes after the shots the said William Bonney was dead."*

[AUTHOR'S COMMENT: Note definitive Jury plus Maxwell identifications of the victim as William Bonney.]

*The jury has found the following verdict: We the jury unanimously find that William Bonney has been killed by a shot*

*on the left breast near the region of the heart, the same having been
fired with a gun in the hand of pat F. Garrett and our verdict is
that the deed of said Garrett was justifiable homicide and we are
unanimous in the opinion that the gratitude of all the community
is due to the said Garrett for his deed and is worthy of being
rewarded.*

*M. Rudolph, President      Anto, Sevedra(signature)*
*Pedro Anto. m. Lucero (signature)*
*Jose Silba (x)        Sabal Gutierrez (x)*
*Lorenzo Jaramillo (x)*

*All said information I place to your knowledge.*

*Alejandro Segura Justice of the Peace (signature)*

[AUTHOR'S COMMENT: This is a legally binding document
confirming victim identification. To reopen   the case is double
jeopardy. Further confirmation of jurymen's certainty, is that
no indictment was subsequently made with the District
Attorney against Garrett for a murder.]

Investigators remembered Deputy Poe's statement and Sheriff
Garrett's statement as to where Poe had been that night.

[AUTHOR'S COMMENT: The hoaxers hope the reader believed
their faked contention that Poe spent the night at Rudolph's.
What follows is more fakery to manufacture "inconsistencies."]

Earlier that evening

[AUTHOR'S COMMENT: The time was afternoon, as quoted by
the hoaxers earlier, and tagged by me to prepare for this
switcheroo where they need night for their fake argument.]

Garrett had dispatched Deputy Poe to interview M. Rudolph in
Sunnyside, seven miles north of Fort Sumner. Poe says he left
Rudolph and rode to meet Garrett and McKinney. All records
show that the shooting took place about midnight and Historian
Philip I. Rash [sic] sets the time at 12:30 AM on July 15th. If this
were true then the time does not allow for the statement of Poe
and the coroner's jury report to both be true.

[AUTHOR'S COMMENT: Their hoaxers' time switcheroo is done to discredit the Coroner's Jury Report: their bugbear. But, even if granted them, it does not work because of the length of the ride. Poe could cover the 7 miles to Sunnyside in 1½ hours. Puenta de la Glorietta was 4 miles north of Fort Sumner on the way. So Poe's return journey to meet his companions was only 3 miles, or about 45 minutes: easy to meet them by evening, a fact he and Garrett confirmed. No time inconsistency exists.]

If, after the shooting, Garrett had to get some order to the scene, locate a rider to ride to Sunnyside to get Rudolph,

[AUTHOR'S COMMENT: The above Coroner's Jury Report clearly states that the appointment - and probable contacting - of Rudolph was a legal duty performed by the appropriate official: Justice of the Peace, Alejandro Segura, certainly <u>not</u> Garrett, a suspect as to justifiability in Billy Bonney's killing.]

and the rider then had to get his horses [sic] caught, saddled and ready to go all of which would take the better part of an hour,

[AUTHOR'S COMMENT: Timing here is faked. Maxwell had a stable and workers. A horse could be readied quickly.]

the time would be 1:30 am.

[AUTHOR'S COMMENT: The hoaxers are creating another straw man argument about "inconsistency" by time fakery. Yet they know that the Coroner's Jury met sometime during daytime of the 15th. There was no need for middle-of-the night urgency; and no evidence that it occurred.]

It would take a rider who was in shape, on a good horse, and riding fast, an hour and a half to cover the seven miles to Rudolph's ranch, putting the time at 2:30 am. Adding an hour for the rider to wake Rudolph up and for Rudolph to catch his horse and saddle the horse the time would be 3:30 am. If Rudolph was in good shape, on a good horse it would be another hour and a half on the return trip to Fort Sumner putting the time at 4:30 am. Add another hour to put together a jury, and the time is now 5:30 am. This is if everyone worked smoothly.

In the jury's report we find the words:

*... a jury to investigate the case and the above jury convened in the home of Luz B. Maxwell and proceeded to a room in the said*

*in said house where they found the body of William Bonney alias "Kid"...*

Either the jury found the Kid in the Maxwell's home, or he was not given to the women to put on the carpenters workbench as Poe says, or the jury report is deceptive.

[AUTHOR'S COMMENT: The hoaxers hope they convinced readers of that conclusion. But there was enough time to carry the corpse from the Maxwell house, across about 300 yards of Parade Ground, to the carpenter's shop. In the morning, it could be returned to the Maxwell's house for the jurymen.]

Deputy Poe also says:

*The next morning we sent for the justice of the peace,*

[AUTHOR'S COMMENT: Here the hoaxers undo their fakery of the night riding by giving this quote about the next morning.]

*who held an inquest over the body, the verdict of the jury being such as to justify the killing, and later, on the same day, the body was buried in the old military burying ground at Fort Sumner.*

If the Kid's body was taken to the carpenter shop then the jury did not find the body at Maxwell's house as stated and makes investigators wonder why they would lie in the report.

[AUTHOR'S COMMENT: This fabrication leads to a "lie" accusation. But nothing indicates that the body was not brought to the house from the carpenter's shop. But the hoaxers are still struggling to discredit the Coroner's Jury Report by "contradictions," though, of course, that is irrelevant to establishing the victim's identity.]

Deputy Poe says something else that raised investigators suspicions when he writes about the shooting itself:

[AUTHOR'S COMMENT: This fast switcheroo distracts from the sly misstatements slipped past. And though the hoaxers never say what is "suspicious" in Poe's quote – which is merely repeating Garrett's description - they are setting the stage for their fake "investigation" to be described next.]

*An instant later a shot was fired in the room, followed immediately by what everyone within hearing distance thought was two shots fired, the third report, as we learned afterward, being caused by the rebound of the second bullet which had struck the adobe wall and rebounded against the headboard of the wooden bedstead.*

[AUTHOR'S COMMENT: Let us take stock now. Nothing so far indicates a victim other than profusely identified William Bonney. Also, the hoaxers have not given the promised "contradictions." Later, as their hoax foundered, they did a desperate switcheroo, contradicting this whole document: they stated that William Bonney *was* shot, was laid out on the carpenter's bench, but just played dead!]

[AUTHOR'S COMMENT: Note that the second bullet site is in the bed's headboard. But the hoaxers will soon do fake forensics on a washstand instead! So next follows a faked CSI-style investigation.]

On August 29, 2003, Deputy Sederwall of the Lincoln County Sheriff's Department

[AUTHOR'S COMMENT: Note Sederwall is in official capacity as "Deputy Sederwall." Years later, he call this a "hobby."]

located the carpenter bench where the Kid's body was placed on July 14, 1881.

[AUTHOR'S COMMENT: Error: earliest morning of July 15ᵗʰ]

[AUTHOR'S COMMENT: Since the bench will later become central to the hoax's next phase, it should be noted that the one here, in possession of Maxwell family descendents, was first identified in the late 1920's by historian, Robert Mullin, and photographed by historian, Maurice Garland Fulton. There is no to prove it is the one on which Billy was laid out; as will be discussed in detail later in this book.]

On September 13, 2003, investigators located all the furniture that was in Pete Maxwell's bedroom the night of the shooting, July 1881.

[AUTHOR'S COMMENT: Though this information is irrelevant to the claim of whether Billy was Garrett's victim, this Maxwell furniture - including the carpenter's bench - became pivotal to the survival of the hoax. But the furniture's certain provenance is unprovable. Maxwell family Fort Sumner holdings were sold at public auction on January 15, 1884, and bought by Lonny Horn, Sam Doss, Daniel Taylor and John Lord in partnership with the New England Cattle Company which transferred its operations there. The Maxwell house (with the fateful bedroom) was torn down about 1887, and some of the timber was used to build the Pigpen Ranch south of Melrose, New Mexico.

Pete Maxwell died in 1898. His brother-in-law, Manuel Abreu, lived in the area, and *may* have taken some furniture. In the 1920's, making a little museum from Billy the Kid, the family claimed to have Pete Maxwell's bedroom furniture and the carpenter's bench - as pictured in a 1930 article. So all one can say is that about 50 years after the killing, Maxwells assembled alleged Billy the Kid-related objects for profit.]

Among these items is the headboard of the bed that was in Maxwell's room that night. There is no bullet hole in the headboard.

[AUTHOR'S COMMENT: That finding, though irrelevant to the murder victim, contradicts Deputy Poe's eye-witness statement that the headboard was hit; thus, invalidating the furniture's authenticity! In fact, the fakery is greater. The headboard in question is missing its entire center, being only an outside rim of a frame. There is no place for a bullet hole!]

In a statement made by Deluvina Maxwell she says the following:

*... There was a washstand with a marble top in Pete Maxwell's bedroom, which Garrett had seen in the moonlight*

[AUTHOR'S COMMENT: A hoaxer slip. Earlier, they denied that Garrett could have clearly seen Billy, yet here they confirm moonlit visibility. Note that they are trying to validate the washstand for its fake investigation to follow - while the headboard was actually the object shot.]

*and shot at, thinking it was Bonney trying to get up. It was an old Spanish custom that the night before the burial of a person, people would take turns staying with the body and reciting prayers. William Bonney had a proper funeral. The people took turns and stayed through the night.*

[AUTHOR'S COMMENT: A hoaxer slip: confirming corpse identity by eyewitnesses.]

*He was buried in the old government cemetery in Fort Sumner. For many years Deluvina left flowers on his grave in the summer time.*[15]

[AUTHOR'S COMMENT: The last sentence is not Deluvina's quote; but it is accepted that she did that for 40 years – unlikely if the body was not her beloved Billy's.]

([15]Deluvina Maxwell's story as related to Lucien B. Maxwell grandchildren, unpublished.)

[AUTHOR'S COMMENT: Note that unreliable reports by grandchildren are the only "proof" of washstand validity. Also, the story is irrelevant to victim identity - though it repeats, to hoaxer detriment, the vigil and corpse witnessing. As to further fakery, the unconvincing washstand is as tiny as a child's toy.]

Deluvina lends credibility to the story of the Kid's body being laid on the carpenter bench.

[AUTHOR'S COMMENT: Here is a hoaxer slip that ends their case: Billy's corpse on bench!]

She also mentions, *"There was a washstand with a marble top in Pete Maxwell's bedroom, which Garrett had seen in the moonlight and shot at, thinking it was Bonney trying to get up."* In the items investigators located on September 13, 2003 was that wash stand.

[AUTHOR'S COMMENT: This washstand is unsubstantiated as from Pete Maxwell's bedroom - as is the rest of the furniture. And Deluvina apparently only said a washstand was "shot at," not shot. And Deputy Poe said the bed's headboard was hit. But what follows is a fake mimicking of crime scene investigation based on faked "certainty" of washstand provenance.]

The was stand was dark in color and 29 1/2 inches wide, with a splash board on the back that measured 5 inch at the middle and tapered down to the ends in a decorative curve. From front to back the wash stand measured 16 inches. It stood 29 inches with three drawers with rusted locks on each drawer. There was what appeared to be a bullet hole through the stand.

Deputy Sederwall removed a .45 caliber pistol round from his deputy weapon and noticed the round was just a little bit bigger than the hole. The night of the shooting Sheriff Garrett was shooting a Colt Single Action Army Revolver, Serial Number 55093, caliber .44/40.[16] ([16]Typed letter from P.F. Garrett dated April 16, 1906. James H. Earl Collection, from County Clerk's office, El Paso, Texas.)

[AUTHOR'S COMMENT: Note that there is no bullet, just holes. Claiming .44/40 ammunition is fakery to match Garrett's known weapon's caliber. Actually there is no link to Garrett or to Maxwell's bedroom. There is even no link to anyone being shot, since accidental discharges happened in New Mexico where owning guns was common from the 19th century to the present – the time frame for "shooting" the tiny washstand!]

The bullet pierced the left side of the washstand, both sides of the drawer and exited out the right side of the stand.

The bullet struck the left side of the stand 22 1/4 inches on the center up from the bottom and 6 1/2 inches on the center of the back of the stand. The bullet exited to the right side 20 1/2 inches on the center up from the bottom and 6 1/2 inches on center from the back of the washstand. On the inside of the left side panel the wood was somewhat splintered indicating that was where the bullet entered the stand. On the right side panel the outside of the panel was splintered indicating the exit of the bullet.

The owner of the washstand, whose name investigators do not wish to release at this time

[AUTHOR'S COMMENT: Periodically the hoaxers nervously claimed secrecy, then forgot, and gave names.]

says it was inherited along with the bed from Maxwell's bedroom. The discovery of this evidence makes Deluvina's statement believable.

[AUTHOR'S COMMENT: Historically real or not, the furniture examination is irrelevant to Garrett's victim.]

Many questions remain. Why would the coroner's jury report and the eye witness reports be so at odds?

[AUTHOR'S COMMENT: They are not at odds; and no discrepancy has been demonstrated. But the hoaxers are heading again into a straw man argument.]

A hint can be found in a document discovered in July of 1989 by Joe O. Bowlin.

[AUTHOR'S COMMENT: This is a low blow to a dead man. Joe Bowlin, with his wife Marlyn, founded the Billy the Kid Outlaw Gang to "preserve, protect, and promote the history of Billy Bonney and Pat Garrett." This hoax would have been anathema to Joe Bowlin. What follows misstates a book Bolin published posthumously for its author, Paco Anaya.]

The document is a story, according to Louis Anaya of Clovis, New Mexico as told to his father, Paco Anaya, a friend of Billy the Kid.

[AUTHOR'S COMMENT: Note the admitted friendship of Paco Anaya and Billy. It will catch the hoaxers in another slip-up.]

This story was translated from Spanish and then printed in book form. In this transcript you will find the following:

*Also, I will have to tell you a lot in reference to the reports that Pat Garrett made about the sworn declaration that appears in the records of the Secretary of State and more, concerning what he said about the Coroners Jury that investigated the death of Billy the Kid when Pat killed Billy.*

*In this report, I find that the Coroners Jury that investigated the death of Billy the Kid when he was dead is not part of the same report that acted as a Coroners Jury, neither the form or the verdict of the Coroners Jury. The verdict is recorded in the office of the Secretary of State in Spanish, and they (the jury) are not the same men. There are two that did not even live in Fort Sumner.*[17] (*[17]Anaya, A. P. I Buried Billy.* Creative Publishing Company. 1991.)

Paco Anaya goes on to list the members of the Jury that he remembered holding the inquest over the body. They are not the same as the jury report as is held up as proof that Garrett killed the Kid.

[AUTHOR'S COMMENT: This fast one is for another straw man. There are many other corpse identifications for Billy. In fact, most have accidentally been quoted herein by the hoaxers!]

One of the differences is Illeginio Garcia [sic - poor legibility - unclear spelling] as the Jury President and not M. Rudolph.

Paco Anaya says that Garrett wrote the first version in English himself. Anaya says that Garrett later came back and wrote another report in Spanish with the help of "Don Pedro Maxwell and Don Manuel Abrea," [sic - Abreu] Maxwell's brother-in-law.

This makes the investigators ask, if Garrett wrote the verdict is that why the words are found, "...*we are unanimous in the opinion that the gratitude of all the community is due to the said Garrett for his deed and is worthy of being rewarded"*?

It should be noted that in the Coroners Jury Report that Garrett puts forth

[AUTHOR'S COMMENT: Note the switcheroo. Garrett did not put forth the Coroner's Jury Report. It was a legal document done under Justice of the Peace, Alejandro Segura. Garrett was the *subject* of their investigation. The document might have been available to him after the inquest. It surely would not have been available to humble citizen Anaya.]

it is interesting to note that two of those listed were in Garrett's wedding, Sabal Gutierrez is his brother-in-law, and Garrett admits in his statement that Rudolph is a close friend.

[AUTHOR'S COMMENT: Note the lie. Garrett did not pick the jurymen; the Justice of the Peace did. With continuing sly innuendo, the hoaxers end their discussion of the Coroner's Jury Report here, but have done nothing to show that Garrett murdered anyone but Billy. A hoaxer hope is that the reader be misled by fake "suspicions" about the Report; and somehow think that makes uncertain victim identity. But their ploy is even more flawed. The reader would then have to postulate a preposterous conspiracy including Justice of the Peace Segura; Milnor Rudolph; the other jurymen; Peter Maxwell; and his brother-in-law, Manuel Abreu; and Deluvina, all to help Garrett get away killing the unknown victim (seen by 200 townspeople who need to be in on the conspiracy too)!]

[AUTHOR'S COMMENT: As bad, is the hoaxers' use of Paco Anaya. Like many old-timer accounts, his was written long after the events; in this case, in 1930, forty-nine years later. He would not have been privy to the Coroner's Jury information; and his inaccuracies are explained by age and time. In fact, his entire memoir completely garbles Lincoln War history. But key here is that he knew Billy well, saw his body, and named his book *I Buried Billy!* Again the hoaxers contradict themselves by giving a very certain identification of the dead and buried victim as Billy.]

[AUTHOR'S COMMENT: Next is the hoaxer' last try: using fellow hoaxer David Turk for "ricochet validation" by useless hearsay, given gloss of his fancy title.]

David Turk, Historian for the United States Marshal's Service has pointed out other documents

[AUTHOR'S COMMENT: Note that only one document is presented, though its inclusion hints at Turk's larger role as an active hoax participant - including possible assistance in writing this Probable Cause Statement, since he came from Washington, D.C. in December of 2003 when it was being written, supposedly by Deputy Sederwall.]

bringing into question Garrett's involvement in the Kid's escape.

[AUTHOR'S COMMENT: Note the switcheroo. Who said Billy escaped? Up to now he has been a corpse.]

Mr. Turk has produced a Works Progress Administration, Federal Writer's Project interview where the following statement was taken:

*The people around Lincoln*

[AUTHOR'S COMMENT: The murder was 150 miles from Lincoln; and Turk's old-timer claims has only weak hearsay knowledge. But this technique characterizes other slip-shod and pretender-oriented writings of Turk, which played a part in the hoax – like his "U.S. Marshals Service and Billy the Kid" pamphlet.]

*say Garrett didn't kill Billie (sic) the Kid. John Poe was with Garrett the night he was supposed to … said that he didn't see the man that Garrett killed.*

[AUTHOR'S COMMENT: Besides the fact that Poe's statements all refer to seeing the victim, Poe did not know Billy.]

*I can take you to the grave in Hell's High Acre, an old government cemetery, where Billie (sic) was supposed to be buried and show you the grave.*

*The cook at Pete Maxwell's was always putting flowers on the grave and praying at it. This woman thought a lot of Billie (sic), but after Garrett killed the man at Maxwell's home her grandson was never seen again*

[AUTHOR'S COMMENT: "Grandson" was the victim? This makes no sense, and is historically untrue.]

*and Billie (sic) was seen by Bill Nicholi an Indian scout. Bill saw him in Mexico.*[18] ([18]Frances E. Tolly [Totty], comp. "Early Days in Lincoln County," Charles Remark Interview. February 14, 1938, Works Progress Administration, Federal Writer's Project, Folklore-Life Histories, Manuscript Division. Library of Congress.)

[AUTHOR'S COMMENT: So this sole document saying Garrett did not kill Billy is only an old-timer recollection, 57 years later, by someone unconnected to the event, and titled as "folklore." This old-timer just "thinks" someone saw Billy in Mexico. It should be noted that, by 1938, Billy the Kid was famous, and slews of old-timers were fabricating connections to him. In fact, old-timer unreliability is illustrated in the following Overton affidavit, attached to this Probable Cause Statement.]

[AUTHOR'S COMMENT: Next comes the conclusion. Note hoaxers' faking their unproved contentions as proved.]

Discovering the headboard of Maxwell's bed that does not have a bullet hole in it, as Deputy Poe says it did, leads investigators to question if Poe was in fact in the room after the shooting of William Bonney as he said.

[AUTHOR'S COMMENT: More obvious is that this headboard is unsubstantiated as historically real, and is missing its entire center. Anyway, saying "if the headboard was not shot, Poe was not in the room" is not only illogical, but has nothing to do with victim identity.]

However, the discovery of the Maxwell wash stand with the bullet hole through it indicates someone was shot in Maxwell's room on the night of July 14, 18821.

[AUTHOR'S COMMENT: Why? A shot washstand does not mean a shot person - or anything at all about who Garrett shot.]

The question remains as to who is in William H. Bonney's grave at Fort Sumner.

[AUTHOR'S COMMENT: No question remains. The hoaxers made it up. A probable cause statement had to justify Garrett as a murder suspect of a victim other than Billy. They failed by no motive, no evidence, and Billy established as the body.]

Investigators believe with the conflicts of Sheriff Pat F. Garrett and Deputy John Poe and the fact that these statements are at odds with the Jury Report as shown above,

[AUTHOR'S COMMENT: This is fakery. The "conflicts" do not exist; and had nothing to do with whom Garrett shot.]

coupled with the evidence discovered by deputies,

[AUTHOR'S COMMENT: What evidence? The hoaxers have some antique furniture, which, even if real, is irrelevant as to victim identity. And their period quotes are either irrelevant or misrepresented.]

probable cause exist [sic] to warrant the court to grant investigators the right to search for the truth in criminal investigation 2003-274 through DNA samples obtained from Catherine Antrim.

[AUTHOR'S COMMENT: Without any probable cause of a murder, the hoaxers have headed to their objective: exhumation of Billy and his mother.]

[AUTHOR'S COMMENT: Signatures follow; typed and written.]

Steven M. Sederwall: Deputy Sheriff, Lincoln County (12/31/03)

Tom Sullivan: Sheriff Lincoln County (12/31/03)

[AUTHOR'S COMMENT: The signature date is noteworthy, being three months after the hoaxers' exhumation case began. Even on December 17, 2003, their attorney, Sherry Tippett, was urging, by letter, for its completion for her brief for the Silver City judge. Was completion delayed while awaiting writing assistance? That possibility will be discussed later.]

\* \* \* \* \* \* \*

# OVERTON AFFIDAVIT

Adding to the "Probable Cause Statement for Case # 2003-274" is a two page, typed, old-timer affidavit by a Homer Overton. Note that Pat Garrett's widow, Apolinaria Gutierrez Garrett, died in 1936, four years *before* Overton's alleged conversation with her in 1940 (b.1861 - d.1936)! She is buried in the Masonic Cemetery in Las Cruces, New Mexico, where Pat Garrett also lies.

Overton's confabulations include fabrications of a Pat Garrett report to Texas Rangers, a corpse with blasted face, and, of course, Garrett's murder of someone other than Billy the Kid.

Overton's claims also insult Pat Garrett's widow's reverential protection of Garrett's legacy. After Garrett's death in 1908, she even legally fought and reclaimed from a saloonkeeper his revolver used to kill Billy the Kid. She was the last person in the world to tell random, 9 year old child, Homer Overton, that Pat had not shot the Kid - even if she had not been four years dead!

**\* \* \* \* \* \* \***

December 22, 2003

Tom Sullivan
Lincoln County Sheriff
P.O. Box 278
Carrizozo, NM 88301

Tom,

It was good talking to you on the phone and, as promised, I am sending this letter as promised to present this Statement of Facts.

Fact: I was born in Pecos, Texas in the year 1931 and lived there until the later [sic] part of 1941. In the summer of 1940, I was invited to spend the summer with Bobby Talbert and his mother, who had moved from Pecos to Las Cruces, New Mexico earlier that year.

**[AUTHOR'S COMMENT: Time specificity of Overton's age plus the date fixes Overton in Las Cruces in 1940 – not earlier.]**

The time I spent there was wonderful, but one thing happened that summer that made the summer unforgettable.

Bobby's next door neighbor was a lady who introduced herself as Mrs. Garrett, the widow of Pat Garrett. Mrs. Garrett would invite us over to have iced tea with mint leaves in it, and told us stories about her life with Pat.

I recall her having a parrot that had belonged to Pat which she said was very old. She told us some parrots live to be over 100 years.

That afternoon, she brought out a gun to show us and said it had belonged to Pat. As I recall, the gun appeared to be a Colt single action revolver. At that point I asked her if that was the gun used to kill Billy the Kid. At this point she got an unusual look on her face and stated that she was going to tell us something we would have to promise to keep a secret, and never to tell anyone. We both promised, and until this day I have never told anyone but my immediate family.

Mrs. Garrett proceeded to tell us the following facts concerning her husband and Billy:

Mrs. Garrett said, "Pat did not shoot Billy". She said there was a very close relationship between Pat and Billy, almost like a father and son relationship. She further stated that the night Pat was supposed to kill Billy, that they were in Ft. Sumner and had made a plan to make it look like Pat killed Billy so Billy could go to Mexico and live with no one looking for him any more. She said that Pat had seen a drunk Mexican lying in the street on his way to talk to Billy. So they planned to use the Mexican and claim that he was in fact Billy the Kid. She didn't state if the Mexican was dead or not, but said that they shot him in the face so he couldn't be recognized. They dressed him in Billy's clothes and Pat signed a paper for the Texas Rangers stating that he had killed Billy the Kid and that this was his body. The Mexican was then buried in Fort Sumner and identified as Billy.

Mrs. Garrett struck me as being very sincere when she told us this and she stated that she had never told anyone before. I have kept this secret for sixty-three years and feel it is time to disclose this story. I hope it will be helpful to you in your quest to find the truth about Billy, as I believe what Mrs. Garrett told us that day was the absolute truth.

All that I have told you is as I recall it related to me sixty-three years ago when I was nine years old. It made such an impression on me that I have remembered it in detail these sixty-three years.

Sincerely,
Homer D. Overton
AKA: Homer D. Kinsworthy
CONTACT INFORMATION

Witnessed by: Jerry Raffee, NOTARY
on December 27th 2003


SEAL AFFIXED

# FAKING HISTORY IN THE
# BILLY THE KID CASE

*HOAXBUST: The Billy the Kid Case hoaxed a Pat Garrett friendship with Billy to provide a motive for his murdering an "innocent victim" for the Kid's escape. But no friendship existed. Hoaxed too was validity of a Maxwell family carpenter's bench with "the Kid's blood DNA" to circumvent need to exhume Billy and his mother for DNA. But putting Billy on that bench needed rewriting the hoax with Billy "playing dead" when on it.*

## FAKING FRIENDSHIP OF GARRETT AND THE KID

Pat Garrett's biographer, Leon Metz, told me: "At best, Pat Garrett was Bonney's passing acquaintance. Of course, he killed him." That was confirmed by historians, Frederick Nolan, Robert Utley, Robert Mullin, Maurice Garland Fulton, Walter Noble Burns, and Philip Rasch. And the corpse killed by Garrett was profusely and legally identified as Billy Bonney.

But the hoax needed "friendship" for Garrett's murder motive. And that "friendship" had to turn Garrett into the most evil lawman ever: as an accomplice to the Kid's jailbreak killing of his deputy guards by providing the weapon on April 28, 1881; and as a murderer himself, on July 14, 1881, of the innocent victim to help the Kid escape again. That "friendship" had to make Garrett risk being hanged for those crimes. It also made Garrett a conspirator (with Deputies Poe and McKinney, Peter Maxwell, Deluvina, and 200 townspeople) to hide his murders; and it made him a hypocrite for accepting rewards for killing he Kid. The hoaxers needed a Garrett so attached to Billy, that murders made sense. Needed was the greatest man-to-man love story ever told.

Even the hoaxers balked. So they soon shape-shifted the case to "protecting Garrett's reputation from people accusing him of murder" - omitting they were those "people;" and that real murder cases are not filed to prove the suspect is innocent!

As to a relationship, Pat Garrett would have met the Kid in about February of 1878 after leaving Texas buffalo hunting and settling in Fort Sumner; where Billy occasionally came. Garrett, tall and decade older, played poker with Billy in that town's saloons, getting nick-named by locals as "Big Casino" and "Little Casino." That was it. Then, from 1880 to 1881, Garrett repeatedly tried to kill Billy by shooting. That was not friendly.

Garrett was elected Lincoln County Sheriff on November 2, 1880, with the mandate to get Billy the Kid dead or alive. Garrett was also made a Deputy U.S. Marshall by Secret Service Operative Azariah Wild, in the Territory to stop an alleged counterfeiting ring and to terminate Billy as its supposed leader.

White Oaks men, a third of Lincoln County's population, who voted Garrett in as sheriff, first tried the killing. On November 22, 1880, their posse, under Lincoln County Deputy Will Hudgens, ambushed Billy and cohorts at nearby Coyote Spring. Accidentally, they only shot horses. They tried again on the 27th, ambushing Billy's group at the Greathouse Ranch. This time they accidentally killed fellow posseman, Jim Carlyle. Billy escaped.

Garrett's own posse killed better. On December 19, 1880, they ambushed Billy and his companions in Fort Sumner, and shot dead Tom O'Folliard. The others escaped. At December 22, 1880's dawn, at Billy and group's hide-out cabin in Stinking Springs, Garrett shot dead Charlie Bowdre, mistaken by him as the Kid by wearing Billy's sombrero. Then Garrett captured the bunch for Billy's certain hanging trial. (Note that if "friendship" was real, this was the best time for Garrett to let Billy escape.)

So, in reality, by December of 1880, Billy was not dead because Garrett had accidentally killed O'Folliard and Bowdre instead.

As an aside, the pretenders, used by the hoaxers for "survival suspicion," did not claim Garrett friendship; but used accidental-shooting-of-my-friend for their Billy the Kid murder scenes.

Ironically, this maligning of Garrett would end up being the hoaxers' biggest mistake. They forgot about living descendants of Garrett's eight children. Years later, they would take action.

## FAKING THE CARPENTER'S BENCH WITH BILLY

Original hoax history involved only Garrett's innocent murder victim in the Kid's grave, with need to dig up Billy and his mother to "prove" that. But hoaxers' back-up plan for faking the Kid's DNA relied on the carpenter's bench used in the dead Kid's vigil. Deputy Sederwall said in the "Probable Cause Statement" that he had found it. So he claimed shot Billy left "blood DNA" on it.

But that needed a new hoax for a new victim: Billy! Worse, Billy on the bench meant *he* was dead: regular history - ending fame, fortune, and a presidency. Worse, using that bench for CSI needed its "chain of custody." But the Maxwells only came up with the bench 45 years after Billy's killing - to earn money from a little "Billy the Kid" museum for Fort Sumner tourists.

None of that stopped the hoaxers from collecting "blood DNA" from the bench or re-writing their own hoax history.

## HOAX SHAPE-SHIFTING FOR BENCH

Using the bench for "Billy-blood-DNA" had a big historical problem for the hoax: Billy-as-corpse. Steve Sederwall proved himself a conning master by proclaiming: "Dead men don't bleed." So his shot Billy survived, but bled on the bench! Hoax loyalist reporter, Julie Carter, for her October 6, 2005, *RuidosoNews.com* article "Follow the Blood: In the Billy the Kid Case, Miller Exhumed," [APPENDIX: 7] quoted Sederwall:

> "Whoever was laid on that, whether it was Billy the Kid or not," said Sederwall, "he left his DNA." The investigators said the amount of blood found on the bench indicated that whoever was on that bench must have been still alive. **"Dead men don't bleed," explained Sederwall. "and we witnessed a large amount of blood."** [author's boldface]

Sederwall made up "blood." But he could not stop his new concoction's absurd implications. Did Garrett tell his friend Billy, "This will hurt; but you'll thank me later: BANG!? During the 200 townspeople's vigil, did Billy (painfully) climb off the bench, while Garrett switched in the innocent victim? Why did the townspeople not notice a new corpse? Why did no pretender the hoaxers planned to dig up have this story?

Sederwall wisely never elaborated. And tangled innocent-dead-victim-and-shot-living-bloody-Billy-on-the-bench added to public befuddlement, and assumption that it all made sense.

## SHAKEY MAXWELL FURNITURE HISTORY

Maxwell family history validating the bench is problematic. That the Kid was laid out after midnight on July 15, 1881 on a Fort Sumner carpenter's bench is given by Deputy John William Poe's quote, used in the "Probable Cause Statement for Case # 2003-274;" and is from Poe's 1933 book, *The Death of Billy the*

*Kid*: "[S]everal women pleaded for permission to take charge of the body ... They carried it across the yard to a carpenter shop, where it was laid out on a workbench, the women placing lighted candles around it according to their ideas of properly conducting a 'wake' for the dead." Then the bench likely continued its use in the shop.

But just three years later, on January 15, 1884, the Maxwells lost Fort Sumner in auction to a Lonny Horn, Sam Doss, Daniel Taylor, John Lord, and the New England Cattle Company. Their mansion was torn down in about 1887. Some Maxwells, including Lucien Maxwell's widow, Luz, moved into a house two miles to the town's southeast, built by her son-in-law, Manuel Abreu (who had married two Maxwell daughters: Amelia, who died; then Odelia).

It strains credulity that in plummeting fortunes, Maxwells saved the carpenter's bench. Billy was not a saint with holy relics! In fact, the Maxwell's only came up with it and other Billy the Kid objects 45 years later for first historians: Maurice Garland Fulton, Walter Noble Burns, and Robert N. Mullin. Stella Abreu Miller, enterprising teenaged daughter of Odelia Maxwell Abreu, made a little museum for them; possibly asking still-living Deluvina and Paulita Maxwell about comparable objects from the old days.

Deputy Sederwall located all that Maxwell furniture in the Albuquerque home of Manuel "Mannie" Miller, Stella's son, who moved from Fort Sumner in 1944, and brought the furniture there in 1959. He died in March of 2011. Soon after, I met his nephew, Kenny Miller, Stella Abreu Miller's grandson, the new caretaker. Kenny Miller showed me the objects in their garage-like converted chicken coop; and gave me photos of them. Included was young Stella's home-made sign about "outlaw" Billy the Kid - not what Billy's day's Maxwells would have called him - and indicating her pandering to tourists. Stella Abreu Miller wrote:

> FOR YOUR INFORMATION
> THIS MUSEUM IS OWNED BY THE NIECE AND NEPHEW OF PETE MAXWELL. IT WAS IN HIS HOME WHERE BILLY THE KID WAS KILLED BY SHERIFF PAT GARRETT WE WILL ASSURE AND NOT MISREPRESENT ANY ONE WHO
> IS INTERESTED IN THE SOUTH-WEST AND ITS NOTORIOUS OUTLAW BILLY THE KID. THERES NOT JUST ONE OR TWO ANTIQUES BUT SEVERAL THINGS OF INTEREST DATED BACK 18-81
> AND TERRITORIAL DAYS.

Maurice Garland Fulton photographed Stella's bench there in 1926. By 1937, her museum closed; but a reporter, Dee Blythe, wrote "Billy the Kid Landmarks Fast Vanishing: Historic Spots

Hard to Find; Markers Needed" for the *Clovis, New Mexico Evening News-Journal*. With photos, it stated:

> Nearby [a post office] is the house of Manuel Abreu and Mrs. Stella Miller, children of Mrs. Odelia Abreu, youngest of the daughters of Pete Maxwell. They have treasured quite a few relics of the old days, particularly with reference to Billy the Kid, but these relics are all jumbled together into one small room of the house.
>
> The collection includes the carpenter's bench on which Billy the Kid's body was laid to cool, the bed beside which Pat Garrett sat talking to Pete Maxwell that fateful night; a rifle once owned by the Kid; a washstand that was struck by Garrett's second shot; the lamp Deluvina Maxwell held to see if the Kid was dead ...
>
> Last year, for awhile these relics were on display in a building on highway 60 in Fort Sumner [Stella Miller's museum]; but the arrangement was unsatisfactory and they were brought back to their out-of-the-way resting place.

What I saw put in question Sederwall and Sullivan's claims.

The headboard, compared to the 1937 photo, had lost its carved top third; and still had no center, being only an oval rim. [Figure: 1] It *had no place* for "Garrett's second shot" as in Poe's 1933 *The Death of Billy the Kid*: "[T]here were only two shots fired, the third report, as we learned afterward, being caused by the rebound of the second bullet, which had struck the adobe wall and rebounded against the headboard of a wooden bedstead."

The washstand was an unconvincing toy-like miniature, with two holes - called bullet holes by Stella Abreu Miller.

The carpenter's bench, 3 crude planks with legs and 7 feet long, had faint brown stains and drips on its underside - like rust.

Nevertheless, the hoaxers did ricochet validation of the bench with "official historian" Professor Paul Hutton. From May 12, 2007 to July 22, 2007, Hutton put the washstand, bedstead, and carpenter's bench in a Billy the Kid show in the Albuquerque Museum of Art and History. He labeled the bench falsely as having "human blood," and attributed that to Dr. Henry Lee.

But key Maxwell family truth was told me by Kenny Miller: "The family has no doubt that Pat Garrett killed Billy the Kid."

And most important, was that the bench, real or not, was forensically useless for Billy the Kid DNA - except for hoaxing. Of course, forensic hoaxing was being done wildly.

**FIGURE: 1.** Photo of Maxwell family headboard examined by Dr. Henry Lee - lacking any center. (Courtesy of Kenny Miller)

# FAKING FORENSICS FOR BILLY THE KID CASE BY DR. HENRY LEE

*HOAXBUST: The Billy the Kid Case hoaxers devised a clever scam: use forensic DNA results to claim that Billy the Kid survived Pat Garrett's shooting on July 14, 1881. But required was keeping secret all DNA records to conceal that the claims were fake. Needed was a complicit forensic expert; publicity-hound Dr. Henry Lee filled the bill. Required also was keeping secret that no verifiable DNA of Billy the Kid or any kin existed on the planet. After that, the hoaxers could say anything they wanted about the Kid not being in his grave; or any chosen pretender being him. So a key for forensic hoaxbusting was getting the hoaxers' DNA records.*

## *DNA: THE HOAXERS' HOLY GRAIL*

Billy the Kid was a media magnet; but DNA was media magic. For their hoax to succeed, the Billy the Kid Case hoaxers had to get deoxyribonucleic acid (DNA) to make "high-tech CSI forensic" claims about any conclusion they made up about Pat Garrett as a murderer, or of any old-timer pretender having been Billy. Their impassable obstacle was that no valid DNA source existed!

Nevertheless, on their fake DNA shopping list were New Mexico graves of Billy the Kid and his mother, Catherine Antrim; an old carpenter's bench claimed by Maxwell family descendants about 45 years after Billy's death; and Billy the Kid identity claimants: "Brushy Bill" Roberts and John Miller - plus about two dozen other imposters to dig up to keep TV programs rolling.

And Governor Bill Richardson's "official historian" for the Billy the Kid Case, Professor Paul Hutton, had hooked Sheriff Tom Sullivan and Deputy Steve Sederwall up with a TV documentary-making production company, Bill Kurtis productions, for "media circus" programs (which Hutton would also write and co-produce). Bill Kurtis manufactured what scholarly forensic experts called "show-biz forensics" - showy, with shaky to sham science. And, when the hoaxers made contact with him, Bill Kutis's expert for his razzmatazz was Dr. Henry Lee, already on Kutis's payroll for a History Channel series titled "Investigating History."

Dr. Lee also used a laboratory for his DNA extractions and matchings: Orchid Cellmark, near Dallas, Texas. Thereby, Lee could stay hands-on for hoaxing DNA and hiding records.

## DR. HENRY LEE WAS THE PERFET DNA MATCH

Dr. Henry Lee was a perfect DNA match for the Billy the Kid Case hoax. He chose cases by their limelight wattage. And he had national name recognition by helping O.J. Simpson walk free in his 1996 murder trial. As to having professional reputation for veracity, that was another story.

Prosecutor, Vincent Bugliosi, in his book, *Outrage: The Five Reasons Why O.J. Simpson Got Away With Murder,* called Henry Lee "nothing short of incompetent." Bugliosi was avoiding "liar." An example from *Outrage* was Lee's testifying that "crime-scene" shoe "imprints" on murder victim Nicole Simpson's walkway did not match O.J. Simpson's incriminatory, "size-12 Bruno Magli bloody shoe prints" - also at the scene. But the "prints" Lee used, according to Bugliosi, had been hardened into the concrete during its laying "ten years earlier!"

Valuable Dr. Lee resurfaced for the 2007 murder trial defense for music impresario, Phil Spector; accused, and ultimately convicted, of fatally shooting actress, Lana Clarkson. But Attorney Sara Caplan - in Spector's first defense team - testified to the judge, Larry Paul Fidler, that, at the crime scene, Lee bottled dead Clarkson's torn-off fingernail, which indicated possible struggle - not Spector's defense's claim of her committing suicide. Then that fingernail disappeared. Judge Fidler declared destruction of evidence. The CNN.com AP headline of May 25, 2007 was: "Famed expert's credibility takes a hit at Spector trial."

That Dr. Henry Lee was part of the Billy the Kid Case hoaxers' team from 2004 onward, is also a good indicator of his unscrupulousness. Wearing a cowboy hat in photo, Lee even pops up in 2010 as a member of the hoaxers' "posse" in past-Deputy Steve Sederwall's website called billythekidcase.com.

Lee's joining the Billy the Kid Case was announced with fanfare by hoax-backing *Albuquerque Journal* reporter, Rene Romo. On August 2, 2004, Romo splashed, "Forensic Expert on Billy's Case: Questions Remain on Outlaw's Fate" [APPENDIX: 8]. Romo declared:

> Dr. Henry Lee, one of the nation's leading forensic scientists ... has added the Billy the Kid slaying to his case files ... "This is an extremely interesting case of some historical importance,' Lee said in an interview ... 'That's why I agreed to spend some of my own time to work with them ... It's basically a worthwhile project and legitimate."

So famous Dr. Lee called the Billy the Kid Case "a worthwhile project and legitimate." What else was the public to think - not knowing about the hoaxers' trick of ricochet validation?

Rene Romo stressed Lee's "own time," because, by then, the hoaxers were trying to conceal their obvious use of taxpayer money. But was Lee paid? Yes.

Romo states: "Lee's expenses were paid by Illinois-based Kurtis Productions, headed by Bill Kurtis, host of the History Channel series 'Investigating History.' "

Lee's profit motive was expanded in the August 12, 2004 *Lincoln County News* article by Doris Cherry: "Forensics 101 for 'Billy." [APPENDIX: 9] She quoted Sheriff Sullivan:

> "Along with Sullivan and Lee were a crew from Curtis [sic] Production Company filming for the History Channel and Court T.V. Dr. Lee also has a show produced by Curtis [sic] Production."

So Billy the Kid DNA was to be churned out by Lee and Kurtis for their forensic enterprise. No wonder Lee called the project "worthwhile." He was joining an exhumation franchise.

But the public was fed a different bill of goods via the press. By April 13, 2006, misled reporter, Leo W. Banks of the *Tucson Weekly*, in "The New Billy the Kid?" had Lee pleading; as in: "Everybody wants a piece of the Kid, even a celebrity like Henry Lee ... when he heard about the Kid dig-up efforts, he called Sederwall to volunteer his services."

The Billy the Kid Case hoaxers plugged Lee mercilessly.

Rene Romo's August 2, 2004 *Albuquerque Journal* article even used their "Probable Cause Statement's" quoted historian (and secret fellow hoaxer):

> "You're getting the top guy ... I think that will go a long way to finding out what happened in Lincoln," said David S. Turk, a historian with the U.S. Marshals Service ... who is cooperating on the case.

Added was that a Calvin Ostler, a Utah Medical Examiner - would participate. Unmentioned, was that Ostler was Lee's business partner. So Lee-Turk-Ostler did ricochet validation, without public awareness that they were all in cahoots for tabloid-level documentary-making with Bill Kurtis and Professor Paul Hutton - with a waiting talking-head: Bill Richardson.

## LEE FINDS "BILLY" AND "BLOOD" ON THE BENCH

The insurmountable problem for Dr. Lee (if he was doing a legitimate forensic investigation) and for his fellow Billy the Kid Case hoaxers, was getting "reference DNA." "Reference DNA" has 100% certainty of being from the individual in question; and is the only DNA valid for identity matching.

But by the time Lee joined, the New Mexico Office of the Medical Investigator had declared the graves of Billy and his mother useless for DNA because of their uncertain locations.

However, DNA forensics were not Lee's worry. His worry was *DNA film footage.* Anything linked to Billy the Kid sufficed. If graves of Billy and his mother were blocked, the list had one item: the carpenter's bench. To use that bench for fake DNA had made the hoaxers switch their fake history from Garrett's shot innocent murder victim on that bench, to shot playing-dead-Billy on it.

But the bench needed feigned "validation" - since it had a fatal gap of zero provenance from 1881 to 1926. Ricocheting validation fell to the hoax's "official historian" Professor Paul Hutton and to "Probable Cause Statement" hoax historian, David Turk. On April 19, 2006, hoax-cheerleader reporter, Julie Carter, in *RuidosoNews.com*, reported in "Digging up bones":

> UNM History professor Paul Hutton and U.S. Treasury [sic - Marshals Service] historian Dave Turk have both authenticated the bench.

Since that bench had to provide "Billy the Kid's blood" for DNA, guess what Dr. Lee allegedly found. HE FOUND BLOOD!!! Next, guess if that was true. No!

Rene Romo's August 2, 2004, *Albuquerque Journal's* "Forensic Expert on Billy's Case" gave the new hoax scripture:

> Lee, assisted by Calvin Ostler ... performed tests on the bench that Sederwall believes to be the one on which the Kid's body was laid out after Garrett gunned him down. Preliminary results indicated **trace evidence of blood**, [author's boldface] but, without further testing, it is not certain whether the blood was human, Lee said.

On August 12th, reporter Doris Cherry, for her *Lincoln County News*, "Forensics 101 for 'Billy,' " wrote:

Dr. Lee proved the good odds by utilizing a laser to bore into the wood of the bench to take samples and he took scrapings from the top and underneath of the bench. "Then he swabbed it with the chemical that changes color to indicate the presence of blood," Sullivan said.

The hoaxers were just hoaxing. Their "blood" was not proven - and never would be. Luminol is a non-specific chemical that fluoresces with iron-containing substances. Besides blood, it lights up for rust, paints, and cleaning agents - all more likely on a possibly random carpenter's bench than blood. And no other testing would *ever be done* by that hoaxing group to verify blood - or to connect it to Billy Bonney (which was impossible).

Aware of the problems, the hoaxers bolstered their "blood" claim. First, faking preservation of 123 year old blood was needed. Doris Cherry's "Forensics 101 for 'Billy," quoted Sederwall:

> "The focus of attention for Dr. Lee was an old bench ... The bench has been in the Maxwell family descendents since 1881 and has been stored out of weather, protecting the blood evidence ... **Only once was the blood exposed to the elements, when a family member who took the bench without family approval returned it to the Maxwell family home in Fort Sumner and left it outside to get rained on once.** [author's boldface] So the odds of finding blood evidence were very good."

That "rained on" part was bad for blood, but Sederwall's mouth had a life of its own, and truth tended to slip out.

He kept on talking. For an October 6, 2005 *RuidosoNews.com* article, loyalist Julie Carter wrote "Follow the Blood: In the Billy the Kid Case, Miller Exhumed." [APPENDIX: 7] Carter stated:

> The Maxwell compound and everything in it was reportedly washed away in a flood of 1906. The photo of the bench was taken in 1926 by historian Maurice Fulton ... Since 1959, they [Maxwell family] had stored the historical furniture and household items in an old chicken coop.

Ooops! Added to unknown location from 1881 to 1926 is possibly "washed away" in a 1906 flood! Then "a bench" is in the 1926 photo op, but had a storage gap till 1959 and the "chicken coop" [sic - Manuel Miller's back yard building].

Next the hoaxers got carried away by blood. Romo's original "trace," in his August 2, 2004, "Forensic Expert on Billy's Case," started bleeding like stigmata. In Doris Cherry's "Forensics 101 for Billy," Sullivan stated that Lee "found a lot of blood." For Julie Carter's "Follow the Blood," Sederwall says, "We witnessed a large amount of blood;" and he creatively added: "an upper chest wound." By April 13, 2006, "blood" was almost dripping off the bench. Leo Banks of the *Tucson Weekly*, in "The New Billy the Kid," reported that Sederwall said the bench was "saturated!"

Then, as old cartoon character, Porky Pig, said, "Th-th-that's all, folks." You just heard, in its entirety, Dr. Henry Lee's "discovery" of the "bloody bench reference DNA of Billy the Kid" on a carpenter's bench lacking any forensic chain of custody!

## *"BLOOD OF BILLY THE KID" GETS A DNA LAB*

Next, Dr. Henry Lee had to turn the fake "blood of Billy the Kid" into fake "DNA of Billy the Kid." By his admission, Lee sent his bench swabbing and scraping specimens to his primary forensic laboratory: Orchid Cellmark. Reporter, Doris Cherry, in her August 12, 2004, "Forensics 101 for 'Billy' " stated:

> Each swab and all scrapings from the bench were sealed in preparation to shipping to the Orchard Selmark [sic - Orchid Cellmark] Lab in Dallas. Sullivan said Dr. Lee uses the lab for most of his work, and the lab is also famous for its forensic work to determine DNA of the 9-11 victims.

Guess if Orchid Cellmark Lab extracted human DNA. OF COURSE THEY DID! Guess if Orchid Cellmark Lab tests for blood. NO. THEY ONLY DO DNA!

Not mentioned to the public, is that any object left in an environment with humans accumulates human DNA; and that controls were necessary to rule out Sederwall, Sullivan, Lee, Ostler, and Maxwells as DNA sources (meaning getting DNA from them all for comparison with Lee's DNA samples). Soon, the rightfully nervous hoaxers called the lab's name "secret."

In fact, Orchid Cellmark had "secrets." On August 9, 2004, I had contacted its then director, Mark Stolorow, explaining the Billy the Kid hoax. He was amused. On August 18th, we spoke again. Stolorow was defensive. Orchid Cellmark, he told me, was under a "gag order" on the case. Dr. Lee was now in charge!

And three months later, Orchid Cellmark was caught faking DNA computer data on another case. That scandal appeared on November 18, 2004, in the internet blog "TalkLeft.com," as "Fraud alleged at Cellmark, DNA Testing Firm." It concluded: "Bottom line: A lot of defendants will be seeking retesting by an independent lab when the prosecution is relying on results by Cellmark." That scandal left Orchid Cellmark reduced to one lab in Farmers Branch, Texas (called "Dallas" by the hoaxers).

Mark Stolorow was replaced as director by Dr. Rick Staub. Staub apparently had steel-wired nerves like the hoaxers. Later, when they needed someone on site in Arizona for their illegal secret exhumation, Staub showed up himself with his bone bag to illegally transport remains across state lines back to Texas. After all, Dr. Staub was being filmed - Bill Kurtis Productions was making another TV program for the hoaxers!

## DR. LEE GIVES PAT GARRETT A MEAN MAKE-OVER WITH THE MAXWELL FAMILY WASHSTAND

Dr. Henry Lee's faking of "Billy bench DNA" was just his warm-up. He was on a forensic (pay)roll. Pat Garrett as demonic murderer was next. As with fabricated shot Billy on the possibly fabricated bench, there was no valid physical evidence at all to investigate. But there was more Maxwell family furniture: there was the punctured, bulletless, child-size washstand from Stella Abreu Maxwell's Billy the Kid Museum via Mannie Maxwell to Deputy Steve Sederwall.

The key historical issue is that on July 14, 1881 Pat Garrett fired a second shot at Billy Bonney in the darkened Peter Maxwell bedroom. Deputy John William Poe recorded where that second bullet went: the headboard of Maxwell's bed. In his 1933 *The Death of Billy the Kid*, Poe wrote:

[A] shot was fired in the room, followed immediately by what everyone within hearing distance thought were two other shots. However, there were only two shots fired, the third report, as we learned afterward, being caused by the rebound of the second bullet, which had struck the adobe wall and **rebounded against the headboard of a wooden bedstead.** [author's boldface]

Hoax helping reporter Rene Romo continued the saga of Dr. Lee's "sleuthing" in his August 2, 2004 *Albuquerque Journal*'s "Forensic Expert on Billy's Case." Lee used that washstand. (Lee simply ignored the headboard from the furniture collection. Recall that it lacked its center, and was just a rim.) And Lee's forensic "analysis of the washstand involved "alien invasion illogic" of "ifs" with that fake object that merely had two holes of uncertain origin from an unknown time. Romo stated:

> Lee and the investigators also examined a washstand that was purportedly struck by a bullet when Garrett shot the Kid in a bedroom of the outlaw's friend, Pete Maxwell, in Fort Sumner ... Lee and the investigators used laser technology Saturday to determine the trajectory of the bullet as it entered the left side of the washstand and exited the right at a downward angle. Given the washstand's likely location in the room, the investigation has already cast some doubt on Garrett's account of the fatal shooting, Sederwall and [Calvin] Ostler said.
>
> "The evidence we are seeing does not corroborate the popular legend," Ostler said. "Something's askew" ...
>
> One simple explanation that Lee offered is that Garrett may have shot defensively at the Kid as he fled and struck the washstand from the side instead of head on. Garrett's official story may have omitted that embarrassing detail. "You don't want to paint yourself as a chicken," Lee suggested.

This rendition proves that a career alternative for Dr. Henry Lee is stand-up comic. Based on non-validated furniture, unknown location in a non-existent room, no bullet for dating, no provable relationship of the washstand to Garrett or to Billy or to Peter Maxwell, and its irrelevancy to proving anything about any murder victim, Lee creates a crime scene, positions Garrett in the room, and declares him a "chicken!" No wonder O.J. Simpson walked free. But that was less funny.

Deputy Steve Sederwall was soon spouting Dr. Lee's freshly minted Pat Garrett mythology in Julie Carter's October 2005, "Follow the Blood":

> "Using high-tech lasers and other modern crime scene methods, investigators learned that the shooting of the Kid in Pete Maxwell's bedroom was not in the way history has portrayed it. Tests indicate that Garrett fired his second shot from the doorway while on his knees and with his left hand on the floor, firing back over his shoulder ... Being blinded by his

first shot, it appears he was in a great hurry to get out of the room and fell to the floor." He [Sederwall] added: "To find the furniture from Maxwell's bedroom was great. But to have Dr. Lee recover usable evidence was truly a historical find."

## DR. LEE'S DEPUTY KILLING "INVESTIGATION"

Next on peripatetic and crooked Dr. Henry Lee's agenda for the hoaxers (and presumably for future TV viewing - which came to pass in March of 2010 using the deputy killing "investigation" here) were the April 28, 1881 jailbreak killings of Deputies Robert Olinger and James Bell by Billy Bonney: the Billy the Kid Case hoax's sub-investigation from the "Probable Cause Statement."

As may be recalled, the connection to the Billy the Kid Case hoax's "Garrett as murderer" was to manufacture his murder motive of "friendship," by making up that Garrett gave Billy the deputy killing murder weapon. Since there now exists no weapon, and since the Garrett "friendship" was fabricated by the hoaxers, Lee's job for them was to manufacture doubt about the jailbreak circumstances to raise "suspicion" about history's actual information about the shooting of James Bell.

In that context, one may recall that the "alien invasion illogic" of that Probable Cause Statement's sub-investigation was that *if* Garrett gave the Kid the murder weapon, he was a friend; and would, thus, help Billy escape again on July 14, 1881 by killing an innocent victim for the Fort Sumner grave.

Dr. Lee's forensic investigation for the Bell killing ranks as the hoax's most silly forensics, since it has nothing at all to do with the sub-investigation, Deputy Bell, or reality. And its conclusion is very funny on its own.

Apparently, if one points a camera at Dr. Henry Lee, then points to a place, he will find blood. The lawmen hoaxers took him to the old Lincoln courthouse, the site of the Bell killing. Of course, Lee tested for blood. Of course, he found "blood."

Lee's report on his "investigation," dated February 25, 2005, was obtained years later during litigation against the hoaxers. Done on August 1, 2004 as "Examination of Lincoln County Court House," it gives a photograph of what is called the "target area," which is "at the top landing of the stairs." Ignored, and necessary for a control sampling, is that Deputy Bell historically was shot by Billy, and possibly bled, at the *bottom* of the stairs. But the entire wooden staircase has been replaced since Billy's day.

Present for the "investigation" with Lee were Deputy Steve Sederwall, Sheriff Tom Sullivan, Sheriff Gary Graves, and, surprisingly, hoaxer U.S. Marshals Service Historian David Turk - taxpayer funded all the way from Washington, D.C. Not as surprising was the presence of the man paying Henry Lee for the fake forensics: Bill Kurtis of Bill Kurtis productions, Mr. Media Circus himself.

Lee's report misstates that the staircase was "repainted." The one Lee had for his crime scene reconstruction of April 28, 1881, was actually *replaced* in the 1980's. And Lee's report has a photo of the "target area" showing brown drips on the upper wall under the stairway. The stains look like dripping rusted water.

To test those stains, Lee used O-tolidine, like Luminol, a chemical that shows a change in presence of iron compounds - like rust. But cagy Lee calls the possible rust stains *"blood-like* stains;" and states that they merit "presumptive blood tests." So, in his report's "Conclusions," Lee states - you guess - "those stains could be bloodstains."

And, as the forensic expert doing a Deputy Bell CSI investigation with blood recovery, Lee should obviously have asked initially if there existed Bell remains or Bell kin for DNA matching. The answer is no. But Lee slyly concludes misleadingly: "Further DNA testing could reveal the nature and identity of that blood like stains." [sic - on Lee's grammar]

As to "identity of that blood like stains," no test in the world could "reveal the nature and identity," since there existed no Bill DNA for any matching.

And, as to the drips on the "target area," if one faces the long, first floor wall below the stairway in question, its entirety rains down Lee's rusty stain marks. A second floor Battle of the Alamo would have been needed to get enough blood for all that dripping - rather than the more likely rusty leakage before a roof repair in the 1980's.

By the next day, August 2, 2004, in the *Albuquerque Journal's* "Forensic Expert on Billy's Case," Rene Romo already was privy to "the truth." You guess. There was Deputy Bell's blood!!

And that "blood" allowed forensic expert Lee to reconstruct the crime scene of Bell's killing - though neither blood nor a link to Bell existed!

Lee and the investigators Sunday afternoon also found several positive indications of blood residue below floor-boards at the top of a stairwell in the old Lincoln County courthouse.

Such evidence could support Sederwall's theory that the Kid fatally shot deputy J.W. Bell there, at the top of the stairs, in his infamous escape from the Lincoln County jail. That version would also contradict Garrett's account that the Kid, at the top of the stairs, shot Bell who was at the bottom of the stairwell.

*Lincoln County News* reporter Doris Cherry followed suit with her August 12, 2004 "Forensics 101 for 'Billy' ":

Sullivan said that after studying the courthouse and the shooting he contended Bell was really killed at the top of the stairs, not near the bottom of the stairs as legend has it.

Doris Cherry did note Sheriff Sullivan's admitting that, lacking any Bell kin, DNA testing could not confirm "blood" as his.

So what was the conclusion of the hoaxers' deputy shooting investigation? Deputy James Bell had been shot on *the top, versus bottom, of a stairway*. This "conclusion" was based on no proof of actual blood, no relationship to any shooting, no existing stairway from the period in question, and no connection at all to Deputy James Bell!

And Deputy Steve Sederwall himself appeared in a National Geographic International TV program, produced by British Parthenon Entertainment for the Discovery ID channel, to give the world this Lee top-of-stairs "revelation" on March 13, 2010.

Again, Porky Pig says, "Th-th-that's all, folks."

## GHOST OF LEE'S DEPUTY KILLING "INVESTIGATION"

Dr. Henry Lee old Lincoln courthouse floorboard investigation kept on reappearing for a decade like the ghost of Christmas past. As the sub-investigation for Case 2003-274's "Probable Cause Statement," it was shape-shifted by the hoaxers during my investigations of them into their entire murder case; to make it seem as if the murder being investigated by the Billy the Kid Case was just the Kid's killing of his deputy guards, and not Sheriff Pat Garrett's alleged killing of the innocent victim. This switcheroo was done in an attempt to conceal the DNA records which the hoax was now generating. And the above revealed shenanigans do prove why these crooks were very motivated to hide their sham handiwork of "forensic DNA."

# FAKING FORENSICS IN BILLY THE KID CASE BYPSEUDO-CSI

*HOAXBUST: To debunk the fake forensics of the Billy the Kid Case hoax, I used forensic experts. The graves of Billy and his mother were invalidated for DNA by uncertain locations. The carpenter's bench was worthless because of unprovable provenance, no provable blood, 123 year old blood being useless for identity matching, and blood also being useless since no reference DNA of Billy the Kid existed for its validating. Saying "dead men don't bleed" to claim bench blood from live Billy, is false, since blood does drain from a corpse. And if identity matching resulted, it could be from coincidence alone, since DNA matching is statistical, and requires historical corroboration. And pretenders were automatically canceled out for lack of playing-dead-on-the-bench death scene stories. Eventually, my getting Orchid Cellmark DNA records proved the hoaxer DNA claims were fabrications.*

## *DEBUNKING THE CARPENTER'S WORKBENCH*

Dr. Henry Lee could not legitimately use the carpenter's bench to start "a forensic chain of evidence," because it lacked 100% certainty of being the crime scene object or being stored to protect a forensic sample like blood. Maxwell family claims are undermined by: 1) unlikelihood of its being saved after the sale of Fort Sumner in 1884; 2) possible storage by Pete Maxwell's sister's husband, Manuel Abreu, being disrupted by flooding; and 3) a 45 year gap before Maxwell descendants presented it to historians; 4) later exposure to outside elements and rain. And its hoaxing also required the falsity that a corpse does not "bleed."

## DEBUNKING BENCH "BLOOD"

*FAKING BLOOD:* Blood was the only possible Billy tissue for getting DNA. But Dr. Lee did not prove it by using Luminol. Tom Mauriello, author of a textbook on forensic science, professor of criminology at the University of Maryland, and a director of a crime lab, said Luminol's non-specificity cannot prove blood.

And Orchid Cellmark Laboratory does not test for blood; only doing DNA extraction from samples. No other testing for blood was done on Dr. Lee's samples.

*FAKING LINK TO BILLY:* Even granting the fake blood claim, the hoaxers cannot link their "blood" to Billy. They need *his* reference DNA to match with bench DNA. And his certain DNA does not exist. His only kin, his mother, Catherine Antrim, is useless by her uncertain gravesite and its OMI block.

Forensic expert Tom Mauriello also noted that carpenters cut themselves. And if shot Billy had left blood, the people doing his vigil, or the carpenter the next day, would have washed it off.

Also, DNA cannot be dated or reveal its tissue of origin. Brian Wraxall, a 40 year forensic DNA expert trained in Scotland Yard, and Chief Forensic Serologist at Serological Research Institute in Richmond, California, said the "bench DNA" could be that week's sneeze by then-Sheriff Sullivan.

And there also existed another potential shot corpse for bench "blood." Gunslinger, Joe Grant, on January 3, 1880, tried to shoot Billy in Fort Sumner's Hargrove's Saloon; but, as Billy said, he "got there first." Joe Grant may have been laid out there too.

*FAKING MATCHING VALIDITY:* Even granting the fake blood, and fake link to Billy the Kid, identity matching with very old blood is a problem. Dr. Edward Blake, a DNA forensic expert at Forensic Sciences Associates in California, said he knows of no small blood sample, significantly older than 50 years, that has been used successfully for identity matching with current DNA technology. That leaves any match claim questionable. And if Dr. Henry Lee wanted to prove otherwise, he would have to do the research to prove that antique blood can be valid for matching.

## DEBUNKING SURVIVING SHOT BILLY

Even granting the fake bench, fake blood, and fake Billy link, one comes to the "surviving Billy" of "dead men don't bleed." (Comically, "Bell's stairway-top blood" proves he was *alive* there!)

*BLEEDING CORPSES:* To continue their hoax, the hoaxers needed surviving Billy – so they claimed: "dead men don't bleed." (Of course, that also faked that there was any blood on the bench.)

But the dead *do bleed* by drainage, as confirmed by retired L.A.P.D. ballistics detective, Jimmy Trahin; and Dr. Harry Bonnell, a forensic pathologist in San Diego, California.

And dead Billy's blood would more likely drain out in Maxwell's bedroom or in the vigil walk to the carpenter's shop.

How do the dead bleed? Forensic pathologist in the San Antonio, Texas Office of the Medical Examiner, Dr. Vincent DiMaio, a gunshot wound expert and author of definitive books on the subject, who has done more than 9,000 autopsies and reviewed more than 30,000 in his career, said blood leaves a corpse's bullet-torn vessels because the circulatory system is under pressure: blood pressure. So elasticity of vessels under pressure squeezes blood out. That free blood - up to 3 liters in a fatal chest wound like Billy Bonney's - can get out, depending on exit wound size and corpse manipulation.

*EXIT WOUNDS:* For "bleeding on the bench," an exit wound was necessary. But was an exit wound necessarily present?

Dr. Vincent DiMaio said no. Even at close range, a .44/40 bullet - like from Garrett's single action revolver - does not always make one. That alone eliminates the "bloody bench" scenario.

Dr. Bill Bass elaborated. He is the forensic pathologist who created "Death's Acre" for the Department of Anthropology at the University of Tennessee, to study corpses for crime investigations. Non-exit can include lodging in bone. Also, if Garrett's gun barrel was begrimed by black powder, its internal rifling groove for creating effective bullet spin would not work; and the bullet entering victim Billy could wobble, causing tilted entry and internal lodging. Again, there would be no exit wound.

What about a big exit wound? They "bleed" more. Dr. Bill Bass noted that an exit wound is usually larger than an entrance wound, since a bullet creates a flaring cone of destruction. So *quite dead* Billy could have had a big back hole for blood leakage either before or after being on a carpenter's bench.

*PLAYING DEAD*: By claiming "dead men don't bleed to get a live Billy bleeding on their carpenter's bench," the hoaxers were stuck with Billy "playing dead" throughout the townspeople's night vigil and the Coroner's Jury inquest in the morning.

But can someone in his shot situation play dead? "Impossible," said Dr. Vincent DiMaio. Being shot in the chest causes involuntary hyperventilation: rapid, *visible* gasping because of lung damage. So the hoaxers' ploy of "Billy playing dead while bleeding on the bench" bites the dust.

Remaining for the hoaxers was only a conspiracy theory of the whole town and coroner's jury covering up live and escaping Billy. But then Garrett would not have needed to shoot him at all.

## "BILLY" DNA MATCHING AS A "LOTTERY"

Deputy Steve Sederwall, adroit in creating populist imagery, used a "lottery" metaphor for DNA matching of an exhumed pretender's remains to their bench DNA. Rene Romo quoted Sederwall in the *Albuquerque Journal* of November 6, 2005 in "Billy the Kid Probe May Yield New Twist" [APPENDIX: 10]:

> "Wouldn't it be a coincidence if someone we dug up in Arizona, and who died in 1934 [sic - 1937] and claimed to be Billy the Kid, bled on the bench? That's like winning the lottery ... That would be so coincidental, I would challenge anyone to prove it's not him [Billy the Kid].' "

But Sederwall's "DNA lottery" is unwinnable; and not just because of unprovable bench, unprovable Billy blood, and no pretender having the bench scenario.

Bench DNA itself is the problem as Sederwall's "lottery ticket." To "win," its "numbers" must match a pretender's numbers. Here is why that is unattainable.

*BACKGROUND:* DNA is a double-stranded molecule, with thousands of genetic codes strung like beads in sequences along its lengths. For DNA matching, specific bead sequences - "markers" — have been picked for identity comparisons. If all are the same in different samples, it is *possible* the person is the same.

For DNA from a cell nucleus, 13 to 16 markers are used. For DNA from mitochondria - vesicles in cell fluid - *only one marker* is used. Orchid Cellmark used *mitochondrial* DNA from its samples.

*DEGRADATION AND CONTAMINATION:* A lottery ticket needs to be intact. But bench DNA strands would degrade; fragmenting like chopped spaghetti. And objects exposed to people, over years, accumulate *their* DNA too. It chops up too. All pieces mix together. That contamination, according to Dr. Elizabeth Johnson, a California DNA expert (who exposed a Houston, crime lab, DNA scandal), means it is impossible to separate out one person (like Billy) from the muddle.

At best, a "marker" *not matching a pretender's*, would show *no identity*. But identity is *impossible* to claim. So Sederwall's "lottery," has only "shredded tickets" mixed like confetti. No single ticket can be assembled to match anyone else's "ticket."

*MITOCHONDRIAL DNA:* A real lottery ticket has big odds against a 100% match. Mitochondrial DNA's single marker makes the reverse: a match of one in hundreds; instead of the one in trillions with DNA from the nucleus. So approximately one in 500 people can be the hoaxers' "Billy the Kid" by coincidence alone!

Dr. Simon Ford, president of Lexigen Science and Law Consultants in California, said it is, thus, impossible to use DNA to claim certain identity - even with a 100% match.

So, with mitochondrial DNA, history must be added to improve odds. In the pretenders' cases, none of their histories matched "bleeding on bench," or even being on the bench. So any match using bench DNA is invalidated by their history alone.

Worse, mitochondrial DNA testing is so sensitive, according to Dr. Bill Shields, a mitochondrial DNA expert and professor of biology at Syracuse University in New York, that even a few contaminating cells can skew results - by being read themselves as if *they* were the sample. So, in Sederwall's lottery, *he* could be the DNA ticket compared to a pretender's DNA ticket!

Worse, mitochondrial DNA comes only from a mother. The hoaxers also wanted to match Catherine Antrim to pretenders. But their Arizona pretender, John Miller did not claim her as his mother, invalidating that matching used for him.

*INHIBITORS:* DNA - the "lottery ticket numbers" - can be misread as false positives by lab machinery if "inhibiting substances" come from the bench - wood residues, paint, grease, and coal oil (kerosene) - said Mark Taylor, a forensic DNA expert and President of Technical Associates Inc. in Ventura, California.

## HOAXER HOPE

"Winning" the "lottery" can be "rigged" by semantics. Dr. Elizabeth Johnson noted that "match" does not mean "100% identical." It just means "comparison." So the hoaxers could claim a "match" if only a few base pairs between samples were the same. By 2005, they did declare a pretender "match" as "80%." That means *no* identity. But I named that the "Doomsday Document."

Simpler for the hoaxers was hiding all their DNA records for years, while fabricating DNA claims - until I finally got DNA records of Dr. Henry Lee and Orchid Cellmark Laboratory and could lay bare the audacity of the Billy the Kid Case's forensic DNA hoaxing.

# BILLY THE KID CASE'S
# HIDDEN FORENSIC DNA RECORDS

*HOAXBUST: The Billy the Kid Case hoaxes concealed all their forensic DNA records so as to hide the total fakery of their DNA claims. During open records litigation, and by subpoena, I finally got a copy of Dr. Lee's specimen recovery report and many Orchid Cellmark Laboratory DNA extraction records. Of course, these records proved that the hoaxers had been hoaxing all their forensic DNA claims.*

## DR. HENRY LEE'S REPORT FOR CASE 2003-274

On May 1, 2006, Dr. Henry Lee responded by letter to my investigation of Billy the Kid Case forensics on State of Connecticut Department of Public Safety letterhead with himself listed as "Chief Emeritus." He stated:

> [T]he Lincoln County Sheriff's Department contacted me. They requested a forensic expert to perform preliminary identification and scene reconstruction ... We examined a wooden bench, and floorboards at the courthouse.
>
> I completed my examination of the evidence and submitted my report to the Lincoln County Sheriff's Department. ...
>
> Since I did not conduct any DNA testing on the evidence and the Lincoln County Sheriff's Department sent samples directly to a private laboratory for analysis, I am sorry but I do not have answers to your questions regarding DNA.

Lee, an active hoaxer, was trying to throw me off. He concluded, "If you want a copy of the report, you should contact the Lincoln County Sheriff's Department directly."

Completing that shell game, Sheriffs Tom Sullivan, followed by Sheriff Rick Virden, of course, denied having the report.

Lee also lied that the Sheriff's Department sent the samples he had collected from the bench and courthouse "directly to a private laboratory." In fact, it would emerge 6 years later, that Lee's partner, Calvin Ostler, also present for Lee's "examination," did that. Also, Lee kept secret his lab's name.

Lee had reason for concealment. His report was like his "footprints in 10 year old concrete" for O.J.'s crime scene: fakery.

## DR. HENRY LEE'S REPORT

On January 31, 2012, after years of my open records litigation, the law enforcement hoaxers handed over a copy of Dr. Lee's 25 page report, dated February 25, 2005, and titled "Forensic Research & Training Center Forensic Examination Report." [APPENDIX: 11] Its header listed "Requested by: Lincoln County Sheriff's Office, New Mexico; Investigation History Program, Kurtis Production." "Local Case No." was "2003-274." The "Report to:" was Steve Sederwall, Lincoln County Sheriff's Office, New Mexico." Recorded for the "forensic investigation team" were: "Calvin Ostler, Forensic Consultant, Riverton, Utah;" "Tom Sullivan, Sheriff, Lincoln County, New Mexico;" "Steve Sederwall, Deputy Sheriff, Lincoln County;" and none other than "David Turk, US Marshall [sic], United States Marshall [sic] Service."

The report's sections were titled: "Item # 1 Workbench," "Item # 2 Washstand," and "Examination of Lincoln County Court House."

Lee's "Results and Conclusion" section was inadvertently funny, but shows that *Albuquerque Journal* reporter Rene Romo correctly quoted Lee's faked "findings." And the report proves Lee as an active hoaxer. Lee wrote [with retained grammatical errors]:

After a detail examination of the evidence and review of all the results of field testing, the following conclusion was reached.

1. Brownish dark stains were observed on different areas of the workbench. These areas were subjected to chemical presumptive blood tests. Some of those samples give a positive reaction. These results indicate the presence of Heme or Peroxidase like activity with those stains testing positive, which suggest that those stains could be bloodstains. Further DNA testing could reveal the nature and identity of these blood-like stains.

**[AUTHOR'S COMMENT: Lee is hoaxing by omitting more obvious rust staining; then implying DNA testing could reveal their "nature and identity." But Orchid Cellmark does not test for blood. And finding DNA would not even connect it to the stains, since no controls were done for DNA from non-stained areas. Nor were control specimens taken from all present to check for contaminating DNA. Lastly, Lee is faking that "[f]urther DNA testing could reveal the nature and identity of these blood-like stains." There exists no reference DNA of Billy the Kid or any of his kin to compare with any DNA found.]**

2. Two bullet holes were located on the side panels of the Washstand. The hole on the left side panel is consistent with a bullet entrance hole while the hole on the right side panel is consistent with a bullet exit hole. However, it is not possible to determine when those bullet holes were produced at this time.

[AUTHOR'S COMMENT: Lee has no proof the washstand is from the "crime scene." However, he feigns taking seriously the wee object - measured by him at 30" high x 28 ¾" long x 16" wide - and makes up room dimensions and its placement to create a fake shooting scene for Pat Garrett, as follows.]

The angles produced in the examination tell us two things:

First, the bullet was fired from no more than 41" from the floor given the reported limitations of the room. The room was reported to be 20' by 20'; the maximum distance is assumed to be 20'. If the firearm was a maximum of 41" off the floor it is unlikely that the shooter was standing. It is more likely the shooter was kneeling, squatting, or close to the floor.

Second, the horizontal angle is such that if the Washstand was positioned so that the back was against the wall, the shot could not have been fired from more than approximately 40 inches from the Washstand, because the wall would have been in the way. The angle of trajectory intersects the back plane of the Washstand at approximately 45 3/16", and no more than 46".

3. No bullet hole and no observable damage, no sign of bullet ricocheted type of defects were found on the Headboard. No blood or biological materials were observed on the Headboard.

[AUTHOR'S COMMENT: Sneaky Lee omits that the remaining rim-like headboard has no center - no place for any bullet!]

4. The floor boards on the 2nd floor stair landing area of the court house have been repaired. Different types of wood and nails were used in this area.

5. Various stains were observed on the surface and underside of the floorboards. Chemical tests for the presence of blood were positive with some of these stains. These results indicate presence of Heme or Peroxidase like activity with those stains tested positive, which suggests that those stains could be bloodstains. Further DNA testing could reveal the nature and identity of those blood-like stains.

[AUTHOR'S COMMENT: Lee omits rust stains' possibility]

## *ORCHID CELLMARK RECORDS FOR CASE 2003-274*

For years, the hoaxers hid their Orchid Cellmark DNA records. But, on April 20, 2012, by subpoena, 133 pages of those records were obtained for Dr. Henry Lee's specimen recoveries and for the exhumed Arizona bodies. Still missing are the hoaxers' claimed matching results of Lee's bench specimens to their pretender remains and random man from Arizona.

These Orchid Cellmark records exposed hoaxing beyond just fabricated DNA claims. The law enforcement hoaxers had lied that: 1) the DNA records did not exist; 2) that Dr. Lee's investigation was not part of Case 2003-274; 3) that Orchid Cellmark's carpenter's bench DNA of Billy the Kid justified exhuming bodies for DNA matching - to see if any old-timer identity claimant had been surviving Billy the Kid (meaning Garrett murdered the innocent victim); 4) that the Arizona exhumations were not part of Case 2003-274; and 5) that mixed DNA samples were useful for future DNA separations.

In truth, the Orchid Cellmark records proved the following:

1) EVIDENCE BAGS LABELS: [Figure: 2] Dr. Lee's specimen bags were labeled for "Chain of Custody" with both Case No. 2003-274 and Orchid Cellmark No. 4444 (with numbering like "4444-0001B" for each specimen, like "underside bench") showing they were the same case.

2) CHAIN OF CUSTODY: Lee's floorboard and carpenter's bench specimens were recorded by date, as were the bone and tooth specimens from the Arizona exhumations

3) ARIZONA EXHUMATIONS AS PART OF CASE 2003-274: [Figure: 2] Listed together for Case No. 4444 were Lee's specimens and Arizona exhumation specimens as: "Laboratory Report - Forensic Identity - Mitochondrial Analysis."

4) NO TESTING WAS DONE FOR BLOOD: Orchid Cellmark only does DNA extractions and matchings. It does not test for blood. No other testing for blood was done by the hoaxers.

5) USELESS RESULTS: DNA extractions yielded junk results. Samples were either inconclusive or mixed. **There never was "DNA of Billy the Kid" (or blood) from the bench.** [author's boldface]

6) CONTACT PERSON: [Figure: 3] Forensic labs use a contact person to simplify records access for everyone else doing a case. The records list Calvin Ostler, co-signer of Dr. Lee's report, as "Submitting Agency." To hide the records for years, the hoaxers denied knowing that Ostler was their contact.

7) MIXED DNA SAMPLE SEPARATIONS: Because the hoaxers claimed "two DNA samples" from the bench, I got consultation on mixed samples from Lexigen President, Dr. Simon Ford. He stated:

> Mixed DNA results are very common in forensic casework. Unfortunately there is no laboratory technology available to reliably separate out the DNA from different types of cells (apart from sperm cells, which are a special case and presumably not relevant to your case). Furthermore, based on DNA technology alone, there is no way of knowing from which kind of cell a particular DNA profile originated. **[AUTHOR'S NOTE: This confirms that no blood is proven by the Orchid Cellmark DNA findings]** That's why labs still supplement DNA testing with microscopy and the old fashioned serological tests for blood, saliva etc. What all this means is that when you extract DNA from a forensic sample that contains biological material from more than one person, then the resulting DNA profile will contain the DNA profiles of all the individual contributors superimposed one on top of another and the only solution to make sense of it all is to attempt to resolve the mixed DNA profile through interpretation.
>
> There are two stages to interpreting a DNA profile. The first stage is to determine whether or not a particular person can be included or excluded as being a contributor to the profile ("matching"). This is based on comparing the evidence DNA profile with the reference DNA profiles from the persons involved in the case. **[AUTHOR'S NOTE: There is no "reference DNA" in the Billy the Kid Case.]** In some mixed samples this stage can be somewhat subjective ... Some mixtures are easy to resolve - others impossible.
>
> For example, it is impossible to know with any certainty exactly how many contributors are present in a mixed DNA profile. This is because individual contributors to the mixture may share genetic markers. Rather than saying that a DNA profile is a mixture of two contributors **[AUTHOR'S NOTE: As the hoaxers claimed with the bench specimens in my litigation]**, in many situations it is more accurate to say that a DNA profile is a mixture

of AT LEAST two contributors. If a scientist is confident that there only appears to be two (and no more) contributors to a DNA profile, then it is more accurate to say "there is no affirmative evidence of more than two contributors" than to say the mixed DNA profile is from two contributors.

Factors which make interpretation of mixed DNA profiles more difficult include; samples with very little DNA, samples with old (degraded) DNA and samples that contain inhibitors (from the surface upon which the stain is deposited). **[AUTHOR'S NOTE: All possible in the Billy the Kid Case samples]** My guess is that you will encounter all of these in your case. These factors can lead to loss of parts of the DNA profile, known as dropout. Dropout is particularly challenging in mixed samples. The more contributors to a mixture the more difficult it is to interpret. If there is a very large number of contributors (say five or more), it can be impossible to make sense of the profile.

8) COST OF MIXED SAMPLE SEPARATIONS: As last-ditch cover-up of their faked DNA claims, Steve Sederwall eventually claimed they had needed "$50,0000" to separate mixed DNA. (court testimony on January 21, 2011 and February 4, 2013). But consultation with Lexigen President, Dr. Simon Ford, indicated quite different pricing:

Most labs charge about $1,000 for testing an evidence sample or reference sample. Some labs have a surcharge of between $300 and $500 for "difficult" samples, such as bone or tissue. The interpretation (matching and statistical calculation) is usually included in the cost of the testing.

## *BIG PICTURE FOR FAKED FORENSICS*

My obtaining the DNA records was the last nail in the coffin of the Billy the Kid Case's faked forensics. But the big picture was that the Billy the Kid Case hoaxers' years of covering up these records had been forensically meaningless. Even if they had gotten records of excellent DNA extractions - which they had not - without reference DNA of Billy the Kid or his kin - which did not exist - those results could not establish a claim for having "DNA of Billy the Kid." And the same forensic uselessness applied to Dr. Henry Lee's floorboard specimens for the Deputy James Bell-floorboard sub-investigation for claiming "DNA of Bell," since there were neither Bell remains nor Bell kin for reference DNA.

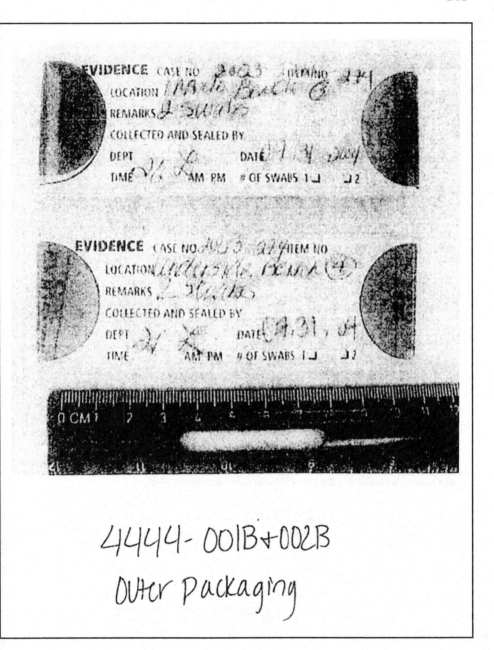

**FIGURE: 2.** Chain of Custody Evidence Bag; for Dr. Henry Lee's Lincoln County Sheriff's Department Case No. 2003-274 carpenter's workbench specimens; received for its Orchid Cellmark Case No. 4444

142

4444. Evidence Received:

| Accession # | Sample Description | Receipt Date/Method of Delivery |
|---|---|---|
| 4444-001A | Wood shavings "Lincoln County Courthouse #1" | 8/4/04 FedEx |
| 4444-002A | Wood shavings "Lincoln County Courthouse #2" | |
| 4444-001B | Swabbing from "underside of bench #3" | |
| 4444-002B | Swabbing from "underside of bench #4" | |
| 4444-003B | Wood shavings "underside of bench #3" | |
| 4444-004B | Wood shavings "underside of bench #4" | |
| 4444-005 | Reference hair - BTK? | 1/31/05 USPS |
| 4444-006 | Jaw bone from south grave | 5/19/05 Hand delivered to Orchid Cellmark (Stemmons Frwy) by Rick W. Staub (RWS) |
| 4444-007 | Casket wood from south grave | |
| 4444-008 | Paper/cloth material from south grave | |
| 4444-009 | Skull and mummified brains from south grave | |
| 4444-010 | Pelvis from south grave | |
| 4444-011 | Left femur from south grave | |
| 4444-012 | Mandible and teeth from north grave | |
| 4444-013 | Right femur from north grave | |

2. Results:

Mitochondrial DNA from specimen 4444-002A, 4444-005, 4444-011, 4444-012, and 4444-013 was amplified and sequenced at Hypervariable Regions I and II of the Mitochondrial Control Region. Sequence data are presented as variations from the Revised Cambridge Reference Sequence (rCRS). Bases not specifically listed are consistent with rCRS.

HVI (16024 – 16365)

| | 16153 | 16223 | 16266 | 16292 |
|---|---|---|---|---|
| 4444-011 | * | T | * | T |
| 4444-013 | A | * | G | * |
| rCRS | G | C | C | C |

(*) consistent with rCRS

FIGURE: 3. Orchid Cellmark Laboratory Record; "Laboratory Report" for all specimens of Case No. 2003-274 to undergo mitochondrial DNA analysis under Orchid Cellmark Case No. 4444

# CHAPTER 5:

# FIGHTING HOAXER EXHUMATIONS OF BILLY THE KID AND HIS MOTHER

SIXTH JUDICIAL DISTRICT COURT
STATE OF NEW MEXICO
COUNTY OF GRANT

NO. MS 2003-11

IN THE MATTER OF CATHERINE ANTRIM

PETITIONER'S BRIEF IN CHIEF IN SUPPORT
EXHUMATION

Comes now P...

Ste...

and...

by an...

Chief...

HISTO...

P...

Antrim o...

Investigati...

Case No. 0...

investigati...

inno...

"B...

FILED
DISTRICT COURT O...
GRANT COUNTY, N...

04 JAN -5 PM 2...

SIXTH JUDICIAL DISTRICT COURT
STATE OF NEW MEXICO
COUNTY OF GRANT

NO. CV 2003-11

IN THE MATTER OF CATHERINE ANTRIM

PETITION TO EXHUME REMAINS

...titioners Tom Sullivan, Sheriff of Lincoln County, Steve
...f of Lincoln County and Gary Graves, Sheriff of De
...heir attorney...

DISTRI
GRANT

03 OCT 1...

## Billy the Kid's DNA sparks legal showdown

### Sheriffs and mayors face off over digging up remains from the Old West

## Lincoln County deputy sheriff sends his own letter to governor

Lincoln County Deputy Sheriff
Steven M. Sederwall has sent to
Gov. Bill Richardson a reply to an
open letter from Silver City officials
asking the governor to "disassociate
ate from Messrs. Sederwall,
Sullivan and Graves and the 'Billy
the Kid' case."

"I would like to respond to Silver City's misleading concern,"
Sederwall said in his reply. The
village of Silver City questions why
a criminal investigation...
after being...

Sederwall allege that he and his co-
petitioners, Lincoln County Sheriff
Tom Sullivan and De Baca County
Sheriff Gary Graves, have found the
carpenters bench on which Billy's
body was laid after his death "for
the women to mourn his passing,"
as well as many other artifacts.

"We are examining those and...
facts for evidence, at...
Sederwall...

"There is no bullet in the headboard.
However, a bullet hole is found in
the washstand."

Sederwall said the statement of
Silver City's open letter that "not a
single one of our town officials has
ever been asked for geo... input, or...

TENTH JUDICIAL DISTRICT COURT
STATE OF NEW MEXICO
COUNTY OF DE BACA

No. CV-04-00005

IN THE MATTER OF WILLIAM H.
BONNEY aka "BILLY THE KID"

10th JUDICIAL DISTRICT
DE BACA COUNTY NEW MEXICO
FILED IN MY OFFICE

JUN 2 4 2004 11:30AM

DIANE ULIBARRI
DISTRICT COURT CLERK

VILLAGE OF FORT SUMNER'S MOTION TO DISMISS
AGAINST PETITIONERS SULLIVAN, SEDERWALL,
AND GRAVES FOR LACK OF STANDING

COMES NOW the Village of Fort Sumner, by and through its attorneys, Kennedy
... Herb Marsh, Jr., and hereby moves the Court for an order
...oners Sullivan, Sed... ...s on grounds that
... result, together
...d," this matter
Fort Sumner

TENTH JUDICIAL DISTRICT COURT
STATE OF NEW MEXICO
COUNTY OF DE BACA

No. CV-04-00005

IN THE MATTER OF WILLIAM H.
BONNEY aka "BILLY THE KID"

VILLAGE OF FORT SU...
DISMISS AGAINST WILLIAM...

10TH JUDICIAL DISTRICT COURT DE BACA COUNTY

## CASE DOCKET
### CASE NO. D-1027-CV-2004-00005

RE: WILLIAM H BONNEY

Location: Fort Sumner
Judicial Officer: Hartley, Teddy L.
Filed on: 02/26/2004
Case Number History:

CASE INFORMATION

File Date 02/26/2004
Filed By GRAVES, GARY
SEEDERWALL
SULLIVAN, TO...
STEVE; BONNE...
WILLIAM H

Cause of Action
Miscellaneous

Statistical Closures
09/24/2004 Stipul...

DATE

## Billy the Kid's Life and Death May Be Put to the DNA Test

### THE NATION

### Officials want to exhume the body of the outlaw's mother to test a Texas man's claim that he was Bonney. If so, Pat Garrett didn't kill the Kid.

January 18, 2004 | Richard Benke | Associated Press Writer

ALBUQUERQUE, N.M. — In a sworn statement, a 72-yea...
Garrett's widow told him 63 years ago that her husb...
Garrett's friend -- but that Garrett and the Kid sh...

The affidavit of Homer Overton was offered as ev...
Kid's mother, Catherine Antrim, to compare her DN...
claimed until his death in 1950 that he was William...
Billy the Kid.

A hearing on the exhumation petition is scheduled Jan...
buried. City officials there oppose disturbing the grave.

...ty Sheriff Tom Sullivan, Deputy Steve Sed...
... are asking for the exhumation. ...
... Ollie "Brushy Bill" Roberts, a H...

SIXTH JUDICIAL DISTRICT
STATE OF NEW MEXICO
COUNTY OF GRANT

IN THE MATTER OF CATHERINE...

### BILLY THE KID'S UNOPPOSED...
### REQUEST FOR EXPEDITE...

COME NOW, Bill Robins, III and David S...
Cloud, Lubel & Greenwood, LLC, and seek to inte...
estate of William H. Bonney, aka "Billy the Kid...

Defendant...
Intervene...

Petit...

SIXTH JUDICIAL DISTRICT COURT
STATE OF NEW MEXICO
COUNTY OF GRANT

No. MS 2003-11

IN THE MATTER OF CATHER...

REP...
SIL...

COMES NOW...

"Silver City"), by an...

Baked, Thomas...

...killed Bonney...
...Garre...

# READYING SHOVELS FOR
# BILLY THE KID AND HIS MOTHER

*HOAXBUST: When the Billy the Kid Case began in 2003, the hoaxers expected an easy slam-dunk: dig up Billy the Kid and his mother, claim no DNA match, start a media empire by exhuming pretenders, and say this adds up to pardoning the Kid and becoming U.S. President. That misbegotten plan did not count on me. And I did not count on the corrupt collusion of public officials that would make their plot near unbeatable.*

## *WHERE ANGELS FEAR TO TRED*

There is a 1969 movie cartoon named "Bambi Meets Godzilla." Created by a Marv Newland, it lasts under two minutes. On screen, Bambi nibbles grass. A clawed scaly foot descends. SPLAT! Credits roll. It has been voted one of the 50 greatest cartoons of all time. It symbolizes my odds of winning in all that follows here - and what a fool I was rushing in and believing otherwise.

After I read the Billy the Case hoaxers' June 5, 2003 *New York Times* article, "122 Years Later, The Lawmen Are Still Chasing Billy the Kid," I called New Mexicans who had been consultants for my novel, being sure they had organized opposition to the exhumations. They had done nothing.

Fort Sumner residents told me that Lincoln County Sheriff Tom Sullivan and his deputy, Steve Sederwall, had already been there. Big middle-aged men of six feet two and five respectively - together with local, jowly, De Baca County Sheriff, Gary Graves - they had announced the exhumation of Billy the Kid. In that first assault, was included Marlyn Bowlin, founder, with her deceased husband, of the Billy the Kid Outlaw Gang. Because her souvenir shop with small "Billy the Kid Museum" had a 99 year lease and was adjacent to the half-acre cemetery with Billy the Kid's gravesite, the hoaxers thought she controlled the grave. She did not. Fort Sumner did. But they terrified Marlyn, as they did other townspeople. She is dead now. To the end, she made me keep secret her name as their opponent for fear of their revenge.

Hoaxers' intimidation proved irrelevant. No Fort Sumnerite had any idea how to help or to hinder them. Anyway, the locals turned into Noah's neighbors watching ark-building: "It won't happen." And the little local paper, the *De Baca County News*, showed no interest in the subject. Its owner, Scot Stinnett was at the time preoccupied with sexual and financial irregularities of their Sheriff Graves - not Billy the Kid. Marlyn Bowlin said Stinnett was good only for reporting high school volleyball scores.

Then hoax focus switched to Grant County's Silver City with a rumor circulating that Billy's mother would be exhumed first, and on July 14, 2003 (her son's death anniversary). Like in Fort Sumner, residents were paralyzed but angry. I called then-Silver City Museum historian, Susan Berry. She confirmed what I knew: Catherine Antrim had been re-buried in Memory Lane Cemetery. Susan Berry had records confirming that her first burial in 1874 was in floodlands in downtown Silver City. In 1881, all cemetery remains were disinterred by a wealthy John Miller (coincidentally with the same name as the Kid pretender), who bought the land for his house. Without scrutiny, he reburied remains out-of-town. It was possible that Catherine Antrim's bones were gone after 7 flooded years. Susan Berry told me I was the first to call about the graves. I told her I would not be the last.

Later, I heard that a local woman in her nineties remembered a wooden grave marker for Catherine Antrim at Memory Lane's entrance (the old part of the cemetery). The current granite gravestone, in the cemetery's new part, was placed in 1947 for tourists. And study of that plot showed it was just an overlapping grid of multiple burials. That uncertainty should have legally ended the exhumation following objection of the state Office of the Medical Investigator (OMI). The hoaxers ignored all that.

Uneventfully, July 14th passed. The next date floated by the hoaxers and the anxious rumor mill for assailing Catherine Antrim's gravesite was Billy's November 23rd birthday. Since it was only me against them, I had to do something before the hoaxers came up with other Billy the Kid anniversaries.

## GETTING LEGAL MUSCLE

Necessary was an attorney to oppose the hoaxers' exhumation petitions in Grant and De Baca Counties district courts - for free. Back then, Fort Sumner's mean per capita income was $13,000. In Silver City, it was $24,000. No one could pay.

Meanwhile, I decided people might rally by owning a symbol of opposition. Using my jewelry-making skills, I created white bronze tokens having Billy the Kid in relief and "Fort Sumner, July 14, 1881." Also, I made white bronze bolo ties with a Billy the Kid figure detailed enough to see cartridges in his gunbelt. A foundry error made twelve of those silver Billys turn gold. One of those golden bolos would coincidentally turn the tide my way.

But the November 23, 2003 date for exhuming Catherine Antrim was approaching. In the Albuquerque phone book, I found the Kennedy Han Law Firm. Attorneys Mary Han and Paul Kennedy, civil rights powerhouses located in a restored Spanish-style mansion, accepted the case pro bono (with me paying costs); and added handsome junior attorney, Adam Baker. Fate's elevator had seemingly whisked me to the top.

Almost as quickly, the lawyers told me they could not proceed. They needed a client with "standing": someone with legal justification to be in court. Kin had standing. There were none. (The hoaxers claimed standing by being law enforcement officers.)

But Mary Han told me that the mayors of Silver City and Fort Sumner had legal obligation to protect their cemeteries - *if willing*. Fort Sumner's Mayor, Raymond Lopez, I knew, was in the "it won't happen here" contingent. I had given him a golden bolo anyway. And Marlyn Bowlin was trying to inspire him.

Anyway, Silver City was more critical. I had heard that a Councilman, Steve May, opposed exhumation. The history of Billy the Kid and Pat Garrett would depend on him - and his mayor.

## BAMBI BECOMES DAVID (AS IN GOLIATH)

I called Councilman Steve May. He hated Billy the Kid - "a juvenile delinquent from his town's past," he said. That was a bad start. But he felt obligated to protect "sanctity of graves from a publicity stunt." He contacted the mayor, Terry Fortenberry. An ex-policeman, taciturn Fortenberry agreed to represent the town. Then, Silver City Town Attorney Robert Scavron and local lawyer, Tom Stewart, joined. We were ready for court - just in time.

Then one of my golden bolos played its part. On October 1, 2003, Governor Bill Richardson went to Fort Sumner on an official visit. Using his Richardson's Implied Rule: "The public are suckers," he told Mayor Lopez that "no exhumation will happen here." And he admired the mayor's golden Billy the Kid bolo.

So Mayor Raymond Lopez gave it to him, saying, "This is for your promise not to dig up Billy."

As the Kansas City Athletics and Wen Ho Lee could attest: Richardson lies. At that moment, Richardson knew his compatriots would be filing for exhumation of Catherine Antrim in 9 days - step one to Billy's grave. So, in 9 days, hot-tempered macho Mayor Raymond Lopez was shouting, "Liar! Goddamn liar!" And I got a second mayor willing to stand for his town.

Later, a skilled Texas attorney and judge, Herb Marsh, joined my case. He was a Lincoln County War history buff.

My backers were impressive, though Davids against Goliaths.

## A HIDDEN SILVER CITY HERO

Some heroes are too heroic to seek credit. Silver City's Grant County Sheriff Raul Holguin was one. Three years into hoax-fighting, on August 29, 2006, I called him on a hunch: Hadn't the hoaxers needed him for the Antrim exhumation?

In his peaceful voice, Raul Holguin said he had been approached in 2003 by Fort Sumner's hoax participant, De Baca County Sheriff Gary Graves. "I was appalled," deeply religious Holguin said. "It was clearly a publicity stunt. The woman deserved to lie in peace." To Gary Graves he had said, "I predict that you will regret what you're doing." That came true.

## PREPARING FOR CONFRONTATION

In those days, I demanded anonymity because I am a coward and believed that if the hoaxers knew just one person was behind all the opposition they would kill me. Secondly, all I could do realistically was educate my side's participants.

So I did write-ups. For example, DNA matching was key. To demonstrate legitimate matching, I made a hand-out showing Catherine Antrim with "red DNA." Billy Bonney would need "red DNA" to "match" hers. Soon I got a call from Silver City. A rumor was circulating that Billy's mother had *special DNA*: it was red! And I realized how vulnerable people were to misinformation; to say nothing of how gossip spread like wildfire in New Mexico's multi-generational communities.

Also, I knew we needed experts to testify that the murder case was a hoax; thus, lacking justification for exhumations. World-renowned British Frederick Nolan was the historian of choice. A witty genius, he agreed to fly to America to be a witness (if I paid for his ticket). It was ironic that the hoax forced me to contact Nolan. His research set historical foundation, but I had avoided him personally as not comprehending (or not facing) Santa Fe Ring influence; thus, portraying old-fashioned "Billy as outlaw," not the freedom fighter of my revisionist view.

Leon Metz, Pat Garrett's biographer with *Pat Garrett: The Story of a Western Lawman*, also offered me his support.

Later, my consultants were renowned DNA scientists, forensic anthropologists, forensic pathologists, criminalists, and ballistic experts. Not a one doubted that I was facing a hoax.

### *ONE JOURNALIST*

Public opinion was needed too. The *Albuquerque Journal* was - as people in Billy's day would have muttered - "just a Ring tool."

I heard that a Santa Fe journalist named Jay Miller was interested. He was an avuncular curmudgeon and native New Mexican; and had gone to high school in Silver City, where his father, J. Cloyd Miller, had been president of Western New Mexico University, and where the library is named after him. For over 20 years, Jay Miller saw himself as a gadfly to politicians with his syndicated column, "Inside the Capitol." His dry acquiescence to me was: "I've already lived a full life."

Under his name, but with my writing, we ran articles debunking the hoax. Eventually, without asking me, Jay Miller used them for his 2005 book: *Billy the Kid Rides Again: Digging for the Truth*. At the time, I did not think it odd that he claimed my writing and expertise as his own. And I was happy to stay anonymously hidden.

Later, from 2004 to 2006, I again used Jay Miller's journalistic credibility to write open records act requests for hoaxers' records; and he proxied by signing them (allowing me to keep secret).

In the final analysis, even with some bumps in the long road to follow, Jay Miller would turn out to be the only member of the press to risk taking a clear stand against the dangerous and increasingly vindictive and desperate hoaxers.

*FLOW OF INFORMATION*

Though New Mexicans maintained their learned helplessness going back to Santa Fe Ring victory in the 1878 Lincoln County War, they also retained a corollary: passive-aggressive gossip. Many became my eyes and ears. Yet most information came from the over-confident hoaxers themselves - in press, blogs, and eventually a billythekidcase.com website! That let me be one step ahead, organizing before hoaxers arrived. Garrulous Deputy Steve Sederwall spilled the beans so often that I facetiously and privately nicknamed him an "honorary opposition member."

Back then, the Billy the Kid Case was so absurd that I expected its quick demise. I was wrong - for unexpected reasons.

# PREPARING FOR BILLY THE KID CASE "MEDIACIRCUS" EXHUMATIONS

*HOAXBUST: For months, the Billy the Kid Case hoaxers secretly prepared their exhumation "media circus" by trying to force OMI rubber-stamped permits; and then used compliant press to counteract my opposition to their district court cases.*

Months before their exhumation petitioning, the hoaxers had on-board a Silver City attorney named Sherry Tippett: the unnamed lawyer at Richardson's hoaxer meeting reported in the *New York Times* on June 5, 2003. Tippett passed away 9 years later, and was eulogized in *The New Mexican* on May 17, 2012 as being for civil rights and gun control. Missing from its reporter Steve Terrell's piece, was Tippett's role in the Billy the Kid Case hoax: she fired the starting gun for hoax exhumations.

Sherry Tippett was a cog in the hoaxers' plan to coerce the Office of the Medical Investigator (OMI) into issuing exhumation permits. With Sullivan and Sederwall, she had met with OMI staff; and then fabricated in writing their exhumation permission which had actually been denied!

And Tippett's boss was not the hoaxer sheriffs, but Richardson himself. Richardson had also assisted by having his appointed University of New Mexico President David Harris remove the OMI's staff attorney to block their using legal opposition to intervene against the hoax's exhumation petitions.

On July 11, 2003, Attorney Sherry Tippett sent her "Memorandum RE: Exhumation of Catherine Antrim" to Richard Gay, Richardson's Assistant to the Chief of Staff. It said:

> This is a summary of the work I have performed to date on the exhumation of Catherine Antrim from Memory Lane Cemetery in Silver City. Initial research of city records indicates that Mrs. Antrim died on September 16, 1874 and was buried in the old Silver City cemetery, the cemetery was traded for a larger tract east of town which was owned by a John Miller. Mrs. Antrim's body was moved to its present location at Memory Lane Cemetery. Research conducted by Dr. Debra Komar, of the Office of Medical Investigations [sic] (OMI) now indicates that the body of Mrs. Antrim can be moved without disturbing any other bodies in the cemetery.

**[AUTHORS NOTE: Lying about Komar is also in Tippett's exhumation petition. In response, OMI Doctors Komar and Zumwalt got an attorney and filed opposing affidavits and a Komar deposition for use in my Kennedy Han legal case.]**

> I attended a meeting with OMI staff in Albuquerque on July 3, 2003, and again on July 9, 2003. At the July 9th meeting, OMI attorney Angela Martinez was present and several legal issues were discussed. Ms. Martinez agrees with my interpretation of In Re Johnson, 94 NM 491, 612 P.2d 1302 (1980) and Sec. 24-14-23 (D) NMSA (1978) and we concur that the OMI has the discretion to issue a permit to disinter Mrs. Antrim under state law and that the court order is not required prior to issuing the permit.
>
> However, OMI will not issue the permit without a letter from the Governor requesting that Mrs. Antrim be disinterred. To date OMI has not received such a letter.
>
> After the permit is issued, the closest relative of Mrs. Antrim could object to the exhumation, claiming a "quasi-property" right in the body and file Petition for a Temporary Restraining order to the District Court. I am unaware of anyone who has such a qualifying relationship who would object to the exhumation. A Mr. Albert Garcia of Santa Rosa claims to be a great grandson of Billy the Kid, however he is strongly in favor of the exhumation.

**[AUTHORS NOTE: Garcia's kin claims are unsubstantiated. He was eventually abandoned in the exhumation attempts.]**

OMI has been extremely helpful on this project and they are ready to proceed with the exhumation when your office is ready to go. **[AUTHOR'S NOTE: Repeat lie]** They will need a one-week lead time to prepare. The contact at OMI is Dr. Debra Komar, Forensic Pathologist. Dr. Komar is very experienced in the area of disinterment and has worked for the United Nations in Bosnia and Serbia in disinterring mass graves ...

Thank you for the opportunity to work on this project. It has been very exciting and will no doubt benefit Grant County as well as the state of New Mexico.

Newspaper ink was hoax life-blood. To my opposition, the hoaxers unleashed reporters. For example: On October 11, 2003, the AP for the *Silver City Sun News* inadvertently summarized the Billy the Kid Case hoax in one headline with: "Authorities call for exhumation of Billy the Kid's mother to solve mystery."

On November 18, 2003, for msnbc.com Alan Boyle wrote: "Billy the Kid's DNA sparks legal showdown: Sheriffs and mayors face off over digging up remains from the Old West." Take-home was dumb local officials were against truth by DNA. Boyle writes:

Tradition says Billy the Kid ... was killed by Sheriff Pat Garrett back in 1881 and buried in Fort Sumner, N.M. But in 1950, a Texas man named "Brushy Bill" Roberts claimed that he was the real Billy the Kid and that someone else had been shot in his place. He said he had lived incognito for decades but was finally seeking a pardon for his crimes. Roberts died later that year, and is now buried in Hamilton, Texas.

As if that wasn't complicated enough, there was yet another claimant to the famous name: John Miller, who died in 1937 and is buried in Prescott, Ariz.

So which story is correct. Back in June, two New Mexico sheriffs and the mayor of Capitan, N.M. proposed a 21st century solution: Exhume the remains of all three gravesites, and match the DNA against samples taken from the body of Billy the Kid's mother, Catherine Antrim, who is buried in Silver City, N.M. The results would confirm one of the stories ...

But the mayors of Fort Sumner and Silver City say they won't let the bodies buried in their towns be disturbed, and that sets the stage for a legal showdown ...

By solidifying its claim on the Billy the Kid story, Fort Sumner and New Mexico could give their tourism trade a boost, [Sheriff] Graves said. That angle is one reason why New Mexico Gov. Bill Richardson supports the use of DNA analysis to solve the mystery.

On January 18, 2004, Tippett, before being reeled in for failings in the Silver City exhumation, had filed her January 5, 2004 "Brief in Chief for the Exhumation of Catherine Antrim." Its exhibits were the "Probable Cause Statement for Case # 2003-274, and the Homer Overton Affidavit (which I then obtained as already mentioned). Overton's Affidavit plus Tippett's garbled hoax version - with *both* Billy and Pat shooting "a drunk" for grave-filler - were in a January 18, 2004 article by a Richard Benke for *The Nation*, titled "Billy the Kid's Life and Death May Be Put to the DNA Test: Officials want to exhume the body of the outlaw's mother to test a Texas man's claim that he was Bonney. If so, Pat Garrett didn't kill the kid." Richard Benke wrote:

ALBUQUERQUE, N.M. – In a sworn statement, a 72 year-old man says Sheriff Pat Garrett's widow told him 63 years ago that her husband did not kill Billy the Kid – Garrett's friend – but that Garrett and the Kid shot a drunk in his place.

The affidavit of Homer Overton was offered as evidence for exhuming the body of the Kid's mother, Catherine Antrim, to compare her DNA with that of a Texas man who claimed until his death that he was ... Billy the Kid ...

A coroner's jury concluded in 1881 that Garrett killed Bonney with a gunshot to the left breast. But according to Overton's affidavit, Apolinaria Garrett - Pat Garrett's widow - told Overton, then 9, and his boyhood friend Bobby Talbert that Garrett and Bonney shot a drunk lying in a Fort Sumner street, putting the bullet in his face to make him unrecognizable so his body could pass for Bonney's.

Overton ... gave the Dec. 27 affidavit filed in court in Silver City a week ago. The affidavit says the boys visited Apolinaria Garrett in the summer of 1940, about 32 years after her husband was fatally shot near Las Cruces.

"I believe what Mrs. Garrett told us that day was the absolute truth ... It made such an impression on me that I have remembered it in detail these 63 years," Overton's affidavit says. Sullivan, sheriff in the county where Bonney was convicted of murdering one of Sullivan's predecessors in the 1870's, has said it is important to determine the truth of such stories ...

"There are a number of people who believe that. And now that we have the tools to determine the truth, don't we have the responsibility?" Tippett said.

Later, I wrote a Jay Miller article ridiculing the Overton Affidavit about Garrett's dead widow's confidings. After that, it disappeared from Case 2003-274's file and any hoaxer mention.

# LAW IN THE LAND OF ENCHANTMENT

*HOAXBUST: Attempting exhumations, the hoaxers faked law in their district court petitions by ignoring fatal opposition by the Office of the Medical Investigator; having no legitimate murder case to investigate; having no justifiable law enforcement standing to be in court; having no living suspect to convict; and having no graves to yield valid DNA. Then they added the dead Billy the Kid as an actual exhumation petitioner - with an illegally appointed attorney representing him. And the taxpayers paid for all that!*

For tourists, New Mexico is supposed to be "The Land of Enchantment." Residents know the real motto is "Pay-to-Play."

District court permission was needed to open graves. Billy's mother's gravesite meant Grant County; Billy the Kid's gravesite meant De Baca County. His mother was first. The judge in Grant County was Henry Quintero. An ambitious attorney, he had wanted a judgeship. He got it on February 8, 2003 from Governor Bill Richardson. Quintero would be needed 9 months later.

The hoaxers had also tried to seduce Silver City officials by promising a "media circus" at exhumation - though destroying their history by the hoax promised a *brief* "circus." The hoaxers' own "circus" arrived earlier, with their TV film crew secretly driving tire-tracks all over Catherine Antrim's grave and adjoining plots. That mess would end up being a big mistake.

## *FIRST HOAX ATTORNEY: SHERRY TIPPETT*

A sign of hoaxer confidence was that they had started small in Silver City with local attorney, Sherry Tippett, used, as already discussed, to try strong-arming the OMI for permits.

Tippett initiated the exhumation circus by her filing, on October 10, 2003, in Grant County's Sixth District Court: "Case No. MS-2003-11, In the Matter of Catherine Antrim: Petition to Exhume Remains." [APPENDIX: 12] It locked in case definition: "For purpose of determining the guilt or innocence of Sheriff Pat Garrett in the death of William Bonney aka 'Billy the Kid.' " It also had Tippett's fabricated exhumation permission from OMI Forensic Anthropologist, Dr. Debra Komar. The legal word for all that - if proved - is "perjury." Attorney Sherry Tippett had fired the first hoaxer shot - into her foot.

Tippett also denied that other graves would be disturbed. In fact, there *was* a contiguous grave - since 1989. And its tire-track "disturbance" by the hoaxers' film crew had outraged its occupant's sister, Joani Amos-Staats, who joined her own Petition to Silver City's Petition in Opposition. Besides potential for perjury, Tippett had another failing: underestimating the OMI.

The OMI knew the case was a hoax. Its head, Dr. Ross Zumwalt, privately hired an attorney, William Snead (since Richardson had cut-off their attorney). Snead sent Tippett, on January 12, 2004: "Response of Office of Medical Investigator to Petition to Exhume Remains of Catherine Antrim" [APPENDIX: 13], implying her mendacity with "contrary to the statements contained in the [her] petition ..." A parting dig from the OMI was that "the petitioner's alleged investigation ... is a very great waste of public resources and a distraction of the OMI from its mandated work." Snead added affidavits from Drs. Komar and Zumwalt [APPENDIX: 14], stating that the sought DNA was worthless by virtue of Catherine Antrim's much-moved remains.

Also, plot boundaries overlapped *almost a dozen individuals*, whose remains could not legally be disrupted. [Figure: 4] And Dr. Komar gave a 450 page deposition, to the same effect, to Attorney Adam Baker. All that should have ended exhuming the mother. "Strangely," Judge Henry Quintero continued the case.

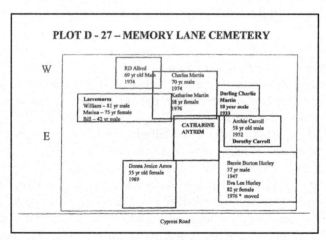

**FIGURE: 4.** Map of Catherine Antrim gravesite with overlapping plots invalidating sought DNA. (OMI Exhibit from "Sixth Judicial Court, State of New Mexico, County of Grant. No. MS 2003-11, "In the Matter of Catherine Antrim. Affidavit of Ross E. Zumwalt, M.D." January 9, 2004)

## THE KENNEDY HAN-MARSH ATTACK

My fight began with legal arguments against the exhumation of Catherine Antrim. On October 31, 2003, Attorneys Paul Kennedy and Adam Baker, with Silver City lawyers, Thomas Stewart and Robert Scavron, filed "Response in Opposition to the Petition to Exhume Remains." It called the hoax a hoax. They said that investigating the "guilt or innocence" of Pat Garrett was "unlawful, unnecessary, and sensationalistic." They concluded:

5. The proposed exhumation of Catherine Antrim would serve no legitimate law enforcement purpose, because there is no legal controversy that the person shot and killed by Sheriff Pat Garrett on or about July 15, 1881, was the notorious criminal Billy the Kid; that said shooting constituted a justifiable homicide; and, that any present investigation into the matter is untimely, futile, precluded by law, and an unjustifiable intrusion upon the public fisc.

6. The absence of a necessary and indispensable party, to wit, the New Mexico Department of Health, is fatal to the Petition.

"Strangely," Judge Henry Quintero continued the case.

## SHERRY TIPPET'S COUNTERATTACK

Attorney Sherry Tippett answered our attorneys in her "Petitioners Response in Opposition to the Town of Silver City's Motion to Intervene." Seven pages of legal gobbledygook, it cites irrelevant cases - like foster parents having "no legal parental right to the children."

Tippett also dredged up Elbert "Bert" Garcia of Santa Rosa, New Mexico, whose unsubstantiated belief that he is Billy's descendent - via his grandmother - was the subject of his book, *Billy the Kid's Kid*. In it, Garcia provides no kinship "proof;" and further diminishes his credibility by providing a photo of the Kid's "family heirloom," a bolo tie - though the bolo was invented in 1940! Tippett stated for the Court, "Mr. Garcia was and remains strongly in favor of the exhumation." Not provable kin, he lacked standing. His opinion on exhumation was irrelevant.

Tippett also continued her m.o. of making things up, arguing that Silver City's Mayor Fortenberry had no standing. She attained a sentence by sentence score of 100% false by concluding:

That the Town has no substantial, protectable significant and direct interest in this matter is clear. Managing the cemetery does not provide a property interest in the body. Only heirs to Catherine Antrim have such an interest in the body and, as mentioned earlier, the only alleged descendent of Ms. Antrim [Elbert Garcia], is strongly supportive of the exhumation.

Wherefore, Petitioners Sederwall, Sullivan and Graves request that the Town's Motion to Intervene be denied.

But 100% falsity seemed to look 100% fine to Judge Quintero.

## TIPPETT'S SWAN SONG

Even the hoaxers realized Tippett was pushing their luck. She was soon replaced by their big gun: Attorney Bill Robins III. Eventually, I obtained her swan song: a four page December 17, 2003 letter with two attachments, to Sederwall, Sullivan, and Graves. It shared her planned answers to Judge Quintero's Order of December 9, 2003; giving the impression that Quintero sought a shield of legal blather. For example, he asked disingenuously: "Assuming there is a legitimate investigation, who will be charged if there was a crime?" Also, Tippett was asking for a new Probable Cause Statement - dissatisfied with what she had gotten. She stated: "I need you to do a sizeable amount of work in preparing the probable cause segment of the brief." Much later, I located the discarded version, which I called the "Seventy-Seven Days of Doubt Document." Ultimately it would help crack the hoax.

In that letter, Tippett also complained of local anger: "I mentioned to Tom [Sullivan] that I experienced clear hostility the day after the Hearing (December 9th) while grocery shopping at the Silver City Food Coop. It seems that certain segments of the population find this issue very offensive and thinks [sic] that it is purely driven by profit." Was she worried? Guess! She concluded: "All the interesting facts and data you have discovered on the life and death of Billy the Kid are certainly fodder for stories we can pass on to our grandchildren AFTER WE WIN THIS CASE ON JANUARY 27 TH. [sic - Tippett's capitalizations]

Sherry Tippett was so confident that she enclosed her pre-printed senate "Memorial" for a (now-deceased) Silver City official, secretly working against his own constituents to get senate backing for the case. [APPENDIX: 15] Tippett wrote in her letter:

As I mentioned to Steve [Sederwall] and Tom [Sullivan] on the telephone, I met with Sen. [Benny] Altamirano, the state Senator who represents Silver City, last weekend ... He told me that if I prepared a Memorial supporting the Investigation, he would introduce it and carry it this session and make sure it is passed. I don't need to tell you that Sen. Altamirano is Chair of the Senate Finance Committee, the longest running state Senator in New Mexico history and a very well respected [sic - missing word] in the New Mexico Legislature.

So another player danced in Richardson's ring-around-the-rosie, all hold hands! And Altamirano heralded worse to come.

## *ATTORNEY BILL ROBINS III EMERGES*

Attorney Bill Robins III stepped out from the hoax's shadows to replace Sherry Tippett by being more outrageous.

The *New York Times* article of June 5, 2003 had foreshadowed him under a "Dallas" law firm connected to Governor Richardson. In fact, Bill Robins III was second partner in a Houston one; with reported, yearly, personal injury, product liability, and medical malpractice settlements of up to $300 million. He and his firm, Heard, Robins, Cloud, Lubel & Greenwood LLC, also were Richardson's big political donors for his gubernatorial and presidential bids. And, in 2004, they were also presidential candidate John Kerry's top donors in his September quarter. They were kingmakers. Richardson knew it.

The case was getting "curiouser and curiouser;" and not just by replacing a flyswatter with a nuclear warhead, but because Richardson himself stepped forth, following his *Between Worlds* book's axiom: "If hit, hit back harder."

Mary Alice Murphy, in the *Silver City Daily Press Internet Edition* of November 17, 2003 stated in "Billy the Kid Hires a Lawyer": "A spokesman at the law firm of Heard, Robins, Cloud, Lubel and Greenwood, of Houston and Albuquerque [sic - Santa Fe and Hobbs], confirmed Gov. Bill Richardson has appointed Bill Robins as Billy the Kid's attorney."

Notice "appointed." The public (as suckers) were supposed to think "pro bono" - as in no taxpayer money used. (Who was paying Judge Quintero, his court, and two sheriffs' departments, people?) But "appointment" is the key. It was illegal. Judges appoint attorneys for indigent clients. A governor cannot. It violates constitutional separation of executive and judicial branches, and commits *ultra vires,* meaning "abuse of power."

Notice also Attorney Robins's client: dead Billy the Kid! Silver City got the message: Bill Richardson was steam-rolling them.

"Strangely," Judge Henry Quintero took no notice that his court now had an illegal attorney whose client was a corpse.

But in Richardson's pay-to-play world, what was Bill Robins's "play?" Robins's press comments hint. On November 19, 2003, the AP reported on the Internet from Silver City:

> Robins says he's excited to represent the Kid. His first duty as Billy's lawyer will be to intervene in the Silver City case to exhume the body of Billy's mother, Catherine Antrim. DNA testing is supposed to show whether Antrim was related to Ollie "Brushy Bill" Roberts. If Antrim is related to Roberts, that would mean Billy the Kid is buried in Hico [sic - Hamilton], Texas - not Fort Sumner.

The day before, msnbc.com's Alan Boyle had printed: "Billy the Kid gets a lawyer: 122 years after shootout, attorney to gather information for a pardon." There it was again: linking the exhumations to a pardon. Reporter Boyle wrote:

> "The true story about Billy the Kid needs to be told," Robins said, "and therefore it seems to me that it would be appropriate and proper for this exhumation to go forward ... If the DNA doesn't match, and Billy the Kid was not ever buried in Fort Sumner, and in fact he did live to a ripe old age, that says a lot about what Pat Garrett did ...
> "I'm hoping that this investigation will ultimately lead to a conclusion that Billy the Kid will be pardoned," Robins said.

What did Attorney Robins mean by "The true story about Billy the Kid needs to be told?" What did he mean by Billy's living "to a ripe old age?" Was he a loony "Brushy Bill" believer? The *New York Times* article had elevated "Brushy" also. On Robins's firm's website in 2004, he called himself an amateur historian of - you guessed it - "Billy the Kid." But who was his "Kid?"

Was Governor Richardson handing big donor Robins the iconic history in exchange for a presidency? That seemed too crazy to be possible. My bet was a two part publicity stunt: dig then pardon. Though it did seem that Attorney Robins might be an odd-ball!

## *ATTORNEY BILL ROBINS III CHANNELS THE DEAD*

When Attorney Bill Robins III entered Judge Henry Quintero's court, he enhanced the concept of a "handicapped client." For Billy Bonney, challenged by death's muteness, Robins would utter his words - apparently by channeling!

"Strangely," all this made sense to Judge Henry Quintero.

On November 26, 2003, Robins presented "In the Matter of Catherine Antrim: Billy the Kid's Unopposed Motion For Intervention and Request For Expedited Disposition" [APPENDIX: 16], thus contributing a Billy the Kid Case hoax milestone. His legal words meant that Billy the Kid himself was asking for his mother's exhumation - pronto!

To distract from that preposterousness, Robins's Petition first claims to be on behalf of "the estate" of Billy the Kid - though Billy had no estate (meaning property or probate action).

And that façade of legalize is immediately abandoned; and Billy himself - called "the Petitioner" - declares magically via Robins's words:

Billy the Kid supports the exhumation and wishes to provide this Court with a brief outlining the basis for his concurrence and asks leave to do so. In addition, in the event that the Town is allowed to intervene, **Billy the Kid would also like the opportunity to address the Town's arguments in opposition to the exhumation and asks leave to do so as well.** [author's boldface]

So, Bill Robins III - like demon-possessed Linda Blair in "The Exorcist" - channels the spirit Kid demanding: "Dig up my mom! And if Silver City objects, I'll personally tell them where to get off." Missing only was Robins's spinning head.

"Strangely," none of this perturbed Judge Henry Quintero.

This four page Robins filing also revealed a hidden agenda of extending exhumation goals to "Texas and Arizona" (read pretenders "Brushy Bill" Roberts and John Miller), because, as Robins fabricates, "this version [conventional history] has been questioned;" though the only questioners are himself, Billy the Kid Case hoaxers, and "Brushy" believers. Robins states:

The investigation is at least partially directed at the determination whether Billy the Kid was indeed shot by Pat Garrett or whether he survived to live a long life in either Texas or Arizona. The truth that is sought to be ascertained thus goes to the very fact of the Kid's life and death. Since whether he is truly buried in New Mexico can only be proven with the extraction and comparison of Ms. Antrim's DNA with that of his own, **or of anyone who laid claim to his identity** [author's boldface] the investigation and this proposed exhumation ... should be allowed.

Next came newly-minted Judge Henry Quintero's move. Robins's acts and statements were both absurd and illegal. Mayor Terry Fortenberry's lawyers had given arguments fatal to the case. Quintero acted: He set a December 8, 2003 Hearing for "more input from each side." Why was Quintero stalling?

On December 1, 2003, enraged Richardson got on KOBTV to say that *he* wanted the DNA ("DNA expert," thus, joining his "baseball-draft" persona). Television, instead of telephone, addressed the recalcitrant judge. But Quintero kept rescheduling.

Finally, on April 2, 2004, Henry Quintero filed a brilliant legal decision - for himself: "In the Matter of Catherine Antrim, Decision and Order." [APPENDIX: 17] He declared the case "not ripe;" meaning *unless* the Petitioners *first* got DNA from the Fort Sumner grave, they had no reason to dig up Catherine Antrim! It was the wisdom of King Solomon - if King Solomon had been a crook. Quintero, protecting himself from the crazy proceedings in his Court, also craftily sent the Petitioners exactly where they wanted to be all along: the grave of Billy the Kid.

But Quintero added a limiting stipulation: "Only if the Petitioners are successful in locating the Kid's burial site and collecting his DNA, may they again petition this Court for a review of Catherine Antrim's matter." That meant the DNA for matching *had to come from Billy Bonney's Fort Sumner grave.*

We, in the opposition, heard Quintero's real message: the law in New Mexico was no deterrent to the hoaxers. Quintero even concluded: "This matter is dismissed *without* prejudice." That meant the Petitioners would be welcomed back in his court - along with dead Billy the Kid and Catherine Antrim's fake DNA.

And Fort Sumner was next.

## DÈJÁ VOUS ALL OVER AGAIN IN FORT SUMNER

Technically, when the hoaxers hit Fort Sumner in 2004, the exhumation of Billy the Kid was blocked by legal precedent for over 42 years. A prior exhumation attempt had been stopped by a judge; and all the same reasons remained.

That case, Petition No. 3255, begun in 1961, had been filed by a Lois Telfer, alleging Billy kinship, but seen as a publicity-seeker. Her petition was "For the Removal of the Body of William H. Bonney, Deceased, From the Ft. Sumner Cemetery in Which He is Interred for Reinterment in the Lincoln, New Mexico, Cemetery."

But Billy's grave is contiguous to Charlie Bowdre's. And Bowdre's father's brother's descendant, Louis Bowdre, was still alive. Louis Bowdre went to Fort Sumner to testify his opposition on grounds of disrupting his deceased relative's remains. On April 6, 1962, District Judge E.T. Kinsley, Jr. agreed and blocked any exhumation. [APPENDIX: 18]

Ignoring that Kinsley decision, Attorney Bill Robins III and his co-conspirators were coming back for a re-run.

Unbeknownst to them, however, I took the precaution of contacting Louis Bowdre; by then, in his 80's and blind, but still willing to fight. After Louis Bowdre's death in 2005, his role as family historian passed to a younger generation. And that person told me, with fervor that echoed passionate Charlie Bowdre himself: "I will protect my grandfather's wish to my dying day."

## THE FORT SUMNER EXHUMATION FORAY

Attorney Bill Robins's petition stated that "Honorable Bill Richardson, Governor of the State of New Mexico," had appointed him "to represent the interests of Billy the Kid in the investigation." Dead Billy was about to request *his own* exhumation. But what would a Fort Sumner judge make of that zombie stumbling there all the way from Judge Quintero's court?

Filed by Robins on February 26, 2004 in the Tenth Judicial Court of De Baca County, it was "Case No. CV-2004-00005, In the Matter of William H. Bonney, aka 'Billy the Kid,' Petition for the Exhumation of Billy the Kid's Remains." [APPENDIX: 19]

With Robins, another firm member signed: David Sandoval. Since Robins only had a Texas law license, by law he needed Sandoval - with a New Mexico license - to be in court with him.

A new player signed also: Attorney Mark Acuña of the Albuquerque, Jaffe law firm. The clever reason for adding Mark Acuña would soon emerge; though never who paid him.

Robins's petition also elucidated pretender exhumation plans. He claimed in "IV. Historical Background":

11. This was also a time whose history was **not accurately nor completely written** [author's boldface] ... Perhaps the most significant lingering question involves whether Billy the Kid was indeed shot by Sheriff Pat Garrett in an ambush **one dark night** [author's boldface] in Ft. Sumner **or whether the Kid went on to live a long and peace-abiding life elsewhere.** [author's boldface]

12. The debate has been sparked at various times in the past by at least two individuals who laid claim to his identity. **Ollie** [author's boldface] "Brushy Bill" Roberts resided in Hico, Texas and claimed to be Billy the Kid. John Miller, in Arizona also died still claiming he was Billy the Kid. Co-Petitioners are in the initial phases of pursuing exhumations of these individuals as well.

13. **The Sheriff-Petitioners' investigation has certainly fueled debate as to whether or not Pat Garrett's version of events surrounding his claimed killing of Billy the Kid is in fact historically accurate. The investigation has renewed questions as to whether Billy the Kid lies buried at the fabled grave-site in Ft. Sumner.** [author's boldface] Allowing the exhumation of the remains at Ft. Sumner grave site for extraction of DNA to be compared with that of Ms. Antrim's will likely finally provide definitive answers to this historical quandary.

At the time, this just seemed like familiar hoax-talk. My take was that references to pretenders were the only argument the hoaxers had for a surviving Billy. Later, those boldfaced words above, plus some other documents, would illuminate Robins's role. Ultimately, all that would crack the Billy the Kid Case hoax.

## *A TICKET TO HADES*

Governor Bill Richardson, Attorney Bill Robins, and the colluding lawmen - Sheriffs Tom Sullivan and Gary Graves, and Deputy Steve Sederwall - still had a hurdle: Fort Sumner's long-seated judge: Ricky Purcell. Purcell had an inconvenient reputation for fair-minded honesty.

So Robins made his bid for Hades. He used the plaintiffs' option of removing a judge without cause. And the hoaxers knew who would replace him. Robins wrote, on March 5, 2004, demonically croaking Billy's words - "Remove Ricky Purcell":

## NOTICE OF EXCUSAL

COMES NOW Co-Petitioner, William H. Bonney aka "Billy the Kid," by and through counsel Bill Robins III and David Sandoval, and pursuant to 1978 NMSA Section 38-3-9 exercises his peremptory challenge and excuses the Honorable District Judge Ricky D. Purcell from this proceeding.

Dead Billy the Kid alone was positioning Richardson's pawn, Judge Teddy L. Hartley, appointed February 8, 2003 - the same day as Judge Henry Quintero - and whose family's political contribution to Richardson allegedly bought Teddy that judgeship. The hoaxers felt they were back in a slam-dunk position.

They were wrong. Opposition solidarity was growing.

Mayor Raymond Lopez had attended the Catherine Antrim exhumation Hearing. The Kennedy Han law firm had stayed with the case, requesting only modest compensation. To pay their bill, Mayor Lopez announced he would "stand on a street corner selling cupcakes." His inspired citizens contributed to a special fund.

Then the adroit Texas attorney, Herb Marsh, stayed with Adam Baker pro bono. So we were ready for the arriving hoaxers.

## *A BAKER-MARSH LEGAL BARRAGE*

The Baker-Marsh barrage began on April 12, 2004 with a magnificently crafted, hefty stack of opposition filings, and with Mayor Raymond Lopez standing for the case.

"Village of Fort Sumner's Unopposed Motion to Intervene," established the right of Fort Sumner to act against the exhumation of Billy the Kid.

Then was "Response in Opposition to the Petition for the Exhumation of Billy the Kid's Remains," which refuted the validity of dead Billy the Kid as a Petitioner, refuted the authority of Attorney Robins to represent the "interests" of a dead person in that context, and refuted the pseudo-historical claims of a Garrett murder. Baker and Marsh also denied the forensic value of DNA from both graves; and cited the Petitioners' failure to obtain OMI permission. They emphasized that the unsubstantiated Probable Cause Statement's contentions did not justify exhumations. They recommended the petition's dismissal *with prejudice* - meaning that it could never be repeated in Fort Sumner.

There was more.

Filed on June 24, 2004 was their "Village of Fort Sumner's Motion to Dismiss Against Petitioners Sullivan, Sederwall, and Graves for Lack of Standing." [APPENDIX: 20] The men, they said, were just acting as "amateur historians," and not "law enforcement officers" ... Petitioners are merely engaged in an academic exercise aimed at sifting through the stories that surround the 'legend of Billy the Kid' to discern fact from fiction - a monumental task already accomplished through years of research by a number of qualified ... historians on the subject." Baker and Marsh added that, *even* as law enforcement officers, the Petitioners had no statutory authority for the exhumation. Only the Medical Investigator had that right. The same document exposed the underlying legal hoaxing: a dead man - like Pat Garrett - cannot be prosecuted since he does not exist.

Also, false was the hoaxers' contention of "no statute of limitations on murder." New Mexico once *had* that statute of limitations on murder, necessitating that such a murder case to be tried only in that period: 1953 to 1968.

They concluded:

> Sullivan, Sederwall, and Graves are no different than any other citizen who might walk into a courthouse to file a petition to exhume the remains of a person with whom they have no factual or legal connection whatsoever. Clearly, the law of standing would be thrown on its head if an action for exhumation could be maintained under these circumstances. The Court should therefore dismiss the Petition as to these Petitioners, because they do not have standing to litigate the issues in this case.

In short, the Billy the Kid Case had no legal basis; and the Petitioners had no standing. The implication, not needed there, but relevant years later, was that Sullivan, Sederwall, and Graves were committing law enforcement fraud.

There was more.

On the same June 24th filing date, dead Billy the Kid as a client was attacked with their "Village of Fort Sumner's Motion to Dismiss Against William H. Bonney Under Rule 1-017(A)."

[APPENDIX: 21] The grounds for dismissal were that Billy the Kid "was not a real party [being dead] ... to assert the claims."

Added was that Attorney Bill Robins III was in Court solely to represent a dead person, namely Billy the Kid, and therefore had no real client to justify being in the case.

Adam Baker and Herb Marsh jabbed that Attorney Robins's claim of standing was so absurd "that it would cast a grave shadow of doubt on the integrity of the courts and of our system of justice were it to be cognizable at law."

Then Baker and Marsh showed the kind of courage a whistleblower dreams of, while demonstrating that they were uncowed by political posturing: they attacked Governor Bill Richardson himself. Addressing "integrity of the courts," in their "Village of Fort Sumner's Motion for Proof of Attorneys' Authority to Act on Behalf of William H. Bonney," they declared Robins's *appointment by Richardson to be illegal.* They stated:

> 1. Here, Attorney Bill Robins III and David Sandoval have entered their appearance in this lawsuit on behalf of "Co-Petitioner Billy the Kid," who died in 1881, under an alleged "appointment from Governor Bill Richardson" to represent the interests of Billy the Kid in the [other Petitioners'] investigation.
>
> 2. **Governor Richardson is without the constitutional or statutory authority to make said appointment.** [author's boldface]

"Strangely," Judge Ted Hartley ignored everything by Baker and Marsh. He set a Hearing for September 27, 2004 at 1:30 PM.

## SILVER CITY FIGHTS BACK

Silver City citizens had anxiously watched Fort Sumner's courtroom shenanigans by the hoaxers. They acted, writing a petition to Governor Richardson on June 21, 2004.

It was signed by Mayor Terry Fortenberry, Town Councilor Thomas A. Nupp, Town Councilor Steve May, Town Councilor Gary Clauss, Town Councilor Judy Ward, Town Manager Alex Brown, Executive Director of the Silver City/Grant County Chamber of Commerce Cissy McAndrew, Director of Silver City Mainstreet Project Frank Milan, and Director of the Silver City Museum Susan Berry. [APPENDIX: 22]

They wrote:

We must ask why the Governor's office has taken a partisan position against Grant and De Baca Counties when every expert historian of the life and times of Billy the Kid has labeled the case as pure bunk ... when the state's own Office of Medical Examiner has denied a permit for exhumation of the bodies based on DNA results being useless.

Richardson did not respond. But he remembered. When Silver City later requested funds to expand Memory Lane Cemetery for lack of new graves, Richardson line-vetoed their $250,000.

But for that Silver City petition, Steve Sederwall did ricochet validation with Richardson in the *Silver City Daily Press* of June 25, 2004. The unnamed reporter quoted Sederwall:

> Lincoln County Deputy Steven M. Sederwall has sent to Gov. Bill Richardson a reply to an open letter from Silver City officials asking the governor to disassociate from Messrs. Sederwall, Sullivan and Graves and the Billy the Kid Case."
>
> "I would like to respond to Silver City's misleading concerns," Sederwall said in his reply. "The village [sic] of Silver City questions why a criminal investigation is reopened after being closed 122 years ago by a legally embodied coroner's jury. It has been reopened because the physical evidence, documents and the coroner's jury report itself cause us to believe the records cannot be true."

## THE HOAXERS STRIKE

Then, in court, the hoaxers struck back. On July 30, 2004, Attorney Robins presented: "In the Matter of William H. Bonney aka Billy the Kid", Stipulation of Dismissal with Prejudice." [APPENDIX: 23] He, thus, removed himself, freeing Judge Ted Hartley from his ridiculed claims of a dead but talking client.

Attorney Mark Acuña took over. But Baker and Marsh had denied Sullivan's, Sederwall's, and Graves's Court standing. So, on July 26, 2004, Acuña presented "Petitioner's [sic] Response to the Village of Ft. Sumner's Motion to Dismiss." [APPENDIX: 24] In it, Acuña just repeated, 13 times in five pages, that they *were* "law enforcement officers." Getting carried away, Acuña created the funniest hoax document. As "law enforcement officers," he argued, they did the case "for the benefit of the public" to protect people from a murderer. He added that, if the lawmen did not chase suspects, they would risk being kicked out of office!

## SOMEONE SPEAKS FOR PAT GARRETT

By this point, people had forgotten that the Billy the Kid Case was about Pat Garrett. One man had not: William F. Garrett. He had come to every exhumation hearing, encouraged by Marlyn Bowlin, who kept him abreast on the case. And his "letter to the editor" in the *De Baca County News* of May 6, 2004 *did* speak for the dead. [APPENDIX: 25]  He wrote:

> Fort Sumner has and has had the Kid. We all know that ... And Pat? Pat did his duty and that is that. Those two sheriffs and others doing this dastardly deed are not helping to lift our fair state, they are doing otherwise ... I know these things because Pat was my great uncle and my respect goes to him and all the good people in the pursuit of honesty and dignity.

## NUTTY ILLEGALITIES IN A NUTSHELL

With no valid exhumation petitioners, with no real murder committed, with a fraudulent murder investigation, with an exhumation-blocking precedent case, without valid DNA anywhere, Attorney Mark Acuña and his clients Sheriff Tom Sullivan, Deputy Steve Sederwall, and Sheriff Gary Graves optimistically awaited Judge Ted Hartley's September 27, 2004 Hearing - certain of victory.

# CHAPTER 6:

# BILLY THE KID CASE HOAX PLAYERS

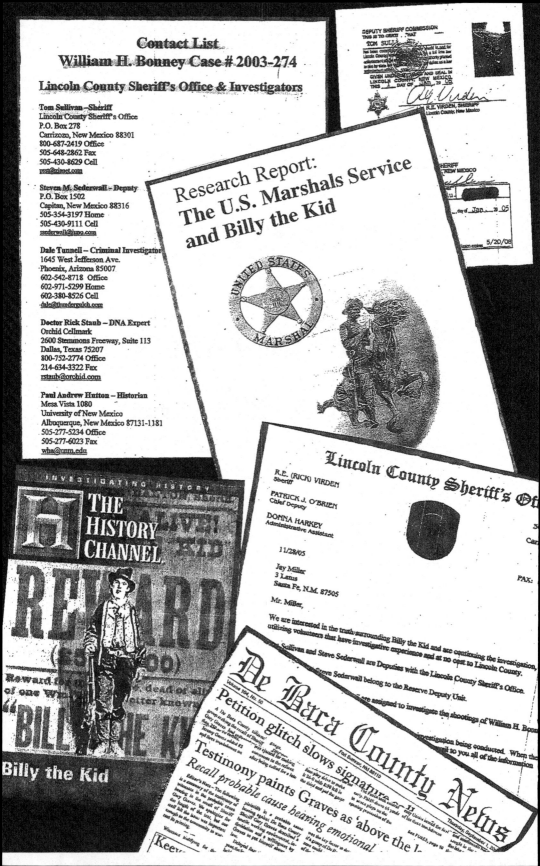

# Contact List
## William H. Bonney Case # 2003-274

### Lincoln County Sheriff's Office & Investigators

**Tom Sullivan - Sheriff**
Lincoln County Sheriff's Office
P.O. Box 278
Carrizozo, New Mexico 88301
800-687-2419 Office
505-648-2862 Fax
505-430-8629 Cell
pssti@zianet.com

**Steven M. Sederwall - Deputy**
P.O. Box 1502
Capitan, New Mexico 88316
505-354-3197 Home
505-430-9111 Cell
ssederwall@juno.com

**Dale Tunnell - Criminal Investigator**
1645 West Jefferson Ave.
Phoenix, Arizona 85007
602-542-8718 Office
602-971-5299 Home
602-380-8526 Cell
dale@thunderguch.com

**Doctor Rick Staub - DNA Expert**
Orchid Cellmark
2600 Stemmons Freeway, Suite 113
Dallas, Texas 75207
800-752-2774 Office
214-634-3322 Fax
rstaub@orchid.com

**Paul Andrew Hutton - Historian**
Mesa Vista 1080
University of New Mexico
Albuquerque, New Mexico 87131-1181
505-277-5234 Office
505-277-6023 Fax
wha@unm.edu

## Research Report:
## The U.S. Marshals Service and Billy the Kid

UNITED STATES MARSHAL

### DEPUTY SHERIFF COMMISSION
THIS IS TO CERTIFY THAT
TOM SULLIVAN

R.E. VIRDEN, SHERIFF
Lincoln County, New Mexico

5/20/06

## THE HISTORY CHANNEL.

INVESTIGATING HISTORY

REWARD

Billy the Kid

## Lincoln County Sheriff's Of

R.E. (RICK) VIRDEN
Sheriff

PATRICK J. O'BRIEN
Chief Deputy

DONNA HARKEY
Administrative Assistant

11/28/05

Jay Miller
3 Lanns
Santa Fe, N.M. 87505

Mr. Miller,

We are interested in the truth surrounding Billy the Kid and are continuing the investigation, utilizing volunteers that have investigative experience and at no cost to Lincoln County.

Sullivan and Steve Sederwall are Deputies with the Lincoln County Sheriff's Office.

Steve Sederwall belong to the Reserve Deputy Unit.

are assigned to investigate the shootings of William H. Bon

investigation being conducted. When the
to you all of the information

## De Baca County News

Volume 104, No. 50                   Fort Sumner, NM 88119                   Thursday, September 1, 20

### Petition glitch slows signature

### Testimony paints Graves as 'above the l

### Recall probable cause hearing emotional

# BILLY THE KID CASE PLAYERS AND PLAY

*HOAXBUST: My early hope was to end the Billy the Kid Case hoax by my open records requests' exposures. That failed by their records concealment, but I discovered more players and more of their play. They were a frightening bunch, acting above the law and confident in their cronies. Richardson's cohorts were thugs, lugs, losers, loonies, and dubious donors - with everything to gain.*

## *RICHARDSON DONS MORE MASKS*

Governor Richardson, to his other fake personas, had added "latter-day Governor Lew Wallace" setting things right by a pardon (by digging Billy up?). He intoned presidentially in *Time* magazine on June 21, 2004, "I have to decide whether to pardon him. But not right away - after the investigation, after the state gets more publicity." (Meaning: "Till I get more publicity.")

His best persona was "governor; it being inconceivable that a governor would try to destroy his state's tourism and history.

## *SULLIVAN'S AND SEDERWALL'S MORPHING*

Tom Sullivan's and Steve Sederwall's favorite spin was: "We're "cops" doing gritty "CSI forensics;" as opposed to "ivory tower," armchair academicians "making things up." Facing opposition, they became "martyrs," with a mantra: "Why are they so afraid of the truth?" That was in Sullivan's October 21, 2005 letter to the *RuidosoNews.com* editor, which whined:

> Frederick Nolan dismisses the modern day law enforcement technologies we have used to recreate the crime scene in Pete Maxwell's bedroom on the night that Pat Garrett allegedly shot "the Kid" as nothing but "stunts."

And now Robert Utley refers to us as "loony guys" and "two nut cases." I am surprised that he would stoop to that level showing his true colors. These two so called "historians" are upset that we were able to prove what actually happened in Pete Maxwell's bedroom and what actually happened in the stairwell in the Lincoln County Courthouse in the day Bell was killed. They are also upset that we located the furniture in Pete Maxwell's bedroom and the bench that the "kid's" body was laid upon after he was shot.

Our investigation contradicts their theories written in their books. It appears that our critics all suffer from the same "kindergartenmentality." [sic]

**Why are they so afraid of the truth?** [author's boldface]

Frederick Nolan says that we have no right to conduct an official investigation since we are no longer in law enforcement.

Steve and I were both sworn in as sheriff's deputies by Sheriff Rick Virden shortly after he took office. Once again Nolan failed to do his homework.

I respect true historians as Dr. Paul Hutton, Don Cline, Leon Metz and Bob Boze Bell all who have looked at our investigation with an open mind.

Here, Sullivan even shape-shifted Garrett's historian, Leon Metz, from opponent to advocate. But even their cited historian, Don Cline, in his book, *Alias Billy the Kid*, refuted their hoax:

John W. Poe ... said, "It seems too bad that people will circulate erroneous and false stories about this occurrence [Billy's killing by Garrett] but I suppose it is one of the things that will have to be endured."

Sullivan, however, as will be seen, was right about Professor Paul Hutton, their "official historian;" and about Bob Boze Bell, *True West* magazine's Editor-in-Chief - both fellow hoaxers.

## WE'RE TOURISM PROMOTERS

The favorite hoaxer shape-shift was New Mexico Tourism Department representatives. That left out an obvious tourist response: "Why should I visit someplace where nothing happened, everybody lied, and with a grave of an unknown cowboy?"

The tourism ploy appeared in a September 23, 2004 article in the *Lincoln County News* under "Lincoln County 'War' Heats Up Over 'Billy,' " after County Commission Chairman Leo Martinez publicly reminded then-Sheriff Tom Sullivan that, a year before, he promised "the state Dept. of Tourism would provide funds." But Tourism Secretary Mike Cerletti, to my open records request through Jay Miller, denied any Tourism Department involvement.

The hoaxers' tourism ploy was presented in an *MSNBC News* Internet article of November 21, 2003 by reporter Alan Boyle:

> Why wouldn't Lopez and his counterpart in Silver City, Terry Fortenberry, want to have the tests done, particularly if the results could well back the mainstream view that Billy the Kid was indeed killed and buried in their locale? That is what De Baca County Sheriff Gary Graves, who works in Fort Sumner, is wondering ...
>
> That angle is one reason Gov. Bill Richardson supports the use of DNA analysis to solve the mystery. "We want to get to the bottom of it," Richardson said in a Voice of America report. "And if it means New Mexico gets a little attention, so be it. I'm the governor, I want to see people fascinated by Billy the Kid. And that means fascination with New Mexico."

# THUG HISTORY: MIGHT MAKES RIGHT

*HOAXBUST: The Billy the Kid Case hoax made thugs and lugs "historians." Taking to the role like fish to land, they confused brawn over brains, and tried to power through by intimidation or faking - all they had to work with, since they had no real evidence.*

### *INTIMIDATION BEATS SCHOLARLY RESEARCH*

When the Billy the Kid Case began in 2003, cowboy-costumed Sheriffs, Tom Sullivan and Gary Graves, and towering Deputy Steve Sederwall, bullied Fort Sumner locals with: "We've got the Governor, the biggest attorneys, and big money behind us."

After Fort Sumner's Mayor, Raymond Lopez, announced that he would oppose them, he told me he got this Sederwall call: "Get your head out of your ass. We're getting this [the exhumations] done whether you want it or not."

Feisty Lopez answered: "I've been beaten up by smaller men than you, and I'm still not afraid."

The hoaxers lacked academic image. An example was Attorney Bill Robins III's crude and constant spitting of his slimy, brown, chewing-tobacco dribble into a clear glass during his Silver City exhumation hearing on Catherine Antrim; and almost making the court reporter vomit.

Little things were revealing. Sederwall and Sullivan attacked Silver City after a June 2004 disinvite by its officials for the big local event: the Millie and Billy Ball (the invitation apparently came from their attorney, Sherry Tippett). Reporter, Levi Hall, in the June 12, 2004 *Las Cruces Sun* wrote: "Sederwall said he no longer had any plans to help Silver City and was going to let the whole town 'drain dry.' " The duo also snarled to Mary Alice Murphy and Melissa St. Aude in the *Silver City Daily Press* of June 10, 2004. Sederwall is quoted: "Tom and I will go on as if Silver City doesn't exist ... We're going to call the governor and tell him we're not going to Silver City."

Sullivan, a three time sheriff, then sheriff's deputy, showed his lack of gravitas in the December 27, 2007 affidavit of my process server DeWayne Zimitski. Zimitski wrote: "Mr. Sullivan came to the door ... and told me ... "to get off his fucken property."

Sullivan's and Sederwall's letterhead for my 2006 open records request said: "You believin' Us Or Them Lyin' Whores."

Locally, Sullivan was seen as an alcoholic lout with a bad back. By rumor, in the 1980's he got that bad back when driving off with a woman (with her being voluntary or involuntary seems uncertain). Her male relatives caught up, and allegedly beat the proverbial crap out of him. Sullivan was rescued by his deputies, who later got promotions. Possibly being sheriff was not enough fun. For the Billy the Kid Case, Sullivan became an actor for nine months in 2004 for movie about it - collecting his sheriff's' 24 hour per day on-duty pay. He played Sheriff William Brady.

### *ACTIONS SPEAK LOUDER FOR SEDERWALL*

The hoaxers were not just bluff. Steve Sederwall, erstwhile hat maker and a lawman in Texas and California - privately called "snake" by locals - was arrested in 1983 in Oklahoma for alleged "assault and battery" in "Case CRM-83-55 State of Oklahoma versus A.B. McReynolds, Jr., John (Nick) Moore and Steve Sederwall." Its February 9th Affidavit by a Ray Kirkland stated:

I investigated an Assault and Battery upon one Darryl Gene Williams and ascertained that A.B. McReynolds, Jr., John (Nick) Moore and Steve Sederwall assaulted and hit, acting in concert with each other, the said Darryl Gene Williams. That this incident took place at Christ's Forty Acres in Honobia, in LeFlore County, Oklahoma, and was without just or excusable cause.

Sederwall, not convicted, when facing this in a 2008 Lincoln County sheriff's election, allegedly stated both that it was a *different* "Steve Sederwall" *and* that "*he* was the arresting officer."

But the indubitable Steve Sederwall, in New Mexico, allegedly verbally attacked a political opponent - a widowed mother, Debra L. Ingle - by naming her a "whore and cocaine dealer" - shortened glibly to "cocaine whore." Her 2004 Lincoln County case in Twelfth District Court was for defamation as "Ingle vs Sederwall (and Village of Capitan) No. D-1226-CV-200400147." Sederwall lost, and the county paid damages. The county footed other Sederwall legal bills for filed claims according to the October 16, 2008 *Lincoln County News*, which during his Capitan mayorship resulted "in over $350,000 in payments to plaintiffs."

As to me, Sederwall worked behind-the-scenes. In September of 2009, he called the publisher of the first edition of this book, titled *MegaHoax*; but failed to stop its publication. And the publisher told me about the intimidation. Sederwall repeated that maneuver in November of 2012, after my advertisement for all my Billy the Kid books came out in *Wild West* magazine. He contacted Editor-in-Chief Greg Lalire, and came away with the promise that my books on the hoax would not be reviewed there. But Lalire did accept my ads; and informed me about the call. Sederwall had also tried double-barrels: having his fellow hoaxer, U.S. Marshals Service Historian David Turk (translate into: branch of Homeland Security) contact Greg Lalire with the same implied threat.

Also, Sederwall may have contributed his Debra Ingle approach for an article maligning me in fellow hoaxer Bob Boze Bell's *True West* magazine of August/September 2010. I was portrayed as a conspiracy theorist blocking Billy the Kid Case truth, and as a crazy mutilator of Lincoln County horses. (That horse theme may have come to Sederwall from his past job with the Bureau of Land Management dealing with horse abuse cases.)

## *GARY GRAVES WINS "MOST UNPOPULAR THUG"*

### RECALL AS SHERIFF

De Baca County Sheriff Gary Graves's worst thuggery was not connected to the Billy the Kid Case. On his own, he made New Mexico history by being the first (and only) sheriff ever recalled.

Grave's come-uppance began with the September 13, 2004 De Baca County Tenth Judicial Court "Case No. CV-04-00019,

In the Matter of De Baca County Sheriff Gary Graves. Petition for Order Allowing Recall Vote." It was filed by five men (Dennis Cleaver, Jay Paul, Allen Sparks, Ellis Jones, and Rex Pope) and local attorney, Steve Doerr. Graves was accused of malfeasance and misfeasance; using public property as his own; threatening, harassing, and intimidating residents; violating prisoners' rights at the De Baca County Detention Center; not keeping financial records; and misappropriating money and property entrusted to his sheriff's office.

On September 14, 2004, Fort Sumner's *De Baca County News* printed: "De Baca County Citizens' Committee Files Petition for Recall of Sheriff Gary Graves." It said: "Spokesman Dennis Cleaver said the recall is an effort to restore law enforcement and end more than 21 months of intimidation and harassment of De Baca County citizens."

Graves's Sheriff's Association refused to represent him. Guess who did? From Texas, came Attorney Bill Robins III! Was it recompense for Graves's Billy the Kid Case hoaxing? Was it pro bono? Those answers are unknown. But the results are known.

The hearing for the recall of Sheriff Gary Graves, under Judge Joe Parker, was documented by Scot Stinnett, owner of the *De Baca County News*. Stinnett's headline on September 1, 2005 was: "Testimony paints Graves as 'above the law.' " Graves's head dispatcher/administrative assistant, Linda Boyd, gave incidents called "sickening" (alleged sexual comments), and scary (in which Graves sped his county vehicle with her and her son inside).

Attorney Robins so harassed Linda Boyd in cross-examination, that she vomited into a waste basket (demonstrating that Robins had other ways of making women vomit besides tobacco-spitting).

De Baca County Jail Supervisor Lynita Lovorn testified that Graves bound prisoners with duct tape. He allegedly also seized $2,000 from a Mexican woman following a traffic stop, gave her $50 travel money, and kept the rest.

Robins accused Lovorn of lying. Graves's deputy, A.J. Haley, vouched for that lying. But A.J. Haley had traveled from Utah to be "deputized" by Graves specifically to testify on his behalf! Judge Parker kicked out A.J. Haley's testimony.

The Billy the Kid Case came up only in prosecution questioning as to whether Graves was continuing it. He said yes.

After two days of testimony, Judge Parker ruled that the citizens group could proceed with recall.

The tiny Fort Sumner population voted 576 to 150 to oust him. Attorney Robins appealed the recall in both the Appellate and Supreme Courts of New Mexico - and lost.

But what happened to Graves? It being New Mexico, he was re-employed in a police department in another part of the state.

## HAPLESS AS HOAXER

De Baca County Sheriff Gary Graves was enlisted by the Billy the Kid Case hoaxers as on-site lawman for the Kid's exhumation. But once signed on, it seems that the whole shebang gave Graves the heebie-jeebies. For example, his parallel Sheriff's Department Case No. 03-06-136-01 disappeared; and was never found again!

A rogue cop (which led to his recall), he did not help things by defying his County Commissioners' letter of September of 2003 from Chairman Powhatan Carter III, Joe Steele, Tommy Roybal; and County Clerk Nancy Sparks. It said:

> The De Baca County Commissioners are in full support of the Village of Fort Sumner's stand against exhuming the Body of Billy the Kid. We feel this is a waste of time and especially money.

Ignoring the fact that Graves was kicked out of office for his own thuggish demerits, his fellow Billy the Kid Case hoaxers shape-shifted him to their ultimate "martyr for their truth."

Before his recall troubles, Graves was way over his head with his hoaxer shape-shift into "history buff" for hoax-backing *True West* magazine. Reporter Jana Bommersbach's "Breaking Out More Shovels: Fort Sumner's sheriff commits to exhuming the Kid," appeared in their January/February 2004 issue. She began: "If anyone knows Billy the Kid, it's the sheriff in the town that claims to hold the outlaw's grave." Graves sang his song:

> "You've got your die hards that are scared of their shadow and say leave it alone," says Sheriff Graves in his soft twang during a phone interview from his home. "The mayor says he wants nothin' to do with it" ... "I'm not anybody's 'yes-man,' " Sheriff Graves says. "I think it's great."

Then Graves hit a wall. Wildly, he guessed that the case was to decide if Garrett killed Billy "legal" or "illegal" - whatever that meant. If "illegal," then Garrett was "a murderer!" Having marching orders, Graves trudged on, giving his own fantasies.

> "I don't think he killed him in the Maxwell house," the sheriff says. "And I think they held him until dark and then killed him."
> He suspects Garrett came gunning for Billy, [Both Graves and Bommersbach seem to think Billy was tracked only for killing the deputies] not so much to catch a cop killer as to protect himself and his complicity with the outlaw. "I think Pat Garrett was afraid people would hear the real story," he says.
> "I kind of feel ol' Pat Garrett might have been behind the escape," says Graves, as he notes the lingering suspicions that the sheriff had planted a gun to help Billy.

As if recalling lines, Graves then becomes a "researcher":

> Why does the sheriff feel the story is a legacy of lies? He says he's uncovered two major points that fuel his suspicions:
> * While Billy the Kid was in Fort Sumner, he was involved with Pat Garrett's sister-in-law.
> * Garrett's long-rumored friendship with the Kid is allegedly underscored by paperwork that has the men buying property together.

Obviously, this "paperwork" - unknown before that moment - never appeared. And "researcher" Graves finished his unintended demolition of the Billy the Kid murder case by adding that he did not believe the stories of "Jim" [sic - John] Miller or "Brushy Bill."

Forgetting his punch line for exhumation, he ended: "[T]he real Billy the Kid was killed in his town some 120 years ago."

Maybe his recall from the craziness ended up being his relief.

## SHERIFF RICK VIRDEN KEEPS IT UP

After Sheriff Sullivan's term ended in 2004, his Undersheriff, Rick Virden, was elected Sheriff; and immediately deputized Sullivan and Sederwall to continue the Billy the Kid Case.

With over 30 years in State Police, as Sheriff in Otero County, and Undersheriff in Lincoln County, Rick Virden took corruption in stride. He was also a possible robber - of railroad ties: the worst kept crime secret in Lincoln County. To me, stealing road ties seemed like a bank robber handing a teller the note: "Don't move. I'm taking the furniture." As Sheriff, Virden solved no real cold case murders - like the "Cotton" and Judy McKnight killings (some locals even implicated him). Much later, I found out first hand that he had surprisingly powerful, frightening friends.

Virden learned my name in 2006 by my open records request to him; and, with Lincoln County Attorney Alan Morel and Sullivan and Sederwall, reported me (as a terrorist?) to the U.S. Marshals Service (presumably hoaxer Turk again) for doing it.

## "LITTLE WEASEL" LINCOLN LAWYER ALAN MOREL

As the Billy the Kid Case hoax progressed, Lincoln County Attorney Alan Morel - called by some locals "the little weasel" - proved central in its cover-ups. From 2003, he faked open records responses with its lawmen, mislead his County Commissioners about the liability, and finally contributed to years of unnecessary open records litigation. Morel was a thug on the level of Sederwall, Sullivan, and Virden; participating with them in October of 2006 in reporting me indirectly to Homeland Security for doing an open records request, apparently hoping to stop me by intimidation.

About my huge potential litigation bill by 2013, Morel allegedly told his County Commissioners, "It's not our worry. It comes from taxpayers." And I heard that after a March 9, 2010 hearing in my litigation, that he joked to a local woman that I would never get the records because he had them at his home." (No one seems to keep secrets in Lincoln County.) When on the stand himself in my case on February 4, 2013, I got the chance to see his conscienceless shenanigans under oath.

## EVEN THE HOAXERS' PHOTOGRAPHER WAS ROUGH

A photo-credit for a Lionel "Lonnie" Lippman came in an article on the hoaxers' Arizona exhumation. The picture has Steve Sederwall holding John Miller's (or William Hudspeth's) skull. Lippman, now deceased, was Sederwall's friend. "Lonnie" had also served time in jail. According to the Texas Department of Public Safety Conviction Records Database, Lionel Whitby Lippman had a trio of arrests in Bexar County's San Antonio. The first was on February 17, 1970 for "vehicular theft;" the second, on July 7, 1970, for "assault with attempt to commit rape;" and the last, on June 11, 1973, for "forgery and passing." So "Lonnie" fit right in.

# OFFICIAL HISTORIAN: PAUL HUTTON

*HOAXBUST: A University of New Mexico history professor and self-proclaimed Old West expert, Paul Hutton used his media connections to advance the hoax. Then he hypocritically denied connection to any of it. He did more damage to the history than all the hoaxers combined. And his first production came out on TV in August of 2004, before Judge Ted Hartley made any ruling.*

Paul Andrew Hutton, appointed by Governor Richardson as "official historian" for the Billy the Kid Case, was both: the hoax's primary one, and a real historian, as a University of New Mexico professor, advertising his Old West expertise. He is also the executive director of the Western History Association, and promoted in Wikipedia as: "Dr. Hutton has appeared in, written, or narrated over 150 television documentaries on CBS, NBC, Discover, Disney Channel, TBS, TNN, A&E, and the History Channel." So he was a great media contact for Richardson's bunch.

But when I investigated his "official historian" role for the Billy the Kid Case, surprisingly, Hutton responded that he was not their historian. So Hutton recycled a Groucho Marx question: "Who are you going to believe, me or your own eyes?"

## HUTTON GETS ANNOUNCED

In hoaxer "eyes," Paul Hutton certainly was one of their own. As announced by Bill Richardson himself, in his June 10, 2003 press release [APPENDIX: 4], Paul Hutton was present at his first hoaxer meeting in the governor's "Round House" capitol building, along with Sheriff Tom Sullivan, Deputy Steve Sederwall, Sheriff Gary Graves, and Attorney Sherry Tippett.

Richardson's press release left no role doubt:

> I have also asked University of New Mexico Professor of History and Executive Director of the Western History Association, Doctor Paul Hutton, to serve as our historical advisor.

When *True West* magazine's Editor-in-Chief Bob Boze Bell began promoting the hoax, Paul Hutton, his friend and editorial board member, was featured. *True West* August/September 2003 issue's "Digging Up Billy," by Jana Bommersbach, says:

> Gov. Richardson has offered state aid for the investigation and has appointed Paul Hutton, a renowned Western historian from the University of New Mexico and True West contributing editor, to assist as the official historian.

On June 11, 2003, reporter, Anthony DellaFlora, headlined the *Albuquerque Journal's* front page with: "State Not Kidding Around: Governor won't mind if probe of notorious 19th century N.M. outlaw boosts tourism." It said, "University of New Mexico history professor Paul Hutton, executive director of the Western History Association, also will aid in the investigation." [APPENDIX: 6] DellaFlora quoted Hutton talking about the Kid's "escape": 'The real question is, who helped him." That was intended to mean Garrett as a murderer.

And in the Lincoln County Sheriff's Department file was a "Contact List" for "William H. Bonney Case # 2003-274." Under "Investigators," and following "Tom Sullivan - Sheriff," "Steven M. Sederwall - Deputy," was "Paul Andrew Hutton - Historian," with his University of New Mexico address. [APPENDIX: 26]

## HUTTON'S HISTORY CHANNEL PROGRAM "INVESTIGATING HISTORY: BILLY THE KID"

Paul Hutton also arguably achieved the most hoax damage. Unintentionally, he also preserved, like in one chunk of amber, all the major hoaxers united. His fulfillment of "official historian" was literal: He wrote and co-produced the hoax history for the world. It was in the form of his 2004 History Channel program validating the Billy the Kid Case. Titled "Investigating History: Billy the Kid," Paul Hutton's TV creation used hoax tenets, hoax reenactments, and all the major hoaxers masquerading as a "documentary." It is still shown around the country, guaranteeing hoax "immortality."

Paul Hutton's co-producer for "Investigating History: Billy the Kid," was none other than Bill Kurtis (the same Bill Kurtis paying the hoax's forensic expert, Dr. Henry Lee; filming the John Miller exhumation; and apparently planning on making the Billy the Kid Case hoaxers' Lincoln County Sheriff's Department Case 2003-274 his ongoing, fake DNA, exhumation franchise).

And Hutton set all this up. As Steve Sederwall said in a deposition for my open records litigation on June 26, 2012:

> [T]he way I met Bill Kurtis was through Paul Hutton. Paul Hutton wanted me to be on some investigative history … I said, "You know, I'm looking at bringing Henry Lee out here … Tell Kurtis I'll let him film it if he wants to, or whatever, if he can get Henry out here." So he [Hutton] jumped on it.

For his "Investigating History: Billy the Kid" TV program, Paul Hutton earned his appointment as "president-maker," featuring Governor Bill Richardson as an "historical investigator" bringing together "experts" to decide on pardoning Billy the Kid. And the "experts" were the other hoaxers and "Brushy" believers.

As usual, at that stage, I assumed that pardon focus was just a publicity stunt to diffuse the more bizarre stunt of Garrett as a murderer. Instead, complicit Hutton was doing his bidding to hit the hoax's bull's eye. It would take me years to recognize that. However, that makes "Investigating History: Billy the Kid" an invaluable parade of hoax, hoaxers, and hinted horror.

In addition, Hutton tried to cover-up Pat Garrett's investigation in Case 2003-274, which was being subjected to my relentless assaults. But concealing it, left the hoaxers' DNA quest irrationally attached to pardoning. Nevertheless, "Brushy Bill" and pretender exhumations were advertised. Since Hutton's house of cards was all lies, it made little difference what he presented. And evidencing some vestige of guilt-producing conscience, he concealed himself in the "Investigating History: Billy the Kid" credits, by hiding "writer" and calling himself on the "Governor's pardon team." And amusingly, he gave himself the most screen time, subtitled as "Professor, University of New Mexico."

But Paul Hutton boastfully confirmed his real role in the production when tempted by innocence of a *University of New Mexico Campus News* reporter, Carolyn Gonzales, for her February 16, 2004 article titled "Hutton writes wild frontier stories for History Channel." Carolyn Gonzalez, with her inadvertent scoop, stated about Professor Hutton:

> His role has evolved into fulltime scriptwriting for "Investigating History" … Hutton pitched the idea of the series to the History Channel after working with Governor Bill Richardson to try to verify the Kid's identity through a DNA comparison with his mother … Richardson, who dubbed Hutton "Doc," appointed him historian on the Billy the Kid issue.

For his "Investigating History: Billy the Kid," Hutton also contributed a hoax mantra: "the mystery of Billy's murder." In full hoaxer mode, when interviewed on April 24, 2004 by a Rick Nathanson for the *Albuquerque Journal* weekly television guide, "Entertainer," about his program, Hutton was quoted:

> "And people are always intrigued by mystery, and this has always been one of the great mysteries of the Old West. The great mystery in this case is, of course, who is buried in Billy the Kid's grave in Fort Sumner."

And from Hutton's presentation, reporter Nathanson derived the key hoax mantra about Garrett's being "Billy's good friend."

Then, for Rick Nathanson, Hutton straddled the fence. Nathanson paraphrases:

> "I'm pretty sure that Pat Garrett shot Billy the Kid that night at Pete Maxwell's house in Fort Sumner and that Billy was buried there the next day."

Left out for reporter Nathanson, is that Paul Hutton's actual program is unambiguous hoax promotion to the contrary.

## EXPOSÉ OF PAUL HUTTON'S "INVESTIGATING HISTORY: BILLY THE KID"

*HOAXBUST: The 2004 History Channel program by Paul Hutton, is a major hoax creation, on the order of the "Probable Cause Statement;" and it disseminated irrevocable hoax damage to a national level. It belies any Hutton shape-shift into non-hoaxer, since he was writer, co-producer, and on-camera narrator. It also reveals this professor's historical ignorance, while claiming "Old West expertise." And though using the hoax's claim of Pat Garrett not killing Billy, it claimed the investigation was being done to determine a governor's pardon for Billy. Also, it foreshadowed an ongoing TV series of pretender exhumations seeking "Billy." And, unbeknownst to the public, the varied talking heads were just the hoaxers doing ricochet validations. And "Brushy Bill" Roberts was promoted as a credible claimant for the Kid's identity as survival "evidence" for the Garrett murder.*

## *OVERVIEW*

Paul Hutton's "Investigating History: Billy the Kid" is the hoax's ultimate ricochet validation trick, since almost all hoax participants come on-screen to vouch for the Billy the Kid Case. The line-up had: Governor Bill "Remember-Me-For-President" Richardson, Sheriff Tom Sullivan, Deputy Steve Sederwall, Attorney Bill Robins III, Bob Boze Bell of *True West*, and "Brushy Bill" believer and author, W.C. Jameson.

The context is hoax-skewed re-enactments of Billy the Kid history; with Paul Hutton's bug-eyed, unctuous face-time making hoax pronouncements!

Spliced in are historian, Robert Utley's brief token comments (Garrett was not Billy's friend; Garrett shot Billy; Billy is buried in his grave), which are ignored.

Final credits present "Frederick Nolan," under "Footage/Photos;" though, Nolan told me his name was used without his participation or knowledge.

For the program, the Billy the Kid Case appears as jumbled hoax tenets - the Billy body was not identified, friend Garrett helped Billy escape, tourist interests prevented exhumations for DNA. Concluding is that the "homicide investigation's" purpose as assisting Governor Richardson's decision on pardoning Billy.

Also, the Billy the Kid Case is shape-shifted into a "homicide investigation" of Billy's Lincoln County War killings - to see if Billy "deserved" the posthumous pardon for committing them.

Hutton's scamming leaves a future problem: The hoaxers would need Garrett as the killer of "the innocent victim" to justify more TV programs: their pretender exhumations to come - and not Billy as a Lincoln County War killer. But Hutton apparently chose to delay that preposterous murder claim, along with its fake forensics, since the carpenter's bench goes unmentioned.

Added are new elements to support the pardon spin.

Billy becomes their "good guy." Hutton misstates history to create a sense of injustice by falsely saying Billy was the "only one" blamed for the Sheriff Brady killing. And Sullivan, for the only time in the case, says, "I'm not sure the Kid was all that bad."

Garrett, however, is the "bad guy" (tracking Billy only "for the reward," says Hutton; killing him "in cold blood," says Attorney Bill Robins - accidentally removing the basis of the entire Billy the Kid murder case!) So absent here, is the frequent hoaxer spin, in other contexts, of "doing the case to protect Garrett's honor!"

This case morphing from "bad Garrett's" murder to "good Billy's" pardon, necessitated humorous shape-shifts of Sheriff Sullivan to the "discoverer" that Billy was promised a pardon; of Hutton and Bob Boze Bell to "historians" on the "Governor's pardon team," who had "been gathering information for years;" and of Bill Robins (now from Santa Fe, not Texas) being a lawyer helping Governor Richardson with pardon legalities (Robins's exhumation cases being omitted!). Sederwall is just a Capitan Mayor wondering if "Brushy Bill" was Billy. Richardson, a recurrent, on-screen, inflated head like a hot-air balloon, declares his commitment to "science," "tourism," and New Mexico.

Since all the hoaxers, except Richardson and Robins, are in cowboy costume, there are droopy or stringy mustaches throughout - leaving the impression that Old West characters were all jive-talkers; and making one anticipate that all would soon start singing: "Come a ti yi yippie yippie yay."

## THE PROGRAM

Advancing the Billy the Kid Case hoax's agenda constitutes the program: fabricate doubt about the Fort Sumner death scene; make Garrett into a liar; and denigrate the subject's legitimate historians. Thus, the film begins with a re-enactment of Shadow Billy approaching the dark Maxwell house, while the narrator (Hutton as writer) intones: "This is one of the most controversial moments in the history of the Old West: history's version of the last seconds of Billy the Kid."

With that hoax lie as a starter, one can almost hear bottom-of-the-barrel-historian Paul Hutton's scornful hissing of "hissstory;" since what will follow is his error-filled historical ignorance, and his apparent avoidance of hissstory books. He continues: "Pat Garrett fires into the darkness ... Billy the Kid is dead when he hits the floor - or is he?"

The answer you will get from the professor is hoax-speak "suspicion," based on the Probable Cause Statement's technique of "ifs" followed by faking history to create a straw-man for knocking down.

So Hutton, on screen, will say, in his wheedling tone - after "doooubting" a successful shot in a dark room: "The story is alllmost toooo good. The idea that the Kid ... would come strolllling into this room unarmed and right intooo the hands of the law enforcement official ... is just toooo bizarre."

What is bizarre, is that, in front of a national audience, this professor had the gall to make it all up: In truth, Billy was armed; he could be seen in the brightly moonlit doorway; and he, most surely, was sent into that fatal ambush, since his intent had been to go to the opposite side of the building to cut a steak.

But to complete Pat Garrett's character assassination, Paul Hutton fabricates that Garrett lied about Billy's being armed, because "Garrett took a lot of heat for killing the Kid without giving him a chance." (What "heat?" Was Hutton hoping for a duel; for the OK Corral?)

Hutton lies that the history is "Garrett's version;" says that the only murder eye-witness was Pete Maxwell, "who was never interviewed" (omitting Maxwell's Coroner's Jury statement, and the townspeople as the corpse's eye-witnesses), and says Poe "contradicted" Garrett's statement (Poe was merely initially unsure that Garrett had shot Billy, whom he could not recognize.)

This hoaxing (as will be listed below with other examples) is, however, odd. Though it promoted the Billy the Kid Case hoax at large - Garrett as a heinous accomplice to Billy's murder of the deputies and murderer of the innocent victim directly - it is not featured in this production with all its fake DNA glory (though bad public officials interfering with some sort of a DNA investigation for some sort of truth-finding does appear).

One can postulate that this program was intended to set the stage for an ongoing Paul Hutton "Investigating History" series with Bill Kurtis in which a "bad Garrett" was needed to allow "good Billy's escape" so the pretenders could live on to provide a treasure trove of possible graves for shovels and filming.

Indeed, the John Miller exhumation in Arizona was intended to be their "Part Two" (and was in Kurtis's can by May 19, 2005). It was halted only because my ongoing hoax exposé intervened, making their Bill Kurtis film footage crime scene evidence!

Professor Paul Hutton's shocking (given his academic credentials) continual errors of historical facts rely on his TV viewers' equal ignorance to avoid exposing of his incompetence (as well as unscrupulousness).

For example, as early information, Hutton says Billy's mother died when he was 12 (actually 14½); and he calls the outlaw, Jessie Evans, Billy's "old side-kick" (Billy rode with Jessie one month, September of 1877, before being hired by John Tunstall.).

As to errors in the lead-up to the Lincoln County War, Hutton, strangely mimicking "Brushy Bill" and his authors, thinks John Tunstall and Alexander McSween were in partnership in Tunstall's Lincoln store (actually that was the Santa Fe Ring's frame-up lie for killing Tunstall); and says the James Dolan House filed a civil case against Tunstall (that two part case was against McSween; was filed by the Fritz heirs; was both a civil breech of contract and a criminal embezzlement; and Tunstall's property was attached by falsely alleging partnership with McSween).

After Tunstall's murder, Hutton narrates that Sheriff Brady was shot in revenge (when he was actually ambushed by the Regulators to protect McSween returning to town that day); says "only" Billy was charged with Brady's shooting (when the murder defendants included all the shooting Regulators).

For the Lincoln County War, Hutton - still strangely in line with "Brushy Bill's" pseudo-history - thinks the McSween side lost because of being "divided up" throughout the town (when they were strategically well placed in both the east and west, held the town for five days; and lost only because of military intervention - with that military intervention simply left out by Hutton).

When Paul Hutton finally gets to the pardon, it remains oddly muddled as to how the investigation of "bad Garrett" and Billy the Kid's killing people during the Lincoln County War would lead to a posthumous one from Richardson.

Nevertheless, Hutton continues with presentation of his own historical ignorance. He calls Governor Lew Wallace's Amnesty Proclamation "for everyone;" when Billy's tragic fate was based on the fact that it excluded for amnesty those already indicted - like him.

As to Billy's own potential Wallace pardon, Hutton claims Billy's testimony in the 1879 Grand Jury *failed* to indict Dolan for the Huston Chapman murder because the district attorney was Dolan's friend. This is a *very big* Hutton error, missing the only possible reason in Hutton's historical mess to *justify giving Billy the pardon: namely that he both testified and got Dolan indicted, as well as Billy Campbell, and Jessie Evans as an accessory.* Also, the D.A. just cross-examined; the jurymen indicted.

As to Pat Garrett's sheriff's election, Hutton says erroneously that he was chosen for that job by Governor Lew Wallace (when the truth is that Garrett was elected; though "favored" by the Santa Fe Ring and Secret Service Operative Azariah Wild - all nothing to do with Lew Wallace); and says Garrett wanted to be sheriff to get the $500 reward (when Garrett just wanted a job; and Wallace's first reward for Billy the Kid was offered over a month *after* Garrett won the election - on December 22, 1880).

About Pat Garrett's Stinking Springs capture of Billy the Kid, Hutton wrongly says it was the day after Garrett's ambush of Billy's group at Fort Sumner (which killed Tom O'Folliard on December 19, 1880). It was days later - on December 22nd.

As to Billy's jail letters to Wallace, Hutton says they were written in the Lincoln County courthouse jail, when they were from the Santa Fe jail. (This mistake strains belief that Hutton actually teaches history or has any interest in the "Old West.")

**But the most egregious and most permanently damaging part of Hutton's TV concoction is his Billy the Kid Case hoaxer-mode re-enactment scene having Pat Garrett place the jailbreak revolver in the outhouse for Billy's murder of the deputy guards. No one accused Garrett of this horrific crime before the hoax. Paul Hutton made it irrevocably real by that scene.** [author's boldface]

Ongoing errors continue in other re-enactment scenes. For example, after Brady is shot, Billy runs out to steal *Brady's* Winchester carbine; when Billy was getting *his own Winchester*, confiscated earlier by Brady during Billy's brief unjust arrest.

Blatant hoax-jive is throughout Hutton's production. But the take-home message for the victimized viewers is that: Everything about known Billy the Kid is "suspicious;" "Brushy Bill" Roberts may be Billy the Kid; and Governor Bill Richardson with legal experts - like Attorney Bill Robins III - is working to get to the bottom of it ... and pardon Billy the Kid. In conclusion, "Investigating History: Billy the Kid" was pure Billy the Kid Case hoaxing, with an added pardon twist.

# SPECIFIC HUTTON HOAXING

***HOAXING MURDER SUSPICIONS***: Hutton omits historical evidence that Billy's killing was well documented, and that Billy's corpse's identification was profuse. Instead, Hutton gives lies: This is "the beginning of a mystery that still haunts the West today." "Poe said, 'Pat you shot the wrong man.' " "This is Pat Garrett's version ... but questions linger." "The only other eye witness, Pete Maxwell, never gave his version of the story." "Was it really the Kid shot ... the story seems unlikely." "The Kid's reputation was so fearsome that no one wanted to go inside to identify the body." "The line between fact and legend is elusive."

***HOAXING DEATH ESCAPE:*** Hutton, on screen, proclaims: "Some suggested that it was more likely that Pat Garrett, Billy's friend, let him go ... burying someone else in his place" (here fabricating both fake friendship and "innocent victim.") Doing the ricochet trick, Bob Boze Bell (subtitled as "Editor, True West Magazine") comes on screen to state snidely that: "Friends of Pat Garrett conducted what they called an autopsy. But there were no photographs." Boze Bell adds that those "friends" said in the report that Garrett deserved the reward. (In truth, the Coroner's jurymen were not Garrett's friends. Their report said he deserved "thanks," not a reward. The body was examined by the jurymen.) Boze Bell says Garrett did the killing in "secrecy," and buried the body the next day. (This misinformation hides legal validity of the Coroner's Jury report by substituting an ambiguous "autopsy report;" by preposterously wanting a camera, when they were unavailable in those days; and by implying that burying a rotting corpse a day after death was peculiar.) Do not miss that these fabrications echo W.C. Jameson's and Frederick Bean's in their own "Brushy" book: *The Return of the Outlaw Billy the Kid.*

***HOAXING GARRETT FRIENDSHIP:*** This necessary part of the Billy the Kid Case hoax (though irrelevant to the pardon) gets no supporting evidence from Hutton, who merely falsely proclaims it, then fakes the gun-placing re-enactment. While you see that happening, Hutton narrates: **"Pat Garrett put the gun in the privy because he and the Kid were old friends and he wanted to help him escape."** [author's boldface]

*HOAXING "BRUSHY" AS BILLY:* "Brushy" gets a big plug. The screen fills with his first book: *Alias Billy the Kid.* Hutton narrates: "Over the years that story has gained some credence." W.C. Jameson, a "Brushy" believer and author, lies onscreen that the "Coroner's Jury Report was never found," and that there was "no evidence jurymen saw the body." Sederwall adds, "If 'Brushy Bill" is Billy the Kid, it comes down to this ... Garrett had to have let him escape in Fort Sumner."

*HOAXING LAW ENFORCEMENT CASE:* Hutton announces that the "investigation" would solve if Billy was really killed by Pat Garrett and if Governor Bill Richardson should pardon him based on Governor Lew Wallace's promise.

*HOAXING EXHUMATION BLOCKADE:* Sullivan, with sheriff's badge, says he tried to settle the matter, but was "opposed by tourism interests" in Silver City and Fort Sumner, which he calls "obstruction of justice." Billy Sparks, Richardson's spokesman, says: "People want to prevent any truth that is not their truth." A Dennis Erickson, Ph.D. Science Policy Advisor in Richardson's Office, says there are ways of locating graves through "ground-penetrating radar." (Concealed is OMI blockade, irrelevance of that radar, and uncertain gravesites.)

*HOAXING PARDON:* Sullivan, shape-shifted to a "researcher" who found a "wrinkle in the historical record," says "Wallace reneged on his promise to pardon Billy which could have ended the Lincoln County War." (So Sullivan "discovered" a Wallace pardon promise!! But, oops, the War had ended the year before!) Hutton intones:: "New Mexico Governor Bill Richardson is ready to make things right." Balloon-headed Richardson declares: "I might pardon him." And he wants the truth "through science" (which makes no sense.) Bill Robins, bulbous-nosed and emoting sincerity, appears as an attorney seeking pardon evidence, saying Billy "should never have been charged."

*HOAXING TOURISM BOOST:* Richardson says, "When I traveled around the world, there was curiosity about the wild West and I know that's tourism, that's economic development for us." (So Richardson is doing this case for the world and for New Mexico. Remember him for president! And forget that he is willing to destroy his state's history to promote himself.)

# PAUL HUTTON'S CARPENTER'S BENCH SCAM

Dr. Lee's carpenter bench scam became part of Professor Paul Hutton's "job" as Richardson's "official" Billy the Kid Case hoax historian. So in 2004, Hutton shape-shifted to "authenticator" of the unauthenticatable bench (with co-hoaxer, U.S. Marshal's Service Historian David Turk). Hutton continued bench promotion in 2007 for his Albuquerque Museum of Art and History Billy the Kid show, with its curator, Deb Slaney. There, Hutton labeled it as having "human blood" attested to by Dr. Lee!

## PAUL HUTTON AS PROBABLE CAUSE STATEMENT AUTHOR

As "official" hoax historian and writer-producer of the 2004 History Channel program featuring it, Professor Paul Hutton seemed a likely contributor to the Probable Cause Statement.

That was why, on February 6, 2006, I - with journalist Jay Miller as my proxy - sent Hutton a query letter. Hutton did not respond. The letter was repeated on March 20th, saying the case merited an answer. Hutton returned it scrawled with: "Dear Mr. Miller: I have no comment on your questions or any interest in answering them."

But Paul Hutton was a *state paid* historian at the University of New Mexico. So, on June 15, 2006, he next got my open records request via Jay Miller. Hutton answered on June 20th, with the letter already cited, implying that Richardson and *True West* lied in calling him the "state historian;" and saying he was not the Probable Cause Statement's author.

So, if not author, his "attitude" was a possible contribution. That is in his Billy the Kid article, "Dreamscape Desperado," from the June 1990 *New Mexico Magazine*. There, Paul Hutton thrusts out a Dr. Strangelove hand. From his topic of the Kid's changing media image, suddenly flies out: "It is frustrating for the academics when their own work goes unnoticed while the Kid, just as he challenged the establishment a hundred years ago, mocks them by his hold on the public's imagination." Hutton may have disliked being "unnoticed" himself. So anything goes in his anti-intellectual, dreamscape, "Investigating History," TV program, with him playing professor - with more screen-time than Billy the Kid - as he and the other hoaxers merrily drifted, smashing truth in their self-aggrandizing rampaging fun.

## PAUL HUTTON'S PERSONAL INNOCENCE SPIN

Notwithstanding all evidence to the contrary, by June 20, 2006, Paul Hutton adamantly denied any connection to the Billy the Kid Case or to being its "official historian." In Old West jibing, that kind of fence riding merits only a sore crotch.

In answer to my inquiry written through journalist Jay Miller, Hutton wrote: "I was never the 'state historian' (as *True West* put it) on this project and had absolutely nothing to do with the production of any written materials on it outside of some initial talking points I emailed the governor's office before the first press conference." [APPENDIX: 27]

About his 2004 TV program, Hutton added: "As for my work on the History Channel and how I came to any conclusions in the Billy the Kid program, that is really none of your business." Not taking chances, Hutton added that the Billy the Kid Case was a "positive effort to promote our state nationally."

There was actually no doubt about Paul Hutton's choosing to be the hoax historian. Jay Miller had contacted Paul Hutton's mentor: historian, Robert Utley. No confidentiality was requested, so Jay Miller e-mailed me Utley's September 16, 2004 answer:

> I am truly disappointed in your governor. He was my congressman back in the 1980's, and I have admired him ever since. Of course I am a card-carrying member of ACLU, but he should be held accountable for the dumb things he is doing in the Billy dustup. When his aid tried to enlist me as "historical advisor," I told him to tell Richardson to stay out of this or he would get in deep doodoo. So they got Paul Hutton, my protégé, who loves the outrageous.

So Paul Hutton can add Robert Utley to his list of "liars."

When I spoke with Utley himself in November of 2005, he bemoaned that betrayal of historical ethics by the man he called his "protégé": Paul Hutton.

One thing I can predict: Professor Paul Hutton will shape-shift into a backer of whichever side prevails in the Billy the Kid Case's evolution. It is just too early for that hypocrite to decide. But Paul Hutton's inexcusable and permanent damage to the history of Billy the Kid and Pat Garrett cannot be denied or reversed.

# SECRET HISTORIAN: DAVID TURK

## *FINANCING DAVID TURK*

Hoax participant, U.S. Marshals Service Historian David Turk, is the only historian quoted in the Probable Cause Statement with his fake "proof" by useless hearsay of an old-timer quoted about a post-death Billy the Kid sighting. Also, since its footnotes are obscure National Archive documents on microfilm (like the Azariah Wild Secret Service Reports), Turk may have provided them to Steve Sederwall, an admitted writer of it.

Later, by ricochet validation, Turk vouched for the Dr. Lee carpenter's bench DNA scam, by "validating" the bench; and was also present at Lee's old Lincoln Courthouse Deputy Bell murder forensic CSI sham (where he was called an actual U.S. Marshal).

But Turk's ultimate hoax role took me years to learn. Tracking his use of taxpayer money for the Billy the Kid Case was its lead-in, and done under the Freedom of Information Act (FOIA), since he did his hoaxing as a public official.

Using Jay Miller for my August 5, 2004 FOIA records request to Turk, as stipulated it went to their General Counsel, Arleta Cunningham. It was titled: "Re. David Turk, Historian for U.S. Marshal's Service, FOIA on Sederwall/Sullivan/Graves/Billy the Kid Case." A copy went to Turk's boss, U.S. Marshal's Service Director Benigno Reyna. It spelled out the hoax. Requested was Turk's job description and salary; any contracts between him and Lincoln County law enforcement to work as their historian; and documentation of his costs and payments.

A year passed. (Repeat: A year passed!)

On June 22, 2005, a William E. Bordley, Associate General Counsel/FOIPA Officer, sent "Freedom of Information/Privacy Act Request No. 2004USMS7634, Subject: David Turk, Historian U.S. Marshals Service, FOIA on Sederwall/Sullivan/Graves/ Billy the Kid Case." Turk's duties were listed as: "Conducts historical research in order to prepare and edit historical articles for publications and exhibits on USMS history ... Develops fact sheets, brochures, pamphlets, and books on the history of the USMS. Research is conducted both on and off site." Participating in a filed, New Mexico, murder case stretched that job description!

The eye-opener was Turk's taxpayer funding for doing it. In New Mexico from December 5, 2003 to December 9, 2003, he traveled to Silver City, Lincoln, Las Cruces, Santa Fe, Ruidoso, Albuquerque, and Tijeras; spending $848.42 of taxpayer money for travel, lodging, car rentals, and cell phone, while collecting $1,967.00 of his yearly salary of $84,127.00.

As to Turk's hoax participation, Attorney William Bordley used double-talk:

> Regarding Item 6 of your request, Mr. Turk's role in this matter is to research and gather information relative to the Billy the Kid case to ascertain the historical accuracy of the U.S. Marshals Service involvement in the events relating to the Billy the Kid case.

I called Bordley on that gibberish. My Jay Miller, July 25, 2005 letter was "Follow-up on your response titled Freedom of Information Act Request No. 2004USMS7634 Subject: David Turk, Historian U.S. Marshals Service, FOIA on Sederwall/Sullivan/Graves/ Billy the Kid Case." I asked: Why was Turk involved in a New Mexico murder case? Did he author its Probable Cause Statement? That answer came in a month.

On August 24, 2005 a Mavis DeZulovich FOI/PA Liaison, Office of Public Affairs, responded with a tantalizing tidbit:

> Mr. Turk is not the author of the Lincoln County Sheriff''s Department Probable Cause Statement 2003-274. **However, mention is made in that document to information contained in a research report authored by Mr. Turk entitled:** *The U.S. Marshals Service and Billy the Kid.* [author's boldface]

So Turk's quote for the Probable Cause Statement had come from *his own* research report! Was "Garrett-as-murderer" David Turk's personal agenda? That needed my investigation. And Turk's New Mexico dates ultimately became the clue.

### TURK AS A PROBABLE CAUSE STATEMENT AUTHOR?

David Turk seemed a possible author-contributor to the Probable Cause Statement; but only chance gave an answer.

My FOIA investigations into his Billy the Kid Case finances had put Turk in New Mexico in early December of 2003, when Attorney Sherry Tippett was pressuring for a Probable Cause Statement. Did Turk help Sederwall write it by December 31st?

The hoaxers hid Turk's contribution. When, through Jay Miller, I sent Sheriff Tom Sullivan, on August 18, 2004, a request of all records pertaining to Turk, Sullivan refused them by claiming Turk's records for Case # 2003-274 were exempt by being part of that ongoing criminal investigation. That meant there *were* Turk records and that he had participated!

Turk's bosses were also wary. Department of Justice's Mavis DeZulovich had identified Turk's "research report" titled: *The U.S. Marshals Service and Billy the Kid.*

The plot thickens. David Turk is the U.S. Marshals Service's *only* historian. Pat Garrett is a famous Deputy U.S. Marshal. One would expect Turk, the historian, to scoff at a baseless case which painted Garrett as an insane murderer of an innocent victim, and accomplice to killing his own deputies, just to save a notorious outlaw - and certainly not to back it. And Turk's "evidence" was only useless hearsay. Was Turk a dim bulb? A kook? Turk's *The U.S. Marshals Service and Billy the Kid,* probably had the answers. I had to get a copy.

An adventure began. In April of 2006, I called the U.S. Marshals Service's Publication Department. They said it was Turk's personal report. I had to call him. But their Service is part of scary Homeland Security; and weird Turk might have a scary agenda. (As discussed, by October of 2006, the hoaxers did later report me to "the U.S. Marshals Service" - assumedly Turk - as intimidation for my open records request to Sheriff Rick Virden.)

So I got an out-of-state P.O. Box as a made-up "Wilma Jordan." Then I called, using a Polish accent from my Billy the Kid novel. On Internet photos, Turk looked plain and boyish.

ME: (*Using a crib sheet for the accent*) Dis iz Vilma Chordan. I vant to oder de pamplet on Pad Garred and Billy de Kid.
TURK: (*With boyish voice*) It's in revisions with my department. It may take a month.
ME: Vat iz de cost?
TURK: Free. Your taxpayer dollars paid for it.

"Wilma Jordan" called back on June 2, 2006. Now Turk himself was doing "revisions;" and delay was indefinite. Wilma asked, "Zo, do you tink Pad Garred *did nod shood* Billy de Kid?"

Bull's eye! "The facts do not fit together," Turk said.

"Vy is dis your interest?" Wilma asked.

Turk said because it involved murders of U.S. Marshals when Billy escaped in October of 1880. Dim bulb flashed. "Wilma," like Pandora, could not resist temptation. She said they were *Deputy* Sheriffs, and it was *April* 28th of 18-*81*.

On June 15th, "Wilma" wrote Turk, wanting more information on why Garrett did not kill the Kid. And she wanted that report.

Turk's answer, on July 3, 2006, was intended to scare the stuffing out of nosy "Wilma Jordan": he had tracked her down, and supplied her address! Amazingly, there *really was a Wilma Jordan*! It was *her* address! (I hope she does not have a Polish accent.) This proves that some Homeland Security tax dollars go to employee research to protect their own backside's security.

And Turk directed "Wilma" to a Steve Sederwall, with his telephone number provided! And, of course, there never came a copy of *The U.S. Marshals Service and Billy the Kid.*

There was something else. I learned that, subsequent to this interchange, Steve Sederwall himself was asking around if anyone knew about a Polish woman who had called David Turk. At least I got confirmation that I had done the accent right!

On August 8, 2006, via Jay Miller, my FOIA request to the U.S. Marshal's Service asked for *The U.S. Marshals Service and Billy the Kid.* It also queried how Turk had "authenticated" the carpenter's bench.

On August 31, 2006, a Nikki Cedric from their Office of Public Affairs responded:

> Mr. Turk ... has seen the said workbench; *however, he did not state that any particular person was on the bench. This is for the lab to determine.* The bench does match descriptions given in other sources and he believes it to be the one described.

And Nikki Cedric stated that the pamphlet would be sent "when it is ready for distribution." It never came.

On September 11, 2006, through Jay Miller, I tried: "Re. Follow-up to your August 31, 2006 response to my Freedom of Information Act request No. 2004USMS7634 in reference to David Turk, Historian for the U.S. Marshals Service; and request for clarification." I asked if Turk had provided the sources for the Probable Cause Statement. Responses ceased forever.

February of 2007 brought hope. David Turk published *"Billy the Kid and the U.S. Marshals Service"* in *Wild West* magazine! I got it. "Revised" seemed "expurgated" to just U.S. Marshals in the Lincoln County War period.

But it had a peculiarity. After the conventional death scene, a Dr. Strangelove hand lunges for Turk, who fakes Garrett as sole witness, and babbles like a Billy the Kid Case hoaxer about Billy's post July 14, 1881 survival. Turk writes:

> That traditional account [of the killing] - as told by Garrett himself (with the help of a ghostwriter) in the *Authentic Life of Billy, the Kid* - has been questioned many times over the years with some accounts suggesting that the Kid got away to live another day or decades, and others indicating that somebody else besides the Kid died in Maxwell's bedroom.

Finally, on September 3, 2008, the mystery was solved - as a part of my long, open records case litigation.

For his deposition on September 8, 2008, Sheriff Rick Virden's file for Case 2003-274 was subpoenaed. Though it was thoroughly expurgated of the forensic DNA records I was after, its last 26 pages were the actual, David Turk, *The U.S. Marshals Service and Billy the Kid*!

The date on that pamphlet's cover - illustrated with a galloping Old West rider and a big marshal's badge - was December 2003: the signing date of the Probable Cause Statement!

That cover stated, along with "United States Marshals Service Executive Services Division": "Research Report, Submitted by David S. Turk."

Page one gave me what I wanted in its title: "Research Report: The U.S. Marshals Service and Billy the Kid. **To Be Added in its Present Entirety, with Exhibits, to Lincoln County, New Mexico Case # 2003-274.**" [author's boldface]

So David Turk was quoted for the Billy the Kid Case's Probable Cause Statement; and he authored his own secondary Probable Cause Statement. By the latter, Turk had created his own, major, Billy the Kid Case hoax document! And its style implies him as a possible contributing author to the actual Probable Cause Statement - and certainly as providing National Archive documents used for it.

## U.S. MARSHALS SERVICE AND BILLY THE KID

*HOAXBUST: Lacking any historical evidence, U.S. Marshals Historian David Turk backs the Billy the Kid Case hoax premise of Pat Garrett as murderer of an innocent victim. His report irrelevantly discusses U.S. Marshals in the Lincoln County War period (including Pat Garrett). No Garrett-Billy friendship is indicated. Abruptly, based on a few WPA interviews from the 1930's (of people unconnected to the event), Turk concludes that Billy's killing "fueled speculation over the precise outcome." And noteworthy is the peculiarity and impropriety of the U.S. Marshals Service paying an employee to participate in a New Mexico Sheriff's Department murder investigation - to say nothing of participating in a hoax that was intended to destroy the reputation of one of America's most famous Deputy U.S. Marshals.*

*David Turk seemed to be aware of the risky and heretical nature of the document, as evidenced by his years of effort in concealing it. And when it was published in Wild West magazine in 2007, it was heavily expurgated to conceal its original purpose. And Turk's role as a direct participant in Case # 2003-274 was kept secret by him and the U.S. Marshal's Service.*

Below is the dissection of *The U.S. Marshals Service and Billy the Kid*. Called a "Research Report," it has a cover, 9 pages of text; "Endnotes" (bibliography); and "Exhibits" consisting of a Turk article titled "How much did it cost to find Billy the Kid?"; a "National Police Gazette" May 21, 1881 article on Billy's escape; and a May 30, 1881 letter from Attorney Sidney Barnes (one of Billy's prosecutors) about Billy's Mesilla trial and his later escape.

Turk's general information on U.S. Marshals is irrelevant to the Billy killing, and is omitted here.

And the only parts of Turk's "Research Report" that appear in the Probable Cause Statement are Turk's Frances E. Totty, WPA quote about "Billie" being seen after the death date; and "Endnote" sources, like Secret Service Operative Azariah Wild's reports. But David Turk's report - that he tried so hard to hide from me (and Wilma Jordan!) - was in the 2003-274 case file, as "probable cause" that Pat Garrett was a murderer.

**\* \* \* \* \* \* \***

# Research Report:
# The U.S. Marshals Service
# and Billy the Kid

Submitted by David S. Turk, Historian
December 2003

**"Research Report: The U.S. Marshals Service and Billy the
Kid. To Be Added in its Present Entirety, with Exhibits, to
Lincoln County, New Mexico Case # 2003-274."**

## Purpose of Research [Page 1]

There is renewed interest in examining the crimes and final
resting place of William H. Bonney, also known as Henry Antrim,
Henry McCarty, or Billy the Kid.

**[AUTHOR'S COMMENT: The only "renewed interest" was
from the Billy the Kid Case hoax and conspiracy theorists.]**

Two Sheriffs' Offices in New Mexico reopened an
investigation, with the approval of the Governor of New Mexico. In
September 2003 Steve Sederwall, Mayor of Capitan, and Deputy
Sheriff, Lincoln County, New Mexico, contacted me on research
matters relating to the Lincoln County War.

**[AUTHOR'S COMMENT: Turk claims Sederwall as contact.]**

Given the integral role of the U.S. Marshals Service, and the
dual roles between our two institutions during the time of Billy
the Kid, and further that Pat Garrett was a Deputy U.S. Marshal
during the pursuit of the Kid, and that another Deputy U.S.
Marshal (and Lincoln County officer), Robert Olinger, was shot
and killed by the Kid during his escape, it is relevant to the
agency's historical interest to research those portions of the case
pertinent to it to ensure accuracy.

**[AUTHOR'S COMMENT: The report gives no information to
doubt conventional history. It does not "ensure accuracy!"]**

The primary investigation of Lincoln County, New Mexico
State No. 2004-274 [sic] is being conducted by Lincoln County

Sheriff Tom Sullivan, De Baca County Sheriff Gary Graves, and Steve Sederwall, but the following findings add significantly to the data being collected in revisiting Billy the Kid.

[AUTHOR'S COMMENT: No reason is given for "revisiting Billy the Kid," except death rumors 56 years after the event.]

## Overview of Research Focus [Page 1]

The following research relates to the prominent roles of the U.S. Marshals Service in the Lincoln County War ... Finally, there is a study on the deaths of Deputy Marshal Olinger and Lincoln County Officer J.W. Bell, followed by Billy the Kid's subsequent escape. The Works Progress Administration interviewed several Lincoln residents during the late 1930's in this regard ...

[AUTHOR'S COMMENT: The oddness of this statement is easy to miss; but each part is irrelevant to the others. Out of nowhere, will come Turk's suspicions that the Kid was not Garrett's murder victim.]

## Deputy U.S. Marshal Garrett and His Agency Status [Page 4]

[AUTHOR'S COMMENT: This page, about Garrett's U.S. Marshal status has Secret Service Agent Azariah Wild's praise of Garrett to his Chief. All is irrelevant to Garrett's murder victim.]

## Key Event: Billy the Kid's Escape and the Deaths of Bell and Olinger [Page 8]

On April 28, 1881, [sic - missing word] made his famous escape from Lincoln. Accounts of the events were recalled later by witnesses. A contemporary news account from *The National Police Gazette* dated May 21, 1881, followed a generally accepted recollection pattern with some minor inconsistencies. Deputy U.S. Marshal Olinger and guard J.W. Bell ... were holding the Kid in the jail. Olinger dined at a local establishment, and during his absence the shackled prisoner hit Bell with handcuffs. He then grabbed Bell's revolver and shot him in the chest ... Just as he [Olinger] entered a small gate leading through the jail fence, the Kid shot him with a double-barreled gun, filling his breast of shot and killing him.

[AUTHOR'S COMMENT: Note that the *National Police Gazette*, published in New York, was merely a crime-oriented tabloid of its day, and not a legitimate historical source. And Turk presents a Billy escape without Garrett's participation.]

## Differing Accounts on Death of Billy the Kid [Pages 8 - 9.]

Deputy U.S. Marshal and Lincoln County Sheriff Pat Garrett pursued Billy the Kid for several months after the deaths

[AUTHOR'S COMMENT: About 2 ½ months.]

of Deputy Olinger and J.W. Bell. The end of the chase appeared to be at Pete Maxwell's ranch on July 15, 1881 [sic].

[AUTHOR'S COMMENT: Here is "Dr. Strangelove's hand with Probable Cause Statement's sly innuendo. Note "appeared to be." And the date is wrong!]

What occurred at the Maxwell Ranch fueled speculation over the precise outcome. There appears [sic] to be many questions to answer.

[AUTHOR'S COMMENT: This is full-blown conspiracy theory, with vague "suspiciousness." No evidence is given.]

According to the WPA interview of Francisco Trujillo in May 1937, Garrett was negotiating capture of the Kid with Pete Maxwell himself. Josh Brent's father was one of the Sheriff's deputies, stating that Garrett said "that he sure hated to kill the boy, but he knew it was either his life or the boy's life."

[AUTHOR'S COMMENT: The Billy the Kid hoaxers omitted this hearsay from the Statement. But, as a hoax connoisseur, I say they missed a great hoax quote – even though it is groundless! It was a chance to fake the Pat-Billy friendship.]

Yet another resident stated,

The people around Lincoln say Garrett didn't kill Billie [sic] the Kid. John Poe was with Garrett the night he was supposed to ... [sic] said that he didn't see the man that Garrett killed. Ican [sic] take you to the grave in Hell's Half

Acre, a old government cemetry [sic], where Billie [sic] was supposed to be buried to show you the grave.

The cook at Pete Maxwell's was always putting flowers on the grave and praying at it. This woman thought a lot of Billie [sic], but after Garrett killed the man at Maxwell's home her grandson was never seen again and Billie [sic] was seen by Bill Nicoli? And indian scout. Bill saw him in old Mexico.

[AUTHOR'S COMMENT: This "fuzzy factoid" was put in the Probable Cause Statement with attribution to Turk.]

The recollections took a legendary bent, even extending to events that occurred after those at the Maxwell ranch. Josh Brent stated that Garrett told his father that after he killed the Kid, "that a fellow from the east wrote him and said that he would pay $5000.00 for the trigger finger of the boy."

[AUTHOR'S COMMENT: Irrelevant pseudo-historical filler like in the Probable Cause Statement.]

### Other Related Fact [Page 9.]

A sidelight from this period was the debunking of one widely-held story that Billy the Kid killed twenty-one men by the age of twenty-one. U.S. Attorney Barnes stated in a letter to the Attorney General, dated May 30, 1881, that while the Kid "has killed fifteen different men & is only twenty one years of age."

[AUTHOR'S COMMENT: Again, irrelevant hearsay by one of Billy's Mesilla prosecuting attorneys, who had no way of knowing the information; but providing irrelevant historical filler like in the Probable Cause Statement.]

\* \* \* \* \* \* \*

Though it is now certain that U.S. Marshals Historian David Turk contributed to the Billy the Kid Case hoax, he is as much a conspiracy theorist as a hoaxer. His damage is from prestige of his title. A clue as to his link with the Billy the Kid Case's use of "Brushy" is in his February of 2007 *Wild West* magazine's "*Billy the Kid and the U.S. Marshals Service*" where he postulates "decades" of survival after Garrett's killing of a questioned victim.

# MAGAZINE HISTORIAN: BOB BOZE BELL

An unexpected Billy the Kid Case hoaxer was *True West* magazine's Editor-in-Chief Bob Boze Bell, since he authored 1992 and 1996 history books titled: *The Illustrated Life and Times of Billy the Kid*. His text summarized Frederick Nolan's books, with his own illustrations. The only hint of his historical hostility is that his Billy pictures rate as the largest number of ugly paintings done by one person of another. Since Boze Bell is appearance challenged, this may be his revenge. More revenge was his backing of the Billy the kid Case hoax - knowing it was one.

## *TRUE WEST MAGAZINE HOAX COVER-UP*

Glossy *True West* magazine, appealing to Old West aficionados, backed the hoax enough to be renamed: *Fake West*.

But, at the start of my hoax opposition, I knew only that one of its owners, Bob McCubbin, a past president of El Paso Gas and a major Billy the Kid collector, played host to Frederick Nolan when I brought him from England to testify against the hoax. I assumed McCubbin's publication reflected his academic appreciation.

And McCubbin referred me to Bob Boze Bell in October of 2005, when I relinquished my cowardly anonymity after the hoaxers revealed their secret Arizona exhumation of pretender, John Miller. I wanted *True West* to do a hoax exposé.

On October 25, 2005, I called Bob Boze Bell. After my explanation, there was silence. Then Boze Bell said: "But Sederwall and Sullivan are my friends. How could I write that?" I said I would be the author. He said: "Keep it short."

While waiting for a response to my article, I sent for *True West's* five magazines with Billy the Kid case articles; four of which were by Janna Bommersbach - and realized my mistake. *True West* had backed the Billy the Kid Case hoax all along!

Bommersbach's first article was in the August/September 2003 edition as "Digging up Billy. If Pat Garrett didn't kill the Kid, who's buried in his grave?"

The title was the message. Who said Garrett did not kill Billy? Who said there is a question of who is in his grave? Like subliminal advertising, this was a month before the Silver City foray. Bommersbach added, "And of course, *True West* will be there. Be there? Hell, we'll buy the shovels." She concluded:

Most significantly, it's not some splinter or kooky group that wants to do the exhuming and genetic testing. It's the highest authority in New Mexico, Gov. Bill Richardson. Two other major driving forces are the current Lincoln County Sheriff Tom Sullivan and Capitan, New Mexico Mayor Steve Sederwall ... Gov. Richardson wants to know if the Kid deserves a pardon ... And all this adds up to not only a chance to clarify and perhaps correct American history, but also a great tourism boom for New Mexico.

One could respond: Why *aren't* a governor, a sheriff, and a mayor "kooky" for calling themselves historians?

In the next *True West* issue, October/November 2003, came "From Shovels to DNA: The inside story of digging up Billy." Richardson was again paraded:

Gov. Richardson said, "By utilizing modern forensic, DNA and crime scene techniques, the goal of the investigation is to get to the truth. In the process, the reputation of Pat Garrett, still a hero to Lincoln County law enforcement, hangs in the balance."

By *True West*'s January/February 2005 magazine, Janna Bommersbach was pitching carpenter's bench DNA. She ends:

Let us not forget that Gov. Richardson endorsed the project, saying the search for the truth was a worthy cause and promising his office's cooperation.

Into *that* lions' den, I had gone! The lioness to whom I was assigned was named Meghan Saar. She e-mailed me on January 31, 2006 - wanting me to include the hoaxers, writing:

All parties in this article should be given the opportunity to respond; the article feels very biased and skewered toward one direction, and I feel this may be because not all parties were asked to comment.

I withdrew my article, citing *their* bias. Then I learned that Paul Hutton was their contributing editor, that he was Bob McCubbin's best friend, and that "Investigating History: Billy the Kid" had been filmed in McCubbin's home library as background for talking-head Hutton. When I confronted McCubbin, he denied having "editorial control." By 2010, I would be on their cover as a Boze Bell hideous painting, with an article about my "craziness."

# Closers of Open Records

## LINCOLN COUNTY ATTORNEY ALAN MOREL

Already discussed, Lincoln County Attorney Alan Morel is arguably the most blameworthy hoaxer, since he is paid by his county to protect them from taxpayer frauds like misuse of the Sheriff's Department by the Billy the Kid Case hoax. From 2003 to 2007, however, Morel inappropriately refused all my records requests (earlier ones through Jay Miller) pertaining to Sheriff Tom Sullivan, Deputy Steve Sederwall, or Sheriff Rick Virden. That lead to my litigation, beginning in 2007, and still ongoing.

## THE SECRET HOAX ALLY: AG PATRICIA MADRID

The enforcer of the open records act is the state's Attorney General, who also issues New Mexico's open records compliance guide. At the start of the Billy the Kid Case hoax, that person was Democrat, Patricia Madrid. Naively, through Jay Miller, I sent complaints to her about Sheriff Tom Sullivan's total open records non-compliance and law enforcement fraud.

In response, Patricia Madrid and her deputy attorney general, Stuart Bluestone, used stonewalling. Since Sheriff Sullivan had provided no records at all for his entire murder investigation, her action could have ended the impasse. So she ignored Miller's complaints from 2004 till the 2006 end of her term.

Why had Attorney General Patricia Madrid protected the hoaxers? She was not Bill Richardson's "friend." But they shared "friends." That was enough, as can be seen in Newmexicomatters.com's "RichardsonWatch" of December 19, 2006," under "AG won't investigate governor's hires." It stated :

Attorney General Patricia Madrid announced Friday that she won't investigate the hiring practices of Gov. Bill Richardson, which Republicans say have resulted in illegal and unauthorized hirings. The GOP lawmakers in March requested an investigation of Richardson's hiring of at least 65 people as 'temporary' exempt employees. Many of the people are politicians and members of political families.

Who was the linking "friend?" Attorney Bill Robins III! He was a big political contributor for Madrid's upcoming Congressional campaign! On January 23, 2003, Madrid gifted Robins and his firm with a state contract. His big bucks to her had followed. That was exposed in the May 14, 2005 Internet *Daily New Mexican* by AP reporter Barry Massey as "Casinos, contracting lawyers fund Madrid." Massey also implicated Governor Richardson, since he had appointed "the state investment officer," and was himself chairman of the "Investment Council." Massey stated:

> Gambling interests and lawyers contracting with the state are the top contributors to a political committee affiliated with Attorney General Patricia Madrid ...
>
> Bill Robins, a partner in a Houston law firm that also has offices in New Mexico, contributed $25,000 last August ...
>
> Madrid saw no problems in accepting contributions from the law firms that contract with the state. "It's not like ... they are parties that I am suing on behalf of the state. It might be improper to take money from people like that. But we're all on the same side here," she said in an interview.
>
> Robins and his law firm also have been significant political contributors to Democratic Gov. Bill Richardson, who appoints the state investment officer. The governor is chairman of the Investment Council.
>
> Robins gave $31,000 to Richardson's re-election committee and the Texas law firm contributed $20,000 during the past year. They also were contributors to Richardson's 2002 campaign and his former political committee.

But on August 8, 2006, Jay Miller and I confronted Madrid's conflict of interest (using the Massey article), asking if it was the reason for her stonewalling.

It was titled "Re. FOIA/IPRA Request with regard to your relationship with Attorney Bill Robins III and/or his law firm Heard, Robins, Cloud, Lubel & Greenwood LLP."

Her response came from an Elizabeth Kupfer, on August 28, 2006. Ignoring all questions, it merely provided a copy of Madrid's Robins employment contract titled "Contract No. 04-305-P625-0015, Budget Activity No. 305/P625 State of New Mexico Office of the Attorney General Professional Services Agreement."

It did yield a little gem showing that Bill Robins III had signed it for the firm on January 21, 2003 - plenty of time for him to get things geared up for that year's Billy the Kid Case.

Madrid, however, sent out a feeler to Jay Miller. Her Deputy Attorney General, Stuart Bluestone, called him, feigning surprise at a "stonewalling" accusation. (Hypocrite Bluestone himself had stonewalled our same complaints since 2004!) So on September 1, 2006, Miller sent both Madrid and Bluestone my packet of 75 *pages documenting all their mutual stonewalling.* Of course, that was the last we heard from either of them. But my "Calendar of Complaints to Attorney General Patricia Madrid" is my testament to corrupt public officials' stonewalling technique of exhausting an opponent by labor, futility, and time. [APPENDIX: 28]

In 2006, Patricia Madrid's pervasive corruption was raised by her political opponent, Republican incumbent, Heather Wilson, as they competed for the congressional seat. Madrid lost. And Heather Wilson never responded to my information on the hoax.

## *ASSISTANT AG SMITH COVERS FOR SEDERWALL*

Patricia Madrid's Assistant Attorney General, Mary Smith, protected Deputy Steve Sederwall differently. She closed an open records violation case against him before I ever made one!

Through Jay Miller, I had written to Attorney General Madrid about a "maturing problem" of Sederwall's records turn-over refusals. Smith was given Miller's letter. She called Sederwall. He said the case was his hobby. Smith closed "the case," writing to Miller that private citizens are immune to open records law.

Assuming merely Sederwall's manipulation, through Miller, I sent Smith a formal complaint on August 10, 2004, clarifying that the Billy the Kid Case was a murder investigation and Sederwall was its commissioned Deputy Sheriff.

Nine months later - repeat, nine months later - on May 17, 2005, came Smith's response. Ignoring Miller's information, she had a new punch line: Sederwall had no records; so there were no records to report. Case closed! Again!

Then came a September 23, 2004 *Lincoln County News* article by Doris Cherry titled: "Lincoln County War heats up over Billy." It had Sederwall's public confession of having and concealing the records: "He (Miller) can go to hell because I will not turn the (documents) over because once they are turned over they become public documents." On May 6, 2006, that article and a new complaint went to Smith - copied to Attorney General Madrid. Lacking any excuse, they responded by the great silence - forever.

# SECRET PRIVATE DONORS

*HOAXBUST: Another Billy the Kid Case hoaxer tactic was claiming that the case got money from secret private donors - so that made it private. That was untrue. First, private donors do not pay for sheriffs' murder cases. Second, private money entering public coffers becomes public (to prevent bribery). Third, taxpayers were paying through the nose: for the Lincoln and De Baca County Sheriff's Departments and Sheriffs, and for the Grant and De Baca County District Court exhumation cases, and for the OMI. And Lincoln County Attorney Alan Morel got his taxpayer salary while covering up their records. But who were their "private donors?"*

### *"SECRET DONOR" ATTORNEY BILL ROBINS III*

The role in the Billy the Kid Case of Attorney Bill Robins III took a long time to uncover. And, like with U.S. Marshals Historian David Turk, clues came from following the money.

By 2004, by coincidence, I discovered that Attorney Robins was *paying into* the Billy the Kid Case, because I was paying Kennedy Han law firm costs for opposing exhumation petitions.

For a Catherine Antrim exhumation hearing, historian Frederick Nolan was coming from England to testify. His airfare and hotel costs were mine. Just days before that Hearing, in November of 2003, Attorney Sherry Tippett requested an extension. Unsure if it would be granted, Frederick Nolan had to come anyway.

Judge Henry Quintero did give the extension; but for her short notice, he sanctioned Attorney Tippett to pay Nolan's bills.

The Kennedy Han Controller, Lisa Kemper, sent me an April 28, 2004 fax titled "In the Matter of Catherine Antrim":

This is to confirm our receipt of payment in the amount of $830.59, issued by Heard, Robins, Cloud, Lubel and Greenwood LLP, deposited on March 1, 2004, as payment in full for reimbursement of travel and lodging expenses incurred by Mr. Frederick Nolan. We issued our Trust Check #1670 on the same date to Mr. Nolan for the same amount.

Thus, Attorney Tippett was reporting to Governor Richardson, while being taken care of by his primary political backer.

So when Sheriff Tom Sullivan concealed Tippett's cost coverage in one of my open records requests as being from a "secret private donor," it was Bill Robins doing the donating.

Later, I discovered a "Private Fund" checking account of Sullivan's and Sederwall's for Case # 2003-274. Was Robins behind that? Later the evidence came in: he was paying into it. But was Robins also paying his co-counsel, David Sandoval, and Attorney Mark Acuña? What about paying Orchid Cellmark Laboratory or Dr. Henry Lee? What about paying for some of the secret lawyers who would consult against my open records violation litigation? Those remain hoaxer secrets.

But, of course, Attorney Robins's biggest and known "private donations" were to Governor Bill Richardson himself.

## ANOTHER SECRET DONOR: JOHNNY COPE

It is unlikely that I will ever find out all the direct hoax participants - and a Johnny Cope is a good example of why. He had no logical connection - only one "friend" helping another. Johnny Cope's name came up during my ongoing open records quest, when a copy of a $500.00 check he had paid into the "Billy the Kid Investigation" (then wrote it off as charity!) turned up in an unsolicited June 21, 2007 "Memorandum" by Deputies Sullivan and Sederwall to Sheriff during my open records requesting. As a Richardson political backer, was Johnny Cope a pay-to-player?

New Mexico power broker, Johnny Cope, was in an *Albuquerque Journal* article on July 8, 2007 by a Thomas J. Cole: "Tycoon Backs Gov. All the Way: Hobbs businessman has helped raise millions, but he's had his share of controversy." Cole wrote:

> The wealthy Hobbs businessman is a deal-maker, mover-and-shaker and kingmaker in state government and politics. He is also tight - make that very tight - with Gov. Bill Richardson ... A self-made millionaire many times over, Cope is a Richardson ATM, contributing lots of his own money and helping the governor raise millions more for his gubernatorial and presidential campaigns ...
>
> But his rise to the top hasn't been without troubles; business setbacks, a drug problem [cocaine] that led to jail time and a couple of stormy marriages that involved allegations of abuse. He has also found himself under scrutiny in connection with a couple of state deals. One involved his work as a prison contractor; the other a failed attempt by Cope and business associates to line up a $30 million loan guarantee for

a fish farm in southern New Mexico **[AUTHOR'S NOTE: Backed by Richardson along with state guarantee that taxpayers would cover losses!]** ...

Because no good deed goes unnoticed in politics, Richardson made Cope chairman of the powerful commission that oversees state road work. Later Cope tried to use that Transportation Commission money to by Richardson a $4 million dollar jet. That was stopped, though Richardson did get one for $5 million with Legislative approval and used also by Cope.

Cope, according to reporter Cole, also seemed to have a finger in every money-making pie in the state - either as facilitator or owner: including commercial buildings, a $393 million train line called the Belen-to-Albuquerque-to-Santa Fe Rail Runner Express [a reputed boondoggle], a spaceport, a prison in Hobbs, a Waste Isolation Plant, Louisiana Energy Services planned multi-billion dollar uranium enrichment plant, and his hoped-for fish farm.

Also, Cope matched the hoaxers' thuggery. Reporter Thomas Cole wrote about his ex-wives: "Jean Vanise Cope reported to police in September 1989 that Cope came to her home upset over a child custody matter and threatened several times to kill her ... During a separation, Rebecca Cope [next wife] ... told police Cope had been drinking, became upset with her ... choked her and struck her in the face [Cope denied the allegations]."

Balding, horse-toothed Cope is shown in his office "decorated with baseball memorabilia" and is said by Cole (without irony) to share "his passion with the game with Gov. Bill Richardson."

Johnny Cope, according to reporter Cole, also owned Hobbs Rental Corp, an oilfield services company.

It was that company's check, signed by Johnny Cope, that was in the "Memorandum's" "Attachment 2" as "Charitable Contributions;" and made out to Heard, Robins, Cloud, Lubel & Greenwood LLP for "Investigative Fund 2003-247" [sic] c/o the Robins law firm at their Santa Fe address. Below Cope's check on "Attachment 2's" page, Attorney Robins, from his Santa Fe office address, wrote his own check for $3,000 to "Investigative Fund 2003-247" [sic] with sub-heading "For Billy the Kid investigation."

So Johnny Cope was funneling money into the Billy the Kid Case. One more thing: Cope is rumored to do business with an R.D. Hubbard, a major power-monger discussed later. Another thing: Bill Robins's law firm has a branch in Hobbs, New Mexico. Does Attorney Robins represent Cope and Hubbard? Who knows?

# "BRUSHY" BELIEVER: JANNAY VALDEZ

As a hoax hopeful loyalist of "Brushy Bill" as Billy the Kid, Dr. Jannay Valdez followed the Billy the Kid Case, tying to help when he could, and ranting in his inimitable way. He had authored a 1995 book with "Brushy" believer, Judge Bobby E. Hefner, titled *Billy the Kid: Killed in New Mexico - Died in Texas*.

Frederick Nolan, with his historian's pre-eminence, was a Valdez target. Insults worsened when Nolan planned to testify against the hoaxers in Judge Ted Hartley's Fort Sumner hearing. So Nolan got what he considered a death threat from Jannay Valdez, which he reported to the FBI; and came anyway. That Valdez e-mail came on September 12, 2004, titled "RE: Billy the Kid (Brushy Bill Roberts)."[APPENDIX: 29] It stated:

> You, Nolan, are narrow-minded, closed-minded, non-American, and insulting the dignity of the old. You are a poor excuse for being a decent person. Brushy Bill Roberts was/is Billy the Kid, and some day you will have to deal with the truth. Stay where you belong ... in snobville ... I challenge Nolan to stay in England, leave America alone (we fought to leave England) to write about HIS kings and Queens, and leave Billy the Kid and our tax Money to us – Americans.

Jannay Valdez also responded fervently, on December 28, 2005, to Jay Miller's anti-hoax book, *Billy the Kid Rides Again*, in an Amazon.com Customer Review titled "Perpetuating Pat Garrett's Lie." Valdez wrote:

> Miller's attacks on Tom Sullivan and Steve Sederwall are unnecessary and false. I know them personally and they are fine gentlemen. What newspaper would allow this "writer" to be on its payroll? Miller, Utley, and Nolan have defiled the fields of anthropology, archaeology, history, and scientific DNA testing. What do these anti-truth-in-history fanatics have in common? They insult those who disagree, and they put down those who seek the truth, even attacking the credibility of prominent individuals working on this case. The only thing Ft. Sumner has to fear is the truth itself - they don't have the body of Billy the Kid, they have an empty grave and they know it! Miller, Nolan and Utley "know-it-alls" would have us quit digging all mummified remains; quit digging up ancient cities and dinosaurs, quit seeking our origins, our past, the secrets of humanity. Take a shovel and 2 hours at

"Billy the Kid's grave" (with permission, of course), and all of this could be settled. These anti-truth-in-history flakes continue to scream about the cost of this investigation. The only reason this has cost any significant amount of money is because of the unnecessary resistance of the officials at Silver City and Ft. Sumner! I'll provide the shovels and help dig; Steve, Tom, Gary, and many other REAL historians would gladly volunteer all costing NM nothing. So, the real investigation question should be: Why is the truth about Billy the Kid's death being stifled? I call all their accusations a smokescreen because they have personal and financial reasons besides an agenda particularly aimed at those who are seeking the truth. Let's get to the punch line: Santa Fe, Silver City, and Ft. Sumner (the triangle of the Santa Fe Ring cover-up) are not interested in the truth, rather they want to perpetuate the lie Pat Garrett told years ago.

# THE DARK SAHADOW: R.D. HUBBARD

In June of 2003, right after the *New York Times's* "122 Years Later, The Lawmen Are Still Chasing Billy the Kid," the name R.D. Hubbard was one of the first I heard connected to the Billy the Kid Case. When I called Marlyn Bowlin in Fort Sumner, she told me she had heard that "R.D. Hubbard is offering a million dollars for the body of Billy the Kid."

Randall Dee "R.D." Hubbard was almost invisible in the Billy the Kid Case hoax. While Attorney Bill Robins III may have had thoughts of Billy the Kid as "Brushy Bill" Roberts; R.D. Hubbard may have dreamt of Billy the Kid as a casino.

And the money and might behind Hubbard made Bill Robins and Bill Richardson look like puny players.

When Jay Miller released my "Inside the Capitol" article about a Hubbard connection to the Billy the Kid Case hoax, Miller got a call from a man, refusing to give his name, but saying he was from Capitan and Sicily. He said, "Stay away from R.D. Hubbard."

Miller, proceeded to pleasantly converse about life in Capitan versus Sicily with the assumedly confused thug enforcer.

"I think that was a death threat, Jay," I later told him.

The Jay Miller article in question explored why R.D. Hubbard might have wanted Billy's body for a million dollars.

R. D. Hubbard is a mega-rich, nationally known, racetrack and casino owner, who had become a major New Mexico real estate developer with connections to Bill Richardson. He also contributed generously to politicians in both parties. In 1999, when CEO of California's Hollywood Park racetrack and casino, he was listed as one of George W. Bush's "115 Pioneers," meaning donating "at least $100,000 for his presidential campaign."

But Hubbard had a problem: a 2002 indictment in Indiana for racketeering and prostitution: allegedly providing hookers to lure high rollers. For that, his casino there was fined according to a Pat Andrews, Chairman of GRIEF (Gambling Research Information & Education Foundation), who presented a June 25, 2003 *Indianapolis Star* article: "Casino fined $2.26 million over allegations of prostitution." [APPENDIX: 30]

On December 4, 2002, *Albuquerque Tribune* reporter, Ollie Reed Jr., stated under "Board approves Hubbard license": "Renewal of Hubbard's New Mexico license was in doubt because of allegations of improprieties at an Indiana casino, which forced Hubbard to surrender his gambling license in that state, pay a fine of $740,000 and agree not to seek a gambling license in Indiana in the future."

Hubbard did not need Indiana for his "future." To him, Richardson played Statue of Liberty: "Give me the wretched refuse of your teeming shore." As "refuse," Hubbard became pay-to play treasure according to an *Albuquerque Journal* op-ed piece on December 16, 2002, by a Dr. Guy C. Clark, executive director of the New Mexico Coalition Against Gambling. It was titled: " 'Dollar Bill' Richardson." [APPENDIX: 31] The "play" was getting a casino/racetrack in Hobbs, New Mexico. Clark stated:

> Because he received a large majority of the votes for Governor in this month's general election, does Governor-elect Richardson deserve a "honeymoon" of immunity from criticism? Unfortunately, many of Richardson's plans and activities already indicate a policy of "pay to play" in his administration ... Transition chairman and co-chairs are heavily represented by gambling interests from the tribal casinos and racetracks ...
>
> The ongoing battle over a possible Hobbs racetrack is another indication of our new governor's predisposition. Governor Johnson basically dismantled the racetrack commission this week because it appeared that they were going to approve a new racetrack for Hobbs, possibly with R.D. Hubbard as the owner ...
>
> Attorney General Patricia Madrid indicated that adding a racetrack would not violate compacts or disconnect revenue sharing. But then, AG Madrid has received tens of thousands in

campaign contributions from gambling interests, including R.D. Hubbard.

Governor-elect Richardson said that the new track in Hobbs was fine with him ... There are some petitions carried and surveys taken that strongly refute the support for a casino in Hobbs, but the gambling "industry" certainly is in favor of a casino there, and they have contributed heavily to our Governor-elect's campaign. Mr. Hubbard alone contributed over $10,000 to his campaign.

One may recall that Attorney General Patricia Madrid had been accused by reporter, Barry Massey, in his May 14, 2005 *New Mexican* article: "Casinos, contracting lawyers fund Madrid." Among the "casino interests" was R.D. Hubbard.

Once entrenched in New Mexico's casino and horseracing, R.D. Hubbard took on the Billy the Kid theme. He purchased the Lincoln County Heritage Trust Museum in historic Lincoln, as well as the Ruidoso Museum of the Horse; which he re-named the Hubbard Museum of the West. In Ruidoso, where he owned the Ruidoso Downs racetrack and casino, he offered a gimmicky "Billy the Kid gang membership," copying the Billy the Kid Outlaw Gang (to the helpless anger of Marlyn Bowlin). In the Ollie Reed article, banker, Tom Batton, plugs Hubbard as turning "the Lincoln County Cowboy Symposium into a national attraction." (Tom Batton is one of the Lincoln County Commissioners who covered up the Billy the Kid Case hoax.)

But how did any of that connect R.D. Hubbard to Billy the Kid's body? Actually, it was the only part of Billy tourism that Hubbard did not own. Possibly he needed it!

In 2004, it was rumored that R.D. Hubbard was secretly - thus illegally avoiding open bidding - negotiating with Governor Richardson for 80 acres of water rights with their attached, and mostly vacant, huge Fort Stanton property. (Recall that the fort's commander, in Billy Bonney's day, changed the outcome of the Lincoln County War by marching on Lincoln with his troops.)

Richardson marched on Fort Stanton in 2005.

According to the annual report of the New Mexico Historic Preservation Division, in a January article, "Preservation and Planning at Fort Stanton," "Governor Richardson and the state legislature saw the opportunity to save a valuable New Mexico resource in the last legislative session and approved nearly

$1 million to fund emergency repairs and planning that will lead to much needed maintenance and the eventual re-use of Fort Stanton." The "eventual re-use" seems to have been another Bill Richardson pay-to-play. Local buzz was of using the Fort Stanton property for a Hubbard-owned casino with a Billy the Kid theme (though illegal, since New Mexico requires non-Native American casinos to have a race track also).

Could R.D. Hubbard have had a Graceland-type fantasy with Billy's relocated grave as that Billy casino's centerpiece? (Historic Lincoln town - with Hubbard's museum there and the famous old courthouse of Billy's escape - is just nine miles away. Why not get your Billy the Kid tourism, plus fun gambling, plus paying respects to the Kid's corpse, without leaving Lincoln County for that long ride to bleak Fort Sumner's Billy grave?)

Jay Miller's article exposing that scheme (earning the "Sicilian call") may have ended that. Soon, "the state" helpfully purchased Hubbard's, now unwanted, Lincoln and Ruidoso museums. Hubbard's "Billy body" for "Graceland grave" seemed over. But did Hubbard stay on as a "secret private donor" to the Billy the Kid Case? That is secret; but it would have been a "friendly" gesture.

Richardson certainly had been "friendly." A local told me about Richardson's other scheme to get R.D. Hubbard water for his real estate and golf course development in Capitan, New Mexico. It involved Richardson's attacking another New Mexican icon: Smokey the Bear, a subsequently famous cub rescued in 1950 from a forest fire in the Capitan Mountains' Lincoln National Forest, just north of Lincoln town. Dying in 1976 in the National Zoo, Smokey was buried in Capitan with grave-marker: "This is the resting place of ... Smokey Bear ... symbol of wildfire prevention and wildlife conservation."

None of that moved Governor Bill Richardson. I was told that he was behind the purposeful setting of the 2004 Peppin Fire, started by a supposed "controlled burn" in the Capitan Mountains' Lincoln National Forest, which destroyed about 64,000 acres.

That premeditated deforestation was to create rain run-off for Hubbard's development. And to prepare for the holocaust stampede of escaping wildlife, Richardson secretly issued bear hunting permits a year earlier, *so all the Capitan bears could be slaughtered* to prevent their infesting the human-inhabited valley below. SO, BYE BYE FUTURE SMOKEYS, GOOD BYE!

In 2004 also, Richardson's manipulations got Hubbard bigger casino profits as reported in the *Albuquerque Journal* of June 26, 2004 as "New Racing Schedule Tramples Horsemen." [APPENDIX: 32] The upshot was the Governor's "overhaul" of the five-member racing commission to decrease the racing season from 70 to 47 days. Racetracks, as required for non-Native American casino licenses in the state, are the money losers. Lessening track days, increased overall profits for that "friend" of the "Gov."

For that play, Hubbard seems to have paid. An op-ed page, signed only by a K.B., in the December 13, 2005 *Albuquerque Journal* said: "After a big fundraiser in California hosted by his pal, casino owner R.D. Hubbard, and the gas refund checks, I think Bill Richardson has mastered the gentle political art of getting votes from the poor and campaign funds from the rich."

That "gentle political art" may have also sluiced money, flowing from Randall Dee Hubbard, to Johnny Cope, to Bill Robins, to Bill Richardson, to Billy Sparks, to Sheriff Tom Sullivan's hot palm, to backhoers of John Miller and William Hudspeth graves; as the Billy the Kid Case hoaxers followed their yellow brick road to "Brushy Bill" Roberts, fame, fortune, and the U.S. presidency.

# CHAPTER 7:

# BILLY THE KID CASE
# HOAX TAKE-OFF AND
# CRASH LANDING

ENTH JUDICIAL DISTRICT COURT
TATE OF NEW MEXICO
OUNTY OF DE BACA

N THE MATTER OF WILLIAM H. BONNEY,
ka "BILLY the KID"

NO.

TENTH JUDICIAL DISTRICT COURT
COUNTY OF DE BACA
STATE OF NEW MEXICO

IN THE MATTER OF WILLIAM H.
BONNEY a/k/a "BILLY THE KID"

No. CV-04-00005

10th JUDIC
DE BACA COU
FILED IN

JUL 0

DIANE UL
DISTRICT COU

**NOTICE OF HEARING**

A hearing in this case is set before the HON. TEDDY L. HARLEY as follows:

Date of Hearing: September 27, 2004

Time of Hearing: 1:30 p.m.

**STIPULATION OF DISMISSAL**

COME NOW ...Sandoval, coun...

Adam Baker, cou...

the New Mexico...

prejudice all c...

each party to...

Resp...

Hear...
Gree...

By:...

# Lincoln County "War" Heats Up Over 'Billy'

## Capitan Mayor Tracks His Kind of
### Tells Jay Miller where to go: wonders why commissioner has his panties in a wad.

**To County Commission Meeting**

by Doris Cherry

Had words been bullets there would have been several casualties in the Lincoln County Courthouse Tuesday when Lincoln County Commissioner Leo Martinez demanded Sheriff Tom Sullivan immediately cease his active investigation of the murder of deputy James Bell, allegedly killed by Billy the Kid some 123 year old murder case. Words not healed since Sullivan defeated the active murder case during the Lincoln County Commission meeting on Tuesday, September 21 in Carrizozo. The

case was filed in the Lincoln County Sheriff's Office in April 2003. Martinez had requested to be on the agenda to discuss the "Billy the Kid Investigation—Hoax or Fact."

At the conclusion of the lengthy and sometimes very heated discussion Martinez challenged Sullivan to produce accountability for his time and potential public money spent on the case, and for Sullivan to redefine his priorities and exhibit self discipline in deciding between public and private duties.

But in the end, Martinez provided his comments in a written statement. "It is my impression that the time has come to give Sheriff Sullivan an ultimatum," Mar-

he has followed the situation closely as a student of history and his impression is that of Capitan do in their dint is their own business. "If there is wrong doing go to the district attorney and file the charges, then it becomes the charge problem," Simpson said to Martinez.

This county commission has no authority to tell the sheriff what to do in his spare time," Simpson said.

Billy the Kid case should cease to be a function of Lincoln County, and that as Sheriff, Tom Sullivan should immediately cease and desist. "If the Billy the Kid case is a private action, and Sheriff Sullivan refuses to cease and desist in its pursuit, then he should resign immediately," Martinez said "If Sheriff

tines read. "The conducting of the Billy the Kid Case in the Lincoln County Sheriff's Department and the manner in which it was conducted was wrong."

"I therefore state that the Billy the Kid case should be used in the service of private gain, and it was inappropriate for having private money pay for an active investigation that was filed as a criminal case.

Sullivan has accrued personal profit from the Billy the Kid case he should be required to turn over such profits to Lincoln County."

"Public office should not influence investigations. Martinez said in keeping up with the "supposed" investigation of the case, he has concluded that the county needs to take a position since the county commission has been mentioned in court documents and articles. "The last article

in the sheriff's office, because this could lead to anyone with money being able to influence investigations.

# LINCOLN County News

SINCE 1905

50c

VOLUME # 99, NUMBER 38

THURSDAY, SEPTEMBER 23, 2004

11

CARRIZOZO, NM 88301

TENTH JUDICIAL DISTRICT COURT
STATE OF NEW MEXICO
COUNTY OF DE BACA

No. CV-04-00005

IN THE MATTER OF WILLIAM H.
BONNEY aka "BILLY THE KID"

DIANE ULIBARRI
DISTRICT COURT CLERK

## STIPULATION OF DISMISSAL WITH PREJUDICE

COME NOW Petitioners Gary Graves, Tom Sullivan, and Steve Sederwall, by and through their attorneys The Jaffe Law Firm (Mark Anthony Acuña), and the Village of Fort Sumner, by and through its attorneys, Kennedy & Han, P.C. (Adam S. Baker) and Herb Marsh, Jr., and hereby stipulate to the dismissal with prejudice of the Petition filed herein pursuant to Rule 1-041.A.(1)(b) of the New Mexico Rules of Civil Procedure.

Each party will their own costs and attorneys' fees relative to the action hereby dismissed.

Respectfully submitted,

MARK ANTHONY ACUÑA
THE JAFFE LAW FIRM
Attorneys for Petitioners Graves,
Sullivan, and Sederwall
P.O. Box 809
Albuquerque, NM 87103
(505) 242-9311

ADAM S. BAKER
KENNEDY & HAN, P.C.
Attorneys for the Village of Fort Sumner
201 Twelfth Street, N.W.
Albuquerque, NM 87102
(505) 342-8662

# Kid's Mom May Stay Burie

■ Silver City wins a round to block exhumation for outlaw's DNA

BY RENE ROMO
Journal Southern Bureau

SILVER CITY — Silver City officials won an important round Monday in their fight to block efforts to dig up the remains of Billy the Kid's mother.

State District Judge Henry Quintero gave the city legal standing in the case.

He also rescheduled a full-day hearing on the main issue — whether or not to permit the controversial exhumation — for Jan. 27.

This summer, the sheriffs of Lincoln and De Baca counties opened a criminal investigation into the death of William Bonney also Billy the Kid, to resolve claims that Lincoln County Sheriff Pat Garrett killed someone other than the famous outlaw at Fort Sumner on July 14, 1881.

Over the years, other men claiming to be Billy the Kid surfaced in Prescott, Ariz., and in Hico, Texas, saying they had eluded Garrett and lived to old age in secret. Investigators

extract ...

# FULL SWING SCAM

*HOAXBUST: By 2004, the Billy the Kid Case hoaxers had adjusted to my unexpected legal opposition; and, confident in their corrupt judges, Henry Quintero and Ted Hartley, for future exhumations, they advanced their media thrust.*

P.T. Barnum, said, "Without promotion, something terrible happens: nothing." The Billy the Kid Case hoaxers knew that. And even before his September 27, 2004 Fort Sumner exhumation Hearing, Judge Ted Hartley earned his Richardson appointment by giving the hoaxers months to publicize their "law enforcement investigation." That benefited Ted Hartley too. Good public opinion would lubricate his opening Billy Bonney's grave for no legal reason at all. So the media was the message.

For the press, the hoaxers shape-shifted to cops fighting elitist academicians, or to tourism promoters - or, conversely, to victims of tourist-greedy local officials trying to stop them. Audaciously, they were defending Garrett against those calling him a murderer. Or their case only investigated Billy's deputy murders - ignoring that this made their intended exhumations irrelevant. And even if Billy's and his mother's graves were legally blocked, Plan B was faking "Billy the Kid blood DNA" from their carpenter's bench.

So, by 2004, the hoaxers' were emoting Deputy Steve Sederwall's jaunty mantra from his May 2003's "Capitan Mayor's Report": "[I]t is a crazy idea but won't it be fun." Fun differed. It was media access. It was getting respect as historical researchers and CSI cops. It was lording over hapless New Mexicans and legitimate historians. It was protection by a political/judicial/big-money umbrella. It was hope for "Brushy Bill" Roberts's believers.

But the hoaxers' greatest fun was keeping a secret no one could guess - until too late. It centered on the gubernatorial posthumous pardon - not on DNA at all!

# TURNING POINT:
# ANOTHER LINCOLN COUNTY WAR

*HOAXBUST: Just when Billy the Kid Case hoaxers seemed about to prevail, a brave Lincoln County hero emerged to confront them with a threat so serious that he turned the tide of the hoax.*

When De Baca County Sheriff Gary Graves's recall was still a year away, Judge Ted Hartley's hearing fast approached its September 27, 2004 date. I felt hopeless. Then occurred what the local papers called the Second Lincoln County War.

### A LINCOLN COUNTY HERO

The Second Lincoln County War was fought on almost the same turf as the first. It occurred on September 21, 2004.

Lincoln County Commission Chairman Leo Martinez had enough. In his County Commissioners' meeting, with Sheriff Sullivan and Deputy Sederwall shouting obscenities, Martinez read a statement titled "Observations Regarding the Lincoln County Sheriff's Department's Use of Authority and Management of Priorities." [APPENDIX: 33] Martinez drew the line in the sand.

Leo Martinez asked his County Commissioners to stop Sheriff Sullivan's pursuit of the Billy the Kid Case, which he called a "criminal investigation" which "meets none of the criteria for a real law enforcement matter."

Martinez's punch line was money. He said that Sullivan's doing the case as Sheriff by definition brings in county liability; further increased by deputizing Sederwall. Three years later, with my beginning litigation, these words would appear prophetic.

Commissioner Martinez's list of improprieties included Sullivan's lack of authorization by the County Commissioners to do the case; his improper use of departmental resources and sheriff's time; and his incurring open records act requests which all amounted to the county paying without giving authorization.

Referring to (my) Jay Miller open record's investigations, Leo Martinez reported Sullivan's refusal to disclose Billy the Kid Case finances, and his claim of "secret private donors." Martinez stated, "One is left with the impression that if one pays our Sheriff enough money in Lincoln County, they can control law enforcement. Private funding is not to be used for operating costs in a criminal investigation." That meant vigilante law.

Martinez made his demands:

- I would therefore state that the Billy the Kid Case should cease to be a function of Lincoln County, and that as Sheriff participating in the case Tom Sullivan should immediately cease and desist.

- If the Billy the Kid Case is a private action, and Sheriff Sullivan refuses to cease and desist in its pursuit, then he should resign immediately. [The threat was recall of Sullivan]

## *FALLOUT FROM THE MARTINEZ BOMBSHELL*

Press attended Chairman Leo Martinez's meeting. Only the *Albuquerque Journal's* Rene Romo kept a valuable partisan silence. But hysteria seized the local papers.

The next day, September 22, 2004, a huge, *Ruidoso News* front page headline was: "Showdown in the County Seat: shouting match erupts at County Commissioners meeting over investigation of Billy the Kid." [APPENDIX: 34] Reporter, Dianne Stallings, stated:

> Shouting and pounding the podium, Lincoln County Sheriff Tom Sullivan attempted unsuccessfully Tuesday to drown out questions from County Commissioner Leo Martinez over his publicity-generating investigation of two 123-year old murders ...
> Sullivan [said], "I don't tell you how to make burritos. Don't tell me how to run the sheriff's department. This is nothing but a personal attack."

That "personal attack" was really Sullivan's own racist slurs about Leo Martinez running a Mexican restaurant. And Sullivan and Sederwall bluffed franticly: denying use of public money or even their law enforcement roles; while, at the same time, saying their case was a sealed, ongoing, criminal investigation!

Then what happened? Sullivan's County Commissioner buddy, Rick Simpson, ended the meeting. Stallings wrote:

> When he [Martinez] called for a motion to sever any association, no other Commissioners responded.

Irrespective of the spineless and/or complicit Commissioners, Sullivan and Sederwall realized they were in trouble.

And the press did not stop. The next day, September 23rd, the *Lincoln County News* weighed in with Doris Cherry's "Lincoln County War heats up over 'Billy: Capitan Mayor Tracks His Kind of ' ------- ' To County Commission Meeting. Tells Jay Miller where to go; wonders why Commissioner has his panties in a wad."

Doris Cherry had added the raw dialogue of the thugs running the case. Tom Sullivan was reported as saying Leo Martinez's questioning "smells of Jay Miller ... a sleaze-bag reporter from Santa Fe;" and challenging Martinez: "Are you calling me a liar?"

Steve Sederwall shamelessly accused Martinez of "an attempt to grandstand to get his name in the papers." Later came Sederwall's: "I don't understand why Martinez has his panties in a wad [about the case]" - fighting words. But Martinez was not putting up his dukes; his words were landing the punches.

Cherry's reporting also documented the hoaxers' switcheroo of case definition, as well as an accidental confession of concealing public documents (blabbing Sederwall, as usual!). She wrote:

> After Martinez read his three page written statement, county commissioner Earl Hobbs asked Sullivan if the case had been filed as a murder investigation. Sullivan answered yes and said the murders of James Bell and Robert Olinger in 1881 were never solved ... "We don't care about the myth or legend, we just looked at Bell as a police officer who was murdered, " the mayor [Sederwall] said.
> **"The sheriff has no documentation," the mayor said. "I have them." He then went on to say that he will not release the documents, not as mayor or as a commissioned reserve deputy. 'He (Miller) can go to hell because I will not turn the (documents) over because once they are turned over they become public documents.' "** [author's boldface]

Cherry also has Leo Martinez saying "that a year ago [in a County Commissioners' meeting] Sullivan said the investigation would be done on his time and the state Dep. of Tourism would provide the funds."

In response, Sullivan simply lied that the Attorney General, Patricia Madrid, had already answered Jay Miller's complaint to her about his [Sullivan's] non-compliance with financial reporting.

And when Martinez brought up the OMI's block of Catherine Antrim's exhumation, Sullivan, realizing failure of his lie that the case was the deputy murders, declared: "The director is wrong."

One thing was obviously right, Tom Sullivan and Steve Sederwall had been blindsided. The hoax depended on the silence of Lincoln County's lambs. And speaking of "panties," they had been caught with theirs down.

What happened to Leo Martinez after that? This was Lincoln County, after all. He sacrificed his political career. When he ran again for County Commissioner that November, the locals elected a Sullivan-Sederwall man, Tom Batton - their politician friends making sure to back him with bucks. And Batton covered up the hoax through his tenure. And the local man behind the entire hoax cover-up, though present at the Martinez meeting, would stay untouched and active: Lincoln County Attorney Alan Morel.

## THE MARTINEZ EFFECT

But Leo Martinez had an immediate effect: Tom Sullivan realized he had only one option. Talk of Sheriff Gary Graves's possible recall was in the air. If that happened to him, he would lose his retirement benefits. And Lincoln County citizens were on the verge of realizing that they had been paying his bills - and might pay more in the future.

So just three days before Judge Ted Hartley's Hearing, on September 24, 2004, the "law enforcement petitioners" - Graves, Sullivan, and Sederwall - filed in his De Baca County Court, through their attorney, Mark Acuña, to withdraw *with* prejudice their Billy the Kid exhumation case! [APPENDIX: 35]

"With prejudice" meant they could *never* meet Judge Henry Quintero's stipulation of getting DNA from the Billy the Kid grave in order to exhume Catherine Antrim.

## PREMATURE CELEBRATING IN FORT SUMNER

With the good news of the collapse of the hoaxers' exhumation case, Fort Sumner had a victory banquet celebration. To keep my anonymity, I did not attend. But I had flown Frederick Nolan over from England for the Judge Ted Hartley hearing. And Attorneys Herb Marsh and Adam Baker were there.

Marlyn Bowlin, afraid people might assume she was the gift-giver, nervously set out big, bronzed, Frederick Remington, cowboy statue reproductions which I had purchased anonymously for Baker and Marsh, and had added personalized plaques. And to Frederick Nolan was given a presentation box (again from me, but anonymously) with engraved silver front, having all the Billy the Kid mementos I had crafted for anti-hoax participants.

Scot Stinnett, in his *De Baca County News*, exulted on September 30, 2004, "Rest in Peace, Billy! Exhumation case dismissed." He continued:

> Calling it a "big day for the Village of Fort Sumner," Mayor Lopez congratulated a room full of Billy the Kid supporters Monday [September 27th] during a victory celebration at City Hall ...
>
> "Saying the truth won," Nolan said the efforts of those fighting to prevent the exhumation "sends a message that there are people who care about history; that there are people who want to get it right and there are people who will fight for it ..."
>
> Adam Baker of Albuquerque, the lead attorney for the Village in the case, said, the "sheriffs are done in Fort Sumner."

Herb Marsh gave a speech thanking me as "the mystery woman." That spilling-the-beans made me as anxious as was timid Marlyn Bowlin. My job was not over. I could not risk being identified. And the hoaxers had managed to gate-crash some of their backers into that celebration.

And Marlyn Bowlin's fears proved not unfounded. On that September 27, 2004 day of festivities, violence did occur. An unidentified assailant attacked the Billy the Kid grave at night. Marlyn Bowlin found the damage the following morning - and told me to keep it secret. In apparent mad frenzy, the thick chain with which she locked the protective cage surrounding the Billy the Kid "Pals" gravesite had been cut, with what needed to be a specialized tool. The flower bouquet in a vase, placed inside earlier by Frederick Nolan and the other guests, was stomped and strewn far-and-wide. And the heavy chain and lock had been hurled over the high perimeter wall. One hopes the person attained lasting catharsis. Marlyn Bowlin suspected Jannay Valdez - though I could not believe he would have come all the way from Texas. But Marlyn Bowlin was terrified. And I was so scared of all the hoaxers and "Brushy Bill" fanatics that I thanked my lucky stars for my anonymity plan. And Marlyn told me to keep secret the vandalism for fear of encouraging more from the hoaxers.

# ANOTHER TURNING POINT:
# PRETENDER FOCUS

The others in that September 27, 2004 festivity thought the hoax was over. I did not. The Billy the Kid Case hoaxers still had their carpenter's bench malarkey; and they had Billy the Kid imposters, "Brushy Bill" Roberts and John Miller, who were now like money in the bank.

In fact, the hoaxers were just eight months from backhoeing John Miller's and William Hudspeth's Arizona graves: the long way around to "Brushy Bill" Roberts's grave in Hamilton, Texas. Everything for the hoaxers now depended on the pretenders.

By *True West*'s January 2005 magazine, with the New Mexico exhumations having failed, reliable hoax-friendly writer Janna Bommersbach, was pitching the next step under "Kid Exhumation Nixed: Billy and his mom rest in peace, Nobody is going to dig up Billy the Kid. Nor his mom." For damage control on the truth - that being: exhumations had been blocked for invalid DNA and law enforcement fraud - Bommersbach blamed opponents; Jay Miller getting the worst as a "controversial columnist," along with Steve Sederwall's "sleazebag reporter" quote lifted from the Leo Martinez County Commission meeting confrontation of September 21, 2004.

But *True West*'s mission in the article was to ricochet validate the fake bench-Billy-DNA. So to deal with my Jay Miller article which had already debunked Dr. Henry Lee's carpenter's bench forensics, Bommersbach used a Dr. Philip Keen, chief medical examiner in Phoenix, Arizona, to ruminate meaninglessly about whether "blood could last" (leaving out that no verified blood was found). Then Bommersbach ends with a sanctimonious seal:

> Let us not forget that Gov. Richardson endorsed the project, saying the search for the truth was a worthy cause and promising his office's cooperation.

Billy the Kid's pretenders were obviously the next battleground for yet another Lincoln County War.

# CHAPTER 8:

# DEBUNKING BILLY THE KID'S PRETENDERS

# Billy the Kid's PRETENDERS

Brushy Bill and John Miller

### Gale Cooper

GELCOUR BOOKS

## Lincoln County Sheriff's Office

TOM SULLIVAN
Sheriff

RICK VIRDEN
Undersheriff

DONNA HARKEY
Administrative Assistant

April 30, 2003

Charles Ryan, Director
Arizona Department of Corrections
1601 W. Jefferson
Phoenix, AZ 85007

Dear Director Ryan:

Lincoln County Sheriff's Department is currently conducting an investiga
of two law enforcement officers in Lincoln County, New Mexico. These t
Robert Olinger and J.W. Bell, were killed by William H. Bonny, a.k.a. Billy
from the Lincoln County Courthouse, April 28, 1881. Lincoln County Sher
Bonney to Ft. Sumner, New Mexico, where he killed The Kid on July 14, 18
ended the case against Bonney.

In 1935 a man was buried in Prescott, Arizona by the name of John Miller. In
"Wherever Happened to Billy the Kid" by Helen Airy was published. In Airy's b
claim that Miller was William H. Bonny.

On November 27, 1950, William (Brushy Bill) Roberts along with his attorney app
governor of New Mexico advising the governor that he was William H. Bonney. R
the governor with twenty-two pieces of evidence to prove he was in fact Billy the Ki
weeks later Roberts was dead, buried in Hamilton, Texas. His grave is reported to
"Authentic Grave Site of Billy the Kid". Roberts claim was that Lincoln County Sher
killed someone else and buried that man under the name of Billy the Kid. If Roberts
true this would make Pat Garrett a murderer.

On April 28, 2003, I along with Deputy Steve Sederwall pulled case number 2003-278 i
investigation of the murder of the two law officers that Bonny killed on his escape. Our
investigation shall look at, among other things, where William H. Bo
buried anywhere other then Ft. Su

## LINCOLN COUNTY SHERIFF'S OFFICE
### LINCOLN COUNTY, NEW MEXICO

Case: *William H. Bonney, a.k.a. William Antrim,*
*a.k.a. The Kid, a.k.a. Billy the Kid*

An Investigation into the events of April 28, 1881 through
July 14, 1881- seventy-seven days of doubt.

Just minutes after twelve, noon, on April 28, 1881, two lawmen lay dead, in the yard o
the courthouse in Lincoln, New Mexico, from gunshot wounds. In less time then it t
the New Mexico breeze to clear the gun smoke, history was clouded with the myth o
shooting and escape of William H. Bonney, a.k.a. Billy the Kid from the make-shif
where he awaited a date with the hangman.

The following is a thumbnail sketch of the most widely excepted account of the e
the escape, capture and shooting death of William H Bonny a.k.a. Billy the Kid.

### The Last Days of William H. Bonney

On August 17, 1877, in George Atkin's cantina near Camp Grant, Arizona, W
Bonney, who answered to "The Kid" found himself in an altercation with Fr
"Windy" Cahill over cards or Cahill's woman, no one is quite sure as newsp
. It's reported that Windy Cahill called The Kid a "pimp", and in respo
"sonofabitch". Infuriated, Cahill reportedly grabbed The K
Cahill's stomach, sending a hot round into his b
len horse. Cahill died the next d
Kid to be "crimin"

# PRETENDERS FROM THE GET-GO

*HOAXBUST: Bill Richardson wanted to be President. Sheriff Tom Sullivan and Deputy Steve Sederwall wanted fame and fortune from a "Billy the Kid" exhumation industry. All that linked their Billy the Kid Case to Billy the Kid's pretenders.*

Sheriff Tom Sullivan could barely wait to start digging up bodies. After filing his Lincoln County Sheriff's Department Case No. 2003-274 on April 28, 2003, he wrote on April 30, 2003 to Arizona Department of Corrections Director Charles Ryan.:

> In 1935 [sic – 1937] a man was buried in Prescott, Arizona by the name of John Miller. In a 1993 book, *"Whatever Happened to Billy the Kid"* by Helen Airy was published. In [Helen] Airy's book she made the claim that Miller was William H. Bonney.
>
> On November 27, 1950, William (Brushy Bill) Roberts along with his attorney approached the governor of New Mexico advising the governor that he was William H. Bonney ... Just a few weeks later Roberts was dead, buried in Hamilton, Texas ... Roberts claim was that Lincoln County Sheriff Pat Garrett killed someone else and buried that man under the name of Billy the Kid. If Roberts claims are true this would make Pat Garrett a murderer.
>
> On April 28, 2003, I, along with Deputy Steve Sederwall, pulled case 2003-278 [sic- 274] in the investigation of the murder of the two law officers that Bonney killed in his escape. Our investigation shall look at, among other things, where William H. Bonney was buried. If Bonney is buried anywhere other than Fort Sumner, and either Miller or Roberts turns out to be William H. Bonney, history changes, and Sheriff Pat Garrett committed a murder. Our investigation has led us out of our county and into other New Mexico counties, as well as Texas and Arizona ...

# It Was Hard To Be Billy

*HOAXBUST: The old-timer pretenders, "Brushy Bill" Roberts and John Miller, used by the Billy the Kid Case hoaxers for "survival suspicion," became awkward after Billy's and his mother's exhumations were blocked. The hoaxers needed to use the fake carpenter's bench "blood DNA of Billy the Kid" for matchings, but the pretenders had no "death scenes" of being laid out and "playing dead." Also, the main history books were written decades after they died, so the pretenders lacked fodder to make up lives as Billy.*

After withdrawing from Fort Sumner, the hoaxers' visions of fame, fun, profit, and presidency stood on the shoulders of two crazy old men, "Brushy Bill" Roberts and John Miller, and their odd-ball authors. The Billy the Kid Case, billed as state-of-the-art CSI, thereby became a throwback to 1950's historical ignorance, and pretenders' insanity. "Modern forensics" was overkill.

"Brushy Bill" Roberts canceled out as a twenty years too young "Billy the Tot." John Miller bit the dust as a ten years too old, "Billy the Codger." Worse, the pretenders did not match the hoax's contentions of the Garrett friendship murder and the playing dead on the bench. So toppling the pretenders, toppled the hoax. That became my next task. By 2010, I published *Billy the Kid's Pretenders: Brushy Bill and John Miller*, debunking them.

Oliver "Brushy Bill" Roberts and John Miller had moxie as well as madness, since minimal Billy the Kid history was known in their day. And their first authors faked that their man knew things *only real Billy* would know; and their photos matched his. But the books proved no special knowledge or photo-identity.

Pretender ignorance was embarrassing. If someone claimed to be you, but were younger than you by two decades, or older by a decade; did not know where you were born; did not know that you had a brother, a mother who died of TB, or a mean step-father; did not know that you were jailed, as a boy, for theft, and escaped to Arizona; did not know that your committing murder there forced your escape back to New Mexico Territory; were unaware that your boss gifted you a ranch on the Peñasco River, or that you gave a deposition about his murder to a presidential investigator; did not know that you fought a political ring in a grass-roots war, in which they were ignorant of its preliminary massacre of Hispanics, its weaponry, its participants, or its locations;

had minimal knowledge about your attempted governor's pardon for wartime murders; did not know that you had a devoted attorney trying to protect you from hanging and who was almost assassinated; did not know that you were pursued by the Secret Service; did not know the details of your capture or hanging trial; did not know why your jailbreak escape led you to Fort Sumner; called themselves outlaws, when you considered yourself a freedom-fighting soldier; could not speak Spanish like you; were illiterate unlike you; and differed from you physically, would you find it hard to argue against them? That sums up the pretenders.

Also, by lacking the facts, the pretenders' tales also lacked Billy Bonney's motivations or traumas: the stuff of real identity.

But pretenders, "Brushy Bill," John Miller, and the modern Billy the Kid Case hoaxers, relied on Mark Twain's observation: "The most outrageous lies that can be invented will find believers if a man only tells them with all his might."

## MEETING THE REAL WILLIAM BONNEY

*HOAXBUST: The real Billy Bonney was intellectually brilliant; and he left a big paper trail of writings and words proving it. Barely literate imposters, "Brushy Bill" Roberts and John Miller, could not approximate him. In 2012, I published Billy the Kid's Writings, Words, and Wit to document in entirety Billy's productions. The pretenders are an insult to his true legacy.*

Real Billy Bonney might have become the maniacal killer of legend, if forced to face the pretenders. Their mediocrity insulted his identity. Billy left plenty of proof. From 1878 to 1881, he wrote letters and a bill of sale in excellent Spencerian penmanship. He gave a deposition, on June 8, 1878, about John Tunstall's murder to Investigator Frank Warner Angel; and testified for the prosecution, on May 28th and 29th of 1879, in a Court of Inquiry for potential Court Martial of Commander N.A.M. Dudley. Billy's eye-witness testimony in the April, 1879 Lincoln Grand Jury - for his supposed Governor Lew Wallace pardon deal - yielded successful indictments of killers.

And Billy's full-length tintype, taken when he was about 20, has impeccable provenance of Dan Dedrick, to whom he gave it; and who willed it to an Elizabeth Upham, a family member by marriage. And it had stayed in the ownership of that same family.

# WRITINGS OF WILLIAM BONNEY

Billy Bonney's most famous letter sets the hoaxbusting stage. Written about March 13, 1879, to Governor Lew Wallace, it was the first of many to the Governor. Billy's articulateness and ability to spell even "indictments," contrast the pretenders' low literacy.

As to Billy's history, the letter is also of great importance. It was written after the governor had issued an amnesty proclamation on November 13, 1878 for the fighters in that year's Lincoln County War. Those already indicted did not qualify. Billy had been indicted for the murders of Sheriff William Brady, Deputy George Hindman, and Andrew "Buckshot" Roberts.

So this letter was Billy's bold and brave offer to testify as an eye-witness against Santa Fe Ring murderers of Attorney Huston Chapman in exchange for the Governor's annulling those indictments. It began their pardon deal negotiation. Billy wrote:

*To his Excellency the Governor*
*General Lew Wallace*

*Dear Sir I have heard that You will give one thousand $ dollars for my body which as I can understand it means alive as a Witness. I know it is as a witness against those that murdered Mr. Chapman. if [sic] it was so as that I could appear at Court, I could give the desired information, but I have indictments against me for things that happened in the late Lincoln County War and am afraid to give up because my Enemies would kill me. The day Mr. Chapman was murderded [sic] I was in Lincoln, at the request of good Citizens to meet Mr. J. J. Dolan to meet as Friends, so as to be able to lay aside our arms and go to Work. I was present when Mr. Chapman was murderded [sic] and know who did it and if it was not for these indictments I would have made it clear before now. If it is in your power to Annully [sic] those indictments I hope you will do so so a[s] to give me a chance to explain. Please send me an annser [sic] telling me what you can do. You can send annser [sic] by bearer.*

*I have no wish to fight any more indeed I have not raised an arm since Your proclamation. as [sic] to my Character I refer to any of the Citizens, for the majority of them are my friends and have been helping me all they* could. I am called Kid Antrim but Antrim is my stepfathers name.

Waiting for an annser [sic] I remain
Your Obedient Servant,
W.H. Bonney

Billy wrote again to Lew Wallace on March 20, 1879 to arrange his feigned arrest so that he would not be killed by the Ring before testifying. It was written from his safe haven of the Hispanic town of San Patricio, reflecting his bi-cultural allies. It also reflects his courage as well as his literary skill - epitomized by his elegant quotation: "I am not afraid to die like a man fighting but I would not like to be killed like a dog unarmed."

This is the letter:

Thursday 20th 1879

General Lew Wallace:

Sir. I will keep the appointment I made, but be Sure and have men come that You can depend on. **I am not afraid to die like a man fighting but I would not like to be killed like a dog unarmed.** [author's boldface] tell Kimbal [Sheriff Kimbrell] to let his men be placed around the house and for him to come in alone: and he can arrest us. all I am afraid of is that in the Fort We might be poisoned or killed through a Window at night. but You can arrange that all right. tell the Commanding Officer to watch Lt. Goodwin he would not hesitate to do anything. there Will be danger on the road of Somebody waylaying us to kill us on the road to the Fort. You will never catch those fellows on the road. Watch Fritzes, Captain Bacas ranch and the Brewery. they Will either go to Seven Rivers or to Jicarillo Mountains. they will stay around close until the scouting parties come in. give a spy a pair of glasses and let him get on the mountain back of Fritzes and watch and if they are there there will be provisions carried to them. it is not my place to advise you, but I am anxious to have them caught, and perhaps know how men hide from Soldiers better than you. please excuse me for having so much to Say

and I still remain Yours Truly,

W H. Bonney

*P.S.*

*I have changed my mind. Send Kimbal to Gutiereses just below San Patricio one mile, because Sanger and Ballard are or were great friends of Camels* [Billy Campbell's] *Ballard told me today yesterday to leave for you were doing everything to catch me. it was a blind to get me to leave. tell Kimbal not to come before 3 oclock for I may not be there before*

Billy also knew proper legalize, as seen in his October 24, 1878 Bill of Sale for a horse to a Dr. Henry Hoyt.

It began: *"Know all persons by these presents that I do hereby sell and deliver to Henry F. Hoyt one sorrel...."*

It ends with his most famous signature: "WHBonney," artistically linking H and B of "William Henry" with "Bonney."

## DEPOSITION OF WILLIAM BONNEY

In a deposition given to President Rutherford B. Hayes's investigator, Frank Warner Angel, Billy, then 18, described, in meticulous detail, the murder of his boss, John Henry Tunstall. Billy also proudly identified himself as having a ranch on the Peñasco River along with another Tunstall employee, Fred Waite.

Lacking that deposition, discovered years later by historian Frederick Nolan, pretenders had to invent a Tunstall murder scenario. And Billy's Peñasco ranch was unknown to them.

## COURT TESTIMONY OF WILLIAM BONNEY

As daring as proposing his own pardon to Governor Lew Wallace, was Billy's volunteering, in early 1879, to testify against Colonel Nathan Augustus Monroe Dudley, the commander of Lincoln's local fort, whose Ring-partisan march on the town had caused murderous defeat of Billy's side. This testimony, not part of the Wallace pardon deal, was Billy's own anti-Ring agenda.

Billy gave his two day testimony at Fort Stanton's Court of Inquiry, siding with the potential Court Martial of N.A.M. Dudley.

Billy's testimony details the July 19, 1878 turning point in the Lincoln County War, when Dudley, violating the Posse Comitatus Act, brought his soldiers, a howitzer cannon, and a Gatling gun to aid, by intimidation, Lincoln County's Ring-partisan sheriff, George Peppin. And Billy's testimony alone should have yielded Court Martial.

To be noted in the testimony, is that Alexander McSween, during the besiegement of his house, gave Billy letters from Commander Dudley *to read*. ("Brushy Bill" claimed illiteracy.)

Also noteworthy in the testimony are Billy's precise mind and meticulous descriptions. An issue for debunking the pretenders is the key element in Billy's testimony: that he saw three white soldiers fire a volley at himself and others fleeing the burning McSween building. That information made Dudley guilty of treason But the pretenders did not know that; nor were they aware of the outrage Billy must have felt at Dudley's exoneration.

In the transcript below, the "Recorder" is the military prosecutor, who was assisted by Attorney Ira Leonard, also in the courtroom. (So Leonard would have seen Billy's testimony - possibly cementing his loyalty to Billy.) "By Col. Dudley" refers to Dudley's attorney, Henry Waldo, the Territory's best trial lawyer.

In Billy's first day of testimony, on May 28, 1879, he responded as follows:

*Q. by Recorder. Where were you on the 19th day of July last and what, if anything, did you see of the movements and actions of the troops in that city, state fully?*

*Answer: I was in the McSween house in Lincoln, and I saw soldiers come from the post with sheriff's party, that is the sheriff's posse joined them a short distance below there, the McSween house. Soldiers passed on by and the men dropped off and surrounded the house, the sheriff's party. Shortly after the soldiers came back with Peppin, passed the house twice afterwards. Three soldiers came and stood in front of the house, in front of the windows. Mr. McSween wrote a note to the officer in charge asking what the soldiers were placed there for. He replied saying that they had business there, that if a shot was fired over his camp, or at Peppin, or at any of his men, that he had no objection to blowing up, if he wanted, his own house. I read the note myself, he handed it to me to read. I saw nothing further of the soldiers until night. I was in the back part of the house. When I escaped from the house three soldiers fired at me from the Tunstall store, outside corner of the store. That's all I know in regards to it ...*

*Q. By Col. Dudley. In addition to the names you have given, are you also known as the "Kid?"*

*Answer. I have already answered that question; Yes Sir, I am; but not "Billy Kid" that I know of...*

**[AUTHOR'S NOTE: Billy does not use "Billy the Kid"]**

*Q. By Col. Dudley. Whose name was signed to the note received by McSween in reply to the one previously sent by him to Col. Dudley?*

*Answer. Signed N.A.M. Dudley, did not say what rank, he received two notes, one had no name signed to it.*

**[AUTHOR'S NOTE: Confirmation that Billy could read.]**

*Q. By Col. Dudley. Are you as certain of everything else you have sworn to as you are to what you have sworn to in answer to the last proceeding question?*

*Answer. Yes Sir.*

*Q. By Col. Dudley. From which direction did Peppin come the first time the soldiers passed with him?*

*Answer. Passed up from the direction of where the soldiers camped, the first time I saw him.*

*Q. By Col. Dudley. What direction did he come from the second time?*

*Answer. From the direction of the [Wortley] hotel from the McSween house.*

*Q. By Col. Dudley. In what direction did you go upon your escape from the McSween house?*

*Answer. Ran towards the Tunstall store, was fired at, and there turned towards the river.*

*Q. By Col. Dudley. From what part of the McSween house did you make your escape?*

*Answer. The Northeast corner of the house.*

*Q. By Col. Dudley. How many soldiers fired at you?*

*Answer. Three.*

*Q. By Col. Dudley. How many soldiers were with Peppin when he passed the McSween house each time, as you say?*

*Answer. Three.*

*Q. By Col. Dudley. The soldiers appeared to go in company of threes that day, did they not?*

*Answer. All that I ever saw appeared to be three in a crowd at a time after they passed the first time.*

**[AUTHOR'S NOTE: Billy, only 19, cannot be shaken by bullying Attorney Henry Waldo.]**

*Q. By Col. Dudley. Q. By Col. Dudley. Who was killed first that day, Bob Beckwith or McSween men?*

*Answer. Harvey Morris, McSween man, was killed first.*

*Q. By Col. Dudley. How far is the Tunstall building from the McSween house?*

*Answer. I could not say how far, I never measured the distance. I should judge it to be 40 yards, between 30 and 40 yards.*

*Q. By Col. Dudley. How many shots did those soldiers fire, that you say shot from the Tunstall building?*

*Answer. I could not swear to that on account of firing on all sides, I could not hear. I seen them fire one volley.*

**[AUTHOR'S NOTE: Illustrated are Billy's precision in answering, and his observation of a "volley" - meaning firing in unison, under orders.]**

*Q. By Col. Dudley. What did they fire at?*

*Answer. Myself and Jose Chavez ...*

Billy resumed his testimony the following day: May 29, 1879; and further identified the shooting soldiers. In a fair court, a Court Martial could have resulted from this testimony alone. And Billy would have had anger at the injustice when the courts three biased judges ultimately cleared Dudley of wrongdoing.

*Q. by Court. Were the soldiers which you say fired at you as you escaped from the McSween house on the evening of July 19th last, colored or white?*

*Answer. White troops.*

*Q. by Court. Was it light enough so you could distinctly see the soldiers when they fired?*

*Answer. The house was burning. Made it almost light as day for a short distance all around.*

## *LOST TESTIMONY OF WILLIAM BONNEY*

Billy fulfilled his part of a the believed, Governor Lew Wallace, pardon deal by testifying as an eyewitness in the April 1879 Lincoln County grand jury against Attorney Huston Chapman's murderers - James Dolan, Billy Campbell, and Jessie Evans.

By doing that, Billy knew he was also implicating the Santa Fe Ring, whose local "boss" was Dolan; and thereby risking his life in his anti-Ring crusade. And Billy's testimony achieved those men's murder indictments (James Dolan and Billy Campbell for murder; Jessie Evans for accessory to murder).

That court record is missing. A compelling guess is that it fell victim to what appears to have been Santa Fe Ring expurgations of their incriminating records.

Nevertheless, a letter from Attorney Ira Leonard to Governor Lew Wallace confirms not only that Billy gave that testimony, but that, while giving it, he endured harassment by Ringman District Attorney William Rynerson. As in the Dudley Court of Inquiry, Billy obviously could not be thrown off course by another bullying lawyer. And, unbeknownst to the pretenders, Billy's motive was zealous, continuous, and brave opposition to the Santa Fe Ring.

# A LEGEND IN HIS TIME

Billy Bonney generated mythology when still alive. Examples are fabricated pre-death sightings of him, and even fabricated deeds after his jailbreak on April 28, 1881

In reality, after his April 28, 1881 jailbreak, Billy hid out in Fort Sumner and its sheep camps, and presumably secretly made whoopee with Paulita Maxwell.

But those false sightings heralded Billy's future, false, "post-death sightings" and "deeds."

For example, the following appeared in the *Santa Fe Daily New Mexican* in May of 1881, the month after Billy's jailbreak:

> On May 5, 1881: "There was a report on the streets last night that the Kid was then in Albuquerque, and was bound for Santa Fe. It was also said that he had killed another man there, but the rumor thus far lacks confirmation."

# OLIVER "BRUSHY BILL" ROBERTS GETS A BOOK

*HOAXBUST: The only "identity" between Oliver P. Roberts and Billy Bonney was the name "Bill;" which Roberts picked for his moniker: "Brushy Bill." The rest of Roberts's bid to be Billy used known historical names and his pseudo-history built around those names; plus Roberts's own authors' fakery. Though favored by the Billy the Kid Case hoaxers as their "surviving Billy," "Brushy" did not claim their Garrett-friendship-playing-on-dead-bench-scenario; thus, canceling their justification to exhume him. And "Brushy Bill" is discredited by his own history - being under 2 years old at Billy Bonney's death - and by Billy Bonney's real history, which "Brushy" did not know. But "Brushy's" attractiveness to the Billy the Kid Case hoaxers came from his modern conspiracy theory followers being their ideally gullible audience.*

## GAINING FELLOW TRAVELERS

Oliver P. "Brushy Bill" Roberts's transformation into Billy the Kid arose from three clever eccentrics, each now dead. Their 1955 book, *Alias Billy the Kid*, became "Brushy's" followers' bible.

The first strange person was "Brushy Bill" himself, a creative confabulator with at least 12 aliases with life stories, all of famous characters - Billy the Kid being just one. "Brushy" claimed he was in Jesse James's gang, Roosevelt's Rough Riders, and Buffalo Bill Cody's wild west show. His list also included being a Pinkerton Detective, a bronco rider, Bell Starr's friend, a Deputy U.S. Marshall, a rancher in Mexico, and a Pancho Villa associate.

The second oddball was Charles Leland Sonnichsen, an actual historian listed as first author, and introduced as being convinced by "Brushy's" "knowledge." Post-publication he tried to dissociate from the book's derision by calling himself only its proof-reader.

Lastly, was the most venal and least honest: William V. Morrison, the amateur historian second author, who called himself an attorney, but was not; claimed falsely that he was a descendant of Lucien Maxwell's oldest brother, Ferdinand; and is idolized by "Brushy's" followers as a martyr for the truth. But Morrison' is a true hoaxer, who coached mentally unstable "Brushy," and sought maximum publicity by petitioning for a New Mexico governor's pardon for "Brushy" as Billy the Kid.

Morrison's "Brushy"-as-Billy hoax took work. He even included his sources as footnotes, apparently hoping they seemed corroborating, instead of cribbing. Included are Billy's famous letters to Governor Lew Wallace and Attorney Edgar Caypless - which give "Brushy" near-verbatim quotes - 70 years post-writing (and even made more clumsy by claiming a "friend" as their writer)! Used also were Pat Garrett's *Authentic Life of Billy the Kid*, Walter Noble Burns's *The Saga of Billy the Kid*; works by historians Robert Mullin and Maurice Garland Fulton, and by Billy's contemporaries: Charlie Siringo, Jim East, and George Coe.

Added were archival documents - like a page of Billy's Court of Inquiry testimony (not the informative ones cited above).

Also, in 1949, Morrison interviewed Lincoln County residents, then brought "Brushy" himself to tour Lincoln town in 1950.

Lastly, were "Brushy's" own taped products. There were also "Brushy" scribblings, which Morrison did not use, since he calls "Brushy" illiterate to remove suspicion of his studying-up. But tellingly, when historical sources ran out, so did "Brushy's" "memory" - or his confabulations took over.

Over 30 years after publication of *Alias Billy the Kid*, "Brushy Bill's" niece, Geneva Pittmon, became his nemesis. Since "Brushy" was born less than two years before Billy was killed, he and Morrison had added 20 years to his life. But Geneva Pittmon knew her uncle, called him emotionally unstable, and refuted his claim with the family Bible. On December 16, 1987, she sent the co-founder of the Billy the Kid Outlaw Gang, Joe Bowlin, a letter and a copy of the family Bible's genealogy page. She concluded: "My uncle was *Not Billy the Kid* ... He was born Aug 26, 1879." [APPENDIX: 36]

In response, "Brushy's" later believers craftily replaced "Brushy's" Hamilton, Texas, tombstone to give a birth date of December 31, 1859. But no explanation was offered for Geneva Pittmon's "conspiracy" to discredit their man!

## *LOSING A PARDON; GAINING A BOOK*

Initially, William Morrison's scheme worked. He and "Brushy" got New Mexico Governor Thomas Jewett Mabry's ear on Thursday, November 30, 1950. That day, a United Press reporter named Sexson Humphreys wrote from Santa Fe, "Pardon My 6-Shooters: Billy the Kid? Governor to Decide; 'Pardon Me,

I'm Alive,' Says Billy the Kid." Reporter Humphreys, making factual errors compatible with his day's lack of information, wrote:

> A page out of the old West comes to life today when a grizzled old man who claims to be the fabulous outlaw, "Billy the Kid," matches wits with the Governor of New Mexico.
>
> Governor Thomas Mabry will get out of a sickbed to confer with several distinguished historians and "Billy" over his application for a pardon in connection with the 1878 murder of Sheriff William Brady.
>
> It has long been presumed that the legendary gunman was shot to death by Sheriff Pat Garrett on July 14, 1881. But periodically since that date "Billys" have come forth to claim ownership of the silver six-guns that killed 21 frontiersmen.
>
> The latest claimant ... had been both verified and denied by elderly Southwesterners who claim to be former companions of "The Kid" ...
>
> Governor Mabry has indicated he wants to meet the new Billy and decide once and for all if the notorious gunman is still alive, or in a grave near Ft. Sumner, N.M., where hundreds have gazed on him for many years.
>
> The latest Billy came suddenly to life when an El Paso law firm last week wrote Mabry seeking a pardon "because the applicant, now past 90 years of age, wishes to spend his remaining days in peace."
>
> The lawyers claimed Billy had not really been killed by Sheriff Garrett, but only wounded ... and later escaped to old Mexico where he lived up to now, they said.
>
> The 1878 [sic] death of Billy the Kid is "nothing but legend," says an attorney who asks New Mexico Governor Thomas J. Mabry for a pardon for him. The attorney, Ted Andress **[NOTE: for whom William Morrison wrote the petition]**, says ... he surrendered because the territorial governor, Crawfordsville's Lew Wallace, of "Ben Hur" fame, promised him a pardon. But the pardon was never given and Billy under conviction for murdering a sheriff, broke for freedom. The "legend" is that he was killed in the escape attempt, but the petition says that he was only wounded and ... that it was a companion who was killed.

Assembled by Governor Mabry were kin of Pat Garrett, of "Kip" McKinney, and of William Brady; as well as historians. "Brushy" was unconvincing to all these experts.

Governor Thomas Jewett Mabry concluded: "I am taking no action, now or ever, on this application for a Pardon for Billy the Kid because I do not believe this man is Billy the Kid."

Mabry's pronouncement should have ended the game. But "Brushy" did Morrison a favor. He died a few months later. So William Morrison kept his foot in the door of Billy the Kid fame. He wrote in third person about himself for *Alias Billy the Kid*: "He was convinced that Roberts was really what he claimed to be and made up his mind that this man should have a hearing even if it had to be posthumous." In other words, freed of the old coot's limitations, Morrison could make up a better version himself.

First, Morrison needed validation. He turned to historian C.L. Sonnichsen, and performed a trick of "he-knew-things-never-printed" by saying that "Brushy" said "negro soldiers from Fort Stanton took positions on the hillside and joined in the firing that day when the Murphy men burned down McSween's house."

This interaction proves that Sonnichsen (and, of course, "Brushy") did not know the actual history. The Lincoln County War, from July 14, 1878 to July 19, 1878 (the day Morrison is referring to) had profuse eye-witnesses. So it is known that Commander N.A.M. Dudley's *all-black, 9th cavalrymen were never on the south foothills, and never fired.* All Dudley's soldiers were encamped at the east part of Lincoln, with a few non-shooting troops at the McSween house or with Sheriff George Peppin. On the foothills and shooting were only Peppin's white possemen.

But unknown to "Brushy," Dudley had also brought white infantry and officers. When real Billy testified in the Dudley Court of Inquiry, he stated he saw three *white* soldiers fire a volley at himself and others fleeing the burning McSween house. So they were either infantrymen or officers - not black cavalrymen.

But duped C.L. Sonnichsen came on board. William Morrison was in the book-writing business.

## OVERVIEW OF "BRUSHY'S" MORRISON BOOK

*Alias Billy the Kid* has 90 pages of text and 8 pages of photographs. It reads like "Through the Looking Glass," with historical names and basic events drifting in topsy-turvy chaos of "Brushy's" compensatory confabulatory creations - all wrong.

After the authors' introductory comments, the rest is "Brushy's" "own words" with Morrison narrating. Appendices mix real Billy's documents with "Brushy's."

A Publisher's Forward presents Morrison's hoaxed "suspicion": "Was Billy the Kid really shot to death by Sheriff Pat Garrett on that July night in 1881, or was someone else the victim?"

Used is Morrison's mantra: "Brushy" knew things "never printed." The Publisher states, "It was generally believed, for example, that there was a federal charge outstanding against Billy the Kid. Brushy Bill said the case 'was thrown out of court.' Legal records, when found, proved Brushy Bill's statement." But this "never printed" information is lifted from Billy's available letter to one of his attorneys, Edgar Caypless - cited by Morrison!

The "Prologue" has Morrison's punch line purpose: "Brushy Bill" wanted the "Billy the Kid" pardon - even posthumously.

## MORRISON BEGINS WITH THE PHYSICAL

To sell "Brushy" as Billy, Morrison starts with appearance. Meeting "Brushy" in Texas in 1949 (when Roberts was 70), Morrison writes that he "was amazed to see a man 90 years old in excellent physical condition."

For likeness, "Brushy" and Morrison used the famous Billy the Kid tintype. So they claim "Brushy's" "*left ear*" protruded "noticeably farther from the head than the right ear." In the tintype, Billy's rakishly tilted hat pushes out his *right* ear. But "Brushy" and Morrison were unaware that a tintype is right-to-left reversed. So they put the "funny" ear on the left. Saying "Brushy" was toothless avoided Billy's protruding teeth.

"Brushy" also shows Morrison a hip scar, saying it "was from the time I run into the street in Lincoln to take the guns off the body of Sheriff Bill Brady. Billy Matthews ran behind an adobe wall and fired. His shot went through the flesh of this hip and then hit Wayte [sic - Waite]." The story and names are famous, but the specifics are all wrong. It was Billy and the Regulators who ambushed Brady *from behind an adobe wall*. Jacob Basil "Billy" Matthews, a Deputy Sheriff, next fired at them from *inside the Cisneros house*. Billy's shot friend was Jim "Frenchie" French, not Fred Waite (another known Regulator). And the *single* firearm recovered by Billy was his Winchester '73 carbine, confiscated by Brady in deputized Billy's brief arrest after Tunstall's murder; though "Brushy" says they were pearl-gripped .44 revolvers.

"Brushy" adds from movie Westerns, "I wore my pistols in the scabbard with the butts toward the back. I fanned the hammer at times." Double-holstered guns and fanning were not used by Billy.

Weird hands was another false Billy myth manufactured by attributing his jailbreaks to slipping from wrist shackles. That became a pretender prerequisite. So "Brushy" flexes his thumbs to "slip through handcuffs." Added are "Brushy's small hands": another myth belied by real Billy's muscular ones in his tintype.

Ambidextrousness, a known Billy trait, is claimed by "Brushy," but ruined by his favoring the left, repeating his tintype error, where Billy's *right* hand cocks at his Colt revolver's butt - showing real Billy favored the right!

## *"BRUSHY" MANGLES HISTORY*

In *Alias Billy the Kid*, Morrison quotes "Brushy": "I done wrong like everyone else in those days." Illiteracy met 1950's readers' expectations; but was not real Billy's articulateness.

There was a bigger predicament: alleging to be a first-person account, "Brushy Bill" and Morrison lacked information to create one. Instead, "Brushy" fills in with errors. And he is quoted for 44 pages in "Brushy Bill's Story."

In the 1950's, Billy Bonney's known history started in 1877 (when he was 17). So childhood was needed. "Brushy" jumps in: "I was born at Buffalo Gap [Texas] on December 31, 1859." Why not Billy's birthday, November 23rd; or birthplace, New York? Morrison says "Brushy" made up those details, because "that's what bad men did in those days!"

Sixteen long blank years remained for the dynamic duo. Not till 1993, would Billy's adolescence in Silver City and Arizona be known from Jerry Weddle's *Antrim is my Stepfather's Name*. So necessity mothered "Brushy's" wild inventions.

A Kathleen Bonney - related to "Brushy's" *real* mother who died when he was "three" - takes him to Silver City. (Morrison/"Brushy" were unaware of the historical "Catherine McCarty Antrim;" or that she died when Billy was 14½; or that "Bonney" was merely Billy's made-up alias from 1877 onward.)

Missing also are real Billy's early crises: his 1875 Silver City chimney escape from Sheriff Harvey Whitehill's jail after arrest for clothing and revolver theft from a Chinese laundry; and his subsequent life in Arizona with imprisonment for horse rustling and escape, followed by his killing of blacksmith "Windy" Cahill.

Instead, "Brushy" placidly leaves Silver City "to see his people" in Texas, where, as a "cowboy," he adventures in Indian Territory; Dodge City, Kansas; and even Chihuahua, Mexico!

With relief, Morrison jumps to 1877, with a return to New Mexico Territory - "from Mexico" "Brushy" says wrongly; not knowing Billy fled hanging in Arizona for Cahill's murder by return to New Mexico. "Brushy" picks up at Billy's known crossing of the Guadalupe Mountains to reach the Pecos River settlements. But when there, "Brushy" states: "Jim and John Jones were working for Chisum, so I went to work for them - I think up at Bosque Grande. Frank McNab [sic - MacNab] was foreman."

Only the names are historical; everything else is made up. The Jones boys worked for Chisum prior to 1877. By Billy's arrival, they ranched cattle and operated a Roswell general store with their father, Heiskell. Billy never worked for them. MacNab was a cattle detective with Hunter and Evans, which had bought John Chisum's huge herd. Bosque Grande was Chisum's original ranch and was not connected to Billy until 1880, when Billy sold rustled stock to its new owner, Dan Dedrick (to whom he gave the famous tintype). In actuality, Billy arrived in August of 1877; and by the next month, he joined the outlaw gang of Jessie Evans, and was sighted when doing a stagecoach hold-up with them.

But "Brushy" says: "I went to work with them [the Joneses] at Murphy's Seven Rivers camp that winter." But the Murphy-Dolan cow camp was south of Seven Rivers; and Billy did not work there.

By October of 1877, real Billy was hired by John Tunstall to work on his Feliz and Peñasco River ranches.

Available sources did allow "Brushy" to name some Tunstall employees, when he belatedly gets to his Tunstall job. There, "Brushy" gets wrong the McSween-Tunstall attachment order from the Fritz insurance case - unaware of the Santa Fe Ring - attributing it to "trouble about McSween's law fee," instead of the Ringmen's malicious accusation of embezzlement - known to Billy.

John Tunstall's murder is threadbare and errorful, since it lacked Frank Warner Angel's still undiscovered Report with specifics - including Billy's own deposition. Found by historian Frederick Nolan in 1954, and cited in 1956 in his article "Sidelight on the Tunstall Murder," it was too late for "Brushy," dead by 1950; or for William Morrison's 1955 concocted Alias Billy the Kid.

"Brushy" follows conventional history until Sheriff William Brady's ambush murder, where he hits an ignorance wall and pulls a "pearl-handled .44 off his body" - when it was really Billy's Winchester '73 carbine retrieved. Also, "Brushy" has no idea why Brady was murdered, so he fabricates a motive: "Sheriff Brady was gunning for me with warrants for cattle stealing."

"Brushy" is unaware that the Regulators killed Brady only a month and a half after he headed Tunstall's murder posse; and did so to protect Alexander McSween, returning to Lincoln for his

April 1878 embezzlement trial. And real Billy's rustling began months later in 1878, after the Lincoln County War was lost.

Before "Brushy" massacres that war, he gets a Morrison pitch: "The three-day battle in Lincoln, July 17, 18, and 19, 1878, was the end of the struggle for the McSween faction. It was a bloody business, and Brushy Bill Roberts described it as if every detail had been burned into his memory with a branding iron."

This was empty promotion. First of all, the war began on the 14th - so it was six days long. And "Brushy's" "every detail" are just known superficialities - plus black shooting soldiers. Even Commander Dudley's terrifying Gatling gun is missed!

But Morrison apparently had the Dudley Court of Inquiry's transcript page listing those escaping from McSween's burning house. So "Brushy" gets some right!

Lew Wallace next enters as the past governor's replacement. And "Brushy"/Morrison crib the Attorney Huston Chapman murder from real Billy's letter to Lew Wallace.

Next is the Wallace-Billy meeting. With the "he-knew-things-never-printed" trick, Morrison adds "Brushy's" quote: "We didn't meet like they say we did in the daytime at Patron's."

All that is false. First of all, it has never been said that the initial Wallace meeting was at Juan Patrón's Lincoln house -  or in the daytime. It was on March 17, 1879, at night, and at the Lincoln house of Justice of the Peace John "Squire" Wilson.

Then trouble strikes again: no records until December 12, 1880 with real Billy's letter to Lew Wallace about the killing of Jim Carlyle at the Greathouse Ranch; a murder of which Billy was accused, though he wrote that Carlyle was mistakenly shot by his fellow possemen. So "Brushy," not unexpectedly, gets this right. Morrison even refers to that letter!

But the location of the Greathouse Ranch was unknown until the 1980's. So "Brushy" "forgets" its location.

Known history gets the dynamic duo through Garrett's sheriff election and his capture of Billy, but an embarrassing gaffe comes because neither know why Billy was pursued; guessing the Carlyle murder; when it was for murders of Sheriff William Brady, Deputy George Hindman, and Andrew "Buckshot" Roberts.

Billy's Mesilla hanging trial, however, gets color from Billy's known letter to Attorney Edgar Caypless, "remembered" by "Brushy" as its near quote: "In April I pleaded to the federal indictment and it was thrown out of court." But left out, is the victim: Andrew "Buckshot" Roberts - not in Billy's letter.

A story about Billy's famous bay mare is then mutilated by ignorance. In reality, Garrett's posseman, Frank Stewart, had stolen her from Billy at the Stinking Springs capture. Billy wanted to sell her to pay for a new attorney after Ira Leonard withdrew from his trials in Mesilla - as Billy described in a letter. Billy even made a replevin (rustling and recovery) case against Frank Stewart with Attorney Edgar Caypless.

But "Brushy"/Morrison fill in their blanks by saying the mare ended up at a Scott Moore's, because "Brushy" (as Billy) "owed him money for board." Actually, Scott Moore was the person to whom Frank Stewart illegally sold the mare, and was the owner of Moore's luxurious Hotsprings Hotel in Las Vegas, New Mexico - not a place Billy "boarded."

Historically, after Billy's hanging trial in Mesilla, the next big event was his famous escape from the Lincoln County courthouse-jail. Morrison notes that he took "Brushy" there in August of 1950. But the "Brushy"/Morrison escape story, though conventional, leaves "Brushy" unable to "remember" his escape route, claiming "everything had changed." In truth, that rural area remains almost identical to Billy's day. The problem is that *no one knows* Billy's route. The duo had again run out of script.

But they knew Billy crossed the Capitan Mountains to his friend Yginio Salazar; except it is spelled "Higinio;" a mistake Yginio's bi-lingual, literate friend, real Billy, would not make.

Spewing historically familiar names, "Brushy" finally gets to Fort Sumner, where information again ceases. He says, "I knew Celsa and Pat's wife, who were sisters to Saval Gutierrez."

This is a *big* mistake. They were sisters, but Celsa was *married* to Saval, her cousin. Since "Brushy" and Morrison are unaware of this relationship - clearly known by the real Billy, who even began his death-walk from their house - they have Celsa wanting to run off to Old Mexico with "Brushy Bill!"

This "Brushy"-Morrison error, nicely revealing hoaxing underpinnings, arises from the known fact that Saval was Pat Garrett's "brother-in-law." "Brushy" and William Morrison are unaware that it was brother-in-law *by marriage*.

Next, "Brushy" claims he hid out at the Yerby Ranch. That name from a Billy-Wallace letter. But it is unlikely. Yerby had employed Charlie Bowdre, but was not Billy's friend. Furthermore, Pat Garrett had already recovered Billy's allegedly stolen mules at Yerby's in December of 1880, making it a high-risk location to hide out.

## *"BRUSHY'S" ODD DEATH SCENE*

Then comes the Fort Sumner death scene: "Brushy's" unique creation. Killed is an "innocent victim" mistaken for him (as Billy the Kid). That victim is his claimed partner, a Billy Barlow, who, oddly, is shot *on the back porch* of the Maxwell house.

No attempt is made by Morrison to reconcile the famous, Old West, death scene in the Maxwell bedroom. "Brushy" embellishes by claiming himself shot in the jaw and shoulder (though not by whom). And Celsa Gutierrez aids his escape, while "they were passing off his [Barlow's] body as mine."

No "Billy Barlow" has been historically found; though *he* would be the modern Billy the Kid Case hoaxers' carpenter's bench-blood-DNA source - according to "Brushy!"

## *"BRUSHY" HEADS OFF INTO THE SUNSET*

After the death scene, a hoaxbuster is grateful, since the story becomes Oliver P. Roberts's own life, is irrelevant, and the repellant task of reading his deranged tale ends.

## *A PICTURE FOR "BRUSHY" IS WORTH NOTHING*

Since "Brushy Bill" was not Billy the Kid, William Morrison's photo section in *Alias Billy the Kid* lacks relevance, but is made ludicrous by Morrison's choices.

For example, for Katherine Ann [sic] Bonney, is a picture commonly used for Billy's mother. But, unknown to Morrison, it was fake. To quote from Frederick Nolan's *The West of Billy the Kid:* "The original was owned by the George Griggs family, who exhibited it at their Billy the Kid Museum. It was called the Kid's mother sometime in the late 1930's, when Eugene Cunningham, author of the book, *Triggernometry*, identified it as such to photographic collector Noah H. Rose in order to obtain from Rose another photograph ... he eventually confessed that he had no idea who the woman was."

Other photos are of Lincoln County War participants, an illustration of the Billy tintype, a revolver of "Brushy's," a revolver claimed taken from Billy "when he surrendered to Garrett," the towns of Lincoln and Fort Sumner, the Lincoln courthouse, the Maxwell mansion, and Fort Sumner's barracks.

Then come "Brushy" photos," the first, taken six months before his 1950 death. He looks in his seventies - which he was. Another shows him at "about age 30" on a horse, proving he sat straight.

Last, is a bizarre collage "comparing ears." John Jones - cut from his group photo with other Seven Rivers boys - appears as "Billy at seventeen." Jones's ears do not match "Brushy's" big flappy ones in his photos at fourteen, twenty-seven, fifty-five, and eighty-five (in "new tombstone" years). And real Billy's tintype, showing one ear, is different. And a 1989 professional analysis denied a photo-match of "Brushy" and real Billy.

## APPENDICES, UNDERPINNINGS, AND END

*Alias Billy the Kid* "Appendices" reveal Morrison's "tools." Present are Billy the Kid letters, Governor Lew Wallace's Amnesty Proclamation; Billy's 1979 change of trial venue; Billy's 1881 hanging trial documents; Wallace's hanging instructions to Garrett; the translated Coroner's Jury Report (surprisingly present, since its existence was denied); Morrison's unsuccessful search for a "coroner's verdict;" and a December 13, 1880 Wallace reward notice for "the Kid." Affidavits swear that Garrett did not kill the Kid, that "Brushy" is the Kid, and that Billy was seen after his death date. (Also, the Indiana Historical Society has a letter donated by Morrison, of his typed copy of Billy's first letter to Wallace, which he got from the grandson, Lew Wallace Jr.; who held it back from his donation to the Society of other Billy letters.)

As a reader bonus, the book concludes with "Brushy" quotes.

"Brushy" says, "Jesse [sic - Jessie] Evans knew that Garrett didn't kill the Kid." [Oops! Shouldn't "Brushy" have said *"me?"*] In fact, Jessie Evans knew nothing. In 1881, he was in jail in Huntsville, Texas. And he had fled the Territory in March, 1879, escaping his Fort Stanton jailing for Huston Chapman's murder.

"Brushy" also says: "Jim East, I knew him too. He was a friend of mine." This is laughable, since Texan Jim East was a Pat Garrett posseman involved in Billy's Stinking Springs capture.

About Governor Lew Wallace, Roberts concludes: "I done everything I promised him to do."

The real Billy prompt-letter of March 4, 1881 to Lew Wallace said beautifully: "I have done everything that I promised you I would, and you have done nothing that you promised me."

In the end, the Morrison-Sonnichsen-"Brushy Bill" book only proves a pig's ear cannot make a silk purse.

# "BRUSHY BILL" GETS MORE AUTHORS

Forty years after William V. Morrison's hoaxed book, *Alias Billy the Kid*, Morrison and "Brushy Bill" Roberts got true-believer authors. In 1997, W.C. Jameson and Frederic Bean, conspiracy theorists, published their *The Return of the Outlaw Billy the Kid*, a hefty 256 pages. As Jameson admits in its beginning, "This amazing story captivated me such that for the next twenty-eight years I investigated it at every opportunity."

Jameson and Bean, converted by Morrison's "he-knew-things-never-printed" trick - and apparently avoiding the mass of history books on Billy Bonney written since Morrison's day - decided to let "Brushy" talk through Morrison's records and convince people himself. Adding "forensic science" - meaning photo-comparisons - they were sure "Brushy" as Billy would be clinched.

Their plan was disastrous. It revealed "Brushy's" atrocious errors in his tapes and scribblings - concealed by Morrison. So Jameson and Bean actually exposed the hoax's underpinnings.

## BILLY THE KID CASE HOAXERS JOIN JAMESON

Frederick Bean is dead, but W.C. Jameson, a country music singer, was listed by the Billy the Kid Case hoaxers as one of their "historians." In their 2004 History Channel program plugging their own hoax (as real history), W.C. Jameson appears to earnestly plug "Brushy" as Garrett-surviving Billy the Kid.

Earlier, in November of 2003, Billy the Kid Case hoax-backing, glossy *True West* magazine had promoted Jameson in a stacked debate titled "Was Brushy Bill Really Billy the Kid? Experts face off over new evidence." Set-up was Leon Metz, Pat Garrett's biographer, against W.C. Jameson, spewing Morrisonisms, as follows:

> On one side, passionate supporters of the historical status quo assert Roberts was a fraud, yet to date they have provided no logical, definitive proof ... Roberts was an illiterate man, yet he was astonishingly intimate with the people, geography, architecture and events of Lincoln County, New Mexico, in the late 1870s-early 1880s – an intimacy that could have come only from being present and involved ...
>
> After Roberts' image was compared to the only known photograph of Billy the Kid, one researcher concluded that

William Henry Roberts was, in all likelihood, Billy the Kid, and as such, history needed to be rewritten ...

Jameson's *True West* interview, like his *The Return of the Outlaw Billy the* Kid, is like repeating bull charge again and again at Morrison's obstacles: "Brushy's" wrong age, Billy's missing Silver City years, Billy's literacy, the strange death scene, and the failed photo-likeness. It was sound and fury signifying nothing.

## HISTORICAL IGNORANCE IS BLISS

Pervasive historical ignorance of Jameson and Bean, that left them prey to Morrison's hoaxing, is clear in *The Return of the Outlaw Billy the Kid*'s initial overview, apparently from William Morrison's records. One example, all errors, is presented:

> At one point, Murphy retained lawyer McSween to collect on a $10,000 life insurance policy on partner Fritz, who died while on a trip to Germany. McSween collected the money but refused to hand it over to Murphy. Under orders from Murphy, Sheriff Brady attempted to seize some of Tunstall's cattle as partial payment.
>
> Tunstall decided he needed to confer with Brady and arrange an appointment with him in Lincoln. On 18 February 1878 John Tunstall, riding a buckboard and accompanied by several of his hired gunmen, including Billy the Kid, headed for Lincoln. As they approached the town of Ruidoso, the gunmen spotted a flock of turkeys and set off in pursuit. Seconds later, a group of men led by Jesse [sic] Evans rode up to Tunstall in the wagon and shot him dead.
>
> Tunstall's hired hands, led by Dick Brewer, vowed vengeance and organized themselves into a vigilante group they called the Regulators.

Here are the dramatic mistakes - which real Billy would not make about obvious events, for which he was eye-witness:

1) **Murphy did not hire McSween**. McSween was hired to represent the interests of the Fritz estate by Emil Fritz's siblings, its Administrators: Charles Fritz and Emilie Fritz Scholand.

2) **McSween only collected part of the life insurance settlement;** the rest was retained by the New York City law firm, Donnell and Lawson, as fee for their own collection services.

3) **McSween refused to hand over the money to Dolan, not Murphy.** By 1878, Murphy was dying of alcoholism and had retired. The money was for Fritz's heirs; not Dolan. Dolan made a legal claim to it; but it was rejected by the Probate Court.

4) **Sheriff Brady did not attempt to seize Tunstall cattle as partial payment.** The mistake is "payment." The insurance money was used for the fake embezzlement case again McSween; with Tunstall added falsely as "his business partner." That criminal complaint was filed in February of 1878. The Grand Jury was not until that April. To guarantee the $10,000 until the trial's outcome, a Writ of Attachment (meaning appraisal) of both men's property was made. Tunstall's cattle were appraised; not seized.

5) **Tunstall did not head to Lincoln on February 18, 1878 to confer with Sheriff Brady.** Tunstall knew the attachment would be done that day on his 600 cattle at his Feliz Ranch, 50 miles from Lincoln. Believing his horses were exempt, and to avoid clashing with Brady's possemen, he proceeded to Lincoln with his men and the horses. On that trip, he was murdered.

6) **Tunstall did not ride on a buckboard.** Tunstall was on horseback with his men. Fred Waite was sent to Lincoln with the buckboard on another road. Tunstall's horse was killed with him.

7) **Tunstall's men were not gunmen per say.** They were his ranch hands at his Feliz River and Peñasco River properties. At this stage, there was no overt fighting.

8) **They were not approaching the town of Ruidoso.** It did not exist then. They were less than an hour from the Ruidoso *River*, homestead ranch of Tunstall's foreman, Dick Brewer.

9) **The murder did not occur at a wagon.** (see 6).

10) **The Regulators were originally not an outlaw vigilante group.** After Tunstall's murder, his men were legally deputized to arrest his murderers by Lincoln County Justice of the

Peace John "Squire" Wilson. After they were illegally named "outlaws" by Governor Axtell in his March 9, 1878 Proclamation, they continued with their mission, calling themselves Regulators.

Total erroneousness continues unabated.

Sheriff Brady's murder is described as for "vengeance," rather than to protect McSween from Brady's assassination that day.

The Blazer's Mill murder of Andrew "Buckshot" Roberts by the Regulators is wrongly called when they "sought sanctuary" there; when, in fact, Blazer's Mill was a Murphy-Dolan stronghold; and the Regulators were there seeking stolen Tunstall stock there.

The dramatic final day of the Lincoln County War is shrunk to a Sheriff Peppin deputy setting fire to McSween's house - with the military intervention and Gatling gun lost in "translation." Billy is called the Regulator head; but he never was.

The Huston Chapman killing - which Billy witnessed - lists Jessie Evans as the murderer, but Evans was only an accessory by presence. (The fatal shots were fired by James Dolan and Billy Campbell - to which real Billy testified and got their indictments.)

Dates and events are revealed to have been utterly jumbled by "Brushy" - even with Morrison's coaching - but now not benefiting from Morrison's more canny editing in his *Alias Billy the Kid*.

So incidents taken from Billy's letters to Lew Wallace in 1879 and 1881 get mixed up.

Real Billy's June 17, 1879 "escape" from his Patrón house "arrest," is called "a short time later" to his January 10, 1880 killing of Joe Grant (actually January 3, 1880). And that killing is attributed to "an argument;" when it was "Texas Joe" Grant's unprovoked, gunslinger attempt to shoot Billy in the back.

Garrett's 1880 election as sheriff leads to "Brushy's" confabulated version of Garrett's tracking of Billy - even falsely adding Garrett to the Jim Carlyle murder's White Oaks posse.

The Stinking Springs capture misses Charlie Bowdre's unforgettable death scene ambush of being shot by Garrett and tumbling into the huge gully concealing Garrett and his possemen.

Skimmed over is the Mesilla hanging trial, Billy's courthouse jail escape, and his destination of Fort Sumner.

In Fort Sumner, there is a funny fabrication of Peter Maxwell betraying "Billy" to Pat Garrett because of "the outlaw's affections for his servant girls!"

Then Jameson and Bean embarrassingly mix up "Brushy's" and Morrison's back porch murder scene with the conventional bedroom one for real, dead, identified Billy!

## CONSPIRACY OF HISTORIANS

Their book's core is Jameson's and Bean's "great conspiracy" of historians; because conspiracy is the only explanation for such true-believers. They state: "There exists a confederacy of Billy the Kid researchers and writers, an informal alliance composed of a number of adherents to the prevailing and accepted theories regarding the death of the outlaw ... The alliance dismissed Roberts ... The truth is, however, their efforts were never supported by valid scientific and historical research."

But Jameson and Bean have no evidence for that "conspiracy." They merely say that historians "repeat themselves" - meaning reuse accepted documentation. For motives, they say historians want to maintain the *status quo*; refuse to admit being wrong for so long; and, thus, perpetuate "myth and misinformation."

## CONSPIRACY OF GARRETT

Since W.C. Jameson and Frederick Bean believe that Roberts-Billy survived the Fort Sumner murder, it follows for them that *someone* made up existing history. So maybe it was Pat Garrett!

Offered is that Pat Garrett was "an aspiring political figure." That is both untrue and unfathomable as to motivation.

Meaningless swipes say Pat Garrett was "overrated," "never succeeded in anything," and Billy was "a thousand times braver." From that blather, Jameson and Bean somehow conclude that Garrett "was a man of questionable veracity and integrity."

Or, maybe, they postulate, Garrett wanted the reward money. For that foray, they say Garrett "was denied his territorial reward for killing the Kid by the territorial legislature" because of an unidentified corpse. But this is false. That $500 reward was Lew Wallace's personal one, and was paid to Garrett belatedly because Wallace had left the Territory in mid-1881 to be Ambassador to Turkey. And the corpse was not unidentified. It was profusely identified as Billy's - including by the official coroner's jury.

Garrett's and Poe's lying about how they knew Billy was in Fort Sumner is also a focus. Though irrelevant to victim identity, that lying is probably historically true, but would have been done to conceal Peter Maxwell's possible, traitorous assistance in Billy's fatal ambush in the town where Billy was loved by residents.

Then Jameson and Bean use Poe's widow's quote about Poe's initial concern that Garrett killed the wrong man. It is irrelevant, since Poe could not recognize Billy, and even corrected himself.

Bizarre hearsay quotes from William Morrison, and by people unrelated to the events, are used. Presented is that McKinney's grandson told Morrison that Garrett had said "the Kid got away;" or that someone in a Texas saloon had made a telephone call (note the modern timing) to a business to say he had overheard McKinney tell Garrett the same thing!

## CONSPIRACY OF CORONER'S JURYMEN

The next conspiracy ruminations by W.C. Jameson and Frederick Bean focus on the Coroner's Jury Report. Its clear-cut identification of dead Billy is any pretender's biggest headache.

So Jameson and Bean attack that document by contriving irregularities, which they call "suspicious."

They say: "For reasons never completely explained, this coroner's jury report never made it to the official records of San Miguel County. In fact, Justice of the Peace Segura never made an entry regarding the report in his own books."

So one intended "conspirator" is Alejandro Segura.

But, as Justice of the Peace, Alejandro Segura would have stored the Report in his courthouse office or his home. Records like those, years later, were taken to Santa Fe, and, at times, temporarily or permanently lost. The former happened to Billy's Coroner's Jury Report, which, as the authors acknowledge, was found in a storage box in the 1930's. So nothing untoward happened to the Coroner's Jury Report.

As to Segura's record keeping, the implication is only that he was careless; or that some of his other records got lost.

(One is tempted to spoof Jameson and Bean with the fact that the Lincoln County Coroner's Jury Report for murdered Sheriff William Brady has never been found. By their "logic," Brady too "escaped" like their "Roberts-Billy!")

Next, "suspicions" escalate. Jameson and Bean say: "Like the shooting, the inquest has also been shrouded in confusion and mystery." What "confusion and mystery?" They state that "the inquest was handled quickly." Why not? It was hot July; the body would rot. They offer: "The body was not put on public display."

For whom would a decaying corpse be displayed in rural New Mexico Territory? And they omit the 200 townspeople's nighttime vigil for Billy's corpse in the carpenter's shop.

Then Jameson and Bean also want photos of dead Billy; forgetting rural people, back then, did not have cameras.

Their "clincher" is alleging *two* Coroner's Reports prepared at different times. "Evidence" is a non-referenced newspaper interview with an A.P. Anaya. But he is the same "Paco" Anaya, whose own book is named *I Buried Billy* (not *I Did Not Bury Billy!*). Jameson and Bean are merely garbling Anaya's tale with the fact that there is a Spanish version of the Report.

Then they lie: "To date no one has ever seen a copy of the document." But in their own bibliography is the book containing its photocopy: *Violence in Lincoln County*! They even quote its author - historian, William Keleher - who described how the original Spanish version was found in the 1930's. Slyly, they note that Keleher gives Billy's famous "quién es?" quote in English. But they are merely reading Keleher's own 1957 translation.

Jameson's and Bean's fretting follows about misspelling of signers' names; or that Garrett forged the report.

All this misinformation yields their non-sequitor conclusion: "There is, in fact, *no legal proof of the death of Billy the Kid*" [their italics]. Thus, Jameson and Bean contend, a conspiracy must have concealed the corpse's identity.

## *CONSPIRACY OF BURIAL*

Next up for conspiracy is the burial; beginning falsely with Jameson and Bean claiming few witnesses.

Then they provide a fake witness. They state that an S.M. Ashenfelter, reporter [sic - owner] at the Grant County *Herald*, wrote in July of 1881 that the corpse was dark-skinned and bearded. Since Grant County would have put Ashenfelter about 250 miles from the almost immediate, Fort Sumner burial - after the night's unheralded ambush killing - Ashenfelter apparently fantasized an "outlaw" description for his article.

But Jameson and Bean solemnly, and with what they later call "scientific style," cite a book on sexual maturity (with "SMR's - Sexual Maturity Ratings") to compare Ashenfelter's corpse to fair beardless Billy, to show the impossibility of his transformation to Ashenfelter's hirsute fantasy (while forgetting Billy Barlow, *their* purported victim, "looked like" their fair "Roberts-Billy")!

Feeble funny hearsay survival tales follow. A William Morrison quote says a man in 1914 said Garrett did not shoot Billy. Another man, in 1980, recalls "his uncle" (an unsubstantiated participant) dug the grave, and an "armed guard" prevented anyone looking in the casket.

Of course, Jameson's and Bean's foregone conclusion is: "The facts stated above cause grave doubts about the identity of the body in the casket."

## MOTHERS OF ALL CONSPIRACY THEORIES

By the end of *The Return of the Outlaw Billy the Kid,* W.C. Jameson and Frederick Bean launch conspiracy theories that knock the breath from you.

Here goes:

1) **All Fort Sumner people were in a conspiracy.** They tricked Garrett into believing he had killed Billy, because they were "friendly and sympathetic to the Kid." They perpetuated "the masquerade well into the twentieth century because they knew the Kid was still alive." This is "Brushy's" own scenario. Jameson and Bean state: "According to Roberts, the two (Jesus Silva and Deluvina) decided to perpetuate a deception, perhaps allowing Garrett to believe the victim was, in fact, the wanted outlaw." More than absurdity ruins this: it requires Garrett's not recognizing Billy. But Garrett knew Billy since 1878; captured him at Stinking Springs; and transported him by train to Las Vegas, then Santa Fe, for jail. And, as Lincoln County Sheriff, Garrett imprisoned Billy in his courthouse-jail to await hanging.

2) **All of New Mexico is in a conspiracy.** The reason given is "tourism." If Billy was a Texan (meaning "Brushy"), the loss would be "millions of dollars each year." So, Governor Mabry had been in cahoots with all the assembled historians and descendants to call "Brushy" an imposter for economic reasons.

3) **The Lincoln County Heritage Trust was in a conspiracy.** The reason given is that their 1989 photo-analysis (discussed below) refuted "Brushy Bill" as Billy the Kid. Again, it was tourism dollars that made the director, Bob Hart, lie to protect his job; and the Trust was a big business.

4) **Historical conferences and a television program on "Prime Time Live"** (date not provided) **were conspiracies.** The reason given is that historians denied "Brushy" was Billy; and TV presenter, Sam Donaldson, was "a resident of Lincoln County." Apparently, that circled back to tourism dollars.

## A FAMILY TREE GROWS FOR "BRUSHY"

If conspiracy is heart and soul of W.C. Jameson's and Frederick Bean's *The Return of the Outlaw Billy the Kid*, "Brushy Bill" is its meat. To flesh him out, and to address his actual mismatch to Billy, these authors soldier into nonsense not dared by William Morrison.

Dealing with "Brushy's" being under two years old at Billy's death - the Geneva Pittmon knowledgeable niece problem - reveals Jameson and Bean to be as creative as they are unacademic.

They simply dispense with Pittmon by calling *her* "Brushy Bill" relative - Oliver P. Roberts - not *the actual* "Brushy Bill!"

*Their* "Brushy Bill" - from a *different family* - is Oliver *L.* Roberts! Anyway, *his really real* name was "William Henry."

How did they prove this? They do not say; but like Morrison's "P," "L" was born in Buffalo Gap, Texas! They add that since Billy could ride and shoot, he could not have been from New York!

"L's" new family comes with a family tree. He even has *another family Bible* from a Martha Vada Roberts Heath and "genealogical papers" from a Eulaine Emerson Haws of Tyler, Texas. This tree has a "Cherokee wife" with two marriages. Her first was to a "Bonney," to produce "Catherine Bonney." Her second, to a "William Dunn," yielded Mary Adeline Dunn, whose son, "William Henry Roberts" (their "Brushy Bill"), came from marrying a James Henry Roberts. In case the reader missed the point, beside this Dunn-Roberts son is added "aka Billy the Kid."

What happens to the new name "Oliver *L.* Roberts?" It is abandoned. "Brushy" will be called "William Henry" for their book.

Jameson and Bean do admit that this family tree is "reconstructed" - leaving contemplation of how reconstructed by them, when their Catherine Bonney has, as husbands, a "Michael" McCarty (also called "Edgar" elsewhere by them), and then a William Antrim. Note that the names McCarty" and "William Antrim" have now been updated from real Billy's mother's relationships (at least they glanced at new history books); but this "Catherine" is not their "Roberts-Billy's" mother.

Remaining in mystery, is "Brushy's" new tombstone, birth date of December 31, 1859, *since no dates are given for anyone - the point of family Bible notations!*

Later, Jameson and Bean make the confused claim that by using the name Bonney for Billy's mother, "Brushy" solved the mystery of where the name arose; thus, forgetting their own claim that their "Brushy" mother was a "Dunn," not a "Bonney!"

## LITERATE ILLITERATE "BRUSHY"

W.C. Jameson and Frederick Bean call "Brushy" "semi-literate" to use his jottings; though William Morrison stuck to "Brushy's" being illiterate.

And even "Brushy" knew that he could not claim writing the famous and articulate Billy the Kid letters. So "Brushy" made a creative confabulation, saying about Billy's first letter to Wallace: "I had a friend who spelled it out in a letter for me, what I wanted from Governor Wallace."

This "friend" ploy fails. Billy, using modified Spencerian penmanship, wrote his letters in different locations from 1879 through 1881; including solitary confinement inside the Santa Fe jail! So that "friend" had to be "Brushy's" actual shadow!

Score zero for that Jameson and Bean try; and a touchdown for their own discrediting their man as Billy.

## "BRUSHY" STUFFS HIS FOOT INTO HIS MOUTH

Probably the most calamitous decision of W.C. Jameson and Frederick Bean for helping "Brushy" was to turn him loose. William Morrison had wisely edited out "Brushy's" biggest gaffes.

"History," right from "Brushy," lays bare his utter ignorance about causality of events, dates, and participants - and the failure of Morrison's coaching. Worse, it demonstrates how "Brushy" confabulated his tales around historical kernels.

And in the service of helping their man, Jameson and Bean, though averse to legitimate history books, read enough to add a few facts - whose omission by Morrison had been too glaring. But that help only worsens their own absurd constructions.

So "Brushy's" childhood has a fabricated "New York Children's Aid Society" caring for "Billy" (What happened to being from Buffalo Gap, and not being from New York, where people cannot shoot?); the Dunn mother death; and "Brushy's" being taken in by her half-sister, "Catherine Ann Bonney," who relocates him to Colorado and "several other locations" (unnamed).

Catherine Ann Bonney then marries a William Antrim in New Mexico. Humorously, child Billy then meets, in Silver City, child Jesse [sic - Jessie] Evans: the Ringman gunslinger of the Lincoln County War (whose youth was actually in Kansas).

Their "Billy" then wanders the West, meeting every famous outlaw, including Bell Starr and the James brothers (sticking with "Brushy's" own grandiose delusions).

But with a post hoc Jameson-Bean fix, "Brushy" bounces back to Arizona in 1877 to murder a "Windy" Cahill; but is incorrectly described as arrested.

Back somehow in New Mexico Territory, "Brushy" calls himself "Billy the Kid," which real Billy never did.

Jameson and Bean quotations, right from their man, yield a window into the chaos of "Brushy's" mad mind. For Lincoln County War history, he ruinously states:

> I remember how it all started ... Lawyer McSween had been hired by the Murphy bunch to prosecute some of the Chisum cowboys for rustling cattle, but when he found out the Chisum boys were only taking back Chisum cows that were stolen by Murphy's men, [McSween] switched sides and joined up with John Tunstall. The Murphy-Dolan Ring operated a store where they sold supplies to the ranches, and then John Tunstall came along and opened his own store. That's where the trouble really started, between the two stores. McSween formed a partnership with Tunstall when he worked the case for Emil Fritz.

Everything stated is wrong.

- Emil Fritz was dead. McSween represented his estate.

- McSween had no partnership with Tunstall.

- McSween had been a Murphy-Dolan lawyer, but for their mercantile business.

- The "Murphy bunch" were themselves stealing Chisum's cattle for their beef contracts with the Mescalaro Indian reservation and Fort Stanton.

- McSween was not working for Murphy and Dolan in late 1876, when Tunstall came; having quit earlier because of distaste for their corruption.

- The Fritz life insurance money case (a) had nothing to do with Tunstall, and (b) was being done by McSween prior to Tunstall's arrival. It became the McSween embezzlement case precipitating Tunstall's murder and the Lincoln County War.

Next comes "Brushy's demolition of pre-war and war episodes.

For the Emil Fritz, life insurance money, embezzlement case, Lawrence Murphy is faked as initiating the attachment of property; though that was done, via Judge Warren Bristol, by Fritz's siblings, who were goaded to do so by James Dolan. Meanwhile, Murphy was merely at his ranch dying of alcoholism.

For John Henry Tunstall's murder scene, "Brushy's" errors place him incorrectly in a wagon; have Roberts-Billy falsely as a witness of the murder itself, and mistakenly have James Dolan present in the on-site posse.

In the post-murder period, when the Regulators pursued Tunstall's assassins, "Brushy's" ignorance has the Regulators - after their capture of William "Buck" Morton and Frank Baker - head west to Lincoln, from that distant Pecos River location, by "the north road, over the mountains." Perhaps "Brushy" got this misconception on his 1950 cribbing trip to Lincoln, courtesy of William Morrison. But he is wrong. The east to west Capitan Mountains may have *looked to "Brushy" like a barrier* to the town, but the road used by the Regulators was a military one, skirting the mountains' eastern terminus, and over flatlands (where, unbeknownst to "Brushy," Morton and Baker were killed).

The Brady murder scene repeats the Morrison book's errors; as does the murder scene of "Buckshot" Roberts, in Blazer's Mill. "Forgotten" by "Brushy," were "Buckshot's" horrific killing of Dick Brewer by a shot to the head, mangling of George Coe's hand, and blasting of John Middleton's chest.

For the Lincoln County War, "Brushy" is unaware of which buildings McSween's men occupied. Nor does he know their assailants. His guessed attackers are Sheriff Peppin "accompanied by several deputies." In actuality, there were almost 50 men from Seven Rivers and Mesilla in Peppin's posse.

Most dramatically, missing - as was in Morrison's book - is the most terrible event of the War: when Commander Dudley brought to Lincoln, with his troops, a howitzer cannon and a Gatling gun. And Dudley personally told McSween that those weapons might be used to blast down his house. All trapped inside the besieged house, including Billy, would have heard that terrifying threat.

Unaware of real military specifics, "Brushy" sticks to his made-up shooting, black soldiers.

"Brushy" states, for the burning building escape: "We opened the back door and looked out just as Bob Beckwith and some of them niggers started to come in." These mistakes are glaring. Bob Beckwith, deputized to serve McSween's arrest warrant, entered the back yard after Billy and others had fled the scene. Bob Beckwith was only with Sheriff Peppin's white possemen. And no troops "came in." Dudley had kept them in his encampment at the northeast end of town. The only shooting soldiers that day were the three, secret, white ones, firing a volley; and seen by Billy in his escape as being behind the adjacent Tunstall store.

And, for Billy's burning building escape, "Brushy" mixes up the crossed *Bonito River* with the Peñasco, 100 miles to the south!

"Brushy" next makes a mess of the Lew Wallace period.

First comes Attorney Huston Chapman's murder, with ungrammatical "Brushy" saying: "Me and Tom were standing right there and saw the whole thing." But what "Brushy" "saw" is wrong: Chapman with Alexander McSween's widow, Susan. In fact, Chapman was alone; in town as hired by Susan McSween for her murder and arson case against Commander Dudley.

For the Billy-Wallace-pardon-meeting, "Brushy's" version reveals Morrison's hoaxing, via Jameson's and Bean's giving the reader "Brushy" flubbing his coaching. Billy's letter to Wallace states that Wallace *offered* a $1000 reward *for his capture*; and Billy offers to testify about the Chapman murder in exchange for a pardon annulling his Lincoln County War murder indictments.

But "Brushy" states: "Wallace had offered a thousand dollars *to the outlaw* if he would turn himself in and testify about the illegal activities of the Dolan faction." "Brushy" continues, "He also wanted me to testify against Colonel Dudley in his court-martial at Stanton." The Dudley testimony was *not* part of the pardon deal, and real Billy - who did testify - knew it was not a Court Martial, but a Court of Inquiry for *possible* Court Martial.

"Brushy's" Wallace fabrications spiral downward from there. Jameson and Bean say for him: "Before leaving, Wallace promised to pardon the Kid if Billy would agree to stand trial for the killing of Sheriff Brady. He even promised to have his own personal lawyer, Ira E. Leonard, represent the young outlaw." These thirty-seven words equal: give-up-"Brushy." Everything is wrong:

1) **Wallace wanted "Billy" to stand trial for the Brady murder**. No. The pardon was to *avoid* standing trial for that murder. More subtly, Wallace and Billy would have known that a trial, with the courts controlled by the Santa Fe Ring, would only have ended in Billy's certain hanging.

2) **The "exchange" for the pardon.** The actual "exchange" was to be Wallace's pardon for Billy's testifying in the Lincoln Grand Jury as an eye-witness to the Chapman murder.

3) **Ira Leonard was *not* Wallace's "personal attorney."** He was widow McSween's attorney, replacing murdered Chapman. Later, he was Billy's first attorney in Billy's Mesilla hanging trial.

"Brushy's" total confusion then reigns. He names Albert Jennings Fountain as Billy's attorney for the 1879 pardon-related legalities. But Fountain was Billy's, April, 1881, court-appointed one (after Ira Leonard withdrew) for Billy's Mesilla hanging trial.

Billy's June of 1879, feigned "escape" from Juan Patrón's house-jail arrest is mixed up with the November 28, 1880 murder of Jim Carlyle at the Greathouse ranch. So "Brushy" has the latter event's White Oaks posse incorrectly tracking Billy after that Patrón house "escape" - which lacked any tracking of Billy.

The Mesilla murder trial has "Brushy" say about the Sheriff Brady murder: "They pinned the whole affair on me." In fact, Billy had co-defendants - John Middleton, Henry Brown, Frank MacNab, Fred Waite, and Jim French - but they had already fled the Territory. But ignorant of the disastrous wake they were leaving, Jameson and Bean sailed on.

## GARRETT GETS THE "BRUSHY" TREATMENT

"Enter Garrett" - as the authors say - and then let "Brushy" get everything wrong.

"Brushy" claims Pat Garrett knew Billy from Texas, though Garrett had left the buffalo range there in early 1878; and Billy had only deposited rustled stock in Texas late in 1878, and possibly through 1880.

"Brushy" also says that Garrett worked at Fort Sumner's Beaver Smith's Saloon, when it was at Hargrove's Saloon.

And "Brushy's" erroneous guess that Garrett tracked down Billy because of the Jim Carlyle killing is repeated.

For Garrett's murder of Billy's friend, Tom O'Folliard, "Brushy" falsely includes in the posse a Tip [sic] McKinney. Tossed in is that McKinney was O'Folliard's cousin. Nothing is true. McKinney was not related to Tom O'Folliard; his nick-name was "Kip;" and he was on no Garrett posses. He was one of Garrett's two deputies present at Billy's killing.

Garrett's Stinking Springs capture of Billy also bites the dust with "Brushy" calling Billy's fellow captives Regulators, when that group had disbanded two years earlier. Except for past-member, Charlie Bowdre, the other captives were actually petty criminals: "Dirty" Dave Rudabaugh, Billy Wilson, and Tom Pickett.

## DEATH SCENES GALORE

Jameson's and Bean's foray into "Brushy's" discrepant death scene, unintentionally shows why Morrison was circumspect. "Brushy," it appears, elaborated his errors to absurdity - and without reconciliation to the historical one. But Jameson and Bean deposit the different versions throughout the text; so a reader with a memory disorder might not notice. [APPENDIX: 37]

If one does remember, one receives: (1) a victim in the bedroom shot accidentally by Garrett, and concealed by Garrett's staying "locked in the murder room" with Poe and McKinney as "guards;" (2) a bedroom victim, rumored in town as "not Billy the Kid;" (3) a shooting of Billy Barlow, *near* Maxwell's bedroom *and* the hanging beef by someone unidentified, while "Brushy," running out, is wounded in the jaw, back, and scalp; (4) a vertiginously confusing rendition with Garrett and Poe quoting the bedroom shooting and the carpenter shop vigil over the body; accompanied by "Brushy's" contradictory quotes of a dead Billy Barlow being on a back porch with unclear murderer; (5) a Jameson-Bean version with a Maxwell bedroom murder by Garrett, and Maxwell and Deluvina viewing the body, but with nit-picking of Garrett's and Poe's reporting; and (6) a rumor-anecdote of a 1944 interview with

Attorney Albert Jennings Fountain's son, who says Garrett told him a different story - but confirming that Garrett shot the Kid!

Leaving out that the historical death scene is well confirmed, that Billy's body was identified by 200 townspeople and the Coroner's Jury, and that Billy Barlow is not real, "Brushy's" own errors in his long verbatim transcripts are the undoings of his confabulated death scenes.

The phase of the moon alone destroys "Brushy's" creations. He is unaware of the near-daylight from the almost full moon on July 14, 1881. So "Brushy" confabulates: "It was dark that night, but there was enough moonlight to make shadows."

That "dark" night would later become my clue to identifying "Brushy's" believers, who would repeat his devastating error.

Weird attacks occur with a barrage of gunfire which injures "Brushy" – but they stayed unknown in the actual small town.

Also, "Brushy" does not know the configuration of the Maxwell house, or the location of its side of beef. (It was at the north porch: the opposite side of the mansion from Maxwell's room, at the south porch.) So, in his death scene version (3), he wrongly calls the beef "hanging near Maxwell's bedroom;" and in version (4) he puts the hanging beef wrongly at the back (west) porch, which he calls the "trap" - ignoring the real Maxwell bedroom trap at the southeast.

"Brushy" also has no idea of the Maxwell property's or Fort Sumner's lay-out. Thus, after hearing "pistol shots," he describes running "from Silva's [the foreman] into Maxwell's backyard" to shoot. In fact, that very long journey to the back of the Maxwell would have put "Brushy" nowhere near Maxwell's bedroom or the hanging beef - though he says he encountered assailants there.

So, unaware that the town lay around an open parade ground, "Brushy" presents his flight "into the gallery of a nearby adobe house;" when, in fact, there was no "nearby" house. Flight would have required crossing the west perimeter of the parade ground, occupied by the mansion and covering the 300 yard open square, to end up at residential buildings at the east or south sides.

Naïve that "Brushy's" renditions made no sense, and ignoring the historical record as usual, Jameson and Bean proclaim: "None of the so-called facts relating to the death of Billy the Kid at the hands of Sheriff Pat Garrett have ever been supported by concrete, or even competent, evidence."

## *RESEARCHING LIFE AFTER DEATH*

Calling themselves "researchers," W.C. Jameson and Frederick Bean check "Brushy's" claims about his post-July 14, 1881 life. That life continues pre-July 14, 1881 confabulations. "Brushy" had provided Morrison with every famous name he could come up with as his next set of associates.

But dead serious Jameson and Bean seek evidence of "Brushy's" being a Buffalo Bill Cody performer, a Pinkerton detective, a bronco rider, and a U.S. Deputy Marshal; or being recognized by the Dalton Gang as Billy the Kid (who had no way of recognizing Billy); or riding with Roosevelt as a Rough Rider; or going to Mexico, where its President in 1899 seized his ranch in a gunfight; or returning to the United States to organize his own wild west show; or returning to Mexico to fight in the Mexican Revolution; or riding with Pancho Villa.

Predictably, Jameson and Bean discovered nothing. But they surmise that their drawing a blank was because "Brushy" used aliases - though avoiding Billy the Kid was enough! And "Brushy" could have stuck with good ol' Oliver P. (or L.) Roberts.

## *JAMESON AND BEAN AND SHERLOCK HOLMES*

Jameson-Bean "research" continues with "Evidence For and Against William Henry Roberts as Billy the Kid;" though that begins with their conclusion that one could guess: "There exists a great deal of evidence that leads to a conclusion for some that William Henry Roberts was, in fact, Billy the Kid."

Their "investigation" will involve: (1) physical similarities with the tintype; (2) "Brushy's" revelations; (3) anecdotal evidence; and (4) identification affidavits.

## PHYSICAL SIMILARITIES AND REVELATIONS

"Physical similarities" between "Brushy" and Billy the Kid's tintype parrot William Morrison's book, but preview Jameson's and Bean's own photo-analysis to come.

"Revelations" are the "he-knew-things-never-printed" trick. Added will be Lincoln town itself, from "Brushy's" 1950 field-trip there with Morrison; as well as "Brushy's" miscellaneous (already debunked) claims, like "shooting black soldiers," and the federal versus territorial indictment for the Mesilla hanging trial.

# LINCOLN REVELATIONS

About the town of Lincoln, real Billy's memories would have been profuse and detailed, since the most dramatic events of his life happened there. And the town is intact to this day. Billy could have walked around the Tunstall store and showed the location of its adobe wall's Brady ambush; pointed out the location of "Squire" Wilson's house, where he met with Governor Wallace; showed Juan Patrón's house with its feigned arrest room; and located the Wortley Hotel to the west and the Isaac Ellis house to the east.

But "Brushy's" Lincoln "revelations" concern only two sites: the Lincoln County courthouse-jail and the McSween house. Unrecognized by Jameson and Bean, "Brushy's" descriptions only show the failure of his 1950 "educational tour" around town by William Morrison.

As to the courthouse, Jameson and Bean praise "Brushy's" statement about the commonly known, later addition of outside stairs to the second story balcony. But when it comes to esoterica, "Brushy" puts the south-west armory room - from which Billy stole weapons in his jailbreak - incorrectly in the northwest room where other prisoners were held. No critical details - like the location of the ring chaining Billy to the floor, or the east window ledge for ambushing Deputy Bob Olinger, or the stairway on which Deputy James Bell was shot - are present.

The McSween house fares no better; though Jameson and Bean inscrutably state, "Roberts' intimacy with the layout of the McSween house and yard could only have come from personal experience." (Having been burned down, its lot is now bare, and its floor plan is unknown.)

And "Brushy's" "intimacy" yields only that the kitchen had a window, the corral had a fence, and there was a woodpile. For filler, he concocts Lincoln County War siege events; but gets them wrong. He has "Murphy men ... just across the river" - where no attackers were.

Missing are any intimate specifics of July 19, 1878: the holocaust day in which the McSween house was burned around Billy; his fellow fighters; Alexander McSween; his wife; and her sister, Elizabeth Shield, with her five children. What rooms did they stay in? Where did the fire start? Where was the gunpowder keg that exploded in the blaze? From what room did they escape? Where did they run? Where did Billy see the shooting white soldiers? Obviously, all this intimate information is missing.

# MISCELLANEOUS REVELATIONS

W.C. Jameson and Frederick Bean provide more "Brushy" confabulated "revelations" than Morrison had dared to reveal.

About the start of the Lincoln County War, they write: "Roberts told Morrison that, following the killing of Tunstall, he, and several of the Regulators, escorted Alexander McSween to his house in Lincoln. After fighting off the sheriff's posse, most of the Regulators took refuge in McSween's house while the remainder sought shelter at Tunstall's store."
Everything is wrong. Fused are the Tunstall murder day of February 18, 1878 and the first War day of July 14, 1878.
On that War day, when 60 McSweens rode into Lincoln, a few Regulators, including Billy, joined McSween, already in his house. The other Regulators were in Tunstall's store, the Montaño building, the Patrón house, and the Isaac Ellis building. And they did not take "refuge." They were strategically positioned from west to east to hold the town peacefully. Then fighting began with Seven Rivers and John Kinney's men joining Sheriff Peppin's side.

The "revelation" of the escape from the courthouse-jail is a freebie for "Brushy," since no one knows how Billy did it. So "Brushy" claims his thumb trick for slipping out of handcuffs. (Noteworthy for foiling the Billy the Kid Case hoaxers use of "Brushy" as their potential "Billy," "Brushy" *does not* claim Garrett as friend and accomplice.)

The Jim Carlyle murder "revelation" is lifted from the Billy-Wallace letter already discussed.

A "revelation" incident after the Stinking Springs capture - historically related by Garrett posseman, Jim East - portrays Billy's farewell to the Maxwell family. "Brushy's" telling joins known information to his elaborations. He has "an Indian servant girl" take him to the meeting, and, oddly, give him her scarf - for which he gifts her with the famous tintype! This mish-mash draws on Walter Noble Burns's *The Saga of Billy the Kid*, where Maxwell family servant, Deluvina, knits Billy a scarf - another indication that Roberts could study-up. But real Billy would have used her name; the tintype had already been given to Dan Dedrick; and East's real punch line was Billy's farewell to his truelove, Paulita.

As to that Maxwell family farewell story being a "revelation," Jameson and Bean say the Jim East letter, from which it came, was unknown until 1949. That is wrong. In 1920, Charles Siringo, another Garrett posseman from Texas, had it in his book, *The History of Billy the Kid*. It was available to "Brushy"/Morrison.

Tiny tales make next "revelations."

In one, a Severo Gallegos, in old age, claims to have helped Billy catch the horse for his courthouse-jail escape, and tie a rope to the saddle - unaware that it was a *blanket* tied to the saddle so Billy's severed ankle chains would not frighten the animal.

Another anecdote has a Mrs. Bernardo Salazar, say that Yginio's cousin cut off of Billy's leg irons after the escape.

These "revelations" further expose Morrison's hoaxing techniques. In 1949, he conducted interviews in Lincoln. The Gallegos and Salazar anecdotes, collected then (as Morrison cites in *Alias Billy the Kid*), clearly became "Brushy's" "coaching."

## ANECDOTAL EVIDENCE

After "revelations," comes "anecdotal evidence," which would be polite to call preposterous.

One learns that, once, on a Texas street, a mother called to her child, "Billy!" And Roberts turned. (The authors forget that *they and he* claimed his name was both "Brushy *Bill*" and "William!")

Another tale is that, in 1990, the grandson of a one-time Pinkerton detective, said, in 1945, his grandfather cried out to Roberts, "Bonnie [sic] ... you're under arrest." (This proves that in 1945 there were at least two eccentrics in Texas.)

And, in 1983, an unnamed Texan wrote a letter saying that Garrett's blind daughter told him Pat did not shoot Billy.

Similarly, in 1948, someone told someone in Las Cruces, New Mexico, that Billy was not shot by Garrett, because he saw him in Mexico in 1914. He knew Billy, he said, when they lived in Silver City from 1868 to 1871. (Real Billy lived there from 1873 to 1875.)

Yginio Salazar is cited as believing Billy had not been killed. That is true. Yginio, however, had no first-hand knowledge, living 150 miles from Fort Sumner, in Las Tablas. His belief was based on a visit he received, in old age, from a teacher from Mexico - not "Brushy." That pretender, with forgotten name, disappeared. By then, Yginio was an unreliable morphine addict, from pain of the two, Lincoln County War bullets, still in his back.

# AFFIDAVITS

Five identification affidavits follow; proving merely - like William Morrison did in *Alias Billy the Kid* - that you could get random people, unrelated to the historical events, to swear that "Brushy" was Billy.

# CONCLUDING EVIDENCE

Jameson and Bean end chivalrously with "Evidence Against William Henry Roberts as Billy the Kid." As can be surmised, this is a short section.

They proclaim that the "only available evidence" that Billy Bonney died on July 14, 1881 is "Garrett's word" that he had killed him.

So their foregone conclusion is: the case "for Roberts being Billy the Kid is considerably stronger than the case against."

# *PIECE DE RESISTANCE: PHOTO-COMPARISON*

W.C. Jameson and Frederick Bean's 1990 "Photo-Comparison Study," as their "scientific research," was the basis of Jameson's boasting that "history needed to be rewritten" in his 2003, *True West* magazine article, "Was Brushy Bill Really Billy the Kid? Experts face off over new evidence."

For that "Photo-Comparison," "Brushy" would be compared to Billy in the famous tintype. This is a good place to recall that Morrison's book had pictures of young Roberts - like young Billy in the tintype. But Jameson and Bean gave their photo-expert "Brushy's" death-year picture for the comparison!

Jameson's and Bean's precautions were unnecessary. They had found their own version of the Billy the Kid Case hoaxers' forensic expert, Dr. Henry Lee. Jameson's and Bean's man was Dr. Scott T. Acton, at the Department of Electrical and Computer Engineering and the Laboratory for Vision Systems and Advanced Graphic Laboratory at the University of Texas.

But there was a starting-gate problem. A year before their photometric analysis, one had already been done by a Thomas G. Kyle for the Lincoln County Heritage Trust: the museum which, at that time, housed the Billy tintype. Kyle had concluded that "Brushy" was not Billy based on eye position, nose, chin, and ears.

To Jameson and Bean, as cited earlier, that explanation meant conspiracy: either "economic" for tourism or historical for "status quo." So they question Thomas G. Kyle's equipment and statistical methods. Then they get mean, saying that, for Kyle, the whole thing had been "more like a hobby." Finally, eyeballing the photos of "Brushy" and Billy the Kid themselves, they conclude that the ears should not have been used!

Then comes their "good guy" in "The Acton Study."

Jameson and Bean enthuse about Dr. Scott Acton's "state of the art facilities," and inventory his equipment. Embarrassingly revealed, thus, is Acton's shockingly old computer system from 1972 and 1976, and unimpressive 92% success rate (with "success" not being defined).

Helpfully, Jameson and Bean provide Acton's data, along with his quote that "the similarity between the facial structure of Roberts and the man in the ... tintype is indeed amazing."

Amazing is Acton's conclusion. His fakery starts with "mouths." Old "Brushy's" photo has a fish-tail mustache, whose blunt-cut length *covers his mouth*. Yet, in Acton's "mouth breadth" measurements, Billy gets an 80 to "Brushy's" 82. And Billy's "mouth" is as unreal as "Brushy's," since Acton used the deteriorated tintype in which dark spotting mars the mouth.

It gets worse. Acton created - and the authors dutifully reproduce - a "restoration of the Dedrick-Upham photograph of Billy the Kid." Instead of *correcting* the mouth's spotting defects, Acton uses them to elongate real Billy's small mouth! And "Brushy's" "restoration" uses his mustache's shadow to manufacture a long mouth. These "mouths" yield the "80 to 82!"

Wisely, Acton follows the Jameson-Bean "law," and omits Roberts's ears, unlike Billy's; though in Billy's Acton-restored tintype, generously added is real Billy's missing left ear, along with added rolled rims on both ears - emulating "Brushy's!"

All this leaves one with an opinion of Dr. Scott T. Acton, identical to Jameson's and Bean's opinion of Thomas G. Kyle. And Morrison's photos of Roberts at 27 and 14, look nothing like Billy.

Jameson and Bean finish unexpectedly subdued, claiming only that the men are "a very close match."

Amusingly, pretender John Miller's author also "proved" *he* was Billy by *her* photo-analysis and reconstructions!

In short, at the end of the Jameson and Bean game, the score remained: "Brushy" zero.

# "BRUSHY" AND THE BILLY THE KID CASE HOAXERS

*HOAXBUST: The Billy the Kid Case hoax's flirtation with "Brushy Bill" Roberts began from day one. As the pretender with the most publicity and believers, he provided "survival suspicion" for the hoaxers' Pat Garrett as murderer. But by using "Brushy," the hoaxers permanently elevated his long-discredited claims.*

## *"BRUSHY'S" SECOND ACT*

Oliver "Brushy Bill" Roberts was elevated to mainstream from loonybin by the Billy the Kid Case hoaxers right from their first national announcement on the June 5, 2003 front page of the *New York Times*, with headline declaring "122 Years Later, The Lawman Are Still Chasing Billy the Kid." In it, "Brushy Bill" believer, Jannay Valdez, owning a Canton, Texas, museum for "Brushy" as "Billy," is quoted: "I'm absolutely convinced that Garrett killed someone else and that Brushy Bill was the Kid."

After that, "Brushy's" name kept popping up in hoaxers' press. And the hoax's "official historian" Professor Paul Hutton's 2004 TV fake documentary for the Discovery Channel titled "Investigating History: Billy the Kid," "Brushy" gets plugged by author-believer, W.C. Jameson. And, though I saw "Brushy" as only a hoaxers' ploy for "survival suspicion" since they had no actual history for support, I worried that they might make "Brushy" "Billy the Kid" if their other publicity stunts failed.

As already cited, "Brushy" appeared in the exhumation petitions of Attorney Bill Robins III. For example, on February 26, 2004, Attorney Robins, with Attorneys David Sandoval and Mark Acuña (to provide the New Mexico law licenses which Robins lacked, being from Texas), filed the "De Baca County District Court Case No. CV-2004-00005, Petition for the Exhumation of Billy the Kid's Remains." [APPENDIX: 19]

"Brushy" makes his grand entrance under its topic "IV. Historical Background." With hoaxer style, Robins leads in with vague "suspicion," followed by pseudo-history hinting at "Brushy" as surviving the July 14, 1881 Garrett shooting. "Brushy" is, thus, used by Robins to argue for Billy's exhumation as follows:

This was also a time whose history was not accurately nor completely written ... For generations now, the life of Billy the Kid has been the subject of historical debate. Perhaps the most significant lingering question involves whether Billy the Kid was indeed shot by Sheriff Pat Garrett in an ambush **one dark night** [author's boldface] in Ft. Sumner or whether the Kid went on to live a long and peace-abiding life elsewhere.

Who says that a "lingering question" about the killing exists, except conspiracy theorists and hoaxers? And only "Brushy" himself called the ambush on a "dark night;" saying: "It was dark that night, but there was enough moonlight to make shadows."

Attorney Robins continued in that petition:

The debate has been sparked at various times in the past by at least two individuals who laid claim to his identity. **Ollie** "Brushy Bill" Roberts [author's boldface] resided in Hico, Texas and claimed to be Billy the Kid. John Miller, in Arizona also died still claiming he was Billy the Kid. Co-Petitioners are in the initial phases of pursuing exhumations of these individuals as well.

The investigation [Billy the Kid Case] has renewed questions as to whether Billy the Kid lies buried at the fabled grave-site in Ft. Sumner. Allowing the exhumation of the remains at Ft. Sumner grave site for extraction of DNA to be compared with that of Ms. Antrim's will likely finally provide definitive answers to this historical quandary.

There exists no "historical quandary;" but dear "Ollie" was definitely being plugged by Attorney Robins as a real contender.

## "BRUSHY" IS BIG IN THE CASE NO. 2003-274 FILE

### SECRET "SEVENTY-SEVEN DAYS OF DOUBT" PAPER

More evidence of the Billy the Kid Case hoaxers' use of "Brushy Bill" Roberts came in my 2007, ongoing, open records violation litigation against Lincoln County Sheriff Rick Virden, and his deputies: Sullivan and Sederwall. While refusing all requested forensic records, Virden, on September 3, 2008, gave an expurgated version of his Case # 2003-274 file for a deposition. Almost a third of its 192 pages were articles on "Brushy Bill!" And it had a heretofore secret document: a precursor of the eventual Probable Cause Statement for Case # 2003-274.

Significantly, in that precursor, "Brushy's" "survival" is given as *key* "evidence" of Garrett's not killing Billy - meaning that "Brushy's" fabrication *was originally* the hoaxers' probable cause that Pat Garrett was a murderer! That made "Brushy's" creation, Billy Barlow, Garrett's innocent victim, and the corpse in Billy the Kid's Fort Sumner grave.

That secret "Brushy"-backing document was titled: "Lincoln County Sheriff's Office, Lincoln County New Mexico, Case: William H. Bonney, a.k.a. William Antrim, a.k.a. The Kid, a.k.a. Billy the Kid: An Investigation into the events of April 28, 1881 through July 14, 1881 - seventy-seven days of doubt."

I called it the "Seventy-Seven Days of Doubt Document." Abandoned, it had no date. "LATEST" is handwritten on its front page, as if drafts were attempted. Typed-in for future signatures are: "Tom Sullivan: Sheriff, Lincoln County Sheriff's Office; and Steven M. Sederwall: Deputy Sheriff, Lincoln County Sheriff's Office." Since the final Probable Cause Statement for Case # 2003-274 has no mention of "Brushy Bill" Roberts and John Miller, something must have spooked the hoaxers into hiding this initial pretender thrust, since John Miller is half-heartedly there too.

## AUTHORING "SEVENTY-SEVEN DAYS OF DOUBT"

Though the author is a mystery, the sentiment is of a "Brushy" believer. "Brushy" is even called "William Henry," not Oliver P. Roberts's actual name, as in W.C. Jameson's and Frederick Bean's construct for their *The Return of the Outlaw Billy the Kid.*

The "Seventy-Seven Days of Doubt Document" dove-tails with Silver City Attorney Sherry Tippett's already-cited, December 17, 2003 letter to Sullivan, Sederwall, and Graves about her needing their "preparing the probable cause segment of the brief." So, by that December 17th, the "Seventy-Seven Days" version seems to have been rejected. And by January 5, 2004, she had the final version (plus the Overton affidavit) used as "Plaintiffs' Exhibits 1 and 2" for her "Billy the Kid's Pre-Hearing Brief" for the Catherine Antrim exhumation. And that final Probable Cause Statement is utterly different from the "Seventy-Seven Days," which is simplistic and footnoteless - clearly by a different author.

More important, that "Seventy-Seven Days Document" points to a hoax formulation of "Brushy Bill" as Billy - with exhumations to prove it. And the final and used Probable Cause Statement entirely conceals that purpose - relying on future faked DNA to achieve that end.

So who was its author? What about Jannay Valdez? But the "Seventy-Seven Days Document" contains a mistake "Brushy" aficionado and museum owner, Valdez, would not make: getting wrong William V. Morrison's "contact person" to "Brushy."

It states:

> Joe Hines told Morrison his name, Hines, was an alias. Hines claimed his real name was Jesse [sic] Evans and he was a survivor of the Lincoln County War.

Inner circle believers say Hines's real name was Jimmy McDonald, not Jessie Evans. And the contact person for "Brushy" was J. Frank Dalton (who they think was Jesse <u>James!</u>).

What about Steve Sederwall? Even before his 2003 "Mayor's Report" he knew it was a "Brushy" case. In early 2003, he told Judge Bob Hefner, a major "Brushy" advocate, that the Billy the Kid Case's plan was to compare the mother's DNA with "Brushy's." But Sederwall is unlikely. He knew enough to avoid mistakes like incorrectly calling Paulita, Peter Maxwell's "teenage daughter" - not his sister. And Sederwall later said he wrote the actual Probable Cause Statement (though it seems he got help).

The obvious potential writer of the "Seventy-Seven Days of Doubt Document is amateur historian Attorney Bill Robins III, since needed was a "Brushy Bill" advocate formulating a murder case against Pat Garrett: a perfect fit.

But was Robins also a contributor to the actually used Probable Cause Statement? He did mimic its verbiage a month before its December signing. Louie Fecteau's *Albuquerque Journal*, "No Kidding: Governor Taps Lawyer for Billy," of November 19, 2003, has Robins say: "[I]t was hard to tell who the good guys were." The Probable Cause Statement starts: "[I]t was hard to tell who the good guys were."

And the "Seventy-Seven Days Document," like starry-eyed W.C. Jameson, showcases "Brushy," with his "dark moonless night" of the Barlow murder - and survival.

My bet is for Bill Robins as authoring the "Seventy-Seven Days of Doubt Document." And, as such, it is a testament to his belief that "Brushy" was Billy the Kid.

Since the "Seventy-Seven Days of Doubt Document" would later help my cracking the Billy the Kid Case hoax, it is presented in full below. It is also important for its long quote from "Brushy" himself, showing the floridness of his confabulations for a murder scene and for his invented victim, Billy Barlow.

**************

## LINCOLN COUNTY SHERIFF'S OFFICE
## LINCOLN COUNTY, NEW MEXICO

**Case: *William H. Bonney, a.k.a.* William Antrim, a.k.a. The Kid, *a.k.a.* Billy the Kid**

**An Investigation into the events of April 28, 1881 through July 14, 1881 - seventy-seven days of doubt.**

Just minutes after twelve, noon, on April 28, 1881, two lawmen lay dead, in the yard of the courthouse in Lincoln, New Mexico, from gunshot wounds. In less time then [sic] it took the New Mexico breeze to clear the gunsmoke, history was clouded with the myth of the shooting and escape of William H. Bonney, a.k.a. Billy the Kid from the make-shift jail, where he awaited a date with the hangman.

The following is a thumbnail sketch of the most widely excepted [sic] account of the events of the escape, capture and shooting death of William H. Bonney a.k.a. Billy the Kid.

### The Last Days of William H. Bonney

On August 17, 1877, in George Atkin's cantina near Camp Grant, Arizona, William H. Bonney, who answered to "The Kid" found himself in an altercation with Francis P. "Windy" Cahill over cards or Cahill's woman, no one is quite sure as newspapers report both. It's reported that Windy Cahill called The Kid a "pimp", and in response The Kid dubbed Cahill a "sonofabitch". Infuriated, Cahill reportedly grabbed the Kid and The Kid shoved his pistol into Cahill's stomach, sending a hot round into his belly. With Cahill on the floor, The Kid fled on a stolen horse. Cahill died the next day. A coroner's jury headed by Miles Wood found the shooting by The Kid to be *"criminal and unjustifiable"*. The Kid now being a bona fide outlaw drifted across the line into New Mexico's Lincoln County where he signed on as a cowboy working for London born rancher John Tunstall.

Tunstall and his lawyer friend Alexander McSween had decided to challenge the chock-hold [sic] monopoly L.G. Murphy & Company had on Lincoln County. Murphy and his associates, with the backing of the "Santa Fe Ring" ran Lincoln County as they pleased and verticality [sic] unchecked until Tunstall's challenge. The Santa Fe Ring, with their powerful political and financial backing and through Murphy controlled the sheriff, maintained a buddy-buddy relationship with the military and appropriated by means both legal and illegal most of the government money out of the Mescalaro Apache Indian Agency near Fort Stanton. When Tunstall wouldn't back down and his challenge became to [sic] powerful for the Murphy faction to turn their heads to, Tunstall was killed. His death on February 18, 1878 fanned the spark that raged into the white-hot flame that became the famed and bloody Lincoln County War.

As history goes Bonney was insignificant as a man, but there exist [sic] no better example of how legends of the west are born and continue to grow. By participating in a number of bloody shootouts, included [sic] the assassination of Lincoln County Sheriff William Brady and one of his deputies, on April 1, 1878, Bonney was catapulted from his status of an unknown drifter to the undisputed leader of the Tunstall-McSween faction and into history becoming bigger the [sic] life.

**[AUTHOR'S NOTE: Though starting when Bonney was 17 ½ (not his last days!), this flaunted "historical knowledge" is fake. Billy was never the leader of the Tunstall-McSween faction. The writer tries to blur history and "legend," to fabricate that actual history was legend. Beyond that, everything is irrelevant to any probable cause statement.]**

After newly elected Lincoln County Sheriff Pat Garrett captured Bonney at Stinking Springs, east of Fort Sumner, just before Christmas 1880, Bonney was held in the jail in Santa Fe for several months and then taken to La Mesilla, New Mexico for trial.

The Dona Ana County, District Court records reveal on April 13, 1881, William H. Bonney was convicted of the April 1, 1878 murder of Lincoln County Sheriff William Brady. United States District Judge, Warren Henry Bristol, of the Third Judicial District, sentenced Bonney to be confined in Lincoln County until Friday, May 13, 1881.

Looking down from the bench, the judge proclaimed, *"between 9 a.m. and 3 p.m., William Bonney, alias Kid, alias William Antrim, be taken from such prison to some suitable and convenient place of execution within said county of Lincoln, by Sheriff of such county and that then and there, on that day and between the aforesaid hours thereof, by the sheriff of said county of Lincoln, he, the said William Bonney, alias Kid, alias William Antrim, be hanged by the neck until his body be dead."*

On April 21, 1881, Bonney was transported back to Lincoln under heavy guard. Because Lincoln had no adequate jail Bonney was incarcerated in the upstairs of the old Murphy-Dolan store, recently bought by the county to be used as the courthouse. A staircase led up to a hallway that ran north to south across the middle section of the building. The room ahead and to the left of the hallway was being used as the sheriff's office. Off the sheriff's office, with access only through the sheriff's office was the room where Bonney was confined.

With no bars on the windows of this room, Sheriff Garrett had special leg shackles made, and Bonney was chained to the hardwood floor at all times. In addition, Garrett assigned Lincoln County Sheriffs Deputy J.W. Bell and Deputy United States Marshall [sic] Bob Olinger, to guard the prisoner twenty-four hours a day. On the floor Bonney's guards drew a chalk line across the center of the room, a line which Bonney was forbidden to cross or he would be shot by the guards.

On Wednesday, April 27, 1881 Sheriff Pat Garrett left Lincoln on a tax-collecting mission to White Oaks, New Mexico. Just after twelve, noon, the next day, Thursday, April 28, Deputy United States Marshall [sic] Olinger escorted all the prisoners with the exception of Bonney to the Wortley Hotel, across the street from the courthouse, for their midday meal, leaving Deputy Sheriff Bell in charge of Bonney.

No eye witness record can be found of the escape of Bonney with the exception of the following statement made by the courthouse caretaker Gottfried Gauss, published in the *Lincoln County Leader* on January 15, 1890, nearly a decade later.

*I was crossing the yard behind the courthouse, when I heard a shot fired then a tussle upstairs in the courthouse, somebody hurrying downstairs, and deputy sheriff Bell emerging from the door running toward me. He ran right into my arms, expired the same moment, and I laid him down, dead. That I was in a hurry to secure assistance, or perhaps to save myself, everybody will believe.*

*When I arrived at the garden gate leading to the street, in front of the courthouse, I saw the other deputy sheriff Olinger, coming out of the hotel opposite, with the four or five other county prisoners, where they had taken their dinner. I called to him to come quick. He did so, leaving his prisoners in front of the hotel. When he had come up close to me, and while I was standing not a yard apart, I told him that I was just after laying Bell dead on the ground in the yard behind. Before he could reply, he was struck by a well-directed shot fired from a window above us, and fell dead at my feet. I ran for my life to reach my room and safety, when Billy the Kid called to me: "Don't run, I wouldn't hurt you – I am alone, and master not only of the courthouse, but also of the town, for I will allow nobody to come near us." "You go," he said, "and saddle one of Judge (Ira) Leonard's horses, and I will clear out as soon as I have the shackles loosened from my legs." With a little prospecting pick I had thrown to him through the window he was working for at least an hour, and could not accomplish more than to free one leg. He came to the conclusion to wait a better chance, tie one shackle to his waistbelt, and start out. Meanwhile I had saddled a small skittish pony belonging to Billy Burt (the county clerk), as there was no other horse available, and had also, by Billy's command, tied a pair of red blankets behind the saddle ...*

*When Billy went down the stairs at last, on passing the body of Bell he said, "I'm sorry I had to kill him but I couldn't help it." On passing the body of Olinger he gave him a tip with his boot, saying, "You are not going to round me up again." And so Billy the Kid started out that evening, after he had shaken hands with everybody around and after having a little difficulty in mounting on account of the shackle on his leg, he went on his way rejoicing.*

There are numerous theories about the killing of Deputy J.W. Bell. One is that he was coming up the stairs when shot. Another theory is Bell was running down the stairs and was at the bottom of the stairs and heading to the doorway when Bonney shot him. Garrett's testimony seems to be the most solid. Garrett says, *"Bell was hit under the right arm, the bullet passing through his body and coming out under the left arm. The ball had hit the wall on Bell's right, caromed passed through his body, and buried itself in an adobe (wall) on the left. There was no other proof besides the marks on the walls."*

Garrett later said of Olinger, that he was *"hit in the right shoulder, breast and side. He was literally riddled by thirty-six buckshot."* Each pellet weighed four grams - nearly a quarter pound of lead in all hit Olinger.

It's hard to determine how many shots were fired at Bell from Bonney's pistol. In the 1920's Maurice G. Fulton saw the building and states there were *"any number of bullet holes"*. Fulton had a photograph taken in the 1930's prior to the restoration, which shows three.

With only two people on the stairway that day numerous versions of what happened have been brought forth, and debated. One theory in the Kid's escape is that he slipped his irons, which were double the usual weight, over his small wrists and hands. He turned on Bell striking the deputy over the head with the irons and grabbing the deputy's pistol. This theory could have come from the following article.

In the *Grand County Herald's*, May 14, 1881 edition an article appeared quoting an "anonymous bystander" as testifying about the Kid's escape. *He had at his command eight revolvers and six guns. He stood on the upper porch in front of the building and talked with the people who were in Wortley's, but he would not let anyone come towards him. He told the people that he did not want to kill Bell but, as he had to. He said he grabbed Bell's revolver and told him to hold up his hands and surrender; that Bell decided to run and he had to kill him. He declared he was "standing pat" against the world; and while he did not wish to kill anybody, if anybody interfered with his attempt to escape, he would kill him.*

In this statement the "anonymous bystander" claims Bonney says he took Bell's pistol from him and used it to kill the deputy. In Garrett's book *The Authentic Life of Billy the Kid,* Garrett writes this about the escape:

*From circumstances, indications, information from Geiss (also spelled Gauss – the courthouse caretaker) and the Kid's admissions, the popular conclusion is that:*

*At the Kid's request, Bell accompanied him down stairs and to the back corral. As they returned, Bell allowed the Kid to get considerably in advance. As the Kid turned on the landing of the stairs, he was hidden from Bell. He was light and active, and with a few noiseless bounds, reached the head of the stairs, turned to his right, put his shoulder to the door of the room used as an armory (thought locked, this door was well known to open by a firm push), entered, seized a six-shooter, returned to the head of the stairs just as Bell faced him on the landing of the stair-case, some twelve steps beneath, and fired. Bell turned, ran out into the corral and towards the little gate. He fell dead before reaching it. The Kid ran to the window at the south end of the hall, saw Bell fall, then slipped his handcuffs over his hands, threw them at the body, and said: "Here, damn you, take these, too."*

Garrett's account seems to have to [sic] many holes to be taken as truth in this matter. At the beginning of Chapter XXII, where this account is found Garrett begins, *On the evening of April 28, 1881, Olinger took all the other prisoners across the street to supper, leaving Bell in charge of the Kid in the guard room.* It is a known fact that the escape did not happen in the evening as Garrett writes but just after noon.

Frederick Nolan, in his commentary notes at the side of the page in this book, points out the following: *The "popular" conclusion set forth here - that Bell would have allowed the Kid latitude and time he needed to perform these maneuvers - has already been examined. That he could have moved "noiselessly" when wearing manacles and leg irons defies belief. And would Billy have waited until after killing Bell before he "slipped his handcuffs over his hands?" Either the Kid struck Bell over the head with his handcuffs, grabbed Bell's gun and killed him with it, or, far more plausibly, someone hid a pistol in the outhouse privy, which Billy retrieved and, when they got inside, killed Bell with it.*

When Garrett describes The Kid shooting Olinger he says that ... *Olinger appeared at the gate leading into the yard, as Geiss appeared at the little corral gate and said, "Bob, The Kid has killed Bell."* At the same instant the Kid's voice was heard above: "Hello, old boy," said he. "Yes, and he's killed me too," exclaimed Olinger, and fell dead with eighteen buckshot in his right shoulder and breast and side.*

It is doubtful that Olinger would have time to say the words that

Garrett contributes [sic] to him before the Kid cut him down, making Garrett's account difficult to be taken as true accounting of the events.

[AUTHOR'S NOTE: Though lacking sly finesse of the final Probable Cause Statement, this author likewise uses Garrett's ghostwritten, dime-novel-style book to discredit him. But it is irrelevant to Garrett as a murderer.]

Garrett also says about The Kid in his account – *He took deliberate aim and fired the other barrel, the charge taking effect in nearly the same place as the first; then breaking the gun across the railway of the balcony, he threw the pieces at Olinger, saying: "Take it, damn you, you won't follow me any more with that gun."*

This doubtful this happened. [sic] The account of The Kid breaking Olinger's shotgun on the balcony is not found elsewhere. Added to the fact that Olinger's shotgun was a Whitney, serial number SN903, and is now on loan to the *Texas Ranger Hall of Fame* in Waco, Texas from the James H. Earl Collection; the shotgun is in tact [sic].

[AUTHOR'S NOTE: Error. The Deputy Olinger, Whitney, double-barrel shotgun is broken at its waist, and repaired, at some unknown time, by a wrapping of copper wire. Its curator at the Texas Ranger Museum, attesting to the description, is Don Agler. This is another irrelevant attempt to discredit Garrett.]

The version which seems the more popular, is that Bonney, retrieved a pistol that had been hidden in the outhouse by a "friend." History has theories but no firm answers to the identity of the "friend" who put the pistol in the outhouse.

[AUTHOR'S NOTE: Error. This seems to be a confusion of the Bell killing with Olinger's, for which the Whitney was used.]

After the Kid shot and killed both of his guards he gather [sic] weapons, and left Lincoln about 3 p.m. on a stolen horse. The Kid's whereabouts from the date of his escape until just before his death, as nearly every aspect of the case, is still debated. The Kid later showed up in Ft. Sumner, New Mexico. Pete Maxwell's teenage daughter, Paulita,

[AUTHOR'S NOTE: Error. Paulita was Peter Maxwell's sister. Also, using Paulita contradicts the "love tales" of "Brushy Bill" (Celsa) and John Miller (Isadora), and eliminates them as Billy contenders!.]

was supposedly in love with the Kid and he with her, which seems to be the most likely motive for him to return to Ft. Sumner.

On the night of July 14, 1881, after searching the area around Ft. Sumner Lincoln County Sheriff Pat Garrett and his deputies John Poe and Thomas C. "Kip" McKinney were about to ride back to Lincoln. Before leaving they thought it a good idea to check with Pete Maxwell. In Garrett's account of this he takes credit for wanting to check with Maxwell before giving up the chase, Deputy Poe differs with Garrett. In Deputy Poe's account written in 1919 we see the events through his eyes.

*Garrett seemed to have but little confidence in our being able to accomplish the object of our trip, but said that he knew the location of a certain house occupied by a woman in Fort Sumner which the Kid had formerly frequented, and that if he was in or about Fort Sumner, he would most likely be found entering or leaving this house some time during the night. Garrett proposed that we go to a grove of trees near the town, conceal our horses, then station ourselves in the peach orchard at the rear of the house, and keep watch on who might come or go. This course was agreed upon, and we entered the peach orchard about nine o'clock that night, stationing ourselves in the gloom or shadow of the peach trees, as the moon was shining very brightly. We kept up a fruitless watch here until some time after eleven o'clock, when Garrett stated that he believed we were on a cold trail; that he had very little faith in our being able to accomplish anything when we started on the trip. He proposed that we leave the town without letting anyone know that we had been there in search of the Kid.*

*I then proposed that, before leaving we should go to the residence of Peter Maxwell, a man who up to that time I had never seen, but who, by reason of his being a leading citizen and having a large property interest should, according to my reasoning, be glad to furnish such information as he might have aid us [sic] in ridding the country of a man who was looked on as a scourge and curse by all law-abiding people.*

*Garrett agreed to this, and there-upon led us from the orchard by circuitous by-paths to Maxwell's residence, which was a building formerly used as officers' quarters during the days when a garrison of troops had been maintained at the fort. Upon our arriving at the residence (a very long, one-story adobe, standing end to the flush with the street, having a porch on the south side, which was the direction from which we approached, the premises all being enclosed by a paling fence, one side of which ran parallel to and along the edge of the street up to and across the end of the porch to the corner of the building).\, Garrett said to me, "This is Maxwell's room through the open door (left open on account of the extremely warm weather), while McKinney and myself stopped on the outside. McKinney squatted on the outside of the fence, and I sat on the porch.*

*It should be here that up to this moment I had never seen Billy the Kid, nor Maxwell, which fact in view of the events transpiring immediately afterward, placed me at an extreme disadvantage.*

*It was probably not more than thirty seconds after Garrett had entered Maxwell's room, when my attention was attracted, from where I sat at the little gateway, to a man approaching me on the inside of and along the fence, some forty or fifty steps away. I observed that he was only partially dressed and was both bareheaded and barefooted, or rather had only socks on his feet, and it seemed to me that he was fastening his trousers as he came toward me at a very brisk walk.*

*As Maxwell's was the one place in Fort Sumner that had considered above suspicion of harboring the Kid, I was entirely off my guard, the thought coming to my mind that the man approaching was either Maxwell or some guest of his who might be staying there. He came on until he was almost within arm's length of where I sat, before he saw me, as I was partially concealed from his view by the post of the gate.*

*Upon seeing me, he covered me with his six-shooter as quick as lightening, sprang onto the porch, calling out in Spanish "Quien es" (Who is it?) - at the same time backing away from me toward the door through which Garrett only a few seconds before had passed, repeating his query, "Who is it?" in Spanish several times.*

*At this I stood up and advanced toward him, telling him not to be alarmed, that he should not be hurt; and still without the least suspicion that this was the very man we were looking for. As I moved toward him to reassure him, he backed up into the doorway of*

*Maxwell's room, where he halted for a moment, his body concealed by the thick adobe wall at the side of the doorway, form* [sic] *whence he put his head and asked in Spanish for the fourth time who I was. I was within a few feet of him when he disappeared into the room.*

*After this, and until after the shooting, I was unable to see what took place on account of the darkness of the room, but plainly heard what was said on the inside. An instant after the man left the door, I heard a voice inquire in a sharp tone, "Pete, who are those fellows on the outside?" An instant later a shot was fired in the room, followed immediately by what anyone within hearing distance thought were two shots. However, there were only two shots fired, the third report, as we learned afterward, being caused by the rebound of the second bullet, which had struck the adobe wall and rebounded against the headboard of a wooden bedstead.*

*I heard a groan and one or two gasps from where I stood in the doorway, as of someone dying in the room. An instant later, Garrett came out, brushing against me as he passed. He stood by me close to the wall at the side of the door and said to me, "That was the Kid that came in there onto me, and I think I got him". I said, "Pat, the Kid would not come to this place; you have shot the wrong man".*

*Upon saying this, Garrett seemed to be in doubt himself as to whom he had shot, but quickly spoke up and said, "I am sure it was him, for I know his voice to* [sic] *well to be mistaken". This remark of Garrett's relieved me of considerable apprehension, as I had felt almost certain that someone whom we did not want had been killed.*

The next day Billy the Kid was buried in Fort Sumner. Or was it the Kid in the grave?

**[AUTHOR'S NOTE: Poe's initial uncertainty about Billy's identity, is this writer's only "proof" about victim identity doubt. Omitted are all witnesses and the Coroner's Jury. ]**

## What Happen [sic] to William H. Bonney a.k.a. Billy the Kid?

Soon after the shooting in Maxwell's home on July 14, 1881, the rumor took life that Garrett shot the wrong man and that he knew he shot the wrong man but covered it up.

**[AUTHOR'S NOTE: This Seventy-Seven Days document is transparently tailored to fit the pretenders.]**

Some even say that Garrett had an empty coffin buried the next day in Fort Sumner. Some say Garrett wrote the book *The Authentic Life of Billy the Kid*, in which he demonizing [sic] Billy the Kid, to prop up his waning popularity that was being eroded by the rumor that he killed The Kid in less than a fair fight or that he did not kill The Kid at all.

> **[AUTHOR'S NOTE: These contentions, without sources, appear made up.]**

To this day the rumor still has life that Billy the Kid never died that night.

> **[AUTHOR'S NOTE: Nothing has been presented to support that "rumor."]**

Most everything we know about William H. Bonney a.k.a. Billy the Kid is what is know [sic] about him in during the last three years of his life. The date and place of his birth, who his father was, where he lived, as a child is still a mystery. Most of what we do know and what we call history is flawed by myth. Even where he is buried is the subject of controversy these 122 years later.

> **[AUTHOR'S NOTE: This illogic tries to make Bonney's death uncertain, by manufacturing "uncertainties" in his earlier history.]**

In England is a grave with the name William H. Bonney on the headstone, where is it said [sic] Billy the Kid is buried. The story is that the Tunstall family, in apparition [sic] of his help and loyalty to John Tunstall, brought the Kid back to England where he lived a long life dying of old age.

> **[AUTHOR'S NOTE: This is so bizarre, it seems a delirium, rather than an argument. It does indicate the author lacks ability to sort fact from fiction.]**

> **[AUTHOR'S NOTE: The case for Garrett's murder of an innocent victim ceases here without proof; and the segue is to the pretenders. ]**

## John Miller

[AUTHOR'S NOTE: At this preliminary stage - years before the hoaxers needed John Miller's exhumation to keep their hoax afloat - he was of minimal interest; their focus being "Brushy." This disinterest is reflected in the following cursory text - and was kept secret when they headed with backhoe to John Miller's grave.]

In 1993 Helen Airy published a book by Sunstone Press entitled *What* [sic- Whatever] *Happened to Billy the Kid.* In this book the claim is made that a John Miller who died on November 7, 1937, at six-thirty in the evening, in the Pioneer [sic] Home in Prescott, Arizona and was buried in the Prescott Pioneer home cemetery [sic], was Billy the Kid. In Airy's book Miller is quoted as saying, *"there was a Mexican shot and buried in the coffin that is supposed to be the Kid."*

In her book *What* [sic- Whatever] *Happened to Billy the Kid* these accounts are found:

Page 162 paragraph 2 - *Ann Storrer of Belen writes: "My father, Charlie Walker, grew up around Fort Sumner during the early 1900's. A Mexican he used to work for told him that he saw Billy the Kid at the bullfights in Mexico long after he was supposed to be dead. The rumor around Fort Sumner was that Pat Garrett and Bill [sic] the Kid were good friends and Garrett tried to stop everyone from killing Billy. My father believed there was never a body in the grave.*

Page 162 paragraph 3 and 4 - *Arleigh Nation of Albuquerque supplied the Following story; "A man by the name of Trujillo, who died in 1935 at the age of ninety-five told Nation he worked for Pete Maxwell at the time Billy the kid was supposed to have been killed. He said the day before the shoot-out they dressed up an Indian, who had died the night before, to look like the Kid. The Indian was buried in the grave that was said to have been the Kid's.*

*Nation, who is a Billy the kid Buff, also said a neighbor of his who lived in Lincoln, Mrs. Syd Boykin, told him that the kid stayed as [sic] her home in Lincoln many times after he was supposed to have been dead.*

Airy states that a John Collins claimed to have been a friend of Billy the Kid. Collins says that he helped bury the corpse of the man Garrett killed on July 14, 1881, and it was not Billy the kid.

Arley Sanches interviewed Nadine Brady, of Adelino, New Mexico, and whose grandfather was Sheriff William Brady, who was shot by the Kid, for a story, which appeared in the *Albuquerque Journal* on September 8, 1990. Nadine says one old timer told her Garrett didn't shoot Bonney. He told her Garrett and Bonney were friends and Garrett invented a story to help his friend escape. A wanderer was killed and buried, and Garrett told everyone he had shot Billy the Kid.

Airy says Frank Coe, a friend of Billy the Kid during the Lincoln County War, believed to the day of his death that Billy was still alive, and spent a great deal of time tracing reports that he had been seen.

*The El Paso Herald Post,* June 29, 1926 reported a story that a "government official" re[ported that "Billy the Kid and Garrett framed an escape" from Lincoln, New Mexico. The government official claimed the Kid was still alive in this article.

*The El Paso Times,* July 26, 1964, reported that retired Immigration and Naturalization Service Inspector, Leslie Traylor of San Antonio, Texas claimed Billy the Kid was a man named Henry Street Smith. Traylor said he traced Smith and believes him to be buried under the name of John Miller who died in 1935 in Prescott, Arizona.

[AUTHOR'S NOTE: Airy's John Miller hoax is debunked later in this book. The writer here, however, does not appear to argue for Miller as Billy. And no death scene is presented, that being the purpose of a probable cause statement for a murder case!]

## William Henry Roberts a.k.a. Brushy Bill Roberts

[AUTHOR'S NOTE: Next is the writer's apparent temptation to set-up "Brushy" as heir to Billy's identity. "Brushy" later appeared throughout the hoax, but seemingly for "survival suspicion" and an attention-grabbing publicity. The very fact that this Seventy-Seven Days of Doubt Document" was kept secret, indicated to me hoaxer reluctance to make "Brushy" as Billy their culminating conclusion. But the effusions that follow here - hidden in the ensuing Billy the Kid Case - left open that the hoaxers might let their fake forensics "do that proving" later. And the subsequent problem of "Brushy's" non-bench death scene, presented in detail below, was not yet anticipated; since the hoaxers expected the Billy and mother exhumations to be a slam dunk for DNA - without need for their later switch to bench scenario for DNA.]

Before Sheriff Pat Garrett could clean his pistol the bogus Billy the Kid's began to crop up everywhere. Some were too ridiculous to take notice of and some convinced a few people but were forgotten with the passage of time. Out of all the men to come forward to claim they are Billy the Kid the one that caused the most stir and gained national and even worldwide attention was Brushy Bill Roberts.

To this day Roberts' claim is being taken seriously by many. In Hamilton, Texas, where William Roberts is buried there stands a sign that proclaims that his grave is "The Authentic Grave Site of Billy the Kid." A plaque states that he spent the last part of his life attempting to get a "promised pardon" from the New Mexico Governor. Just weeks before Roberts death he and his attorney [sic - William Morrison, not an attorney] approached the Governor of New Mexico and asked for a pardon for the Kid, who Roberts claimed to be. Dubious of Roberts claims the Governor granted no pardon.

**[AUTHOR'S NOTE: This "Brushy" pardon focus adds credence to the otherwise non sequitor quest for the pardon in the Billy the Kid Case hoax. For that, the Garrett murder "investigation" is irrelevant. But gaining the pardon was the "Brushy"-Morrison goal.]**

The story goes that in 1948, William V. Morrison was working as an investigator for a law firm. Morrison was a graduate attorney [sic - Morrison was not an attorney] and it was said that he had a "good nose for evidence". He was a member of the Missouri Historical Society and a descendant of Ferdinand Maxwell, the brother of Lucien Bonaparte Maxwell and uncle of Pete Maxwell. [AUTHOR'S NOTE: Allegedly this lacks evidence.] Because of this, Morrison possessed a keen interest in New Mexico history.

During this time Morrison was sent to Florida to investigate an inheritance claimant by the name of Joe Hines. Hines' brother, in North Dakota, had passed away and Hines claimed to be the sole inheritor of some property. As Morrison interviewed the old man the story did not match with the facts Morrison possessed. After more questions Joe Hines told Morrison his name, Hines, was an alias. Hines claimed his real name was Jesse [sic] Evans and he was a survivor of the Lincoln County War.

**[AUTHOR'S NOTE: Important Error: This would not be made by someone in the "Brushy Bill" inner circle. Hines claimed to be a Jimmy McDonald, not Jessie Evans. And the contact**

person for "Brushy" was J. Frank Dalton, whom "Brushy's" conspiracy theorist believers consider to have been Jesse James!. This would, however not cancel out Attorney Bill Robins III – or Steve Sederwall trying his best!.]

Morrison being proud of his ancestral connection to New Mexico history mentioned to Hines (Evans) that Billy the Kid worked for the Maxwells at one time

**[AUTHOR'S NOTE: Error: Billy did not work for Maxwell.]**

and added that the Kid was shot and killed in Maxwell's house on July 14, 1881. To that Hines replied, "Garrett did not kill the Kid on July 14, 1881, or any other time." Hines went on to say, "In fact Billy was still living in Texas last year. The reason that I know is that a friend of mine, now living in California stops over to visit with me here every summer. He and Billy and me are the only warriors left of the old Lincoln County bunch.

**[AUTHOR'S NOTE: Besides the fact that everything here is non-historical, real Jessie Evans would not have called himself a Lincoln County War "warrior."]**

Later that year Morrison became acquainted with another man in Missouri who said he knew who all the parties were and gave Morrison an address of a man named O.L. Roberts who lived in Hamilton, Texas. In June of 1948 Morrison drove to Hamilton, Texas and met Roberts. On their first meeting Roberts told Morrison that the Kid was his half brother and was still alive in Old Mexico. The next day Morrison came back to Roberts home and Roberts sent his wife to a neighbor's house saying he and Morrison had business to discuss.

After Mrs. Roberts left the house Morrison claims Roberts pointed his finger at him and said, "Well, you've got your man. You don't need to look any farther. I'm Billy the Kid. But don't tell anyone. My wife doesn't know who I am. She thinks my half brother is Billy the Kid, but he died in Kentucky many years ago. I want a pardon before saying anything about this matter. I don't want to kill anyone anymore, but I'm not going to hang." Morrison goes on to write that Roberts told his story and tears coursed down his cheeks, as he said, "I done wrong like everyone else did in those days. I want to die a free man. I do not want to die like Garrett and the rest of them, by the gun. I have been hiding so long and they have been telling so many lies about me that I want to get everything straightened out before I die. I can do it with some help. The good Lord left me here for a purpose and I know why He did. Now will you help me out of this mess."

Morrison wanted proof that Roberts claims were true and knew the scars the Kid would have on his body. Morrison had Roberts strip and from the scars on Roberts' body Morrison was convinced that he was talking to the true William H. Bonney.

Roberts tells Morrison in detail how he escaped death at the hands of Sheriff Pat Garrett the night of July 14, 1881. In a statement Roberts records the following:

[AUTHOR'S NOTE: The following is an excellent example of "Brushy's" confabulatory style. This text can be found in pages 105-117 of W.C. Jameson's and Frederick Bean's 1997 *The Return of the Outlaw Billy the Kid*. They claimed to have gotten the transcript from *Alias Billy the Kid* author, William Morrison's, step-grandson, Bill Allison.]

[AUTHOR'S NOTE: Do not miss the dramatic validation of "Brushy" that this document represents. His own words are being used in *a real law enforcement case* to show probable cause that Garrett was a murderer.]

*I rode into Fort Sumner from Yerby's a few days before Garrett and his posse rode in. When they rode in that day, I had spent the day with Garrett's brother-in-law, Saval Gutierrez. Nearly all the people in this country were my friends and they helped me. None of them likes Garrett. It was dark that night, but there was enough moonlight to make shadows. Me and my partner Billy Barlow, rode up to Jesus Silva's house when we reached Fort Sumner. We had been staying at the Yerby Ranch laying low for a while. Word was all around that Pat Garrett and a posse were after me. Pat's wife was a sister to my friend Saval Gutierrez, and Saval told me that Pat was after me, that he heard it from his sister.*

*Things were mighty hot in Lincoln County for me right about then, but I wasn't running from it. I meant to have a talk with Pt Garrett and set things straight between us if I could. We used to be friends ... We hid our horses in the barn and walked up to Jesus' back door. Barlow was nervous about being in Fort Sumner with me and I couldn't blame him much. Jesus came to the back door when I tapped on it with the barrel of my six-shooter. When he saw that it was me, he grinned and let us in. I told Jesus we were hungry. We'd been out in the hills all day, scouting around fort Sumner for any sign of Garrett and his posse. "I have nothing but cold frijoles, compadre," Jesus whispered as he closed the door. Barlow made a sour face. "I want some meat," he said, "we have been living on beans and tortillas all week. Ain't you got any beef?*

According to Roberts statement Jesus Silva told Barlow that Pete Maxwell had some meat hanging on his porch. Barlow wanted to get the beef to cook but Roberts told him it was too dangerous and they should not move from the house. Barlow would not listen. According to Roberts statement Barlow took a butcher knife and left the house to head to Maxwell's to get the beefsteak. While Roberts and Jesus were lighting the wood stove they hear [sic] gunfire in the direction of Pete Maxwell's place. Roberts' statement goes on to describe the following events:

*I pulled one of my .44's and ran through the door, trying to see in the dark. Two more shots came from a shadow beside the Maxwell house. I couldn't find a target to shoot at. It was too dark to see. I ran toward Maxwell's back porch. I heard another gunshot and felt something hit me in the jaw. I stumbled and kept on running with a broken tooth rolling around my tongue. I tasted blood and spit the mess out of my mouth as I started emptying my six-shooter at the shadow where I saw the muzzleflash. From the corner of my eye I saw a body lying on the back porch ... I knew it had to be Barlow.*

*My partner had walked right into a trap, and the trap had likely been set for me. I pulled my other .44 and ran toward the porch to check on Barlow, but I ran into a wall of gunfire. I knew I wasn't going to make it to my partner. Too many guns were shooting at me. I didn't have a chance. I turned for a fence across the back of Maxwell's yard and dove for it when a bullet caught me in the left shoulder. I jumped over the fence and landed hard on the far side, with the echo of gunshots all around me, ringing in my ears. I staggered into an alley that ran behind the house, firing my .44 over my shoulder until it clicked empty. My mouth and shoulder were bleeding and I lost track of where I was, but I knew I had to get away from Maxwell's before they killed me. I heard a shout and another gunshot. Something passed across my forehead like a hot branding iron. I was stunned. I lost footing and fell on my face in the darkness.*

*I knew I was hurt bad and wondered if I would make it out of this scrape alive.*

*I forced myself up again, wiping the blood from my eyes with my shirtsleeve as I stumbled headlong down the ally. I didn't know how bad the head wound was, only that it was bleeding and I couldn't see. It wouldn't matter if the found me in the alley just then, they were bent on killing me, to be sure. If I fell again I knew they'd find me and finish the job, so I kept running down the ally as hard as I could, barely able to see where I was going. I heard them shouting to each other behind me, arguing over something, but I was too woozy to think about what they were saying and too frightened to care. The gunshot to my head had knocked me senseless. I kept on staggering and running down the alley, trying to get away. Blood was pouring into my eyes; I couldn't see a thing. I ran past a little adobe shack down the alley from Pete Maxwell's. I supposed all the shooting woke everybody up, because a door opened just a crack when I ran behind the adobe and I could see a lantern light spilling from the doorway across the alley.*

*I stumbled toward the light not knowing what else to do. I needed help and the open door was the only place I could find, hurt like I was. A Mexican woman pulled me inside. She saw the blood on my face and threw her hands over her mouth. She closed the door quickly and helped me to a chair. I sleeved the blood from my eyes, watching her, loading my Colts.*

In Roberts' statement he identifies the woman as Celsa Cutierriz [sic - if the writer is referring to Celsa Gutierrez] who he had known previously. Ms. Cutierriz [sic] helped Roberts and kept him at her home that night. Roberts says that later Ms. Cutierriz [sic] had Frank Lobato saddle his horse and bring it around in the alley so he can [sic] escape. Before Roberts was able to leave Ms. Cutierriz [sic] told him it was rumored about Fort Sumner that Sheriff Garrett was telling everyone he had killed the Kid.

Roberts says, *I started puzzling over what Celsa told me. Garrett was trying to pass off Barlow's body as that of Billy the Kid. I wondered how he figured to get away with it. Garrett knew by now that he'd killed the wrong man in the dark. Billy Barlow looked a lot like me, the same general description, with blue eyes like mine. But in the daylight, a lot of folks who knew me would know they had the wrong body. I couldn't figure it, unless Garrett realized his mistake and was making a try at collection [sic] the reward money that was out on me anyway ...*

Roberts says it was 3 a.m. when Celsa brought his horse up to the house. He says he left with Frank Lobato. Roberts stayed in a camp south of Fort Sumner until his wounds healed and the first of August he rode to El Paso, Texas.

**[AUTHOR'S NOTE: Debunking of this error-filled "Brushy" hoaxing appears earlier in this book, though this expansive dialogue demonstrates excellently the relentless floridness of his confabulations and imagination. Noteworthy for the Billy the Kid Case hoaxers, however, is that this choice of death scene with back-porch-Barlow points to an early phase of their own faking, where they were not yet concealing the major discrepancies between "Brushy's" "death scene" tale and their own.]**

## Questions About the Case

There seems [sic] to be problems with every account of the escape of Billy the Kid from the make shift [sic] jail in Lincoln and the shooting at Fort Sumner by Pat Garrett. In every account there remain questions as to what really happened.

**[AUTHOR'S NOTE: The above uses the hoaxers' technique of "vague, though unfounded, suspicions" instead of actual evidence - which they lacked. What follows is "alien invasion illogic" of "ifs" to attain hoaxed conclusions – here listed as "Questions." It represents the writer's last chance to fake a link of Garrett to a "probable cause" of murder.]**

**[AUTHOR'S NOTE: It is all "alien invasion illogic." For clarity, the illogical transitions are put in boldface. The breath-taking leap of the scam is seen when the "ifs" of the outhouse version, lead to a fake, implied accusation that Garrett presented the armory version to conceal that *he* was the pistol-giving "friend." Missing only is the "what if" of Roswell aliens giving Garrett that gun for placing!]**

1. In the historical account of the escape of Billy the Kid, from the courthouse in Lincoln, **it's believed** that a "friend" placed a pistol in the outhouse for Billy to use in his escape. The identity of the "friend" who placed the pistol in the outhouse has gone nearly unasked. **If** this

version is true, and a "friend" left a pistol in the outhouse to aid in Bonney's escape that "friend" is a coconspirator to the murder of Bell and Olinger. This "friend" also should have been charged with two counts of homicide but remained at large. **Why** didn't Sheriff Garrett pursue the question of the idenenty [sic] of the "friend" who hid the pistol? Garrett says the Kid took the pistol from the armory. **If** the story of the pistol in the outhouse is true did Garrett have a reason to say it was from the armory?

2. **If** Roberts account and claim about the night of July 14, 1881, is to be believed then Lincoln County Sheriff Pat Garrett was not the hero that history portrays him as. Instead, he becomes a murderer who killed Billy Barlow and covered up that killing and passed off Barlow's body as that of Billy the Kid. With the sign in at [sic] Brushy Bill's grave site claiming to the [sic] grave site of Billy the Kid they are in short saying Pat Garrett lied. Did Garrett lie?

[AUTHOR'S NOTE: This earliest version of the Billy the Kid Case hoax relies heavily on Roberts; later discrepancies between the evolving hoax and Roberts's tales would be concealed by the hoaxers. Here, confidence of victory without scrutiny apparently yielded a devil-may-care attitude.]

[AUTHOR'S NOTE: This earliest version of the hoax also is unabashedly vicious in accusing Garrett of heinous crimes. Later, under scrutiny, the hoaxers would claim the case was to protect Garrett's honor against "others" who had accused him!]

3. **If** Roberts claims are believed, it beings up other questions? [sic] He claims in his statement when talking about Pat Garrett, *"we use* [sic] *to be friend"* [sic]. **If** Garrett and Roberts were friends did Garrett and Garrett [sic] allowed The Kid out of friendship to escape from Fort Sumner, *did he also* arrange his escape from Lincoln? Did Garrett question why **his friend, the Kid**, with all the others involved in all the killing was the only one to be convicted and sentenced to hang? The Kid **mentions this** in an interview that was published in the *Mesilla News* on April 15, 1881 when he said, *Think it hard that I should be the only one to suffer the extreme penalties of the law."*

[AUTHOR'S NOTE: Here, long-discredited "Brushy" appears as an authority. "If-ing" with him runs rampant. And the "if-ings" of "alien invasion illogic" that falsely make Garrett both

**Billy's "friend" and "accomplice." In addition, there is a switcheroo, by misusing the words "mentions this" (boldfaced above), when the Kid's words are only referring to his own sense of injustice, not a friendship with Garrett.]**

4. **Did** Garrett arrange having the pistol put in the outhouse by the "friend" **and is this** why he did not search for the coconspirator to the murder of the two lawmen? **If this is the case then** Garrett is also a coconspirator in the murder of those two lawmen.

**[AUTHOR'S NOTE: More "ifs of alien invasion illogic."]**

5. In the Lincoln County Courthouse Caretaker Gauss' statement he quotes Bonney as saying about Bell, *"I'm sorry I had to kill him but couldn't help it."* This statement must raise the question did Bonney, when he produced the pistol he retrieved from the outhouse

**[AUTHOR'S NOTE: Note the switcheroo from the "ifs," now using the outhouse as a fact.]**

order Bell to surrender? Did Bell panic and instead of throwing up his hands, turn and run causing Bonney to shoot him?

**[AUTHOR'S NOTE: Irrelevant question, but possibly inserted to promote the outhouse option to falsely build a Garrett case.]**

6. Other questions come to mind in this investigation, some about Gauss. It should be noted that Gauss had worked with Tunstall, so had Bonney. Gauss and Bonney shared the same table as they took meals, slept on the same floor and spent a great deal of time together when Bonney was in the courthouse under guard. It goes to reason that Gauss was sympathetic towards Bonney. With that in mind it could be pointed out that there were a number of things missing from Gauss's account. Gauss made no reference to how Bell was killed, and leaves out the fact that Bonney used Olinger's own shotgun to kill him. If Bonney retrieved a pistol from the outhouse it had to be prearranged with Bonney and the "friend" as to what date and where to place the pistol in order for Bonney to find it. Since Gauss spent so much time with Bonney would he not have heard something about the plot?

[AUTHOR'S NOTE: The writer here appears less adroit at conning than the author of the final Probable Cause Statement. Inadvertently, he is building a case for Gauss as the gun-placing "friend," negating the argument for Garrett as the colluding accomplice - the purpose of a Probable Cause Statement!]

7. Since the caretaker Gauss worked outside it is not outside the realm of possibility that he saw who put the pistol in the outhouse?

[AUTHOR'S NOTE: This irrelevant question never arose in the Billy the Kid Case hoax, and, as for 6. above, merely means Gauss may have been the weapon-placer.]

8. It is known that Bonney ate his meals at the courthouse and the only time he was allowed to leave was to use the outhouse. Bell and Olinger took turns escorting the prisoners to the hotel for lunch, leaving the other in charge of Bonney. Bonney as well as the others would have known that Olinger would be escorting the prisoners to lunch that day. Bonney was aware that out of the two guards Bell was the one to make his escape move on since Bell was easy going and seemed to get along with him. Bonney also knew that Olinger had killed men in the past and had threatened to kill him. **Had Garrett and the Kid discussed this and chose Bell** as the deputy for Bonney to make his move thinking Bell would just give up giving the Kid an hour to escape while Olinger was eating?

[AUTHOR'S NOTE: "Alien invasion illogic," with highlighted absurd jump.]

9. **If** Garrett was part of the plot for the Kid's escape **is that why** he rode to White Oaks on a "tax collecting" trip, to give himself an alibi?

[AUTHOR'S NOTE: Good example of "alien invasion illogic."]

10. **If Garrett were part of the plot to allow the Kid to escape he would have reason to chase the Kid. He could not afford for the Kid to tell of his involvement in the two killings of the lawmen. Garrett also has a weak link in the plot, that being the "friend" who put the pistol in the outhouse. If Roberts' story is true, is Billy Barlow the one who put the pistol in the outhouse under orders of Garrett? In Roberts' accounting he shows up at Fort Sumner with no one but Barlow. Did he meet Barlow after he**

**rode out of Lincoln and move on [sic] to Fort Sumner?** [author's boldface]

> [AUTHOR'S NOTE: All highlighted – the prize for most absurd "alien invasion illogic," missing only little green men themselves!]

11. If Garrett shot Billy Barlow in the dark, by mistake, on July 14, 1881, and Barlow was the only one who could tell the story of Garrett's involvement other than the Kid, would Garrett not know the Kid would run to keep from hanging?

> [AUTHOR'S NOTE: This incoherent reverie, appears to contradict the Pat-Billy friendship on which the hoax is based. ]

12. In Deputy John W. Poe's statement as he lays out the shooting in Maxwell's house on July 14, 1881, he says "... Garrett came out, brushing against me as he passed. He stood by me close to the wall at the side of the door and said to me, That was the Kid that came in there onto me, and I think I got him.' I said, "Pat, the Kid would not come to this place; you have shot the wrong man.' Upon my saying this, Garrett seemed to be in doubt himself as to whom had shot ..." Did Garrett kill the wrong man by mistake and cover it up?

> [AUTHOR'S NOTE: The writer forgot that backing "Brushy" means no bedroom murder scene – but a Barlow-on-back-porch one. He also forgets "Brushy" had enough ambient gunfire to rival the Alamo.]

> [AUTHOR'S NOTE: Similar to the final Probable Cause Statement, this "question" omits the multiple identifications of Bonney, following this moment of doubt in a darkened room.]

13. Most researchers and historians have accepted without much question, the statement that Billy the Kid was born Henry McCarty, in New York on November 23, 1859. It should be noted that the first time this information comes to light is in Pat Garrett's book *The Authentic Life of Billy the Kid.*

[AUTHOR'S NOTE: Error. This information came out during Billy's lifetime, and while he was being tracked down by Garrett and Secret Service Agent Azariah Wild. Its bibliographic reference is: No Author. "Outlaws of New Mexico. The Exploits of a Band Headed by a New York Youth. The Mountain Fastness of the Kid and His Followers - War Against a Gang of Cattle Thieves and Murderers." December 27, 1880. *The Sun*. New York. Vol. XLVIII, No. 118, Page 3, Columns 1-2.]

In the book the evidence for this claim is sited [sic] to have come from a birth announcement that appeared in the New York Times on November 25, 1859. In 1950 William Morrison the attorney [AUTHOR'S NOTE: Morrison was not an attorney] for William (Brushy Bill) Roberts claims he asked the *New York Times* about the announcement and the Times replied that no information about birth announcements appeared in that issue. A ghostwriter by the name of Marshall Asmon [sic - Ashmun] Upson is credited with writing Garrett's book. It might also be worth mentioning the date November 23, is the birth date of Marshall Asmon [sic - Ashmun] Upson. Is it by chance that Upson and the Kid have the same birthday or by design?

[AUTHOR'S NOTE: Irrelevant, but a clumsy and fake "everything seems suspicious" ploy used as pseudo-evidence.]

14. As stated above most believe Billy the Kid was born in New York. This information also appeared for the first time in Garrett's book. [AUTHOR'S NOTE: See *New York Sun* 1880 article reference above.] It is also believed that Billy the Kid was shot and killed in 1881 at the age of 21. However, according to the United States Bureau of Census, 1880 census, Fort Sumner, San Miguel County, William Bonney says differently. Between June 17 and 19, 1880, while taking census records at the Fort, Lorenzo Labadie, a former Indian Agent, noted the vital statistics of one William Bonney, who was living next to Charlie Bowdre and his wife Manuela, leaving us to believe this to be the William Bonney of Lincoln County fame. What is interesting about the entry is that he gave his age as twenty-five, and his place of birth not New York but Missouri.

[AUTHOR'S NOTE: Irrelevant, but a clumsy attempt at the "suspiciousness" ploy. Also, it is thought that Manuela Bowdre gave the interview and incorrect information.]

The attorney Morrison asked Roberts why Garrett would say he was born in New York. Roberts told him that is what the told the "Coe boys" when he first came to New Mexico. Roberts went on to say he never saw New York until he was a grown man.

[AUTHOR'S NOTE: Morrison was not an attorney.]

[AUTHOR'S NOTE: Irrelevant paragraph since "Brushy" was not Billy Bonney.]

## Conclusion

If history is correct and William H. Bonney a.k.a. Billy the Kid was shot and killed by Lincoln County Sheriff Pat Garrett on July 14, 1881, at the house of Pete Maxwell in Fort Sumner, and was buried the next day in Fort Sumner, then Brushy Bill Roberts is a fake and nothing more than a story teller of the first order.

[AUTHOR'S NOTE: Again, this early document points to "Brushy" as Billy; that direction later became more covert.]

However, if it is not the body of William H. Bonney buried in Fort Sumner then Lincoln County Sheriff Pat Garrett killed the wrong man on July 14, 1881. He covered up that killing with help from others such as Pete Maxwell. If it is not Bonney buried at Fort Sumner then Garrett is a murderer and Maxwell is a knowing coconspirator to that homicide.

[AUTHOR'S NOTE: This is the first Billy the Kid Case hoax attempt at constructing a conspiracy theory. And the Garrett "friendship" appears to be abandoned for use of "Brushy's" "accident" version. Maxwell is added without giving motive or evidence - since neither exist.]

If Brushy Bill Roberts were William H. Bonney then one would have to assume that the body in the grave is that of Billy Barlow as Robert's claims. If that is true Sheriff Garrett could quite possibly be a coconspirator of the double murder of two lawmen that occurred during the Kid's escape from Lincoln.

**[AUTHOR'S NOTE: This illogical jump even leaves "Brushy" behind, since he never claimed a collusive Jail escape plot with Garrett, or that a "friendship" with Garrett related to the escape.]**

The Lincoln County Sheriff''s Department believes, with the unanswered question as to who is buried in Fort Sumner

**[AUTHOR'S NOTE: This is fakery. The victim is not doubted.]**

there remains serious doubt as to what involvement Sheriff Pat Garrett played in the escape of Billy the Kid from Lincoln that resulted I the deaths of two lawmen.

**[AUTHOR'S NOTE: This is fakery. There is no evidence that Garrett assisted the jail escape of Bonney. ]**

If the body of William H. Bonney is buried in Fort Sumner the claims of William Roberts'' and others alleging to have been Billy the Kid are unfounded and the name of Pat Garrett is cleared of any wrong doing in this incident. It is the duty of the Lincoln County Sheriff''s Office to clear this mystery and possible crime off the books of history in a professional manner and to allow the guilt to fall where it belongs.

**[AUTHOR'S NOTE: The pretenders are easily debunked without exhumations. And no one is accusing Garrett, except pretenders and hoaxers – and without basis. ]**

Billy the Kid's mother is buried in Silver City, New Mexico. To exhume her body could provide the DNA to solve this 122-year-old mystery. Her DNA would hold the key to the true answer as to where William Bonney is buried and if Pat Garrett was a murderer or a Sheriff doing his duty.

If those in Hamilton, Texas believe Roberts is in fact Roberts [sic] this DNA should prove their claim. If he is not the town of Hamilton, Texas needs to take down the signs that the grave of Roberts is "The Authentic Grave Site of Billy the Kid." However, if Roberts is William Bonney then history should be rewritten showing what really happened in Lincoln County and Fort Sumner.

If Bonney is buried in Fort Sumner the History stands and the name of Sheriff Pat Garrett would be cleared and he did not kill some incendet [sic] person in Fort Sumner and would appear he had no hand in the escape of William Bonney from Lincoln and the death of Olinger and Bell.

Lincoln County Sheriff, Tom Sullivan and the Lincoln County Sheriff's Office believe it our duty to put this mystery to rest after 122 years of doubt. Since these questions continue to nag at our conscience, and since there is no statute of limitations on Murder we feel this investigation should answer the question of "is Pat Garrett a murderer?" or a Sheriff doing his duty and wrongly accused of a crime?

**[AUTHOR'S NOTE: No probable cause has been established to implicate Garrett as a murder suspect – the purpose of this document.]**

In Pat Garrett's book *The Authentic Life of Billy the Kid* he pens these words - *"Again I say that the Kid's body lies undisturbed in the grave - and I speak of what I know."*

It is the intention of the Lincoln County Sheriff's Office to prove one way or the other if these words are true.

_____

Tom Sullivan: Sheriff
Lincoln County Sheriff's Office

_____

Steven M. Sederwall: Deputy Sheriff
Lincoln County Sheriff's Office

_____

Date

\* \* \* \* \* \* \* \* \* \* \* \* \*

# Summarizing "Brushy Bill"
# Flubbing Billy Bonney

## DEBUNKING OLIVER P. "BRUSHY BILL" ROBERTS

Oliver "Brushy Bill" Roberts's success with the general public, in the face of his easily disproved claims, proves that pretending pays. Besides his hoaxing first author, all he needed to get passionate true believers was sprinkling of historical names, studying his few sources, and kicking-in his fertile mad imagination. But that is not enough to bear historical scrutiny. And the fix-up attempts by his later authors by pasting on some facts from modern history books cannot undo "Brushy's" mistakes. Some of "Brushy's" multitude of disastrous errors of personal history and confabulations are summarized below:

- Birth Date: August 26, 1879 .......... [Billy's Birthdate: November 23, 1859. "Brushy" fabricated December 31, 1859 for himself, but was born on August 26, 1879]

- Birthplace: Buffalo Gap, Texas .......... [Billy's Birthplace: New York City, New York]

- Claims mother, named Mary Adeline Dunn-Roberts, died when he was three .......... [Billy's mother, Catherine McCarty Antrim, died when he was 14 ½]

- Claims his mother's half-sister, Kathleen Bonney, raised him .......... [Unrelated to real Billy's history]

- Named Oliver P. Roberts; self-named "Brushy Bill;" claimed names William Henry Bonney and Billy the Kid .......... [Billy's names: William Henry McCarty, Henry Antrim, William Henry "Billy" Bonney, nickname "Kid." Never used "Billy the Kid"]

- Unaware of Billy's brother .......... [Billy's brother was Joseph, "Josie"]

- Favored left hand .......... [Billy was ambidextrous and favored the right]

- Near illiterate; claiming a "friend" wrote for him .......... [Billy was highly literate and wrote famous letters]

- No claim of bi-lingual skill .......... [Billy spoke fluent Spanish]

- Unaware of life incidents in Silver City .......... [Example: Unaware of Billy's imprisonment for theft and escape from jail chimney]

- Unaware of Billy's Arizona period from ages 15 1/2 to 17 1/2, incarceration for theft, or killing of "Windy" Cahill .......... [Fabricates that Billy visited family in Texas; went to Oklahoma Indian Territory; Dodge City, Kansas; and Mexico]

- Called self an "outlaw" and bad man" .......... [Billy considered himself a soldier, deputy constable, and posseman]

- Unaware of the chronology or specifics of Billy's return to New Mexico Territory in 1877 .......... [Example: Thinks Billy worked for the Jones family]

- Unaware of the Santa Fe Ring .......... [Though central to Billy's history]

- Unaware of the specifics of the Fritz life insurance policy case, and how it legally entangled McSween and Tunstall

- Unaware of McSween's protector: Deputy Sheriff Adolph Barrier

- Error-filled specifics of Tunstall murder .......... [Examples: Unaware of why Tunstall was returning to Lincoln on his murder day; fabricates that Tunstall was in a wagon that day; and is unaware of Tunstall's murder along with his horse]

- Unaware of the original legal status of the Regulators as deputies or possemen to serve Tunstall's murder warrants

- Unaware of the proclamations of Governor Axtell outlawing the Regulators and removing Sheriff Copeland

- For the Morton-Baker capture, thinks the road back to Lincoln crossed the Capitan Mountains .......... [The road skirted the mountains on flatlands; and Morton and Baker were killed there]

- Gets wrong specifics of the Regulators' Sheriff Brady ambush .......... [All fabricated; wrong location, wrong gun taken from body, wrong motive, and wrong fellow-Regulator shot along with Billy. Unaware of concomitant Deputy Hindman killing]

- Unaware that Billy gave a deposition on the Tunstall murder to investigator, Frank Warner Angel

- Gets wrong all Lincoln County War specifics .......... [Examples: Not knowing its cause, who was on each side, which buildings were occupied, town geography, or specifics of the besieged McSween house; unaware that the military was not present until the last day and turned the tide; unaware that the military brought in a howitzer and Gatling gun, and that the commander coerced the Justice of the Peace into writing arrest warrants for McSweens, including Billy; unaware that black troops did not shoot; unaware that white soldiers fired a volley during the escape from the burning building; unaware that there were trapped women and children in the burning McSween house]

- Unaware of Attorney Chapman murder specifics .......... [Wrongly states Susan McSween was present]

- Unaware that Attorney Ira Leonard replaced Chapman

- Unaware of the specifics of Billy's Governor Wallace pardon promise deal .......... [Example: Garbles the Wallace-Billy meeting place, and fabricates erroneously that he, as "Billy," was offered $1000 to give himself up to stand trial for the Brady murder, instead of the truth that the $1000 was a capture award offered by Governor Wallace]

- Unaware that Billy's 1879 arrest and imprisonment in the Patrón house were a feigned part of the pardon for testimony deal with Governor Wallace

- Wrongly makes Billy's 1881 Mesilla trial lawyer - Albert Jennings Fountain - as Billy's attorney in 1879 .......... [Then Billy had no attorney, and was just a witness testifying in the Grand Jury against Chapman's murderers in the Wallace pardon deal]

- Unaware of Billy's successful 1879 Grand Jury testimony

- Unaware of specifics of 1879 Court of Inquiry, including details of Billy's testimony, most importantly: unaware of firing white soldiers .......... [Erroneously calls the proceeding a Court Martial]

- Fabricates an "escape" from that Patrón house imprisonment by "slipping out of handcuffs .......... [Does not realize that no escape was needed. The arrest was feigned. Billy simply left.]

- Unaware of Attorney Ira Leonard as a main pardon advocate in Billy's life, and as Billy's main attorney

- Unaware of counterfeiter Dan Dedrick in Billy's life

- Unaware of the circumstances of Billy's 1880 self-defense killing of Joe Grant

- Unaware of the specifics of the 1880 ambushes on Billy and his companions by the White Oaks posse (thus, unaware of Coyote Spring and ignorant of the location of the Greathouse ranch)

- Unaware of the counterfeiting charge against Billy

- Unaware of Secret Service Agent, Azariah Wild

- Unaware of why Garrett was tracking down Billy (wrongly thinks it was the Carlyle murder)

- Unaware of the specifics of Garrett's Stinking Springs capture of Billy

- Unaware of details of Billy's Mesilla murder trial .......... [Fabricates that witnesses lacked subpoenas]

- Unaware of the episodes or locations of Billy's long incarceration, including near tunneling out, and the hope of partisan rescues .......... [Unaware that the Ring was awaiting railroad completion to prevent rescue during transport]

- Unaware of Billy's replevin case with Attorney Edgar Caypless for the posseman's theft of his bay mare .......... [Or of the theft itself]

- Unaware of all details of Billy's great escape from the courthouse-jail on April 28, 1881

- Unaware of why Billy went to Fort Sumner after his escape

- Claimed love interest: Celsa Gutierrez, incorrectly called Saval Gutierrez's sister (was his wife) .......... [Unaware of Billy's truelove, Paulita Maxwell]

- Unaware of Fort Sumner and Maxwell house lay-out ..... [Fabricates everything incorrectly]

- Says July 14, 1881 ambush was on a dark night .......... [Actual full moon made it as bright as day]

- Said ambush's "innocent victim" was his friend, Billy Barlow .......... [Fabrication]

- Requires a preposterous and gigantic cover-up conspiracy to conceal the July 14, 1881 victim's identity; and involving: Garrett, Peter Maxwell, Deluvina, the six coroner's jurymen, the 200 townspeople, and all legitimate historians – all agreeing Billy Bonney was the corpse

- No photo-match with Billy the Kid's tintype

# JOHN MILLER'S SINGLE SHOT

*HOAXBUST: The only "identity" between John Miller and Billy Bonney was Miller's calling himself "Billy the Kid" to family and friends. Miller himself made few efforts to elaborate his "history" as Billy the Kid; and those tries were confabulated pseudo-history. His biographer, equally unenergetic, added wan hoaxing. Both omitted that Miller was born nine years too early, making him no "kid" in Billy's day. Though used by the Billy the Kid Case hoaxers for "survival suspicion," Miller failed them, lacking their Garrett-friendship-playing-dead-on-bench death scene; thus, removing justification for his exhumation for DNA to match with their fake carpenter's bench DNA of "playing-dead-Billy." Though, of course, they ignored that mismatch for future digging when it was needed to continue their hoax, as well as to keep Bill Kurtis Production's cameras filming.*

Pretender John Miller, dead since 1937, with only one little book and no known believers, was placed on history's stage by the Billy the Kid Case hoaxers after they were blocked in New Mexico courts from Billy's and his mother's graves, and were in need of bones to keep TV cameras rolling for their fake documentaries.

Buried in the Arizona Pioneers' Home Cemetery, in Prescott, Miller is still called "Johnny" in its records; presumably his nickname when a resident in its attached nursing facility - until he died of a broken hip, and was buried in their cemetery.

"Johnny" Miller's biographer was Helen Airy. Her *Whatever Happened to Billy the Kid?* was published in 1993, when she was in her 80's. She is now deceased. Her book is a hoax by virtue of willful misinformation; but her frail effort is more a "hoaxlet." She relies on old-timers. They remember that Miller said he was Billy.

## MAKING A CASE FOR MILLER

As with "Brushy Bill" Roberts, age was John Miller's problem. He was born in December of 1850; nine years before real Billy. John Miller as Billy, would have been older than Billy's boss John Tunstall, who died at almost 25. And John Miller as Billy would have been the same age as Pat Garrett.

In addition, Miller's birthplace was Fort Sill, Texas; which has no connection to real Billy's history. Helen Airy circumvented these starting-gate problems by not mentioning them.

Helen Airy begins *Whatever Happened to Billy the Kid?* with a tiny sly death scene: "It was near midnight on July 14, 1881, when Sheriff Pat Garrett shot someone in Pete Maxwell's darkened bedroom in the old officers' quarters in Fort Sumner, where Maxwell lived."

Why that shot "someone" was not the Kid is not addressed; though later, attributed to John Miller's telling, is a death scene of an accidental killing of an "Indian-dressed-similarly" to him.

Airy, however, implies a cover-up of the victim's identity. What makes her think that occurred? She refers to an unreferenced, unhistorical, and hither-to-fore unknown document for which she has no reference; and claims: "When he was asked to sign an affidavit that it was the Kid he had shot, Garrett refused to sign."

Then she outright malingers: "McKinney and Poe accused Garrett of shooting the wrong man." So, to her own distortion of John William Poe's widow's statement of Poe's initial concern that the victim was not Billy, she adds "Kip" McKinney.

She concludes: "But all through the years since that night, there have been doubts that it really was Billy the Kid's body they buried the next day."

Why doubts? Airy says people "saw Billy" after the death date; some Coroner's Jurymen signed with an X (so?); there was "irregularity" in filing the Coroner's Jury Report (untrue); and the corpse was seen by only a few people (untrue). For her "few people" witnesses, she lists Garrett, his deputies, "immediate family members" (Billy had none), and snidely adds: "supposedly, members of the coroner's jury." Omitting effort of formulating a conspiracy theory, Airy concludes, "Surely there was reason to wonder."

The rest of Airy's, 175 page, *Whatever Happened to Billy the Kid?* is about John Miller's irrelevant life after July 14, 1881; though little flash-backs of totally blighted Billy history are interspersed - and prove nothing.

A concluding fabricated matching of Miller with real Billy's tintype involves ludicrous and disingenuous tweaking for Helen Airy's foregone conclusion.

## *ROMANCE AND MURDER*

In Helen Airy's telling, the "rescue character" is an Isadora (a "petite, dark-eyed Mexican girl," and John Miller's real wife).

Airy writes: "Isadora later told friends and neighbors that some days before the shoot-out at Pete Maxwell's house the Kid [sic - John Miller] had been wounded and she had taken him to her house in Fort Sumner."

Stop. That means Airy's Miller-Billy was shot *some days prior* to the Garrett killing. That ends the modern hoaxer's carpenter's bench scenario - though it did not stop them from digging him up.

Isadora is called the widow of Charlie Bowdre; though that widow's name was Manuela; and Manuela had left Fort Sumner after her husband's murder by Pat Garrett in December of 1880.

But why should we think John Miller was Billy Bonney?

Airy says there were similarities: light eyes, a bad temper, and a tendency to point his rifle at people!

Another Airy "proof" would have been offensive to real Billy. Miller's last shooting victim was his Mexican worker. Billy's bi-culturalism arguably brought Hispanic men to the McSween cause. One can quote a "Teddy Blue" Abbott, a wandering cowboy contemporary of Billy Bonney's, who wrote an old-timer biography titled *We Pointed Them North*. Abbott stated about coming to New Mexico Territory: "The Lincoln County troubles was still going on, and you had to be either for Billy the Kid or against him. It wasn't my fight ... it was the Mexicans that made a hero of him."

As to the physical, Helen Airy touts "remarkable" resemblance of John Miller to Billy.

As evidence, she says Miller wore the same hat as Billy had on in the tintype! That claim is more worthless than it appears, because the tintype hat is likely just the photographers prop. Called the Carlsbad, it first appeared in 1880 as a peculiar, high crowned, short-brimmed style; and was definitely not for riding the range. Real Billy wore a sombrero. It seems that Miller had acquired his tintype facsimile for his own for posturing as Billy.

Of course, Miller had requisite crooked front teeth. Also he did a rope trick involving hand flexibility for "handcuff" slipping. Miller's dark brows are compared to the fake Catherine Antrim photo; though Airy even contradicts that "proof" by stating that John Miller had a Cherokee mother - a possible truth. Wisely unmentioned by Airy is John Miller's long scrawny neck, since Billy had a short thick one.

Pictures of wax busts made for comparative photographs for *Whatever Happened to Billy the Kid?* by a sympathetic artist prove that, by tweaking Billy Bonney and John Miller, a vague resemblance can be achieved; though Billy suffers most in lost attractiveness.

## *OLD-TIMERS HAVE THEIR SAY*

After page 33 of *Whatever Happened to Billy the Kid,* Helen Airy's only "proof" of John Miller as Billy is old-timer recollections. Most of her interviewed old-timers merely say Miller *told them* he was Billy - and Miller's wife, Isadora, vouched for it.

The oddest of the old-timers is a Herman Tecklenburg, who claims *he* knew John Miller in Fort Sumner as Billy the Kid; and was later his "most trusted friend." Tecklenburg seems to have had a follie a deux with Miller; meaning *both* were delusional.

Miller himself, apparently, barely elaborated Billy history - and knew none as seen in his snippets presented by Airy. But Miller did strip to show twelve bullet scars on his chest; though real Billy - other than a leg wound from Deputy Jacob "Billy" Matthews in the aftermath of the Sheriff William Brady shooting - acquired his single non-healing chest wound on July 14, 1881!

A rare elaboration of a John Miller rendition does come from a Frank Burrard Creasy, who prefaced with: "The following is an actual account of Billy the Kid as I know it" - and is Miller's florid fabrication. Creasy states, "The first time anyone really heard the name of Billy the Kid was in 1871, when he was twelve years old. A deputy sheriff apparently insulted Billy's mother for which Billy promptly shot him and fled to the hills."

Frank Burrard Creasy also provided a wildly fantasized, Miller-made death scene:

Pat Garrett, who was the marshal of Lincoln at the time, and a well known bounty hunter, heard that Billy was in town and along with two of his deputies laid in waiting near the side of beef. When the Indian boy stepped up onto the veranda of the house, he was shot down by Pat Garrett, who had apparently mistaken him for Billy. Billy [Miller] told me once that he and the

Indian were dressed alike to confuse people. Pat Garrett was afraid of the reaction of townspeople and immediately buried the body.

Absolutely nothing in the rendition is true. But Frank Creasy even ends Airy's book with the photo of his cherished "gun of Billy the Kid": a single action Colt .45, which John Miller gave to him.

But Creasy had inspired Helen Airy to vehement crescendo:

> To date, American historians maintain Sheriff Pat Garrett killed Billy the Kid in Lincoln County, New Mexico. But according to Creasy's account Garrett killed the wrong man, concealed the error and collected the reward ... For reasons unknown, historians in the United States failed to follow up on the leads Frank Creasy furnished about John Miller's claim that he was Billy the Kid.

And Helen Airy's total historical ignorance shows throughout her book. She even states that Billy was shot in *Lincoln County*, not San Miguel County - from which his Fort Sumner killing (and John Miller's own fabricated death scene) was 150 miles away.

*Whatever Happened to Billy the Kid?* has a little Appendix of misinformation containing tabloid-like *El Paso Times* articles from the 1920's to '60's. For example, Billy the Kid's grave was said to be "marked by a rude cross, that was to prove to Billy's sister that he was still alive." Billy had no sister.

But by 2005, the clock was ticking on how much longer John Miller would repose in the sacrosanct peace of his own grave. The modern Billy the Kid Case hoaxers needed his DNA after there was no hope of getting into Billy the Kid's and Catherine Antrim's gravesites in Fort Sumner and Silver City - leaving them only Dr. Henry Lee's fake carpenter's bench Billy-blood-DNA and a round-about murder case solution for Lincoln County Sheriff's Department Case 2003-274 (*if* a claimant, like John Miller, was actually Billy the Kid, then Pat Garrett must have killed the innocent victim on July 14, 1881 for the grave in Fort Sumner).

# SUMMARIZING JOHN MILLER
# FLUBBING BILLY BONNEY

## DEBUNKING JOHN MILLER

One can say that John Miller is the unluckiest Billy the Kid pretender - if imposters expect to lie in peace in their graves.

And, despite the obvious absurdity of John Miller's claims, comedian George Carlin's warning must be heeded: "Just because you got the monkey off your back, doesn't mean the circus has left town." So, "Johnny" Miller may again rise from the dead, if needed again for another media circus. After all, the Billy the Kid Case hoaxers have their Bill Kurtis Production Company's John Miller exhumation film in the can.

Nevertheless, John Miller's" failure as a Billy the Kid identity claimant is summarized below.

- Birth Date: December (unknown day), 1850 .......... [Billy's Birthdate: November 23, 1859]

- Birthplace: Fort Sill, Texas .......... [Billy's Birthplace: New York City, New York]

- Named John Miller; used "Billy the Kid" .......... [Billy's names: William Henry McCarty, Henry Antrim, William Henry "Billy" Bonney, nickname "Kid." Never used "Billy the Kid"]

- Cherokee mother .......... [Billy had an Irish mother]

- Had only a sister .......... [Billy had no sister. He had a brother]

- Unaware of Billy's childhood and Silver City history

- Stated when Billy was 12 he shot a deputy sheriff .......... [Fabrication]

- Apparently near illiterate .......... [Billy was highly literate]

- Racist (murdered his Mexican worker) .......... [Billy was pro-Hispanic]

- Called self an "outlaw" .......... [Billy considered himself a soldier, deputy constable, and posseman]

- Claimed 12 bullet wounds .......... [Billy only had a thigh wound and a death wound!]

- Unaware of all Lincoln County War history

- Unaware of Dudley Court of Inquiry

- Unaware of Secret Service Agent, Azariah Wild

- Unaware of specifics of Garrett's capture of Billy

- Unaware of Billy's Mesilla trial

- Unaware of all details of Billy's great escape of April 28, 1881

- Love interest: Isabella (his actual wife) .......... [Unaware of Billy's truelove, Paulita Maxwell]

- Claims being shot by an unknown attacker days before July 14, 1881; and his "Indian friend" was the "innocent victim"

- Claims Garrett killed his "Indian friend" near the side of beef, mistaking him for "Billy" .......... [Fabrication]

- Claims the "innocent victim's" body was buried immediately without witnesses .......... [Fabrication]

- Gigantic conspiracy needed to hide July 14, 1881 victim's identity - involving: Garrett, Peter Maxwell, Deluvina, coroner's jurymen, 200 townspeople, future historians

- No photo match to Billy Bonney's tintype

# CHAPTER 9:

# DIGGING UP MORE THAN JOHN MILLER

**Follow the blood: In Billy the Kid case, Miller exhumed**

Julie Carter/For the Ruidoso News
Oct 6, 2005, 07:54 pm

One established absolute fact to date in the ongoing saga of the legend of Billy the Kid is that he is dead. That fact can be written without question because 145 years since he was born would make it so.

The _____ question today is, Where is he dead? Currently, investigators are waiting _____ from a carpenter's work bench last summer (July 2004) _____ exhumed body of John Miller, one of two who _____ the Kid.

_____ one the Kid was laid on by friends in the _____ was shot.

_____ and retired federal cop and Capitan Mayor _____ cial investigation they began in 2003.

_____ legend and knowing that science could now _____ pair set out to do just that.

_____ of the escape of Billy the _____ from the Lincoln _____ will _____ of _____ #2003-274 _____ investigated or _____

Capitan Mayor Steve Sederwall, instrumental in the investigation of the real Billy the Kid, examines the skull of John Miller in Arizona.

---

**Officials could face charges for digging up alleged Billy the Kid**

By JOANNA DODDER The Daily Courier

PRESCOTT  Did New Mexico deputies violate the law by digging up the remains of a Prescott man who claimed to be Billy the Kid?

Local authorities _____
Line _____
Pre _____
John _____
Kid.

Former _____
others _____
blood th _____
Lincoln _____
Sumner, _____

A shoulder _____
consistent _____
Sullivan said _____
also are cons _____

Since Garrett _____
and then let hi _____

He hopes to see _____

Sullivan and other _____
a femur from an un _____
on May 19, 2005. T _____
unmarked grave, jus _____
taped the event.

A Billy the Kid historia _____
filed a complaint with t _____
forwarded it to the Pres _____

"This is some kind of goo _____
crusade," Snell said. "He'_____
always been."

PPD Det. Anna Cahill cont _____
the disinterment, ranging fro _____
County Medical Examiner's O _____
ederal officer involved in the _____
Sullivan. Tunnell hired Fulginiti _____

---

**LINCOLN COUNTY SHERIFF'S DEPARTMENT**

**SUPPLEMENTAL REPORT**

Case #:      2003-274
Date:         Thursday, May 19, 2005
Subject:     Exhumation of John Miller, Prescott, Arizona
Location:    Arizona Pioneers' Cemetery, Prescott, Arizona
Report By:  Steven M. Sederwall

On Thursday, May 19, 2005, at approximately 1:00 pm the following met at the Arizona Pioneers' Cemetery in Prescott, Arizona.

**Investigators:**

Steven M. Sederwall; Lincoln County Sheriff's Deputy
DOB- 09/02/52
Capitan, New Mexico

Tom Sullivan; Sheriff of Lincoln Cou _____
DOB- 04/10/40
Capitan, New Mexico

Dale Tunnell; Arizona State Investiga _____
DOB-
Phoenix, Arizona

Stephen W. McGregor; Ex-Lincoln _____
DOB- 07/16/57
Hannibal, Missouri

Dr. Rick Staub; Orchid Cell Mark, D _____
DOB- 02/15/52
Dallas, Texas

Mike Polino; Yavapai County Sheriff _____
DOB- 06/29/62
Prescott, Arizona

Laura Fulginiti; Forensic Scientist
DOB - 11/09/62
Phoenix, Arizona

Kristen Hartnett; Forensic Scientis _____
DOB - 10/30/77
Phoenix, Arizona

---

**PUBLISHED ON APRIL 13, 2006:**

**A New Billy the Kid?**

The mad search for the bones of an American outlaw icon has come to Arizona

By LEO W. BANKS

Billy the Kid's legend has hovered over the landscape of the American West for 125 years — _____ hype and fantasy, always _____ merel _____

_____
inca _____
enti _____
shot _____
of Tu _____
Grant _____

---

**VARIETY.com**

100 _____    HOME | FILM | TV | INTL. | BUSINESS | MUSIC | HOME ENT | LEGIT | TECHNOLOGY | ...

Visual FX/Animation Resource Guide

Search

---

Posted: Sat., May 20, 2006, 8:31am PT

**Requiem for Billy the Kid**

Jacques Bezoin and Cargo Films presentation of a Cargo Films pro _____
by Caine Leblanc. Executive producer, Bezoin; _____

---

**Men Who Exhumed Billy the Kid Won't Be Charged**

BY Associated Press
October 24, 2006
URL: http://www.nysun.com/a _____

Prosecutors won't seek charges _____
exhumed the remains of a man _____
outlaw William Bonney, also k _____

A former sheriff of Lincoln C _____
Sullivan, and a former mayor _____
Sederwall, dug up the bones o _____
Miller was buried at the state _____
Cemetery in Prescott nearly 7 _____

"It appears officials in charge _____
permission and the people wh _____
recover samples of the remain _____
permission to do so," Bill Fitz _____
the Maricopa County Attorney _____
decision not to seek charges, s _____

Messrs. Sullivan and Sederwal _____
Miller's remains. The samples _____
to compare Miller's DNA to bl _____
bench that is believed to be the _____
placed on after he was shot to d _____

Messrs. Sullivan and Sederwall _____
the Kid's bones since 2003.

They began their quest in Fort S _____
history says the Kid was buried S _____
County Sheriff Pat Garrett gunned him down in 1881.
But at least two men — Miller and Ollie "Brushy Bill"
Roberts of Texas — claimed prior to their deaths _____

---

NEW MEXICO & THE WEST          ALBUQUERQUE, MAY 14, 200 _____

**New Mexicans Dig Up Trouble in Arizona**

BY AMANDA LEE MYERS
- The Associated Press

PRESCOTT, Ariz. — More than 100 years after his death, Billy the Kid can still stir up a heap of trouble.

Two men on a quest to find where the outlaw hero and American legend is buried could face time in the pokey for unearthing remains last May in this central Arizona community.

Tom Sullivan, former sheriff of New Mexico's Lincoln County, and Steve Sederwall, former mayor of Capitan, exhumed ____ who was buried in Prescott nearly 70 years ago. John Miller and Ollie "Brushy Bill" ___

Authorities are considering ____ whether to charge Sullivan and Sederwall with a felony for removing some remains of Miller and of another man buried in an unmarked grave next to him.

The Arizona Pioneers Home Cemetery is the site in Prescott, Ariz., where two New Mexico men exhumed remains last year in their quest to find the body of Billy the Kid. Authorities are considering whether to charge Tom Sullivan and Steve Sederwall.

"This is a simple, straightforward, open-and-shut grave-robbing case," said David Snell, a ____ silly the Kid junkie from Tucson.

In March, Snell wrote a letter to Yavapai County Attorney Sheila Polk that sparked a police investigation into the exhumation. In the letter, he called unearthing the graves a "sordid and reprehensible affair."

He argued that Sullivan and Sederwall acted inappropriately because they didn't have a permit or court order. Sullivan and Sederwall dis _____

agree.

"I'm confident we didn't do anything wrong in Arizona," Sullivan said. "When you commit a crime, you have to have intent. There's certainly no intent to be grave-robbers."

Sullivan and Sederwall have been hunting for the Kid's bones since 2003. They began their very public quest in Fort Summer where history says the Kid was buried after then-Lincoln County Sheriff Pat Garrett killed him in 1881.

But at least two men — Miller and Ollie "Brushy Bill" Roberts of Texas — claimed prior to their deaths that they were Billy the Kid. Their stories pre _____

suppose that Garrett killed the wrong man in Fort Sumner.

After more than a year of fighting to unseal the Summer grave, Sullivan and Sederwall dropped the request and decided to begin the process of elimination in Arizona. They now have a Dallas lab comparing DNA from the bones they dug up to blood found on a bench on which Bru _____ lieve the Kid's de _____ lay.

Sullivan said there are al _____ plans to unearth the grave of "Brushy Bill."

Historians have called fo _____ quest to unearth Billy th _____ ridiculous and say _____ an impossibility that Miller or _____ turn out to be the Kid.

"The guy in Prescott was _____ Billy the Kid," said Bob Stah _____ professor at Arizona State _____ versity who has, for five yea _____ researched the Kid's death _____ terial to write a book ab _____ him.

# ESCAPE TO ARIZONA: HOAX REBIRTH

*HOAXBUST: Blocked from disinterring Billy and his mother, pretender exhumations were the sole option to continue the Billy the Kid Case. Using Governor Richardson's political connections in Arizona, John Miller, buried in Prescott, was dug up first, under a Lincoln County Sheriff's Department Supplemental Report for Case # 2003-274; though Miller lacked the scenario of bleeding on the bench to justify DNA matching with Dr. Lee's bench sample - fake anyway. That exhumation also marked the hoaxers' cross-over into criminality - by digging up John Miller without valid DNA for justification, plus disinterring random William Hudspeth in wanton desecration. When investigated after a criminal complaint to Arizona authorities, and later by open records request, Virden, Sullivan, and Sederwall falsely denied involvement. And in this Arizona exhumation period, the hoaxers hid another media coup.*

After my accidental success in protecting Billy's and his mother's gravesites from Billy the Kid Case hoax ravages, my second "tolling bell" - again a fax, again a newspaper article - came from a friend. Dated October 6, 2005 and by hoax-loyalist reporter, Julie Carter, it was her *RuidosoNews.com's* "Follow the Blood: In the Billy the Kid Case, Miller Exhumed." [APPENDIX: 7] It had "Lonnie" Lippman's photo of his buddy, Deputy Sederwall, holding their trophy skull. Its caption said:

> Capitan Mayor Steve Sederwall, instrumental in the investigation of the real Billy the Kid, examines the skull of John Miller in Arizona.

The skull could also have been William Hudspeth's. The hoaxers had done a secret John Miller exhumation in Arizona.

By then, as of January 1, 2005, there was a new Lincoln County Sheriff, Rick Virden, Tom Sullivan's past Undersheriff. Virden had covertly continued Case 2003-274, deputizing Sullivan and Sederwall for it. Virden proved his hoaxer chops by the next month and on airwaves. He got on Harvey Twite's local "KEDU Community Radio" to assure people that he was *not* continuing the Billy the Kid Case. But he had deputized Sullivan on January 1, 2005, and Sederwall on February 25, 2005 for the case!

It took my records request through journalist Jay Miller to get Sheriff Virden to fess up on November 28, 2005. Virden answered on his official sheriff's department stationery:

> We are interested in the truth surrounding Billy the Kid and are continuing the investigation ... Tom Sullivan and Steve Sederwall are assigned to investigate the shootings of William H. Bonney and Deputies Bell and Olinger. [APPENDIX: 38]

So Rick Virden was actually the initiator of the hoax's exhumation frenzy. During his tenure would be generated all the forensic DNA documents of Case 2003-274. And the hoaxers' desired "media circus" would be achieved.

Rick Virden had been a hoax participant from day one. As Undersheriff, according to a report he wrote on Sheriff's Department stationery on April 28, 2003 for "Case # 2003-274," he waited in the Wortley Hotel, across the street from the old Lincoln courthouse, while his Sheriff, Tom Sullivan, fired a revolver inside. Virden heard it.

That puff piece of investigative faking was the reality of a grand and unsupported pronouncement in Anthony DellaFlora's June 11, 2003 *Albuquerque Journal* article, "State Not Kidding Around":

> Sullivan and others pushing for the investigation hope to determine from modern ballistic tests if the gun used to kill Bell and Olinger belonged to one of the deputies – which would support the argument that Bonney wrested it away from Bell – or if it belonged to someone else, which would point to outside help.

Omitted was the hoaxers' lack of any authenticated gun - or anything else - to prove anything at all about the deputy killings. And hearing the shot meant only that Rick Virden was not deaf.

## MEET JOHN MILLER

From their New Mexico experience, the hoaxers had learned a crucial lesson: avoid courts and medical examiners. Dig; then tell.

With John Miller, needed only was Governor Bill Richardson - and a favor. Richardson knew fellow Democrat Janet Napolitano, then Arizona's governor. John Miller's Prescott grave was in her state-owned and run Arizona Pioneers' Home Cemetery; Miller having died in its associated nursing home. Richardson appeared poised to offer her and Arizona "Billy the Kid," in return for the "media circus" featuring presidentially-hopeful him.

And bulldog-built Napolitano, called extremely corrupt by my Arizona contacts, was ideal. By 2009, as Obama's Homeland Security Secretary, she called Iraq and Afghanistan vets potential terrorists, the insult earning April 16th's *Drudge Report's* headline: "Big Sis Feels Heat for Homeland Warning on 'Radicals.' " By 2013, she would not be immune to whistleblower Edward Snowden's proof of NSA spying on all American citizens.

The concealed John Miller exhumation, done on May 19, 2005, was not announced until that October 6, 2005 with Julie Carter's *RuidosoNews.com* article: "Follow the Blood: In the Billy the Kid Case, Miller Exhumed." That article also had Sederwall's necessary carpenter's bench fakery to re-write the hoax with shot Billy on the bench. So it had his concoctions of "dead men don't bleed," "a large amount of blood [on the bench]" and "chest-wound-pattern [on the bench];" while warily shape-shifting case definition to only the Kid's deputy murders. Then Carter segued to the bench, Garrett as a murderer, and digging up John Miller, stating:

> When the lab [Orchid Cellmark] called and said the DNA was human and it was the same DNA on the three-board-wide bench, Sederwall and Sullivan decided it was time to start looking at the John Miller story a little harder ...**[AUTHOR'S NOTE: Faked here is a "match" of Miller to bench.]**

> With both Sederwall and Sullivan present, the exhumation of Miller took place on May 21 [sic- May 19] ... Miller's samples have been sent to an unnamed laboratory in Texas to extract DNA.

By November 6, 2005, hoaxer reporter Rene Romo's *Albuquerque Journal* article further spun the exhumation;

it emerging later that Governor Napolitano's staff and Arizona Pioneers' Home supervisor, Gary Olson, helped him write it. In his "Billy the Kid Probe May Yield New Twist" [APPENDIX: 10], the case shape-shifted as protecting Garrett! Romo says:

> Sederwall acknowledges that what started out as an effort to defend the honor of Garrett against claims that the famous Lincoln County sheriff did not kill the Kid may have taken a new direction.

The "new direction" was: John Miller is Billy the Kid! Julie Carter's October 6, 2005 "Follow the Blood," had quoted Sederwall in full "martyr for the truth" mode:

> "In the light of the evidence, we see that the history of Billy the Kid will change. Those with monied interest in history remaining the same will not be happy ... As a cop I know when people fight to keep you from looking at something, they are always trying to hide something. The Lincoln County War is still going on."

For reporter Romo, Sederwall showed the rest of his cards:

> "If that DNA matches the work bench, I think the game is over ... If not," he said, "investigators will try to obtain permission to exhume the remains of Roberts, who is buried in Hamilton, Texas."

But, for now, a bone in the hand was worth many underground. Sederwall had to clinch John Miller as Billy. So, as would later emerge, he lied floridly to do it. Romo quoted:

> Sederwall ... said Miller's skeletal remains were intriguing. He said Miller had buck teeth, like the Kid, and an old bullet wound that entered his upper left chest and exited through the scapula.

And TV cameras were turned on again. Sederwall gloated to Romo that Bill Kurtis had an "exclusive deal to publicize them because he helped to pay some costs associated with the investigation." No one seemed to notice the oddity of a TV producer paying into a Lincoln County murder case. And Julie Carter stated that Kurtis's programs were A&E Channel's "Cold Case Files" and "American Justice and Investigative Reports."

Arizona plus Miller's body did not mean the hoaxers abandoned Silver City hopes. For Carter's "Follow the Blood," the hoaxers hid Judge Henry Quintero's stipulation of getting DNA from Fort Sumner's grave exhumation to return to Billy's mother.

Sullivan stated:

> "A judge in Silver City told the investigators to come back if they had enough evidence to warrant the need for Catherine Antrim's (the Kid's mother) DNA. With the DNA results from the blood on the table and soon the results of Miller's DNA, investigators will likely take the judge up on that offer ... The officials in Ft. Sumner and Silver City thought we would just roll over and play dead. We didn't and this case is far from over."

But the hoaxers were keeping more secrets. One was beyond their wildest ambitions; the other made Bill Kurtis's footage potential crime-scene evidence.

### *JOHN MILLER GETS A "BELIEVER"*

The hoaxers' biggest problem was that John Miller had no believers. So, with their ricochet validation trick, one was created. In a report from the Prescott Police Department that I got by open records request, that man was described as a 15 year friend of Sederwall's. His name was Dale Tunnell.

Tunnell emerged on March 13, 2006 - just two days after a still unknown and unanticipated potential disaster for their scheme. Tunnell's Internet article on helenair.com, by a Robert Struckman, was "Bitterroot man hopes to uncover the truth about Billy the Kid." [APPENDIX: 39] A major hoax document, it was a new shape-shift. Struckman's conclusion said it all:

> He [Tunnell] would like to confirm the story put forth by Airy. Like him, she was an amateur historian who bucked the official story. Academics scoffed at her account. "I'd like to prove her correct," he said.

First, however, Tunnell's "credibility" had to be manufactured. He is described as owner of Forensitec *and a Billy the Kid researcher convinced by Airy's John Miller claims.* Tunnell added: "[A] Ph.D. in forensic criminology ... pursuing a second doctorate in general psychology," a "retired federal investigator," "a deputy sheriff in 1974 in Lincoln County," an "investigator with the

Arizona Department of Corrections," and "a federal agent with the U.S. Department of Interior."

I Googled Forensitec and found: "Forensitec - Forensic Psycholinguistic Patterning." Tunnell is listed as "President and founder." What about the Ph.D.? He calls himself "a doctoral learner in General Psychology," and the "World's Foremost Authority in Forensic Language Analysis." This apparently meant he read psychology books and thought he could tell if people were lying (ironic given his hoax participation, his hoax cohorts, and the indication that he was no "doctor" as he claimed).

For Struckman's article, Tunnell, as a "forensic criminologist," hoed rows for his hoaxer buddies: Miller as Billy; and their case weirdly as both a criminal investigation and an amateur pursuit.

Why the shape-shift from the Garrett murder case and its law enforcement glitz? The hoaxers were skitterish. Their exhumation "permission" was shaky; and their "forensic data" fake. So an amateur status claim - they hoped - blocked open records requests.

First, Tunnell had to upgrade John Miller. Struckman stated:

> Tunnell's interest in the famous outlaw was piqued when he read a 1993 book by Helen Airy entitled, "Whatever Happened to Billy the Kid" ...
>
> "Even if it [DNA matching] comes back positive, there will be more work to do," Tunnell said. He hopes to find conclusive documentation placing Miller at or near Fort Sumner in July of 1881 or connecting his wife, Isadora, to a relationship there ...
>
> Tunnell has found enough material to poke holes in the official histories, he said ...
>
> "I want to set the record straight. If Billy the Kid , from 1881 to 1937, lived the life of an honest man, a hardworking fool, then I say he paid his debt to society," Tunnell said.

A credibility gap remained. Hiding the Garrett murder investigation, made exhumation seem like just a favor to Miller: setting *his* record straight! Reminiscent of the hapless hoaxer - ultimately recalled De Baca County Sheriff Gary Graves - Dale Tunnell became confused by the tangled fakery. So he made an unintentionally funny comment to Struckman:

> "It's possible," Tunnell said, "that Garrett conspired with Billy to fake the death. Maybe Billy never laid, wounded, on the carpenter's bench. Maybe another body was buried in Billy's place."

Oops, "Doctor" Tunnell! Without Billy on the bench, there goes "Lee's bloody DNA of the Kid." There goes digging up John Miller solely for a DNA match! Struckman ended with Sullivan:

> After **getting permission** [author's boldface] to exhume Miller's body, DNA samples were taken. The DNA analysis will be done by Dr. Henry Lee, founder of the Forensic Science Program at the University of New Haven and chief emeritus of the Connecticut State Police, Sullivan said.
> What if the DNA matches the wooden bench?
> "We'll change history. I don't know. Arizona would have the real Billy the Kid," Sullivan said.

Note the "getting permission." On that would hang the hoaxers' fate - along with their secret, second, disinterred body. And unbeknownst to Tunnell, he was to be the hoaxers' patsy.

# ARIZONA TROUBLE: LAW MEETS HOAX

## *CRIME MIGHT NOT PAY*

On April 12, 2006, my fax rang. A team member had sent that day's article by a Joanna Dodder in *The Daily Courier* of Prescott, Arizona. Its headline was "Officials could face charges for digging up alleged Billy the Kid." [APPENDIX: 40] An Arizona citizen had made a criminal complaint to the police! A call to one of my legal consultants identified for me the potential crimes as being felonies of disturbing remains and grave robbing.

Given that extremity, for Joanna Dodder, Tom Sullivan and Steve Sederwall ditched their Tunnell-generated amateur historian identities and the Kid's deputy killing case, and shape-shifting back to Lincoln County Deputy Sheriffs doing a murder investigation against Pat Garrett.

> Former Lincoln County Sheriff Tom Sullivan said he and the others plan to compare DNA from Miller's bones with DNA from blood that came from a bench on which Billy the Kid lay after Lincoln County Sheriff Pat Garrett shot him on July 14, 1881, in Ft. Sumner, N.M. ...
> Sullivan and former Capitan, N.M., mayor Steve Sederwall now are commissioned as Lincoln County deputies, Sullivan said. They are in the midst of a 3-year-old investigation into whether Billy the Kid actually is buried in Ft. Sumner ...

Sullivan and his fellow former lawmen are on a mission to find the real Billy using modern-day technology.

And, apparently hoping discovery trumped criminality, they claimed *evidence that Miller was Billy the Kid*!

What evidence? "DNA matching" was supposedly months away. So they repeated their fake skeleton claim from Rene Romo's November 6, 2005, *Albuquerque Journal's*, "Billy the Kid Probe May Yield New Twist." Dodder quotes Sullivan:

> "A shoulder bone from Miller's grave already indicates damage consistent with that of a gunshot wound that The Kid suffered ... The skeleton's protruding teeth and small stature also are consistent with Billy ... Since Garrett was friends with The Kid, he might have shot him and then let him escape."

But now their fakery stakes were much higher. Arizona was the home of Joe Arpaio, "America's toughest sheriff." His pink underwear for prisoners was famous. So the hoaxers ramped up credentials, and spilled secrets for aggrandizement. Their buddy, Dale Tunnell, was shape-shifted to their forensic expert who had hired another one, a Dr. Laura Fulginiti, to be *on site*.

But who had pressed criminal charges? The hero was Arizona amateur historian, David Snell. Dodder quoted Snell: "This is some kind of good ol' boy back-slappin' beer-drinkin' crusade ... He's [Billy's] buried in Ft. Sumner, where he's always been."

Later I learned that on March 11, 2006 - just two days before Tunnell's Miller as Billy article - Snell had filed his complaint.

Having followed the Billy the Kid Case, David Snell had suspected John Miller's exhumation in May of 2005 because of tire tracks in the Arizona Pioneers' Home Cemetery. He also made a complaint to Arizona's Attorney General, Terry Goddard, and did open records requests on the Prescott Police Department after they began their own investigation of John Miller's exhumation.

In that May 2005 period, a Lincoln County resident angry about the Billy the Kid Case called the Supervisor of the Arizona Pioneers' Home Cemetery, Jeanine Dike. Dike allegedly told him that the exhumation had been done with permission from "the governor of New Mexico!"

It would take years for the hoaxers' similar admission - under oath, and with an astonishing addition of copies of very telling checks for Case 2003-274 received at Governor Richardson's office.

For his March 11, 2006 complaint, David Snell wrote with anguished passion to Shiela Polk, the Yavapai County Attorney - the county of the exhumation. [APPENDIX: 41]

I feel it is my duty to report to you that grave robbers are plying their trade in Yavapai County. There individuals' crimes are being committed openly, knowingly, and with contempt for state and county law regarding exhumations. In the course of their nefarious activities, these parties have compromised and ultimately corrupted various officials and public employees. To date, all the parties involved in these crimes have been exempted from any sort of criminal investigation, let alone prosecution ...

Now that these circumstances have been brought to your personal attention, I have every confidence that the good citizens of Yavapai County, and Arizona, can be assured of timely and effective action against these ghoulish scofflaws who loot our people's final resting places for personal gain.

Next stop was the Prescott Police Department, then the City Attorney. Dodder's article stated:

Now Prescott City Prosecutor Glenn Savona is trying to figure out whether someone violated the law and whether the city or state has jurisdiction since the State of Arizona owns the Pioneers' Home Cemetery.

Complicating matters is the fact that the person who apparently gave Sullivan permission to dig up the grave, former Pioneers' Home Superintendent Jeanine Dike, is away on a Mormon mission until June 2007 ...

Dike apparently agreed to let Sullivan and others dig up Miller's unmarked remains under a relatively new state law that allows the action without a court order and permit if it's for "internal management," according to a Prescott Police Department report.

"It doesn't look like the request came for an internal issue," Savona said. That law doesn't allow people to take the remains, either, he added ...

The only other way to legally disinter the body is to get a permit from the Yavapai County Community Health Services Department after getting a court order or family permission

Fulginiti and others told police that Tunnell assured them he had permission to conduct the dig.

So it emerged that the hoaxers intended to claim "permission" was from Superintendent Jeanine Dike.

David Snell wailed, on April 19, 2006, to Julie Carter in her *Ruidoso News* article, "Digging up bones": "I am a one man crusade against stupidity."

I wondered if the hoaxers were sweating - all because of David Snell. Being a coward, and afraid of the hoaxers, I had already made my choice when I learned about the exhumation from the hoaxers' October 2006, Julie Carter, "Follow the Blood" article: Do nothing. But before I knew it, "history's current" swept me back into political sewage flowing from New Mexico to Arizona.

## PILTDOWN MAN REDUX

Threatened by David Snell and pink underwear, the hoaxers proved cool cucumbers. The day after Joanna Dodder's article, on April 13th, they manically tossed, at their next reporter, the full-blown hoax; as they deliriously shouted a version of "We're giving you Billy the Kid!"

This approach would reveal two problems. The first was Piltdown Man's: being made from two skeletons.

The second was this next reporter: Leo W. Banks of the *Tucson Weekly*. Banks called their bluff. In so doing, he uncovered the fact that could land them all in jail. He discovered a second exhumed corpse, who would, a month later, be identified by another reporter as a William Hudspeth.

For Leo Banks, Deputy Tom Sullivan switched hats with Dave Tunnell to became the Helen Airy convert, and was quoted: "Helen Airy's book triggered it for me ... It made a lot of sense. I read it and thought, 'We have another Billy the Kid.' "

But Banks, in his "The New Billy the Kid?" called their roving extravaganza "airship Billy." [APPENDIX: 42] And Banks had heard about its perpetrators, saying: "You might remember the names of the two investigators: Tom Sullivan, a retired sheriff of Lincoln County, N.M., and Steve Sederwall, a former federal cop."

For Banks, however, Sullivan and Sederwall performed their "high-tech forensic" gambit, flaunting famous Dr. Lee and the carpenter's bench - now "saturated with blood." Banks quoted:

"When we found the bench and the other evidence, we thought, 'Let's forget about these other bodies,' " says Sullivan, referring to Catherine Antrim and the Kid. "Let's do Miller. And if that doesn't work, we'll go down to Texas and do Brushy Bill."

Dr. Laura Fulginiti, the hoaxers' forensic front, however, became a liability. To Leo Banks, she debunked Miller's skeleton!

> Fulginiti says the first body she studied had buck teeth and the scapula fracture that caused such a commotion with investigators.
>
> As Sederwall told the *Weekly*, "We were shocked when we got him up. He had buck teeth just like the Kid and a bullet hole in the upper left chest that exited the shoulder blade."
>
> Sullivan made a similar statement, suggesting this might be the man Garrett shot the morning of July 14, 1881.
>
> But when contacted by the *Weekly*, Fulginiti didn't support their enthusiasm. "There was evidence of trauma on the scapula, but I couldn't tell whether it was from a gunshot wound or not," she said.

There was worse. The body with the bad scapula and alleged buck teeth was not Miller's! Fulginiti revealed that it was from the adjacent north grave, also dug up. Worse again, it was the right, not left scapula! And the damage was not from a bullet!

Fulginiti had done research. She learned that John Miller had died shortly after sustaining a hip fracture. One grave's bones had a broken, unhealed hip. Reporter Banks called the first body "Scapula Man;" the second body, "Hip Man" [Miller].

So the hoaxers were substituting "Scapula Man" (William Hudspeth) for John Miller ("Hip Man) for their fables! As well as switching the right scapula as a left one!

It got worse. Leo Banks contacted Orchid Cellmark Laboratory, and made an astounding discovery. Banks wrote:

> The DNA expert present at the exhumation, Dr. Rick Staub, of Orchid Cellmark Labs in Dallas, was unable to extract useable DNA from Hip Man [Miller]. But he did get a usable sample from Scapula Man.

So John Miller's remains had yielded no DNA at all! When confronted by Banks, Sullivan and Sederwall were left awkwardly claiming that their hired forensic expert was wrong.

Nevertheless, it was obvious that, for their own Piltdown Man, the hoaxers had assembled a "John Miller as a Billy the Kid" from a random corpse's bones and DNA matched to Dr. Lee's fake bench blood DNA! It would even emerge from Dr. Fulginiti's report, that John Miller's skull had no buck teeth - it had no teeth at all!

## *HOAXER BELLE INDIFFÉRENCE*

The Arizona digging had been done with thieves' stealth, as Sullivan and Sederwall had admitted blithely to Leo Banks for that April 13, 2006 "The New Billy the Kid?" Banks quoted:

> "People at Fort Sumner wouldn't allow us to exhume Billy's remains, because they're not sure he's there," says the 65-year-old Sullivan, still smarting from the criticism. "Everybody lawyered up, and we ran into a lot of legal B.S."
> **So Sullivan and Sederwall stole into Arizona on stocking feet, working quietly to get Miller's bones out of his grave at Prescott's state-run Arizona Pioneers' Home, snag some DNA and head back home.** [author's boldface]
> "We slipped in there and slipped out fast," Sullivan told the *Weekly.*
> "We all stayed at the same hotel, sort of to keep it quiet. If the media got word, our critics would've gotten together to lawyer the whole thing up, serve people with papers and temporary restraining orders, and all that crap."

Their Pat Garrett as murderer fabrication tripped easily off their tongues at Leo Banks's leading question:

> Was Sheriff Garrett, **a known friend of the Kid**, [author's boldface] outraged at Billy's conviction in the Brady trial and somehow involved in helping Billy escape justice?
> "From a law-enforcement perspective, nothing fits," says Sullivan ...
> Sederwall points with suspicion to the last line of the coroner's report on Billy. "It says Garrett deserves the reward money for killing him," he says. "I've never seen that in a coroner's report before."

They even hyped a return to the Silver City mother's grave:

> "The judge in Silver City said you can't exhume Catherine, because you have nothing to compare her DNA to," says the former sheriff ... They told us to come back if we found more evidence. Then we got DNA from the bloody workbench ..."

Unaware of their ricochet validation trick, Banks used their hoax-promoting, *True West* editor, Bob Boze Bell, who heralded their next underground invasion, saying that he supported using science to find out if Billy is buried in Hico [sic - Hamilton], Texas.

But Leo Banks also quoted legitimate historian Frederick Nolan, who called the Billy the Kid Case a "disgraceful charade."

The hoaxers miscalculated. Good ol' boy anti-intellectualism did poorly in Arizona. Banks's subtitle was: "The mad search for the bones of an American outlaw icon has come to Arizona."

And the legal case loomed. Sulkily, Sederwall told hoax ally, Julie Carter, on April 19, 2006, for her blog, under "Digging up bones, Arizona may protest Miller exhumation":

> "We have done absolutely nothing wrong. We did not violate any law whatsoever and made sure we had all the t's crossed and the i's dotted. We have documents to back up what we went to Arizona to do, **all the way to the state level**. [author's boldface] We went there quietly to do this without any fan fare. It doesn't mean we did it without permission" ... Sederwall said the return of the bones has been part of the deal from the very beginning and concurred with Sullivan that they had permission and assistance for their investigation at the cemetery.

And with usual garrulous disclosure helpful to me, Sederwall admitted to "state level" involvement: one step from fingering Governors Napolitano and Richardson.

It was also his threat: If we go down, so do you. Those politicians had met their match. Much later, Sederwall would demonstrate that his threats were not idle. He was secretly keeping copies of incriminating evidence - against his compatriots!

## RICHARDSON WORKS NEW MEXICO

Governor Bill Richardson did not require threats. Another "Implied Rule" of his is: "Never back down. Advance harder." In fact, he was attempting to recruit back-ups.

Jay Miller told me that, in the January 2006 legislative session, Richardson privately offered *him* the directorship of a *million dollar*, new, tourism division for Billy the Kid (apparently for Miller's supposed expertise from my articles and his book).

And Bill Richardson had asked Miller a startling question: Would he work with Attorney Bill Robins III? Later, that question about a Texas lawyer having anything to do with New Mexico tourism, would reveal a premeditated plan. But understanding the meaning of that question required my cracking the Billy the Kid Case hoax years later.

As to that directorship, Jay Miller answered, "I'm not a Bush journalist. If you do good, I'll report it. And if you do bad, I'll report *that*." Then he refused what many would call a bribe.

Instead, Tourism Secretary Mike Cerletti got $200,000 earmarked for Billy the Kid. So, through a connection, I informed Cerletti of Richardson's possible plot to give either Arizona or Texas Billy the Kid - just for a publicity stunt. I would later learn it was far more pernicious. Anyway, Mike Cerletti did nothing.

### MY NEW TACTIC

After the David Snell complaint, I realized that, owning all the Billy the Kid Case documents, I had to act. But I shared Voltaire's sentiment: "I am very fond of truth, but not at all of martyrdom." So, ruminating that "everybody dies anyway," I settled on waiting alertly and hoping David Snell prevailed.

# RECONSTRUCTING HOAX DIGGING

Emboldened by their huge umbrella of two governors, Sullivan and Sederwall again revealed their strategies, and provided me with a paper trail to reconstruct their Arizona exhumation scam.

Central to their plot had been an apparent loophole in Arizona exhumation law: the supervisor of a state cemetery could approve an exhumation *to identify remains*. The statutory intent was to ensure correct grave markers - not investigating a deceased person's delusional identity claims. Added to impropriety, of course, was having no valid DNA to justify any exhumation. But to advance their scheme, the hoaxers added to their ship of fools.

### ADD SUPERVISOR JEANINE DIKE

The role of "supervisor of a state cemetery" as permission-granter would be assumed by Jeanine Dike, the Supervisor of the Arizona Pioneers' Home and Cemetery in 2005.

The rumor was that the hoaxers were directed to her by Governor Janet Napolitano's Office. Sederwall and Dale Tunnell took Jeanine Dike on: Tunnell as the forensic expert from Forensitec; Sederwall as the cop. Avoiding the name, "John Miller," they told her they had to dig up "William Bonney!"

That they landed Jeanine Dike hook, line, and sinker is seen by her chummy e-mail of May 3, 2005 to Tunnell - as "Dale" - signed as "Superintendent," with "Subject: Disinterment of Wm Bonney."

> I am so glad for you that things are coming together for the forensic study on Wm Bonney. I am asking Dale Sams to contact Mountain View Cemetery and make arrangements for the disinterment and reinterment to take place on May 19, 2005 at 10 AM ... I wish you the best and I hope your anticipated results are correct. It has been a pleasure working with you.

The next day, May 4, 2005, dazzled Dike cleared the way with her employee, Dale Sams, e-mailing him to make arrangements for "disinterment and reinterment."

For billing, she provided Tunnell's Forensitec address. (Another later e-mail from the Pioneer Home's next Supervisor, Gary Olson, to Napolitano's Office, stated that Tom Sullivan had paid the exhumation bills. Three years later, under oath in a deposition, Sullivan revealed who did pay - Bill Richardson.)

The same May 4, 2005, Dale Sams contacted a George Thompson, at an adjoining cemetery, on their Arizona Pioneers' Home's official letterhead with "Governor Janet Napolitano" under Arizona's state seal. The subject was "Disinterment." Sams wrote:

> George: An excavator wants to disinter William Bonney on May 19 at 10 am at the Pioneers' Home Cemetery ... Please have someone there to dig up Mr. Bonney. I'm not sure where he's located but this company believes he's there.

For the merry exhumers, let's all sing with gusto: "Hi-ho, hi-ho, it's off to dig we go,/ Without a clue who is buried where,/ and without having DNA to compare!"

### ADD DR. LAURA FULGINITI

Maintaining the Billy the Kid Case hoax's forensic veneer, the hoaxers, for facsimile forensic validation, or for Bill Kurtis Productions film impact, had hired moonlighting, Maricopa County, forensic anthropologist, Dr. Laura Fulginiti. Another dreamboat for a hoaxer, she took their word about "permission" without checking, shrugged off plowing into an additional and random grave, and noticed nothing amiss by their frenzied and breakneck single day's digging (to maintain secrecy).

*Tucson Weekly's* Leo W. Banks in his April 13, 2006 "The New Billy the Kid?" noted that the graves were in an unmarked field. And none other than Dale Tunnell did the locating! Banks wrote:

> The Miller exhumation began about 1 p.m. on May 19 last year, and didn't end until about 7:30 that night, with investigators examining the last of the remains by flashlight. A backhoe did most of the heavy labor, after which the diggers worked by hand to avoid damaging the coffins or the remains.
>
> But they soon learned that the coffins had already collapsed with age, which had also made the bones extremely fragile. Each piece was carefully photographed, measured and cleaned, then placed on a white sheet on the ground.
>
> Dr. Laura Fulginiti, a well-known forensic anthropologist from Phoenix, supervised the dig. She describes the atmosphere as collegial and charged with excitement as they removed the tobacco-colored bones from the ground.
>
> "At one point, they were holding up the skull and comparing it with pictures of Billy," Fulginiti says. "They recited the story to each other, and when we found something that matched, like the scapula (shoulder) fracture, they were like little kids. They were really invested in this, and that added to the enthusiasm."
>
> But the effort was anything but clear-cut.
>
> In the first place, Miller's grave held no marker or headstone, and neither did the grave closest to his. To determine where Miller's plot should be, the investigators used a map provided by the Pioneers' Home, which pinpointed the location to within 20 square feet.
>
> As Tunnell acknowledges, ground shift and weather patterns can sometimes move bodies underground, and Miller had been 6 feet under almost 70 years. How certain were they of digging in the right place? "Probably upwards of 90 percent," says Tunnell.

Dr. Laura Fulginiti, not scholarly or meticulously ethical like Dr. Ross Zumwalt, ruminated to Leo Banks: "Was it respectful to Miller to dig him up? Part of me says it wasn't, given that the information we had wasn't the best ... From the beginning, I assumed it was another of these Wild West goose chases."

But Fulginiti's report of June 2, 2005, to "Dale L. Tunnell, Ph.D., Forensitec," titled "Re: Exhumation, Pioneer [sic] Home Cemetery, Prescott, Arizona," is invaluable. [APPENDIX: 43]

No hoaxer, Dr. Fulginiti ponderously recorded the absurd:

- For grave location she relied only on "Dr." Tunnell and his associates (presumably Sullivan and Sederwall).
- She documented two, unmarked, separate, adjacent graves, which she named "South" and "North."
- The North Grave, she concluded, was not Miller's. It had a *right* scapula with "extensive healed traumata;" and she denied the hoaxers' on-site claim of a bullet hole. (It would become their "Miller *left* scapula with bullet hole.")
- The Miller, South Grave, skull was "edentulous" (toothless). The hoaxers claimed "buck teeth" in the press.

Lax Dr. Fulginiti even permitted a Yavapai County Deputy named Mike Poling - delivering specimens to her from another case of hers - to use his metal detector for casket location, because the graves were unmarked and locations uncertain. Deputy Poling would prove later to be another lucky break for the hoaxers.

### ADD REVEALING PERPETRATORS AND WITNESSES

The hoaxers made their own self-incriminating document for the John Miller exhumation. Signed by Sederwall on Sheriff Virden's official form, it became available to anyone from the Prescott Police Department - where I got it. It began like this:

## LINCOLN COUNTY SHERIFF'S DEPARTMENT
## SUPPLEMENTAL REPORT

Case # : 2003-274
Date: Thursday, May 19, 2005
Subject: Exhumation of John Miller
Location: Arizona Pioneers' Cemetery, Prescott, Arizona
Report By: Steven M. Sederwall

On Thursday, May 19, 2005, at approximately 1:00 pm the following met at the Arizona Pioneers' Cemetery at Prescott, Arizona.

**Investigators:**

Steven M. Sederwall, Lincoln County Deputy Sheriff

Following Sederwall, was Tom Sullivan as "Sheriff of Lincoln County, Retired," then Dale Tunnell as an "Arizona State Investigator." In line was "Dr. Rick Staub, Orchid Cell Mark [sic], DNA," proving the lab head himself was there for the bones.

The remaining "Investigators" were listed as "Mike Poling, Yavapai County Sheriff's Deputy [note this sly inclusion of this random lawman]; Laura Fulginiti, Forensic Scientist - Anthropologist; Kristen Hartnett, Forensic Scientist - Archeologist; Misty Rodarte, Arizona Pioneers' Administration."

Then came "Others Present." They were Pearl Tenney Romney, Anthony Rodarte, Diana Shenefield, Jesse Shenefield, Russ Hadley, Toby Deherra Jr., Pat Sullivan, Linda Fisher, Billie Martin, Dale Sams, and Clara Enest. All but Pat Sullivan, Tom Sullivan's wife, had Arizona addresses listed.

Lastly, under "Bill Kurtis Productions," were cameraman, Joel Sapatori; and the soundman, Greg Gricus.

As their David Snell-instigated criminal investigation dragged on, Sullivan claimed to Joanna Dodder, for her *Daily Courier* of Prescott article of July 9, 2006, that Supervisor Jeanine Dike had been present too.

The Billy the Kid Case hoaxers' scheme was to blame the exhumation on Jeanine Dike and another unsuspecting person in that crowd of witnesses. What was left out was the person at whom the buck should have stopped, and whose Supplemental Report form was used: Lincoln County Sheriff Rick Virden. Later, that would make Virden the main defendant in real litigation.

## *DUPES SWORN TO SECRECY*

Sullivan and Sederwall built-in a delay with their dupes as they tried to decide whether to ditch John Miller for the real prize: "Brushy Bill" Roberts. So they swore everyone to secrecy!

Everyone complied, as seen in an e-mail sent by Sederwall on July 6, 2005, to Misty Rodarte, present at the dig, and the Arizona Pioneers' Home Administrator. The subject was "Billy the Kid." In full-bore "martyr for truth" mode, Sederwall stated:

> Thanks for calling the other day. It is too funny how these people react to someone looking for the truth. Thanks for not talking to anyone about it that is just what we are doing [sic].
> Here is the update: Rick from the lab called me the other day. They have recovered DNA from the grave to the right as

you stand at the foot of the graves. They are working on the grave on the left now. When they recover DNA from that grave they will compare them both with the work bench we recovered last year. I will keep you up to speed on it and we will not wait. Tell all the wonderful folks out there we said hello.

By August 18, 2005, the new and uneasy Arizona Pioneers' Home Supervisor, Gary Olson, e-mailed Napolitano's Office:

Representatives from APH [Arizona Pioneers' Home] were in attendance during the process - some were asked to sign a confidentiality agreement and asked to remain silent by Sullivan and Sederwall. We have no copy of this form.

For all these reasons, when David Snell first called Arizona Pioneers' Home Supervisor Jeanine Dike to inquire about why the Arizona Pioneers' Home cemetery was covered with tire tracks (the exhuming hoaxers and the filming Bill Kurtis Production crew), she denied any exhumation. The next Arizona Pioneers' Home Supervisor, Gary Olson, did the same. His boss was Governor Janet Napolitano. It had been a crime. Olson knew it. Napolitano knew it.

## COVER-UP AT NAPOLITANO'S OFFICE

On August 18, 2005, Governor Napolitano's Policy Advisor for Health, Anne Winter, panicked, e-mailing Alan Stephens, Napolitano's Chief of Staff, and Tim Nelson, Napolitano's General Counsel: "Re: Pioneer Home, Grave, Billy the Kid and DNA," with worrisome communication from Superintendent Olson:

Hi – you both should be aware of this one. Tim, I've asked Gary the new Superintendent of the Pioneer Home for his contact at the AG office. Given that this home reports to the Governor's Office, what risks do we have? What level of involvement do we need? And, do you have direction for Gary. He's really terrific. He'll be in town Friday if you want to discuss this with him in person. Please advise. Thanks!

ATTACHMENT:

There is suspicion that a former resident of the Arizona Pioneers' Home (APH) who is buried in the Arizona Pioneers' Cemetery may be "Billy the Kid." In this, a couple of former sheriff officers from Lincoln County New Mexico visited APH approximately two years ago and requested information on John C. Miller (supposedly he had paid for a new tombstone for Billy the Kid's mother prior to his death, but had made no outward claim to be Billy the Kid) [Author's Note: John Miller died in 1937. The new Catherine Antrim gravestone was installed in 1947.] Subsequent to approval by then Superintendent Jeanine Dike, these two investigators were given the cemetery plot map and all hard copy and archived information on John C. Miller. **Approximately 6 months ago, Steve Sederwall (one of the investigators) and Tom Sullivan (current New Mexico Lincoln County Sheriff and financial support of this investigation) received permission from the Superintendent Jeanine Dike to exhume the body of Mr. Miller to do genetic testing for comparison analysis to find out if he was Billy the Kid (according to my understanding, Jeanine Dike felt she had the authority to authorize the release of the records and the exhumation of the body since there were no living heirs).** [author's boldface]

**[AUTHOR'S NOTE: Gary Olson shows no doubt that the exhumers were Tom Sullivan and Steve Sederwall. ]**

Subsequent to Jeanine's retirement, APH received the call as to the date this exhumation would occur. This happened on 5/25/05 (between Jeanine's retirement and my arrival) [sic] – and was followed through with pursuant to the prior permission given to do so. **Representatives from APH were in attendance during the process - some were asked to sign a confidentiality agreement and asked to remain silent by Sullivan and Sederwall we have no copy of this form).**

**In this exhumation it was discovered that the graves of Mr. Miller and another had combined through the shifting of the land - and so a sample was taken from each of the graves for the genetic testing.** [author's boldface]

**[AUTHOR'S NOTE: Olson lies about "combined" graves in apparent cover-up attempt of the illegal second exhumation; contradicting on-site expert Dr. Laura Fulginiti's report that the graves were entirely separate.]**

First of all, permission had only been given for Mr. Miller's remains - in this, it was discovered that Mr. Miller had no living relatives which is why permission had been given. However, no one had looked into relatives of the individual in the second grave until recently **(per the Attorney General's Office)** [author's boldface]. To date, one of the grave remains has been analyzed with a negative result; the other result is not in yet ... The APH Cemetery is not considered a private cemetery via statutory definition because the APH Cemetery Statute was changed to allow APH to sell interment rights - making it a public cemetery. Public cemeteries require a permit for exhumations - no permit was obtained for the above exhumation.

**The Attorney General's Office feels that Mr. Snell will not give up on this** [author's boldface], and since the History Channel was allowed to film it may show up on TV at some point. **The AG's office is still working on this one** [author's boldface].

The problems are: an exhumation permit was not obtained if the APH is in fact a public cemetery; the relatives if any of the individual in the second grave were not contacted/informed and an authorization obtained from them; exhumation remains are somewhere in New Mexico or beyond being analyzed; do we need to get them back and does the Superintendent have the authority to release records and/or give permission for an exhumation if no heirs exist?

This was Governor (and future Homeland Security head) Janet Napolitano's crooked cover-up for fellow governor, Bill Richardson, in action.

But the crucial statement was from Arizona Pioneers' Home Supervisor Gary Olson: "The Attorney General's Office feels that Mr. Snell will not give up on this."

## COVER-UP AT YAVAPAI COUNTY DEPARTMENT OF COMMUNITY HEALTH

Another cover-up attempt came by letter, on March 30, 2006, to Governor Napolitano's in-house Policy Advisor for Health Anne Winter, on official stationary, as "Re: Disinterment of bodies at Arizona Pioneer's [sic] Cemetery, Prescott May 19, 2005." It was from a Marcia M. Jacobson. She stated:

As Director of Yavapai County Department of Community Health Services, I am the appointed local registrar with the responsibility and authority to issue disinterment-reinterment permits pursuant to A.R.S. Title 36, Article 2, and 36-327. A concerned citizen recently brought a matter to my attention that warrants report to you as Governor Napolitano's Policy Advisor for Health and the official responsible for oversight of the Arizona Pioneer's Home and Cemetery in Prescott ...

As reported to me and confirmed through our independent review, a disinterment was conducted May 19, 2005 to a body at Arizona Pioneer's Cemetery pursuant to authorization granted by then Superintendent Jeanine Dike. This authorization was granted without having first obtained a disinterment-reinterment permit from my office pursuant to A.R.S. 36-327. The disinterment was reportedly conducted with some publicity as the purpose of the operation was apparently to confirm or disprove that the remains were that of William H. Bonney a/k/a "Billy the Kid."

Irregularities in the disinterment process were compounded when another body was uncovered and, rather than stop and seek any type of authorization for disinterment for a second body, work continued and specimens of unknown quantity or type were removed from each of the two bodies for scientific testing. It is unclear at that point who was responsible for allowing that disinterment of the second body proceed [sic]. It is our understanding that Jeanine Dike had retired as Superintendent sometime prior to the disinterment operation and the current Superintendent, Gary Olson, had not yet commenced his service. Our review of the matter has confirmed the foregoing through the attached correspondence and other related documents including an interview with the **Yavapai County Sheriff's Office Detective Mike Poling, who was at the site for the primary purpose of delivering specimen to Dr. Laura Fulginiti for her examination and testing in a completely unrelated matter.** [author's boldface]

While this matter technically constitutes a violation punishable as a Class 1 misdemeanor through A.R.S. 36-344 and would be punishable as a Class 4 felony through A.R.S. 32-1364(B) if committed with malice or wantonness, my responsibility lies primarily in fulfilling my responsibility and authority to issue disinterment-reinterment permits and not necessary to insure that criminal prosecution or enforcement be initiated ... I, however, would recommend that appropriate policies or procedures are implemented to ensure that such incidents do not recur at a later time.

**With this notification, I will consider this matter closed.** [author's boldface]

But determined and brave David Snell foiled Marcia Jacobson. The "matter" was not closed.

## THE CORPSES ARE OUT OF THE BAG

Rumors about David Snell's not backing off, and Snell's badgering of Arizona Attorney General Terry Goddard for the truth, broke through the Sullivan-Sederwall confidentiality agreement's cover-up. Arizona Pioneers' Home Supervisor Gary Olson communicated with Snell in an October 3, 2005 letter:

> You recently asked the Arizona Pioneers' Home if a body in its cemetery had been exhumed for the purpose of determining whether the body could be identified as Billy the Kid. I understand that you have also been making inquiries to the Attorney General's Office.
>
> The purpose of this letter is to correct information previously provided to you by the Arizona Pioneers' Home. In our conversation, I told you that nothing of that nature had occurred since my arrival at the end of May. I further understand that another representative from the Arizona Pioneers' Home told you that no bodies had been exhumed. While I was not employed by the Arizona Pioneers' Home prior to the end of may, I understand that an exhumation at the Pioneers' Home cemetery did occur earlier this year for the purpose you noted.
>
> I apologize for the misinformation.

David Snell smoldered, then sent his enraged letter to Yavapai County Attorney Shiela Polk on March 11, 2006, initiating the criminal investigation of the John Miller exhumation.

# BATTLEGROUND ARIZONA:
# LONG ARM OF THE LAW

With Democratic Governors Janet Napolitano and Bill Richardson in a fix, I thought Republicans would rally. So I acted.

In April of 2006, I called Arizona State Senator and Senate President Ken Bennett, a Prescott resident. He accepted my written information on the Billy the Kid Case hoax, repeatedly promised to assist, and did nothing. By 2009, Ken Bennett had become Arizona's Secretary of State, leaving open the possibility that ambition for political advancement might have been in proportion to his stonewalling a crime in his own backyard.

In 2006, Len Munsil, Janet Napolitano's gubernatorial opponent, accepted documents from me, and was then silent. New Mexico Congresswoman, Heather Wilson, running against then New Mexico Attorney General, Patricia Madrid (who was covering-up the Billy the Kid Case for Richardson interests), said the Billy the Kid Case hoax was too complicated for her campaign. John Dendahl, Bill Richardson's gubernatorial opponent, agreed with Heather Wilson with regard to his own campaign.

My only hope was Arizona law enforcement. So I became a fearful and secret informer.

## *PRESCOTT POLICE DETECTIVE ANNA CAHALL*

At the Prescott Police Department, David Snell's complaint was assigned to Detective Anna Cahall as Case # 06-12767. I reached her by phone on April 13, 2006. But, a week before, she had already sent her report to the Prescott City Attorney, Glenn Savona. And for it, she had relied on Sullivan and Sederwall for information! I got a copy of her report. Sullivan and Sederwall had added tricky things to their usual hoax double-talk. Anna Cahall's report stated:

> On 4/5/06 I contacted Steven Sederwall. He told me he, as a Deputy Sheriff, and Sheriff Tom Sullivan opened a 'historic homicide investigation' (Lincoln County S.O. DR # 2003-274) in 2003 looking into a homicide committed by Billy the Kid. As part of this investigation, information was received that Johnny Miller, buried in the Arizona Pioneer Home Cemetery, had claimed to have been Billy the Kid. Sederwall contacted Tunnell, a former coworker of his, who contacted an attorney and made arrangements for the disinterment in Prescott. Sederwall said he believed it was permissible for the Arizona Pioneer Home to disinter remains in an effort to positively identify them, and he believed they were doing everything with the appropriate permission. **He ... assumed Det. Poling was present as a law enforcement representative, as he saw him provide a metal detector** ... [author's boldface]

**[AUTHOR'S NOTE: This Deputy Poling misrepresentation became crucial; though the Dr. Fulginiti and Marcia Jacobson reports had made clear that Poling was a random visitor.]**

**Sullivan said he relied on Tunnell to make arrangements for the operation in Prescott, and he just attended to observe it.** [author's boldface]

So Deputy Anna Cahall had met the kings of conning, and was conned. To Prescott City Attorney Glenn Savona she reported that the "suspects" were Jeanine Dike and *Dale Tunnell*! Hilariously, the "witnesses" were Tom Sullivan and Steve Sederwall! They had sold down the river not only their sucker, Jeanine Dike, but their buddy, Dale Tunnell.

Detective Cahall seemed bright and friendly, so I faxed her hoax information. She laughed at the switch from "perpetrators" to "witnesses," and assured me that her assigning names as "suspects" was "just paperwork." There was one shadow. She complained about feeling too much "political pressure."

I requested confidentiality. She agreed - as did all the others to come. So I was more a whistlepeeper than a whistleblower.

## THE PRESCOTT CITY ATTORNEY

Next in line for my information presentation, was Prescott City Attorney Glenn Savona. His report, based on Detective Anna Cahall's investigation prior to my communications to her, was ignorant of Sullivan's and Sederwall's roles. Savona focused on Jeanine Dike, addressing his letter of April 13, 2006 to Yavapai County Attorney Shiela Polk as Re: Police Department DR#2006-12767 Arizona Pioneers' Home Cemetery." [APPENDIX: 44]

Savona concluded that the violations were felonies, and stated: **"There is nothing in A.R.S. 36-327 authorizing the removal of body parts [out of state] for any reason."** [author's boldface]

But since Savona handled only misdemeanors, he passed the case up to the Yavapai County Attorney, Dennis McGrane.

## THE HOAXERS' SPECTACULAR ANNOUNCEMENT

As their Arizona troubles grew, the Billy the Kid Case hoaxers had concealed their media coup. It was finally announced by Steve Sederwall on April 24, 2006 in the blog of hoax-promoting *True West* magazine Editor-in Chief Bob Boze Bell as follows:

> The Wild is back in the West. This past year a French film crew made a film about investigation #2003-274 'The Billy the Kid Investigation'. The film was selected for the Cannes Film Festival. The Film maker is taking (Tom) Sullivan and I to Cannes ... We may have put the Kid on the front pages of the New York times [sic] but now we have taking [sic] our bandit buddy to Cannes. We should blend in France. Does it get any funnier?

This giddy mood remained for good reason.

Hoaxer mouthpiece, Julie Carter, on May 5, 2006, on her website, wrote: "Culture shock: The cowboys and the Kid go to France" [APPENDIX: 45]. The 90-minute French-made film was "Requiem for Billy the Kid;" was directed by an Anne Feinsilber, and would be shown at the Cannes Film Festival on May 19th.

Director Anne Feinsilber's inspiration, Carter said, had been the June 5, 2003 *New York Times* article! After contacting Sullivan and Sederwall, she had raised almost a million dollars for her Cargo Films production!

And Tom Sullivan had become an actor: he played Sheriff William Brady! (Julie Carter reported that Sullivan had spent nine months in 2004 - when sheriff - filming on taxpayer money when he was supposed to be Sheriff 24 hours per day. What "fun!")

I was miserable. Like a pandemic virus, the Billy the Kid Case hoax was about to infect the world.

Only one small intervention was possible for me. Sullivan and Sederwall had asked Governor Richardson to name them "Ambassadors of New Mexico" for Cannes. I had someone warn Richardson about risking his gubernatorial re-election by destroying his state's state tourism through naming Arizona's John Miller as Billy the Kid. So Richardson granted the hoaxers no titles; and they promised to make no DNA announcements.

But I learned later that what Richardson had rewarded them with instead was gigantic.

## *WILLIAM HUDSPETH COMES A'HAUNTING*

As Cannes Film Festival "Requiem for Billy the Kid's" showing loomed, ghosts of exhumed victims nipped at hoaxers' heels.

On May 13, 2006, Mark Shaffer of the *Arizona Republic* wrote, for the Internet, "N.M. pair may face charges in grave case."

In it, Shaffer named the second corpse: William Hudspeth.

For reporter Mark Shaffer, Sullivan and Sederwall shape-shifted into tourism promoters - albeit Arizona's. And their buddy, Dale Tunnell, became a "forensic scientist" - possibly unaware that he was also "the suspect." But the perpetrators were obvious.

> Last year, a pair of former New Mexico law enforcement officers had the body of Miller and a man identified as William Hudspeth, who was interred next to him, exhumed from the Pioneers' Home Cemetery. Bones and teeth were taken to a Dallas laboratory for DNA analysis.
>
> The Yavapai County Attorney's Office is reviewing a Prescott Police Department investigation to determine if criminal charges will be filed in the exhumation of Miller and Hudspeth because a permit was not obtained.
>
> Dennis McGrane, chief deputy Yavapai County attorney, said Friday that his office is seeking outside legal help in the case ...
>
> Former Lincoln County, N.M., Sheriff Tom Sullivan and his partner, former federal officer and Capitan, N.M., Mayor Steve Sederwall, don't believe that Sheriff Pat Garrett ambushed and killed Billy the Kid in Fort Sumner, N.M., on a July night in 1881. They contend the Kid could have lived out his years peacefully using the alias John Miller.
>
> Sullivan and Sederwall sold the History Channel on their theory and camera operators from the channel filmed the exhumation.
>
> Sullivan said that he came up with the bloody bench that the outlaw purportedly died on "through good police work," and now it's just a matter of making a DNA match.

As if placating Arizona prosecutors via the press, Deputy Sullivan and "scientist" Tunnell offered Billy the Kid to Arizona.

> "It's a believable story," Sullivan said. "You look at the likenesses in those pictures and the fact that they were both good with a gun, had blue eyes, were good dancers and expert horsemen and made frequent trips to Mexico. I look at Brushy Bill and say, 'Uh, I don't know about him,' but I think a good case can be made about John Miller.' "
>
> Sullivan said he hopes to have DNA results on the bodies and bench by this summer while pushing for more exhumations.
>
> Dale Tunnell, a forensic scientist who assisted in Miller's exhumation, said New Mexico has staked a good chunk of its tourism future on Bonney being buried in Fort Sumner and "a group of people there have banded together to protect that gravesite at all costs.

"If someone can prove that William Bonney is not buried there, they can turn out the lights of that town. And I'm thinking Prescott could be the big beneficiary of that," Tunnell said.

The hoaxers were confidant; but I was too, certain that the evidence I gave the prosecutors would lead to indictments - and would end the Billy the Kid Case hoax at last without my ever being revealed.

# HISTORY IN BALANCE: TO JAIL OR CANNES

## *ON TO THE YAVAPAI COUNTY PROSECUTOR*

It was April 21, 2006 when I called Chief Prosecutor Dennis McGrane's Yavapai County Attorney's Office. The switchboard referenced the case by suspects: "Jeanine Dike and Dale Tunnell."

I was transferred to Office Supervisor, Carol Landis. Friendly, she said the Cahall and Savona paperwork had not arrived; but she would pass along my information. And their decision could come in 30 days. By April 24th, still lacking records, she added that a seven year statute of limitations applied to those felonies.

Concerned about the suspect names, the next day, I told Carol Landis about the switch. Then I asked about "government pressure." She said it was "pretty tough."

On May 2nd, I learned the case had been assigned to Deputy Attorney Steve Jaynes. So I faxed him, as well as Chief Attorney Dennis McGrane, information on the Billy the Kid Case, on Sullivan's and Sederwall's roles in the exhumations, on the lack valid bench DNA, and on roles of Richardson and Napolitano.

On May 18th, I called Deputy Attorney Steve Jaynes, and got bad news. He had transferred the case to Maricopa County because of "a potential conflict of interest": Yavapai County Sheriff's Department Detective Mike Poling had been present! If there was litigation, his Office needed to represent him. I explained that Poling had just delivered unrelated specimens to Dr. Fulginiti. Jaynes said everyone present could be a suspect.

So the "thirty days to make a decision" estimated by Supervisor Carol Landis went down the tubes.

## FRENCH FILM FESTIVITIES

Sullivan and Sederwall made it unscathed to the "Festival de Cannes" for the most prestigious film festival in the world.

It ran from May 17th to the 28th of 2006. "Requiem for Billy the Kid" was one of twenty eight films under "hors compétition" (not for competition), right along with Al Gore's "An Inconvenient Truth" on global warming.

Screened on May 19th, it was listed as the first film for director-writer Anne Feinsilber. As narrator, was actor, Kris Kristofferson: the actor who played "Billy the Kid" in Sam Peckinpah's famous Western, "Pat Garrett and Billy the Kid."

Anne Feinsilber's message was pure Billy the Kid Case hoax: doubt existed about Billy's killing; and the pretenders might be real Billy. Arbiters of historical "truth" were now Deputy Tom Sullivan and Deputy Steve Sederwall - as they called themselves.

The catalogue stated: "The premise of the film is an investigation into the often-challenged circumstances that led to the death of the 21-year old outlaw in the hands of Sheriff Pat Garrett on July 14, 1881." Perched on this pedestal of "documentary cinema" were the fake "friendship" of Garrett and Billy, and "tens of thousands" visiting "Brushy's" rarely visited grave. Sullivan and Sederwall spun their case as "saving Garrett's honor," fast-talking around Richardson's muzzling of their DNA announcement to make themselves law enforcement heroes.

## CROWING FROM CANNES

Surprisingly, in their heady whirl, our opposition was on Sullivan's and Sederwall's minds. A Lincoln couple, unaware that the men had their address, got two postcards from Cannes.

One, in color, had boats on the Mediterranean, fireworks, and "Cannes;" the other had "Le Fiestival de Cannes." Written in French, the postcards were signed: "Tom and Steve."

Translated, the first chortled: "We're at Cannes. Nobody recognizes Nolan or Utley or Jay Miller but they recognize the two shurffs" [sic- joke for sheriffs]. The second taunted: "It's during adversity you realize who your friends are ... thanks for the loyal fight (support) which has led us here."

The snide postcards indicated that thugs tire of too much "smiley face" - even in the midst of glory.

## "REQUIEM" SPELLS REQUIEM

Director Anne Feinsilber's film got wide and good publicity. On May 21st, from *Variety* magazine, came the review of "Requiem for Billy the Kid" by a Todd McCarthy. He said:

> With Sam Peckinpah's Billy, Kris Kristofferson re-enlisted to portray the Kid delivering his account of what happened between him and Pat Garrett in 1881, pic goes on a photogenic search for the "truth" about the young killer. Seems there has always been a rumor that Billy escaped and lived to a ripe old age, and Tom Sullivan, who was sheriff of Lincoln County when pic was shot in the fall of 2004, describes his efforts to exhume the body of Billy's mother for DNA, efforts shot down by a judge whose motives Sullivan describes as baldly financial.

A May 25th review by Dave McCoy of MSN Movies, as "L 'Ouest Américain," said: "Feinsilber follows up on a rumor that Pat Garrett shot the wrong man and Billy the Kid actually isn't buried where it's said he is."

Anne Feinsilber's damage was further evidenced on a May 6, 2006 Internet version of *The Hollywood Reporter* in reviewer, Ray Bennett's, "Bottom line: A story well told." He wrote:

> History has it that Sheriff Pat Garrett, a reformed villain, gunned down William Bonney, also known as Billy the Kid, at Fort Sumner, where his grave has a much-visited marker. Some say, however, that the friendship between Garrett and Bonney led the lawman to let the outlaw go and another man's body lies beneath his headstone. Could Billy the Kid have lived to see two world wars and driven a car? Feinsilber sets out to discover the truth and she finds several people in New Mexico whose grandparents were said to have known Bonney. Competing factions would like to exhume the bodies of Billy and his mother Catherine, who died of tuberculosis when Billy was 14, in order to prove once and for all when he died. Such myths fuel tourism, however, and the mystery has remained unsolved.

With this Billy the Kid Case hoax victory, Pat Garrett became a "reformed villain," the friendship between Garrett and Billy was real, a stranger's body very likely lay in Billy's grave, the exhumation would have solved the questions "once and for all," and the "mystery" was being left unsolved to "fuel tourism."

Anne Feinsilber, in one fell swoop, had arguably done more damage, than any other person in the world, to almost 80 years of historical work. Her total "research" seems to have been listening to hoaxers Sullivan and Sederwall gabbing, talking to some addled old-timers, and hiring Hollywood actors. A "requiem for real Billy" is what this dupe created.

Feinsilber's contagion of disinformation continued.

The hoaxer's Lincoln County reporter, Julie Carter, enthused on June 9, 2006 for *RuidosoNews.com* under "The cowboys are back in town, film in six months." After gushing that "The pair did a dozen interviews while they were in Cannes, including two live television interviews, two live radio interviews and more with a variety of newspapers and magazines," Carter concluded: "Producers hope to host a film debut and make a county event of its first American showing. Sullivan said after that it will probably be released to PBS and then followed by DVD sales. Sederwall and Sullivan gifted the director with their black cowboy hats before they left. 'It was the right thing to do,' said Sederwall."

One wonders if Sederwall's gift Stetson to Feinsilber was the one he wore for his Miller skull photo for Carter's exhumation article. If so, Anne Feinsilber got a fitting souvenir of her damage.

Julie Carter's article also demonstrated that, by June 9th, the hoaxers euphoria had swelled to grandiosity. Their spin of "doing it for New Mexico tourism," had inflated to "doing it for the French economy!" Thus, Carter quoted:

> Sederwall said he was amazed at the amount of money The Kid brought to France and to Cannes by the way of the film. Not just what it cost to initially shoot the movie, but the entourage of 15-20 people directly connected with the film that was housed in expensive hotels and villas overlooking the Mediterranean, fed three meals a day of the finest foods and chauffeured in limousines wherever they wished to travel.

All the while, Frederick Nolan's telephone calls to the BBC to present historical truth as counterpoint to the hoax went ignored.

## ROLL OUT THE RED CARPET

A New Mexico heroes' welcome was the hoaxers' wish. Loyal Julie Carter tried a shoutout in her June 9, 2006, "The cowboys are back in town": "They're baaaaaack. And both Tom Sullivan and Steve Sederwall said the people of Cannes and all of France treated them like royalty."

A stranger communication appeared in a June 2, 2006 *RuidosoNews.com* letter to the editors by an Emily C. Smith, calling herself a "research historian from Hayden Lake, Idaho." She spoke oddly like Sederwall; and one wonders who "*we*" were in Idaho. "We" also presented "Brushy Bill" as mainstream and suggested that New Mexico and Texas should share Billy the Kid. "Emily Smith" also pushed for red carpet treatment:

> What an honor for two of New Mexico's finest citizens to be invited to the prestigious Cannes film Festival in France for showing of their documentary on May 20, [sic] 2006.
>
> Tom Sullivan, Lincoln County retired sheriff, and Steve Sederwall participated in the making of a Western documentary, *Requiem for Billy the Kid*, directed by Anne Feinsilber. The film investigates the questioned death of Billy the Kid by Pat Garrett on July 14, 1881.
>
> In their quest for evidence that focused totally on finding the truth, Sullivan and Sederwall's reputation gathered notoriety worldwide until they were contacted by Feinsilber two years ago and agreed to do the documentary ...
>
> Old myths perpetuated by a book authored by Pat Garrett himself and a handful of in-the-box-thinking historians would have us believe Billy was killed by his friend, Pat Garrett, at Pete Maxwell's in Fort Sumner.
>
> In-depth, official sheriff's criminal investigation over the past four years has revealed strong supportive evidence to the contrary.
>
> One trail of thought supported by documented evidence from such notables as Dr. Wm. V. Morrison, Dr. Jannay Valdez, Judge Bob Hefner, research historian and author Brett Hall, et al., suggests Billy lived to be an old man of 90, dying in the street of Hico, Texas, under the assumed name of Brushy Bill Roberts.
>
> How wonderful it would be if New Mexico and Texas would partner to creatively embrace the ongoing criminal investigation of the legend of Billy the Kid, for Billy belonged to both, and there is much for each to share and to profit in both his life and his death.
>
> We should be proud of the dedicated and hard work these two men have exhibited in their continuing determination in extracting the truth against all odds.
>
> They have earned and rightly deserve the "red carpet" treatment they received recently in France and we would hope the same would occur upon their arrival home as well. Congratulations, Tom and Steve, for representing the State of New Mexico while preserving and presenting its fine history in a tremendous job well done.

My ray of hope from Sederwallian-Emily from Idaho was the indication that their interest in non-entity John Miller was waning after big-time Cannes; while big-time "Brushy" tempted. Also, the Arizona criminal investigation was continuing.

And Governor Bill Richardson stayed silent. No red carpet rolled out. He knew too much else could have rolled out with it.

### RICHARDSON'S FAUSTIAN BARGAIN

Governor Bill Richardson had kept a low profile in the Arizona fiasco, but, behind-the-scenes he had done something terrible and illegal. It was a Faustian bargain that gave the hoaxers the upper hand. If they went down legally in Arizona, so would he. Therefore, next in line for a major moral test was the Maricopa County Prosecutor. But in August of 2006, I was unaware of all those high stakes.

# POLITICAL LOGJAM AT PROSECUTOR'S OFFICE

The Arizona exhumation case went international. On May 17, 2006, in Gulfnews.com, AP reporter, Amanda Lee Myers, wrote "Billy the Kid Still 'Wanted." Though Sullivan and Sederwall got spin as "cops," and David Snell was a "Billy the Kid junkie," Myers knew trouble was afoot. She stated:

> More than 100 years after his death, Billy the Kid can still stir up a heap of trouble. Two men on a quest to find where the Wild West outlaw turned American legend is buried could face time in jail for unearthing remains last May in the central Arizona community of Prescott.
>
> Tom Sullivan, former sheriff of Lincoln County, New Mexico, and Steve Sederwall, former mayor of Capitan, New Mexico, exhumed the body of a man who was buried in Prescott nearly 70 years ago. John Miller had claimed to be William Bonney, also known as Billy the Kid.
>
> Authorities currently are considering whether to charge Sullivan and Sederwall with a felony for removing some remains of Miller and of another man buried in an unmarked grave next to him.
>
> "This is a simple, straightforward, open-and-shut grave-robbing case," said David Snell, a Billy the Kid junkie from

Tucson. In March, Snell wrote a letter to Yavapai County Attorney Sheila Polk that sparked a police investigation into the exhumation. In the letter, he called unearthing the graves a "sordid and reprehensible affair."

He argued that Sullivan and Sederwall acted inappropriately because they did not have a permit or court order to dig up the remains or permission to take samples from the second grave.

Sullivan and Sederwall disagree.

"I'm confident we didn't do anything wrong in Arizona," Sullivan said. "When you commit a crime, you have to have intent. There's certainly no intent to be grave-robbers" ...

Sederwall said he will not rest until he knows beyond a doubt when, where and how Billy the Kid died, saying he is just seeking the truth. "To the living we owe respect; to the dead we owe the truth," he said. "We're going to find the truth. We're cops that's what we do. We get into a case, and man, I'm going to finish it."

The hoaxers' Cannes vacation was over. Facing the music, they were dancing to the new tune of possible pink underwear.

## *ENTERING MARICOPA COUNTY*

On June 9, 2006, I learned the name of the woman on whom could rest Billy the Kid history's fate. The switchboard told me that Case # 2006020516 had been assigned to Maricopa County Prosecutor, Deputy Attorney Jonell Lucca.

Taking my call, Jonell Lucca sounded much like pleasant Detective Anna Cahall. Having in hand my documents, she listened about Sullivan's and Sederwall's switch of themselves to witnesses - and interjected intelligent questions. Then I asked what the next step was. Her response took me aback.

Jonell Lucca said the issue *was not about history* (though I had addressed only legalities), but whether *a permit was necessary for the exhumation*. She would consult with her colleagues.

I thought, "What if that's an excuse not to indict?" But I reassured myself that she was checking state statutes. And there was no possible legal argument to permit digging up the second and random man: William Hudspeth.

On June 26, 2006, I told Lucca about the case's politics. She said *all the attorneys* had to meet about the case. I was impressed. But a Silver City official told me: "Get real. They're trying to figure out how to bury it." Still, I had hope. The guilt was too obvious. And noting could justify digging up William Hudspeth.

## "BRUSHY BILL'S" BUDDY WEIGHS IN

Jannay Valdez tried to help "Brushy" by helping the hoaxers. In a June 9, 2006 letter to the editor of *RuidosoNews.com*, he plugged John Miller's exhumation under "Digging Up the Truth About Billy." After all, if the Arizona troubles passed, the hoax's next stop would be "Brushy's" Hamilton, Texas grave - in likely company of Bill Kurtis Productions or even French film crews. So Jannay Valdez raved in his inimitable way:

> I am involved in this Billy the Kid issue, concerning whether he was killed in 1881, or not. I am so proud that New Mexico has three heroes – Tom Sullivan, Steve Sederwall, and Gary Graves, who have staked their lives and careers on investigating some of the issues about BTK and looking for the truth. May I ask these outrageous skeptics; "What's wrong with finding the truth?" Do those who oppose finding the truth, fear the truth? I'll bet the TRUTH would devastate them.
>
> John Miller's grave was almost forgotten, until these men revived it. Professor Bob Stahl at Arizona State University is correct. Miller is not BTK. But, in the name of historical research and fact-finding, his grave was dug up, and I applaud the heroes for seeking any/or all clues to find the truth. That's something that is lacking with some of NM's "historians." These heroes are lawmen, who know how to solve crimes and gather information, as opposed to armchair "historians" who call themselves "historians" yet find EXCUSES to oppose finding the truth.

## THE HOAXERS RETURN BONES

The next news was that the hoaxers had returned the bones (what was left of them) - like bank robbers returning the money.

Joanna Dodder, wavering on whose side to take, reported on July 9, 2006 in *The Daily Courier* as "Back at Rest: Bones of Billy the Kid return to Prescott."

For this go-around, Dodder was in damage-control mode. She omitted entirely the exhumation's legal case; even though, on April 12, 2006, her own article for *The Daily Courier* had been "Officials could face charges for digging up alleged Billy the Kid." Sullivan and Sederwall were now shape-shifted to "retired" amateur historians. And scammed by the carpenter's bench malarkey, Joanna Dodder wrote:

> Thursday's reburial was without fanfare. Pioneers' Home Superintendent Gary Olson said he was never able to find living relatives of the two men.
>
> A lab that's helping former New Mexico officials investigate the death of the infamous Billy the Kid mailed the bones of Miller and Hudspeth back to the Pioneers' Home ...
>
> So far, they've dug up only Miller and his neighbor. They said the planned to compare his DNA with DNA from blood on a bench where they believe Billy laid after Garrett shot him.
>
> Sullivan and Sederwall have since retired from public life as elected officials ... As they continue their pursuit, they continue to draw quite a bit of interest, including unwanted interest from those who think the investigation is pointless ...
>
> "We'll make a comment when the time is right," Sullivan responded when asked if the DNA results on Miller are in."

On July 14, 2006, the 125th anniversary of Billy's death day, a devil-may-care reporter, Bruce Danials, on ABQnewsSeeker of ABQjournal.com, presented "O Fair New Mexico;" writing:

> Today's the day (in 1881) Pat Garrett shot Billy the Kid.
>
> Or did he? A couple of former New Mexico lawmen – former Lincoln County Sheriff Tom Sullivan and former deputy and Capitan Mayor Steve Sederwall are on a well publicized quest to find out whether "Billy" and Garrett may have planted a ringer in the Fort Sumner grave and the legendary outlaw lived to a ripe old garrulous age in Texas or Arizona ...
>
> The last we heard (according to this story from the Associated Press that appeared last May in the Arizona Daily Star), Sullivan and Sederwall in their zeal got themselves crosswise with some folks in Prescott Ariz., where they exhumed the remains of one Billy claimant named John Miller, who'd been buried some 70 years ago. But since they also had removed the remains of a man buried next to Miller, they were threatened with charges of grave-robbing ... What A state!

## *BREAKING THE LEGAL IMPASSE*

By mid-July of 2006, and with no legal decision having been made, I enlisted Arizona public opinion through a Ryan Flahive, an historian at the Prescott, Arizona, Sharlot Hall Museum. Flahive was shocked, gleaning from the newspapers only the preposterous claim that John Miller had been Billy the Kid. He referred me to the local Cemetery Association chairperson, Pat Atchison, who was equally shocked. Violation of William Hudspeth's grave was the clincher for her.

On September 1, 2006, Ryan Flahive and Pat Atchison wrote to Deputy Attorney Jonell Lucca:

> As members of the Prescott historical community, we are watching this case intently. We are concerned that this case may compromise the protection and integrity of our historic cemeteries if an example is not made against illegal exhumation.

At my next phone call, Attorney Jonell Lucca's assistant, Laura, gave me a message from Lucca that the entire office was meeting on August 21st. And an announcement about prosecution would be made on the week of the 28th.

So, on August 11th, I faxed for all the participants in that meeting: "Overview of Billy the Kid Case Promulgators."

Next came fate. By August 17, 2006, Attorney Lucca took sick, and missed the week of the 28th. Through Laura, Jonell Lucca gave me the message: "No decision has been made yet."

"Maybe," I thought, "I can help them by breaking a political-legal logjam by exposing Richardson, Napolitano, and Lincoln County Sheriff Rick Virden through open records requests." Jay Miller had drawn the line at that bunch, saying, "I still want to be able to visit Lincoln County."

And I could investigate Dr. Henry Lee too. Jay Miller had already proxied questions to him from me (and got Lee's May 1, 2006 letter about his report having been sent to the Lincoln County Sheriff's Department).

The next steps would involve more exposure - of me. Living with fear had become my way of life. Even a coward like me can get used to fear. But it does not feel good. You need to enjoy adrenalin more: like someone who chooses to do extreme sports - or a real hero.

# CHAPTER 10:

# IDEALISTICALLY

# I INVESTIGATE

# INJUSTICE

**State of New Mexico**
*Office of the Governor*

Bill Richardson
*Governor*

October 13, 2006

Gale Cooper, M.D.
P.O. Box 328
Sandia Park, New Mexico 87047

Dear Dr. Cooper:

This letter is i...
office on...

---

**STATE BAR OF ARIZONA**

November 2, 2007

Gale Cooper
P.O. Box 328
Sandia Park, NM 87047

RE:   File No: 07-0060
      Jonell L. Lucca, Respondent

Dear Dr. Cooper:

We are in receipt of your correspondence dated March 21, 2007. Your
numerous questions regarding the State Bar's prior decision to dismiss
attorney Jonelle Lucca. Please consider this letter as the State Bar's res...

We can... ...cifically respond to every issue raised in your March 21,
...merous to address individually here. Please be assured,
...e carefully read and considered before a decision is made...

...raise are outside the jurisdiction of the State Bar. As an...
...granted the authority to exercise prosecutorial discretic...
...decide which cases to prosecute, and is ultimately acco...
...rt of the prosecutor's decision-making process includes...
...esses or the likelihood of obtaining a conviction. Abs...
...State Bar, as a disciplinary agency, cannot override or...
...ation of prosecutorial discretion. Thus, insofar as you...
...on not to charge a particular crime, the State Bar lacks...
...sion.

...27, 2007, request for production of certain State Bar...
...e Bar Lawyer Regulation Records Manager. Additio...
...ay in responding to your concerns; and thanks you f...
...ter.

...riz.R.S.Ct., the State Bar file may be expunged in t...

Consumer Assistance Program

...lation Records Manager

---

## THE DRIED BEAN

### "YOU BELIEVIN' US OR THEM LYIN' WHORES"

Mr. Alan Morel: Attorney at Law
Lincoln County Attorney
P.O. Box 1030
Ruidoso, New Mexico 88355-1030

September 30, 2006

Dear Mr. Morel:

Lincoln County Sheriff Virden forwarded an FOIA request on the Billy the Kid signed by
Gale Cooper. We will do out best to answer these questions for you and give you some
background on this case.

When we (Sheriff Tom Sullivan and I) opened this case to examine the death of two
Lincoln County Deputies there had been no official investigation. Those upset with our
investigating hold up Sheriff Pat Garrett's 1882 book *"The Authentic Life of Bil...*
*Kid"* to say Garrett's account is fraudulent in fact, since he was the Sheriff, should stand as the off...

However, ...one who has come out publicly against our investigation...
...Kid an annotated edition" by Oklahoma...
...this text is farrago...

---

**Alan P. Morel, P.A.**
*Attorney at Law*

700 Mechem Drive, Suite 12
Post Office Box 1030
Ruidoso, New Mexico 88355-1030

September 29, 2006

Gale Cooper, M.D.
P.O. Box 328
Sandia Park, New Mexico 87047

RE:   *Freedom of Information Act/Inspection of Public...*
      *dated September 22, 2006, to Lincoln County Sh...*

Dear Dr. Cooper:

On September 28, 2006, the Lincoln County Sheriff, Rick...
Information Act/Inspection of Public Records Act Request...
been forwarded to me for review and response. I am the at...
as such, represent the various elected officials of Lincoln...
believe that your request is excessively burdensome or...
respond, until October 13, 2006.

Very truly yours,

Alan P. Morel, P.A.

*Alan Morel*

Alan P. Morel

APM/wm
Enclosures: a/s
c:   Sheriff Rick Virden
     Tammie J. Maddox, Lincoln County C...
     Thomas E. Stewart, County Manager...

---

JANET NAPOLITANO
*Governor*

**STATE OF... OFFICE OF THE GOVERNOR**
1700 WEST WASHINGTON STREET, PHOENIX, AZ 85007

November 13, 2006

Gale Cooper, M.D.
P. O. Box 328
Sandia Park, NM 87047

Dear Dr. Cooper:

Enclosed please find records responsive to your request dated September 22,
2006. We are providing you with a total of 23 pages. Fees for this request have been
waived.

Please contact me if you have any questions.

Sincerely,

Michael R. Haener
Deputy Chief of Staff

Enclosures

cc:   Nicole Davis
      Tim Nelson

# JUST FOR JUSTICE:
# I ABANDON ANONYMITY

*HOAXBUST: In 2006, I naively believed that regulatory watchdogs and prosecutors sought justice. It did not occur to me they were in mutual protection societies. My hope was to help the Maricopa Prosecutor resist political pressure and prosecute. That would end the hoax. But I was aware of my new level of danger.*

The first I heard of open records law was from an out-of-state political contact of Marlyn Bowlin's. It is a nemesis of crooked public officials. Federally, it is called the Freedom of Information Act (FOIA). Each state crafts its own version. New Mexico's is the Inspection of Public Records Act (IPRA). The contact told me they are called "sunshine laws" for shedding light on wrongdoings. He taught me how to write a request for records. New Mexico's IPRA Section 14-2-5 states grandly as its "Purpose of Act":

> [A]ll persons are entitled to the greatest possible information regarding the affairs of government and the official acts of public officers and employees ... to provide persons with such information is an essential function of a representative government and an integral part of the routine duties of public officers and employees.

Any citizen is entitled to get records of public officials. The Lincoln County Sheriff's Department Billy the Kid Case # 2003-274 was purely a public law enforcement case. From 2004 to 2006, I had requested its records through Jay Miller for Sheriffs Tom Sullivan and Rick Virden; their Deputy, Steve Sederwall; and for Tourism Secretary Mike Cerletti. Of course, concealing records is the other side of the coin for public officials up to no good.

So Sullivan, Sederwall, and Virden had refused all Case 2003-274 records by illegally claiming they met the IPRA exception for an ongoing criminal investigation (to prevent suspects escaping - and dead Garrett was going nowhere). But even doughty Jay Miller refused to confront for me the next bunch of crooks higher up the ladder. I was on my own for records requests to get hoped-for proof for Attorney Jonell Lucca's hoped-for indictments.

When I told Silver City Town Councilman Steve May about my planned investigations, he said, with customary formality, "If they kill you, Dr. Cooper, I'd like your Chihuahua."

At least, there would be "witnesses." I planned profuse Cc's with my requests. I never imagined that all those Cc's could be complicit "friends": as in "us against them": "them" being citizens.

## FIRST, THE WORST:  GOVERNOR BILL RICHARDSON

On September 22, 2006, after my IPRA request departed to Governor Richardson by certified mail, I got the proverbial lightness of being, professionally known to psychiatrists as "counterphobia" - meaning brain-freeze to deny panic.

My request's preamble defined the hoax. My requested records were about taxpayer money spent on the Billy the Kid Case and the Arizona exhumations; plus all communications from and to his Office from the Sheriffs, Attorney Bill Robins III, Governor Janet Napolitano, and "official historian," Paul Hutton.

The Cc's went to everyone except God: New Mexico U.S. Attorney David Iglesias; New Mexico Attorney General Patricia Madrid; New Mexico Tourism Secretary Mike Cerletti; John Dendahl, New Mexico Republican Candidate for Governor; Arizona Governor Janet Napolitano; Maricopa County Chief Prosecutor Andrew Thomas; Maricopa County Deputy Attorney Jonell Lucca; New Mexico  Senator Jeff Bingaman; New Mexico Senator Pete Domenici; New Mexico Congresswoman Heather Wilson, 1st Congressional District; New Mexico Congressman Steve Pearce, 2nd Congressional District; New Mexico Congressman Tom Udall, 3rd Congressional District; Arizona Senator John McCain; New York Senator Hillary Rodham Clinton; Massachusetts Senator John F. Kerry; Illinois Senator Barack Obama; House Democratic Leader Nancy Pelosi; Senate Democratic Leader Harry Reid; and Honorable Al Gore.

Richardson's response came on October 13, 2006, via a Marcie Maestas. All responses were: "no records."

But Marcie Maestas, feigning compliance, enclosed what must have seemed innocuous documents. They were gems. There was Richardson's June 10, 2003 press release [APPENDIX: 4], putting himself in the case's center, naming Paul Hutton as its "official historian," and identifying Case 2003-274 as a Pat Garrett murder investigation. Another record gave Richardson's judgeship appointments for Henry Quintero and Ted Hartley - February 8, 2003 - in time to OK the planned Billy/mother exhumations.

The biggest surprise was about Silver City Attorney Sherry Tippett. It had her already cited, July 11, 2003 memo to Bill Richardson that indicated *he* was her "boss" for the case.

As to the Cc's, the sole answer came on October 12th from New Mexico Senator Pete Domenici, saying to keep him "apprised of the issues." (I did; and I never heard from him again.)

Unfortunately, nothing was useful for Attorney Lucca.

## NEXT: GOVERNOR JANET NAPOLITANO

On September 22, 2006, I also sent Governor Janet Napolitano a FOIA. Cc's went to Maricopa County Chief Prosecutor Andrew Thomas; Maricopa County Deputy Attorney Jonell Lucca; Governor Bill Richardson; New Mexico Congresswoman Heather Wilson; Yavapai County Sheriff Steve Waugh; Arizona Attorney General Terry Goddard; Arizona State Senate President Ken Bennett; Arizona State Senator Karen Johnson; Len Munsil, Republican Candidate for Arizona Governor; Arizona Senator John McCain; Arizona Senator John Kyl; and Arizona congressmen Rick Renai, Trent Franks, John Shadegg, Ed Pastor, J.D. Hayworth, Jeff Flake, Raul Grijalva, and Jim Kolbe from 1st to 8th congressional districts respectively.

Requested were records about her Miller/Hudspeth exhumation involvement. Enclosed were the cover-up writings by her Policy Advisor for Health Anne Winter and then Yavapai County Health Services Director Marcia Jacobson.

Napolitano cannily got an extension to after the gubernatorial election - and responded on November 13th when re-elected. Then, she simply ignored my requests. As to my Cc's, just her state's senator, John McCain, answered on October 27, 2006; saying only it was her "jurisdiction," so my mailings should be sent to her.

But Napolitano's responder, a Michael Haener, did give me her internal e-mails about the John Miller exhumation from October and November of 2005. Omitted were the obviously incriminatory lead-ups, "permissions," or follow-ups. And I did get a hoaxer e-mail to her about their John Miller "DNA results" as well as her Office's participation in press reporting.

So revealed was her involvement in Rene Romo's hoax-serving November 6, 2005 *Albuquerque Journal* article: "Billy the Kid Probe May Yield New Twist." It started with Romo's October 19, 2005 e-mail to Arizona Pioneers' Home Supervisor Gary Olson about the exhumation. The next day, Gary Olson e-mailed Anne Winter: "Subject: Re. John Miller." Olson wanted direction:

> Anne, I thought you and the Governor may want to know about this request. Let me know your thoughts. Gary.

That day, internal damage control e-mails followed. Winter e-mailed the Governor's Chief Counsel Tim Nelson and Chief of Staff Alan Stephens under "Subject: FW: re. John Miller":

> Do you have any issue with his [Olson's] talking about this? Remember there was the legal issue that they dug up two bodies.

Five days later, Policy Advisor for Health Anne Winter e-mailed the Governor's press liaison, Jeanine L'Ecuyer, under "Subject: FW: re. John Miller" for direction:

> I will be sending you a few  e-mails on this issue. I would like you to be in on this and get your thoughts. apparently, billy the kid [sic] was at the Pioneer's [sic] Home and was exhumed for DNA testing. Gary Olson the superintendent (reports to me) is getting media requests. Please advise on how to handle.

Proving the hoaxers' were in Governor Napolitano's loop, was Sederwall's Cc of Romo's article to Orchid Cellmark's Director Rick Staub, to Emily Smith (the Idaho roll-out-the-red-carpet lady), and *True West's* hoax-promoting editor, Bob Boze Bell.

On November 7th, Anne Winter and Olson still worried about media. Winter e-mailed L'Ecuyer, Alan Stephens, and Tim Nelson:

> Gary Olson of the Arizona Pioneer Home was just interviewed by KPNX. I was informed that he called Tim  when he couldn't get ahold of me. The interview was very high level and they acknowledged that all of this activity occurred prior to

Gary's arrival. Nothing controversial was asked. He showed them where the cemetery is, but would not tell them where the unmarked grave was ... He thinks it will air tonight. Let me know if you have any questions.

Earlier, on October 17, 2006, Supervisor Gary Olson e-mailed Policy Advisor for Health Anne Winter with "Subject: RE: the kid":

[T]his article looks to me like it may be trying to persuade the New Mexico municipal courts to reverse their denial/blockage on digging there.

Then there was the diamond: An e-mail revealing the hoaxers' claimed DNA matching results - which Richardson had blocked from Cannes' disclosure! I named it the "Doomsday Document." Dated September 8, 2005, five months after the Arizona exhumations, it was sent by Policy Advisor for Health Anne Winter, to General Counsel Tim Nelson and Chief of Staff Alan Stephens under subject: "Billy the Kid." Only one line, it asked:

80% DNA match ... do you guys remember this issue?

Arizona thought it was getting Billy the Kid. Unfortunately, nothing good was present for Prosecutor Jonell Lucca. But I did get a feeling for Lucca's behind-the-scenes "political pressure."

## INVESTIGATING VIRDEN AND GETTING ATTACKED

I dreaded most Lincoln County Sheriff Rick Virden, picturing him calling Sullivan and Sederwall and asking, "Who the hell is Gale Cooper?" All would know my name for the first time.

And I would have to face complicit Lincoln County Attorney Alan "little weasel" Morel as a possible responder for Virden. And Morel had illegally refused all records from my Jay Miller IPRA requests on Sheriffs Sullivan and Virden from 2004 to 2006 by fake use of IPRA's exception for criminal investigations.

From Virden, I requested the forensic DNA records from Dr. Henry Lee and Orchid Cellmark Laboratory for Case # 2003-274. Attempting to block their repeated fake use of the criminal case exception, I added that *if* Virden used it, he should show why it applied - with his case's lacking a live suspect or a crime scene at risk. And I requested his records on the Arizona exhumations of John Miller and William Hudspeth.

Cc's went to Governor Janet Napolitano; Maricopa County Chief Prosecutor Andrew Thomas; Maricopa County Deputy Attorney Jonell Lucca; Yavapai County Sheriff Steve Waugh; and New Mexico U.S. Attorney David Iglesias.

On September 29, 2006, came Attorney Alan Morel's scary response: "We believe your request is **excessively burdensome or broad** [author's boldface], and we need additional time to respond." Morel had already threatened Jay Miller with an harassment case for doing the IPRA requests on Sullivan.

The actual Virden response, on October 11, 2006, made every effort to intimidate me by collective fury, threats, and retaliation from Virden, Morel, Sederwall, and Sullivan. [APPENDIX: 46] Moments like this test cowardice. I realized that when you add "Hamster Girl" to "coward," you get a stubborn coward. I would not retreat, though I was in abject terror.

Alan Morel's mailing was thick, though he denied existence of any requested records. But to legitimize Case # 2003-274, he provided the deputy cards for Sullivan (issued January 1, 2005) and Sederwall (issued February 25, 2005). Those sealed Virden's lie to "KEDU Community Radio's" Harvey Twite, in February of 2005, about his *not continuing the Billy the Kid Case.*

The Arizona exhumation made Sheriff Virden most nervous. He denied authorizing Sullivan or Sederwall for it, adding that they "advised him" that they did "not personally perform any exhumations in Prescott, Arizona, or elsewhere." (None knew I had their "Lincoln County Sheriff's Department Supplemental Report" from Deputy Anna Cahall of the Prescott Police Department, linking Case # 2003-274 to John Miller's disinterment; and signed by Sederwall as Lincoln County Deputy.)

Then Virden's game got rough. (Remember that they had not heard of me, and must have thought I was a random, ignorant, and vulnerable citizen.) Alan Morel labeled attachments as an "Exhibits," as if for litigation *against me.* He wrote:

I have also attached to this response two e-mails from Steven M. Sederwall to Jay Miller, dated September 19, 2006, and September 20, 2006 as Exhibit 3. **I do not believe they are responsive to any of your requests for records** [author's boldface], but I decided to include them, as they were provided to me by Mr. Sederwall.

Sederwall's thuggish September 19, 2006 e-mail stated:

> Jay, Is there a reason you're obsessed with our investigation? ... I am sure your [sic] aware this story is not what history claims, are you worried it will destroy New Mexico's cash cow?

Morel's letter continued:

> In addition, I have attached a copy of a letter dated September 30, 2006, with the heading 'The Dried Bean,' which was written to me on September 30, 2006. This correspondence is attached as Exhibit 4. Although I do not believe that the enclosed correspondence is responsive to any request for public records that you forwarded to me [sic - to Sheriff Virden], I have, nevertheless, attached the correspondence, **as it has already been forwarded to outside parties - namely the U.S. Marshal** [sic] **Service** [author's boldface] and Jay Miller.

"Exhibit 4" was frightening by intent. The U.S. Marshals Service is a branch of Homeland Security. The hoaxers had reported me for doing an IPRA request - as if I was a terrorist! I guessed the recipient was fellow hoaxer U.S. Marshals Service Historian David Turk. Later, it emerged how far David Turk was willing to abuse his public powers to protect all of their hoax.

That "Exhibit 4" letter was to Morel, dated September 30, 2006, and co-signed by Sullivan and Sederwall. Its obscene letterhead was: "The Dried Bean: 'You Believin' Us or Them Lyin' Whores'. " [APPENDIX: 47] So I was a "lyin' whore," in recycling of Sederwall's defamatory "cocaine whore" given to Debra Ingle. Addressing the exhumation, Sullivan and Sederwall blatantly lied about their involvement, culminating with:

> None of the 'promulgators' [them] so much as entered the grave of Mr. Miller. We did however examine some of the remains with our eye. [Author's note: Sederwall's hands are "eyeball-holding" John Miller's skull in the newspaper photo!]

However, this hoaxer pack was uncertain whether *I was Jay Miller*. So their tirade of misinformation in "The Dried Bean" letter calls me "Miller/Cooper," or just "Miller." Assuming my ignorance, they even boldly lied that historian Frederick Nolan backed them.

But I got what I wanted for Attorney Jonell Lucca: written denial by Virden, Sullivan, and Sederwall, along with their county attorney, that they had any DNA records to justify their Arizona exhumation of John Miller for "DNA matching."

## INVESTIGATING DR. HENRY LEE

Open records law did not cover privately employed Dr. Henry Lee. But the American Academy of Forensic Sciences (AAFS) Ethics Committee did. And I had evidence for an ethics complaint.

I had already questioned Lee - in my Jay Miller request for his records of March 27, 2006 - about his forensic claims quoted in Rene Romo's and Doris Cherry's articles. [APPENDIX: 48]

The question - on which Attorney Lucca's prosecution hinged - was: Do you claim "reference DNA of Billy the Kid" from your carpenter's bench specimens sent to Orchid Cellmark Lab?

On May 1, 2006, Dr. Lee answered on official stationery of State of Connecticut Department of Public Safety, Division of Scientific Services, under his title "Chief Emeritus" [APPENDIX: 49] Not disavowing his alleged quotes, he used the cagey language for which he was known:

> Since I did not conduct any DNA testing on the evidence and the Lincoln County Sheriff's Department sent samples directly to a private laboratory for analysis, I am sorry but I do not have answers to your questions regarding DNA.

Lee was unaware that past Orchid Cellmark Director Mark Stolorow told me their case was Lee's. But Lee confirmed his sending his report to the Lincoln County Sheriff's Department.

On June 15, 2006, I again wrote to Lee through Jay Miller [APPENDIX: 50], including the newspaper articles connected to the exhumations, by stating:

> As you are aware, these are very serious questions, since, based on the claim of having valid reference DNA of William Bonney for identity matching, two exhumations have been performed in Prescott, Arizona ... As you would also recognize, the claiming of true reference DNA from that carpenter's bench would involve many unusual assumptions and problems for a forensic DNA expert. So ... you might *not* have made the claims at all, and should have the opportunity to clarify that fact.

Dr. Henry Lee chose non-response.

So on August 8, 2006, Lee got urging by letter from me via Jay Miller. [APPENDIX: 51] It stated:

If your role was as pivotal as indicated by the articles, your response is important to clarify public awareness of this most serious case. And if your participation and/or conclusions were misrepresented, that is equally important to make known.

Nothing came back from sly Dr. Lee.

Given Lee's reputation among attorneys and forensic experts for lack of veracity, it was surprising to me that he never had an AAFS Ethics Complaint - then not realizing that professional groups protect their own; and whistleblowers, not the crooks, get their opprobrium,.

I sent my Ethics Complaint on October 2, 2006, after I spoke by phone with the chairman of the five member Ethics Committee, Haskell Pitluck, a retired judge. When I asked Pitluck if it would be hard for them to take action against their "media star," he was silent.

My complaint against Dr. Lee had six thick evidence folders (with duplicates for the five members plus Lee). I stated that Case 2003-274 was a historic-forensic hoax; and that Dr. Lee had ethical violations by willfully fabricating conclusions about: (1) the carpenter's bench as having blood, its victim feigning death, and the victim being Billy the Kid; (2) the Pat Garrett crime scene by using the meaningless tiny washstand as evidence for a made-up room and crime scene; and (3) the Deputy James Bell stairway shooting by Billy Bonney without having any way to link it to the scene, the Kid, or to Bell; while making unsubstantiated claims of blood.

I further opined that given such flagrant improprieties, all of Dr. Lee's other forensic findings in all his past court cases were suspect.

Cc's went to Attorney Jonell Lucca and her Chief Prosecutor Andrew Thomas. My bet was that slippery Dr. Lee would deny "reference DNA of Billy the Kid," and would accuse the other hoaxers of all claims. That should clinch for prosecutors that there had never existed "reference DNA of the Kid" to justify the perpetrators' John Miller exhumation.

But before the Ethics Committee could respond to me, something astounding happened in Arizona.

# COUNTDOWN TO ARIZONA'S DECISION

## *PLAYING BEAT THE CLOCK*

Now certain I could make a difference with my Dr. Henry Lee ethics complaint, I sent Prosecutor Jonell Lucca my Bill Richardson, Janet Napolitano, and Sheriff Virden records request responses: all showing forensic and political improprieties.

Meanwhile, since Governors Richardson and Napolitano were campaigning for re-election, I hoped for press coverage: my Plan B to stop the hoax by public opinion.

I had already revealed the Billy the Kid Case hoax to a Bob Johnson, Executive Director of the New Mexico Foundation for Open Government ("FOG"). When I called now, he referred me to the *Albuquerque Journal's* Editor-in-Chief, Kent Walz; saying that, Rene Romo notwithstanding, Walz would report fairly.

So I called Kent Walz that October of 2006. Coldly he said that *even if* the Billy the Kid Case was a hoax, it was too hard to explain to the public. He added: "What difference does it make if they dug up a few Arizona graves?"

Kent Walz referred me to his State News Desk reporter, John Robertson. Robertson said he was "dealing with more important things: the election." I said that New Mexicans needed to know about Richardson's hoaxing *for the election.* He ignored that.

Contacting Ollie Reed of the *Albuquerque Tribune*; Mark Evans of the AP; the editorial department of the *Arizona Republic*; Ben Hansen, Editor-in-Chief of the *Daily Courier* of *Prescott*; and a D. Ceribelli at the *New York Times* Executive Editors Desk, yielded zero articles. My hoax exposure remained voiceless.

## *RICO AND FBI*

After you jump into cold water - or, I suppose, into a sewer - something happens: you get used to it, and can keep swimming.

I decided that a crime which could help Prosecutor Jonell Lucca was RICO. RICO stands for Racketeer Influenced and Corrupt Organizations Act of 1970 against organized crime. By 1997, it was broadened to any conspiracy for the same criminal objective; stating: "If conspirators have a plan which calls for some conspirators to commit the crime and others to provide support, the supporters are as guilty as the perpetrators." That could fit the Billy the Kid Case hoaxers.

The FBI investigates RICO cases; and a state's U.S. Attorney prosecutes them. In New Mexico, the U.S. Attorney was David Iglesias, a Republican appointed by President Bush; seemingly outside Democratic cronyism of this Santa Fe Ring-style hoax.

I called the Albuquerque FBI office. When I said "Governor Richardson," the screener told me to address my complaint to Squad 5, " for the highest division of white collar crime."

My presented evidence to Squad 5 had 14 folders and the title: "RICO complaint against New Mexico and Arizona public officials promulgating together Lincoln County Sheriff's Department Case # 2003-274 and De Baca County Sheriff's Department Case # 03-06-136-01 ('The Billy the Kid Case')."

I had not stopped working since writing my September records requests. On October 10, 2006, after I mailed it, I slept 48 hours.

On October 18th, I called back. To my delight, the operator said my complaint was with Squad 5's head: Supervisory Special Agent Mark Humphrey. I fantasized his clipped sentences, tight with power. Instead, he sounded like an accountant. (It being white collar crime, he may have been.) We spoke for quite a while.

HUMPHREY: You need big sums for a jury to convict. My job is to give the U.S. Attorney a case he can win.
ME: I thought *you* investigate. You're my last hope.
HUMPHREY: I'll keep reading.
ME: (*Thinking to myself*) The hoax may be a perfect crime: too elaborate for the press; too puny for a jury.

But I sent Attorney Jonell Lucca a copy of my RICO complaint, sure that this back-up would bolster her gumption.

## ARIZONA SHOCKER

On October 20, 2006, an envelope arrived with "Lucca" typed above "Maricopa County Attorney Andrew Thomas." I assumed it was to thank me, or to explain more delay. It was neither.

On departmental stationery with "Maricopa County Attorney" in Old English lettering, dated October 17, 2006, titled "RE: State v. Jeanine Dike & Dale Tunnell," and signed by

Attorney Lucca, it said:

> Dear Dr. Cooper: This letter is to inform you that the Maricopa County Attorney's Office has declined to file charges against Jeanine Dike and Dale Tunnell as there is no reasonable likelihood of conviction in this case. There is no further information regarding the decision. Thank you for your interest in the case.

Racing through my mind was: "You knew Sullivan and Sederwall were the suspects. You knew that you did not even need the Billy the Kid Case. You had William Hudspeth for a case." Jonell Lucca had folded.

It occurred to me that all my evidence may have merely convinced the Prosecutor's Office of the need for cover-up.

But why had Lucca revealed her tricks: switching suspects, concealing Hudspeth? Why had she given me advance warning? Was it her conscience's last squeak? What was I supposed to do?

I called an opponent of the hoax in Lincoln County. She wept.

## *RICHARDSON'S RING POWER*

Then I realized that Jonell Lucca's capitulation had been foreshadowed. I owned an  e-mail copy (obtained by attorney's demand from a public official). It was dated May 16, 2006 - just before the Cannes Film Festival. Written by keyed-up Steve Sederwall, it could bring down Richardson and Napolitano. It was signed with a smiley face symbol and "Steve." He stated:

> Well we have the governor reaching out to the Arizona [sic- missing word] to stop this investigation. They thought we had the DNA [sic - illegible word follows] and they tried to get the FBI to get John Millers bones back with a warrant and get the DNA. They think we are going to announce that John Miller is the kid in France. We will not give them a break. They are now trying to get is [sic - us?] worked up about grave robbery charges. But being good cops we have all the docs that show the state of Arizona did the dig not us. How funny. if [sic] they do something stupid and file on us we sue and Arizona well [sic] be the state of Tom and Steve.

I would have given my kingdom for the first missing word. Was it "governor?" Was it "prosecutor?" Either way, obstruction of justice was Bill Richardson's Faustian bargain for Sederwall's and

Sullivan's Cannes Film Festival DNA silence. And it proved that the Santa Fe Ring extended into Arizona.

## LUCCA'S LIES

For the press, completing her exhumation cover-up, Prosecutor Jonell Lucca switched her suspects back to Sullivan and Sederwall. Through her prosecutor's office spokesperson, Bill Fitzgerald, Jonell Lucca confirmed that *they* had been absolved!

That hoaxer victory was announced on October 22, 2006 in *The Daily Courier* of Prescott - my information to its editor-in-chief, Ben Hansen, ignored. The reporter was Joanna Dodder, now concealing her own reporting on the exhumation crimes. Her article was: "Officials won't file charges in Billy the Kid grave case." Presented were Lucca's lies. Dodder stated:

> The Maricopa County Attorney's Office has decided not to prosecute people who dug up the bones of a man who claimed to be Billy the Kid.
>
> Former Lincoln County, N.M., Sheriff Tom Sullivan, former Capitan, N.M. mayor Steve Sederwall and others dug up the bones of John Miller and the remains of the man buried next to him at the state-owned Pioneers' Home Cemetery in Prescott in May 2005.
>
> Maricopa County won't seek charges against anyone involved in the disinterment, Attorney's Office spokesman Bill Fitzgerald said Thursday evening.

From the Internet's *New York Sun*, came an October 24, 2006 AP article titled "Men Who Exhumed Billy the Kid Won't Be Charged." So John Miller was now called *Billy the Kid*!

The same day was a near-repeat in the "Metro Section" of the *Albuquerque Journal* as: "Billy the Kid Case Dropped." (If only *that* had been true!) Ignored was my information to Kent Walz. His paper, again celebrated the hoaxers - now without concern that their case was too complicated for the public to understand.

That day came also the *New York Times's* "Arizona: No Charges Sought for Exhuming Remains," repeating the AP and closing the circle of its hoax-backing from its 2003 article.

The day before, on AOL News, an unnamed AP reporter wrote "PRESCOTT, Ariz. - Prosecutors won't seek charges against two men who exhumed the remains of a man who claimed to be the outlaw Billy the Kid." Added was a dramatic quote:

Sederwall refused to disclose the results of that DNA test Monday, for fear of provoking attacks from historians. He said, "What I know is not what's written in history."

And the "Doomsday Document" took on horrible implications.

By May 13, 2007, Sederwall jumbled the Arizona exhumation case into double-talk for the Internet's "Billy the Kid Discussion Board." To a "Billyondabrain" (with typos intact), he wrote:

We did not dig in Phoenix it was a different county. That's because a state investigator worked that part of the case, the state of Arizona their equipment, their employees, and a deputy sheriff from that county was right there the entire time. This all brewed up during their elections and we took the hit on it. But there is a lot more behind the scenes that no one sees.

Behind the scenes, the hoaxers were trying to decide who should be "Billy the Kid." It would depend on the availability of "Brushy Bill" Roberts's Texas grave to their shovels.

# ALONE AGAINST THE RING: I FIGHT BACK

### *NEW DIRECTIONS*

I rallied. There was still the FBI and RICO. I called one of my Lincoln County sources, bemoaning my need for financial information to give Agent Mark Humphreys.

"What about their Billy the Kid fund?" he asked.

"What fund?!" I exclaimed.

"I have a copy of its check," he said. "In 2006, Sederwall and Sullivan had a write-up in the paper about a fella stealin' it."

He faxed to me a page from the November 25, 2006 *Ruidoso News*. On it was that check from the First Federal Bank of Capitan, with: "TOM T. SULLIVAN, STEVEN M. SEDERWALL, CASE #2003-274 PRIVATE FUNDING; P.O. BOX 544, CAPITAN, NM, 88316, 505-354-2664."

With this new evidence, I called Mark Humphrey. His weary voice perked up. I sent him the check on October 30, 2006, and added the hoaxers' U.S. Marshals Service threat against me. I felt safer; though realistically, Humphrey was no protection at all.

## ANSWERING LUCCA

On a roll that October 30, 2006, I wrote questions to Attorney Lucca, copying her boss, Chief Prosecutor Andrew Thomas. [APPENDIX: 52] Why did she change suspects? How could she condone exhumations without "reference DNA of Billy the Kid?"

Jonell Lucca never responded. What could she have said?

## TAKING ON ATTORNEY ALAN MOREL

My roll continued.

Attorney Alan Morel had made himself a weak link in the Ring's chain. As Lincoln County Attorney, he was taxpayer paid to stop public officials' crimes - not back them. (Later, a local told me: "Morel says his job is to keep the sheriff out of prison.")

On November 13, 2006, I sent a complaint against Morel to the New Mexico Bar Association for professional misconduct of purposeful defamation and libel of me; purposeful harassment to inflict emotional pain and suffering on me; and violation of the Inspection of Public Records Act, in conspiracy with Sheriff Rick Virden, to withhold public records. Emphasized was Morel's attempt to frighten me from exercising my rights under IPRA.

To vouch for me, I attached an e-mail from Frederick Nolan, which he sent me on November 4, 2006, in response to Morel's and the others' using his name in their "Dried Bean" letter. He wrote:

> As someone who has from its inception opposed the hoax this letter calls an "official investigation," I wish to have it placed on record that I object strongly to the writers' twisting my words out of context to suggest that I support it, and vigorously contest their claim that with the "information" they hold "the 'myth and legend" of Billy the Kid "will surely be destroyed."
>
> I would also add that I have myself been the recipient of harassment in the form of written threats of violence from associates of these men and have referred those documents to State and Federal law-enforcement agencies.

## BLOCKED AND BLOCKED AGAIN

Things were looking up. Special Agent Mark Humphrey, after getting the "Private Donor" check, suggested that I send my complaint to U.S. Attorney David Iglesias.

On October 30, 2006, I mailed it to Iglesias and his Assistant U.S. Attorney, Mary Higgins. Iglesias responded fast: he killed my case! His letter of November 16, 2006 stated: "It does not appear from a review of the enclosed documents that a federal criminal statute is implicated by the activities described." What happened?

The next month, President Bush fired Iglesias (with seven other U.S. Attorneys). Iglesias cried "racism." My contacts told me Iglesias went down for possibly incompetent, or possibly willful, blocking of all prosecutions involving Governor Bill Richardson.

My next blow came on December 11, 2006 from the New Mexico Bar Association. Special Assistant Disciplinary Counsel attorney, Christine E. Long, denied my Morel complaint. She stated: "In neither the September 29, 2006, nor the October 11, 2006, letters from Mr. Morel does there appear to be any violation of the Rules of Professional Conduct. It is truly unfortunate that you feel threatened or harmed by Mr. Morel, but there is simply no evidence that he was doing anything other than making a good faith effort to comply with your request for information. Accordingly, this office will be closing its file in this matter."

Anyway, I thought, my Dr. Lee complaint is an iron in the fire.

## PERSISTING IN ARIZONA

Awaiting the AAFS Ethics Committee, I tried disciplinary action against Attorney Lucca. There was a loophole in her suspect-switching ploy: a new complaint could be made against Sullivan, Sederwall, and Virden. But the way needed paving.

On January 5, 2007, I filed an Arizona Bar Association complaint contending that Attorney Lucca had yielded to corrupt political influence, had obstructed the course of justice, and had perverted the course of justice by switching suspects and by ignoring or concealing evidence against Sullivan and Sederwall. [APPENDIX: 53] It was 52 pages long, with 12 folders of evidence.

## BLOCKED AGAIN TIMES TWO

On February 27, 2007, the State Bar of Arizona's Staff Bar Counsel-Attorney Ariel I. Worth, responded. She ignored my specifics, and rejected my complaint: "Based on the information submitted, it is unlikely the Lawyer Regulation Office will be able to carry its burden of proof in a disciplinary proceeding."

My March 21, 2007 letter requested that Attorney Worth address my allegations. So she made up a new rejection on November 2, 2007: denial of her Bar's jurisdiction. But she offered no other "jurisdiction" for presenting my allegations.

Meanwhile, I tried another approach: contacting Arizona's Attorney General Terry Goddard - to whom David Snell had first complained about the John Miller exhumation. Goddard's January 5, 2007 "Guest Opinion" interview to the *Arizona Star*'s had been promisingly titled: "Public Officials not above the law." He had written: "Although the Legislature and the courts, not the attorney general, set the standards for official conduct, it is my job to make sure the standards are clear and public officials are held accountable."

On March 21, 2007, I sent Terry Goddard my Attorney Lucca case, titled: "Presentation of alleged prosecutorial improprieties relating to the exhumation of remains of John Miller and William Hudspeth at the Arizona Pioneers' Home Cemetery."

I got no response. Later, I heard that Terry Goddard was a Napolitano loyalist.

### LESSONS FOR A GRIM FUTURE

I had done everything a citizen could do to stop the multiple crimes of the Billy the Kid Case. All regulatory agencies failed me.

My only success to date had been protecting the Billy the Kid and Catherine Antrim graves. My conclusion is: it is worse to be dead in Arizona than New Mexico - if the dead want to lie in peace.

Meanwhile, I had to face the now unleashed Billy the Kid Case hoaxers' next foray: the Hamilton, Texas, grave of "Brushy Bill" Roberts. And they knew about me by name.

# CHAPTER 11:

# HOAX RESURECTION AND THE DOOMSDAY DOCUMENT

# Lincoln County Sheriff's Office

R. E. (RICK) VIRDEN
Sheriff

PATRICK J. O'BRIEN
Chief Deputy

DONNA HARKEY
Administrative Assistant

300 CENTRAL AVENUE
P. O. BOX 278
CARRIZOZO, NM 88301

(505) 648-2342
(800) 687-2419

FAX: (505) 648-2862

Hamilton Texas
Mayor Roy Ramsey

Mayor Ramsey,

This letter will inform you that Tom Sulliv[...]
deputies with the Lincoln County New M[...]

They have been investigating case #2003[...]
personally and has been conducted on th[...]

Mr. Mayor, should you have any questi[...]

R.E. Virden
Lincoln County Sheriff

---

## AMERICAN ACADEMY OF FORENSIC SCIEN[...]

410 North 21st Street • Colorado Springs, CO 80904 • (719) 636-1100 • Fax (719) 63[...]

Haskell M. Pitluck
573 Lake Avenue
Crystal Lake, Illinois 60014
Phone: (815) 459-7192
Email: pitluck@mc.net

Gale Cooper, M.D.
P.O. Box 328
Sandia Park, New Mexico 87047

May 9, 2007

Dear Dr. Cooper,

This letter is to advise you that the Ethics Committee of the American Academy of Forensic Sciences has completed its investigation of the complaint you have filed against Dr. Henry C. Lee. The Committee has reviewed all of the materials which you were kind enough to provide with your complaint as well as Dr. Lee's report dated, February 5, 2005.

Dr. Lee's report is very clear in what he did. Nothing in that report constitutes any deviation from our ethical standards. The issues raised in your complaints address issues that are outside of what Dr. Lee actually did in his tests. Some of those issues have to do with what other individuals did and Dr. Lee is not responsible for those actions.

Based upon our investigation, the Committee has unanimously concluded that Dr. Lee's work in this matter is not in violation of the Academy's Code of Ethics and Conduct.

I am sorry that it took us so long to conclude our investigation. However, after we received a copy of Dr. Lee's report, we all met in person in Chicago recently to discuss the case.

We have closed our file. Thank you for your attention to this matter.

Very truly yours,

Haskell M. Pitluck, J.D.
Chair, Ethics Committee

Federal ID Number: 87[...]

---

## Tim Nelson

**From:** Anne Winter
**Sent:** Thursday, September 08, 2005 3:00 PM
**To:** Tim Nelson; Alan Stephens
**Subject:** Billy the Kid

80% DNA match....do you guys remember this issue?

Anne Winter
Policy Advisor For Health
Office of Governor Napolitano
1700 West Washington
Phoenix, AZ 85007
602-542-1626
awinter@az.gov

# BILLY THE KID'S DNA LOTTERY

*HOAXBUST: The Billy the Kid Case hoaxers had emerged unscathed from my efforts to stop them. They had press and TV galore, Dr. Henry Lee's fake bench DNA, and Orchid Cellmark's fake DNA from the John Miller exhumations. They were poised to manufacture any "Billy the Kid" they wanted. And their "Doomsday Document" gave one possible direction. Everything depended on the AAFS Ethics Committee stopping Dr. Henry Lee from backing their scam.*

## HEEEER'S MILLER, THE BILLY WINNER ... OR NOT

Freed from risk of pink underwear, the hoaxers had to decide: would John Miller win the "Billy the Kid lottery?"

I knew they were tempted. I had their September 8, 2005 e-mail, "Subject: Billy the Kid," to Governor Janet Napolitano's Office: my so-called "Doomsday Document." It had made a stir with Anne Winter, Napolitano's Policy Advisor for Health; Tim Nelson, Napolitano's General Counsel; and to Alan Stephens, her Chief of Staff. It had said:

80% DNA match ... do you guys remember this issue?

Governor Napolitano got it for a reason: Arizona was being felt out for a new tourist attraction: the grave of Billy the Kid. So Napolitano got the hoaxers' dog and pony show of "modern high-tech forensics" with "DNA matching proof" that John Miller was "Billy the Kid."

Napolitano's response is unknown. But, as already mentioned, before Cannes, in May of 2006, Richardson had prevented his fellow hoaxers from making that DNA announcement there. They were left only with chortling "that history is not as written."

Of course, the hoaxers were hoaxing Napolitano. Their fake presentation relied on a layman's "lottery mentality" in which 80% sounded like a big winning number. In fact, 80% in DNA matching would mean *no match*. In other words, if 20% of the genetic markers in two, compared, DNA samples are different, it means the two people are different. (Anyway. the DNA in question was from William Hudspeth, not John Miller - as well as from fake bench DNA!)

But I knew the hoaxers were poised to confuse the public. Their "Miller as Billy" could be doomsday for the history.

Two years later, I also saw a plus to this e-mail: the "Doomsday Document" proved that the hoaxers admitted to having Case # 2003-274 forensic DNA records.

But back then, my only built-in salvation to endure anxiety of the history coming to unjust ruin was knowing that the hoaxers' hope was for publicity-grabbing "Brushy" as their Billy the Kid.

## HEEER'S "BRUSHY," THE KID WINNER?

I wondered, "When would Texas be attacked?" Sederwall - my "honorary opposition member" - did not let me down. Soon there was a newspaper interview from him.

Using his Lincoln County Deputy Sheriff title, he had gone to Hamilton, Texas - site of Oliver "Brushy Bill" Roberts's grave - requesting exhumation permission from the mayor and Town Council. Sederwall was offering *them* Billy the Kid.

And Sheriff Rick Virden was right on board. On official letterhead, at the start of their "Brushy" grave invasion - though forgetting to date that May 2007 letter - he wrote to Hamilton, Texas's Mayor, Roy Rumsey - misspelling it as "Ramsey":

> This letter will inform you that Tom Sullivan and Steve Sederwall are both commissioned deputies with the Lincoln County New Mexico Sheriff''s Department. They have been investigating case # 2003-274 ... Mr. Mayor, should you have any questions please do not hesitate to contact me.

The *Roswell Daily Record*, using a Stephenville, Texas, article, wrote on May 2, 2007, "Billy the Kid Exhumation a Possibility."

With Sederwall's standard gibberish - this time with Garrett himself placing "the bleeding body on a bench" - the article presented a new hoax direction: Going back to Billy's mother!

**Sederwall said if DNA is allowed to be obtained from Roberts, investigators will pursue exhuming the body of Catherine McCarty Antrim ... Sederwall has already obtained Miller's DNA.**

Why was their "Billy bloody bench DNA" abandoned? Was "Brushy's" lack of a carpenter's bench death scene too well known in Texas? (But notice Sederwall's admission of having "Miller" DNA.) Those questions, were mine. The hoaxers were still trying to decide who should be Billy.

On May 4th, Steve Sederwall presented their decision: He demoted John Miller on the Internet's "Billy the Kid Discussion Board." To a Loretta, Sederwall stated:

> Billyonthebrain asked why we did not release the match on the bench and Miller. Good question. Miller's story is that Garrett didn't shoot him but shot someone else and he was wounded 'some days before the shooting' found in 'Whatever Happened to Billy the Kid' by Helen Airy. That would say that if Miller's story is the truth as written, just like Brushy Bill his DNA would not have hit the bench.

So the next hoaxer "historical" shape-shift was: John Miller could not have been the Kid. (And forget that we already dug him up based on Helen Airy's book "convincing" us.) Do not miss that this was a real "confession" for any honest Arizona prosecutor, proving that the John Miller exhumation was unjustified.

On May 4, 2007 the *Albuquerque Journal*, again interested in Billy the Kid – when it came from the hoaxers and not from me - printed "Manhunt for Real Billy the Kid Goes On: Deputy hopes DNA will finally reveal outlaw's true identity." In it, Sederwall blew smoke for the reporter:

> Those (Hamilton City) people want to know, they are not afraid ... You talk to Fort Sumner and they want to pull pistols on us. You talk to Hamilton City and they're like, "Sure, we'd like to know."

I knew Sederwall was blowing smoke, because I had spoken to those "Hamilton City" people. Mayor Roy Rumsey told me he had said to Sederwall: "If Roberts is Billy the Kid, I'm Pancho Villa!" And Rumsey had demanded to see their "DNA papers."

For Mayor Rumsey; the Town Councilors; and other Hamilton officials - Justice of the Peace James Lively, Judge Randy Mills, and City Administrator Bill Funderburk - I provided documents demonstrating the Billy the Kid Case hoax.

Their May 10, 2007 Town Council meeting to decide about exhumation was even graced by Jannay Valdez, who gave his heartfelt pitch for his beloved "Brushy." Then the Council members voted. Exhumation was unanimously opposed.

On May 11, 2007, the *Houston Chronicle* reported "Texas town denies request to exhume Billy the Kid claimant." In it, Jannay Valdez wheedled: "We dig holes in Africa to find ancient cultures. All we want is just a fingernail snip."

And hypocritical hoax historian Paul Hutton fence-rode for a May 5, 2007 article by a Thomas Zorosec in the Houston Chronicle under "DNA Could solve mystery of Billy the Kid." Calling himself "a history professor ... specializing in the American West," Hutton said the Roberts family Bible proved "Brushy" was born too late; and there is "ample evidence that Garrett shot and killed the famous pistolero." (Of course, this left out that writer/ co-producer Hutton had omitted all that in his 2004 "Investigating History: Billy the Kid;" and had, in fact, had argued for "Brushy's" plausibility, and re-enacted a murderer Garrett placing Billy's jailbreak revolver in the outhouse.) But for this two-faced article, Hutton still hugged his fellow hoaxers. He said Sederwall and several former lawmen he is working with [sic - all were *active* lawmen] are serious investigators 'and they're having fun. It's a fun story, and that's the right attitude to have about it.' "

Hutton and crew might be having fun. I was not. Next, I heard that Sederwall approached the Hamilton District Judge. So I lined up a pro bono attorney; informed Mayor Roy Rumsey; and gave information to Hamilton City Attorney Connie White and assistant to Dallas Chief Medical Examiner, Dr. Jeffrey Barnard.

But suddenly the hoaxers stopped. Maybe they realized that Catherine Antrim's DNA would be another hopeless quest. Sederwall and Sullivan had already failed in their IPRA request to get OMI Forensic Anthropologist Dr. Debra Komar's notes on that grave. And, as to the carpenter's bench, my AAFS Ethics Committee investigation seems to have made Dr. Henry Lee run to for the hills when he heard "Billy the Kid bench DNA" from the Billy the Kid Case "investigators."

And Mayor Roy Rumsey took care of the "Brushy Bill's" grave angle. On September 12, 2008, he faxed me: "RE: Lincoln County Sheriff's Department 2007 attempt to exhume Oliver Roberts." He stated: "The city of Hamilton considers this matter closed." "Brushy" was blocked from Billy the Kid Case hoaxers.

## HEEEER'S THE FORENSIC EXPERT ... OR NOT

I was certain that the AAFS Ethics Committee, responsible for integrity of researchers and court testifiers, would end the charade of "Billy bench DNA." But six months had passed from my complaint. So on April 10, 2007, I wrote to the Academy's President, Dr. Bruce Goldberger, to prod the process.

On May 4, 2007, Dr. Goldberger faxed that I would know the committee's decision in two weeks. On May 9th the letter arrived from Haskell Pitluck. It concluded:

> Based upon our investigation, the Committee has unanimously concluded that Dr. Lee's work in this matter is not in violation of the Academy Code of Ethics and Conduct.

With my massive evidence, how could they justify that?

Coordinating with wily Dr. Lee was the answer. Recall Lee's letter to Jay Miller about his bench report. Lee gave only that report to the Committee - dated, according to Pitluck, February 5, 2005. [Note that this is in Sheriff Virden's tenure. Note also that Lee's report discussed earlier in this book was dated February 25, 2005. Possibly Pitluck had a typo. Possibly Lee and the hoaxers are still hiding another report.] Pitluck stated to me:

> Dr. Lee's report is very clear in what he did. Nothing in the report deviates from our ethical standards.

What about Lee's fake forensic conclusions about the bloody bench; the shot washstand, the "chicken-Garrett" murder scene; and the top-of-stairs Bell murder - all quoted in articles? The Ethics Committee's mincing legalize stated:

> The issues raised in your complaints address issues that are outside of what Dr. Lee actually did in his tests. Some of those issues have to do with what other individuals did and Dr. Lee is not responsible for those actions.

So Lee's out was that all those "quotes" and conclusions were not his. That took care of Lee's so-called DNA of Billy the Kid! (Of course Lee was calling the hoaxers and reporters liars.)

I persisted. On May 30, 2007, I sent Pitluck my response, with a yes-no listing of Rene Romo's *Albuquerque Journal* quotes, asking if Lee denied making them. [APPENDIX: 54]

On June 2, 2007, Haskell Pitluck continued nose-thumbing me. Their "unethics" committee had circled the wagons around their media star. Pitluck stated:

> The items you raise in your letter of May 30, 2007 are outside the scope of what Dr. Lee did and Dr. Lee is not responsible for the actions or statements of others.

To pin that down, on June 19, 2007 I requested clarification; essentially asking if everyone but Lee was a liar. [APPENDIX: 55] Pitluck's testy response of July 6, 2007 was:

> We make no assumptions as you attempt to attribute to us in your letter of June 19, 2007. Any assumptions that you make are strictly your own and not those of the Ethics Committee. We stand on our previous determination and our file remains closed.

Actually, Lee could not afford another scandal. That May, he was caught allegedly destroying evidence for the Phil Spector murder trial. Steve Davis, a Los Angeles detective on that case, told me, "This should put an end to Dr. Lee." It did not.

Lee's fake Billy the Kid Case forensic handiwork lived on with Professor Paul Hutton, whose Albuquerque Museum of Art and History Billy the Kid show ran from May 12, 2007 to July 22, 2007. With Steve Sederwall at its opening ceremony, and named "Dreamscape Desperado" after Hutton's Billy the Kid article of June 1990 for *New Mexico Magazine*, it featured the carpenter's bench, falsely labeled with blood as follows:

> Maxwell family tradition holds that Billy the Kid's body was laid on this bench prior to his burial. Blood drips are visible beneath the bench near its center point. The blood was sampled and identified by forensic expert Henry Lee, who determined it was human.

I wrote to the museum's Curator of History, Deborah Slaney, on July 30, 2007, about those bench claims. She answered, on August 6th, that the "analysis" of the bench was by exhibit curator, Paul Hutton.

The last loose end was to address Haskell Pitluck and

Committee's: "statements of others" unfairly attributed to saintly Dr. Lee. That meant the *Albuquerque Journal*.

On June 19, 2007, I sent Lee's accusation of fabricating his words to the paper's owner, Tom Lang; Editor-in-Chief, Kent Walz; and reporter, Rene Romo.

Only Walz responded. His August 13, 2007 letter stated:

> You contend Dr. Lee "apparently denied making" comments attributed to him in Mr. Romo's report. Please be advised that to my knowledge Mr. Lee has not contacted anyone at the Journal to dispute the comments attributed to him in any way.

So, to quote everyone involved in claiming the carpenter's bench yielded DNA of Billy the Kid: "I NEVER SAID THAT!"

We are back in the "Land of Enchantment" where disembodied words appear, without human source, in newsprint.

# CHAPTER 12:

# MY LAST CHANCE: ENFORCING IPRA

**BARNETT LAW FIRM, P.A.**

AMY B. BAILEY
MICKEY D. BARNETT
PHILLIP W. CHEVES
DAVID A. GARCIA, OF COUNSEL

1905 WYOMING BLVD N
ALBUQUERQUE, NM
FAX (505)
PHONE (

April 24, 20

CERTIED MAIL
RETURN RECEIPT REQUESTED
AND FIRST CLASS MAIL
Sheriff Rick Virden
Lincoln County Sheriff's Office
PO Box 278
Carrizozo, NM 88301-0278

Re:    Request for Inspection of Public Records

Dear Sheriff Virden:

This office represents Gale Cooper, M.D. Pursuant to the Inspection of
Records Act, Section 14-2-8 *et seq.* NMSA 1978, this letter is our written re
the public records identified as follows:

1.    Please provide any and all records and reports of raw da
or conclusions provided in any form at all to the Lincoln County Sher
Department by Dr. Henry Lee as the stated "forensic expert" utilized by t
Lincoln County Sheriff's Department for promulgation of Lincoln Count
Sheriff's Department Case # 2003-274 with regard to any and all DNA
tests and procedures are to be considered

---

STATE OF NEW MEXICO
COUNTY OF SANDOVAL
THIRTEENTH JUDICIAL DISTRICT COURT

CAUSE NO. D 1329 CV 2007-01364

GALE COOPER and DE BACA COUNTY NEWS, a New Mexico corporation,

Plaintiffs,

-vs-

RICK VIRDEN, LINCOLN COUNTY SHERIFF and CUSTODIAN OF RECORDS
OF THE LINCOLN COUNTY SHERIFF; and STEVEN M. SEDERWALL, FORMER
LINCOLN COUNTY DEPUTY SHERIFF; and THOMAS T. SULLIVAN, FORMER
LINCOLN COUNTY SHERIFF AND FORMER LINCOLN COUNTY DEPUTY
SHERIFF,

FIRST AMENDED COMPLAINT FOR DECLARATORY
JUDGMENT ORDERING PRODUCTION
IN RECORDS AND INFORMATION

---

## Memorandum

To:        Rick Virden, Lincoln County Sheriff
From:      Steven M. Sederwall & Thomas T. Sullivan
Subject:   Billy the Kid Investigation
Date:      Thursday, June 21, 2007

On April 28, 2003 we began a quest for the truth, looking into the *"escape of Willia
and the double homicide of James Bell & Robert Olinger."* We chose this as a priv
and did not want to burden the county financially. The idea was to bring modern s
police investigative methods to uncover the truth of the escape of the Kid and the
deputies. We had planned to file a report with the Sheriff at the end of the investi
which the public could then access if they so desire.

---

# Attachment 2

*Checks handed to Sheriff Sullivan in the State Capital by Billy Sparks*

HOBBS RENTAL CORPORATION

Vendor:   INVESTIGATIVE FUND 2003-247
Item to be Paid - Description
CHARITABLE CONTRIBUTIONS

Check Date:   Aug 1, 2003
Check Amount: $500.00

Amount Pa
500

Heard, Robins, Goud
Lubel & Greenwood, LLP

SEP 17 2003

Received

HOBBS RENTAL CORPORATION
P.O. BOX 805   250-3085
HOBBS, NEW MEXICO 88241

WESTERN COMMERCE BANK

PAY    Five Hundred and 00/100 Dollars

TO THE     INVESTIGATIVE FUND 2003-247
ORDER      C/O HEARD, ROBINS ETAL
OF         300 PASEO DE BERALTO, STE. 200
           SANTA FE, NM 87501

DATE
Aug 1, 200

#021142# C11220192OC 03 18 1455#01

BILL ROBINS
710-694-026
300 PASEO DE PERALTA, STE 200
SANTA FE, NM 87501-2501

1131

Date 9/10/03

Pay to the
Order of    Investigative Fund 2003-27 2     $ 2000.00

Bank of America

C10700032?C 004274736630C 1131

---

INSPECTION OF
PUBLIC RECORDS
ACT
COMPLIANCE
GUIDE
FOURTH EDITION

Office of the Attorney General
Civil Division
P.O. Drawer 1508
Santa Fe, NM 87504-1508
(505) 827-6000
www.ago.state.nm.us

PATRICIA A. MADRID
Attorney General

State of New Mexico
Office of the Attorney General

---

1    THIRTEENTH JUDICIAL DISTRICT
2    COUNTY OF SANDOVAL
     STATE OF NEW MEXICO
3
4    GALE COOPER and DE BACA COUNTY NEWS, a
     Corporation,
5
6          Plaintiffs
7    vs.

---

## Suit Targets Investigation Into Billy the Kid's Death

Copyright © 2008
Albuquerque Journal

BY CHARLES D. BRUNT
Journal Staff Writer

Legal wrangling over DNA
analyses could have Billy the
Kid rolling in his grave
wherever it may be.

Scot Stinnett, publisher of
the De Baca County News, and
Gale Cooper, a retired psychi-

artist and amateur historian
from Cedar Crest, are suing
current and former Lincoln
County lawmen they say are
withholding public records
about DNA evidence collected
during an investigation into
events leading up to the Kid's
presumed death in 1881.

Legend has it that the Kid,
William Bonney, was gunned

See BILLY on PAGE A9

THE ASSOCIATED PRESS
William Bonney, Billy the Kid,
is believed to be depicted in
this photo from about 1880.

DWI Search

OPER VS LINCOLN COUNTY

| CASE DETAIL | | | |
|---|---|---|---|
| CASE NUMBER | CURRENT JUDGE | FILING DATE | COURT |
| D-1329-CV-200701364 | Eichwald, George P. | 10/15/2007 | BERNALILLO DISTRICT |

| PARTIES TO THIS CASE | | |
|---|---|---|
| PARTY | PARTY | PARTY |

# HIGH NOON IN LINCOLN COUNTY: IPRA SHOWDOWN

*HOAXBUST: One Achilles heel of the Billy the Kid Case was its public nature: done by public official lawmen for their filed murder case. So their records were public. Another Achilles heel was that their hoax rested on DNA claims. And if IPRA requests for the forensic DNA records of Case # 2003-274 were denied, enforcement was available by litigation. That could topple the hoax. But the hoaxers would fight like trapped rats.*

After the Arizona prosecutor's office, FBI, Bar Associations, and American Academy of Forensic Science Ethics Committee refused to take action on Billy the Kid Case hoaxers' wrongdoings, I still would not back down. The hoaxers had to be exposed.

One way was by IPRA requests for their forensic DNA records. But I needed an attorney, since my own requests had been arrogantly ignored. And, though my legal fight against the Billy/mother exhumations contended that the Pat Garrett murder investigation was fraudulent, Case # 2003-274 was still done as law enforcement by public officials. So their records were public and subject to Inspection of Public Records Act ("IPRA") law. And IPRA's purpose is to root out abuses like those in Case # 2003-274.

So the forensic DNA records seemed key to hoaxbusting.

Dr. Lee had confirmed that he sent his carpenter's bench report to the Lincoln County Sheriff's Department. The hoaxers had boasted in press of the rest: Orchid Cellmark Labs got DNA from Lee's bench specimens and the Arizona remains, and got DNA matchings of bench DNA to Miller's and Hudspeth's DNA.

An attorney could request those records in my name. And the custodian of the records under IPRA law was the Lincoln County Sheriff responsible for Case # 2003-274: Rick Virden. IPRA, under

Section 14-2-6(A), defines "custodian" as "any person responsible for the maintenance, care or keeping of a public body's public records, regardless of whether the records are in that person's actual physical custody or control."

The attorney had to be pro bono. The Kennedy Han group said no, having already done enough free work for Billy the Kid.

# ATTORNEY MICKEY BARNETT

John Dendahl, Richardson's past gubernatorial opponent, saved the day after I asked him for help, by referring me to his friends: Albuquerque attorney, Mickey Barnett; State Senator Rod Adair, a Pat Garrett history buff; and Albuquerque Attorney Pat Rogers, an IPRA expert. And Barnett and Rogers were Republican operatives - up to the Bush/ Cheney level. They would be immune to Democrat "Boss" Richardson's Santa Fe Ring cronyism.

First, I called State Senator Rod Adair. An internet photo showed him as having a shock of white hair. His District 33 included most of Lincoln County. He spoke for hours about Billy, Garrett, and Lew Wallace. He hoped to build a Pat Garrett park - with a Garrett statue - in Roswell; later seeking its funding in the 48th legislative session in 2008. I sent Adair a hoax write-up. He did say one strange thing: "Oh, no! Not Rick Virden!"

"Unfortunately yes," I had answered. "He's at the center. All the forensic DNA records were generated during his tenure."

Later, I learned that Rick Virden, an influential local Republican, had gotten Rod Adair his senate seat by bringing Lincoln County into Adair's close election against a Rory McMinn.

## *THE BARNETT LAW FIRM*

In February of 2007, I made an appointment with Attorney Mickey Barnett. His plain Albuquerque office was in a little downtown strip mall. A fair wiry man, in a green-and-mustard plaid jacket and mustard pants, he looked like a used-car salesman. But his piercing blue eyes and cocky manner would look impressive in court - if things came to that. Barnett included his associate, Phil Cheves, who looked like a twin. He took the case pro bono; and wanted no retainer agreement. (I would pay costs.) On April 24, 2007, his firm, through Phil Cheves, sent out their Virden records request on my behalf. I was no longer alone.

I wrote up the list of records for them. I could not predict that this request letter would potentially cost taxpayers millions of dollars; or that it would yield my greatest betrayal in my fight to save Billy the Kid history. But that was 5 years away. The letter was titled "Request for inspection of public records." It stated:

Dear Sheriff Virden:

This office represents Gale Cooper, M.D. Pursuant to the Inspection of Public Records Act, Section 14-2-8 *et seq.* NMSA 1978, this letter is our written request to inspect public records identified as follows:

1. Please provide any and all records and reports of raw data and or conclusions provided in any form at all to the Lincoln County Sheriff's Department by Dr. Henry Lee as the stated "forensic expert" utilized by the Lincoln County Sheriff's Department for promulgation of Lincoln County Sheriff's Department Case # 2003-274 with regard to any and all DNA findings. Furthermore, all tests and procedures are to include any and all DNA results from Dr. Henry Lee's scrapings and swabbings of the carpenter's bench on which the Billy the Kid Case promulgators contend that the shot William Bonney was laid out. Said findings are to also include DNA results from the remains removed respectively from the graves of John Miller and William Hudspeth done solely for the purpose of advancing the Billy the Kid Case investigation. Said findings are also to include DNA results from DNA matchings of the remains removed from the graves of John Miller and William Hudspeth and the DNA sample(s) taken from the above-mentioned carpenter's bench. Such documentation is to include papers, notes, letters, print-outs, graphs, tapes, e-mails, recordings and/or other materials, regardless of physical form or characteristics, that are maintained or held by or on behalf of you in your capacity as Lincoln County Sheriff or by and/or for the Lincoln County Sheriff's Department.

2. Please provide any and all records and reports of raw data and or conclusions provided in any form at all to the Lincoln County Sheriff's Department by Orchid Cellmark as the stated forensic lab utilized by Dr. Henry Lee and by the Lincoln County Sheriff's Department promulgation of Lincoln County Sheriff's Department Case # 2003-274 with regard to any and all DNA analysis. Said findings are to include any and all DNA results derived by Orchid Cellmark from Dr. Henry Lee's scrapings and swabbings of the carpenter's bench on which the Billy the Kid

Case promulgators contend that the shot William Bonney was laid out. Said findings are to also include DNA results from the remains removed respectively from the graves of John Miller and William Hudspeth done solely for the purpose of advancing the Billy the Kid Case investigation. Said findings are also to include DNA results from DNA matchings of the remains removed from the graves of John Miller and William Hudspeth and the DNA sample(s) taken from the above-mentioned carpenter's bench. Such documentation is to include papers, notes, letters, print-outs, graphs, tapes, e-mails, recordings and/or other materials, regardless of physical form or characteristics, that are maintained or held by or on behalf of you in your capacity as Lincoln County Sheriff or by and/or for the Lincoln County Sheriff's Department.

In this letter, the term "public records" has the same meaning as defined at Section 14-2-6(E) NMSA 1987 [sic -1978], and shall include, without limitation, all documents, papers, letters, books, maps, tapes, photographs, recordings, e-mails, telephone messages, voice mail messages, daily agendas, calendars, schedules and transcripts or notes.

**Each category of documents requested above in numbered paragraphs one through eleven [sic] is to be deemed a separate request to inspect the records identified in the category, to the same extent as if eleven separate requests had been delivered instead of this single letter.** [author's boldface] Accordingly, should the custodian of the records sought purport to determine that any category of documents requested above is excessively burdensome or broad pursuant to Section 14-2-10 NMSA 1978, such determination shall apply only to the particular category named and shall not serve to delay inspection of the other categories.

Pursuant to Section 14-2-8(C), we seek access to the records both for ourselves and for Gale Cooper, M.D. Our address and phone number is set forth above.

In the event that you are not the custodian having possession of or responsibility for the records, please forward this request to the custodian pursuant to Section 14-2-8(E).

We appreciate your consideration. Please call me if you wish to discuss this letter.

Sincerely,
BARNETT LAW FIRM, P.A.
BY: *Philip W. Cheves*

Importantly, Sheriff Virden never denied being custodian of Case 2003-274 records. And the legal issue, in boldface above, of "each category" being a "separate request" would, years later, be crucial in the subsequent litigation.

Lincoln County Attorney Alan Morel answered for Rick Virden, on April 27, 2007 with a new "little weasel" trick: he switched the definition of 2003-274 to "an investigation into the escape of William H. Bonney and the murder of two Lincoln County Deputies, namely James W. Bell and Robert Olinger on April 28, 1881." As such, the case *had no DNA documents!*

Morel and the other hoaxers still were unaware that I knew all about the case. I had Morel's May 19, 2004 IPRA response to Jay Miller refusing records by the IPRA exception of calling the case "an ongoing criminal investigation" into Garrett as murderer.

But Morel, now lying, added that the deputy murder investigations were by Sullivan and Sederwall and: "The Lincoln County Sheriff's Department is unaware of what information Mr. Sullivan and Mr. Sederwall may or may not have responsive to your request." Morel even gave their telephone numbers!

Attorney Alan Morel's ploy was undone by my clarifying the issue to Mickey Barnett; and his sending a June 8, 2007 repeat request: "Fully documented by multiple, New Mexico, Exhumation Petitions ... this case is *solely* a murder investigation into whether past Lincoln County Sheriff Pat Garrett murdered an innocent victim instead of William H. Bonney aka 'Billy the Kid." The Barnett firm called the deputy murders its *sub-investigation.*

Unbeknownst to the hoaxers, I had Virden's response letter of November 28, 2005 to Jay Miller confirming his deputizing Sullivan and Sederwall "to investigate the shootings of William H. Bonney and Deputies Bell and Olinger." (And Virden had used the "law enforcement" exception to deny records!) [APPENDIX: 38]

To make sure that Virden and Morel realized that the jig was up, the Barnett firm called the DNA documents "the stated justification for exhuming two bodies in Arizona in 2005."

Revealed by Alan Morel's responses was that he and his fellow hoaxers were in a legal bind: using IPRA exceptions admitted both that the case and its records were public and existed. So the hoaxers were now left only with silly lies, shell games with the records, and hoping that I was ignorant. That made victory seem easy. And I kept on writing summaries for Barnett and Cheves to keep them informed about Billy the Kid Case hoaxer tricks.

## THE JUNE 21, 2007 HOAX "MEMORANDUM"

On June 22, 2007, Attorney Morel responded, starting the hoaxers' shell games that continue to the present. He said Virden had no records! Sullivan and Sederwall did; but would not give them back! (Contemplate a four year murder investigation where deputies take *all forensic records* and the sheriff is left helpless.) A waggish follower of mine said: "You've got your headline: 'Sheriff of Lincoln County Loses DNA of Billy the Kid.' "

Feigning retrieval attempt, Morel enclosed his request letter to Sullivan and Sederwall - and their refusal. As humorist, Will Rogers had said, "A holding company is a thing where you hand an accomplice the goods while the policeman searches you." (Omitted was that Virden could easily contact Dr. Henry Lee and Orchid Cellmark Lab on his own to get the requested records.)

Also, the well-practiced bunch - Sullivan, Sederwall, Virden, and Morel - enclosed a document dated June 21, 2007, titled "Memorandum, Subject: Billy the Kid Investigation," and addressed to "Rick Virden, Lincoln County Sheriff," from "Steven M. Sederwall & Thomas T. Sullivan." [APPENDIX: 56] It was signed by Virden, Sullivan, and Sederwall.

A major hoax document, it is seven, single spaced pages, plus "Attachments 1-11." It was their four-pronged illegal strategy to hide the records. And, in its desperation, it was willing to reveal shocking secrets to pass the buck of culpability. But all was irrelevant to IPRA law. They had to give me the records - and had no statutory reason for refusal. The rest was smoke and mirrors.

## PRONG ONE: PSEUDO-HISTORY

Prong One was a new hoaxer shape-shift to "conspiracy theorists" who were victims of a campaign to discredit their "investigation." Culprits were "the state" and historians and local officials protecting "tourism" based on "myth and legend": Frederick Nolan; Jay Miller; Silver City and Fort Sumner officials; me; Hamilton, Texas politicos; and the OMI's Dr. Debra Komar!

Sullivan and Sederwall wrote: "We wondered if the fear of harming New Mexico's tourist industry had caused the state to apply pressure to Dr. Komar and told her not to talk to us, in hopes this case would die and the myth would live." The recall of Sheriff Gary Graves - not based on the Billy the Kid Case – thus, became revenge for Graves's Billy the Kid Case participation.

Attachments to feign their pseudo-history research (comparable to the fake footnotes in their 2003 "Probable Cause Statement") were an odd mélange of Sederwall posing at "Brushy's" grave; "Brushy's" death certificate; a "Miscellaneous Incident Report for Case #03-274" about the Kid's escape; a letter from Mayor Raymond Lopez to Governor Richardson; a July 20, 2003 statement from then-Sheriff Graves; a note by historian, Marcie [sic - Maurice] Fulton saying "Ft. Sumner claims it is the Kid's grave, is not possible" [inadvertently removing justification for their exhumation attempt there!]; and a flyer for a Hamilton, Texas Billy the Kid Museum - "Brushy" again.

## PRONG TWO: BLAME RICHARDSON

And on page one, Richardson's Faustian bargain with the devilish hoaxers now claimed his soul. Sederwall, with blackmailer's skill, used his collection of copied records. The blame for the Billy the Kid Case was to be on Richardson - with proof:

On September 1, 2003, the Governor, behind the scenes, supported the investigation, by instructing Billy Sparks to hand Sheriff Sullivan three checks, from private backers, totaling $6,500.00. [Its Footnote 2 states: "Three checks handed to Sheriff Sullivan in Governor's office by Billy Sparks"] Standing at the threshold of the Governor's office, Sparks said, *"The governor wants to insure this investigation goes forward"*... The Governor also asked investigators to contact Ft. Sumner and get them *"on board."* [their italics]

Attachment 2 was that "Footnote 2." Its two pages, titled "Checks handed to Sheriff Sullivan in the State Capital [sic] by Billy Sparks," started on August 1, 2003 for "Investigative Fund 2003-247" [sic - 274] and "Billy the Kid Investigation." (If a governor secretly paying-off a sheriff to do a fake murder investigation is not bribery, then pigs can fly.)

One check stub showed its write-off as: "Charitable Contributions." That "charity" was "The Lincoln County Sheriff's Department!" Or was it the Sullivan-Sederwall Pocket Charity? Did these "charitable" contributions dove-tail with the 2006, Sullivan and Sederwall, "Private Donor" account for Case # 2003-274? The signers were the "powerful attorneys" who "forced them" to try the Fort Sumner exhumation: Attorney Bill Robins III and his firm, Heard, Robins, Cloud, Lubel & Greenwood LLC. One pre-printed check, from the "Hobbs Rental Corporation," was signed by a Johnny Cope (a big Richardson political donor).

## PRONG THREE: CALL CASE A PRIVATE HOBBY

The "Memorandum" was also Sullivan's and Sederwall's shape-shift into private amateur historians doing Lincoln County Sheriff's Department Case # 2003-274! So they called its records (thus, confirming they existed!) their private property. They stated: "The letter from Dr. Gail [sic] Cooper's attorney is her attempt to gain information we have spent years gathering to add to a book she is attempting to sell ... We will continue our investigation. Later, we shall make the decision if and when we will release the information." Not lost on me was a snitch about my book-writing. They were asking around about "Gail" Cooper.

## PRONG FOUR: RESIGN AS DEPUTIES

Lastly, in that June 21, 2007 "Memorandum," Sullivan and Sederwall quit. They wrote: "Now, we choose to put an end to the harassment and political pressure by tendering our resignations as Deputies of Lincoln County Sheriffs [sic] Department, effective this date." (Thus, they admitted being deputies, not hobbyists!).

### *MY NEW ALLY*

Scot Stinnett, born in Portales, New Mexico, had inherited the little, Fort Sumner *De Baca County News* from his father. In it, he covered Sheriff Gary Graves's recall, but not the Billy the Kid Case hoax. But over the years, I had kept him informed of its developments. He was also an open records advocate. Twenty years before, he was a founding member of the Foundation for Open Government (FOG). On September 11, 2007, when my Barnett case was headed to litigation after Virden's refusals extended to June 26, 2007, Stinnett asked if he could join as my co-plaintiff. Though he did not know older Mickey Barnett, he said they had gone to the same high school. And he thought my litigation could become precedent law. I felt less alone by the day.

But I had forgotten that Marilyn Bowlin, long before she died, had told me: "Keep away from Scot Stinnett." And she had refused to say why. By 2012, I would have my own horrible reasons.

## THE FOUNDATION FOR OPEN GOVERNMENT

For years, I hoped that FOG would save the day. In 2004, I heard about them from Jay Miller, who had kept its Executive Director, Bob Johnson, informed about our IPRA requests. In 2006, Johnson put me in contact with *Albuquerque Journal* Editor-in-Chief, Kent Walz. Johnson had also participated in writing the IPRA statute and in founding FOG.

So in August of 2007, I called Bob Johnson about Attorney Alan Morel's responses to the Barnett law firm; and asked: "How could Morel dare to claim that Virden has no DNA records?"

He chuckled: "Because they're all liars."

Back in October of 2006, when Rick Virden refused my own IPRA request, Bob Johnson had told me that FOG might join me if I litigated against those lawmen. So I told Barnett and Cheves. And they approached Johnson and FOG.

Then Johnson balked, telling me he felt uneasy about "affecting the Richardson administration." (Later, I learned that hoax-backing Kent Walz was on FOG's Executive Committee; and Walz's brother was a Richardson backer.) On August 15, 2007, Bob Johnson sent Mickey Barnett an equivocating letter, saying FOG might join an appeal: a toothless offer at that stage.

Three days later, on August 18th, the *Albuquerque Journal* ran Rene Romo's front page, "Seeking Billy the Kid, Minus Badges, Deputies Resign to Hunt for Billy." It was an apologia for beleaguered *private citizens*, Sederwall and Sullivan, pressured by a Gale Cooper, "a researcher in the Albuquerque area," into giving up their badges. (Huh? Private citizens with badges?) Had Romo contacted me? Had Walz set things straight? Had Bob Johnson run my impending litigation past Walz? You guess.

Those deputy resignations had already been reported on August 16th by Julie Carter in *RuidosoNews.com* under "Lincoln County deputies resign commissions for Kid case." For her interview, Sullivan and Sederwall played their "Richardson paid us off card." The *Albuquerque Journal* omitted that *little* fact.

On August 25th, I learned Bob Johnson had died suddenly of a stroke at 84. His eulogizing, eulogized FOG. FOG board member, Attorney Marty Esquivel (who, it would turn out, was in the law firm that would defend Virden), stated on FOG' web site: "Bob tenaciously reminded public servants that sunshine laws were not matters of convenience ... he reminded us all that democracy does not work behind closed doors."

By January of 2008, I called FOG's new Executive Director, Attorney Leonard DeLayo, and sent him my case's overview and a request for FOG's action. I got no response at all.

Scot Stinnett, however, told me he had known Kent Walz for 20 years, and would present our litigation to FOG's board; and thought he could get FOG to join us. I felt like I had a champion. It would be years before it was clear that Stinnett could not guarantee FOG, did not know IPRA law that well, and would work to undermine my precedent-setting litigation and my credibility.

## HEADING TO COURT

I wrote the records request drafts for Attorney Barnett. All records were refused from April 27, 2007 to June 26, 2007 by Virden. But Morel forgot something that I would not realize for five years: he never wrote a specific IPRA letter of records denial. That was legally improper - to say nothing of the fact that all the refusals had no legal basis either. All that meant I was an "injured party": meaning I got no records in my IPRA records request phase. That entitled me to enforcement of my rights by litigation.

It is true that Attorney Barnett was no Clarence Darrow. Each time we met, he would ask me, "Explain again how Dr. Lee connects to DNA." But when it was time to litigate, he said with blue eyes blazing, "I don't take a case unless I expect to win." That seemed more than good enough.

What did I hope for? I wanted the records for my exposé to halt the Billy the Kid Case hoax. Did I know IPRA law? No. I left law to Stinnet and Barnett - as I had with the Kennedy Han firm.

So the Billy the Kid Case went "on trial" on October 15, 2007, with the Barnett firm's filing of Sandoval County District Court Cause No. D-1329-CV-07-01364 as: "Verified Complaint for Declaratory Judgment Ordering Production of Certain Records and Information." Plaintiffs were Gale Cooper and the *De Baca County News*. Defendants were "Lincoln County and Rick Virden, Lincoln County Sheriff and Custodian of Records; and Steven M. Sederwall, Former Lincoln County Deputy Sheriff; and Thomas T. Sullivan, Former Lincoln County Sheriff and Former Lincoln County Deputy Sheriff." The Complaint listed the illegally withheld records from my original records request of April 24, 2007. The judge was George P. Eichwald, a native New Mexican and not a Governor Bill Richardson appointee.

By November 1, 2007, Barnett removed Lincoln County to stop possibility of our case being heard there by biased judges.

Response came from the Albuquerque law firm that would represent Virden for years: that of a Henry Narvaez, specializing in defending public officials and living off unlimited taxpayer money from a state insurance fund paid into by each county, and called Risk Management. Virden's lawyer from that firm was a Nicole Werkmeister. Sullivan and Sederwall were represented by a comparable firm of Attorney Kevin Brown, who appeared for them. On March 5, 2008, Attorney Werkmeister filed a "Motion to Dismiss Based on Improper Venue and Failure to State a Claim."

Our Hearing was on March 26, 2008 in the cavernously empty, glass-fronted, Sandoval County District Courthouse. Present in the bright, panel-walled courtroom were unassumingly sweet Judge Eichwald and his court reporter. At the plaintiff table sat Attorney Barnett, me, and Scot Stinnett - whom I met then in person for the first time. He was clean-shaven and attractively fit; and wore a black Stetson and blue jeans. To court his wife he had learned to rodeo-ride. He looked ready to get on a horse right then.

At the defense table, were long-brown-haired, girlish Attorney Nicole Werkmeister for Virden; and hawk-faced scowling Attorney Kevin Brown for Sullivan and Sederwall. The defendants did not come - and only came later when forced by subpoenas.

Werkmeister argued, without evidence, that the Billy the Kid Case was a private hobby with Lincoln County as the venue.

Mickey Barnett gave fiery opposition, calling Case # 2003-274 public and law enforcement. He argued that since IPRA was statewide, its litigation could be in my county: Sandoval.

We won!

Judge Eichwald kept our case in his court, adding that it interested him. He granted our taking defendants' depositions.

## LET THE SUNSHINE LAWS SHINE IN

Things got better. On July 16, 2008, Scot Stinnett went to a FOG Executive Committee lunch meeting at the *Albuquerque Journal* building, to request their joining. On August 12th, he e-mailed me to say, "I talked to Kent Walz about the FOG deal. He said he will speak to other board members this week and expects to join." On August 22nd, Attorney Barnett's e-mail to me said everything by its subject: "FOG is in." He wrote: "They will submit an IPRA in a couple of weeks." Winning seemed possible.

## PREPARING DEPOSITIONS

Depositions meant I would meet the three men who had terrified me for years. When I learned that the setting had no metal detectors (and concomitantly heard that Sederwall had allegedly gotten a concealed weapons permit), I wanted a body guard. Barnett and Stinnett scoffed at this. I hoped that fear denial was not a lingering (unrealistic) code of the Old West.

I wrote the depositions - an immense effort for which I read a legal bible on cross-examinations. Each defendant had 60 pages of questions with 64 folders of evidence (of which I had to make copies for each party and the court reporter). I knew my opponents would be shocked. Everything, from their Probable Cause Statement to exhumation petitions, was there in official form - with them as sheriff or deputy sheriff for Case # 2003-274 - not "hobbyists!" There were also Morel's records refusals using IPRA's "criminal investigation" exception, newspaper articles where they called themselves "cops" with DNA, Dr. Lee's letter saying his report went to their Sheriff's Department, Governor Napolitano's e-mails about their John Miller's exhumation, and the "Lincoln County Sheriff's Department Supplemental Report" for Case # 2003-274, linking them to John Miller's 2005 exhumation.

## LINCOLN COUNTY PANIC

On August 9, 2008, Lincoln County Manager Tom Stewart e-mailed his County Commissioners, feigning surprise about the litigation's financial fall-out. Since Stewart knew about the years of IPRA records refusals, and heard Chairman Leo Martinez warning the Commissioners about liability from the Billy the Kid Case, only Tom Stewart's surprise was surprising. He wrote:

County Commissioners,

For the first time I can recall as county manager, we have run out of insurance coverage on a case. The e-mail below from our insurer advises that the county must pay directly all further costs associated with this case. Our county attorney wanted me to ensure that I advised you that the county's insurance coverage of $10,000 has been used in the case of Gale Cooper and DeBaca County News, a New Mexico Corporation v. Rick Virden, Lincoln County Sheriff and Custodian of Records of the Lincoln County Sheriff; and Steven M. Sederwall, Former Lincoln

County Sheriff; and Thomas T. Sullivan, Former Lincoln County Sheriff and Former Lincoln County Deputy Sheriff, Thirteenth Judicial District Case No. D1329-CV-07-1364. The county will be forced to pay the attorney's fees and costs incurred in connection with defending all the defendants in this cause of action until settled or until there is a trial on the merits.

Thanks,
    Tom Stewart
    Lincoln County Manager

Tom Stewart attached the e-mail from their claims examiner:

Tom,
    I'm sending you a letter advising that the IJ $10,000 limit for attorney fees is gone. I also paid above the limit in the amount of $2037.96 because I thought they paid here then asked for reimbursement from the Counties upon file completion, that's my error in not knowing their billing procedure here. Anyway, my letter will advise you the limit is gone and ask for reimbursement of the $2037.96.
    I've sent an e-mail to the two attorneys on this matter, Kevin Brown and Nicole Werkmeister advising them to bill the County direct. Kevin is the lead attorney and had done the bulk of the work and has the strategy going. I apologize for my error and if you have any questions, please call me.
    The suit stems from a public information request, Morel said.

Thank you.
    Kerry Kent
    ML Claims Examiner

Tom Stewart then became Paul Revere. He contacted *Ruidoso News* reporter, Dianne Stallings. She wrote, on August 13, 2008, "Billy the Kid Case straps county for insurance." Stallings printed the e-mails and quoted Attorney Alan Morel:

The suit stems from a public information request, Morel said. The county has given up all records in its possession, but the plaintiffs contend Sullivan and Sederwall have not, yet while they collected the information they held themselves out as sheriff and/or deputies acting within the scope of the county.

Morel, as usual, was lying: Lack of possession was no excuse; Virden had to recover records not in his direct possession.

The Sullivan-Sederwall hobbyist claim was a lie. They had to turn over their public records. And Virden still had to get those records from them or directly from Dr. Lee and Orchid Cellmark.

And now citizens were grumbling. Would financial pressure from Lincoln County help us? It did achieve something: The defendants did not dare to delay their depositions.

And those three lawmen were in a risky game with those taxpayers: calling their Sheriff's Department records their hobby, while having the county pay their legal bills as public officials. "Richardson's Implied Rule": "The public are suckers," seemed about to be disproved. There might be a new joke slogan: "Come to Lincoln County to conduct hobbies. Taxpayers will pay your bills."

## *DEPOSITIONS OF SULLIVAN AND SEDERWALL*

The depositions of Tom Sullivan and Steve Sederwall were both on August 18, 2008, in a Ruidoso office building, AM and PM respectively. Scott Stinnett and I were there with Attorney Mickey Barnett. Attorney Kevin Brown represented his clients in the hot, windowless room, where we sat around a conference table with the male transcriptionist at its head. I politely brought cookies, and put out water. No cookies were eaten.

Bigger Steve Sederwall entered with big Tom Sullivan, both having western-style garb and mustaches. Inappropriately, I thought, Sederwall took a chair in a far corner to hear Sullivan's deposition (and prepare himself).

From that spot, bulky Sederwall, 6'5", addressed me. "How's your book selling?" he asked in his incongruously soft mellifluous voice. His eyes were small and colorless in a doughy face like a mask. But he was smiling. Few knew my novel had just come out. This was a masterful sentence by a master con, conveying knowledge, hinting help, menacing damage. It was my test.

I smiled back and answered, "How *kind* of you ask," equalizing ambiguity. My fear, I realized was gone.

The deponents had a strategy. Attorney Kevin Brown had already written to Mickey Barnett with blithe contradiction that the records were not public; and that Sullivan and Sederwall did not have them (ignoring their claim of possessing them in their June 21, 2007 "Memorandum"). But Brown had apparently not showed them the evidence folders. Their ability to dodge blatant truths would now be tested.

# SULLIVAN ON THE HOT-SEAT

Tom Sullivan almost immediately, growled out their defense plan: The case was his hobby. For the documents that proved otherwise, he either refused to answer, or threw the papers back at Barnett, or threatened to leave. But there were Morel's records refusals, like this May 19, 2004 response to Jay Miller:

> Sheriff Sullivan maintains that the case involving Billy the Kid is an ongoing criminal investigation and, as such, the records you requested pertaining to the investigation are not subject to disclosure at this time pursuant to the Public Records Act, Sec. 14-2-1, Subparagraph A 4.

And there were then Sheriff Sullivan's years of lawman boasting; as in Rene Romo's December 9, 2003, *Albuquerque Journal's* "Kid's Mom May Stay Buried":

> This summer, the sheriffs of Lincoln and De Baca counties opened a criminal investigation into the death of William Bonney aka Billy the Kid to resolve claims that Lincoln County Sheriff Pat Garrett killed someone other than the famous outlaw at Fort Sumner on July 14, 1881.

And, at the start of Case # 2003-274, there had been my first attempt to get a copy of their "Probable Cause Statement" through an attorney, Randy Harris. Sheriff Sullivan, on October 8, 2003 (only five days after the Catherine Antrim exhumation attempt began), on his official letterhead, had sent Attorney Harris an official form-letter "Denial" for the "Billy the Kid Case." Checked was: "This is an ongoing investigation and until the investigation is completed and closed they will not be available for release, as per Section 14-2-1 (A) (4) of the Inspection of Public Records Act which protects law enforcement records."

Of course, there was also the comedy document: Attorney Mark Acuña's July 26, 2004, "County of De Baca, State of New Mexico, Tenth Judicial District, In the Matter of William H. Bonney A/K/A 'Billy the Kid' Cause No. CV-04-00005" [APPENDIX: 24], in which Acuña's five page filing called Sullivan, Graves, and Sederwall "law enforcement officers 13 times *to deny that they were* "*hobbyists!*" As Mark Acuña had stated - with my boldface:

Sederwall, Sullivan, and Graves, all joined in on the Petition to Exhume the remains of Billy the Kid as Co-Petitioners and in their capacity as **law enforcement officers** engaged in an on-going investigation ...

Petitioners assert that they maintain standing in the instant action as **law enforcement officers** engaged in the investigation of criminal violations, namely, the alleged killing of Billy the Kid by the legendary Sheriff, Pat Garrett.

But Sullivan was not clever enough to sham. He even confirmed that the John Miller exhumation "Supplemental Report" was his official form. But when asked about the e-mail from Arizona Pioneer Home Supervisor Gary Olson, saying that Sullivan had paid for Miller's exhumation, Sullivan surprisingly said the *payment had been by Governor Richardson*, continuing the shell game of shifting blame - with unexpected disclosures.

## NEXT THE MASTER: SEDERWALL

At his turn, Steve Sederwall showed that his morning's presence had honed his world-class conman's skills. Leaning affably back in his chair, he embodied relaxed beneficence. As comedian George Burns said, "You've got to be honest. If you can fake that, you've got it made."

And, periodically, Sederwall addressed me with: "Just tell me what you want to know;" or "I'll tell you after this is over."

For his deposition, he was in fine form. For example, when handed Attorney Sherry Tippett's first Antrim exhumation petition of October 10, 2003 listing him as a Co-petitioner and a Lincoln County Deputy Sheriff [APPENDIX: 12], he acted utterly surprised, asking how his name got there. He said he was just a hobbyist interested in Deputy James Bell's murder.

But, for contrast, here is the "other Steve Sederwall" speaking to the June 25, 2004 *Silver City Daily Press* under "Lincoln County deputy sheriff sends his own letter to governor." It was his response to the local officials' cease and desist petition to Governor Richardson, already described. No hobbyist for it, Sederwall is in maximum cop-mode.

Lincoln County Deputy Sheriff Steven M. Sederwall has sent to Gov. Bill Richardson a reply to an open letter from Silver City officials asking the governor to "dissociate from Messrs. Sederwall Sullivan and Graves and the 'Billy the Kid' case.

"I would like to respond to Silver City's misleading concerns," Sederwall said in his reply. "The village of Silver City questions why a criminal investigation is reopened after being closed 122 years ago by a legally embodied coroner's jury. It has been reopened because the physical evidence, documents and the coroners jury itself cause us to believe the records cannot be true."

But Sederwall outdid himself with the incriminating "Supplemental Report." He turned it sideways and looked at his own signature. He announced: "It's a forgery. That's my signature, but I never signed this." He pointed to lines across the copy. (It was from Prescott Police Department Detective Anna Cahall.) "It's been pasted together," he declared. (How some "forger" knew everyone present, with birthdates and addresses, in a secret exhumation with a signed confidentiality agreement, was your problem; not his.)

About his hobby ploy, Sederwall affably said that - though he *had been* a deputy sheriff - the Billy the Kid Case was done only *when he was not one.*

"How could you tell the difference?" Attorney Barnett asked, and got an unperturbed response that he just knew.

Sederwall had already floated this "two-headed Janus" plan of being deputy/hobbyist at the same time." It connected to his "quitting as deputies ploy" from the June 21, 2007 "Memorandum." Loyalist Julie Carter had presented it to the public in her August 16, 2007 *RuidosoNews.com* "Lincoln County deputies resign commissions for Kid case." Sederwall was quoted: "The original investigation was numbered and logged in through the sheriff's office, but was a private venture as to not burden the county financially." So, according to Sederwall, the real murder case, with law enforcement's power and legal standing to exhume human remains, was public and private at the same time!

Suddenly, in mid-deposition, Sederwall stood and announced, "Let's go to my car. I have what you need."

"Gun!" I thought, recalling his weapons' permit; and said I'd wait there. But Barnett and Stinnett went with him, returning with a few unimportant papers from Sederwall's car.

I had given Attorney Barnett a hint before the deposition. It was the Aesop's fable of the fox and the crow. A fox sees, high in a tree, a crow with a beakfull of cheese. "Your voice is so beautiful," says the fox. "Please sing." The flattered cawing beak opens. The cheese falls to the waiting jaws. So Attorney Barnett permitted his ramblings. Suddenly, Sederwall, sang. He said *he had the Dr. Lee carpenter's workbench report,* describing it in detail. One could almost feel his attorney kicking him under the table. That confession later gave his side considerable trouble.

Also, Sederwall had a vicious outburst. To Scot Stinnett he growled: "[I]f we keep pressing this thing somebody's gonna turn the lights out in Fort Sumner." It had taken me years to realize that Sederwall was a con-artist with a compulsion to tell the truth to boast his knowledge. He was revealing the hoax's biggest secret; one that would, indeed, "turn the lights out in Fort Sumner." But at the time, it just sounded to me like a random thuggish threat. It was actually the key to cracking the Billy the Kid Case hoax.

After his deposition, Sederwall waited at the door to give me his "special information" as he had offered. I said to him, "We are not going to talk, Mr. Sederwall."

Scot Stinnett later saw him pacing in the parking lot, as if waiting for me. And much later, Sederwall would announce in court that he and I had actually met and discussed the case.

### *FINALLY FOG GOES PUBLIC*

On August 28, 2008, the *Albuquerque Journal* announced that FOG was joining my case - omitting that Editor-in-Chief Kent Walz's hoax-backing and FOG's inaction had arguably necessitated that litigation. At least hoax reporter, Rene Romo, was not assigned. A Charles D. Brunt wrote, "Suit Targets Investigation Into Billy the Kid's Death." [APPENDIX: 57] Brunt began with parroting the Billy the Kid Case hoax:

> Legal wrangling over DNA analyses could have Billy the Kid rolling in his grave - wherever it may be ... With backing from Gov. Bill Richardson, two Lincoln County lawmen launched an investigation several years ago seeking to determine whether it really was the Kid who was shot by Garrett and buried in Fort Sumner.

Nevertheless, reporter Brunt communicated the legal questions and that those questions were confirmed by FOG, called the "government watchdog."

Brunt wrote:

Scot Stinnett, publisher of the De Baca County News, and Gale Cooper, a retired psychiatrist and amateur historian from Cedar Crest, are suing current and former Lincoln County lawmen they say are withholding public records about DNA evidence collected during an investigation into events leading up to the Kid's presumed death in 1881 ...

The New Mexico Foundation for Open Government - a nonprofit government watchdog - is the latest player to enter the saga that so far has included the exhumation of two bodies in Arizona and analyses of their DNA by celebrity forensic scientist Dr. Henry Lee.

"Our primary interest is in the reason they (the records) are not being produced," NMFOG executive director Leonard DeLayo said earlier this month ...

Stinnett and Cooper say the current sheriff has a duty under the Inspection of Public Records Act to obtain and produce the records, which they say include:

Lee's analysis of DNA derived from blood on a carpenter's bench where Billy the Kid's body supposedly was placed after being fatally wounded by Garrett the night of July 14, 1881, in Fort Sumner ...

Lee's analysis of DNA taken from the graves of John Miller - who claimed he was Billy the Kid - and William Hudspeth in Arizona; and information regarding any payments to Lee. Hudspeth's remains, buried alongside Miller's, were unintentionally unearthed during the May 19, 2005, exhumation at Arizona Pioneers' Home in Prescott, where Miller died in 1937.

According to court documents, Cooper filed several requests under New Mexico's public records law seeking records held by current Lincoln County Sheriff Rick Virden, former Sheriff Tom Sullivan and former Deputy Steven Sederwall.

The lawmen have refused to produce the requested documents, claiming they either don't have them or that the records they possess are private documents not subject to disclosure ...

DeLayo said NMFOG's executive committee has directed him to move toward joining the plaintiffs in the litigation.

"Our interest is in the continuity of record keeping, and that when you generate a document during an investigation, it's public information," DeLayo said. "You don't take it with you, and you don't claim that you did it on your own time."

The suit is filed in the 13th Judicial District Court in Sandoval County.

## *VIRDEN'S DEPOSITION*

Sheriff Rick Virden's deposition was scheduled for September 8, 2008 in Attorney Mickey Barnett's office. Three strange things happened in the preceding week.

The first, and least strange thing, happened on Thursday, September 4th, when I was in Attorney Mickey Barnett's office, preparing his partner, David Garcia, who would conduct the deposition. Legal assistant, Lori, had given me a copy of FOG's IPRA records request letter from Attorney Leonard DeLayo, dated that day. It requested the same forensic records as I had first requested on April 24, 2007.

Second, Lori gave me a thick folder which had arrived the day before. Its September 3rd cover letter was from Attorney Nicole Werkmeister for Virden. Obtained by subpoena by Attorney Barnett for the upcoming deposition, it was the 192 page file of Lincoln County Sheriff's Department Case # 2003-274! Except it lacked all forensic documents. And Werkmeister, forgetting their "hobbyist" ploy, wrote that it met the IPRA exception for a criminal investigation!

But it had gems. There were Attorney Sherry Tippett's communications to the hoaxers about the Antrim exhumation; and a Case # 2004-274 "Contact List" with addresses and phone numbers; with Sullivan and Sederwall as Sheriff and Deputy, Professor Paul Hutton as historian, and Orchid Cellmark Director Rick Staub "for DNA." [APPENDIX: 26] And it had a strange preponderance of "Brushy" articles. I named it the "Turn-Over."

The third strange thing happened next. It seemed horrible. Attorney Barnett stopped me in the hall. He said, "I just heard from Rod Adair. He told me to kill the case."

"Are you continuing?" I asked.

"Of course," he said and walked away.

Monday morning, September 8, 2008, to Attorney Mickey Barnett's conference room, came Attorneys Nicole Werkmeister and Kevin Brown, and Sheriff Rick Virden. A graying, reedy, tall, small-headed man, with big western buckle and tooled leather holster, Virden stood stiffly awaiting the transcriptionist, and said to me, "I'm fourth generation from Lincoln County."

I knew that. I responded, "So your family must have been there in Billy the Kid's days?"

He almost shouted, "They didn't know anything about Billy the Kid. I don't know anything about Billy the Kid." Apparently that summed up his coaching. (And he was not risking ancestors.)

A "Sederwall" Rick Virden was not. His deposition was "I don't knows" and "I don't remember." So he "did not know" his filed case was about Pat Garrett or exhumations. All documents - including his own signed letter deputizing Tom Sullivan and Steve Sederwall - he "did not remember."

He did remember a letter from his "Turn-Over." On official letterhead, it confirmed that, as Undersheriff and in the Wortley Hotel, he heard the gunshot fired by Sheriff Sullivan (in the fake deputy murder sub-investigation). Attorney David Garcia got him on that one. Was he on salary on that day? He was. That alone ended their: "We didn't use taxpayer money for the case."

When Virden was handed the incriminating "Lincoln County Sheriff's Department Supplemental Report" for the John Miller exhumation, Attorney Brown loudly interrupted and lied that it was an established forgery.

Mild-mannered Attorney David Garcia was no match for them; and eventually just gave up with Virden's "I'm an Alzheimer's victim" technique. So Garcia did not ask the obvious punch line: If your deputies absconded with all your forensic records, Sheriff, why didn't you just ask Orchid Cellmark and Dr. Lee for copies?

Afterwards Attorney Garcia said to me, "If they are claiming this was a hobby, and if Sullivan and Sederwall resigned their deputyships last year, why is Brown being paid by Risk Management, which is for public officials?"

I thought things were proceeding very well. I was wrong.

### FATEFUL MEETING WITH THE GREAT PAT ROGERS

Next, Attorneys Mickey Barnett and David Garcia invited me to a meeting with Attorney Pat Rogers, their good friend (and John Dendahl's best friend). For 9 AM, Friday, September 12, 2008, it was at Rogers's multi-floor Modrell Sperling law firm in Albuquerque. I assumed we would be getting his expert IPRA input. I even bought a new dress. Neither Scot Stinnett nor I saw a need for his attendance and long drive from Fort Sumner.

Barnett and Garcia had breakfast with Rogers first. I was early, alone in a 10th floor conference room and admiring the shelves of Native American pottery, when Attorney Pat Rogers entered alone: silvered, Mitt Romney handsome, and debonair.

Then my attorneys came, with Mickey Barnett bringing my mass of evidence folders, assumedly for reference.

We sat at the long conference table, Mickey Barnett at the head, the other two men facing me. Barnett did not introduce me. So I began to present my dramatic evidence. Barnett irritably interrupted with: "He doesn't need that."

Then Barnett announced, "Rod Adair told me to kill the case." No one responded.

Rogers asked me what I wanted. I said a judge's ruling that the forensic records were public; and his order for their turn-over.

Then we entered the "Twilight Zone."

Rogers spoke, not as a consultant, but for FOG. He said he planned to *revise* Attorney Leonard DeLayo's request, and ask *only for the Dr. Lee report*, admitted to by Sederwall. That sounded OK to me. My own litigation could handle the Orchid Cellmark Lab records, with their DNA extraction results.

Then Pat Rogers said ... drum roll ... *and the records custodian will be listed as Sederwall.*

All three men were staring at me hostilely.

I may be a coward, but tenacity makes me hard to intimidate. To the state's expert on IPRA law, I said, "A reserve deputy is not the custodian of forensic records of a sheriff's murder investigation. Sheriff Virden is the custodian by IPRA definition."

Attorney Barnett looked like he wanted to strangle me. Attorney Garcia looked like he wished he were elsewhere.

Attorney Rogers placatingly said it was just a consideration. He kept my evidence files when the meeting soon ended.

When I described this odd turn of events to a Lincoln County official, he said, "That was a hostile take-over of your case done for Adair. They want Virden off the hook - and Sederwall on it."

"I know Rod Adair," I said. "I'll call him."

"Just so you know," my source said, "he surreptitiously records calls. It's legal in New Mexico."

Visualizing Barnett and Rogers as major Republican operatives, President Bush's water-boarding torture came to mind.

That afternoon, I told Scot Stinnett. He soon e-mailed me: "Spoke to Pat Rogers ... And Pat is preparing an IPRA for FOG that would supersede - and exceed - what FOG has already done ... Keep your chin up. Things are going well, in my mind at least." Marlyn Bowlin's warning about Stinnet never came to my mind.

## *STATE SENATOR ROD ADAIR TO VIRDEN'S RESCUE*

On Monday, September 15, 2008, I called Senator Rod Adair, and was amused when he fumbled with something I assumed was for recording. I said, "Mickey said you told him to kill my case."

"I never used those words," he said for his possible machine.

"Tell me what you want," I said.

"I want Virden to win the sheriff's election," Adair said.

That explained things. Sederwall, as an Independent, was running against Republican Virden for sheriff. I said, "My case can't affect that. We won't be in court before November 2nd."

"What did you think of Virden?" Adair asked, meaning his deposition.

"He's a despicable liar," I answered. "All the forensic records were generated during his tenure."

## *SNATCHING DEFEAT FROM VICTORY'S JAWS*

My opponents knew that truth was dawning like the red sun over the great high desert of New Mexico, with law shining into darkness of political machinations. Unfortunately, my opponents were my own lawyer and his friends.

So things moved quickly for my case - as in downward. Those crony's were about to do a Bambi meets Godzilla on me. Except Godzilla's foot spoke as e-mails: "Blame Sederwall - or else."

On September 25th, their drama began. I was forwarded a September 22nd e-mail - originally from Rogers to Barnett and Garcia - titled "Docs for editing," requesting elaboration of my evidence. Its deceptively cheery note from David Garcia said: "Hi Dr. Cooper, FYI, can you answer Pat's questions? David."

One question was: "June 5, 2003 NY Times article quotes Sederwall, any other helpful info?" *They wanted me to do the work for framing Sederwall!*

Rogers had added: "I have an outline/rough draft of an approach and a letter that has been sent to NMFOG exec comm. [sic] for review." That Executive Committee meeting was for October 1st - five days away. I was being railroaded into Rod Adair's "kill the case" scheme.

To the Barnett firm, on that September 25th, I responded by e-mail: "I will review this."

For perspective on the Adair-Barnett-Rogers "Twilight Zone," note that IPRA law makes a custodian responsible for their records, whether or not they are in "that person's actual physical custody." So saying Sederwall has them, can make him their thief, not their custodian. But that was the bill of goods I was being sold.

On September 28th, I e-mailed Barnett a polite letter to protect myself by documentation. [APPENDIX: 58] I repeated our *pro bono* relationship and Adair's case termination request. Attached was Attorney Rogers's e-mail with my interpolated responses. I made clear that I refused to call Sederwall the Records Custodian. My hope was that they would all back off. They did not. They simply cut me out of the loop.

Therefore just Scot Stinnett was sent the copy of Pat Rogers's communication to Attorney Leonard DeLayo in an e-mail dated September 30, 2008. Rogers stated:

> If Dr. Cooper (or anyone) wants to provide any written suggestions or analysis of any perceived shortcomings with the strategy, the letter, or PJR [sic- him] generally, I will present the same to the board, tomorrow. If a suit is necessary, I had anticipated joinder, but that is not necessary, **if Dr. Cooper opposes.** [author's boldface]

Note, that Rogers had not told *me* so I could "oppose" anything! The scaly foot was descending. And their ultimatum meant my accusing Sederwall or losing FOG.

Pause and think. With this plot, who lost the most? FOG! By backing a plot by public officials to pass incriminatory documents to an accomplice, they were destroying the power and intent of IPRA law - which, back then, I naively thought mattered to them. But in retrospect, major hoax backers were on FOG's board. And it did not occur to me that Scot Stinnett was not fighting for me.

Attorney Pat Rogers ended his e-mail with double-talk to conceal that obvious fact about a records custodian:

> While I actually share most if not all of Dr. Cooper's views about the constellation of other people involved in this saga, including but not limited to the private 'contributors' and Governor Richardson, I don't favor a larger, broader, more substantive request or involvement by FOG.

So Sederwall or no one. And my IPRA case was not against Richardson or "private donors." I responded by e-mail to Pat Rogers, stating my total opposition, and assuming he would remove FOG at the October 1st, Executive Committee meeting.

Rogers answered by e-mail at the startling time of 4:40:27 AM, as "Re: Second Response to Your FOG Proposal":

> I disagree with your legal analysis and your conclusion that my recommended course would create a fatal flaw. As indicated, my views remain, Sederwall created/is maintaining the documents.

The scaly foot lowered. Do not miss a new word that Attorney Rogers slipped in: "created." Rogers was not only faking Sederwall as Records Custodian, he was saying that Sederwall was responsible for *generating the forensic records of the murder case.*

Look closer at how Pat Rogers was trying to kill my case. By IPRA law, records generated by a deputy are public *and under the custodianship of the sheriff.* But naming Sederwall both the custodian and records generator, achieves a hoped-for loophole for Virden. It segues into Sederwall's sham hobbyist claim of his records being immune to IPRA law - since a real murder case would only have *Sheriff Virden* as its records custodian.

Rogers's pre-dawn e-mail to me continued:

> As stated in my memo to Leolard [sic - DeLayo], if you did not want me/FOG to proceed for any reason, I recommend we respect that decision. I will make it clear to the FOG board that I have no problems with another FOG attorney taking over.

Obviously, there was no "other attorney" at FOG who would touch it, though I had Cc'd all these e-mails to FOG President, Charles "Kip" Purcell; Kent Walz; and Leonard DeLayo.

Attorney Leonard DeLayo had shown his coarse disdain for "citizen Gale" in his September 29, 2008 e-mail response to my Cc: "Hey [no name], FOG does not represent you." (So much for DeLayo's *Albuquerque Journal* effusion that "NMFOG's executive committee has directed him to move toward joining the plaintiffs in litigation.")

"Hey, Sir, DeLayo, I AM one of those plaintiffs," I thought.

So the scaly foot descended.

But there was silence on October 1st. I assumed that Godzilla had stomped out my Bambi case with FOG. I was wrong. The descending foot simply ignored me and proceeded with their nefarious plan to stamp out my entire case.

On October 9, 2008, without my knowing, Attorney Rogers, for FOG, sent a records request to Sederwall, through Attorney Kevin Brown; and a separate one to Attorney Alan Morel for the "Lincoln County Custodian." One can imagine the clique of Adair, Virden, Morel, Sullivan, Barnett, Rogers, and the rest of FOG, snickering as my case was going splattt. Even Attorney Brown and Sederwall must have been pleased - knowing Sederwall was legally untouchable. So Brown sent a letter to Rogers saying:

> I would also note that Mr. Sederwall is not a custodian of records under the definitions of the statute.

The Barnett firm waited to October 20th to e-mail me those documents. On October 27th, I responded by letter to Attorney Rogers, reiterating my disagreement, and my assumption that FOG had withdrawn. I repeated that FOG had damaged my case.

Attorney Rogers had done worse. His Sederwall request was ambiguous, causing Attorney Brown's October 16th letter to call FOG's case *mine*, and stating *I* was against Lincoln County ("Cooper v. Lincoln County, et al").

But I was more vocal and difficult than Pat Rogers must have calculated. My October 27th letter to him, with Cc's to FOG and Mickey Barnett, accused him of putting me in "harms way" both legally (using my name to unjustly accuse Sederwall) and physically (given Sederwall's unpleasant track record with possible attempted murder in Oklahoma).

I also wrote to Attorney Kevin Brown on November 17, 2008 as "Re: My response to your letter of October 16, 2008 to Attorney Patrick Rogers, and my dissociation from the referenced Foundation for Open Government communications."

Attorney Kevin Brown merely asked the Barnett firm to stop their client from communicating directly with him.

Attorney Mickey Barnett completed a squoosh to the Godzilla splat. On October 1, 2008, he had e-mailed me:

> Gale, I am sorry to say you have really taken the wind out of my sails and almost made none of this worth the effort … I am a professional and will proceed but believe you to be flat wrong.

After that stomp, Bambi heard from Barnett in a February 23, 2009 withdrawal letter - blaming me. [APPENDIX: 59]

By 2012, Barnett's attack on me would be far worse. And Scot Stinnett would join him in the attack!

Meanwhile, in 2008, in Lincoln County, Rick Virden won the Sheriff's election, beating Sederwall; and getting a second term.

On November 10, 2008, Attorney Pat Rogers sent me a letter withdrawing as FOG's attorney for the case so he would not "cause me distress." Subsequently - I assumed with Roger's doing - FOG refused to back me; though, to document FOG's corruption, I continued to send requests to join. All this led to my concluding that FOG should redefine its acronym to "For Our Guys."

## Attorney Pat Rogers Follow-up

By 2012, operative Pat Rogers had become Chairman of the Republican National Convention. And Susana Martinez was New Mexico's governor, allegedly through his, Rod Adair's, and Mickey Barnett's "kingmaking" - and they actually ran the government. So Rogers ended up high enough for others to notice he was a rat.

On August 25, 2012, a Snejana Farberov had a Dailymail online article about him: " 'This State is Going to hell': GOP leader in trouble after blasting New Mexico governor for dishonoring General Custer by meeting with Native-Americans." It had his June 8, 2012 leaked e-mail to Martinez's staff. Farberov wrote:

> "Such a blatantly racist statement against our native people is offensive from anyone, but to come from a national GOP leader and lobbyist for some of the country's largest corporations is indefensible," Progress Now New Mexico's executive Director Pat Davis said ...
>
> This is not the first time Rogers has found himself in trouble over emails. In July [2012], he was forced to step down from the board of the New Mexico Foundation for Open Government after he was criticized for using personal email accounts to contact state government officials.

The "trouble over e-mails" was serious - and familiar to me. On July 2, 2012, New Mexico investigative reporter, Heath Haussamen, for his nmpolitics.net blog wrote: "Lawyers tenure on sunshine group board needs to end." Haussamen had picked up on Rogers's manipulations with Governor Susana Martinez. They looked like pay-to-play. Haussamen wrote:

**Pat Rogers has spent much of his legal career fighting for government transparency, but his recent actions helped create the appearance that the Martinez administration's controversial contract with the Downs at Albuquerque was an insider deal.**

Rogers is an excellent sunshine lawyer who is a past president of the New Mexico Foundation for Open Government (FOG), a current board member, and a 2004 recipient of the organization's Dixon Award for fighting for open government.

But, as I wrote last week, Rogers' recent actions helped create the appearance that the Martinez administration's controversial contract with the Downs at Albuquerque was an insider deal.

Rogers represented the Downs in the process. He's also the Republican National committeeman for New Mexico and a former general counsel for the state GOP.

This is what the Downs deal looks like: A company that gave lots of money to Republican Gov. Susana Martinez's 2010 campaign won a state contract after hiring a GOP insider (Rogers) who was communicating privately about the contract, before it was awarded, with people close to Martinez.

### Sending e-mails to private addresses

Since publishing last week's column, I've obtained an additional three Rogers e-mails that contribute to the insider appearance of the deal, bringing the total to six.

Among the six Rogers e-mails, which were obtained and released by the left-leaning Independent Source PAC ... are two that relate to compliance with the Open Meetings Act. Rogers sent two e-mails to Dan Mourning, the general manager of Expo New Mexico and overseer of the lease contract process, on Nov. 1, weeks before the State Fair Commission voted to award the Downs the contract.

He sent them to Mourning's personal e-mail address, not his government address.

In the first, Rogers advised Mourning that the State Fair Commission's Open Meetings Act resolution didn't allow members to participate in meetings by telephone. He also wrote that he would have some additional notes on Commissioner Charlotte Rode's "flagrant open meetings act violations." Rode has been the most vocal critic of the way the Martinez administration handled the lease process.

Less than an hour after that first e-mail, Rogers sent additional notes in a second e-mail. Rogers then forwarded both e-mails to Martinez's deputy chief of staff for boards and commissions, Ryan Cangiolosi, using Cangiolosi's Martinez campaign e-mail address rather than his government address.

Rogers also forwarded the e-mails to Martinez's political adviser Jay McCleskey, who is not a state employee.

Rogers sent the other four e-mails provided by Independent Source PAC to Cangiolosi's campaign e-mail address. He also sent two of them to McCleskey. They all appear to relate to the Downs deal, and at least one indicates a chummy relationship: In it, Rogers referred to "Mr. McCluskey" kissing Albuquerque Journal reporter Charles Brunt's "posterior" and being involved in "the erosion of the executive branches' authority and majesty."

In that same Sept. 1 e-mail he sent to Cangiolosi and copied to McCleskey, Rogers also wrote that his "position is that Hossie needs to run everything" – an apparent reference to State Fair Commissioner David "Hossie" Sanchez of Albuquerque that leaves little doubt about the topic of the e-mail, especially given that Brunt covered the Downs deal.

### Appearance of an insider deal

Martinez's spokesman says Cangiolosi's e-mails were illegally intercepted and he never received them. But whether one of the people close to Martinez received the e-mails isn't the point of this column. Rogers' actions are.

I was concerned several years ago when Rogers became the GOP's national committeeman from New Mexico. He was a member of the FOG board's executive committee at the time, and I wondered how he would be able to juggle heavy involvement in a nonpartisan government watchdog organization with such a partisan position.

Now my concern has risen to a level that compels me to speak out ... [T]hese e-mails show that Rogers was also communicating about potential Open Meetings Act violations and other issues related to the contract with people close to Martinez privately – hidden from the government sunshine for which he's spent so much time fighting. That contributes to the appearance that this was an insider deal.

### Sunshine group under a cloud

As a journalist who has focused often on government transparency and as a member of FOG, I believe Rogers' continued membership on FOG's board of directors casts a cloud over the organization.

I hate to say it, because Rogers has spent much of his career fighting for government transparency and done lots of good work, but, for the sake of the integrity of the organization, Rogers' membership on the FOG board needs to come to an end.

To me, Heath Haussamen sounded like he just landed in another Roswell alien spacecraft. He acted like that the names "Richardson" and "Martinez" were not interchangeable. By 2008, with my one Billy the Kid Case exposé, even I knew that New Mexico had neither ethics nor a two party system. Santa Fe Ring politics is bipartisan. Both sides are "friends." And email misuse and possible pay-to-play had riled up Haussamen, but never my hot potato Billy the Kid Case - which revealed all.

How did Rogers's FOG buddies respond to Rogers "the Rat?" On July 20, 2012, Board President Terri Cole e-mailed members: "The New Mexico Foundation for Open Government tonight accepted the resignation of longtime board member Pat Rogers. His letter is below. We appreciate Pat's service over many years to FOG and his dedication to the First Amendment. We understand and appreciate his decision."

What did Pat Rogers e-mail FOG? The same smarmy m.o. as his quitting letter to me about not wanting to "cause distress." Except now he side-stepped Haussamen's pay-to-play find as being from "virulent partisans." To the Executive Board he gave his hypocritical self-justification on July 2, 2012:

Dear Ms. Cole and Members of the NMFOG Executive Committee:

Although I appreciate the effort of the NMFOG Executive Board to discuss Mr. Haussamen's concerns about my continuing membership in NMFOG, it is clear that this, my prompt resignation will allow NMFOG ... to concentrate on your critical First Amendment and open government mission to avoid further distractions by an issue that has become improperly politicized.

... In calling for my resignation, Mr. Haussamen also notes that my services as New Mexico's National Committeeman to the Republican National Committee gave him concerns, as well: "I wondered how he would be able to juggle heavy involvement in a non-partisan government watchdog organization with such a partisan position."

... In addition to open government, I believe that political participation, competition, debate and principled dissent are also vital to the health of our society ... My clients, as NMFOG did, receive zealous representation all within the bounds of the law and professional ethics ...

Best regards,
Pat Rogers

# SILENCE OF THE STINNETT

On October 7, 2008, during my Pat Rogers crisis, I asked Scot Stinnett to call his "20 year friend," Kent Walz about keeping FOG involved as to our IPRA litigation. Stinnett said, "I don't know him well enough." And, as far as I knew, Stinnett had done nothing to stop Mickey Barnett's and Pat Rogers's attempt to throw my case by their attempted trick of dismissing custodian Rick Virden, and claiming fatally that reserve deputy Sederwall was the records custodian for Sheriff's Department murder investigation Case # 2003-274. Back then, Stinnett's inaction raised no suspicion for me. It should have - big time.

# LITTLE ORPHAN CASE

I needed help.

So I contacted Rod Adair's political opponent, Rory McMinn. He told me that Rod Adair and Pat Rogers had done similar one-two dirty-dealing punches on him, as they had on me - with Rogers threatening him with litigation so as to halt his senate seat campaign ads against Adair. (And Adair won.)

I also got more feedback about Adair and the Billy the Kid Case hoaxers from past Lincoln County Commissioner Leo Martinez. He said his defeat for re-election to the County Commission was by combined efforts of Adair, Virden, and Sullivan. The winner as Chairman was banker, Tom Batton; who compliantly left the Billy the Kid Case alone.

Locals did not trust their Senator Adair. Some thought he used his profession as a demographer to skew polls and for partisan alteration of county boundaries for gerrymandering. And some opined as to whether he owed Governor Bill Richardson (not just Virden) protection from my case. (Recall his bid for a Pat Garrett park)

Other people had ideas about Attorney Mickey Barnett's having, as a major client, PNM, the New Mexico utility company. Richardson controlled its board. Was Richardson being protected by Barnett also? My case had dragged on for almost two years. Was that just a convenient delay for my opponents (meaning both sides) to outlast me - since I paid all costs?

I needed another attorney.

In one firm, after my long and explicitly accusatory interview with a junior partner, his final handshake was dripping wet. Their expected rejection letter manufactured an unspecified "conflict of interest."

Another attorney, a Democrat, told me, "New Mexico is a 'small' state. After Barnett and Rogers, no one will take your case." I understood. The attorneys were all "friends" too.

And strangely, Scot Stinnet said he could not help me find an attorney. I did not take stock of the facts: His mother worked as a local paralegal. He knew many attorneys - especially from the Sheriff Gary Graves recall. He had not contributed a cent to the case. He had done nothing to prevent the FOG debacle. He was protecting nether me nor the case. So I used him as my sounding board to vent my frustrations about New Mexico's corruption. I was a fool.

As Will Rogers quipped: "Last year we said, 'Things can't go on like this; and they didn't. They got worse."

# CHAPTER 13:

# NEW LAWYERS, NEW HOPE

H JUDICIAL DISTRICT COURT
S SANDOVAL
NEW MEXICO

PER and DeBACA COUNTY NEWS, a New Mexico

Plaintiffs,

NO. D-1329-CV-07-1364

RDEN, LINCOLN COUNTY SHERIFF and CUSTODIAN OF RECORDS
LINCOLN COUNTY SHERIFF; and STEVEN M. SEDERWALL, FORMER
N COUNTY DEPUTY SHERIFF; and THOMAS T. SULLIVAN, FORMER
LN COUNTY SHERIFF AND FORMER LINCOLN COUNTY DEPUTY

FF,

Defendants.

ORDER GRANTING PLAINTIFFS' MOTION FOR SUMMARY
JUDGMENT AND DENYING DEFENDANT VIRDEN'S CROSS-
MOTION FOR SUMMARY JUDGMENT AND ORDER GRANTING
LEAVE TO FILE INTERLOCUTORY APPEAL

THIS MATTER having come before the Court on November 20, 2009 on

laintiffs' Motion for Summary Judgment and Defendant Virden's Cross-Motion f

Summary Judgment and the Court having received

of Counsel and otherwise being fully advised.

THE COURT FINDS:

1. Defendants Sullivan and Sederwall were a

of Defendant Lincoln County Sheriff at all times pert

2. Defendant Lincoln County Sheriff opened

the investigation which is the subject of this cause of a

mentary or otherwise; res

---

State of New Mexico
County of Sandoval
Thirteenth Judicial District Court

Gale Cooper and De Baca County News,
a New Mexico Corporation,
Plaintiffs

v.

No. D-1329-CV-2007-01364

Rick Virden, Lincoln County Sheriff and
Custodian of Records of the Lincoln County Sheriff; and
Steven M. Sederwall, Former Lincoln County Deputy Sheriff; and
Thomas T. Sullivan, Former Lincoln County Sheriff and
Former Lincoln County Deputy Sheriff,
Defendants

Order on Hearing of January 21, 2011

This Matter has come before the court on January 21, 2011, on Plaintiff's Motion for

Mandatory Order of Disclosure and Production. The ___ received and considered the

evidence and having heard the ___

The Court ___ the double homicide of

___ the Lincoln County

___ e made, generated,

___ ocuments under the

___ recoveries in the

---

1  THIRTEENTH JUDICIAL DISTRICT
2  COUNTY OF SANDOVAL
   STATE OF NEW MEXICO
3
   GALE COOPER and DE BACA COUNTY NEWS, a New Mexico
4  Corporation,
      Plaintiffs,                    D-1329-CV-07-1364
5
6      vs.
7  LINCOLN COUNTY and RICK VIRDEN, LINCOLN COUNTY SHERIFF and
   CUSTODIAN OF RECORDS; and STEVEN M. S___  FORMER
8  LINCOLN COUNTY DEPUTY SHERIFF; and T___VAN,
   FORMER LINCOLN COUNTY SHERIFF AND FO___
9  DEPUTY SHERIFF,
      Defendants.
10                        ___ANSCRIPT OF PROC

---

LINCOLN COUNTY SHER
"BILLY THE KI

THE MUR
AC
**
PROB
arrett is a m

S
elped Billy

---

# FORENSIC RECORDS FOR CASE #2003-274

## Orchid Cellmark Lab

CARPENTER'S WORKBENCH
**DR. LEE'S DNA COLLECTION**

### DNA EXTRACTION

DNA OF
BILLY THE KID

DNA OF
JOHN MILLER

DNA OF
WILLIAM HUDSPETH

### DNA MATCHING

BILLY + MILLER
**MATCH RESULTS**

BILLY + HUDSPETH
**MATCH RESULTS**

**EXHUMATIONS**

JOHN MILLER

WILLIAM HUDSPETH

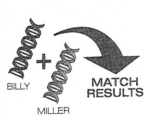

# Knights in Shining Legal Armor

*HOAXBUST: More surprising to me than learning the pervasiveness of New Mexico corruption, was realizing that I was an optimist. That, added to my being Hamster Girl, kept me going as I struggled against impossible odds to keep my litigation alive.*

### *MAYBE FAIRYTALES DO COME TRUE*

Returning to squashed Bambi, one can feel relief that cartoons are not reality-bound - and sometimes life is not either. Visualize pancake-flat Bambi reassembled by animation's magic into an airplane - like pilot Chesley "Sully" Sullenberger's engineless plane miraculously landing, on January 15, 2009, on the Hudson River. And you will have an idea of what happened to me next.

My months of searching settled on young attorney, Blair Dunn, from a family of New Mexico politicians. He liked my case. He also had an old-timer mentor: Attorney Martin E. "Ed" Threet. Blair got Ed Threet to join. Threet's father had been on New Mexico's Supreme Court. For a time, Threet and Dunn became my fairytale knights in shining armor.

Our first meeting was on March, 2, 2009, at a Macaroni Grill in Albuquerque. Little, wiry, spry Threet had eyes that "twinkled." Ramrod straight, he said to me, "I used to be as tall as Blair [6'9"], but this is what years as a lawyer in New Mexico does to you." That was the first "Threetism" I heard. When we left our meeting, Threet effortlessly carried out my pounds of evidence folders. Blair told me Threet was in his 90's. Threet told me 15 years less.

My little cartoon plane, having nose-dived straight down, now seemed to sweep upward into the blue heavens. At that moment, I would have thought myself daft to doubt Threet's and Dunn's sincerity or their immunity to my unscrupulous defendants' manipulations.

# NERVEWRACKING SUMMARY JUDGMENT HEARING

By August of 2009, with Scot Stinnett still on board, Ed Threet and Blair Dunn filed our "Motion for Summary Judgment": a request that Judge George Eichwald rule in our favor. The defendants counter-filed for a decision in their favor.

On November 20, 2009, Ed Threet with Blair Dunn drove me to the Sandoval County District Courthouse, with its glass-walled vistas to the distant mountains where I lived. In the dark-paneled bright courtroom were Attorneys Nicole Werkmeister and Kevin Brown - but no defendants.

To my surprise, Brown and Werkmeister had copies of this book's first edition, titled *MegaHoax*, for my signing. Brown asked me to write "to hawk-face": what I had called him. I signed it to "Attorney Kevin Brown;" thinking that comedy always lurks.

There was another surprise. Apparently confident of winning, the hoaxers had tipped off a local TV station, Channel 7. So in the jury area assembled men with cameras and microphones.

As we waited our turn, Threet sat between Dunn and me. Every time the judge denied Summary Judgment on another case, tall Blair would look over little Threet's head to my worried eyes. So Threet said a Threetism: "Don't scream until you're shot."

Finally we all entered court-side. For weeks, I had prepared evidence folders for this. And Threet's and Dunn's inspiring words from the transcript should go down in New Mexico history.

**\*\*\*\*\*\*\*\*\*\*\*\*\*\***

THE COURT: Okay. I read these motions and they are rather interesting, and I guess, to make a long story short, what the plaintiffs are claiming is that defendants have certain information that they're not turning over. And basically there's no rule or no law stating that the defendants are entitled to keep these because they're all brought - or this information was gathered as these people were acting in their official capacity as Sheriffs or workers from the Lincoln County Sheriff's Department. I think that's basically what you're going to argue, is that correct?

MR. THREET: That is correct, Your Honor.

THE COURT: Who's going to argue the motion?

MR. THREET: May it please the Court, I will argue the opening and Mr. Blair Dunn will argue the – any reply that we have to the argument of opposing counsel.

THE COURT: Okay. Mr. Threet?

MR. THREET: May it please the Court. The Court has summarized very succinctly the case and the issues presented. And this, of course, is on a summary judgment, but, may it please the Court, it appears to me that there is an issue here for all of us to consider, and that is the importance of this particular matter to the State of New Mexico. The issue, ultimately, will be solved by the statutes. But overriding everything is a question concerning two things: Responsibility of law enforcement to respond pursuant to the statute. That, above all, is a question for the Court to ask.

However, in addition to that, there is a question concerning the importance to the State of New Mexico as a part of its heritage. Where this could be now forthcoming could solve and add to our history, it apparently has been withheld. Those of us who have grown up in New Mexico find ourselves entwined in the history. As an example, in my own family, when my mother and father moved from Arkansas out to Las Cruces, they moved in next door to the widow of Pat Garrett. When I went to school in Las Cruces, I went to school with the grandchildren of Oliver Lee, Bob and Seto. All of us seemed to, at some time or another, be entwined in this history, and it's important to all of us.

With that, may it please the Court, I feel like that what we have lined out indicates, without a doubt, there can be no doubt of the people that investigated this case, that it is established that what they did, the steps that they took. And, may it please the Court, they have admitted that they have information in their possession.

Likewise, we have a Sheriff who seems to feel that he has no further responsibilities under the law because he has, in some fashion, turned over or allowed his deputies to take possession of certain facts in evidence.

I don't know exactly the best way to look at this, but I can only tell the Court that if we start out, the issues that we bring up - and, of course, the matters on summary judgment are known to counsel and to the Court. There is no need for me to repeat that. The statute involved is very, very clear as to what the duties are on the public disclosure. And in that it's also defined as what the custodian is. And Section 14-2-6 in the definition. "As is in the inspection of public records, 'custodian' means any person responsible for the maintenance, care, or keeping of a public body's public records regardless of whether the records are in the person's actual physical custody and control." That means the custodian has an overriding duty and responsibility to the people of the State of New Mexico to maintain records that are uncovered that should be examined not only for the present case but to guide future examinations and to provide the fabric of this State's history.

Now, I think, may it please the Court, if we look at this matter, it becomes clear. The case is 2003-274. A copy of that probable cause statement -- buying the title that it is in the Lincoln County Sheriff's Department probable cause statement sets out - and I'm sure the Court has read it - clearly what the purpose of this investigation would be. And it is signed by Mr. Steven Sederwall, Deputy Sheriff, and Mr. Tom Sullivan, Sheriff. It was issued in December of 2003.

In addition to that, Your Honor, as Exhibit A to the Complaint that was filed herein, there is a memorandum from Sederwall and Tom Sullivan to Mr. Rick Virden, the Lincoln County Sheriff, dated July - June 21st, 2001 [sic -2007]. That becomes a part of what the Court must consider. This talks about what was being done, talking about, also, what steps had been taken and what had been – and recites certain newspaper articles. This is the seminal document, may it please the Court, and it's interesting that there are many contributors to the costs of this matter. But under these circumstances, may it please the Court, those costs have to be considered as public funds because the Sheriffs - or the deputies could not have taken them in any other way and have conducted a formal investigation.

We go next then to a very interesting document, and this becomes the crux of what we're looking for, that is our Exhibit B. That is a letter, May 1, 2006, to Mr. Jay Miller from Dr. Henry C. Lee. It's from the State of Connecticut, Department of Public Safety, Division of Scientific Services. And Dr. Henry C. Lee is Chief Emeritus, and if I can recall correctly, that is a gentleman who was involved also in the O.J. Simpson case, may it please the Court. And he is writing to Mr. Miller, and here's what he says.

"In response to your letter, dated March 27th, 2006, regarding forensic consultation in the New Mexico Billy the Kid case. To set the record straight, the Lincoln County Sheriff's Department contacted me. They requested a forensic expert to perform preliminary identification and scene reconstruction. This was a pro bono forensic consultation case. We examined a wooden bench and floorboards at the courthouse. I completed my examination of the evidence and submitted my report to the Lincoln County Sheriff's Department. If you want a copy of the report, you should contact the Lincoln County Sheriff's Department directly."

Now, stopping right there, this is information that came to the Sheriff's office. And what this is, Your Honor, is a bench, and DNA secured from a bench where supposedly the body of Billy the Kid was laid out and from which, perhaps, if we can get the reports, can be determined that the DNA that appears on that bench matches the DNA of Billy the Kid's mother.

And this is being done in regard pursuant to an open case, a cold case surely, involving Pat Garrett - but a cold case - but an open case because there's no statute of limitations, as we have pointed out, on a question of murder.

But he goes on, "Since I did not conduct any DNA testing on the evidence and the Lincoln County Sheriff's Department sent samples directly to a private laboratory for analysis, I am sorry, but I do not have answers to your questions regarding DNA."

So we have now two sources. And if you read the position taken by Sheriff Virden, he's raising his hands and he says, I don't have those. But then he says, I think my deputies do. And they say, well, that's a private hobby. Well, may it please the Court, that's simply something that stretches your mind to a point of snapping.

The Sheriff could contact Lee, could contact the laboratory, Orchid Cellmark, to find out what that was, saying for whatever reason, I don't have them in here. I need to complete my records. Would you please send them to me? But he hasn't done a thing. But yet the statute makes him the custodian. It makes him have the responsibility.

All we're asking the Court to do is to look at these people and say, you know, our legislature made a decision that it's important to the population of this state, to the citizens of this state, for you to be able - for an official to be able to keep records, and for the citizens to view those records. All we want to do is to exercise a right granted to us by the legislature. We are being obstructed every step of the way.

They are saying we are not part of the Sheriff's office, we weren't doing this with the Sheriff's. But yet, may it please the Court, it's very interesting, as shown by the Exhibit C, Lincoln County Sheriff's Department Supplemental Report, there is an Information [sic – exhumation] of Jay [sic – John] Miller conducted in Arizona. And look who the people there were - and I would say this was one of the suspected people of - that might be - the decedent was - of Billy the Kid. Look who's there. Steven Sederwall, Lincoln County Sheriff's Deputy, Tom Sullivan, Sheriff of Lincoln County, retired. May it please the Court, they were there. They were doing it.

Now, our Exhibit B, in the Petition, "To exhume the remains of the mother of Billy the Kid." Here is a very interesting petition from those records over there. "Comes now Petitioner Tom Sullivan, Sheriff of Lincoln County, Steve Sederwall, Deputy Sheriff of Lincoln County, and Gary Graves of De Baca County, through their attorney, Sherry Tippett, and petition this Court to issue an order." And what is the purpose of this? For the purpose of determining that guilt or innocence of Sheriff Pat Garrett in the death of William Bonney, also known as Billy the Kid. Catherine Antrim is the undisputed mother of William Bonney."

Well, may it please the Court, they are over there participating in this. And what did we find? We don't find anything. They haven't - certainly they have described - what they were and their official capacity. They were Sheriffs and Deputy Sheriffs.

Likewise, on our Exhibit E, the Tenth Judicial District Court, State of New Mexico, County of De Baca. "In the Matter of William H. Bonney, a/k/a Billy the Kid, petition for the exhumation of Billy the Kid's remains." Starts off, the Co-Petitioners are Gary Graves, Sheriff of De Baca County, Tom Sullivan, Sheriff, Steve Sederwall, Deputy Sheriff. And, may it please the Court, these are in their official capacity and they are receiving information. And, may it please the Court, Virden - Sheriff Virden is the custodian, according to law, but he says he doesn't have it.

We go again to our Exhibit F, "In the Matter of William H. Bonney a/k/a Billy the Kid -" and we - this is their attorney citing it "- prior to the filing of the Petition for Exhumation of the remains of Billy the Kid a/k/a William H. Bonney, Sullivan, Sederwall, and Graves, acting in their capacity as law enforcement officers, initiating an investigation into case 2004-274, filed in Lincoln County." And they -- again, the purpose of the case was to determine the guilt or innocence of Sheriff Pat Garrett for the death of Billy the Kid. And they describe what they did. In there it says - and this is very important, I believe. "The principal purpose of opening the investigation in the case was to determine the guilt or innocence of Sheriff Pat Garrett in the death of Billy the Kid initially. As part of their ongoing investigation, Sederwall, Sullivan, and Graves, in their capacity as law enforcement officers, petitioned the Sixth Judicial District Court for the exhumation of the remains of Billy the Kid's mother, Catherine Antrim." Now - and it says what the purpose of this exhumation was. Again, may it please the Court, what are we looking at? Is there any question that these people were operating, obtaining information in their position as an officer of the law of the State of New Mexico?

Then we go on to a very interesting letter written by Mr. Alan P. Morel concerning the documents. And it says - and this is on Page 1, in response to Item 2, he says, "Sheriff Sullivan advised me that he did issue a Deputy Sheriff's card to Mayor Sederwall. The County of McKinley [sic – Lincoln] does not have a copy of the card that was issued to Mayor Sederwall, and as such, a copy of the same would have had to be obtained from Mayor Sederwall who is the Mayor of Capitan,

New Mexico. The Lincoln County Sheriff's Office advised me that Mayor Sederwall was issued a Deputy Sheriff's card, which is identified on a list as number 147." Again, Lincoln County has no copy of the card and the card is in the possession of Mayor Steve Sederwall."

Again, we are tracking information in their hands, may it please the Court. We go on to Exhibit H, which is a denial letter in which there is a request for -- to look at the records, and it says, Billy the Kid case. This is from Tom Sullivan. He says, "We cannot permit inspection of these records because they are protected from disclosure by the reasons checked below." And this is "other" - other than an ongoing investigation - and until the investigation is completed and closed, they will not be available for release as per --" and then they cite the statutes. Well, may it please the Court, I doubt that this investigation is still going on, and I see no reason whereby they would be obstructing this when this happened over a hundred years ago.

Now, I don't know what they're trying to do here, Your Honor. Then they have a letter here from the Lincoln County Sheriff's Office, and the official description of Tom Sullivan and Sederwall are contained there. Then, again, another letter from Mr. Morel. He says this, "As a result of your latest request for public records -" and I'm looking at the second paragraph "- I decided it was time to speak with Sheriff Rick Virden and Lincoln County Manager Tom Stewart regarding the potential liability to the County of Lincoln as it relates to the entire matter. While I'm not at liberty to discuss the entire attorney/client privilege communication that occurred between my clients and myself, I can tell you that it was the respective decision of my clients to formally request from Mr. Sullivan and Mr. Sederwall any and all public records that they have in their possession related to Case 2003-274. I have attached to this correspondence, as Exhibit A, copies of two letters that I have prepared to Tom Sullivan and Steven Sederwall, dated June 21, 2007. Both Mr. Sullivan and Mr. Sederwall received originals. Other than the signatures of myself and Lincoln County Manager, Tom Stewart, and Lincoln County Sheriff, Rick Virden, they are identical."

And what does he say happened? May it please the Court - and we have the letters there - two people to whom they were directed, have themselves refused to turn over. They haven't said, no, we don't have it. They have it. They are not going to turn it over.

Then, may it please the Court, it would appear to me that if we take a look at Tom Sullivan's responses to the Request for Production of Documents, and this case says, "Please provide any and all DNA results from Dr. Henry Lee's scrapings and swabbings of the carpenter's bench pertaining to Lincoln County Sheriff's Department, Case Number 2003-

274." Response. "This is a request for documents that are not public records; therefore, defendant objects to this request on the grounds that it's not calculated to lead to the discovery." There is a series of questions each time - they don't say we don't have it. They say that these are not public records.

Now, Your Honor, the track of the history of the matter simply is that - the fact that the only way they came into possession of this information and these records is the fact that they were acting as Deputy Sheriffs. And they have - Sheriff Virden has two things, two ideas that he could go after. He could either file requests of demands that these two people deliver records or he could go ahead and write to Henry Lee and he could write to Orchid Cellmark, give me these, I need them to complete it. They won't do anything.

Now, one of the things - and the - it is very interesting that in Rick Virden's response to our Motion for Summary Judgment, he says that this case - in his introduction - this case involves the investigation of Billy the Kid's murder. Now, may it please the Court, he ends up by saying, well, there's nothing really that shows that Sheriff Virden has or does not have any duty in regard to these records. Well, may it please the Court, he has a duty, he has – the statute sets forth the duty. All he has to do is look at the statute and follow the law.

What also is bothering me, Your Honor, it appears to me that years ago, at the early inception of this country, a question concerning the right of the press, the reporters to have information was established. What is occurring here, Your Honor, is not only just to the public, as may be voiced in a court action, but we have people here who are an important part of our fourth state of government, the press. They're being denied this. This is not fair and this is not right. This is against the law.

And, may it please the Court, we go on. And I'm about done, but - and I apologize if I've taken too long, but it's something that I think is very important, and that is, we have the right to - we have the right to know. It is important. I have three children and a grandchild. This is part of my family's heritage. It is a part of my heritage. It's a part of the Court's heritage.

And may it please the Court, I am sorry if I get a little bit fired up, but when a public officer ignores a public law, I begin to get a little bit upset. I've been in this business 50 years. This is my 50th year practicing law. I have not been in a case in which I've seen a law enforcement officer deny the right that a person has to look at records. I would point out in the depositions that are attached as copies - one of the Deputies saying yes, now, when I was working for the Sheriff, we didn't find that much, but since that time, I found it. Your Honor, if these people initiated the efforts and got the beginning of the foundation of the investigation while in the public employ of the State of New Mexico, those records, regardless if it was before or after a date of termination, those records are susceptible to being discovered.

And the Sheriff being the custodian, regardless of his position - and that's what the statute says. The statute says, in fact, that the custodian means "any person responsible for the maintenance, care, or keeping of the record of the public body's public records, regardless of whether the records are in that person's actual, physical custody and control." That's an affirmative duty to go ahead and secure these documents so that the public can view them.

Your Honor, I submit, there are no questions here. There are no questions; there are duties, and we ask the Court to enforce those duties. Thank you, Your Honor.

THE COURT: Ms. Werkmeister?

**[AUTHOR'S NOTE: Werkmeister will now begin defense lies used for years in the litigation: claiming the custodian's IPRA responsibility is only for records in direct possession; ignoring the list of requested records, and calling them one Dr. Lee report and maybe one Orchid Cellmark report; and denying records existence (ignoring IPRA's burden on the custodian, not the requestor, to establish existence). She will use the possession argument to claim that since Virden possesses no records, he should be dismissed from the case. Of course, that would end the case – in the same way Barnett and Rogers tried; since an IPRA case needs the custodian as a defendant – plus any others connected to the records. But Werkmeister tries a shell game of switching recovery responsibility to Sederwall, because he admitted to having a Lee report.]**

MS. WERKMEISTER: Thank you, Your Honor. I take real issue with Mr. Threet's characterization of the Sheriff's Department of Lincoln County as somehow obstructing this records request. Lincoln County has turned over every shred of document it has relating to the Billy the Kid investigation. It is not withholding a single piece of paper. Everything that Lincoln County has is in the plaintiffs' possession at this point.

What is at issue here are two documents, this report by Dr. Lee, and a report that may or may not exist, generated by Orchid Cellmark Laboratories.

And let's look at the Dr. Lee report for a second. We know where that report is. It was testified to by Mr. Sederwall in his deposition that he has a copy of, and it was testified to by Sheriff Virden that he does not have a copy of it, and the Sheriff's Department has never had a copy of it. And while I understand Mr. Threet to be arguing that the Sheriff's Department should have a copy of it, that doesn't change the fact that they do not and that they never did. And, furthermore, they've already tried to obtain that copy by specifically requesting in writing that Defendant Sederwall turn it over, and he's refused. So the Sheriff's Department has bent over backwards in this case to try and get the plaintiffs what they want. And we're in the position, at this point, of saying, we simply cannot produce something that we don't have and never did.

This Orchid Cellmark Lab's report, we don't even know if it exists or not. There's not been any evidence in this lawsuit that the laboratory has generated any report. Sheriff Virden testified - and his deposition testimony is attached to our motion. And, by the way, Your Honor, there are cross-motions for summary judgment here, and so we're going to be asking for the dismissal of this lawsuit on behalf of the Sheriff's Department because we also filed a motion for summary judgment in addition to the plaintiffs. But Sheriff Virden testified that he doesn't know if this laboratory report exists. He's never seen it, never heard of it, certainly has never had a copy of it. And I think the same testimony was made on behalf of the other individual defendants in this case. So I haven't seen anything that this lab report even exists. Certainly, the Sheriff's Department doesn't have a copy of it.

Now, with regard to the Dr. Lee report, Exhibit B, I think to Mr. Threet's motion, was a letter from Dr. Lee saying, I sent my report to the Sheriff's Department. Well, we obviously don't have a copy of the letter that Dr. Lee sent because that's what's in dispute, and we don't have the address on the letter to see where it was actually sent. But we do have Mr. Sederwall's testimony, sworn testimony under oath in his deposition, that that letter that Dr. Lee referred to, in Exhibit B to Mr. Threet's motion, was sent to his home address, and that he has it.

So I'm a little curious in this case why there hasn't been a simple motion to compel filed seeking Your Honor's ruling as to whether the plaintiffs are legally entitled to see this Dr. Lee report. It would be a very simple matter to file a motion to compel. It could have been done at the outset of this lawsuit, and there's really no reason to drag Lincoln County through this lawsuit because, regardless of whether Ms. Cooper is legally entitled to Dr. Lee's report or not, Lincoln County doesn't have a stake. If she's legally entitled to it, then Mr. Sederwall would have to turn it over pursuant to court order. If she's not, she's not. Lincoln County doesn't have to be in this lawsuit for that determination to be made.

And the same is true with regard to the Orchid Cellmark Lab's report. That could be subpoenaed by the plaintiffs. Again, there's no reason to drag Lincoln County through this lawsuit in order for those documents to be produced if there is a legal basis or if there's a legal entitlement for plaintiffs to obtain them.

This issue as to whether the documents are public or private and whether this was a public investigation or whether Mr. Sederwall and Sullivan were investigating this matter in their capacities as private citizens, that's really a red herring with regard to the claims against Lincoln County. And I'm saying Lincoln County, Your Honor. The lawsuit was actually filed against Sheriff Virden as Records Custodian for the Sheriff's Department of Lincoln County. So when I say Lincoln County, I'm really talking about the Sheriff in his official capacity.

But this issue of public versus private records is really a red herring with regard to the claims against Lincoln County because it doesn't matter whether they are public or private. And let me just say that there are issues of fact with regard to whether they are public or private documents. And we have cited in our Brief, evidence from both the individual defendants testifying that they completed this investigation in their capacity as private citizens. And we've also cited evidence that not a dime of Lincoln County money was spent on this investigation. There have been invoices and receipts and checks produced in discovery in this case, and not a single one points to a single penny coming from Lincoln County for this investigation.

So even if we pretend that that issue is appropriate for summary judgment, and even if we assume that they were public records, as the plaintiffs contend, the Sheriff's Department is still in the position of not being able to turn over records that it doesn't have and that it never did have. Mr. Threet is arguing that the Sheriff's Department should go out and get these or contact Defendant Sederwall and say, turn them over. Well, we've done that. We wrote a letter requesting these records, and they refused. So there is no legal precedent, no legal basis for this Court to require Lincoln County to somehow go out and, I don't know, file a lawsuit against former County officials, or file a lawsuit to compel third parties to produce documents that Lincoln County never had possession of in the first place.

So the bottom line in this case, with regard to Lincoln County, Your Honor, is that, one, we've turned over all the documents we had. We're not withholding anything. But we don't have the two documents that the plaintiffs want. Number 2, we can't give them something that we

432

don't have. And there's no legal basis to compel us to file a lawsuit against third parties to get something that we never had in the first place.

And I think, most importantly, Your Honor, the dismissal of Lincoln County from this lawsuit is not going to prejudice Ms. Cooper's rights in any way to get these documents if she is legally entitled to them. And I think that's an issue for the Court to decide. But Lincoln County - if the Court decides that she is legally entitled to get these documents, then she can get them without the presence of Lincoln County in the lawsuit because it's not the County that's going to produce the documents since they don't have them.

And so, for all those reasons, Your Honor, we would ask that Lincoln County or Sheriff Virden, as Records Custodian, be dismissed from the lawsuit and that our cross-motion for summary judgment be granted. Thank you.

THE COURT: Mr. Brown?

**[AUTHOR'S NOTE: Brown tries to blur everything as "myth and rumor;" and argues that Sullivan and Sederwall are just private citizens, ignoring their deputizations, and further claiming that as a "reserve deputy" Sederwall was not really a deputy. Brown also falsely links lack of deputy salary as meaning not being a public official. Brown also ignores all law enforcement documents in evidence, and claims the only evidence against his clients is hearsay and newspaper articles. He calls the incriminatory Supplemental Report on John Miller's exhumation just a Prescott Police Department "police report." And he calls the records private property. Brown also accuses me of doing the case to write a book, ignoring that IPRA requires no reason for requesting records, and that IPRA's intent includes exposés.]**

MR. BROWN: Thank you. Your Honor, the story of Billy the Kid is one of the most fascinating legends in the State of New Mexico. And like all legends, it's intertwined with myth and rumor, and that's what this case is, it's intertwined completely with myth and rumor.

In 2004, Tom Sullivan left as Lincoln County Sheriff. Steve Sederwall was never a public employee, he was a Reserve Deputy. He was never paid. This suit was filed in 2007, three years after Tom Sullivan left. The suit named Lincoln County and the custodian of the records, as it should, and it improperly named Sullivan and Sederwall as defendants.

The facts - we're here on a motion for summary judgment, so it's really pretty simple. The facts which the plaintiffs relied upon are primarily newspaper articles, a lot of hearsay, a lot of conclusions, a lot of statements which they made, which are not supported by the record.

Mr. Threet mentioned Exhibit C, which was a document - a police report in 2005, and it alleges or makes - and it makes an allegation that Sederwall and Sullivan were working as deputies at that point in time. Factually - and I've cited all this - there's been no foundation, and Sederwall even said he's never seen that and he believed it was a fraud.

Everything else which was cited occurred in 2003 - 2003, when Sullivan was Sheriff at the time. All those records were left, it's undisputed, with Lincoln County, with the custodian of the records. And it's my understanding that Mr. Virden - or Sheriff Virden produced everything he said he had.

Now, with all due respect to Mr. Threet - and what our actual response to the Request for Production was – and I'll just read one because it was the same thing on all of them, "This is a request for documents that are not public records, therefore, defendant objects to this request on the grounds that it is not calculated to lead to the discovery of relevant information." The part that was left out, "without waiving this objection, defendant states he has no such documents." That was the answer to every request for document that was made, so it's Sullivan and Sederwall's position that there are no documents which have been requested, and so - at summary the judgment stage, we have clearly a statement or a dispute of fact. But the case against Sullivan and Sederwall should be dismissed because it's pretty clear that they aren't custodians of the record. Under the Public Records - Inspection of Public Records Act, the custodian is Lincoln County and Sheriff Virden.

And I think what this case is about is selling a book. And Ms. Cooper has written a book, and in that book she recognizes the defense of Sullivan and Sederwall, because she says, "I may be a coward, but I'm hard to intimidate." The state's expert on IPRA law -- I said to the state's expert, I said, "A reserve deputy is not the custodian for forensic records of a Sheriff's murder investigation." Virden is the custodian of the IPRA definition. Again, she says - describing what's going to happen when she makes that argument -"Sederwall: I'm not the Records Custodian under the IPRA law." Judge: He's not the Records Custodian under the IPRA law. You lose, Cooper and Tinnett [sic - Stinnett]. Thanks for (inaudible) [sic – throwing] the case, Mickey and Pat."

Basically, they've sued two people who weren't in office, weren't public employees after 2004, they're not records custodian, and the claims against them should be dismissed because of that, and summary judgment that the plaintiff seeks should be denied because of disputed facts. Thank you.

THE COURT: Let me hear your reply.

434

[AUTHOR'S NOTE: By quoting from *MegaHoax,* Brown gave us the chance to enter it as an exhibit. Dunn kept his reply simple: IPRA law required Virden's records recovery as custodian; his deputies generated public documents; and ample evidence proved the records existed.]

MR. DUNN: May it please the Court. Preliminary, if I could, since they've cited to the book, we can possibly go ahead and enter the book into the record.

THE COURT: Okay.

MR. DUNN: May I approach?

THE COURT: You may. Just give it to my reporter.

MR. DUNN: To start with, I think that it's important to simplify what has been stated by opposing counsel by pointing out that basically the situation we have is that each of them is turning to the other and pointing at one another saying, no, that's your job as official records custodian. And no, that's your job because you were doing this on your own.

There really is no dispute between the plaintiffs and the defendants it seems. It's almost a feud between the defendants themselves over who should actually have these documents. I don't think that anybody can say that these documents don't exist, in good faith. One of the things that has been failed to be mentioned so far is the fact that these forensic documents were the basis for violating the graves of two individuals and violating the sanctity of burial in Arizona. They went and dug up bodies. As we pointed out in the documents, that was their basis, their entire basis as law enforcement officers, for digging up bodies. And that fact alone has to make you wonder about how our government officials are acting.

To boil down their two arguments, I guess I would start by pointing out that Sheriff Virden's argument is that I don't have them. We've turned over everything we have. But that does not alleviate his duty as a custodian of records. As Mr. Threet read, it doesn't matter. Regardless of whether the records are in the person's actual physical custody and control, those records are supposed to be maintained by Sheriff Virden.

It's interesting that they point out that he sent a letter to Sederwall and Sullivan asking for these documents, but they never requested the documents from Orchid Cellmark or from Dr. Lee, when very clearly they could have obtained copies that direction. What we have is a shell game where each side is trying to blame the other side and move it away and keep them from getting it.

The other argument that the other side brings up, and it's important to note, this wasn't their official capacity. Every single document that they use to obtain any sort of information in this case, which is an open case, which is part of the Public Records Act, and any documents generated thereof, was always done on official letterhead or they held themselves out to be County Sheriffs or Deputy Sheriffs, however that is. All of the petitions to exhume bodies used their official titles. And until our case, they never claimed it was not a murder -- or they never claimed it was an investigation, meaning that they fully held it out to be an ongoing investigation until this case, and then suddenly when this case was filed, it became a hobby. They never said that prior to the filing of this case. It's important to note the timing of that because, very clearly, they were treating it as an official case until somebody wanted the official documents.

And, you know, it's also disingenuous the argument that no taxpayer money has been spent on this. As we've noted, they dug up bodies. We've had several cases. They've used up court's time in De Baca and Grant County and elsewhere to try to exhume bodies or to look at this.

It is very much a case, and it's not just a couple documents, but it's the whole entirety of the case where they have tried to obstruct people from obtaining the documents that they obtained as part of an official investigation.

I guess it all kind of ties back into the purpose of our government officials. And as Mr. Threet gets fired up, that's part of the same for me. It's - when we elect a Sheriff to be the custodian of records, he has a duty to maintain those records. It is his duty to then provide those records to the public. It's entirely disingenuous and contrary to our system of governance in this country for our officials to use their titles and then not comply with the statutes that bestow responsibilities upon them.

And the argument that you can get these through some other medium, through a request to do discovery here or anything else, that does not take away or does not exempt Sheriff Virden from his custodial duty to obtain these documents under the Public Records Act. Our government - the legislature established that Act for the purpose of allowing the public to get those documents without having to jump through these hoops. He has failed in his duty.

That is the simplest explanation of this case, that it is an open records case, these are public documents, were generated in the course of investigation and should be turned over. It's no more complex than that.

**[AUTHOR'S NOTE: The Court's ruling followed.]**

THE COURT: On the Defendant's Motion to Dismiss, I'm going to deny that motion. On Plaintiff's Motion for Summary Judgment, I'm going to find that Sheriff [sic – Deputy] Sullivan
and Deputy Sederwall were, in fact, acting in accord with state law. They were, for lack of a better word, they were employees of the County - of Lincoln County Sheriff's Department. Even if Steven Sederwall was a Reserve Deputy, the Sheriff has the authority to grant commission cards making him then an actor for Lincoln County.

I'm also going to find that this investigation, when it was opened, has continued by the Lincoln County Sheriff's Department. Anything that comes out of it is, in fact, public record.

I'm going to order that all information that was   received, including Dr. Lee's report and any lab report, if it exists, be turned over to the plaintiffs. And this is a  direct order to Mr. Sederwall, if he has it, he is to turn it over to the Lincoln County Sheriff's Department and turn it over to counsel.

In the event that that does not occur and we need an evidentiary - a further evidentiary hearing on that matter, this Court will, in fact, have that evidentiary hearing.

So I'm going to grant your motion for summary judgment.

MR. THREET: Thank you, Your Honor.

**************

We won!

Outside the courtroom, the TV crew waited. Into a microphone, I said, "This is an important day for New Mexico history."

When Blair and I got back in Threet's car, Threet startlingly gave the loudest yell I ever heard. Until then, I had not realized how much attorneys like to win.

Later, when I asked Threet how Attorneys Brown and Werkmeister had dared to lie so much, he uttered another Threetism: "If you have the facts, pound the facts. If you have the law, pound the law. If you have nothing, pound the table." Of course, at the Summary Judgment Hearing, he had given a Threetism for the ages: "We [the people] have the right to know."

What I did not realize until years later, was that the granting of Summary Judgment should end a case. It meant the defendants had to turn over the records to the plaintiffs - or face contempt of court. But that ball of declaring contempt is the judge's to play.

## PRESENTMENT HEARING

On March 9, 2010, Attorney Ed Threet and I were back in court for a "Presentment Hearing": meaning our demanding the records' turn-over. There were TV crews from Channels 7 and 13, and grim-faced Attorneys Werkmeister and Brown without clients. As was the emerging pattern, Scot Stinnett did not come; and the defendants never came unless they were witnesses.

And on February 18, 2010, Attorney Brown had sent Threet a Dr. Henry report provided to him by Sederwall, claiming it fulfilled the records request. But it was just an unrequested Lee report about DNA sampling of the old Lincoln courthouse's floorboards for the faked "blood" of the Deputy Bell killing sub-investigation. We returned it as irrelevant to the requests.

But before the March 9th hearing began, Attorney Brown displayed that report to a TV camera, saying it was the case's requested document. The problem was not just the lie; but, as usual, Sederwall's mouth. In his August 18, 2008 deposition, as may be recalled, he said he had Lee's *carpenter's bench report*, which he had described in detail. So, in court, Threet read Sederwall's own words, and added one of his own: "dissimulating."

Judge Eichwald's ruling repeated turn-over. Threet told me it was another win. And the two TV crews interviewed me and Threet. But the resulting Channel 13 Internet article was utterly garbled: stating *I* questioned Garrett's shooting of the Kid!

## THE JUDGE'S ORDER

By March 12, 2010, the judge signed his order "Granting Plaintiff's Motion for Summary Judgment and Denying Defendant Virden's Cross-Motion for Summary Judgment." It stated:

THIS MATTER having come before the Court on November 20, 2009 on Plaintiffs' Motion for Summary Judgment and Defendant Virden's Cross-Motion for Summary Judgment and the Court having received evidence and having heard argument of Counsel and otherwise being fully advised.

THE COURT FINDS:

1. Defendants Sullivan and Sederwall were acting either as employees or agents of Defendant Lincoln County Sheriff at all times pertinent to this cause of action.

2. Defendant Lincoln County Sheriff opened the investigation and continued with the investigation which is the subject of this cause of action.

3. All evidence, documentary or otherwise, resulting from this investigation is public record.

IT IS THEREFORE ORDERED THAT:

1. Plaintiffs' Motion for Summary Judgment is granted and Defendants are ordered to turn over to Plaintiffs all information which has been collected as result of the investigation which is the subject of this cause of action.

2. An evidentiary hearing will be held in the event that either party is not satisfied with the nature of the information that the Court ordered to be turned over.

3. Defendant Virden's Cross-Motion for Summary Judgment is denied.

4. This decision does not practically dispose of the merits of the action, involves a controlling question of law as to which there is substantial ground for the difference of opinion, and an immediate appeal from this order may materially advance the ultimate termination of this litigation, therefore leave to file an interloculatory appeal is granted.

George P. Eichwald
District Judge

Threet told me that offering an appeal was customary. And we could present more proof in our requested evidentiary hearing.

## *THE FOG COMES ON LITTLE CAT FEET*

Carl Sandburg, who wrote poetically about fog, would not have been inspired by New Mexico's FOG - Foundation for Open Government. As may be recalled, they had already tried to squash my case in 2008, in the forms of their attorney, Pat Rogers, and their Director, Leonard DeLayo. I had not heard from them since; my case apparently assigned to permanent limbo.

But by 2010, things had changed. DeLayo was replaced by non-attorney Sarah Welsh. So, on March 2, 2010, I called her and explained the political stalemate with her board (still the same people back then, including Pat Rogers); and sent her a copy of *MegaHoax* and an overview of the Billy the Kid Case hoax and the IPRA litigation.

On March 19, 2010, I made a formal request for FOG to join my case as "friend of the court" (amicus curiae); and I provided our "Motion for Summary Judgment" and Judge George Eichwald's March 12, 2010 "Order" for records turn-over. I heard nothing.

On March 25th, I called. Welsh said FOG's board did not want to join "just to pat the judge on the back." They wanted a legal reason. I put her in touch with Attorney Threet. Threet gave her a "legal reason": FOG could join an "ongoing matter."

There was again silence. On April 23rd, I called Sarah Welsh. She said FOG *might* join if we filed a "Motion for Contempt." Left hanging, of course, was that FOG *had already joined me* in 2008. Then, Sarah Welsh vaporized into silence of little, FOGy, cat feet.

So FOG averted giving my case the publicity of their joining the litigation, which could have ended it through public outcry. But that would have perturbed their "friends."

And still - though I had done all the work for the litigation and had paid all the costs - it did not occur to me that it was odd that my co-plaintiff, Scot Stinnett - there because he was a FOG founder and member, who cared so much about IPRA law - had done nothing to bring in his organization. Instead, I continued to call Stinnett and rant about New Mexico's corruption.

# THE FIFTH DIMENSION

Modern quantum physics debates the number of dimensions in our universe. Four are known: three spatial dimensions, and a fourth for time. But I discovered the fifth dimension. It is "legal time;" and it flows unrelated to fourth dimensional time.

Albert Einstein dramatized his principles of relativity by dramatized scenarios, spoofed here as: "If Ann was on a spaceship traveling from Earth at almost the speed of light; and Bill stayed on Earth; after Ann's month on the spaceship, Bill's descendants would be in their fourth generation. This proves time is relative."

So here goes for fifth dimensional "legal time," which does not require leaving Earth, since it occurs right here: "If Gale was told in Sandoval County District Court on November 20, 2009 that the defendants would have 30 'legal time' days to turn over to her the forensic DNA records of Case # 2003-274, and by her January 21, 2011 evidentiary hearing - 427 fourth dimension days later - the defendants had not turned over a single record; then the 30 'legal time' days had not yet expired. This proves that Gale will need life-extension for those 30 'legal time' days to be up, so she can learn if records were handed-over by future descendants of the defendants.

In regular time, Attorney Ed Threet sent a letter of demand to Attorneys Nicole Werkmeister and Kevin Brown for the records first requested for me on April 24, 2007. According to it, the defendants had 14 days to send those records. Odds on that bet were so bad that no bookie would have taken it.

The next step - after turn-over did not happen - would be going to that evidentiary hearing ruled on by the judge.

And I contented myself with concluding that, to date, my case had proved that my defendants definitely, positively, and beyond any reasonable doubt, did not want me (or anyone) to see the forensic DNA documents of their Billy the Kid Case. And I could guess why.

But before an evidentiary hearing occurred, and in preparation for it, I accidentally cracked the Billy the Kid Case hoax.

# CHAPTER 14:

# CRACKING THE
# BILLY THE KID CASE
# HOAX

SIXTH JUDICIAL DISTRICT COURT
STATE OF NEW MEXICO
COUNTY OF GRANT

FILED
DISTRICT COURT OF
GRANT COUNTY, N.M.

04 JAN -5 PM 4:09

*Sylvia Ozaraga*
CLERK
DEPUTY

NO. MS 2003-11

IN THE MATTER OF CATHERINE ANTRIM

BILLY THE KID'S PRE-HEARING BRIEF

COME NOW, Bill Robins, III and David Sandoval, of the law firm of Heard, Robins,

Cloud, Lubel & Greenwood, LLC, and on behalf of the estate of William H. Bonney, aka

"Billy the Kid", file this Pre-Hearing Brief and state as follows:

I. INTRODUCTION

The Court asked undersigned counsel to brief several questions as follows:

1. The Governor's Right to Assign an Attorney to Represent
the Interests of Billy the Kid and the Associated Zone of Public
Interest;

2. Who is the Real Party in Interest Represented by Counsel;

3. What Stake Does That Party Have in Intervening in This
Cause;

4. Billy the Kid's Interest as Defined in the Law Relating to

*the Removal of*

*llows: Point One provides*

*on 1, Point Three addresses*

*Point Five supports th*

---

# LINCOLN COUNTY SHERIFF'S OFFICE
# LINCOLN COUNTY, NEW MEXICO

Case: *William H. Bonney, a.k.a. William Antrim,
a.k.a. The Kid, a.k.a. Billy the Kid*

An Investigation into the events of April 28, 1881 through
July 14, 1881- seventy-seven days of doubt.

Just minutes after twelve, noon, on April 28, 1881, two lawmen lay dead
the courthouse in Lincoln, New Mexico, from gunshot wounds. 
the New Mexico breeze to clear the gun smoke, history was c
shooting and escape of William H. Bonney, *a.k.a.* Billy the Kid
where he awaited a date with the hangman.

The following is a thumbnail sketch of the most widely excepted a
the escape, capture and shooting death of William H. Bonny *a.k.a.*

## The Last Days of William H. Bonney

On August 17, 1877, in George Atkin's cantina near Camp Grant, Arizona
Bonney, w
"Windy"
both. It's
dubbed Ca
Kid shove
Cahill on t
jury heade
*unjustifiab*
Mexico's
rancher Jol

Tunstall an
hold mono
associates,
and vertica
powerful p
maintained

---

LINCOLN COUNTY SHERIFF'S
DEPARTMENT
Case #2003-274
Probable Cause Statement

In the struggle dubbed the "Lincoln County War", investigators soon learned that nothing
was as it seemed. As they poured through the volumes of information, documents,
paperwork, reports, county records, books and examine newly discovered evidence, it
became apparent no clear lines could be drawn as to who was working with or for whom.
What first appeared to be clear quickly became clouded as new information was
uncovered, it's difficult to judge who the "good guys" and the "bad guys" were. One
... that the Lincoln County Sheriff's Department would be on the side of the
... a duly sworn posse of Lincoln County Deputies, that shot and killed
... investigators in clean conscience can only categorize us as an

---

Welcome to the

VILLAGE OF
CAPITAN

Web site

CAPITAN VILLAGE HALL NEWS

P.O. Box 246, Capitan, NM 88316     Phone: 505-354-2247     Fax: 505-354-2713

Village Home Page | Notice Index

# Revelation Via "Billy the Kid's Pre-Hearing Brief"

*HOAXBUST: In retrospect, three of its constants should have enabled me to crack the Billy the Kid Case hoax: saying Garrett did not kill the Kid, promoting "Brushy Bill" Roberts, and linking exhumations to a governor's pardon for Billy. I had believed they were separate publicity stunts. In fact, they were inextricably connected to destroy Billy the Kid history. When I understood why, I cracked the Billy the Kid Case hoax. But first I needed a missing document. I got it by accident when preparing for possible Threet and Dunn depositions for the upcoming evidentiary hearing.*

## *YOU CAN GET THERE FROM HERE*

Even if the Billy the Kid Case hoaxers had handed over the forensic DNA records of Case # 2003-274 in my IPRA litigation, those could not have cracked the Billy the Kid Case hoax - meaning exposing its motive. Those DNA records only would expose the hoaxed forensic DNA claims and the illegality of John Miller's exhumation - but not why those records were generated.

But preparing for the evidentiary hearing, I began to write depositions. One would be for an attorney rumored to be hiding the DNA records for the defendants (Alan Morel). Another would be for a past attorney participant (Bill Robins III). So to be ready for attorney-style evasions to questions, I did extra research on the "Probable Cause Statement for Case # 2003-274" and its Homer Overton Affidavit. Originally, I got them in early 2004 from the Kennedy Han law firm attorneys. They told me they had been "Plaintiffs' Exhibits 1 and 2" for Attorney Sherry Tippett's January 5, 2004 "Brief in Chief for the Exhumation of Catherine

Antrim." I had wanted them; and did not care about getting her whole Brief, deciding it would just be her same malarkey; like in her October 10, 2003 "Exhumation Petition for Catherine Antrim." But now I wanted to have it, simply to be prepared for attorney deponents wanting to see the source of those plaintiff exhibits.

So I called Silver City Attorney Robert Scavron, part of the anti-exhumation Kennedy-Baker legal team, for a copy. He could not find it. Instead, in a storage box, he found a 15 page pleading also dated January 5, 2004, but titled "Billy the Kid's Pre-Hearing Brief." Scavron faxed it to me on Tuesday, March 23rd.

Anticipating not much, I waited till Friday, March 26th to read it. Tippett was not the writer! "Billy the Kid's Pre-Hearing Brief" was by Attorney Bill Robins III. [APPENDIX: 60; with excerpts below] Though it was another Robins channeling of dead Billy for Judge Henry Quintero, *it argued for Robins's appointment to the Billy the Kid Case by Governor Bill Richardson for the sole purpose of pardoning Billy the Kid.*

## *MY REVELATION OF MARCH 27, 2010*

The next morning I awoke to a eureka moment. I had cracked the hoax! It was 6 years, 9 months, and 22 days since that June 5, 2003 *New York Times* article announcing: "After 122 Years, The Lawmen are Still Chasing Billy the Kid." I now knew the premeditated outcome of the Billy the Kid Case hoax!

Key was Robins's "Billy the Kid's Pre-Hearing Brief," written too early for the smug perpetrators to be secretive. So Robins had outlined his and Richardson's strategy and goal for the Billy the Kid Case! *And the pardon did require the exhumations.*

I had not cracked their scheme earlier because it was unthinkable; and because it needed Robins's "Pre-Hearing Brief."

### HERE IS THE SCHEME!

**Catherine Antrim's DNA was intended to match "Brushy Bill" Roberts's DNA to "prove" that *he* was Billy the Kid! And since "Brushy" - *as Billy the Kid* - had lived a "long and law-abiding life," *he* would deserve the governor's pardon!**

**So the Billy the Kid grave had to be dug up to "prove" it had the "innocent victim" (by no DNA match to Antrim); so "Brushy" could be pardoned as the Kid to make good**

pardons denied by Governors Lew Wallace and Thomas Jewett Mabry. And, if "Brushy" was dug up, his DNA would match any DNA the hoaxers wanted: from Catherine Antrim or from the carpenter's bench to seal the deal.

So Pat Garrett *had to be a murderer*, because "Brushy" *could not die on July 14, 1881*. That made "Billy Barlow," "Brushy's" creation, the innocent victim.

So their "Brushy-Billy the Kid" would lie forever in a Hamilton, Texas, grave, under the name Oliver L. Roberts.

So the actual DNA records had to be hidden, so the hoaxers could claim fake matchings. And once their fake version became mainstream, it would be untouchable by anyone. "Brushy Bill" Roberts would be Billy the Kid!

## HERE IS THE MOTIVE!

The Billy the Kid Case is a bizarre pay-to play. Oddball "Brushy" believer, Attorney Bill Robins III - Governor Bill Richardson's top donor - was buying himself the two prizes that "Brushy" and his author, William Morrison, had lost: "Brushy's" identity as Billy the Kid, and "Brushy's getting the Kid's gubernatorial pardon.

And the Billy the Kid Case's conspiracy theory backers, Jannay Valdez and W.C. Jameson - on-board for a show of credibility - would finally fulfill their delusional dreams.

So the Billy the Kid Case hoaxers had never intended to pardon real Billy Bonney! That was why a link between pardoning and exhuming Billy made no sense to me. But the link was obvious once the hoaxed murder scenario and the hoaxed DNA matchings made "Brushy" Billy the Kid. Then Governor Richardson could "set history straight" - with national and international "presidential" headlines - and pardon Billy the Kid as "Brushy Bill" Roberts.

So the doomsday in Arizona's Doomsday Document was the plot to fake and to hide DNA matchings. That was why, for AOL News in Prescott, Arizona, on October 23, 2006, Sederwall had announced: "What I know is not what's written in history." And he was not talking about dug-up John Miller then in the news. He was previewing "Brushy." He was impatiently and grandiosely jumping the gun to boast about the "new history" to be written by him and his colleagues for their Billy the Kid Case hoax.

## PUZZLE PIECES UNITE

With that revelation, the Billy the Kid Case claims fell into place for me, as the hoaxers' chorus of "One for all, all for one," became "'Brushy for all, all for Brushy."

In retrospect, "Brushy" as Billy was *the only outcome* which fit together the hoaxers' pseudo-history of: (1) Pat did not kill Billy; (2) exhumation would show that Billy was not in his grave and had survived; (3) "Brushy" had led a long and law abiding life; and (4) Richardson's pardon would, indeed, be based on his Billy the Kid Case "investigation," which would "prove" "Brushy" was Billy.

But that plot had never been publicly presented in toto. They had not dared! They knew "Brushy Bill" had been mocked as an imbecilic fraud since Governor Mabry had kicked out his pardon quest in 1950. But the Billy the Kid Case was just a re-run.

In retrospect, hoaxer hints were like subliminal advertising for a "Brushy Bill" pardon. And, in retrospect, those hints, made by all the central hoaxers, prove they were complicit in that nefarious scheme to swindle New Mexico out of its history.

The puzzle pieces follow in chronological order.

### SEDERWALL'S MAYOR'S REPORT

Steve Sederwall, with then Sheriff Tom Sullivan, was first to announce a "Brushy" focus. It was in his May 2003 Capitan "Mayor's Report" [APPENDIX: 5] Using "Brushy" as a justification for Case 2003-274, Sederwall claimed that Billy Barlow was in the Fort Sumner grave, and claimed that these "possibilities" justified a murder investigation against Pat Garrett, as follows:

This investigation came about after Sheriff Sullivan and I talked about a man by the name of Brushy Bill Roberts. In 1950 Roberts ["Brushy Bill"] came to the Governor of New Mexico with his attorney [sic - William Morrison, not an attorney]; saying he was Billy the Kid. He said that Pat Garrett shot a man by the name of Billy Barlow and buried his body claiming to be that of Billy the Kid. Roberts said he lived out a life within the bounds of the law under an assumed name and wanted a pardon that was promised to him by Governor Wallace.

On the surface of this story you would say "so what?" But if you look at this man's claim he is saying our Sheriff Pat Garrett is a murderer. Garrett knew the Kid and killed someone else.

What this says also is that Pete Maxwell who said the body is of The Kid is a co-conspirator in a murder. There is no statute of limitations on Murder [sic], so the Lincoln County Sheriff"'s Office has opened a case to pursue the investigation. If Brushy Bill Roberts is Billy the Kid then history changes.

## *NEW YORK TIMES* ANNOUNCEMENT

Then came the hoaxers' June 5, 2003 *New York Times* "After 122 Years, The Lawmen are Still Chasing Billy the Kid," [APPENDIX: 3] with "Dallas" attorney [really *Houston* Attorney Bill Robins III], and Jannay Valdez as a contributing "historian":

> Officials in New Mexico and Texas are working out plans to exhume and conduct genetic tests on the bodies of a woman buried in New Mexico who was believed to be the Kid's mother and a Texas man known as Brushy Bill Roberts, who claimed to be the Kid and died in 1950 at the age of 90. If test results suggest that the two were related, it would add new evidence to a long-held alternative theory that Garrett shot someone other than the Kid and led a conspiracy to cover up his crime.

And that article had included that inexplicable link to the pardon - which would turn out to be for "Brushy":

> Beyond renewing interest in the Kid saga, the possibility that testing could enlarge Garrett's reputation or destroy it has even caught the fancy of Gov. Bill Richardson of New Mexico, who has offered state aid for the investigation and a possible pardon that an earlier New Mexico governor had once promised to the Kid for a murder he committed.

## GOVERNOR RICHARDSON PRESS RELEASE

For that *New York Times* article and others, Governor Bill Richardson issued a June 10, 2003 press release. In retrospect, it had tell-tale "Brushy" features: faking "lingering questions" about the history, faking Pat Garrett as murdering an innocent victim, and linking the pardon to that "investigation." Richardson stated:

> Case number 2003-274 seeks to answer key questions that have lingered for over 120 years surrounding the life and death of Billy the Kid ... By utilizing modern forensic, DNA and crime scene techniques, the goal of the investigation is to get to the truth. In the

process, the reputation of Pat Garrett, still a hero in Lincoln County law enforcement, hangs in the balance. The question is did Sheriff Garrett kill Billy the Kid at Fort Sumner, New Mexico on July 14. 1881? ... As Governor, I will examine the events surrounding the alleged offer of a pardon to Billy the Kid by former New Mexico Governor Lew Wallace. I will evaluate the evidence uncovered and make a decision.

## "SEVENTY-SEVEN DAYS OF DOUBT" DOCUMENT

On September 3, 2008 the Probable Cause Statement authorship plot thickened with Sheriff Rick Virden's "Turn-Over" of his subpoenaed file for Case # 2003-274. Besides the final Probable Cause Statement, the file had its heretofore unknown precursor titled "Lincoln County Sheriff's Office, Lincoln County New Mexico, Case: William H. Bonney, a.k.a. William Antrim, a.k.a. The Kid, a.k.a. Billy the Kid: An Investigation into the events of April 28, 1881 through July 14, 1881 - seventy-seven days of doubt." I named it the "Seventy-Seven Days of Doubt Document." Its typed-in signers were Sheriff Sullivan and Deputy Sederwall. It is presented in full in this book's "Pretender" section, and hypothesized to be authored by Attorney Bill Robins III.

The "Seventy-Seven Days of Doubt Document" featured "Brushy Bill" Roberts, and concluded that Pat Garrett's killing of the innocent victim - named as "Brushy's" creation Billy Barlow - gave probable cause to investigate Sheriff Pat Garrett for murder. It stated:

> If Brushy Bill Roberts were William H. Bonney then one would have to assume that the body in the grave is that of Billy Barlow as Roberts claims. If that is true Sheriff Garrett could quite possibly be a coconspirator of the double murder of two lawmen that occurred during the Kid's escape from Lincoln ...
>
> Billy the Kid's mother is buried in Silver City, New Mexico. To exhume her body could provide the DNA to solve this 122-year-old mystery ... However, if Roberts is William Bonney then history should be rewritten showing what really happened in Lincoln County and Fort Sumner.

Created by the hoaxers in 2003 before my opposition was encountered, "Seventy-Seven Days" did not fear using "Brushy's survival" as legal "proof" that Garrett killed someone else on July 14, 1881. Later, this theme went defensively underground.

# ATTORNEY SHERRY TIPPETT
# SPILLS THE BEANS TOO

In Attorney Sherry Tippett's January 18, 2004 article about the Homer Overton Affidavit (with Case 2003-274's Probable Cause Statement and an exhibit for her January 5, 2004 Brief in Chief to exhume Catherine Antrim), she promoted "Brushy Bill" for *The Nation* reporter Richard Benke for his "Billy the Kid's Life and Death May Be Put to the DNA Test: Officials want to exhume the body of the outlaw's mother to test a Texas man's claim that he was Bonney." About "Brushy," Benke then wrote:

> A hearing on the exhumation petition is scheduled Jan. 27 in Silver City, where Antrim is buried. City officials there oppose disturbing the grave.
> Lincoln County Sheriff Tom Sullivan, Deputy Steve Sederwall and DeBaca County Sheriff Gary Graves are asking for the exhumation. They want to know if Antrim's DNA shows any relationship to Ollie "Brushy Bill" Roberts, a Hico, Texas, man who long claimed to be the Kid ...
> In oral histories recorded during the 1930's under the Federal Works Progress Administration, several interviewees said they doubted that Garrett shot Bonney, she said.

# *TRUE WEST* UNDER BOB BOZE BELL

By November of 2003, *True West* magazine, under Editor-in-Chief Bob Boze Bell, besides promoting the Billy the Kid Case hoax, was showcasing *The Return of the Outlaw Billy the Kid's* true-believer author, W.C. Jameson, in a debate with Pat Garrett's biographer, Leon Metz, in the article: "Was Brushy Bill Really Billy the Kid?" Jameson was quoted:

> On one side, passionate supporters of the historical status quo assert Roberts was a fraud, yet to date they have provided no logical, definitive proof ... Roberts was an illiterate man, yet he was astonishingly intimate with the people, geography, architecture and events of Lincoln County, New Mexico, in the late 1870s-early 1880s – an intimacy that could have come only from being present and involved ...
> After Roberts' image was compared to the only known photograph of Billy the Kid, one researcher concluded that William Henry Roberts was, in all likelihood, Billy the Kid, and as such, history needed to be rewritten ...

# ATTORNEY BILL ROBINS III

Attorney Bill Robins III left his own trail of "Brushy" hints. On November 19, 2003, after he joined the Antrim exhumation case, from Silver City came the newspaper statement:

> DNA testing is supposed to show whether Antrim was related to Ollie "Brushy Bill" Roberts. If Antrim is related to Roberts, that would mean Billy the Kid is buried in Hico [sic - Hamilton], Texas - not Fort Sumner.

The day before, msnbc.com's Alan Boyle had linked exhumations and pardon in: "Billy the Kid gets a lawyer: 122 years after shootout, attorney to gather information for a pardon":

> "The true story about Billy the Kid needs to be told," Robins said, "and therefore it seems to me that it would be appropriate and proper for this exhumation to go forward ... If the DNA doesn't match, and Billy the Kid was not ever buried in Fort Sumner, and in fact he did live to a ripe old age, that says a lot about what Pat Garrett did ...
> "I'm hoping that this investigation will ultimately lead to a conclusion that Billy the Kid will be pardoned," Robins said.

So Robins implied that "the *true* story about Billy the Kid" was not in recorded history. And he slipped in the possibility of "Brushy" as surviving "Billy," having lived "to a ripe old age."

By November 26, 2003, Attorney Robins, speaking for dead Billy the Kid, presented to Silver City Judge Henry Quintero his own urging to do the exhumation - first requested by Attorney Sherry Tippett - with his "In the Matter of Catherine Antrim: Billy the Kid's Unopposed Motion For Intervention and Request For Expedited Disposition" [APPENDIX: 16]. As justification for disinterring the mother, Robins alleged pretender survival :

> The investigation is at least partially directed at the determination whether Billy the Kid was indeed shot by Pat Garrett or whether he survived to live a long life in either Texas or Arizona ... Since whether he is truly buried in New Mexico can only be proven with the extraction and comparison of Ms. Antrim's DNA with that of his own, **or of anyone who laid claim to his identity** [author's boldface] the investigation ... should be allowed ...

Bill Robins III repeated his pro-"Brushy," "long and peace-abiding" argument for the exhumation in Fort Sumner. There, on February 26, 2004, he, with Attorneys David Sandoval and Mark Acuña, filed the "Tenth Judicial Court of De Baca County Case No. CV-2004-00005, Petition for the Exhumation of Billy the Kid's Remains." [APPENDIX: 19]

"Brushy Bill" Roberts makes his grand entrance under its section "IV. Historical Background," with "Brushy's" "one dark night" confabulation about the actually bright-mooned murder scene; and that "dark night" murder scene is a "Brushy" believer give-away. In retrospect, Robins's errors revealed his reading of "Brushy" literature plus his avoidance of actual Billy Bonney history. For this petition, Robins stated:

For generations now, the life of Billy the Kid has been the subject of historical debate. Perhaps the most significant lingering question involves whether Billy the Kid was indeed shot by Sheriff Pat Garrett in an ambush **one dark night** [author's boldface] in Ft. Sumner **or whether the Kid went on to live a long and peace-abiding life elsewhere**. [author's boldface]

Attorney Bill Robins III continued in that "Petition for the Exhumation of Billy the Kid's Remains" with an affectionate tip of his hat to "Ollie," rather than Oliver Roberts, stating:

The debate has been sparked at various times in the past by at least two individuals who laid claim to his identity. **Ollie** "Brushy Bill" Roberts [author's boldface] resided in Hico, Texas and claimed to be Billy the Kid. John Miller, in Arizona also died still claiming he was Billy the Kid. Co-Petitioners are in the initial phases of pursuing exhumations of these individuals as well.

Robins, in this same document, called "historical quandary" the July 14, 1881 killing of Billy the Kid - a "quandary" existing only for "Brushy" believers. Robins stated:

The investigation [Billy the Kid Case] has renewed questions as to whether Billy the Kid lies buried at the fabled grave-site in Ft. Sumner. Allowing the exhumation of the remains at Ft. Sumner grave site for extraction of DNA to be compared with that of Ms. Antrim's will likely finally provide definitive answers to this **historical quandary**. [author's boldface]

Thus, contemplate this mind-twister: When Attorney Bill Robins III's spoke for dead Billy the Kid, channeled, talking, dead Billy was actually channeled, dead, talking "Brushy Bill" Roberts! So dead 'Brushy" was seeking *his* pardon, while *pretending* to be real Billy Bonney, by using demon-possessed Attorney Bill Robins's tongue in Silver City and Fort Sumner courts! Wow!

## PROFESSOR PAUL HUTTON

The hoax's most blatant promotion of "Brushy Bill" as Billy was by its "official historian," University of New Mexico history professor Paul Hutton, who authored and co-produced the August 2004, History Channel program, titled "Investigating History: Billy the Kid." Interviewed, on April 24, 2004, for the *Albuquerque Journal*, Hutton set the stage with reporter Rick Nathanson:

> And people are always intrigued by mystery, and this has always been one of the great mysteries of the Old West. **The great mystery in this case is, of course, who is buried in Billy the Kid's grave in Fort Sumner.** [author's boldface]

Hutton's TV program features "Brushy's" credibility as Billy. As William Morrison's *Alias Billy the Kid* looms on-screen, Paul Hutton narrates: "Over the years that story has gained some credence." And W.C. Jameson appears to give the lies that the "Coroner's Jury Report was never found," and that there was "no evidence jurymen saw the body." Sederwall, as a "Capitan Mayor," adds, "If "Brushy Bill" is Billy the Kid, it comes down to this ... Garrett had to have let him escape in Fort Sumner."

As to the pardon, narrator Hutton states: "New Mexico Governor Bill Richardson is ready to make things right." Then, Richardson himself says: "I might pardon him." But *that* will be based on [Attorney Bill] Robins's "investigation."

## GOVERNOR RICHARDSON TO JAY MILLER

As mentioned, in January of 2006, Richardson offered journalist, Jay Miller, the directorship of a million dollar tourism division for Billy the Kid if he could work with Attorney Bill Robins III. Why a Texas attorney was part of the Kid's tourism becomes clear with a premeditated "Brushy" as Billy goal. "Brushy's" Texas was to join New Mexico's Old West tourism!

# EMILY FROM IDAHO

After Tom Sullivan and Steve Sederwall returned to New Mexico from the Cannes Film Festival - with its showing of Anne Feinsilber's "Requiem for Billy the Kid" movie inspired by Case # 2003-274's pretender claims - the hoaxers' attempts to solicit red carpet treatment were linked to making public their "Brushy" plan. The mouthpiece of that thrust was Emily-from-Idaho.

On June 2, 2006, in a *RuidosoNews.com*, letter to the editors, Emily C. Smith, calling herself a "research historian from Hayden Lake, Idaho," sounding much like Sederwall, presented a bizarre scenario as apparent sweetener for "Brushy" as Billy: New Mexico and Texas would share the Billy the Kid history.

To be recalled is that, by June 2, 2006, Steve Sederwall and Tom Sullivan were confident of being freed from their Arizona, John Miller, exhumation legal woes. Next on their agenda was trying to dig in "Brushy's" grave. So Emily-from-Idaho was giving an advertisement that proved to be the goal of the Billy the Kid Case hoax:

Tom Sullivan, Lincoln County retired sheriff, and Steve Sederwall participated in the making of a Western documentary, *Requiem for Billy the Kid*, directed by Anne Feinsilber. The film investigates the questioned death of Billy the Kid by Pat Garrett on July 14, 1881 ...

Old myths perpetuated by a book authored by Pat Garrett himself and a handful of in-the-box-thinking historians would have us believe Billy was killed by his friend, Pat Garrett, at Pete Maxwell's in Fort Sumner.

In-depth, official sheriff's criminal investigation over the past four years has revealed strong supportive evidence to the contrary.

One trail of thought supported by documented evidence from such notables as Dr. Wm. V. Morrison, Dr. Jannay Valdez, Judge Bob Hefner, research historian and author Brett Hall, et al., suggests Billy lived to be an old man of 90, dying in the street of Hico, Texas, under the assumed name of Brushy Bill Roberts.

How wonderful it would be if New Mexico and Texas would partner to creatively embrace the ongoing criminal investigation of the legend of Billy the Kid, for Billy belonged to both, and there is much for each to share and to profit in both his life and his death.

## U.S. MARSHALS SERVICE HISTORIAN DAVID TURK

When I finally got a version of U.S. Marshals Service Historian David Turk's *"Billy the Kid and the U.S. Marshals Service"* in a February 2007 *Wild West* magazine, I confirmed Turk's conspiracy theory inclinations about Billy the Kid's killing. His "Brushy" hint concerns an escapee living for "decades" post-Garrett killing. It was shades of Attorney Bill Robins III's mention of a survivor's "long and law abiding life!" Turk wrote:

> That traditional account [of the killing] - as told by Garrett himself (with the help of a ghostwriter) in the *Authentic Life of Billy, the Kid* - has been questioned many times over the years with some accounts suggesting that the Kid got away to live another day or decades, and others indicating that somebody else besides the Kid died in Maxwell's bedroom.

And David Turk's contribution to the "Probable Cause Statement" for Case 2003-274 reflected "pretender beliefs by implicating Garrett, and presenting the Kid's escape and survival:

> Historian for the United States Marshal's Service has pointed out other documents bringing into question Garrett's involvement in the Kid's escape.
>
> Mr. Turk has produced a Works Progress Administration, Federal Writer's Project interview where the following statement was taken:

> *The people around Lincoln say Garrett didn't kill Billie (sic) the Kid. John Poe was with Garrett the night he was supposed to ... said that he didn't see the man that Garrett killed ...*
>
> *The cook at Pete Maxwell's was always putting flowers on the grave and praying at it. This woman thought a lot of Billie (sic), but after Garrett killed the man at Maxwell's home her grandson was never seen again and Billie (sic) was seen by Bill Nicholi an Indian scout. Bill saw him in Mexico.*

But it took Sheriff Rick Virden's September, 2008 turn-over of his Case 2003-274 file, to get Turk's long-hidden and undoctored original: "U.S. Marshals Service and Billy the Kid." That left no doubt that Turk was an off-the-wall conspiracy theorist as well as a direct hoax participant. And "Brushy" as Billy was his goal.

# SEDERWALL AND SULLIVAN "MEMORANDUM"

On June 21, 2007, Deputies Tom Sullivan and Steve Sederwall presented their long apologia "Memorandum" [APPENDIX: 56] to Sheriff Rick Virden in attempt to block my IPRA request for their forensic DNA records.

Besides the "Memorandum's" total misinformation, was the theme that the Billy the Kid Case was to determine if the Kid lay in Fort Sumner or in Hamilton, Texas, as "Brushy." Its multiple "Attachments" featured "Brushy" as their "research." And Governor Richardson and Attorney Robins are accused by Sederwall and Sullivan of being perpetrators of the scheme.

It is excerpted below (with its original italics):

Governor Bill Richardson was prompted to call a press conference. On Tuesday, June 10, 2003 he told the world of his intentions; *"I am announcing my support and the support of the state of New Mexico for the investigation into the life and death of Henry McCarty, also known as William Bonney"... The question is did Sheriff Garrett kill Billy the Kid at Fort Sumner, New Mexico on July 14, 1881"* The Governor went on to say, *"If we can get to the truth we will"...*

On September 1, 2003, the Governor, behind the scenes, supported the investigation, by instructing Billy Sparks to hand Sheriff Sullivan three checks, from private backers, totaling $6,500.00. [Footnote 2: Three checks handed to Sheriff Sullivan in Governor's office by Billy Sparks] Standing at the threshold of the Governor's office, Sparks said, *"The governor wants to insure this investigation goes forward"...*

Without contacting us and immediately after the judge ruled, Attorney Bill Robins filed to exhume the Kid in Ft. Sumner ...

During the investigation the village of Fort Sumner, the town of Silver City and the city of Hamilton, Texas, in an effort to protect tourism, fought the investigation so DNA could not be recovered.

In the case of Hamilton, Texas, Brushy Bill Roberts died under the name of Oliver L. [sic] Roberts and his date of birth, on his official death certificate sets out he was born on December 31, 1868 [Footnote 7: Death certificate of Ollie L. Roberts], which would make the man 12 years old in 1881 when the Kid shot and killed James Bell and Robert Olinger.]

Roberts died a pauper and was buried at county expense and above his grave was placed a homemade marker of cement.

[Footnote 8: Old Tombstone of Ollie L. Roberts] However, the investigators found a new tombstone on a grave located in the middle cemetery [sic] on the first row, in a very prominent place. We wondered if that grave is empty and there only for tourists. We wondered if the man was in fact buried in the back of the cemetery.

The new marker was donated and placed by the owner of the Billy the Kid Memorial Museum in Hamilton. [Footnote 9: New Tombstone for "Henry William Roberts"] Roberts name has changed from Ollie L. Roberts as listed on his death certificate and old tombstone to *Henry W. Roberts* on the new tombstone. As well, his date of birth has changed from December 31, 1868, to December 31, 1859. This would make him 21 in 1881 rather than 12 and would coincide with the history of Billy the Kid ...

Even though Ft. Sumner and Hamilton know, in their hearts, Billy the Kid can have only one grave, they continue to fight the discovery of the truth and continue the fraud in the name of commerce.

## STEVE SEDERWALL'S DEPOSITION

Then, in his August 18, 2008 deposition, there was Steve Sederwall's strange threat to Fort Sumner resident, Scot Stinnett: "[I]f we keep pressing this thing [the Billy the Kid Case] somebody's gonna turn the lights out in Fort Sumner."

Again Sederwall "The Mouth," was hinting at the truth. If the Billy the Kid Case hoax had prevailed, the tourist industry of Fort Sumner would have ended, being based primarily on the grave of Billy the Kid being there - not in Texas!

## SHERIFF RICK VIRDEN'S "TURN-OVER"

Though concealing the forensic records of Case # 2003-274 from my IPRA records requests from April of 2007, on September 3, 2008, by subpoena demand, Sheriff Rick Virden turned over 192 pages which he alleged was his complete file.

Though expurgated of more than its forensic records, that "Turn-Over" shockingly turned out to be predominately about "Brushy Bill;" with articles, his tombstone photos, and photos of the Hamilton, Texas, gravesite. Why "Brushy" would have been featured in a murder investigation against Garrett now was clear. As dramatic, there was no information on the historical William Bonney.

## *ATTORNEY ROBINS'S PRE-HEARING BRIEF*

Attorney Bill Robins III's January 5, 2004 "Billy the Kid's Pre-Hearing Brief" presents "Brushy" as pardon-worthy Billy. (In entirety it is in APPENDIX: 60.) It shams legalities and Robins's standing in answer to Judge Henry Quintero's questions for clearing obstacles to exhuming Catherine Antrim.

By fakery, Robins argues: (1) that his appointment is legitimate (actually it was illegal as representing a corpse and by improper appointment by Richardson); (2) that dead Billy should be present in court (incarnated as Robins) to protect his "interests" - called his "legacy;" (3) that, for his "legacy," dead Billy wants his "death" clarified by exhumations; (4) that once the exhumations prove he was "Brushy Bill," Billy can get a pardon for having led a "long and law-abiding life;" (5) that Billy's mother wanted to be dug up also to "help Billy" get his "Brushy" pardon (presumably Robins could hear her voice from beyond also); (6) that the precedent-setting exhumation denial of the 1961-1962 Lois Telfer petition to dig up Billy should be ignored; and (7) that Robins's standing was justified to get "Billy" his pardon as "Brushy" – because that was what Governor Richardson intended.

The following excerpts reveal how the "Pre-Hearing Brief" cracked the Billy the Kid Case hoax for me.

**************

### BILLY THE KID'S PRE-HEARING BRIEF

COME NOW, Bill Robins, III and David Sandoval, of the law firm of Heard, Robins, Cloud, Lubel & Greenwood, LLC, and on the behalf of the estate of William H. Bonney, aka "Billy the Kid"

**[AUTHOR'S COMMENT: The Kid had no "estate," meaning posthumous property. This is sham legalize before Robins switches to representing dead Billy himself!]**

file this Pre-Hearing Brief and state as follows ...

### Point One
### Initial Discussion as to the Nature of This Proceeding

This is an interesting proceeding in that the relief sought here is not exclusively judicial ...

458

Petitioners [Sheriffs Sullivan and Graves and Deputy Sederwall - and Billy the Kid!] should thus be commended for bringing this Court into the picture and in doing so, offering the town of Silver City, a relative of another descendent buried in the cemetery, and the legal interests of Billy the Kid, an opportunity to participate in the process.

The questions the Court asked briefed, however, suggest the possibility that the court may not allow Billy the Kid to be heard.

As will be shown clearly, Billy the Kid's interests are real, legitimate, proper for consideration, and we respectively ask the Court to recognize them as such ...

To the extent that the Court remains concerned with the presence of Billy the Kid in this litigation,

it is a matter that can be more properly addressed pursuant to legal requirements of standing and intervention, which the discussion below shows the Kid satisfies ...

This inherent power must also allow the Governor to appoint attorneys to address his concerns and/or further his interests outside his immediate circle.

**[AUTHOR'S COMMENT: Robins ignores division of powers: the executive branch Governor cannot appointment to a judicial branch. A judge alone appoints to a court. But this lie leads to Robins's non sequitor leap to pardon power.]**

The governor has the "power to grant reprieves and pardons." N.M. Const. Art. V Sec. 6. Undersigned counsel intends on seeking a pardon for Billy the Kid. Certainly Governor Richardson is within his inherent appointment power to hire counsel to advise him on the merits of such a pardon.

**[AUTHOR'S COMMENT: Robins omits that pardon advising is irrelevant to court standing. His fake argument is that the governor wants to pardon Billy, so he needs him in court.]**

That the power extends to pardons of long-dead individuals is clear because our Constitution extends that power to pardon offences under the Territorial Laws of New Mexico. N.M. Const. Art. XXII Sec 5. (Footnote: Posthumous pardons are not unusual. In fact, Lenny Bruce was pardoned by Governor Patake in New York just last month.) ...

**[AUTHOR'S COMMENT: Posthumous pardons are possible, but that is irrelevant to proper standing in this court of either dead Billy or illegally appointed Robins. But Robins's fake reasoning for his presence follows; and it inadvertently cracks the Billy the Kid Case hoax.]**

The Governor has apparently deemed it necessary and appropriate to seek guidance from undersigned counsel on matters related to the Kid and potential pardon ... The governor's pardon power gives the state an interest [sic- in] legal matters involving a potential candidate for pardon ...

**[AUTHOR'S COMMENT: Robins shows Richardson's goal in is the "potential pardon" for "the Kid;" though this argument is irrelevant to Robins standing or to dead Billy's standing.]**

### Point Three
### What Interests Are of Importance Here

A. *The Law of Standing*

As has been established, this is an action in equity. New Mexico's Supreme Court wrote: "The equity right of intervention in proper cases has always been recognized. The equitable test is, 'Does the intervener stand to gain or lose by the judgment ...' "

> **[AUTHOR'S COMMENT: The actual and failed test is that Robins has no client to have any interest – or to be in court.]**

Billy the Kid's interest here is his legacy.

> **[AUTHOR'S COMMENT: This begins Robins's segue into channeled Billy wanting his pardon.]**

As noted in previous briefing the very question of his life and death will be impacted by the results of the Petitioners' investigation.

> **[AUTHOR'S COMMENT: Robins is entering "Brushy" territory by adding "death." Billy's killing by Garrett *should* be irrelevant to pardon - unless Billy survived *July 14, 1881*! ]**

### B. *The Planned Request For Pardon Confers Standing Here*

Undersigned counsel intends to ask Governor Richardson that he pardon Billy the kid for the murder conviction of Sheriff Brady on several known bases including the fact that then Territorial Governor Lew Wallace reneged on his promise to pardon the Kid.

> **[AUTHOR'S COMMENT: Until now Robins seemed to be talking about Billy Bonney's pardon. Now he segues to pretenders - as if one *is* Billy. So the pardon he is discussing is not for real Billy at all!]**

There were at least two individuals that laid claim to Billy the Kid's identity years after his alleged shooting by Garrett. **Both of them apparently led long and peaceful and crime-free lives ...** [author's boldface]

The reasons that the exhumation is sought is to disinter the remains of Billy the Kid's mother for the extraction of Mitochondrial DNA.

As such, Ms. Antrim presents the only source of such DNA. Should the exhumation be denied, Billy the Kid will be forever denied the opportunity to make use of modern technology to shed light on his life and death.

> **[AUTHOR'S COMMENT: Do not miss that Robins's argument assumes Billy's historical death was questionable to justify his needing "the opportunity ... to shed light on his [Billy's] life and death."]**

**Should the DNA extracted from Ms. Antrim confirm that one of the potential Kids was in fact Billy the Kid, undersigned counsel will be able to make an even stronger argument for pardon by citing to the long years of law abiding life**. [author's underlined boldface]

[AUTHOR'S COMMENT: ABOVE IS THE SENTENCE THAT CRACKED THE BILLY THE KID CASE HOAX FOR ME.   It reveals the hoax's plot: prove the pretender by faking DNA, then pardon him as "Oliver "Brushy Bill" Roberts as being Billy the Kid.]

*C. A Comparison of Interests ...*

[AUTHOR'S COMMENT: Now "Billy" - as "Brushy" - will join "his" mother to "speak" about desiring to be dug up.]

As expected, the Mayor here opposes the exhumation and is positioned to present evidence in support of its objection. Whether or not that truly represents the interests of Ms. Antrim can never be known. Given the identity of the decedent and the time that has passes since her death, the Mayor cannot possibly have any direct evidence of Ms. Antrim's wishes. As such, the evidence that is presented by the Mayor can be viewed as best, supposition, or at worst, utterly unreliable.

[AUTHOR'S COMMENT: Do not miss the bizarreness of this argument. The Mayor has to protect remains in that cemetery. But Robins says the Mayor needs to mind-read corpse Catherine to find out *if she really wants to be dug up*. Or better, Robins implies, the Mayor should channel her himself - so she can speak her mind right in Court!]

One is left to question why such a party with such a remote interest and lack of express knowledge about the decedent's wishes is conferred standing while the interests of Billy the Kid go unheard if this Court denier him standing. Allowing such a party to appear and present evidence while denying the same opportunity to a party that has been appointed to represent the interests of the decedent's son does not seem prudent nor fair.

[AUTHOR'S COMMENT: This argument is so crazy that a reader might rationalize that it cannot be so crazy. It is. Robins is saying that dead Billy is more credible to let his wishes be known, than the live Mayor's obligation to protect the cemetery. And, according to Robins, he himself can tell the wishes of the dead; unlike the supernaturally limited Mayor. By this craziness, is concluded that corpse Billy the Kid has standing - meaning he is better justified to speak in Court by channeling than is the Silver City Mayor!]

## Point Four
## The *Telfer* Case and Impact on This Case

The *Telfer* case is of no major consequence here ...

Even if the body buried in Ft., Sumner cannot possibly be exhumed for comparable DNA, a denial here is not called for. As has been mentioned there are at least two other individuals who claim to have been the Kid. Surely *Telfer* would not be a binding precedent to deny exhumations of grave sites in Texas or Arizona.

[AUTHOR'S COMMENT: Robins returns to getting into pretender graves. But his argument makes no sense. Why should Catherine Antrim be dug up to compare with men easily debunked by history alone?]

## Point Five
## Exhumation is Proper

The Sheriffs invoke the jurisdiction of this Court in an attempt to exhume the remains of Catherine Antrim ...

The leading exhumation case in New Mexico is *Theodore*, 57, N.M. 434 and sets forth as follows ...

[AUTHOR'S COMMENT: The *Theodore* case has noting to do with the Antrim exhumation at hand. It is about digging up and relocating a body. Robins uses it for fake legalize to lead into fake "Factors of Public Interest."]

1st Factor Public Interest, Billy the Kid's name is forever tied to New Mexico and to that of another legendary figure of the Old West, Sheriff Pat Garrett. A commonly held version of history paints a picture of an ambush in which Garrett killed the Kid in Ft. Sumner where most believe the Kid still lies at rest. This version has been questioned. It is the investigation into whether Garrett killed the Kid that has prompted these investigators to seek exhumation.

[AUTHOR'S COMMENT: This hoaxer talk for "Brushy as Billy," as in: "This version [historical] has been questioned."

Now transparent is the Billy the Kid Case hoax's components of fake murderer Garrett, fake exhumations, and fake pretenders' credibility.]

2nd Factor, the Decedents wishes. In spite of Silver City's position to the contrary, we simply do not know what the decedent's wishes would be. Given the present circumstances, however, where her remains could possibly provide critical evidence to be used by modern day advocates to clear her son's name, one might easily surmise that Silver City's dogged attempt to resist exhumation would not be appreciated by Ms. Antrim.

[AUTHOR'S COMMENT: Here Robins is channeling Catherine Antrim to express "her wishes": she wants to "clear her son's name." The outrageousness of this preposterous argument from beyond the grave should not be missed: Catherine Antrim, channeled by Robins, wants to be dug up to "prove" that her son, Billy Bonney, was actually never-murdered "Brushy Bill" Roberts!]

3rd Factor, Surviving Relatives Wishes. There are no relatives of Ms. Antrim currently before the Court ... The closest party currently before the Court is in fact Billy the Kid as represented by the undersigned counsel. As is apparent from the arguments set forth in this brief, the kid's [sic] interests would be furthered by the exhumation ...

[AUTHOR'S COMMENT: Here Robins is shamelessly channeling dead Billy the Kid to say that HE wants his mom dug up! Like his mom, dead Billy apparently "wants his name cleared;" meaning he wants it proved that his name is "Brushy Bill," with a long, law abiding, and pardon-worthy life under his erstwhile belt!]

Billy the Kid believes that the evidence adduced at the exhumation hearing will certainly support an order of exhumation here.

[AUTHOR'S COMMENT: Oops, Robins has crossed into the "Exorcist" movie's territory. Robins has now "disappeared" entirely as an entity in the court; and only dead Billy, as "Brushy Bill," is talking now. The very creepy thought is that Bill Robins III may not be faking. Does he really think he IS "Brushy Bill" Roberts incarnate, writing the very words you have just read?]

### III. CONCLUSION

The foregoing has established that the undersigned counsel may legally and properly appear in these proceedings on behalf of, and to represent the interests of Billy the Kid. They are ready to present testimony and evidence to further support their interests that the exhumation of the Kid's mother, Ms. Catherine Antrim be allowed to proceed.

[AUTHOR'S COMMENT: Only in his feverish and delusional "Brushy Bill" dreams, has Bill Robins III established anything at all "legal" to justify his own being in the Grant County District Court representing an exhumation petitioner, or established anything resembling sane in his channeling of dead Billy the Kid as a client. One is even left wondering if Robins's phrase "They are ready ..." means himself and his dead buddy "Ollie" Roberts (creepily hovering in non-dead limbo as "Billy") are both "ready." Or Robins just means that he and his co-counsel, David Sandoval (present with his New Mexico law license and signature because Robins had only a Texas one), are ready. In that latter scenario, "ready" has to include being immune to embarrassment and deserved ridicule for being responsible for this absurd document and for the entire idiotic Billy the Kid Case hoax.)

Respectfully submitted this *5th* day of January, 2004.
Heard, Robins, Cloud, Lubel & Greenwood, L.L.P.

By: *David Sandoval*
Bill Robins III
David Sandoval
Address and Telephone Numbers
**ATTORNEYS FOR BILLY THE KID**

[AUTHOR'S COMMENT: Really - in their own boldface - Attorneys Robins and Sandoval signed this legal document as a deadman's lawyers! And, do not miss that this means for true-believer Robins, that he is actually dead "Brushy Bill" Roberts's attorney.]

[AUTHOR'S COMMENT: For irony, APPENDIX: 61 has Attorney Sherry Tippett's January 5, 2004 Brief in Chief, which led me accidentally to this Robins brief, filed on the same date. And Tippett's would not have cracked the hoax for me!]

# BILL ROBINS III AS HOAX PUPPETEER

Once the hoax was cracked, Attorney Bill Robins's strange role became clear. Geppetto carved Pinocchio, a marionette, but really wanted a living boy. Attorney Bill Robins III was the Geppetto of this Pinocchio hoax to turn wooden faker "Brushy Bill" Roberts into flesh-and-blood William H. Bonney.

Of course, Robins's actual puppet had to be potential United States president, insatiably ambitious, Governor Bill Richardson. And the strings were made of money.

I do not believe Bill Robins is a hoaxer. My bet is for his being a "Brushy" true-believer. For the Billy the Kid Case, Robins must have believed that he could achieve what no one else could: buy for "Brushy" the fulfillment of that old codger's delusion of fame and a pardon. And he, Bill Robins III, would be part of that new history.

In that sense, Bill Robins III was as much a statistical impossibility as the Billy the Kid Case promoter, as I was as that case's opponent - both of us there by unlikely attributes.

To desire and to create his pay-to-play pardon scheme - which, I believe, birthed the full-blown Billy the Kid Case hoax - Bill Robins required a combination of law degree; personal wealth; dedication to Democratic Party politics; an amateur historian's interest in the Old West, but not its history books; the mind-set of a conspiracy theorist; a conversion experience to fervid "Brushy" believer; and PR instincts to make the entire stunt of national value to his candidate, Bill Richardson.

"Anyone can buy Richardson," I had heard. And Bill Robins III was far from anyone. He was Richardson's major donor (along with his firm, Heard, Robins, Cloud, Lubel & Greenwood LLP).

What Robins apparently purchased for himself, by political contributions and outright payments, is startling and chilling. It begins with a governor, proceeds to an attorney general, and ends up with a filed murder investigation along with its law enforcement officers. Added were a history professor, judges, other attorneys, "show biz" forensic experts, and TV producers. And, as the Richardson tourism post offered to Jay Miller in 2006 implied, Robins may even have "bought" himself a place in New Mexico's "Billy the Kid" tourism.

Excluding campaign donations to Richardson for his two terms as governor and for his presidential bid, my access to Robins's direct pay-offs for the Billy the Kid Case was limited. The Sullivan-Sederwall "Memorandum" payments came to $6,500.00. Robins had bailed out Attorney Tippett for almost $1000. Later, seemingly *pro bono*, he represented hoaxer-Sheriff Gary Graves against his De Baca County recall. Someone, possibly Robins, paid (through Governor Richardson) for the Arizona Miller/Hudspeth exhumations.

As to Attorney Bill Robins's role besides dollars in the Billy the Kid Case, one can guess that its structure was the product of his brilliant mind. (His résumé lists him as graduating summa cum laude from University of Houston Law School.) Without any legal access to the graves of Billy and his mother, it was sheer genius to structure a real cold case murder investigation in order to position complicit sheriffs and a deputy to use that case's law enforcement status to claim court standing for necessary exhumations to "solve" the crime - and to access "Brushy's" grave.

And, if Robins and Richardson had brain-stormed, the obvious sheriff to prosecute *past* Lincoln County Sheriff Pat Garrett would be *the current one*: Tom Sullivan. (Or they may have built on Sullivan's and Sederwall's ongoing gambit of the deputy murders.) The sheriff in the county of Billy's grave, Gary Graves, completed the picture. It was a group marriage made in Heaven's opposite.

And everything pointed to Bill Robins III's premeditated plan of attaining the posthumous pardon for "Billy the Kid." Unabashedly, Robins admitted in the *Albuquerque Journal's* November 19, 2003, "No Kidding: Governor Taps Lawyer for Billy," by Louie Fecteau: "I think Billy should have gotten a pardon a long time ago by Lew Wallace, so I'm going to be advocating that the governor (Richardson) pardon the Kid."

But that pardon, as has been presented here, was for "Brushy Bill" as "the Kid [who] went on to live a long and peace-abiding life elsewhere;" as Robins had presented in his February 26, 2004, Fort Sumner "Petition for the Exhumation of Billy the Kid's Remains" [APPENDIX: 19].

Bill Robins III's slips of "Brushy Bill's" confabulated "one dark night" for the Garrett killing of the Kid, "Ollie" for Oliver Roberts, and history as "Pat Garrett's version," have been discussed. And that "Pat Garrett's version," with its shades of conspiracy theory, links Robins to William V. Morrison, W.C. Jameson, Frederick Bean, Judge Bob Hefner, and Jannay Valdez - all convinced that the history was "Garrett's version" - and is wrong.

# PARDON FOR "BILLY THE KID"

## CURRENT OF HISTORY

On April 23, 2010, the bell tolled again for me; this time as my own ringing telephone calling a Santa Fe contact about my having cracked the hoax. After listening, he said to me, "Then you should know this: Governor Richardson asked Jay Miller to call people to feel out their reaction to his pardoning Billy either in July during the Old West History Association Roundup meeting or on October 8th through 10th, during the "Cowboy Symposium."

The latter venue was apparently preferred because the Albuquerque balloon festival coincided; and Richardson liked the idea of using its international press presence to promote his scheme – fitting, since both locales would then have hot air. And I did not miss that Jay Miller had not called me, keeping a secret.

I was beside myself. By then, "Billy the Kid Case panic" had given me post traumatic stress disorder from years punctuated by bursts of terror at each new hoaxer move.

Trembling, I called Jay Miller, to whom I had not spoken in years; but with hope that my revelation from "Billy the Kid's Pre-Hearing Brief" would alarm him about the pardon's risk. He acted shocked that the hoaxers would hand Texas New Mexico's history; and said he would try to help.

By the next morning, I was hopeful. If Richardson made Jay Miller the pardon "feeler," maybe he was actually feeling *him* out! Did my past anti-hoax articles through Miller leave Richardson leery about new ones exposing his pardon scheme? Was Jay Miller now positioned to be the dragon slayer? I called Miller back.

He promised to tell Richardson that his "feeling out" had revealed anger as well as troubling concern about pardoning "Brushy Bill" Roberts instead of Billy Bonney.

I asked Miller if he would partner my articles to reveal: (1) damage already done to the history by Richardson's hoax (doubting the killing of Billy, doubting the validity of the Fort Sumner burial, making "Brushy Bill" credible as Billy); (2) my litigation and its hidden DNA records; (3) taxpayer money was being wasted to cover-up the hoax; and (4) exposing the hoax's pardon plot as manufacturing "Brushy" as Billy the Kid.

Miller said he would consider it after speaking to Richardson.

## *DESPERATE DAYS AND DESPERATE MONTHS*

Billy Bonney had been desperate to get his 1879 governor's pardon from Lew Wallace to save his own life. I was desperate to prevent the 2010 "Billy the Kid" pardon by Governor Richardson to save the life of real Billy's history.

Meanwhile, the hoaxers, their enablers, and duped Billy the Kid aficionados were all scampering to the pardon precipice to Governor Richardson's chant of: "Run, run, run; fun, fun, fun."

And by the time the Billy the Kid aficionados heard Richardson intoning: "My Billy the Kid Case investigation has proved that I should pardon the Kid for having led a long and law abiding life;" they would be tumbling down the precipice, hearing from above: "Texas gets Billy a s 'B r u s s h y y y.'"

One question remained: Could tiny tugboat (me) - going bump, bump, bump, bump, bump, against a huge warship (Richardson's hoax juggernaut) - actually turn that behemoth from its direction. Time would tell. But I knew I could not rely just on Jay Miller.

# CHAPTER 15:

# FIGHTING THE FAKE
# PARDON FOR A FAKE
# BILLY THE KID

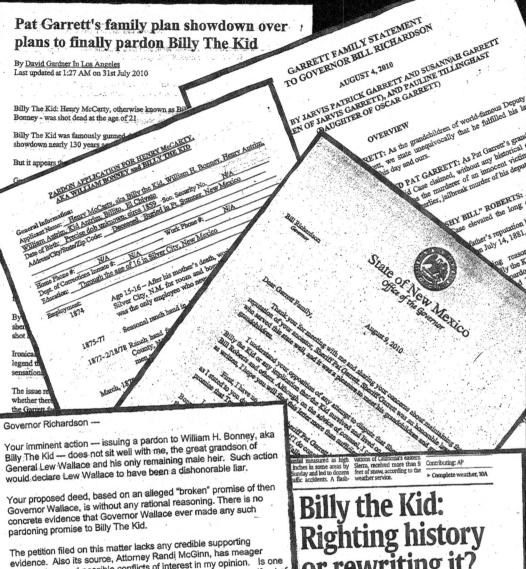

# Pat Garrett's family plan showdown over plans to finally pardon Billy The Kid

By David Gardner In Los Angeles
Last updated at 1:27 AM on 31st July 2010

Billy The Kid: Henry McCarty, otherwise known as Bi...
Bonney - was shot dead at the age of 21...

Billy The Kid was famously gumm...
showdown nearly 130 years a...

But it appears th...

## GARRETT FAMILY STATEMENT TO GOVERNOR BILL RICHARDSON
### AUGUST 4, 2010
BY JARVIS PATRICK GARRETT AND SUSANNAH GARRETT
...EN OF JARVIS GARRETT, AND PAULINE TILLINGHAST
DAUGHTER OF OSCAR GARRETT)

#### OVERVIEW

...RETT: As the grandchildren of world-famous Deputy
...ett, we state unequivocally that he fulfilled his la...
...is day and ours.

...D PAT GARRETT: As Pat Garrett's gran...
...Case claimed, without any historical...
...the murderer of an innocent victim...
...rlier, jailbreak murder of his depu...

...HY BILL" ROBERTS:...
...ase elevated the long...
...father's reputation...
...n July 14, 1881,...
...ng reaso...
...lly the K...

## PARDON APPLICATION FOR HENRY McCARTY, AKA WILLIAM BONNEY and BILLY THE KID

General Information: Applicant Name: Henry McCarty, aka Billy the Kid, William H. Bonney, Henry Antrim,
William Antrim, Kid Antrim, Billito, El Chivato — Soc. Security No. N/A
Date of Birth: Precise dob unknown, circa 1859 — New Mexico
Address/City/State/Zip Code: Deceased. Buried in Ft. Sumner, New Mexico

Home Phone #: N/A — N/A — Work Phone #: N/A
Dept. of Corrections Inmate #: N/A
Education: Through the age of 16 in Silver City, New Mexico
Age 15-16 — After his mother's death, wo...
Silver City, N.M. for room and boa...
was the only employee who nev...

Employment:
1874
1875-77 — Seasonal ranch hand in...
1877-2/1878 Ranch hand f...
County, N...
men...
March, 187...

### Dear Garrett Family,

Thank you for meeting with me and sharing your concerns about maintaining th...
...reputation of your ancestor, Sheriff Pat Garrett. Sheriff Garrett was an honorable la...
...who served this state well, and it was a pleasure to meet his grandchildren and...
...grandchildren.

I understand your opposition of any attempt to disparage the good name of...
Billy the Kid or any implication that the Kid survived and lived on...
Bill Roberts and others. Although, on the advice of counsel, I can...
...as written. I hope you will find this letter more than sufficient...

First, I have no...
...as I stated to you de...
promise that T...

*Bill Richardson Governor*

## State of New Mexico
### Office of the Governor

August 9, 2010

---

Governor Richardson —

Your imminent action — issuing a pardon to William H. Bonney, aka Billy The Kid — does not sit well with me, the great grandson of General Lew Wallace and his only remaining male heir. Such action would declare Lew Wallace to have been a dishonorable liar.

Your proposed deed, based on an alleged "broken" promise of then Governor Wallace, is without any rational reasoning. There is no concrete evidence that Governor Wallace ever made any such pardoning promise to Billy The Kid.

The petition filed on this matter lacks any credible supporting evidence. Also its source, Attorney Randi McGinn, has meager qualifications and possible conflicts of interest in my opinion. Is one to believe Ms. McGinn thought up the petition all by herself out of her compassion for someone who may have taken as many as 22 lives in federal territories two centuries back? This is not a petition. It is a deceit.

Lew Wallace was an American hero of his time. His honors are many. His statue is one of the just 100, two for each state, in the National Statuary Hall in the United States Capitol, his representing the State of Indiana.

You may have walked across that impressive rotunda. New Mexico's representatives there are Chavez and Pope, each of who would m...

---

...dall measured as high
inches in some areas by
Sunday and led to dozens
affic accidents. A flash-

vations of California's eastern
Sierra, received more than 9
feet of snow, according to the
weather service.

Contributing: AP
▶ Complete weather, 10A

## Billy the Kid: Righting history or rewriting it?

**New Mexico's governor asks public to weigh in on 130-year-old case**

By Oren Dorell
USA TODAY

Gov. Bill Richardson of New Mexico is trying to reach back more than 130 years to decide whether to pardon Billy the Kid, one of the most notorious gunslingers...

for John Tunstall, a newcomer who tried to compete with a group of businessmen and bankers who had operated a monopoly supplying local townsfolk with supplies and who controlled local government and the sheriff's office. McGinn says.

Tunstall was killed by a posse sent by Sheriff Brady, starting the so-called Lincoln County War, which killed 40 to 60. Bonney and his fellow ranch hands, deputized by a justice of the peace, formed their own posse and brought several murder suspects to jail. As a grand jury convened, Brady and his men arrived to dismiss the jury on a technicality.

Billy the Kid, circa 1880. The young outlaw was shot to death in July 1881 by Sheriff Pat Garrett.

---

## For 2nd Time in 131 Years, Billy the Kid Is Denied Pardon

By MARC LACEY

PHOENIX — In his final weeks in office, Gov. Bill Richardson of New Mexico flew to Cuba and North Korea on free-ance negotiating trips and then traveled back in history, to the Old West, to decide whether to pardon a notorious outlaw.

When Mr. Richardson announced in Santa Fe, N.M., on Friday, his last day in office, that he would not pardon Billy the Kid, he prompted sighs of relief

from descendants of those who hunted down the young gunman. He also underscored the expansive view he has long held of himself as a politician and diplomat.

"If one is to rewrite a chapter as prominent as this, there had better be certainty as to the facts, the circumstances and the motivations of those involved," Mr. Richardson said in announcing that he would not tamper with the history of a man whose life was spent "pillaging, ravag-

ing and killing the deserving and the innocent alike."

At issue was a pardon that Lew Wallace, a territorial governor, apparently offered Billy the Kid in 1879 if the outlaw would testify before a grand jury about a killing he had witnessed. The Kid testified, but Mr. Wallace never followed through.

Mr. Richardson, a history buff who has a replica of Mr. Wallace's office chair in his desk, said his reading of the historical record convinced him that a par-

don was offered, but he said he lacked enough evidence to know why Mr. Wallace had decided against the deal.

Mr. Richardson said he also factored into his decision that Billy the Kid, who also went by the names Henry McCarty and William H. Bonney, killed two lawmen after the deal fell through and he had 'escaped from jail.

Mr. Richardson's very public contemplation of a pardon provoked strong reactions in the

state — even more so . be-cause people who claim family links to the central characters in the drama still live there.

While considering the pardon, Mr. Richardson discussed the matter with three grandchildren and two great-grandchildren of Sheriff Pat Garrett, who shot Billy the Kid to death in 1881.

They had opposed the propo... pardon, as did Mr. Walla... great-grandson William... lace.

"Best to leave history alo... Susannah Garrett, a gr... daughter of the sheriff, sa... an e-mail. "May he res... peace."

Mr. Richardson said on A... "Good Morning Ameri... where he announced his ... sion, "It's living history."

...of an innocent, one-armed
lawyer. Bonney was later convicted in Brady's murder, then killed two
sheriff's deputies in an escape.

...cide by year's end.

...murder charge against him.
Wallace wrote back, saying, "I
have authority to exempt you from prosecution if you will testify to what you say...

# DESCENDANTS VERSUS HOAXERS

*HOAXBUST: The Billy the Kid Case hoax's intended gubernatorial pardon of "Brushy Bill" Roberts seemed inevitable. Richardson's publicity machine swung into action in July of 2010, with six months left to his term. I had one hope: Would impacted descendants - Pat Garrett's and Lew Wallace's - help me?*

It was beyond my ability to stop the Billy the Kid Case hoax's climactic and self-justifying 2010 pardon by Governor Bill Richardson of pretender "Brushy Bill" Roberts as Billy the Kid. But that pardon scheme also slammed two descendant families by making Sheriff Pat Garrett a murderer and Territorial Governor Lew Wallace a liar. My task was to engage their descendants to trump Richardson by what he feared most: media exposé.

# PAT GARRETT'S DESCENDANTS

## *SHERIFF PAT GARRETT'S REAL DNA*

My cracking the Billy the Kid Case hoax did not end the hoax. That took real DNA and coincidences that started in June of 2010. Coincidences began because I had no media voice to warn people that Governor Richardson's Billy the Kid pardon was the culmination of his seven year scam to pardon pretender, "Brushy Bill" Roberts. My only avenue was attending the "Wild West History Association Roundup" of July 19-22, 2010 to prophesize doom to its 300 attendees as a vendor of my *MegaHoax* book.

Terrifyingly, that meant being in Lincoln County's town of Ruidoso: home base of my defendants, Virden, Sullivan, and Sederwall. And a major Wild West History Association member was the hoax's "official historian," Professor Paul Hutton himself.

Gaining entry required contacting that "Roundup's" organizer, Bob McCubbin (one of three owners of *True West* magazine in its hoax-disseminating phase, and host of his home as film location for Paul Hutton's hoaxing TV program: "Investigating History: Billy the Kid"). Reverting for me to his 2003 anti-hoax stance (calling it "an insult to history"), McCubbin acted friendly and chatty; assuring me that Paul Hutton would not be attending. And John Henry Tunstall's family was coming from London. And Paulita Maxwell's granddaughter might come too. Then McCubbin said: "The grandchildren of Pat Garrett will be coming too."

"What!!!?" I exclaimed. "Grandchildren of Pat Garrett!!!? Where do they live?"

McCubbin said - probably regretting his slip - "Albuquerque and Santa Fe." So, knowing my years of fighting a Garrett hoax, he had concealed that Garrett's kin lived mere miles from me.

And they were grandchildren - not great-grandchildren as one would expect - because Pat Garrett had eight children; with the youngest, Jarvis, being only three when Garrett was murdered in 1908. Jarvis remarried late in life, and had these two children, whom fate had now potentially picked to save Pat's reputation.

Granddaughter, Susannah Floyd Garrett, lived in Santa Fe. I e-mailed her. Her e-mail answers all ended with a poignant, pre-printed, Albert Camus quote: "Live to the point of tears."

Susannah and I planned to meet for lunch on June 30th at Old Town Santa Fe's La Fonda restaurant - the starting point of Billy the Kid and Pat Garrett history; where Alexander McSween and John Henry Tunstall first dined in October of 1876, when it was the Exchange Hotel; and Tunstall was persuaded to set up his fateful mercantile and ranching business in Lincoln County.

More was happening. Apparently, I was again caught in that mysterious "current of history." From June 21-27, 2010, I was a vendor of my Billy the Kid books at the Single Action Shooting Society's "End of Trail" show near Albuquerque. Society members came dressed in Old West outfits to its re-created Western town for shooting contests and exhibits.

At my booth, with its life-sized blow-up photo of Billy the Kid, stopped a slim black-mustached man in a black Stetson, whose hatband was centered by a diamond and ruby-studded star badge. He said: "You might be interested to know that I'm Pat Garrett's grandson."

I answered: "What a coincidence! I'm meeting with your sister next week." So it appears that nothing could have stopped me from meeting real Garretts right then.

His name was JP Garrett - Jarvis Patrick. JP and I talked about the hoax; and I gave him a *MegaHoax* book. We planned to meet for dinner on July 8, 2010 in preparation for our attending the "Wild West History Association Roundup" together.

## OLD WEST ROYALTY

Gentle, wise Susannah Garrett and soft-spoken, clever JP Garrett - unaware about the  hoax's insult to Pat Garrett and to their family name - wanted to end it. And they said that another Garrett grandchild - Pauline "Polly" Tillinghast, a daughter of Pat's son, Oscar - would be coming from Florida to the "Roundup."

JP chose for our first meeting the Albuquerque area, hacienda-style El Pinto restaurant. As taciturn as Pat was reputed to be, JP spoke with the power of Old West royalty and said: "We'll make a petition against the pardon for the 'Roundup.' We'll know what side they're on. We'll contact Richardson. And tell him to stop."

After my seven years of fighting by slow erosion, JP's battering ram approach was breathtaking.

The Garretts - JP, Susannah, and Polly - and I, e-mailed each other frenetically, to devise the anti-pardon petition and to write a Garrett family letter to Bill Richardson in pardon opposition.

At the "Roundup," about a hundred attendees signed that petition, which called the pardon a publicity stunt insulting Pat Garrett, and intending to make "Brushy Bill" Billy the Kid.

After the "Roundup," things moved breathtakingly fast. But before the "Roundup," things moved quickly too.

## BIG BAD NEWS IN INDIA AND PAKISTAN

Without me or the Garretts realizing, our window of opportunity to save the history was just weeks. Richardson's publicity machine had been on the move beyond that "informal survey" by Jay Miller. India and Pakistan bit first! And the pardon was - just as I had predicted - linked to hoax premises of Garrett as a murderer, "Brushy" as Billy, and faked DNA.

On July 11, 2010 India's *Press Trust of India Hindustan Times* and Pakistan's *Daily Express* printed "Billy the Kid 'to be pardoned.'" It stated:

Billy the Kid was 19th century America's most infamous frontier outlaw who killed 21 men in Lincoln County War. Now, the Wild West's "Robin Hood" may get a posthumous pardon, 129 years after he was supposedly gunned down by Sheriff Pat Garrett, a media report said. Experts and historians believe the outlaw may not have been the man who died in Fort Sumner, New Mexico, on July 14, 1881, in a shoot-out that has become part of frontier folklore and material for Hollywood producers.

**Instead, many now believe Garrett, a lawman who is ranked alongside Wyatt Earp, accidentally killed the wrong man and lied to cover up his mistake.**

**On hearing reports of his death, it is thought the Kid, born Henry McCarty, but also known to have used the names Henry Antrim and William H Bonney, retired as a gunslinger and fled to Texas where he outlasted both world wars and died, at the ripe old age of 90, in 1950.**

**Now, the myth surrounding the gambler, cattle rustler and outlaw, who has no known family survivors, could be laid to rest at last as forensic experts want to exhume the body of the man buried in Hamilton under the assumed name of Ollie "Brushy Bill" Roberts, the** *Daily Express* **reported.**

**Above the grave is a monument that unequivocally identifies Roberts as Billy the Kid. And, if it proves to be accurate, New Mexico Governor Bill Richardson has pledged that he will grant a formal pardon to the fugitive of many names, the report said.**

**He said: "The evidence that will clinch this will be if genetic tests match samples from another grave in Silver City, New Mexico, we believe contains the body of Billy the Kid's mother Catherine Antrim."** [author's boldface]

## *RELIABLE ROMO AND ALBUQUERQUE JOURNAL*

On Saturday, July 24, 2010, came Richardson's bigger salvo; fired right after the "Wild West History Association Roundup" and on the *Albuquerque Journal's* front page by hoaxmaster reporter, Rene Romo as: "Gov. Weighs Pardon for Billy the Kid." Romo's job was to sell the pardon and do damage control spin for its Billy the Kid Case hoax to counter by misinformation my years of exposé - concealed by him. Romo wrote:

RUIDOSO- The history of Billy the Kid is fueled with enduring debates: Was he a hero fighting for justice in a corrupt landscape? Or was he a scoundrel, unworthy of respect, who sank to the level of his enemies?

It might seem politically questionable for Gov. Bill Richardson, on his way out of office, to wade into the debate, but the governor appears to be doing just that. And think of the field day his critics will have if the governor pardons a serial cop killer.

The Governor's Office confirmed that, during the spring meeting in Santa Fe, Richardson asked syndicated columnist Jay Miller to put out feelers to historians and others enthralled with the history of the Lincoln County War and to assess the reaction to a pardon for the Kid.

After the Lincoln County War, Gov. Lew Wallace offered to pardon the Kid if he testified about heinous crimes. The Kid did, but Wallace never held up his end of the bargain, and the outlaw subsequently killed two Lincoln County deputies in his infamous escape from the Lincoln County jail.

A spokeswoman for the governor said last week that there's nothing new about Richardson's consideration of the pardon and the idea just "came up" during the meeting with [Jay] Miller.

But someone close to the highly publicized Lincoln County investigation of the Kid's 1881 slaying told me he was contacted in recent months by someone from the Governor's office asking for his reaction to the idea of a pardon.

Richardson first talked about a pardon back in 2003 during a press conference in Santa Fe to announce the Lincoln County Sheriff's Department had opened an investigation into the Kid's slaying on July 14, 1881, by Sheriff Pat Garrett.

The idea, investigators said, was to try to refute, by DNA evidence, claims by several men, such as John Miller and Brushy Bill Roberts, widely regarded as imposters who professed to be the Kid after the historical record said the outlaw had been killed. Those claims, the thinking went, cast doubt on Garrett's character, and modern forensic tools could lay the stories to rest.

**[AUTHOR'S NOTE: Romo spins the hoax as a murder case against Garrett *absurdly to prove him innocent of murder.* Also added is damage-control anti-pretender spin.]**

In any event, publicity about a new investigation was said to be good for New Mexico tourism.

**[AUTHOR'S NOTE: The lie is omits that casting doubt on the history and its sites destroys tourism.]**

But critics lambasted the case. Officials in Silver City and Fort Sumner fought off legal efforts to dig up the remains of the outlaw's mother and the Kid himself in the hunt for DNA. They said the investigation just fed doubts about established history and undermined the value of Billy's Fort Sumner grave as a tourist site.

**[AUTHOR'S NOTE: Romo slyly conceals the true obstacle – unavailable real DNA - while using the hoaxer's basic excuse of recalcitrant local officials.]**

There are even disagreements about whether a pardon would boost state tourism today.

"Leave him (Billy the Kid) alone," said former Mayor Juan Chavez. "As far as pardoning, what good will it do now? He's dead."

The investigation has since ground to a halt, beset by lawsuits and the rebuffed attempt to dig up the remains of Brushy Bill.

**[AUTHOR'S NOTE: "Lawsuits" meant my IPRA litigation for their fake DNA records. Romo also conceals that "Brushy's" exhumation was refused because the hoaxers refused to provide any DNA to justify it.]**

Rene Romo was apparently at the "Wild West History Association Roundup," because he quotes attendees to make the pardon path appear as clear sailing for Richardson. Not quoted were Garretts or me. So, for the public, there was no inkling that with the pardon came destruction of the iconic history.

## BOB BOZE BELL BRINGS IN TRUE WEST

Hoax backer and *True West* magazine Editor-in-Chief Bob Boze Bell, had also laid pardon scam groundwork in his August 2010 edition by smearing me. That piece of hoaxer offal was available on the main table at the "Roundup" for attendees.

Its glossy cover headlined: "Digging Up Billy. What Happened?" Boze Bell's cover painting was lurid, with a skeletonized Billy the Kid sitting in his dug-up grave's coffin, surrounded by camera-wielding men and one, witchy, shrieking, long-blond-haired woman: obviously intended to slam me.

Inside was the six page article, by a Mark Boardman, titled "The Lunacy of Billy the Kid." For it, Boardman did not interview me. He credited Jay Miller with legitimate historical interests.

I was the "lunacy," as a conspiracy theorist with an "unhealthy obsession," who insanely mutilated the investigators' horses! (And no one - like Jay Miller or Frederick Nolan - wrote to *True West* to set straight the record about my saving the history.) And for that article, obviously, no mention was made of the hoax - or Richardson's and *True West's* central roles in it.

## GARRETT FAMILY ONSLAUGHT BEGINS

Bill Richardson, Rene Romo, Bob Boze Bell, Mark Boardman, and the eager hoaxers, could not have anticipated what their final pardon thrust of the Billy the Kid Case hoax would yield.

Sunday, July 25, 2010, the day after Romo's pardon publicity piece, the Garretts e-mailed their letter to Governor Richardson. Arguably, that marked the day the Billy the Kid Case hoax got its near-fatal blow. It stated:

REPRESENTATIVES OF THE GARRETT FAMILY

The Honorable Bill Richardson
Governor of the State of New Mexico
490 Old Santa Fe Trail, Suite 400
Santa Fe, NM 87501

Re: Possible pardon for Billy the Kid

Dear Governor Richardson:

As grandchildren of Pat Garrett, we have watched with outrage and sadness the seven year progression of the Billy the Kid Case. It came to a head in the *Albuquerque Journal* article of July 24, 2010, titled "Richardson Weighs Pardon for Billy the Kid." It is time for our response.

Before we express our opinion as to whether Billy the Kid should be granted a pardon for the crimes for which he was convicted, it is necessary to make an important distinction. Is it Brushy Bill that will be pardoned or is it William Bonney, alias Billy the Kid?

In your 2003 press release you declared your support of re-opening the investigation of the death of Billy the Kid with the use of current forensics. The case is numbered 2003-274. In that case, probable cause is claimed for the following allegations against Pat F. Garrett:

- A cold case murder investigation to be undertaken (with tax payer money) against Pat F. Garrett for the alleged murder of an innocent victim, instead of William Bonney AKA Billy the Kid, on July 14, 1881.
- Garrett as an accomplice to a double murder of Deputies Olinger and Bell claiming that Garrett hid the murder weapon for Billy's escape.
- Garrett as Escape Abettor of a condemned murderer after premeditating the murder of his own deputies, he aided and abetted the jail break escape.
- Garrett conspired to conceal his alleged crimes along with his deputies John W. Poe and Thomas McKinney and six Coroner's jurymen and the townspeople to conceal the identity of the innocent victim buried on July 15, 1881 in the Billy the Kid grave.

From the beginning, Governor Richardson, we feel as many historians feel, that you have created your own version of the facts that has nothing to do with the real history of the State of New Mexico. We are well aware that you and your associates have provided no information at all to justify a pardon. In fact, the case's only mention of a pardon was related to the long discredited Texas man named Oliver Brushy Bill Roberts. He was not Billy the Kid. In 1950 the New Mexico governor, Thomas J. Mabry, refused a pardon based on lack of evidence.

Now, if we are talking about the real Billy the Kid and NOT Brushy Bill Roberts, the comments of the historians, as quoted in the Albuquerque Journal article on Saturday, July 24, 2010, may have merit. We were at the Wild West History Association conference too. We agree this was a difficult time period in our state's history, and perhaps Billy took part of the heat for it as the identified gang leader. People feel he got treated unfairly because he was the only person tried for Brady's murder; all involved were indicted--but Billy was the only one who was still around. All the rest were either dead or had left the territory. However, Lew Wallace did not follow through with the pardon and perhaps the reasons why need to be appropriately researched and debated. There is plenty of history to make an intelligent determination regarding the question of a pardon. The real question to ask is: If Billy the Kid was living amongst us now, would you issue a pardon for someone who made his living as a thief and, more egregiously, who killed four law enforcement officers and numerous others?

In the meantime our grandfather has been accused of murder and conspiracy in the escape of Billy the Kid as set forth in public record case # 2003-274 along with other charges. Because Pat Garrett is deceased, he has not had the benefit of legal representation in these unfounded allegations. This is an abomination as well as an inexcusable defamation of a great man. This charade has done nothing but create doubt. In fact, we consider it to be a case of public slander. Therefore, we urge you to stop this pardon. Severe and irreparable damage has already been done by your public support of the 'Billy the Kid case' to our grandfather's reputation and to our family name. The history of New Mexico has been permanently disfigured by the element of doubt alone.

We are attaching signatures from a petition against your pardoning of Billy the Kid as Brushy Bill Roberts that was signed during the Wild West History Association meeting of last week. Almost 100 signatures were obtained on the petition many of whom are well known historians. A pardon for Billy is premature, but an apology to us should take place now. Please respectfully respond that you will drop this action. As Pat F. Garrett said, "Let those who doubt will".

Respectfully submitted,

Jarvis Patrick Garrett (signed)
Susan Floyd Garrett (signed)
Pauline Garrett Tillinghast (signed)

It was Cc'd to Tourism Secretary Michael Cerletti.

## *GARRETTS MERIT BIGGER PRESS*

For years, Bill Richardson had ridden Billy the Kid's coattails, but ignored famous Sheriff Pat Garrett. That was a big mistake.

On Thursday, July 29, 2010, there was to be a lunch at the La Fonda restaurant for the Tunstall and Garrett families and historian Frederick Nolan (back from that "Wild West History Association Roundup"). With inspiration born of urgency, that morning I called Santa Fe Associated Press reporter, Barry Massey, who, over the years, I kept informed about the Billy the

Kid Case hoax. I told him about the Garrett family letter. At his request, Susannah Garrett e-mailed it to him. Soon, with his photographer, he was at the La Fonda lunch to do an article.

Out by the next day, July 30, 2010, Massey's article started salvation of the true history. Titled: "Billy the Kid to be Pardoned, 130 Years Later? Lawman's Grandchildren Outraged; "Would You Issue a Pardon For Someone Who Made His Living As A Thief?" The accompanying photographs, taken at the restaurant, were of JP and Susannah Garrett; and of Billy in his tintype. Massey even included me and *MegaHoax*. He wrote:

> The showdown between frontier lawman Pat Garrett and notorious outlaw Billy the Kid has fascinated the American public for nearly 130 years with its classic, Old West storyline. As it turns out, the feud isn't completely over.
>
> New Mexico Gov. Bill Richardson is considering granting a posthumous pardon to Billy the Kid, angering descendants of Garrett who call it an insult to recognize such a violent outlaw.
>
> Three of the late lawman's grandchildren sent a letter to Richardson this week that asked him not to pardon the outlaw, saying such an act would represent an "inexcusable defamation" of Garrett.
>
> "If Billy the Kid was living amongst us now, would you issue a pardon for someone who made his living as a thief and, more egregiously, who killed four law enforcement officers and numerous others?" the Garrett family wrote.
>
> The issue has resurfaced because Richardson asked a New Mexico columnist earlier this year to check with historians to measure their support for issuing a pardon. The governor plans to meet with Garrett family members next week to discuss the issue.
>
> Garrett shot Billy the Kid down on July 14, 1881. Garrett tracked him after the outlaw escaped from the Lincoln County jail in a famous gun battle that left two deputies dead.
>
> The Kid's status as an Old West folk hero grew as countless books, films and songs were written about the gunslinger and his exploits. According to legend, he killed 21 people, one for each year of his life, but the New Mexico Tourism Department puts the total closer to nine.
>
> The pardon dispute is the latest in a long-running fight over whether Garrett shot the real Kid or someone else and then lied about it. Some history buffs claim Billy the Kid didn't die in the shootout with Garrett and landed in Texas, where he went by "Brushy Bill" Roberts and died of a heart attack at age 90 in 1950.

Richardson joined the tussle in 2003 by supporting a plan by then-Lincoln County Sheriff Tom Sullivan to reinvestigate the century-old case.

The governor said he was willing to consider a pardon for the Kid - something the outlaw hoped for but never received from New Mexico territorial Gov. Lew Wallace.

"Governor Richardson has always said that he would consider making good on Governor Wallace's promise to Billy the Kid for a pardon," Richardson spokeswoman Alarie Ray-Garcia said Thursday. "He is aware of the Garrett family's concerns and will be meeting with them next week."

Susan Floyd Garrett of Santa Fe is one of the grandchildren who signed the letter to Richardson. She said the family decided to speak out because a pardon represents a "defamation of character" to their grandfather. She described the Kid as a "gangster."

"Everybody wants to mythologize Billy the Kid," she said.

Garrett and her brother, Jarvis Patrick Garrett, met Thursday with descendants of another key figure in the Kid's story - John Henry Tunstall, a rancher whose murder in 1878 triggered a bloody feud known as the Lincoln County War. Billy the Kid, also known as William Bonney, worked as a ranch hand for Tunstall.

Hilary Tunstall-Behrens of London, a great-nephew of Tunstall, said he's not backing a modern-day pardon for the Kid.

"I wouldn't join the cause," said Tunstall-Behrens, 83. "There is so much strong feelings."

Gale Cooper, an amateur historian who lives near Albuquerque, said a pardon by Richardson would be the "culmination of the hoax that contended Pat Garrett was a nefarious killer and Billy was not buried in his grave."

Cooper has written a book, "MegaHoax," to debunk claims that Garrett killed someone other than the Kid.

## RICHARDSON CONTACTS GARRETTS

Within days of Barry Massey's article, the Garretts got their invitation to meet with Richardson on August 4, 2010 in his Governor's office in the "Round House" capitol building. That was the same room in which he; his complicit law enforcement officers; his "official historian," Professor Paul Hutton; and their first attorney, Sherry Tippett, met in June of 2003 to launch their Billy the Kid Case hoax.

Again the Garretts and I wrote feverishly. We prepared the following "Family Statement" to present at that meeting:

## GARRETT FAMILY STATEMENT
## TO GOVERNOR BILL RICHARDSON
## AUGUST 4, 2010

### SUBMITTED BY JARVIS PATRICK GARRETT AND SUSANNAH GARRETT (CHILDREN OF JARVIS GARRETT), AND PAULINE TILLINGHAST (DAUGHTER OF OSCAR GARRETT)

### OVERVIEW

REGARDING SHERIFF PAT GARRETT: As the grandchildren of world-famous Deputy U.S. Marshal and Sheriff Patrick Floyd Garrett, we state unequivocally that he fulfilled his lawman duties and was a role model for honesty in his day and ours.

REGARDING BILLY THE KID CASE AND PAT GARRETT: As Pat Garrett's grandchildren, we are aware that your seven year Billy the Kid Case claimed, without any historical or forensic evidence whatsoever, alleged that Pat Garrett was the murderer of an innocent victim instead of Billy the Kid; and was the accomplice to the Kid's earlier, jailbreak murder of his deputy guards.

We oppose those accusations as utterly false.

REGARDING BILLY THE KID CASE AND "BRUSHY BILL" ROBERTS: As Pat Garrett's grandchildren, we are aware that your Billy the Kid Case elevated the long debunked, Texas imposter, "Brushy Bill," to a possible Billy the Kid.
We state that such characterization insulted our grandfather's reputation by implying that he was a hypocritical liar who had not actually shot Billy the Kid on July 14, 1881, but claimed credit.

REGARDING PARDON OPPOSITION: For the following reasons, as Pat Garrett's grandchildren, we unequivocally oppose your proposal to pardon Billy the Kid: 1) Billy the Kid was the acknowledged murderer of four lawmen and others; 2) such pardon has implicit in it the validation of Billy the Kid Case claims against our grandfather; and 3) during the seven year duration of the Billy the Kid Case, or in any other venue held by you, no historical evidence has been presented to justify said pardon.

We state that a pardon given to Billy the Kid in those circumstances would needlessly damage New Mexico's iconic Old West history, of which our family is a part.

## RESOLUTION

We, as the grandchildren of Sheriff Pat Garrett, here meeting with you to protect his honor and our family name, solemnly and cordially request:

1) that you withdraw your pardon plans for Billy the Kid based on insufficient evidence;

2) and that you offer us an apology for the Billy the Kid Case accusations made against Pat Garrett, and which, thereby, negatively impacted our family name.

The day before the meeting, the Garrett's were forbidden to bring me as their "historical expert," on word from Alarie Ray-Garcia, Richardson's replacement for Billy Sparks (who, in 2003, had handed Sheriff Tom Sullivan $6,500 in "bribery" checks for Case 2003-274 at the governor's office). Her message was: If Gale Cooper came, the governor would refuse to meet with them.

If Richardson hoped to trick the Garretts by isolating them from me, it was too late. I even armed them with the following list:

## SOME COMMON BILLY THE KID CASE
## HOAXER TRICKS

Throughout the seven year duration of the Billy the Kid Case, the hoaxers made many different switcheroos when cornered: they use historical-sounding doubletalk, reverse their own statements, or blame a fellow hoaxer.

Some tricks that might come up in the Wednesday meeting follow. But no argument against them in the meeting. One should merely recognize, if Richardson or Robins (if there) tries them; but one should just stick to the points on the Garrett Family Statement.

TRICK: The Billy the Kid Case was done to clear Garrett's reputation.

TRUTH: You don't open a real murder investigation with a real probable cause statement (meaning the suspect appears guilty enough to be indicted) to prove someone innocent.

TRICK: There exists historical doubt about whether Garrett killed Billy.

TRUTH: All legitimate historians called the case a hoax. There is complete historical documentation that Garrett killed Billy.

TRICK: This was a legitimate forensic investigation to seek the truth.

TRUTH: There was never any valid DNA of Billy Bonney or his mother available to do a forensic investigation. They knew it. The "investigation was entirely fake.

TRICK: It wasn't me, it was him that's to blame.

TRUTH: All the hoaxers participated together, and needed the combination of their various public offices to make the hoax work.

TRICK: Ricochet verifications: one hoaxer would verify information of another – while the public didn't know they were in cahoots.

TRUTH: Know the list of major hoax players – there were many minor ones (Bill Richardson, Attorney Bill Robins III, past Sheriffs Tom Sullivan and Gary Graves, past Deputy Steve Sederwall, current Sheriff Rick Virden, University of New Mexico professor Paul Hutton, U.S. Marshals Service historian David Turk, and forensic expert Dr. Henry Lee).

TRICK: The Billy the Kid Case was done to promote NM tourism.

TRUTH: Casting doubt on the validity of the state's Old West history, vilifying famous Pat Garrett, saying that Billy is not buried in his grave, and claiming a Texas pretender was Billy, does not help NM tourism.

TRICK: Billy the Kid deserves a pardon.

TRUTH: No investigation at all was done about the real Billy Bonney and the pardon. The investigation focused only on Pat's not killing him; and on "Brushy Bill's" deserving a pardon for "a long and law-abiding life."

## SHOWDOWN IN SANTA FE

On August 4, 2010, Billy the Kid/Pat Garrett history was being made, instead of being hoaxed.

For the 11:30 AM Richardson meeting, JP Garrett brought his son, Brandon; and Polly Garrett Tillinghast brought her daughter, Laura; though Susannah's daughter, Anissah, had to stay home with their new sick kitten (on such tiny turns as feline diarrhea hinge historical events).

For their presentation, I had made folders with the "Garrett Family Statement," as well as copies of their letter to him. In addition, I had provided Richardson's own, June 10, 2003 press release accusing Pat Garrett of being a murderer.

Outside the governor's office, I waited with reporter Barry Massey, Jay Miller, and a French film crew. An hour passed.

The Garrett family emerged - without Richardson - giving interviews. JP Garrett, ever audacious, in their meeting, had even asked Richardson to sign his anti-pardon petition!

And Bill Richardson, also audacious, had blamed his accusing Garrett and promoting "Brushy Bill" on Steve Sederwall and Tom Sullivan (just like they had blamed him in their June 21, 2007 "Memorandum" for *forcing them* to do it)!

All indication was of victory: Richardson had backed down on the hoax's Garrett and "Brushy" claims.

But as a world-class negotiator, Bill Richardson grasped, in a death-grip, his last straw: blaming Lew Wallace. He told the Garretts that he *might* still grant the pardon based on that past governor's "promise" of pardon to Billy the Kid. Effectively Richardson negated their power to stop him.

## REAL MEDIA FRENZY

The media frenzy that Richardson almost achieved for himself and his pardon plot, now focused full blast on the Garrett family's showdown. Associated Press reporter, Barry Massey, led the pack with his Wednesday August 4, 2010 "NM gov meets with lawman Pat Garrett's descendants," with photo of Susannah and JP Garrett.

Massey wrote:

SANTA FE, N.M. – Nearly 130 years after Pat Garrett tracked down and killed Billy the Kid, the legendary lawman's descendants are lobbying against a posthumous pardon for the Wild West outlaw.

Three of Garrett's grandchildren and two great-grandchildren met with New Mexico Gov. Bill Richardson and his staff Wednesday to voice their objections to a pardon for the Kid, who was born William Henry McCarty but also went by the name William Bonney.

Jarvis Patrick Garrett of Albuquerque asked Richardson to sign a petition in opposition to a pardon. The governor declined but told the Garretts he's made no decision about a pardon.

"As far as I am concerned, as soon as I get his signed signature on my petition, then I'll be satisfied," Jarvis Patrick Garrett, a grandson from Albuquerque, said after the meeting.

He's gathered about 100 signatures on the petition, which was circulated at a Wild West History Association conference last month in New Mexico.

Family members said Richardson told them he was considering a pardon because he was interested in why Territorial Gov. Lew Wallace didn't follow through on a promised pardon after the Kid testified about killings that happened during the so-called Lincoln County War.

The bloody feud in southern New Mexico broke out in 1878 between two factions vying for control of mercantile and cattle trade. The Kid was later convicted of killing a sheriff during one of many gun battles between the opposing sides.

Garrett shot the Kid on July 14, 1881. Garrett tracked him to a ranch near Fort Sumner after the outlaw escaped from the Lincoln County jail in a shootout that left two deputies dead. The Kid was in jail awaiting his execution by hanging.

The Billy the Kid legend has grown because of Hollywood films, books and historical skeptics who claim that Garrett shot the wrong man and that the real Kid escaped and lived to an old age.

"There are many people who want to do revisionist history and we as Garretts don't want that to happen. We hear these lies. It's hurts us," said Tillinghast.

Alarie Ray-Garcia, a spokeswoman for Richardson, said the governor asked to meet with the Garretts to hear their concerns and "found the family to be very gracious." She confirmed that Richardson has made no decision concerning a pardon.

The Garrett family oppose a pardon because they say it would cast doubt over the honor of their grandfather and the veracity of historical accounts that he shot the outlaw.

"We have a tendency unfortunately in this country to glorify criminals," said Pauline Garrett Tillinghast of Tampa, Fla.

Richardson waded into the historical fray in 2003 by supporting a plan by southern New Mexico lawmen to reopen the case and the governor said he was willing to consider a pardon for the outlaw. Critics called it a publicity stunt. However, efforts to exhume the body of the Kid and his mother were dropped because of opposition in several New Mexico communities.

The Garretts spoke out after learning that Richardson again was considering a pardon before his term ends this year.

Although Richardson made no pledge about dropping the pardon, Tillinghast said she was relieved that Richardson told the family he considered their grandfather an honorable lawman and he accepted the traditional historical account about the Kid's death.

## *RICHARDSON RESPONDS*

Proved was that Governor Bill Richardson was no match for Old West Royalty. Five days after his Garrett family meeting - and after world-wide media trouncing - on his official stationery with statehood seal of 1912, Bill Richardson wrote a letter to the Garretts granting what they demanded.

## State of New Mexico
### Office of the Governor

Bill Richardson
*Governor*

August 9, 2010

Dear Garrett Family,

Thank you for meeting with me and sharing your concerns about maintaining the reputation of your ancestor, Sheriff Pat Garrett. Sheriff Garrett was an honorable lawman who served this state well, and it was a pleasure to meet his grandchildren and great-grandchildren.

I understand your opposition of any attempt to dispute that Sheriff Garrett killed Billy the Kid or any implication that the Kid survived and lived on as claimed by Brushy Bill Roberts and others. Although, on the advice of counsel, I cannot sign your petition as written, I hope you will find this letter more than sufficient to your request.

First, I have no doubt that Sheriff Pat Garrett killed Billy the Kid. Secondly, and as I stated to you during our meeting, if I do consider a pardon it will focus on the alleged promise that Territorial Governor Lew Wallace made to the Kid.

I appreciate your expression of trust that, if a gubernatorial pardon of William Bonney, a.k.a. Billy the Kid, is considered, that my office will be fair in its review of the historical record.

Sincerely,
Bill Richardson (signed)
Governor of New Mexico

### *"BRUSHY" BELIEVERS HOLD HOPE*

Since "Brushy Bill" Roberts's believers are sure Garrett did not kill the Kid, and that he survived as "Brushy," they knew Richardson's pardon would mean "Brushy's" at last!

They weighed in on August 14, 2010 with a *Fort Worth Star-Telegram* article by reporter, Chris Vaughn, called "Texas Town seeks New Mexico pardon for Billy the Kid."

HICO, Texas - The corner of Texas 6 and Pecan Street, in downtown Hico, is a curious place for a political rally aimed squarely at New Mexico Gov. Bill Richardson ...

Standing in front of a Billy the Kid statue, in which a likeness of the Kid is aiming a revolver at the antiques store down Pecan Street, Hico Mayor Lavern Tooley brought whatever pressure she could bear on Richardson's consideration of a pardon for the Kid, whose name was William H. Bonney, Patrick [sic] McCarty or Bill Roberts, depending on which version of history you're buying.

"In recent weeks, descendants of Pat Garrett met with you, Gov. Richardson, to make their case against a pardon," said Tooley, a school nurse by career. "I am asking for an opportunity to make the case for a pardon and explain how Billy came to spend his final years in Hico. We would be honored to entertain you as a guest of the city of Hico ..."

The folks here ... contend that Garrett shot the wrong man and that Billy the Kid died of old age in 1950 after escaping from Fort Sumner, moving to Texas and assuming the name "Brushy Bill" Roberts.

A cemetery in Hamilton, 20 miles south of Hico, has Roberts' grave, declaring that Roberts lies there.

Two towns, two Billy the Kid museums, both wanting a piece of the tourism that comes with his legend.

## NEW YORK TIMES FOR DAMAGE CONTROL

On August 15, 2010, six days after Richardson's apparent capitulation to the Garrett family, he returned to square one - the *New York Times* - now for damage control. And he shape-shifted. Once he was "a baseball draft choice for the Kansas City Athletics;" now *he* was "a history buff" for reporters Marc Lacey and Rick Scibeli (first dupe reporter, Michael Janofsky, no longer worked there). They wrote: "Old West Showdown Is Revived."

SANTA FE, N.M. — Billy the Kid is dead and buried. So is the lawman who shot him. But in this city of adobe homes and historical plaques, the past and present are sometimes as hard to separate as the Kid's finger was from his trigger.

**Gov. Bill Richardson a history buff** [author's boldface], has a special chair in his office, a facsimile of the one that a predecessor, Lew Wallace, used in the late 1800s. Mr. Richardson, his time in office dwindling fast, also has a piece of unfinished business from the Wallace administration on his desk: the proposed pardon of Billy the Kid.

In opening a review of the former territorial governor's deal to grant clemency to Billy the Kid, Mr. Richardson has revived the classic Old West showdown between the Kid and the sheriff who arrested him - and later shot him - nearly 130 years ago.

The governor sat down with three of Sheriff Pat Garrett's grandchildren and two great-grandchildren in his office recently and listened to what he described as their "heated" defense of their ancestor.

"This is our history, and it's important to New Mexico and we can't arbitrarily alter it," said Susannah Garrett, 55, a granddaughter of the sheriff.

Historical documents show that Mr. Wallace struck a deal with the Kid that if he would testify before a grand jury about a killing he had witnessed, the governor would grant him a pardon for his many crimes. Billy the Kid did testify but the pardon never came, something the outlaw grumbled about as he managed to escape the law, get caught and then escape again, only to be gunned down in the dark by the frontier lawman in 1881.

Pardons are granted by governors across the country, especially departing chief executives like Mr. Richardson, who has served eight years in office and is prevented by term limits from running again.

But the proposed clemency for Billy the Kid, who also went by the names Henry McCarty and William H. Bonney, is provoking strong reactions in this history-minded state - even more so because people who claim family links to the central characters in the drama still live here ...

This time around, Garrett descendants, fearful that their ancestor's reputation is being besmirched, are waging a public campaign to urge the governor to abandon the pardon and back the sheriff. They were particularly upset by an investigation that Mr. Richardson initially supported into whether their ancestor shot the wrong man.

"If Billy the Kid were living amongst us now, would you issue a pardon for someone who made his living as a thief and, more egregiously, who killed four law enforcement officers and numerous others?" the Garrett family wrote to Mr. Richardson last month.

But no modern-day cop killer has the romanticism attached to him that Billy the Kid does. Despite the strong objections by some, the governor is holding out the possibility of an 11th-hour pardon, which he acknowledges would be rooted both in history and publicity ...

"It will be based on the facts, on the documents, on the discussions between Lew Wallace and Billy the Kid," Mr. Richardson said in his office this week. "It's a question of whether as a governor, I would be fulfilling my obligations in the area of pardons by fulfilling this promise that was never kept."

He added, "Admittedly, this also gets good publicity for the state."

The governor's critics say it also draws more attention to Mr. Richardson, whose presidential ambitions were quashed and who had to withdraw from consideration for a post in the Obama administration because of a conflict-of-interest investigation that has since been closed ...

New Mexico leaves pardons solely up to the governor's discretion - "unrestrained by any consideration other than his conscience, wisdom and sense of public duty," the state's executive clemency guidelines say ...

Mr. Richardson says his mail shows the state about evenly split on the issue.

## JAY MILLER TRIES TO HELP

On June 23, 2010, cautiously not taking sides, Jay Miller submitted my write-up for his syndicated column, "Inside the Capitol" and his blog, insidethecapitol.blogspot.com. Titled by him, "Kid's Pardon a Publicity Stunt," it was my total exposé in one shot - but Miller took no sides. Scot Stinnett reprinted it in his next day's *De Baca County News* as "Billy the Kid historian says pardon all part of the hoax." Though he was my co-plaintiff in the anti-hoax litigation, Stinnett buried it on the third page - without mention of his own role!

Jay Miller's article stated:

SANTA FE – I recently wrote of Gov. Bill Richardson's request that I sample public sentiment concerning a pardon for Billy the Kid. Thus far, the sentiment has ranged from excitement to disgust. The following example of the latter was received from Dr. Gale Cooper, author of "MegaHoax: The Strange Plot to Exhume Billy the kid and Become President."

In the good old days (1878-2002), Billy the Kid aficionados had only one problem: to decide if he was an outlaw or a rebel with a cause.

In 2003, everything changed because of Gov. Bill Richardson's quixotic scheme to hijack Billy's history as a publicity stunt for his planned presidential run; and as an apparent favor for his major donor, Attorney Bill Robins III, an Old West buff seemingly attached to pretender "Brushy Bill" Roberts (two years old at Billy's death).

Called the Billy the Kid Case, the stunt was a real murder investigation filed in Lincoln and De Baca Counties against Pat Garrett. Why? Garrett was accused as the murderer of an innocent victim instead of Billy, on July 14, 1881, to fill the Fort Sumner grave. Why? Because "Pat Garrett did not kill Billy the Kid" grabbed headlines. Was it true? No. Billy's corpse had enough eye-witnesses (including coroner's jurymen) to rival Abraham Lincoln's lying in state.

So the endeavor was actually the most elaborate historic-forensic hoax ever perpetrated. And in its seven years, it produced no evidence to contradict established history ...

What was done? As the country's only governor selling his state's iconic history for a bowl of political porridge, Richardson – with recruited lawmen and with Bill Robins III appointed as the attorney bizarrely "speaking" for dead Billy – sought to exhume Billy and his mother to "compare DNA?"

Omitted for the public was that their grave sites were just tourist markers, and the state Medical Investigator refused digging permits based on silliness. So legal opposition in Silver City and Fort Sumner stopped that phase.

But it did not stop the hoaxers' digging. TV programs and a movie were at stake. So backhoed were Arizona pretender, John Miller, and a random man buried beside him, William Hudspeth, to compare their DNA with alleged DNA of Billy the Kid.

Where did the hoaxers get Billy's DNA? Creatively fabricating, they claimed acquisition of Billy's blood from a carpenter's bench on which Billy was allegedly laid out (abandoning their "innocent victim" ploy, and floating humorously that Billy had merely "played dead"). Flashy forensic expert, Dr. Henry Lee, used to swab the bench, and under American Academy of Forensic Sciences Ethics Committee investigation, denied making any conclusions attributed to him by the hoaxers.

What happened to the "DNA matching results?" They are concealed by the hoaxers; even defying a three year open records case. Why? Apparently the "results" are of fake Billy-bench-DNA matched to random man William Hudspeth's (no DNA came from John Miller)! ...

What about "Brushy Bill" Roberts's bones? In 2007, local officials laughed the hoaxers out of Hamilton, Texas: location of his gravesite.

Gov. Richardson is in the last gasp of his hoax: pardoning Billy. Or is it Billy? As Attorney Bill Robins III states in his exhumation petitions: "he" deserves a pardon for having led a "long and law-abiding life" as "Brushy Bill." Real Billy had a short none. And law-abiding was not his strong suit.

The only pardon in question, is whether New Mexicans should pardon Bill Richardson for seven years of using their taxpayer dollars for sheriffs' departments, district courts, and public attorneys to oppose open records act requests in an attempt to give to Texas New Mexico's Old West Billy.

## "BIG BILL" RICHARDSON'S LAST TRICK

By August of 2010, the Billy the Kid Case hoax was stripped of Garrett as a murderer and calling "Brushy" Billy the Kid. What had taken me 7 years of trying, was done by the Garrett family in about 7 weeks. But Bill Richardson held his last card: the alleged "pardon promise" of Territorial Governor Lew Wallace - the last man Richardson felt free trash as a way of getting himself into Old West history's pantheon.

And, possibly Richardson believed that his big donor, Attorney Bill Robins III, would be satisfied with a secret pay-to-play finale in which "pardoning Billy the Kid" *really* meant pardoning his man: Ollie "Brushy Bill" Roberts.

But now I had a modus operandi myself: real DNA wins! Next in line for me to contact were the descendants of Lew Wallace. I had news for them.

# LAST DITCH LAWYER FOR
# LAST DITCH PARDON

## *SUDDEN PARDON PETITION OF RANDI McGINN*

Bill Richardson's "Wallace pardon promise" had a built-in problem. With only a few months left in office, he lacked a stitch of evidence. His original plot - which I had cracked - would have used faked DNA either to deny that Billy was in the Fort Sumner grave (mother to Kid DNA matching) or to "prove" carpenter's bench Billy-blood-DNA matched "Brushy's." So the pardon was to be a setting right of Governor Thomas Mabry's "Brushy" rejection. Proving a Wallace "pardon promise" was a new kettle of fish.

So Richardson cheated, relying on his "Implied Rule" that the public were suckers; and got someone to submit *their own* pardon petition based on *their own* arguing of a "pardon promise."

Recruited by Richardson was his own attorney; who had allegedly defended him in his pay-to-play grand jury trial: Randi McGinn. In his deposition of January 6, 2011, Attorney Bill Robins said she was also *his* friend. McGinn also is married to Attorney Charlie Daniels, whom Richardson appointed as a state Supreme Court judge in November of 2007. (To be noted is that from 2003 to 2007, I asked Daniels to represent me in hoax opposition, and kept him up-to-date on the hoax. So Daniels knew about the hoax when his wife joined it.) Of course, Bill Richardson and Randi McGinn kept their hand-in-glove relationship secret. So, out of nowhere, appeared a Randi McGinn - shape-shifted in the press as an "amateur historian" who requested the pardon!

A more obvious petitioner was Attorney Bill Robins III. But by then, Richardson knew what I would do with that! So Robins may have been "channeled" by McGinn as her Petition's author.

On December 14, 2010 - only seventeen days to December 31, 2010's end of Richardson's term, and last chance to redeem his Billy the Kid Case hoax as "research" for the pardon - Attorney McGinn, on her Albuquerque law firm's official letterhead of McGinn, Carpenter, Montoya & Love, P.A., via hand-delivery to Shammara Henderson, Legal Counsel Office of the Governor, presented, by letter and attachments totaling six pages, her "Application for Pardon for Henry McCarty, aka William Bonney or Billy the Kid." It is a major hoax document, on the order of the "Probable Cause Statement."

McGinn's cover letter stated:

Dear Ms. Henderson:

Enclosed please find an application for Henry McCarty, who was known in New Mexico by the name of William Bonney and later became known as Billy the Kid.

Please let me know if I need anything further to advance this pardon application.

Best regards,
Randi McGinn

**\*\*\*\*\*\*\*\*\*\*\*\*\*\***

## PARDON APPLICATION FOR HENRY McCARTY, AKA WILLIAM BONNEY and BILLY THE KID

**General information:**

Applicant Name: Henry McCarty, aka Billy the Kid, William H. Bonney, Henry Antrim, Kid Antrim, Billito, El Chivato

Date of Birth: Precise dob unknown, circa 1859 Soc. Security No. N/A

Address/City/State/Zip Code: Deceased. Buried in Fort Sumner, New Mexico

Home Phone #: ___N/A___ Work Phone #: ___N/A___

Dept. of Corrections Inmate #: ___N/A___

Education: Through the age of 16 **[sic-15½]** in Silver City, New Mexico

Employment:

| | |
|---|---|
| 1874 | Age 15-16 **[sic-14½- 15½]** – After his mother's death, worked as a hotel employee, Silver City, N.M. for room and board and for landlord who said he was the only employee who never stole anything.**[sic-also worked at butcher shops]** |
| 1875-1877 | Seasonal ranch hand in Arizona Territory at various ranches **[sic- also a cook and petty rustler]**. |
| 1877-2/18/78 | Ranch hand for John Tunstall at the Rio Feliz Ranch in Lincoln County, N.M., until Mr. Tunstall was killed **[sic- also a Tunstall employee after the murder]** by a "posse" **[sic- was a real posse under Brady]** of armed men sent by Sheriff William Brady on February 18, 1878 |
| March, 1878 | Member of a posse called "the Regulators" to capture and arrest the men who murdered John Tunstall. Arrest warrants for the killers issued by Justice of the Peace John Bautista Wilson were withdrawn by Governor Samuel B. Axtell. |

**Crime location:**

List conviction: Only one of the 6-7 suspected shooters to be tried and convicted of murder in the shooting death of Sheriff William Brady on April 1, 1878, as Brady walked down the streets **[sic-one street]** of Lincoln, New Mexico with 3 other men to inform the assembled grand jurors [sic- no Grand Jurymen were assembled; a notice was allegedly to be posted at the court] that the grand jury investigation into the death of John Tunstall was canceled **[sic – was never canceled]** and would not occur that day. One other man, George Hindman, was also shot and died. Present to testify as witnesses before the grand jury about the killing of John Tunstall were some of the Regulators, John Middleton, Fred Waite, Frank McNab **[sic- MacNab]**, Henry Brown, Jim French, William Bonney and Rob Widenmann **[sic – they were in town to do the ambush murder; the Grand Jury was not yet in session]**.

Although 5 men were ultimately indicted for the killing of John Tunstall by the Grand Jury which re-convened **[sic-convened]** on April 13, 1878 – Jesse **[sic-Jessie]** Evans, Miguel Segovia, Frank Rivers, James J. Dolan, and Billy Matthews – none of these men were ever tried or convicted. Nor was any other person ever tried and convicted of any of the dozens of killings which occurred during the Lincoln County War between February, 1878 and March, 1879 **[sic - Lincoln County War was between July 14, 1878 to July 19, 1878]**.

Sentence: Death by hanging. Date sentenced: April 13, 1881

Date(s) probation/parole ended: N/A Shot by Sheriff Pat Garrett on July 13, 1881 **[sic- July 14, 1881 ... most famous date in the history!!!]**

List additional conviction(s) on the lines below:

None. However, killed 2 men, deputies Jim [sic- James] Bell and Bob Olinger, during his escape from custody on April 28, 1881, while awaiting imposition of the death sentence at the jail on the second floor of the Lincoln County courthouse. Shot dead by Sheriff Pat Garrett before he could be tried on those crimes. **[sic – omits other murders]**

**Questions:**

Have you met all sentencing requirements? N/A

Are you requesting restoration of firearm privileges? No State reasons __

**Additional attachments:**

1. Factual Statement of historical basis for gubernatorial pardon     and clemency.

*Randi McGinn*                          *December 14, 2010*
Pardon Applicant                        Date

**************

## Factual Basis to Pardon Billy the Kid

A promise is a promise and should be enforced. It is particularly important to enforce promises and deals made by government officials, law enforcement officers or the governor of a state made in exchange for a citizen risking his life to testify against a criminal who committed murder.

Such a promise was made by New Mexico Governor Lew Wallace **[sic – Billy thought there was a "promise;" he was likely tricked]** to the man known in New Mexico as William Bonney, aka Billy the Kid, at the end of the Lincoln County War **[sic - a year later, if made]**. Mr. Bonney kept his end of the bargain by testifying before a grand jury against the men who murdered attorney Huston Chapman on February 18, 1879. Governor Wallace did not keep his end of the deal **[sic - "deal" may have been a "trick"]**, which was to pardon Mr. Bonney for all outstanding charges, including the impending indictment related to the death of William Brady **[sic - indictments were for "Buckshot" Roberts, William Brady, George Hindman]**. This injustice should be corrected.

On February 18, 1879, the anniversary of the murder of John Tunstall, Mr. Bonney's former employer and mentor, both sides in the year-long Lincoln County War **[sic – the War lasted 6 days in July of 1878]** met to negotiate a truce **[sic – the Dolan-Billy meeting was merely a peace meeting between *them*]**. The new governor, Lew Wallace, who replaced the old, corrupt governor, Sam Axtell, on October 2 **[sic- October 1st]**, 1878, had issued an amnesty proclamation on November 13, 1878, which pardoned all offences committed during the Lincoln County War, except for those with pending prosecutions. With an indictment **[sic – indictments]** pending against him for the April 1, 1878 dea6ths of Sheriff Brady and Mr. Hindman [sic – and the April 4, 1878 murder of "Buckshot" Roberts], William Bonney was one of the few Lincoln County residents who was not given retroactive amnesty for the dozens of killings which had been committed during the conflict     **[sic - none of the McSween-side fighters were given amnesty; they left the Territory]**.

Both sides of the Lincoln County War – those on the Dolan/Murphy "House" side and those from the Tunstall/McSween/Chisum side – met after the Governor's amnesty proclamation to negotiate a treaty. **[sic - This is made up. The February 18, 1879 meeting was of Dolan and some of his men and Billy and some of his friends.]** The prime mover behind the meeting, the person who wanted peace in Lincoln County, was William Bonney, who sent a letter to the other side proposing a truce. **[sic - This is made up. The February 18, 1879 meeting was proposed by Dolan, following pressure from Susan McSween's lawyer, Huston Chapman, who was threatening litigation against Commander Dudley. Dolan, thus, first made a peace offer to her; then to Billy as arguably representing the Hispanic faction in the War.]** At the meeting, the parties agreed that the fighting would end and none of the parties would testify against any of the others, on pain of death. Unfortunately, after the written treaty was signed [sic - **This is made up**], Jesse [sic - **Jessie**] Evans and Jimmy Dolan broke out whiskey to celebrate and, in short order, there were 20 [sic - **This is made up**] armed, drunken cowboys [sic - **Dolan was no cowboy, Evans and Campbell were outlaws**] stumbling down Lincoln's one street. The only sober one was William Bonney, who did not drink alcohol.

Into this drunken celebration walked a one-armed lawyer named Huston Chapman, who was coming back from a neighbor's house [sic – **he was in town representing Susan McSween. He was coming from her house to Juan Patrón's, where he was staying**]. He was confronted on the street by drunken Billy Campbell, from the Murphy/Dolan House [sic – **Campbell was one of Jessie Evans's outlaw gang**], who pulled out his pistol, pressed it to Chapman's chest [sic – **Dolan did that**], and demanded that he "dance." When Chapman refused, he was shot from the front by Mr. Campbell and from behind by Jimmy Dolan. [sic - **This is incorrect. Dolan shot Chapman point-blank in the chest, igniting his coat; and Campbell fired at Chapman as he fell. The shots were from Chapman's front.**] He was set on fire and burned in the street where he lay.

The death of the lawyer, Chapman, finally convinced Wallace to travel to Lincoln, which he did two weeks after the shooting. Although the federal troops at the Governor's disposal were quickly able to capture Campbell, Dolan and accomplice Jesse [sic – **Jessie**] Evans, and hold them in the fort, he could not find anyone to testify against them. It was then that the Governor received a letter from W.H. Bonney stating that Mr. Bonney had been present and was an eyewitness to the shooting of the lawyer, Chapman, and, despite the risk of death, was willing to testify against the killers if the Governor would annul the pending charges against him, including the indictment for the murder of Sheriff Brady [sic – not asked for specifically in Billy's letter].

Governor Wallace wrote back to Mr. Bonney and asked to meet him at a private residence, indicating that: "I have the authority to exempt you from prosecution if you will testify to what you say you know." [**Note: This is not a promise of anything. It is Wallace's statement of his authority. It may also have been a purposefully misleading trick to imply a promise.**]

Mr. Bonney came to the private, nighttime meeting. [sic – **Justice of the Peace John Wilson was present.**] At that meeting, after representing that he had the power to give him absolute protection, Governor Wallace promised Mr. Bonney that, if he testified fully against Billy Campbell and the other shooters before the grand jury meeting in 2-3 weeks, "In return for y7our doing this, I will let you go scot free with a pardon in your pocket for all your misdeeds." [sic – **This is made up. The actual conversation is unknown. The quote is taken from a fictional article Lew Wallace wrote in 1902 – 23 years later – for *New York World Magazine*, titled "General**

Lew Wallace Writes a Romance of 'Billy the Kid' Most Famous Bandit of the Plains." It has no correct facts – even stating that the meeting occurred in Santa Fe.]

Several hours after this meeting and agreement [sic – typical hoaxer style of first making up information, later presenting it as true. McGinn – or whoever wrote this – has not proved any pardon agreement], Jimmy Dolan, Jesse [sic – Jessie] Evans and Billy Campbell "escaped" from the Fort Stanton guardhouse. [sic – Only Evans and Campbell escaped. The date was the next day: March 18th. Dolan was released legally, by habeas corpus, on April 13th.] After the escape, Mr. Bonney wrote another letter to Justice of the Peace John Wilson, where the governor was staying [sic – Wallace was staying in the Montaño family home to the east of Wilson's; the meeting was in Wilson's], asking him to find out whether, now that the prisoners had escaped, the governor was still interested in their deal. [sic – This is a lie. Billy did not cite a "deal." Billy's total letter stated: *"San Patricio Thursday 20th 1879 Friend Wilson. Please tell You know who that I do not know what to do, now as those Prisoners have escaped. So send word by bearer. a note through You it may be he has made different arrangements if not and he still wants it the same to Send :William Hudgins: as Deputy, to the Junction tomorrow at three Oclock with some men you know to be all right. Send a note telling me what to do WHBonney P.S. do not send Soldiers"*] Governor Wallace responded:

> *The escape makes no difference in arrangements. To remove all suspicions of understanding, I think it better to put the arresting party in charge of Sheriff Kimball, who shall [sic - will] be instructed to see that no violence is used. This will go to you tonight.*

[sic - Actually, with lawyer's slyness, Wallace had decisively crossed out, in his own unused draft, *"I will comply with my part if you will with yours;"* as if taking no chances by putting a "promise" in writing. So Wallace actually wrote in his first and unsent draft: *"The escape makes no difference in arrangements. ~~I will comply with my part if you will with yours~~. To remove all suspicions of ~~arrangement~~ understanding, I think it better to put the arresting party in charge of Sheriff Kimball, who will be instructed to see that no violence is used. This will go to you tonight.*]

Mr. Bonney wrote back [sic – The version provided edits and corrects Billy's grammar and punctuation]:

> *Sir. I will keep the appointment I made but be sure and have men come that you can depend on. I am not afraid to die like a man fighting but I would not like to be killed like a dog unarmed.*

*Tell Kimbal to let his men be placed around the house and for him to come in alone: and he can arrest us All I am afraid of is that in the Fort we might be ... killed through a window at night. But you can arrange that all right ... It is not my place to advise you, but I am anxious to have them caught, and perhaps know how men hide from soldiers better than you."*

Based on the plan devised with Governor Wallace to protect the safety of their eyewitness, Sheriff George Kimball **[sic – Kimbrell]** made a mock arrest of Mr. Bonney on March 23, 1879 **[sic – March 22, 1879]**. Shortly thereafter, Mr. Bonney kept his word and testified before the grand jury which, with an eyewitness, indicted Billy Campbell, Jimmy Dolan and Jesse **[sic –Jessie]** Evans for the murder of lawyer Huston Chapman.

Despite his promise **[sic – no promise has been proven here]**, Governor Wallace returned to Santa Fe without granting William Bonney a pardon. After getting the testimony he needed for the indictment, the local District Attorney William L. Rynerson did not enforce the governor's promise **[sic – the pardon had to be in writing; Wallace never put it in writing, as he did for Billy Matthews, for example]** and immediately pressed the prosecution of his eyewitness, William Bonney, even changing venue out of his hometown, Lincoln, where he was well liked by much of the citizenry. Mr. Bonney was out of jail at the time the indictments were returned in another county and was never pursued by Sheriff Kimball **[sic – Kimbrell]**, who knew firsthand of the Governor's broken promise. **[sic – This is made up. Kimbrell favored the McSween side, including Billy. There is no evidence he was privy to a pardon promise - only the fake arrest.]** Over the next 21 months, while the local and national press gave him the catchy nickname, Billy the kid, and built him into a Western legend, Mr. Bonney started a small ranch near Portales, New Mexico. **[sic – It is inexplicable where this made-up ranch came from. In Billy's December 12, 1879 letter to Wallace, Billy states: *"I had been at Sumner Since I left Lincoln making my living Gambling…"*.]**

**[sic - Omitted by McGinn – or whoever wrote this sorry mess – is Wallace's March 31, 1879 letter to Secretary of the Interior Carl Schurz, during the actual period of the alleged pardon "deal," and when Billy was in the fake arrest in jailer, Juan Patrón's house. Wallace showed his attitude of scorn and distaste about Billy, stating: *"A precious specimen nick-named "The Kid," whom the Sheriff is holding here in the Plaza, as it is called, is an object of tender regard. I heard singing and music the other night; going to the door, I found the minstrels of the village actually serenading the fellow in his prison."*]**

On December 13, 1880 **[sic - December 22, 1880 in the *Las Vegas Gazette*]**, Wallace announced a reward of $500 for the capture of the man now known as Billy the Kid. By December 24, 1880 [sic - **December 21, 1880**], Sheriff Pat Garrett and his posse had tracked William Bonney to Stinking Springs, near Ft. Sumner, where he was captured and taken into custody.

On January 1, 1881, William Bonney wrote the governor from jail asking him to come and see him/. When there was no response to the request or a second note on March 2, he wrote a third letter on March 4, 1881 [sic – **with Billy's grammar again corrected by the writer**]:

> *Dear Sir:*
>
> *... I expect you have forgotten what you promised me, this month two years ago, but I have not, and I think you had ought to have come and seen me as I requested you to. I have done everything that I promised you I would, and you have done nothing that you promised me.*
>
> *... I am not treated right by (his jailor)* [sic - **U.S. Marshal John Sherman's name is given by Billy, not his jailor's**]. *He lets every stranger that comes to see me through curiosity in to see me, but will not let a single one of my friends in, not even an attorney. I guess they mean to send me up without giving me any show ...*

There was no response to that or a fourth letter. By that time, because the story of "Billy the Kid" had captured public attention and there was pressure not to pardon an "outlaw," the governor did not keep his promise.

One month later, on April 8, 1881, Mr. Bonney was put on trial for the murder of Sheriff Brady with a recently appointed public defender, Colonel A.J. Fountain, who had just quit his job as a newspaper editor. He was convicted on April 13, 1881 [sic - **April 9, 1881**] and sentenced to death [sic - **April 13, 1881**].

The Old West wasted no time in carrying out death sentences and there was no appeal. [sic - **Billy attempted appeal with Attorney Edgar Caypless, but could not sell his horse, stolen at Stinking Springs by a Garrett posseman. The issue was money to hire Fountain for the appeal.**] Three days after his sentence, Mr. Bonney was moved to Lincoln to be hanged. There, he was held in custody in the building owned by "the House" [sic - **the House had already been sold by 1880 to Lincoln County for a new courthouse-jail**], the powerful business faction behind the killing of his former boss, rancher John Tunstall. Shortly before he was to be executed, On April 28, 1881, while Sheriff Pat Garrett was out of town, William Bonney escaped, in the process killing 2 deputies, Jim [sic – **James**] Bell and Bob Olinger, who were left to guard him. [sic – **They were Billy's regular guards that jail.**]

On July 13, Sheriff Pat Garrett carried out the death sentence [sic - **This is the most bizarre error in this document, ending suspicion of a typo** when July 13<sup>th</sup>, rather than 14<sup>th</sup>, was used earlier – missing the most famous date in Billy the Kid's history!] when he tracked Mr. Bonney to where he was hiding at the Maxwell house [sic - There is no evidence that Billy was hiding in that house, and approached it from another location] near Ft. Sumner [sic - in Fort Sumner] and shot him. William Bonney was dead at 22 [sic -21].

Submitted by: Randi McGinn             December 14, 2010

*Sources of Historical Information:*
*Joel Jacobson, "Such Men as billy the Kid"*
*Frederick Nolan: "The Billy the Kid Reader," The West of Billy the Kid"*
*Mark Lee Garner, "To Hell on a Fast Horse"*
*Pat F. Garrett's, "The Authentic Life of Billy the Kid" (additional author –*
     *Frederick Nolan*
*Interview with Drew and Elise Gomber*
*Review of Historical records, visits to scene and museums.*


## *DEBUNKING McGINN'S FAKE PARDON PETITION*

Given to the public on Richardson's gubernatorial website to justify his secretly planned pardon, the McGinn Petition - as annotated above - used familiar Billy the Kid Case hoaxer m.o. of guise of expertise (here legalize), unestablished premises used as truths, misinformation (like using Wallace's 1902 fictional newspaper "Romance of Billy the Kid" as a "pardon in the pocket" proof), faking use of historical references (here a bibliography), and historical errors. A one trick pony, it failed simply by arguing "a promise is a promise," without proving a promise ever occurred.

It is also odd in its repeat error of July 13 (rather than 14<sup>th</sup>), 1881 as Billy's death date. Even the most amateur "historian" (and the other hoaxers) would get that right. But it is a mistake that could have been made by the historically ignorant person to whom the date was meaningless, since it was not "Brushy's" bad day: Mr. Dark-and-moonless-night - Attorney Bill Robins III.

McGinn's "promise" ploy also tries to address the probable scenario of Billy being misled by sly Wallace. So McGinn calls a "trick" a promise. Not only is a trick not a promise, but all historical evidence shows that Lew Wallace never intended a pardon. An attorney so brilliant as to be presidentially appointed as prosecutor for the Abraham Lincoln murder trial, he would certainly know the territorial pardon law in 1879 - when Billy requested "annuly" of his indictments. The 1897 *Compiled Laws of New Mexico*, defined pardon under Section 3457: "Any person against whom prosecution shall have been commenced under the laws of this territory for an offence against the law, any such person may be surrendered *or* not surrendered, at the discretion of the governor, before he shall have been tried or set at liberty, or if he shall be sentenced or punished for the same." And that pardon had to be in writing to a court to effect indictment annulment or sentencing pardon. Wallace never did that.

But Lew Wallace did make clear his non-pardon intent.

On December 22, 1880, Wallace printed in the *Las Vegas Daily Gazette* his "Billy the Kid: $500 Reward." Billy was not yet captured by Garrett at Stinking Springs, so had not been tried. Obviously, Wallace did not annul Billy's indictments. .

Also on April 28, 1881, coincidentally Billy's jailbreak day, Wallace, unaware of that, gave the owner-editor of the Las Vegas *Gazette*, J.H. Koogler, his "Interview with Governor Lew Wallace on 'The Kid.'"

> The conversation drifted into the sentence of "the Kid." "It looks as though he would hang, Governor." "Yes, the chances seem good that the 13th of May would finish him." "He appears to look to you to save his neck." "Yes," said Governor Wallace smiling, "but I can't see how a fellow like him should expect any clemency from me." Although not committing himself, the general tenor of the governor's remarks indicated that he would resolutely refuse to grant "The Kid" a pardon. It would seem as though "the Kid" had undertaken to bulldoze the governor, which has not helped his chances in the slightest.

Two days later, on April 30, 1881, Wallace wrote Billy's death warrant - not a pardon - for Sheriff Pat Garrett, as follows:

*To the Sheriff of Lincoln County, New Mexico, Greeting:*

*At the March term, A.D. 1881 of the District Court for the Third Judicial District of New Mexico, held at La Mesilla in the County of Doña Ana, William Bonney alias Kid, alias William Antrim, was duly convicted of the crime of murder in the First Degree; and on the fifteenth day of said term, the same being the thirteenth day of April, A.D. 1881, the judgment and sentence of said court were pronounced against the said William Bonney, alias Kid, alias William Antrim, upon said conviction according to law: whereby the said William Bonney, alias Kid, alias William Antrim,*

*was adjudged and sentenced to be hanged by the neck until dead,
by the Sheriff of the said County of Lincoln, within said county.*

*Therefore, you the Sheriff of the said county of Lincoln, are
hereby commanded that on Friday, the thirteenth day of May, A.D.
1881, pursuant to the said judgment and sentence of the said court,
you take the said William Bonney, alias Kid, alias William
Antrim, from the county jail of the county of Lincoln where he is
now confined, to some safe and convenient place within the said
county, and there, between the hours of ten o'clock, A.M. and three
o'clock, P.M., of said day, you hang the said William Bonney, alias
Kid, alias William Antrim, by the neck until he is dead. And make
due return of your acts hereunder:*

> *Done at Santa Fe in the Territory of New
> Mexico, this 30th day of April, A.D. 1881.
> Witness my hand and the great seal
> of the Territory.*
> *Lew Wallace*
> *Governor New Mexico*

On May 3, 1881, when Wallace was aware of Billy's Lincoln
courthouse-jail escape - and again could have saved him - Wallace
printed in the *Daily New Mexican* his repeated "Billy the Kid.
$500 Reward."

On May 18, 1881, came out Wallace's interview for the
*St. Louis Daily Globe-Democrat* as "The Thug's Territory:
Stage Robbers and Cut-Throats Have Things Their Own Way in
New Mexico. Gen. Lew Wallace Anxious to Punish the Crime that
is So Prevalent - A Chapter About 'Billy the Kid.'" It stated:

DEMING, N.M. May 9, 1881. – Your correspondent ... visited
Santa Fe, and had a pleasant talk with Governor Lew Wallace ...
the Governor gave a very interesting sketch of the life of "Billy
the Kid,"

**The most noted and desperate character in New Mexico,
and who was sentenced to be hanged on the 13th inst., but
escaped by killing his guards and defying the entire
populace of Lincoln to take him, and Governor Wallace has
offered a reward of $500 for his recapture, and has a posse
consisting of seventy-five men on his trail.**

**"I deem him," said the Governor, "the most dangerous
man at large, and I hope that I will have the pleasure of
seeing him meet his just deserts for the many crimes he
has committed."** [author's boldface]

## *PRESS RELEASE FOR PARDON PETITION*

On December 16, 2010, Richardson sent out a press release to resuscitate his hoax with Attorney Randi McGinn's Petition. It was titled: "Governor Bill Richardson to Consider Billy the Kid Pardon Petition." He added a new ploy to make it go down better: calling it a "limited pardon" - only for the Sheriff Brady killing. To slip all that through, Richardson and McGinn shape-shifted to Old West history aficionados. It stated:

SANTA FE – Governor Bill Richardson today announced his office has received a formal petition for the pardon of Billy the Kid which he will consider and make a decision before the end of the year. Governor Richardson is seeking input on the petition and has set up a website and email address where history buffs, experts, and other interested parties and the general public can weigh in on its merits.

The petition centers around the widespread belief that Territorial Governor Lew Wallace promised Billy the Kid a pardon in return for damning testimony The Kid gave during a murder trial. The petition is narrow in scope and does not argue for a blanket pardon of all of Billy the Kid's activities …

"As someone who is fascinated with New Mexico's rich history, I've always been intrigued by the history of Billy the Kid and, in particular, the alleged promise of a pardon he was given by Territorial Governor Lew Wallace," Governor Richardson said. "I will diligently review this new petition and all the facts available regarding an agreement between Billy the Kid and Governor Wallace before rendering any decision" …

Independently, nationally prominent trial attorney Randi McGinn was designated to review both the history and prior petitions to ascertain whether there was sufficient basis for the matter to be seriously considered. Ms. McGinn, a New Mexico resident and western history enthusiast, agreed to undertake this voluntarily and at no cost to taxpayers. After concluding her review, Ms. McGinn submitted a formal petition on December 14, 2010 …

"I look forward to hearing what others have to say about the petition. I also hope that it will spark renewed interest in New Mexico's history and how the days of Billy the Kid and the Lincoln County War helped shape our state," Richardson added.

By December 21, 2010, J.P. Garrett wrote directly to Attorney Randi McGinn; who, one can imagine, was surprised. He stated: "I'm just an ordinary person, I don't know the law and just rely on common sense." He made clear his opposition to a pardon. He added that since New Mexico Territory was under federal law, and

Lew Wallace was federally appointed by President Hayes, a pardon had to be federal - via President Obama - not on a governor's level.

Randi McGinn answered sanctimoniously the same day by e-mail, and tried to snow JP with fake legalize, while avoiding his state versus federal argument, as follows:

Mr. Garrett –

I too am just an ordinary person. Graduate of Alamogordo High School, in the heart of Billy the Kid territory. **[AUTHOR'S NOTE: Alamogordo is not in Billy's "territory," being far south-east and across a mountain range from Lincoln.]**

New Mexico law, which is based on common law which existed in territorial days **[AUTHOR'S NOTE: She is side-stepping the territorial versus federal jurisdiction which JP rose]**, requires that the government or its officials (including a governor), must keep promises made to obtain testimony, whether the person making the promise meant the promise or was trying to "trick" the person into testifying. **[AUTHOR'S NOTE: She is herself trying to trick JP, in the same way she argued in her petition: using the "promise" as existing, but not proving that fact.]** That is true whether the promise is made to a good man or an outlaw. **[AUTHOR'S NOTE: Irrelevant comment]** The letter in which I passed on the cite to the pertinent New Mexico case law is re-copied below for your distribution list:

Mr. Garrett -

Thank you for your e-mail and for joining this fascinating historical debate on whether Governor Wallace promised M. Bonney a pardon in exchange for his testimony before the grand jury in the killing of lawyer Huston Chapman.

You are correct, there were 3 pending charges at the time of the promise. **[AUTHOR'S NOTE: McGinn repeats the typical hoaxer switcheroo of giving a made-up claim, and thereafter using it as established.]** However, the federal charges involving the death of Andrew Roberts … were dismissed for lack of jurisdiction before trial. The court then proceeded on only the state [sic – territorial] charge involving the death of Sheriff Brady, for which Mr. Bonney was convicted. I have not found any documents indicating that Mr. Bonney was ever tried for the charge involving Deputy Hindman …

This is why the petition seeks only to enforce the limited promise made by Governor Wallace **[AUTHOR'S NOTE: Switcheroo again of a made-up claim subsequently used as established]**, i.e., to grant a pardon for the one charge upon which Mr. Bonney was convicted – the killing of Sheriff

506

Brady. **[AUTHOR'S NOTE: This is a switcheroo and a lie: claiming a Wallace pardon promise, then calling it a limited "one charge" pardon – to match Richardson's next ploy to save the hoax.]** ...

My review of the historical record led me to believe that the Governor promised to annul the pending charges in exchange for Mr. Bonney's testimony before the grand jury. **[AUTHOR'S NOTE: McGinn is just paraphrasing Billy's March 13, 1879 proposal letter to Wallace.]** Mr. Bonney kept his promise, the Governor did not. **[AUTHOR'S NOTE: Switcheroo again of a made-up promise claim used as established]**

Whether trick or not, New Mexico law requires that such a promise to obtain testimony must be enforced. _State ex. rel. Plant v. Sceresse_ 84 NM 312 (1972). **[AUTHOR'S NOTE: This is fake legalize because she never proved a promise occurred. Also, she cites modern law _ex post facto_; Lew Wallace was bound by law of his day. As to that modern case - which she must have guessed JP would not look up – she is still faking. That NM Supreme Court appeal was about <u>an actual promise made by an Assistant DA to murder suspects</u>, that their testifying would not incriminate them. But he did not keep the promise. The decision stated: "[T]he Court dealt with a guilty plea resting ... on a promise by the prosecutor, later breached, that no sentence recommendation would be made. Of 'plea bargaining,' the Court said: when a plea rests in any significant degree on a promise or agreement of the prosecutor, so that it can be said to be part of the inducement or consideration, such promise must be fulfilled.' " This case does not make a trick a promise! It merely prevents a promise being used as a trick.]**

Thank you for your input on this matter. Would love to meet with you about all this at some point.

Best Regards,
Randi McGinn

Do not miss that McGinn's rigmarole was unnecessary. Richardson had said that! In his August 15, 2010, _New York Times_ "Old West Showdown Is Revived," he was quoted: "New Mexico leaves pardons solely up to the governor's discretion - 'unrestrained by any consideration other than his conscience, wisdom and sense of public duty,' the state's executive clemency guidelines say." So what was going on with a McGinn petition?

My bet was for a "Brushy" move: re-running the Mabry, 1950, pardon request, also based on a Wallace "pardon promise."

At this point, things looked bad for my stopping the Billy the Kid Case hoax. Smug Randi McGinn and smug "Big Bill" Richardson made clear that they were unfazed by Garretts, and were ready to play their Wallace card to win the game.

# LEW WALLACE'S DESCENDANT

## *GOVERNOR LEW WALLACE'S REAL DNA*

Governor Bill Richardson's mistake, even after facing the outraged Garrett family, was forgetting that there might be more, real, living, Old West DNA in the form of Wallaces.

Lew Wallace and his wife Susan had one son: Henry. Henry had two sons, one having died in World War II. The other, Lew Wallace Jr. had a son, William, and two daughters.

After my Garrett family success, I labored to find these great-grandchildren - fast. At the Indiana Historical Society, one repository of Lew Wallace's papers - including Wallace's Billy the Kid letters - no Wallace family contact had occurred for 15 years.

But from a past consultant for my Billy the Kid docufiction novel, I learned that they were alive. After many dead ends -like calling every Wallace in a possible geographic area - I located great-grandson, William N. Wallace, the last male descendant.

With trepidation, I phoned. Everything depended on him.

William N. Wallace, an author and retired *New York Times* journalist in his 80's, was imperious and abrupt (as was probably Lew himself); but was indignant about the insult to "the General," as he called his ancestor. Amusingly, William N. Wallace also referred to Richardson's office as being in the "Palace of the Governors" (as had been Lew Wallace's). And William N. Wallace's e-mail name was a *Ben-Hur* character; all leaving me feeling like I had passed through a worm-hole back to the 19th century and had contacted Lew Wallace himself.

By December 16, 2010, William N. Wallace had written to Richardson - having received from me, on August 14th, e-mailed historical "talking points" on the pardon issue (including his great-grandfather's statements), a copy of Richardson's August 9, 2010 letter to the Garrett family, and the McGinn pardon petition. He also utilized my referral to Santa Fe AP reporter Barry Massey; enlisted a "German Worldwide TV outfit;" and planned an interview with the *L.A. Times.*

So ink was barely dry on Bill Richardson's promotional *New York Times's* "Old West Showdown Is Revived," when he, Alarie-Ray Garcia, Eric Witt, and Mike Cerletti got William N. Wallace's letter. Professional journalist Wallace had written grandly:

508

Governor Richardson –

Your imminent action – issuing a pardon to William H. Bonney, aka Billy the Kid – does not sit well with me, the great grandson of General Lew Wallace and his only remaining male heir. Such action would declare Lew Wallace to have been a dishonorable liar.

Your proposed deed, based on an alleged "broken" promise of then Governor Wallace, is without any rational reasoning. There is no concrete evidence that Governor Wallace ever made any such pardoning promise to Billy the Kid.

The petition filed on this matter lacks any credible supporting evidence. Also, its source, Attorney Randi McGinn, has meager qualifications and possible conflicts of interest in my opinion. Is one to believe that Ms. McGinn thought up this petition all by herself out of her compassion for someone who may have taken as many as 22 lives in federal territories two centuries back? It is not a petition. It is a deceit.

Lew Wallace was an American hero of his time. His honors are many. His statue is one of the just 100, two for each state, in the National Statuary Hall of the United States Capitol, his representing the state of Indiana.

You may have walked across that impressive rotunda. New Mexico's representatives there are Chavez and Pope, each of who would make far more effective objects of tourism enhancement than the questionable pardon of Billy-the-Kid, a convict. Your other motives in issuing the pardon are unclear to me.

Why would a retiring governor choose to defame a distinguished predecessor 130 years later?

By your intended action, you desecrate, defile, debase and dishonor an American hero in favor of a convicted murderer.

Furthermore such an action may have no legal standing because New Mexico, at the time of Governor Wallace, was a territory, not a state, and thus under federal jurisdiction.

I intend to make public my views. (My distribution list is competitive.)

My background: Yale University Bachelor of Arts degree (major in American history); New York City Journalist, 1949-1999 (*New York Times*, 1964-1999); published author of 11 books.

William N. Wallace

## *REPORTER MASSEY WRITES AGAIN*

Santa Fe AP reporter, Barry Massey, followed his Garrett family article with an August 21, 2010 William N. Wallace one headlined: " 'Billy the Kid' pardon effort draws Wild West showdown." It popped up in remote corners like Wilkes-Barre, Pennsylvania's *The Times Leader*. Massey wrote:

SANTA FE, N.M. (AP) — New Mexico Gov. Bill Richardson has stirred up a historical hornet's nest with his talk of pardoning the Old West outlaw Billy the Kid.

The latest to come out against it is a descendant of the territorial governor who once met with the Kid but never granted him clemency 130 years ago.

William N. Wallace, great-grandson of Civil War Gen. Lew Wallace, said he sees no solid historical foundation for Richardson to offer a posthumous pardon for the Kid, also known as William H. Bonney and Kid Antrim.

"There was nothing in my lifetime knowledge of Gen. Lew Wallace, my great grandfather, that ever suggested that he intended to give William H. Bonney ... a pardon," the 86-year-old Wallace said in a telephone interview from his home in Westport, Conn.

Richardson is considering a pardon to make good on an alleged promise by Gov. Wallace to provide some form of clemency for the Kid in exchange for his testimony about killings during the Lincoln County War ...

The historical record surrounding the supposedly promised pardon - like many events during New Mexico's turbulent frontier days - is ambiguous and open to conflicting views.

There's no written documents "pertaining in any way" to a pardon in the archive of Wallace's papers maintained by the Indiana Historical Society, according to staff members who sent an e-mail and letter to Richardson last week.

"If Gen. Wallace did not intend to give William H. Bonney a pardon, there is no reason why Gov. Richardson should consider giving William H. Bonney, a murderer, a pardon," said Wallace's great-grandson, a retired New York Times sports writer.

Descendants of Sheriff Pat Garrett - the lawman who shot and killed the Kid on July 14, 1881 - met with Richardson earlier this month to oppose a pardon. The governor told them he accepts historical accounts of the Kid's death.

Richardson has made no decision, said chief of staff Eric Witt. Before the governor would issue any pardon, Witt said, he'd start a formal inquiry and solicit comments from historians and others. The governor's term runs through Dec. 31.

Wallace went to New Mexico in 1878 to help bring an end to the violence of the Lincoln County War. After arriving, he offered general amnesty to those involved in the bloodbath unless they already were under indictment.

That excluded the Kid, who faced murder charges, including for killing a Lincoln County sheriff.

A tantalizing part of the pardon question is a clandestine meeting that Wallace had with the Kid in Lincoln in March 1879.

Letters written by the Kid leave no doubt the Kid wanted Wallace to at least grant him immunity from prosecution if he agreed to testify about killings he had witnessed.

The letters suggest the Kid was looking for a way out of a life of crime. Wallace, in arranging the meeting, responded to the Kid: "I have authority to exempt you from prosecution if you will testify to what you say you know."

The Kid delivered on his testimony. But Wallace never granted any form of clemency, even after the Kid was later convicted of murder and sentenced to hang.

As the Kid awaited his execution in 1881 - and as Wallace prepared to leave New Mexico to become ambassador to Turkey - the Las Vegas, N.M., Gazette asked the outgoing governor about prospects that he would spare the Kid's life.

Wallace replied, "I can't see how a fellow like him should expect any clemency from me."

The Kid escaped from the Lincoln County jail but Garrett tracked him to a ranch near Fort Sumner, N.M.

In the early 1900s, a few years before Wallace died, a pardon for the Kid resurfaced in newspaper articles in which Wallace described his secret meeting with the Kid. Wallace, by then, had achieved literary fame as the author of the historical novel, "Ben Hur."

Wallace's great-grandson questions the accuracy of the newspaper accounts, saying a number of facts are wrong. They describe the meeting between Gov. Wallace and the Kid, for instance, as taking place in Santa Fe rather than Lincoln.

"I am smelling a rat right off the bat," William Wallace said.

Doug Clanin of Anderson, Ind., who retired after serving as editor of the Wallace papers for the Indiana Historical Society, said Gov. Wallace became quite famous and in his later years was adept at "improving on old stories" as he entertained audiences on a lecture circuit.

Historian Frederick Nolan, who lives in London and has written extensively about the Lincoln County War, said in an e-mail that "there does not seem to me to be the slightest doubt that Wallace indeed made some kind of promise to the Kid" and that was at least immunity from prosecution, which could have set aside two indictments for murder.

As for a posthumous pardon, Nolan said, "Speaking for myself, I'd sort of like to see the Kid pardoned because - at the time the 'arrangement' was made - he surely merited at least as much consideration as all the others who took advantage of Wallace's amnesty. But the moment passed and so, I think, did the Kid's entitlement to a whitewash."

### RICHARDSON'S REGRESSIVE ATTEMPTED SAVE

Refusing to be thwarted, Richardson reverted to his earliest hoax approach: "pardon hearings." A September 6, 2010 *NY Times Opinion Section Contribution* by an ignorant but hostile historian named Hampton Sides - a Martin Luther King Jr. and Kit Carson author - wrote "Not-So-Charming Billy." Sides describes a "pardon hearing" planned for November in Lincoln, with period costumes and Richardson presiding as judge (presumably with his hoaxers giving canned testimony). It never happened.

### WILLIAM N. WALLACE'S POTENTIAL LAST SALVO

On September 16, 2010, William N. Wallace e-mailed me about his planned final salvo if Richardson continued to the bitter end, stating: "Ms. Cooper - Barry Massey of the AP has ready from me a reaction quote should Gov. Richardson go ahead with the pardon, a condemning quote. Massey has informed the governor's staff that he has the quote and will use it."

So Bill Richardson, unaccustomed to intimidation, had to weigh consequences of his scam. He wanted a political life after December 31, 2010. Was the hoax worth his future?

# UP TO THE END: DECEMBER 31, 2010

December 27, 2010 was the rumored date of Richardson's pardon announcement. But the only word that day came from an uncertain press. For "CBS News," reporter Edecio Martinez wrote "Billy the Kid to be Pardoned 130 Years Later?" From its text, Richardson's pressure was clear: "Descendants of Old West lawman Pat Garrett and New Mexico Territorial Gov. Lew Wallace are outraged that Gov. Bill Richardson is considering a pardon for Billy the Kid, saying Wallace never offered a pardon, and a petition seeking one is tainted because it comes from a lawyer with ties to Richardson." For what it was worth, Randi McGinn shape-shifted for that reporter from amateur historian enthusiast to a lawyer seeking weird work - now, no longer *pro bono*, but for pay: "McGinn said her only tie to the administration is that she volunteered to look into the pardon issue for a fee."

So my message of shenanigans had finally gotten a public voice. But could a man with no conscience be stopped?

On December 29, 2010, an AP staff writer named Mark Guarino wrote: "Outgoing New Mexico Gov. Bill Richardson is considering a pardon for celebrated outlaw Billy the Kid. An informal e-mail poll shows support. But time is running out." For this article, "official" hoax historian, Paul Hutton resurfaced to justify pardon (omitting his 2004 "Investigating History: Billy the Kid" in which "Brushy" was likely the "Billy" to be pardoned).

On December 29, 2010, Richardson floated his last-ditch oddball solution via reporter Glen Levy at TIME NewsFeed.com as "Will Billy the Kid Be Pardoned? Governor Has Until Friday." For it, Richardson's Deputy Chief of Staff Eric Witt - one of the talking heads in Hutton's hoax History Channel program - states: "We're not offering a blanket pardon for everything he did."

December 30, 2010 brought FoxNews.com's Kelly David Burke with a cautious "Billy the Kid Pardon?" And Burke documents, without catching the irony, that Richardson - with only one day to go - says: "I want to see "some concrete evidence ... on whether ... the pardon promise, potentially a promise by Governor Lew Wallace, was valid and documented."

Left with only drama of time running out, on December 30, 2010, Richardson, through Alarie Ray Garcia, gave his press release titled "Governor Richardson to Announce his decision on Billy the Kid Pardon Request Tomorrow." Deflecting fall-out to Randi McGinn's "request," it stated: "Governor Bill Richardson will announce his decision regarding a pardon of Billy the Kid tomorrow, Friday, December 31st live on ABC's Good Morning America. The announcement is expected at approximately 7:10 am ET/5:10am MT."

On that day, reporter Jessica Hopper reported for "ABC Good Morning America": "Gov. Bill Richardson: 'I've Decided Not to Pardon Billy the Kid.' " Hopper's article proved that my fear of Richardson's using the pardon to validate his eight year Billy the Kid Case "investigation" had been correct. She wrote:

> In 2003, Richardson, a history buff, first said that he would consider pardoning the famous outlaw. He finally made up his mind today. "It was a very close call. I've been working on this for eight years. The romanticism appealed to me to issue a pardon, but the facts and the evidence do not support it and I've got to be responsible especially when a governor is issuing pardons," Richardson said. Richardson said that Billy the Kid's decision to continue to kill after the pardon wasn't granted to him impacted his decision.

After my Garretts-Wallace onslaught, I pictured historically imbecilic Richardson asking around: "What's my excuse for no pardon? Oh! The Kid killed deputy guards? I'll use that."

On December 31st, FoxNews.com printed: "Richardson Declines to Pardon Outlaw Billy the Kid." In it was JP Garrett's quote that "Richardson appointed McGinn's husband to the state Supreme Court;" and William N. Wallace's: "McGinn has 'meager qualifications' and possible conflict of interest."

Again, on December 31st, Kathryn Watson of *The Washington Times* headlined: "Alas, no pardon for Billy the Kid: New Mexico's Richardson says close call." For her, Richardson was a "history buff" denying pardon based on the deputy killings. With hypocrisy lost to all but me, Richardson intoned: "We should not neglect the historical record and the history of the American West."

Also, on that last day, the *Los Angeles Times*, with a Rick Rojas, gave Richardson's final spin: "No Pardon for Billy the Kid. New Mexico Gov. Bill Richardson says, 'The Romanticism appealed to me ... but the facts and evidence did not support it.'" For that, Richardson had "Albuquerque lawyer Randi McGinn" fall on her sword with an ungranted "pardon petition." McGinn shape-shifted for this by claiming no regrets - and spookily channeling Bill Robins III: "It's great being Billy the Kid's lawyer."

## BITTER "BIG BILL" BLURTS ONE LAST LIE

By January 1, 2011, loser Bill Richardson was nasty. *New York Times* reporter, Marc Lacey, gave his final spin as: "For 2nd Time in 131 Years, Billy the Kid is Denied Pardon;" and quoted: "If one is to rewrite a chapter as prominent as this, there had better be certainty as to the facts, the circumstances and the motives of those involved," Mr. Richardson said in announcing that he would not tamper with the history **of a man whose life was spent 'pillaging, ravaging and killing the deserving and the innocent alike'.**" [author's boldface] Apparently, spoil sport "Big Bill" was now just a "history *bluff*."

Billy himself might answer Richardson - his worst enemy since Santa Fe Ring bosses of his day - as he did a *Mesilla News* reporter on April 16, 1881, three days after his hanging sentence: "I think it a dirty mean advantage to take of me, considering my situation and knowing that I could not defend myself by word or act. But I suppose he thought he would give me a kick down hill."

I would add: "Billy had dodged his most dangerous bullet yet."

# MY PYRRHIC PARDON VICTORY

My painful moral dilemma was over: stopping what I most wanted - the pardon – so as to protect Billy Bonney's history from Bill Richardson's Billy the Kid Case hoax. My consolation was that this "pardon" was not for real Billy or for real reasons.

Billy Bonney deserved better than Attorney Randi McGinn's hoaxed last-minute "Pardon Petition." The never-granted Wallace pardon is legally, politically, morally, and psychologically one of the most complex quandaries in Old West history; and can only be resolved by revisionist understanding of the 19th century Santa Fe Ring's oppression. Available to sort it out, are 19th century contemporary documents and authoritative history books.

McGinn's "Pardon Petition" proved that Bill Richardson had been as much a tragedy for real Billy as was Lew Wallace. Richardson squandered his eight year opportunity as Governor to tackle that pardon issue with the best historical and legal minds; squandered the chance to bring legitimate attention to New Mexico's actual history and tourist opportunities; and, maybe, squandered the opportunity to grant that pardon for real reasons comprehensible to the public.

But anti-intellectual bully Bill Richardson was just a modern Santa Fe Ringman, believing his cadre of ignorant thugs, greedy bottom feeders, and hired lackeys could power through his pardon agenda by corruption and chicanery; not expertise or enlightenment. A justified pardon needed a different governor and a real Billy the Kid - and not the lazy publicity-stunt Billy the Kid Case hoax.

The pardon press made clear that Richardson only achieved a shouting match based on movie-lore and misinformation. Nevertheless, one can still say that Billy Bonney prevailed. That December 31, 2010, FoxNews.com wrote in their "Richardson Declines to Pardon Outlaw Billy the Kid": "Richardson's office received 809 e-mails and letters in the survey [the special website] that ended Sunday, with 430 favoring a pardon and 379 opposed. Comments came from all over the world."

The time might come again for real Billy's chance. My own book, *Pardon for Billy the Kid: An Analysis,* was then almost done; and it had the necessary information for people to decide for themselves on a pardon based on actual facts.

However, I was not holding my breath for Richardson's Republication replacement, Susana Martinez. She contributed her two cents through the December 31, 2010 *The Washington Times* article by Kathryn Watson. "Ms. Martinez said the state had better things to do than waste time deliberating over the possible pardon of a notorious dead outlaw, and called the pardon issue a waste of time." Martinez apparently was bored by her state's tourist base. But after all, she was just a pawn positioned by Republican political operatives State Senator Rod Adair, Attorney Pat Rogers, and Attorney Mickey Barnett (attempted saboteurs of my litigation to protect that history). Martinez was aided by Richardson's corruption record - far exceeding his Billy the Kid Case hoax - which tainted the Democratic opponent, Diane Denish (who apparently was tainted anyway). I was told Martinez was also corrupt; but as just a Doña County District Attorney, she had limited chances for plunder. But, her ambition, like Richardson's, was the U.S. Presidency.

## DOING THE SHERIFF AND "THE GENERAL" PROUD

On December 31, 2010, JP Garrett e-mailed me: "yea!!! no pardon!!!" More sensitive Susannah Garrett, aware of my cruel choice, extended her sympathy. Subsequently, the Garretts refused to join or to publicize my IPRA litigation. Thus, I was left only with their months of world-wide press vilification of Billy.

That December 31, 2010, William N. Wallace e-mailed: "Ms. Cooper - Your persistence, in rallying the troops, enabled common sense. Thank you. Bill Wallace." This was our last contact. He died on August 11, 2012 of acute myeloid leukemia, never aware of my conflicted feelings.

## THE CURRENT OF MONEY

### HISTORIAN FREDERICK NOLAN

Historian, Frederick Nolan was depressed by the hoax and supportive of me when the Billy the Kid Case began, flattering my opposition as being "caught in a current of history." Years later, with my court blocking of the Billy-mother exhumations and my exposing the faked DNA by my IPRA litigation, Nolan apparently heard the all-clear sounded and joined the current of money - that meant the media-grabbing hoaxers.

For his pardon statement to AP reporter Barry Massey for the August 21, 2010 " 'Billy the Kid' pardon effort draws Wild

West showdown," Nolan, aware the hoax needed the pardon, was quoted from an e-mail: "[T]here does not seem to me to be the slightest doubt that Wallace indeed made some kind of promise to the Kid and that was at least immunity from prosecution, which could have set aside two indictments for murder [sic – three]."

But on August 13, 2010, Nolan was less "certain" about that pardon promise, e-mailing me: "To the best of my knowledge no contemporary of the Kid's ever mentioned his 'deal' with Wallace - nothing even in the extensive interviews with the Coes (and others) by Evarts Haley."

Massey quoted Nolan taking no chances: backing Richardson's pardon, but saying it was too late: "Speaking for myself, I'd sort of like to see the Kid pardoned because - at the time the 'arrangement' was made - he surely merited at least as much consideration as all the others who took advantage of Wallace's amnesty. But the moment had passed and so, I think, did the Kid's entitlement to a whitewash."

At the "Wild West History Association Roundup," Nolan had taken no chances with me either with the hot topic. Organizer Bob McCubbin had already refused me any speaking time. Nolan refused to either mention my anti-hoax work or to give me even minutes of his hours of time at the podium to do it myself.

Why? He and McCubbin were hiding from me that right after the "Roundup," a PBS TV crew was arriving. They were making a program *with Richardson* for his hoax pardon. When I learned about that crew, Nolan and McCubbin refused to give me any contact information to them. I was kept out of the program.

Any doubt about the current of money for Nolan was removed on February 19, 2010 in his exuberant e-mail to me and 35 others, titled "Fame at last!" It said:

> The Billy the Kid program 'staring' Bob Boze Bell, Drew and Eloise Gomber, Steve Sederwall and Frederick Nolan will air on the Discovery ID Channel on Saturday March 13th at 10pm EST. Just look at the company our Billy is keeping!

So, Nolan added his legitimizing presence to Billy the Kid Case "stars" Bob Boze Bell and Steve Sederwall under the hoax-talk title: "History Mysteries." And Drew Gomber was in Paul Hutton's hoax TV program to say he doubted Garrett's version of the killing. I was told Nolan did it for money. To me, Nolan rationalized, "I wanted to make sure the correct history was presented." And if his "fame at last" was his joke, it was not funny.

# JOURNALIST JAY MILLER

People were surprised by my certainty that Jay Miller backed my Richardson hoax opposition, since Miller was apparently in a conflicted position of being a lobbyist for education funding. I did not put two-and-two together - even with his writing a middle-of-the-road book using my articles and taking credit for my work in the defamatory 2010 *True West* magazine article (and never setting it straight). Suspicion broke through, when Richardson appointed him pardon feeler, and Miller kept that secret from me. By the time of the fierce pardon thrust, I lost my faith in Miller.

Though I had provided Jay Miller with the historical details of the pardon issue, as well as its dove-tailing with the hoax, he chose to side with Richardson, merely quoting my hoax exposé as if it was a random responder to his pardon poling. For his own article on August 30, 2010, he legitimized the McGinn-Richardson "promise-is-a-promise" Petition ploy, stating: "When is a promise not a promise? That is what Gov. Bill Richardson needs to decide as he debates whether to fulfill the promise of a pardon former Gov. Lew Wallace may have made to Billy the Kid."

Just how far Miller would drift with the current of money was indicated by his September 6, 2010 e-mail to me, which politely is bizarre. Miller wrote: "Steve Sederwall evidentially wants to peddle your books on his soon-to-be-finished website. I won't give him your contact info so he wants me to give you his email address ... FYI, I have some of mine [the book written using my articles] left over from my last purchase so I told him he could sell those." (Note that Miller knew I was in my third year of litigation against Sederwall and the other law enforcement hoaxers.)

# REPORTER BARRY MASSEY

For the years after his AP office mate had been fired, I kept Barry Massey informed of Billy the Kid Case hoax progression and my opposition. But he wrote only articles about the pardon, and never clarified its the hoax connection. After that, he returned to writing nothing about the Billy the Kid Case or my litigation. A clue might be the fate of that office mate, who planned to expose the Billy the Kid Case hoax. Apparently, news that interested Massey most was that he had a job. But like the Garrett family, Barry Massey, by press, could have empowered my fight and provided the protection that making it public would have brought.

# FALLOUT FOR FUTURE

## *ACCOSTED BY SEDERWALL*

My fear about going to the "Wild West Roundup" was being attacked by my thuggish IPRA litigation defendants - Rick Virden, Tom Sullivan, and Steve Sederwall - who, after all, represented the local law enforcement! I made no secret of my anxiety to Bob McCubbin and others. The mean response was to place my booth away from anyone else at the entrance. So I was alone.

When the "Roundup" began, Sederwall arrived, and immediately walked around my table to lean his gigantic bulk over seated me. "Are you afraid now?" he asked with pinwheel eyes. I could feel his breath.

But I am a psychiatrist as well as a coward. And my specialty was extremes of deranged behavior. I said, looking up, "Here to see the show?" He answered that he was not staying long. "Some men can get a lot of pleasure pretty fast," I teased. He seemed thrown off, but spent a long time wandering around the large hall and staring at me from different angles. Since I was at the entrance, I slipped out and got security for back-up. When Sederwall finally left, he returned to my table. I said to him, "I want you to know that no matter what happens in my opposition to the hoax, I will not blame you. I blame Richardson."

Each night, security walked me to my car. Later, in his inimitable way, Sederwall presented this interaction in a deposition and court testimony as having had "meetings" with me.

I was developing terrible enemies and no discernable friends.

## *STRANGE DEATH OF ATTORNEY MARY HAN*

On November 18, 2010, my first attorney, Mary Han, was found dead at her townhouse garage. The Medical Investigator declared suicide by carbon monoxide intoxication. Many favored murder. At her death, she was doing a trial against her enemy, the Deputy Chief of the Albuquerque Police Department - and was in the process of withdrawing. Her opposing attorney told me that he felt he would have lost against her. By August 16, 2013, New Mexico Attorney General Gary King, with a reputation for his own corruption and apparently assisting cover-ups in my own IPRA litigation, told KOB Eyewitness News 4 reporter, Erica Zucco, for her article "AG questions suicide ruling of civil rights attorney," that Han's death should be labeled "undetermined," that the "suicide" ruling was made too quickly, and that "high-ranking police and city officials ... interfered with the investigation." The city attorney's office called "[t]he Attorney General's involvement and action in his case highly suspicious." All this just illustrates how the state's crooked officials name-call each other for political fodder. And it did nothing for dead Mary Han.

What about Mary Han's law partner, Paul Kennedy? He had done my own anti-lawmen exhumation case. A major Republican, he had been appointed by new Governor Susana Martinez as her personal attorney; then appointed to the state Supreme Court (where he subsequently lost in the election). What about Paul Kennedy and me? He had ended the Billy-mother hoax exhumations and embarrassed Lincoln County Republican darlings: Sheriffs Sullivan and Virden. He must have been wised-up by his own cronies: Rod Adair and Pat Rogers. When corruption is all-pervasive, there is no two party system. This was not Richardson's Democratic hoax. It was bi-partisan.

After all, the big picture with Mary Han, was that she was fighting corrupt lawmen and politicians - for me and afterwards - until she was eliminated.

### NOT ALONE AMIDST MY ENEMIES

"At least I have Scot Stinnett on my side," I thought; not reckoning that, to date, he had contributed no work, no money, no FOG's joining, and no help getting a lawyer. I had long forgotten Marlyn Bowlin's warning; and she was dead since 2008.

But whistleblowing's cruel price - ostracism (or worse) - was dawning on me as I next faced my IPRA case litigation with its upcoming evidentiary hearing. But I felt confident that DNA records would be the hoaxers' last stand. And little Napoleon Ed Threet and sincerely youthful Blair Dunn were attorneys who had shown that they could hold their own against the Billy the Kid Case hoaxers.

I imagined that the hoaxers were feeling desperate - as they lost ground of fake exhumations, fake pardon, and fake "Brushy Bill" Roberts - and I tried not to imagine what all that could make them do. It would turn out, that they had a plan beyond any possibility of my guessing.

# CHAPTER 16:

# LAWYER GAMES

STATE OF NEW MEXICO
THIRTEENTH JUDICIAL DISTRICT COURT
COUNTY OF SANDOVAL

GALE COOPER and DE BACA COUNTY NEWS,
A New Mexico Corporation,

Plaintiffs,

vs.                                    D-1329-CV-2007-01364

RICK VIRDEN, Lincoln County Sheriff and
Custodian of the records of the Lincoln County
Sheriff's office, and STEVEN M. SEDERWALL,
former Lincoln County Deputy Sheriff, and
THOMAS T. SULLIVAN, former Lincoln
County Sheriff,

Defendants.

## SUBPOENA FOR PRODUCTION OR INSPECTION TO LABORATORY CORPORATION OF AMERICA

SUBPOENA FOR

[✓] DOCUMENTS OR OBJECTS
[ ] INSPECTION OF PREMISES

TO: LABORATORY CORP...

---

TRANSCRIPT OF PROCEEDINGS

On the 17th day of January 2012, at ap
this matter came on for a hearing, befo
e George P. Eichwald, Judge of the Thi
District, State of New Mexico.
Plaintiff, Gale ...oper, appeared in per
Record, Willia...
...e, NM 87104.
...i o Gran

---

THIRTEENTH JUDICIAL D...
COUNTY OF SANDOVAL
STATE OF NEW MEXICO

GALE COOPER and DE BACA COUN...
a New Mexico Corporatio n,
Plaintiffs,

vs.                      D-1329-CV-2007-

RICK VIRDEN, LINCOLN COUNTY SHERIFF, et
Defendants.

TRANSCRIPT OF PROCEEDINGS

On the 31st day of May 2012, at approximate,
...atter came on for a Motio n Hearing, before the
George P. Eichwald, Judge of the Thirteenth
...strict, State of New Mexico.
...intiff, Gal e Cooper, appeared in person and by
..., william. F. Riordan, 2740 Rio Grande Blvd,
... 87104.
...Baca County News, appeared in person
...trick Griebel & Jeramy Theor...
...B, Albuquerqu e, N...
...eared in...

---

# Forensic Research & Training Center

## Forensic Examination Report

Date of Request: May 22, 2004
Requested By: Lincoln County Sheriff's Office, New Mexico
Investigation History Program, Kurtis Productio...
Local Case No. 2003-274
Date of Report: February 25, 2005
Report to: Steve Sederwell
Lincoln C...

Int...

---

# Forensic Research & Training Center

## Forensic Examination Report

Date of Request:   May 22, 2004

Requested By:   Steve Sederwall, and Bill Kurtis Productions

Date of Report:   February 25, 2005

Report to:   Steven M. Sederwall

## Examination of Lincoln County Court House:

On Sunday, 8/1/04, the forensic investigation team examined the old Lincoln County Court House in Lincoln, New Mexico. Present at the scene were Steve Sederwall, Tom Sullivan, David Turk, Bill Kurtis, and Gary Wayne Graves. The target area of examination is located on the top landing of the stairs of the old courtroom.

1. The staircase has been repainted several times over the years.

2. The $2^{nd}$ floor hallway floor was recovered with wooden floor board. The... floor boards were removed. Th...

---

THIRTEENTH JUDICIAL DISTRICT COURT
COUNTY OF SANDOVAL
STATE OF NEW MEXICO

D-1329-CV-200...

GALE COOPER & DE BACA COUNTY NEWS,
Plaintiffs,

vs.

LINCOLN COUNTY, RICK VIRDEN, et al.,
Defendants.

TRANSCRIPT OF PROCEEDINGS

On the 21st day of September 2012, at
...:30, this matter came on for a hearing, befo
...norable George P. Eichwald, Judge of the
...dicial District, State of New Mexico.
The Plaintiff, Gale Cooper, appeared in
...nsel of Record, William Riordan, 2740 Rio
...uquerqu e, NM 87104.
The Pla...

# Attorneys Threet and Dunn

*HOAXBUST: As the Billy the Kid Case hoax progressed, I would not have been surprised by any dirty trick played by my opponents. But it did not occur to me that there was another way they could win: through my own attorneys.*

## JUDGE GEORGE EICHWALD'S ORDER

On March 12, 2010, Judge George Eichwald filed his "Order Granting Plaintiff's Motion for Summary Judgment and Denying Defendant Virden's Cross Motion for Summary Judgment." I may have been traumatized by Attorney Mickey Barnett's betrayal, but Attorneys Ed Threet and Blair Dunn were winning. (After Dunn moved out of state, Threet took over as lead attorney.) And if the defendants gave no records, we had an upcoming evidentiary hearing to give the Court my huge amount of documentary proof.

## A DR. HENRY LEE REPORT TURN-OVER PLOY

Judge Eichwald's order stimulated a new defense strategy: feign document turn-over.

### CONFIRMING LEE'S REPORTS' EXISTENCE

Dr. Henry Lee, in his May 1, 2006 letter to Jay Miller, said he had sent his report on "a wooden workbench and floorboards at the courthouse" to "the Lincoln County Sheriff's Department."

Sederwall, in his August 18, 2008 deposition, said he had Lee's bench report; but called it his private property, though admitting to know its Orchid Cellmark DNA results. Sederwall had responded to Attorney Barnett's questions:

Q. In the report that you have a copy of, is it from Dr. Lee?

A. Uh-huh.

Q. And is it contemporaneous in time with this letter? Or would it have been prior to the letter, because it says it has been sent?

A. I guess I'm not following. The report is about the workbench that I called him to have him do ...

Q. All right. And what did that report say? ...

A. ... It was measurements. It was that sort of thing ...

Q. Do you remember, how many pages was the crime scene investigation, was it like two or three pages or ten pages?

A. Oh, probably ten or twelve ...

Q. With the evidence sent to Orchid Cellmark by Dr. Lee or by someone associated with this, do you have any knowledge as to whether that generated any DNA results? ... Did it?

A. Yes, sir ...

## SEDERWALL TURNS OVER A LEE REPORT

On February 18, 2010, Attorney Ed Threet called me saying he had gotten the Lee report from Sederwall's lawyer, Kevin Brown. I drove with pounding heart to Threet's Albuquerque office. He handed me nine pages, with color photos. Dated February 25, 2005, it was Lee's unrequested floorboard report seeking "blood" at the old courthouse steps. Brown's cover letter stated:

> Our position is that the document Mr. Sederwall obtained from Dr. Lee is not a public record ... However to resolve this matter, I am enclosing the document Mr. Sederwall obtained from Dr. Lee. This should resolve all claims against both Mr. Sederwall and Mr. Sullivan ... If you do not believe all claims against both Mr. Sederwall and Mr. Sullivan are now resolved ... please return the document to me without making any copies.

The title was "Forensic Research and Training Center Forensic Examination Report: Examination of Lincoln County Courthouse." Its header stated that it was "Requested By: Steve Sederwall, and Bill Kurtis Productions." It stated:

> On Sunday, August 1, 2004, the forensic investigation team examined the old Lincoln County Court House in Lincoln, New Mexico. Present at the scene were Steve Sederwall, Tom Sullivan, David Turk, Bill Kurtis, and Gary Wayne Graves.

A "Results and Conclusions" section documented:

Various stains were observed on the surface and the underside of the floorboards. Chemical tests for the presence of blood were positive with some of those stains. These results indicate the presence of oxidase activity with those stains tested positive, which suggests those stains could be bloodstains. Further DNA testing could reveal the nature and identity of that blood like stains [sic].

Signers were "Dr. Henry C. Lee, Chief Emeritus, Connecticut State Forensic Laboratory, Distinguished Professor, University New Haven" and Calvin D. Ostler, Forensic Consultant, Crime Scene Investigator" (Lee's business partner, and in the Utah Medical Examiner's Office).

Lee was hoaxing with O-Tolidine, a non-specific tester for iron compounds (like blood or rust), though he said "blood like" stains. And he wanted DNA testing, knowing there were no Deputy James Bell remains for identity matching. And he hides that the room's walls are covered by brown drippings - clearly past water damage from a leaking roof or broken pipe. If he called that blood, not rust, he needed a group massacre, not just shot Bell!

I told Threet to return the report as unrequested. But it seemed odd that Sederwall had said in his deposition that he had a 12 page Lee bench report, not this 9 page floorboard one. And why were the law enforcement titles left off everybody's names?

## LEE'S REPORT AT THE PRESENTMENT HEARING

On March 9, 2010 we had a Presentment Hearing to demand records and to say that no requested record had been turned over. Virden lied through Nicole Werkmeister that he was not "required to produce documents that we are not in possession of."

Sederwall lied through Kevin Brown about the Lee report:

I didn't want to disregard the Court's ruling, and so I obtained the particular document that Sederwall had that we were talking about. I presented it to Mr. Threet, and I said, I think this is going to resolve all the matter. If you disagree, return it back to me and we'll just go further. It was returned back to me, and I was told that this isn't what you requested and there's something else. Well ... **I will state to the Court, the document which I have here, which I would mark as an exhibit or do whatever, is the only document that Sederwall received.** [author's boldface]

## VIRDEN TURNS OVER A LEE REPORT

On April 6, 2010, by fax, Attorney Threet sent me an April 6, 2010 fax from Attorney Werkmeister. She turned-over the same Lee floorboard report, with cover sheet stating: "Attached is the Forensic Examination Report from Dr. Lee ... Please be advised that this report was never in Lincoln County's possession, and the only reason we have a copy of it is because Mr. Brown provided it to us." On April 12, 2010, she sent a second letter:

> This letter is to follow up my phone conversation with Mr. Threet this morning regarding a document pertaining to the Billy the Kid investigation that he believes has not been produced. [In] Mr. Sederwall's deposition he testified that he received a copy of Dr. Lee's report 'about the workbench' ... Mr. Sederwall testified that it was perhaps 10 [sic – 12] pages in big font ... The report Mr. Brown produced seems to fit the above description, with one exception. It is a report authored by Dr. Lee that is 9 pages long in big font. However it appears to be an examination of floorboards rather than a workbench.
>
> Could Mr. Sederwall simply have been mistaken ... about the nature of the report? ...
>
> [I]f the only remaining dispute in this case is about whether there exists a second report ... we could either have an evidentiary hearing and allow Judge Eichwald to decide, or ... Mr. Threet could subpoena Dr. Lee and have him produce any reports he authored dealing with Billy the Kid.

Werkmeister was playing games by her "possession only" lie, saying Sederwall meant floorboard not bench, and making a Lee report the only requested record. She also wanted us to subpoena records - when IPRA requires her client's records recovery.

## HEARING ON MANDATORY DISCLOSURE

On September 9, 2010, our hearing was to get the judge to demand records turn-over. Threet got tough, stating: "This is a question concerning the failure of the Defendants in this case to abide by the order of this Court. It is a case of indirect contempt ... They have admitted that they have them. They are deliberately attempting to frustrate the order of this Court."

Threet brought up Sederwall's website: "A website currently under construction will have all of Sederwall's case information available ... That type of a situation, Your Honor, is simply to make a profit." Threet even suggested punishments:

> The Court can, in fact, issue a monetary fine based upon the days that they do not produce these reports. And, lastly, the Court can exercise its powers of contempt and incarcerate the Sheriff and his deputies. When they can come to the front page of the Ruidoso News and refuse to tell people who are trying to get this information, Your Honor, it's one of the most shameful, flagrant contemptuous actions toward the Court I know. We ask the Court, we ask the Court to require these people to answer.

Defense for Virden argued by irrelevant open records cases from Louisiana and Tennessee, while ignoring New Mexico's IPRA statute requiring records recovery. Defense for Sullivan and Sederwall hid their dates of deputyship, called Case # 2003-274 their "hobby;" switched case definition to the deputy murders; and claimed Lee's report was not public. Brown stated: "[O]ur position is ... that Steve Sederwall is an amateur historian."

Judge Eichwald took no action for contempt, but ordered the evidentiary hearing because of a "loggerhead." He said, "I stated that an evidentiary hearing will be held in the event that either party is not satisfied with the nature of the information that the Court has ordered to be turned over."

## VIRDEN'S SHAM RECOVERY ATTEMPTS

The evidentiary hearing was set for January 21, 2011. So Virden scrambled (three years late) to sham records requests.

On October 26, 2010, he wrote on official letterhead to Dr. Lee, using my litigation's number (not Case 2003-274) for subject, and asking for the unrequested floorboard report. He stated:

> It is my understanding that on May 22, 2004, Steve Sederwall requested you to review evidence that came from a forensic investigation of the old Lincoln County Courthouse in New Mexico in connection with the death of Billy the Kid. You reviewed the evidence and generated a 9 page report dated February 25, 2005, signed by you and Calvin Ostler, Forensic Consultant. If you generated any other reports as a result of your

review, I would appreciate you providing copies to me. I am happy to pay for any reproduction costs. Thank you very much for your cooperation.

On November 12, 2010, Lee wrote back on official stationery:

This letter is in response to your letter dated October 26, 2010. My only report issued in regards to the death of Billy the Kid was issued on February 25, 2005. No other report has been issued by me in regards to this case.

Did Virden request Lee's report? No. But on November 22, 2010, Werkmeister sent Threet copies of this sham requesting.

On the same October 26, 2010, Virden also wrote on official letterhead to Orchid Cellmark Lab (not using Director Rick Staub as a contact, though his own file for Case 2003-274 gave all Staub's contact information). Merely doubletalk, and titled by my litigation case's number (not Case 2003-274), it stated:

It is my understanding that in the spring or summer of 2004, Steve Sederwall sent a blood sample(s) to Orchid Cellmark Lab gathered from a forensic investigation of the old Lincoln County Courthouse in New Mexico and possibly related to the death of Billy the Kid. If you reviewed the blood sample(s) and generated any reports, or have in your possession any documents related to the blood sample(s) sent to you by Steve Sederwall, I would appreciate you providing copies to me. I am happy to pay for any reproduction costs. Thank you very much for your cooperation.

On November 2, 2010, Virden called Orchid Cellmark's Customer Liaison for Forensics Joan Gulliksen, falsely saying that Sederwall had sent specimens to their Lab (as if their client). Gulliksen told him therefore needed Sederwall's written permission for records release. She followed up by letter:

Orchid Cellmark is in receipt of your letter requesting DNA documents relating to Billy the Kid. The case file is confidential and available only to our client. For those documents to be handed over, I would need written permission on Letterhead from our client authorizing us to release those documents.

Again, Virden did no follow-up - even though he could have contacted Director Staub directly, or gotten the contact information from Dr. Lee, or used the actual client's name - Calvin Ostler - from the Lee report. Nevertheless, Werkmeister included this exchange in her November 22, 2010 response to Threet as meeting her client's IPRA recovery requirement.

Do not miss the absurdity of Virden's requests. He is an almost 40 year lawman (state police and in this sheriff's department since 1997) saying he has no idea how recover the missing and total forensic records of his department's most famous murder investigation. The following is my fictional sample of a valid request to Director Rick Staub, not Virden's shamming:

> As the Sheriff conducting Lincoln County Sheriff's Department Case 2003-274, an investigation into the death of Billy the Kid, I am writing to you as the Orchid Cellmark contact listed in my file for that case's DNA records. I have standing in this case, but your own client of record may be either Dr. Henry Lee or Calvin Ostler, who performed initial DNA specimen recoveries and sent those specimens to Orchid Cellmark.
>
> To complete my case file, I am requesting Orchid Cellmark's records for my case: DNA extractions from Dr. Lee's specimens from an old workbench, DNA extractions from exhumed Arizona remains of a John Miller and a William Hudspeth, and DNA matching results of the bench to those remains.
>
> Please contact me if you need further information.

## SEDERWALL TURNS OVER ANOTHER LEE REPORT

On November 10, 2010, with looming evidentiary hearing, Sederwall shockingly pulled another Dr. Lee report out of a hat - this time, the carpenter's bench report! Its cover letter was to Attorney Threet from Attorney Brown (keeping a "straight face" after telling the judge in the March 9, 2010 presentment hearing that Sederwall had *only one* report). It stated: "Enclosed please find a copy of another report dated February 25, 2005 which deals with the examination of furniture by Dr. Lee."

Oddly, this report differed from the floorboard one, having ornate title font and no "Results and Conclusions" - a report's purpose. Titled "Examination of furniture from Pete Maxwell's of July 15, 1881," and 16 pages long, its signatures were of Lee and

530

Calvin Ostler. Its header had no law enforcement information; and "Requested by" was expanded from the floorboard report's "Steve Sederwall, and Bill Kurtis Productions" to "Steve Sederwall, Capitan, New Mexico, paid for by Investigating History Program, Kurtis Production." Its introduction stated:

At the request of Steve Sederwall of Lincoln County, New Mexico, Bill Kurtis and Jamie Schenk of Kurtis Production, Dr. Henry Lee went to New Mexico on July 31, 2004 to assist in the re-investigation of the case of Billy the Kid. The forensic investigating team participating in re-investigation consist the [sic] following individuals: were Steve Sederwall, Investigator; Tom Sullivan, Investigator; Dr. Henry Lee, Chief Emeritus of the Connecticut State Police Forencic Laboratory; Calvin Ostler, Forensic Consultant, Riverton, Utah; Kim Ostler, Crime Scene Assistant, Riverton, Utah; David Turk, U.S. Marshall [sic], United States Marshall Service [sic]. In addition, Mike Haag, Firearm examiner from Albuquerque Police Department Crime Lab, also provided valuable technical assistance in the investigation.

The forensic investigation team arrived at the Manny Miller residence, located at (address removed), Albuquerque, New Mexico, at 18:20 hours on Saturday, July 31, 2004. Upon arrival we were presented with three pieces of evidence: a worktable, a washstand, and a headboard. Investigator Sullivan, Investigator Sederwall, and members of Bill Kurtis Productions had removed the three pieces of evidence from a storage building ...

This time, Lee's testing for blood used Luminol (another agent like O-Tolidine for iron compounds - like blood or rust - with rust being more likely on a carpenter's bench.)

And it had something fatal for the hoaxers on page 9:

Swab samples of area number "3" and area number "4" were collected for DNA testing. Two swabs were taken from each area and placed in two separate swab boxes, one box was labeled for area number "3" and one box was labeled for area number "4". **These two samples were transferred to Lincoln Sheriff Department.** [author's boldface] In addition, scraping samples were also taken from these two areas. These samples were placed in two evidence envelopes [AUTHOR'S NOTE: Remember these envelopes] **and were transferred to Lincoln Sheriff Department.** [author's boldface]

## *THREET MAKES ME A STRANGE OFFER*

Before Virden's sham records requests, something strange happened to me on the way to the evidentiary hearing. It involved Attorney Ed Threet. On September 14, 2010, he faxed me his letter titled "Re: Billy the Kid." It stated:

> Henry Narvaez has again repeated his assurance to me that if we will agree to dismiss Virden from the case, although not giving up our rights to attorneys' fees and costs, he will have Virden get the information from Dr. Henry Lee and Orchid Cellmark Laboratories. Please give me the authority to do this as I think it is a good thing to do, it will short circuit all this terrible situation as far as time is concerned. What I don't have is the correct address for Dr. Lee and for Orchid Laboratory. Please get this back to me if you would. And let me know if I have the authority to proceed.

This was troubling. Narvaez headed Werkmeister's law firm. Threet's "again repeated assurance," was the first I heard of a "deal." IPRA law *means* the custodian must get requested records. If anything, this offer admitted that Virden had avoided getting records - *and could!* Asking me for addresses was absurd. It was Virden's job. And ending "this terrible situation" was odd. We were about to win in the evidentiary hearing; and had won Summary Judgment. I faxed back a response draft for Threet:

> It is the position of my clients that, beginning in 2007, they have repeatedly made their records request to Lincoln County Sheriff Rick Virden for the forensic documents of Lincoln County Sheriff's Department Case # 20030274. Those records requests also repeatedly listed the requested records.
>
> As their admitted records custodian, it remains to Sheriff Virden to obtain those requested records from any source or sources he chooses.
>
> As public records, and as per the order of Judge George Eichwald, they must be turned over to the plaintiffs.
>
> At this time, the plaintiffs see no reason to forego the mandated evidentiary hearing.

Threet sent it verbatim to Attorney Narvaez on September 27, 2010. Later, the meaning of that Threet letter would become horribly clear.

Back then, I rationalized that Threet was no IPRA expert. But his letter to me was too similar to Mickey Barnett's and Pat Roger's trying to get me to dismiss Virden - because dismissing the custodian ends the litigation. So I called an attorney I met at one of my book signings. But she refused to take my case (if the need arose) because, from her experience, Judge Eichwald was too timid to rule against public officials. I was not as negative. I liked his thoughtful manner, letting both sides have a chance.

Only after the evidentiary hearing, did I realize that Threet had, indeed, tried the Barnett/Rogers trick on me. I realized only because I had been making separate IPRA requests to Association of Counties Rick Management: the taxpayer fund reimbursing the Narvaez and Brown law firms monthly for representing Virden, Sullivan and Sederwall. I was requesting their billings as public records, but the copies I got back had blank-outs of some service descriptions. After the usual stonewalling, I got the missing services (assuming they would reveal more lawyers working secretly for the defense). I was wrong and shocked.

On the October 31, 2010 Narvaez Law Firm billing, filled in were secret meetings *with Attorney Threet*! They stated:

> 09/09/10 HFN  Appearance at hearing before Judge Eichwald to consider plaintiff's motion for an order holding Defendants in contempt for failure to produce records and documents, **and post hearing meeting with attorney Ed Threet regarding possible settlement.** [author's boldface] 2.70 hours  $378.00
>
> 09/13/10 HFN  **Conference with Ed Threet regarding the parameters for the upcoming evidentiary hearing and the possible dismissal of Sheriff Virden from the lawsuit.** [author's boldface] 2.10 hours  $294.00

I too was getting monthly bills from Attorney Threet for his time spent on the case. (I paid all case costs.) These bills had no mention of those Narvaez negotiations behind my back.

By February 21, 2011, I fired Threet.

The next attorney gave me Threet's file boxes. So certain had Threet been of tricking me into dismissing Virden, that among his papers - ready to go - was the following secret, never used document faxed to him on September 20, 2010 by the Narvaez law firm:

## STIPULATED ORDER OF DISMISSAL WITH PREJUDICE

THIS MATTER came before the Court on the parties' stipulation of dismissal with prejudice. Plaintiffs, having agreed to dismiss Defendant Rick Virden, Lincoln County Sheriff and Custodian of Records of the Lincoln County Sheriff's Department ("Sheriff Virden"), with prejudice and the Court being fully advised,

The Court hereby FINDS that this matter should be dismissed as against Virden.

IT IS THEREFORE ORDERED THAT this lawsuit, and all matters which were or could have been raised in the lawsuit against Sheriff Virden, whether or not actually raised, are hereby dismissed with prejudice, **each party bearing their or his own fees and costs.** [author's boldface]

Do not miss that Threet had lied in his September 14, 2010 fax-letter to me about attorney fees and my costs being covered. Maliciously, he had intended to leave me footing the bills for the litigation! Their plan was apparently more than destroying my case: it was vengeful destruction of me personally for doing that case. Then I recalled that Threet had told me that 30 year younger Henry Narvaez had been his protégé. Narvaez was Werkmeister's boss. That is what friends do for each other.

## *LEAD-UP TO EVIDENTIARY HEARING*

But back in September of 2010, I only knew that Threet's faxed letter seemed odd. And I labored for months to make copies from my hundreds of documents for folders of 80 exhibits - including the 192 page Virden case file turn-over (all times 7; with copies for me; each defense lawyer; Threet and Dunn; the judge; and my co-plaintiff, Scot Stinnett). Papers covered all surfaces in my house. It was done by Hamster Girl super-power.

And, at my request, Threet and Dunn made a "Motion to Exceed Page Limit for Exhibits" to enter my huge exhibit pack into the court record at the evidentiary hearing.

I also made color 2'x3' display boards for court, diagramming the pure law enforcement nature of the case and the Lee and Orchid Cellmark records requested. [APPENDIX: 62 and 63] And I hired a videographer for the "history-making" event.

As to Threet, he was to get depositions from Lincoln County Attorney Alan Morel, Attorney Bill Robins III, and Governor Bill Richardson; and subpoena Virden, Sullivan, Sederwall, and Morel as witnesses to insure their attendance at the evidentiary hearing.

But I started to get uneasy as time was running out. On December 8, 2010, I faxed a letter to Threet stating:

> I am deeply concerned that three months have elapsed since the granting of the Evidentiary Hearing, and the subpoenas for the depositions of Attorney Morel, Attorney Robins, and Governor Richardson have not been served. And now the short time-frame leaves them much opportunity for evasion. Please fax me an explanation of the service problems and your planned action.

## THE DEPOSITIONS: RICHARDSON, MOREL, ROBINS

The prospect of the depositions was exciting: after seven years, I could question central hoaxers under oath. For Threet, I wrote long question lists with exhibits. But Threet delayed deposition subpoenas. Finally, Richardson's counsel answered his December subpoena and refused deposition by claiming executive privilege; and Morel claimed attorney-client privilege - falsely, since questions involved his public document IPRA responses. But Threet let Morel off the hook by leaving no time to argue back. The evidentiary hearing was to be on January 21, 2011.

### ATTORNEY BILL ROBINS III

Attorney Bill Robins III did come to his deposition in Santa Fe on January 6, 2011. He was surprisingly short. Dark-haired and blocky. He looked more imposing in photos. Threet ignored my questions, calculated to trap. Instead, even after Robins said he was a history major interested in Billy the Kid, Threet let him claim that David Sandoval (present in court only for his New Mexico law license) did the case; never asking why he then came from Texas at all, or how he represented a dead client. As to his checks contributed to Case # 2003-274, Robins said Richardson solicited money from many people; but was not asked why. As to "Brushy," he denied knowing he had wanted a pardon. As to the Sullivan-Sederwall June 21, 2007 "Memorandum" blaming him for seeking the Kid's exhumation, he blamed them right back for it.

I had one odd observation. Periodically, Robins turned his face to me, and his blue eyes became blank-gray while his features froze corpse-like. I wondered if he had petit mal epilepsy. Much later, I remembered that death-stare: on my murder case clients, engrossed in describing to me their killings. Robins had been glancing at me with lethal hatred of the "murder face."

Threet left me in an agony of lost opportunity by what I considered his lack of preparation. Later, I remembered Threet's telling me that, before the deposition that he had a good talk with Robins, "who had a Texan sense of humor." Their joke was on me. Threet squandered my only chance with Robins. But I felt that the evidentiary hearing would nevertheless end the litigation.

## LAST CHANCE TO PREPARE FOR COURT

On Monday January 17, 2010, Threet and Dunn met with me at Threet's office. Exhausted by months preparing write-ups, thousands of pages of exhibit copies and full-color exhibit boards [APPENDIX: 62, 63], I filled the conference room. I also asked Threet if he subpoenaed Virden, Sullivan, Sederwall, and Morel as witnesses. He said he would. (Back then, the fact that only three days remained to do that, raised no red flags for me.) I was so sure of winning that I did not factor in the one way to lose: treachery.

## EVIDENTIARY HEARING OF JANUARY 21, 2011

My confidence in winning at the all-day evidentiary hearing, made me invite enough people to fill the large spectator area.

But layman's ignorance made me miss a key fact: an evidentiary hearing has to get your evidence into the court record. Why? First, it proves your position. Second, if the case is appealed (possible here), nothing new can be added from the district court's records! That key fact would color the upcoming hearing. Keeping out my evidence was the only way to throw my case. January 21, 2011 would be the worst day of my life.

I arrived early with Threet and Dunn to set up my evidence packs and display boards. We took our places at the long plaintiffs' table, I was to the left (with Scot Stinnett at the short end), giant Blair Dunn in the middle, and little Ed Threet most to the right.

Just before Judge George Eichwald entered, Blair Dunn whispered to me, "Threet just said he's doing nothing today. I have to do it. Can you help me?"

Back then, I was unaware of my right to request a continuance if my lead attorney was indisposed and my other one unprepared. Or I could go *pro se* (represent myself) - but would have been too afraid for that anyway. Miserably, I said to Blair, "Yes."

It was obviously Blair's first trial. Attorney Kevin Brown and the court reporter had to tell him how to label exhibits. But knowing few, he entered almost none. For an opening statement, he read my display boards (meant for cross-examinations). Even I could not understand my own case from Blair's presentation.

Threet slept, head to chest, the whole day; with Blair poking him not to fall over (like the tea party Dormouse in *Alice's Adventures in Wonderland*.) Threet did awake for a hearty lunch. Back then, I did not know it was odd for a judge not to call a near-unconscious lead attorney to the stand to ask if he was OK.

As to witnesses, just Virden and Sederwall deigned to come - since Threet had subpoenaed no one. Sullivan and Morel were no-shows. Blair Dunn's father was a spectator, and ominously sat with Virden. They had gone to school together. Later, Blair asked me if he had been too hard on Virden since his dad cared. He had no need to worry.

The motion to enter my 80 folders - called together Exhibit B - was never brought up by Dunn or the judge. So all my wonderful evidence was kept out: even my listing of the requested records; or that Virden was ultimately responsible for their recovery.

## SOME SAD SPECIFICS

If my piles of evidence had been used in cross-examining the witnesses, hammered home for Judge Eichwald would have been the defendants' shell games with the easily recoverable records, their contempt of the Court's order for records turn-over, and IPRA law's obligation for the custodian's records recovery.

Instead, smelling blood, the defense went wild.

For Virden, Attorney Nicole Werkmeister rehashed her past arguments contradicting IPRA law: She said: (1) "do these DNA documents even exist" **[NOTE: The custodian has to request them and find out]**; (2) Plaintiffs could have subpoenaed Orchid Cellmark or Dr. Lee to get the records" **[NOTE: The purpose of the law is that custodian has to get the records]**; and (3) "There's a very technical definition under the Public Records Act, and basically it entails possession." **[NOTE: A lie. IPRA Section**

**14-2-6(A), defines "custodian" as "any person responsible for the maintenance, care or keeping of a public body's public records,** *regardless of whether the records are in that person's actual physical custody or control."*]
(4) Defying the Court's past Order, she asked: "[A]re they public records?" She used Virden's September 3, 2008 turn-over of the 2003-274 file, which had no forensic documents, to argue if he had no records there, he had no other obligation. (5) She concluded: "So we hope after you hear the evidence in this case, your Honor, you will find that number one, these documents don't exist. And number two, if they do exist, the Sheriff never had them, and couldn't possibly turn over, and he's gone beyond what the public records act requires in this case to try to obtain them."

Attorney Kevin Brown, for Sullivan and Sederwall, ignored the Court's Order as to their being public officials and called them hobbyists and called Case # 2003-274 just the deputy murder investigation. Then Brown segued into his intended clinchers. He said Sederwall's work with the carpenter's workbench was private, and its specimens were sent to Orchid Cellmark by report signer Calvin Ostler (unintentionally proving they knew Ostler was the client!). Brown then smugly gave the Court **the workbench report as Exhibit E and the floorboard report as Exhibit F** [author's boldface]. Brown added, "[O]nce we start talking about DNA, its existence or creation of documents, we are going to be getting into a recognized exception in the Public Records Act, which is trade secret privilege."

Blair Dunn's cross-examination of Virden was disastrous for my side. Blair did not pin down Virden's custodial requirement for records recovery, and he let him shift blame to Sederwall:

> Q. …Did you ask him [Sederwall] to send a letter to the lab asking that they release whatever they had to you?
> A. No, I did not.
> Q. May I ask why, sir?
> A. I felt like I had done my part trying to get records that I'm not even sure exist.
> Q. If anything did exist, you could have simply obtained it by asking Mr. Sederwall to send a letter …

As to the Orchid Cellmark records, Blair Dunn did not know enough to counter Rick Virden's sham recovery attempts:

Q. Sheriff Virden, can you describe in more detail any attempts you made to secure these records, any efforts at all you made?
A. Contacted Orchid Cellmark. We contacted Dr. Lee's office. Prior to this, early on, myself and the attorneys contacted Mr. Sullivan and Mr. Sederwall about records ...

Dunn was even worse with master con Sederwall, who said he had provided the Lee reports, switched the case definition, and said Lee was working for *his* hobby case. Finally, Dunn gave up - letting Sederwall lie unchecked. It is worth hearing Sederwall in action:

Q. Can you describe what Dr. Lee did at that time? Did he take any samples of anything ?
A. Could I describe it?
Q. Did he take any sample - forensic samples?
A. Yes, sir ...
Q. What happened to those?
A. Cal Ostler took them and told me he would send them on to Orchid Cellmark.
Q. And they were part of case 2003-274; is that correct?
A. No, sir.
Q. ...Is it fair to say, that the case 2003-274, in part, concerned whether or not Sheriff Pat Garrett shot Billy the Kid?
A. The way I saw 2003-274, was Sheriff Sullivan opened up a case or pulled a call sheet number, and it was a follow-up on the escape and homicide of James Bell and Robert A. [sic-Olinger] ...

But Dunn inadvertently got testimony from Sederwall that would occupy the following year. It concerned the Lee reports given as Exhibits E and F. The punch line is: Sederwall acted as if they were genuine! And Sederwall followed the "hobby" script, which confused Dunn even assisted. Sederwall stated:

Q. Exhibit E [sic –F], please - Requested by" it says, "Steve Sederwall, Capitan, New Mexico, paid for the investigation history Curtis [sic] Production ?" ... [D]id you actually request Dr. Lee to come out or request a report from him?

A. Dr. Lee called me is how that went down. He called me, and I
told him if we did anything like this, we would try to get him
involved, that would be great, because this whole thing was
done by - we call it posse. It is done on their own time and
their own dime. And Dr. Lee, when we found the workbench
and the other items, and then we wanted to do a CSI down at
the courthouse, so we called him …

Q. So did you personally ever receive a copy of Exhibit E?

A. Yes, sir.

Q. How did you receive it?

A. Dr. Lee mailed it to me … At my house.

Q. When you received a report at your house, when you did this,
you weren't acting as a Lincoln County investigator, were
you? [AUTHOR'S NOTE: The stupidest question asked by
any of my attorneys. This is the defense's argument!]

A. No, sir.

Q. When you received the report, who did you think it
belonged to?

A. It belonged to me. It was sent to me.

Dunn's other questioning let Sederwall portray himself in a
central role; though Dunn missed that Sederwall confessed access
to Orchid Cellmark information - which meant records existed and
were recoverable! Sederwall responded:

Q. Did you have any discussions with them about DNA which had
been sent to them from the workbench?

A. Yes, sir … Rick Staub called me about it … He's one of the
owners of Orchid Cellmark … He told me they had DNA on
the workbench from that scraping … Later on, he told me that
it was blended, that there was two DNA.

As to the Arizona exhumation, Dunn did get Sederwall to say
he knew the DNA was sent "to Cellmark," and was taken there by
Rick Staub. Dunn then forgot my warning that Sederwall made up
that the "Lincoln County Sheriff's Department Supplemental
Report" for the John Miller exhumation was a forgery. So Dunn
gave it to Sederwall, who delightedly called it a forgery for Court!

In re-direct, Attorney Brown asked Sederwall a question that
held defense's doom - though I did not yet know it: "Q. Is there
anything in your possession that she's asked that you haven't
turned over? A. No, sir. I don't have anything on DNA, nothing."

Amazingly, Judge Eichwald's ruling still favored us; but he based his judgment on what was presented. Thus, he focused on Sederwall; said Virden had turned over all records in his possession (leaving out obligation for records recovery). And he had received almost none of my pile of exhibits. And, like our side, he believed that the Dr. Lee reports were genuine. Eichwald's later Order would repeat his ruling verbatim. He stated:

THE COURT: Here's what I'm going to find and rule. I'm going to find the investigation in this case of Billy the Kid and the double homicide of James Bell and Robert Ollinger [sic] and the investigation of the death of Billy the Kid are related. I'm going to find these investigations were under the auspicious of the Lincoln County Sheriff's Department Office. I'm going to find that any report, lab results, and anything coming out of this investigation are public documents. I'm going - Dr. Lee's has already been turned over, and that in reviewing Dr. Lee's report, they are pretty comprehensive, and I don't - there's no need to go over any of Dr. Lee's reports or order any new information to be turned over to Plaintiffs. **I'm going to also order that Mr. Sederwall instruct Orchid Cellmark Laboratory, in writing, to provide a complete copy of the entire file, to include any findings or lack of findings, to Sheriff Virden, who will, in turn, provide a copy to Plaintiff's counsel.** [author's boldface] I'm going to also allow counsel for Mr. Virden to take an appeal on this matter. I'm not sure this is the time or the court, but should Mr. Brown deem the necessity to take an interlocutory appeal, I'm going allow it ... **Another finding I'm going to make is Sheriff Virden, in my opinion, has turned over everything that he has in his possession.** [author's boldface] My biggest concern now is the Orchid Cellmark report. Let me also say, I'm not sure who the client is for the lab. It may be Mr. Sederwall, it may be Arizona. I don't know who it is. You may get a letter back from the lab saying that he's not your client. However it turns out, it turns out.

As we left the courtroom, my confused spectators asked me if I had won or lost. I stumbled out in horror. Threet, now and thereafter, with no sign of that day's "sleeping-sickness," said we had won. I knew *he* had won: damaging my case as much as possible after he had failed to trick me into doing the damage myself - by exactly the same tactic as done by Mickey Barnett and Pat Rogers.

By February 17, 2011, the on-site KRQE reporter, Jeff Todd, wrote his "Trial seeks truth in Billy the Kid case," and was even unsure of who was "trying to prove Billy the Kid died in New Mexico." Todd also was unclear that it was an open records case! It was Threet and Dunn's take-home gibberish for any observer and for the judge - and a gift to the defense, their "friends."

## FIRING THREET AND DUNN

I had trustingly entered the courtroom like a lamb to slaughter; completely underestimating the depth of moral degradation in New Mexico. On February 12, 2011, I sent my termination letter to Threet. [APPENDIX: 64] On April 13, 2011, I e-mailed Dunn a termination also, unsure if I could trust him. Later, Scot Stinnett, told me Threet and Dunn had contacted him about representing him separately. Until then, I did not know that a co-plaintiff was not like a partner. But Stinnett stuck with me. And I felt consoled by his presence. It did not occur to me that Threet and Dunn had been attempting another way to destroy my case: through Scot Stinnett. So that option still remained.

Vindictive Ed Threet sent the judge his withdrawal that May, omitting being fired, and stating "he and Plaintiff Gale Cooper can no longer cooperate or communicate." So his passing swipe was to discredit me. (Only much later, did I realize that Threet had oddly made no mention of an "uncooperative" Scot Stinnett.)

## SEDERWALL'S NEXT BOGUS RECOVERY PLOY

By February 5, 2011, Sederwall shamed compliance with Judge Eichwald's ruling that he must get the Orchid Cellmark records. Through Attorney Kevin Brown, Dr. Rick Staub was sent a letter with no identifying information and a reference to a non-existent "event which occurred on July 21, 2004." No Orchid Cellmark response was ever presented. Brown had written:

I represent Steve Sederwall who is a defendant in a suit brought by Gail [sic] Cooper regarding the production of certain DNA results. I have been ordered by the Court to write you and have you produce any DNA results you have from an event which occurred on July 21, 2004. I have enclosed a copy of a report of the event for your convenience.

# ATTORNEYS TIWALD AND RIORDAN

Ahead was a possibly insurmountable hurdle - as intended by Threet and the defendants - my finding a new attorney. Only my Hamster Girl super-power saved my case. Every weekday, for months, from morning to evening, I called each attorney in the Albuquerque yellow pages. By that coincidence, I also learned that under "Civil Rights," the attorneys all represented defendants, not plaintiffs like me. They followed the bucks by protecting the "civil rights" of New Mexico's crooked public officials - like mine - who got a free legal ride on taxpayers covering their attorney bills.

Anyway, I was known myself. Most of the other attorneys I called had been forewarned: over-eager secretaries told me "we have a conflict of interest" as soon as I gave my name, but not my case! Icy dread was non-stop. What if I could find no one? I would lose by default by not filing necessary papers. Scot Stinnett, lifelong New Mexico resident and a journalist, still said he had no lawyer contacts, and did nothing at all to help.

Finally, in June of 2011, I cold-called an attorney named John Tiwald. He said his wife was part of Billy the Kid history. Her family had owned the Tunstall store! And she had grown up in the house whose back-yard held the bodies of those killed in the Lincoln County War: like John Tunstall and Alexander McSween!

I met with John Tiwald and his office manager wife, lugging in the cart with my hundreds of pages of exhibits and write-ups. Attorney Tiwald, a small, bony, tense man, said he had no time for my case. But his wife insisted. He relented reluctantly.

By August, an Old West aficionado and collector referred me to his friend: retired state Supreme Court Judge William "Bill" Riordan. He said Riordan was so impressive that he believed that he had won a case of his own simply because Riordan sat in the spectator area so that his judge saw him. People called Riordan "Judge," in awe.

Rotund Bill Riordan joined on the condition that John Tiwald did most of the work, because he was semi-retired and occupied with doing mediations. He also insisted on a big retainer - (the first lawyer to ask for that, since IPRA grants attorney fees). I asked Stinnett to help me pay Riordan. He said he could not.

But the case was resurrected! (And to make Attorney Riordan's payments, I lived mostly on potatoes.)

## *LEE REPORTS SHOCKER*

After I got Attorneys John Tiwald and Bill Riordan, something unexpected happened in Tiwald's office, with Riordan present. Tiwald had gotten some legal records I asked for.

As a layman, I could only get only the transcripts (for which I was paying); but an attorney had to get the evidentiary hearing's exhibits. I had asked Tiwald to get them so I would what Blair Dunn had gotten into the record. I was trying to decide how to save the case and get in more of my missing evidence.

The pile was small. The defense had entered very little also - since they had no evidence! But I was struck by defense Exhibits E and F. (E was Lee's 16 page carpenter's bench report, and F was Lee's 9 page courthouse floorboard report.) The defendants had no way of knowing I have near-photographic memory. I exclaimed, "This floorboard report is completely different from the floorboard report Sederwall turned over to Threet on February 18, 2010 and gave to Werkmeister on April 6, 2010!" [Figure 5 and Figure 6]

This different Exhibit F floorboard report used the same ornate font used in the Lee bench report's title, and which Sederwall had turned over on November 10, 2010 (and then gave to the Court as Exhibit E). I thumbed through the reports. Neither Exhibits E nor F reports had a "Results and Conclusions" section - though that first Lee floorboard report had one! From my papers I took out that first Lee report to show Tiwald and Riordan.

Then, with all laid out together, I realized that the Lee and Ostler signatures were superimposable - cut and pasted (as Sederwall had accused for the "Supplemental Report" for the John Miller exhumation - apparently knowing the technique!). SO THE DEFENDANTS WERE FORGING DR. LEE REPORTS! No wonder that since 2010 Sederwall had been pulling them like rabbits from a magician's hat. He was re-working them in repeated fix-ups for court and to mimic compliance.

Just when I thought my case was fatally damaged by Threet's and Dunn's keeping out my evidence, I had found a bombshell. It proved defendants' perjury of giving false records as genuine, and proved evidence tampering (criminal violations). And proved was that the defendants *had turned over no requested records at all*. Again, winning seemed possible. This information should finally make patient Judge Eichwald angry, and make him act.

But what was in the real Dr. Henry Lee report or reports?

# Forensic Research & Training Center

## Forensic Examination Report

Date of Request:     May 22, 2004

Requested By:        Steve Sederwall, and Bill Kurtis Productions

Date of Report:      February 25, 2005

Report to:           Steven M. Sederwall

**Examination of Lincoln County Court House:**

On Sunday, 8/1/04, the forensic investigation team examined the old Lincoln County Court House in Lincoln, New Mexico. Present at the scene were Steve Sederwall, Tom Sullivan, David Turk, Bill Kurtis, and Gary Wayne Graves. The target area of examination is located on the top landing of the stairs of the old courtroom.

1. The staircase has been repainted several times over the years.

2. The 2$^{nd}$ floor hallway floor was recovered with wooden floor board. These floor boards were removed. The original floor was exposed. Photograph #1 shows an overall view of hall floor after the removal of new floor board.

3. Photograph #2 shows the target area, which is at the top landing of the stairs where presumptive blood tests were done. The area measured approximately 28 7/8" deep by 43 ½ "wide.

4. Figure 1 is a sketch diagram shows the general dimensions of this staircase.

5. Photograph # 3 depicts the location and condition of the floor boards in the target area.

Page 1 of 9

**FIGURE: 5.** First Dr. Henry Lee floorboard report turned over by defendants on February 18, 2010. as allegedly "original."

# Forensic Research & Training Center

## Forensic Examination Report ©

Date of Request:    May 22, 2004

Requested By:       Steve Sederwall, Capitan, New Mexico, paid for by
                    Investigation History Program, Kurtis Production

Date of Report:     February 25, 2005

Report to:          Steven M. Sederwall

## Examination of Lincoln County Court House:

On Sunday, 8/1/04, the forensic investigation team examined the old Lincoln County Court House in Lincoln, New Mexico. Present at the scene were Steve Sederwall, Tom Sullivan, United States Marshal's Historian David Turk, Producer Bill Kurtis, and Gary Wayne Graves of De Baca County, New Mexico. The target area of examination is located on the top landing of the stairs of the old courtroom.

1. The staircase has been repainted several times over the years.
2. The 2nd floor hallway floor was recovered with wooden floorboard. These floor boards were removed. The original floor was exposed. Photograph #6 shows an overall view of hall floor after the removal of new floor board.

Page 1 of 9

EXHIBIT
F

**FIGURE: 6.** Allegedly same "original" Dr. Henry Lee floorboard report as February 18, 2010 version; and given to the Court by defendants as Exhibit F on January 21, 2011.

*PRESENTMENT HEARING*

We got a Presentment Hearing on September 23, 2011. Brown gave his bogus Sederwall Orchid Cellmark request letter. Tiwald and Riordan brought up that there were discrepancies in the Lee reports. But Judge Eichwald's sole act was to accept our proposed Order: a verbatim repeat of his January 21, 2011 ruling at the evidentiary hearing.

# ADDING ATTORNEY GRIEBEL

By then in my case, I was writing first drafts of the legal filings for Tiwald and Riordan, both of whom were complaining about not having enough time. Also, the court required that attorneys file their papers by e-mail. Tiwald delayed because of his schedule. Riordan had limited ability with computers. So I sought a lawyer to help them.

In October, another lawyer recommended a Patrick Griebel. First I met with Griebel, then with his law firm associates in their modern-looking office. All were young and vigorous. They even projected some of my write-ups on their big conference room's high-tech screen. Griebel was tall, with edgy, reddish, gel-spiked hair and pointy nose; so he looked like a humanized hedgehog.

On November 2, 2011, Scot Stinnett and I signed Patrick Griebel's representation agreement, which was pro bono. That let me free John Tiwald from the burden of my case. Riordan stayed on; with assurance that Griebel's well-staffed office could shoulder most of the work. My hope was fast returning.

# ATTORNEYS GRIEBEL AND RIORDAN

My honeymoon period with Patrick Griebel was short, ending the same month. Initially, his work seemed excellent. The crisis began when I checked the court docket and found, unbeknownst to me, Scot Stinnett listed as having filed a motion for payment of fees to the past (fired) attorneys (Barnett, Threet, and Dunn).

This was confusing. Plaintiffs' attorney fees are awarded *at the end of an IPRA case.* Our case was not over. And this would distract from the tampered Lee reports. Also, a fee request would likely throw the case into appeal. So, thinking the docket was in error, I e-mailed Griebel on November 16, 2011.

But Griebel's response was a return to the Twilight Zone (which I had first entered in my September 12, 2008 meeting with Pat Rogers and Mickey Barnett). Griebel fired off abusive and irrational e-mails to me into the night. He also demanded a large sum of money and a new retainer canceling the one of 14 days before. He seemed "on something," manic, or enraged. I forwarded the e-mails to Stinnett (who did nothing). By morning, Griebel tried to minimize his outbursts. But I had enough.

## FIRING ATTORNEY PATRICK GRIEBEL

On November 21, 2011, I sent Attorney Griebel my termination letter, Cc'd to Scot Stinnett and Attorney Bill Riordan, and titled: "Re: Immediate termination of services for Sandoval District Court Cause No. D-1329-CV-07-1364." It stated:

This letter constitutes an immediate termination of your legal services, those of Albuquerque Business Law, and any individual contracted by you or your firm for the case of Gale Cooper and the De Baca County News vs Lincoln County Sheriff Rick Virden et al (Sandoval District Court Cause No. D-1329-CV-07-1364).

I will send [a courier service] on Monday November 21, 2011 to pick up the two boxes of case documents I delivered to your office last Tuesday, as well as any other documents generated at your firm.

Below are my reasons for this decision, which arose after consideration of your e-mails to me from November 16th and 17th of 2011. For reference, I included quoted statements where relevant:

OVERVIEW: You were referred to me by [attorney name] on October 18, 2011 for possible representation for my ongoing open records violation case against Lincoln County law enforcement officials. The following pertains to our contacts:

1. On our first contact on Wednesday October 19, 2011, by telephone, you volunteered that you understood that cases like mine were on a contingency basis. Acceptance of contingency is why I continued our discussions.

2. On Monday October 24, 2011, we met for lunch, along with Pat Garrett's grandson, Jarvis Patrick Garrett, to further discuss the case, and to address his joining as a co-plaintiff.

3. On Monday October 27, 2011, I met for an in-house lunch with you; members of your firm; and my then attorneys, John Tiwald

and William Riordan, to discuss my case. Later that day you phoned me to say that your firm would take the case on a contingency basis. The contingencies were Attorney William Riordan's continuing as consultant, and Attorney Tiwald's discontinuing participation.

4. To comply, I sent e-mails to Attorney Riordan and Attorney Tiwald (with his termination based only on his not having enough time to devote to the case). You told me that I could add to that termination letter assurance that his fees would pre-empt those charged by your firm in any court hearing on the matter. (That generosity, of course, impressed me).

5. On Wednesday November 2, 2011, my co-plaintiff, Scot Stinnett, and I each separately signed a services agreement with your firm. It made clear the contingency nature of the case. We then had a lunch meeting with you, your firm, and Attorney Riordan to discuss planning issues. Communicated was that your contract worker, Jeremy Theoret, would do much of the hands-on work. It was agreed that my long experience with Case # 2003-274 and its open records requests, as well as my knowledge of Cause No. D-1329-CV-07-1364, would be used.

6. At that November 20th meeting, it also emerged that the Findings and Conclusions of Law document was due in two days. It was agreed that Attorney Riordan and I would prepare it for firm review - which we did.

7. At that November 20th meeting, I also learned that our response to the defendants' responses to the Tiwald/Riordan Motion for Supplementing the Record and Sanctions addressing the defendants' forged/altered forensic documents was due on November 9th.

8. On Monday and Tuesday of November 7th and 8th of 2011, Jeremy Theoret, myself, and you prepared that response to the defendants' responses. I felt that document was superlative. On Wednesday the 9th, it was sent to the court; and I got copy. But it had been altered; and an erroneous and potentially deleterious statement blaming the forensic lab had been added.

9. My response to that error was to inform you by e-mail and to request a brief phone call to fine-tune communications by giving me sign-off. That time was set for Friday the 18th.

10. On Tuesday November 15, 2011, as requested, I delivered to your office case pleadings and other relevant documents (two boxes) so that Jeremy Theoret could begin review.

11. On Wednesday November 16, 2011, you e-mailed me that a Hearing on fee settlement for my case had been scheduled for January 17, 2012. Since my checking the court record indicated that filing was by a plaintiff, I asked why that had been done by our side - concerned that the judge could end the case (especially if our forged document motion had not yet been heard). You e-mailed that you had not done that filing.

12. Then all hell broke loose.

ALTERED FINANCIAL REQUIREMENTS: The evening of that Wednesday November 16th, you sent e-mails which made financial demands differing from our signed agreement of November 2, 2011. Most dramatic, was a demand for $5,000.00. Threateningly and humiliatingly, you also stated that you had told Jeremy Theoret and Laurie Scott to cease all work on my case.

UNPROFESSIONAL LANGUAGE: That same evening of Wednesday November 16th, to the early morning of Thursday the 17th, you sent other e-mails which I construed as unprofessional, abusive, and unjust. (And we have had no phone contact at all since they were sent.) They are as follows [and signed by him]:

I am now starting to understand why you have had 5 different lawyers.

We did not request the hearing. We received the notice today. Does that answer your uninformed question?

And my first name is not "attorney." it's Patrick. Please don't refer to me as "attorney Griebel" any more.

I will call you on tomorrow at which point I will decide if I will stay in this case or not. You seem unwilling to learn how these things work and you seem to be having a very hard time understanding your role as it relates to our role, and while I am a patient teacher, my patience with you is starting to wear thin. You don't seem to get it. And I am too busy with paying clients for this case unless we get things perfectly straight. I'll be in touch tomorrow.

---

Also... When we chat tomorrow, we will need to come to an agreement on a retainer that will need to be paid to our firm to cover my hard costs pending payment from the defendants. It will be at least $5,000 with a $2,500 reserve payable immediately.

By copy of Jeremy and Laurie, I am asking them to cease further work until your new engagement letter is executed and funds have cleared. We have many, many other matters to attend to which we will now do pending execution of our new arrangement.

---

Your expectations and understanding of the process are way, way off base, so now I'm investing my time an MY money in your case and am starting to recognize that I am probably making a huge mistake. I think it is probably related to yet another artificial aspect of this case: you have no financial skin in the game. Sort of like a spoiled 16 year old who gets a brand new convertible BMW for her birthday... And you're complaining about the color of the seats... Daily. You will need to put some skin in the game. What can you do?

ACCUSATION OF MY IGNORANCE: I make no claim of legal training. But in answer to your e-mailed remark about the fee Hearing - "We did not request the hearing. We received the notice today. Does that answer your uninformed question?" - I got my information from the court; and understood that the hearing was requested by plaintiff 2 (Scot Stinnett). You and Attorney Riordan are our only lawyers; all others having gotten formal terminations. See below for the Hearing information:

Miscellaneous

| Party Name | Party Type | Party # |
|---|---|---|
| COOPER GALE | P | 1 |
| | | |
| DE BACA COUNTY NEWS | P | 2 |
| LINCOLN COUNTY | D | 1 |
| VIRDEN RICK | D | 2 |
| SEDERWALL STEVEN M | D | 3 |
| SULLIVAN THOMAS T | D | 4 |

Register of Actions Activity

| Event Date | Event Description | Event Result | Party Type | Party # | Amount |
|---|---|---|---|---|---|
| 11/16/2011 | NTC: OF HEARING | | | | |
| | Notice of Hearing | | | | |
| 11/10/2011 | REQUEST FOR HEARING/ SETTING | | | | |
| | Attorney's Fees | | | | |

CONCLUSION: For litigation, a client needs - besides good representation - treatment with dignity, and agreements honored.

1. After our first conversation; after the delightful meetings with you, your bright colleagues, and the staff; after the meticulous and clever work done by Jeremy Theoret and you in preparing the Supplement-Sanctions response; I thought I had finally found lawyer heaven.

2. But just two weeks after my signing your services agreement, your unaccountable hostility arose: fee demands; and abusive, unprofessional, and unjustified e-mailed attacks.

3. Also, later that Thursday the 17th, you blamed *me* by e-mail for *your* outbursts – attributing them to my questions about the fees Hearing (which seemed more like rationalization of abuse, than accepting responsibility for it).

4. I have zero tolerance for abuse. And my trust ended with your attempts to change our contingency payment agreement, only weeks after its signing, to one of seemingly high fees. (Furthermore, that implied possible future sudden and threatening demands – no matter what revised agreement was made now.)

5. So I have no choice but to end any connection to you and your firm.

Please keep any future communication to writing to insure clear communication.

Next, within days, Scot Stinnett informed me that he was staying with Griebel. Marlyn Bowlin's warning finally came back to me: Do not trust Scot Stinnett. In retrospect, Stinnett had done nothing for the litigation - no bringing in of FOG, no major IPRA arguments, no work, no money, and no press (he owns a paper!). And now that I had a new angle to defeat the defendants, Stinnett sprang into action: for the fired lawyers. I smelled a rat: him.

And Attorney Riordan also did not protect me, though he stayed on the case. He had his own issue with me - possibly not entirely different from Attorney Griebel's. In the Tiwald period, he wanted to quit. He said, "You are the smartest client I've ever had. And I don't like it." I thought he was joking. He was not.

On the ever-darkening road I was traveling, my enemies were as likely to be on my own side as my opponents' side. Destruction of state history got no reaction. A trouble-maker did: hatred. I was frightened and miserable. But I would not back down.

# Thrown into the Court of Appeals

Of course, the premature fee request - as I had predicted - gave the defendants a chance to take the district court case to the New Mexico Court of Appeals on April 9, 2012, by Attorney Brown, soon followed by Attorney Narvaez. And - as I expected - they argued not just that it was too early to settle fees, but that fees were moot since *the whole case should be thrown out by the Appeals Court.* And they presented their false arguments of private hobbyists' records, records not existing, and the Sheriff having turned over what was in his pocket.

Attorney Bill Riordan refused to represent me there. So I had to go *pro se* and learn how to write appeals briefs. I alleged that the defendant-appellants were arguing beyond the scope of their limited fee appeal; that the fee request was not mine; and that resolution could come simply by awaiting case completion in district court. I requested dismissal of the appeal. The Appeals Court refused. Scot Stinnett seemed about to destroy my case.

Meanwhile, the hearings on the tampered Lee reports awaited. Griebel and Stinnett joined Riordan for that matter.

# Just Attorney Bill Riordan

It was a relief that Attorney Riordan continued representing me. Of course, he wanted more money. Upcoming in January was the hearing I hoped would end my case. Big, ovoid, bald, and with too-small feet that hurt, Riordan looked like Humpty-Dumpty; but got respect. Plus, he seemed above politics. That was enough.

### *HEARING ON LEE REPORTS AND ATTORNEYS' FEES*

On January 17, 2012, for the Hearing on the "Plaintiffs' Motion to Supplement the Record and a Request for Sanctions, and Co-Plaintiff's Motion For Attorney Fees," the courtroom looked like my personal nightmare. Present were all my fired attorneys (or firm members) - people I had hoped never to see again. John Tiwald came too in case fees were settled. My worry had been how to respond to enemies. I learned the courtroom answer (where facing adversaries is common): everyone becomes invisible and does not interact. But we were a funny scene, with standing room only on the plaintiff-side; and the defense side having just scowling hawk-faced Attorney Kevin Brown (he had to deal with forgery!) and girlish long-haired Nicole Werkmeister.

Riordan gave Judge Eichwald the three different Lee reports; stating that none were "original;" all were forged or tampered. Defense for Virden ignored his IPRA responsibility to turn over genuine records, and passed the buck: "[H]e never had a copy of Dr. Lee's report, and, in fact, he didn't even know it existed prior to this litigation. So what he ultimately produced is what he obtained from Defendant Sederwall in this litigation." Repeated was their IPRA law lie: "All that the statute requires ... he can't produce something he never had possession of." Brown was left with just double-talk to avoid nasty words like "forged."

When it came to arguing for the past attorney fees, Riordan made the first move. He had been excited during our drive to court, saying he had an obscure rule he hoped to use. (As an aside, if one wants to question a witness, they have to be subpoenaed to attend, as well as presented with evidence that would be used. That risks concocting lies.) But Riordan did a stealth maneuver, based on the fact that the past attorneys were already present! He asked the judge for under five minutes to question Mr. Threet.

Threet took the stand assuming it was about fees (and likely worried about the issue of being fired and not deserving them). Riordan asked him if, in the course of his representation of me, he sent and received communications. He had. So Riordan said he wanted to make an Admission Against the Evidence (that means entering an Exhibit that a witness is likely to be honest about, because to do otherwise would be self-incriminating.) That granted, Riordan entered into the record Threet's September 14, 2010 letter to me saying that Virden *could get the Lee and Orchid Cellmark records if dismissed.* Threet admitted he had written it. The judge looked like he would explode. Then Attorney Tiwald argued that fee payments were actually punitive sanctions.

Judge Eichwald ruled. He delayed decision as to the Lee report, but stated: "Mr. Sederwall is to produce all original reports within five days." And he admonished the defense clients against playing "hide the ball." As to attorney fees, Eichwald stated: "The four attorneys who are no longer in the case, I'm going to award their attorneys' fees." That meant an almost unprecedented fee award of 100%. It seemed that retired Supreme Court Judge Riordan emboldened sweet and timid Judge George Eichwald.

## *SEDERWALL'S NEXT LEE REPORT TURN-OVER*

To my surprise, Sederwall came up with yet another Lee report (discussed earlier). On January 31, 2012, Riordan and I, along with a lawyer from Griebel's firm, met in Attorney Kevin Brown's office. Brown kept a straight face. This was the fourth "only one report" he was giving to us. This one was 25 pages, with black-and white photos; and came with the same envelope Sederwall had been presenting since 2008 as holding his "one" Lee report. [APPENDIX: 11]

Titled "Forensic Research & Training Center Forensic Examination Report," it was in yet another font. The eye-opener was its heading and "Introduction" on pages 1 and 2. After repeating the "May 22, 2004 request date shared by the other "Lee reports," it gave the law enforcement information expurgated from the others, including case number and lawman titles [in author's boldface below]:

Requested By: **Lincoln County Sheriff's Office, New Mexico**
          Investigating History Program, Kurtis Production
**Local Case No. 2003-274**
Date of Report: February 25, 2005
Report to: **Steve Sederwall**
          **Lincoln County Sheriff's Office, New Mexico**


### Introduction

At the request of **Steve Sederwall of Lincoln County Sheriff's Office, Lincoln County**, Bill Kurtis and Jamie Schenk of Kurtis Production, [sic – and] Dr. Henry Lee went to New Mexico on July 31, 2004 to assist in the re-investigation of the case of Billy the Kid. The forensic investigation team participating in re-investigation consist [sic –of] the following individuals:

Dr. Henry Lee, Chief Emeritus of the Connecticut State Police
    Forensic Laboratory
Calvin Ostler, Forensic Consultant, Riverton, Utah
Kim Ostler, Crime Scene Assistant, Riverton, Utah
**Tom Sullivan, Sheriff, Lincoln County New Mexico**
**Steve Sederwall Deputy Sheriff, Lincoln County New Mexico**
David Turk, US Marshal, United States Marshall [sic] Service

In addition, Mike Haag, Firearm examiner from Albuquerque Police Department Crime Lab, also provided valuable technical assistance in the investigation.

The forensic investigation team arrived at the Manny Miller residence, located at (address given here, not removed like in Exhibit E version), Albuquerque, New Mexico, at 18:20 hours on Saturday, July 31, 2004. Upon arrival we were presented with three pieces of evidence: a worktable, a washstand, and a headboard. The three pieces of evidence had been removed from a storage building at the rear of the residence by **Sheriff Sullivan, Deputy Sederwall**, and members of Bill Kurtis Productions. Each item was inspected visually and macroscopically. The following were found:

This report repeated Lee's giving his samples to the Lincoln County Sheriff's Department. And it had the "Results and Conclusion" section which was removed from "Lee reports" Exhibits E and F. It had only Lee's claim of "blood-like" stains (as far as Lee dared hoax in writing); and did not claim conclusive blood, like the hoaxers had stated all along for the press.

Riordan stayed skeptical. It still was not original or a duplicate of the original, since Lee's scrawled signature (likely done with a Sharpie) did not match the one on Lee's May 1, 2006 letter to Jay Miller or the copy-and-pasted ones on the other "Lee reports." And Calvin Ostler's signature line was unsigned.

But it was closer to the original. It was one report - as Lee had always claimed - and combined his investigations into: "Item #1 Workbench," "Item #2 Washstand," "Item #3 A piece of Headboard." And it showed why my defendants wanted to hide it: they were making up its conclusions to keep exhuming bodies.

## SUBPOENAED ORCHID CELLMARK RECORDS

In what seemed to be his ongoing effort to dismantle my IPRA litigation - or sheer ignorance of IPRA law - my co-plaintiff, Scott Stinnett, and his wild attorney, Patrick Griebel, next abandoned IPRA law and subpoenaed themselves my requested DNA records from Orchid Cellmark Laboratory. By April 20, 2013, they got some of them - an impressive total of 133 pages, including the DNA extractions from Dr. Henry Lee's bench and floorboard samples; and DNA extractions from the Prescott, Arizona, remains of John Miller and William Hudspeth.

Proved was that Case # 2003-274 records existed and were recoverable; and that Orchid Cellmark considered Case # 2003-274 as combining Lee's specimens and Arizona exhumation specimens – labeling all as their Case No. 4444. And a photo of Lee's chain of custody bags for his carpenter's bench samples even had both case numbers.

The subpoena was good because it proved the hoaxing, since there was no testing for bench blood, and DNA findings were "inconclusive" junk (no DNA of Billy the Kid!). And Lee's report's co-signer, Calvin Ostler, was listed as Orchid Cellmark's client.

The subpoena was bad, because it risked my litigation by getting records (though Virden was in noncompliance). And still outstanding were original Lee report(s) and Orchid Cellmark's DNA matching results of Lee's bench DNA to the two dead Arizona men's DNA. So my litigation remained unassailable.

In response to the records, the hoaxers did their usual *Albuquerque Journal* Rene Romo damage control. This time it was joined by Attorney Griebel and Scot Stinnett doing their own back-patting. (As usual, I was not contacted.) On April 29, 2012, Romo printed "Fight Won, Questions Remain: Billy the Kid DNA Report [sic] Released." It spun that the DNA records did not put "to rest" claims of "Brushy" and John Miller. It had Sederwall give hoax contentions (possibly for Judge Eichwald's eyes); and then it falsely declared my litigation ended. Was that "Fight Won" and case ended also sabotage betrayal by Stinnett? The truth was that no records had been turned over, forgeries were given, and the case of total IPRA violation was continuing. But Romo wrote:

> LAS CRUCES – It took five years and a dogged court fight, but a historian and a De Baca County weekly newspaper have finally obtained records spawned by Lincoln County's much-publicized investigation of Billy the Kid's death and criminal exploits through the state's public records law.
>
> But the documents, 163 pages of a Texas Laboratory's analysis of DNA material collected from an Arizona grave site and scraped from a bench upon which the outlaw's bloody body was said to rest, do not clear up any lingering questions about the Kid's death.
>
> Nor does the analysis, produced by Orchid Cellmark of Dallas put to rest claims by two men – Ollie "Brushy Bill" Roberts of Hico, Texas, or John Miller of Arizona – that they were the real Billy the Kid and had not been killed by Sheriff Pat Garrett on July 14, 1881, in Fort Sumner.

The modern examination of the Kid's murder of two Lincoln County deputies in early 1881 and his death that year was started by former Capitan Mayor Steve Sederwall, Lincoln County reserve deputy, and then-sheriff Tom Sullivan.

Then, on April 24, 2007 Gale Cooper, a retired psychiatrist and amateur historian, filed a written request for investigation records under the state Inspection of Public Records Act.

**[AUTHOR'S NOTE: Here, the hoaxers, Griebel, and Stinnett agree to the truth that I requested the records. Later, Stinnett would lie that he was the requestor.]**

A lawsuit followed later that year, with Cooper and the De Baca County News as plaintiffs.

**[AUTHOR'S NOTE: At this time, Griebel and Stinnett truthfully say Stinnett joined my case as a plaintiff for litigation. Later they would make up a different story.]**

Sederwall and Sullivan argued that they conducted the investigation as private citizens, using their own funds, and so any documents generated by the case were their private hobby.

But Cooper and the news weekly argued successfully that, because the investigation was conducted under the Lincoln County sheriff's department, all records were public.

The plaintiffs received a ruling declaring the records public from state District Court in Sandoval County in March 2010. They obtained another ruling in January 2011 ordering Lincoln County Sheriff Rick Virden, who said he did not physically possess the requested records, to produce them.

The DNA files were finally produced earlier this month

**[AUTHOR'S NOTE: Here is the switcheroo to "produced," as if the defendants had handed them over in the litigation.]**

after the De Baca County News' new attorney, Patrick Griebel of Albuquerque Business Law, sent the Texas laboratory's parent company, Laboratory Corp. of America, a subpoena.

De Baca County News publisher Scott [sic] Stinnett said the importance of the legal victory is in upholding the principle that public records must be produced upon request, even when a records custodian claims the files are not in their possession.

**[AUTHOR'S NOTE: Stinnett's quote is odd and false for an "IPRA man," since plaintiff's subpoenaing records is no "legal victory" and sabotages IPRA's intent that records must be turned over by the responsible public officials.]**

If that principle is not upheld, Stinnett said, "Any public official can just give them (records) to someone and say 'I can't get them.' "

"These are my concerns," Stinnett said, "that the Inspection of Public Records Act is not only upheld, but strengthened by case law that shows if you're a public official and screwing around with public records, you are going to pay the price."

To date, the defending law suit has cost nearly $101,000, [sic] according to an attorney with the New Mexico Association of Counties, which administers a self-insurance pool that covers Lincoln County's legal expenses.

Sederwall said last week that he never saw written records by the laboratory, Orchid Cellmark of Dallas. Sederwall said that after realizing the DNA material had limited value, he told the lab to stop its work.

**[AUTHOR'S NOTE: Oops! As usual, Sederwall "the mouth" talks too much – here proving his direct contact with Orchid Cellmark and its records - as had custodian Virden.]**

Sederwall said that one of his initial goals was to defend Garrett's reputation. Claims by Miller and Roberts, decades after the Kid's death, that they were the true outlaw presumed that Garrett killed the wrong man and lied about it. But in the course of the investigation, Sederwall began to question Garrett's accounts of several incidents, irritating some historians and Fort Sumner officials.

Then-Gov. Bill Richardson embraced and publicized the investigation in a Santa Fe news conference.

But Sederwall and Sullivan were stymied when they proposed exhuming the remains of the outlaw's mother, Catherine Antrim, in Silver City, and the Kid's in a Fort Sumner cemetery and Roberts' remains in Texas.

**[AUTHOR'S NOTE: Arizona exhumations are omitted.]**

Fort Sumner officials complained that, because the precise location of the outlaw's remains was uncertain, the investigation would undermine the town's claim to be the Kid's final resting spot and damage tourism.

**[AUTHOR'S NOTE: Sederwall's double-talk to hide why exhumations were really blocked by accusing officials' of a tourism agenda, so as to appear as a "martyr for the truth."]**

"There are Pat Garrett fans, and there are Billy the Kid fans," Sederwall said last week. "Neither one of them wants questions asked, because they want history to remain the same."

Unable to get the outlaw's DNA from a grave, in the summer of 2004, Sederwall and Sullivan turned to a bench from the Maxwell House [sic] where the Kid was killed and on which his body was reportedly laid after he was gunned down.

**[AUTHOR'S NOTE: Oops. Romo has a dead Kid on the bench - accidentally ending Case 2003-274's murder investigation! Apparently, Sederwall had not dared to float for Romo his "dead men don't bleed" - so Billy "played dead." This hoax switcheroo from graves to bench was always hard for Sederwall to pull off because it is so transparently silly.]**

Forensic scientist DR. Henry Lee, with a Utah investigator, took swabs and wood shavings from the bench for DNA analysis.

However, the swabs and shavings did not provide enough DNA to generate a complete DNA sequence that could be compared to another. "No conclusions with regard to this sample can be reached," says a 2004 report by Orchid Cellmark.

**[AUTHOR'S NOTE: This not "enough DNA" and no "complete sequence" for comparison is Sederwall's new hoax add-on after the fiasco of the Orchid Cellmark DNA results. The truth is that the samples were uselessly mixed DNA and there existed no reference DNA to establish any identities. But sly and determined Sederwall, is still trying to keep the door open, as if getting "more DNA" was a solution.]**

Television producer Bill Kurtis, who met Sederwall while working on the "investigating History" series on Billy the Kid for the History Channel, wrote the Journal in an email: "At no time did Lee or Steve Sederwall state to me that the DNA was from Billy the Kid."

**[AUTHOR'S NOTE: If no one said there was Billy DNA, why did you, Bill Kurtis, think they dug up John Miller for DNA matching with Billy DNA – as your crew was filming in Arizona? This is a ricochet validation fail!]**

Plaintiffs in the case are seeking legal costs for the years-long fight that could exceed $150,000, Griebel said. Plaintiffs also seek damages against Lincoln County Sheriff's Department that, at the rate of $100 per day since the initial records request was filed, could exceed $180,000.

**[AUTHOR'S NOTE: This Griebel calculation of damages is far less than the actual amount. Demonstrated is that Stinnett does not know IPRA law, or was doing damage control.]**

## SECOND HEARING ON FORGED LEE REPORTS AND SUBPOENAED ORCHID CELLMARK RECORDS

On May 31, 2012, was the hearing on "Second Motion to Supplement the Record and a Request for Sanctions." Bill Riordan said Sederwall's Lee report given January 31, 2012 was still not "original" because it lacked signatures and color photos. But he forgot the punch line of its proving that that forged versions removed law enforcement headers. He requested defendant depositions as sanctions at their expense, and at the courthouse when Judge Eichwald was present, "so we can get the questions answered about how all of these versions were made up."

Then Attorney Griebel entered the 133 pages of subpoenaed Orchid Cellmark records, proving they existed.

Virden's defense was left only to repeat the not-in-his-possession lie, and try to extend it to those recovered records:

Are you required to send letters affirmatively and go out and acquire such documents? I would submit that that is not a reasonable interpretation of IPRA. That is not a burden that the courts want to impose on custodians of public records. I would submit it would be a reasonable burden for custodians to go out and search what is in their custody, possession, and control, and produce it.

Attorney Brown, for Sederwall and Sullivan, had to bluff, saying Sederwall "went through all his stuff" and found the report "which was a combined report, initially, in the mail." Brown said "Sederwall is not the custodian ... There's no legal basis for sanction at this time." Brown was trying to eliminate Sederwall's responsibility for perjury and records tampering!

Judge Eichwald ruled only that we could repeat depositions: "I'm going to order the deposition to be taken of all Defendants. The only limit I'm placing on the deposition is that it be limited to - it's pretty broad, actually - anything having to do with the DNA evidence or evidence that is subject of this case." But he was soft on the defendants. As to the cost of the depositions (thousands of dollars) he said: "[A]t this point the parties bear their equal share and will be assessed after the depositions are taken." (That meant *me* paying.) But he did say: "My concern is this, folks, I hope the Defendants aren't playing a shell game with the Court." That meant Sederwall still had to give a genuine Lee report.

## *ANOTHER SEDERWALL LEE REPORT TURN-OVER*

On June 7, 2012, Sederwall "found" another Lee report, which Attorney Kevin Brown turned over to Attorney Riordan. It was a CD having the January 31, 2012 turned-over, 25 page, Lee report. This one had color photos and no signatures at all.

In his cover letter of June 7, 2012, Brown stated: "Because the issue of color photographs was raised by Mr. Riordan at the last hearing, I have enclosed a CD containing an electronic version of the 25 page report with color photos."

## *SEDERWALL AND VIRDEN REPEAT DEPOSITIONS*

The court-ordered depositions as potential sanctions were scheduled for June 26 and 27, 2012 in the jury room next door to Judge George Eichwald's chambers in the Sandoval County District Courthouse. Sullivan, claiming ill health, and had been excused. As usual, I wrote the questions, this time modifying my approach for Attorney Riordan to a few pages per topic, with topics as separate labeled folders with their exhibits. (It was another chance to get in my evidence!) Sederwall was on the first day; Virden on the next. Attorney Jeremy Theoret from Patrick Griebel's office would also question. Scot Stinnett, did not come.

## STEVE SEDERWALL DEPOSITION, JUNE 26, 2012

It was the first time I had been in a jury room. Claustrophobic jurors must suffer. Windowless, the narrow, long, gray-walled space was filled by a long table slab. At the far end was a counter with a sink and coffee pot, which the transcriptionist filled. After that was a bathroom. The entrance at the other end was also the only door out. At one point, the bailiff even locked us in because its courtroom was in use.

Present with Steve Sederwall, was a court reporter, Attorney Kevin Brown, and Attorney Henry Narvaez. I had only seen Narvaez a few times in court. Close-up, that small neat man resembled a ventriloquist's dummy with painted-on dark hair and painted-on smile. Sitting across from me, he smilingly said to call him "Henry," that he was a Billy the Kid fan, and after the case he wanted me to show him around historical sites. He seemed so slimy that I half expected to see his glistening trail leading into the room from that one door.

Automatically awe-inspiring Attorney Riordan made all the difference. As soon as Kevin Brown opened his mouth to object (as he had interrupted Attorneys Barnett and Garcia in 2008), Riordan attacked. He called in Judge Eichwald and complained of improper interference. As usual, Eichwald just listened benevolently; but after he left, Brown stopped his tactic.

Big Sederwall was no match for broad Riordan, who made his lies look awkward and elicited near confessions. Riordan had joined Sederwall's billythekidcase.com website (by paying $25.00), and been outraged. Riordan's questioning exposed Sederwall's profiteering from Case # 2003-274 records as follows:

Q. Let's talk about those newspapers and whatnot. You mentioned MSNBC, do you recall how many hits that got?

A. Billy Sparks said there was over 24 million hits in less than 24 hours ...

Q. ...That commission card was given to you, you posted it on your Web site, and you put the words across, 'Billy the Kid case," right?

A. Um-hmm.

Q. Dos Sombreros, is that you and Sullivan?

A. That's me ... That's my - that's the name of my private detective agency ... Key word there, private ...

Q. Let me show you Exhibit 20. That's a report from the Metropolitan Forensic Science Center of Albuquerque, New Mexico, isn't it? ... And it references Case Number 2003-274, Lincoln County; is that correct? ... And it states that these requests were made by Lincoln County Sheriff's Office: Steve Sederwall, and Institute of Forensic Science, Dr. Henry Lee; correct?

A. It does say that yes, sir.

Q. And it has to do with the dresser and the furniture, right? ... And that was part of the official investigation of 2003-274?

A. It was part of the investigation. As far as official, I don't know if would tack that name on it ...

Q. Do you have any idea how many people joined?

A. I don't have a clue ... I don't handle that at all ...

Q. Where does the $25 go to? ... You get the profits of this $25, does that come to you?

A. ... I think it goes to Pay Pal and it goes to another fund ...

Q. When you say there's credit cards, that this money was paying off credit cards, whose?

A. My credit card ...

Q. But you don't got the checks? ...How do you pay your credit
card with this money if you don't get the check?

A. My wife or somebody does it ...


Wilting under Riordan's questioning were Sederwall's calling
Case # 2003-274 private, switching Case # 2003-274's definition to
deputy murders, and pretending no involvement in exhumations,
as follows:

Q. To your knowledge are there some Lincoln County Sheriff's
Department criminal investigations that are official and some
that are not official?

A. No, there's call sheet numbers ...

Q. Was the probable cause statement that you drafted part of the
record for 2003-274?

A. I assume it was. He [Sheriff Sullivan] asked me for it and
I handed it to him ...

Q. Do you know if it was going to be used in any of the lawsuits in
which exhumation was requested?

A. I don't remember if that -- I don't know if it came up or not ...

Q. Well, case number 2003-274 was a Sheriff's Office official
investigation, wasn't it?

A. It was a case - yeah, if you'll look at the call sheet, it was to
investigate - Tom pulled that when we fired a gun off in that
courthouse. It says, "The investigation of the murder of Bell
and Olinger. It doesn't say a damn thing about digging up
Billy the Kid and all this nonsense. [NOTE: Sederwall is
omitting the Probable Cause Statement] ...

A. I know Sherry Tippett, but I don't know if she represented me.
I don't know. [Petitioners attorney for exhuming Billy and
mother]

Q. Weren't you a petitioner in the petition to exhume the remains
of Catherine Antrim?

A. My name was on it, yes, sir.

Q. Did you know that your name was on it?

A. I was aware of that later.


To Riordan, Sederwall did not dare use his "forgery" ploy for
the "Supplemental Report" on the John Miller exhumation:

Q. I think that previously you were asked about the supplemental report document in your deposition, and you said that you didn't know whether or not this was your signature on it, do you recall that?

A. That does appear to be my signature.

Riordan's carpenter's bench questioning went for blood - Sederwall's, not Billy the Kid's! Riordan established that the murder investigation was for the Kid's killing; that Sederwall investigated the bench as a deputy; brought out Sederwall's lies about blood on the bench [unsupported by Dr. Lee's report]; and had Sederwall admit to knowing bench DNA results as follows:

A. ... There's two DNA on this workbench. There's blood running down the edges of it. As an investigator, I've been to crime scenes, and when there's that much blood, somebody's heart's pumping. And I know there is nothing about this story that makes sense, nothing. There is nothing about this story that adds up.

Q. Which story?

A. The story of the Kid being killed ..

Q. [Reads from Probable Cause Statement] "On August 29, 2003, Deputy Sederwall of the Lincoln County Sheriff's Department located the carpenter bench where the Kid's body was placed July 14, 1881. On September 13, 2003, investigators located all the furniture that was in Pete Maxwell's bedroom the night of the shooting, July, 1881." That's what it reads, isn't it?

A. Yes, sir.

Q. Then would you look at the very last paragraph on the last page ... The third line from the bottom. It reads "Probable cause exists to warrant the Court to grant investigators the right to search for truth in criminal investigation 2003-274 through DNA samples obtained from Catherine Antrim" ... So the case -- the probable cause statement in this case shows, obviously, that it was an official case of the Sheriff's Department. The probable cause statement is in case numbered 2003-274 ... And the document states that you were acting as the Deputy Sheriff involved in case 2003-274 at the time you did these things, right? ... [Y]ou were commissioned at that time by Sheriff Sullivan, weren't you? ... And then you were later commissioned by?

A. Yes, sir.

Riordan cornered Sederwall on his deputy versus hobbyist scam, eliciting Sederwall's most quote-worthy lie: not feeling like a deputy in his mind! Riordan's questioned as follows:

Q. This is a letter to [Jay] Miller from Virden. It says that you - Tom Sullivan and Steve Sederwall are assigned to investigate the shootings of William H. Bonney and Deputies Bell and Olinger?

A. Yes, sir ...

Q. And he goes on to conclude in his letter, because apparently, this is in request to some documents, it says, "You acknowledge in your letter there is an ongoing investigation being conducted." This is in November of 2005. "When the investigating officers conclude their investigation, I will gladly avail you of all the information you requested in case 2003-274." Is that what the letter says?

A. Yes, sir ... I've never - this is the first time I've seen this letter ... Rick Virden never gave me an assignment other than, can you go watch a horse barn, and help transport prisoners, and work the Lincoln Days ...

Q. Okay. I'm moving on to the investigation. That commission card was given to you, you posted it on your Web site ... And the document states that you were acting as the Deputy Sheriff involved in case 2003-274 at the time you did these things, right?

A. That's what the document says, yes, sir ...

Q. With the probable cause statement that I just read you and the questions and answers, we know that you were acting as a Deputy Sheriff at the time you went with Henry Lee to get the scrapings, weren't you? ...

A. **In my mind, I was, not that night, acting as a Deputy Sheriff.** [author's boldface] ... Because I'm a Deputy Sheriff, doesn't mean that I am acting on their behalf. I was not. I wasn't sent up there to do this. I was just looking. I'm a Deputy Sheriff, yes. I'm also a grandpa ...

Q. The question is to you, sir. This case 2003-274 was an official investigation of Lincoln County Sheriff's Office, you admitted that?

A. Yes.

Q. You were a Deputy Sheriff of the Lincoln County Sheriff's Office. You admitted that. This probable cause statement says in there that you as a Deputy Sheriffs went and located those items, and now you're saying you were acting on your own time; is that you are saying?

A. It says, "Deputy Sederwall of the Lincoln County Sheriff's Office." Okay. That identifies me.

Q. As a Deputy?

A. That's right. As a man, too, as an investigator.

Sederwall, having painted himself into the hobbyist corner, went wild with claiming Dr. Lee and Orchid Cellmark's Rick Staub contacted him and asked him what to do!

A. Henry calls me and says, "If you need some CSI work done, I will do it. [**Note this contradicts Lee's report and Orchid Cellmark's specimen bag labeling for 2003-274**] ... Well, I had already lined up Orchid Cellmark. Rick [Staub] and I talked back and forth ... I said, "Lee had called me." [He] said, "If you need any kind of CSI work, I will do it pro bono." [Later] Rick Staub asked me, "What do you want to do about this DNA?" He said, "It's blended." I said, "What do you mean, it's blended?" [on the bench] ... Then he says it's going to cost X number of dollars to get it separated. I said, "Okay." I think I could have come up with that money. I could have found it. But I just told him, "Let it go. I don't want nothing more. I don't want it ...

Q. Why was Rick Staub even talking to you? ...

A. I was the first guy to talk to him about this ... I set it up ...

Sederwall then had a "Dr. Strangelove moment" under Riordan's questioning, and admitted to knowing that Calvin Ostler was Orchid Cellmark's client of record:

A. ... So, when Lee was coming out here, I called him [Staub] and said, "They may be sending you some stuff, is that okay?" He [Staub] said, "No problem." He told me send it to him or something, and I relayed that to Cal {Calvin Ostler]. I don't know if he sent it to general delivery, or if he sent it to Staub himself ... I set it up, and when Ostler came out and did the thing, Ostler -- they did the scraping, I never touched it. I said, "I've never sent DNA to a lab, you do that." And he said, "Yeah, I'll do that, no problem" ...

Q. Speaking of Mr. Ostler, he's the one who picked up the evidence at the scene and apparently sent it to Orchid Cellmark; is that your understanding?

A. Yes, sir ...

**Q. Who do you believe was the client for Orchid Cellmark?**

**A. Ostler.** [author's boldface]

About the forged Lee reports, Riordan had Sederwall read aloud discrepancies, till he admitted that his first-obtained report - "original" - had law enforcement information. Sederwall stated:

**A. Let me define "original." This is first ... report that someone, either Henry Lee - and it had his return address on it - his secretary, somebody put in the mail to me in that envelope. When you say the original, this is the first report I got.** [author's boldface]

Griebel's firm attorney pressed about rewritings, getting Sederwall's admission of his wanting law enforcement information removed:

Q. And you objected to that and wanted it [law enforcement information] removed?

A. I did mention to him [Dr. Lee], yes.

Q. But he didn't remove it, did he?

A. I don't know. I don't know.

Riordan asked outright about forgery of the other reports: "Did you make up that report?" Sederwall responded:

A. No, I did not make up the report. The report has been **massaged, it's been changed, it's been worked on. That's what's been done.** [author's boldface]

Riordan went after the various reports' Lee-Ostler signatures, getting Sederwall's evasions as follows:

Q. Did you cut and paste the signatures on any of the other exhibits that we have here ...?

A. I don't know if they've been cut and pasted or not.

Q. I'm just asking if you did it?

A. Not that I recall.

# RICK VIRDEN DEPOSITION, JUNE 27, 2012

For Virden's deposition, Attorney Henry Narvaez came, but Brown sent a firm attorney. As with Sederwall, Virden seemed compelled to be truthful under Riordan's questioning. (Gone was Virden's global "amnesia" from his 2008 deposition with the Barnett law firm.) But there was a problem: Riordan had to leave at noon for a mediation. But by then, Riordan and I had a system, with me seated next to him to hand documents. Though I could tell he had not studied all my questions, and would pause uncertainly, I would hand a folder - and he would pick right up.

Under Riordan's questioning, tall slim Virden confirmed his almost 40 years in law enforcement; said he was an Undersheriff participant when Case # 2003-274 began; admitted to being the custodian of the records in question; agreed the IPRA statute said the custodian had to recover records not in possession; stated he commissioned Sederwall and Sullivan as deputies for Case # 2003-274; identified Case # 2003-274 documents on Sederwall's billythekidcase.com website as being his Sheriff's Department's property; and agreed that the Lee reports were altered to remove law enforcement information. Riordan's questioning also proved that all the information Virden needed to get the records was in his 2008 Case # 2003-274 turn-over file: with "Contact List," with "Probable Cause Statement" confirming exhumations and DNA; and with the Sullivan-Sederwall "Memorandum" of June 21, 2007 saying they had the records from the bench and exhumations.

Given all that, Virden looked foolish for not getting the forensic records. But he had been given a new excuse: I did what Attorney Alan Morel told me. Riordan's questioned as follows:

Q. … Why did you wait three years or more from the time you got the memorandum, June 21, 007, until this letter of October 26, 2010 … [C]an you explain why three years went by when there was information contained in the file about where to get DNA information? …

A. I believe this letter [records refusal with "memorandum"] was generated by my attorney. I don't know why we waited three years.

Q. But you were the custodian from 2005, of the records at the Lincoln County Sheriff's Office?

A. That's correct … I rely on my counsel, Alan Morel.

Q. Any reason why you didn't ask the District Attorney to get those records, or have your attorney get the records for you?

A. I depended on my attorney to take care of these.

Q. But your attorney is not the records custodian, is he?

A. No, he's not.

Q. And it's not his obligation to obtain any of the records, is it? ... [T]he statute says that you are the records custodian and you are to turn them over, right? ...

A. Yes, sir.

Virden even refuted Sederwall's hobbyist claim under Riordan's questioning:

Q. When you heard that Sederwall and Sullivan were claiming that the documents they obtained while they were investigating this case, were private property, were you surprised at that?

A. Mr. Sederwall doesn't - nothing he does surprises me ...

Q. And have you ever had any other Deputies obtain documents during an investigation and told you they were private property?

A. No, sir, I have not.

Q. Did that upset you when you found out that he was claiming that they were his private property?

A. It concerned me, yes, sir ...

Q. Now, you're probably aware from the numerous documents you've seen in this case, and the interrogatories and your deposition, that Mr. Sederwall is making a claim that he was not an official deputy when he did a lot of things in this case; is that right? ...

Q. And to the extent that the documents would show the Sheriff's Department number on it, or maybe say they are addressed to him as a Deputy Sheriff, you would presume from just from looking at the faces, that those are official documents? ...

Q. ... And they should be in your file, what we call the turn-over file?

A. I would hope so.

Devastatingly for the defense-side, Virden confirmed that Orchid Cellmark's Case No. 4444 was his Case # 2003-274. And he confirmed that the "Supplemental Report" for the John Miller exhumation showed that Rick Staub of Orchid Cellmark had gotten the DNA samples.

Putting the lie to Virden's feeble excuse of not knowing if the records existed, Griebel's firm attorney, Jeremy Theoret, questioned about the chain-of-custody photos of evidence bags collected by Lee, then labeled by Orchid Cellmark as follows:

Q. Okay. I'm going to show you some documents from there that I'm marking as [Exhibit] 50 … There are three different pages here. Are you able to read on the one that says on the bottom 4444-002B? Do you have that one?

A. Yes, sir.

Q. And just looking at this picture, do you have any idea what that is? Can you describe that? What does that look like?

A. It says it's evidence.

Q. Evidence. Can you read the case number there?

A. It appears to say 2003-274.

Q. Okay, can you read what it says under location?

A. I don't know.

Q. If I said, "it was underside bench 4," would that seem accurate to you?

A. Yes, that's right, yes.

Q. And do you see the date? Can you read that?

A. It appears to be July 31, '04. [Date of Lee specimen recovery, same as Lee report's]

Q. Okay. That's correct. Underneath everything, what does it say right there?

A. Chain of custody.

Q. How about the next page, it says 4444-001B. Can you read that, what does it appear to be?

A. Evidence case No. 2003 – I don't know what the next is. Off to the side it says 274.

Q. And the location? … If I said it was inside bench three, would that seem accurate to you?

A. Yes, that seems accurate.

Q. And the date there, can you read that?

A. The date is July 31, 2004.

Q. Okay. I'm not sure if you can read the last one as well. The reference is 4444-001B and -002B, outer packaging. Are you able to read any of that at the top line there, the case number?

A. I would say it's "2003-274."

Q. 2003-274. Does that appear accurate to you again?

A. Yes.

All 133 pages from Orchid Cellmark were entered as an exhibit by Griebel's lawyer, and were used in questioning to confirm that Lee's carpenter's bench and floorboard results, and the Arizona exhumations' results were all part of Case # 2003-274 - meaning they had been Virden's responsibility to recover.

And questioning showed Virden's records recovery attempts had been shams. Griebel's attorney asked [author's boldface]:

Q. Did you ever think to pick up the phone and dial up old Henry Lee and say, "Dr. Lee, I got your letter here, it's a little confusing to me," and have a telephone conversation with him?

**A. Once I wrote the letter, the attorney handled it.**

Q. So you figured you don't have any obligation? You know the documents exist once you signed the letter?

**A. I let the attorney handle it. ...**

Q. You could have called Henry Lee also, couldn't you?

A. I could have.

Q. Just like you could have called Cal Ostler when you found his name on something. You didn't call him either?

A. No, sir.

By day's end, Griebel's attorney got Virden's confession:

Q. [Y]ou were the custodian from 2005, of the records at the Lincoln County Sheriff's Office? ... And there was a case file in there, an official Lincoln County Sheriff's Office Case 2003-274? ... And contained within that file was information that would have led you to DNA evidence, or DNA materials, or documents that were requested by the Plaintiffs in this case, correct?

A. It appears so, correct.

## RIORDAN SHOCKER

Attorney Riordan had miscalculated the length of Virden's deposition, but had to leave by noon for a mediation. I stayed to help him pack his materials after the room emptied for lunch. Like a bear that shows no facial expression before attack, rotund Riordan walked to the room's far end and closed the door. I thought he wanted privacy to exult in our victorious depositions with near confessions from Sederwall and Virden.

Instead, his round face turned red in a fit of rage, and shouting, he lumbered straight for me, seated at the far end of the long table. I took stock. I was locked in a sound-proof room, with no way out, with a potentially violent, big man. "I'll never do a deposition with you again!" he bellowed. "You interrupted me." (That meant handing him folders and exhibits - but he had not objected and had needed those prompts to get in the information.)

The psychiatrist in me swung into action. My specialty was extreme mental illness and murder. This was no first in terms of danger - except, of course, for treating your lawyer like your patient. Step one is to stay calm. Step two is neutralizing aggression by anxiety or guilt. I had heard gossip about his affairs with clients. I went for sexual guilt: "I thought you were going to praise me. But I feel like you just punched me in the balls!" I said indignantly. I then added vulnerability, hoping for inhibition: "I worked so hard. Now I feel like crying. I know you hate me. "

Silently, he stopped. I stayed seated. Still angry, he stuffed papers into his carrier. I stood to help. His flailing hand struck me in the groin. (I was wearing a long skirt.) We said nothing. I decided it was unconscious. Finally, without apology, he left.

That afternoon, I asked Patrick Griebel's attorney, who had to continue the questioning alone, if he could include my question/exhibit folders that Riordan had missed. He did.

## HENRY NARVAEZ SHOCKER

That afternoon, slimy Attorney Henry Narvaez sized up the new playing field: my Rottweiler had departed. The depositions had devastatingly condemned Sederwall and Virden. So when Griebel's attorney finished in late afternoon, Narvaez acted. He told Griebel's lawyer that he just needed to check with the judge.

When Eichwald entered, Narvaez announced with his painted-on smile: "We're ready to mediate!" That slippery move was to preempt our evidentiary hearing for entering the depositions' admissions and exhibits. Also, mediation's confidentiality could conceal the defendants' criminality forever.

Griebel's attorney did not object. Judge Eichwald told Narvaez to submit a formal request. I had to act, even though addressing a judge without my attorney could give up my representation. I said, "Attorney Riordan had to leave. I'm not going *pro se*, but I'm sure he would say that the depositions' information needs to be heard in court." Eichwald just nodded benevolently and left.

## ANOTHER RIORDAN SHOCKER COMES NEXT

The evening of June 27th, I e-mailed Attorney Riordan about Narvaez's mediation move. The next day, Riordan e-mailed me an excuse (not an apology) for his behavior as having felt rushed because of needing to leave the deposition early.

After that, Riordan seemed back on track, using the paralegal I hired for him to do precedent case research for the evidentiary hearing (despite Narvaez's mediation request). And Griebel had also requested a Status Conference (for progress update).

On the morning of August 27th, the paralegal told me that Riordan wanted to meet with both of us to discuss her cases the following morning. That evening, Riordan abruptly quit by e-mail:

> Dr. Cooper. When I talked to [the paralegal] the other day, I suggested that she and I and you meet perhaps tomorrow to discuss the research for the case that would be the most efficient. I also asked her if she could draft a brief on the subject and she was, in my opinion, not sure that she could do it, but she did not say no. I have been thinking of what is ahead. I think now may be a good time for me to get out of this case ...
>
> I am in my declining years of practicing law and ending my legal career. I do not need this fight.
>
> You need to find other counsel, or represent yourself ...
>
> I am attaching a copy of my draft billing to date.
>
> Please find someone to take this over ASAP. Bill Riordan

That e-mail also fairly justified his own achievements:

> You may recall when you first met with me that you said that after Threet's lack of action in the hearing that your case may very well be over. I feel like I was responsible for engineering the comeback, obviously with your knowledge of the facts and documents. You are in a much better position that you were ...
>
> One of the reasons that I have stuck with this case to the extent that I have is that you have been through a lot of attorneys. From what I know, your changes ... have been necessary and reasonable. I know from my experience as an attorney and Judge, when a litigant has so many changes in attorneys, they [judges and other lawyers] tend to think that there is a problem with the client. I was trying to help you get past that.

But he made clear that he resented my input (and lack of reverential awe):

> I have spent 43 years practicing law. I have experience as a trial Judge and Supreme Court Justice. I think I know haw [sic] they [judges and lawyers] think. I am frankly somewhat insulted when you ignore my advice. [AUTHOR'S NOTE: I had refused Riordan's advice to mediate the Brown-Narvaez appeal on my Co-Plaintiff's attorneys' fees motion, because Brown and Narvaez were insisting on getting the entire district court case thrown out – not just the fee request.]

I pleaded with Riordan to stay on as my lawyer for the upcoming Status Conference, and to explain to Judge Eichwald his work-load problems as reason for withdrawing - and not me (as had damaging Attorney Threet). He agreed to that.

That night of August 27, 2012, I was too terrified to sleep. There was no way I could get another attorney. How could I conduct an evidentiary hearing on my own? It was like a multi-day trial, with witnesses' cross-examinations, entering evidence, and making objections: the courtroom choreography learned by going to law school and law practice experience. And how could I write all the necessary court documents on my own?

For the third time - Barnett, Threet, now Riordan - when I was close to certain victory, brought me to near certain defeat. Had someone called Riordan during that August 27th day? I would never know. But I did find out that it was a violation of his Professional Code of Ethics to abandon a client mid-case. And, not only had he fabricated my refusals to "follow his advice," he had made no provision to get me another attorney.

## STATUS CONFERENCE, SEPTEMBER 21, 2012

On September 21, 2012, Attorney Riordan came to the Status Conference, and exerted his usual impressive influence.

Judge Eichwald began the hearing by complying with tricky Attorney Henry Narvaez's mediation request, stating:

> [W]hat I intend to do is send you folks to mediation, and see what can be mediated, if anything. If it all can't get mediated, fine. If some of it can get mediated, that's better. If everything can get mediated, that's the best result you can get.

Of course, Attorneys Narvaez and Brown eagerly agreed.

But Riordan came prepared, carrying a thick red law book. He requested an evidentiary hearing *before that mediation* by quoting "Rule 32(F) on depositions": "[I]t is desirable in the interest of justice and with due regard to presenting the testimony of witnesses orally in open court to allow ... the depositions to be used." Riordan added, "And we really need, from our standpoint, to get those depositions and exhibits in evidence." He also requested again that the defendants pay for those June 26th and 27th depositions as sanctions. Riordan further requested adding Attorney Alan Morel as a defendant after the information acquired in Rick Virden's deposition.

Judge George Eichwald ruled that: (1) Riordan was to request an evidentiary hearing on the evidence from the depositions; (2) that the evidentiary hearing would be held within the next 45 days; (3) at least 15 days before that hearing, counsels should confer to stipulate as to that evidence from the depositions (agree what was admissible); (4) that mediation be held between January and February of 2013; (5) that the order for the May 31, 2012 hearing could be submitted in Court by Riordan, but pending approval by the other parties; (6) that Plaintiff Cooper pay for the depositions at present, but with that payment to be reassessed at the evidentiary hearing (as usual, the defendants were spared penalty by Judge Eichwald ... and I had to pay).

Riordan waited till the end to request withdrawal. Eichwald refused! I asked to speak and said that Attorney Riordan simply did not have the time for the case; but we had all appreciated his contributions. So Riordan was permitted to withdraw.

I asked Judge Eichwald if he would be comfortable with me as *pro se.* He looked like he was about to cry. A lifeline of validation for him had just been cut off. Eichwald told me to try and find an attorney. In reality, I had 88 days left to become one.

# CHAPTER 17:

# PRO SE MEANS ALL ALONE

THIRTEENTH JUDICIAL DISTRICT COURT
COUNTY OF SANDOVAL
STATE OF NEW MEXICO

GALE COOPER and DE BACA COUNTY NEWS,
a New Mexico Corporation,

　　　　　　Plaintiffs,

vs.　　　　　　　　　　　　　　No. D-1329-C

RICK VIRDEN, LINCOLN COUNTY SHERIFF and CUSTODIAN
OF THE RECORDS OF THE LINCOLN COUNTY SHERIFF'S OFFICE;
and STEVEN M. SEDERWALL, FORMER LINCOLN COUNTY DEPUTY
SHERIFF; and THOMAS T. SULLIVAN, FORMER LINCOLN COUNTY
SHERIFF AND FORMER LINCOLN COUNTY DEPUTY SHERIFF,

　　　　　　Defendants.

PLAINTIFF GALE COOPER'S PROPOSED FINDINGS O...
AND CONCLUSIONS OF LAW

Plaintiff Gale Cooper ("Plaintiff Cooper"), acting pro se, propo...

Findings of Fact and Conclusions of Law.

---

THIRTEENTH JUDICIAL DISTRICT COURT
COUNTY OF SANDOVAL
STATE OF NEW MEXICO

GALE COOPER and DE BACA COUNTY NEWS,
a New Mexico Corporation,

　　　　　　Plaintiffs,

vs.

RICK VIRDEN, LINCOLN COUNTY SHERIFF and CUSTODIAN
OF THE RECORDS OF THE LINCOLN COUNTY SHERIFF'S OFFICE;
and STEVEN M. SEDERWALL, FORMER LINCOLN COUNTY DEPUTY
SHERIFF; and THOMAS T. SULLIVAN, FORMER LINCOLN COUNTY
SHERIFF AND FORMER LINCOLN COUNTY DEPUTY SHERIFF,  No. D-1329-C...

　　　　　　Defendants.

PLAINTIFF GALE COOPER'S MOTION TO COMPL...
PRODUCTION OF THE REQUESTED FOREN...
LINCOLN COUNTY SHERIFF'S DEPART...

COMES NOW, Plaintiff Gale Cooper ("Plaintiff C...
to compel Defendants Rick Virden ("Virden"), Steve S...
("Sullivan") to honor the Summary Judgment rul...
Plaintiff Cooper her requested forensic DN...
...ase No. 2003-274 ("Case 2003-274"...
...cords, have defied custodial du...
...uty/agents, and have...
...er. And record...
...blic Reco...

---

THIRTEENTH JUDICIAL DISTRICT COURT
COUNTY OF SANDOVAL
STATE OF NEW MEXICO

Case No. D-1329-CV-2007-
01364

GALE COOPER and DE BACA COUNTY NEWS,
a New Mexico Corporation,　　　　　JS

　　　　　　Plaintiffs,

vs.

RICK VIRDEN, LINCOLN COUNTY SHERIFF and
CUSTODIAN OF THE RECORDS OF THE LINCOLN COUNTY
SHERIFF'S OFFICE; and STEVEN M. SEDERWALL,
FORMER LINCOLN COUNTY DEPUTY SHERIFF; and
THOMAS T. SULLIVAN, FORMER LINCOLN
COUNTY SHERIFF and FORMER LINCOLN
COUNTY DEPUTY SHERIFF,

　　　　　　Defendants.

PLAINTIFF GALE COOPER'S ENTRY OF PRO SE APPEARANCE

COMES NOW, Plaintiff Gale Cooper, to enter her appearance as pro se in the

above entitled and numbered cause of action.

Respectfully submitted,

_Gale Cooper_ 11/12/12
Gale Cooper,
Plaintiff
P.O. Box 328
Sandia Park, NM 87047
(505) 286-8483

I hereby certify that a copy of the foregoing
was faxed to the above Court on this
12th day of November 2012 and its filed copy
was mailed to the following:

Attorney Patrick Griebel
1803 Rio Grande NW Suite B
Albuquerque, NM 87104
Attorney for Co-Plaintiff DeBaca County N...

---

FILED IN MY
DISTRICT COUR...
8/19/2013 1...
CRYST...

---

Court of Appeals of New Mexico

STATE TOOMEY v. CITY OF TRUTH
OR CONSEQUENCES

STATE of New Mexico ex rel. Deborah TOOMEY, an individual, Plaintiff–Appellan...
v. CITY OF TRUTH OR CONSEQUENCES, Mary Penner, Sierra Community Cour...
and Jay Hopkins, Defendants–Appellees.

No. 30,795.

---

NOTICE OF MOTION HEARING

NOTICE IS HEREBY GIVEN that a hearing in this case has been set before the Honorable Georg...

Date of Hearing:　Friday, 13th day of December, 2013 at 5:00 AM
Place of Hearing:　Sandoval County Judicial Complex, Courtroom 2013
　　　　　　　　　1500 Idalia Road Building A
　　　　　　　　　Bernalillo, NM 87004
Matter to be Heard:　Plaintiff Gale Cooper's Repeat Request for Hearing on...
　　　　　　　　　Sanctions against Defendant
Length of Hearing:　1 Hour
Comments:

If this hearing requires more or less time than the court has designated, or if th...
please contact us immediately as continuances may not be granted on late not...
Americans with Disabilities Act. Counsel or PRO SE persons may notify th...
...ast five (5) days before ANY hearing so appropriate accommodations m...

THERESA VA...
CLERK OF TH...

CERTIFICATE OF SERVIC...
of Sandoval County,...

---

IN THE COURT OF APPEALS
OF THE STATE OF NEW MEXICO

GALE COOPER and DE BACA COUNTY NEWS,
a New Mexico corporation,　　　　No. 32,060

　　　　　Plaintiffs-Appellees,

vs.

LINCOLN COUNTY and RICK VIRDEN, LINCOLN
COUNTY SHERIFF and CUSTODIAN OF RECORDS;
and STEVEN M. SEDERWALL, FORMER LINCOLN
COUNTY DEPUTY SHERIFF; and THOMAS T.
SULLIVAN, FORMER LINCOLN COUNTY SHERIFF
and FORMER LINCOLN COUNTY DEPUTY SHERIFF,

　　　　　Defendants-Appellants.

COURT OF APPEALS OF NEW MEXICO
FILED

APR 2 4 2013

_Wendy F. Jones_

ON DIRECT APPEAL FROM THE
THIRTEENTH JUDICIAL DISTRICT COURT,
The Hon. George P. Eichwald, District Judge
No. D-1329-CT-2007-01364

...MOTION FOR DISMISSAL WITH PREJUDICE

...re # Gale Cooper, Plaintiff-Appellee De B...
...ck J., Griebel and Jeremy J...
...through their...

# FACING THE IMPOSSIBLE

*HOAXBUST: It seemed like I would lose, after all my years of fighting, not because of my wily opponents, but because of my own side - though, in truth, they were not necessarily distinguishable. What I did not know, was that worse betrayal was about to come.*

## *POST- TRAUMATIC STRESS DISORDER AND ME*

If your attorneys become indistinguishable either from your opponents' lawyers or from psychiatric patients, you are in big trouble. I had been mercilessly and unjustly battered by sudden betrayals from my own side during my years of IPRA litigation. Post-Traumatic Stress Disorder is a physiological response to psychological traumas by pathological resetting of your fight or flight thermostat, so your bloodstream keeps getting flooded by adrenalin and cortisol. I got it. So, following Attorney Bill Riordan's quitting, came unremitting, 24 hour, icy dread as I had to face the equally impossible tasks of finding a lawyer, or becoming one, for the most important hearing in my case.

## *REAL IPRA LAWYERS AND A BIG SURPRISE*

By this next crisis, my case was well enough known publicly for me to get its records reviewed by IPRA specialty lawyers - who refused to take it. But what they found shocked me - and it was not just that my attorneys' filings showed ignorance of IPRA law; or that the inappropriately premature fees request led to the appeal; or that subpoenaing Orchid Cellmark records had been a questionable approach, since it abandoned IPRA law.

The jaw-dropping shock was that my co-plaintiff, Scot Stinnett, had no standing (no right) to be in the litigation! All those years, I had trusted his expertise in IPRA law. And I had been touched, on September 11, 2007, when he offered to join my litigation. But he - and Attorney Mickey Barnett, who let him join - made the most basic mistake in IPRA law. To enter IPRA enforcement litigation, you have to be an *injured party* in the IPRA records request phase. *Injury meant that your written records request was improperly denied in writing.* (Now I understood why, on September 4, 2008, FOG Attorney Leonard DeLayo filed a separate records request to join the litigation.)

These IPRA expert attorneys showed me that IPRA's Section14-2-8(C), Procedure for Requesting Records, stated:

> A **written request** [author's boldface] shall provide the name, address and telephone number of the person seeking access to the records sought with reasonable particularity.

And IPRA's Section14-2-12(D), Enforcement stated:

> The court shall award damages, costs, and reasonable attorneys' fees **to any person whose written request has been denied** [author's boldface] and is successful in a court action to enforce the provisions of the Inspection of Public Records Act.

Scot Stinnett had made no records request at all! However, an attorney could request records for a client (like Barnett did for me); or an attorney could request records on behalf of an unnamed client (who wanted to stay secret). But Barnett had made no records request either in Stinnett's name or his own (for Stinnett). I was Barnett's only client as a records requester from April 24, 2007 to June 26, 2007. And the implication was dire.

If Stinnett had no right to be in the litigation, it meant Griebel had no real client; thus, no right to his attorney fees!

What was I to do? By then, I had lost all trust and respect for Scot Stinnett. I owed him nothing for his faked expertise, faked promise of help, and indications of sabotaging of my case.

And I had other problems. The trial-like hearing was set for December 18, 2012. I had no lawyer. But this being New Mexico, Land of Crooks, one of the lawyers who confirmed Stinnett's lack of standing for me, apparently decided to earn "friendship points" by violating my confidentiality and informing Attorney Kevin Brown; who filed, on November 3, 2012, a motion to dismiss Stinnett for lack of standing (likely hoping to end the case - though I had standing). I would later learn all that by accident.

At the end of September, I called the University of New
Mexico law school's bookstore, and bought textbooks for courses on
law, evidence, and trials; and books of New Mexico statutes -
about 6,000 pages to digest for representing myself. And I made
pathetic calls to the few attorneys who would answer questions:
"How do you title a motion?" (Answer: "It took me years to realize
that you just make them up.") "Do you raise your hand to object?"
(Answer: No. Stand and start talking.) "What is a ¶?" (Answer:
Symbol for a numbered paragraph.) "How do you find exhibits in
boxes of over a hundred when cross-examining a witness?"
(Answer: Use a paralegal. Oh, that's right. You don't have one.)

# THE AMAZING DEBORAH TOOMEY

In July of 2012, I had heard that an IPRA case impacted mine.
New Mexico's Court of Appeals Case No. 30,795 had backed *pro se*
appellant Deborah Toomey against corrupt Truth or Consequences
officials. Filed on July 26, 2012, it reiterated IPRA's requirement
for a custodian's retrieval of records held on their behalf by an
outside entity (further negating Virden's "they're not in my
possession" ploy). Judge Linda Vanzi, Chief Judge Celia Foy
Castillo, and Judge Cynthia A. Fry stated:

> [T]he dispositive question is whether ... [the requested
> records] were made on behalf of the City so as to constitute
> public records within the meaning of IPRA ... [P]ublic bodies
> contract with private entities to provide a wide range of
> services ... To allow such entities to circumvent a citizen's right
> of access to records ... would thwart the very purpose of IPRA
> and mark a significant departure from New Mexico's
> presumption of openness at the heart of our access law ...
> Plaintiff has prevailed in her action here.

As to IPRA itself, feisty Deborah Toomey's September 8, 2008
"Emergency Petition for Writ of Mandamus" for "extraordinary
relief" to the New Mexico Supreme Court on her District Court
Case Nos. D-0721-CV2009-98 and -99, had audaciously alleged
failure of her district court judge to perform his "ministerial duty,"
thereby committing "abuse of discretion." She had stated:

The starting point for any case involving the New Mexico Inspection of Public Records Act ... is to understand the fundamental importance of the statute. "The liberties of a people never were, nor ever will be, secure, when the transactions of their rulers may be concealed from them." (Patrick Henry, American colonial revolutionary.) Every state in the United States has a public records statute like the IPRA, and the basic assumption behind every act is the same: it is a bedrock principle of democracy and a necessity for liberty that the people have a right to know and do know what their government is doing.

Her July 8, 2011, "Appeal from the Seventh Judicial Court County of Sierra, Case No. D-0721-CV-2009-159, Brief in Chief," stated:

IPRA is not simply about the disclosure of a document. "People have a right to know that the people they entrust with the affairs of government are honestly, faithfully and competently performing their function as public servants." *State of New Mexico ex rel. Newsome v. Alarid*, 90 NM 790 568 P2d at 1241 .... Nowhere in Newsome does our Supreme Court place a burden on the party requesting documents. Instead, Newsome clearly places the burden ... upon the custodian to justify why the records sought to be examined should not be furnished." *City of Farmington v. The Daily Times*, 2009-NMCA-057, 146 N.M. 349, 210 P.3d 246 at 13. Defendants did not meet this burden nor claim an exception when they denied Plaintiff-Appellant's request ...

It is clear the Legislature intended to enforce disclosure by imposing a cost for nondisclosure. *Board of Comm'rs v. Las Cruces Sun-News*, 2003-NMCA-102, 134 NM 238, 76 P.3d 36. The obfuscation and destruction of public records committed by Defendants-Appellees should not be rewarded; it should be punished.

Attorney Bill Riordan, with a retirement home near Truth or Consequences, had told me he heard that Toomey was a "crazy person." Given his feelings about me, I knew I had to contact her.

My first call to Deborah Toomey was my game-changer. Brilliant, she quoted law from memory. And she ended my *pro se* self-pity. She said: "America is unique. Our *pro se* rights are precious and are protected by our First Amendment: "[T]o petition the government for a regress of grievances."

In October, we met at the Macaroni Grill Restaurant, which I picked for ironic overlap with my Threet and Dunn horror-story, which began there. Deborah Toomey was a compact woman, with short-cropped auburn hair whose white forelock was her only adornment. She seemed military in zeal and no-nonsense talk. She had graduated U.C. Berkley with a BA in political science. During college she worked as a paralegal; but instead of going into law, she became the world's 17th woman Microsoft Certified Systems Engineer - building computer infrastructure. Her career was cut short by near-death: a medication reaction caused liver failure. With weeks to live, she found a holistic healer. Her total recovery was medically inexplicable. But she retired, in 2006, to Truth or Consequences for its "best hot springs in the country."

Toomey did more than soak. Seeing the city's corruption, she swung into action with speeches, attendance in town meetings, and exposé litigation. As she wrote in her January 13, 2012, "Motion for Summary Judgment" in her district court case that led to her successful appeal: "There has been no truth or consequences in Truth or Consequences. Plaintiff prays there will be both."

Deborah Toomey, with her idealism and skillful pleadings, contrasted the moral and intellectual vacuum in which I had fought for a decade. That environment was ideal for the law enforcement hoax; but not for defeating its good ol' boys and gals gorging at taxpayer feeding troughs. And the apathetic biased press kept that status quo. As to Toomey, Santa Fe AP reporter Barry Massey's July 31, 2012 article on her Appeals victory minimized any credit. Titled "Court: Records Act Applies to Contractor," she is tacked on at the end without name - just as a "community activist." Credit went to FOG, via its *amicus curiae* attorney, Dolph Barnhouse. (When I called Barnhouse myself after Riordan quit, he had his secretary refuse my case.) So my experience was not unique. The difference was that Toomey won.

Deborah Toomey also showed me a Public Comment speech she gave on May 26, 2009 - Memorial Day - to Truth or Consequences Commissioners. It was titled "I Remember." She said it was her "declaration of war" against local corruption. To me, its was like water in the desert. Here are excerpts:

In honor of all those who have defended and progressed American democracy, liberty and justice, I remember.

On this day of memory, I honor just a few of my heroes: Benjamin Franklin, Thomas Jefferson, Thomas Paine and all the founding fathers that set down in writing and principle the right and duty to dissent. I remember ...

On this day and every day, I am proud to say I am a patriot. My pride in country is not based upon a fervent nationalism but is based upon a lifelong study of the history and political theory of the United States of America ...

At University, my love of country led me to study political science with a concentration in theory. I learned the factory worker is governed by the same rule of law as the local sheriff; the local sheriff is governed by the same rule of law as our President. No one is above the law in this nation, including our leaders. This simple principle is what makes the United States of America different; this is what makes us "better"— the rule of law. Let's not forget that ...

As Justice Brandeis said in 1928: "Our government is the potent, the omnipresent teacher. For good or for ill, it teaches the whole people by its example. Crime is contagious. If the government becomes a law-breaker, it breeds contempt for law - it invites anarchy." We cannot allow anarchy and despotism to destroy our democracy, to destroy the United States of America. I agree with Pres. James Madison that "despotism can only exist in darkness." Let us shine the light of truth ...

On this Memorial Day, I remember. I think back through these past two centuries of the men and women who gave of themselves to protect America and to further freedom. We dishonor them when we ignore our history and principles—our rule of law ...

"All tyranny needs to gain a foothold is for people of good conscience to remain silent." (Thomas Jefferson) Do not remain silent. Do not remain in the dark.

Honor our past. Honor our future. In honor of Memorial Day, for every soldier and citizen who has looked into the light and shouted LIBERTY AND JUSTICE FOR ALL, I quote John Quincy Adams: "Posterity: you will never know how much it has cost my generation to preserve your freedom. I hope you will make good use of it."

Make good use of it. Don't give up on it now. Demand the rule of law. Demand prosecution.

What became of Deborah Toomey? By March of 2014, disgusted with her city's inaction, a local press abusive to her, and the rampant corruption, she left New Mexico, a victim of the state's natural selection for mediocrity and moral atrophy.

# BEING *PRO SE* AND FILING BRIEFS

Going in person to Sandoval District Court, on November 14, 2012 I filed my "Plaintiff Gale Cooper's Entry of Pro Se Appearance" and my "Pre-Evidentiary Hearing Brief." [APPENDIX: 65] The same day, I filed my "Motion to Dismiss Co-Plaintiff De Baca County News Based on Lack of Standing" (unaware of Attorney Kevin Brown's earlier filing).

That last document began my fight within the fight as Scot Stinnett and Mickey Barnett responded through Attorney Patrick Griebel. Stinnett and Barnett had two choices: admit their mistake or lie. That was easy. They boiler-plated an affidavit claiming my case had been Stinnett's all along! Here is Stinnett's September 16, 2012 Affidavit, with its lies in my boldface:

I, SCOT STINNETT, being first duly sworn, do hereby depose and state as follows:

1. My name is Scot Stinnett. I am over the age of 18 and I make these statements from personal knowledge and am competent to testify to the matters herein.
2. I am principal of the De Baca County News in Fort Sumner, New Mexico.
3. I am a Plaintiff in the action captioned above.
4. Previously, I was a registered lobbyist for the New Mexico Press Association and served as President.
5. I was recently inducted into the New Mexico Press Association Hall of Fame.
6. Former Governor Garrey Carruthers appointed me to the New Mexico Open Records Task Force.
7. In 1990-1991 The New Mexico Open Records Task Force drafted what became codified as the Inspection of Public Records Act ("IPRA") in 1993.
8. I was a charter Member of the Foundation for Open Government ("FOG").
9. I have been a Plaintiff in and prevailed in prior IPRA cases.
10. Prior to the Barnett Law Firm becoming involved in this case, Gale Cooper approached me regarding matters related to IPRA and this case, **asked me to be a Co-Plaintiff with her, and I agreed.** [AUTHOR'S NOTE: On September 11, 2007, Stinnett, to my surprise, offered to join the impending litigation.]

11. I advised Ms. Cooper regarding how to proceed in an IPRA case.

12. Prior to April 24, 2007, Mickey Barnett of the Barnett Law Firm telephoned me about the case, having received my contact information from Ms. Cooper, and asked me questions about the case and about Ms. Cooper. [AUTHOR'S NOTE: If so, I was never told]

13. **Prior to April 24, 2007, I was asked by Mr. Barnett if I would be a party to a lawsuit if an IPRA request was made and denied, and I agreed**. [AUTHOR'S NOTE: Lie.]

14. On April 24, 2007, Mickey Barnett of The Barnett Law Firm sent by Certified Mail Return Receipt Requested and First Class Mail a written request for Inspection of Public Records to Sheriff Rick Virden of the Lincoln County Sheriff's Office, pursuant to the Inspection of Public Records Act ("IPRA") Section 14-2-8 *et seq.* NMSA 1978, a true copy of that written request is attached hereto.

15. That letter stated that the Barnett Law Firm represented Gale Cooper, MD.

16. **At the time the written IPRA request was made, The Barnett Law Firm also represented me in my role as principal for the De Baca County News with respect to the request.** [AUTHOR'S NOTE: Lie. As Barnett's client, would have had to be told. I was not. As Stinnett's friend, Stinnett would have been told by him. I was not.]

17. **The written IPRA request was also made on behalf of the De Baca County News, although the representation of the De Baca County News by The Barnett Law Firm was not disclosed in the April 24, 2007 letter.** [AUTHOR'S NOTE: Lie. Not only was Stinnett not a client, he could not piggy-back on my request under my name. And, if a requestor, he could be kept secret from the requestee(s), but not from me.]

18. **The De Baca County News was represented by the Barnett Law Firm when the IPRA request was made and denied and has been a party to this action at all materially relevant times: from the time before the April 24, 2007 written IPRA request was made; at the time the written April 24, 2007 IPRA request was made as well as when subsequent written requests were made); at the time the written IPRA request was denied;** [AUTHOR'S NOTE: All lies] and at the time that the above captioned action was commenced.

Further, Affiant sayth naught.

Since they were lying, Stinnett and Barnett had no proof at all that Stinnett had been a request phase client. And there was no contract, since Barnett did my case as a favor to John Dendahl.

And I did have proof of the lies: (1) All requests from April 24, 2007 to June 26, 2007 were in my name; (2) by NMRA Rules of Professional Conduct, Barnett needed my permission to add a client; (3) Barnett and Stinnett would have told me about adding Stinnett; (4) I made all payments; (5) Barnett's monthly billings in the request period had only me as his client; (6) in that request period Stinnett gave IPRA suggestions to me, which I wrote up for Barnett; (7) my own notes showed Stinnett asked me on September 11, 2007 about his joining my litigation (and that I told Barnett that day); (8) my *MegaHoax* book, published in 2010, gave Stinnett joining only at litigation; and (9) my November 14, 2012 Affidavit swore that I was the sole request phase client.

So on November 27, 2012, I filed my "Motion for Legal Action Against Attorney Mickey Barnett and Scot Stinnett for Production of False Affidavits Claiming Standing of the De Baca County News to Refute Plaintiff Gale Cooper's Motion to Dismiss Co-Plaintiff De Baca County News Based on Lack of Standing" with 89 pages of Exhibits and my own affidavit as to being the sole records requestor client. On December 26, 2012, I also filed my "Opposition Reply to Virden's Objection to Plaintiff Cooper's Pre-Evidentiary Hearing Brief." [APPENDIX: 66]

That Scot Stinnett episode was like entering a purgatory inhabited only by moral zombies. Stinnett knew my decade of labors and sacrifices to protect the history on which Fort Sumner depended. For years, he had not only been a source of IPRA perspectives, but also recipient of my anguished calls about hoax inroads, or yet another attorney's folding. Stinnett would remain the most hurtful of my Billy the Kid Case contacts. It was now clear that hardest would be stomaching my revulsion at them all.

My "Pre-Evidentiary Hearing Brief" and my "Opposition Reply to Virden's Objection" to it, summarized my arguments for Judge Eichwald. I had taken possession of my case. At last, my case had a chance - even if I went down fighting.

There was one coincidence that would be my salvation. When I told an attorney about my motion to dismiss my co-plaintiff, he said, "It won't matter what you argue. The judge won't do it. That would mean getting rid of your co-plaintiff's attorney too. And no judge wants to be left in court with just a *pro se*."

# Evidentiary Hearing Day 1:
# December 18, 2012

*HOAXBUST: The second evidentiary hearing's objective was to get into the court record the near confessions by deponents Sederwall and Virden, along with the exhibits Threet and Dunn had kept out. But first I had to argue my motion to dismiss my co-plaintiff. That would be harder and more horrible than I anticipated.*

On December 18, 2012, I arrived at the Sandoval County district court with so many boxes of evidence and display boards with easels that I hired a man to carry them. I also brought a videographer, by now essential with the press black-out. And I had subpoenaed as witnesses Virden, Sederwall, and Lincoln County Attorney Alan Morel. It felt refreshing to no longer helplessly await a next betrayal or an unprepared presentation by my attorney. But there was no way to stop my fear of the unknown. Could I function like a lawyer with just a few months of preparation? Inexplicably, however, a feeling of "being home" - being where I belonged - returned when I entered the courtroom.

## HEARING ON DISMISSAL OF SCOT STINNETT

First heard in the all-day proceeding would be my motion to dismiss my co-plaintiff, Scot Stinnett. In retrospect, I should have anticipated fierce attack. Firstly, New Mexicans fight Old West style - rough and unintellectual. Secondly, Patrick Griebel was abusive – why I fired him. Thirdly, Stinnett and Barnett were desperate: Stinnett really had no standing. Fourthly, I thought they would just repeat their Affidavits' boiler-plated lies about Stinnett being Barnett's client all along. Character assassination did not occur to me. Fifthly, I thought their lack of any evidence, coupled with my own motions with hundreds of pages of exhibits to the contrary, would make a difference; unaware that judges do not necessarily read beforehand. And there was my double-bind: I felt inhibited about arguing aggressively, and having the judge hate me - as had Attorney Riordan. It was a hard way to start.

My novice failing would be getting flabbergasted at the audacious lies under oath, instead of using them as my opportunities for impeachment. And the judge's conclusion may have been foregone anyway - as I had been forewarned.

In summary, Attorney Patrick Griebel came with a strategy (with my cynical asides added here). First was to paint Stinnett as one step from sainthood or winning a Pulitzer Prize for journalism; as being a cornerstone of state's open records law and FOG; as being elected that year to New Mexico Press Association's Hall of Fame (the first I head it, and wondered if all his hoax-backing reporter cronies liked his making a mess of my case); as best friend of Barnett since childhood; and as fighting for Fort Sumner's Billy the Kid tourism; and, of course, the person who did my case instead of me. But the real and sole issue was that Stinnett was not Barnett's client in the records request phase.

For that, Griebel misrepresented a 1977 Appeals Court case - *San Juan Water Users vs. KNME TV* - which lets a lawyer keep secret a client's name when doing a request in their own name. Griebel left out that Stinnett *had to be a client to begin with; and secrecy was for opponents, not another client in the case.*

Next was Barnett as a surprise phone witness (I should have been informed), repeating Stinnett's client lie; and purposefully defaming me as having such a bad reputation (with "quitting" lawyers) that he only took my case because of Stinnett's presence.

And the defense attorneys, Henry Narvaez and Kevin Brown, knowing I would continue the case myself, had no motive to fight hard. Instead they basked in my denigration by Griebel, Stinnett, and Barnett, damaging my case by damaging my credibility.

The following are annotated boldfaced transcript excerpts.

### SCOT STINNETT EXAMINED BY PATRICK GRIEBEL

Q. Mr. Stinnett, please describe your role at the De Baca County News.

A. I'm the president of our corporation, which is called Pecos Publishing, it's a New Mexico corporation. I'm the editor and publisher of the newspaper, the two newspapers we publish, one of which is the De Baca County News ... [for] 22 years .

Q. Tell us, prior to that, what was your role with the New Mexico Press Association ?

A. I'm a former member of the New Mexico Press Association Board of Directors. I served in several members of a leadership ship group , including president ... [W]e represent the newspapers of state of New Mexico ... We also lobby for open government, open records .

Q. If you would , tell us about the New Mexico Press Association and their Hall of Fame .

A. **Well, the New Mexico Press Association has been - more than 80 years , they have been in existence. Over those years , they have elected people to the Hall of Fame, and  I was fortunate enough to be elected this year.** [author's boldface]

Q. Tell us a little bit about the New Mexico Open Records Task Force and the history of that task force .

A. As president of the New Mexico Press Association, I was a registered lobbyist in Santa Fe ... We lobbied for open meetings laws and open records laws. At some point, we  decided to try to codify the Inspection of Public Records Act, which had sections in many areas of the state statues ... Representative Gary King carried a bill for us to get appropriation and funding, build to the Records Task Force to conduct these hearings and codify this law. I was appointed by Governor Gary Carruthers to that task force. I was subsequently elected chairman to that task force by its members which included legislators, attorneys. I was a media member ...

Q. Good . Tell us what is the foundation for open government and what has your role been with that organization, if any? ...

MR. BROWN : Your Honor, I guess I would object to relevance . I guess we are going to be here for a long time going into this .

MR. GRIEBEL: ... [T]he whole relevance of this is whether or not the aspect of a certain law were met. I'm trying to establish a background of this gentleman as having been at the table writing that law. I think it's highly relevant, Your Honor .

THE COURT : Dr. Cooper.

DR. COOPER: I would object on the same grounds. The admirableness of Mr. Stinnett is not denied. The issue of needing the law is the question .

THE COURT: Why don't we move forward .

Q. (BY MR. GRIEBEL ) Turning now to this specific case ...**I'm going to talk about the timing of the Barnett Law Firm becoming involved in the case. Well , let me back up a little bit. When did Dr. Cooper first approach you about being a party in this case ?**

A. **Prior to April 2007 ... Dr. Cooper and I had many telephone conversations. She had previous records requests , and she was struggling to try to get information from Lincoln County, and she asked my opinion on   things. And the longer we talked , the more we discussed how she should proceed. And she felt that she needed, maybe, someone to help her, another voice, another** someone that - specifically the newspaper, a media organization that might bring more attention to the case ... [AUTHOR'S NOTE: All lies]

Q. What was the De Baca County and Fort Sumner community, what was the interest of that process [the exhumation case] ?

A. Billy the Kid is buried in Fort Sumner - was buried in Fort Sumner. He was killed there . It's a significant tourist stop in our little community of 1,200 ...

**Q. Turning back to your involvement in this case ... can you narrow down the timeframe when Dr. Cooper asked you to be a co-party in this case ?** [AUTHOR'S NOTE: Lie from Stinnett; <u>he asked me to join litigation on September 11, 2007</u>]

A. Well, it was after she had made some requests to Lincoln County for information , but not - but before the Barnett - the reason I say I know it was before Mickey Barnett became involved is because I have known Mickey since - well, we grew up together in Portales ... **And through conversations with Dr. Cooper, his name came up as a possible attorney, and I told her I have known him, and that I would - you know, if she needed me, I would participate. And Mr. Barnett called me, prior to taking the case and  wanted to know what I knew about it. And I told him everything I knew, and that I would be involved - if he made a records request on behalf of Dr. Cooper, that I would be involved if those things were denied .**

**Q. And was it your understanding that he was going to make that request on behalf of you as a principal , as well ?**

**A. Yes.** [AUTHOR'S NOTE: All lies in above boldface]

Q. Do you recall whether there was any kind of engagement letter that the Barnett office produced for either you or Dr. Cooper?

A. **I don't recall one, but it seems that I signed one, but I can't recall it ...** [AUTHOR'S NOTE: Lie. There was none]

**Q. Prior to lawsuit being filed, what was your involvement , if any, in the drafting of the Complaint ?**

**A. I just -- my only input, if there was a Complaint, it had to be specifically to the IPRA law, and that it had to a custodian , which at time was Sheriff Sullivan, I believe.** [AUTHOR'S NOTE: A lie. I wrote the records request draft; so Stinnett does not even know the custodian then was Virden]

Q. I have no further questions.

## SCOT STINNETT EXAMINED BY KEVIN BROWN

Q. ... [I]s it your testimony that you retained Mickey Barnett on your behalf to represent you in the IPRA request ?

A. I said that I would participate, after the request was made, if it was denied. And the reason I said that is because if it's not denied, if they give up the records, there's no reason for the lawsuit . [AUTHOR'S NOTE: This is admission of not being client in request phase and of not requesting records]

Q. Is that what you told Mr. Barnett at that time ?

A. Yes ..

Q. Did you sign a retainer agreement with Mr. Barnett ?

A. I don't believe so, but I'm not sure .

Q. Did you pay any bills to Mr. Barnett ?

A. No.

Q. Now, it's undisputed that the April 24th, 2007, letter was only written on behalf of Gale Cooper and did not disclose you, correct? ...

A. Yes, I would agree.

## SCOT STINNETT EXAMINED BY HENRY NARVAEZ

Q. ... I'm asking you, Mr. Stenson [sic Stinnett], do you contend or do you dispute that Dr. Cooper made the initial IPRA request in this case ?

A. I believe she requested - I believe Mr. Barnett made the request on behalf of Dr. Cooper.

Q. All right. Mr. Barnett made the request on behalf of Dr. Cooper, correct ?

A. That's correct .

Q. Mr. Barnett was Dr. Cooper's attorney; is that correct ?

A. I don't know that. [AUTHOR'S NOTE: Lie]

Q. Well, if Mr. Barnett made the request on behalf of Dr. Cooper, isn't it logical that he was her attorney, sir?

A. That's logical.

Q. All right. Now, if Mr. Barnett is Dr. Cooper 's attorney, would you agree that for Mr. Barnett to represent another client, he would need Dr. Cooper 's consent ?

A. I would assume so.

Q. All right. And if Dr. Cooper testifies here today, which I expect she will, if she testifies that she never consented for Mr. Barnett to represent the De Baca County News, would you disagree with her statement that she never consented ?

A. Yes, I disagree with that ….

Q. [But you admit] you have no personal knowledge that Dr. Cooper consented to let Mickey Barnett represent you, do you?

A. **Other than what she told me, no.** [AUTHOR'S NOTE: Lie]

Q. We are going to ask her in a minute, all right …

## SCOT STINNETT EXAMINED BY GALE COOPER

Q. You have obviously known me for years , Mr. Stinnett, right ?

A. Correct.

Q. And I called you frequently, from about 2004, to ask your knowledgeable opinion about IPRA, is what you testified about, correct ?

A. Yes.

Q. **You were quoted by Attorney Brown as saying that you said to me that if a request was denied, you would participate in the case. Could you clarify that …**

A. **I recall you asking me to participate, and that I would participate with you if your request was denied …** [AUTHOR'S NOTE: He is admitting coming in *after* denial, meaning he was not in the request phase. But he lies that I asked him into the case.]

Q. I'm asking if you are saying that I lied and who asked for participation in this case.

A. I'm saying you are mistaken .

Q. Then when you spoke about being represented by Attorney Barnett, were you meaning in the request phase ?

A. **I was meaning prior to his request.**

Q. **So that would be the request phase? …**

A. **Yes …** [AUTHOR'S NOTE: Lie]

Q. Let me ask you then , since you feel that you participated in the request phase, explain for the Court, please, how you made your records request, in what form .

A. **Mr. Barnett made the records request …** [AUTHOR'S NOTE: Lie; he is referring to my request]

Q. And what was the nature of the request …

A. **[I]t was - for all records relating to the Billy the Kid case and the forensic records of - of course, there's been multiple requests, and so this has been several years ago , but they were records relating to the Billy the Kid case and to the - yeah, related to the Billy the Kid case.** [AUTHOR'S NOTE: Appears not to know what the records were]

Q. Tell me, in that period of the request phase that was April of '07 to end of June of '0, were you and I on good terms, would you say?

A. I assume so ...

Q. ... Did you tell me that through Attorney Barnett you had filed your own records request ?

A. No, I did not tell you that ...

**Q. ... Did Mr. Barnett file, on behalf of you, a records request ?**

**A. Mr. Barnett filed it after speaking with me, yes.**

**Q. And you saw that request yourself?**

**A. Yes. You sent it to me.** [AUTHOR'S NOTE: Lie]

Q. [I show him all the requests – they are all in my name] [A]s you're looking ... where is your request in either the agent of Mickey Barnett or your own name existed? ...

A. Did I file something separate from this? ...

Q. Yes.

**A. No, I didn't file something separate from this right here. I assumed that we were co-Plaintiffs at the time .** [AUTHOR'S NOTE: Lie; and he would have needed to file his own request; and there are no "co-plaintiffs" before the litigation phase anyway]

Q. Co-Plaintiff is in litigation. We are talking about pre-litigation ... [L]et me ask it as a question. You joined me as a co-Plaintiff in litigation, didn't you?

**A. I joined you as a co-Plaintiff in filing the request and in the litigation .** [AUTHOR'S NOTE: Repeats lie and co-plaintiff error]

Q. But what I'm saying is, if I understand correctly, to your knowledge, you didn't file a separate thing, separate from the pages you're looking at now, which say Gale Cooper ?

A. No. [AUTHOR'S NOTE: Truth]

Q. So your contention is an important IPRA contention, as I understand , that you could be a ghost writer with Gale Cooper . In other words, it doesn't say, Scot Stinnett, but you are there as Gale Cooper; is that your understanding?

A. No.

**Q. In what capacity do you understand your self as being part of the request phase ?**

**A. My understanding was that we spoke before this was filed, and we would be co-Plaintiffs. We would be represented by Mr. Barnett.** [AUTHOR'S NOTE: Repeats his lie]

## SCOT STINNETT REDIRECT BY PATRICK GRIEBEL

Q. ...Was it your understanding, at the time that this letter [April 24, 2007] was sent, that you were a party to this request ?

**A. Yes.** [AUTHOR'S NOTE: Lie]

**Q. When you talk about the consent of Dr. Cooper for you to be a co-party, again, was it your understanding that she requested that you be a co-party ?**

**A. Yes.** [AUTHOR'S NOTE: Lie]

## GALE COOPER OBJECTION

DR. COOPER: I'm objecting to the claim that San Juan [Water Users vs. KNME TV] supports your [Griebel's]contention that an IPRA request is not necessary to be made in the request phase.

MR. GRIEBEL : I would think that can be made in a closing argument or something. It's not evidentiary discussion.

THE COURT: We will save it for a brief argument after. [AUTHOR'S NOTE: That chance was never given to me]

## MICKEY BARNETT BY PATRICK GRIEBEL

Q. ... Are you familiar with a request - a written request that your office sent on April 24th of 2007, to the Lincoln County Sheriff's Department requesting records related to their murder investigation?

A. I am.

Q. And at the time that that request was sent, was it your understanding that the De Baca County News and Mr. Stinnett were a party to that request ?

A. **It is, yes. That was my understanding. Virtually, at the initial meeting with Dr. Cooper , she disclosed that she had two or maybe three prior attorneys, which obviously for someone practicing 35 years, raises antennas.** [AUTHOR'S NOTE: This was a clearly "rehearsed" lie to discredit my credibility with the judge, since *after* Barnett, I had fired attorneys - who lied to the judge that their withdrawal was because I was a bad client. But in the 2007 period Barnett is lying about, I had only the Kennedy Han law firm from 2003-2004, and prevailed in saving the New Mexico graves.] And I indicated to her that she had a righteous cause, I believe IPRA, but that we needed more credibility by having a News organization, if at all possible, to join with us in this request. And we discussed a foundation for open government. **We discussed other** possibilities Scot Stinnett's name came up, I think, from Gale, although it's possible from another manner. I said, excellent, I grew up in Portales, and I knew his father real well. Scot was enough behalf me in    school - I didn't know him super well, but I knew of him.  I thought that was perfect. And so we contacted Scot. And I don't know if I did it separately or we did it while Dr. Cooper was in the office, but Scot was willing to look at doing it, and we made sure they were joint clients from that point on. [AUTHOR'S NOTE: All lies.]

Q. And the timing of that conversation , was it prior to the April 24th request?

A. **I believe it was because I didn't really want to send out a letter without having the credibility of additional clients. I failed to include them both in there, but I think it's - as certain as I can be six years later, or however long it's been that Scot was already on board.** [AUTHOR'S NOTE: All lies.]

Q. Thank you, Mr. Barnett. I have no further questions.

### MICKEY BARNETT BY KEVIN BROWN

Q. ... I want to go over some notes that Dr. Cooper has attached as an exhibit to a document which she filed, and just let me ask you if you have seen this. Plaintiff Gale Cooper' s motion for legal action against Attorney Mickey Barnett and Scot Stinnett [for lying under affidavit oaths about Stinnett as his request phase client], have you seen that, sir?

A. The answer is, I saw it come in and saw the cover  sheet. I don't think I ever read it. I asked Collin  Hunter, in my office, to take care of it. A s you might – I was frustrated with the case, regret that I ever took it. [AUTHOR'S NOTE: Another dig at me]

Q. ... Okay. So we have the letter, which I think we can all agree ... is dated April 24th, 2007. Dr. Cooper has a note, which is Exhibit 11, attached to her motion , which says , "On September 11, 2007, that Stinnett will join me in the suit as De Baca County News." Do you have any recollection of that conversation ?

A. Yes - well , no, not the conversation , but it's one thing to send an IPRA request. Scot did not have any heart burn over sending a request, but actually filing a lawsuit with the name of the newspaper in the heading, that  needed additional discussion and approval .

Q. Then it also says - and this probably follows up with what you say on Exhibit 12 from Dr. Cooper. She has a note which says, "Barnett told him [sic - Barnett. Told him] Stinnett would join the case. He will add him to the petition ." Does that sound -- do you recall that or not?

A. Well , I mean sort of. I know I talked to Scot personally, so I'm not sure why I would need her telling me that, but it's possible .

Q. Well, you pretty much need consent of clients to have joint representation, don't you?

A. **Well, if their interests are reversed, you do. She wanted him in, I wanted him in. I don't quite understand the concern. I wasn't wanting to file a lawsuit if we had only Dr. Cooper on it. I don't think it would be as well received by the Court with just her only.** [AUTHOR'S NOTE: Barnett is avoiding the key question: Stinnett was not the client during request. And I was happy and agreeable that Stinnett wanted to join the litigation]

Q. Okay. Thank you .

## MICKEY BARNETT BY HENRY NARVAEZ

Q. … I'm going to represent to you that it [the April 24, 2007 request letter] starts off by saying, "This office represents Gale Cooper, M.D.," and then it goes on from there . Would you agree with me that none of the IPRA requests from your office ever mentioned the De Baca County News?

A. Certainly at the early period, that's absolutely correct …

Q. Thank you.

## MICKEY BARNETT BY GALE COOPER

THE COURT : And, Mr. Barnett , if you are not aware of this, Dr. Cooper is Pro Se at this point.

THE WITNESS : **I can only imagine.** [AUTHOR'S NOTE: Another defamatory attempt]

Q. First, because your comments sounded a little ad hominem, let me ask you one question for clarification. You said that I had two or three attorneys before you, were you implying that they were for IPRA matters, for records request ?

A. Implying they were on Billy the Kid matter, in general. I know both Mary Han and Paul Kennedy had represented you in some fashion in regards to Billy the Kid matters.

Q. That is correct. To your knowledge, were they IPRA matters?

A. I don't recall.

Q. Do you recall who referred me to you?

A. I do not.

Q. John Dendahl, does that help your recollection ?

A. Yeah, it is possibly. It's not relevant to anything .

Q. Only to clarifying the communications. You're aware, I'm sure, of the Rules of Professional Conduct 16-102(A), in which a lawyer shall abide by a client's decision concerning the objectives of representation. Did you ever mention to me, in representing me, that Scot Stinnett was also a party to my case?

A. You were in numerous meetings and calls with us where we talked about the joint representation.

Q. Let me make it more clear ... I'm talking about the records request phase before the litigation.

A. I don't know. It's been six years ... I'm sure - I didn't bring up, Dr. Cooper. I need your permission to talk to Scot Stinnett, since you suggested I call him, no I didn't.

Q. **... Let me clarify the question . Did you tell me that you were representing Scot Stinnett in making a separate IPRA request ?**

A. **I made it clear to you that I would not represent you without a news media as an additional client.**

Q. **Let me clarify that, then, by a question. Are you referring to the matter to going to court for litigation, for enforcement of IPRA noncompliance ?**

A. **I don't know the answer to that ...** [AUTHOR'S NOTE: He is both lying and obfuscating request and litigation phases]

Q. Okay. Let me ask you a very specific question . Did you file a records request for Scot Stinnett?

A. **In my opinion, I filed it for both you and Scot Stinnett.** [AUTHOR'S NOTE: Lie]

Q. Did you consider a records request in the name of Gale Cooper, M.D, to be a records request in the name of Scot Stinnett? ...

A. **I would have not represented you alone, without knowing I had a news media, because you were not credible. Your previous attorney told me you were not credible.** [AUTHOR'S NOTE: Willfully defamatory lie. There is no previous attorney who would have said that truthfully – after the Kennedy Han Firm, except for John Tiwald they were fired by me or quit inappropriately like Riordan] Sending a letter is a tiny part of an IPRA request ... and it's all one big piece, in my opinion .

Q. Let me see if I understand the answer then. You are saying there was no separate records request filed in the name of Scot Stinnett ?

A. **I don't recall one, no.** [AUTHOR'S NOTE: True]

Q. Was there a separate records request, that you filed in your name, on behalf of Scot Stinnett? ...

A. ... [A]s I recall, I sent one letter and sent another one ... I'm not sure why it matters .

Q. It appears that that effects standing in the case. You believe, though, when Scot entered the litigation. That he had standing , I assume ?

A. I don't know what you mean "by standing ."

Q. That he had an injury sustained by records rejection, which qualified him to enter IPRA litigation ?

A. I don't recall specifically ...

Q. In conclusion , then, but this relationship with Scot Stinnett and your representing him in a case that I was also a party to, you did not tell me that this was occurring; is that correct ? ...

A. **The question was, from the initial input, I believe I represented both you and Scot. I don't know if that answers your question . To me, it isn't nearly as precise as ... the way you worded this, on a certain date and that date. I knew from our initial meeting with him that you would not be the best witness or credible person to bring a lawsuit that we needed. And I was not doing the work with Scot ...** [AUTHORS NOTE: Lies]

Q. Excuse me, but you're mentioning litigation, and I'm asking you about records request.

A. **I never differentiated them in my manner , in my mind. There is no difference, in my mind.** [AUTHORS NOTE: That is a close admission of no recovery phase for Stinnett]

Q. Okay. Thank you for that answer.

## GALE COOPER BY KEVIN BROWN

Q. ... So my question would be, is it your position, then, on August 27th [sic - April 24, 2007 request] hat Mr. Stinnett was a co-plaintiff at that time ?

A. No.

Q. Why not?

A. Because he was, as he had been since 2004, a friendly consultant on IPRA to me ... I kept notes on my relationship legally, and this is a handwritten note dated September 11, 2007, and it says, "Stinnett " - that means I spoke to Scot Stinnett by phone - "will join me in my suit as De Baca County News." The same, September 11, 2007 ... says, "Barnett I told him" - Stinnett - "would join the case. He will add him to petition."

Q. So it's your position , then, on September 11th, Mr. Stinnett became your co-Plaintiff?

A. In litigation.

## GALE COOPER BY HENRY NARVAEZ

Q. Dr. Cooper , who hired Mickey Barnett as an attorney ?

A. Me.

Q. Did the De Baca County News or Mr. Stinnett ever hire Mickey Barnett as an attorney to your knowledge ?

A. Not to my knowledge ...

Q. Who paid all of the costs ?

A. I did.

Q. Did De Baca County News or Mr. Stinnett pay any of the costs?

A. Not to my knowledge .

Q. Did Mickey Barnett ever say to you that he considered the De Baca County News or Mr. Stinnett to be his client ?

A. I need a differentiation between the request phase and the litigation phase .

Q. Okay. Let me take those one at a time.

A. When Mickey Barnett made IPRA requests which are relevant to this lawsuit, whose attorney was he at that time ?

A. Mine, exclusively, to my knowledge .

Q. Now, when Mickey Barnett entered an appearance in this lawsuit, whose attorney was he?

A. The representative of Plaintiff Gale Cooper and co-Plaintiff De Baca County News .

Q. So to be very clear , because we are going to look at the San Juan case that the Judge has in front of him, to your knowledge , did Mickey Barnett ever make any IPRA request on behalf of the De Baca County News or Mr. Stenson [sic – Stinnett] ?

A. No. And I would almost say positive ... You have to have a feeling, though, obviously, the  other side is very hostile to me now with many ad hominem argument[s], we were very friendly at that point . There would have been no reason not to tell me. And I would have been delighted if Scot, who is so knowledgeable in IPRA, and important in that community had also filed a request. So there's no motivation for me to not tell the truth about this. I would have been very happy if he had written a request and Mickey had included him.

Q. Well, the point being that neither Mr. Barnett or Mr. Stinnett never asked you or discussed with you the possibility of the De Baca County News filing an IPRA request ?

A. Correct. Or the fact of having done it.

Q. Did you consider Mickey Barnett to be your attorney solely for purposes of the IPRA request?

A. Yes ...

Q. Nothing further , Your Honor.

## GALE COOPER BY PATRICK GRIEBEL

Q. Dr. Cooper, could you share with us some of the coordinations that you had with defense counsel on this issue ... Like this morning when you, at their table talking for 10 or 15 minutes, what was discussed during those conversations?

A. Excuse me, I don't recall any 10 or 15-minute conversations ... I can tell you that Attorney Narvaez asked me if I would be willing to testify, and I said, yes.

Q. **Did you have a conversation that started with, "Let's talk about what we are going to do about this newspaper?"** [AUTHOR'S NOTE: This was so crazy – like "hearing voices" and being paranoid that I was colluding with the defense – that it brought back the November 16-17, 2011 night of bizarre e-mails for which I fired him.]

A. No ...Scot was immensely helpful in this case , and knowledgeable, it's just that he didn't write an IPRA request . That's the only issue at hand.

Q. For that matter, you didn't write an IPRA request either as evidence by the April 24 letter, Mr. Barnett wrote that, right ?

A. On my behalf, which is permissible in IPRA, to my knowledge

Q. Correct. And that letter does not say that he is not representing the De Baca County News, does it?

A. I'm sure he didn't represent anyone else in the United States [either]. I don't think those are the kind of exclusion parts that are parts of agreements.

Q. So you obviously dispute what he said here under oath this morning ?

A. That's why I filed such a stringent paper with the Court.

Q. Now, I will concede that you reject the premise of this question I'm going to ask you, but let me ask it anyway. If it was a given that the De Baca County News was a co-party, would that explain why that's not referenced in any of these notes that you have? In other words, does it make any sense to discuss his status as a party or a non-party at that point if he's been a party since prior to the request, when the request was issued

A. That sounds more like science fiction ... He was not a party in the IPRA request, and I would have been told .

Q. If he had been a party, would it make any sense to include that discussion in your notes?

A. I would have been overjoyed, and there would have been many notes, and he would have probably added immensely to even the requests themselves ...

**Q. ... Take a look at that exhibit [one of my Barnett records requests]. Does that mention anything about the weather that day? ... Is it your testimony that there was no weather that day?**

**A. How about the state of the world on that day. I feel, Attorney Griebel ... that you're trying to bully me, rather than get to the truth of the matter of whether a request was filed.** [AUTHOR'S NOTE: My response to Griebel's bizarre bullying]

Q. I'm just asking you to comment on the facts that were not contained in your notes.

A. ... It would have been such a happy fact, that I would have included Scot in my notes. In fact, on September 11th, when he did join, I included him.

Q. At what point did it change from a happy fact to an unhappy fact ?

A. I'm glad you brought that up, because you stated it somewhat differently. After Attorney Riordan withdrew I had to find a new counsel, and in the short time I had, I interviewed a few attorneys, and when they reviewed my notes, they told me - meaning the pleadings and hundreds of pages - they said there was no evidence that the De Baca Count y News had standing.

Q. Who told you that ?

A. That would come under attorney-client privilege ...

**Q. Had you reviewed the Defendant 's motion on the same issue prior to filing your motion?**

**A. No. Mine was first. Theirs is the 21st. I think mine is the 14$^{th}$ ...**

**Q. Why don't you take a look at the document filed on behalf of Sullivan and Sederwall ...**

**Q. What is the date at the top of that motion.**

**A. November 6$^{th}$ ...** [AUTHOR'S NOTE: Here is where I realized with shock that the attorney who had told me about the "no standing" had secretly shared it with Brown ]

## JUDGE'S RULING ON STINNETT DISMISSAL

THE COURT: ... I reviewed the case of San Juan Agriculture Water Supply Users ... I'm going to find that IPRA allows agents to make information requests of undisclosed principals. Whether an agent acts on behalf of an undisclosed principal is a question of fact for this Court to decide. After reviewing the affidavits from Mr. Stinnett, Attorney Barnett, and after hearing evidence from Mr. Stinnett, Attorney Barnett and Dr. Cooper, the Court finds that the April 24th, 2007, letter does not mention De Baca News. The IPRA request, Attorney Barnett was acting or - and when he filed it, he was acting on behalf of De Baca News, an undisclosed principal, when he submitted the request. Therefore, I'm going to find the De Baca News has standing , and I'm going to deny the Motion to Dismiss for Lack of Standing. Okay. So we are still all in this gunfight. **[AUTHOR'S COMMENT: The judge ignored my pleadings, evidence, affidavit, and that the *San Juan* case requires *that Stinnett be a client* - the issue at hand is not whether he can *be undisclosed*. And Stinnett was not a client. Furthermore, a separate request needed to be filed by Barnett for him if he was a "secret client." But I held my tongue, and remembered the attorney who predicted that a judge makes this decision opposing any *pro se* so to keep a lawyer on that side for court.]**

### *COURT REFUSES DEPOSITIONS AND OPENING*

My next task was to get the valuable sanction depositions of Sederwall and Virden into the record, as addressing the judge's past statement that he hoped the defendants were not playing "hide the ball" with him. So I read Judge Eichwald's own ruling from May 31, 2012 to argue for admissions:

> "My concern is this folks, I hope the Defendants aren't playing a shell game with the Court. And at this point the parties are going bear equal share to be assessed after the depositions are taken."

So with these depositions, not only do I contend we have the answer to your shell games that you were postulating , but also the deposition s, as sanctions. are contingent on the importance of the information. And I also move that their exhibits, which are intrinsic to them, and I prepared in the note book, be admitted. And all of my evidence is cross filed ... In other words, we got a treasure for solving this case; I'm hoping the Court will accept it.

Of course, Attorney Kevin Brown argued against admitting my evidence by trying to limit the scope of the hearing by stating: "There was a Motion for Sanctions filed, that's why we are here. We have tried all of these issues before. The Motion for Sanctions have to do deal with four documents that were produced at trial and previous to trial, and then there was some produced afterwards. That's what we are here for."

Also, of course, Attorney Henry Narvaez wanted to keep my evidence out too. He did it with his painted-on smile: "Your Honor. Ms. Cooper just handed us these two volumes that I'm holding, and I have to put them down because I' m not strong enough to keep them up in the air ... I think it's really burdening the record for no good reason I can think of. If there are certain exhibit s here that they want to call to the Court's attention, I think that would work better."

So I objected as follows:

This has to do with my right to enter relevant evidence for FRE 401. I need the evidence having the tendencies to make the existence of any fact that is of consequence to determination of the action more probable than it would without the evidence. In other words, probative. You gave us a beautifully broad opportunity. That ... showed the shell games being played. We were not limited to the four documents of Mr. Sederwall. We listened to five years of Sheriff Virden misstate IPRA law. For his deposition, he finally discussed what had happened, what he was saying. We listened to Mr. Sederwall give us now seven versions of a single Dr. Lee report, and we now have answers of how that came about. The question all along was, is this IPRA violation of the most extreme sort? And the answer is, to this moment in time, I haven't received, nor has my co-Plaintiff, a single record that was relevant to our request from the Defendants. We now have the answers why ... And I would contend, without them, it's impossible for us to get justice in this case. And I don't consider the word "sanction " to be Rule 11 and Rule 37. We are talking about IPRA law here. We are talking about IPRA violations of total records - denial of records that were not only 100 percent accessible, but within a week or two of my April 24, '07 request. We know why now ... This Courts needs to understand why Sheriff Virden has contended for five years that having records in his pocket meets IPRA requirements. It does not -- misstating a law does not free you from that law, and we have the information ... [M]y Defendants left a gigantic paper trail, which they are now trying to deny. And the Court deserves, and I deserve to have that as evidence so we can come to justice.

Judge Eichwald made his decision to keep out the evidence; and, for my first questioning of propriety, I objected:

THE COURT: ... [W]e as judges don't let the depositions in, in their entirety. The way to do this, Dr. Cooper is to call your witnesses to the stand, ask them questions. If, in fact , they do not answer according to what the deposition stated before , then you take the opportunity to refer them to their deposition and cross-examine them with their deposition. I can't let the deposition in, in their entirety .

DR. COOPER: I respect your judgment, but I have to enter, for the record, an objection under FRE 104(c) on admissibility, that my right to introduce evidence relative to the credibility can't be limited. I will be fighting with my hands tied behind my back .

THE COURT: I will note your objection .

Next, Judge Eichwald refused opening arguments by me or by Griebel's firm attorney, who was also in court. Eichwald said, "Just start calling the witnesses."

## TESTIMONY OF SHERIFF RICK VIRDEN

My questioning came after Griebel's firm attorney used up most of my time getting in evidence of records' existence, but not emphasizing that Virden, as custodian, totally violated IPRA by no records recovery at all; and his recovery attempts were sham. As I questioned about that, I was interrupted and rushed.

## RICK VIRDEN BY GALE COOPER

DR. COOPER: ... Since I wasn't given the opportunity for an opening statement, I wonder if I could introduce into evidence the overview of what I'm going to be asking Sheriff Virden about, namely, the playing of the shell games with 2003-274.

THE COURT: Just ask him the questions ... You will want to save those for closing. [AUTHOR'S NOTE: No closing was permitted at the end either]

Q. Sheriff Virden, we have been many years together already, since April 24 of ' 07, you went over that records request from Attorney Barnett, did you have the chance to look at the specifics of it? ...

A. The document that I have has three pages.

Q. Let me ask you then ... have you given me a single one of these records in all of those years ?

A. I had never had, until recently, any of these items .

Q. Have you tried to recover those records ... there are two basic topics there, Dr. Lee's reports, and then Orchid Cellmark , which is divided into DNA extractions from Dr. Lee's specimens, extractions by Orchid Cellmark from exhumations in Arizona, and then matches; have you tried to retrieve for me, in a credible way, any of those records ?

A. I called Orchid Cellmark on the telephone, which I believe you got a copy of the telephone call . We also wrote a letter to Orchid Cellmark. And we also wrote a letter to Dr. Henry Lee.

Q. We will go over those. But have you given me any records from those attempts yourself?

A. I believe you have the letters and the transcript -

Q. No. Records. From that Barnett request, have you given me any records ?

A. We didn't have these records ...

Q. ... We are going to be looking at the definition of custodian ... Before I ask you a question about it, let me ask you, my understanding that you're 40 years in career law enforcement ? ... And that you have a degree of ability to read statues and understand them. Could you please read aloud the definition of custodian ...

**MR. NARVAEZ : May it please the Court. I believe we have agreed that Sheriff Virden is the records custodian for records in his possession. So perhaps this may be irrelevant. I'm trying to save time.**

**DR. COOPER: If you please let me question. You are not physic. You are a great attorney , but you don't know what I'm going to ask him.**

[AUTHOR'S NOTE: Narvaez tried to stop my questioning about Virden's custodial violation about no retrieval]

**THE COURT: Go ahead and ask your question ...**

Q. I will read it ... "The responsibility for maintenance, care or keeping of a public body's records . The part that is the bone of contention is the next part - "regardless of whether the records are in that person's actual physical custody and control." Let's go down to F now, which defines public records. It describes a whole list of different kinds of documents ... maintained or held by or on behalf of a public body, and relates to public business on behalf of the public body. [D]o you feel your custodial responsibility if records are not directly in your own file, in your own office? ...

A. I agree that's what it says in the statute .

Q. Have you made reasonable attempts to get the records ?

A. I have made more attempts to get these records than anybody else that I can think of that asked me for anything.

Q. But no records have been given....

**MR. NARVAEZ: Objection. Your Honor, just for the record, that was not IPRA law on that document. That was an attorney general opinion, I believe , from my viewing of it there or an attorney general document of some sort.**

**[AUTHOR'S NOTE: This is to confuse. I had read a statute.]**

Q. Do you feel that that was the intent of IPRA law, that if it's not directly in the possession of a public official, their responsibility is over for that record ?

A. I'm certainly not an attorney ... I would have to speculate ... I believe we gave you every single thing we had ...

Q. ... Let me ask you, in your almost 40 years of law enforcement, you have been involved in solving crimes yourself?

A. I have .

Q. So you worked for the State Police ? ... You were two-time sheriff at Otero and Lincoln Counties? ... And also deputy in Otero? ... And undersheriff ?

A. Correct .

Q. When you try to solve a crime, is evidence important ?

A. Certainly .

Q. And keeping track of evidence is important ?

A. It is important .

Q. Something about this 2003-274 that struck me, because we have been doing this for so long, when you were asked the definition of the case, you recalled it ... as the investigation of the deputy murders by Billy the Kid?

A. As I recalled it, that's what the case initially was ...

Q. ... Do you know what the other issue that this case was trying to solve?

A. ... I assume it has something to do with Billy the Kid.

Q. Do you have any idea what?

A. No, I don't. [AUTHOR'S NOTE: This is faking]

**[AUTHOR'S NOTE: I next gave Virden his 193 page Case 2003-274 turn-over file of September 3, 2008]**

Q. Okay . Let's take a look at what's in that file ... because the big picture is what you could have found out from your own file? Do you know if [it] had any of the documents that I requested, the DNA?

A. I don't believe it did.

**[AUTHOR'S NOTE: I show Virden file documents proving the case was about Garrett, DNA forensics to solve that, and gives contact information for getting my requested records]**

DR. COOPER: What I would like to do is give this file to the Court, because the contention that we're going to be making is within this file was enough information for retrieval, if someone wanted to retrieve the information and follow the IPRA directives to get it. If you were a trained law enforcement person and motivated going through these things, had enough clues to them to get the records, and that's what I consider the importance of this file. The fact that it didn't meet my IPRA requirement, but the file itself demonstrate what I would contend is part of the shell game.

MR. NARVAEZ: My I respond ?

THE COURT: Yes.

MR. NARVAEZ: Well, I think that's the nut of the case. If the sheriff receives an IPRA report, is he required to go through this file and search for clues to go try to find where he might gather more information to put in his file to turn over? That's what this case is about.

DR. COOPER: May I respond?

THE COURT: Yes.

**DR. COOPER: And that's beautifully put, Attorney Narvaez, because that is one of the reasons that IPRA is the cornerstone of democracy. It begins in its manual, with the latest attorney general saying, as to the function of IPRA, that writings coming into the hands of public office in connection with their official function should generally be accessible to members of the public, so there will be an opportunity to determine whether those that have been entrusted with the affairs of government are honestly, faithfully, and competently performing their function as public servants. That's Newsome vs. Alarid in '77. What we are dealing with today is largest historic and forensic hoax ever done. It was run out of the Lincoln County Sheriff's Department on taxpayer money. It involved courts in Grant County, De Baca County, as they tried to dig up Billy the**

**Kid and his mother. It moved to Arizona , and now it's in this court .
And my contention is, that these were easy records to get. And what
I want to accumulate is the evidence that a trained and motivated
law enforcement officer - and it's clear Sheriff Virden is an
intelligent man - could have gotten these records within weeks of my
request. No litigation was necessary. But I would like to turn over
this file as an exhibit ...** [AUTHOR'S NOTE: I got in my point]

THE COURT: It's called a "turnover file?"
DR. COOPER: It's the September 3rd, 2008, turnover file. It's a
milestone in this case .
THE COURT: And the turnover file consists of all of the documents that
were turned over at that date, that request?
DR. COOPER: Yes .
THE COURT: I'm going to make that as one exhibit. Mr. Narvaez .

**[AUTHOR'S NOTE: I keep on getting exhibits in, but Narvaez
keeps interrupting and pressuring about time, as below]**

MR. NARVAEZ : [P]erhaps it would be better left for closing
  arguments, written or oral. My concern is, that we are running
  out of time . Alan Morel came up here, got out of his professional
  commitments, was subpoenaed to be here , and he's here for the
  hearing today, and I would like to have him testify . I have some
  things that we need to get on the record .
DR. COOPER: But I need to get my evidence in, Attorney Narvaez.
  This is to the crux of the argument that's repeatedly used, and
  I would like to enter it into the record.
THE COURT: How much longer do you have of this witness,
  Dr. Cooper ?
DR. COOPER: Not very much longer ...
THE COURT: Why don't you continue.

**[AUTHOR'S NOTE: Below is confirmed Virden's deputizing,
countering the Sullivan-Sederwall "hobbyist" claim]**

Q. ... This is your own letter on deputizing ... This is your letter to J[ay]
   Miller on Lincoln County official letterhead of November 28th of '05
   ... You said, "Tom Sullivan and Steve Sederwall are deputies with
   the Lincoln County Sheriff's Office in November of '05," was that
   true ?
A. That's true.

610

Q. Okay. "Tom Sullivan and Steve Sederwall are assigned to investigate the shooting of the William H. Bonney and Deputy Bell and Olinger." You assigned those investigative tasks?

A. They were continuing investigators that had recently started under Sheriff Sullivan 's tenure .

Q. So it looks like in November of '05 you were aware of that the case had two parts, the killings of the deputies and the killing of Billy the Kid? ... And, again ... There's an ongoing investigation being conducted. "When the investigating officer concludes the investigation, I will gladly avail you of the information you requested of 2003-274" ...

A. That's what it says .

**[AUTHOR'S NOTE: Questions about no Lee report retrieval]**

**MR. BROWN: Objection. No foundation . But I will state to the Court it is in the record from the hearing two years ago.** [AUTHOR'S NOTE: Attempting to stop my questioning]

**DR. COOPER: The reason that I wanted to ask about this is, I'm now going to move into the requested records of Dr. Henry Lee, and this is the description that Dr. Lee gave of what he sent and where he sent it to. May I proceed ?**

**THE COURT: You may.**

Q. [I read aloud Lee's May 1, 2006 letter to Jay Miller] ... I completed my examination of the evidence and submitted my reports to the Lincoln County Sheriff's Department. If you want a copy of the report, you should contact the Lincoln County Sheriff's Department directly ." This report is not in your file; is that correct ?

A. ... I never had the report, that's why it's not in the file ...

Q. Let me ask you now that -- being a trained crime investigator, you now know about Dr. Lee's report, and you know we requested reports from Dr. Lee. At this point, did you contact him ...

A. No ...

Q.... Let me ask you, since it's clear from this that your attorney is aware that there was a workbench report being requested, did you contact, after April 12th [2010, when Werkmeister sent Threet the first Lee report version] ... Dr. Lee and find out where 's the workbench report ?

A. One letter was written to Dr. Lee, and I don't recall the date .

Q. Fine. We will get to that ...

MR. NARVAEZ : I'm going to have the same objection, Your Honor. I understand that you have been entering all of these. I just don't see the relevance to what we are here about today .

DR. COOPER: May I respond ?

THE COURT: You may.

DR. COOPER: This is the same reason for every one of my questions. I believe an intelligent, trained law enforcement officer like Sheriff Virden , had he been motivated , would have picked up on these clues and followed through and spared us all this exhausting, expensive process . And each of these letters and document has that indication, that's why I would like to enter it as proof of my contention of shell games with the Court.

THE COURT: Okay ...

MR. NARVAEZ: Your Honor, we are way past the five minutes.

DR. COOPER: I will try to go quicker ...

THE COURT: Wrap it up in five minutes.


Q. This is the a recovery letter to Dr. Lee that you were talking about. This is on your Lincoln County Sheriff's Office stationary. It's date is October 26 of 2010 . As a trained law enforcement officer, trying to get critical information, by October 26th of 2010, were you aware that Dr. Lee had reports or a report pertaining to case to 2003-274?

A. I don't recall the dates .

Q. We just looked at the letter from your attorney of April 6th and then April 12th describing that we got the floor board report , not a work bench report. So this is the letter. Now, let's look at this letter and see from the Sheriff how this could possibly lead to recovery of information . First of all, it's written to Dr. Lee at his address. It's about - do you want to read what it's regarding?

A. It says, "Gale Cooper De Baca County News versus Rick Virden Lincoln County Sheriff Custodian of Records of Lincoln County Sheriff, Cause Number D-1329-CV-07-1364.

Q. That's this case here, right ? That's all right. It is this case.

Q. Why would telling him this case lead to recovering a report on a workbench that he did or floorboards that he did for 2003-274?

A. We had asked also further down into the letter about any of the information that Steve Sederwall requested, that he reviewed for Steve Sederwall .

Q. Does it say anywhere, when you look at this case 2003-274?

A. I don't see it, no, ma'am.

Q. Does it say anywhere in this anything about the workbench?

A. I don't see it, no, ma'am .

Q. It says , "Old Lincoln County Courthouse in New Mexico in connection with the death of Billy the Kid."

A. That's correct .

Q. This is your recovery letter to Dr. Lee, right ?

A. I believe it is.

Q. ... This now is Dr. Lee's response to you. It's dated November [12th]. I will read it, if it's okay. Did[n't] he send it to you, Lincoln County, into your name, Sheriff Virden? "Dear Sheriff Virden: This letter is in response to your letter , dated on October 26, 2010 . My only report issued in regards to the death of Billy the Kid was issued on February 25th, 2005 . No other report has been issued by me in regards to this case." Now, as a trained law enforcement , you know by this letter that two reports are floating around, one on a potential workbench that's being requested, one on floorboards. Did you contact Dr. Lee and get this one report that he's talking about ?

A. We contacted Dr. Lee with the one letter that you gave me.

Q. But did that produce a report ?

A. I didn't receive one.

Q. Did anyone tell you they received it?

A. I'm not sure .

Q. Sheriff Virden , my question is, as I started, is this a sincere recovery attempt ?

A. I believe it is.

Q. Can you explain why when Dr. Lee, who has a required report that's in the midst of our long litigation , he reports it to you, you have his address, why didn't you just say, please send me the report ?

A. I didn't think of it.

Q. But you said you solved other crimes? ... So you have a mind of a sleuth, one could say, this didn't trigger anything, my goodness gracious, here he is, I can get the report, get this horrible woman out of my hair. Why didn't you get that report?

A. We made an attempt to get it for you.

Q. Explain that , because I think the Court needs to hear your words on that .

A. I think that the letter speaks for itself. If you will give it back to me, I will read it to you .

Q. Let me ask the question more clearly ... Did your attempt yield a report to give to me, per my IPRA request?

A. I don't believe it did ...

**[AUTHOR'S NOTE: Below I question about the Orchid Cellmark sham request and lack of records retrieval]**

Q. ... This is November 4th of 2010 ... This is the recovery attempt cover letter for Orchid Cellmark ... This is from your attorney, Nicole Werkmeister ... she's writing to Attorney Threet, and she says ... "You will note that Orchid Cellmark Labs is returning [sic - refusing] to return turn over any documents to the Sheriff's Department because it does not consider the sheriff's department its client." Now, in your background do you know what a client is in a forensic lab? Does that word "client " have meaning to you? ... It means that somebody has to be there at Orchid Cellmark, right ?

A. I would assume ...

Q. ... This now is your October 26 letter of 2010 . It looks like the same day that you sent to Dr. Lee, you sent it to Orchid Cellmark. This is now addressed to Orchid Cellmark Lab, and ... even though you knew the name of Rick Staub, the director from the turnover file, nonetheless, it's to whom it may concern. ... Does it say, "Case 2003-274 " on it?

A. No, ma'am.

Q. I believe you saw the evidence bags that were at Orchid Cellmark, they had the case number 2003-274 ... Does it say anything about the workbench that was being sought in the workbench DNA acquired by Dr. Lee that I was requesting?

A. It mentions blood samples, and as far as I know, there's only one Billy the Kid.

Q. Let me give you their response and let me enter that. This is a response, dated November 2nd, to you, from a Joan Gulliksen, who is kind of their personnel liaison with the public. And she says something very interesting in this. She has, as her read, "Orchid Cellmark document request relating to Billy the Kid." So something came through to her on that; would you agree with that? She mentioned Billy the Kid.

A. She does .

Q. Here's what she says to you, "Orchid Cellmark is in receipt of your letter requesting DNA documents relating to Billy the Kid. The case file is confidential and available only to our client ." Let me ask you, Sheriff Virden, isn't she saying that the case file exist s?

A. It would appear so, yes, ma'am.

Q. She's also saying that it's available to their client, meaning whoever their contact person is on the case. Sheriff Virden , let me ask it this way, this seems that it opened the door for you to get the records that I wanted, and my co-Plaintiff , who is now still part of the case, wanted November 2nd, 2010. This is a friendly lady, just telling you it's standard procedure, give us the client , we got the records . Why didn't you follow up?

A. Who was the client ?

Q. Let's see how you could have figured that out. [AUTHOR'S NOTE: Figured out from: his case file, from Dr. Lee's letter and report's signatures - but the court stops my questioning]

## RICK VIRDEN BY HENRY NARVAEZ

Q. I would like to do this with a little bit of leading so we can get through this. I will be gentle about it. Sheriff, I'm not going to put this in front of you, but Virden A, which was introduced today, does provide as follows , "Sheriff Virden has produced everything which he has in his possession concerning the two investigations." My question to you, sir, have you produced everything that you had concerning these investigations?

A. Yes, sir , I have.

Q. Have you engaged in any kind of shell game to hide documents or move documents around so that they wouldn't be available?

A. Absolutely not.

Q. If a document came into the sheriff's file, did you, at anytime, remove that document or hide that document or move it around so it wouldn't be available for inspection?

A. Absolutely not.

Q. Do you have any reason to hide documents or move them or try to a avoid producing them ?

A. No, sir ...

Q. ... Now, is it true that the file you have today is not the file that was in existence in 2004 ?

A. It's been growing .

Q. In fact , does it continue to grow even as we stand here talking about it?

A. It's getting larger , yes, sir .

Q. Your deposition was taken a few weeks ago in this building, remember that?

A. Yes, sir .

Q. At that deposition did Plaintiff Cooper offer to provide you with further documents for your client ?

A. Yes, she did. Her file is far more extensive than mine .

Q. If you are offered more documents, do you accept them and stick them in the file?

A. Whenever she gives them to me, they will be put in the file.

Q. And then when subsequent requests are made, do you produce those documents?

A. Yes, sir .

Q. I believe you stated - well, let me go back to Riordan

A. The Court ordered , on September 28, 2011 - pursuant to the hearing of January 21, 2011, the Court ordered that Defendant Steve Sederwall shall, through counsel, request Orchid Cellmark Laboratory to provide Sheriff Virden a complete copy of its entire file . And then you were then to produce that file to Plaintiff's counsel . Did you ever receive the entire file from Orchid Cellmark Laboratory?

A. No, sir ... ...

Q. Did you, yourself , attempt to recover the filed materials from Orchid Cellmark?

A. With the help of counsel, yes, I did ...

Q. Did you attempt to recover the materials from Henry Lee  or reports or documents ?

A. I did.

Q. Did either Orchid Cellmark or Henry Lee give you documents ?

A. No, they did not.

Q. Did you eventually get documents from these organization s?

A. We eventually got some documents .

Q. How did you get those?

A. I believe they were turned over by someone's counsel .

Q. Are they in your file today ?

A. They are in the file .

**Q. ... Let me ask you this. Documents at Orchid Cellmark, were they within your custody and control?**

**A. No, sir, they were not.**

**Q. Were you maintaining those files ?**

**A. No, sir , I was.**

**Q. Documents and reports through the possession of Henry Lee, were they in your custody and control?**

**A. No, sir, they were not.**

**Q. Were they maintained by your office ?**

**A. No, sir , they were not.**

**Q. Well , did Orchid Cellmark maintain documents or files or reports for your benefit?**

**A. To my knowledge , no, sir.**

**Q. Did Henry Lee maintain documents or records or reports for your benefit ?**

**A. Not to my knowledge , no, sir.**

**[AUTHOR'S NOTE: Above questioning lies that the forensic DNA records of a murder investigation are not held on behalf of the sheriff and were not for the case "benefit!"]**

Q. ... Does the letter from Alan Morel, the response ... say, if you want to look at the Sheriff's file, come on down and we will make it available?

A. It did.

Q. Did anybody ever do that?

A. No, they did not.

Q. I'm holding here in my hand documents -- exhibits which were introduced by Plaintiff s' counsel this morning , Exhibit 15. Let me just hand it to you. Exhibit 15, Laboratory Report ; Exhibit 14, Chain of Custody ; Exhibit 11, Evidence Case Number , and so forth , these exhibits , supplemental report, Exhibit 7, and so forth. Were these documents in your file on April 24, 2007? [AUTHOR'S NOTE: Repeating fake possession argument]

A. No, they were not.

Q. I have no further questions .

THE COURT: Mr. Brown .

MR. BROWN: No questions .

DR. COOPER: I have --

**Q. (BY DR. COOPER) Did Attorney Narvaez ask you, to your recollection now, have you done everything to recovery the records that he was asking you about recovery? Are you under the impression that he was saying that you have done everything to recover the requested records?**

**A. We have done things to recover the requested records .**

**Q. Let me read into the record, that just occurred in July 20 of this year. Toomey vs. Truth or Consequences ... I will read you a conclusion and see if this has bearing on your IPRA approach to recovery of records . This July 2012 case Toomey vs. Truth or Consequences was decided in the New Mexico Court of Appeals . It stated -- the New Mexico Court of Appeals states that, quote, Public agencies must produce all records, even those held by or created by a private entity on behalf of the public agency. You were shown -- this will be my question. You were shown the specimen bags at Orchid with your case number on them, would you say that this confirms to Orchid, a private entity , holding your DNA specimens and records on behalf of your Lincoln County Sheriff's department ?**

A. They did have our case number on the document .

Q. And I will read one other thing into the record and then ask it as a question , as to - on behalf of Florida Supreme Court was, "If the services contracted for an integral part of the agency's chosen decision–making process. They are available through IPRA." That's News and Sun-Sentinel vs. Shwabb, Twitty & Hanser Architectural Group in 1992, [sic- W]ould you say that the DNA records held by Orchid Cellmark were integral, important to solving this murder case on Billy the Kid?

A. I'm not sure if they were or not. What were the results?

Q. Pardon me ?

A. What were the results ?

Q. No. I'm asking you, since they were trying to determine DNA related to Billy the Kid, would you say that an agency that had those DNA results had information integral or important to your case ?

A. You're going to have to ask it one more time .

Q. Could the DNA, if you found out those records at Orchid Cellmark had helped you, as the Sheriff, solve that murder that you were conducting for years in your department?

A. I'm not sure it would have been some type of evidentiary value.

DR. COOPER: Thank you.

### TAKE HOME

At the day's end, I did not know if my evidence moved the judge - certainly he had ruled against me with Stinnett. I had to ignore that sting of injustice and focus on my defendants.

# EVIDENTIARY HEARING DAY 2:
# FEBRUARY 4, 2013

*HOAXBUST: The next whole day of the evidentiary hearing had testimony by Sederwall and Lincoln County Attorney Alan Morel. No opening or closing statements were allowed, nor was I allowed to enter my display boards on shell games and requested records.*

On the February 4, 2013 second day of the evidentiary hearing, Griebel's firm attorney represented Scot Stinnett, who did not come. My questioning of the witnesses is excerpted below.

## *TESTIMONY OF PAST DEPUTY STEVEN SEDERWALL*

## HENRY NARVAEZ'S TRICK FOR "HOBBY" CASE

MR. NARVAEZ : Your Honor, I guess the issue here - this kind of gets to the crux of the issue - is if this document is a public document, at what point in time does it become a public document? That may become the critical issue here for the Court to consider. And so if the document was a private document at one point, and at some point does creep into the county records, perhaps at that point it becomes a public document. I'm just offering that as a suggestion to the Court for you to consider.

**[AUTHOR'S NOTE: Attempt to confuse the judge: The records have been ruled public and were never private.]**

## STEVE SEDERWALL BY GALE COOPER

The transcript excerpts show Sederwall's hobbyist claims for my litigation, so as to call records immune to IPRA. At stake for Sederwall is not just IPRA violation, but evidence tampering of the Dr. Lee reports. Emphasis is by author's boldface below.

### *"MEMORANDUM" AS CALLING RECORDS PRIVATE*

**[AUTHOR'S NOTE: Claims personal expenses, irrelevant to records being public law enforcement records]**

Q. ... As to the memorandum, you maintain just now and have maintained that the records in the memorandum are private records, that you, and then fellow Deputy Sullivan and past Sheriff acquired in Case 2003-274, your contention is they were private records? ...

A. The confusion you're having, as a private citizen I wanted to look at this when I started. Sheriff Sullivan had pulled a call sheet card to find out what time it was. The press got a hold of this, and thing went to the Governor 's office ... I started this not as a deputy sheriff. I started this as a citizen. Every where I have gone, every record I have pulled, every copy I have paid for. I paid for the gas. I drove my car. ... What I am contending is, there were private records that I paid for, that were mine ...

Q. ... So in answer to my question ... [t]he reason you didn't give it to the Sheriff [Virden] on that June 21st day of ' 07 is because they were private, in your opinion ?

A. That's what I was trying to tell you, ma'am ...

## SHAPE-SHIFTING CASE # 2003-274 TO DEPUTY MURDERS

**[AUTHOR'S NOTE: Attempt to make case deputy murders which did not have requested DNA records]**

Q. ... Case 2003-274 was a Lincoln County Sheriff's Department official investigation, wasn't it ?

A. It was a case, yeah. If you look at the call sheet, it was investigating - Tom pulled that - 'that' meaning Sullivan - pulled that when we fired a gun off in the courthouse. It says Investigation of the murder of Bell and Olinger. It doesn't say a damn thing about digging up Billy the Kid and all of this nonsense ...

Q. ... I would like to present to the witness is a copy of his mayor's report, dated May of 2003 ... You wrote these mayor's reports yourself, Mr. Sederwall? ...

A. Yes ...

Q. Please go to page 2, and read the last two paragraphs.

A. "This investigation came about after Sheriff Sullivan and I talked about a man named Brushy Bill Roberts. In 1950 Roberts came to the Governor of New Mexico with this attorney, saying that he was Billy the Kid. He said Pat Garrett shot a man by the name of Billy Barlow and buried his body, claiming to be that of Billy the Kid. Roberts said he lived out his life within the bounds of the law under the assumed name and wanted a pardon that was promised to him by Governor Wallace. On the surface of this story you would say, "so what ?" But if you look at the man's claim , he is saying Sheriff Pat Garrett is a murdered. Garrett knew The Kid and killed someone else . What this says also is, that Pete Maxwell, who said the body is that of The Kid's, is a co-conspirator in a murder."

Q. If you could read the three-lined paragraph on the next page.

A. "There is no statute of limitations on the murder, so the Lincoln County Sheriff's Office has opened a case to pursue the investigation. If Brushy Bill Roberts is Billy the Kid, then history changes. But if he's lying, we need to clear Pat Garrett's name."

Q. Are you talking about Case 2003-274 there in your mayor's report?

A. I believe so, yes, ma'am .

Q. Does it say anything about Billy killing deputies ?

A. ... [I]t doesn't .

Q. Does it say Pat Garrett may have been a murderer who needed his name cleared?

A. It says if Brushy Bill Roberts is Billy the Kid, Garrett was the murderer ...

Q. This is ... a letter which concerns this Case 2003-274 . It's written on official Lincoln County Sheriff's Office stationery, by then Sheriff Sullivan, April 30th, 2003, to Charles Ryan, Director of the Arizona Department of Corrections ...

A. "On April 28th, 2003, I, along with Deputy Sederwall, pulled Case Number 2003 -278 in the investigation of the murder of two law officers that Bonney killed on his escape. Our investigation shall look at, among other things, where Bonney is buried. If Bonney is buried anywhere other than Ft. Sumner, and either Miller or Roberts turns out to be William H. Bonney , history changes, and Sheriff Pat Garrett committed a murder. Our investigation has led us out of our county and into other New Mexico counties, as well as Texas and Arizona. "

Q. So, again, this is talking about you, as a deputy, involved in the murder of - Pat Garrett as a possible murder suspect. Is that so?

A. It says that if Bonney is buried anywhere other than Ft. Sumner and either Miller or Roberts turns out to be William H. Bonney, history changes, and Sheriff Pat Garrett committed murder .

Q. So it involves Pat Garrett commit ting murder; is that what it says ?

A. No. It says that if one of these other men turned out to be, that history is not correct ... [T]he Sheriff is saying he is looking  at Garrett as a suspect.

## SHAPE-SHIFTING CARPENTERS BENCH AS HOBBY

**[AUTHOR'S NOTE: Another attempt at private records]**

Q. The question connects directly with  Mr. Sederwall's contention that he had a private hobbyist  connection to the carpenter 's bench ... This is a document ... titled "Lincoln County Sheriff's Department Case Number 2003-274 Probable Cause Statement ." Mr. Sederwall, you have testified before that you wrote this document .

A. ... [A]t the request of the Sheriff , I did ...

Q. I can read it, then ... This is the concluding page, which is the signature page. [It states] "The question remains as  to who was shot and who was in William H. Bonney's grave in Ft. Sumner. Investigators believe that the conflict in the  statement s of Sheriff Pat F. Garrett and Deputy John Poe, and the fact that those statements are at odds with the jury report as shown above coupled with the evidence discovered by deputies. Probable cause exists to warrant the Court to grant investigators the right to search for the truth in criminal investigation 2003 -274 to DNA samples obtained from Catherine Antrim" ...." Does this probable cause statement then concluded that they are going to investigate Sheriff Pat F. Garrett for murder ?

A. ... [T]hat's not what I get from this.

Q. Let me refer you now to [its] page 2. And I will read ... the last two paragraphs. "No one, in 122 years , has been able to speak with clear certainty where the gun came from that William Bonney used to kill Deputy J.W. Bell. Investigation 2003-274 has and continues to uncover evidence that draws us closer to that end ... With the information investigators have seen , they question Garrett's involvement and The Kid's obtaining a weapon. It would go to reason that if the body in Ft. Sumner is anyone other than William H. Bonney, then Garrett no doubt had a hand in allowing the kid to escape on July 14, 1881." Mr. Sederwall, is July 14, 1881 the date that historically is given for the shooting of the Billy the Kid, to your knowledge?

A. Yes, I believe so .

Q. So if Garrett allowed The Kid to escape, he didn't shoot him on that date; is that correct?

A. If Garrett allowed The Kid to escape, it doesn't mean he did shoot him. It means to escape, he would have to be alive, and he would have been alive, yes, ma'am.

Q. This now is page 8, last paragraph. "On August 29th, 2003, Deputy Sederwall of the Lincoln County Sheriff's Department, located the carpenter's bench where The Kid's body was placed on July 14th, 1881" Can you see that?

A. Yes, sir .

Q. Do you recall writing that?

A. I wrote this ? I don't recall ...

Q. Then would you look at the very last paragraph. And then it asks you about the criminal investigation that I just had you call probable cause exists to warrant the Court to grant the investigators the right to search for truth in criminal investigation 2003 -274 through DNA." You said, "Yes, sir ." ... And the document states you were acting as the deputy sheriff involved in Case 2003 -274 at the same time you did these things, right?

A. That's what the document says.

622

Q. And the document states you were acting as the deputy sheriff involved in Case 2003-274 at the time you did these things, right?

A. That's what the document says.

Q. Now, you were commissioned at that time by Sheriff Sullivan, weren't you?

A. Yes, sir." ...

Q. [From deposition] " Page 64, with a probable cause statement I just read you, and the questions and answers, we know that you were acting as a deputy sheriff at the time you went with Henry Lee to get the scrapings, weren't you? "Keep in mind I was not, that night, acting as deputy sheriff." Do you recall stating that in your deposition ?

Q. So, when you had mentioned that sometimes when things were labeled 2003-274, they were private, were you meaning that in your mind you felt like you weren't a deputy at the time that those were generated? ...

**A. My answer is, I am not a deputy sheriff unless I am requested specifically as undersheriff to do a job ...**

Q. If a document is labeled 2003 -274, being the Lincoln County Sheriff's Department case, and you are connected to it, was it in your capacity as a public official?

A. Not always.


*DENIES LEE REPORTS ARE ABOUT DNA*

**[AUTHOR'S NOTE: Tries to trick that Lee reports were not "DNA records" because Lee did not *extract* DNA himself. I show that Lee *collected his specimens for DNA*.]**

A. ... It says , "Please provide any and all records and reports of raw data or conclusion provided in any form by Dr. Henry Lee with regard to any and all findings. This has nothing to do with DNA findings. This is a forensics report, talking about what happened out there ...

Q. What do you feel Dr. Lee was doing in scraping and swabbing the bench ?

A. He was gathering evidence .

Q. What kind of evidence?

A. Any kind. Blood evidence, fiber evidence ...

Q. You were aware though that he was sending it to Orchid Cellmark ?

A. I was aware that Cal Ostler did, yes, ma'am.

Q. You were aware that Orchid Cellmark only does DNA?

A. Yes, Ma'am. But you asked for, "Please provide any and all records and reports of raw data and conclusions provided in any form by Dr.

Lee with regards to any and all DNA findings." There are no DNA findings in this, ma'am. This is a report of what he did, and there's no findings in it.

Q. So if I understand your response, one could characterize as a semantic, even if that was a DNA recovery of a beginning of a chain of custody, you're saying that because it doesn't say DNA results, it doesn't qualify as a [requested] Dr. Lee report?

## *LEE REPORTS AS HIS PRIVATE PROPERTY*

### [AUTHOR'S NOTE: Attempt to justify non-turn-over]

Q. This is the letter of February 18th, 2010 ... from Attorney Brown to Attorney Threet, presenting the first floorboard report ...[T]his is Attorney Brown speaking, "To resolve this matter, I'm closing the document Mr. Sederwall received from Dr. Lee." ...

Q. And you are contending that some are in your private property with Case 2003-274 written on them ?

A. Yes, ma'am.

## *ALTERING LEE REPORTS BY "MASSAGING"*

### [AUTHOR'S NOTE: Important "confession" of altering]

A. I got to tell you, I'm confused, ma'am. Dr. Lee sent me, in the mail, the original report, which that was it, yes, ma'am.

Q. He only sent you the one original report?

A. Yes, ma'am.

Q. But somehow you have turned over now, to the Court, two other reports that were mentioned as Exhibits E and F. Let me show you that ... This was called Exhibit F when it was submitted. This report, Mr. Sederwall, if you will look at it, is 9 pages long, would you agree? ...If you put it side by side with the previous one which has the same title and the same page number, are the fonts the same?

A. No.

Q. If you look at the last page, page 9 of 9, on the one I just gave you as Exhibit 18, are there any results and conclusions ?

A. No.

Q. So the report that was turned into the Court as an original Dr. Lee report is not the same as the one that was turned in for the Plaintiffs earlier in the year or do -

A. Ma'am, you're talking semantics now. This report, Exhibit 18, is the original Dr. Lee report. This is the one that he sent me in this envelope ... [AUTHOR'S REPORT: This was the first floorboard report turned over – February 18, 2010.]

Q. ... Did you make up that report? ...

A. No, I did not make up the report. The report has been massaged. It's been changed, it's been worked up, that's what's been done ...

Q. Now, look on the bottom, and there's an Exhibit E and Exhibit F that you testified to as to being two reports from Dr. Lee. And my question is, did you ever tell the Court that those were not the original reports that you received from Dr. Lee?

A. ... [N]one of this is the original report that I received from Dr. Lee ...

Q. **When you received the original report from Dr. Lee with 2003-274 on it, did you object and want it removed?**

A. **We discussed it, yes, ma'am.**

Q. **Is that case number on any of the other reports you have two floorboard reports and one furniture report? ... So if one only saw the reports that were first given to the Court as floorboard courthouse and furniture, one would have no way of knowing they were connected to 2003-274, would one? ...**

A. I believe they would or the Court wouldn't have them ...

Q. **And when your attorney handed them over, did he make clear that they had, as you had said, been massaged ?**

A. **I don't know.**

Q. **Huh?**

A. **I don't know, but it's obvious .**

Q. **... [I]'s obvious it's been massaged. I just wanted to clarify that.**

## *ALTERING LEE REPORTS FOR COURT EXHIBITS*

### [AUTHOR'S NOTE: Removal of Case 2003-274 connection]

Q. ... I want to go back to some of the questioning that you had with your attorney, Attorney Brown, just now. Ask as an overview of what my questioning is directed to, we are here for a reason today. We are here because of a serious accusation that the Plaintiff s' side is making of attempts to mislead the [court] and to alter records and total IPRA non-compliance, and I think we have gotten a very good example presented by Mr. Sederwall concerning the evidentiary hearing of January 21st of 2011 ... **Do exhibits E and F, which you have before you, in any way indicate to the Court that this had to do with Dr. Lee's work with Case 2003-274? When you look at**

Exhibit 19, the workbench, and then my Exhibit 18 of the floorboards, is there anything that would indicate Case 2003-274 for the Court. This was presented to the Court that it had to do with Case 2003-274.

A. I don't understand your question, ma'am ...

Q. On Exhibit E. Look for the 19-page report on the workbench, which says "E" on the header. It says it's done for Steve Sederwall ... Is there any place on the header that indicates Case 2003 -274?

A. No ...

Q. Is there any place on that front page that calls you Lincoln County Deputy? ... Is there any place that says it's for the Lincoln County Sheriff's Office?

A. No, ma'am.

Q. ... Were these reports presented to the Court, in the form we see them, to substantiate that this was just your hobby?

A. No, ma'am.

Q. How could the Court tell that these were not the original documents which you later gave to us?

A. ... I don't understand your question.

Q. Let me say it a different way. Your attorney had previously sent copies of these reports to the Plaintiffs side , are you aware of that?

A. No.

Q. We read those into the record, the February 18th, 2010, report, in which your attorney said he felt it met the requirement; do you recall that, today ?

A. He said that - no, I don't recall it.

Q. Do you recall my reading from the transcript of that hearing on January 21st, 2011, about Exhibits E and F?

A. No, I don't recall. It's probably in the record .

Q. That was this morning. Do you have a little bit of memory problem?

A. No, ma'am. I will just tell you the truth . I'm sick of this ...

Q. Okay ... So my question is, these are not the same as the original report that you contend was the first report that you contend was the first one you got from Dr. Lee, correct, E and F?

A. You're asking me?

Q. Are they the same, in terms of identifying a Case 2003-274 for the Sheriff's Department ?

A. We have been discussing that for years, no, ma'am, they are not the same. The substance is the same. The headers are different ...

Q. Mr. Sederwall , let me ask you if you would agree or disagree. My contention is, the substance is the opposite, and supports your false claim that this was a hobby .

A. What was my false claim?

Q. That this was a hobby, rather than an investigation from the Sheriff's Department .

A. Your question is what now?

Q. Are these self-serving reports with the information removed?

A. No, ma'am.

## ALTERING SUBSTANCE OF LEE REPORTS

Q. Just one last question, is about the substantive differences and the meat - it's just a "yes" or "no." So you feel that removing the deputy and sheriff titles, the case number, the Sheriff's Department results did not constitute a major change as to the meat of these Dr. Lee reports?

A. As I have explained , ma'am, the meat of the report is talking about, say, a bullet hole or whatever, that's what I'm talking about, the meat of the report . His findings, what he did, that's the meat of the report, ma'am, that's what I'm referring to.

Q. ... In the context of this case, changing those things couldn't lead one to think differently about a  document, as opposed to official to non-official, couldn't it?

A. Ma'am , these were not turned over to the Sheriff . They are not official nothing. They were given to you, because  my attorney said you're looking . I said, just give them anything they want. I don't care . As I offered to you when this start ed. I told you you can come look at our files. This is not in the Sheriff's report.

Q. ... So you are saying that your attorney chose these documents to give to the Court on that day?

A. No, ma'am, that's not what I'm saying. ... I sent them to him, my attorney, and I told them just exactly what I told you years ago, whatever you want, what is it you want, I will give it to you ...

Q. What we wanted, since this is an Inspection of Public Records Act case, and you were a deputy in answer ... what we wanted was the original requested documents or true duplicates.

A. I understand.

## CALVIN OSTLER AS ORCHID CELLMARK'S CLIENT

[AUTHOR'S NOTE: Establishing that he knew client to get Orchid Cellmark records – and did not]

Q. ... You had stated that you knew Calvin Ostler was the client for Orchid Cellmark Lab?

A. I found that out, yes, ma'am.

Q. Did you ever tell Sheriff Virden that ...?

A. I don't recall talking to the Sheriff about it, no, ma'am.

## TESTIMONY OF ATTORNEY ALAN MOREL

Lincoln County Attorney Alan Morel was a key hoaxer and central to Case 2003-274 records concealment from 2003 to the present. For testimony, he attempted various lies, not knowing I was behind all past requests. And Griebel's firm attorney caught him on his Barnett records refusal of May 11, 2007 when he lied that there were no records "whatsoever" for Case 2003-274; but on September 3, 2008, by subpoena, Virden turned over 192 pages. So "little weasel" Morel calmly said he "misspoke!"

## ALAN MOREL BY GALE COOPER

### ME ANNOUNCING ALL IPRA REQUESTS WERE MINE

**[AUTHOR'S NOTE: Revealing my IPRA work since 2003]**

Q. Your timeline [he made a "calendar" for court jumps ... to '06, which was my September request. Do you realize there were other IPRA requests going back to '03, '04 during that period ?

A. Absolutely.

Q. Do you know the case of San Juan Water Users District vs. KNME TV? ... And it allows agency relationships. And so through the agents of Randall Harris, an attorney in Clovis , and the journalist, Jay Miller, I wrote earlier IPRAs to you, and I would like to show you your responses. This is based on your statement that you never withheld any records. "We turned over any records. We have made records available." Did I quote correctly from your recollection ?

A. I do recall having received prior IPRA requests.

Q. Do you recall ever turning over any records between '03 and '06? ...

A. ... I do acknowledge that I did received some. Actually, I think the Sheriff may have responded to one of those ...

Q. This is a letter on your letter head, dated May 19, 2004, to Jay Miller, titled "Freedom of Information Act Request, dated May 13th, '04."

628

[AUTHOR'S NOTE: Immediate defense push-backs! Narvaez objects as to relevance; then wants the request (I have it). Morel says the IPRA request is attorney client privilege (lie – it is a public record), I gave court courtesy copy of IPRA Compliance Guide. Then Brown asks for bathroom break]

Q. Attorney Morel, if you could read that entire paragraph, because the result of this was no records were produced? ...

MR. NARVAEZ: ... I object, again, on the grounds of relevance.

THE COURT: Dr. Cooper .

DR. COOPER: ... This part that I was going to have him read constituted the refusal of the [deputy] card and the reasoning for it. And since the request asked for many documents, it included the refusal for, in fact, all documents. The big picture on this case is, I have been involved for ten years , no documents have been produced, but an incredible number of excuses. When I talked about shell games, it's impossible, because there are constant excuses. The argument here is, we can't give you records, because it's a criminal investigation. The argument now that we're here five years in this court, it's a hobby or I don't have them or [mis]statements of IPRA law. I wanted to demonstrate to the Court that there is no way of getting records from Lincoln County Sheriff's Department on Case 2003-274, and the motive , I feel, is concealed [sic - concealment].

**THE COURT: Let me just state something, okay. The frustration that you feel is the frustration that I feel. The frustration all along has been that but for opening this case by the Sheriff's Department through the Sheriff's Department of Lincoln County conducting a criminal investigation, and then morphing into some type of, for lack of a better word, hobby, has been a frustration of this Court. We are not going to get into that. Is I don't see how someone in a criminal case can take evidence and make it part of their personal collection. That's the frustration that I feel. I think it's the frustration that you are feeling.**

DR. COOPER: **You felt this morning and heard Mr. Sederwall saying he may have written he was a deputy, but he didn't feel like a deputy, in his mind.**

THE COURT: **That's for me to decide, not you.**

DR. COOPER: I know, but it's frustrating. But given the fact that it's mutually frustrating, is it not  appropriate to question Attorney Morel on his responses at that period ?

THE COURT: I don't think so.

DR. COOPER: But may I state for the record that the excuse back then used IPRA exception number 14-2-14 [sic – 14-2-1(4)] for criminal investigation.

**[AUTHOR'S NOTE: I enter as an exhibit all my Barnett records requests from April 24, 2007 to June 26, 2007]**

Q. These are all of the records that the Barnett firm received, beginning with April 24 of 2000 [sic-2007] … No records were produced. Does that jog your memory? In fact , that's why we are in litigation. But if I tell you that no records were yielded by that, would that jog your memory as to whether they were or weren't?

A. Actually, some records were forwarded to you, Dr. Cooper, in my June 22nd, 2007 response to Mr. Cheves .

Q. Which record, do you recall ?

A. Actually, I attached the memorandum the day after I received –

**[AUTHOR'S NOTE: Good example of Morel's cagy lying]**

Q. … **I mean requested records.** If you go back to the first page of the April 24th '07 records request, and if you look at the first huge paragraph on the bottom, those are all Dr. Lee's records, and the second page are all the Orchid Cellmark records , were any of those records ever turned over? …

A. At this time, they were not turned over, because they were not in my possession.

**[AUTHOR'S NOTE: Audacity to use possession argument]**

Q. … If you now look at the IPRA guide … under 14-2-11, Procedure for Denied Requests … [u]nder A, I will read that … "Unless a written  request has been determined to be excessively burdensome or  broad, a written Request for Inspection of Public Records … that has not been permitted within 15 days of receipt by the Office of the Custodian may be deemed denied." …

A. **Actually, I responded to you on April 27th, three days after your request … On April 27, 2007, I responded to your April 24, 2007 letter, and I invited you to come to Lincoln County to review any records we have . I can't give you something I don't have.**

Q. That's a very important statement … We are at the heart of this case, the beating heart. But before that, let me just finish this. Under B, if you can read what that says …

A. "If a written request has been denied, the custodian shall provide the requester with a written explanation of the denial . The written denial should describe the record, set fort h the names and titles or positions of each person responsible for the denial, and be delivered or mailed to the person requesting the record within 15 days after the request for inspection was received."

Q. ... [M]y question is, and you have before you the entire communication, where is the denial that's requested by IPRA? The formal denial describing the records sought, not by me, but the records sought, repeated, the names and titles of each person responsible for the denial and when it was delivered?

A. Okay. Your April 24, 2007, correspondence to me has two paragraphs ... Three days later, I responded to you, and I said , response to item number 1, referring to your letter . "Neither Sheriff Virden or County of Lincoln maintains any public record responses to your request number 1." We did not have any record I didn't deny them, I just don't have them .

Q. ... If you could show me where that long list of records that I requested is denied, one by one.

A. Response to item 1, referring to your letter. I don't need to reiterate every single thing. I have identified the exact paragraph that you requested, and then stated we don't have any records responsive. I believe that's responsive.

Q. And the second, the names, the titles, and positions of each person responsible for denial?

A. I signed the letter. It's my responsibility .

Q. I think they refer to the people in connection to the records, the record holders or custodian ... You are claiming that by signing it, you constitute the denier?

A. If I will sign a letter, I am responsible for my response, yes ...

## FAKE POSSESSION ARGUMENT

Q. The core question, then, is possession ... [I]t's been repeated over and over in this court. You were read, by Attorney Theoret, the IPRA definition of custodian under 14-2-6(A), whether the records are in that person's physical custody or control, and public records F, under that, describes the records held on or on behalf of any public body. Do you  maintain that the records that I am requesting were not recoverable unless they were in the direct possession of the Lincoln County Sheriff's Department?

A. No, Dr. Cooper, that's not what I'm saying. What I am saying is, each time I received an IPRA request, I looked for records that were responsive ... And every time I received that request, I talked to people who I thought had records that may be responsive.

**[AUTHOR'S NOTE: He is purposefully ignoring the statute, and evading that no written records requests were made to Dr. Lee or Orchid Cellmark; instead he is playing the shell game of "the deputies took the records"]**

Q. The "people" being the deputies, at that time, Sederwall and Sullivan? ...

A. Yes. In each one of our responses, I have identified those two gentlemen as possibly having records responsive to your request. I can't go --

Q. I'm not asking that, excuse me. You said you also were conscientious in looking over the entire files, so you were also aware of the name of Orchid Cellmark Lab?

A. Yes. And I forwarded it to the attorney, the very next day I got it, after I received it.

**[AUTHOR'S NOTE: This is made up. No such request exists.]**

Q. Were you aware of the name Dr. Henry Lee?

A. **I'm not sure when I became aware of Dr. Henry Lee because I never saw any of those records early on.**

**[AUTHOR'S NOTE: A lie. He himself answered my April 24, 2007 records request for Lee and Orchid Cellmark records.]**

Q. Let's look at that. Barnett requested April 24th, '07 ... Do you see his [Lee's] name there ?

A. I do.

Q. **At that time, since the deputies were claiming that they didn't want to give records, did you, in that period, contact Dr. Lee?**

A. **Actually, Dr. Cooper, at this time, I didn't know that that's what they were maintaining. That didn't occur until back in June of 2007.**

**[AUTHOR'S NOTE: Double-talk about deputies, not sheriff's requirement to get them from Lee and Orchid Cellmark.]**

Q. The 21st?

A. This was April of 2007. I went to state in my response to you, the investigation, for the most part, is being conducted by two individuals ... When I did tell you who I thought might have the records, I said, "A former Lincoln County Sheriff and current special deputy of the Lincoln County Sheriff's Department and Steve Sederwall, who is the current special deputy with the Lincoln County Sheriff's Department. The Lincoln County Sheriff's Department is unaware of what information Mr. Sullivan and Mr. Sederwall may or may not have within their possession relating to your request." I then gave you both of their telephone numbers.

**[AUTHOR'S NOTE: Focus on the deputies, not the sheriff's custodial responsibility for recovery. Also, tries to make records requestor me responsible for records recovery.]**

Q. ... I'm glad you brought that up, because let me ask you if you feel that was my responsibility, this is an aside, to contact Mr. Sederwall or Sullivan to recover records ?

A. I believe that the law requires that if I have records that are not exempt I have to turn them over to you. And if I know where there may be records, I need to tell you, the custodian of those records. I did that.

**[NOTE: This repeats his lie that IPRA requires only possession, not recovery of requested records. Then he fabricates "need to tell." The true custodian "need" - requirement - is to make actual records request(s).]**

Q. Let me just quote this . "Additionally saying records not existing burdens or requests to approve . This is contrary to the Supreme Court decision, and it's the Newsome [sic-vs.] Alarid case ." That's quoted right in the IPRA manual. Instead Newsome clearly places the burden upon the custodian to justify why records sought to be examined should not be furnished ... Attorney Morel, there's been a certain pattern which has been repeated. We don't know how to get them, they are too hard to get. I told you to call Sederwall and Sullivan. [T]his isn't he spirit of the law. **Do you feel that the obligation for records recovery is on the requester ?**

A. **Dr. Cooper, I think it depends on what records they are and where they are. Again, we may just simply agree to disagree as to what the government 's responsibility it is, to actually go get records that may be public records held by a third person, that I don't even know were there. I have requested the records.**

**I told you where you may be able to find the records. I have written to request the records. I don't know what else I can do.**

**[AUTHOR'S NOTE: Repeats possession only misstatement of IPRA. Adds lies of "requested the records," and not knowing where records are - when my April 24, 2007 records request lists Lee and Orchid Cellmark!]**

Q. Let me then go back to my line of questioning that I started with when I interrupted you, and you were talking about Sederwall and Sullivan. At that April 24th time or when you got that shortly afterwards, did you contact Dr. Lee?
A. No, I did not.

**[AUTHOR'S NOTE: This is the IPRA violation.]**

Q. Did you contact Orchid Cellmark Lab?
A. No, I did not.

**[AUTHOR'S NOTE: This *is* the IPRA violation.]**

Q. Did you review the file for 2003-274 to see if such contact information was available?
A. I reviewed those files on multiple occasion s in responding to IPRA requests, not necessarily to look for information that you didn't request in your IPRA request. I looked for the documents you requested, that's what the law requires, that's what I did, and then I responded truthfully as to what was said in the record.

**[AUTHOR'S NOTE: Repeats possession only argument]**

Q. You had already been questioned by Attorney Theoret concerning what 's already in evidence called contact list for case 2003-274, listing all of the information about the director of Orchid Cellmark, Orchid Cellmark 's address, his cell phone number, his personal number, his FAX, left out only a biography . But I would like to show you this - and this is just a courtesy copy - are you aware - because it addresses your understanding of IPRA of **Toomey vs. Truth or Consequences case, just decided this past July last year?**
A. **Actually, I taught a little seminar on it at the New Mexico Association of Counties about two weeks.**
Q. **Good. So you know about it, obviously?**

**A. Yes.**

Q. The New Mexico Court of Appeals stated that public agencies must produce all records, even those held by or created by a private entity on behalf of the public agency ... Are you aware that Orchid Cellmark is, if not the largest, one of the largest DNA laboratories in the country ?

A. I'm going to claim complete ignorance as to Orchid Cellmark .

Q. Are you aware that Dr. Lee is one of the most famous forensic experts in the country?

A. I recall his name coming up in the O.J. Simpson case .

Q. Let me -- because our time is short. And the issue that I'm after is retrievable, which is the core of this litigation. You had talked to them about Dr. Lee, and this has already been entered in evidence as 12. This is a recovery letter from Dr. Lee -- to Dr. Lee, the October 26$^{th}$ [2010] from Sheriff Virden. This is Lee's rather prompt response of November 12 [2010]. Please read aloud Dr. Lee's response .

A. "Dear Sheriff Virden. This letter is in response to your letter, dated October 26, 2010. My only report issued in regards to the death of Billy the Kid was issued on February 25, 2005. No other report has been issued by me in regards to this case. Best wishes, Henry Lee."

Q. Were you shown that letter as someone working along with your Sheriff? Are you aware of that letter? ...

A. ... I believe I did, but I can't tell you when I did.

Q. Dr. Lee says, am I correct in that statement, that he does have a report?

A. Yes, he does .

Q. Are you aware that the Sheriff never requested that report from Dr. Lee?

MR. NARVAEZ : Objection, Your Honor, I don't believe that's accurate. I believe that Henry Lee report was requested on behalf of Lincoln County and the Sheriff.

**[AUTHOR'S NOTE: Attempt to mislead. This is the first Lee request - 3 years after litigation started. When Lee wrote back that he had the report, Virden never requested it.]**

Q. Let me read, then, from the deposition, maybe that will clarify ... This is the deposition of Rick Virden ... And he wrote back -- he, being Lee -- wrote back and said there was only one report? "ANSWER: That's what his response is, yes, sir. "QUESTION: But I don't think he sent you a copy of it, did he? "ANSWER: No, sir. "QUESTION: Did you ever think to pick up the phone and dial up old Dr. Henry Lee and say, ' Dr. Lee, I got your letter here ... and have a conversation with him. "ANSWER: Once I wrote the letter, the attorney handled it. By that he was referring to you.[my statement to witness Morel]. So you figure you don't have any obligation, you know, the documents exist once you signed the letter? "ANSWER: I let the attorney handle it." "You could have called Henry Lee also, couldn't you? I could have ... "Just like you could have called Cal Ostler."

MR. NARVAEZ: ... Your Honor. We are out of time.

**[AUTHOR'S NOTE: Again Narvaez interrupts just at my impeachment. And the judge permits that by stopping me.]**

THE COURT: Dr. Cooper, I'm going to have to call time.

## ALAN MOREL BY HENRY NARVAEZ

Q. I'm going to be brief. It's late in the day. But I want to ask you, Mr. Morel, you're familiar with IPRA, so I'm going to get right to the chase. Is Henry Lee a custodian under IPRA?

A. In my opinion, no.

Q. Why not?

A. He is not a holder of records for Lincoln County. He is a third-party who may have records, however they got there. But the reality is, the custodian has to be somebody associated with my county, who has responsibility for those records.

**[NOTE: Lee as "custodian" is absurd and untrue. The issue is that, by his own admission, Lee is holding a requested report or reports *on behalf of* Virden's Lincoln County Sheriff's Department Case # 2003-274.]**

Q. Same question for Orchid Cellmark. Is Orchid Cellmark a custodian under IPRA?

A. In my opinion, no.

Q. For the same reasons?

A. Yes, sir .

Q. The Court has expressed that ... that Sheriff Virden has provided everything in his file at all times. My question is this, if the Court has a concern ... that there is some kind of shell game going on here, that documents are getting moved around in and out of the Sheriff 's file or out of Lincoln County files. My question to you, as County Attorney during all of this time that's applicable is, to your knowledge have any files been moved in or out of the Sheriff 's file in an attempt to avoid producing those documents?

**[NOTE: This is a repeat of the fake possession claim as being the only requirement - and making it seem as if the court agreed to it - plus a misstatement of the actual shell games really being played with the requested records, by misstating definition of shell games.]**

A. I have reviewed those files on four or five occasions, responding to IPRA requests, and on each occasion they were very similar, with very few new added documents. The problem is, the documents under the IPRA request were simply never in the files at the Lincoln County Sheriff's Department. They may have been somewhere else in Lincoln County, but they were not in my possession and control, and I can't give you something I do not have.

Q. Well, let me ask you this. Since the recent Truth or Consequence case has been mentioned, and since you are familiar with that case, let me ask you, is there anything in the Truth or Consequence case that's applicable here, and if so, how is it applicable ?

A. I like that case. I think it's a reasonable case. Counties have a lot of actors, we have hospitals, we have all kinds of institutions that conduct our business, and if they have significant contact with the county, then I think their records probably do become public records. That's not the situation here. It wasn't -- in that case they didn't give up the records. They actually had them and could have given them up, and they ended up destroying one tape. In this instance, I didn't have the records. I asked for the records, and I couldn't get the records.

**[AUTHOR'S NOTE: This is the "deputies took them" ploy.]**

I think it's a completely different scenario. Orchid Cellmark, nor Dr. Henry Lee has sufficient contacts with Lincoln County to be considered a custodian of record.

**[NOTE: This audacious fakery of the IPRA statute fabricates that if records are "held on behalf of" an entity, the *holder* becomes custodian. "Held on behalf of" actually means where the custodian must retrieve records not in his direct possession - here from Lee and Orchid Cellmark.]**

Q. Sir ... assume, for purposes of this question, that Sullivan or Sederwall have documents, and on June 21 of 2007, you hand them the letter - in fact , that's the evidence here . You hand them the letter and say, "Give me those documents." What more could you have done, looking back on that, sir, under oath here to this Court, what more could you have done?

**[AUTHOR'S NOTE: This is a set up for the deputies being the only source of the records. The correct answer to the question would be to get the records from the records holders: Lee and Orchid Cellmark.]**

A. We were going to request that they turn over their deputy cards, but they actually volunteered them to me at the beginning of the meeting. They knew they weren't going to keep the records and keep their cards. They are not employees. I cannot discipline them. I can't fire them. There isn't a thing which I can do to them, that's the problem.

**[AUTHOR'S NOTE: This is a lie. He could have subpoenaed the records.]**

Q. Let me ask you that . On June 21, 2007, were Sullivan or Sederwall employees of Lincoln County?

A. On what date is that ?

Q. On June 21, 2007, the date that you handed them the letter and they gave you that memorandum ?

A. I think the second thing, handing over cards , they had zero further contact or association with my county .

Q. Okay. What more could you have done when they gave you their cards on June 21, 2007?

A. Absolutely nothing .

Q. I pass the witness . I guess we are done, Your Honor. May Mr. Morel be excused?

## ALAN MOREL BY COURT

THE COURT: I have a couple of questions, a follow-up to those. When Mr. Sederwall and Sullivan turned in their deputy commissions on that day, but they have records that belonged or were made on the behest of the Sheriff, why doesn't the county then force them to turn over those documents.

**[AUTHOR'S NOTE: This is ominous. The judge focuses on "the deputies took them," not IPRA law requiring records recovery from where they are held "on behalf of."]**

THE WITNESS: Your Honor, that's a great question. Other than going over there with a gun or filing a lawsuit, I really didn't know how to get the documents.

THE COURT: I know it's not within the realm of this lawsuit, but perhaps another legal action.

**[AUTHOR'S NOTE: This too is ominous by the judge. My case is IPRA with records recovery violations - the lawsuit itself.]**

THE WITNESS: I guess I just question whether IPRA actually forces - the government goes and sues somebody to get a record ...

**[AUTHOR'S NOTE: Morel is manipulating the judge to focus on just the deputies.]**

THE COURT: That may be a question for another day.

MR. NARVAEZ: I think it's a question for this day, and it's going to be a question for our courts. So I will ask you, Attorney Morel, as attorney for Lincoln County, in your opinion, does IPRA require Lincoln County, as of June 21, 2007, to file a lawsuit and/or to subpoena your ex-employees to get documents that are responsive to a pending IPRA request?

**[AUTHOR'S NOTE: Narvaez is manipulating the judge's focus to only the deputies. Also, Narvaez's question is fake: my records requesting began in April 24, 2007 (not June 21, 2007); and no action was taken against the deputies.]**

THE WITNESS: Under the current law, I don't believe so.

THE COURT: I guess my question would be better phrased is, are there other laws, other than IPRA, that
could have forced these two to produce these documents outside have IPRA law?

**[Author's NOTE: This is an IPRA case, and the answer exists in IPRA.]**

THE WITNESS: I think there's some cause of action that could have been filed, but the question is, is that a burden that the government has. That's a huge burden, Your Honor.

**[AUTHOR'S NOTE: Morel is faking. Taxpayer cost was stamps for letters to Lee and Orchid Cellmark requesting the records; and, given their responses on November 12, 2010 and November 2, 2010, requesting the actual records.]**

THE COURT: That was the only question. You may step down.

## *JUDGE'S RULING ON EVIDENTIARY HEARING*

Judge George Eichwald's only ruling was mediation and the mediator: a local attorney and retired judge, George Perez.

THE COURT: Here's what I'm going to do, folks. Here's what I want to do today. I am going to order mediation. Mr. Narvaez, I think , had suggested this way back in the summer. Who would be appropriate?

DR. COOPER: I want to object.

THE COURT: That's fine, but I'm going to order it anyway.

MR. NARVAEZ: I think we all agreed that George Perez would be a great mediator.

DR. COOPER: May I state the grounds for my objection?

THE COURT: I have the prerogative to set this matter for mediation . Here's the deal on that, okay. I'm sending the parties to mediation. You have to appear in good faith to the mediation. If you resolve the case in mediation , you are going to save yourself a big old headache in giving me findings and conclusions … I want Mr. Narvaez to prepare the appropriate order, okay … In the event that you settle the matter , then what I want is a letter saying that the matter was settled. Dr. Cooper, let me tell you what settlement is, okay, that includes any sort of monetary sanctions and so forth … In the event that you do not settle, then what I want is, within 30 days of me being notified that you did not settle the case, then I want proposed findings and conclusions …

MR. NARVAEZ : May I make a further suggestion, Your Honor? … that the mediation should include a global proposition such that matters currently on appeal be included, so that if there is a settlement reached, we settle everything connected globally with this case.

THE COURT: It would only make sense … Let me state also that the parties will be equally responsible for … George Perez' fee. It will be split by five or six ways, so it will not be a whole lot.

**[AUTHOR'S NOTE: Given the defendants' total IPRA violation, contempt, and evidence tampering, was Judge Eichwald hoping to bury my case by mediation and no ruling?]**

# COURT-ORDERED MEDIATION: MARCH 26, 2013

The court-ordered mediation with attorney and retired judge George Perez was on March 26, 2013 at the Sandoval County District Courthouse. There were so many parties that most of the second floor rooms were used. As I demanded, I had my own room.

Mediation is confidential. Its outcome is not. My past (mostly fired) attorneys - including Attorney Patrick Griebel for my co-plaintiff - got almost $200,000; $125,000 of which went to Griebel. "Strangely," co-plaintiff Scot Stinnett settled out - with no recorded payment. (I had heard about a plaintiff scam of splitting attorney's fees. I do not know if Stinnett did that. But I no longer need Marlyn Bowlin's warning about Stinnett. I have my own.)

Do not miss that Stinnett bowed out. As self-proclaimed open records hero, who joined my litigation because IPRA "needed more precedent cases" (from higher courts), as a recipient of Judge Eichwald's blessing to stay as a "real co-plaintiff," and as a brand-new Press Association Hall of Famer, he bowed out. He bowed out without accomplishing anything for IPRA - and having done nothing to help me in the litigation. He and Mickey Barnett, however, had done all they could - by their lying Affidavits and lying testimony - to destroy my credibility in the ongoing litigation. It seems for Stinnett FOG only means "For Our Guys."

And by that mediation, defense attorneys Henry Narvaez and Kevin Brown had pocketed almost $350,000 from taxpayers through Lincoln County's Risk Management insurance fund covering legal liability of its public officials. (I had done IPRA requests on their billings throughout the litigation.). For example, how about the Narvaez billing on April 25, 2012 for $105.00 for "Phone conversations with Sheriff Virden ... and Rene Romo from ABQ Journal?" So taxpayers even paid for hoaxer press.

Defense billings, added to mediation settlements, came to over half a million dollars for Lincoln County lawmen to cover-up their decade of law enforcement fraud and forensic/historic hoaxing.

Also, my defendants agreed to dismiss their appeal (since it had been based on past attorneys' fees, now paid out.)

I did not settle. I would continue my litigation alone. And it was obvious that enduring injustice was its price - as well as controlling nausea at dealing with the unsavory group.

# PUBLIC FORUM

*HOAXBUST: After the mediation's taxpayer bleeding, the hoaxers used media for damage control, but their loss was obvious, because plaintiffs' attorneys got paid off. But the hoaxers hid their own huge costs. So I sent an open letter outlining the case to people who could make a difference - if they cared about taxpayers' money.*

## *HOAXERS USE ALBUQUERQUE JOURNAL SPIN*

By June 11, 2013, the hoaxers' damage control was on the *Albuquerque Journal's* front page by reporter Scott Sandlin, with "Billy the Kid case costs taxpayers nearly $200K: Billy the Kid lives on in battle of public records." Of course, I was not contacted; but Scot Stinnett and Patrick Griebel featured themselves.

Stinnett gave a bold-font exit quote: "These guys were trying to rewrite the history of my town for their personal gain. And they were using the Lincoln County and De Baca County Sheriff's Offices to do it." Stinnett helpfully omitted that "these guys" were still doing it. The hoaxers gave usual lies (as in: blood on the bench! "Brushy" and Miller as Billy! tourism interests stopped the truth! misstated requested records! misstated IPRA custodial requirements!). Surprising was Griebel's firm's misinformation - as if channeling Sederwall (as in: records obtained settled nothing "definitively!" Sederwall's fake claim of "$50,000" needed for mixed DNA separations is true! and the word "hoax" is hidden!).

Taxpayer drain from the mediation settlements had to be spun, as in the $200.00 headline, (it was public information) - so concealed is that almost $350,000 had already been scarfed-up by attorneys for Virden, Sullivan, and Sederwall. Nevertheless, payment of plaintiff attorneys' fees obviously confirmed plaintiffs' winning. Reporter Sandlin did the best she could with her biased agenda for "Billy the Kid case costs taxpayers nearly $200K," as follows (with my boldface):

> Lincoln County has paid $125,000 in attorney fees to a weekly newspaper for violating the Inspection of Public Records Act in a lawsuit over documents relating to an investigation into Billy the Kid's death and whether he was buried in Fort Sumner.
>
> The settle agreement represents only the payment to the De Baca County News, which sued along with retired

psychiatrist and East Mountain resident Gale Cooper in 2007, according to an attorney for the newspaper.

Four other law firms previously involved in the case were paid another $70,000 combined ...

Cooper had filed written requests for records pertaining to a DNA analysis by celebrity forensic scientist Dr. Henry Lee of blood left on a carpenter's bench where the Kid's body purportedly was placed after he was shot in 1881. Cooper also wanted Lee's DNA report of two others who had claimed to be Billy the Kid.

One theory explored by the much ballyhooed investigation, which started with the backing of then-Gov. Richardson, was that Sheriff Pat Garrett shot someone else after the Kid's escape from the Lincoln County jail. That person was buried in Fort Sumner while Billy the Kid escaped to Texas and lived his days as Brushy Bill Roberts.

Billy the Kid's grave is Fort Sumner's main tourist attraction and still draws a steady stream of visitors.

De Baca County News publisher Scot Stinnett joined with Gale Cooper in seeking the records in the lawsuit, naming Lincoln County Sheriff Rick Virden, ex-Deputy Steven Sederwall and ex-Sheriff Tom Sullivan as defendants.

Sederwall and Sullivan have said in court documents and continue to maintain that the investigation they opened in 2003 into Billy the Kid's death was "conducted" as private citizens and not in their capacity as sheriff's department officials.

They claimed they had no records subject to the state Inspection of Public Records Act.

But Jeremy Theoret, who along with Patrick Griebel of Albuquerque Business Law represented the De Baca County News, said it was clear from evidence that the investigation, which had a Lincoln County case number, was public record.

13th Judicial District Court Judge George Eichwald entered an order in March 2010 finding that "Sullivan and Sederwall were acting either as employees or agents of defendant Lincoln County Sheriff at all times pertinent.

(The) sheriff opened the investigation and continued with the investigation which is the subject of this (lawsuit).

"Lincoln County fought us for five years over this and provided lawyers for the defendants," Stinnett said. "They ended up paying all these fees to us and as part of our settlement we insisted they pay other attorneys who had previously worked on the case. That was another $70,000."

The De Baca County News and Cooper eventually parted ways, but both proceeded with the action.

**Theoret said his client eventually obtained a report from one of the defense attorneys, and a later version of it**

**later surfaced.** [AUTHOR'S NOTE: Falsely credits Stinnett with getting the Lee reports, then leaves out that they were forged]

**Eventually, he said, plaintiffs obtained documents from Orchid Cellmark, a lab in Dallas, but nothing was settled definitively.** [AUTHOR'S NOTE: Hoaxing was shown!]

"The documents said there was DNA evidence on the bench where Billy reportedly had been laid out but **it was blended (from more than one person) and it would cost $50,000 to unblend them," Theoret said**. [AUTHOR'S NOTE: Theoret is quoting hoaxing Sederwall, not Orchid Cellmark's DNA records!]

Lincoln County defendants have continued to assert in pleadings that they did not have reports.

In a pleading submitted to the appeals court last April asking for the court to take the case, the defense said that one of the questions presented was, "Are documents that the sheriff has never used, created, received, maintained, held or even had knowledge of public records under IPRA?"

Theoret said that a New Mexico Court of Appeals case against the city of Truth or Consequences establishes that "anything maintained or created on behalf of a government entity is public."

Cooper, meanwhile, now self-represented, has filed documents asking for damages, costs, and sanctions against the defendants. Sederwall's and Sullivan's attorney, Kevin Brown, filed a response Friday asking for her motion to be dismissed until the court has entered its findings and conclusions.

Theoret said he suspects the attorneys fees may be the highest anybody has had to pay under IPRA.

"I think the attorney fee provision is important in IPRA cases. It is really a strong enforcement tool," he said.

Stinnett, a longtime public records advocate and Member of the Foundation for Open Government, publishes a 1,200 circulation newspaper in a county of 2,200 people.

"These guys were trying to rewrite the history of my town for their personal gain. And they were using the Lincoln County and De Baca County Sheriff's Offices to do it."

The upshot was that Griebel (and maybe Stinnett) walked away with cash-stuffed pockets; and left me with parting gifts of repeating hoax claims themselves, and leaving untouched the critical issue of IPRA damages (different from attorney's fees and costs, and the teeth in enforcement litigation). But it was good riddance to be freed of the lot - including my past fired attorneys. With Scot Stinnett present, I really had enemies at both plaintiff and defense courtroom tables. Finally, being alone felt good.

## *MY LETTER TO LINCOLN COUNTY COMMISSIONERS*

My next move was to expose the hoax where should matter: the complicit Lincoln County Commissioners. By name, they were Jackie Powell, Preston Stone, Mark Doth, Dallas Draper, and Kathryn Minter (who, before taking office, had read *MegaHoax* and lied to me that she would end the money-draining hoax and end Attorney Morel's contract). Cc's went to Governor Susana Martinez (put in her job by corrupt Attorneys Mickey Barnett and Pat Rogers and past-State Senator Rod Adair!), Attorney General Gary King (called corrupt, then blocking my IPRA investigation of the defense attorneys' billings, and in his own litigation to destroy IPRA's power!), and New Mexico U.S. Attorney Ken Gonzales (called corrupt, and had refused to take action on the Billy the Kid Case law enforcement fraud!) - all a disreputable bunch.

I sent a copy to the only paper that might print it: *The Lincoln County News*. And it was an exhibit for the addendum to my motion for my own costs, damages, and possible sanctions.

On June 18, 2013, I sent "Re: Open letter to Lincoln County Commissioners about Lincoln County Sheriff's Department Case No. 2003-274 and Sandoval County District Court Cause No. D-1329-CV-1364, Gale Cooper and De Baca County News vs. Rick Virden, Lincoln County Sheriff and Custodian of the Records of the Lincoln County Sheriff's Office; and Steven M. Sederwall, Former Lincoln County Deputy Sheriff; and Thomas T. Sullivan, Former Lincoln County Sheriff and Former Lincoln County Deputy Sheriff." I stated (with boldfacing for emphasis):

This letter is sent to you because of my deep concern about the unchecked ravages to taxpayers and to Old West history resulting from your Lincoln County Sheriff's Department Case No. 2003-274 ("Billy the Kid Case") - a decade-long historic/forensic hoax and law enforcement fraud – that led to Sandoval County District Court's ongoing, 5½ year, Inspection of Public Records Act ("IPRA") litigation (Cause No. D-1329-CV-1364) for its unjustified and total open records violations.

**OVERVIEW**: Since 2003, Case 2003-274's Sheriff and Deputy promulgators have hijacked the Lincoln County Sheriff's Department for their fraudulent murder investigation against Pat Garrett; have misused their law enforcement authority in De Baca and Grant County District Courts by their unjustified exhumation attempts on Billy the Kid and his mother; have relied on Lincoln County Attorney Alan Morel to conceal their incriminatory records by illegal blocking of all IPRA records requests; and are currently in total IPRA non-compliance in Sandoval County District Court's IPRA violation litigation - **where they have already cost taxpayers over a half million dollars in plaintiff and defense attorneys' fees; and may ultimately cost taxpayers over $1,500,000.00.**

**And not one penny of public money should have been wasted for this self-serving, publicity-stunt, which had no place in a Sheriff's Department; and which should have been forbidden at its outset by the County Commissioners and the County Attorney.**

I predict that the Billy the Kid Case will become the poster child for betrayal of public trust by public officials, who chose cronyism and cover-up instead of exercising moral oversight.

**ABOUT ME:** I am a Harvard educated, M.D. psychiatrist, specialized in forensic murder case consultation. In 1999, came to New Mexico to write about Billy the Kid, and researched over 40,000 pages of archival documents and books to publish my *Joy of the Birds*; *Billy and Paulita*; *Billy the Kid's Writings, Words, and Wit*; *Billy the Kid's Pretenders: Brushy Bill and John Miller*; and *MegaHoax: The Strange Plot to Exhume Billy the Kid and Become President*.

Qualified to oppose the Billy the Kid Case hoax, from 2003 to 2004, I engaged the Kennedy Han Law Firm to stop the exhumations of the Kid and his mother. From 2004 to 2006, I wrote, for journalist Jay Miller, exposé articles. From 2003 to 2006, using an attorney and Jay Miller as agents, I wrote IPRA records requests. In 2006, I made my own IPRA request. On April 24, 2007, having gotten no requested records, I hired an attorney for IPRA records requests. In October of 2007, total and unjustified denials of records led to litigation. In November of 2012, I went *pro se* for that litigation, for which I have paid most of the plaintiff-side costs.

**ABOUT THE BILLY THE KID CASE:** In 2003, Case 2003-274 was filed by Sheriff Tom Sullivan, who deputized for it Capitan Mayor Steve Sederwall, and used Undersheriff Rick Virden. It is a murder investigation against Sheriff Pat Garrett, falsifying probable cause that he was a killer of an innocent victim, on July 14, 1881, to enable Billy the Kid's escape to a life of freedom. A sub-investigation is the Kid's jailbreak murders of his deputy guards, with fabricated claim that Garrett provided the Kid's murder weapon. Garrett was to be "convicted" by forensic DNA matchings of the exhumed Kid and his mother (to prove the innocent victim lay in the Kid's grave).

But Case 2003-274 had zero evidence to support its murder claim; the graves are invalid for forensic DNA (so exhumation permits were refused by the OMI); and history proves Garrett did kill the Kid. The Billy the Kid Case is just an attention-grabbing scam for personal profit by its law enforcement promulgators; who used it to make TV programs, a movie, and a website. And their claim of its promoting tourism is preposterous; since calling the history false, and saying the Kid is not in his grave, only damages tourism. (Would you visit the grave of the unknown cowboy?)

**ABOUT THE COVER-UP:** Since 2003, only one Lincoln County public official, Commissioner Leo Martinez, tried to stop the hoax; telling the County Commissioners, on September 21, 2004, that the Sheriff must be stopped. He was not backed. And, from the start, Lincoln County Attorney Alan Morel covered-up the hoax by refusing my IPRA records requests by the IPRA exception for criminal investigations (used to prevent suspects' escaping ... But Garrett was dead since 1908!).

**ABOUT THE HOAX'S PROGRESSION:** By 2004, the exhumations of the Kid and his mother were blocked. So the law enforcement hoaxers shamelessly re-wrote their hoax. Sederwall claimed that, as a deputy, he found the carpenter's bench on which the shot Kid was laid out (recall that the first hoax version said the innocent victim, not the Kid, was shot!). Dr. Henry Lee was used to get specimens of "the shot Kid's blood DNA" from that bench. But shot-Kid-on-bench meant conventional history – attracting no TV programs. So the hoaxers said the Kid "played dead" on the bench! All this malarkey is debunked by the bench being forensically invalid (surfacing in Fort Sumner over 45 years after the Kid's killing); by blood not being proven (Lee used only a preliminary chemical that fluoresces with rust – more likely than blood on a carpenter's bench); and by bench DNA being useless anyway, since no verified Kid DNA exists for identity matching. Nevertheless, Lee's fake "Billy blood DNA" was sent to Orchid Cellmark Lab in Texas for DNA extractions. (On May 1, 2006, Lee wrote to Jay Miller - answering a letter I wrote with Miller – stating that he had sent his bench report to the Lincoln County Sheriff's Department.)

In 2005, Virden became Sheriff, and immediately deputized Sullivan (January 1, 2005) and Sederwall (February 25, 2005) to continue the Billy the Kid Case against Garrett.

By May 19, 2005, the hoaxers got Arizona's permission to exhume Billy the Kid pretender John Miller (ten years older than the Kid - and no kid) for DNA for identity matching. (Exhibit 1) The murder case "logic" was: if Miller - as the Kid - survived to old age, then Garrett killed the innocent victim. For good measure, the hoaxers also dug up an adjacent random man. (What if that random man was your grandfather?) Bones of both men were taken to Orchid Cellmark for DNA extractions to match with bench DNA. (Thus, being matched was fake Kid bench DNA to a faking old-timer and to a random man!).

By May of 2007, the hoaxers headed to the Hamilton, Texas, grave of pretender, Oliver "Brushy Bill" Roberts – under two years old at the real Kid's death; but the hoaxers' chosen recipient of Billy the Kid's identity because he is a conspiracy theory darling and a ticket to publicity. But I informed Texas officials about the hoax; and "Brushy" stayed buried.

My litigation, started in October of 2007, seems to have stalled the hoax ... for now.

**ABOUT THE LITIGATION:** To date, my Defendants - Virden, the records custodian, and Sullivan and Sederwall as his deputies – have turned over **not a single requested record**; though all are accessible to them. I requested, on April 24, 2007, four record categories: (1) report(s) of Lee's bench DNA specimen recoveries; (2) Orchid Cellmark's DNA extractions from Lee's bench specimens; (3) Orchid Cellmark's DNA extractions from the exhumed Arizona men; and (4) Orchid Cellmark's matchings of bench DNA to the exhumed men's DNA. (Exhibit 2) (Exhibit 3)

**DEFYING IPRA LAW:** The defendants merely played records shell games. (Exhibit 4) Virden refused records by falsely claiming that IPRA's custodial responsibility covered only records in direct possession. (IPRA also requires recovery of records not in direct possession. This was upheld by the New Mexico Court of Appeals in *Deborah Toomey vs. City of Truth or Consequences* in 2012.) Virden also used non-IPRA excuses: "My deputies took the records;" and "I'm not sure the records exist." In turn, Sullivan and Sederwall called Case 2003-274 their private hobby with "trade secret records." And Attorney Morel switched from IPRA's "criminal investigation" exception – because that confirmed the records were public – to backing the fake "direct possession" and the fake "hobbyist" claims. By Virden's sworn deposition, Morel also told Virden not to get the records. Virden also denied getting Lee's report at the Sheriff's Department.

**APPARENT BRIBERY:** In a June 21, 2007 "Memorandum" to my attorney in the pre-litigation, records request phase, Sullivan, Sederwall, and Virden blamed Case 2003-274 on Governor Bill Richardson; and provided apparent bribery checks which Sullivan got at Richardson's office. And a "Private Donor Fund" checking account for Case 2003-274 existed in Sullivan's and Sederwall's names. (The $6,500 in Richardson checks were from Attorney Bill Robins III and his law firm - major Richardson political donors - and Johnny Cope.) (Exhibit 5)

**VIRDEN TURN-OVER:** Under subpoena duces tecum for his September 8, 2008 deposition, Virden turned over his Case 2003-274 file, claiming it proved the requested records were not there - and ignoring his IPRA records recovery requirement. But that file had records – like a "Contact List" and that June 21, 2007 "Memorandum" - which gave enough information to retrieve the requested records.

**DEFYING THE COURT**: On November 20, 2009, the judge granted Summary Judgment to the plaintiff side; and ruled that Virden, Sullivan, and Sederwall had created the records as public officials, that the records were public documents, and that they must be turned over. The Defendants ignored the judge's order. After an Evidentiary Hearing on January 21, 2011, the judge repeated his turn-over order. The Defendants have ignored it to the present. This defiance of the Court adds potentially sanctionable Defendant offences under NMRA Rule 11.

**EVIDENCE TAMPERING**: In 2010, Sederwall presented to the Court and to the Plaintiffs Lee's alleged reports. I demonstrated that those reports were forged/tampered. Under Court order, on January 31, 2012, Sederwall turned over a Lee report which revealed that the other versions had re-written headers to conceal that Lee's work was for Case 2003-274 and for *Sheriff* Sullivan and *Deputy* Sederwall. (Exhibits 6 and 7) Evidence tampering is sanctionable under NMRA Rule 37. (And, as records custodian, Virden is ultimately responsible for turning over genuine records.)

**PROOF OF RECORDS EXISTENCE**: On April 20, 2012, by subpoena, my co-plaintiff got 133 pages of Orchid Cellmark's DNA records. That proved records' existence and indicated the Defendants' cover-up motive; since Lee's bench DNA and the exhumed remains' DNA were "inconclusive" junk – putting the lie to the Defendants' having the Kid's DNA (and proving that the Arizona exhumations were criminal - lacking the Kid's DNA for justification).

**SHAM RECORDS RECOVERY ATTEMPTS**: Three years into litigation, on October 26, 2010, Virden finally wrote request letters to Lee and Orchid Cellmark. Both wrote back that they had records. But Virden never asked for them! In his June 27, 2012 deposition, Virden blamed Attorney Morel's advice; while admitting he himself was responsible as records custodian.

**SETTLEMENT**: IPRA law provides for payment of a prevailing plaintiff's costs, attorney fees, and damages. Court-ordered mediation, on March 26, 2013, resulted in the Defendants paying fees of Plaintiff attorneys (totaling almost $200,000.00). And my co-plaintiff settled out of the case.

**MY CONTINUING LITIGATION**: I did not settle, and filed a Motion for my Costs and Damages. (Exhibit 8) IPRA law grants plaintiff's Damages "up to $100.00 per day," starting 15 days after improper denial. Improper denials are for the four sets of records I requested on April 24, 2007. So IPRA's money clock started ticking - at $400.00 per day – on May 9, 2007. It stopped ticking on April 20, 2012 when my co-plaintiff's subpoena got Orchid Cellmark's DNA extractions from Lee's bench specimens, and Orchid Cellmark's DNA extractions from the two exhumed men. That left Lee's DNA bench specimen recovery record(s), and Orchid Cellmark's matchings of bench DNA to the exhumed men's DNA. That kept IPRA's money clock ticking for them.

Maximum damages of $100.00 per day are justified, since the Defendants could have gotten my requested records at my April 24, 2007 request. The New Mexico Court of Appeals backs IPRA Damages to encourage prompt compliance, as shown by its decisions for *Rio Grande Sun News vs. Jemez Mountains School District,* 2012; and *Daniel Faber vs. Gary King, Attorney General,* 2013.

**ABOUT POSSIBLE FUTURE LITIGATION:** Additional IPRA violations have occurred during the litigation in the form of Risk Management's blanking-out of Defense attorneys' paid services for billings (already exceeding $320,000 in taxpayer money - and ongoing without a ceiling). As public records, they cannot be concealed. So I have made a complaint about that to AG Gary King.

**ABOUT WRONGDOINGS:** County Commissioners and the County Attorney, having oversight responsibility for Case 2003-274, are, thereby, culpable for the Billy the Kid Case's law enforcement fraud and taxpayer debacle. Virden, Sullivan, and Sederwall used color of their law enforcement authority to make a mockery of the Lincoln County's Sheriff's Department and to desecrate graves - all for a self-serving hoax. And they violated IPRA law to cover-up their offences. Here is Lincoln County's roster of shame:

- Sheriffs Virden and Sullivan, and their Deputy Sederwall were permitted to conduct the fraudulent Billy the Kid Case murder investigation; conceal its records; tamper evidence and ignore court-orders; and saddle taxpayers with their huge legal bills from IPRA litigation.

- For a decade, Attorney Alan Morel covered up incriminatory Billy the Kid Case records by IPRA violations and by prolonging litigation by encouraging records withholding.

- Throughout the litigation, Sullivan and Sederwall lied that Case 2003-274 was their private hobby, and called its law enforcement records their "trade secrets;" but have billed the taxpayers as public officials for **over $150,000 in their legal defense bills** in that litigation.

- Throughout the litigation, Virden refused all records by misstating custodial responsibility as records possession, preposterously claiming he had no DNA records of his solely forensic DNA murder case; and refusing records' retrieval; thus costing taxpayers **over $150,000 for his legal defense bills - plus the plaintiffs' attorney bill settlement of almost $200,000.**

- In 2010, Sederwall made a website called billythekidcase.com; in which he sold, for $25.00, Case 2003-274 records (Exhibit 9) - while records' existence was denied in the litigation!

- The Billy the Kid Case has irreparably diminished national and international public trust in New Mexico's Pat Garrett and Billy the Kid history by fake TV documentaries and a movie.

- The Billy the Kid Case is New Mexico's most egregious IPRA violation case; bleeding taxpayers horrifically to cover-up a massive Lincoln County law enforcement scandal.

**CONCLUSION:** **Arguably the most elaborate historic/forensic hoax ever perpetrated, Case 2003-274's fraudulent murder case against Pat Garrett - involving sham forensics and outrageous IPRA violations - has cost taxpayers over $500,000; and may go to $1,500,000.**

**\*\*\*\*\*\*\***

I heard from no recipient. According to a source in Lincoln County, Attorney Alan Morel told local officials to do nothing since it would not affect them because taxpayers would pay.

## *THE TINY LINCOLN COUNTY NEWS WEIGHS IN*

From Carrizozo, the eight page *Lincoln County News* did cover my County Commissioners letter. Owner, Peter Aguilar, with reporter, Doris Cherry, published, on June 27, 2013, as a front page story: "Modern Billy the Kid 'Cases' Cost Public Plenty: County Shells Out Bucks for Failing to Release Information." (The rest of that front page had a reprint of the June 11, 2013 *Albuquerque Journal* article.) Doris Cherry wrote:

> The story of Billy the Kid has been romanticized since first written about by Pat Garrett in the 18880's. But William "Billy" Antrun [sic] "Bonney" was a real person, an intelligent orphan caught up in the turbulent times of territorial Lincoln County and New Mexico, where outside money fueled the stampede of land and water grabbing carpetbaggers – scenarios that sometimes continue to this day.
> The newest chapter about Billy the Kid officially started on April 28, 2003, when then Lincoln County Sheriff Tom Sullivan filed incident report no. 3560 (which became the official LCSO

Case # 2003-274), "homicide investigation (escape)" with narrative "follow up investigation, escape of William Bonney and double homicide of James Bell and Robert Ollinger [sic]" in the Lincoln County Sheriff's Office.

It was this report *THE NEWS* found while conducting a routine "sheriff's report" beat. Sullivan then told *THE NEWS* he just wanted to find the truth about Texan Brushy Bill Roberts who claimed to be Billy the Kid, and who claimed that Garrett helped him escape from Fort Sumner. And as a side-line the case would help boost tourism.

Now 19 years later, this modern Billy the Kid murder case has caused Lincoln County – through Risk Management – to shell out more than $500,000 in attorney fees, and more than $200,000 in lump sum penalties to an author, and a publisher of a small New Mexico newspaper – on behalf of Sullivan, and Sheriff Rick Virden, both of whom in 2007 refused to turn over requested information involving the DNA testing for the Billy the Kid Case records, in violation of the New Mexico Inspection of Public Records Act (IPRA).

Ultimately, the case became a murder investigation against Pat Garrett, because it alleged Garrett had on July 14, 1881, killed an innocent victim instead of Billy, and allowed Billy, his friend, to escape. The investigations for the case involved a "reenacted shooting," in the old Lincoln Courthouse, of the Kid's murder of guards during his jailbreak.

Sullivan and his friend then Capitan mayor Steve Sederwall whom Sullivan deputized, would call in experts to do DNA testing of bones exhumed from the Kid grave in Fort Sumner and his mother's grave in Silver City, in order to prove who really lay in the Kid's grave, and later DNA testing of Arizona men [sic] who also claimed to be Billy the Kid.

While the case brought new attention to Billy the Kid, and thus Lincoln County, it also brought some harsh criticism from some who saw the "case" as a way for an elected official to gather, under his official title, information about Billy the Kid that would ultimately be used for his own personal gain.

Then Lincoln County Commissioner Leo Martinez questioned the investigations, but was the lone voice on that board, and later lost his bid for election. In stepped Dr. Gale Cooper, historian and author from Sandia Park, NM. "I was determined to stop those historical hijackers," Cooper told *THE NEWS* about Sullivan and Sederwall and their Billy the Kid case. Cooper, who has researched Billy the Kid since 1998 for her docu-fiction novel about Billy and Paulita Maxwell, as well as a book on the Kid's writings [sic – and *MegaHoax*], got involved after reading the New York Times, June 5, 2003 front page story. It was about the newly opened Billy the Kid case, with Garrett called a murderer and a Brushy Bill as the Kid who never died in Fort Sumner in 1881. "There was no historical evidence for any of their claims," Cooper said. "The Billy the Kid Case is an elaborate historical, forensic, legal hoax for personal gain, and for name recognition for then Gov. Bill Richardson."

So in 2003 Cooper began a pursuit for what should have been public information gathered under an official case number by public officials. From 2003 to 2006, Cooper made several requests for public information for the information gathered under the case, in particular DNA reports. Cooper said the requests were forwarded to Lincoln County Attorney Alan Morel who forwarded from the sheriffs office refusal to release information, citing the IPRA exception for ingoing "criminal investigation.

"Getting no response to her request for information, even with the help of columnist Jay Miller, Cooper eventually joined with Scott [sic] Stinnett, publisher of the De Baca County News in Fort Sumner, as parties to an IPRA lawsuit. Both had requested [sic – in the lawsuit] four different items of information from the Lincoln Country Sheriff's Office [sic – Virden] relating to and concerning the Billy the Kid Case DNA investigations, testing and reporting. (Information requests continued to be denied based on the IPRA exception for "ongoing investigations [sic – not so] for a case being conducted with "private funds" by men claiming to be hobbyists and all information was intellectual property.

On November 20, 2009, Judge George Eichwald of the 13th Judicial Court in Sandoval County ordered that Sullivan and Sederwall [sic – and Virden] were public officials who had generated public documents – in particular reports from tests by Orchid Cellmark Lab, of supposed DNA evidence collected from a bench alleged to have been used to lay out Billy's body, and DNA extractions from exhumed bodies in Arizona, all done for Case # 2003-274.

Still no information was provided as ordered. So on March 10, 2010, the same judge ordered the evidence resulting from the investigation as public record, and he ordered Virden, Sullivan and Sederwall to turn over to Cooper and Stinnett, all information collected as a result of the investigation. The order was ignored, and no information was turned over. So Cooper and Stinnett went to court again and the judge ordered a hearing on January 2012 [sic – 2011], after which he again ordered the information to be provided.

According to Cooper, Sederwall started turning in reports from Dr. Henry Lee who had conducted the original DNA tests, however, the reports were suspected to be tampered with. So in May 2012, the judge ordered depositions be taken from Virden, Sullivan and Sederwall to explore the records withholding and tampering. Cooper told THE NEWS that Sederwall admitted to removing information linking Dr. Lee's report to Case No. 2003-274 and Virden admitted that he made no attempts to get the requested DNA reports from Lee and Cellmark. "At that point we [sic – the] defendants requested mediation (on the IPRA fines and penalties), which the Court ordered in September 2012," Cooper added.

"IPRA provides for payment of prevailing plaintiff's costs, attorney fees and damages," Cooper told commissioners in her letter to them. "Court-ordered mediation, on March 26 [sic – 27], 2013, resulted in the defendants paying fees of the plaintiffs' attorneys (totaling almost $200,000)."

Also based on that mediation, Judge Eichwald in April of this year, ordered the lump sum payments for attorney fees be paid to attorneys for Cooper and Stinnett. Cooper was paid a total of     $55,139.40 [sic – for the fees] and Stinnett was paid $125,000. The lump sum payments do not include fees paid to defense attorneys for Virden (Henry Narvaez, Albuquerque) and Sullivan and Sede3rwall (Kevin Brown, Albuquerque), both of whom Virden re-deputized after Sullivan's term ended in order to continue the Billy the Kid case investigations, or for Lincoln County Attorney Alan Morel on behalf of the county.

The lump sum payments come from the New Mexico association of Counties Risk Management Division. Lincoln County, a member of NMAC, pays into the risk management multi-line pool according to how many individuals per department participate. According to Cooper, [sic – some of] the IPRA violations filed by herself and Stinnett stopped on April 20, 2012 when a subpoena filed by Stinnett against Orchid Cellmark Lab got the reports on the DNA tests from the bench specimens and the exhumed Arizona men (which showed testing as inconclusive). But those reports did not include all the DNA bench recovery records [sic – and DNA matching results], so Cooper said she is continuing her IPRA litigation and its subsequent daily accruing fees, acting as her own counsel in the case.

Cooper is advising the Lincoln County Commissioners about the situation in an "open letter" dated June 18, 2013, regarding Lincoln County Sheriff's Case 2003-274, and her case in the Sandoval County 13th District Court Cause No. D-1329-CV-1364.

"This letter is sent to you (commissioners) because of my deep concern about the unchecked ravages to taxpayers and to Old West history resulting from your Lincoln County Sheriff's Department Billy the Kid Case - a decade-long historic/forensic hoax and law enforcement fraud – that led to the district court's ongoing, five and a half years, IPRA litigation for its unjustified and total open records violations," Cooper writes to commissioners. In the letter, Cooper defends the continuing

IPRA fines on the original information requests, since the defendants could have provided the public information as she requested in April of 2007.

"The New Mexico Court of Appeals backs IPRA damages," Cooper states in her commissioners' letter. "To encourage prompt compliance." Also in her letter to the commissioners Cooper states that additional IPRA violations have occurred by Risk Management blanking-out the billings for defense attorneys, which she claims exceeds $320,000, about which she made a complaint with attorney General Gary King.

"Throughout the litigation," Cooper wrote to the commissioners, "Virden refused all records by misstating custodial responsibility as records possession, preposterously claiming he had no DNA records of his solely forensic DNA murder case, and refusing records' retrieval 9claiming it was an ongoing investigation yet being 122 years old there are no living witnesses to the crime [sic – this parenthetical is not in the letter, but added here]); thus costing taxpayers over $150,000 for his legal defense bills in that litigation."

Using their official titles Sullivan and Sederwall extended their investigations into DNA testing with attempted exhumations of Billy's mother and an actual exhumation in Arizona of another alleged Billy make believe. When exhumation requests were denied in Silver City and Fort Sumner in order to obtain DNA from Billy's mother's bones in Silver City, and to dig Billy's grave in Fort Sumner, a work bench allegedly from the Maxwell ranch used to lay Billy after he was shot by Garrett appeared. It tested positive for blood [sic – sigh. It is impossible to get through that there was no blood]. DNA testing was done and Sullivan and Sederwall claimed it showed a possible match to an Arizona man claiming to be Billy the Kid. But how could Billy's blood be on the bench if he was allowed to escape from Fort Sumner? [sic – Cherry missed the hoax's switcheroo to "playing-dead Billy."]

All the while, the two maintained they were conducting the investigations using private funds, and never any public funds. To support this claim, in information obtained by *THE NEWS*, in 2003 three checks were given to Sullivan at the State Capitol in Santa Fe by then Gov. Bill Richardson's staffer Billy Sparks. The first check was dated Aug. 1, 2003, for $500 from a business – Hobbs Rental Corporation, owned by Bill Robbins [sic – Robins, and he was not the owner] – paid to the "Investigative Fund 2003-247," c/o Heard, Robbins [sic], et al, Santa Fe. Checks were issued from a Bill Robbins [sic] account on Aug. 26, 2003 for $3,000 to the "Investigative Fund 2003-247" and on Sept. 12, 2003 for $3,000 check dated Sept. 12, 2003 owned by Bill Robbins [sic] of Hobbs.

At the time, Richardson and even Fort Sumner mayor Raymond Lopez were interested in the investigation as a way to boos tourism to the state and the little town of Fort Sumner whose claim to fame is the location of Billy's grave. [sic – this is Cherry's addition]

When De Baca County Sheriff Gary Graves entered into the "official investigations" in Fort Sumner, the publisher of the De Baca County News began to challenge the investigations and made an official request for public information [sic – this is untrue; I made the request!] and columnist Jay Miller began to question [sic – via my articles written for him!].

Cooper told *THE NEWS* that the irony of this public information case is Sullivan and Sederwall themselves sought public records information with the New Mexico Office of the Medical Investigator (OMI) concerning the Billy the Kid Case and were denied.

"The actual records requested – the results of DNA testing – were obtainable within weeks of my records request on April 24, 2007, which would have cost the county nothing," Cooper said. "Risk Management – meaning taxpayers – have paid two defense firms for Virden and Sullivan and Sederwall for a sum that would be about $350,000 by 2013," Cooper added. "For defendants claiming to be hobbyists, not public officials.!"

"The defendants ignored Judge Eichwald's order in 2009, so he ordered a hearing in January 2011, after which he repeated his order to turn over the records," Cooper added. In May 2012, depositions were again ordered by the judge from Virden, Sullivan and Sederwall concerning records withholding and records tampering (involving the DNA testing).

At that time Sederwall admitted to removing information linking a DNA report to the sheriff's department or Case 2003-274. Virden admitted he never made valid attempts to get the requested records – waiting three years before writing letters for the DNA information, claiming he acted on Morel's advice. Sullivan and Sederwall through their attorneys filed an appeal of Judge Eichwald's order in the New Mexico Court of Appeals. The appeals Court on April 24, 2013 ultimately denied that appeal when it approved a motion for dismissal filed by Cooper and De Baca County News.

"This Billy the Kid case almost cost New Mexico its old West history, and to date I have not received a single, genuine, requested forensic DNA records from the defendants," Cooper concluded.

While the records from the Case 2003-274 have never been released, Sederwall in 2010 owned a website whereby one could purchase a $25 membership to gain access to the case details. [sic – case records] He also was featured in a 2010 Discovery channel program about the Billy the Kid case.

*The News* left a message on Sederwall's home phone asking for a comment, but he had not returned the call by deadline.

*The News* contacted Morel's office twice and received a call back on the second day. Morel would not give details of Cooper's IPRA case as he said it continues in litigation. He did say the IPRA issue was settled by all parties, except for Cooper, who is carrying on her claim. Morel explained that Risk Management attorneys are doing the negotiation and will be providing legal counsel for the county in Dr. Cooper's case that has been scheduled to convene in the 13th District Court in November [sic]. "We try to amicably resolve all our legal issues," Morel concluded about Dr. Cooper's litigation.

*Sullivan was not available for comment, so The News* contacted Sullivan and Sederwall's attorney Kevin Brown for comment, who by dead-line had not returned the call.

Editor's Note: At the time Sullivan opened the Ollinger [sic] and Bell murder case, there was at least one unresolved murder that was committed during Sullivan's 1980s term as Lincoln County Sheriff – the 1985 murders of Cotton and Judy McKnight which were never solved and thus continue to be open murder cases in the Lincoln County Sheriff's Office. McKnight, a rancher in the Picacho area, was Lincoln County Commissioner serving with Ben Hall and John Allen Hightower in the late 1970's.

Doris Cherry's well-meaning *Lincoln County News* piece was somewhat garbled. (The case, with hoaxer switcheroos and lies, was hard to understand.) But eventually, Judge George P. Eichwald would need to understand it for justice to be done.

# Barnett Bar Association Complaint

On January 19, 2013, I sent the New Mexico Bar Association: "Complaint Against Attorney Mickey Barnett By Client Gale Cooper." It had my pleadings about Scot Stinnett's lack of standing, and hundreds of pages of exhibits showing Barnett unethically claimed adding a client to my case without telling me, and of his perjury. Its rejection was on February 22, 2013 by an Attorney Anne J. Taylor. I appealed on March 8, 2013. Rejection was repeated on April 12, 2013 by Attorney Curtis R. Gurley.

As to that Bar Association, perspective comes from Bill Richardson's lawyer, Carlos William Fierro. For his 2008 hit-and-run, totally drunk, headlights-off, vehicular homicide, he got a few years in prison, *but only a suspended law license; not disbarment.*

# JUST ME BACK TO COURT:

My hearing for my May 23, 2013 "Plaintiff Gale Cooper's Motion to Request Award of Her Costs and Damages From Defendants, and To Request Award of Sanctions Against Defendants," and its June 30, 2013 "Addendum" with the case summary exhibit of the letter to the Lincoln County Commissioners, was not scheduled for months. A pattern had emerged of Judge George Eichwald building in tremendous delays.

My hearing was finally scheduled for a December 13, 2013, having added another year to my case. I had requested an hour and a half, and was given only one hour by Judge George Eichwald. And my "bill" for the defendants would be almost a million dollars in costs and per diem penalties - and that left out in calculation the sanctions which they deserved.

So Judge Eichwald would have to decide if fifth dimension legal time of 30 days for the defendants' records turn-over - which he started on November 20, 2009 with his Summary Judgment in my favor - had run out at last.

For this hearing I would be entirely alone against my defendants. I anticipated that they would fight with every crooked trick in their armamentarium. They possessed nothing else. But I had faith that timid Judge Eichwald could now rule. The defendants' audacious violations had blown the case to gigantic proportions. But I did not factor in the last person who could still save the day for the hoaxers: Judge George P. Eichwald himself.

# CHAPTER 18:

# HOAX LAWYERS, JUDGE, AND ME

Defense attorneys: Left, Henry Narvaez; Right, Desiree Gurule; Rear Alan Morel,
Evidentiary Hearing 11, December 18, 2013

Judge George Eichwald and court reporter, Evidentiary Hearing 11, December 18, 2013

The author in Evidentiary Hearing II, December 18, 2013

# A DREAM

I had been terrified in 2006, when journalist Jay Miller refused to do open records requests on Governors Richardson and Napolitano and Sheriff Virden, forcing me to do them myself - and be exposed. That caused an unusually vivid dream.

From my house, the unpaved road down the mountain has precipitous drop-offs, steep descents, and occasional deep drainage ditches to the sides. During snow season, from October to April, my tire tracks are sometimes alone on the road's white expanse. Risk of sliding off and not being found had haunted me.

My dream was like reality. Driving down the winter mountain, I lost control of my sliding car, and became marooned in a deep side ditch, wondering if bears and coyotes would eat me. Then I realized that my car was filled with women from my life: my mother, her sister, and dead grandmothers. Invisible, they were laughing. They said we should lower the windows and get out. In the ditch, I realized my car was an unfamiliar electric blue sedan. At their instruction, we reached through its open windows to the roof and lifted. Effortlessly, the car rose. Then we were back inside the car and driving on the road. They were laughing. "It's the Chelon Point," they said. In the white landscape, I drove effortlessly on the brilliant-white sunlit road. My fears of being trapped now seemed foolish and mistaken. It was all so easy.

Later, on the internet I sought the word "Chelon." I found nothing. But memory of the effortless current stayed with me.

Now, as I prepared for the upcoming December 13, 2013 hearing that would be my showdown all alone with the hoaxers, I finally understood Frederick Nolan's "current of history;" and I realized that I had entered it in 1998 when my fascination with Billy the Kid led to my docufiction novel, *Joy of the Birds*, that became *Billy and Paulita* in a later edition.

My journey in New Mexico had begun with coincidences blurring my life with that of Billy Bonney and his fellow freedom fighters. By 2000, I had written about the completion of Billy's path, and his accepting the current of his own destiny. He could have avoided Fort Sumner and death after his great escape. But he refused to let fear dictate his life. He wanted to be with Paulita. By 2003, I had put these words into his mouth as he spoke to Charlie Bowdre soon before they went to their Stinking Springs ambush: "I'd bet, even after I'm dead, our War will fire up some new Regulator who'll keep it going if we haven't won yet."

So I became the Regulator I had predicted years before.

# STANDING ALONE

*HOAXBUST: My showdown in the Billy the Kid Case would involve arguing for justice: my statutory right to receive penalties of costs and damages under New Mexico's open records law, as well as to get sanctions against the defendants for contempt of ignoring court orders and for evidence tampering by forgeries. The sums of money involved were unprecedented and astronomical. I was certain that my defendants would fight desperately and dishonestly. And the judge would be morally tested.*

### *ARGUING FOR JUSTICE*

When Judge George Eichwald's schedule changed, he moved my hearing to December 18, 2013, giving me its entire afternoon. That also made the day the one year anniversary of my first *pro se* court appearance at the second evidentiary hearing. But now my co-plaintiff and his attorney were gone. There would just be me against the defense attorneys.

My argument would be for my costs and damages under New Mexico's Inspection of Records Act (IPRA) law, and additional sanctions for contempt and evidence tampering. That law is in plain language intended for laymen. Costs and damages for a prevailing plaintiff are spelled out for the civil statutory penalties.

IPRA's Section 14-2-11(A, B, C) requires a written denial letter within 15 days, which must give: a proper IPRA explanation for denial (like use of an exception); a listing of the requested records, and a listing of those responsible by names and titles; or be subject to per diem fines of up to $100 per day. My defendants had never presented that letter. Also they had no proper grounds for denying me the requested records.

And the improperly denied records totaled four by categories: (1) Dr. Henry Lee's report(s) on DNA and the carpenter's bench; (2) Orchid Cellmark's DNA extractions from Lee's bench specimens; (3) Orchid Cellmark's DNA extractions from the two Arizona exhumations; and (4) Orchid Cellmark's matchings of bench DNA to exhumed remains' DNA. So the $100 per day penalty had kicked in 15 days after my April 24, 2007 request date and was accruing at $400 per day.

IPRA's Section 14-2-12(D) states: "The court shall award damages, costs and reasonable attorneys' fees to any person whose written request has been denied and is successful in court action to enforce the provisions of the Inspection of Public Records Act." Fees of my past attorneys had already been settled in the March 26, 2013 mediation (in tacit admission of defendants' guilt). My costs and damages remained for the hearing.

I planned to present precedent law. Besides *Deborah Toomey vs. Truth or Consequences* nailing down that a custodian must retrieve records held "on behalf of" a public entity, there were other cases; one just ruled on in the 2nd Judicial District Court in which the judge's decision had similar IPRA issues to my case, and even was about a sheriff (the Bernalillo County Sheriff).

But law was not my worry, lawyer games were. I anticipated filibustering interruptions and spurious objections spewing the same misinformation as those defense attorneys had used in the second evidentiary hearing to confuse the judge. Courtroom rough and tumble would be my real test.

So I planned a surprise that would complete my fated "coming out": I would reveal, by bringing in the almost thousand page, earlier proof of this book, that I was behind all aspects of Billy the Kid Case opposition. It was impossible to lie to me. And with irony not missed by me, my original frightened quest for anonymity would end in my total exposure.

And I would quote from IPRA law's magnificent and poignant idealism of its creating legislators: "It is declared to be public policy of this state, that to provide persons with such information is an essential function of a representative gov. and an integral part of the routine duties of public officers."

I would quote from the benchmark 1977, New Mexico Court of Appeals case, *Newsome v. Alarid*, which corroborated IPRA's intent to let citizens determine if their public officials are honestly performing their function as public servants. And there could be no defendants more willfully in IPRA violation than were mine.

As to my costs and damages, they were breathtaking and unprecedented. Only my defendants' and their attorneys' sociopathic arrogance and reliance on corruption had permitted them to accrue to this level. As of that December 18, 2013, my costs were $19,594.56, and the penalties of $400 per day reached $966,000. That totaled $985,594.56 owed to me.

And I had a trick up my sleeve. The defendants had been so sure of doing a Bambi Meets Godzilla on all-alone me that they had not even bothered to respond properly to my "Motion for Costs, Damages, and Sanctions" (after all, in the mediation they had paid $125,000 to get rid of my co-plaintiff's attorney, and possibly him). So Attorneys Henry Narvaez and Kevin Brown jointly had merely answered my motion by a silly paragraph, referring me and the judge to their own "Findings of Fact and Conclusions of Law." This was not only preposterously saying we should make up their arguments for them, but it made no mention of the costs, damages, and sanctions. That error came under New Mexico Rules Annotated (I now owned the big red book that Attorney Riordan had brought to court himself), with Rule 1-007.1 which says that "[i]f a party fails to file a response within the prescribed time period the court may rule with or without a hearing." That meant the hearing was unnecessary. Judge Eichwald was free to award me the full amount of the costs and damages I requested. Of course, I was under no illusion that this timid judge could behave so boldly. But impetus would be added.

## A DEATH IN THE FIFTH DIMENSION

There was another matter. An October 22, 2013 article by Dianne Stallings in the hoax-backing *Ruidoso News* was titled: "Former Lincoln Co. Sheriff Tom Sullivan Dies in Texas," and was reprinted the next day by the *Albuquerque Journal*. Both publications made the Billy the Kid Case his sentimental send-off. In a photo, cowboy-hatted Tom Sullivan sits with bloated Bill Richardson and their tintype blow-up at their first publicity-stunt meeting at the Santa Fe Round House capitol.

For this cover-up article, Dianne Stallings simply lied. She knew better, having reported for the *Ruidoso News* Commissioner Leo Martinez's confrontation of Sullivan in her October 22, 2004 "Showdown in the County Seat: shouting match erupts at County Commissioners meeting Tuesday over investigation of Billy the Kid." Moreover, I was told that when the *Ruidoso News's* new editor-in-chief, Terrance Vestal, wanted to cover my litigation, she stopped him. For Tom Sullivan's undeserving eulogy, Dianne Stallings wrote:

Near the end of his last term

**[AUTHOR'S NOTE: A lie. Sullivan's term ended in 2004. He began the Billy the Kid Case in mid-2003]**

and for several years after leaving office

**[AUTHOR'S NOTE: A lie. He was deputized by Virden to continue the case in 2004; only quitting it in 2007],**

Sullivan joined the former mayor of Capitan

**[AUTHOR'S NOTE: A misstatement. Sederwall was also continuously a deputy for the case from 2003 to 2007]**

to investigate the death and burial place of Billy the Kid, a major player in the Lincoln County War. The endeavor, encouraged by then-Gov. Bill Richardson, received international attention.

Dianne Stalling's also sprinkled laudatory quotes, which are ironic, considering Sullivan's actual legacy of corrupt misuse of his sheriff's department and near-destruction of his state's iconic history. But Ruidoso Police Chief Joe Magill stated: "He was very reputable and honest." And former Ruidoso Police Chief Wolfgang Born (in office during the hoax) "recalls Sullivan as a symbol of the old West." The latter is true; if "old West" means its reality, not its mythology, in New Mexico Territory: Secret Service assisted, political murder of Billy Bonney vilified as outlaw "Billy the Kid;" strangle-hold of the Santa Fe Ring on the Territorial citizens; and the murder of John Henry Tunstall by past Lincoln County Sheriff William Brady to end Tunstall's mercantile and ranching competition with the Santa Fe Ring.

Be that as it may, I was concerned that the defense would belabor that fact of a deceased defendant to distract the judge. So I planned to move immediately to dismiss Tom Sullivan, preempting any shenanigans. Equally corrupt Rick Virden and Steve Sederwall were enough for my defendant list.

# MY DAY IN COURT

As usual, I came early. Alone in the empty courtroom, I absorbed its familiar, odd feeling of coming home. Eventually, Attorney Henry Narvaez and Attorney Desiree Gurule (for Kevin Brown) took their seats at the defense table. I later realized that Judge George Eichwald was watching from behind the scenes, because he praised us on interacting politely (small talk). With Narvaez and Gurule, was Lincoln County Attorney Alan Morel; present, I assumed, to assist or to watch my coup de grâce.

My ruminations on "currents of history" and my "Chelon Point" dream had not converted me to non-coward. I was thinking: "What if I start coughing and can't stop? What if my mind goes blank? What if I faint?"

My videographer, coming late, set up in the jury area. None of people I had asked to come kept their promise for that dangerous exposure. The spectator area stayed empty.

Then Judge Eichwald emerged. Things evolved differently than I anticipated: better. I spoke first. There was silence: no objections or interruptions! This was the first time they had seen me in action. They seemed shocked. And experiencing no impediment, I took off. I spoke from the heart. I spared no accusations of my defendants or their attorneys. "Little Weasel" Morel must have left early. He was gone when it was over.

## *MY WORDS*

There was another trick I planned to break through my opponents' press blackout keeping New Mexicans ignorant of my important case. I would put that hearing's video on YouTube and in my galecooperbillythekidcase.com website under *Cracking the Billy the Kid Case Hoax.*

And I positioned a wastebasket at the podium. Soon I would tear up IPRA law and throw it out, saying it was useless if I could not get my just ruling: about a million dollars in penalties, plus more as sanctions for evidence tampering and contempt.

Below is the transcript (with added boldface).

**[AUTHOR'S COMMENT: It had errors only in my parts, reversing my meanings or making my arguments gibberish. The court reporter did some corrections, but not all I requested. Later, I realized that this hamstrung transcript could present a big problem.]**

DR. COOPER: ... [Today has to do] with enforcement of statutory civil penalties on what's arguably the most extreme case of Inspection of Public Records Act or IPRA violation in the history of this state. In the six-year litigation that I have been present in and in which I am a Plaintiff, all of the records that I have requested have been willfully and wrongfully withheld. That was done in defiance of the IPRA statute, in defiance of orders and defiance of my fundamental right to inspect public records. That failure to give me records is completely unjustified. No valid IPRA exception was used for my denials, and no IPRA deadline was met. In IPRA law, that's it. There's no other safe haven. My co-Plaintiff, whose subpoena, proved that the requested records did exist. The fact is that I could have gotten those records within the 15-day time period of my first records request on April 24th of '07. There was no reason that I wasn't given those records. This litigation was not necessary. And during this litigation, at any day, I could have been given the records right up to the present. **If I can't get enforcement for IPRA penalties in a case like this, I can take this beautiful cornerstone of democracy, the IPRA manual, and get rid of it, because no other citizen should go through what I have had to go through on this other case. The law would have no teeth and no value. [AUTHOR'S NOTE: I tear up the law into a waste paper basket.]**

Now, I didn't need a reason to request these records, but I have one, a very big one. I'm exposing the murder case in Lincoln County called 2003-274, called by its promulgators, the Billy the Kid case. I'm exposing it as a law enforcement fraud and DNA hoax jeopardizing Billy the Kid history and doing it by a legal [sic - illegal] exhumation with fraudulent DNA. The purpose was a publicity stunt to prove that Pat Garrett didn't kill Billy the Kid, even though that's not true. The reason I bring that up is two-fold. One, it speaks ... to the motive of what has happened for the past six years. The Defendant[s] simply didn't want me to see the records. The records are not compatible. The actual DNA records, with the claims that they were making, the claims that would allow them to claim they had the DNA of Billy the Kid, the reference DNA, and conduct a legal exhumation using it.

Since I have been questioned so often in this Court, this is my next edition that I brought, that I would like to put with my other ones, if the Court will accept it. This is called, Cracking the Billy the Kid Hoax. This is the case that we are dealing with. It's almost 1,000 pages of labor on my part exposing this ... **[Accepted by Court only as a courtesy, but refused as part of record]** In this book and in this case, I want to make clear to the Court, my extensive knowledge is definitely his [sic –as] expertise as came up in the February 4th evidentiary hearing of this year and behind all of the IPRAs that were ever done in this case, that's ten years ... [with] six years in this court. I've been given no records, just deputy cards, once. But the excuses were different.

In addition, I'm behind blocking the exhumation of Billy the Kid and his mother. And I brought the Kennedy Law Firm in 2003 and in 2004, to achieve that.

That brings us to the records that I asked for, because they are not random, and they make sense as to why they are difficult for the Defendants to give to me. They were the only way that they could continue case 2003-274, after I blocked the exhumation[s]. The premise had been that Pat Garrett didn't kill Billy, and that would solve their murder. And our records, preserved, are their proximate [probable] cause statements [statement] and their petitions for exhumation. But after those graves were blocked, they were going to say that the DNA of Billy and his mother didn't match. Well, they had no DNA. They had to come up with it. So central to continuing the hoax was the carpenter's bench on which Billy the Kid, they alleged, had been laid out, bled, and preposterously was only playing dead for the coroner's jury, and for all of the townspeople of Fort Sumner, and he headed off into the future as one of the claimants to his identity. They were going to use DNA from the carpenter's bench to match the claimant, and thus indirectly solve the murder, because the claimant was claimed to match that DNA that Pat hadn't killed Billy on July 14th of '81, Billy survived, and Pat was, again, the murderer of an innocent victim, which is what brought case 2003-274 about.

So the records I asked for, quite purposefully, were Dr. Lee's specimens for DNA that he collected from the carpenter's bench as the first unfulfilled records request. Second, was Orchid Cellmark Laboratories DNA extractions from Dr. Lee's specimens. Third, was Orchid Cellmark's DNA extractions from Billy the Kid claimants [who] were dug up in Arizona, one being John Miller, and the other being a random man buried beside him. And the forth, was matching of Orchid Cellmark DNA from the bench to the claimants ... Those records are listed ... in my initial complaint in this court, and were in my request. My April 24th, 2007, request of those four items.

As to IPRA law in precedent cases, they support the maximum penalties that I'm requesting today. IPRA is a very idealistic law and made for citizens. In Section 14-2-5 it

states, "It is declared to be the public policy of this state, that to provide persons with such information, such information is an essential function of a representative government, an integral part of the routine duties of public office [sic - officers]."The landmark in New Mexico is a Court of Appeals case in 1977, *Newsome vs. Alarid*, and it says in short that IPRA intends to let citizens determine if the public officials are "honestly" performing their function as public servants. Implied in that is a welcome to be a whistle-blower and to root out dishonesty in performing their function as public servant.

This Court has already made its decision for liability for me. Summary Judgment was given to me on November 20th of '09, with its order being March 12th of 2010. It stated that my requested records were public and created by the Defendants as a public official. On September 28 of 2011, those material facts were elaborated, and the order by you, Your Honor, stated that Billy the Kid's killing by Pat Garrett and the deputy killings by Billy the Kid was a single case, 2003-274, by the Lincoln County Sheriff's Department. Importantly, my Defendants, in six years, have given me and this Court no contrary evidence, whatsoever.

There's some named authorities for the damages and for the violation itself. One that is very important, because it goes to the heart of ... one of the arguments that the Defendants have presented, that case is a New Mexico Court of Appeals from last year *Toomey vs. Truth or Consequences*. There the Court ruled that, "Absent an express exemption from disclosure, public agencies must produce all records, even those held by or created by" -- I repeat, "held by or created by a private entity 'on behalf of' the public agency." Well, since our IPRA law is silent on exactly the meaning on "behalf of the" and "the test factors," our court of appeals sought Florida law, that's the Supreme Court case in 1992 called *News and Sun-Sentinel vs. Schwab, Twitty & Hanser*. And what they were looking for was deciding factors, two of the factors are applicable here. "Whether services are an integral part of the public agency's decision-making process"; and the second is, "For whose benefit the private entity is functioning." And the Court cautioned, when they made this decision, that it's immensely important that an avenue not by opened for potential defendants to contract with private agencies to conceal records that they would like to hide. In this case, ... this DNA was the only remaining way, the integral part of the sheriff's department solving the murder of Pat Garrett and the innocent victim, and for whose benefit, it certainly was the sheriff's department, since Orchid Cellmark is the biggest lab in the country. They are not doing research on Billy the Kid. More importantly, both Dr. Lee and Orchid Cellmark identified they were going to [do] case 2003-274.

Now, *Rio Grande Sun vs. Jemez Mountains Public School District* again, last year, and the New Mexico Court of Appeals addressed the purpose of damages, stating that "Granting Plaintiff's costs and damages encourage, 'Socially beneficial litigation.' I would say saving the history of New Mexico in regard to the iconic Old West Billy the Kid and Pat Garrett and saving its intendant [sic - attendant] tourism certainly brings it socially beneficial.

*Board of Commissioners of Dona Ana County vs. Las Cruces Sun News*: our court of appeals, in 2003, "The legislature's punitive intent in imposing a cost for non-disclosure is evident." Punitive here is taken to mean deterrent.

*San Juan Agricultural Water Users Association vs. KNME-TV*, in 2011, a Supreme Court case said that "IPRA's damages provisions are considered as effective remedies and are intended to 'Encourage' public entities, prompt compliance and facilitate enforcement." That's the key, prompt compliance. It's the only teeth in IPRA.

*Fabor* [sic – Faber] *vs. King,* this year, stated in the Court of Appeal's judgment that prevailing Plaintiff is entitled to per diem damages from the first day of non-compliance with the records request until the day of proper denial or compliance.

Now, as to the broader motion of sanctions for impropriety, which I also brought up in my motion - I will just cite one case, and that's *United Nuclear Corporation vs. General Atomic,* and that's our New Mexico Supreme Court, 1980, "When a party has displayed a willful, bad faith approach to discovery, it is not only proper, but imperative that severe sanctions be imposed to preserve the integrity of the judicial process and the due process rights of other litigants." The importance of IPRA, you are not doing it for yourself. I didn't join the State to my case, but I could have easily been any citizen in New Mexico, standing before you and trying to exercise my rights. What about the Defendants? This United Nuclear case talks about willful, bad faith. What I have gone through, what this Court has gone through, which is willful withholding, with no statutory basis or facts. It was done by misstated law, false statements, double-talk, and shell games.

I want to give everyone a copy of this, because it's only a fraction of what I am going to refer to. [Chart of the shell games played] ... These are the shell games ... Defendant Virden is the undisputed records, custodian. He produced no records whatsoever. All of the records that I have asked for are generated in his tenure, beginning in 2005. He gave me no proper written denial. IPRA is very specific on exactly how a denial has to be, to be valid. He used no IPRA exception. He ignored this Court's orders. All of his responses were unreasonable, which is a polite word. This Court saw me questioning Defendant Virden on - exactly a year, December 18th of last year, about the turnover file that I had subpoenaed from him under subpoena duces tecum for his September 2008 deposition. After claiming he had no records. He produced 193 pages. Of course, they had no DNA records, but what I pointed out to him, they had a contact list that was passed down from his predecessor, Tom Sullivan, who started the case having all of the necessary information to get me the record within 15 days, a daytime [sic - ?] limit. And IPRA is kind to people receiving requests, and you can ask for a burdensome request, to have extra time, you have to ask in the 15 days; that was never done. They just said that the records couldn't be found, which is not anything to do with IPRA. But what happened, it got worse, three-and-a-half years after my request, three years into this litigation, under pressure from this Court. I would contend that Mr. Virden began to make gestures, which ... were to look like records requests. On October 26 of 2010, he sent one letter to Dr. Lee and, again, I questioned him in this court - to Dr. Lee and to Orchid Cellmark - how does he identify the case with this litigation number, not 2003-274, what did he ask for. He had the list in my request - he had to [sic- the] list in my complaint. He knew what the records were. He asked for floorboard reports, which I didn't request, about Dr. Lee, and any actual reports on blood, which they had fabricated anyway, and I certainly didn't ask for it. Okay. But he said Billy the Kid, so they knew what he was talking about. They second guessed it, and he got answers. And those were submitted to the Court. On November 12, 2010, Dr. Lee said, yeah, I have a report, and Orchid Cellmark said, yeah, we have a report or reports, just get in touch with a client of record, our client, and get them released. So there they were. The reports existed. What did Sheriff Virden do? Nothing. Nothing. That had nothing to do with IPRA at all. That has to do with trying to trick me and this Court. What Sheriff Virden would like us to believe is that a 40-year law man veteran, four-time sheriff, state police department worker, he had no idea how to get his own lost DNA records. DNA is totally common nowadays in solving crimes. They were the only way to solve his crime, he has no idea what to do about it. He said the records didn't exist. IPRA doesn't ask for your opinion, it just says, get the records.

So my co-Plaintiff last year, apparently - I didn't participate in this - decided to create the material fact that the records did exist, so he subpoenaed Orchid Cellmark, and they gave some of the records, but it was a big pile, 133 pages. This Court has them, and the Defendants have them. And it was clear that Orchid Cellmark labeled them dually 2003-274, that's the sheriff's department case, and 44444 as their internal case.

So what did I get, instead; for six years, absurd excuses. "My deputies took the records, and they won't give them back." That's not an IPRA excuse. It's barely an adult excuse. They called IPRA law possession only. The definition of custodian under 14-2-6(a) is only 31-words long. And it says very clearly, as the *Toomey* case established, that the custodian is responsible for the records, regardless of whether there is actual, physical, custody and control. And it's further expanded under public records themselves in Section 14-2-6, as in which public records are defined as records, even if they are held on behalf.

We have just had shell games. They are shell games of switcheroos and changing the words. A very good example is criminal exception. The four years I did IPRAs before this case, all of my records were denied based on using the criminal exception, which is 14-2-1-A-4. We have that preserved in the record, in a request letter that I did for my agent/journalist Jay Miller, a letter to him by Sheriff's Virden, dated November 28th of '05. And that's the letter which he confirms that he deputized Mr. Sederwall and Sullivan to do the Billy the Kid case, 2003-274. He denied me all records based on the criminal exception. Well, why wasn't it used here? Because it admits that they are public records. So they have to concoct the preposterousness of "My deputy took them, and I don't know how to get them."

These people could not possibly be that foolish and conduct themselves in life, certainly not in their jobs. We saw where under questioning by my attorney, Bill Riordan, you saw my past attorney, Martin Threet question - and that was in one of the hearings, that was the hearing on sanctions and past attorneys' fees on January 17th of last year. We had Attorney Threet read the letter that he sent to me on September 12th of 2010. The letter said, "Henry Narvaez" - who is then Virden's attorney and still is, "Henry Narvaez assured me that if you dismiss Sheriff Virden, he will get you the records that you want." IPRA is not about, let's make me deal. IPRA is simply, get me the records. I refuse to do that.

Well, they submitted findings and conclusions to this Court, which in the light of the summary judgment are more for the use of the Court and optional, but they are very good summary - that was April of this past year - of the stand that's being taken by Defendant Virden in purported dispute with me and the Court, apparently. What it is is merely fabricated fact, fabricated into a law, and no case law at all. Possession only is claimed. They preposterously say, why didn't I come to the sheriff's department and look at the records, when there were no records in the Sheriff's Department. IPRA can come and visit and look in our files, in our pocket of the custodian. IPRA is, if we have the records, you can either see them or we'll send you a copy. That's not IPRA law. The findings and conclusions opine about Dr. Lee and Orchid Cellmark's DNA. IPRA isn't about opining. It's not the custodian giving their opinion about the records. It's producing the records. Then they have a very nice example of the shell game, they do a reversal. They say that Virden is not Lee's or Orchid Cellmark's records custodian. He's not. They're his agents, generating and holding, on his behalf the DNA records of case 2003-274. He is a custodian of the records. That's a game. Then oddly, they deny that records exist in that findings and conclusions of when they have, in hand, Dr. Lee's admission that he has it, as well as my co-Plaintiffs, 133 pages that are not even the totality.

What about Defendant Sederwall? This Court has already ordered, but I will go over it again. He's a commissioned deputy for 2003-274. The games that were played around that involved NMSA Section 14-41-9, which had to do with his responsibility. As a deputy, he is authorized to discharge all of the duties that belonged to the Sheriff as if they were executed by the Sheriff himself. Another game that was played, there were shell games there, too, that he wasn't compensated. UJI, 13-401 NMRA states, "An agent is a person who represents the principal with or without compensation." And this Court wasn't taken in by that. But just to emphasize Mr. Sederwall's records responsibility, he is listed as the deputy on all the official documents, the exhumation petition for which all of my Defendants claim standing, based on being law enforcement, and for the Arizona exhumation of John Miller. He even, in the recovery phase before this litigation, admitted to withholding the records from me. That was his memorandum, which is preserved in the record of June 21$^{st}$ of 2007. But how did he justify that? He fabricated, for the first time, from my request - and I knew, because I did all of the IPRA[s] - that he was a hobbyist all along. Well, what about the evidence for it? In six years, they said it over and over again, we don't have a stitch of evidence. Hundreds of pages of my exhibits showing the official capacity ... An important example which shows the game in action was my questioning Defendant Sederwall this past February 4th, in the evidentiary hearing, about the critical element of the records. I'm requesting the carpenter's bench. He admittedly wrote the proximate [sic - probable] cause statement for case 2003-274. So he wrote - and I had him read that, as Lincoln County Deputy Sheriff. He found the carpenter's bench - the Maxwell family, in whose house Billy died, claimed to have it - and Mr. Sederwall contacted their family. It says, "Deputy, carpenter's bench wrote the report, how did he get out of that?" That's one of the records. He said he didn't feel like a deputy in his mind. It is important to remember that, because it's impossible to get these Defendants to fess up.

As to IPRA itself, it gives no leeway. You can recall, as I said earlier, 14-2-5, says, "In responding to an IPRA request, it's a integral part of routine duties of public officers."

It doesn't say, "Just the records custodian." Anyone who is part of the production, holding any relation to the records can became a Defendant, and that's why they are in my case. Poor [deceased] Mr. Sullivan and Defendant Sederwall. This was his job, to keep those records, and turn them over, much as it was Defendant Virden. 14-2-11(b) and its very careful stipulation of how to write a denial letter, which they never did, states, "Each person responsible for the denial has to be listed." I got no such letter. But Mr. Sederwall was certainly responsible. Dramatically even admitted the forging and tampering Dr. Lee's report to remove the case 2003-274 information, as well as the law enforcement title, his being deputy, and Tom Sullivan, who was the Sheriff at the time of the investigation by Dr. Lee removing his Sheriff's title. That was stated in his deposition of June 26th of last year, that was a Court ordered deposition. That's a very important statement and not just in the attempt to trick me and the Court. I was given those forged documents as real, and this Court was given different versions of those documents as real. He started turning them out in 2010, like pulling rabbits out of a hat as this Court pressured. But the important thing beyond tampering with evidence is the willful attempt to trick me and the Court. Those are not random alterations. Those are alterations that support his false contention that he was a hobbyist, and that the carpenter's bench report was not done for the Lincoln County Sheriff's Department. What did he call that? "Massaging," okay. You are not supposed to massage records. You are supposed to give originals or exact duplicates of originals.

As did the findings and conclusions that were also presented this April - they are also a good summary. They are as untruthful about the facts and law as Defendant Virden, but they have the personal lies. They lie he is not a deputy for the workbench, lie that salary abrogates responsibility or lack of it. Claim that the four reports that I got from Dr. Lee constituted meeting an IPRA requirement and for report turnover. I am going to address the fourth report, which is called original in the findings and conclusions. It's not original. Mr. Sederwall, himself, in his deposition on the 26th of June last year, said it was the first report he got from Dr. Lee. It has the law enforcement information on it and the case number on it, but it was unsigned. My attorney, then, Bill Riordan, brought that up in our hearing last year on sanctions, that was the May 31st of 2012 hearing - that it was not an original, it was unsigned, and also it was a reproduction, because the photographs weren't in color. That pressure made them produce yet another version of this - time on CD, which did have the color pictures and the law enforcement, but had no signatures at all. The big picture was, there was no fulfilling of my request. We all know that Dr. Lee not only told Sheriff Virden that he had the records, but he told me, indirectly, in one of my IPRAs, to a journalist, Jay Miller, in a letter of May 1st, 2006, he wrote, "I sent my letter to the Lincoln County Sheriff - my report on the carpenter's bench and the floorboards to the Lincoln County Sheriff's Department." It subsequently disappeared into the ether when I made my request. They lie that the exhumation was private. I had given this Court, as an exhibit, the supplemental report from Lincoln County Sheriff's Department exhumation of John Miller on May 19th, 2005, where the investigator was listed as Deputy of the Lincoln County Deputy Steven Sederwall and he signed the report. "Where did I get it from? I got it from the Prescott Police Department. I was participating with them in the investigation of that as a criminal case, and the deputy assigned to it, Anna Cahall, sent me the copy, which she got from Mr. Sederwall. Because in that phase they were purporting and putting themselves forth as cops and law enforcement. That was before my case. They say that he is not the records custodian, that's true and irrelevant. They say he is not Orchid's clients [sic – client] of record, that's true and irrelevant. The relevant thing that he admitted in his June 26 deposition, he knew who the client was all along. It's Calvin Ostler, who assisted Dr. Lee, and is his partner in doing that forensic business. Calvin Ostler, himself, could just have been called by the Defendant Sederwall at any time, and we wouldn't have had to go through this preposterousness. What about Calvin Ostler himself? There's been a constant attempt to mystify the clients [sic – client] of record. When I was testifying in the evidentiary hearing on January 21st of 2011, you noted that you have a lot of experience with DNA cases, so you would know that a client is merely a formality. The contact person - because many of the law enforcement departments are huge, 20 or 30 people sheriff's department, all of whom needs the records of police departments - and one person for their records takes care of that. It's pro forma. Calvin Ostler had no authority in case

2003-274, other than being the agent and the Sheriff and being part of the chain of custody, because the client mails in the specimens, as well as giving the release. The big picture is, his name should have been given from the start of the 15 days, and I had should have had the reports years ago. They state, oddly, that I have not shown that these are public records, which is just plain perplexing. And one could say they have not shown that they are not public records. They also, oddly, say the records do not exist, and that they are trade secrets, and I think that is a hint to what's going on. This case, in its overall scope, was an attempt to privatize public records, keep them secret and profit from them. And I don't have to make a big jump. This Court has seen Mr. Sederwall's website called thebillythekiddcase.com, in which he was selling, for a $25, membership, in which he would send you records of case of 2003-274. What's the magnitude of that implication? In his deposition on June 26th of last year, that's when the case started, that would be in '03, Billy Sparks, Governor Richardson's spokesperson, said they got 24 million hits. Multiply 24 million times 25.

My past attorney, Ed Threet, used to say to me about the Defendants, if you have the facts, you pound the facts. If you have the law, you pound the law. If you got nothing, you pound the table. I've had to listen to six years of table pounding for unjustified referrals [sic - refusals] and spend my life with this.

I'm now going to talk about the enforcement. This is enforcement for total defiant and willful noncompliance. I met the IPRA request and requirement of a written request. IPRA sets up an award of statutory penalties for wrongful denial of my four records requests, and that's based on the legislature's intent to enforce transparency by setting strict timelines with penalties. There was no safe haven for my Defendants.

I do want to alert the Court to a technical thing, though, and that has to do with Rule NMRA 7.1 My Defendants, when I filed my findings and conclusions, this May, filed no adequate response to it. They filed a joint response brief of June 7th, 2013 ... It does not mention my motion. Instead, oddly, it merely refers me and the Court to their findings and conclusions, which I have already addressed. As if the Court and myself were supposed to make up the argument for them. There is no argument. It's only one page addressing this. And that has very important implications. If you fail to make an adequate response that comes under 7.1(d), which states, "If a party fails to file a response within the prescribed time period, the Court may rule with or without hearing." Though it doesn't bear directly on a District Court, just to see the magnitude of that position, the U.S. District Court of New Mexico in local Rule 7.1(b) provides that failure to file a response in opposition to a motion filed constitutes consent to grant the motion. I contend that this Court is free to make my uncontested award, but I leave that to the Court, and I just want to give the argument on enforcement.

*Faber vs. King,* of this year, in the Court of Appeals, the opinion stated that when IPRA damages are requested, it helps the higher courts and, in fact, it focuses to say what the damages mean, are they compensatory? Are they punitive? What are the damages?

Well, they are statutory damages, and IPRA gives enough information to know what they intend. Section 14-2-(a)(a) calls them penalties. And there's a penalty if the written response ... is not properly answered. An oral request for records doesn't have a penalty. Section 14-2-10 goes over remedies pursued if the custodian does not permit records to be inspected in a reasonable amount of time. 2,415 days and counting is not a reasonable amount of time. 14-2-11 A, B, C made clear the specifics of the denial letter that's required, and it's very serious, because the denial letter is the stand that's being taken by those responsible for the records. It has to be produced in 15 days. It has to have an explanation, and that doesn't mean "My deputies took them." It has to be a compatible IPRA explanation for why the records weren't given. The records have to be listed, and those responsible for the records have to be listed. By the way, in this case, I got no such letter. But more importantly, the Defendants have repeated, over and over, that they have no idea what the records I requested are. When they are arguing the request, at times they call it one record of Dr. Lee. There has never been a statement by the Defendant as to the records. Anyway, non-complying subjects the Defendants to per diem fines of up to $100 per day per records requests. And I'm contending that by "up to," $100 is appropriate in this case.

Section 14-2-12(d) makes clear that this Court has the authority to act in this civil matter of IPRA enforcement stating "The Court shall award damages costs and reasonable attorney fees to any persons whose written request has been denied and is successful in a court action to enforce the provision of the inspection of public records act."

Now, "shall" is an important word. It's mandatory. *Derringer vs. State,* in our Court of Appeals, in 2003, stated, "The Plaintiff is awarded mandatory cost fees and damages. If the Plaintiff is successful in an action, damages are not discretionary, but arise from violating this statute." That's very important. They arise from violating the statute. Damages flow from the statute. You don't have to prove damages. You don't have to prove compensation. This is a penalty for violating the law. What about the damages? They have to be sufficient to achieve IPRA's purpose. They have to be a debtor [sic – deterrent] to stop the commission of IPRA violation. To use old west imagery, I would say my Defendants are now like a horse with a bit in their teeth. They are running wild. Apparently, they feel they will not be touched by any penalty.

As to my attorney's fees under 14-2-12(d), those were settled, all of my past attorneys, on March 26th of this year, in the mediation. My ongoing costs as of today, and those are going to continue if the case continues, they are $19,594.56. The per diem damages - and arguably there's never been anything like this in IPRA law in New Mexico, and there probably won't be again - are calculated based on the 2,415 days since my records request ... But let me call attention of the Court to my records request, through my agent attorney, Mickey Barnett, of April 24 of '07. I had him write in it, "Each category of documents requested above is to be deemed a separate request to inspect the records identified in the category, to the same extent as if separate requests had been delivered instead of a single letter." That's one of the reasons I gave you Judge Campbell's decision letter. The case was so similar. His wording of that was for the Jennifer Baker [sic – Vega] Brown case. The requests were made in a single writing, but were 16 discreet requests. He elaborates on that later, in his decision letter, which is very meticulous in sorting out the issues of noncompliance. He states that "Arguments by the Defendants against the maximum per diem damages appear to shirk responsibility and shift it to the very citizens for whom IPRA's policy of transparency exists." Because after all, that's what this is all about. These are our public servants. What they are doing with the taxpayer money has to be transparent.

I want to address, though, the subpoena records that my co-Plaintiff did. He received them from Orchid Cellmark on April 20, of 2012 of last year, and he got two of the categories - at least what they released to him at that point - addressed two of the categories which were Orchid Cellmark Labs extractions from Dr. Lee's DNA and Orchid Cellmark's DNA extractions from the two exhumed bodies from Arizona. I might as well note here, because there was not a good place to put it. As I mentioned in the findings and conclusion, they said that the exhumation is private. It's listed under case 2003-274 as 4444, under Orchid Cellmark's DNA records. They weren't busy trying to conceal it in 2005. And so Dr. Lee's and the exhumation are all appropriately under the case. Anyway, he got the records. What does that mean in terms of my settlement? And I want to address it, because it's a little bit subtle. First of all, *Derringer vs. State*, in New Mexico Court of Appeals, in '03, stated, "IPRA does not provide for damages pursuant to an action brought after a public body has complied with the act." Well, that's the key issue, my Defendants did not comply. My co-Plaintiff spared [sic – despaired] of IPRA and went outside of it, exactly what IPRA is set up, to spare Defendants. But that doesn't mean it's compliance. It just means that we proved to this Court that they were lying that the records didn't exist. So they are still in noncompliance. What about the fact that I have the records now; does that have any bearing? IPRA is pretty clear on that. There's no burden on a request [sic – requester]. I could have had the records all along and requested them- which I didn't - but I could have. Section 14-2-A C in IPRA states, "No person requesting records shall be required to state the reason for inspecting the records." That was elaborated on in *City of Farmington vs. The Daily Times*, in Court of Appeals, in 2009, in our state, addressing the landmark case of *Newsome vs. Alarid* of 1977. Nowhere in Newsome does the Supreme Court place the burden on the party requesting the documents. Instead, Newsome clearly places the burden upon the custodian to justify why the records sought to be examined should not be furnished. And that's the issue, the records sought to be examined. There was no reason that they shouldn't have been furnished.

That brings my total of $100 a day from the first day of noncompliance to today, per request, to a total of $966,000 ... So we have the cost of $19,594.66, and the per diem damages as $9,666. And those damages would be categorized as *Faber vs. King* requested as statutory civil penalties of per diem damages as mandatory fines for noncompliance.

To finish the IPRA section, though, I want to bring up something that I haven't seen brought up anywhere else, and that's an elephant in IPRA's room. And I think it has a bearing on the Court's evaluating damages in the case as egregious as this one, and that's the disparity of the resources. IPRA's guide says invitingly, "The legislature widely created a large number of private Attorneys General to help enforce the act. It is imperative to enforce their right to inspect records." Well, "imperative" means necessary and obligatory. So what happens if you become a whistleblower and IPRA invitingly offers you? Well, the Plaintiff is not on a taxpayer salary with the Attorney General, just a layman personally and financially overburdened by conducting litigation of this sort. Meanwhile, public official Defendants hiding records can get attorneys paid from an unlimited taxpayer pool forever. There's no ceiling at all. I have been doing parallel IPRAs payments on this case. There's no incentive to stop. Forever. The only incentive is the coercive betterment [sic – deterrent] of the statutory per diem damage penalty to enforce prompt compliance in this case. It's not prompt, but hopefully forces compliance, and otherwise public officials with something to hide will use exhausting stonewalling as a defense tactic, which is exactly what I have gone through and what this Court has been exposed to. My hope is that this Court will now end the accrual of more per diem penalties and more of my costs. I would say that it's time for us all to move forward from this litigation.

As to the non-IPRA sanctions. We had hearings last year on January 17th and May 31st about the forged records. The magnitude of that can't be underestimated. I contend it was willfully done for concealment of evidence directly to this Court. Starting in September 9th of 2010, my attorney Martin Threet brought up the issue of NMRA Rule 11 Contempt for the total defiances of this Court's orders for records turn over. The tampering comes under Rule 37 for discovery abuse of evidence tampering and obstruction of justice as presented to me and this Court as genuine or authentic of records tampering [sic – tampered or] forged to willfully conceal their connection in case 2003-274 and its law enforcement titles. I want to finish with a quotation from the U.S. Court of Appeals in Denver,

Colorado in the case called *Garcia vs. Berkshire Life Insurance Company of America.* It was a 2009 case. And the quote is, "It is hard to imagine that appellant would not have retrieved this information immediately had it consisted of beneficial rather than damaging material." I prepared an order for the Court as a suggestion and which goes over all of these issues. May I give a copy?

THE COURT: Go ahead and present and provide it to counsel ...

(NOTE: Court in recess at 2:31 p.m., and reconvened at 2:40 p.m.)

THE COURT: Okay. You may be seated. Mr. Narvaez ...

MR. NARVAEZ: Your Honor, I represent Lincoln County and the Sheriff of Lincoln County, Rick Virden ... As far as I know, Sheriff Virden is not sued in his individual capacity. So I represent the Sheriff and the County. **[AUTHOR'S NOTE: This is untrue. Virden was sued in individual capacity]** And our legal position is very distinct and apart from the other Defendants Sederwall and Sullivan. That's why we have separate attorneys. Your Honor, the Amended Complaint -- the First Amended Complaint here mentions IPRA requests on April 24, 2007 and May 9, 2007. Those are the IPRA requests at issue before Your Honor as put forth in the Complaint. **[AUTHOR'S NOTE: Untrue. He leaves out multiple requests from April 24 to June 26 of 2007]** Now, I'm glad that Ms. Cooper brought before you the recent case in the Second Judicial District involving Plaintiff Vega Brown and Defendant Bernalillo County, because this case emphasizes my legal position on behalf of Lincoln County and the Sheriff of Lincoln County before you today. If Your Honor will look at page 4 of the opinion, which we received today from the Plaintiff, from Dr. Cooper, I will read the following language from that opinion by Judge Campbell at the bottom of the page, Your Honor, citing the statute. "A custodian who does not deliver or mail a written explanation of denial within 15 days after receipt of a written request for inspection is subject to an action to enforce the provisions of IPRA, and the requestor may be awarded damages. Such damages shall, paragraph 1, be awarded if the failure to provide a timely explanation of denial is determined to be unreasonable. 2, not exceed $100 per day." It doesn't say $100 per day, it says, "not exceed." "3 accrue from the day the public body is in noncompliance until a written denial is issued. And 4, be payable from the funds from the public body." That's at Section 14-2-11.

**[AUTHOR'S NOTE: Narvaez next lies that IPRA law is possession only, and says I should have come to the office to "look for" records. Then he tries to talk down $100 per day penalties.]**

Now here, Your Honor, the IPRA requests of 4-24-07 was timely responded to by the County, by attorney Alan Morel. And the IPRA request of 5/9/07 was likewise timely responded to. His first response was sent on 4/27/07. And the second response was sent on 5/1107. So each response was

682

set within three or four days of the IPRA request. The response is that we don't have the records you are seeking, because they were seeking DNA records which were not in the Sheriff's Office or records of the Sheriff's Office. The response also says -- and Mr. Morel certainly made it clear, "If you want to come and look at anything in the Sheriff's file, you are welcome to do so." So unlike, the case in Bernalillo County, Lincoln County made timely responses with explanations. So there is no legal basis, Your Honor, for granting up to $100 per day. It's not here as a matter of law against Lincoln County or the Sheriff of Lincoln County. Now, the Court -- this Court held a hearing - one of many, at least four or five hearings - in January of 2011, Your Honor held an evidentiary hearing. Following that evidentiary hearing, this Court issued an order finding specifically that Sheriff Virden had turned everything over he had that related to the investigation. Under those circumstances, Your Honor, there is no basis for making any award for damages against Lincoln County or the Sheriff of Lincoln County. And that's all we are here about today, damages and costs, because there is no claim for attorneys' fees here before you today. All of the attorneys' fees have be settled and paid. So when it comes to Lincoln County, this is a very simple case.

**[AUTHOR'S NOTE: Misleading doubletalk follows about the requests, the "deputies took them," or "what were we to do."]**

One of the IPRA requests, which is not included by the way in the First Amended Complaint, was an IPRA request on 4-14-2007. June 14, of 2007. And those IPRA requests were sent to Sullivan and Sederwall. And Alan Morel, sitting here today, testified before Your Honor in regards to that IPRA request or requests that were saying they were identical of June 14, 2007. Alan Morel sent a letter from the Sheriff. The Sheriff and Alan Morel hand delivered the letter to Sullivan and Sederwall that said, "Look, we got this IPRA request. Give us everything in your possession. We want to put it in the Sheriff's Office file, and we want to turn it over, give it to us." And that letter was dated June 21. And on June 22, when they met to the deliver the letter, Sullivan and Sederwall instead turned in their Sheriff's commission cards. What was Lincoln County to do at that point? What does the law require Lincoln County to do? What more could Alan Morel do? ... Could he have tried to issue a subpoena to Sullivan and Sederwall? Is that what IPRA requires? Does IPRA require you to grab the employee who turns in his resignation in effect and say, "Give me those files or I am going to"-- I am going to what? I am going to fire you. They can't fire you. They quit on you. What can you do, Your Honor, I put it to you. I think all you can do is tell them, "You've got to give it to us or else," and then they quit. I don't know that the law requires Lincoln County to do anything further to protect the taxpayers of Lincoln County from this type of lawsuit.

[AUTHOR'S NOTE: Narvaez vilifies me as victimizing taxpayers by my suit. He omits that he and Attorney Brown have already gotten almost $400,000 from taxpayers by prolonging the litigation.]

What more can the officials of Lincoln County do to protect the taxpayers? I cannot think of anything else that can be done. If Your Honor or Plaintiff can think any of something else, I would like to hear it. But I haven't heard it yet. And we had that hearing before you, Your Honor. Alan Morel sat here and said, "As the attorney for Lincoln County, I did all I could do. What more could I do?"

[AUTHOR'S NOTE: Narvaez next misstates the DNA and uses his "only possession" lie of IPRA law for records recovery.]

Now, the information sought in these IPRA requests related to DNA information. Again, it was not in the Sheriff's possession ... The Court asked us to send letters, and we did send letters. We sent letters to Orchid and to Lee. Those were sent on or about October 26, 2010. Orchid Cellmark responded on November 2, 2010 to the Sheriff and said, "We are sorry, but this is confidential information available only to our client, and you are not our client," so they wouldn't give it to us. And Orchid Cellmark and Henry Lee are both out of the state; they are not in New Mexico. Henry Lee, likewise, declined to provide the information. [AUTHOR'S NOTE: A lie] Eventually, this information was obtained after subpoena duces tecums were served on them by attorneys in the lawsuit. [AUTHOR'S NOTE: Misstates the Stinnett subpoena as including Lee] So okay, was Lincoln County required to serve subpoenas upon Orchid Cellmark and Henry Lee, two out-of-state actors, to obtain the requested information which was not in the file of the Sheriff of Lincoln County? I do not believe that would be the legal requirement of the IPRA act, Your Honor, and no one is suggesting that ...

[AUTHOR'S NOTE: Next, Narvaez argues against my costs by ignoring their calculation. He is also trying to omit damages.]

Your Honor. There is no evidence about costs of $19,500 as claimed by the Plaintiff. I am not saying she doesn't have such costs. I am saying, I don't know, there's no such evidence. There certainly is no basis for an award of $100 a day or any award or any penalty or any fine against Lincoln County and the Sheriff. And let me say, there is no basis for awarding such a penalty or fine that the taxpayers of Lincoln County will be forced to bear. Under these circumstances, Your Honor, we would respectfully request that you enter the findings and conclusions which we have submitted and which are in accordance with the evidence submitted in this case and the law of this case, and which are consistent with your finding following the January 2011 hearing that the Sheriff produced everything in his file. Thank you ...

MS. GURULE: Good afternoon, Your Honor. Desiree Gurule, on behalf of Defendant Sederwall ... Your Honor, the joint response to Dr. Cooper's motion filed on May 23rd, 2013, was filed for two reasons in the manner it was. The first reason was, that in regard to this new May 23rd, 2013 motion, there are no new evidence or no new facts or no new proceedings which have occurred before the Court in this very long course of litigation which would merit a new motion or a new finding before the Court in regard to either fact or law, other than what has already been proposed or submitted to the Court pursuant to the order requiring proposed findings of fact and conclusions of law by the State in April this year, which all parties have complied with. There is no argument by    Sederwall that that's not been the case. However, what Mr. Sederwall argues is, that this May 23 motion, and then the later addendum filed 7-1 of 2013, served the purpose of effectively constituting a supplementation, if you will, to Dr. Cooper's purposed findings of fact and conclusions of law, which were initially filed in February ... **[AUTHOR'S NOTE: She tries to negate their error of no response to my motion at hand]**

Mr. Sederwall, with the position stated and now expounded upon by Mr. Narvaez, that in this case the proper custodian of records was the Sheriff's Department and the Sheriff itself. And in this case, as Dr. Cooper admitted just now in her argument, Mr. Sederwall and Mr. Sullivan were not custodians **[AUTHOR'S NOTE: She is misstating my argument by leaving out that I proved their legal records responsibility]**, despite the fact that a records request was submitted to them. And as Your Honor has ruled previously that Mr. Sederwall was acting as an agent of the County at this time, and he was investigating, we would only ask, Your Honor, that the Court consider the time frame of when the incidents occurred, when the actions were allegedly taken in regard to inspection investigation ... **[AUTHOR'S NOTE: The time frame was all records produced in their tenure]** And, again, to consider, Your Honor, that in regard to these four requests made by Dr. Cooper, that the County not only timely responded and replied to each request, but also upon a ruling by the Court, did produce everything that it had. **[AUTHOR'S NOTE: She repeats the "possession only" misstatement]** And, as I believe everyone agrees in this case or in the argument here today, the proper client with regard to the Orchid Cellmark record was not any of the named parties to this litigation and both

**[AUTHOR'S NOTE: This is irrelevant to recovery obligation ]**

**[AUTHOR'S NOTE: Next, records recovery attempts are misstated as having actually occurred]**

Your Honor has been provided with evidence, that both the County Defendants represented by Mr. Narvaez and Defendants represented by our office made attempts to seek those materials from Orchid Cellmark upon the

Court's direction to do so, and were not given any information, other than, "We can't respond to you, because you are not our client." Furthermore, our office made multiple calls to Orchid Cellmark -- and this is also in regard, as well, attempting to seek this information or at least speak with the representative, Dr. Lee, who never returned calls to us. So we got one letter, I believe, was just the basics of it, just saying, "No, you are not our client; we won't give you anything." So even at the point that the Court ordered for all Defendants to try to get these records - and that was done, we didn't go through the subpoena process, but we did follow the Court's order and direction in obtaining the materials to the best that we could do, as our clients were not actually the clients who apparently submitted records requests - excuse me, not records request, but materials and/or requests for analysis or at least a review of those materials which have now been produced to all parties via subpoena by De Baca County News, who is no longer a party as you know ... **[AUTHOR'S NOTE: This is doubletalk]**

So finally, Your Honor, I would just ask that in consideration of the records request as a whole, who the custodians actually were, and the timely responses to each, as well as the later Order of Production by the Court and fulfillment of that production, I would simply ask for the Court to consider the whole scope of each particular request. They are not very broad. Each one requests - needs to meet a type of materials. And I would argue that each of those materials has been provided to the Plaintiff ... **[AUTHOR'S NOTE: A lie. No requested records were provided]** I don't believe there's anything further that could be provided. So to argue that the continuing violation is accruing in an ongoing matter, I just don't believe that's accurate. **[AUTHOR'S NOTE: Doubletalk follows]** I would argue that first off, the potential for a penalty should not even be considered or approved, because the County did timely address the request. Secondly, if the Court finds that that was not the case, and that the penalties might be appropriate, that the penalties only be entered up to the point that compliance occurred. And third, Your Honor, that there is no further compliance to be had, and therefore -- in regards to these requests, and therefore, there should not be an assessment of continuing penalties to any party, and especially not to Mr. Sederwall. As the Court has ruled, he was agent of one entity, and it would not be appropriate - or I don't think the IPRA statute requires or allows for penalties assessed by multiple custodians of records for the same entity. So I would request, Your Honor, that you just consider the proposed findings of fact submitted by all parties and evaluate the actual request and consider whether penalties should be, first of all, assessed at all. And secondly, whether compliance has occurred, and when and by which entities - at the point of compliance, Your Honor. And finally, I would just request that the Court consider Dr. Cooper's motion - not a new motion for any set of costs, but more just as supplementation to her proposed findings of fact and conclusions of law.

[AUTHOR'S NOTE: Next comes obscuration of Sederwall's tampering and forging of the Dr. Henry Lee report.]

I also argue, Your Honor, that there's no basis in this case for Rule 11 sanctions or Rule 37 sanctions. The Court has allowed hearings in that regard and allowed evidentiary ... testimony, and there just has not been any basis shown for such sanctions. Thank you, Your Honor.

THE COURT: Okay. Dr. Cooper.
DR. COOPER: Well, this is the first time I've ever done anything like this, so I have the responses of a layman, not of an attorney. And my overall response to my colleagues here is amazement. As if you repeat the same misinformation and lies, over and over again, it somehow makes them true, which is the overall thing.

IPRA law is tremendously simple. It's made for a layman like me, and I see no evidence that the attorneys or the responsible Defendants ever read it. They seem to be winging it and making it up ... I don't mean to be insulting, but it's absolutely perplexing for a layman to listen to it.

Let me go over the specifics -- actually, let me back up, first. I already went over the findings and conclusions for both of the parties and showed that there was no basis, in fact or law, and - or anything - and then what we have heard is merely a repeating of what was there. And let me just say one other overall thing. My costs and damages certainly are a unique addition. This Court, in Summary Judgment, has granted me the liability which leads to the damages and costs and that's what we are here to decide today. To say that it's part of my findings of fact and conclusions of law is just not to the point.

But let me address the specifics of what Attorney Narvaez said first. We specifically sued Sheriff Virden, in his individual capacity - Lincoln County, after the first Complaint on March 15th of '07 [sic – October 15, 2007] Mickey Barnett should be removed, and that's why we submitted the Amended Complaint on November 1st. My Defendants were sued in an individual capacity as a public official. And that was Attorney Barnett's decision, so it's not quite clear to me what Attorney Narvaez was arguing for Lincoln County [as a defendant].

As to the series of arguments that followed on the *Vega Brown* case that were used by both Attorney Narvaez and Attorney Gurule, I am not just contending damages under 14-2-11 A-C. I'm contending that for the point of enforcement, IPRA is very clear that it's 14-2-12(d), where damages are inclusive of, first, improper denial by a letter - an improper denial letter, then improper denial itself. That doesn't make the damages double up. It just reinforces that Plaintiff can get enforcement under either impropriety or both, which is what the *Faber vs. King* case argued. So the improper denial letter is irrelevant. The important thing though is, is it relevant in the final 14-2-12? But in my case, it's perfect; it's both. They kept on writing back with various excuses to Attorney Barnett's office, but they never produced a letter of denial. That is in the record, the total back and forth from April 24th of '07 to June 26 of '07. There's no denial letter. It's just, "The deputies took them. The deputies resigned. The deputies say they have them, but they're trade secret." It's just a bunch of stuff that has nothing to do with IPRA, but has to do with a whole purpose of this case, the hopes that I will just go away, and they can get away with what they have been doing for ten years, which is riding roughshod over the law, over the Sheriff's Department, over their own taxpayers. And it's not just me and these attorneys accruing taxpayer bills, before that, that Sheriff's Department was in Grant County, De Baca County, constantly using taxpayers resources. I'm saying they have to pay the piper finally. They can't talk their way out of it.

And in 14-2-12, as Attorney Narvaez said, is not irrelevant, it's key to settling this case. They are in total violation. They mentioned, as they did in surprising disingenuousness in their findings and conclusions, that I didn't come to the office and look for the records. That's not IPRA. That's not reasonable. This is not law that has me searching through offices in Lincoln County. They are supposed to give me the records. Either give me the records to look at them or give me the records if I want to pay for copies. That never occurred. And timely must be real. Something has to be done. And IPRA is, again, a very simple law. You have 15 days. You have 15 days to give the records, 15 days to write that very specific denial, which has the explanation, which means, IPRA give[s] me an exception. No exception was given. Give me the records listed; that was not done. Give me the people who are responsible; that was not done. IPRA says, if you haven't done it in 15 days, you are in improper records denial.

IPRA gives only one way out, ask for a burdensome amount, extra amount of time within that 15 days. There's no such letter in my pack of responses. That was never asked for. 15 days was the time limit, nothing happened. But it doesn't matter, because nothing has happened since now.

I'm just dismayed when both of the attorneys are talking as if anything was fulfilled in terms of giving records. Again, it's astounding to me, as a layman it is repeated over, and over as Attorney Narvaez and as Attorney Nicole Werkmeister, who came to this Court before, repeated he has nothing else in his pocket, Judge. What is he going to do if it's not in his pocket? That's not IPRA, that's trying to fool this Court. It doesn't matter what's in his pocket. I don't want to hear if it's hard for him. He doesn't know what to do. Sheriff Virden even asked Attorney Threet if he'd get them the address for Attorney Lee. **These people are fooling around - fooling around with my life, fooling around with the Court, and fooling around with their own taxpayers, and thinking they can get away with it. This is what it looks like when corruption is out of control, people feel untouchable. And for a Plaintiff, for someone who's exposing it like me, there's nowhere to turn. The only thing that's available to stop these wildly out**

**of control Defendants is a penalty that won't be forgotten in Lincoln County**. [author's boldface]

**Again, you got to hear, "My deputies took them and didn't give them back." The switcharoos and shell games. What was he going to do? The deputies said, "Well, what was he going to do in 15 days?" It was totally simple, write a letter to Orchid Cellmark, write a letter to Dr. Lee, give Dr. Cooper the records. It's that simple. This is an attempt at obfuscation to turn a totally simple case characterized by absolutely inconceivable arrogance of Defendants, and a sense of immunity to a law that is totally simple.** [author's boldface]

As Attorney Narvaez has said now for a few years, I have got to listen to him, "What more could the Sheriff do?" Well, you could start by reading IPRA law, and it tells you exactly what to do: you have to get the records. Read *Toomey vs. Truth or Consequences*. It's more available to them than me. They have more access to online things than I do. Read it. It says you have to get them if they are held on behalf -- it doesn't want to listen to you whining about subpoenas, and it's hard, and how do I get the address. It's irrelevant. DNA is not in the Sheriff's possession. It's not in his pockets. He doesn't carry around DNA. Thanks, I thought I [sic – he] did. Come on. **We're grownups here. I'm just a layman. This is silly. Somebody's got to do the Emperor's new clothes. They are naked -naked, violating the law.** [author's boldface] Does it mean that we have to send letters? Of course it means you have to send letters. That's what IPRA says. Get them however you can. If they are in your possession, you get them. Okay.

What about your order where you said you believe they are not in the Sheriff's possession, right, so you have to get them. That's all that it means. You establish, as a material fact, that you believe that it's not in his office. They want me to come and look around, but you believe, and I believe it was in his office. I personally believe they expurgated the file, because I know all of the records that were in the file, since I did the litigation against them in Grant County and De Baca County, and there are a lot of records missing, not just the DNA records. But whatever you said that, okay, they are not. That means he has to get them. Like I said only 31 words, half of them say the records that are in his possession. The other half says he has to get them if they are held on behalf of him, as Dr. Lee did.

I am amazed at the audacity of the defense, though, because we even have the letters from Dr. Lee and from Orchid saying, we got them, and we will give them to you, and then the Sheriff does nothing. What did the Sheriff say in his deposition? Attorney Morel is here. The Sheriff, in his deposition. On June 27th of last year, said, "Attorney Morel told me not to do anything else. Attorney Morel told me to stop." Why? **Attorney Morel is part of this. I might as well say the truth. Attorney Morel covered up all of the records for four years by using criminal exception, and now he is playing different games. It's all games. Lincoln County got caught with**

**their pants down by permitting this hold** [sic – hoax] **to be conducted through the Sheriff's Department, on taxpayer money, now it's time to pay the piper for having done that**. [author's boldface] And the last outpost that they are holding onto is these records.

As to adopting his findings and conclusions of his client - this is still Attorney Narvaez - they are diametrically opposed to your own orders, and they also make absolutely no sense, in terms of law or truth or fact. As to my costs, which was perplexing to me, which made me think they don't even read not only the law, but my motions, that he doesn't know how my costs were calculated. I don't know what to say. It's spelled out in my request for costs and damages. And I ... deserve to be paid. I have been burdened for all of these years, financially.

And there's an attempt to plea for the taxpayers that Attorney Narvaez did. They had six years to think about the taxpayers if they were concerned about liability. Not a cent. Maybe postage had to be paid on this case within the first 15 days.

Mr. Sederwall has brought up - and it's always been perplexing to me - even though everybody is saying he is a hobbyist and not responsible, a fortune has gone out to paying his legal bills. The only thing I can say, the Tourism Department should be promoting hobbyists, as this is the ideal state, because you will get all of your legal fees paid. Mr. Sederwall has clearly been this treated by this Court and everyone else as a public official who is just blowing smoke. Then Attorney Narvaez has all of the materials have been presented to him. Not a stitch has been presented to me. I have no idea if this is supposed to be convincing to you ... This makes no sense to me as a layman ...

I have not gotten the requested records, and IPRA says up to an appropriate denial or compliance, that's the only thing that stops the clicking of the ticking of clock. It's a question of what should we do? What should we do? [the defense claims] Do we go against the deputies? It's not my problem. It's not my burden. It's their problem. That's a spurious attempt to mislead the Court, because if Mr. Sederwall absconded with poor deceased Tom Sullivan, with all of the records from their file - or in fact never even put them in the record - in the file and kept them at home, which some deputies can do, all the Sheriff had to do was get on the phone with Orchid Cellmark. Rick Stout [sic – Staub] was directly involved in this case. He was at the exhumation in Arizona to pick up the bones. Call him, "Hey, Rick. I'm in this legal case, I found out that I lost my records, please send me another copy. Oh, the cop [sic – case] client. Tell me who is the client, and I will contact Calvin Ostler." This is not a complicated thing. Now, the thought that my costs and damages should be considered as findings and conclusions seems very silly to me. Liability was decided. We have just been waiting, as we went through the revelation that they were also turning out manufacturing records like hot cakes with Dr. Lee, who had just been waiting after the liabilities for all of the costs and damages. So here it is today. It is not findings and conclusions. This is the time to pay the piper.

Okay. As to Attorney Brown's law firm for Mr. Sederwall. Now, I felt that this extensive verbiage on the Joint Response essentially said nothing. They did not respond to my costs and damages. They didn't even respond arguing their own findings. They simply referred us to look at them. Are we supposed to make it up? It isn't even relevant. They have to respond. They didn't. I win automatically by Rule 7.1(d)NMRA.

Again, Sederwall isn't a custodian, but he's still responsible. Nobody has stopped him. They were not trade secrets. He had to turn them over. This is the game. If you want to measure the arrogance of these Defendants - beside my having to listen to this for six years, I did - Mr. Sederwall, in the midst of this litigation, took out a website to sell these documents. These people are out of control.

Then the representative for Mr. Sederwall said some kind of double-talk about time frames and when materials were produced. No materials were produced. The time frame never happened. No deadline was met. That, again, Mr. Sederwall ... made his own sham records request on February 5th of 2011,again prodded by you. And this Court shouldn't lose sight of the fact they had to prod for years before they did anything - anything at all. 2010 is when the forged records started being produced. What did Mr. Sederwall do? He wrote a - he knew the client, but he left that out - and he just wrote some kind of general letter to Rick Stout [sic – Staub], and never gave me any copies of either that side or any response at all. So I have no idea what they are talking about, but it doesn't matter. It doesn't say that a records requester has to know every single step that was taken to get the records. I just want the records as I am entitled to under law.

And as to Mr. Sederwall and the records, he clearly had a direct line to Dr. Lee. All he had to do is call him, say, "Okay, I have the CD. They need the original. This is just the copy that I was using as a template for a business, a Dr. Lee report business, but give me an original so they will go away and liability will not continue to accrue."

They can say from today until tomorrow that they don't want my costs to accrue and they don't want their liability to accrue, but it does. It's daily, per diem. And why $100? Of course, it's up to $100. It can't be worse than my Defendants ... That's why IPRA has a maximum. In fact, there's a argument that by not defining damages under 14-2-12(d), they can conceivably more than $100 - not less, but more. They said that my costs and damages are no new facts. I'm not arguing the case. It's very clear this is noncompliance. I'm presenting the way of ending the case and stopping the accrual of the damages. I have not heard any argument that has to do with IPRA made by my Defendants - in fact, ever, but today. And I feel that I have argued correctly my costs and damages. And if it's my unfortunate fate to continue arguing this in higher courts, I will, and the damages will continue to accrue. My hope is that we can finish today.

MR. NARVAEZ: May I respond briefly on behalf of both defense attorneys?

THE COURT: She has last say though. Go ahead.

MR. NARVAEZ: **[AUTHOR'S NOTE: Narvaez continues his misinformation campaign]** I will be brief, Your Honor. 14-2-7 sets fourth the designation of custodian and duties. "Each public body shall designate at least one custodian of public records who shall, A, receive and respond to requests to inspect public records. B, provide proper and reasonable opportunities to inspect public records. C, provide reasonable facilities to make or furnish copies of the public records during usual business hours." So on a couple of points here. Lincoln County appointed the Sheriff to be the records custodian. And Dr. Cooper candidly admitted to you and made that statement that Sederwall and Sullivan were not records custodians, and they are not ... So the Sheriff is the custodian, and he must either, under B, provide proper - he either has to provide copies or under B provide proper and reasonable opportunities to inspect the public records ... There is no claim that the responses were untimely ... Now, the Court further has found that the Sheriff provided everything in his possession relating to the investigation ...

I believe the Court is bothered by the fact that Sederwall accumulated documents, decided they were his as a hobby and didn't turn them over. That bothered the County also. So that the request – the IPRA request that came in, in June of 2007, triggered the letter to Sederwall and Sullivan saying, "Give us these documents. We will stick them in the file and turn them over." They resigned. **[AUTHOR'S NOTE: Doubletalk misinformation follows]** I believe that those requests are the only ones that were directed to Sederwall and Sullivan. A, they are not custodians. B, that IPRA request in June 2007 is not before the Court in this lawsuit.

**[AUTHOR'S NOTE: Next, Narvaez tries damage control by telling the judge what to think - believing he can get away with it ]**

Judge, I think where we are at, when you are looking at potential damages here under 14-2-11, when the claim is that there was not a timely response, the statute specifically mentions up to $100 to be awarded - that's when there is not a timely response ... That is not the case that we are here on today. There was a timely response. That's what we urge you to consider.

**[AUTHOR'S NOTE: Next comes misstating the law by misstating the word "reasonable" to argue against maximal penalties]**

Looking at 14-2-12, enforcement, I believe, and I would urge the Court to consider that 14-2-12 would be the statute that you should consider here today, and that is where the Court shall award damages, costs, and reasonable attorney fees to any person whose written request has been denied. We responded. We said, "We don't have the materials. You can come in and look at the file." If you feel that for any reason the request by Dr. Cooper was denied, we think that 14-2-12 would be the section that the legislature intended for you to consider. Now, it doesn't say, "up to $100 per day ... **[AUTHOR'S NOTE: A lie. It does say that]**. You can consider anything you want, but I think it's significant that this one is not mandatory like Section 11 is **[AUTHOR'S NOTE: A lie – 14-2-12 is mandatory.]**, and this one doesn't mention any number. I think, as an attorney, you ought to try to read the sections consistently, and reading them consistently, in my mind, I believe that Section 11 was intended to apply to a situation where there is no reply, where the request is just ignored. I believe Section 12 is intended to apply to enforcement, the situations where there is a denial that is unreasonable. And I believe under those circumstances the legislature intended for the Courts to look at damages, costs, and reasonable attorney fees.

The attorney fees have been paid. **[AUTHOR'S NOTE: Here comes the switcheroo with the word "reasonable," lifted from "reasonable attorney's fees"]** I think the Court should consider what are reasonable damages and costs. Dr. Cooper says they are 19,590 **[AUTHOR'S NOTE: A breathtaking lie – trying to leave out $966,000]**. The Court may consider that request, and the Court might even consider, if it decided to use, some of the Doctor's other figures. She said $966,000 based upon $100 a day. The Court could decide to use that and apply a figure, for example, of $1 a day and make that $9,660. **[AUTHOR'S NOTE: Backtracking to try to mislead the judge into minimizing damage penalty – but observe that no argument is given for reduction from maximum]** I think the Court has some discretion here, but I think the Court should determine, first, that the denial was unreasonable. I think the Court would be hard pressed to make that determination, if the Court had determined that the Sheriff did everything that he could to produce what he had, to invite Dr. Cooper to come in and inspect the records, as is provided for in IPRA. **[AUTHOR'S NOTE: Next, Narvaez becomes condescending, making transparent his assumption that the judge is an idiot or complicit]** I think that in light of the fact that it's now the law of the case that Sederwall and Sullivan are not records custodians, I think that it would be incumbent on the Court to proceed under Section 12 alone.

And I think, Judge, that on behalf of the Defendants, we would ask you to do the following for all of our benefits. We would ask you to enter findings and conclusions and not make any ruling upon the motion that's before you today by Dr. Cooper, but to first consider a requested findings and conclusions and enter the Court's findings and conclusions, and then make any award, if any, based upon those findings and conclusions.

**[AUTHOR'S NOTE: Narvaez gives the judge a way out by urging ignoring of my hearing's arguments for costs and damages]**

We think that would to be to all our benefit, including the Court of Appeals in Santa Fe.

**[AUTHOR'S NOTE: Narvaez adds this threat – while gleefully counting additional thousands of dollars from an appeal!]**

Thank you.

THE COURT: Dr. Cooper.

DR. COOPER: Before I address directly what Attorney Narvaez said, I want to point out on findings and conclusions. Under NMRA Rule 52(a), they are unnecessary in this case. They are unnecessary in decisions on motions under Rule 56 Summary Judgment. This Court has already decided what facts are material to the genuine issue at hand. In fact, this Court decided several times on March 12th you decided - 2010 - and on September 28th of 2011 you decided that these records were public and had to be turned over, and the nature of the records. That has not been complied with, but the findings and conclusions were optional all along, and this Court's orders constitute findings and conclusions. Those were the relative – the necessary material fact for this Court making its decision on my behalf and granting me liability.

Attorney Narvaez is now to address that seems again to still be repeating optimistically misinformation. 14-2-7, which designates custodian responsibilities, merely says that, "It's a responsibility of a public body to make available public records for inspection." If you asked for specific public records, those are the records that have to be given to you or there has to be an IPRA compatible denial of those records. I was not given any. I was not offered the opportunity to see the actual records. Though for some strange reason Attorney Narvaez makes it seem as if that trip to Lincoln County to search out the Sheriff's Office would have been worth it for me, because maybe in some nook and cranny, the Sheriff had ordered the records. It's silly. The opportunity to inspect just means inspect the records that were requested.

I do want to read, though, because there's a misusing of the law for 14-2-11, Procedure for denied requests. This has not been met, no matter how many times Attorney Morel or Attorney Narvaez would like to say that it was. In fact, on February 4th of this year, I questioned Attorney Morel. I gave him the packet of back and forth with the Barnett Law Firm and himself to have him try and find that so-called denial letter. It isn't there.

Under 14-2-11(a), it says, "Unless a written request has been determined to be excessively burdensome or broad, that means exceeding the 15 days, a written request for inspection of public records that has not been permitted within 15 days of receipt by the office of the custodian may be deemed denied. The person requesting the public records may pursue the remedy provided in IPRA."

Well, it's not just a general, I don't have the records, tough luck, in 15 days. Obviously what the Defendants are talking about is an attempt to find loopholes that the legislators who wrote this law were well aware. The purpose of this law is not to let potentially dishonest public officials have evasions. "It's not in my possession." Or "My secretary has it at home." "The dog ate it." You are not allowed, under IPRA, to make excuses. So the denial is a legal document showing your due diligence in the terms of the request. B, "If a written request has been denied, the custodian shall provide the requester with a written explanation of the denial." Nowhere is that in any letter, and you can't even construe it from the multiple back and forths from April until June of '07. There is no IPRA denial justification in writing or anywhere else even made, to this very moment, in this courtroom ... IPRA is not difficult. It means an exception. There are only eight exceptions under 14-2-1(a), eight exceptions. They meet none of them, and they use none of them. "The written denial shall" - shall is a mandatory word in law - "shall, A, describe the records sought." That's after the written explanation. That's not in any document re-typing [sic - ?] the records sought. That's why they try to get away from misstating the records for these six years. "Two, set forth the names and titles or positions of each person responsible for the denial." And that doesn't mean, "my deputies took them." And "Three, delivered or mailed to the person requesting." "C" - and this is the particular damage on that - "a custodian who does have to deliver or mail a written explanation of denial within 15 days after receipt of a written request for inspection is subject to action to enforce the provisions of the Inspection of Public Records Act, and the requester may be awarded damages. Damages shall" - that's mandatory - "1, be awarded if the failure to be provide[d] a timely explanation of denial is determined to be unreasonable." That's the second closing of the gate of loopholes for dishonest record holders with something to hide. It can't be unreasonable. "My deputies took them. I don't know how to contact the forensic lab." "I'm 40 years in the business, but I just don't know. I'm not too swift." They don't ask for that. "2, Not to exceed $100 per day." There's a reason it goes from little to big. Violations go from little to big, and you can't get bigger than this. "3, Accrue from the day the public body is in noncompliance until a written denial is issued." They still haven't done it, because there's nothing to say ...

But Attorney Narvaez, to get back to him, is trying to blur that to minimize 14-2-12, which is the punch line that IPRA has been building up to. 14-2-8 says, they are a penalty. 14-2-11 says, even if you write an improper letter of denial, you are in trouble with per diem damages. And 14-2-12 is paying the piper. Under "D, if your written request has been denied, the Court shall award damages." And Attorney Narvaez oddly - and I just don't know what to make of it when the Defendants make up things - he said, "It's not mandatory." I read it right here. He said that in *Derringer vs. State of New Mexico* in the New Mexico Court of Appeals, 2013, that the "shall" - the Court "shall award damages is mandatory." ... [A]nd that was decided by our Court of Appeals. If we want to go back there, they will decide it again. "The Plaintiff is awarded mandatory costs, fees, and damages if the Plaintiff is successful in action." Damages are not discretionary and arise from violating the statute. That's scary. It's intended to be scary. Per diem is scary.

Now, for big - like Water Safety Act - those kind of penalties are $10,000 a day. These kind of civil penalties are intended to coerce the violator to stop violating. In *Spear vs. McDermott*, the Court of Appeals here in 1996, "Coercive measures are to stop a violator from violating the law." I don't think my Defendants like that. They are squirming now. This is the payday.

What about my costs? I have no idea why Attorney Narvaez chose to quibble about my costs that are listed, other than being vindictive or punishing, but my costs are established. They are straightforward. They come to me for having done this litigation. What they really don't want to talk about is $966,000 and counting, up tomorrow $400 more. They are mandatory. He tries and I guess when you do the best you can, to apply "reasonable" - which is only put in IPRA connected to the attorney fees, because they don't want the attorneys to run wild either. **By the way, I've been supporting, it feels like, two law firms for six years talking about attorneys fees** [author's boldface] – but anyway. "The Court shall award damages, costs and reasonable attorneys' fees." It doesn't say "reasonable costs" or "reasonable damages." They have already established that it's per diem, and they are assuming that that will encourage prompt compliance. They never thought of Defendants like mine, who just thumb their noses at Courts and law and me.

He tells you to try a dollar a day. Maybe we will try ten cents a day. Are we trying to make a deal now with IPRA? Trying to get off the hook. And then he says that we should just forget about my costs and damages and just enter findings and conclusions. They are not necessary. This Court has decided. Liability has been decided for me in sum of the [sic – summary] judgment. It's been repeated. I should now get the recompense that the law has established.

THE COURT: I'm not going to give you a decision. I think I have an idea where I am going. But I do need to enter findings and conclusions. **[AUTHOR'S NOTE: Ominously, the judge seems to be taking the**

**direction which Narvaez dictated. Is he discounting my hearing arguments?]** You have already submitted them before, Dr. Cooper.

You know what I need for you folks to do is re-summit them to me. Once findings and conclusions get filed, I cannot alter them. It's easier for me, if I just have yours. I put them in the file, and I can work with them ... I want the same ones that I had before.

MR. NARVAEZ: I was going to ask that very question, in light of today's hearing, if we could make a couple of slight additions for addendums. **[AUTHOR'S NOTE: Narvaez's slyly tries to change his past document]** THE COURT: No. And when I give my decision, I will also incorporate what I did today. But I need the findings and conclusions. Dr. Cooper, I'm going to just make one ruling today, that any award - if I give you any award, will be – at the most, will be through today. Let me tell you the reason why. I may not get to the final decision for 90 days or so. It's no fault of any, but mine. I will give you a decision, so I don't want to - assuming I was to award per diem, as you are requesting, all right, it would not be the Defendants doing that, I didn't get to them for 90 days, so it will go as far as today, just so you know that.

DR. COOPER: May I respond to that?
THE COURT: Sure.
DR. COOPER: Any decision is obviously yours, but my response for the record would be an objection, because it goes against the statutory requirements for per diem, and it merely requires a proper measure of denial or compliance. You can decide. Obviously, I'm not the one to say, but I, for the record, want to say that the violation, nonetheless, continues, but - so that's my own clarification. In other words, I feel like I would be accepting something that wasn't my own argument, but it's the Court's discretion to cut off.
THE COURT: You made your record.
DR. COOPER: Thank you ... If I can say one other thing.
THE COURT: Sure.
DR. COOPER: I included new findings and conclusions in my proposed order. **[AUTHOR'S NOTE: They included my hearing arguments]**
THE COURT: I saw the order. But I'm working off the proposed findings and conclusions. **[AUTHOR'S NOTE: Those were about 9 months old. Is he ignoring me?]** You folks have a Merry Christmas and Happy Holidays. I appreciate the civility in this case. It's been going on for a long time, but it's been civil. Mr. Narvaez, he has been doing this for a long time. **[AUTHOR'S NOTE: Is this a crony nod to Narvaez?]** He's been in some dogfights where they walk in the door and can't even talk to each other. At least you are civil to each other. You have your issues, but it's not personal.
(NOTE: Court in recess at 3:50 p.m

# WAITING GAME

After my hearing, when I told a New Mexican retired sheriff that the defendants had to pay about a million dollars in penalties, he repeated what Silver City's County Commission Chairman Steve May had said years before: "They'll kill you first."

By then, I was at last immune to that fear. I accepted and understood what I had written for my *Billy and Paulita* novel for December 15, 1880 (seven days before the Stinking Springs capture of Billy and Pat Garrett's slaying of Charlie Bowdre). I have Billy say to Charlie Bowdre that death is "your final weapon. Once you're willing to die, nothing can stop you."

But there were more practical matters like digging out my house from its archeology of paper layered all over, going down to 2003, and needing to be filed.

And I decided that Judge George Eichwald must be unhappy. In *Billy and Paulita*, I have older and wiser John Tunstall employee, Fred Waite, tell Billy: "Lincoln County is a moral proving ground. Evil here's so powerful it breaks people where they're weakest." Would Eichwald break? He had given himself three months to rule, though legally he had only 60 days. My hope was that he wanted extra time to study my long case.

But when I told a Lincoln County old-timer about Eichwald's delay, he said, "Check if he's up for re-election in 2014. He's probably just stalling till after it." So I looked up Thirteenth District Court of Sandoval County Judge George P. Eichwald on the internet.

## *JUDGE GEORGE P. EICHWALD*

When contemplating New Mexico corruption, it is best to brace for the worst, then hope for something better.

Indeed, according to "Judgepedia," George P. Eichwald was up for "retention" - meaning being kept on as a district judge. From 1989 to 2004, he had been in private law practice. On August 8, 2004 he was appointed as a district judge, being elected as such by the people on November 2, 2004. He was retained in 2008. His term expired in 2014.

"Judgepedia" stated that Eichwald's undergraduate and law degrees were from the University of New Mexico - that hotbed of provincialism and cronyism which also harbored "official" hoax historian Professor Paul Hutton in its history department; and had a Richardson-appointed President named David Harris, who had tried to coerce New Mexico's Office of the Medical Investigator into rubber-stamping the hoax's Billy/mother exhumations.

A site called "New Mexico Judicial Performance Evaluation Commission (JPEC)" had a 2008 evaluation for George Eichwald:

> Judge Eichwald received high scores from both attorneys and court staff in each area of the evaluation. Among attorneys, he received high scores for being courteous to all participants, for having a dignified demeanor, and for avoiding arrogance. Among court staff, Judge Eichwald's scores are among the highest in the district. Some of the resource staff (e.g. law enforcement and probation officers) gave the judge somewhat lower scores in displaying a basic sense of fairness and treating all participants equally. Judge Eichwald indicated a willingness to improve in these areas.

So Eichwald was "courteous." What about his "lower scores" for "fairness?" Did he favor public officials?

According to my own sources, George Eichwald's origin was from a poor, antique, New Mexico town called Cuba, where a Mexican population had mingled with German settlers. He now lived in Corrales, a rich suburb of Albuquerque. Could he be influenced by Santa Fe Ring politics of favor?

Certainly, Eichwald would be morally tested. Everyone else in my litigation had folded. I could not guess as to his ruling.

But after recovering from my hearing ordeal, I began training on my home gym like a career athlete. Fighting the Billy the Kid Case might end up being an endurance ultramarathon. As one Lincoln County contact said to me: "They'll keep this going till you die." (Translation: "The defense lawyers will pocket a million dollars themselves, rather let you have a penny.")

# GUESS WHAT THE JUDGE DID

As Eichwald's 90 day's March 18, 2014 approached for the ruling, I called a lawyer to ask about him. He said he detested Eichwald as making decisions ignoring laws and protecting public officials. Because before litigation begins an attorney can remove a district court judge without cause, this lawyer said he had a list of judges he automatically removed. Eichwald was number one.

Tuesday, March 18, 2014 passed. Weeks passed. George P. Eichwald made his choice: HE DID NOT RULE AT ALL!

I took stock with new calm of my Chelon Point dream's reminder of destiny's current. So I called an Hispanic Corrales resident who knew Eichwald. I said he seemed nice. She sneered, "Niceness is just George's front. He's a boss, a "majordomo" - like in the old-style Mexican patronage system. Soft-spoken is their façade. Behind the scenes, George rules with an iron fist. He'll never let you win." She added: "This is where I'd give up. They'll just keep beating your head against the wall."

I answered, "I'd say I've beaten *their* heads against the wall. I'm stopping their hoax."

When this woman - whom I barely knew - sent me reading references on the Hispanic patronage system, to my surprise she signed her e-mail: "Love." It was like water in the desert.

# WALKING THE WALK

Convinced, by then, that regulatory agencies were just mutual protection societies, I was still willing to walk the walk of confronting corruption. I called the New Mexico Judicial Standards Committee. A clerk answered. I asked, "How long does your complaint process take?" She said, with a slip of honesty, "It takes a few months for your claim *to be denied.*" Outcome was a foregone conclusion! And their complaint process was as much work as an actual Court of Appeals case.

But the first step to inducing a ruling was getting intervention of Eichwald's District Court Chief Judge: Louis McDonald. On March 26, 2014, I wrote to McDonald, citing state Rule 1.054.1, giving 60 days for ruling. But when I checked with McDonald's office, his assistant said he refused to take action. And he refused to put that in writing.

So on April 2nd, I wrote to McDonald quoting New Mexico's Code of Judicial Conduct's Rule 21-212 that his supervisory duties were intended to keep "public confidence in the judicial system."

On April 4th, District Court Staff Attorney Jennifer Romero replied for McDonald, saying that Eichwald was too busy with other cases (translation: "Shut up, Peon. The law doesn't apply to you.") Ignoring that ploy, I wrote back to McDonald that the 60 day law was to help a busy judge like Eichwald "to prioritize." And if I did not get a ruling, I would have to go to "higher courts." But I knew that they were all stonewalling me.

"Higher courts" meant first requesting a Writ of Mandamus from the state Supreme Court, asking for its over-riding power (called "superintending control") to make Eichwald rule. If that state Supreme Court refused, the next step was the U.S. Supreme Court. I had a constitutional right of "due process" to get a ruling.

A Lincoln County resident had once told me that Lincoln County Attorney Alan Morel had told his County Commissioners: "She [me] can't be allowed to win. It would set an example."

This attitude could be a disaster ... for the adversaries I had been fighting for over a decade! With Santa Fe Ring's arrogance of power going back to the days of Billy the Kid, the corrupt public officials had turned their hoax that Pat Garrett did not kill the Kid into my million dollar litigation whose judge finally did the unthinkable - possibly propelling their Billy the Kid Case to the U.S. Supreme Court. The hoaxers and their cronies were creating a scandal big enough to break their own Santa Fe Ring. I just needed to record their Lincoln County War rerun. This time around, the good guys might win.

On May 12, 2014, I mailed my 11 page "Writ of Mandamus or Superintending Control" with multiple exhibits. Copies went to Judges Eichwald and McDonald; the defense attorneys; and, as required, to Attorney General Gary King. As Attorney General, King was IPRA's designated protector. This being New Mexico, corrupt King was instead currently attempting to destroy IPRA in an appeals court case of his own, made because he had been found guilty in a district court of concealing his *own public records*! That case was *Faber v. King*. It was about to loom large in my life.

# AT THE FINISH LINE

### THE SHOCKING RULING

My Writ of Mandamus proved to be magic. Right after Judge Eichwald got his copy of it from me, he ruled. His filing date of May 15, 2014 is the day I won the Lincoln County War - if winning means moral victory.

Titled "Findings of Fact and Conclusions of Law and Order of the Court," it was a Jekyll and Hyde ruling of 10 pages. (APPENDIX: 67) Since I was still as phobic as on the June 5, 2003 day I read the *New York Times* article announcing the Billy the Kid Case hoax, I circled its big brown envelope for a day before reading, afraid of enduring more outrages. But its first 8 pages, listing "Facts" and "Law" were great: total condemnation of my defendants and complete confirmation of all my accusations.

Eichwald's "Facts" confirmed that the Billy the Kid Case was murder investigation No. 2003-274 done by the Lincoln County Sheriff's Department against Pat Garrett as a killer of an innocent victim; with sub-investigation of Billy the Kid's double homicide of Deputies Bell and Olinger. That "Garrett murder" was to be solved by DNA matchings. Exhumations of the Kid and his mother had been legally blocked, so had yielded no DNA. Eichwald then correctly listed my requested DNA records as: 1) Dr. Lee's carpenter's bench specimen recoveries for DNA; 2) Orchid Cellmark's DNA extractions from Lee's specimens; 3) Orchid Cellmark's DNA extractions from exhumed John Miller and William Hudspeth; and 4) Orchid Cellmark matchings of bench DNA to the DNA of the two exhumed men.

Eichwald verified that Virden and Sederwall (dead Sullivan having been dismissed) had done the case as public officials; and had refused to turn over the requested DNA records from April 24, 2007 to June 26, 2007, while admitting possession by Deputies Sullivan and Sederwall, but claiming 'trade secrets" of a private hobby; and with Virden not trying any recovery by himself.

Confirming that my enforcement litigation started on October 15, 2007, Eichwald continued incriminations. In their August 18, 2008 depositions, he stated, Sederwall and Sullivan admitted to knowing the records existed, and that Sederwall had the bench report. He stated that Virden's Case 2003-274 file's turn-over on September 3, 2008 showed that it proved the DNA investigation, and had contact information for getting its records.

And Eichwald held fast to his past rulings: "Summary Judgment" granted to the plaintiffs on November 20, 2009 had called the records public and had demanded their turn-over. And his later orders had repeated that.

Eichwald did not avoid the forgery issue, enumerating the multiple versions of "Lee reports" turned over by Sederwall to me, and to the Court, in the Evidentiary Hearing of January 21, 2011. He concurred that they were tampered to hide their link to Case 2003-274, as argued in my 2012 hearings for sanctions.

Eichwald also noted that Virden waited three years to make records requests; then failed to follow-up and get the records from Lee and Orchid Cellmark; though the De Baca County News's subpoena of the Orchid Cellmark records proved records existed.

Eichwald stated that the Sederwall and Virden depositions of June 26th and 27th of 2012 confirmed records tampering and three year delays with sham records recoveries - as were further confirmed in the Evidentiary Hearing of December 18, 2012 and February 4, 2013.

Eichwald concluded his list of "Facts" with my unsuccessful court-ordered mediation.

As to substantiating "Law," Eichwald quoted the IPRA statute's intent to provide citizens with the greatest possible information. He added its statement that 'No person requesting records shall be required to state the reason for inspecting records.' " And he stated that the records here had been withheld without statutory justification and their denial had been done improperly. But strangely, he omitted IPRA law's daily penalty of "up to $100 per day" (per record; and I had four categories of records; meaning $400.00 per day); stating only that improper denial "subjects the custodian to monetary damages."

Eichwald denied Virden's IPRA argument that recovery pertains only to records "in direct physical possession" as not supported by law. Eichwald argued that *Toomey v. Truth or Consequences* "clearly stated 'public agencies must produce all records, even those held by or created by a private entity 'on behalf of' the public agency.' The DNA records of Lee and Orchid Cellmark were held on behalf of Lincoln Sheriff's Office by Lee and Orchid Cellmark, and are intrinsic to solving its Pat Garrett murder Case 2003-274."

Eichwald denied Virden's claim of ignorance of records existence, since it was not an IPRA law exception. And Virden's case file had proved the DNA investigations and had given contact information for records, his deputies admitted records existence, and Lee and Orchid Cellmark admitted to having records. Eichwald also said Virden waited three years to attempt records' recovery, though the law had "time based damages," and precedent law stated those damages were "to encourage public entities' prompt compliance with records requests."

Eichwald also held the commissioned deputies responsible for the records as Virden's "agents;" denying their argument that they were hobbyists. He added that Sederwall had even been selling Case 2003-274 records on his billythekidcase.com website.

Sederwall was called to task for making a non-specific court-ordered request to Orchid Cellmark which left out the client name of Calvin Ostler, which Sederwall admittedly knew. And

Eichwald detailed Sederwall's tampering of Lee records to hide their connection to Case 2003-274.

Eichwald concluded unequivocally: "The Defendants' actions and/or inactions in responding to Plaintiff's IPRA requests are in violation of IPRA law and subject to sanctions."

Next came Eichwald's job: judging. At that point, things got strange. Dead Billy the Kid "talking" to Judges Henry Quintero and Ted Hartley was absent; but someone new got channeled.

First Eichwald erred that IPRA damages for a denied request are covered only by its section that does not repeat the "up to $100 per day" penalty. Then he ignored that penalty, stating there was "no standard" in IPRA for deciding an "amount of damages."

Where did Eichwald get that malarkey? He was channeling crooked Attorney General Gary King in his rogue *Faber v. King* case as if it was the sole law, while concealing that it was being appealed in the Supreme Court for making a false argument that damages were like in a car accident: nominal, compensatory, and punitive; while hiding IPRA law's actual *statutory* damages (meaning per day penalties for violating that *statute*). Attorney General King's corrupt motives had been to deny Attorney Dan Faber's victorious plaintiff her $100 daily damages (totaling about $60,000) *against him*, and to end IPRA damages for all future plaintiffs - thus, destroying IPRA law itself by protecting future crooks from significant penalties for violating open records law.

So *Faber v. King* looked great to Eichwald. So his punch line to his litany of my defendants' crimes was a vindictive punch to *my* stomach for whistleblowing. The "majordomo" had emerged. Eichwald, channeling Gary King, called my IPRA damages "nominal," meaning "a trivial sum of money." So for my correct IPRA claim of about $1 million, Eichwald awarded me $1,000!

Eichwald then added "punitive damages" as apparent sanctions for the defendants' "malicious, willful, reckless, wanton, or in bad faith" conduct for forging. Do not miss that this is separate from IPRA law. Eichwald cited a different law: UJI 13-1827; and awarded me $100,000. Adding more worms to tempt my taking his hook, he also granted me my costs (about $20,000), and topped off my past fired attorneys' "fees which have not previously been paid."

And Eichwald told me I won, writing: "IT IS THEREFORE ORDERED Judgment be entered in favor of Plaintiff Cooper against Defendants."

Do not miss the appearance of impropriety: For years of cover-up, the defendants' attorneys had already pocketed about a half million dollars. The plaintiffs' attorneys got $200,000 for trying to throw my case. And the defendants got no punishment at all. Would you rather be a whistleblower or a crook in New Mexico? Wasn't Gale Cooper the only one punished by Judge Eichwald?

## ALBUQUERQUE JOURNAL TO THE RESCUE

Nevertheless, the ruling was in favor of Plaintiff Gale Cooper. Since the days of Billy the Kid, the Santa Fe Ring never conceded any defeat at all. So by May 20, 2014, the hoax-backing *Albuquerque Journal* did damage control; assisted by none other than my despicable non-co-plaintiff, Scot Stinnett, astoundingly doing spin for the hoaxers. Replacing retired, hoax-biased reporter, Rene Romo, was his equivalent, a Lauren Villagran, who wrote "Award Ends Suit Over Billy the Kid Records."

Stinnett's and Villagran's apparent motive was faking that my case was over; repeating Romo's equally fake April 29, 2012 "Fight Won, Questions Remain: Billy the Kid DNA Report Released." Re-run also was Cooper-bashing of *Albuquerque Journal* reporter Scott Sandlin's June 11, 2013, "Billy the Kid case costs taxpayers nearly $200K: Billy the Kid lives on in battle of public records;" which painted me as sucking money from poor Lincoln County - omitting that Lincoln County officials' had created their own bill by years of covering up for their crooks.

Shockingly, it was Scot Stinnett who now presented the newest hoax-resuscitating switcheroo: the claim that the DNA records revealed by my case were "inconclusive" (instead of the useless junk they actually were); implying that, if freed from Gale Cooper's clutches, the promulgators could eventually get "conclusive" DNA to prove Pat did not kill Billy.

Lauren Villigran wrote:

> The legendary outlaw Billy the Kid is still causing trouble for Lincoln County more than a century after his death.
> A New Mexico court has awarded an author $100,000 in punitive damages in a lawsuit she brought against the Lincoln County Sheriff's Office over access to records regarding an investigation into Billy the Kid's death. The award brings to an end a legal battle of more than seven years that has left Lincoln County taxpayers on the hook for nearly $300,000 in fees and damages.

In 2007, author and amateur historian Gale Cooper and a weekly newspaper sued for access to documents related to the investigation, launched by a Lincoln County sheriff and two deputies more than a decade ago with the aim of using genetic testing to determine whether the story of the Kid's killing at the hands of Sheriff Pat Garrett in 1881 was true or a fabrication.

After years of litigation, the documents were delivered, although they offered no conclusive evidence to prove or disprove the generally accepted story of the Kid's death at Garrett's hand. Then-Sheriff Rick Virden denied having the records, while the deputies, who had recently resigned their posts, admitted to having the records but called them "private hobby trade secrets," according to a court order.

District Judge George Eichwald last week awarded to Cooper the punitive damages, plus $1,000 in nominal damages and yet-undetermined plaintiff costs. Cooper could not be reached for comment on Monday.

The weekly De Baca County News previously settled its claims against the former sheriff and deputies, which included the county paying $125,000 in attorneys' fees on top of a combined payment of $70,000 to four other attorneys previously involved in the case.

Scot Stinnett, publisher of the De Baca County News, said the awarding of attorneys' fees is critical to ensure that "a small paper like mine, or an individual like Gale, or anyone out there who doesn't have the means to hire an attorney on a retainer" won't be denied access to public records.

"If such a precedent is not in place," he said, "governmental agencies will just deny an IPRA request and dare someone to sue, as has been done many times in this state."

Lincoln County taxpayers have had to pay the tab: The new punitive and nominal damages bring the total cost to at least $296,000. Lincoln County Manager Nita Taylor said she did not yet know the total cost to the county, which is home to Billy the Kid landmarks and about 20,000 residents.

## AP INTERVIEWS ME AFTER 11 YEARS

The Santa Fe AP's Barry Massey interviewed me for his May 21, 2014 "Author Awarded $100,000 in Lawsuit Over Records on Legendary Outlaw 'Billy the Kid.' " Though he muffled impact by leaving out the Billy the Kid Case hoax and my saving the Billy the Kid history from it, he did show that I had won, that the defendants had displayed willful bad faith behavior, and that the judge's award of $1,000 was unjust and potentially appealable.

Massey wrote:

BERNALILLO, N.M. (AP) - A New Mexico court has awarded an author $100,000 in a lawsuit she brought against the Lincoln County sheriff's officials for wrongfully withholding records related to the death of legendary outlaw Billy the Kid.

But Gale Cooper of Sandia Park said Tuesday that she's considering appealing part of the damages that were awarded last week by District Judge George Eichwald in Bernalillo.

Cooper's legal battle with the southern New Mexico sheriff's office started in 2007.

She and a weekly newspaper in Fort Sumner, where Billy the Kid is buried, sued after being denied documents from an investigation the sheriff's office started in 2003.

The law enforcement officials planned to use DNA testing to determine the veracity of historical accounts that Lincoln County Sheriff Pat Garrett killed the Kid in 1881.

The investigation was looking into whether Garrett shot someone else and the real Billy the Kid escaped to Texas and lived out his days as Brushy Bill Roberts.

After years of litigation, some documents were delivered to Cooper and the De Baca County News. However, there was no evidence to discredit the generally accepted story of the Kid's death at Garrett's hand.

Cooper said she pursued the lawsuit to debunk the investigation and expose a "self-serving hoax" about the Kid's death that threatened to damage New Mexico's history.

The judge awarded Cooper $1,000 in "nominal damages" because officials withheld records requested under the Inspection of Public Records Act.

Cooper said she was considering an appeal of that portion of the ruling because the law provides for damages of up to $100 a day from when the sheriff's office first failed to comply with the law - about 6 ½ years in her case.

The judge also awarded $100,000 in punitive damages because the conduct of former Sheriff Rick Virden and two ex-deputies was "willful, wanton and in bad faith." There had been alterations to some documents that were released, the court pointed out.

"This didn't have to cost taxpayers a dime other than postage," Cooper said.

The lawsuit could have been avoided, she said, if the sheriff's office had complied with the records law and had mailed the documents soon after they were requested.

Lawyers for the former sheriff's officials didn't immediately return telephone messages seeking comment.

The newspaper previously settled its claims, and $195,000 was paid for its attorneys' fees. Lawyers for the sheriff's officials also have received several hundred thousand dollars in fees, according to Cooper.

## FIRST "TRUTHY" ARTICLE EVER

One publication was bull's-eye accurate. Greg Lalire, Editor-in-Chief of *Wild West* magazine, past recipient of threats against publishing articles about me from Steve Sederwall and U.S. Marshals Service Historian David Turk, bravely wrote "Author Wins 'Kid' Lawsuit" for the October 2014 edition. This was my first true moment of victory: People were told the truth.

Lalire stated:

> After about 6½ years, New Mexico author Gale Cooper has achieved victory in her lawsuit against what she calls "a Lincoln County law enforcement fraud and forensic hoax claiming Pat Garrett never killed Billy the Kid." Back in 2003 Lincoln County Sheriff Tom Sullivan and Deputy Steve Sederwall began an investigation into whether in July 1881 the county's sheriff of the time, Garrett, truly killed the young outlaw in Fort Sumner, New Mexico Territory. They claimed they would show through exhumations for DNA acquisitions and matching that Garrett murdered an innocent victim instead of the Kid and that the Kid lived a long life as "Brushy Bill" Roberts or some other claimant to the Kid's identity. Rick Virden, elected sheriff in 2005, deputized Sullivan and Sederwall to continue that investigation. Two years later, the deputies resigned but turned over none of their DNA records despite Cooper's requests, and Sheriff Virden did not make those public records available. Cooper's long legal battle began. In the original suit, the *De Baca County News* joined Cooper, but the newspaper settled in a March 2013 mediation that also included Lincoln County paying the plaintiffs' attorneys' fees of about $200,000. And the defense attorneys for the lawmen ultimately collected more than $450,000. Sullivan died in October 2013.
>
> In May 2014, a New Mexico court awarded Cooper $100,00 in "punitive damages"(because the conduct of Virden and the two deputies was deemed "willful, wanton and in bad faith") plus $1,000 in "nominal damages" (because the officials withheld records requested under the Inspection of Public Records Act). Cooper states she might appeal, since the open records law provides for up to $100 a day per record from when the sheriff's office first failed to comply with the law ... Cooper points out that the taxpayer burden of her lawsuit could have been avoided by the lawmen's complying with the open records law back in 2007. "This didn't have to cost taxpayers a dime other than postage for mailing me the records," says Cooper ... "My litigation ends the 'Billy the Kid Case,' " Cooper adds. "I feel satisfied that I saved the history of Pat Garrett and Billy the Kid from a publicity-stunt hoax."

### *THE NEW NECESSARY CAUSE*

I had won. Judge George Eichwald's condemnation of my defendants was now a public confirmation of Billy the Kid Case promulgators' dishonesty.

But Eichwald's unjust IPRA damages ruling created a new cause: protecting New Mexico's open records law.

Scot Stinnett, self-styled IPRA expert and Foundation for Open Records (FOG) member, had concealed that ruling's disaster to open records for reporter, Lauren Villagran's, May 20, 2014, *Albuquerque Journal* article. And uselessly partisan FOG itself, not only had refused to back my case, but had refused to join Faber's cause in the Court of Appeals to defeat Attorney General Gary King in his horrible *Faber v. King* threatening IPRA law.

So my life stretched before me as in the Chelon Point dream, in a continued journey of appealing Judge Eichwald's IPRA damages decision. The ultramarathon of my fight against the Santa Fe Ring would continue along this new turn in my road.

But as I told a Lincoln County resident: "I was willing to save your Pat Garrett and Billy the Kid history. And I did. Now I'm willing to fight for your open records law. And I will. But I draw the line at fighting your solid waste problems."

# THE GAME OF CROOKS

Fighting the Billy the Kid Case hoax taught me that public official crooks are "one trick ponies." Stonewalling is the trick. Doing nothing but delaying endlessly defeats most adversaries, who give up or eventually die. Bolstering stonewalling are shell games of passing the buck or hiding incriminating evidence. The Game of Crooks is played best where cronyism is rampant - like in New Mexico with its flourishing Santa Fe Ring; so every direction their adversary turns meets only roadblocks.

But there are uncomfortable attendant observations: You know *you are winning*, if the Game of Crooks switches from stonewalling to character assassination. (I got that courtesy of hoax-backing Bob Boze Bell's *True West* magazine; my non-co-plaintiff, Scot Stinnett; and my fired lawyers, Mickey Barnett and Patrick Griebel. And Billy Bonney himself got branded as "outlaw.") Then, you "know" *you won* when assassination turns real. That is how Billy "learned" he hit the bull's-eye in his personal anti-Santa Fe Ring war. You get very brief satisfaction!

# LIVING IN THE
# LAND OF DISENCHANTMENT

This big book reduces to one sentence: The Billy the Kid Case hoax is a symptom of a state being throttled by total corruption.

Lost is democracy's intent: checks and balances. So the Billy the Kid Case hoax is a poster child for lawbreaking officials seeking personal profit from public office, while hiding their lawbreaking by hiding its records on the public dime.

Abuse of privacy alarmed whistleblower Edward Snowden. Abuse of power trumps that, because it leaves public official crooks free to pursue private agendas. For *DailyMailOnline.com*, reporter Meghan Keneally wrote on September 27, 2013: "NSA employees used phone tapping to spy on their girlfriends and 'cheating' husbands: Investigation into abuses of power at NSA."

Abuse of power is what the Billy the Kid Case was all about: using two sheriff's departments for a fraud, burdening three district courts with litigation, digging up bodies for a publicity stunt, faking forensic DNA, defying open records law for cover-ups, obstructing justice with complicit judges, using the U.S. Marshals Service to intimidate and blacklist, controlling the press, and consuming taxpayer money in what started as a ludicrous bid for a U.S. presidential candidacy.

As in a tyranny, there was nowhere for a citizen to turn to stop the abuses. Having failed were New Mexico's U.S. Attorney and Attorney General; the FBI; state Bar Associations; the American Academy of Forensic Sciences; press; and district court litigation. If you include Bill Richardson's other crimes, cover-ups progress to Attorney General Eric Holder in the Department of Justice, and likely, President Obama.

And being a whistleblower made me ostracized, defamed, and fearing physical aggression: just how the Lincoln County War Regulators felt. My judge's unjust ruling in my IPRA case - added to judicial "strangeness" of channeled dead Billy as a client in courts of judges, Henry Quintero and Ted Hartley - brought to mind other outrages going back to the days of Billy the Kid.

The father of Ring-murdered John Henry Tunstall had sought $200,000 in reparations because his son had been killed by U.S. officials, and his property had been stolen by the Ring. So the father was stonewalled until his death; payment was never made. And Attorney Huston Chapman had been murdered by local Ring boss, Jimmy Dolan. Billy Bonney's testimony got Dolan indicted. So Ringman Judge Warren Bristol quashed Dolan's indictment; and Dolan got away with murder. And Ring-biased Fort Stanton Commander N.A.M. Dudley got praised by his partisan Court of Inquiry Judges for marching on Lincoln, instead of being indicted for murder and arson and being Court Martialed and hanged. And what happened to Sheriff George Peppin after he led the massacre at San Patricio? Nothing at all. And there was the last of the Regulators, Billy Bonney himself: vilified as an outlaw before being killed in the name of the law.

Adding to my many coincidences that began with my purchase of Pat Garrett's *The Authentic Life of Billy the Kid*, was that in the six years leading up to the 2014 publication of this edition, was the worst drought in New Mexico since the 1880's, when Billy Bonney was alive to see it. In my novel, *Billy and Paulita*, for September 11, 1880, I have Charlie Bowdre say to Billy and Tom O'Folliard, "Goddamn drought ... I's turnin' intah Hell here." Hell foreshadowed Charlie's, Tom's, and Billy's Santa Fe Ring murders to come.

But historical hell in New Mexico is not fiction. The famous letter, written February 14, 1878 by Ringman District Attorney William Rynerson to "Friends [John] Riley and [James Dolan]," four days before their pre-meditated murder of John Henry Tunstall, stated: "Shake that McSween outfit up ... and then shake it out of Lincoln." Above that, Rynerson wrote: "It must be made hot for them all, the hotter the better; especially is this necessary now that it has been discovered that there is no hell."

The Santa Fe Ring took care of that. Their clique of public official "friends" made a hell on earth enduring in New Mexico to the present moment. And it reeks to high heaven.

My hope is that the modern Game of Crooks has finally inflated the Billy the Kid Case into such gigantic monstrosity that its cover-up is now impossible. And because of my labors, New Mexico's Billy the Kid and Pat Garrett history is, at last, safe from the hoaxers' destruction.

So all that I had been through brought me to this conclusion: I made the right decision to move to New Mexico to write about Billy the Kid. Not only are most of his historic sites intact, but preserved in amber are Santa Fe Ring players that made his history happen. All one needs to do is keep one's eyes open, keep recording, and fight the good fight against them.

# CHAPTER 19:

# SHOVELGATE:
# HOAX TO SCANDAL

"WHO STOLE THE PEOPLE'S MONEY?" — DO TELL . N.Y.TIMES.

'TWAS HIM.

# SHOVELGATE

*HOAXBUST: Arguably the most elaborate historic-forensic hoax ever perpetrated, the Billy the Kid Case always rated as a scandal by its law enforcement fraud, use of taxpayer money for private gain, apparent bribery and pay-to-play, cover-ups by public officials and watch-dog organizations, and open records violations. Surprising was how many people it took to make it all possible, proving enablers are the secret to crooked public officials' success.*

## *BLAME GAME*

A typical hoax cavorts into the madcap. A scandal slinks into crime. A scandal's fashionable tail is "gate" - as in Richard Nixon's Watergate. So the Billy the Kid Case hoax was "Shovelgate" from its start. And its perpetrators, Governor Bill Richardson and his cohorts, planned to dig up graves for no legitimate reason; but sought to attain fame, fortune, a new Billy the Kid, and, most strangely, the presidency of the United States.

Eventually, their exhumed random man, William Hudspeth, alone should have sent them to single room habitations with clanging doors - to say nothing of prosecution for conspired fraud against taxpayers exceeding a million dollars.

Shovelgate bled New Mexican's coffers for two Lincoln County sheriffs and their staff; a De Baca County Sheriff; the Office of the Medical Investigator; the Lincoln County Attorney; Grant County District Judge Henry Quintero and his staff; De Baca County District Court Judge Ted Hartley and his staff; mayors and public officials in Silver City and Fort Sumner; Sandoval County District Judge George Eichwald and his staff; New Mexico Risk Management fund; and a state-paid university professor. Coming next might be New Mexico's higher courts.

For Shovelgate's Arizona taxpayer outlay, there was then-Governor Janet Napolitano; her staff; and the staff of the Arizona Pioneers' Home, whose cemetery had two graves desecrated.

In Hamilton, Texas, the mayor, his staff, and council people were forced to use public money to counter hoax onslaught there.

And, out of Washington, D.C., the U.S. Marshals Service used federal tax money to pay for its historian, David Turk's, hoax participation and publications. So no taxpayer in the United States was left out of contributing to Shovelgate.

Shovelgate also cost money for cover-ups; hiding public records. Into that moral quicksand, sank lying public officials. Records were hidden by Billy the Kid Case hoaxers' violating open records law, initially by calling records exempt as part of an ongoing criminal investigation; later, for my litigation, reversing and saying records were from a private hobby with trade secrets.

Shovelgate's power came from being inconceivable. It may have had a governor and presidential candidate in a pay-to-play scheme, a law enforcement scam, illegal exhumations, skimming of public coffers, colluding public officials, and two judges allowing a corpse to be a plaintiff, and one judge ruling to punish me for whistleblowing the whole shebang; but it reduced to: a scandal is only a scandal if people get scandalized.

With Governor Bill Richardson's access, the hoaxers were inundated with positive publicity in newspapers, television, and film with their headline-grabbing story: "Pat Garrett did not kill Billy the Kid. We'll prove it by high-tech, forensic, CSI DNA!"

Worse, no one could conceive that a governor, law enforcement officers, Dr. Henry Lee, Orchid Cellmark Lab, three district court judges, the biggest prosecutor's office in Arizona, lawyers, a university history professor, the History Channel, and a Cannes Film Festival nominated movie, were all faking.

Worse, Billy the Kid Case pronouncements were in awe-inspiring specialist jargon on official documents of a real murder investigation and with real exhumation petitions. DNA forensic science was flaunted with swabbings, bullet trajectories, high-tech lasers, CSI chemicals like Luminol, and DNA matching results.

Worse, it was inconceivable that those "high-up" people would put energy into hoaxing history. And, as a scandal, it was equally inconceivable. A scandal is selling a senate seat, or soliciting sex in the oval office (from someone not your wife). Pretending to be an historian is under the radar.

Worse, who could believe that all this effort was exerted to make a deluded long-discredited pretender, "Brushy Bill" Roberts, Billy the Kid - and then to posthumously pardon him for murders committed in 1878!

Worse, who could conceive that "Brushy Bill" Roberts pardoned as Billy the Kid would be adequate pay-to-play for a top political donor with enough bucks to back a presidential bid?

Worse, it seemed impossible that Shovelgate's illegalities were shielded by all watch-dogs: Bar Associations, New Mexico's U.S. Attorneys and Attorney Generals, the FBI, the American Academy of Forensic Sciences Ethics Committee, and the New Mexico Foundation For Open Government.

That was the brilliance of Shovelgate. It was too absurd to be suspected. So public credulity reigned. And TV "documentaries" and a movie gave it immortality.

Shovelgate's best cover-up was the big umbrella of Governor Bill Richardson; who came as a package deal with other officials, judges, lawyers, and lackeys. For years, Richardson shielded Billy the Kid Case crank pseudo-history from actual historians, from his own state's Office of the Medical Investigator, from district courts, from Arizona's Maricopa County prosecutor, and ultimately from the world in his "pardon" thrust.

For perspective, one can contemplate a comparable historical hoax - like saying Abraham Lincoln was not shot by John Wilkes Booth and had merely pretended to be dead. It would have been ended in weeks by legitimate historians and insulted citizens. But it turned out that the dysfunctional Billy the Kid subculture did nothing; and citizens' "history" came from "Young Guns" movies.

Bill Richardson's luck helped.

What if Arizona Attorney Jonell Lucca had prosecuted? What if a 2006 New Mexico gubernatorial candidate had made the Billy the Kid hoax a campaign issue? What if the *Albuquerque Journal* or *True West* magazine had exposed, rather than backed, the hoax? What if TV documentary makers vetted their productions?

Ironic is that Richardson's own bitter cohorts - lawmen, Sullivan, Sederwall, and Virden - in their 2007 "Memorandum," poked the hole in his umbrella by claiming Richardson and Robins made them do the hoax (as was substantiated by Attorney Bill Robins III's own "Billy the Kid's Pre-Hearing Brief"). So Steve Sederwall's 2008 deposition testimony that the Billy the Kid Case could turn "out the lights in Fort Sumner" was true.

Shovelgate failed: There was no disinterred Billy the Kid, no U.S. presidency, no "Brushy Bill" pardoned as Billy Bonney. Whom did Richardson blame? An odd answer appeared in hoaxer mouthpiece, *True West* magazine's May, 2007 article by University of New Mexico graduate student, Jason Strykowski, titled: "A Tale of Two Governors ... And one Kid." Strykowski, (possibly not coincidentally) was in the department of "official" hoax historian and *True West* editorial board member, Paul Hutton. Strykowski said Richardson's quest for "truth and tourism" had been ruined by "citizens of Silver City and Fort Sumner;" and by Billy's outlaw "infamy" (whatever that meant). Confirming his utter ignorance - or foolish prompting - Strykowski added that Governor Lew Wallace had likewise tried to "help" Billy, but was also thwarted.

For 2010, Richardson's Lieutenant Governor, Diane Denish, was predicted to win election as governor (New Mexico voted Democratic). In September of 2009, Denish ignored my records requests about the Billy the Kid Case. Her major political donor was Bill Robins III. She lost. Republican Susana Martinez won; backed by Pat Rogers, Mickey Barnett, and Rod Adair; and by voters' disgust at Bill Richardson's overall corruption.

Susana Martinez's apathy about Billy the Kid history showed in a December 31, 2010 *Washington Times* article where she called the Billy pardon issue "a waste of time." And after her pay-to-play taint from Pat Roger's e-mail fiasco, she mimicked Richardson's fake personas (like his being a veteran-backer). Her "champion of the handicapped" got her a letter to the editor of *People* magazine on August 19, 2013, stating:

> It's amazing how Governor Martinez, who uses her sister's special needs as part of her political forum, doesn't seem to have time to talk to the New Mexico disabled community in regards to the drastic funding cuts that have been made. My daughter ... is one of the many who will suffer.

Susana Martinez had no interest in stopping the ongoing Billy the Kid Case hoax - or its tourism toll. To my Cc to her of my 2013 "Open letter to the Lincoln County Commissioners," there was no response. And she is eyeing the U.S. presidency, while proof of her corruption mounts - as in her department head appointments of those totally unqualified (shades of Richardson's Billy Sparks).

So the beat goes on - to the tune of the Santa Fe Ring.

# SHOVELGATE VILLAGE

*HOAXBUST: As the queerest example of political pay-to-play and misuse of sheriff departments, the Billy the Kid Case hoax left New Mexico's Old West history in tatters, and TV documentary watchers so befuddled that Billy the Kid might have been living on the shores of Loch Ness or abducted by Roswell aliens. Hijacking Billy the Kid Case history to become rich and president kept it comic, as did its astounding numbers of grimly colluding players.*

The evolving Billy the Kid Case hoax became as contorted as a sidewinder snake in convulsions. Nevertheless, its objective was simple: fake DNA matching to make pretender "Brushy Bill" Roberts "Billy the Kid;" then pardon him as Billy. That plot combined crooked politics, crooked law enforcement, crooked forensics, crooked courts, crooked journalists, crooked attorneys, crooked donors, and crooked enablers - for that crooked purpose.

So it proved that it takes a village to do a hoax that big.

Then it ran amok, extending its population of protectors to Arizona, Texas, and up to Washington, D.C. From sheriffs' departments chasing a dead suspect for a murder he did not commit, to New Mexico judges entertaining ghost clients in their courts, to lawmen disinterring bodies for fun, to a criminologist and a lab doing show-biz forensics, to public officials' covering up, to a press writing what they were told, it took many to create Shovelgate. Then it took many more to protect the hoaxers from deserved penalties or slammers - while taxpayers footed the bills.

## *TOURING SHOVELGATE VILLAGE*

The village that raised Shovelgate was first built by Thomas Benton Catron in the days of Billy the Kid, in a land of enchantment, where a magic force called "friendship" joined all its residents, like links of a chain - called by non-residents: the Santa Fe Ring. But Shovelgaters all feared one magic word: "No." If said by even one person, it could break the spell and crumble their village to dust. So no one ever said "No."

Modernizer of Shovelgate Village was Governor "Dollar Bill" Richardson; who expanded its population, all adhering to his "Implied Rule," cribbed from antique robber baron, "Boss" Tweed: "What are you going to do about it?"

Evergreen was also Tweed's "Fingering Game," illustrated by cartoonist Thomas Nast as a circle of fat men, each pointing to his neighbor and saying: "Who stole the people's Money? Twas him." So all Shovelgaters played the "Fingering Game" whenever questioned by citizens - called "Crazy Troublemakers."

The **"SHOVELGATE VILLAGE COVENANT,"** called "Our Probable Cause Statement," starts with their in-joke: "No one from the Governor to the Sheriff of Lincoln County is beyond suspicion of deception and covering up the true facts in this case."

In-jokes abounded. Their **ANTI-TOURISM DEPARTMENT** even erected a billboard of innocent children dancing ring-around-the-rosie, under: "THERE'S NO SUCH THING / AS THE SANTA FE RING!" And their historic, roadside markers announced: "TO BILLY THE KID'S GRAVE" - some with an arrow to Texas, saying: "BRUSHY BILL WENT THATAWAY." Others, pointing to Arizona, have: "JOHN MILLER WENT THATAWAY."

Tourist warnings do apply. Shovelgate Villagers act like a snobby "ruling class" to outsiders, whom they consider "peons." Also off-putting, can be pervasive sewage odor, unnoticeable to "insiders;" but can require using anti-emetics for a prolonged stay.

But Old West charm comes from Shovelgaters earning monikers, as had Billy "the Kid" Bonney; when he lived there in olden days. Back then, Billy got a spoilsport reputation by being part of the "Lincoln County War troubles;" during which bullets entered some Ringmen and sent them to a place that might deserve a book titled: *Some People You Will Meet in Hell.*

A drive along Conman Way, to Shovelgate Village's exclusive, members-only, gated center, called **"HOAXWAY HAVEN,"** has residences of "Dollar Bill" Richardson; Attorney Bill "Pay-to-Play" Robins III; former Sheriff Tom "Hobby Cop One" Sullivan, now dead; former Deputy Sheriff Steve "Hobby Cop Two" Sederwall; past Sheriff Gary "Recall" Graves; past Sheriff Rick "Railroad Tie" Virden; U.S. Marshals Service Historian David "Homeland Security Attack" Turk; UNM history professor, Paul "I'm Not Their Historian" Hutton; Dr. Henry "Where Do You Want Blood" Lee; Dr. Rick "Bone Bag" Staub of Orchid Cellmark "No Questions Asked" Lab; Bob "Fake West" Boze Bell; Dale "Call Me Doctor" Tunnell; and Attorney Randi "Pseudo-Pardon" McGinn.

Each person in this in-crowd owns a framed copy of the tintype of Billy the Kid, created by photometric alteration of Dr. Scott T. Acton of the Department of Electrical and Computer Engineering and the Laboratory for Vision Systems and Advanced Graphic Laboratory at the University of Texas (DEACEALVSAAGLUT for short), to match "Brushy Bill" Roberts. Dr. Acton, using the latest technology of 1976 in 1997, also restored its missing figure of Pat Garrett - supposedly removed in 1881 by conspiracy of everyone on the planet - and now tenderly kissing his beloved "Brushy" as Billy. "*Best Friend's Forever*" was added in gold, paid for through a charity write-off by Johnny "Fish Farm" Cope.

Governor, Susana "See No Evil" Martinez - invited in by the Adair-Rogers-Barnett triumvirate to be presumptive Ring head - has a windowless house to prove she sees nothing bad in Shovelgate Village. So she uses e-mails to keep up her pay-to-play.

*FRIENDS JOURNAL,* the main newspaper, has headlines like: "Billy the Kid Still Asking To Be Dug Up;" and "Just Because 'Brushy Bill' was Two at Billy the Kid's Death Does Not Rule Him Out. Two Year Olds Can Be Rough: Ask Any Mother." Its supplement, "ENTERTAINMENT WORLD: Your Fiction is Our Reality," has ads for Bill "No Vetting" Kurtis's History "Made Up" TV Channel; and for French film-maker, Anne "Billy Killer" Feinsilber's *Requiem for Billy the Kid.*

Other residents are service providers. Their houses cum workplaces have bold signs, leaving no doubt as to their roles.

**"STONEWALLING MASONRY,"** with slogan "We're Impenetrable," houses New Mexico's past Attorney General Patricia "Ms. Corruption" Madrid; past Deputy Attorney General Stuart "What Stonewalling" Bluestone; and past Assistant Attorney General Mary "Record Hider" Smith; and current Attorney General Gary "Kill IPRA" King.

**"LOOK CLEAN WHITEWASHERS,"** with motto, "Political Machines Are Our Specialty," needed a multi-floor structure for New Mexicans: Judges Henry "Thanks For Appointing Me" Quintero, Ted "Thanks For Appointing Me" Hartley; and Judge George "Won't Rule" Eichwald; past Spokesman Billy "Illiterate" Sparks; past Richardson Science Policy Advisor, Dennis "Use Los Alamos Radar" Erickson; Richardson's past lawyer Carlos William "I Should Have Said He Was Driving" Fierro; Manny "Take the Rap" Aragon; and past New Mexico U.S. Attorneys David "Richardson's Not that Bad" Iglesias, Greg "Mouth Sealed" Fouratt, and Ken "Don't Prosecute Friends" Gonzales.

"SPECIALTY SANITIZING," with big sign saying, "We Sweep Your Dirt Under the Rug," has a high-rise for population overflow. Offices have past Lincoln and Chavez Counties State Senator Rod "Kill the Case" Adair; New Mexico Anti-Tourism Secretary Mike "Don't Rock the Boat" Cerletti; past Arizona Governor Janet "Big Sis" Napolitano; her Policy Advisor for Health, Anne "Panic" Winter; her Chief of Staff, Alan "Cover Our Ass" Stevens; her General Counsel, Tim "Feign Law" Nelson; Director of the Yavapai County Department of Community Health, Marcia "Case Closed" Jacobson; Arizona Pioneers' Home Supervisor Gary "Cover-Up" Olson; Maricopa County Deputy Prosecutor Jonell "Folding" Lucca; Arizona Attorney General Terry "Talk is Cheap" Goddard; New Mexico Bar Association Attorneys Christine "I'm For Morel" Long, Anne "I'm for Barnett" Taylor, and Curtis "I'm for Barnett Too" Gurley; Arizona State Bar Attorney Ariel "I'm For Lucca" Worth; the entire American Academy of Forensic Sciences Ethics Committee with Haskell "Lee's Our Media Star" Pitluck; and all the Cc'd politicians in New Mexico and Arizona - with special accommodations for past Arizona's State Senate President Ken "I'm Holding out for Secretary of State" Bennett, and former New Mexico Republican Party Chairman Allen "Do Nothing" Weh. Going from office to office saying "Silence is golden" are past Republican Party Chairman Harold "Make a Deal" Yates and Republican X ("Shallow Throat."). Ever-expanding quarters are needed for all the Lincoln County Commissioners since 2003 (except for Leo Martinez - whom they would kick out anyway).

**KROOK, SLEAZIE, OVERBILLIT & PURJURLY FIRM,** has many convenient branches, since it employs most New Mexico lawyers. Shovelgaters have been delighted with services of Bill "Pay-to-Play" Robins III, now deceased Sherry "Make It Up" Tippett, Mark "Lawmen Lawmen Lawmen" Acúna, Alan "Little Weasel" Morel, Kevin "Hawk-Face" Brown, Henry "Slime Trail" Narvaez, Nicole "It's Not In His Pocket" Werkmeister, Pat "The Rat" Rogers, Mickey "Throw the Case" Barnett, Ed "Snoozy Conscience" Threet, and Patrick "My Name Isn't Attorney" Griebel. A special in-site cafeteria, "The Pig-Out" is run by Steve "They Bill I Pay" Kopelman and the rest of his New Mexico Association of Counties Risk Management, who continuously fill huge troughs with cash for the slobbering lawyers to gorge themselves without limit.

**"YE OLD PETSHOP,"** advertising: "All newspaper-trained," provided pocket-pet reporters to now dead Tom Sullivan, Steve Sederwall, and Rick Virden, with Julie "Ruidoso News" Carter; Dianne "Ruidoso News" Stallings; and "Albuquerque Journal Runts": Rene Romo, Scott Sandlin, and Lauren Villagran. "Dollar Bill's" pocket-pets had fancier pedigrees: Mike "Researchless New York Times" Janofsky, and Kent "Albuquerque Journal Head" Walz. Following Pandering Piper  Bob "Fake West" Boze Bell, were *True West's* adoptable vermin: Janna "We'll Bring the Shovel's" Bommersbach; Megan "Hoax News or No News" Saar; and Mark "Cooper's A Lunatic" Boardman. Huddled in cages were debarked watchdogs: Steve "Know Nothing" Terrell of the *Santa Fe New Mexican,* KOB TV's Larry "Don't Investigate" Barker, and Mike "How the West Was Lost" Rivero.

The **"FOR OUR GUYS (FOG) MARCHING BAND"** conducts parades on Conman Way, always playing the popular "Oh, Close Those Open Records, Lord;" and singing:

> If one gets ............. TRUMPETS BLAST!
> A records request,
> Hug your friend;
> Ignore the pest ....... DRUMS POUND!


Past loyalists are always welcome at Shovelgate Village.

**"DUPES BRIGADE,"** has an open invitation - with required signed promise never to say "William Hudspeth" - extended to Dr. Laura "Ditzy" Fulginiti; and past-Pioneers' Home Supervisor Jeanine "Dazzled" Dike with her merrily loyal staff: Misty "Keeping Secrets" Rodarte and Dale "Backhoe" Sams.

**"LET'S PLAY COWBOY COOK-OUT CLUB"** has a designated re-enactment field, with authentic horse droppings and chuck-wagon cooking; and is big enough to host the Billy the Kid Outlaw Gang (with past President Ron "Contact List" Hadley, and with slogan modified from founders Joe and Marlyn Bowlin to: "Don't Preserve, Don't Protect, Just Promote Us"); the Wild West History Association with Bob "Do the Hoax in My House" McCubbin; and the rest of the Billy the Kid and Pat Garrett aficionado subculture, which has its own motto: "History, shmistory. Who cares?"

At **"PROPHET CORNER,"** the junction of Conman Way and Liars Lane, stands Jannay "Just A Fingernail" Valdez, tirelessly waving his big placard, lettered: "REPENT AND DIG! BRUSHY BILL OLIVER L. NOT P. WILLIAM HENRY 1859 NEW TOMBSTONE ROBERTS IS BILLY THE KID."

Nearby, is the village's tiny **"HALL OF FAME,"** with just one honoree: Scot "Imaginary Co-Plaintiff" Stinnett. He is specially singled out by Shovelgaters for doing absolutely nothing to offend any of them - when he actually had the opportunity to do otherwise. Display cases for his Billy the Kid Case litigation contributions are, as expected, entirely empty. But a framed wall certificate says:

### WITH APPRECIATION FROM ALL THE FIRED BUT PAID LAWYERS

### REMEMBER THE WORDS BENEDICT ARNOLD COULD HAVE SAID: " 'TRAITOR' DEPENDS ON WHOSE SIDE YOU'RE ON."

And on the fire-charred Capitan Mountains, re-named in the gubernatorial tenure of "Dollar Bill" Richardson," and thanks to his efforts, as **"BEARLESS MOUNTAINS,"** at a burned-out promontory called "Smokey's Last Stand," sits R.D. "It's All Mine" Hubbard, watching Shovelgate Village below; as water cascades down the treeless slopes to fill his vast and ever-expanding system of interconnected sewers.

Last of all, living in Shovelgate Village, but hidden under piles of books and thousands of papers, is an embedded terrified reporter: me; surviving, so far, only by Hamster Girl super-power.

Outside the boundaries of Shovelgate Village, graze flocks of sheep as far as the eye can see. Shovelgaters call them **"TAXPAYERS."** They are considered to be an endless food source that can be cheaply sustained on pulp fiction. But herd control may have been overestimated and yielded a false sense of security. Sheep do stampede. The day may come for a new cartoon called "Govzilla Meets Sheep." In it, an arrogant man or woman struts on screen. Millions of sheep gallop across. Credits roll.

# Concluding Without Ending

*HOAXBUST: A good hoax never dies; it just maintains opportunities for enterprising tricksters and gullible trickstees.*

In America, things worse than Shovelgate are happening. But now you have a sub-grass-roots explanation of why: From bottom to top the same crooks are all hand-holding friends.

My insights came from following Mark Twain's research advice: "If you hold a cat by the tail, you learn things you cannot learn in any other way." This is what I learned:

- Fighting City Hall is an extreme sport.

- If you are an American taxpayer: Congratulations! You own the Billy the Kid Case hoax. You paid for it.

- If you are a believer in "Brushy Bill" as Billy the Kid": Congratulations! If people call you crazy now, you have a come-back: Past-Governor Bill Richardson and the Lincoln County Sheriff's Department say I'm not.

- If you are a believer in John Miller as Billy the Kid, try not to get lonely. Remember: one is better than none.

- If you are a sheriff in search of fun and a "media circus," file a murder investigation against Pat Garrett, and locate unprotected cemeteries for graves to dig up. (It does not matter whose graves they are.) This opportunity is now available since the Lincoln County Sheriff's Department is currently in hiatus from that, having returned to their tradition of solving no murders at all.

- If you have a deceased relative who thought he or she (you never know) was Billy the Kid, contact Dr. Henry Lee for a Billy the Kid DNA sample. Decide before-hand if you want, or do not want, them to be the Kid. Orchid Cellmark Lab needs that information for its matching results; the *New York Times* needs it for their reporter; and Bill Kurtis Productions needs it to stage their next History Channel program.

- If you have a deceased relative, and merely want to speak with them, contact Attorney Bill Robins III for channeling.

- If you are kin to William Hudspeth, you may have won the death lottery. Check with an attorney (not connected to any New Mexico one) on legal pursuit of "body snatchers." Good luck!

- If you are an honest Democrat or Republican political aspirant, a move to New Mexico may get you in office. Currently there is only the Fear and Favor party. So voters sentimental about democracy might vote for you.

- If you are currently indicted for a pay-to-play scheme (or are Rod Blagojevich), and want to feel regret, feel regret that you were not Governor Bill Richardson of New Mexico.

- If you want to commit the perfect crime, copy the Billy the Kid Case by choosing one too silly to be taken seriously.

- If you can think of no way to spend your life - and enjoy endless work, no discernable rewards, defamation, and persistent personal danger - consider becoming a political whistleblower. You can even be one for the Billy the Kid Case hoax. Odds are, it will never end.

- If you are one of the Billy the Kid Case promulgators still hanging on, and are unsure how to revise your hoax yet again, you could consider using some of your "bench-blood-DNA-of-playing-dead-Billy-the-Kid-Pat-Garrett-friend" to clone Billy. The South Korean stem cell scientists may help - if you would settle for a four-legged furry Billy that looks like a puppy. And your public followers have already proved that they would accept anything you say - as long as it is in newspapers or magazines, on TV, or in a movie.

- If you think that "Billy the Kid" and "President of the United States" are unrelated topics, you did not read this book.

# APPENDIX

# ANNOTATED DOCUMENTS LIST

**APPENDIX: 1.** Billy the Kid Case Hoax and Its IPRA Litigation by Gale Cooper

**APPENDIX: 2.** Mike Gallagher and Dan Boyd. "In the Clear: Feds Criticize Gov's Office But Skip Indictments." *Albuquerque Journal.* August 28, 2009.

**APPENDIX: 3.** Michael Janofsky. "122 Years Later, The Lawmen Are Still Chasing Billy the Kid." *New York Times.* June 5, 2003.

**APPENDIX: 4.** Governor Bill Richardson press release. June 10, 2003

**APPENDIX: 5.** Steve Sederwall. "Mayor's Report." *Capitan Village Hall News.* May, 2003. [Excerpt, pages 2-3]

**APPENDIX: 6.** Anthony DellaFlora. "State Not Kidding Around: Governor won't mind if probe of the notorious 19th century N.M. outlaw boosts tourism." *Albuquerque Journal.* Front Page. June 11, 2003.

**APPENDIX: 7.** Julie Carter. "Follow the Blood: In the Billy the Kid Case, Miller Exhumed." *RuidosoNews.com.* October 2005.

**APPENDIX: 8.** Rene Romo. "Forensic Expert on Billy's Case: Questions Remain on Outlaw's Fate." *Albuquerque Journal.* Front Page. August 2, 2004.

**APPENDIX: 9.** Doris Cherry. "Forensics 101 for 'Billy." *Lincoln County News.* Front Page. August 12, 2004.

**APPENDIX: 10.** Rene Romo. *Albuquerque Journal.* "Billy the Kid Probe May Yield New Twist." November 6, 2005.

**APPENDIX: 11.** January 31, 2012 Court-Ordered Defendant Turn-Over of Dr. Henry Lee's "original" report (has the law enforcement titles and connection to Case No. 2003-274) "Forensic Research & Training Center Forensic Examination Report." February 25, 2005.

**APPENDIX: 12.** Attorney Sherry Tippett. "Sixth Judicial District Court, State on New Mexico, County of Grant. Case No. MS-2003-11. In the Matter of Catherine Antrim: Petition to Exhume Remains." October 10, 2003.

**APPENDIX: 13.** Attorney William Snead. "Response of Office of Medical Investigator to Petition to Exhume Remains of Catherine Antrim." January 12, 2004.

**APPENDIX: 14.** Ross Zumwalt, M.D. "Sixth Judicial Court, State of New Mexico, County of Grant. No. MS 2003-11 In the Matter of Catherine Antrim. Affidavit of Ross E. Zumwalt, M.D." January 9, 2004.

**APPENDIX: 15.** Attorney Sherry Tippett. Pre-printed for State Senator Benny Altamirano. "Senate Memorial Number ____." Attached to her letter dated December 17, 2003.

**APPENDIX: 16.** Attorneys Bill Robins III and David Sandoval. "Sixth Judicial District Court in Grant County. No. MS 2003-11. In the Matter of Catherine Antrim: Billy the Kid's Unopposed Motion For Intervention and Request For Expedited Disposition." November 26, 2003.

**APPENDIX: 17.** Judge Henry Quintero. "Sixth Judicial District Court, State of New Mexico, County of Grant. No. MS 2003-11, In the Matter of Catherine Antrim. Decision and Order." April 2, 2004.

**APPENDIX: 18.** Tenth Judicial District Judge E.T. Kinsley, Jr. "Decree for Lois Telfer's "Case No. 3255, For the Removal of the Body of William H. Bonney, Deceased, From the Ft. Sumner Cemetery in Which He is Interred for Reinterment in the Lincoln, New Mexico, Cemetery" (Filed in 1961). (Incorporating Louis Bowdre's "Motion to Intervene" of 1961.) Filed April 9, 1962.

**APPENDIX: 19.** Attorneys Bill Robins III, David Sandoval, and Mark Acuña. "Tenth Judicial Court of De Baca County. Case No. CV-2004-00005, In the Matter of William H. Bonney, aka 'Billy the Kid.' Petition for the Exhumation of Billy the Kid's Remains." February 26, 2004.

**APPENDIX: 20.** Attorneys Adam Baker and Herb Marsh. "Village of Fort Sumner's Motion to Dismiss Against Petitioners Sullivan, Sederwall, and Graves for Lack of Standing" June 24, 2004.

**APPENDIX: 21.** Attorneys Adam Baker and Herb Marsh. "Village of Fort Sumner's Motion to Dismiss Against William H. Bonney Under Rule 1-017(A)." June 24, 2004.

**APPENDIX: 22.** Silver City Petition to Governor Bill Richardson. Signed by: Mayor Terry Fortenberry, Town Councilor Thomas A. Nupp, Town Councilor Steve May, Town Councilor Gary Clauss, Town Councilor Judy Ward, Town Manager Alex Brown, Executive Director of the Silver City/Grant County Chamber of Commerce Cissy McAndrew, Director of Silver City Mainstreet Project Frank Milan, and Director of the Silver City Museum Susan Berry. June 21, 2004.

**APPENDIX: 23.** Attorneys Bill Robins III and David Sandoval. "County of De Baca, State of New Mexico, Tenth Judicial District. Cause No. CV-04-00005. In the Matter of William H. Bonney aka 'Billy the Kid.' Stipulation of Dismissal With Prejudice." July 30, 2004.

**APPENDIX: 24.** Attorney Mark Acuña. "County of De Baca, State of New Mexico, Tenth Judicial District. Cause No. CV-04-00005. In the Matter of William H. Bonney A/K/A 'Billy the Kid.' Petitioner's [sic] Response to the Village of Ft. Sumner's Motion to Dismiss." July 26, 2004.

**APPENDIX: 25.** William Garrett. *De Baca County News* Letter to the Editor. May 6, 2004.

**APPENDIX: 26.** No Author. "Contact List, William H. Bonney Case # 2003-274" No Date.

**APPENDIX: 27.** Paul Hutton. Letter to Jay Miller denying being the Billy the Kid Case historian. June 20, 2006.

**APPENDIX: 28.** Jay Miller. "Calendar of Complaints to Attorney General Patricia Madrid" sent to Attorney General Patricia Madrid and Deputy Attorney General Stuart Bluestone. September 1, 2006.

**APPENDIX: 29.** Jannay Valdez. To Frederick Nolan. E-mail "RE: Billy the Kid." September 12, 2004.

**APPENDIX: 30.** GRIEF (Gambling Research Information & Education Foundation) blog. "Dockside must be watched closely." April 15, 2003. (Quoted from the *Indianapolis Star*.)

**APPENDIX: 31.** Dr. Guy C. Clark, Executive Director of New Mexico Coalition Against Gambling in *Albuquerque Journal* op-ed " 'Dollar Bill' Richardson." December 16, 2002.

**APPENDIX: 32.** No author listed. "New Racing Schedule Tramples Horsemen." *Albuquerque Journal.* June 26, 2004.

**APPENDIX: 33.** Lincoln County Commissioner Leo Martinez. "Observations Regarding the Lincoln County Sheriff's Department's Use of Authority and Management of Priorities." September 21, 2004.

**APPENDIX: 34.** Dianne Stallings. "Showdown in the County Seat: shouting match erupts at county Commissioners meeting over investigation of Billy the Kid" and "KID: Question of who is paying sparks debate." *Ruidoso News.* September 22, 2004.

**APPENDIX: 35.** Attorney Mark Anthony Acuña. "Tenth Judicial District Court, State of New Mexico, County of De Baca. No. CV-04-00005. In the Matter of William H. Bonney aka 'Billy the Kid.' Stipulation of Dismissal With Prejudice." September 24, 2004.

**APPENDIX: 36.** Geneva Pittmon. Letter to Joe Bowlin and Copy of Roberts Family Bible. Sent December 16, 1987.

**APPENDIX: 37.** W.C. Jameson and Frederic Bean. *The Return of the Outlaw Billy the Kid.* 1998. [Death scenes]

**APPENDIX: 38.** Lincoln County Sheriff Rick Virden (letter on official letterhead). To Jay Miller. "We are interested in the truth surrounding Billy the Kid." November 28, 2005.

**APPENDIX: 39.** Robert Struckman. "Bitterroot man hopes to uncover the truth about Billy the Kid." helenair.com. March 13, 2006.

**APPENDIX: 40.** Joanna Dodder. *The Daily Courier* of Prescott, Arizona. "Officials could face charges for digging up alleged Billy the Kid." April 12, 2006.

**APPENDIX: 41.** David Snell. "Letter to Shiela Polk, Yavapai County Attorney." March 11, 2006.

**APPENDIX: 42.** Leo W. Banks. *Tucson Weekly.* "The New Billy the Kid? The mad search for the bones of an American outlaw icon has come to Arizona." April 13, 2006

**APPENDIX: 43.** Dr. Laura Fulginiti. "Re: Exhumation, Pioneer Home Cemetery, Prescott, Arizona for "Dale L. Tunnell, Ph.D., Forensitec." June 2, 2005.

**APPENDIX: 44.** Prescott City Attorney Glenn Savona. To Shiela Polk, Yavapai County Attorney (with copies to Detective Anna Cahall and her boss, Chief Randy Oaks). "Re: Police Department DR#2006-12767 Arizona Pioneers' Home Cemetery." April 13, 2006.

**APPENDIX: 45.** Julie Carter. "Culture shock: The cowboys and the Kid go to France." May 5, 2006.

**APPENDIX: 46.** Lincoln County Attorney Alan Morel letter to Gale Cooper. "Re: Freedom of Information Act/Inspection of Public Records Act Request dated September 22, 2006, to Lincoln County Sheriff Rick Virden." October 11, 2006.

**APPENDIX: 47.** Tom Sullivan and Steve Sederwall. Letter to Attorney Alan P. Morel. "The Dried Bean." September 30, 2006.

**APPENDIX: 48.** Jay Miller. Letter to Dr. Henry Lee. "Re. Forensic consultation in the New Mexico Billy the Kid Case." March 27, 2006.

**APPENDIX: 49.** Dr. Henry Lee. Response to Jay Miller. May 1, 2006.

**APPENDIX: 50.** Jay Miller. "Letter to Dr. Henry Lee, Re. Follow-up on your letter of May 1, 2006 responding to my request of March 27, 2006 for information on your forensic consultation in the New Mexico Billy the Kid Case." June 15, 2006.

**APPENDIX: 64.** Gale Cooper termination letter to Attorney Martin E. Threet: "Re: Termination of legal services for Gale Cooper and the *De Baca County News* vs Lincoln County Sheriff Rick Virden et al case." February 21, 2011

**APPENDIX: 65.** Gale Cooper. "Plaintiff Gale Cooper's Pre-Evidentiary Hearing Brief." November 14, 2012. (Copied to Attorneys Patrick Griebel for the De Baca County News, Henry Narvaez for Sheriff Virden, and Kevin Brown for Sullivan and Sederwall)

**APPENDIX: 66.** Gale Cooper. "Addendum to Plaintiff Cooper's Opposition Reply To Virden's Objection to Plaintiff Cooper's Pre-Evidentiary Hearing Brief." November 14, 2012. (Copied to Attorneys Patrick Griebel for the De Baca County News, Henry Narvaez for Sheriff Virden, and Kevin Brown for Sullivan and Sederwall)

**APPENDIX: 67.** Judge George P. Eichwald. "Findings of Fact and Conclusions of Law and Order of the Court." May 15, 2014.

# PRIMARY DOCUMENTS

## APPENDIX: 1. Gale Cooper. "SUMMARY: Billy the Kid Case Hoax and Its IPRA Litigation." 2014.

### OVERVIEW

My 6½ year Inspection of Public Records Act ("IPRA") litigation case arose from Lincoln County Sheriff's Department Case # 2003-274 ("Billy the Kid Case"), and was in Sandoval District Court as *Gale Cooper and the De Baca County News vs Lincoln County Sheriff Rick Virden et al* (Tom Sullivan and Steve Sederwall). It will also be in appelate courts. At stake is New Mexico's Old West history and IPRA law.

### BACKGROUND

The Billy the Kid Case is a real murder case, filed in 2003 in Lincoln County, against past Lincoln County Sheriff and Deputy U.S. Marshal Pat Garrett as suspect; claiming that, on July 14, 1881, in Fort Sumner, he heinously murdered an innocent victim as grave-filler to enable his prisoner, Billy the Kid, to escape. That murder case also claimed, in its Probable Cause Statement, that Garrett, on April 28, 1881, provided the Kid's jailbreak gun; and was, thus, an accessory to the Kid's murders of his two deputy guards (James Bell and Robert Olinger). Backed by no historic or other evidence at all - and ignoring massive historic evidence substantiating that Pat Garrett did kill Billy the Kid - the Billy the Kid Case is an elaborate historic/forensic/legal hoax for personal gain of its law enforcement perpetrators; and was also intended to garner for its backer, then New Mexico Governor Bill Richardson, national name recognition for his planned presidential run in 2008.

Thus, conducting the Billy the Kid Case were Richardson; one of his top political donors, Attorney Bill Robins III (backing Richardson's runs for governor and president); three sheriffs (Tom Sullivan, Gary Graves, Rick Virden); two deputy sheriffs (Tom Sullivan, Steve Sederwall); forensic expert Dr. Henry Lee; University of New Mexico history professor Paul Hutton, appointed by Richardson as its "official historian;" the *Albuquerque Journal* and the *Ruidoso News*; and glossy *True West* magazine. How could anyone doubt that combined prestige?

I did; and was determined to stop those historical hijackers.

That determination began on June 5, 2003 when the Billy the Kid Case was announced on the front page of the *New York Times*. Garrett was called a murderer; and long-discredited Texas pretender, "Brushy Bill" Roberts, was put forth as the Kid. Proof was to be by forensic DNA.

I was shocked. My research since 1998 on Billy the Kid had convinced me that the history was true (40 thousand pages of archival documents and books for my docufiction novel *Billy and Paulita*). I am also a Harvard educated, M.D. psychiatrist, specializing in forensic murder case consultation. So I also had available forensic consultants and the knowledge and zeal for hoaxbusting this law enforcement fraud, and fraud against New Mexico taxpayers.

## HOAXING NEW MEXICO EXHUMATIONS

Billy the Kid Case's fake forensics started with a scheme to exhume Billy and his mother (his only known kin) to compare their DNA; allegedly to determine if Billy himself or Garrett's "innocent victim" lay in Billy's Fort Sumner gravesite. But there was a problem: there exists no valid DNA of Billy or his mother on the planet. The mother (Catherine Antrim) is not likely in her Silver City grave; and Billy is probably elsewhere in Fort Sumner's cemetery. That is why the New Mexico Office of the Medical Investigator ("OMI"), from the case's start, said the DNA would be invalid and refused to issue exhumation permits to the perpetrating lawmen: Sullivan, Sederwall, and Graves.

Those hoaxers ignored the OMI. In 2003 and 2004, they claimed court standing for their exhumation petitions (in Grant and De Baca Counties) via their law enforcement titles and their filed murder investigation against suspect Garrett.

So I brought in the Kennedy Han Law Firm for Silver City and Fort Sumner to block exhumations based on: a) invalidity of a filed murder case against dead man (Garrett); b) irrefutable historical proofs that Garrett had killed the Kid (so was not a murderer); and c) that their Probable Cause Statement, claiming to "establish" Garrett's guilt, was just fakery of misinformation and double-talk.

Later, to public accusations of their insulting famous lawman Garrett, the hoaxers said they were doing the case to "protect his reputation;" though a murder case is to prove a suspect's guilt. Likewise, the hoaxers preposterously said they were promoting tourism by a case that would have destroyed New Mexico's Old West history!

But the hoaxers' Billy/mother exhumation cases in Fort Sumner and Silver City were legally blocked by attorneys I hired. Surprisingly, the hoaxers kept their hoax going by inventing more preposterous claims.

## HOAXING DNA FROM A CARPENTER'S BENCH

The Billy the Kid Case hoaxers needed Billy's DNA. So they manufactured some by claiming - without proof - to have obtained the carpenter's bench on which shot Billy was laid out ...

Stop. Billy laid out? But their murder case had claimed Garrett *did not shoot* Billy. And, if Billy was laid out, he was dead - and conventional history (Garrett killed Billy the Kid) held.

The hoaxers saw this "problem" also. So they created a new absurd tale in which shot Billy merely "played dead" when laid out during his wake. (Presumably, Pat massacred the innocent victim while shot Billy somehow snuck painfully off the bench during his body's night-long vigil by 200 Fort Sumner townspeople, who oddly did not notice a new dead boy substituted in his place.)

That carpenter's workbench became the source for fake Billy DNA.

To get that "Billy bench DNA," the hoaxers brought in Dr. Henry Lee (who also helped fake forensics for O.J. Simpson's own murder case problems). Lee sprayed Luminol on the carpenter's bench (which had no provable link to Billy, since it first surfaced in Fort Sumner in 1926 - 45 years after Billy's death). Luminol fluoresces with any iron compounds, including blood (and rust - more likely on a carpenter's bench!). So the bench fluoresced! And the hoaxers claimed that Lee found the blood of Billy the Kid on it! Lee's bench swabbing and scrapings were sent, for DNA extraction, to a Texas lab: Orchid Cellmark. Omitted by the hoaxers was that: a) any object exposed to people can have DNA on it; b) there was never any testing to prove there was blood on the bench; and c) it was all irrelevant since there was no verified Billy DNA to match to bench DNA. Bench DNA could have been from a sneeze by Dr. Lee!

But since it was a hoax, the hoaxers soon lied that: a) Dr. Lee had found "blood;" b) the "blood" was Billy's; and c) the lab had extracted Billy the Kid's DNA from the "blood." And the hoaxers took the necessary precaution of concealing all those Lee and Orchid Cellmark records from my years of open records requests, as they made up the results.

With this fake Billy bench blood DNA, in 2005, the hoaxers (with addition of Rick Virden as the new sheriff, who retained Sullivan and Sederwall by deputizing them as investigators for the Billy the Kid Case) were off and running to do "DNA identity matching." The murder investigation's new scheme was to say that if a Billy the Kid claimant, buried elsewhere, was real Billy (by matching the bench DNA), then Billy the Kid was not buried in his Fort Sumner grave. That would prove indirectly that Garrett killed the innocent victim, so was guilty in their murder case against him. (This was frightening - if one cared about real history - since any conclusion at all could be fabricated and presented by the hoaxers, who hid all DNA records from outside scrutiny.)

## ARIZONA EXHUMATIONS

On May 19, 2005, Sederwall, Sullivan, and Virden, under a "Lincoln County Sheriff's Department Supplemental Report," exhumed an Arizona, Billy the Kid pretender named John Miller, who had been a decade older than the real Kid - no kid; and, when alive, knew no Billy history! They also dug up a random man buried beside John Miller - William Hudspeth - because the graves were unmarked. (The hoaxers were out of control, committing felony violation of graverobbing with certainty of protection by Governor Richardson and then-Arizona Governor Janet Napolitano.) Bones of Miller and Hudspeth were sent to Orchid Cellmark Lab where DNA extractions and alleged DNA matchings with the bench DNA were done to "decide" if Miller was Billy. In 2006, a criminal complaint was filed for those exhumations by an Arizona citizen; but corrupt politician backers quashed it. Anyway, the hoaxers' still wanted Texas pretender, Oliver "Brushy Bill" Roberts, to be Billy the Kid.

## "BRUSHY'S" UNAVAILABLE CORPSE

Though Oliver "Brushy Bill" Roberts was a month shy of two years old when the Kid was killed, the Billy the Kid Case hoax scenario was as follows: Garrett did not kill Billy, who became "Brushy Bill," whom Governor Bill Richardson would then pardon for "his long and law-abiding life." (Note that Texas was to receive New Mexico's Old West history; and Richardson would arguably be the first governor to send his state's tourist industry to another state.) That bizarre scheme ended in 2007 when Texas officials blocked "Brushy's" Hamilton, Texas, grave (apparently taking no chances with DNA and their "Brushy" tourism).

By then, I realized that the Billy the Kid Case was a pay-to-play by Richardson for his political donor Attorney Bill Robins III, a "Brushy Bill" believer wanting a pardon for "Brushy Bill" as Billy the Kid.

## PUBLICITY AND PROFIT

The hoaxers had successes. In 2004, they made and appeared in a hoax-promoting History Channel program titled "Investigating History: Billy the Kid," which called Billy's killing a "mystery;" and which even "re-enacted" Garrett providing a revolver for the Kid's jailbreak (which was all lies, but not surprising, since Richardson's appointed "official historian," professor Paul Hutton, who wrote and co-produced it). Richardson got screen-time as pursuing "truth" for a pardon. In 2006, a movie, "Requiem for Billy the Kid," by a duped French director had Garrett as a murderer and was in the Cannes Film Festival, where hoaxers Sullivan and Sederwall were honored. (Sullivan spent 9 months of his sheriff's tenure being an actor in that movie.) The hoaxers continued to make TV documentaries - and Sederwall made a website in 2010 (billythekidcase.com) - to promote their false claims.

## PARDON FOR "BRUSHY BILL" AS "BILLY THE KID"

In 2010, in his last year as New Mexico Governor, Bill Richardson attempted to give a posthumous pardon as promised for "Brushy Bill" Roberts in the Billy the Kid Case hoax. That pardon was also intended to validate the entire hoax " murder investigation" itself. I blocked that thrust by bringing in Pat Garrett and Lew Wallace descendants. And Richardson left office with his hoax and fake pardon unfulfilled.

## IPRA REQUEST AND LITIGATION FOR CASE # 2003-274 FORENSIC DNA RECORDS

But the law enforcement hoaxers continued. To expose and to stop them, I used their public officials' status which subjected them to open records law (Inspection of Public Records or IPRA). So from 2003 to 2006, with an attorney and journalist as my agents - then by myself - I requested their forensic DNA records of Case 2003-274. All turn-over was refused by Lincoln County Attorney Alan Morel claiming IPRA's exception of records-blocking for an ongoing "criminal investigation."

In 2007, I made my IPRA requests by through a law firm. The requested records were: 1) Lee's report(s) of DNA specimen recoveries from the workbench; 2) Orchid Cellmark Lab's DNA extractions from Lee's bench samples; 3) Orchid Cellmark Lab's DNA extractions from bones of John Miller and William Hudspeth; and 4) matching results of the bones' DNA to the bench DNA.

Obviously, the hoaxers did not want me to see their DNA records, which would reveal that their DNA claims had been fake.

So Sheriff Virden, using Attorney Morel, began a shell game by claiming his Deputies, Sullivan and Sederwall, took the records and would not give them back. In turn, those two claimed that the murder investigation had been their "private hobby," and the records were their "trade secrets." They added that they possessed no records anyway (completing the shell game).

So, in 2007, my attorneys began IPRA enforcement litigation against Virden, Sullivan, and Sederwall in Sandoval County District Court under Judge George Eichwald, as Cause No. D-1329-CV-2007-1364. Risk Management, defending public officials from a fund of taxpayers' money, thus, began paying two defense law firms (Henry Narvaez's firm for Virden; Kevin Brown's firm for Sullivan and Sederwall) for a sum that would add up to almost a half million dollars by 2014 - while the defendants claimed to be hobbyists, not public officials! (The records were obtainable in days of my request on April 24, 2007 - costing zero dollars!)

On November 20, 2009, Judge Eichwald granted Summary Judgment to the plaintiff side, ordering that the defendants were public officials who had generated public documents for Case # 2003-274, which should be turned over to me and my co-plaintiff (the *De Baca County News*).

The defendants ignored the judge. So Eichwald ordered an Evidentiary Hearing for January 21, 2011. After it, he repeated his prior order for records turn-over.

But in 2010 to 2011, Sederwall turned over forged/tampered Dr. Lee reports to the plaintiffs' and the Court to feign compliance. After I discovered that, 2012 hearings were held for sanctions of evidence tampering, perjury, and contempt. Eichwald took no action.

Also in 2012, my co-plaintiff, Scot Stinnett, went outside of IPRA and subpoenaed Orchid Cellmark's DNA records. Getting records proved they existed, and that their DNA results were junk - proving that the hoaxers had been covering up their fake DNA claims; and had done illegal Arizona exhumations for "matchings," since they had no valid DNA of Billy the Kid for matchings with anyone to check if they were Billy.

In May of 2012, the judge ordered repeat depositions (first done in 2008) on Virden, Sederwall, and Sullivan about the DNA records and tampering. (Sullivan was out-of-state.) In his, Sederwall admitted to removing the law enforcement titles and link of Dr. Lee's report to Case # 2003-274. Virden admitted that he had made no valid attempts to get the requested records - and even waited three years into litigation to write sham request letters to Lee and Orchid Cellmark; though he claimed it was all on Attorney Morel's advice! At that point, the defendants requested mediation, which the Court ordered on September 21, 2012, but with a second Evidentiary Hearing on the DNA documents to precede that mediation.

The Evidentiary Hearing was held on December 18, 2012 and February 4, 2013. I had to go *pro se*, since my attorney had quit. And prior to the hearing I had learned that my co-plaintiff did not have standing, since he had never filed his own records request. In the hearing, I requested his dismissal - which Judge Eichwald refused. In the hearing, much additional evidence was entered for the plaintiff side. But the judge did not rule; and repeated his mediation order.

Mediation on March 26, 2013 resulted in my past attorneys and fake co-plaintiff settling out - implying the defendants conceded defeat.

On December 18, 2013 was my own hearing on IPRA costs and damages, plus sanctions against the defendants. With IPRA's daily penalties, that equaled about a million dollars. Judge Eichwald stated he would rule in 90 days (though law set 60 days).

After 90 days, Eichwald did not rule. I had to seek intervention by his Supervising Chief Judge and a Writ of Mandamus to the state Supreme Court. On May 15, 2014, Eichwald issued his 10 page "Findings of Fact and Conclusions of Law and Order of the Court" in favor of me – with eight pages confirming the defendants' inexcusable violations of IPRA law plus evidence tampering. But instead of awarding the commensurate million dollars in penalties, he gave me $1,000.00! And the defense attorneys had already pocketed almost $500,000.00! As if to obscure the injustice, Eichwald awarded to me "punitive damages" of $100,000.00 for the "bad faith" forging. He was undercutting IPRA law's intent of penalties for non-compliance. Appeals court was my only option.

## TAXPAYER BURDEN

Proved by the Billy the Kid Case hoax is that public officials' corruption is paid for by taxpayers. From 2003 to the present, Lincoln County law enforcement used taxpayer money for its hoaxing Sheriff's Department; the Lincoln County Attorney; the District Courts of De Baca, Grant, and Sandoval Counties; the state Court of Appeals (in 2012); mayors opposing Silver City and Fort Sumner exhumations; payments to defense attorneys of about $500,000.00 and mediated payment to my past attorneys of about $200,000.00. And the next step of appeals courts could enrich defense attorneys by hundreds of thousands.

## CONCLUSION

The Billy the Kid Case hoax would have destroyed New Mexico's Old West history - if not for me. "Brushy Bill" Roberts would have been "Billy the Kid" with a "pardon;" and it would have been unassailably proven by faked and hidden DNA matchings.

APPENDIX: 2. Mike Gallagher and Dan Boyd. "In the Clear: Feds Criticize Gov's Office But Skip Indictments." *Albuquerque Journal.* August 28, 2009.

Gov. Bill Richardson and two top advisors can breathe a sigh of relief over the Justice Department's decision not to pursue indictments in connection with a 1.6 billion highway bond deal, but if they were looking for clear vindication from prosecutors, they didn't get it.

A letter to defense lawyers from U.S. Attorney Greg Fouratt sent late Thursday said the United States "will not seek to bring charges against your clients" arising out of the New Mexico Finance Authority's award of financial work to California-based CDR Financial products.

Fouratt went on to say, however, that the investigation revealed that CDR and its officers made substantial contributions to Richardson's political organizations while the company was seeking the work and the "pressure from the governor's office resulted in corruption of the procurement process so that CDR would be awarded such work."

The three paragraph letter - obtained by the Journal from private attorneys in the case -  said the notification "shall not preclude the United States or the grand jury from reinstituting such an investigation without notification ... if circumstances warrant ..." Fouratt would not comment and would not provide a copy of the letter.

**The letter said," It is not to be interpreted as an exoneration of any party's conduct."** [author's boldface]

Richardson's spokesman Gilbert Gallegos responded late Thursday, saying, "The prosecutor's letter is wrong on the facts and appears to be nothing more than sour grapes."

The investigation cost Richardson a spot in President Barack Obama's Cabinet as commerce secretary. The governor withdrew his name in January when it became clear the probe would not end soon.

**The decision not to pursue indictments was made by the Department of Justice in Washington, D.C., according to attorneys familiar with the case – a development that prompted questions by Republicans in New Mexico about possible political tampering.** [author's boldface]

Richardson's office earlier Thursday issued a statement saying he had been vindicated – although it was before his lawyers received any formal notification and before the Journal informed Gallegos about Fouratt's letter ...

### Contributions

The investigation dealt with whether more than $100,000 in political contributions made by CDR and its principals influenced the company's selection as an adviser to the New Mexico Finance Authority for the GRIP bond program.

It focused on Richardson, his former chief of staff and confidant, Dave Contarino, and UNM Executive Vice President David Harris, who was in charge of the Finance Authority in 2004 when the bond program was initiated ...

Attorneys for Richardson, Harris and Contarino in April signed 90-day waivers of the statute of limitations to have the case reviewed by top prosecutors in Washington, according to attorneys familiar with the case ...

### Explanation sought

**State Republican Party Chairman Harvey Yates Jr. said Attorney General Eric Holder owed an explanation on how the decisions were made** ... [author's boldface]

New Mexico GOP Chairman Harvey Yates Jr. "Was this decision made contrary to the advice of experienced, nonpolitical, career prosecutors and the FBI? If so, what was the justification for ignoring the advice of experienced, nonpolitical prosecutors and FBI investigators?"

Lieutenant Governor Diane Denish (showing skill in speaking out of both sides of her mouth) "Assuming news reports are accurate, this is good news for the people of New Mexico. But the fact remains that public confidence has been eroded by the numerous investigations into possible wrongdoings by other government officials. We need strong ethics reform to make state government more open and accountable, and I will continue to lead that fight."

U.S. Attorney Greg Fouratt "The investigation further revealed that pressure from the governor's office resulted in corruption of the procurement process ... At this time, however, the United States will not seek to bring charges against your clients."

### APPENDIX: 3. Michael Janofsky. "122 Years Later, The Lawmen Are Still Chasing Billy the Kid." *New York Times.* June 5, 2003.

LINCOLN, NEW MEXICO – For more than 120 years, Pat Garrett has enjoyed legendary status in the American West, a lawman on a par with Wyatt Earp, Bat Masterson, even Matt Dillon. As sheriff here in Lincoln County in 1881, Garrett is credited with shooting to death the notorious outlaw known as Billy the Kid, a killing that made Garrett a hero. For years, a patch bearing his likeness has adorned uniforms worn by sheriff's deputies here.

But now, modern science is about to interrupt Garrett's fame in a way that some say could expose him as a liar who covered up a murder to save his own skin and reputation.

Officials in New Mexico and Texas are working out plans to exhume and conduct genetic tests on the bodies of a woman buried in New Mexico who was believed to be the Kid's mother and a Texas man known as Brushy Bill Roberts, who claimed to be the Kid and died in 1950 at the age of 90. If test results suggest that the two were related, it would add new evidence to a long-held alternative theory that Garrett shot someone other than the Kid and led a conspiracy to cover up his crime.

Such skepticism is hardly uncommon. Disputes over major events in the Old West have engaged historians almost since they happened. The debate over Billy the Kid is one of the longest-running.

Beyond renewing interest in the Kid saga, the possibility that testing could enlarge Garrett's reputation or destroy it has even caught the fancy of Gov. Bill Richardson of New Mexico, who has offered state aid for the investigation and a possible pardon that an earlier New Mexico governor had once promised the Kid for a murder he committed.

"The problem is, there's so much fairy tale with this story that it's hard to nail down the facts," said Steve Sederwall, the mayor of Capitan, N.N., who is working with Lincoln County's current sheriff, Tom Sullivan, to resolve the matter. "All we want is the truth, whatever it is. If the guy Garrett killed was Billy the Kid, that makes him a hero. If it wasn't, Garrett was a murderer, and we have egg on our face, big time."

No matter what the genetic testing may show - and it might not show much of anything – it is hard to overstate the prominence of Garrett and the Kid in Western lore, especially here in southeastern New Mexico where their lives converged during and after the gun battles for financial control of the region that were known as the Lincoln County War. The Kid's notoriety grew after he and friends on one side of the conflict killed several men in an ambush, including Garrett's predecessor, Sheriff William Brady. For that, the Kid was hunted down, captured by Garrett, found guilty of murder and taken to the Lincoln jail, where he was placed in shackles to await hanging. He was only 21.

Today the tiny town of Lincoln, population 38, is a memorial to what happened next. More than a dozen buildings, including one that housed the jail, have been preserved as a state monument that attracts as many as 35,000 visitors a year.

Historians generally agree that the Kid, born Henry McCarty and known at times as William H. Bonney, escaped after it became apparent that Gov. Lew Wallace had reneged on a promise to pardon him in exchange for information about another killing in the county war. On April 28, 1881, the Kid managed to get his hands on a gun, kill the two deputies assigned to watch him and leave the area on horseback.

But then the stories diverge, providing fuel for two major theories of where, when, and how the Kid's life ended.

The version embraced here and supported by numerous books and Garrett relatives is that the Kid made his way to a friend's ranch in Fort Sumner, about 100 miles northeast of Lincoln. The ranch owner, Pete Maxwell, was also a friend of Garrett and somehow got word to Garrett that the Kid was in the area. After arriving, Garrett posted two deputies at the door.

As the Kid approached on the night of July 13 [sic], he spoke a few words in Spanish to the deputies, who did not recognize him. But Garrett, waiting inside, knew the voice. When the Kid walked in, Garrett turned and shot him in the heart.

William F. Garrett of Alamogordo, N.M., who is Garrett's grand-nephew, said years of research, including conversations with his cousin Jarvis, the last of Garrett's eight children, convinced him there is "no question about it" that his great-uncle killed Billy the Kid at Maxwell's. Jarvis died in 1991 at the age of 86.

"He was hired to get the Kid, and he got the Kid," Mr. Garrett said in an interview. "uncle Pat was a person of integrity who did his job. He was a law abider, not a law breaker."

But just as the story of Garrett as hero has flourished over the years, so have others, including the tale of Brushy Bill of Hico, Tex. His trip to New Mexico in 1950 to seek the pardon he said he was denied nearly 70 years before gave new life to an alternative possibility, that Garrett had not killed the Kid at all, but a drifter friend of the Kid's named Billy Barlow.

This story holds that Garrett and the Kid may have been in cahoots for some reason and that Garrett had stashed a gun at the outhouse at the jail that the Kid used to kill the deputies and escape. Even if only part of that is true, it would strongly suggest that Garrett killed the wrong man.

**[AUTHOR'S NOTE: From the start, "Brushy" was in the hoax.]**

Speaking with the same person as Garrett's great-nephew, Jannay P. Valdez, curator of the Billy the Kid Museum in Canton, Tex., said he had no doubt that Garrett killed someone else and that Brushy Bill was the Kid. "I'm absolutely convinced," he said here on Monday after meeting with Mr. Sederwall to discuss theories and how to begin the kind of genetic testing that has been used to ascertain lineage of other historical figures like Thomas Jefferson and Jessie James. "I'd bank everything I have on it."

As longtime friends, Mr. Sederwall and Sheriff Sullivan decided they wanted to settle the matter once and for all but could do so only through scientific analysis. To justify the effort that would require much of their time and, perhaps at some point, taxpayer money,

**[AUTHOR'S NOTE: First, the hoaxers admitted to using taxpayer money. Later, under investigation by me, they denied it.]**

They needed an official reason. So in April, they opened the first-ever investigation into the murders of the two deputies shot in the Kid's escape, James W. Bell and Robert Olinger, to examine what happened at the jail and Maxwell's ranch.

**[AUTHOR'S NOTE: Janofsky is parroting the hoax. The deputy murders and Garrett's killing of the Kid are unconnected, but the hoaxers made up that Garrett gave the escape gun.]**

As Mr. Sederwall said, "There's no statute of limitations on murder."

**[AUTHOR'S NOTE: This announces the real murder case; though misrepresented is the statute of limitation on murder in New Mexico – which once did have such a statute.]**

The goal now, he said, is to compare genetic evidence of Catherine Antrim, believed to be the Kid's mother, who died of tuberculosis in 1874 and is buried in Silver City, N.M., and of Brushy Bill, who lived out his life in Texas. A Dallas firm [sic Houston] has agreed to help, and a spokesman for governor Richardson said the state would assist by clearing legal hurdles to gain access to the mother's body.

**[AUTHOR'S NOTE: Note state aid is promised.]**

The Kid was buried at Fort Sumner, N.M., although the whereabouts of the grave are uncertain;

**[AUTHOR'S NOTE: Uncertain location, though true, was later hidden by the hoaxers when trying to exhume. But that invalidated any DNA sought, and should have ended the case.]**

He has no known living relatives. Mr. Valdez said he had already secured permission to exhume the body of Brushy Bill,

**[AUTHOR'S NOTE: This is untrue.]**

who is buried 20 miles from Hico in Hamilton, Texas.

But solving the mystery might not be so simple. For one thing, Mr. Valdez said he was certain that the woman buried in Silver City was but "a half aunt." And even if tests disqualify Brushy Bill as Billy the Kid, other "Kids" have emerged over the years, including a man named John Miller, who died in 1937 and is buried in Prescott, Ariz. Mr. Sederwall said that efforts would be made to exhume his body as well.

The investigators conceded that much is riding on their quest. Sheriff Sullivan, a tall, strapping man who carries a turquoise-handled .357 magnum on his right hip, said he, like so many others in the West, revered Garrett for gunning down the Kid. The uniform patch with Garrett's likeness was his design. Now, the legend is threatened.

**[AUTHOR'S NOTE: Only the hoaxers are threatening!]**

"I just want to get to the bottom of it," said Sheriff Sullivan, who is retiring next year. "My integrity's at stake. So's my department's. So's what we believe in and even New Mexico history. If Garrett shot someone other than the Kid, that makes him a murderer and he covered it up. He wouldn't be such a role model, then, and we'd have to take the patches off the uniforms."

APPENDIX: 4. Governor Bill Richardson press release.
June 10, 2003

### State of New Mexico
*Office of the Governor*

**Bill Richardson**
Governor
For immediate release                    Contact: Billy Sparks
6/10/03                                   telephone number

## GOVERNOR BILL RICHARDSON ANNOUNCES
## STATE SUPPORT OF BILLY THE KID INVESTIGATION

SANTA FE – Governor Bill Richardson today outlined how the state of New Mexico will support the investigation efforts to investigate the life and death of Billy the Kid.

Governor Richardson delivered the following remarks during a news conference today in the State Capitol:

This is an important day in the history of New Mexico and the American West. I am announcing my support and the support of the state of New Mexico for the investigation into the life and death of Henry McCarty, also known as William Bonney. To millions around the world, he was called Billy the Kid. How he captured the world's imagination is well worth exploring. His life, though ended at the age of 21, is part of what makes New Mexico and an American West, unique.

My goal is to shed new light on old history.

I am pleased to be joined here by Lincoln County Sheriff Tom Sullivan, Capitan Mayor Steve Sederwall, DeBaca County Sheriff Gary Grays [sic]. Grant County Attorney Sherry Tippett, University of New Mexico History Professor, Doctor Paul Hutton and State Police Major Tom Branch.

Let me tell you how this all came about.

Last month I was contacted by Lincoln County Sheriff, Tom Sullivan and Capitan Mayor, Steve Sederwall, to support reopening the case. **Case number 2003-274** [author's boldface] seeks to answer key questions that have lingered for over 120 years surrounding the life and the death of Billy the Kid.

This episode in the history of New Mexico and the history of the old west is both fact and legend and continues to stir the imagination and interest of people all over the world.

By utilizing modern forensic, DNA and crime scene techniques, the goal of the investigation is to get to the truth. In the process, the reputation of Pat Garrett, still a hero in Lincoln County law enforcement, hangs in the balance. The question is did Sheriff Garrett kill Billy the Kid at Fort Sumner, New Mexico on July 14. 1881?

This investigation will also seek to shed new light on the events surrounding the escape of Billy the Kid from the Lincoln County Jail on April 28, 1881. The shooting of Deputies J.W. Bell and Bob Olinger by Billy the Kid has never been officially investigated. Where did Billy get his gun and what really happened?

I have contacted the national Labs, Los Alamos and Sandia and have been assured that they will volunteer their support in this effort. Los Alamos Lab can assist us by providing ground penetrating radar, DNA expertise and technical forensic assistance. Sandia Labs will allow their experts to volunteer their time to help us uncover the facts.

The State Police will help supervise the investigation and crime scene analysis of the evidence uncovered in the investigation.

I have also asked University of New Mexico Professor of History and Executive Director of the Western History Association, Doctor Paul Hutton, to serve as our historical advisor. Dr. Hutton has served as President of the Western Writers of America and has won several national honors for his works on western history.

I intend to hold hearings at Fort Sumner, Lincoln, Silver City and Mesilla. I will appoint a defense counsel and a prosecutor to present the evidence.

**[AUTHOR'S NOTE: This more scholarly approach was never done. The Billy the Kid Case relied instead on no evidence and hoaxed claims to the present.]**

As Governor, I will examine the events surrounding the alleged offer of a pardon to Billy the Kid by former New Mexico Governor Lew Wallace. I will evaluate the evidence uncovered and make a decision.

There is no question that this story deserves our attention and that the history of New Mexico and the American West is important to all of us.

If we can get to the truth we will. I have total confidence in the team you see here today to conduct a professional, honest and exhaustive investigation of the facts and report back to me and to the rest of the world what really happened here in New Mexico.

The benefits to our state and to the history of the West far outweigh any cost we may incur. I expect the actual cost to be nominal. Just since this investigation was announced, it has sparked news articles about New Mexico and Lincoln County from New York to London to India. Getting to the truth is our goal. But, if this increases interest and tourism in our state, I couldn't be happier.

I understand that Movie Producer Ron Howard has donated the cabin used in shooting his movie "The Missing", being shot in Santa Fe, to Silver City. The cabin is a replica of a Billy the Kid era home. The cabin will be delivered to Silver City this week.

The potential benefit from this investigation to all of New Mexico is already being felt and is well worth the effort.    #30#

APPENDIX: 5. Steve Sederwall. "Mayor's Report." *Capitan Village Hall News.* May, 2003. [Excerpt, pages 2-3]

... On April 28, 2003, at five minutes after noon, one of our citizens, Sheriff Tom Sullivan fired two shots in Lincoln, New Mexico. The floor under my feet shook at each report of his pistol. The gun smoke hung in the air just as in a western novel would describe it. As I heard the shots a cold chill ran down my back knowing that J.W. Bell heard the shots that killed him.

A 122 years before, just minutes after twelve, noon, on April 28, 1881, two lawmen lay dead, in the yard of the courthouse in Lincoln , New Mexico, from gunshot wounds. Quicker than it took New Mexico breeze to clear the gunsmoke, history was clouded with the myth of the shooting and escape of William H. Bonney a.k.a. Billy the Kid from the make-shift jail where he awaited the date with the hangman.

Sheriff Sullivan and I have opened a case into that shooting in 1881. As part of the investigation Sheriff Sullivan fired off two rounds from a .45 Long Colt to see if the shots could be heard from the Wortley Hotel. To our surprise the black powder rounds loaded for us by Virgil Hall could be heard in nearly every part of town.

This investigation came about after Sheriff Sullivan and I talked about a man by the name of Brushy Bill Roberts. In 1950 Roberts ["Brushy Bill"] came to the Governor of New Mexico with his attorney [sic - William Morrison, not an attorney]; saying he was Billy the Kid. He said that Pat Garrett shot a man by the name of Billy Barlow and buried his body claiming to be that of Billy the Kid. Roberts said he lived out a life within the bounds of the law under an assumed name and wanted a pardon that was promised to him by Governor Wallace.

**[AUTHOR'S NOTE: First known reference connecting hoax claim that Garrett did not kill the Kid, to pretender Oliver "Brushy Bill" Roberts. I first thought it was for "survival" evidence.]**

On the surface of this story [Brushy Bill Roberts's] you would say "so what?" But if you look at this man's claim he is saying our Sheriff Pat Garrett is a murderer. Garrett knew the Kid and killed someone else. What this says also is that Pete Maxwell who said the body is of The Kid is a co-conspirator in a murder. There is no statute of limitations on Murder [sic], so the Lincoln County Sheriff's Office has opened a case to pursue the investigation. If Brushy Bill Roberts is Billy the Kid then history changes. But if he is lying, we need to clear Garrett's name.

**[AUTHOR'S NOTE: Confirming the case as a filed murder investigation, with a "Brushy" emphasis.]**

I feel this investigation will put a positive light on the county, our town and the state in whole. Tom Sullivan and I have been in touch with the Governor's office and he is behind us. People who are conducting DNA on victims of the World Trade Center have agreed to complete DNA tests for us on remains of persons believed to be Billy the Kid. We have a filmmaker creating a made-for-TV story about this investigation. We have recruited some of the best investigators in the country from other states to assist in this investigation. The Sheriff and I feel this should not only clear up a 122-year-old mystery but also bring money into our village ...

Tom Sullivan and I know it is a crazy idea but won't it be fun.

**[AUTHOR'S NOTE: The "fun" mantra repeated through hoax.]**

**APPENDIX: 6. Anthony DellaFlora. "State Not Kidding Around: Governor won't mind if probe of the notorious 19th century N.M. outlaw boosts tourism."** *Albuquerque Journal.* **Front Page. June 11, 2003.**

SANTA FE - With lawmen on his side, Gov. Bill Richardson announced Tuesday he was throwing the weight of the state behind an investigation of New Mexico's most notorious outlaw, Billy the Kid.

Richardson said he hoped that nearly 122 years after The Kid's purported death, investigators and historians could separate fact from fantasy.

He also acknowledged the probe could be a boon to tourism.

"My goal is to shed light on an old story. My goal is to get the truth about the legend of Billy the Kid," Richardson said during a news conference in the packed Cabinet room of the Governor's Office.

Richardson emphasized the probe's cost to taxpayers would be "minimal," since almost all the assistance would be voluntary.

He also acknowledged that the state could benefit from the publicity.

"Getting to the truth is our goal, but if this increases interest in tourism in our state, I couldn't be happier. I know this is good publicity for the state, and I make no bones about improving our image around the world with this investigation," Richardson said.

The investigation likely will include DNA testing using samples from Catherine Antrim, the woman believed to be the mother of The Kid, born Henry McCarty and later known as William Bonney.

Her remains are believed to be in a grave in Silver City.

Richardson also pledged the help of the state police, who will supervise the investigation and crime scene analysis.

He said Los Alamos and Sandia National laboratories will volunteer manpower, and Los Alamos also would provide forensic assistance and ground penetrating radar. The radar is used to locate remains.

**University of New Mexico history professor Paul Hutton, executive director of the Western History Association, also will aid in the investigation.** [author's boldface]

[AUTHOR'S NOTE: Hutton, when investigated by me, falsely denied any connection to the Billy the Kid Case.]

Finally, Richardson said he would appoint a defense counsel and prosecutor to present evidence in hearings planned for Fort Sumner, Lincoln, Silver City and Mesilla, towns that are all part of the Billy the Kid legend.

The probe could take a year, Richardson said.

Although most believe that the Kid's remains are buried in DeBaca County at Fort Sumner, where Sheriff Pat Garrett supposedly shot the outlaw on July 14, 1881, questions have been raised over the years.

DNA testing may not be able to prove Billy the Kid is buried there, but it could eliminate two other claimants - "Brushy" Bill Roberts of Hico, Texas, and John Miller of Prescott, Ariz. - who surfaced well after the Fort Sumner shooting, purporting to be Billy the Kid.

That would help to answer the question of whether Garrett shot the right man, or actually may have been complicit in The Kid's escape, as some history buffs have alleged.

The latest twist on the Billy saga occurred when Lincoln County Sheriff Tom Sullivan and Capitan Mayor Steve Sederwall, also a reserve officer, decided in April to launch their own probe into The Kid's bloody escape from the Lincoln County Courthouse in 1881.

The escape left two lawmen dead, deputies J.W. Bell and Bob Olinger.

Sullivan and Sederwall along with DeBaca County Sheriff Gary Graves, flanked Richardson at Tuesday's news conference. All three lawmen looked like they had stepped out of the Kid's era: cowboy hats, western-style shirts, bolo ties and mustaches.

Sullivan said it was a visit to Hico, where Brushy Bill is celebrated as the real Billy the Kid, that prompted him to open the investigation. He said Hico's claim is contrary to New Mexico history.

Sullivan said Garrett's face serves as a proud symbol of the Lincoln County Sheriff's Office, and he would like to remove the cloud over the famous lawman's name.

Sederwall said he thought it was proper to look into the deaths of fellow lawmen Bell and Olinger. The killings were never officially investigated.

The Kid was being held in Lincoln for hanging after his conviction for the killing of Sheriff William Brady during the "Lincoln County War," a conflict between business groups vying for economic dominance of the county.

After returning from a visit to the outhouse, The Kid shot Bell, then waited for Olinger to return from lunch, before shooting him to death. No one witnessed The Kid shooting Bell, and there are differing stories on how he acquired the lethal weapon, including one version that says an accomplice left a gun in the outhouse for him.

Sullivan believes a bullet, or fragments of it, from the Bell shooting may still be embedded in the wall of the courthouse, and could prove whether Bell was killed by his own weapon or another.

Richardson said the investigation could result in the pardon of Billy the Kid for the killing of Brady and others before the courthouse escape.

In 1878, then-Gov. Lew Wallace had wanted to bring order to Lincoln County, and made a deal with The Kid in Lincoln to pardon him if he would testify to what he knew about the Lincoln County War.

The outlaw testified, but a district attorney refused Wallace's request to drop the charges and Billy the Kid escaped.

Brushy Bill, at 92, came to New Mexico in 1950, claiming to be the Kid and asking that his pardon be given.

Then-Gov. Thomas Mabry rejected the claim and the petition for a pardon ...

"Billy can't be killed," Hutton said wryly. "He's the outlaw of our dreams."

Hutton was part of a 1990 investigation by the Lincoln County Heritage Trust that used computers to compare the one known photo image of Bonny with those of Ollie "Brushy Bill" Roberts, a Hico, Texas man who claimed to be Billy the Kid.

That investigation determined that Roberts claim was false.

However, a Billy the Kid museum in Hico dedicated to Roberts is what prompted Lincoln County Sheriff Tom Sullivan - who has the job once held by the man historians believe killed Bonney - to reopen the investigation.

Richardson maintains that he would pardon Billy "only if a convincing amount of evidence points in that direction."

Richardson said it bothers him that Territorial Gov. Lew Wallace might have promised the outlaw a pardon for the murder of Sheriff William Brady in exchange for testimony in another murder trial ... "I feel a certain responsibility if Lew Wallace made such a promise," Richardson said.

However, even if the Kid might have been owed a pardon by Wallace, there's little chance that the outlaw will be cleared of the subsequent killings of Deputies James Bell and Bob Olinger during his escape from the Lincoln County Courthouse.

Hutton said there's no evidence that someone other than Bonney killed the deputies.

"The real question is, who helped him," said Hutton ...

Sullivan and others pushing for the investigation hope to determine from modern ballistic tests if the gun used to kill Bell and Olinger belonged to one of the deputies - which would support the argument that Bonney wrested it away from Bell - or if it belonged to someone else, which would point to outside help.

**[AUTHOR'S NOTE: There exists no gun – or any other piece of evidence - from the deputy killings to prove anything!]**

## APPENDIX: 7. Julie Carter. "Follow the Blood: In the Billy the Kid Case, Miller Exhumed." *RuidosoNews.com*. October 2005.

One established absolute fact to date in the ongoing saga of the legend of Billy the Kid is that he is dead. That fact can be written without question because 145 [sic - 146] years since he was born would make it so.

The looming question today is, Where is he dead? Currently, investigators are waiting to see if the DNA taken from a carpenter's work bench last summer (July 2004) matches the DNA taken in May from the exhumed body of John Miller, one of two who claimed to be William H. Bonney aka Billy the Kid.

The carpenter's work bench is reportedly the one the Kid was laid on by friends in the Maxwell compound in Ft. Sumner after he was shot.

### [AUTHOR'S NOTE: Hoax switch from innocent victim to Billy.]

Retired Lincoln County Sheriff Tom Sullivan and retired federal cop and Capitan Mayor Steve Sederwall continue to pursue the official investigation they began in 2003.

### [AUTHOR'S NOTE: The hoaxers are concealing their active deputyships under Sheriff Rick Virden.]

Seeing too many holes in the Billy the Kid legend and knowing that science could now prove fact from century old supposition, the pair set out to do just that.

On April 28, 2003, the 122 anniversary of the escape of Billy the Kid from the Lincoln County Court-house, Sullivan and Sederwall opened Lincoln County Case # 2003-274 into the deaths of Bob Olinger and J.W. Bell whose murders were never investigated or prosecuted.

### [AUTHOR'S NOTE: Fake switcheroo of case to deputy murders from their Garrett as murder filing.]

Investigators fired off two black powder rounds to see if the shots inside of the courthouse could be heard from the hotel and as far down the street as the Ellis Store.

### [AUTHOR'S NOTE: This is the deputy murder sub-investigation.]

Later joined by De Baca County Sheriff (Ft. Sumner) Gary Graves, the trio launched a probe into the Kid's escape that led to his slaying in July 1881 in Ft. Sumner. The aim of the investigation has always been to use forensic science and modern police techniques to clear up questions about the Kid's escape and death.

Joining Sederwall and Sullivan in the search for the facts is Bill Kurtis, executive producer of A&E Channel's Cold Case Files, American

Justice and Investigative Reports. Kurtis has had cameras running to document the progress of the investigation including the scraping of material in the bench that has revealed human DNA and **a blood pattern consistent with an upper chest wound** (author's boldface) such as the one the Kid was said to have received from Garrett on July 14, 1881.

"Whoever was laid on that, whether it was Billy the Kid or not," said Sederwall, "he left his DNA." The investigators said the amount of blood found on the bench indicated that whoever was on that bench must have been still alive. **"Dead men don't bleed," explained Sederwall. "and we witnessed a large amount of blood."** [author's boldface]

**[AUTHOR'S NOTE: Here is the hoax switcheroo to shot Billy.]**

When the lab called and said the DNA was human and it was the same DNA on the three-board-wide bench, Sederwall and Sullivan decided it was time to start looking at the John Miller story a little harder.

**[AUTHOR'S NOTE: This is a confusingly worded paragraph seems to be a claim of a Miller and bench match.]**

With both Sederwall and Sullivan present, the exhumation of Miller took place on May 21 in Prescott, Ariz., where he was buried in the cemetery of the Pioneer Home ...

This case has not failed to amaze us at every turn, said Sederwall. John Miller even held some surprises for us. He had buck teeth just as history tells us the Kid had. But we were shocked to see that Miller sported a very old bullet wound that entered the left chest and exited the shoulder blade, the same wound Garrett claimed to have inflicted on the Kid the night in July 1881.

**[AUTHOR'S NOTE: This is hoaxing. Miller's skull was toothless. William Hudspeth's *right* scapula had an imperfection – denied as gunshot by on-site forensic expert, Dr. Laura Fulginiti.]**

Miller's samples have been sent to an unnamed laboratory in Texas to extract DNA ...

**[AUTHOR'S NOTE: Here, Orchid Cellmark Lab is concealed.]**

In his investigation Sederwall found a photo of the carpenter work bench originally thought to be lost. The Maxwell compound and everything in it was reportedly washed away in a flood of 1906. The photo of the bench was taken in 1926 by historian Maurice Fulton.

Our thinking was, said Sederwall, that if they took a picture of it, it was important and someone still has the bench. We also noticed that the museum in Ft. Sumner had a piece of tapestry that was the same tapestry shown in the window of the bench photo. If the tapestry survived the flood, so did the bench.

Tracing down through the generations of the Maxwell family tree, Sederwall found not only a 1936 written reference to the items from the bedroom where the Kid was said to be shot, but in Albuquerque in August 2003 he found direct descendents of the Pete Maxwell family. Since 1959, they had stored the historical furniture and household items in an old chicken coop. The carpenter's workbench was intact as was the entire bedroom set including the wash-stand said to be pierced by Garrett's second bullet shot in the dark at the Kid.

### Enter Dr. Henry Lee.

Dr. Lee is one of the nation's leading forensic scientists with case names attached to his including O.J. Simpson, JonBenet Ramsey and Lacy Peterson. Lee was anxious to aid Billy the Kid to his resume and called the investigators to offer his services.

**[AUTHOR'S NOTE: This is hoaxing of Dr. Lee's "offer."]**

The director of the Connecticut State Police Forensic Laboratory traveled to Lincoln County in July 2004 to conduct tests in both the Lincoln County Courthouse and in Albuquerque on the workbench and wash stand.

Using high-tech lasers and other modern crime scene methods, investigators learned that the shooting of the Kid in Pete Maxwell's bedroom was not in the way history has portrayed it.

Tests indicate that Garrett fired his second shot from the doorway while on his knees and with his left hand on the floor, firing back over his shoulder, recounted Sederwall. Being blinded by his first shot, it appears he was in a great hurry to get out of the room and fell to the floor.

**[AUTHOR'S NOTE: This is a hoaxed crime scene reconstruction.]**

He added: "To find the furniture from Maxwell's bedroom was great. But to have Dr. Lee recover usable evidence was truly a historical find."

### No digging in New Mexico

Attempts to obtain permission to exhume the Kid's body from his Ft. Sumner grave and the body of his mother buried in a Silver City cemetery were blocked by municipal officials in both towns. Investigators had hoped to use modern forensics to scientifically prove or disprove the claims made by Brushy Bill Roberts and John Miller that they were the Kid. Their stories offered the possibility that the Kid did not die on July 14, 1881, in Ft. Sumner.

[AUTHOR'S NOTE: Omitted are OMI reasons for blockage based on invalid DNA from uncertain gravesites.]

A judge in Silver City told the investigators to come back if they had enough evidence to warrant the need for Catherine Antrim's (the Kid's mother) DNA. With the DNA results from the blood on the table and soon the results of Miller's DNA, investigators will likely move to take the judge up on that offer.

[AUTHOR'S NOTE: This misstates Judge Henry Quintero stipulation that return to the Antrim grave required DNA obtained from the Fort Sumner Billy the Kid grave.]

In the light of the evidence, we see that the history of Billy the Kid will change. Those with monied interest in history remaining the same will not be happy, stated Sederwall.

As a cop I know when people fight to keep you from looking at something, they are always trying to hide something. The Lincoln County War is still going on. (author's boldface)

[AUTHOR'S NOTE: Example of the false, but grandiose, pronouncements characterizing hoax press. Ultimately, the hoaxers' DNA claims in the press would be debunked by my getting the actual junk DNA reports from their lab. ]


APPENDIX: 8. Rene Romo. "Forensic Expert on Billy's Case: Questions Remain on Outlaw's Fate." *Albuquerque Journal.* Front Page. August 2, 2004.

LINCOLN - Dr. Henry Lee, one of the nation's leading forensic scientists, has worked on the O.J. Simpson murder trial and the JonBenet Ramsey case. Now he has added the Billy the Kid slaying to his case files ...

"This is an extremely interesting case of some historical importance," Lee said in an interview before arriving at the old Lincoln County courthouse Sunday afternoon. "That's why I agreed to spend some of my own time to work with them ... It's basically a worthwhile project and legitimate" ...

On Saturday at an undisclosed location in Albuquerque, Lee, assisted by Calvin Ostler, an investigator with the Utah Office of the Medical Examiner, performed tests on the bench that Sederwall believes to be the one on which the Kid's body was laid out after Garrett gunned him down.

Preliminary results indicated **trace evidence of blood** (author's boldface), but, without further testing, it is not certain whether the blood was human, Lee said.

Lee and the investigators also examined a washstand that was purportedly struck by a bullet when Garrett shot the Kid in a bedroom of the outlaw's friend, Pete Maxwell, in Fort Sumner ...

Lee and the investigators used laser technology Saturday to determine the trajectory of the bullet as it entered the left side of the washstand and exited the right at a downward angle. Given the washstand's likely location in the room, the investigation has already cast some doubt on Garrett's account of the fatal shooting, Sederwall and Ostler said.

"The evidence we are seeing does not corroborate the popular legend," Ostler said. "Something's askew."

Still, Ostler said, the nightstand's orientation in the room is still indefinite and it is not certain that a bullet from a .44 caliber revolver made the hole.

One simple explanation that Lee offered is that Garrett may have shot defensively at the Kid as he fled and struck the washstand from the side instead of head on. Garrett's official story may have omitted that embarrassing detail. "You don't want to paint yourself as a chicken," Lee suggested.

Lee and the investigators Sunday afternoon also found several positive indications of blood residue below floor-boards at the top of a stairwell in the old Lincoln County courthouse.

Such evidence could support Sederwall's theory that the Kid fatally shot deputy J.W. Bell there, at the top of the stairs, in his infamous escape from the Lincoln County jail. That version would also contradict Garrett's account that the Kid, at the top of the stairs, shot Bell who was at the bottom of the stairwell ...

"You're getting the top guy. Lee thinks it's significant enough to try to find a positive reaction to these tests, and I think that will go a long way to finding out what happened in Lincoln," said David S. Turk, a historian with the U.S. Marshals Service in Washington, D.C., who is cooperating on the case.

**[AUTHOR'S NOTE: David Turk is a fellow hoaxer and contributor to the Probable Cause Statement. This is an example of hoaxer ricochet-style validation of each other.]**

## APPENDIX: 9. Doris Cherry. "Forensics 101 for 'Billy." *Lincoln County News*. Front Page. August 12, 2004.

Sullivan, in his continued search for the true story of William Bonney alias Billy the Kid, had the opportunity to watch as Dr. Henry Lee world famous forensic scientist tested a piece of old furniture which was reputed to have held the body of Billy the Kid ...

Along with Sullivan and Lee were crew from Curtis [sic] Production Company filming for the History Channel and Court T.V. Dr. Lee also has a show produced by Curtis [sic] Production, Sullivan added.

The focus of attention for Dr. Lee was an old bench ... The bench has been in the Maxwell family descendents since 1881 and has been stored out of weather, protecting the blood evidence, Sederwall said. Only once was the blood exposed to the elements, when a family member who took the bench without family approval returned it to the Maxwell family home in Fort Sumner and left it outside to get rained on once. So the odds of finding blood evidence were very good.

Dr. Lee proved the good odds by utilizing a laser to bore into the wood of the bench to take samples and he took scrapings from the top and underneath of the bench. "then he swabbed it with the chemical that changes color to indicate the presence of blood," Sullivan said.

**He found a lot of blood**," (author's boldface) Sullivan added.

After the swabbing and scraping Dr. Lee used duminal [sic - Luminol], which under a florescent light glows in the presence of blood evidence. "At the bottom of the bench there was only a weak positive for blood evidence," Sullivan said. "But as he moved up the middle of the bench it was stronger positive and underneath the bench it was very strong positive."

Each swab and all scrapings from the bench were sealed in preparation to shipping to the Orchard Selmark [sic - Orchid Cellmark] Lab in Dallas. Sullivan said Dr. Lee uses the lab for most of his work, and the lab is also famous for its forensic work to determine DNA of the 9-11 victims ...

Sullivan said that after studying the courthouse and the shooting he contended Bell was really killed at the top of the stairs, not near the bottom of the stairs as legend has it. "We started with the original flooring at the top of the stairs," Sullivan said. "We got weak and strong positive for blood."

"Then we went downstairs and got a ladder and tested the underneath of the boards at the top of the stairs," Sullivan continued, "We got a strong positive."

"The duminal [sic - luminol] lit up with strong positive of blood," Sullivan said ...

Proving this blood evidence is from Bell could be hard to do as no one has been able to find a living descendent of Bell's, Sullivan added.

The blood evidence from the bench is important, because they hope it will provide the DNA evidence for Billy the Kid, said Sullivan ...

However, the district court in Grant County dismissed Sullivan's request to exhume the body of Catherine Antrim with [sic - without] prejudice. "The judge said to bring him Billy's DNA first," Sullivan said.

Soon they may have that DNA, derived from the scrapings and swabs taken from the bench ... Once they have the DNA evidence from the bench, Sullivan and his privately financed attorney Bill Robins will again submit a request to the Grant County District Court to exhume Antrim's body ...

APPENDIX: 10. Rene Romo. *Albuquerque Journal.* "Billy the Kid Probe May Yield New Twist." November 6, 2005.

[AUTHOR'S NOTE: The article was prepared with then Arizona Governor Janet Napolitano's Office and Arizona Pioneers' Home Supervisor Gary Olson to cover-up the illegal exhumations of John Miller and William Hudspeth.]

LAS CRUCES - An ongoing investigation into the fate of Henry McCarty, alias William Bonney, alias Billy the Kid, could still yield a surprising twist in the controversial case.

Without any fanfare, former Lincoln County Sheriff Tom Sullivan and Steve Sederwall last May obtained DNA from the remains of a cowboy, John Miller. Before dying in the 1930's Miller told friends and a son that he was really Billy the Kid.

Miller's remains were exhumed from the cemetery of the Pioneer [sic] Home, a state-owned nursing home in Prescott, Ariz. His DNA is to be examined by a Dallas-based laboratory.

If Miller's DNA matches that of blood traces taken from a 19th century bench purportedly from the Maxwell Ranch in Fort Sumner, Sederwall and Sullivan say they could have a break that upends accepted historical accounts of the Kid's life and death.

The old bench was discovered last year at the Albuquerque home of Maxwell descendents. It is believed to be the one on which the Kid's body was placed after he was shot by Lincoln County Sheriff Pat Garrett on July 14, 1881, in a darkened bedroom of the Maxwell Ranch.

"Wouldn't it be a coincidence if someone we dug up in Arizona, and who died in 1934 and claimed to be Billy the Kid, bled on the bench? That's like winning the lottery," Sederwall said.

"That would be so coincidental, I would challenge anyone to prove it's not him (Billy the Kid)."

**Sederwall acknowledges that what started out as an effort to defend the honor of Garrett against claims that the famous Lincoln County sheriff did not kill the Kid may have taken a new direction.** [author's boldface]

[AUTHOR'S NOTE: Under my investigation and litigation, the hoaxers switched from their Probable Cause Statement accusing Garrett of murder, to claiming preposterously that they were doing a murder case to prove him innocent!]]

Sullivan and Sederwall began their investigation in 2003 when Sullivan was sheriff and Sederwall a reserve deputy. But they were rebuffed in their 2003 and 2004 attempts to exhume the Kid's remains in Fort Sumner and those of the outlaw's mother in Silver City.

The Lincoln County investigators wanted to use the DNA from the Kid's grave, or that of his mother, to validate the widely accepted story of Garrett's killing of Billy the Kid.

But critics in Fort Sumner and Silver City, as well as history buffs around the country, lambasted Sullivan and Sederwall, saying that the Kid's death and burial in De Baca County was well established.

Fort Sumner officials, in particular, fretted that the investigation would undermine the value of the Kid's grave there as a tourist destination.

**[AUTHOR'S NOTE: Hoax damage control: blaming local officials and "tourism," instead of the truth: invalid DNA.]**

In the decades after the Kid's demise, several old men emerged claiming they were Billy the Kid. One would-be Billy was Ollie P. "Brushy Bill" Roberts of Hico, Texas. Another was John Miller, the subject of a book called "Whatever Happened to Billy the Kid" by Helen Airy.

While Sederwall and Sullivan have both been commissioned as special deputies by current Lincoln County Sheriff Rick Virden, Sederwall said their investigation does not use county funds.

Sederwall said he expected the analysis of Miller's DNA to be completed by the end of the year or January.

If Miller's DNA matches what is presumed to be the Kid's on the bench, the news will be publicized by Bill Kurtis, anchor of the A&E Network weekly series "American Justice," Sederwall said.

**He said Kurtis, head of Chicago-based Kurtis Productions, has an "exclusive deal" to publicize the news because Kurtis helped to pay for some costs associated with the investigation.** [author's boldface]

**Sederwall, who is also the mayor of Capitan and a history buff, said Miller's skeletal remains were intriguing. He said Miller had buck teeth, like the Kid, and an old bullet wound that entered his upper left chest and exited through the scapula.** [author's boldface]

**[AUTHOR'S NOTE: This hoaxed skeleton is contradicted by the forensic report of on-site forensic expert, Dr. Laura Fulginiti. The Miller skull had no teeth. And the William Hudspeth skeleton had a damaged right scapula – and no bullet damage.]**

If that DNA matches the work bench, I think the game is over," Sederwall said.

If not, he said, investigators will try to obtain permission to exhume the remains of Roberts, who is buried in Hamilton, Texas.

758

# Forensic Research & Training Center

## Forensic Examination Report

Date of Request: May 22, 2004
Requested By: Lincoln County Sheriff's Office, New Mexico
Investigation History Program, Kurtis Production
Local Case No. 2003-274
Date of Report: February 25, 2005
Report to: Steve Sederwell
Lincoln County Sheriff's Office, New Mexico

## Introduction

At the request of Steve Sederwell of Lincoln County Sheriff's Office, Lincoln County, Bill Kurtis and Jamie Schenk of Kurtis Production, Dr. Henry Lee went to New Mexico on July 31, 2004 to assist in the re-investigation of the case of Billy the Kid. The forensic investigation team participating in re-investigation consist the following individuals:

> Dr. Henry Lee, Chief Emeritus of the Connecticut State Police Forensic Laboratory
> Calvin Ostler, Forensic Consultant, Riverton, Utah
> Kim Ostler, Crime Scene Assistant, Riverton, Utah
> Tom Sullivan, Sheriff, Lincoln County, New Mexico
> Steve Sederwall Deputy Sheriff, Lincoln County, New Mexico
> David Turk, US Marshall, United States Marshall Service

In addition, Mike Haag, Firearm examiner from Albuquerque Police Department Crime Lab, also provided valuable technical assistance in the investigation.

The forensic investigation team arrived at the Mr. Manny Miller residence, located at 1503 Cleave Road, Albuquerque, New Mexico, at 18:20 hours on Saturday, July 31, 2004. Upon arrival we were presented with three pieces of evidence: a worktable, a washstand, and a headboard. The three pieces of evidence had been removed from a storage building at the rear of the residence by Sheriff Sullivan, Deputy Sederwall, and members of Bill Kurtis Productions. Each item was inspected visually and macroscopically. The following were found:

## Item # 1 Workbench

This Workbench is approximately 86 inches in length, 29 inches in width and is made entirely of wood. Figure 1 illustrates the approximate dimensions of the Workbench. The width of the workbench is not consistent throughout the length, and stands an average of approximately 31 inches in height, however each leg is a slightly different length (as shown in Figure 1).

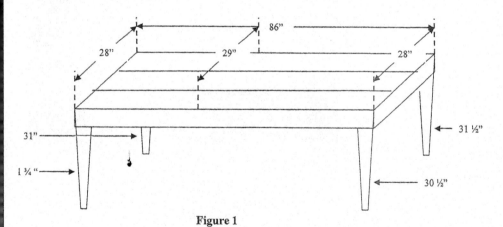

**Figure 1**

The wood comprising the Workbench is secured together with nails. At least four different types of nails were identified on the workbench. The top surface of the Workbench is comprised of three major planks which run longitudinally. Figure 2 shows the assembly of the planks on the surface of the workbench.

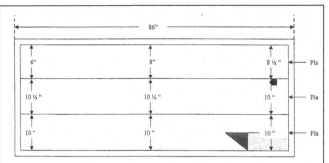

Figure 2 Top of Workbench with plank sizes

Photograph No 1 depicts an overall view of the workbench. There is a defective area on the lower right hand corner of Plank 1. This defective area is marked on the lower right hand corner of Figure 2. A piece of rectangular board has been nailed over the hole to cover this defective area as showing in photograph No. 1. The black triangle immediately to the left of the rectangle represents the end of the hole in Plank 1, which is the area that the board does not cover. The black square on the upper right hand edge of Plank 2 represents a hole in Plank 2.

Page 3

Photo No. 1

Visual and macroscopical examinations reveal several brownish stains. Those areas were further examined under illumination of ALS light source. Some of the stains contain a variety of other colored crusty materials.

Three brown color stains were found on Plank 1. Following are observations of those stains on Plank 1:

Area "1": Located approximately 4" to 11" from the right hand end of the Plank.

Area "2": Located approximately 12" to 22" from the right hand end of the Plank and measuring 4" wide.

Area "3": Located approximately 37" to 48" from the right hand end of the Plank and containing 10 separate spots.

Three stains were located on the top of Plank 2:

Area "1": Located approximately 2" to 19" from the right hand end of the Plank covering the full width of the Plank.
Area "2": Located approximately 29" to 32" from the right hand end of the Plank, one spot measuring approximately 3" in diameter.
Area "3": Located 43" to 50" from the right hand end of the Plank, one spot measuring approximately 2" in diameter.

Four stains were observed on the

Area "1": Located approxi
of the Plank co
appearing to be
Area "2": Located appro
of the Plank a
Plank 2, cons
The white m
Area "3": Located 51'
Plank, appr
weathered
Area "4": Located 7
brownish

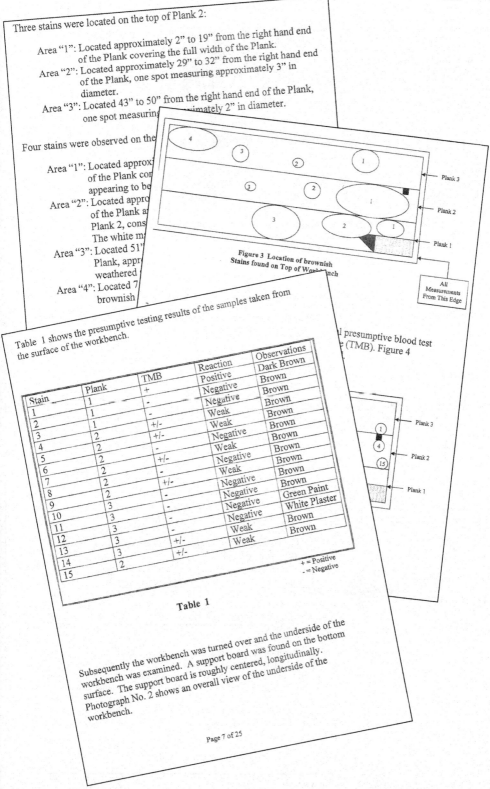

Figure 3 Location of brownish
Stains found on Top of Workbench

Plank 3
Plank 2
Plank 1

All Measurements From This Edge

Table 1 shows the presumptive testing results of the samples taken from the surface of the workbench.

... presumptive blood test
e (TMB). Figure 4

Plank 3
Plank 2
Plank 1

| Stain | Plank | TMB | Reaction | Observations |
|---|---|---|---|---|
| 1 | 1 | + | Positive | Dark Brown |
| 2 | 1 | - | Negative | Brown |
| 3 | 1 | - | Negative | Brown |
| 4 | 2 | +/- | Weak | Brown |
| 5 | 2 | +/- | Weak | Brown |
| 6 | 2 | - | Negative | Brown |
| 7 | 2 | +/- | Weak | Brown |
| 8 | 2 | - | Negative | Brown |
| 9 | 3 | +/- | Weak | Brown |
| 10 | 3 | - | Negative | Green Paint |
| 11 | 3 | - | Negative | White Plaster |
| 12 | 3 | - | Negative | Brown |
| 13 | 3 | +/- | Weak | Brown |
| 14 | 2 | +/- | Weak | Brown |
| 15 | | | | |

+ = Positive
- = Negative

Table 1

Subsequently the workbench was turned over and the underside of the workbench was examined. A support board was found on the bottom surface. The support board is roughly centered, longitudinally. Photograph No. 2 shows an overall view of the underside of the workbench.

762

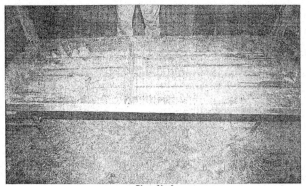

**Photo No. 2**

Various stained areas were noticed. Visual, ALS illumination and macroscopic examinations were conducted. Figure 5 is a drawing representing the areas in which brownish stains were located and samples taken for chemical presumptive blood tests.

Dividing, Support, Board, roughly centered

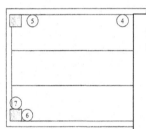

**Figure 5, B**

Table 2 shows the results of chemical presumptive tests for those brownish stains found on the underside of the workbench.

|    | Plank | TMB | Reaction |
|----|-------|-----|----------|
| 1  | 1     | +/- | Weak |
| 2  | 1     | +/- | Weak |
| 3  | 1     | +   | Positive |
| 4  | 1     | +++ | Strong Positive |
| 5  | 1     | -   | Negative |
| 6  | 3     | +/- | Weak |
| 7  | 3     | +/- | Weak |
| 8  | 3     | +   | Positive |
| 9  | 2/3   | +   | Positive |
| 10 | 3/1   | +   | Positive |
| 11 | 3     | +/- | Weak |

**Table 2**

Swab samples of area number "3" and area number "4" were collected for DNA testing. Two swabs were taken from each area and placed into two separate swab boxes, one box was labeled for area number "3" and one box was labeled for area number "4". These two samples were transferred to Lincoln Sheriff Department. In addition, scraping samples were also taken from these two areas. These samples were placed into evidence envelopes and were transferred to Lincoln Sheriff Department.

**AUTHOR'S HIGHLIGHT**

Luminol (a presumptive test reagent for blood) was then prepared and applied to the underside of the workbench. Luminal testing shows a positive indication in area "1" of the underside surface of the workbench and strong positive in areas "3" and "4" of the underside surface of the workbench. The Luminol test was positive on the top surface of the workbench in the general areas of number "2" on Plank 1 and general areas "2" and "3" on Plank 2.

### Item # 2 Washstand

This Washstand measures approximately 28 ¾" long by 16" deep by 30" tall.  Figure 6 is a sketch diagram of the washstand. This washstand is made of wood with a black color finish on it.

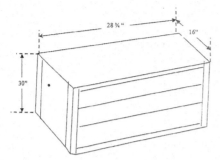

**Figure 6, Washstand**

Photograph # 3 shows the left side panel of the washstand and photograph # 4 depicts a view of the ~~~~~~~~~~~~~~~~~~~~~~~~~~~~~~~~~~~
Visual examination of the external s~~~~~~~~~~~~~~~~~~~~~~~~~~~~~~~~~
holes, one single hole in each end of~~~~~~~~~~~~~~~~~~~~~~~~~~~~~~~~~
examination of these holes indicates~~~~~~~~~~~~~~~~~~~~~~~~~~~~~~~~~
bullet holes.

Photo No. 3          Photo No. 4

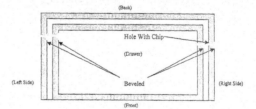

**Figure 7, Washstand**
**Top, Cut Away View**

Figure 7 is a cut away diagram of the washstand.  This diagram depicts the relative locations of the two holes on the side panels of the washstand.

The hole on the left side panel is round and well defined. The hole on the right side panel is chipped and beveled. The left side panel hole is consistent with a bullet entrance hole.

764

The hole on the right side panel is slightly deformed and there is a chip of wood missing which is joining the hole and proceeds down approximately 1 ½" to 2". Figure 8 is a sketch diagram of this hole. The missing chip is approximately the width of the hole and approximately 1/8" deep. This hole is consistent with a bullet exit hole. Photograph 5 depicts a close-up view of this hole.

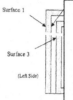

Sodium Rhodizonate test for lead was conducted with the assistance of Mike Haag. Four areas were tested for the presence of lead particles. Figure 9 is a diagram showing the surface areas tested. Surface 1, the exterior surface of the left side panel; Surface 2, interior surface of left side panel; Surface 3, the outside surface of the left side of the top drawer; Surface 4, inside surface of the right hand side panel of the Washstand.

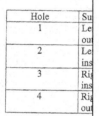

Surface 1

Surface 3

(Left Side)

Subsequently, the top drawer of the Washstand was removed and a laser was set up to reconstruct the angle of the trajectory. The laser used in the ballistic angle reconstruction was a Cao Group, Inc. Prototype Diode Pumped Frequency Doubled Nd:YAG Laser. This laser has a maximum output of 200 milliwatts and produces 532 nanometer light. The laser was placed approximately 20 feet from the outside surface of the left side panel of the Washstand. The laser was then adjusted to project a beam through the entrance holes in the left side panel and to the exit hole in the right side panels of the Washstand. Figure 10 shows the reconstructed trajectory of the shot.

The general bullet path is from left to right with a slight downward and back to front angle. The horizontal trajectory angle was determined to be 5.22 degrees. The vertical angle was determined to be 4.47 degrees.

The results of tests are

| Hole | Su |
|------|----|
| 1 | Le |
|  | ou |
| 2 | Le |
|  | ins |
| 3 | Ri |
|  | ins |
| 4 | Ri |
|  | ou |

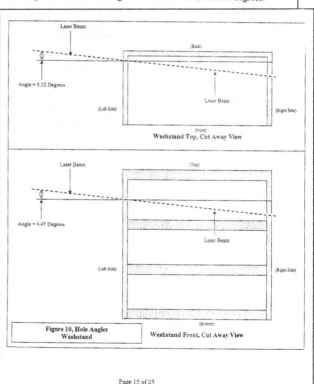

Figure 10, Hole Angles Washstand

Item #3 A piece of Headboard

A piece of Headboard was examined. No blood like stains were observed. No bullet hole was found. No evidence of extensive damage was noted.

## Examination of Lincoln County Court House

On Sunday, 8/1/04. the forensic investigation team examined the old Lincoln County Court House in Lincoln, New Mexico. Present at the scene were Sheriff Sullivan, Deputy Sederwall, Mr. Turk, Bill Kurtis, and Sheriff Gary Wayne Graves of De Baca County, New Mexico. The target area of examination is located on the top landing of the stairs of the old courtroom.

1. The staircase has been repainted several times over the years.
2. The $2^{nd}$ floor hallway floor was recovered with wooden floorboard. These floor boards were removed. The original floor was exposed. Photograph #6 shows an overall view of hall floor after the removal of new floor board.

**Photo No. 6**

3. Photograph #7 shows the target area which is at the top landing of the stairs where presumptive blood tests were done. The area measured approximately 28 7/8" deep by 43 ½ "wide.
4. Figure 11 is a sketch diagram shows the general dimensions of this staircase.

766

Figure 11, Stair Landing

6. Visual examination of the Stair Landing reveals that different types of nails have been used to secure the floor boards. It appears that some of them are newer than others. The floorboards comprising the area also appear to be wood planks of different ages.

depicts the location and condition of the floor get area.

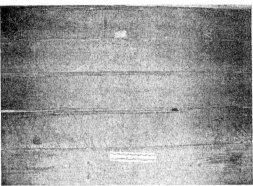

Photo No. 8

Photo No. 7

7. Macroscopic examination reveals a fragment of masking tape, grayish blue paint, hairs, fibers, soil and w

8. Tetramethylbenzideine (a chemical presu blood) was used to test the suspected stain depicts the area of the suspected stains wl blood test.

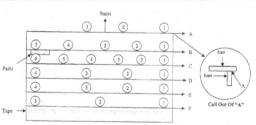

Figure 12, Stair Landing
Sample Location Map

9. The TMB chemical test results are showing in Table 4.

| Space | Sample | Results | Space | sample | Results |
|-------|--------|---------|-------|--------|---------|
| A | 1 | + | D | 1 | - |
|  | 2 | + |  | 2 | - |
|  | 3 | + |  | 3 | W+ |
| B | 1 | - |  | 4 | - |
|  | 2 | - | E | 1 | - |
|  | 3 | - |  | 2 | - |
|  | 4 | - |  | 3 | - |
| C | 1 | - |  | 4 | - |
|  | 2 | - | F | 1 | - |
|  | 3 | - |  | 2 | W+ |
|  | 4 | - |  | 3 | - |
|  | 5 | - | Controls |  | OK |

+ = Positive
- = Negative
W+ = Weak positive

Table 4

10.  Subsequently, the underside of stairs case was examined. Photograph 9 depicts a view of the examination process.

**Photo No. 9**

11.  Visual and macroscopic examinations of the underside of the floor landing area reveal a large number of stained areas where liquids have seeped down through the spaces. Photograph No. 10 shows some of these stained areas.

Photo No. 10

12. Figure 13 is a sketch diagram showing a visual map of the sampling areas for chemical presumptive test for blood.

Stairs

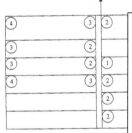

Figure 13, Un
Sample I

Page 22

13. Photograph 11 is a close up view of the major stained area at the under side of the floor boards of the landing area.

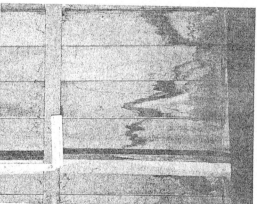

Photo No. 11

14. The suspected areas were tested with presumptive chemical reagent, TMB. Table 5 shows the test results.

| Space | Sample | Results | Space | Sample | Results |
|-------|--------|---------|-------|--------|---------|
| AU | 1 | W+ | CU | 3 | - |
| | 2 | W+ | DU | 1 | - |
| | 3 | - | | 2 | W+ |
| | 4 | - | | 3 | - |
| BU | 1 | W+ | | 4 | W+ |
| | 2 | W+ | EU | 1 | +++ |
| | 3 | - | | 2 | - |
| CU | 1 | +++ | FU | 1 | + |
| | 2 | - | | 2 | - |

+++ = Strong positive

Table No. 5

Page 23 of 25

# Results and Conclusion

After a detail examination of the evidence and review of all the results of field testing, the following conclusion was reached.

1. Brownish dark stains were observed on different areas of the workbench. These areas were subjected to chemical presumptive blood tests. Some of those samples give a positive reaction. These results indicate the presence of Heme or Peroxidase like activity with those stains testing positive, which suggest that those stains could be bloodstains. Further DNA testing could reveal the nature and identity of these blood-like stains.

2. Two bullet holes were located on the side panels of the Washstand. The hole on the left side panel is consistent with a bullet entrance hole while the hole on the right side panel is consistent with a bullet exit hole. However, it is not possible to determine when those bullet holes were produced at this time. The angles produced in the examination tell us two things:

First, the bullet was fired from no more that 41" from the floor given the reported limitations of the room. The room is reported to be 20' by 20'; the maximum distance is assumed to be 20'. If the firearm was a maximum of 41" off of the floor it is unlikely that the shooter was standing. It is more likely the shooter was kneeling, squatting, or close to the floor.

Second, the horizontal angle is such that if the Washstand was positioned so that the back was against the wall, the shot could not have been fired from more that approximately 40 inches from the Washstand, because the wall would have been in the way. The angle of trajectory intersects the back plane of the Washstand at approximately 45 3/16", and no more than 46".

3. No bullet hole and no observable damage, no sign of bullet ricocheted type of defects were found on the Headboard. No blood or biological materials were observed on the Headboard.

4. The floor boards on the 2nd floor stair landing area of the court house have been repaired. Different types of wood and nails were used on this area.

5. Various stains were observed on the surface and the underside of the floor boards. Chemical tests for the presence of blood were positive with some of those stains. These results indicate the presence of Heme or Peroxidase like activity with those stains tested positive, which suggests that those stains could be bloodstains. Further DNA testing could reveal the nature and identity of those blood-like stains.

Dr. Henry C. Lee
Chief Emeritus, Connecticut State Forensic Laboratory
Distinguished Professor, University New Haven

Calvin D. Ostler
(Electronic signature)
Forensic Consultant
Crime Scene Investigator

APPENDIX: 12. Attorney Sherry Tippett. "Sixth Judicial District Court, State on New Mexico, County of Grant. Case No. MS-2003-11." "In the Matter of Catherine Antrim. Petition to Exhume Remains." October 10, 2003.

## IN THE MATTER OF CATHERINE ANTRIM
## PETITION TO EXHUME REMAINS

Comes now Petitioners Tom Sullivan, Sheriff of Lincoln County, Steve Sederwall, Deputy Sheriff of Lincoln County and Gary Graves, Sheriff of De Baca County,

[AUTHORS NOTE: Case is done under law enforcement titles.]

by and through their attorney, Sherry J. Tippett, hereby Petitions this Court to enter an Order directing the New Mexico Office of Medical Examiners (hereinafter "OMI") to disinter the remains of Catherine Antrim for the purpose of obtaining DNA samples. This Petition is made in conjunction with Investigation No. 2004-274 filed in Lincoln County and case number 03-06-136-01 filed in De Baca County, for purpose of determining the guilt or innocence of Sheriff Pat Garrett in the death of William Bonney aka "Billy the Kid."

[AUTHORS NOTE: Under IPRA investigation in 2008, the officials would lie, claiming both that the case was just a "hobby," and was just the investigation of the murders of the deputies by the Kid.]

Catherine Antrim is the undisputed mother of William Bonney. Catherine Antrim is buried in Silver City, NM at the Memorial [sic] Lane Cemetery ...

In the case at hand, there is no known direct descendent of Catherine Antrim or William Bonney alive today.

Section 24-14-23 C NMSA (1978) states that a permit for disinterment and reinterment shall be required prior to disinterment of a dead body or fetus except as authorized by regulation or otherwise provided by law. This statute further states that the permit shall be issued by the state registrar or state medical investigator to a licensed funeral service practitioner or direct disposer. Dr. Debra Komar, Forensic Anthropologist with the OMI has performed a significant amount of research on the burial history and exact location of the remains of Catherine Antrim including visiting Memorial [sic] Lane Cemetery and performing records research in both New Mexico and Arizona. Dr. Komar is confident that Ms. Antrim's remains can be exhumed without disturbing the remains of other bodies laid to rest in Memorial [sic] Lane Cemetery.

[AUTHOR'S NOTE: This claim of OMI permission is untrue and is potential perjury. It resulted in the OMI responding by legal refutation by affidavits and depositions.]

Disturbance of any other remains is unacceptable to the OMI staff. Dr. Komar is a world renowned Forensic Anthropologist who has previously worked for the United Nations in the exhumation of mass buries [sic] in eastern Europe. Several meetings have taken place between the Petitioners, Counsel of Record and OMI Director and Forensic staff as well as UNM Counsel Angela Martinez. All parties are in agreement that an Order should be entered by this court prior to exhumation.

The Petitioner respectfully requests this Order to be entered as soon as possible to begin the exhumation by early to mid November. The coordination of several public and private agencies will be necessary to complete the exhumation.

Respectfully submitted,
Sherry J. Tippett
Attorney for Petitioners

## APPENDIX: 13. Attorney William Snead. "Response of Office of Medical Investigator to Petition to Exhume Remains of Catherine Antrim." January 12, 2004.

COMES NOW the Office of the Medical Investigator, (OMI) through its counsel, William E. Snead, and hereby responds to the Petition to Exhume Remains of Catherine Antrim. OMI provides this response as an organization affected by the relief sought in the Petition. The Petition seeks a court order compelling OMI to disinter the remains of Catherine Antrim.

In the summer of 2003, the Office of the Medical Investigator, (OMI) was asked to respond to three questions in connection with **a criminal investigation** (author's boldface) of the circumstances behind the death of Billy the Kid and any involvement of Pat Garrett. The three questions posed related to the bodies of Catherine Antrim and Billy the Kid: (a) could these bodies be located; (b) could the bodies be recovered; and (c) would the bodies be in a state such that a positive identification could be made.

The OMI, primarily through the work of its forensic anthropologist, Debra Komar, Ph.D. conducted research and investigation in an attempt to respond to the questions posed. The details of the investigative findings are summarized in the attached affidavit by the Director of the OMI, Ross E. Zumwalt, M.D. (attached hereto as Exhibit 1) and the Affidavit of the forensic anthropologist for the OMI, Debra Komar, Ph.D. (attached hereto as   Exhibit 2).

Contrary to the statements contained in the petition, Debra Komar, Ph.D., the forensic Anthropologist referred by petitioner, does not believe that Ms. Antrim's remains can be exhumed without disturbing the remains of other bodies also interred in Memory Lane Cemetery. (author's boldface) In fact, there is very significant probability that, even assuming Ms. Antrim's remains can be identified (although it is scientifically improbable that Ms. Antrim's remains can even be identified), other remains would necessarily be disturbed in any exhumation because of the way other burials have occurred in the cemetery and due to the passage of time, flooding and other natural causes.

Contrary to the petition, the Office of Medical Investigators does not agree that an order should be entered allowing exhumation. (author's boldface) After a detailed and scientific investigation described in the affidavits attached hereto, it is the scientific opinion of the OMI that any such attempted exhumation has very little possibility of contributing any information to the petitioner's alleged investigation, threatens the disturbance of unrelated burials, is a very great waste of public resources and a distraction of the OMI from its mandated work.

APPENDIX: 14. Ross Zumwalt, M.D. "Sixth Judicial Court, State of New Mexico, County of Grant. No. MS 2003-11 In the Matter of Catherine Antrim." January 9, 2004.

## AFFIDAVIT OF ROSS E. ZUMWALT, M.D.

The undersigned Ross E. Zumwalt, M.D. upon oath states:

1. My name is Ross E. Zumwalt, M.D. I am the Director of the Office of the Medical Investigator (OMI), located on the campus of the University of New Mexico Health Sciences Center (HSC) in Albuquerque, New Mexico. A copy of my resume is attached as Exhibit A. My training, education and background qualifies me to make the statements contained in this affidavit.

2. In my capacity as Director of OMI, I was asked to investigate the following questions related to the bodies of William Bonney aka "Billy the Kid" and Catherine Antrim, the mother of William Bonney: (a) whether the bodies could be located; (b) whether the bodies could be recovered; and (c) whether the bodies would be in a state such that a positive identification could be made. The stated purpose of the request was to aid in **a criminal investigation** (author's boldface) of the circumstances behind the death of Billy the Kid and any involvement by Pat Garrett.

**[AUTHOR'S NOTE: Confirmation that the Billy the Kid Case was presented as "criminal investigation."]**

3. Based on research of Silver City cemetery records, the location of the body of Catherine Antrim may not be known to a reasonable degree of scientific probability. According to cemetery records, Catherine Antrim was buried in 1874 in Silver City in a cemetery within the City limits. In 1877, the cemetery in which she was buried flooded. Records indicate that the floodwaters could have disturbed the burial sites within the cemetery. In 1882, as a result of a change in the city ordinance requiring burials outside the city limits, Catherine Antrim's body was removed to a new burial site. It is not certain to a reasonable degree of scientific probability that the body, which was exhumed and moved in 1882, was that of Catherine Antrim. **Accordingly, if the purpose of exhuming Catherine Antrim is to provide a "known" standard for DNA testing, the fact that she cannot be positively identified renders all DNA tests suspect to a reasonable degree of scientific probability.** (author's boldface)

### [AUTHOR'S NOTE: Invalid DNA from mother]

4. If attempt is made to exhume the supposed body of Catherine Antrim from the burial site with her name, it is probable with a reasonable degree of scientific probability that the remains of other individuals will be disturbed. The burial site with Catherine Antrim's name is Plot D-27 at Memory Lane Cemetery. This plot is the resting place of twelve (12) other known individuals. See Exhibit B. In addition to the known individuals within Plot D-27, present cemetery records list two hundred seventy six (276) other individuals known to be buried in Memory Lane Cemetery but whose exact location within the cemetery is listed in the records as "unknown." See Exhibit C. Similarly, cemetery records also indicate that there are at least four hundred fifty five (455) additional individuals who are buried within the Memory Lane Cemetery in "unmarked graves." See Exhibit D. Given the uncertainty of the original location of the aforementioned burials and the fact that the cemetery flooded in 1877; July 1899; July-August 1895, 1892 (twice); August 1904; October 1909, 1913, and 1915; it is impossible to say to a reasonable degree of scientific probability that the remains of some other individual(s) will not be encountered in the process of exhuming the supposed remains of Catherine Antrim.

### [AUTHOR'S NOTE: Illegal disturbance of other remains]

5. Should the exhumation uncover remains, the process of DNA collection will destroy portions of the remains. The process of DNA collection involves cutting and destroying large portions of bone. The amount of bone and the extent of the destruction is dependent upon the number of extractions per test and the extent of preservation of the remains. If independent tests of DNA are performed, which is generally considered to be scientifically sound, or if preservation of the remains is

poor, which given the history is expected to be the case, significant destruction of the recovered remains is scientifically probable.

6. Should the exhumation uncover the supposed remains of Catherine Antrim and DNA samples can be obtained, prior studies show that the probability of successfully extracting mitochondrial DNA (mtDNA) from remains interred in excess of 120 years is extremely low. Support for this principle is found at Stone et al, 2001; Ivanov et al, 1966; Jeffreys et al, 1992; and Gill et al, 1994 (see references). Accordingly, given the age of the remains at this date, it is not certain to a reasonable degree of scientific probability that any DNA will be usable as a standard for comparison to any individual.

7. Because of these technical problems, it has been the long-standing practice of the OMI to decline to disturb any remains that have been buried in an excess of 50 years. Ms. Antrim's remains, as well as those of Billy the Kid, both greatly exceed this threshold period.

8. If the purpose of the exhumation of the remains of Catherine Antrim is to compare her DNA to the remains of the believed Billy the Kid, those remains are not likely to be obtained in my opinion. Based upon research performed by the OMI, the exact location of the Billy the Kid grave is not known, in my opinion, to a reasonable degree of scientific probability.

9. If the purpose of exhuming Catherine Antrim is to compare her DNA to individuals claiming to be potential living descendents of Billy the Kid, it is not possible, to a reasonable degree of scientific probability to do so. The only DNA sample that may be successfully extracted from Catherine Antrim would be mitochondrial DNA (mtDNA). This mtDNA sample provides proof of matrilineal lineage only - in other words, it only passes from mother to child and not from father to child. Billy the Kid would carry his mother's mtDNA; however, his biological children would have received their mtDNA from their own mother and not Billy.

10. If the purpose of extracting mtDNA from the supposed remains of Catherine Antrim is to obtain a sample to compare against Brushy Bill Roberts in Texas, such a comparison, in my opinion, is also scientifically flawed. Based on research to date, I am unaware that Mr. Roberts ever claimed to be the biological child of Catherine Antrim. Thus, a test between his mtDNA and the putative remains of Catherine Antrim would have no scientific basis to a reasonable degree of scientific probability.

11. **Based on the fact that DNA testing of the putative remains of Catherine Antrim would have no probative value and the fact that an exhumation would likely disrupt other burial sites, an exhumation of Catherine Antrim is scientifically unsound in my opinion.** [author's boldface]

FURTHER AFFIANT SAYETH NOT.

Ross E. Zumwalt, M.D.

NOTARIZED

APPENDIX: 15. Attorney Sherry Tippett. Pre-printed for State Senator Benny Altamirano. "Senate Memorial Number ____." Attached to her letter dated December 17, 2003.

## SENATE MEMORIAL
## NUMBER _____

### INTRODUCED BY
### Senator Benny Altamirano

WHEREAS, a Criminal Investigation was filed in Lincoln County on _____ entitled Investigation No. 2004-274 to investigate the death of William H. Bonney and;

WHEREAS, a Criminal Investigation was filed in De Baca County on _____ entitled 03-06-136-02 to investigate the death of William H. Bonney; and,

WHEREAS, DNA testing has provided new scientific tools to aid in the search for the truth in determining the death of William H. Bonney; and,

WHEREAS, the life and death of William H. Bonney is of national as well as international importance as witnessed by hundreds of articles written nationally and internationally since this investigation has been filed; and,

WHEREAS, the life and death of William H. Bonney has played an important role in the history of New Mexico, and in particular, the history of Southern New Mexico;

THEREFORE, BE IT HEREBY ADOPTED THAT THE INVESTIGATION OF THE LIFE AND DEATH OF WILLIAM H. BONNEY alias "BILLY THE KID" IS DEEMED TO BE OF IMPORTANCE TO THE GREAT STATE OF NEW MEXICO AND OF CONSIDERABLE IMPORTANCE TO ITS HISTORY.


APPENDIX: 16. Attorneys Bill Robins III and David Sandoval. "Sixth Judicial District Court in Grant County. No. MS 2003-11. In the Matter of Catherine Antrim: Billy the Kid's Unopposed Motion For Intervention and Request For Expedited Disposition." November 26, 2003.


### BILLY THE KID'S UNOPPOSED MOTION FOR INTERVENTION
### and
### REQUEST FOR EXPEDITED DISPOSITION

COME NOW, Bill Robins, III and David Sandoval, of the law firm Heard, Robins, Cloud, Lubel & Greenwood, LLC, and seek to intervene in this matter on behalf of the estate of William H. Bonney, aka "Billy the Kid", and in support thereof state as follows:

[AUTHOR'S NOTE: William H. Bonney has no "estate." This is just a tricky diversion from dead client Billy being represented as the petitioner - not his estate!]

## I. STATEMENT OF CONCURRENCE
### and
## REASON FOR REQUESTING EXPEDITED DECISION

Undersigned counsel has conferred with Sherri [sic] Tippett, counsel for the parties seeking exhumation, and has obtained her concurrence to this Motion. Billy the Kid's intervention in this matter is unopposed. A proposed order initialed by Ms. Tippett is attached to this Unopposed Motion pursuant to Local Rule.

Billy the Kid is informed that the Mayor of the Town of Silver City ("hereinafter" the Town") has also sought to intervene in the matter. That intervention is opposed and a hearing is set on the matter for December 8, 2003. Billy the Kid requests that the order allowing his intervention be entered prior to the hearing, or in the alternative, that a hearing on this Motion be considered with the hearing on the Town's Motion. *Further, a hearing on the merits of the request for exhumation is set for January 6, 2004. Billy the Kid supports the exhumation and wishes to provide this Court with a brief outlining the basis for his concurrence and asks leave to do so. In addition, in the event that the Town is allowed to intervene, Billy the Kid would also like the opportunity to address the Town's arguments in opposition to the exhumation and asks leave to do so as well."*

[AUTHOR'S NOTE: The "estate" ploy is abandoned. Robins now "channels" dead Billy who "supports the exhumation!"]

## II. INTRODUCTION

This is a unique moment in jurisprudence where law, history, legend, myth, and modern criminology come simultaneously to the forefront in a single proceeding. The individuals implicated here are well-known names in New Mexican history, and that of the Old West; Billy the Kid and Pat Garrett.

William H. Bonney, aka "Billy the Kid" is perhaps the most famous New Mexican of all time. Robins and Sandoval have been appointed by the Honorable Bill Richardson, Governor of the State of New Mexico, to represent the interests of Billy the Kid in the ongoing investigation by several modern-day lawmen that has led to the request before this Court that the remains of Catherine Antrim, the Kid's mother, be exhumed.

[AUTHOR'S NOTE: Richardson's appointment is illegal ultra vires - abuse of power. Richardson is in the executive branch. He cannot dictate to the judicial branch; i.e., appoint an attorney to a court. A judge does that.]

The purpose of the investigation, and the stated reason for the exhumation, revolves around another legendary figure of the Old West, Sheriff Pat Garrett. A commonly held version of history paints a picture of an ambush in which Garrett killed the Kid in Ft. Sumner where most believe the Kid still lies at rest. This version has been questioned.

The investigation seeks to prove or disprove Garrett's responsibility for killing the Kid. The avenue of proof lies in a DNA comparison. The exhumation is to be performed in order to obtain DNA from Antrim's body, for later comparison with DNA of Billy the Kid, and/or those others that at one time claimed to be him. The results of the DNA analysis will shed light on whether Pat Garrett actually killed Billy the Kid, and whether Billy is indeed at rest in a cemetery plot in Ft. Sumner.

Whatever the results of the investigation, the life, death, legend, and myth of Billy the Kid will forever be affected. Further, since the remains of his mother will be disturbed, Robins and Sandoval are called to request an intervention in this matter so that they may serve their client and abide by Governor Richardson's appointment. They seek to intervene in this matter for the purpose of stating their concurrence to the Motion for Exhumation and to otherwise protect the interests of Billy the Kid.

### III. INTERVENTION IS PROPER

Pursuant to the New Mexico Rules of Civil Procedure, a person

> Shall be permitted to intervene in an action: (1) when a statute confers an unconditional right to intervene; or (2) when the applicant claims an interest related to the property or transaction which is the subject of the action and the applicant is so situated that the deposition of the action may as a practical matter impair or impede the applicant's ability to protect that interest, unless the applicant's interest is adequately protected by existing parties.

Rule 1-024. This is known as "intervention of right."

Billy the Kid is entitled to intervene ads of right. Out venerable Supreme Court has noted that relatives and interested parties have an interest in legal actions involving disinterment. *In re Johnson,* 94 N.M. 491, 494 (1980) (recognizing that such an interest gave such parties standing to state their position regarding an autopsy or disinterment.)

**[AUTHOR'S NOTE: This is fakery. Billy, being dead, cannot "intervene." And there are no living kin with legal standing.]**

The investigation is at least partially directed at the determination whether Billy the Kid was indeed shot by Pat Garrett or whether he survived to live a long life in either Texas or Arizona. The truth that is sought to be ascertained thus goes to the very fact of the Kid's life and death. Since whether he is truly buried in New Mexico can only be proven with the extraction and comparison of Ms. Antrim's DNA with that of his own, **or of anyone who laid claim to his identity** [author's boldface], the investigation and this proposed exhumation certainly involves "an interest relating to the subject matter of this action" which his estate should be allowed to protect by intervention.

**[AUTHOR'S NOTE: This misstates "interest" as standing, and reverts back to the fake "estate" claim. It also heralds the hoaxers' plan to dig up the pretenders "Brushy Bill" Roberts and John Miller.]**

## IV. PRAYER FOR RELIEF

WHEREFORE, the Estate of Billy the Kid requests that this Court enter an Order allowing it intervention pursuant to Rule 1-024 of the New Mexico Rules of Civil Procedure.

**[AUTHOR'S NOTE: Returns to false claim of an "estate."]**

Respectfully submitted this 26th day of November, 2003.

> **Heard Robins, Cloud, Lubel & Greenwood, L.L.P.**
> By Bill Robins III
> David Sandoval
> **ATTORNEYS FOR BILLY THE KID**

**[AUTHOR'S NOTE: They list themselves outrageously as "Attorneys for Billy the Kid" – in boldface!]**

## APPENDIX: 17. Judge Henry Quintero. "Sixth Judicial District Court, State of New Mexico, County of Grant. No. MS 2003-11, In the Matter of Catherine Antrim. Decision and Order." April 2, 2004.

### DECISION AND ORDER

THIS MATTER having come before the Court on December 8, 2003, the Court having considered the evidence presented and the briefs submitted by the parties, and the Court having filed its findings of fact and conclusions of law, finds that the Decision should be entered on **ripeness for judicial review** [author's boldface] of exhumation of Catherine Antrim's remains ...

**Due to substantial uncertainty surrounding the recovery of the Kid's remains, only if the Petitioners are successful in locating the Kid's burial site and collecting his DNA may they again petition this Court for a review of Catherine Antrim's matter.** [author's boldface]

APPENDIX: 18. Tenth Judicial District Judge E.T. Kinsley, Jr. "Decree for Lois Telfer's Case No. 3255, For the Removal of the Body of William H. Bonney, Deceased, From the Ft. Sumner Cemetery in Which He is Interred for Reinterment in the Lincoln, New Mexico, Cemetery" (Filed in 1961). (Incorporating Louis Bowdre's "Motion to Intervene" of 1961.) Filed April 9, 1962.

IN RE APPLICATION OF LOIS TELFER,
PETITIONER, FOR THE REMOVAL OF THE
BODY OF WILLIAM H. BONNEY, DECEASED,
FROM THE FT. SUMNER CEMETERY IN WHICH
HE IS INTERRED FOR REINTERMENT IN THE
LINCOLN, NEW MEXICO, CEMETERY.                No. 3255

## D E C R E E

This matter coming on for hearing in open Court at Fort Sumner, New Mexico, this 13th day of March, 1962, petitioner appearing by her attorney, C.C. Chase, Jr., respondents, Board of County Commissioners appearing in person and by Victor C. Breen, District Attorney of the Tenth Judicial District and John Humphrey, Jr., Assistant District Attorney, and respondent, Mrs. J.W. Allen appearing in person  and by her attorneys Victor C. Breen and John Humphrey, Jr., and the intervener, Louis A. Bowdre, appearing in person and by his attorneys, Victor C. Breen and John Humphrey, Jr., and the County having heard the evidence presented and being fully advised in the premises,

FINDS:

1. That Charles Bowdre was killed at Fort Sumner, New Mexico in the year 1880.

2. That the said Charles Bowdre was thereafter buried in the Fort Sumner Cemetery, where his remains now war.

3. That William H. Bonney, alias Billy the Kid, was killed at Fort Sumner, New Mexico, on July 14, 1881.

4. That said William H. Bonney was thereafter buried in the Fort Sumner Cemetery, beside or very near the grave of the said Charles Bowdre, and that the remains of the said William H. Bonney are still buried in the said Fort Sumner Cemetery.

5. **That due to the lapse of time and natural causes, it is no longer possible to locate the site of the graves of the said William H. Bonney, deceased** (author's boldface), and the said Charles Bowdre, deceased.

6. That over the years, large numbers of persons have been buried in the said Fort Sumner Cemetery and that the said Cemetery as it now exists is very thickly planted with graves.

7. That a search for the grave of the said William H. Bonney, deceased, in order to disinter said body, will invariably lead to disturbing the remains of other persons, buried in said cemetery, including the said Charles Bowdre, deceased.

8. That petitioner Lois Telfer is the next of kin of said William H. Bonney, deceased.

9. That intervener, Lois A. Bowdre, is next of kin of said Charles Bowdre, deceased.

WHEREFORE, the Court makes the following

## CONCLUSIONS OF LAW

1. That the court has jurisdiction of the subject matter and of the parties hereto.

2. That the relief prayed for in the petition herein cannot be granted since the site of the grave for William H. Bonney, deceased, cannot be located.

3. That the relief prayed for in the petition herein cannot be granted since a search for the grave of the said William H. Bonney, deceased, in order to disinter said body, will inevitably lead to disturbing the remains of other persons, buried in said cemetery, including the said Charles Bowdre, deceased.

WHEREFORE IT IS ORDERED, ADJUDGED AND DECREED that said Petition of Lois Telfer be, and the same hereby is, dismissed and that the petitioner take nothing and that the action be, and hereby is, dismissed on the merits.

DATED this 6th day of *April*, 1962.

E. L. Kingsley, Jr.
DISTRICT JUDGE

## APPENDIX: 19. Attorneys Bill Robins III, David Sandoval, and Mark Acuña. "Tenth Judicial Court of De Baca County. Case No. CV-2004-00005, In the Matter of William H. Bonney, aka 'Billy the Kid.' " February 26, 2004.

### PETITION FOR THE EXHUMATION OF BILLY THE KID'S REMAINS

COME NOW, Co-Petitioners, and respectfully request that this Court order that the body of William H. Bonney, aka "Billy the Kid" be exhumed, and in support of the Petition state:

### I. The Petitioners

1. The Co-Petitioners are Gary Graves, Sheriff of De Baca County, Tom Sullivan, (Sheriff) and Steve Sederwall (Deputy Sheriff) of Lincoln County, New Mexico. (hereinafter the "Sheriff-Petitioners").

2. Co-Petitioner Billy the Kid is one of the subjects of an investigation being conducted by the Sheriff-Petitioners. Bill Robins III and David Sandoval have been appointed by the Honorable Bill Richardson, Governor of the State of New Mexico, to represent the interests of Billy the Kid in the investigation.

## II. Jurisdiction and Venue

3. Jurisdiction is proper with this Court on the basis of 1978 NMSA Statute 30-12-12.

4. Venue is proper in this County on the basis that the remains that are the subject of this exhumation are located in deBaca [sic] County.

## III. Procedural Background

5. The Sheriff-Petitioners initiated investigation in their respective counties to set the historical record straight as to the guilt or innocence of the legendary Sheriff Pat Garrett in the death of Billy the Kid. The investigative files bear the numbers 03-06-136-01 (*deBaca* [sic] *County*) and 2003-274 (*Lincoln County*).

[AUTHOR'S NOTE: Under IPRA litigation in 2008, the sheriff's would lie that the Billy the Kid Case was their "hobby" and was solely about the deputy murders done by Billy the Kid, not Pat Garrett!.]

6. The remains of Billy the Kid's mother, Catherine Antrim, currently lie in a marked grave located in Silver City, New Mexico. The Sheriff-Petitioners previously filed a Petition to Exhume the remains of Catherine Antrim (hereinafter the "Antrim Petition") which is currently pending before the Honorable District Court Judge Quintero in the Sixth Judicial District. Counsel for Billy the Kid filed a Petition to Intervene in support of that exhumation.

[AUTHOR'S NOTE: Here Robins becomes unabashedly dead Billy's lawyer – to "speak for him" –; though this is illegal and absurd.]

7. The purpose of the Antrim Petition is to disinter her remains to extract vital mitochondrial DNA to then be used to compare with the DNA sought to be extracted from the purported remains of Billy the Kid. Those purported remains of Billy the Kid lie in a cemetery in Ft. Sumner, New Mexico. A hearing on the merits of the Antrim exhumation is scheduled for August 16-18, 2004.

8. Exhumations, DNA extractions and comparisons have become an increasingly common and accepted investigatory method and tool in forensic criminology and historical investigation ...

## IV. Historical Background

9. Billy the Kid is New Mexico's best known Old West figure. He has even been called the best known New Mexican ever. The Kid is no doubt the stuff of legend, myth, and continuing popular attention.

10. The Kid lived during a complex and violent time in New Mexico history which included the "Lincoln County War." It was a time when the distinction between "outlaw" and "lawman" was blurred due to rival political factions having deputized their respective supporters. Billy the Kid himself was deputized during these times.

11. This was also a time whose history was not accurately nor completely written.

**[AUTHOR'S NOTE: This language repeats that in the Probable Cause Statement; and it is double-talk misinformation irrelevant to the murder case at hand: meaning Pat Garrett as a murderer of the innocent victim instead of Billy the Kid on July 14, 1881.]**

For generations now, the life of Billy the Kid has been the subject of historical debate. Perhaps the most significant lingering question involves whether Billy the Kid was indeed shot by Sheriff Pat Garrett in an ambush **one dark night** [author's boldface] in Ft. Sumner or whether the Kid went on to live a long and peace-abiding life elsewhere.

**[AUTHOR'S NOTE: Misinformation to validate intended pretender exhumations. Robins, concocting that "historical debate" exists, is apparently quoting, as if true, "Brushy Bill's" confabulation about the "dark night," when, in actuality, the full moon made it light as day. This moon phase "error" by Robins would eventually help me crack the Billy the Kid Case hoax.]**

12. The debate has been sparked at various times in the past by at least two individuals who laid claim to his identity. Ollie "Brushy Bill" Roberts resided in Hico, Texas and claimed to be Billy the Kid. John Miller, in Arizona also died still claiming he was Billy the Kid. Co-Petitioners are in the initial phases of pursuing exhumations of these individuals as well.

13. The Sheriff-Petitioners' investigation has certainly fueled debate as to whether or not Pat Garrett's version of events surrounding his claimed killing of Billy the Kid is in fact historically accurate. The investigation has renewed questions as to whether Billy the Kid lies buried at the fabled grave-site in Ft. Sumner. Allowing the exhumation of the remains at Ft. Sumner grave site for extraction of DNA to be compared with that of Ms. Antrim's will likely finally provide definitive answers to this historical quandary.

## IV. Claim for Relief
### *Exhumation of Remains*

14. Co-Petitioners repeat and re-allege the foregoing paragraphs 1-13 as if fully set herein.

15. Section 30-12-12 of the New Mexico Statutes grants district courts power and discretion to order the exhumation of remains at a grave site.

16. This Court's power and discretion should be exercised and the exhumation be allowed to proceed for purposes of examining the purported remains of Billy the Kid. And for the extraction of DNA samples from the same.

WHEREFORE, Petitioners request that this Court issue an order allowing the exhumation of William H. Bonney, and all such further relief as the Court deems just and proper.

Respectfully submitted this 24th day of February, 2004.

Heard, Robins, Cloud, Lubel & Greenwood L.L.P.
Bill Robins III, David Sandoval
Attorneys for Co-Petitioner BILLY the KID

**[AUTHOR'S NOTE: The lawyers have only a non-existent dead client.]**


**APPENDIX: 20. Attorneys Adam Baker and Herb Marsh. "Village of Fort Sumner's Motion to Dismiss Against Petitioners Sullivan, Sederwall, and Graves for Lack of Standing" June 24, 2004.**

**[AUTHOR'S NOTE: Statute of limitations on murder issue.]**

"Indeed, the procedural and constitutional problems that would be presented in a posthumous prosecution would bar such prosecution from ever being conducted in a court of law. Additionally, the statute of limitations for murder was fifteen (15) years until the statute was amended in 1997 to eliminate the limitations period for murder. See NMSA 1978, S 30-1-8 (1953), compare MSA 1978, s 30-1-8 (1997). If Pat Garrett were alive, the window of opportunity to prosecute him would have closed by 1968, when the limitations period would have expired under the 1953 statute. Any attempt to prosecute him for murder thereafter would fail on constitutional grounds. See Stogner v. California 123 S.Ct. 2446, 2461 (2003) (holding that 'a law enacted after the expiration of a previously applicable limitations period violates the *Ex Post Facto* clause when it is applied to revive a previously time-barred prosecution.')"

**APPENDIX: 21. Attorneys Adam Baker and Herb Marsh. "Village of Fort Sumner's Motion to Dismiss Against William H. Bonney Under Rule 1-017(A)." June 24, 2004.**

**[AUTHOR'S NOTE: Lack of validity of a dead client.]**

"Regardless of whether Attorneys Robins and Sandoval can demonstrate that they represent "the interests of Billy the Kid," however, the "interests of Billy the Kid" cannot as a matter of law be vindicated by the filing of a law suit by William H. Bonney, because neither William H. Bonney, nor the Attorneys purportedly acting on his behalf, are real parties in interest as requited under Rule 1-017(A).

Rule 1-017(A) states in relevant part:

> Every action shall be prosecuted in the name of the real party in interest; but an executor, administrator, guardian, trustee of an express trust, a party with whom or in whose name a contract has been made for the benefit of another party authorized by statute may sue in that person's own name without joining the party for whose benefit the action is brought."

**APPENDIX: 22. Silver City Petition to Governor Bill Richardson. Signed by: Mayor Terry Fortenberry, Town Councilor Thomas A. Nupp, Town Councilor Steve May, Town Councilor Gary Clauss, Town Councilor Judy Ward, Town Manager Alex Brown, Executive Director of the Silver City/Grant County Chamber of Commerce Cissy McAndrew, Director of Silver City Mainstreet Project Frank Milan, and Director of the Silver City Museum Susan Berry. June 21, 2004.**

Dear Governor Richardson:

Please accept this "open letter" to you as our way of demonstrating our united opposition to all exhumation efforts in Silver City and Fort Sumner.

We all want to promote tourism in "Billy the Kid Country" but not in the district courts of New Mexico. We fear this continued legal battle has the potential to destroy the legend and myth of one of New Mexico's most colorful and notorious characters.

We ask for your consideration of our concerns. It's time to stop the litigation and get on with more appropriate ways of promoting tourism in New Mexico.

## PETITION

We the undersigned elected officials and community leaders of the town of Silver City, Grant County, New Mexico, are deeply concerned regarding the involvement of the Governor in the case of William H. Bonney, a.k.a. "Billy the Kid."

To date the case includes a supposed criminal investigation of murder filed in the Lincoln County Sheriff's office and petitions to exhume the remains of Catherine Antrim (William H. Bonney's mother) in Silver City and the remains of William H. Bonney (Billy the Kid) in Fort Sumner. Petitioners are Lincoln County Sheriff Tom Sullivan, Lincoln County Deputy Sheriff Steve Sederwall, and De Baca County Sheriff Gary Graves. Furthermore, your office has added William H. Bonney - deceased - as a petitioner.

We must ask why the District Court is burdened with specious cases when no basis exists for reopening a criminal investigation when the perpetrator is dead, and the case was closed over 122 years ago by a legally embodied Coroners Jury with some 200 citizens having viewed the deceased's body.

We must ask why not a single one of our town officials has ever been asked for our planning, input, or permission in this matter, or our citizens' wishes of respect for the dead.

**We must ask why the Governor's office has taken a partisan position against Grant and De Baca Counties when every expert historian of the life and times of Billy the Kid has labeled the case as pure bunk; when forensic anthropologists have stated that there could be very little if any chance of any significant evidence being recovered from the exhumation of the bodies; when the state's own Office of Medical Examiner has denied a permit for exhumation of the bodies based on DNA results being useless.** (author's boldface.)

Messrs. Sederwall, Sullivan and Graves have stated that they are promoting tourism - however, Sederwall said he "no longer has plans to help Silver City and was going to let the whole town 'drain dry.'" (Las Cruces Sun News, June 12, 2004) Therefore we must ask why the Governor's office has empowered law enforcement officers to represent themselves as agents of the New Mexico Dept. of Tourism when they have in fact been exposed as having no legitimate basis for a legal case, no expertise in history, and no jurisdiction to represent the State Department of Tourism.

Lastly, we must ask if the Governor's office has considered the implications of the somewhat ghoulish and cynical insensitivity of the Governor stating (in our District Court) that William Bonney wants his mother's remains exhumed?

The original intent of the "Billy the Kid Case" appears to have been to promote interest in all aspects of the life and times of Billy the Kid with the attendant increase in tourism benefiting all the involved areas of the state. Regrettably the case has gone awry and seems to be promoting ill will, financial burden on the taxpayers, and wasted resources of the state, involved counties and municipalities. More importantly, it has the potential to destroy the existing legend and mystery and folklore surrounding Billy the Kid, badly damage the state's tourism industry, severely impact the economy of the state, and damage the reputation of the Governor's office.

Therefore, we respectfully request you dissociate from Messrs. Sederwall, Sullivan, and Graves and the "Billy the Kid Case."

## APPENDIX: 23. Attorneys Bill Robins III and David Sandoval. "County of De Baca, State of New Mexico, Tenth Judicial District. In the Matter of William H. Bonney A/K/A 'Billy the Kid.' Cause No. CV-04-00005." July 30, 2004.

### STIPULATION OF DISMISSAL WITH PREJUDICE

"COME NOW, Bill Robins III and David Sandoval, counsel for William J. [sic] Bonney, and Adam Baker, counsel for the Village of Ft. Sumner, and pursuant to Rule 1-041.A.(1)(b) of the New Mexico Rules of Civil Procedure hereby file this their Stipulation of Dismissal with prejudice all claims brought by and on behalf of William J. [sic] Bonney a/k/a "Billy the Kid," each party to bear its own costs and attorneys' fees."

## APPENDIX: 24. Attorney Mark Acuña. "County of De Baca, State of New Mexico, Tenth Judicial District. In the Matter of William H. Bonney A/K/A 'Billy the Kid.' Cause No. CV-04-00005." July 26, 2004.

**[AUTHOR'S NOTE: "Law enforcement officers" (boldfaced below) is used 13 times in this 5 page pleading. In my later litigation, the hoaxers would call Case 2003-274 their "hobby" – making this document emphasize their lie.]**

### PETITIONER'S [sic] RESPONSE TO
### THE VILLAGE OF FT. SUMNER'S MOTION TO DISMISS

COME NOW Petitioners Sullivan, Sederwall and Graves by and through their attorneys of record The Jaffe Law Firm (Mark Anthony Acuña, Esq.) and for their response to the Village of Fort Sumner's Motion to Dismiss sate as follows:

## INTRODUCTION

Tom Sullivan, Steve Sederwall and Gary Graves are **law enforcement officers**. Prior to the filing of the Petition for Exhumation of the Remains of Billy the Kid, a.k.a. William H. Bonney, Sullivan, Sederwall, and Graves acting in their capacity as **law enforcement officers** initiated Investigation No. 2004 [sic] –274 filed in Lincoln County and Case No. 03-06-136-01 filed in De Baca County. The principle purpose of opening the investigation and the case was to determine the guilt or innocence of sheriff Pat Garrett in the death of Billy the Kid.

> [AUTHOR'S NOTE: The fact that Case No. 2003-274 was a murder investigation against Pat Garrett murder would later be concealed by the hoaxers – both by calling the case only an investigation of Billy the Kid's jailbreak shootings of the deputy guards, or calling the whole case their "hobby."]

Initially, as part of their on-going investigation, Sederwall, Sullivan, and Graves, in their capacity as **law enforcement officers** petitioned the Sixth Judicial District Court for exhumation of the remains of Billy the Kid's mother, Katherine [sic] Antrim. As a part of the on-going investigation, the Petition to Exhume Katherine [sic] Antrim was intended to obtain DNA samples for purposes of comparing those DNA samples with DNA samples that were hoped to be obtained upon the exhumation of the remains of what are thought to be that of Billy the Kid. After filing of the Petition to Exhume the remains of Katherine [sic] Antrim, a second petition was filed in the Tenth Judicial Court for purposes of the exhumation of Billy the Kid's remains and for purposes of obtaining DNA samples to compare with those samples obtained from the remains of Katherine [sic] Antrim. Sederwall, Sullivan, and Graves, all joined in on the Petition to Exhume the remains of Billy the Kid as Co-Petitioners and in their capacity as **law enforcement officers** engaged in an on-going investigation.

Petitioners assert that they maintain standing in the instant action as **law enforcement officers** engaged in the investigation of criminal violations, namely, the alleged killing of Billy the Kid by the legendary Sheriff, Pat Garrett. Moreover, Petitioners assert that as **law enforcement officers** they are duly authorized to investigate the death of Billy the Kid to determine 1) the guilt or innocence of sheriff Pat Garrett, and 2) to determine whether or not foul play was involved if there were violations of criminal statutes or laws. Acting in their capacity as **law enforcement officers** on behalf of the public and the public's best interest, Petitioners further assert that they are the real parties in interest to this suit and, therefore, maintain proper standing to prosecute these claims.

## ARGUMENT

### Petitioners are Law Enforcement Officers Currently Conducting Active Investigations Regarding the Death of Billy the Kid and, therefore, they have Standing.

New Mexico Rule of Civil Procedure 1-017 states in pertinent part that "every action shall be prosecuted in the name of the real party in interest ... for a party authorized by statute may sue in that person's own name without joining the party for whose benefit the action is brought; and when a statute of the state so provides, an action for the use or benefit for another shall be brought in the name of the state.

Moreover, Section 29-1-1 states impertinent [sic] part that ...

"It is hereby declared to be the duty of every Sheriff, Deputy Sheriff, Constable and every other peace officer to investigate all violations of the criminal laws of the state which are called to the attention of any such officer or which he is aware, and it is also declared the duty of every such officer to diligently file a complaint or information, if the circumstances are such to indicate to a reasonably prudent person that such action should be taken, and it is also declared his duty to cooperate with and assist the Attorney General, District Attorney or other prosecutor, if any, if any in all reasonable ways ... Failure to perform his duty in ant material way shall subject such officer to removal from the office and payment of all costs of prosecution."

In the instant case, Petitioners Sullivan, Sederwall, and Graves acting in their capacity as **law enforcement officers** pursuant to Section 29-1-1, were not only authorized to commence the investigation into the death of William H. Bonney, a.k.a. Billy the Kid, but were duty-bound to fulfill their responsibilities as **law enforcement officers** to investigate the circumstances surrounding the death of Billy the Kid. Indeed, Petitioners initiated the investigations into the death of Billy the Kid based upon inconsistent and incongruous facts and information surrounding the death of Billy the Kid and raising suspicion as to the truth of the circumstances surrounding the killing of Billy the Kid. Under the circumstances, Petitioners had a duty to investigate or be subject to removal of office subject to Section 29-1-1.

Furthermore, pursuant to Rule 1-017, Petitioners acting in their capacity as **law enforcement officers**, are real parties in interest to the instant causes of action. Plaintiffs are authorized by statute, that is, Section 29-1-1, to being this action in their own names on behalf of and for the benefit of the public in their capacities of investigating **law enforcement officers**.

## CONCLUSION

Therefore, based upon all the foregoing, it is clear that the Petitioners acting in their capacity as **law enforcement officers** and engaged in an active investigation regarding the death and alleged killing of Billy the Kid by Sheriff Pat Garrett, and of standing in this case and are real parties in interest.

Wherefore, Petitioners respectfully request that the court issue its order denying the Village of Ft. Sumner's Motion to Dismiss as against Petitioners; that the court allow Petitioners to remain in the instant action and for such other further and proper relief as the Court deems just and proper."

Respectfully submitted by:
The Jaffe Law Firm
Mark Anthony Acuña
Attorneys for Petitioners Sullivan,
Sederwall & Graves

## APPENDIX: 25. William Garrett. *De Baca County News* Letter to the Editor. May 6, 2004.

I have heard some real crazy things about your sheriff. He doesn't seem right somehow. You are paying him to be doing a job which he seems to not be doing, and he seems to be acting out of place as an elected official. I've seen kids act more mature than he does.

Somehow he needs to grow up and act more mature and do the job that he is paid for and be mature about it, and what's more he and Sheriff Sullivan in Lincoln are both trying to bring disgrace and stupidity to the Billy the Kid thing because they both seem to be lacking something to do and need attention. What they are really doing is making a mockery and joke and laughing stock out of our fine and reputable state. We do not need or care for that type of attention and most notably neither does the kind city of Fort Sumner. It is disgraceful and ugly stain on the face of law enforcement, Fort Sumner, Silver City, and etc... and these two sheriffs? are credible in this pursuit? Ha, ha who's kidding who?

Fort Sumner has and has had the Kid. We all know that. They are trying to exhume him and his mother in Silver City to prove something that cannot be proven. In the process they are impugning the integrity of those people that signed their name to the Kid's death certificate. They were involved with it on that day of July 14, 1881 when Pat shot him dead at the point there in Pete Maxwell's bedroom. Pete swore to it and so did the others. Pete was an honorable man and so were the others. They are gone now and cannot defend the truth. However, the truth still exists and you have it and so does the world. The Kid is dead and that is that. And Pat? Pat did his duty and that is that. Those two sheriffs and others doing this dastardly deed are not helping to lift our fair state, they are doing otherwise.

Let's leave the Kid alone and the others as well and enjoy what we have and not cast doubt over our fair state and villages. We support Fort Sumner for the fine community that it is and we greatly appreciate its goals and direction. Your sheriff does not deserve our feelings of kindness as long as he proceeds in his present direction.

I know these things because Pat was my great uncle and my respect goes to him and all the good people in the pursuit of honesty and dignity.

I am Wm. F. Garrett
Alamogordo, NM

**APPENDIX: 26. No Author. "Contact List, William H. Bonney Case # 2003-274" No Date.** [AUTHOR'S NOTE: Omitted are addresses and telephone numbers which were included with each listing]

**"Lincoln County Sheriff's Office & Investigators":** Tom Sullivan - Sheriff, Lincoln County Sheriff's Office, Carrizozo, New Mexico; Steven M. Sederwall - Deputy, Capitan, New Mexico; Dale Tunnell - Criminal Investigator, State of Arizona, Phoenix, Arizona; Doctor Rick Staub – DNA Expert, Orchid Cellmark, Dallas, Texas; Paul Andrew Hutton - Historian, University of New Mexico, Albuquerque, New Mexico;

**"New Mexico Governor's Office":** Bill Richardson, Governor of New Mexico, Capital [sic] Building, Santa Fe, New Mexico; Billy Sparks - Director of Communications, State Capitol Building, Santa Fe, New Mexico; Jon Hendry - Marketing Director State of New Mexico, New Mexico Department of Tourism; Santa Fe, New Mexico;

**"Attorney's"** [sic]: Bill Robins III - Attorney at Law, Heard, Robins, Cloud, Lubel & Greenwood, LLP, Santa Fe, New Mexico;

**"Other Numbers to Investigation:** DeAnn Kessler - Monument Manager, Lincoln New Court House [sic], Lincoln State Monument, Lincoln, New Mexico; Ron Pastore - Exhumed Jesse James, Wichita, Kansas; Robert L. Heart, Farm & Ranch Museum, Las Cruces, New Mexico; Ron Hadley - President of Billy the Kid Outlaw Gang, Santa Teresa, New Mexico;

**"Brushy Bill Roberts:** Dr. Jannay Valdez, Desoto, Texas;

**"Media":** Lee Arnone - Film Producer, Capitan, New Mexico; Mia Rue - Lost Pecos Productions, L/L/C., Santa Fe, New Mexico; Mike Janofsky - New York Times, cell phone number only; Roy Freddy Anderson VG Norway's Largest Daily Newspaper, New York, New York; Tim Hurley - Court TV, New York, New York; Scott Wilson, Medical Examiners Office (handwritten in).

## APPENDIX: 27. Paul Hutton. Letter to Jay Miller denying being the Billy the Kid Case historian. June 20, 2006.

Dear Mr. Miller,

I was never the "state historian" (as *True West* puts it) on this project [Billy the Kid Case] and had absolutely nothing to do with the production of any written materials on it outside of some initial talking points I emailed the governor's office before the first press conference. Not a single penny of state money was ever expended on me (not gas money, not even a free lunch) and my work was entirely voluntary. I would have loved to have been more involved but no further services were even requested of me. Sederwall and Sullivan have carried this forward and my impression is that they have no connection with the Governor's office and have received no state funds, but they should answer that for you. I have not read their document [probable cause statement]. The governor is interested in this project as a way to promote New Mexico tourism and I think he is on the right track. Why some people seem distressed over this positive effort to promote our state nationally is beyond me.

As for my work for the History Channel and how I came to any conclusion in the Billy the Kid program, that is really none of your business. As to how you think that particular program reaches any conclusions contrary to Utley and Nolan is a mystery as well. I suggest you view it again - it reaches no conclusions at all. You might also wish to reconsider the tone you use in your letters, as it certainly does not encourage much of a response.

Sincerely,
Paul Hutton

## APENDIX: 28. Jay Miller. "Calendar of Complaints to Attorney General Patricia Madrid" sent to Attorney General Patricia Madrid and Deputy Attorney General Stuart Bluestone. September 1, 2006.

COMPLAINT TO ATTORNEY GENERAL RE. NON-RESPONSE ON FOIA/IPRA REQUEST BY THEN SHERIFF OF LINCOLN COUNTY TOM SULLIVAN:

1. June 1, 2004: My response of a repeat FOIA/IPRA request was made to Lincoln County Attorney Alan Morel, utilized by both then Sheriff Tom Sullivan and the Lincoln County Records Custodian to respond to me. (The irony of using their use of a taxpayer funded attorney while denying use of taxpayer money should be noted.) This response of mine was just one FOIA/IPRA

request among many made to them in this time frame. The requests were sent to Mr. Sullivan, the Lincoln County Records Custodian, and Attorney Morel. All denied any record keeping for the Billy the Kid Case. Additionally, claim was made for the use of "secret private donors" for financing that murder investigation.

2. September 4, 2004: To you, I made a complaint with regard to that FOIA/IPRA non-compliance and requested assistance. I never received a response from you to this date.

3. March 20, 2006: I repeated the above complaint of September 4, 2004 of that FOIA/IPRA non-compliance and requested assistance. That letter was sent directly to Attorney General Madrid. To date, there has been no response.

COMPLAINT RE. NON-RESPONSE ON FOIA/IPRA REQUEST BY THEN MAYOR OF CAPITAN AND ALLEGED DEPUTY SHERIFF OF LINCOLN COUNTY STEVE SEDERWALL:

1. June 1, 2004: FOIA/IPRA Request sent to Mr. Steve Sederwall (First sent May 13, 2004 and repeated because no information was provided.)

2. June 21, 2004: Letter informing Attorney General Madrid about concerns regarding Mr. Sederwall's refusal to provide information pertaining to my FOIA/IPRA Requests.

3. June 24, 2004: Assistant Attorney General Albert Lama informed me that case was referred to Assistant Attorney General Mary Smith.

4. July 8, 2004: I acknowledged Mary Smith's June 24, 2004 letter confirming her assignment, and telling her that I continued to try to obtain the FOIA/IPRA information from Mr. Sederwall and his Records Custodian. (Note that no formal complaint was yet made by me to the Attorney General.)

5. August 3, 2004: Assistant Attorney General Mary Smith sent me a letter denying my "complaint." My assumption was that she had misunderstood the nature on my communications, as well as misunderstood that Mr. Sederwall had performed his actions entirely as a public official.

6. August 10, 2004: I sent a clarification letter to Assistant Attorney General Mary Smith as well as requesting that a formal complaint be made. I received no response.

7. August 28, 2004: On the advice of Bob Johnson, I sent you a complaint to the same effect as that to Assistant Attorney General Mary Smith, and requested assistance. You never responded.

8. May 17, 2005: The response to my August 10, 2004 clarification letter

was sent to me by Assistant Attorney General Mary Smith. Note that it took 8 months for her to reply. And she merely again refused my complaint; and gave appearance of ignoring all its clear-cut documentation.

9. June 13, 2006: I repeated to Assistant Attorney General Mary Smith my request for reconsideration of my complaint, providing new information published by Mr. Sederwall to the effect that he had withheld Billy the Kid Case documents to prevent their becoming "public." To date, I have received no response.

10. August 31, 2006: The above unanswered June 13, 2006 complaint to Assistant Attorney General Mary Smith was sent again to her in the hope that now you might facilitate her timely response on this serious matter.

## COMPLAINT WITH REGARD TO INAPPROPRIATE DEPUTIZING OF THEN MAYOR OF CAPITAN STEVE SEDERWALL:

1. September 3, 2004: Complaint sent to Attorney General Madrid. There was no response.

2. March 20, 2006: Complaint sent again to Attorney General Madrid.

3. May 18, 2006: A response came from John D. Sides, Director, Investigations Division, merely referring me elsewhere.

### FOIA/IPRA REQUEST FOR ATTORNEY GENERAL PATRICIA MADRID:

1. August 8, 2006: Sent to Attorney General Madrid.

2. August 14, 2006: Letter from Records Custodian Elizabeth Kupfer requested an extension.

3. August 24, 2006: Response from Records Custodian Elizabeth Kupfer providing information to only one of the seven Items in my request.

4. September 1, 2006: A repeat FOIA/IPRA Request was sent in attempt to obtain the refused financial information pertaining to the relationship of Attorney General Madrid and her Office with Attorney Bill Robins III and/or his law firm

## APPENDIX: 29. Jannay Valdez. E-Mail to Frederick Nolan.

Public Forum
To: Frederick Nolan "Author"
From: Dr. Jannay Valdez, Billy the Kid Museum, Canton, Texas
Date: September 12, 2004
RE: Billy the Kid (Brushy Bill Roberts)

I want you to know I fully expect you to attend the Katherine [sic] Bonney [sic] exhumation in Silver City. Also, I expect you to OPPOSE any attempt to find the truth concerning Billy the Kid. The truth would devastate you, your poor research, and 123 years of lies. You previously (in 1981), by "Public Forum," insulted the late Dr. William Tunstall [sic – Tunstill; and no relation to Lincoln County War John Tunstall], stating that no serious historian would take Brushy Bill Roberts' claim seriously. You also insulted William V. Morrison. Both authors are Americans, who lived here, breathed Western history, and who did their OWN research, as opposed to "armchair historians" like you. Either author surpasses you in research, dignity, and open-mindedness. You are an insult to Billy the Kid, History, and America. Stay in England and write about your royalty, instead of "looking down your snobby nose" at AMERICAN authors. In your "Public Forum" you referred to Brushy Bill as "that poor, bewildered old man." You, and others like you, have not only insulted Brushy Bill Roberts, but decent, honest men like William V. Morrison and Dr. William Tunstall. You, Nolan, are narrow-minded, closed-minded, non-American, and insulting the dignity of the old. You are a poor excuse for being a decent person. Brushy Bill Roberts was/is Billy the Kid, and some day you will have to deal with the truth. Stay where you belong ... in snobville.

Open Letter To Frederick Nolan

Sheriff Sullivan of Lincoln County, Mayor
Sederwall of Capitan, and Governor
Richardson of New Mexico recently
Reopened an investigation into the murders
Of Deputies Olinger and Bell. Nolan
Referred to them as totally ignorant of
History. They most certainly are not.
Nolan, a British snob, is worried about
American taxpayers' money being wasted.
I challenge Nolan to stay in England, leave
America alone (we fought to leave
England) to write about HIS kings and
Queens, and leave Billy the Kid and our tax
Money to us – Americans.
We have had terrorism and war. Our men
Die daily for the freedom of all people.
Can't we have a little fun with Billy the Kid?

## APPENDIX: 30. GRIEF (Gambling Research Information & Education Foundation) blog. "Dockside must be watched closely." April 15, 2003. (From the *Indianapolis Star*.)

INDIANAPOLIS, IN-The last thing the state needs is more gambling. A case in point: the commission's heavy fine last week against the former chairman of a company that operates a boat on the Ohio River. Former Belterra Resort and Casino Chairman R.D. Hubbard was fined $740,000 over allegations that the casino brought in more than a half-dozen prostitutes from California to entertain 48 wealthy male guests during a weekend golf outing last summer. According to a lawsuit by two former female employees of the casino, which triggered the state investigation, the escorts fondled the male guests and allowed themselves to be fondled. The women who filed the suit said they were ordered to kiss and pat male gamblers and lure rich Arab men to the gambling facility.

## APPENDIX: 31. Dr. Guy C. Clark, Executive Director of New Mexico Coalition Against Gambling in *Albuquerque Journal* op-ed " 'Dollar Bill' Richardson." December 16, 2002.

Because he received a large majority of the votes for Governor in this month's general election, does Governor-elect Richardson deserve a "honeymoon" of immunity from criticism? Unfortunately, many of Richardson's plans and activities already indicate a policy of "pay to play" in his administration.

Campaign contribution information indicates that a large majority of the people Richardson named to be on his transition team were contributors to his election campaign, some on his team contributing in the hundreds of thousands of dollars. Transition chairman and co-chairs are heavily represented by gambling interests from the tribal casinos and racetracks. Is gambling going to be considered the apex of commerce in Bill Richardson's New Mexico?

The ongoing battle over a possible Hobbs racetrack is another indication of our new governor's predisposition. Governor Johnson basically dismantled the racetrack commission this week because it appeared that they were going to approve a new racetrack for Hobbs, possibly with R.D. Hubbard as the owner. Mr. Hubbard made national news recently when he lost his gambling license in Indiana, and he and his company, Pinnacle Entertainment, had to pay about $3 million dollars in fines to avoid being prosecuted for accounting irregularities, and for providing prostitutes for guests at a casino rally.

Governor Johnson said he was opposed to a new casino in Hobbs, because such gambling expansion could disconnect revenue sharing from the tribal casinos. His opposition to the track may also have something to do with the hundreds of thousands he has received in campaign contributions from tribal casinos, who view the new tracks as irritating competition. Attorney General Patricia Madrid indicated that adding a racetrack would not violate compacts or disconnect revenue sharing. But then, AG Madrid has received tens of thousands in campaign contributions from gambling interests, including R.D. Hubbard.

Governor-elect Richardson said that the new track in Hobbs was fine with him, because the people in Hobbs wanted one. There are some petitions carried and surveys taken that strongly refute the support for a casino in Hobbs, but the gambling "industry" certainly is in favor of a casino there, and they have contributed heavily to our Governor-elect's campaign. Mr. Hubbard alone contributed over $10,000 to his campaign.

Are the interests of the people or the influence of the dollars going to be the guiding light in Governor Richardson's new administration? The New Mexico Coalition Against Gambling wonders if our new governor is going to become known as "Dollar Bill Richardson" because of his favoritism towards heavy donors, especially gambling contributors.

## APPENDIX: 32. No author listed. "New Racing Schedule Tramples Horsemen." *Albuquerque Journal.* June 26, 2004.
[With author's boldface]

Any illusion that the Racing Commission holds the interests of the horse racing industry above those of casino profits was shattered Tuesday when the commission approved a 2005 racing schedule horsemen overwhelmingly oppose.

**The five-member commission, appointed in a wholesale overhaul by Gov. Bill Richardson,** approved a shortened summer race schedule sought by the Downs at Albuquerque president Paul Blanchard. Instead of a 70-day season, the Downs will have a 47-day season.

Overall, the commission added 15 days to next year's 256 race dates statewide, but those dates will be split among five tracks instead of four.

The $43 million Zia Park, in which Blanchard is a partner, is under construction in Hobbs and slated to open in November.

New Mexico's casinos make their money in casinos, not from live racing. By scaling back racing, a track/casino operation can boost profits.

**Tuesday's commission meeting was packed by race horse owners and trainers, some of who charged that Blanchard's ties with Richardson played a role in the commission's decision. Blanchard donated $100,500 to Richardson's 2002 campaign, headed his transition team and was later appointed by Richardson to the State Board of Finance.**

**The approval process did nothing to allay the suspicions.** The panel went into closed executive session just after chairman Jack Cole was postponing action on the schedule. When commissioners emerged, they voted 4-0 to approve the schedule.

Horse racing - keeping a faltering industry out of the glue factory - provided the rationale for casino gambling at the tracks. But if horsemen don't have enough race days to support their operations, there won't be any racing - then what's the excuse for casinos?

**APPENDIX: 33. Lincoln County Commissioner Leo Martinez. "Observations Regarding the Lincoln County Sheriff's Department's Use of Authority and Management of Priorities." September 21, 2004.**

OBSERVATIONS REGARDING THE LINCOLN COUNTY SHERIFF'S DEPARTMENT'S
USE OF AUTHORITY AND MANAGEMENT OF PRIORITIES

After much consideration and observation of the year long progression of the Billy the Kid Case, I have decided that its actions by Sheriff Tom Sullivan now require intervention on the part of the County Commissioners.

The Billy the Kid Case is a criminal investigation for murder filed in the Lincoln County Sheriff's Department as Lincoln County Sheriff's Department Case No. 7003-274 Probable Cause Statement. It is signed by both Sheriff Tom Sullivan and Mayor of Capitan Steve Sederwall representing himself as Deputy Sheriff of Lincoln County. In addition, it includes three petitions for exhumations to gather evidence for that murder investigation: two filed in Grant County for the exhumation of Catherine Antrim, mother of Billy the Kid, and one filed in De Baca County for the exhumation of William Bonney aka Billy the Kid. On all these petitions the co-petitioners are Lincoln County Sheriff Tom Sullivan, Mayor of Capitan Steve Sederwall representing himself as Deputy Sheriff of Lincoln County, and De Baca County Sheriff Gary Graves.

It is recognized that any act done by Tom Sullivan in the capacity of his elected role of Sheriff of Lincoln County by definition brings in the County of Lincoln as a responsible party.

It is recognized that the Billy the Kid Case has been conducted as a real criminal investigation by Sheriff Sullivan and has been done exclusively under his title and badge.

It is recognized that in the advancement of the Billy the Kid Case Sheriff Sullivan deputized Mayor of Capitan Steve Sullivan for the sole purpose of participation in the Billy the Kid Case.

It is recognized that despite increasingly negative newspaper coverage which is potentially embarrassing for Lincoln County and its Sheriff's Department, Sheriff Sullivan has persisted with the Case.

It is recognized that the Billy the Kid Case meets none of the criteria for a real law enforcement matter. There is no living criminal to prosecute. The case was closed 123 years ago. Nothing in the case can be construed as acting to protect public safety or apprehending criminals.

It is recognized that Sheriff Sullivan has made public claims of promoting tourism and economic development. Tourism and economic development are not part of law enforcement. Sheriff Sullivan was never authorized by the County Commissioners to participate in promoting tourism and economic development.

It is recognized that Sheriff Sullivan has made claims of using undisclosed private donors for funding of the Billy the Kid Case, as well as pro bono relationships.

Serious concerns have arisen from these findings and have necessitated my response as County Commissioner.

- As to the question Sheriff Sullivan has created with regard to the public versus private nature of the Billy the Kid Case, there is only one answer: it is public. It is being conducted as a public law enforcement matter done by him as Sheriff of Lincoln County.
- The advancement of the frivolous Billy the Kid Case for the past year has demonstrated that Sheriff Sullivan has made a serious misapplication of his priorities, in that a meaningless case has been created and given time, while there has not been a single conviction for a real crime of murder.
- The claim made by Sheriff Sullivan that he has utilized private sources and pro bono work to conduct a criminal case in Lincoln County brings up the most grave concerns of the establishment of dangerous precedent. One is left with the impression that if one pays our Sheriff enough money in Lincoln County, they can control law enforcement. Private funding is not to be used for operating costs in a criminal investigation. That is not how law enforcement is conducted.
- The Billy the Kid Case has risen to a higher priority than the Katina Chavez or Cotton McKnight murder cases. All appearance indicates that the time and effort expended on the Billy the Kid Case have been to the detriment of conducting real law enforcement. The impression has been created of shirking the drudgery of real investigative work for the glamour of publicity-seeking.
- The denial by Sheriff Sullivan that he has not used public money in the Billy the Kid Case has no credibility. He has used his title, his time, the Lincoln County Sheriff's office, his official vehicle, and departmental resources. The very fact that the Billy the Kid Case is filed in the Sheriff's Department and that he has spent a year pursuing it eliminates any arguments to the contrary.
- The claim of Sheriff Sullivan that he has the option of not disclosing private donations to his public coffers is untrue. Private money in cash or kind entering public coffers becomes public money and must be accounted for.

- The deputizing of Mayor of Capitan Steve Sederwall is seen as an act of bad judgment since by definition it makes the County of Lincoln responsible for his acts and creates liability risks. In addition, there appears to have been no justification for the creation of a deputy position for a case not only frivolous but already having two Sheriffs as its law enforcement officers. Question has also arisen as to whether the documentation by Sheriff Sullivan even justified his claim of identifying Mr. Sederwall as his deputy.
- The irregularities and misinformation generated by Sheriff Sullivan through the Billy the Kid Case have created both liability and embarrassment for Lincoln County.

SUMMARY: The seriousness of the situation merits criticism of Sheriff Sullivan because of the liability of the County of Lincoln now incurred by his act of creating and promulgating the Billy the Kid Case and his adding in Mayor of Capitan Steve Sederwall as his deputy and expanding the liability of Lincoln County.

ACTION: It is my impression that the time has come to give Sheriff Sullivan an ultimatum. The conducting of the Billy the Kid Case in the Lincoln County Sheriff's Department and the manner in which it was conducted were wrong.

- I would therefore state that the Billy the Kid Case should cease to be a function of Lincoln County, and that as Sheriff participating in the case Tom Sullivan should immediately cease and desist.
- If the Billy the Kid Case is a private action, and Sheriff Sullivan refuses to cease and desist in its pursuit, then he should resign immediately.
- We can define severe problems arising from Sheriff Sullivan's involvement in the Billy the Kid Case:

  a) Problem of priority
  b) Problem of accountability and budget
  c) Problem of self-discipline in deciding between public and claims

- I want it understood that the manner in which law enforcement was handled in the Billy the Kid Case is not the way law enforcement is handled in Lincoln County.
- I want it understood that if Sheriff Sullivan has already accrued personal profit from the Billy the Kid Case and will accrue personal profit from the Billy the Kid Case, he should be required to turn over such profits to Lincoln County, and should sign an agreement to that effect. Public office is not to be used in the service of private gain.

- I want it understood that the County of Lincoln was irresponsibly left in an embarrassing position to have to learn about the inspection of public records act investigation of Sheriff Sullivan from newspapers, rather than from a forthright disclosure of his problems directly from him.

PROPOSAL: I want to go on the record that we should make an official motion to the board to instruct Sheriff Tom Sullivan that the Billy the Kid Case is not a true law enforcement matter and that the County instructs the Sheriff to stop using his title as well as county assets including time and effort in support of this folly. And this is to be effective immediately.

## APPENDIX: 34. Dianne Stallings. "Showdown in the County Seat: shouting match erupts at county Commissioners meeting over investigation of Billy the Kid" and "KID: Question of who is paying sparks debate." *Ruidoso News*. September 22, 2004.

Shouting and pounding the podium, Lincoln County Sheriff Tom Sullivan attempted unsuccessfully Tuesday to drown out questions from County Commissioner Leo Martinez over his publicity-generating investigation of two 123-year old murders. Like Old West gunfighters, the two exchanged verbal pot shots at the commission meeting, allowing a long-standing animosity between the two of them to fuel a debate over the merits and possible legal problems associated with the investigation into the deaths of two lawmen, supposedly by bullets fired by the outlaw Billy the Kid.

The core of Martinez's attack centered on:

- The origin of private money used to pay for the year-old investigation.
- Whether the sheriff neglected other investigations to pursue the tourist-oriented, community promoting project.
- Whether Capitan Mayor Steve Sederwall, who Sullivan said was a reserve deputy, could sign legal documents that were part of the investigation.
- If using the county attorney's time to respond to Freedom of Information requests, for which the county is charged, amounts to the county paying for a portion of the project without authorization.
- If the county is liable for the actions of the two men during the investigation, because the county's name is attached to Sullivan's elected position.
- Whether allowing someone to contribute private money to pay for an investigation sets a precedent for others to pay a sheriff to pursue cases.

- If a full accounting of the private money can be required when mixed with public coffers.
- If the two men have complied fully with FOIA requests.

Sheriff Sullivan and Sederwall defended their efforts to solve the two previously uninvestigated homicides. Standing at podiums on opposite sides of the commission table, they contended they works [sic] on their own time, drive their own cars and pay for their own expenses. Other private donations came from people interested in the outcome, but who want to remain anonymous, they said.

Sederwall said the documents he compiled came from several public record sources available to anyone willing to do the research. He is not obligated as a private individual to give the information to anyone, he said. On the investigation, he is not acting in the capacity of mayor and as a reserve deputy he would not divulge the details of an on-going investigation, he claimed. Martinez said Lincoln County's name pops up on many legal documents and the commission should take a stand, clearly separating itself from the project. But when he called for a motion to sever any association, no other commissioners responded.

He called the investigation an embarrassment that has attracted negative press lately. He asked the sheriff, who will leave office Dec. 30, to end the project or resign.

"He should stop using his title as well as the county assets on this folly," Martinez said.

Acting chairman Rick Simpson ended the meeting by telling Sullivan he is a student of history. "And it's my impression that the sheriff and Mr. Sederwall are doing this on their own time with their own money and it's their own business," he said. "I think if the law has been broken, someone can go to the district attorney and file charges."

Although Commissioners Maury St. John and Earl Hobbs didn't back Martinez on his call for a motion, they both expressed some reservations.

St John said the sheriff's title does open doors. Hobbs asked for a direct response to Martinez's points.

Sullivan insisted his department has not worked on the project and that it is a personal pursuit.

He took exception to the criticism from Martinez that old murder cases involving the death of two members of the McKnight family and Katrina Chavez from Hondo Valley remain unsolved and the effort would have been better used there. The Chavez case was 10 years old before he was elected sheriff and no physical evidence was left to use for prosecution, he said. The McKnight murders occurred under his watch, but he failed to muster enough votes for a grand jury indictment, he said.

After the meeting, Sullivan fired another round at Martinez, questioning why, if he is concerned about the outstanding cases, he hasn't pushed for more action by the Ruidoso Police Department on the murder of George Lore, a homicide that occurred in December 2001 in his commission district.

At one point Simpson was forced to gavel down Sullivan and Martinez as the commissioner prodded for an admission that county attorney Alan Morel's time equates to dollars.

Sullivan disagreed, saying, "I don't tell you how to make burritos. Don't tell me how to run the sheriff's department. This is nothing but a personal attack."

"I just want you to tell the truth," Martinez shot back. "Using private money to run public investigations is not right."

Sederwall said it was never too late to be interested in the deaths of two people who were employed to protect the county. He noted that the investigation has garnered international coverage and attention, he added.

## APPENDIX: 35. Attorney Mark Anthony Acuña. "Tenth Judicial District Court, State of New Mexico, County of De Baca. No. CV-04-00005. In the Matter of William H. Bonney aka 'Billy the Kid.'" September 24, 2004.

### STIPULATION OF DISMISSAL WITH PREJUDICE

COME NOW Petitioners Gary Graves, Tom Sullivan, and Steve Sederwall by and through their attorneys The Jaffe Law Firm (Mark Anthony Acuña), and the Village of Fort Sumner, by and through its attorneys, Kennedy & Han, P.C. (Adam S. Baker) and Herb Marsh, Jr., and hereby stipulate the dismissal with prejudice of the Petition filed herein pursuant to Rule 1-041 A (1)(b) of the New Mexico Rules of Civil Procedure.

## APPENDIX: 36. Geneva Pittmon. Letter to Joe Bowlin and Copy of Roberts Family Bible. Sent December 16, 1987.

Dear Sir: the reason you are not finding my family is you don't have the right name. My grandfather was H.O. Roberts married to Shara Elizabeth Ferguson on May 14, 1876. Oliver P. Roberts was Brushy Bill's name. I don't know what the P. was for. He was born Aug 26, 1879. I have the family Bible record.

My husband thinks I should not tell you anything unless I know just what are your interest in my family?

A William A. Tunstill [no relation to Lincoln County War John Tunstall; a pro-Brushy Bill as Billy writer] ... is also writing to me asking questions which I have not written. He also has come up with a Ben Roberts as my great grandfather who was from Ken & settled near Austin, 1835.

I would also like for this to be settled as I know

My uncle Oliver was
<u>Not Billy the Kid</u>.

Mrs Geneva Pittmon

\*\*\*\*\*\*\*\*\*\*\*\*\*\*\*\*\*\*\*\*

**The copy of the Bible page said:**

Roberts Family Bible History Written down As Each Child Was Born, Hand Copied in Early Part Of This Century.

Date of Birth

| | |
|---|---|
| H.O. Roberts | May 18, 1852 |

Married May 14, 1876

| | |
|---|---|
| S. Elizabeth Roberts | Feb 24, 1856 |
| S.B. Roberts | Oct. 24, 1871 |
| M.V. Roberts | Sept 3, 1873 |
| A.B. Roberts | Feb. 9, 1877 |
| M.C. Roberts | April 17, 1878 |
| <u>O.P. Roberts</u> | Aug. 26, 1879 ("Brushy Bill") |
| J.W. Roberts | June 27, 1881 |

died Sept 11, 1881

| | |
|---|---|
| L.V. Roberts | June 6, 1884 died |

Sept 30, 1884

| | |
|---|---|
| T.H. Roberts (my dad) | Oct. 3, 1884 died |

June 17, 193(?)

| | |
|---|---|
| Nora M. Roberts | April 29, 1892 |

died May 6, 1892

| | |
|---|---|
| Joseph I. Roberts | Feb. 26, 1895 - |

The first two children were grandpa's by his first wife. They were Samantha and Martha. Then the next ones were Uncle Beny, Aunt Cordelia, Uncle Oliver (two died) then Tom (my dad) and Uncle Irvin.

**APPENDIX: 37. W.C. Jameson and Frederic Bean.** *The Return of the Outlaw Billy the Kid.* **1998. [author's summary of the book's death scenes]**

DEATH SCENE ONE (book page x), in Maxwell's room, is an accidental-shooting-by-Garrett-of-the-wrong-man version. Poe gets dialogue: "Pat, the Kid would not come to this place; you have shot the wrong man." Garrett, called "a vain, self-obsessed, image-conscious sheriff with high political ambitions," stays locked in the murder room, with Poe and McKinney as outside "guards." Jameson and Bean say, "No one ... was allowed to enter except on his orders." This is a Garrett conspiracy without witnesses of the body. They state: "Within minutes, the embryonic elements of the biggest controversy in the history of the American West was talking shape, that of the death of the outlaw Billy the Kid."

DEATH SCENE TWO (book page 27) also takes place in the Maxwell bedroom with Garrett shooting, and is just a rumor-of-the-wrong-victim version. Jameson and Bean state: "Within hours after the shooting in Pete Maxwell's bedroom, it was being whispered about Fort Sumner that the dead man was *not* Billy the Kid. The Kid, according to rumor, had escaped and was hiding not far away at the home of a friend."

DEATH SCENE THREE (book pages 72-73) takes place somewhere near the Maxwell house. It is a killing-Barlow version. And "Brushy" expands his Billy Barlow creation. Cleverly, he covers his tracks by calling the name an alias; and says Barlow was a friend from Muleshoe, Texas ranch work (where real Billy had never been). Since Barlow will be mistaken for Roberts-Billy, he is described as "approximately the same size and general appearance as Billy." (Note the Jameson and Bean blooper of the Grant County newspaperman's "eye witness" account of the victim as swarthy and black-bearded.)

In fine confabulating form, "Brushy" provides a lead-up with Barlow, Roberts-Billy, and Celsa going to a dance in Fort Sumner. (It should be realized that Billy was the most hunted man in America - unlikely to appear in public, to say the least.) After the dance, Maxwell's foreman wants to cook dinner for "Billy" and Barlow. So, for some reason in stocking feet, Barlow walks across the Parade Ground to do real Billy's famous steak cutting from the side of beef (erroneously described as "near Maxwell's bedroom," though it was on the opposite side of the house). Barlow is also shirtless - not any historical description, but Roberts's incurable temptation to embellish.

Barlow is shot by unknowns. Roberts-Billy then, for some reason, runs out to fire at "shadows near the house." This gets him shot by unknowns in the jaw, the back, and scalp.

DEATH SCENE FOUR (book pages 105-117) in the Maxwell bedroom *and* back porch, is vertiginously confused, with Garrett, Poe, and "Brushy" all giving versions. There is the conventional Garrett ambush in the bedroom and a carpenter shop vigil. But dead Barlow is also on the back porch - his murderer unclear.

It has, however, the longest run of direct "Brushy" dialogue, and is an important example of his intricate confabulations. It is additionally important, being repeated in full, in an important and secret hoax document reproduced in the Pretender section in its "Seventy-Seven Days of Doubt Document." According to Jameson and Bean, the source of the transcript was William Morrison's step-grandson, Bill Allison.

Roberts is quoted: "I pulled one of my .44's and ran through the door, trying to see in the dark. Two more shots came from a shadow beside the Maxwell house. I couldn't find a target to shoot at. It was too dark to see." (Though "Brushy's" darkness is necessary for his scene, the historical moon made near-daylight.)

Claiming to have been shot himself - though not by whom - "Brushy" says, "I saw a body lying on the back porch ... I knew it had to be Barlow. My partner had walked right into a trap, and the trap had likely been set for me."

Next, Jameson and Bean have Poe state that "several women pleaded for permission to take charge of the body, which we allowed them to do. They carried it across the yard to a carpenter shop" - thus, accidentally adding identifiers.

"Brushy" here also contributes a buckshot spray of confabulations for the Barlow shooting, possibly giving his compatriot Morrison a pick-and-choose option:

- Garrett had come to town looking for Billy because he "knew Pete and I were friends and that I'd stop by to see him if I was in this country."
- "Was he[Garrett] trying to pass off Barlow's body as mine? We were friends."
- "Garrett knew by now he'd killed the wrong man in the dark. Billy Barlow looked a lot like me."
- "Garrett realized his mistake and was making a try at collecting the reward that was out on me anyway."

DEATH SCENE FIVE (book page 119) a Maxwell bedroom one, is a Jameson-Bean version of a Garrett "plot." They start with: "The only witnesses to the shooting of the man purported to be Billy the Kid in Pete Maxwell's bedroom was [sic] Maxwell himself and Sheriff Pat Garrett." Forgotten is that "Brushy" himself was an "eye witness," attesting to the back porch victim. But, realizing they have made Maxwell one, they offer that he "contributed very little to describing what actually took place in the room," thus omitting his Coroner's Jury statement confirming identity.

Nit-picking Garrett's and Poe's reportings yields nothing. Non-participants, like Charles Rudolph (Coroner's Jury Forman Milnor Rudolph's son), are then added to quibble about the caliber of the victim's gun - or if there was one. Deluvina's entry into the room is mentioned irrelevantly, but adds a body identification!

Billy's asking his famous question, "Quien es? [Who are you?]" is claimed as indicating "it was not the Kid." But that makes no sense. Historically, Billy first asked that of the stranger, Poe, on the south porch, and was a logical question using the language of his probable Mexican disguise. His reassurance was indicated by his continued approach. In Maxwell's darkened bedroom, that same question repeated had a different meaning: sensing possible danger, but avoiding an accidental shooting. The authors also miss the preposterousness of "Brushy's" Billy Barlow asking these people who they were, when just cutting some steak and not anticipating being mistaken for Billy the Kid.

DEATH SCENE SIX (book page 124) is a rumor-anecdote version. It is an interview from 1944 with Attorney Albert Jennings Fountain's son, claiming Garrett told him a *different version* of the killing. That every element his story is incorrect - including the location of the side of beef - is less relevant than *Garrett's telling him unequivocally that he shot Billy*; a point missed by Jameson and Bean when they included that gossip.

## APPENDIX: 38. Sheriff Rick Virden Letter on official letterhead to Jay Miller. November 28, 2005.

Dear Mr. Miller,

We are interested in the truth surrounding Billy the Kid **and are continuing the investigation** [author's boldface], utilizing volunteers that have investigative experience and at no cost to Lincoln County.

Tom Sullivan and Steve Sederwall are Deputies with the Lincoln County Sheriff's Department.

Tom Sullivan and Steve Sederwall belong to the Reserve Deputy Unit.

Tom Sullivan and Steve Sederwall **are assigned to investigate the shootings of William H. Bonney and Deputies Bell and Olinger.** [author's boldface]

As you acknowledge in your letter, there is an ongoing investigation being conducted. When the investigating officers conclude their investigation, I will gladly avail to you all of the information you request in case # 2003-274.

**[AUTHOR'S NOTE: Confirming case as a criminal investigation.]**

R.E. Virden
Lincoln County Sheriff

808

## APPENDIX: 39. Robert Struckman. "Bitterroot man hopes to uncover the truth about Billy the Kid." helenair.com. March 13, 2006.

FLORENCE (Lee) – Blowing snow cast a pall over a small horse pasture outside the kitchen window of Dale Tunnel's rural home. In the distance a line of traffic crawled south on U.S. Highway 93.

Tunnell flipped through a box of papers on a small table in the kitchen, choosing a copy of a letter dated March 27, 1881, from W. Bonney to the governor of Mexico Territory.

"Dear Sir: For the last time I ask, will you keep your promise? I start below tomorrow. Send answer by bearer."

Soon after sending the letter, for which he received no reply, Bonney better known as Billy the Kid killed two deputies in his escape from the Lincoln County (NM) Courthouse. Had he remained in custody, Bonney would likely have been hanged for murder. Instead, he was shot and killed by Sheriff Pat Garrett that July.

The piece of correspondence is one small part of a historical puzzle that Tunnell, a retired federal investigator, has been attempting to solve with a former sheriff, a mayor and others, all from New Mexico.

The group has uncovered new evidence, Tunnell said recently, and has even exhumed the body of a man who died in 1937 and who claimed to be the Kid. DNA samples from the body are being compared with samples taken from blood stains on a carpenter's bench that supposedly held Bonney's body after he was shot by Garrett.

"I want to set the record straight. If Billy the Kid, from 1881 to 1937, lived the life of an honest man, a hardworking fool, then I say he paid his debt to society," Tunnell said.

Tunnell knows quite a bit about honest men, debts to society and crime. He had a long and varied law enforcement career, starting as a deputy sheriff in Lincoln County in 1974. He was also an internal affairs investigator with the Arizona Department of Corrections. In 1966, he retired from his tenure as a federal agent with the U.S. Department of Interior.

Tunnell also earned a Ph.D. in forensic criminology and is pursuing a second doctorate in general psychology. [author's boldface]

About four years ago, he founded Forensic LLC. Six months ago he moved to the Bitterroot Valley. The small firm's main business is training; its clients include the Missoula Police Department. Tunnell also consults with police departments on active investigations. He recently helped solve a New Mexico homicide investigation by studying statements given by suspects and witnesses.

That's his day job. Then there's that box of Billy the Kid artifacts.

Tunnell's interest in the famous outlaw was piqued when he read a 1993 book by Helen Airy entitled, 'Whatever Happened to Billy the Kid: Did He Really Die? Maybe Not!"

According to Airy, Billy the Kid, who had several aliases, survived the 1881 shootout with Garrett and traveled West to Arizona to become a rancher near Zuni Pueblo, using the name John Miller. He died in 1937. Friends and family said he maintained and they agree that he was Billy the Kid.

Lincoln County Sheriff Tom Sullivan and Capitan Mayor Steven Sederwall also found the story intriguing. In 2003, Sullivan officially reopened the case of Billy the Kid's escape from the courthouse. An official investigation had never been conducted into the deaths of the two deputies, J.W. Bell and Robert Olinger.

"I just decided to use modern-day technology to find out what happened," said Sullivan, who has since retired.

Working in their spare time and with their own resources, Sullivan, Sederwall, and Tunnell tracked down documents and materials.

Sederwall did most of the legwork. He used census and genealogy records to find descendents of the people who lived in Fort Sumner when Garrett shot Billy at the home of Pete Maxwell. Sederwall found a washbasin with a bullet hole made by Garrett's second shot, which went wide. He found the carpenter's bench where Billy was taken after the shooting.

The deputies also found the burial plots of the two deputies.

"It's just good police work," Sullivan said.

Then they started looking into John Miller's story.

After getting permission to exhume Miller's body, DNA samples were taken. The DNA analysis will be done by Dr. Henry Lee, founder of the Forensic Science Program at the University of New Haven and chief emeritus of the Connecticut State Police, Sullivan said.

What if the DNA matches the wooden bench?

"We'll change history. I don't know. Arizona would have the real Billy the Kid," Sullivan said.

"If it's a match, it's a done deal," Tunnell said.

If not, there's more work to do, he said. It could mean that Miller was not Billy the Kid. Or that the body exhumed was not Billy's. [sic]

"Even if it comes back positive, there will be more work to do," Tunnell said. He hopes to find conclusive documentation placing Miller at or near Fort Sumner in July of 1881 or connecting his wife, Isadora, to a relationship there.

Airy asserted, and Tunnell believes, that Billy the Kid left Fort Sumner in the months after the shooting with Isadora and that the two married in a small town nearby. Tunnell has found records of a priest with a name very similar to the one Airy collected from oral histories from Miller's family and friends. He has requested marriage records from the priest but has not received them.

Tunnell has found enough material to poke holes in the official histories, he said. Once one point has been debunked, the whole house of cards begins to look flimsy, he said.

"A lot of it is the basis for concluding that the whole episode at Pete Maxwell's house was fabricated," he said.

It's possible, Tunnell said, that Garrett conspired with Billy to fake the death. Maybe Billy never laid, wounded, on the carpenter's bench. Maybe another body was buried in Billy's place.

Tunnell has another motive for his research. He would like to confirm the story put forth by Airy. Like him, she was an amateur historian who bucked the official story. Academics scoffed at her account.

"I'd like to prove her correct," he said ...

### APPENDIX: 40. Joanna Dodder. *The Daily Courier* of Prescott, Arizona. "Officials could face charges for digging up alleged Billy the Kid." April 12, 2006.

PRESCOTT Did New Mexico deputies violate the law by digging up the remains of a Prescott man who claimed to be Billy the Kid?

Local authorities are investigating whether the former sheriff of Lincoln County, N.M., and others violated Arizona law in a Prescott cemetery by digging up and removing the remains of John Miller, who told friends he was William Bonney aka Billy the Kid.

Former Lincoln County Sheriff Tom Sullivan said he and the others plan to compare DNA from Miller's bones with DNA from blood that came from a bench on which Billy the Kid lay after Lincoln County Sheriff Pat Garrett shot him on July 14, 1881, in Ft. Sumner, N.M.

A shoulder bone from Miller's grave already indicates damage consistent with that of a gunshot wound that The Kid suffered, Sullivan said. The skeleton's protruding teeth and small stature also are consistent with Billy, he said.

Since Garrett was friends with The Kid, he might have shot him and then let him escape, Sullivan said.

He hopes to see DNA results within two months.

Sullivan and others removed what they hope are Miller's teeth and a femur from an unmarked grave in the Pioneers' Home Cemetery on May 19, 2005. They also removed a femur from a neighboring unmarked grave, just in case that was Miller. The History Channel taped the event.

A Billy the Kid historian from Tucson named Dave Snell recently filed a complaint with the Yavapai County Attorney's Office, which forwarded it to the Prescott Police Department (PPD).

"This is some kind of good ol' boy back-slappin' beer-drinkin' crusade," Snell said. "He's buried in Ft. Sumner, where he's always been."

PPD Det. Anna Cahall contacted several of the people present at the disinterment, ranging from Dr. Laura Fulginiti of the Maricopa County Medical Examiner's Office to Dale Tunnell, a former federal officer involved in the Billy the Kid investigation with Sullivan. Tunnell hired Fulginiti to help. "It's a Billy Buff War," Cahall concluded

Now Prescott City Prosecutor Glenn Savona is trying to figure out whether someone violated the law and whether the city or state has jurisdiction since the State of Arizona owns the Pioneers' Home Cemetery. He noted that time is running out because officials would have to file any misdemeanor charges within a year of the alleged offense.

Complicating matters is the fact that the person who apparently gave Sullivan permission to dig up the grave, former Pioneers' Home Superintendent Jeanine Dike, is away on a Mormon mission until June 2007.

Sullivan and former Capitan, N.M., mayor Steve Sederwall now are commissioned as Lincoln County deputies, Sullivan said. They are in the midst of a 3-year-old investigation into whether Billy the Kid actually is buried in Ft. Sumner.

In the early 1900s, several aging men claimed to be Billy the Kid, including Miller and "Brushy" Bill Roberts. Sullivan and his fellow former lawmen are on a mission to find the real Billy using modern-day technology.

Miller is the only person they have dug up so far. They haven't been able to obtain a court order to dig up Billy the Kid's mother in Silver City, N.M., Sullivan said.

Miller spent his last days as a resident of the Arizona Pioneers' Home in Prescott. When he died in 1937 at the apparent age of 87, gravediggers buried him at the Pioneers' Home Cemetery here.

The late Helen Airy wrote a book about Miller to back up her theory that he was Billy the Kid. She entitled it, "Whatever Happened to Billy the Kid?" Miller told several people that he was the notorious outlaw of Lincoln County War fame.

Dike apparently agreed to let Sullivan and others dig up Miller's unmarked remains under a relatively new state law that allows the action without a court order and permit if it's for "internal management," according to a Prescott Police Department report.

"It doesn't look like the request came for an internal issue," Savona said. That law doesn't allow people to take the remains, either, he added.

Dike had just retired when the disinterment occurred. Since the new superintendent had not yet arrived to start work, a Pioneers' Home administrative assistant named Dale Sams attended the disinterment, according to police records.

The only other way to legally disinter the body is to get a permit from the Yavapai County Community Health Services Department after getting a court order or family permission

Fulginiti and others told police that Tunnell assured them he had permission to conduct the dig.

"There was no fanfare," Sullivan said. "We just came in and slipped in and slipped out. That's what made them mad."

He admitted that the men didn't want to deal with another court battle like the one they faced in Silver City, where Silver City and Ft. Sumner officials were among those trying to stop them.

"Why don't they want to know the truth?" Sullivan said. "It was like we were treading on sacred ground."

Current Pioneers' Home Superintendent Gary Olson, who started the job just a few weeks after the disinterment occurred, said he will take the written advice of Yavapai Community Health Services Director Marcia Jacobson and create a policy that states people need a permit to dig up Pioneers' Home Cemetery bodies.

Pioneers' Home officials are trying to figure out who else Sullivan and the others dug up at the cemetery, whether they have any relatives and whether the state will demand the return of all the bones, Olson said.

### APPENDIX: 41. David Snell. "Letter to Shiela Polk, Yavapai County Attorney." March 11, 2006.

Dear Ms. Polk,

I feel it is my duty to report to you that grave robbers are plying their trade in Yavapai County. There individuals' crimes are being committed openly, knowingly, and with contempt for state and county law regarding exhumations. In the course of their nefarious activities, these parties have compromised and ultimately corrupted various officials and public employees. To date, all the parties involved in these crimes have been exempted from any sort of criminal investigation, let alone prosecution.

I have been in touch with Mr. Glen Guftason of your staff, who is aware of some of the background on the case. He made it clear, however, that he has very limited scope of involvement in this regard and that his primary focus is on matters which are at least once removed from any formal investigation into specifics of the crimes committed. Mr. Gustafson's efforts notwithstanding, it is now well past the time when a formal inquiry into these matters should have commenced.

Attached are two documents which speak directly to the charges I have outlined. The first is a narrative of events prepared by the Superintendent of the Arizona Pioneers' Home. It was made available to me only after I brought the full weight of the law regarding release of public records to bear. The second attachment is, I think you will agree, one of the more revealing and bizarre pieces of governmental correspondence ever prepared. [These correspondences of Superintendent Gary Olson and the office of Governor Napolitano are addressed later under internal cover-up attempts.]

To further a speedy and decisive resolution of this sordid and reprehensible affair, I am requesting a meeting at which these matters can be reviewed in detail, and where a complete set of documents can be provided. There are several important issues involving culpability and moral turpitude which are not apparent on the surface and which cannot be reduced to a sound bite. I am available to travel to Prescott, Phoenix, or elsewhere to facilitate such a meeting.

Now that these circumstances have been brought to your personal attention, I have every confidence that the good citizens of Yavapai County, and Arizona, can be assured of timely and effective action against these ghoulish scofflaws who loot our people's final resting places for personal gain.

## APPENDIX: 42. Leo W. Banks. *Tucson Weekly.* "The New Billy the Kid? The mad search for the bones of an American outlaw icon has come to Arizona." April 13, 2006

Billy the Kid's legend has hovered over the landscape of the American West for 125 years, a Hindenburg of hype and fantasy, always there to nourish those who merely look up. It will never crash and never burn. The only question is: Where will it go next? In its latest incarnation, Airship Billy has come to Arizona, and it's entirely fitting. After all, unknown to most, the Kid shot his first man right here, about 120 miles southeast of Tucson. It happened on Aug. 17, 1877 at Camp Grant, near Safford ...

The latest twist in the Kid's ever-expanding legend came last May, when two New Mexico men traveled to Prescott to exhume the body of John Miller, a complete unknown whose most memorable life deed was claiming that he, in fact, was Billy the Kid.

Miller died in 1937, which, if his claim is true, means that Sheriff Pat Garrett did not kill Billy with a bullet through the heart in Fort Sumner, N.M., on July 14, 1881, as the official version says.

You might remember the names of the two investigators--Tom Sullivan, a retired sheriff of Lincoln County, N.M., and Steve Sederwall, a former federal cop.

Two years prior to coming to Prescott, they opened an official investigation into Billy's killing of two deputies during his escape from the Lincoln County Courthouse in April 1881.

Their ambitious plans included exhuming Catherine Antrim, the Kid's mother, from her grave in Silver City, N.M., and using modern forensics to compare her DNA to Miller's, and to the DNA of Ollie "Brushy Bill" Roberts of Texas, who also claimed to be the Kid.

A match of either man to Catherine might force historians to rewrite one of the West's most iconic stories. New Mexico Gov. Bill Richardson promised state help in the effort, and in June 2003, *The New York Times* played the investigation on its front page.

The story ignited a worldwide Billy bonfire. The possibilities seemed positively grand. Until they didn't.

The plan, which included the possibility of exhuming Billy himself, generated an angry backlash. Respected Kid historian Frederick Nolan, author of *The West of Billy the Kid*, declared the dig-up effort ridiculous, and its perpetrators ignorant of history. Other critics chimed in accusing Sullivan and Sederwall of behaving like grave robbers and out-of-control cowboys hunting their 15 minutes.

But these cops-turned-history sleuths say the criticism came from people who want to keep the story exactly the way it is--to preserve their reputations and their incomes.

These days, the Kid generates more dollars for New Mexico's Lincoln County than cattle. What happens if he didn't really die there? What happens if he's actually buried in Arizona?

"People at Fort Sumner wouldn't allow us to exhume Billy's remains, because they're not sure he's there," says the 65-year-old Sullivan, still smarting from the criticism. "Everybody lawyered up, and we ran into a lot of legal B.S."

**So Sullivan and Sederwall stole into Arizona on stocking feet, working quietly to get Miller's bones out of his grave at Prescott's state-run Arizona Pioneers' Home, snag some DNA and head back home.**

**"We slipped in there and slipped out fast," Sullivan told the Weekly.** [author's boldface] "We all stayed at the same hotel, sort of to keep it quiet. If the media got word, our critics would've gotten together to lawyer the whole thing up, serve people with papers and temporary restraining orders, and all that crap."

The media blackout wasn't total. Employees of Bill Kurtis Productions, which does popular historical and investigative shows for the cable channel A&E, were on hand to film the exhumation for possible use.

Says Sederwall: "We're just looking for the truth" ...

Bob Boze Bell, executive editor of *True West* magazine, put it well in his book, *The Illustrated Life and Times of Billy the Kid*: "The Kid lived two-thirds of his life in circumstances that remain to this day almost entirely undocumented" ...

It [the killing of Billy by Garrett] sounds open and shut, but Sullivan and Sederwall say that, as cops, Garrett's accounts of Billy's escape and subsequent events raise too many questions.

The sheriff claimed that Billy broke away from Bell, ran all the way up the interior stairs of the courthouse, around the corner to the armory, got a gun, ran back to the top of the stairs and shot Bell, who, after all that time was still only halfway up the stairs in pursuit. How could Billy pull that off, while wearing 17-inch leg irons?

With his jail holding such a prized prisoner, why was Garrett out of town at the time of the escape?

Was Sheriff Garrett, a known friend of the Kid, outraged at Billy's conviction in the Brady trial and somehow involved in helping Billy escape justice?

"From a law-enforcement perspective, nothing fits," says Sullivan, who designed the shoulder-patch likeness of Garrett worn by present-day Lincoln County sheriff's deputies. He told *True West* that his integrity hangs on finding out if Garrett was a liar and a conspirator in a double murder.

Sederwall points with suspicion to the last line of the coroner's report on Billy. "It says Garrett deserves the reward money for killing him," he says. "I've never seen that in a coroner's report before" ...

A cemetery near Hico, Texas, holds the remains of ... "Brushy Bill" Roberts, who made a splash in 1950 saying he was the Kid. His claim drew derisive laughter and wasn't even supported by the family Bible. It listed the year of his birth as 1879, which would've made him a 2-year-old gunman in the Lincoln County war.

But old Brushy won't go away. The town of Hico promotes its ties to the great pretender and hosts a museum dedicated to the proposition that he was genuine. Writers who are not insane keep trying to stand up his story ...

John Miller's claim to being the Kid rests on a 1993 book by the late Helen Airy, called *Whatever Happened to Billy the Kid?*

She traced Miller's life through his years in New Mexico in the early 1880s, then to San Simon, Ariz., around World War I, and later to Buckeye, near Phoenix. Miller arrived at the Arizona Pioneers' Home on March 14, 1937, after injuring his hip in a fall from a roof, and died there eight months later.

The evidence he was Billy? He told numerous friends and family of his secret identity. Plus, he had buck teeth, skill with a pistol and good relations with outlaws and lowlifes. And at his Las Vegas, N.M., wedding on Aug. 8, 1881, he supposedly wore a large-caliber six-shooter and appeared pale and weak with bandages covering a chest wound visible through his flimsy summer shirt.

It's weak stuff, almost as rickety as Brushy's claim.

But Sullivan thought it sounded good. "Helen Airy's book triggered it for me," he says. "It made a lot of sense. I read it and thought, 'We have another Billy the Kid.' "

Then he and Sederwall found additional evidence to work with.

Doing what Sullivan calls "good police work," they found a descendent of the Maxwell family, who had, stored in his chicken coop, the washstand from Maxwell's bedroom, the headboard from his bed and, most significantly, the wooden workbench on which the Kid's body was supposedly laid after being shot.

**This bench was saturated in blood.** [author's boldface] Did this mean they had the Kid's blood? Could it be our mysterious range ruffian, Miller? The famous forensic expert Dr. Henry Lee successfully pulled DNA from the bench, making possible a comparison with Miller's.

"When we found the bench and the other evidence, we thought, 'Let's forget about these other bodies,' " says Sullivan, referring to Catherine Antrim and the Kid. "Let's do Miller. And if that doesn't work, we'll go down to Texas and do Brushy Bill.' "

Although the Prescott exhumation has raised some critical eyebrows, Gary Olson, superintendent of the Pioneers' Home, said Arizona law exempts the facility from normal procedures governing exhumations, and that the superintendent has sole authority over management of the home's cemetery. The superintendent who approved the dig, Jeanine Dike, has since retired and didn't return a call to comment for this story.

But the Pioneers' Home already had one Old West celebrity buried in its cemetery--Doc Holliday's girlfriend Big Nose Kate, who died there in 1940--and Dale Tunnell, the Phoenix investigator who first approached the home on behalf of Sullivan and Sederwall, said Dike thought it would be great to add another.

"The attitude was that it would be a pretty good coup to find William Bonney buried in their cemetery," says Tunnell, who runs a Phoenix company called Forensitec, which specializes in something called psycholinguistics, the analysis of text or conversations to find truth, deceptions or omissions.

**See how everybody wants a piece of the Kid, even a celebrity like Henry Lee? He's worked on just about every high-profile murder case you can name, from O.J. Simpson and JonBenet Ramsey, to the Lindbergh baby and JFK.** [author's boldface]

**But when he heard about the Kid dig-up efforts, he called Sederwall to volunteer his services.** [author's boldface] At the moment Sederwall's cell phone rang, he was riding shotgun on a stagecoach in New Mexico, filling in for a short-handed friend who runs a coach line for tourists.

As the two men talked, the famous Dr. Lee heard the clippetty-clop/jingle-jangle of the coach all the way back in civilized Connecticut, and asked, "What's that *noise?*"

Sederwall chuckled. "You wouldn't believe me if I told you."

The Miller exhumation began about 1 p.m. on May 19 last year, and didn't end until about 7:30 that night, with investigators examining the last of the remains by flashlight. A backhoe did most of the heavy labor, after which the diggers worked by hand to avoid damaging the coffins or the remains.

But they soon learned that the coffins had already collapsed with age, which had also made the bones extremely fragile. Each piece was carefully photographed, measured and cleaned, then placed on a white sheet on the ground.

Dr. Laura Fulginiti, a well-known forensic anthropologist from Phoenix, supervised the dig. She describes the atmosphere as collegial and charged with excitement as they removed the tobacco-colored bones from the ground.

"At one point, they were holding up the skull and comparing it with pictures of Billy," Fulginiti says. "They recited the story to each other, and when we found something that matched, like the scapula (shoulder) fracture, they were like little kids. They were really invested in this, and that added to the enthusiasm." But the effort was anything but clear-cut. In the first place, Miller's grave held no marker or headstone, and neither did the grave closest to his. To determine where Miller's plot should be, the investigators used a map provided by the Pioneers' Home, which pinpointed the location to within 20 square feet.

As Tunnell acknowledges, ground shift and weather patterns can sometimes move bodies underground, and Miller had been 6 feet under almost 70 years. How certain were they of digging in the right place? "Probably upwards of 90 percent," says Tunnell.

**Once in the ground, the investigators found two sets of remains, both white males, resting side by side in graves separated by 3 to 4 feet.** [author's boldface] Which one was Miller? Nobody knew. So they pulled bones from both graves and examined them.

**Fulginiti says the first body she studied had buck teeth and the scapula fracture that caused such a commotion with investigators.**

**As Sederwall told the *Weekly*, "We were shocked when we got him up. He had buck teeth just like the Kid and a bullet hole in the upper left chest that exited the shoulder blade."**

**Sullivan made a similar statement, suggesting this might be the man Garrett shot the morning of July 14, 1881.**

**But when contacted by the *Weekly*, Fulginiti didn't support their enthusiasm. "There was evidence of trauma on the scapula, but I couldn't tell whether it was from a gunshot wound or not,"** she said. [author's boldface]

**[AUTHOR'S NOTE: Fulginiti's report makes clear the hoaxed skeleton.]**

Fulginiti then examined the second body, finding no evidence of a gunshot wound. But she did find a hip injury that was still in the process of repairing at the time of death. This fit with the story from Airy's book that Miller had fallen off a roof just prior to coming to the Pioneers' Home.

Based on this, Fulginiti proceeded on the assumption that *this* man was Miller, and she continues to do so to this day.

Told of Fulginiti's statement, Sullivan responded, "Well, we think it's the other guy."

So who's the right dead guy--Hip Man or Scapula Man?

Truth is, it could be either one. Or neither. The Billy the Kid merry-go-round continues to spin.

It gets better.

The DNA expert present at the exhumation, Dr. Rick Staub, of Orchid Cellmark Labs in Dallas, was unable to extract useable DNA from Hip Man. But he did get a usable sample from Scapula Man.

Did it match the blood on the workbench?

We still don't know.

Orchid has been overwhelmed in their effort to process Hurricane Katrina victims, and hasn't turned its attention to Miller's supposed remains, which they are assessing free of charge. Sullivan expects an answer soon.

The problems the investigators encountered in the Prescott dig-up mimicked the central criticisms they heard in New Mexico. After so long, how can you tell who is buried where?

Eight years after Catherine Antrim's 1874 burial in Silver City, as several Kid Web sites point out, the whole cemetery was moved, and we can't know how diligent the workers were in matching graves with markers in the new location.

Same with Billy. He was buried beside two friends, which would fuzz up the results, as it did with Miller, and his gravesite was said to be unmarked for years following a tremendous flood that washed through the Fort Sumner Cemetery in 1904.

Was the new marker returned to the right place? Did floodwaters mangle bodies and bones underground, or move them to some new location?

Hello, Billy? Are you down there?

Fulginiti says she's glad she took part in an endeavor that's so much a part of history. But she struggles with the question: Was it respectful to Miller to dig him up?

"Part of me says it wasn't, given that the information we had wasn't the best," she says. "From the beginning, I assumed it was another of these Wild West goose chases. But they believed the information and believed they had Billy's blood. So the only way to put the rumor to rest was to do the tests. I give them credit for contacting me and doing it by the book."

Sullivan and Sederwall insist that, through Dr. Lee's work, they've changed history. They say they've proven that Bell and the Kid grappled at the top of the courthouse steps, not halfway up.

Using sophisticated laser tests, they say they've also established that Garrett fired his second shot back over his shoulder as he stumbled in the doorway of Maxwell's room, and that second bullet lodged not in the headboard, as previously believed, but in the washstand.

If these seem like small matters, remember--the word "small" has been banished from the Billy World dictionary. Will the forthcoming DNA results change history? Will we have a "new Billy"? ....

Boze Bell at *True West* supports using science to find out whether Billy is buried in Fort Sumner or Hico, Texas. But he's disturbed by the Miller exhumation. "About five people actually believe Miller is the Kid," Bell says. "It sounds like this investigation has gone off the rails."

In an e-mail from his home in England, historian Frederick Nolan says that even if Sullivan and Sederwall were to acquire the correct DNA from all the correct corpses, it would only confirm what history already knows--that Billy the Kid died in Fort Sumner on July 14, 1881.

**"This disgraceful charade is historical inconsequentiality gone mad,"** Nolan wrote. **"... It's sad to have to, yet again, rev up a steam engine to squash such an insignificant bug. But although it's insignificant, it's also highly toxic."** [author's boldface]

Will negative DNA results mean this is finally over? Will our Billy be allowed to rest? Don't count on it.

Sullivan says he might try to exhume Brushy Bill next, and even return to Silver City to dig for Catherine Antrim's bones.

"The judge in Silver City said you can't exhume Catherine, because you have nothing to compare her DNA to," says the former sheriff, who keeps a framed copy of the *Times*' Page 1 story on his dining-room wall.

"They told us to come back if we found more evidence. Then we got DNA from the bloody workbench and the people in Silver City went, 'Oh ... my ... God!' They called us nutcases and stupid. Well, we're just going to let them sweat for a while ..."

### APPENDIX: 43. Dr. Laura Fulginiti. "Re: Exhumation, Pioneer Home Cemetery, Prescott, Arizona for "Dale L. Tunnell, Ph.D. [sic], Forensitec." June 2, 2005. [AUTHOR'S NOTE: At end is my summary of Fulginiti's evidence.]

RE: Exhumation, Pioneer [sic] Home Cemetery, Prescott, Arizona

On May 19, 2005 at approximately 1230 hours I am asked to assist in the exhumation of the remains of an individual known as Mr. John Miller by Dr. Dale Tunnell, President, Forensitec. The purpose of my involvement is to aid in the exhumation process as well as to assess any skeletal remains recovered. The exhumation takes place at the Arizona Pioneer [sic] Home Cemetery, Iron Springs Road in Prescott Arizona in the presence of Dr. Tunnell, several of his associates, members of the Arizona Pioneer Home staff and Kristen Harnett M.A., AMSU graduate student.

Dr. Tunnell located the alleged gravesite of Mr. Miller prior to our arrival on the scene. The gravesite was located using the line of headstones to the West of the target grave. A standard reference point was established as the headstone of Michael Clancy. At approximately 1400 hours, a backhoe began to remove the sod overlying the alleged grave, which was oriented in an East-West direction, with the head to the West. When fragments of wood began to be removed, the grave was excavated using a shovel. Once the top of the casket and a portion of femur were unearthed, the excavation relied on digging with trowels and by hand. The position of the femur indicated that the remains were supine, with the feet to the East and the skull to the West. The left femoral shaft, minus the head, was removed, examined, and packaged for DNA analysis.

**Dr. Tunnell, in consultation with the cemetery staff and his other associates determined that the adjacent grave to the North was likely that of Mr. Miller and excavation shifted to that gravesite.** [author's boldface]

[AUTHOR'S NOTE: This is the North Grave, claimed to be Miller's; but Fulginiti later disproves that. But exhuming a second grave was automatically illegal.]

The backhoe removed the overlying sod until fragments of wood began to be unearthed. The excavation shifted to shovels and the top of the casket was identified. Excavation proceeded using trowels and hand tools until various aspects of the skeleton were identified and cleared. The skeleton in this grave was also lying supine, head to the West and feet to the East. The casket had collapsed onto the body at some point prior to the exhumation process. **A metal detector on loan from the Yavapai County Sheriff's Office and operated by Det. Mike Poling, YCSO, was used to locate metal items, including nails and casket fittings.** (These items were donated to the Arizona Pioneer Home for their museum).

[AUTHOR'S NOTE: Poling's accidental presence would later affect the legal outcome. ]

Minimal historical artifacts, such as buttons, a possible rivet, portions of wood from the casket and casket fittings were identified as they were unearthed. Skeletal elements were measured for depth and location, removed from the grave and examined (see Forensitec report). Pathological conditions such as osteoarthritis, healed fractures and markers of occupation were noted as follows. The vertebrae exhibited signs of extreme osteoarthritis in the form of lipping of the vertebral bodies, collapse of some of the bodies and osteophytic activity. **There were extensive healed traumata on the right scapula** [author's boldface]

[AUTHOR'S NOTE: So the damaged scapula is in North Grave.]

and the left clavicle, a healed Colles' fracture of the right distal radius, a healed fracture of the second rib and a healed fracture of the left fourth metacarpal. The bone was dark brown in color, friable and dry. There was postmortem damage, both from the collapse of the lid of the casket onto the remains as well as from the removal process. The remains were photographed, samples were harvested for DNA (tooth and femur) and the remains were returned to the grave and reburied.

**Anecdotal historical information suggested that Mr. John Miller had died from complications of a fractured hip while recuperating in the Arizona pioneer Home. The individual in the north grave, while having extensive pathological conditions, particularly in the upper body, did not have discernible pathology of the *os coxae*.** [author's boldface]

[AUTHOR'S NOTE: The North Grave is NOT COMPATIBLE with Miller's history; so the scapula is not his. Fulginiti calls the South Grave Miller's. That makes the North grave Hudspeth's.]

At this point in the exhumation, a decision was made to exhume the *os coxae* of the individual in the south grave to confirm that we had indeed excavated the remains of Mr. John Miller from the north grave. The south grave was excavated by shovel to the point where the remnants of the casket lid were identified. Excavation resumed using trowels and hand tools until the left femoral head was identified.

The head of the femur was misshapen with bony remodeling, suggesting an antemortem injury. Additional excavation revealed the left innominate, which also had extensive remodeling of the acetabulum, ischium and pubis. The ischium tapered to a point with lack of union to the pubis, suggesting a healing fracture of the ischiopubic ramus. **This evidence led the team to believe that the individual in the south grave was, in fact, more consistent with the known facts regarding the Medical history of Mr. John Miller and additional DNA samples were recovered (femur, scalp?, matter from inside the braincase).** [author's boldface]

[AUTHOR'S NOTE: Confirmation of South Grave Miller's.]

**The maxillae and mandible were recovered but were edentulous.** [author's boldface]

[AUTHOR'S NOTE: Miller had NO TEETH. Hoaxers lied and claimed "buck teeth (like Billy the Kid's!")]

There was limited pathology of the vertebrae, ribcage, clavicles and scapulae of the individual from the south grave. Mild osteoarthritis of the vertebral bodies was the only pathology of note. Photographs of the cranium and mandible were taken and the remains were returned to the grave and reburied.

Biological profiles of the two individuals are similar. Both were adult males, consistent with individuals of European (White) descent, and of advancing years. The nasal apertures on both were tall and narrow, with a sharp nasal sill, the malars were retreating and the cranial shape, while fragmentary, was round. The pubic symphyses exhibited characteristics of Suchey-Brooks Phase IV (36-86 years, mean 61.2 years).The symphyseal faces were flat and eroded with marked ventral ligaments. The sternal ends of the ribs; while fragmentary, exhibited long bony extensions, consistent with an Iscan, Loth stage 8 (65 plus). **The individual in the south grave was edentulous.** [author's boldface]

[AUTHOR'S NOTE: Repeat that Miller had NO TEETH.]

The scene was returned to a state approximating that prior to our arrival and was cleared shortly after sundown. Items of evidence collected were distributed to members of the Arizona Pioneer Home Cemetery staff and to Dr. Richard Staub (see Forensitec report).

Laura C. Fulginiti, Ph.D., D-ABFA
Forensic Anthropologist

---

[Author's summary from selections from "Re: Exhumation, Pioneer [sic] Home Cemetery, Prescott, Arizona" to show Fulginiti's important evidence in boldface.]

1) Tunnell is used to set up the location: the south grave. **"Dr. Tunnell located the alleged gravesite of Mr. Miller prior to our arrival on the scene."**

2) Remains are taken from that South Grave. **"The left femoral shaft, minus the head, was removed, examined, and packaged for DNA analysis."**

3) The North Grave is added to the exhumation by Tunnell and "associates," presumably Sullivan and Sederwall. **"Dr. Tunnell, in consultation with the cemetery staff and his other associates determined that the adjacent grave to the North was likely that of Mr. Miller and excavation shifted to that gravesite."**

4) The North Grave is excavated using a metal detector lent by a Yavapai County Detective. He came to deliver specimens from another case to Fulginiti. This would prove important through Sullivan and Sederwall claiming the exhumation was under his auspices. His presence would also affect legal case jurisdiction. **"A metal detector on loan from the Yavapai County Sheriff's Office and operated by Det. Mike Poling, YCSO, was used to locate metal items, including nails and casket fittings."**

5) The North Grave has the damaged scapula as well as other skeletal injuries. **"There were extensive healed traumata on the right scapula and the left clavicle, a healed Colles' fracture of the right distal radius, a healed fracture of the second rib and a healed fracture of the left fourth metacarpal."**

6) The North Grave is canceled out as Miller's. That, in essence, makes its exhumation illegal. **"Anecdotal historical information suggested that Mr. John Miller had died from complications of a fractured hip while recuperating in the Arizona pioneer Home. The individual in the north grave,**

while having extensive pathological conditions, particularly in the upper body, did not have discernible pathology of the *os coxae*."

7) The South Grave is decided to be Miller's - a decision by "the team." The hip injury is found with pelvic damage. And the jaws lack any teeth. **"The head of the femur was misshapen with bony remodeling, suggesting an antemortem injury ... The ischium tapered to a point with lack of union to the pubis, suggesting a healing fracture of the ischiopubic ramus. This evidence led the team to believe that the individual in the south grave was, in fact, more consistent with the known facts regarding the Medical history of Mr. John Miller and additional DNA samples were recovered ... The maxillae and mandible were recovered but were edentulous."**

**APPENDIX: 44. Prescott City Attorney Glenn Savona. To Shiela Polk, Yavapai County Attorney (with copies to Detective Anna Cahall and her boss, Chief Randy Oaks). "Re: Police Department DR#2006-12767 Arizona Pioneers' Home Cemetery." April 13, 2006.**

CITY OF PRESCOTT
LEGAL DEPARTMENT
ADDRESS

Sheila Sullivan Polk
Yavapai County Attorney
ADDRESS

Re: Police Department DR#2006-12767 Arizona Pioneers' Home Cemetery

Dear Ms. Polk:

I have been requested to review whether the actions of Jeanine Dike, the Superintendent of the Arizona Pioneers' Home Cemetery, in May of 2005 were in violation of A.R.S. Statute 36-327. In may of 2005 the remains of two bodies located at the Arizona Pioneers' Home Cemetery were disinterred and portions of those bodies were removed. This action was performed with the consent and approval of Jeanine Dike.

**[AUTHOR'S NOTE: Savona's misunderstanding. Dike was involved only in the Miller exhumation. There was never "permission" for the William Hudspeth exhumation.]**

A.R. S 36-327 makes it a class one misdemeanor to disinter remains without a permit. An exception to the permit was added by the Arizona legislature in 2004, in the event the disinterment and reinterment occurs in the same cemetery for ordinary relocation or for reasons of internal management of the cemetery ...

For purposes of the review relating to the filing of misdemeanor charges, the issue is not whether or not Ms. Dike obtained a permit to disinter rather the issue is whether or not the law *required* Ms. Dike to obtain a permit. The police reports generated by Detective Cahall reveal the purpose underlying the disinterment was to attempt to gather evidence to determine whether or not a person identified as Johnny Miller was not, in fact, William Bonney. Under the circumstances and the limited legislative guidance in interpreting A.R.S. 36-327(B), this Office cannot conclude beyond a reasonable doubt that such purpose was not for "reasons of internal management" of the cemetery ... The consideration of misdemeanor charges only concerns whether or not a permit was requited and not subsequent acts after disinterment.

**[AUTHOR'S NOTE: Savona is unaware that there is no reference DNA to justify disinterment for any "internal management."]**

Ms. Dike is no longer employed as the Superintendent of the Arizona Pioneers' Home. The attachments to the report filed herein indicated that the current Superintendent either has or is in the process of adopting procedures to make sure those at rest at the pioneers' Home Cemetery are to be afforded greater protections from those who desire to disturb them. The Pioneers' Home Cemetery is operated as a public trust through the Office of the Governor and it is their obligation not only to comport with the law, but also honor the respect of persons at peace within their trust and their descendants. The internal management of the Pioneers' Home Cemetery is best addressed with the Superintendent and Governor.

Although a permit, under the "reasons of internal management" exception created in 2004, does not appear to have been required under law, this does not end the legal issues relating to the subject of Detective Cahall's report.

**There is nothing in A.R.S. 36-327 authorizing the removal of body parts for any reason.** [author's boldface] The permit statute does not authorize any further conduct relating to the remains other than moving them to another site within the cemetery. A specific State Statute deals with such conduct. A.R.S. 32-1364(B), titled crimes against the dead, states:

It is unlawful for a person, without the authority of law, to disinter or remove a dead human body or any part of a dead human body from its sepulcher, grave or other interment site, or where the body is awaiting disposition, with malice or wantonness or *with the intent to sell or dissect the body.*

A violation of A.R.S. 32-1364 is a class 4 felony.

It appears from the report, the only reason these two bodies were disturbed was to remove certain body parts and take samples from them for DNA testing. Body parts of the two gentlemen were in fact removed and taken to another state. From the reports generated, DNA was in fact distracted [sic]. This conduct, in accord with Webster's Dictionary, appears to be a dissection which, pursuant to statute can only be conducted "with authority of law."

This office does not have the authority to charge or prosecute alleges violations of law deemed to be felonies by the legislature. Jurisdiction of felony matters rests with the County Attorney. Thus the matter is being sent back to the Yavapai County Attorney's Office for further actions that they deem to be appropriate reference all those involved. [author's boldface]

Sincerely,
Glenn A. Savona
Prescott City Prosecutor

cc. Chief Randy Oaks
    Det. A. Cahall

## APPENDIX: 45. Julie Carter. "Culture shock: The cowboys and the Kid go to France." May 5, 2006.

The south of France is about to meet the Old West and it could be a culture shock for both. Lincoln County Billy the Kid history investigators Tom Sullivan and Steve Sederwall, have been invited to the showing of a Kid documentary at the 2006 Cannes Film Festival.

*Requiem for Billy the Kid*, a French film shot primarily in Lincoln County in 2004, has found a place on the 59th Festival de Cannes film roster in the Cannes Classics heritage films category. Directed by Anne Feinsilber and produced by Jean-Jacques Beineix of Cargo Films, the 90-minute $700,000 movie was filmed in Cinemascope. It features interviews with Sullivan, Sederwall and Kris Kristofferson, who did the Kid's voice-over in the film. The documentary begins with the headstone placement on J.W. Bell's grave in White Oaks, moves to the DNA retrieval from the stairway in the Lincoln Courthouse and on to retracing the Kid's route after his escape.

Off and on for nine months and without compensation, Sullivan and Sederwall aided Feinsilber in her quest to document both the old and the new of the Kid story. They spent hours running horses across a variety of terrain and in different kinds of light for the best of 100 shots to end up on the screen. They recreated the murder of Sheriff Brady, played by Sullivan, and spent days in and around Lincoln and the courthouse.

The idea for the documentary came when Feinsilber was living in New York and saw a story on the front page of *The New York Times* reporting the plans to use DNA testing to discover if the man shot dead by Pat Garrett was actually Billy the Kid. Traveling to Lincoln County, she found what appeared to her to be time standing still. With a sheriff (Sullivan) who wore boots, a star and Stetson, the charisma of the West wooed her to roll the cameras. Feinsilber said she fell in love with the story and decided to make her film a mix of documentary and Western.

Each year more than 1,500 films are submitted to the Cannes Film Festival from more than 100 countries to be considered through juried selection for the limited number of places in the official roster. When *Requiem for Billy the Kid* was chosen for Cannes, Feinsilber contacted Sullivan and said she would like him and Sederwall to come to France for the event. She also hopes to also have Kristofferson at the viewing on May 21.

### Clean jeans and boots

The pair has accepted the invitation and is readying their fancy go-to-meet-high-society-in-Europe clothes, which look remarkably like their no-society-New Mexico cowboy clothes -- clean jeans, starched shirt, polished boots and a big cowboy hat.

Fascination for the story of Billy the Kid is worldwide. Sullivan said over the past two years, since the news of the forensic approach to proving history or changing it, they have been featured in articles from Germany, Denmark, Italy, England, France, Spain, Argentina and Mexico. "As popular as the Kid is in Europe, once people see the film and see the streets of Lincoln, the court house and how it is still the same as it was a hundred years ago, I think there will be many who will want to come to New Mexico to see it first hand," said Sullivan. "This could be a positive influence for tourism to Lincoln County."

In the meantime, Sederwall wants a personal performance from Kristofferson singing "Me and Bobby McGee."

## APPENDIX: 46. Lincoln County Attorney Alan Morel letter to Gale Cooper. "Re: Freedom of Information Act/Inspection of Public Records Act Request dated September 22, 2006, to Lincoln County Sheriff Rick Virden." October 11, 2006.

Dear Dr. Cooper:

Please be advised that your Freedom of Information Act request dated September 22, 2006, to the Lincoln County Records Custodian and Lincoln County Sheriff Rick Virden has been forwarded to me for review and response. By way of information, I am the attorney for the County of Lincoln and, as such, represent the various elected officials of Lincoln County, including the Lincoln County Sheriff. The following represents Lincoln County Sheriff Rick Virden's response to your request for information ...

Prior to responding to your request for information, I met with Lincoln County Sheriff Rick Virden and obtained his verbal and written responses to your requests, which are incorporated herein.

I must point out that I do not agree or disagree with the opinions you expressed in the first three pages of your request for public records ... Your opinions simply aren't relevant to the records you have requested.

**[AUTHOR'S NOTE: I referred to Virden's misuse of the criminal investigation exception.]**

Response Item 1. A copy of a deputy sheriff commission issued to Tom Sullivan on January 1, 2005, is attached ... [Author's Note: Signed by R.E. Virden, Sheriff and by Donna Harkey; expiration date 5/20/08.]

Response Item 2. A copy of a deputy sheriff commission issued to Steven Sederwall on February 25, 2005, is attached ... [Author's Note: Signed by R.E. Virden, Sheriff and by Donna Harkey; expiration date 5/20/08.]

Responses Items 3 and 4. [Author's Note: Denial as "no public records" of law enforcement certification for Sullivan, then Sederwall.]

Responses to Items 5 and 6. Sheriff Virden did not assign or authorize Tom Sullivan to perform any exhumations, whether in Prescott, Arizona, or elsewhere. In speaking with Tom Sullivan (Steven Sederwall), Mr. Sullivan (Steven Sederwall) advised me that he did not personally perform any exhumations in Prescott, Arizona, or elsewhere. By further response, neither Sheriff Virden nor Lincoln County maintains any public records that are responsive to Item 5 (6).

Responses to Items 7 to 23. Neither Sheriff Virden nor Lincoln County maintains any public records that are responsive to Item (7-23).

**[AUTHOR'S NOTE: Items requested records of the Arizona exhumations: forensic reports, funding, and permissions.]**

... I have also attached to this response two e-mails from Steven M. Sederwall to Jay Miller, dated September 19, 2006, and September 20, 2006, as Exhibit 3. **I do not believe they are responsive to any of your requests for records, but I decided to include them,** [author's boldface] as they were provided to me by Mr. Sederwall. In addition, I have attached a copy of a letter with the heading "The Dried Bean," [Appendix: 39] which was written to me on September 30, 2006. This correspondence is attached as Exhibit 4. **Although I do not believe that the enclosed correspondence is responsive to any request for public records that you forwarded to me, I have, nonetheless, attached the correspondence, as it has already been forwarded to outside parties - namely the U.S. Marshals Service and Jay Miller.** [author's boldface]

**[AUTHOR'S NOTE: All attachments seemed for intimidation]**

**APPENDIX: 47. Tom Sullivan and Steve Sederwall. Letter to Attorney Alan P. Morel. "The Dried Bean." September 30, 2006.** [AUTHOR'S NOTE: This is the intimidating main attachment in Attorney Alan Morel's above response to my first Virden IPRA request – in APPENDIX: 46. Each page bottom is labeled EXHIBIT 4, as if in a legal case against me.]

THE DRIED BEAN
"YOU BELIEVIN' US OR THEM LYIN' WHORES"

Mr. Alan Morel: Attorney at Law
Lincoln County Attorney
ADDRESS

September 30, 2006

Dear Mr. Morel:

Lincoln County Sheriff Virden forwarded a FOIA request on the Billy the Kid [sic] signed by Gale Cooper. We will do our best to answer these questions for you and give you some background on this case.

When we (Sheriff Tom Sullivan and I) opened this case to examine the death of two Lincoln County Deputies there had been no official investigation. Those upset with our investigation hold up Sheriff Pat Garrett's 1882 book *"The Authentic Life of Billy the Kid"* to say Garrett's writing, since he was the Sheriff, should stand as the official report. However, Garrett's account is fraudulent in fact.

Frederick Nolan, one who has come out publicly against our investigation, writes in *"The Authenticated Life of Billy the Kid an annotated edition"* by Oklahoma Press [sic] in 2000, *"It will surprise hardly anyone to hear that much of this text is farrago of nonsense."* Nolan goes on to say, *"But careless inaccuracy, slanted historical accounting, deliberate untruth, and downright cover-up are less forgivable, especially when purveyed under the implicit imprimatur of Garrett's name."* A statement with which we investigators agree. This presents a question. Why do the self-proclaimed arm-chair historians including Gale Cooper M.D. and Jay Miller, fear a bright light being shown [sic] on a subject that most agree is a lie?

When we began this case we agreed we would not expend any money from the public coffers or burden the County with this investigation. We do not drive government vehicles, or make copies at the government's expense. We do not sit at a government desk, use government pen or paper or computers, and not ever [sic] a government paper clip has been used. We do not work out of a government office; it is our telephones we use, our paper we write on (this is my letterhead); we use our computers, and our filing cabinets. It is our vehicles with which we use to travel. With our credit cards we pay for meals and lodging. This case has taken thousands of man hours none of which has been billed to anyone including the local, county, state, or federal government, and we have spent thousands of dollars on copying of records, all paid for with our money.

**We have Fulton Collection, Cline Collection, copied files of the National Archives, W.G. Ritch Collection, Lew Wallace Collection, Hailey [sic] Collection as well as many others,** [author's boldface] at great expense, all of which we absorbed. Many historians have answered questions we posed in our search for the truth and many more have blocked our efforts. Using investigative methods we have uncover [sic] a great number of artifacts relating to this case, artifacts passed over and missed by historians and others such as Gale Cooper who *"followed all aspects of the Billy the Kid case."*

We have not entered into contracts as we are men of the west and a handshake has served us well in these matters. In the matter of John Miller Lincoln County provided nothing, not travel monies, not film or camera to take a picture. There is no contract between Lincoln County or anyone. There is no contract between the "promulgators" as Cooper and Miller insist in calling us and anyone. We merely observed the dig and introduced the State of Arizona to the lab we used and advised the lab we would allow our findings to be compared with Mr. Miller. In return the State of Arizona said we could use the comparison of Miller's DNA and our findings in our quest for the truth.

**[AUTHOR'S NOTE: This is their claim of Arizona doing the dig.]**

There was no agreement between Lincoln County and the State of Arizona. None of the "promulgators" so much as entered the grave of Mr. Miller. We did however examine some of the remains with our eye.

What is feared is that the "myth" and "legend" of Billy the Kid as written will change. This is a valid concern, with the information we now hold the "myth" and "legend" will surely be destroyed. This is what drives Jay Miller in his e-mail I have attached.

In any correspondences or written document in a crime investigators search for patters [sic], cadence of the writing, use of words or phrases, similarities and charters [?] in the writings. This is how investigators can know if the writer of a ransom note and a threat letter are from the same writer. In Jay Miller's September 3, 2003 [sic] letter to Stewart Bluestone the New Mexico Deputy Attorney General Miller uses the word "promulgators" in describing us no less than seven (7) times. In his letter to the New Mexico Attorney General Patricia Madrid Miller uses the word "promulgators" as in letters he has written to the [sic] Steve Sederwall in his capacity as Mayor and the United States Marshals Service. In Gale Cooper's letter of September 22, 2006 the word "promulgators" is used ten (10) times. Investigators have combed through the volumes of letters that Miller has sent us in the form of FOIA and have documented a great deal of other structure and phrases that would demonstrate that the Cooper letter and Miller's writings are from the same writer.

Our agreement was to bring our findings to the Sheriff when complete and not burden his office with the matter. In the September 22, 2006 Cooper/Miller letter they write "There cannot be a real murder investigation against a dead man. Pat Garrett died in 1908." Which brings us to wonder why the preachy, wordy letter questioning an investigation that "cannot be a real murder investigation"?

**[AUTHOR'S NOTE: Response to my statement about the inappropriate use of the criminal investigation IPRA exception.]**

Here are the answers to the questions that Cooper/Miller pose.

**[AUTHOR'S NOTE: What follows is a list of 23 numbers (my Items), denying existence of public records; and for Items 5 and 6 about the Arizona exhumations, stating "Lincoln County did not perform one or more exhumations in Prescott, Arizona Pioneers' Home Cemetery at any time in 2005."]**

We feel that Miller has crossed the line into harassment and we have grown weary of his actions. We will be in contact with the United States Marshals Service on this issue also he has papered them with the same long word [sic] letters and they too are weary of these "promulgators".

Sincerely,
Tom Sullivan & Steve Sederwall

Cc: Lincoln County Sheriff Rick Virden
   **United States Marshals Service** [author's boldface]

**[AUTHOR'S NOTE: This appears to be a use of fellow Billy the Kid Case hoaxer, U.S. Marshal's Service Historian David Turk, for intimidation of me, since the Marshals Service is part of Homeland Security. This also demonstrates that Attorney Morel is complicit in that intimidation attempt.]**

   Jay Miller

**[AUTHOR'S NOTE: At this stage, they are not sure if the IPRA request came from Jay Miller, since this is the first they heard about me. So they are adding him for intimidation also.]**

**[AUTHOR'S NOTE: The big picture is that this is not how an appropriate IPRA records response looks. It is merely the collusion of four out-of-control thugs: Morel, Virden, Sullivan, and Sederwall; convinced that they are above the law, and can frighten away any citizen.]**

## APPENDIX: 48. Jay Miller. Letter to Dr. Henry Lee. "Re. Forensic consultation in the New Mexico Billy the Kid Case." March 27, 2006.

I am sending you this letter in my capacity as a journalist who has followed the New Mexico Billy the Kid Case from its inception. Your involvement as the forensic expert hired by its promulgators has been described in numerous articles. Since all forensic information has been presented by the case promulgators rather in quotes from you, I am now writing to make sure that you are in agreement with their statements. In addition, there are some issues that I would like to clarify for myself. Enclosed for your reference are articles which mention your work for the Billy the Kid Case. The following are my questions.

1. Are you working for the Lincoln County Sheriff's Department as a forensic expert in the investigation of the murder of William Bonney aka Billy the Kid and filed in the Lincoln County Sheriff's Department as Case # 2003-274 Probable Cause Statement?

2. The promulgators have stated repeatedly that you found "blood" on a carpenter's bench that possibly held the body of shot Billy the Kid.
   a. Are you also claiming that you found "blood." If that is so, please explain what tests you used to identify your sample as "blood" rather than "human DNA." It should be noted that the promulgators have stated that you used luminol. Since that chemical is non-specific for blood, please list definitive tests.

3. The promulgators have stated that your "blood" DNA sample from the carpenter's bench is from Billy the Kid and is thus valid for purposes of identity matching.

4. Are you also claiming that your DNA sample is from Billy the Kid? If so, please explain on what basis you make that claim. Also explain how you propose to both separate and date mingled DNA strands that have accumulated for at least 125 years so that you can consider your sample valid for the precision needed for identity matching.

5. The promulgators have stated that you will use your carpenter's bench DNA sample for identity matching with DNA from the remains of John Miller. Please define for me what you would call a "match" in terms of the 13 alleles available.

6. Since a criminal investigation is a matter of public record, please send me specifics with regard to your DNA findings to date. Also, please tell me if your specimens as well as the carpenter's bench are available to independent forensic investigators for evaluations.

**APPENDIX: 49. Dr. Henry Lee. Response to Jay Miller. May 1, 2006.**

STATE OF CONNECTICUT
DEPARTMENT OF PUBLIC SAFETY
DIVISION OF SCIENTIFIC SERVICES

Jay Miller
Address

Dear. Mr. Miller:

In response to your letter dated March 27, 2006 regarding Forensic Consultation in the New Mexico Billy the Kid Case. To set the record straight, the Lincoln County Sheriff's Department contacted me. They requested an expert to perform preliminary identification and scene reconstruction. This was a pro bono forensic consultation case. We examined a wood bench, and floorboards in the courthouse.

**I completed my examination of the evidence and submitted my report to the Lincoln County Sheriff's Department.** [author's boldface] If you want a copy of the report, you should contact the Lincoln County Sheriff's department directly.

Since I did not conduct any DNA testing on the evidence and the Lincoln County Sheriff's Department sent samples directly to a private laboratory for analysis, I am sorry but I do not have answers to your questions regarding DNA.

Sincerely,
Dr. Henry C. Lee

**APPENDIX: 50. Jay Miller. "Letter to Dr. Henry Lee, Re. Follow-up on your letter of May 1, 2006 responding to my request of March 27, 2006 for information on your forensic consultation in the New Mexico Billy the Kid Case." June 15, 2006. [AUTHOR'S NOTE: Written by me.]**

Dear Dr. Lee:

Thank you for your helpful responses in your letter of May 1, 2006, answering my request of March 27, 2006 for information on your forensic consultation in the New Mexico Billy the Kid Case. I have enclosed a copy of your letter for your reference. As you may recall, I sent my letter to you in my capacity as a journalist who has followed that case from its inception. Your identification as the forensic expert for its promulgators has been described in numerous articles, which I had enclosed with that first mailing to make sure that you agreed with both the promulgator descriptions of your role, and the press quotations attributed to you.

I took your lack of any denials as agreement with what was written in them.

Your candid letter, however, made me realize that there were important issues that required clarification so that there would be no misunderstandings in this case which, as you know, has by now attracted national as well as international scrutiny.

What struck me most was your concluding response: *"Since I did not conduct any DNA testing on the evidence and the Lincoln County Sheriff"s Department sent samples directly to a private laboratory for analysis, I am sorry but I do not have answers to your questions regarding DNA."* You earlier had said, *"They requested an expert to perform preliminary identification and scene reconstruction ... We examined a wood bench, and floorboards in the courthouse."*

I decided to follow-up on your statements with some clarifying questions. They are as follows:

1. By your responses quoted above, were you simply meaning that you were not doing the hands-on lab work? In fact, that aspect of the bench analysis has frequently been stated by the promulgators as being done by Orchid Cellmark. If that was what you meant, I apologize for imprecision in my question about your participation in the Billy the Kid Case as a forensic DNA expert. Of course, my question was not whether you were running the laboratory machinery to get data print outs.

2. However, did you, in your capacity as a forensic DNA expert, later make any conclusions about alleged human DNA swabbed and scraped by you from the alleged Fort Sumner carpenter's bench?

3. If so, did you state, as newspaper articles seem to attribute to you, that this human DNA was derived from the blood of William Bonney aka Billy the Kid?

4. If so, did you give your opinion as a forensic DNA expert that the sample obtained by you was useful as reference DNA for identity matching; the conclusion being that it was the true DNA of William Bonney aka Billy the Kid?

As you are aware, these are very serious questions, since based on the claim of having valid reference DNA of William Bonney for identity matching, two exhumations have been performed in Prescott, Arizona by the case promulgators. As you would also recognize, the claiming of true reference DNA from that carpenter's bench would involve many unusual assumptions and problems for a forensic DNA expert.

So when I saw your concluding response to me as quoted above, it occurred to me that, in fact, you might *not* have made the claims at all, and should have the opportunity to clarify that fact. By that, I mean - taking your letter's response at face value - you might just have done luminol spraying, swabbing and scraping of the carpenter's bench, checked for fluorescence, and given over your samples to the Lincoln County Sheriff's Department to be sent off to Orchid Cellmark, and done *nothing more* at any subsequent time. So please let me know if that was what you are claiming about *the full extent* of your role in the Billy the Kid Case.

Please let me know, however, if you did continue in the evaluation of data, and made the dramatic conclusion and contention that you obtained actual DNA from William Bonney aka Billy the Kid (from the only tissue that could be claimed as available, namely 123 year old blood), and if you then made that expert conclusion of yours available to the Lincoln County Sheriff's Department for furtherance of their murder investigation filed as Lincoln County Sheriff's Department as Case # 2003-274.

As you must be aware, this unusual and controversial case has been followed in all its facets by highly qualified experts in fields pertinent to every aspect. The forensic contention of obtaining valid reference DNA - if made by you - would, of course, be considered astounding given the nature of a presumably degraded sample with co-mingled DNA of multiple individuals and possible inhibiting factors to certain loci coming from the bench wood or carpenter's chemicals. And if mitochondrial DNA was used (as presumed from a sample too scanty to yield enough nuclear DNA), did you perform the requisite control testing of obtaining DNA of every individual in any contact with the bench - including yourself, all the case participants, the owners, the testers at Orchid Cellmark, and so on?

So, what it comes down to is that if you did make the contention that you had obtained reference DNA from William Bonney aka Billy the Kid, you would have achieved not only an unusual discovery, but entered the realm of real scientific research. And, as you know, the foundation of legitimate science is peer review of data as well as its replication.

In addition, based on the claim of having true reference DNA of William Bonney aka Billy the Kid, the Arizona exhumations were performed. There was no other justification for them other than the promulgators' claim that by having the true DNA of William Bonney aka Billy the Kid, they were going to establish whether a John Miller (a claimant to being this individual) had told the truth. Therefore, if you did make the claim of valid reference DNA, one could say that the only argument for the exhumations was based on your alleged evidence. Since the promulgators are now facing legal scrutiny for the propriety of those Arizona exhumations, of course, additional importance is added to the clear definition of your role and claims in this most serious case.

So this brings me to the other area of my letter of March 27, 2006 in which there may have been a misunderstanding. I requested a copy of your report and your conclusions. For that you referred me to the case promulgators. You stated: *"I completed my examination of the evidence and submitted my report to the Lincoln County Sheriff"s Department.*

*If you want a copy of the report, you should contact the Lincoln County Sheriff"s Department directly."*

I could well understand your response, if your report to them merely stated the descriptions of your on-location procedures in obtaining evidence from the carpenter's bench for transport to Orchid Cellmark for the testing. However, if there exist any notes and reports generated by you beyond recording those basic forensic mechanics, and also if there are reports and written conclusions made by you after receiving back data from Orchid Cellmark with regard to their information obtained from your bench samples, that would also be considered to be part of your own scientific research. And, certainly, if you made the conclusion from this research of yours that you had obtained the DNA from the 123 year old blood of William Bonney aka Billy the Kid, as well as overcoming all the known technical hurdles to that claim, it would a finding of most startling implications to the entire field of DNA forensics. As such, it is entirely scientific in nature, and subject to peer review.

So, as a clarification, I again request copies of your reports and your conclusions as being in the spirit of openness that is the foundation of legitimate scientific research which you seemed to be claiming.

Again, for your reference, I am enclosing the first set of articles I had sent, so that you can inform me of any misrepresentations of your roles and statements.

In particular, bedsides the factors mentioned above, I direct you to the elaborate crime scene reconstruction alleged to you in the enclosed article from the *Albuquerque Journal* dated August 2, 2004 and titled "Forensic Expert on Billy's Case. It addresses the manner of Sheriff Pat Garrett's shooting of William Bonney in the bedroom of Peter Maxwell. According to the article, you derived your description from a wash stand with two bullet holes (and no bullet) through which you shone a laser beam. Since historically no washstand is known to be part of the crime scene; and since the provenance of that wash stand to the scene cannot be established; and since, of course, its location in the room of a building that no longer stands can never be established, the contentions, if truly yours, can be construed as inexplicable. So clarification here too of the correct representation of your claims would be important in understanding the overall thrust of your forensic work for the Lincoln County Sheriff's Department.

Please respond in writing so that there will be no misunderstood communication.

Sincerely,
Jay Miller

**APPENDIX: 51. Jay Miller. Letter to Dr. Henry Lee. "Re. Follow-up to my letter of June 15, 2006 with regard to your forensic consultation in the New Mexico Billy the Kid Case." August 8, 2006. [AUTHOR'S NOTE: Written by me.]**

Dear Dr. Lee:

Because I have received no response from you to my letter of June 15, 2006 with regard to a clarification of your role in forensic consultation in the New Mexico Billy the Kid Case, I am again sending that letter and its attached articles.

As I have informed you in past communications, I am a journalist following the Billy the Kid Case. Your response is most important given the evolution of that case both in New Mexico and Arizona. The crucial issues are as follows:

1. The Billy the Kid Case promulgators have consistently named you as their forensic expert in articles.
2. You are the person to whom is attributed the promulgators' claim of having obtained the DNA of William Bonney aka Billy the Kid from alleged 123 year old blood from an alleged carpenter's bench on which Bonney allegedly lay (but only pretended to be dead while bleeding from a chest wound).
3. Using this alleged "reference DNA," the Billy the Kid Case promulgators have performed two exhumations in Prescott, Arizona with the claim that they could do valid identity matching with it and the remains.
4. These two exhumations are currently being investigated by the Arizona Maricopa County Prosecutor's Office for possible felony indictments for disturbing remains and grave robbing.

If your role was as pivotal as indicated by the articles, your response is important to clarify public awareness of this most serious case. And if your participation and/or conclusions were misrepresented, that is equally important to make known.

**APPENDIX: 52. Gale Cooper. Response letter to Maricopa County Deputy Attorney Jonell Lucca. October 30, 2006.**

Dear Attorney Lucca:

It was so considerate of you to send me the enclosed letter with regard to your decision on the John Miller and William Hudspeth exhumations. That courtesy was certainly in keeping with your generous expenditure of time in discussing the pertinent elements of the New Mexico Billy the Kid Case with me, as well as reviewing its relevant documents which I sent to you.

That said, having come to know your friendly style, and with your knowledge of my ongoing interest in the Billy the Kid Case, I hoped you would clarify my two remaining questions about your investigation. They are as follows:

1) QUESTION REGARDING WHO WERE THE SUSPECTS IN MARICOPA COUNTY CASE # CA2006020516: Why were the suspects listed by you in your communication to me named as "Jeanine Dike and Dale Tunnel," when the suspects most potentially culpable were Tom Sullivan and Steve Sederwall? That this fact was known to the Maricopa Prosecutor's Office was shown by its spokesperson, Bill Fitzgerald, in October 24, 2006 AP articles appearing in the *New York Times,* the *New York Sun,* and the *Albuquerque Journal* as follows:

A former sheriff of Lincoln County, N.M., Tom Sullivan, and a former mayor of Capitan, N.M., Steve Sederwall dug up the bones of John Miller in May 2005. Miller was buried in the state-owned Pioneers' Home in Prescott nearly 70 years `ago.

"It appears officials in charge of the facility gave permission and the people who were attempting to recover samples of the remains believed they had permission to do so," Bill Fitzgerald, a spokesman for the Maricopa County Attorney's Office, which made the decision not to seek charges, said.

Messrs. Sullivan and Sederwall obtained DNA from Miller's remains. The samples were sent to a Dallas lab to compare Miller's DNA to blood traces taken from a bench believed to be the one the Kid's body was placed on after he was shot to death in 1881.

Messrs. Sullivan and Sederwall have been hunting for the Kid's bones since 2003.

When Mr. Fitzgerald performed his duty to inform the press about "the people who were attempting to recover samples of the remains," he makes clear his understanding that they were "Messrs. Sullivan and Sederwall," as well as making clear his understanding of these men's active role in the exhumations. And as Maricopa County Prosecutor's Office spokesman, he makes no reference to an active role in performing those exhumations made by Jeanine Dike and Dale Tunnell, or, more importantly, that *they* were the suspects both considered for indictment and cleared. What remains confusing is how the claim can be made that Messrs. Sullivan and Sederwall are cleared of charges if they were never suspects; though the implication of  Mr. Fitzgeralds's statement, on behalf of the Office, implies that they were, indeed, the suspects (and were cleared).

2) QUESTION ABOUT THE REFERENCE DNA OF BILLY THE KID: Since all issues of the Miller/Hudspeth exhumations (both for permission and performance of the disinterments) relied on the assumption that reference DNA of Billy the Kid existed with certainty,

and was available for comparison with the remains of these two men for the purpose of "establishing identity," was verification of that fact done by the Maricopa County Prosecutor's Office with the only expert qualified to attest to that claim: Dr. Henry Lee? It should be noted that the Orchid Cellmark Director, Dr. Rick Staub, who was present at the exhumation to receive remains for DNA processing in his lab, could only attest to whether he, as representing Orchard Cellmark, had Dr. Lee's DNA sample(s) acquired from a carpenter's bench in 2004. Dr. Staub's only expert claim could be as to whether that DNA acquired from a carpenter's bench in 2004 by Dr. Lee was human or non-human; not whether it was the reference DNA from Billy the Kid. That claim was solely dependent on Dr. Lee, who would have had to inform the Lincoln County Sheriff's Department about the claim. As such, the other source of verification available to the Maricopa County Prosecutor's Office could have been a copy of any or all reports to that Sheriff's Department by Dr. Lee; and then verified by him. If this was not done, it would appear impossible to justify the Miller/Hudspeth exhumations by any individual or entity. And, as I had documented for you, the issue of the "reference DNA of Billy the Kid" claim was considered preposterous by multiple experts in both forensic DNA science and forensic pathology, thus, making the need for verification even more crucial.

Thank you for your attention to this matter.

**APPENDIX: 53. Gale Cooper. Letter to Arizona State Bar Attorney/Consumer Assistance Program. "RE: Inquiry Complaint to Arizona State Bar Concerning Allegations of Legal Misconduct Against Maricopa County Prosecutor's Office's Deputy Attorney Jonell Lucca." January 5, 2007.**

After extensive background information on the Billy the Kid Case as a hoax, the analysis was broken down into "Components of Complaint as Questions for Inquiry of Professional Misconduct of Deputy Attorney Jonell Lucca." They were as follows:

ISSUE 1. Was Attorney Lucca the employee of the Maricopa County Prosecutor's Office responsible for the decision on indictment(s) in the exhumation case?

ISSUE 2. Were the names of Tom Sullivan and Steve Sederwall available to Attorney Lucca as suspects in the exhumation case? And, if so, was there compelling evidence available to Attorney Lucca as to the roles of Tom Sullivan and Steve Sederwall as perpetrators of the exhumations of a John Miller and a William Hudspeth, and actions attendant to those exhumations (removing remains)?

ISSUE 3. Was the possession of "permission" for the exhumation of John Miller a valid consideration for non-indictment in the Arizona exhumation case?

ISSUE 4. Was there any legal justification for the exhumation of John Miller?

ISSUE 5. Was there any legal justification for the exhumation of William Hudspeth?

ISSUE 6. Was adequate information available to Attorney Lucca to comprehend the issues of the New Mexico Billy the Kid Case (which was claimed by the perpetrators as a justification of the John Miller exhumation)?

ISSUE 7. Was adequate investigation performed by Attorney Lucca (or requested to be performed by her) to elucidate any and all issues pertaining to potential indictments in the exhumation case?

ISSUE 8. Was Attorney Lucca under political pressure not to indict the perpetrators of the Miller/Hudspeth exhumations?

ISSUE 9. Was there cover-up done by Attorney Lucca to conceal from the public the improprieties of her decision not to prosecute by using the Maricopa County Prosecutor's Office spokesman Bill Fitzgerald to release misinformation to the press?

**The final "Summary of Complaint for Bar Association Inquiry stated:**

It is the allegation of Gale Cooper, M.D. that Maricopa County Prosecutor's Office's Deputy Attorney Jonell Lucca with full knowledge and purpose committed the legal and ethical misconducts of **obstruction of justice** and **perverting the course of justice** in the exhumation case filed as Maricopa County Case # CA 2006020516 by covering-up the true suspects and by disregarding evidence which established their felonious crimes. To this professional misconduct, the following issues pertain:

1) By naming as suspects Jeanine Dike and Dale Tunnell, Attorney Lucca was purposefully protecting and covering-up the true suspects: Tom Sullivan and Steve Sederwall who were directly responsible for the exhumations of John Miller and William Hudspeth and the stealing of their remains.

2) By allowing (or creating) the press release by the Maricopa County Prosecutor's Office clearing Messrs. Sullivan and Sederwall, Attorney Lucca was defrauding the public into believing that *these two men* had been cleared of charges.

3) By having available to her my extensive documentation of the Billy the Kid Case and its participants, as well as her

prosecutorial power to investigate that information, Attorney Lucca cannot claim ignorance of the true suspects: Tom Sullivan and Steve Sederwall.

4) By virtue of her job as Prosecutor, Attorney Lucca had the obligation to investigate whether there existed true "reference DNA of Billy the Kid": the sine qua non of the investigation since it was the only "excuse" for the John Miller exhumation. There is no indication that this investigation was done, since it is forensically impossible that such definitive documentation exists either with Messrs. Sullivan and Sederwall, the Lincoln County Sheriff's Department, Dr. Henry Lee, Orchid Cellmark, or any other individual or entity.

5) By virtue of the random and wanton desecration of the remains of William Hudspeth, and the robbery and transport of some of those remains outside the state of Arizona, there existed no legal excuse other than obstruction of justice and perverting the course of justice performed by Attorney Lucca to avoid the prosecution of Messrs. Sullivan and Sederwall for these crimes.

6) By virtue of cover-up of the true suspects, Attorney Lucca arguably can be considered as an accessory to their crimes in the exhumation case.

7) By virtue of closing the exhumation case (albeit under false pretenses), Attorney Lucca has created an absurd precedent for Arizona: any amateur historian can, with immunity, dig up graves without true legal, historical, or forensic justification.

8) By Attorney Lucca's refusal to prosecute individuals for the felonious crimes of disturbing remains and grave robbing, she has represented herself, her Prosecutor's Office, and the state of Arizona as unwilling to protect the sanctity of its graves.

9) By Attorney Lucca's refusal to prosecute individuals for the felonious crimes of disturbing remains and grave robbing, she has represented herself, her Prosecutor's Office which employs her, and the state of Arizona which relies on her ethical legal conduct, as putting politics above law or ethics.

It should be noted that in this inquiry/complaint, it has been assumed that Deputy Attorney Lucca has performed willful professional misconduct. There, however, remains the possibility for State Bar investigation that she functioned below the professional level expected of an attorney and of a prosecutor. This professional incompetence would encompass not comprehending evidence and not performing necessary investigations; and, thus, coming to erroneous conclusions about indictments. If this explanation is entertained, it would indicate a lack of suitability for the weighty responsibility attendant to her professional position and professional licensure.

**APPENDIX: 54. Gale Cooper. Letter to Haskell Pitluck, Ethics Committee Chair, American Academy of Forensic Sciences. "Re: Follow-up on the May 9, 2007 AAFS response to my October 2, 2006 Ethics Complaint on Dr. Henry Lee." May 30, 2007.**

Dear Haskell Pitluck:

This letter constitutes a request for clarification of the May 9, 2007 AAFS response to my Ethics Complaint on Dr. Henry Lee.

That response is enclosed, as is a stamped return envelope.

My assumption is that you - as head of the AAFS Ethics Committee, as a member of it who reviewed in full my AAFS Ethics Complaint against Dr. Lee, and as someone who consulted directly with Dr. Lee in evaluating my complaint - are in a position to respond directly to the following request for clarification of that May 9, 2007 response. Thus, I will use "your" to imply both you yourself, as well as the Committee as a whole (including the assumption that any and all of you can now speak for Dr. Lee on this matter of information already presented).

As you know, the Billy the Kid Case, which is the subject of my complaint, has continued from 2004 to date primarily because of the forensic claims attributed to Dr. Lee. My complaint was in regard to those forensic claims, as is this request for clarification.

To facilitate that clarification, I have prepared this communication as a questionnaire. Please check either YES or NO, initial that response, and then sign at the end. My assumption is that your signature can represent the opinion of the Ethics Committee, and also reflects the position taken by Dr. Lee, and explained by him to you when answering the specifics of my complaint.

It should be noted that the newspaper article herein quoted was a part of my Ethics Complaint; as well as provided by me to Dr. Lee in his own copy of that Complaint; as well as presented to Dr. Lee three times by Journalist, Jay Miller, on March 27, 2006, June 15, 2006, and August 8, 2006.

BACKGROUND: AAFS ETHICS COMMITTEE RESPONSE OF MAY 9, 2007

This request for clarification is based on three statements in your AAFS Committee response to me of May 9, 2007. Each appears to reference a report made by Dr. Lee on February 5, 2005 and are numbered by me for reference below.

The need for clarification exists because the vague responses do not clearly or explicitly address the specific issues that constituted my complaint.

The AAFS responses are quoted as follows:

842

RESPONSE 1: "Based upon our investigation, the Committee has unanimously concluded that Dr. Lee's work in this matter is not in violation of the Academy Code of Ethics and Conduct."

RESPONSE 2: "Dr. Lee's report is very clear in what he did. Nothing in the report deviates from our ethical standards."

RESPONSE 3: "The issues raised in your complaints address issues that are outside of what Dr. Lee actually did in his tests. Some of those issues have to do with what other individuals did and Dr. Lee is not responsible for those actions."

## CLARIFICATION QUESTIONNAIRE

The following Items relate to AAFS Ethics Committee response of May 9, 2007 to me with regard to my complaint against Dr. Henry Lee, and pertain to the above Responses 1-3 from that communication.

REGARDING DR. LEE'S AAFS "INVESTIGATION":

ITEM 1: Was the Ethics Committee "investigation," cited in Response 1, based solely on the February 5, 2005 letter presented by Dr. Lee to the Ethics Committee? YES _____ NO _____ INITIAL _____

REGARDING PARTICIPATION BY DR. HENRY LEE IN LINCOLN COUNTY SHERIFF'S DEPARTMENT CASE NO. 2003-274 ("BILLY THE KID CASE"):

ITEM 2: Did Dr. Lee make the following quotation, attributed to him in the August 2, 2004 article in the *Albuquerque Journal* by reporter, Rene Romo, titled "Forensic Expert on Billy's Case: Questions Remain on Outlaw's Fate?"

"This is an extremely interesting case of some historical importance," Lee said in an interview before arriving at the old Lincoln County courthouse Sunday afternoon. "That's why I agreed to spend some of my own time to work with them ... It's basically a worthwhile project and legitimate."
YES _____ NO _____ INITIAL _____

REGARDING CARPENTER'S BENCH BLOOD CLAIMS:

ITEM 3: Did Dr. Lee make the following quotation, highlighted in boldface, about "trace evidence of blood," and attributed to him in the August 2, 2004 article in the *Albuquerque Journal* by reporter, Rene Romo, titled "Forensic Expert on Billy's Case: Questions Remain on Outlaw's Fate?"

On Saturday at an undisclosed location in Albuquerque, Lee, assisted by Calvin Ostler, an investigator with the Utah Office of the Medical Examiner, performed tests on the bench that Sederwall believes to be the one on which the Kid's body was laid out after Garrett gunned him down. **Preliminary results indicated trace evidence of blood, but, without further testing, it is not certain whether the blood was human, Lee said.**

YES _____ NO _____ INITIAL _____

ITEM 4: Did Dr. Lee state, at any time, in writing or by verbal communication to anyone, that "blood," or any other specimen found in his forensic work on the carpenter's bench, belonged to William Bonney aka Billy the Kid?

YES _____ NO _____ INITIAL _____

ITEM 5: Did Dr. Lee state at any time, in writing or by verbal communication to anyone, that the scenario described as "dead men don't bleed" indicated that any specimens he recovered from the carpenter's bench would indicate that William Bonney aka Billy the Kid survived his shooting by Pat Garrett?

YES _____ NO _____ INITIAL _____

REGARDING GARRETT MURDER SCENE CLAIMS:

ITEM 6: Did Dr. Lee establish that the washstand, referred to below, and highlighted in boldface, in the August 2, 2004 article from the *Albuquerque Journal*, by reporter, Rene Romo, titled "Forensic Expert on Billy's Case: Questions Remain on Outlaw's Fate," was an authentic crime scene object in the shooting of Billy the Kid?

Lee and the investigators also examined a **washstand** that was purportedly struck by a bullet when Garrett shot the Kid in a bedroom of the outlaw's friend, Pete Maxwell, in Fort Sumner ... Lee and the investigators used laser technology Saturday to determine the trajectory of the bullet as it entered the left side of the washstand and exited the right at a downward angle. Given the washstand's **likely location in the room**, the investigation has already cast some doubt on Garrett's account of the fatal shooting, Sederwall and Ostler said. "The evidence we are seeing does not corroborate the popular legend," Ostler said. "Something's askew." Still, Ostler said, the nightstand's orientation in the room is still indefinite and it is not certain that a bullet from a .44 caliber revolver made the hole. **One simple explanation that Lee offered is that Garrett may have shot defensively at the Kid as he fled and struck the washstand from the side instead of head on. Garrett's official story may have omitted that embarrassing detail. "You don't want to paint yourself as a chicken," Lee suggested.**

YES _____ NO _____ INITIAL _____

ITEM 7: Did Dr. Lee establish a "likely location in the room" for the washstand referred to in the above quotation, as highlighted in boldface, and appearing in the August 2, 2004 article in the *Albuquerque Journal* by reporter, Rene Romo, titled "Forensic Expert on Billy's Case: Questions Remain on Outlaw's Fate?"

YES _____ NO _____ INITIAL _____

ITEM 8: Did Dr. Lee make the above quotation of "explanation," as highlighted in boldface, about the Garrett shooting of Billy the Kid as attributed to him in the August 2, 2004 article in the *Albuquerque Journal* by reporter, Rene Romo, titled "Forensic Expert on Billy's Case: Questions Remain on Outlaw's Fate?"

YES _____ NO _____ INITIAL _____

REGARDING DEPUTY BELL MURDER SCENE CLAIMS:

ITEM 9: Did Dr. Lee claim, in writing or by verbal communication to anyone, as stated below, and highlighted in boldface, in the August 2, 2004 article in the *Albuquerque Journal* by reporter, Rene Romo, titled "Forensic Expert on Billy's Case: Questions Remain on Outlaw's Fate," that "blood residue" was found in the old Lincoln County Courthouse?

> Lee and the investigators Sunday afternoon also found several positive indications of **blood residue** below floor-boards at the top of a stairwell in the old Lincoln County courthouse. **Such evidence could support Sederwall's theory that the Kid fatally shot deputy J.W. Bell there, at the top of the stairs, in his infamous escape from the Lincoln County jail. That version would also contradict Garrett's account that the Kid, at the top of the stairs, shot Bell who was at the bottom of the stairwell.**

YES _____ NO _____ INITIAL _____

ITEM 10: Did Dr. Lee make any claim, at any time, in writing or by verbal communication to anyone, that his findings in the old Lincoln County Courthouse pertained in any way to the shooting of Deputy J.W. Bell as described above the August 2, 2004 article in the *Albuquerque Journal* by reporter, Rene Romo, titled "Forensic Expert on Billy's Case: Questions Remain on Outlaw's Fate?"

YES _____ NO _____ INITIAL _____

SIGNED: _____

Haskell Pitluck, Chairman AAFS Ethics Committee

DATED: _____

In addition to this Questionnaire, I am requesting a copy of Dr. Lee's report dated February 5, 2005 and cited in the response to in my complaint. Since my complaint process began in October 2, 2006, I would now request the courtesy of a prompt response to clarify your May 9, 2007 AAFS Ethics Committee response.

**APPENDIX: 55. Gale Cooper. Letter to Haskell Pitluck, Ethics Committee Chair, American Academy of Forensic Sciences. "Re: Requested clarification of your responses of May 9, 2007 and June 2, 2007 to my October 2, 2006 AAFS Ethics Complaint against Dr. Henry Lee." June 19, 2007.**

Dear Haskell Pitluck:

This letter constitutes a request for clarification of the May 9, 2007 and June 2, 2007 AAFS Ethics Committee responses to my Ethics Complaint against Dr. Henry Lee.

This letter is necessitated because the language used to justify rejections of that Ethics Complaint was vague and non-specific. Since my complaint was so serious, and its implications far reaching, it is necessary to prevent miscommunication. For your convenience, both letters are enclosed.

In question are the following quotations, written by you as Chairman and on behalf of the AAFS Ethics Committee.

In the May 9, 2007 letter, you stated as follows:

"The issues raised in your complaints address issues that are outside of what Dr. Lee actually did in his tests. Some of those issues have to do with what other individuals did and Dr. Lee is not responsible for those actions."

In the June 2, 2007 letter, rather than answer my detailed questionnaire of May 30, 2007 as to specific, potentially culpable, forensic quotations and conclusions about the Billy the Kid Case attributed to Dr. Lee in a August 2, 2004 article in the *Albuquerque Journal* (and forming a part of my original complaint), you responded only as follows:

The items you raise in your letter of May 30, 2007 are outside the scope of what Dr. Lee did and Dr. Lee is not responsible for the actions or statements of others.

To establish clarity, I will next state what I understand from these above quotations, combined with the other AAFS Ethics Committee contention in the May 9, 2007 letter, i.e.; that Dr. Lee claimed to 1) have provided to the Lincoln County Sheriff's Department for the Billy the

Kid Case solely one forensic document dated February 2, 2005, and 2) to have provided no other participation or conclusions whatsoever in any form.

MY UNDERSTANDING OF AAFS COMMUNICATION TO ME:

The decision was made by the AAFS Ethics Committee to take no action against Dr. Henry Lee for his participation as a forensic expert in the Billy the Kid Case because, for it, he provided only a single document to the Lincoln County Sheriff's Department dated February 5, 2005. This document, as he described to journalist Jay Miller in writing (and included in my original complaint), concerned only obtaining samples from a carpenter's bench and sending those samples to a lab. And Dr. Lee then, nor ever, made any conclusions about those samples. Thus, the AAFS Ethics Committee found a proper use of his forensic expertise in the Billy the Kid Case.

Any further forensic claims made at any time about any or all aspects of the Billy the Kid Case in Dr. Lee's name, including specific quotations and conclusions attributed to him in the press, are categorically denied by Dr. Lee as coming from him either in writing, or verbally, or by any form of communication, and are, according to Dr. Lee, unauthorized statements and fabrications by others, and made without his participation and/or consent. These contentions are supported by the Ethics Committee.

Thus, any statement that the carpenter's bench was found to have human blood on it and/or that the alleged blood represented the reference DNA of Billy the Kid valid for identity matching, though attributed to Dr. Lee, are fabricated attributions to Dr. Lee by another or others. These contentions are supported by the Ethics Committee.

Thus, any statement about the Pat Garrett crime scene reconstruction using an old washstand, though attributed to Dr. Lee, is a fabricated attribution to Dr. Lee by another or others. This contention is supported by the Ethics Committee.

Thus, any statement about the Deputy James Bell murder scene, including human blood present in the old Lincoln County Courthouse, is a fabricated attribution to Dr. Lee by another or others. This contention is supported by the Ethics Committee.

MY REMEDY:

If I do not hear to the contrary in writing from the AAFS Ethics Committee in ten (10) days from receipt of this letter, I will assume confirmation that my above expanded statement of the AAFS Ethics Committee's responses to me is correct and mutually agreed upon.

Sincerely,
Gale Cooper, M.D.

## APPENDIX: 56. Steven M. Sederwall & Thomas T. Sullivan, "Memorandum, Subject: Billy the Kid Investigation." June 21, 2007.

## Memorandum

To: Rick Virden, Lincoln County Sheriff
From: Steven M. Sederwall & Thomas T. Sullivan
Subject: Billy the Kid Investigation
Date: Thursday, June 21, 2007

On April 28, 2003 we began a quest for the truth, looking into the *"escape of William Bonney and the double homicide of James Bell & Robert Olinger.* [Footnote 1: Lincoln County Call sheet pulled by Sheriff Sullivan April 28, 2003.] We chose this as a private venture and did not want to burden the county financially. The idea was to being modern science and police investigation methods to uncover the truth of the escape of the Kid and murder of our deputies. We had planned to file a report with the Sheriff at the end of the investigation, a report which the public could then access if they so desire.

**[AUTHOR'S NOTE: This is a hoax switcheroo from the Garrett murder to the deputy ones. It also begins a shape-shift to a private endeavor of amateur historians, while concealing the actual Case # 2003-274.]**

At the beginning of the investigation, it became known that career law enforcement officers were investigating a century old cold case involving Billy the Kid and the case began to generate a great deal of press.

**[AUTHOR'S NOTE: This is untrue. The publicity came from the contention that Garrett did not kill Billy the Kid, and from Governor Richardson's Press Release to the *New York Times* calling it a real murder investigation with case # 2003-274.]**

With the enormous amount of publicity generated by the investigation Governor Bill Richardson was prompted to call a press conference. On Tuesday, June 10, 2003 he told the world of his intentions; *"I am announcing my support and the support of the state of New Mexico for the investigation into the life and death of Henry McCarty, also known as William Bonney".*

**[AUTHOR'S NOTE: This is a purposefully misleading time inversion; the article and press conference created the publicity.]**

He told the roomful of reporters, *"By utilizing modern forensics, DNA and crime scene techniques, the goal of the investigation is to get to the truth. In the process, the reputation of Pat Garrett, still a hero to Lincoln County law enforcement hangs in the balance. The question is did Sheriff Garrett kill Billy the Kid at Fort Sumner, New Mexico on July 14, 1881"* The Governor went on to say, *"If we can get to the truth we will."*

**[AUTHOR'S NOTE: They are contradicting their starting claim of the deputy investigation. They are also beginning a devil-made-me-do-it accusation of Richardson as the prime mover of the Billy the Kid Case.]**

On September 1, 2003, the Governor, behind the scenes, supported the investigation, by instructing Billy Sparks to hand Sheriff Sullivan three checks, from private backers, totaling $6,500.00. [Footnote 2: Three checks handed to Sheriff Sullivan in Governor's office by Billy Sparks] Standing at the threshold of the Governor's office, Sparks said, *"The governor wants to insure this investigation goes forward."*

**[AUTHOR'S NOTE: Here is the spectacular accusation of Richardson in a "buy a sheriff scheme!" The checks, as copied for Attachment 2, show the Lincoln County Sheriff's Department Case number, or state "Billy the Kid Investigation." The hoaxers are revealing their "secret private donors" and their apparent write-off of as "charity."]**

The Governor also asked investigators to contact Ft. Sumner and get them *"on board."* On Friday, June 13th, Sederwall drove to Ft. Sumner and spoke with Mayor Raymond Lopez. Lopez liked the idea of worldwide attention on his village and felt it would help boost tourist dollars. He handwrote a note to the Governor, on Ft. Sumner letterhead saying, *"Mr. Steve Sederwall and I have talked and feel that we are on the same page on this Billy the Kid deal. He'll bring the information to you on the talk we had."* [Footnote 3: Handwritten note by Mayor Raymond Lopez on Ft. Sumner letterhead]

At the time investigators did not know if DNA could be obtained from a grave after 100 years, so after the Governor's news conference Sederwall met with Dr. Debra Komar an investigator with the New Mexico Office of the Medical Investigator's office [sic] (OMI). During this meeting Dr. Komar said considering the terrain, topography and Climate of Silver City she judged chances of obtaining DNA from Catherine Antrim would be somewhere in the ninety percent range. Dr. Komar said she would begin investigating the graves. She and her boss were excited about working on this historical investigation.

**[AUTHOR'S NOTE: The hoaxers are no longer talking about the deputy murder case, but the Garrett murder one. They are also switching from the Fort Sumner grave to the mother's one. In addition, the Dr. Komar contentions are belied by her affidavit and deposition.]**

On June 17th, 2003, something happened that shocked the investigators. In a Ft. Sumner grocery store, Ft. Sumner's ex-mayor, David Bailey approached DeBaca County Sheriff Gary Graves and told him the Billy the Kid investigation *"had to stop."* Bailey said that if the Sheriff's [sic] were to exhume the grave of the Kid there would be a problem. Bailey said, *"You do not know what you are going to find but I do."*

On Friday, October 10, 2003, investigators were in Grant County District Court requesting a court order to exhume the body of Catherine Antrim, who is known as William H. Bonney's mother. Investigators wanted to obtain her DNA. Attorneys for Silver City and Ft. Sumner opposed the exhumation, so the judge scheduled a hearing on the matter, set for August of 2004.

**[AUTHOR'S NOTE: This is a slipping in of the Garrett murder investigation, but omission of their law enforcement titles. It is untrue that Fort Sumner lawyers were in Silver City to oppose the exhumation there.]**

The same day in a special meeting of the town of Silver City, Councilman Steve May objected to the exhumation by saying, *"Who cares? Who cares if it's Billy the Kid buried in Fort Sumner or if it's Brushy Bill in Texas? We might regret this if the DNA shows it's not Billy the Kid. We could shoot ourselves in the foot."*

Fear quickly spread through the "Billy the Kid" community. Anyone with an interest to protect, museum owners, authors, and entire towns became afraid of what the investigation would uncover and how it would affect their livelihood. The newspapers were full of their fears, libelous accusations and paranoia.

**[AUTHOR'S NOTE: The exhumation blockade is here switched to a "they-are-afraid-of-the-truth-conspiracy" by hiding the OMI's opposition and savvy public hostility to their stunt.]**

*"What will happen if no DNA from that grave matches DNA from the Silver City site? How do we explain that? Might it be better to leave well enough alone?"* – **Jay Miler, syndicated columnist, *Inside the Capital* [sic], July 25, 2003.**

*"I think it would have a truly negative impact if that's not Billy the Kid over there* (Fort Sumner) – **Silver City Councilman Steve May, Silver City Sun News, October 11, 2003.**

*"This is an industry for us,"* Lopez said. *"It's no different from Intel, or Sandia Labs, or Kirkland Airforce Base. It's that big for us. We don't have much to live off other than the legend, so we have to protect it."* – **Fort Sumner Mayor, Raymond Lopez, November 18, 2003, MSNBC News.**

The investigation has the *"potential to destroy the existing legend and mystery and folklore surrounding Billy the Kid, badly damage the state's tourism industry, and severely impact the economy of the state, and damage the reputation of the Governor's Office."* – **Letter to New Mexico Governor Bill Richardson signed by the Silver City Town Counsel** [sic], **June 21, 2004.**

[AUTHOR'S NOTE: This is the Silver City Petition, ignored by Richardson, but apparently given to his fellow hoaxers. It demonstrates Richardson's indifference to historical destruction and the will of his affected constituents. As an aside, it should be noted that the hoaxers refer to destruction of "legend and mystery and folklore," slyly leaving out "true history."]

*Silver City and Fort Sumner face a loss of part of their Billy the Kid legend if DNA analysis is unable to show a match between bones dug up in the two communities." ?"* – **Jay Miler, *Inside the Capital*** [sic], **July 2, 2004.**

*"And if bodies are exhumed and no matching DNA is found, as the Office of the Medical Investigator predicts, the effect on these communities will be considerable, especially on Fort Sumner."* – **Jay Miler, *Inside the Capital*** [sic], **September 19, 2004.**

The comments were published nearly daily. Their words told us they feared the Kid was not buried in Ft. Sumner. Most of the history of the escape of the Kid as well as his alleged killing by Garrett was built on a foundation set forth in Garrett's book. Historian Robert Utley pointed out in his book, *Billy the Kid a short and violent life: "Although not many copies of the Authentic life were sold, it nevertheless had a decisive impact of the Kid's image. More than any other single influence, the Garrett-Upson book fed the legend of Billy the Kid. As the legend blossomed, writers turned to the Authentic life* [sic] *for the authentic details. Ash Upson's fictions became implanted in the hundreds of 'histories' that followed.*

[AUTHOR'S NOTE: Repeat of Utley misquote from the Probable Cause Statement – not about history, but the development of the legend.]

Investigators were searching for the truth in this story and the fact that Garrett was not truthful in his accounts was not brought to the table by investigators but historians themselves. Just as Utley voiced Garrett was not truthful, in an August 8, 2000 interview with the Associated Press, Historian Frederick Nolan made the statement that Garrett's version of the Kid's death *"may have been the biggest lie of all."*

[AUTHOR'S NOTE: This is a misstatement of Nolan, who was, like Utley, commenting on Garrett's book's dime novel style, not denying that Garrett fatally shot Billy. They knew Nolan condemned their hoax.]

Yet when it became know [sic] investigators planned to use science, fear prompted the only thing that could be done to protect the books, museums, throw insults, such as, *"The three sheriffs trying to dig up Billy and his mother are a slippery bunch of varmits."* [sic] – **Jay Miler,** *Inside the Capital* [sic]**, August 9, 2004.**

It was from there that the campaign to discredit the investigation and investigators was launched. Even Nolan saying that Garrett lied, feared his repeated version of the history was being questioned wrote an editor of the *Ruidoso News*. He said, *"This project is a complete and utter nonsense, and I Wouldn't be at all surprised if Sheriff Sullivan and Mayor Sederwall are already wishing they'd never got started on this benighted project."* The next day Nolan garnered more press by appearing on CCN *Live Saturday* with Frederika Whitfield, talking ill of the investigators.

As the unchecked fear spread, investigators were trying to make contact with Dr. Komar at the OMI's office but she refused to return the calls. We were advised by the girl answering the phone that she had instructions not to send our calls to Dr. Komar. The girl stated that Dr. Komar had "lawyered up" and we would have to talk to her attorney. We had never heard of a medical investigator retaining an attorney to deal with investigators.

**[AUTHOR'S NOTE: This is a disingenuousness omission of OMI blockade, and OMI responses to Attorney Tippett's OMI fabrications for their Exhumation Petition. But the hoaxers are expanding their "conspiracy against the truth" to the OMI in what follows.]**

We didn't understand until January 20, 2004, when Bill Robins an attorney appointed by the Governor for the Kid, deposed Dr. Komar. She was asked by Robins, on page 144 lines 7 – 10 of the record, *"You don't think Billy the Kid is buried at Fort Sumner, do you?"* Dr. Komar replied, *"I don't know. I have reason to suspect perhaps not."*

**[AUTHOR'S NOTE: They certainly were not first learning about Robins! By their own Attachment 2, they had been paid by him since August of 2003 to conduct the murder case. Also, misrepresented is Dr. Komar's meaning is that Billy's gravesite cannot yield valid DNA; not that Garrett did not kill Billy.]**

It was at this point we believed Dr. Komar had discovered information, maybe some of the same information we had, about the Kid's grave. We wondered if the fear of harming New Mexico's tourist industry had caused the state to apply pressure to Dr. Komar and told her not to talk to us, in hopes this case would die and the myth would live.

**[AUTHOR'S NOTE: The "conspiracy" involves Dr. Komar and "the state!"]**

852

Since doctor Komar had obtained a lawyer and refused to talk, we wrote a letter to the OMI's office under the *New Mexico Open Records Act* asking for Dr. Komar's records. Unlike our part of the investigation, it was government money that financed her studies and paid her trips to gain information, which we reasoned would make the records public.

**[AUTHOR'S NOTE: The records refusal is misstated into: hiding truth. Note that this claim pertains to 2007.]**

After nearly 5 months of letters back and forth to the OMI's office we were provided with only a list of who was buried in Silver City. We knew that Dr. Komar had more records than the state admitted because she had stated this fact when deposed by Robins. We pointed out the state had paid for her trips and we knew there was more information, we received a response saying, *"The remainder of the material requested in your public records act request is in the possession of Dr. Komar, a faculty member of the University of New Mexico, and constitutes her intellectual property under federal copyright law and the University of New Mexico's Intellectual Property Policy."* [Footnote 5: Letter from Salvatore J. Giammo, Director of Public Affairs HSC Custodian of Public Records, address to Sullivan and Sederwall, dated April 12, 2007]

It became clear the state was hiding information and was not going to share it with investigators. The nagging question remained, what was the information and why did the state feel a need to hide it?

Friday April 2, 2004, the judge in Silver City came out with a surprise ruling, not waiting for the August hearing; his ruling startled investigators would have to provide the court with DNA from Fort Sumner before he would allow the investigators to obtain DNA from Catherine Antrim.

**[AUTHOR'S NOTE: This is a jump back to 2004, to make it seem if the "concealed information" was part of the exhumation case – not the straight-forward OMI rejection based on uncertain grave location and disturbing other remains.]**

What no one realized was that by September 20, 2003, we had located the workbench on which Garrett claimed to have laid the Kid's body. Through our discussions with the CSI experts we felt the Kid's DNA could be obtained from that bench. We also knew historians, from as far back as the 1920's, knew the grave was not located behind the "museum and gift shop" as Ft. Sumner had led tourist [sic] to believe. [Footnote 6: Notes entitled "Bonney Grave, Ft. Sumner", by Fulton found in the Robert N. Mullin Collection, Haley Memorial Library] We also knew that digging into that empty grave would be fruitless.

**[AUTHOR'S NOTE: This statement of Garrett laying the body on bench is a new hoaxer invention. The rest of the paragraph presents a new hoaxer story, contradicting their entire Billy the Kid DNA comparison and murder case of innocent victim thrust**

**with sought exhumation of the "Kid." The switcheroo is to justify use of faked carpenter's bench "blood DNA" instead.]**

Without contacting us and immediately after the judge ruled, Attorney Bill Robins filed to exhume the Kid in Ft. Sumner. The fight was on again with the village of Ft. Sumner filing motions to block Robins' attempt to look in their grave. On Wednesday July 22, 2004, Billy Sparks of the Governor's office called Sederwall at home. Sparks asked if the investigators would *'pull out of Fort Sumner"* and if so the Governor would consider it a *"personal favor."* Sparks said Silver City and Ft. Sumner were putting a great deal of pressure on the Governor to stop the dig because they feared it would destroy their tourism.

**[AUTHOR'S NOTE: This is another surprising attempt of the hoaxers to turn against their fellows – first blaming Richardson's leadership and pay-offs, then including Robins, then making Richardson join the "conspiracy against truth." Noteworthy also, is the avoidance of the use of Dr. Henry Lee's name, giving further credence to the possibility that after my AAFS Ethics Committee investigation, he demanded exclusion from the case.]**

Sederwall called Mayor Lopez and attempted to talk to him about the issue and tell him it was not our desire to harm tourism in New Mexico. When Sederwall identified himself Lopez shouted, *"fuck you!"* and hung up. This was the last time any of the investigators talk [sic] to Mayor Lopez.

**[AUTHOR'S NOTE: This may be an altered rendition of Sederwall's "Get your head out of your ass. We're getting this done whether you want it or not" telephone call threatening Lopez. ]**

That Friday we called our attorney and told him attorney Robins had filed the case on our behalf and we wanted to withdraw it. Which he did and we sat back quietly as Ft. Sumner was shorn in the press throwing a party where Frederick Nolan declared it a victory for "truth."

**[AUTHOR'S NOTE: Omitted, of course, is that the Fort Sumner case had proceeded for months under their attorney, Mark Acuña, that Robins was Billy's, not their, attorney, and they withdrew days before the September 27, 2004 Hearing because of the Leo Martinez and press exposure.]**

During the investigation the village of Fort Sumner, the town of Silver City and the city of Hamilton, Texas, in an effort to protect tourism, fought the investigation so DNA could not be recovered.

In the case of Hamilton, Texas, Brushy Bill Roberts died under the name of Oliver L. [sic] Roberts and his date of birth, on his official death certificate sets out he was born on December 31, 1868 [Footnote 7: Death certificate of Ollie L. Roberts], which would make the man 12 years old in 1881 when the Kid shot and killed James Bell and Robert Olinger.]

> [AUTHOR'S NOTE: This oddity of debunking Roberts's claim, only two months after trying to exhume him as Billy the Kid, is inexplicable, though seems part of the long digression to follow - possibly just feigned "historical research." However, it is also another biting-the-hand-that-fed-them, since loyal Jannay Valdez is betrayed along with Richardson and Robins.]

Roberts died a pauper and was buried at county expense and above his grave was placed a homemade marker of cement. [Footnote 8: Old Tombstone of Ollie L. Roberts] However, the investigators found a new tombstone on a grave located in the middle cemetery [sic] on the first row, in a very prominent place. We wondered if that grave is empty and there only for tourists. We wondered if the man was in fact buried in the back of the cemetery.

The new marker was donated and placed by the owner of the Billy the Kid Memorial Museum in Hamilton. [Footnote 9: New Tombstone for "Henry William Roberts"] Roberts name has changed from Ollie L. Roberts as listed on his death certificate and old tombstone to *Henry W. Roberts* on the new tombstone. As well, his date of birth has changed from December 31, 1868, to December 31, 1859. This would make him 21 in 1881 rather than 12 and would coincide with the history of Billy the Kid.

On May 20, 2005 [sic- May 19, 2003], the only body to be exhumed who claimed to be Billy the Kid was that of John Miller. The state of Arizona exhumed Mr. Miller and the samples were received by Dr. Rick Staub of Orchid Cellmark labs in Dallas for recovery of DNA.

> [AUTHOR'S NOTE: The current reworking of their Arizona exhumation fiasco appears to be this "the state did it" version. Omitted, of course, is that before they faced indictments, the case was conducted under the Lincoln County Sheriff's Department, under their official Deputy titles, and as Case # 2003-274, using Dr. Lee's "carpenter bench DNA."]

Investigators agree the investigation of Billy the Kid has garnered more press and has been more troublesome than any thing we have encountered in the past. Countless letters have been written to the Village of Capitan, Orchid Cellmark, Dr. Henry Lee's office, Lincoln County, the Lincoln County Sheriff, Lincoln Counties [sic] Attorney, the New Mexico Attorney General, the United States Marshal's [sic], newspapers, magazines and to investigators in an attempt to disrupt or stop the investigation. The majority of these letters were written by Dr. Gail [sic] Cooper or Jay Miller.

[AUTHOR'S NOTE: Besides omitting that the "letters" were Freedom of Information Act investigations of them as public officials, there is the interesting inclusion of Dr. Lee. The only way that would be known to the writers - though they seem unaware of the Ethics Complaint - would be communication from Dr. Lee. This is suggestive that Dr. Lee may have told them to stop using his name. This paragraph, however, is the introduction to their attack on me and Jay Miller as unjustly trying to impede their "quest for the truth," with implications of harassment.]

Miller weighed into the fight the first time on June 6, 2003 with an article accusing Governor Richardson of attempting to get publicity for the state for the investigation. Had Jay Miller read the press release, he would know that Governor Richardson admitted that fact up front.

Miller wrote letter after letter requesting files and documents concerning the financing of the investigation but there were no records as it was privately funded by law. Yet, Miller continued to write letter after letter. In a two month period, Jay Miller wrote the United States Marshals office, the Lincoln County Sheriff, the Lincoln County Attorney, James Jimenez, New Mexico Secretary Department Finance and Administration, the New Mexico Governor, and countless others complaining about Sederwall and Sullivan and each rambling letter, required a response. At one point he complained to the Attorney General Sederwall was *impersonating a police officer.*

[AUTHOR'S NOTE: This "secret private donor" ploy was a technique used to inappropriately conceal records, as the hoaxers were well aware. In fact, on these IPRA requests, all documents were concealed.]

The attacks did not center only on Sederwall and Sullivan but on anyone who dared look at the Billy the Kid Case. When Ft. Sumner heard Sheriff Gary Graves was part of the investigative team a campaign began attacking his career. On November 30, 2003 Mayor Ramon [sic] Lopez Mayor of Ft. Sumner was quoted in the paper saying Sheriff Graves was trying to start a "war" with the city over the grave of Billy the Kid. In the end, the Mayor and Ft. Sumner successfully removed Sheriff Gary Graves from office. Sheriff Graves became the first sheriff in New Mexico to be removed by a recall vote and the last sheriff taken out by Billy the Kid.

[AUTHOR'S NOTE: This is entirely misstatement of Graves's recall for malfeasance and misfeasance, unrelated to the Billy the Kid Case. And Mayor Lopez did not participate. It was a citizens' group.]

Both the village of Ft. Sumner and the City of Hamilton, Texas own a grave marked "Billy the Kid" to draw in tourist dollars. The fact remains that a man can have but one grave. Since it is a governmental entity that owns both graves and both governments have fought to keep investigators obtaining DNA from their grave that would prove where Bonney rests, it would go to reason one or both, of these governmental agencies are guilty of perpetrating fraud against the public.

**[AUTHOR'S NOTE: Omitted, of course, is that they have no DNA of Billy the Kid to match with any remains. And Dr. Lee had disavowed any claims.]**

On February 9, 2007, Sederwall and Jay Miller had lunch together in Santa Fe. Without hesitation Sederwall answered any and all questions Miller posed. Miller explained what encouraged him to fight the investigators in the Billy the Kid Case. Miller said he was born in Silver City and knew *"a lot of people up there."* He said he had received a telephone call from someone in Silver City, he chose not to identify, and the caller wanted his help to stop the investigation and the exhumation of the Kid and his mother. Miller said he began to produce the newspaper articles and the massive amount of letters knowing that we would have to answer each of them. He said that a Dr. Gail [sic] Cooper was involved and wrote most of the letters.

Miller admitted if the investigation continued it would jeopardize tourism in both Silver City and Ft. Sumner. The meeting was pleasant and as the men parted company they shook hands. Miller walked away but stopped, turned and said of Catherine Antrim, *"you know she's not in that grave don't you?"*

Even though Ft. Sumner and Hamilton know, in their hearts, Billy the Kid can have only one grave, they continue to fight the discovery of the truth and continue the fraud in the name of commerce. The Governor bending to the pressure from Ft. Sumner and Silver City turned his back on his promise to find the truth. This past week another letter, requiring an answer, came to the Sheriff requesting the information we have gathered in this investigation. We have been told the letter from Dr. Gail [sic] Cooper's attorney is her attempt to gain the information we have spent years gathering to add to a book she is attempting to sell.

**[AUTHOR'S NOTE: Finally revealed is their new tactic for withholding the DNA documents: by calling them proprietary "research." This, however, is untrue. They are public documents of the Lincoln County Sheriff's Department. Also, that this book being "shopped around" was known to very few. They were "researching" me!]**

We will continue our investigation. Later, we shall make the decision if and when we will release the information. Now, we choose to put an end to the harassment and political pressure by tendering our resignations as Deputies of Lincoln County Sheriff's Department, effective this date.

857

857

[AUTHOR'S NOTE: Their quitting as its Deputies, does not change that the documents are part of Sheriff Virden's murder investigation, done officially and are public records.]

Respectively Submitted,
Steven M. Sederwall, Thomas T. Sullivan [written and typed]

---

"MEMORANDUM" ATTACHMENTS 1-11 (with their titles):

[AUTHOR'S NOTE: Though an irrelevant hodge-podge, the treasure is Attachment 2, with its apparent bribery checks.]

ATTACHMENT 1: "Lincoln County Call sheet requested by Sheriff Tom Sullivan on April 28, 2003 as Case began. Not the case description, 'Follow up investigation Escape of William Bonney and double homicide of James Bell & Robert Olinger"

ATTACHMENT 2: "Checks handed to Sheriff Sullivan in the State Capital [sic] by Billy Sparks"

ATTACHMENT 3: "Handwritten letter by Mayor Raymond Lopez to Governor Bill Richardson on Village of Fort Sumner letterhead"

ATTACHMENT 4: "'Statement by DeBaca County Sheriff Gary Graves dated July 20, 2003"

ATTACHMENT 5: "Letter from the Office of Public Affairs of the OMI's office"

ATTACHMENT 6: "Notes by Historian Marcie [sic - Maurice] Fulton found in the Robert N. Mullin collection, indicating that what Ft. Sumner claims is the Kid's grave is not possible"

[AUTHOR'S NOTE: Amusing, since getting into that "not possible" grave for "Billy the Kid DNA" was their case goal.]

ATTACHMENT 7: "Brushy Bill Roberts Certificate of Death showing his name and date of birth has been changed to fit the history of the Kid"

[AUTHOR'S NOTE: Amusing, since they were trying to dig him up as being Billy the Kid.]

ATTACHMENT 8: (photo) "Original headstone of Ollie L. Roberts in Hamilton, Texas Cemetery"

ATTACHMENT 9: (Photo) "New Headstone put up by the owner of the Billy the Kid Memorial Museum, dates and name has changed. Sederwall on the right and Lucas Speer on the left, note the plastic tube under Sederwall's arm directing tourist [sic] to the museum"

[AUTHOR'S NOTE: A strange discrediting of loyalist Valdez.]

ATTACHMENT 10: (Copy) "Flyer found in plastic tube affixed to Brushy Bill's grave in Hamilton, Texas"

ATTACHMENT 11: (Photocopies) "Commission cards of Deputy Steven M. Sederwall and Deputy Thomas T. Sullivan from the Lincoln County Deputy Sheriff office"

**[AUTHOR'S NOTE: Contradiction, since they are claiming the Billy the Kid case as their private hobby in this document.]**

## APPENDIX: 57. Charles D. Brunt. *Albuquerque Journal.* "Suit Targets Investigation Into Billy the Kid's Death." Front page. August 28, 2008.

**[AUTHOR'S NOTE: Damage control article regarding my Barnett IPRA litigation about the Billy the Kid Case. I was not contacted for an interview.]**

Legal wrangling over DNA analyses could have Billy the Kid rolling in his grave - wherever it may be.

Scot Stinnett, publisher of the De Baca County News, and Gale Cooper, a retired psychiatrist and amateur historian from Cedar Crest, are suing current and former Lincoln County lawmen they say are withholding public records about DNA evidence collected during an investigation into events leading up to the Kid's presumed death in 1881.

Legend has it that the Kid, William Bonney, was gunned down by Sheriff Pat Garrett in Fort Sumner. With backing from Gov. Bill Richardson, two Lincoln County lawmen launched an investigation several years ago seeking to determine whether it really was the Kid who was shot by Garrett and buried in Fort Sumner.

The New Mexico Foundation for Open Government - a nonprofit government watchdog - is the latest player to enter the saga that so far has included the exhumation of two bodies in Arizona and analyses of their DNA by celebrity forensic scientist Dr. Henry Lee.

"Our primary interest is in the reason they (the records) are not being produced," NMFOG executive director Leonard DeLayo said earlier this month.

The current Lincoln County sheriff says he doesn't have any records. The former sheriff and a deputy who started the investigation say anything they did was on personal time so any records they might have are their personal material.

Stinnett and Cooper say the current sheriff has a duty under the Inspection of Public Records Act to obtain and produce the records, which they say include:

Lee's analysis of DNA derived from blood on a carpenter's bench where Billy the Kid's body supposedly was placed after being fatally wounded by Garrett the night of July 14, 1881, in Fort Sumner;

Lee's analysis of DNA taken from the graves of John Miller - who claimed he was Billy the Kid - and William Hudspeth in Arizona; and information regarding any payments to Lee. Hudspeth's remains, buried alongside Miller's, were unintentionally unearthed during the May 19, 2005, exhumation at Arizona Pioneers' Home in Prescott, where Miller died in 1937.

According to court documents, Cooper filed several requests under New Mexico's public records law seeking records held by current Lincoln County Sheriff Rick Virden, former Sheriff Tom Sullivan and former Deputy Steven Sederwall.

The lawmen have refused to produce the requested documents, claiming they either don't have them or that the records they possess are private documents not subject to disclosure.

To much fanfare in 2003, Sullivan and Sederwall opened an investigation into the Kid's escape from the Lincoln County Courthouse during which he killed deputies Bob Olinger and James W. Bell - murders that sent Garrett looking for the outlaw in Fort Sumner.

Because the DNA was collected during an official criminal investigation, the plaintiffs maintain the records are public.

Sullivan and Sederwall, who resigned from the sheriff's office in June 2007, say they collected the information on their own time and at their own expense. They say they undertook the investigation to prove whether accepted historic accounts of the Kid's death are accurate or whether they were concocted by Garrett and others.

Under that theory, the Kid escaped and lived out his life elsewhere.

Sullivan and Sederwall have sought to exhume the Kid's remains from his alleged resting place at the Fort Sumner cemetery, those of his mother, Catherine Antrim in Silver City, and another Billy the Kid claimant - Ollie "Brushy Bill" Roberts of Texas - to compare DNA samples that could rewrite history.

Stinnett said Sullivan and Sederwall gave depositions in the lawsuit earlier this month in Ruidoso.

DeLayo said NMFOG's executive committee has directed him to move toward joining the plaintiffs in the litigation.

"Our interest is in the continuity of record keeping, and that when you generate a document during an investigation, it's public information," DeLayo said. "You don't take it with you, and you don't claim that you did it on your own time."

The suit is filed in the 13th Judicial District Court in Sandoval County.

## APPENDIX: 58. Gale Cooper E-Mail to Attorney Mickey Barnett. "SUBJECT: IPRA CASE COMMUNICATION FOR REVIEW." September 28, 2008.

Dear Attorney Barnett,

It seemed a good time to take stock of our IPRA case now that the Virden, Sullivan, and Sederwall depositions are complete.

In addition, I received the September 25th e-mail from Attorney Garcia - and forwarded from Attorney Pat Rogers - to which I want to respond.

But first, I want to say how fortunate I feel that John Dendahl referred me to you on 2007. The integrity and passion to win which he described in you have certainly been proven in action. And your generosity in doing this complex case pro bono is added proof of working not just for a client, but for the benefit of New Mexico.

My additional good fortune was being joined in the case by Scott Stinnett with his *De Baca County News*. His presence as a founding member of FOG demonstrates the importance of this case to open government.

As to the next phase, it seems one in which the correct strategy is paramount. I am sure that you - like me - have never underestimated the political complexities of this case, which in itself is just a simple request for public records produced by public officials.

We could have gotten no more clear proof of that iceberg effect of the shadowy depths of the case, than from that telephone call to you by Senator Rod Adair telling you to kill the case. (And I want to add here how impressed I was yet again by your integrity in not only telling me personally on September 6th in your office, but repeating it in our meeting with Attorneys Pat Rogers and David Garcia.)

Of course, since I knew Senator Adair because of our conversations about the hoax and Billy the Kid history, it was possible to talk to him about his anxieties about the case which appeared to focus on Virden's upcoming sheriff's election - on which our case does not directly impinge. And I hope he was reassured.

And I have been reassured from the start by John Dendahl that Governor Richardson's threats or blandishments could have no effect on you or Attorney Rogers.

I guess you can say that all the above made it worth it for me to spend over a thousand hours and thousands of dollars in preparing the evidence, the depositions, and the overviews and other write-ups for you over the duration of this case. And my hope was to spare you labors and time which I was willing and able to supply.

ACHIEVEMENTS:

- I thought that the depositions went excellently, fully justifying your decision to do them.

- I believe we demonstrated to the defense attorneys and their clients that we are a formidable team.
- The revelation of Lincoln County costs from our case can sway public opinion.
- The addition of FOG can serve to strengthen our position.

NEXT STEPS:

As to the next steps, I have liked all your and Attorney Garcia's suggestions. By that, I mean the following:

- Possibly take Sullivan to court for his refusal to answer questions in his August 18th deposition.
- Subpoena Risk Management for the total payment to Attorney Kevin Brown to document Sullivan's and Sederwall's use of public money while calling the sheriff's department case a private "hobby."
- File a Motion for Summary Judgment.
- Though disappointed, I understood your decision not to depose Richardson ...
- Coordinate with FOG a strategy - be it as two separate cases, or with their joining our case.

ATTORNEY ROGERS E-MAIL RECEIVED 9/25/08:

My responses to the Attorney Rogers e-mail forwarded to me by Attorney Garcia are interpolated with the original, and are in bold-face.

As an overview, it appears to me that issues that Attorney Rogers brought up in our initial meeting on Friday, September , still remain for discussion, since they are repeated. And the issues are worthy ones to consider since this IPRA case has implications for open government law in New Mexico that transcend our specific records request.

The September 25, 2008 e-mail and responses follow. Please note that my interpolated bold-face responses to Attorney Pat Rogers are somewhat based on the fact that it was made clear to me that a) at this stage, the FOG case is completely separate from mine; b) I am not a client of any FOG attorney; c) my supplying evidence folders from my case constituted courtesy only and not my support of FOG arguments or contentions differing from those in my own case.

In addition, I was given by the Barnett law firm a copy of the already-mailed, FOG IPRA request letter written by Attorney DeLayo which requested records compatible with those in my case, but differing from the below suggested request.

**[AUTHOR'S NOTE: Below was their attempt to trick me into incriminating Sederwall as "records custodian," to let Virden off the hook, as requested by their buddy Senator Rod Adair.]**

Hi Dr. Cooper, FYI, can you answer Pat's questions? David

From: Patrick J. Rogers [mailto:patrogers@modrall.com]
Sent: Monday, September 22, 2008 7:45 AM
To: Mickey Barnett; David A. Garcia
Subject: docs for editing

Mickey/David:

I have an outline/rough draft of an approach and a letter that has been sent to NMFOG exec comm for review. I am proposing that we send a new request, for only the Dr. Henry Lee report. I see this as a good case to test the bs about this private investigation switcheroo. I see it as a confusing case as to documents that we cannot prove were actually in the possession of a county custodian. [**COOPER RESPONSE #1: See underlined portion in RESPONSE #4.** I see Sederwall as a county custodian. [**COOPER RESPONSE #2: As I said at the September 16th meeting, it is my contention that Mr. Sederwall, as merely a reserve deputy under Sheriffs Sullivan and Virden, cannot be identified as the records custodian for records of a sheriff's department criminal investigation. At best - if he possesses the records requested - he is their thief. As that attempted designation of Mr. Sederwall applies to my IPRA case, I feel concern that it sets up potential defeat. The reason is that since he is an unconvincing custodian under IPRA law - which implies a justified responsibility over particular records – Mr. Sederwall could use that uncertainty to argue that the records were not public documents, and he had copies for a hobby.**] Presumably the county has not formally designated a custodian for police records? [**COOPER RESPONSE #3: Since IPRA law is untested, I believe that logic can prevail. It appears obvious that the sheriff conducting an official, filed, murder investigation in his own department is the records custodian of the forensic records generated by him or his commissioned deputies to solve that murder.**]

I like the summary and am thinking about some edits and some modifications, and then attaching it as an exhibit to the new FOG letter. I am proposing to release the new FOG letter to the media, in an effort to get Sederwall to provide the copy, before a NMFOG suit or intervention or further damage to the long-suffering taxpayers. [**COOPER RESPONSE #4: It is important for me to clarify my position. I believe that Sheriff Virden has the obligation of recovery of documents which are part of his own criminal investigation – by his own legal action if needed. It was not my job as records requestor. If FOG chooses to move against Mr. Sederwall because of his deposition claim of possessing the Dr. Lee report, I see that action as separate from the contentions of** my case, those contentions being that the forensic records do exist by preponderance of evidence as to their existence and the exhumations done based an their existence. I do not feel that IPRA law demonstrates or requires a records requestor to meet any higher level of proof of records existence for a records request. And it should be emphasized again that the Dr. Lee report, though dealing with initial DNA recovery for the case, is the least significant forensic report generated for Case # 2003-274 in terms of DNA extractions, matchings, and conclusions.]

Can you send me several docs, for editing:

1) Timeline for IPRA Issues in Case (aprox 7 pages)

2) Summary of Lincoln County Sheriff's Department Case ( 1 pager)
*"In 2005, when he became sheriff, Virden... deputized Messrs. Sullivan and Sederwall as its commissioned investigators" Source? [COOPER RESPONSE: Please refer to the records provided to you on September 16th]

Questions/Supporting evidence/docs. The summary is outstanding and very helpful, but often does not contain any reference to the source of the information summarized (see eg Jan and 2005 entries). Can you ask Dr. Cooper to reference and provide (some) of the references, particularly newspaper articles? [COOPER RESPONSE: This appears – if I understand it correctly – to be an attempt to have me assist directly with the FOG case. Further communication about the direction of the FOG case - and my role in it - would be needed.]
June 5 2003 NY Times article quotes Sederwall, any other helpful info? [COOPER RESPONSE: That article is focused on the law enforcement nature of the case – and the Records Custodian then was Sheriff Sullivan, not Mr. Sederwall.]

3) "throughout 2003: informal requests for records ..were refused, based on "ongoing criminal investigation"" Source ? [COOPER RESPONSE: Please refer to the records provided to you on September 12th]

4) "August 2004: Dr Henry Lee is brought in by the Lincoln Cty Sheriff's Dept to perform..." How? Any written docs concerning how he was "brought in"? [COOPER RESPONSE: Please refer to the records provided to you on September 16th:

5) Basis for the Sept 21, 2004 comm meeting? The minutes? Can I get a copy? [COOPER RESPONSE: I own the CD of the entire County Commissioner Leo Martinez meeting. Further communication about the direction of the FOG case would be needed.]

6) What is "Evidence 19" about? The American Academy of Forensic Sciences responds to Dr. Cooper with, inter alia "we have reviewed all of the materials you sent...including Dr. Lee's report dated Feb 5, 2005"???
**[COOPER RESPONSE: This is one response in back-and-forth communication between me and the AAFS Committee in my attempt to get the Dr. Lee report in question (which Dr. Lee had earlier confirmed in writing that he had sent to the Lincoln County Sheriff's Department. The Committee was willing to identify that letter by date, but stated that I had to get it from the sheriff's department, not from them.]**

Best regards, Pat


## APPENDIX: 59. Attorney Mickey Barnett Withdrawal Letter (by Attorney David Garcia). "Re: Cooper v. Virden, Et al., 13th Judicial District Court Cause No. D 1329 CV 2007-01364. February 29, 2009.

Dear Dr. Cooper and Mr. Stinnett:
We had previously suggested a meeting to discuss the above-referenced lawsuit. On February 16, 2009, you e-mailed us requesting clarification of certain matters pertaining to the status of the lawsuit.

**[AUTHOR'S COMMENT: This contact is unclear. My last contact was the above September 28, 2008 e-mail – APPENDIX: 58 - with regard to refusing the Barnett-Rogers pressure to dismiss Virden and call Sederwall the person responsible for the records. At this February 29, 2009 point – as they knew - I was seeking a new attorney.]**

At this point, the litigation is at a standstill, the latest activity having been the depositions taken last fall. The most recent item showing on the Court's docket was filed September 5, 2008.
Our understanding is that the Foundation for Open Government ("FOG") is at this time taking no action either with respect to your lawsuit. We do not anticipate that FOG will involve itself in any matters pertaining to the above-referenced lawsuit. Although we cannot control what FOG does, at this time we are not aware that FOG intends to file any separate lawsuits regarding its own requests under the New Mexico Inspection of Public Records Act ("IPRA") for public records that may be at issue in the above-referenced lawsuit.

**[AUTHOR'S COMMENT: Omitted is that Pat Rogers with Barnett was responsible for this sabotage of FOG – and omitted is that FOG had already filed a parallel request through Attorney Leonard DeLayo on September 4, 2008.]**

With respect to the above-referenced lawsuit, and the depositions that have been taken, a reasonable course of action at this point would be filing of a motion for summary judgment in the IPRA issues in the lawsuit. Specifically, the Plaintiffs should ask the Court to decide summarily whether the documents requested by Plaintiffs that are the subject of the lawsuit are public records and that the records should be provided to the Plaintiffs. The Defendants would then respond to our summary judgment motion and, perhaps, file a summary judgment motion of their own. Although trial courts are sometimes reluctant to grant summary judgment, preferring instead that the parties have their day in court, the issues here are relatively straightforward and the factual background would seem to lend itself to resolution of the IPRA issues by way of a summary judgment proceeding. Although we think our arguments should prevail, obviously we have no way of knowing for sure whether this Court would grant summary judgment, or how the Court might rule.

Regarding the issue of who is "custodian of records" of records we requested, it remains our advice that the word "custodian" is broadly defined under IPRA, § 14-2-6(A). We believe it likely that Mr. Sederwall would, in fact, fall under the definition ...

[AUTHOR'S COMMENT: This is a patently false garbling of the IPRA definition of custodian, and appears to be a self-serving falsity to conceal the attempt to destroy my case by trying to trick me into calling Sederwall the custodian. And the purpose here is to mislead the judge, who gets this withdrawal.]

Dr. Cooper has expressed her concerns that any argument by the Plaintiffs that Sederwall is a "custodian" would allow Sederwall to craft a counter-argument in the litigation which would, at minimum, cause confusion. We do not agree with this analysis and believe that it is important to our IPRA argument that the Plaintiffs retain the ability to argue that Sederwall is a "custodian" and that the IPRA contemplates that an agency may have more than one "custodian" ...

[AUTHOR'S COMMENT: This is false with regard to a sheriff and his filed murder investigation. And IPRA addresses the issue by holding all people who participated in the records generation as responsible for them – without their needing to be a "custodian." This is merely an attempt to deflect their own blameworthiness to me.]

It is clear that Dr. Cooper disagrees with our legal advice with respect to the "custodian" issue ... Accordingly, it would seem that the best course of action at this point would be for our firm to withdraw from representing the Plaintiffs in the above-referenced matter. We are open to further discussion, but at this time we do not believe it is in the Plaintiffs' best interest for us to advance the items requested by Dr. Cooper.

As the Court must approve our withdrawal, we will prepare the necessary papers for our withdrawal and circulate them ... [W]e recommend that new counsel be retained as soon as possible.

Should you have any questions, please feel free to contact our office. Thank you.

> Sincerely,
> BARNETT LAW FIRM, P.A.
> BY: *David A. Garcia*

[AUTHOR'S COMMENT: Note that so-called IPRA expert and my co-plaintiff, Scot Stinnett, has had no input; and is carefully omitted in this blame game. It would take me years to notice that oddity. But the withdrawal letter would also mention me solely - a last-ditch attempt of Barnett to discredit me with the judge and damage my case against Virden.]

**APPENDIX: 60. Attorney Bill Robins III and Attorney David Sandoval. "Sixth Judicial District Court, State on New Mexico, County of Grant. Case No. MS-2003-11." "In the Matter of Catherine Antrim, Billy the Kid's Pre-Hearing Brief." January 5, 2004.**

[AUTHOR'S NOTE: THIS IS THE DOCUMENT THAT CRACKED THE BILLY THE KID CASE HOAX]

<u>BILLY THE KID'S PRE-HEARING BRIEF</u>

COME NOW, Bill Robins, III and David Sandoval, of the law firm of Heard, Robins, Cloud, Lubel & Greenwood, LLC, and on the behalf of the estate of William H. Bonney, aka "Billy the Kid",

[AUTHOR'S COMMENT: The Kid had no estate: posthumous property settled in a probate court. This fakery segues to Robins's revealing dead Billy as his client, though that is in the Brief's title - since dead Billy himself is the petitioner!]

file this Pre-Hearing Brief and state as follows:

### I. INTRODUCTION

The Court asks the undersigned counsel to brief several questions as follows:

1. The Governor's right to assign an Attorney to Represent the Interests of Billy the Kid and the Associated Zone of Public Interest;

2. Who is the Real Party in Interest Represented by Counsel;

3. What Stake Does that Party Have in Intervening in This Cause;

4. Billy the Kid's Interest as Defined in the Law Relating to Standing; and

5. The Effect of *In Re: Application of Lois Telfer, for the Removal of the Body of William H. Bonney*

**[AUTHOR'S COMMENT: These questions by the judge are an hilarious parody of judicial gravitas. Judge Quintero well knows that Governor Richardson had no right to appoint an attorney to his court, knows that Robins has no "real party" as a client, only a ghost; knows that the dead do not appear in court and have no standing; and knows that the Telfer exhumation case in Fort Sumner blocked all future exhumation attempts there by stating that the grave location was uncertain and contiguous remains would be disturbed.]**

The Points and Authorities section below does so as follows: **Point One** provides introductory legal analysis, **Point Two** addresses Question 1, **Point Three** addresses Questions 2, 3, and 4, and **Point Four** addresses Question 5. **Point 5** supports the merits of the Petition for Exhumation.

## II. POINTS AND AUTHORITIES

### Point One
### Initial Discussion as to the Nature of This Proceeding

This is an interesting proceeding in that the relief sought here is not exclusively judicial.

**[AUTHOR'S COMMENT: That is understatement! What follows is just double-talked legalize. But New Mexico taxpayers would be footing its bills for almost a decade.]**

New Mexico allows the state registrar or state medical examiner to issue permits for disinterment. 1978 NMSA §24-14-23D. The statute does not identify who may make such a request nor specify the showing that needs to be made in order to obtain the permit. Rather than proceeding with this simple and non-adversarial process, Petitioners here have invoked this Court's equity jurisdiction for an order allowing the exhumation of Billy the Kid's mother, Catherine Antrim. See, *Hood v. Spratt,* 357 So.2d 135 (Miss. 1978) (request for disinterment "is particularly one for a court of equity") citing *Theodore v. Theodore,* 57 N.M. 434, 259 P.2d 795 (1953).

"[N]ormally a district court would not become involved in such matters unless a protesting relative or interested party files an injunction or takes some other legal action to halt the autopsy or disinterment," *In Re Johnson*, 94 N.M. 491, 494, 612 P.2d 1302 (1980). Petitioners should thus be commended for bringing this Court into the picture and in doing so, offering the town of Silver City, a relative of another descendent buried in the cemetery, and the legal interests of Billy the Kid, an opportunity to participate in the process.

**[AUTHOR'S COMMENT: This sanctimonious fakery implies the hoax is a favor for Silver City - in court to oppose exhumation - and even a favor to dead Catherine Antrim. And Billy has no "legal interests," being dead!]**

The questions the Court asked briefed, however, suggest the possibility that the court may not allow Billy the Kid to be heard.

**[AUTHOR'S COMMENT: At this point, the hoaxers were going through the motions. They had every reason to believe that Judge Quintero was in their pocket.]**

As will be shown clearly, Billy the Kid's interests are real, legitimate, proper for consideration, and we respectively ask the Court to recognize them as such.

**[AUTHOR'S COMMENT: And if you believe a dead man has real interests on earth, Robins and his compatriots probably have a bridge to sell you in New York.]**

A challenge to a governor's appointment power is made in a *quo warranto* proceeding.

**[AUTHOR'S COMMENT: Robins is here faking legitimacy of appointment as dead Billy's attorney. In fact, only the judge can appoint an attorney for a court client - if the client is indigent. Governor Richardson, by appointing Robins here, used *ultra vires*, overstepping his executive power for judicial intervention.]**

*New Mexico Judicial Standards Commission v. Governor Bill Richardson and Espinoza*, 134 N.M. 59, 73 P.2d 197 (2003); see also, 1978 NMSA. §§44-3-1 *et. seq.* (*quo warranto* action proper when "any person shall usurp, intrude into or unlawfully holds or exercise any public office, civil or military, or any franchise within this state.")

The *quo warranto* statute contains specific procedures that the Town has not properly followed, nor could follow because the Town is not a "private person."

869

[AUTHOR'S COMMENT: This fact demonstrates that Robins is misapplying the law to the town with his false argument.]

Standing to bring such a proceeding lies first with the attorney general or district attorney. 1978 NMSA, §44-3-4; *Beese v. District Court*, 31 N.M. 82, 239 P. 452 (1925). Those public officials do not present any challenge here.

A private person can bring a *quo warranto* action only when he has requested the aforementioned public officials to bring action and they have refused. 1978 NMSA, §44-3-4. The only private person in this matter is Ms. Amos-Staadt [sic] and she has not challenged the Governor's appointment, much less shown compliance with the procedural requisites of the *quo warranto* statute.

As noted, the challenge to the Governor comes from the Town of Silver City. It simply has no standing to bring a *quo warranto* proceeding. 1978 NMSA, §44-3-4. The validity of Governor Richardson's appointment of the undersigned counsel is thus not before this Court.

[AUTHOR'S COMMENT: An inappropriately appointed lawyer representing a corpse as client should indeed have been taken up by the Court - and Robins should have been kicked out on his petard.]

To the extent that the Court remains concerned with the presence of Billy the Kid in this litigation,

[AUTHOR'S COMMENT: Robins here switches from the "estate" of Billy the Kid to the dead Kid as client.]

it is a matter that can be more properly addressed pursuant to legal requirements of standing and intervention, which the discussion below shows the Kid satisfies.

[AUTHOR'S COMMENT: Robins advances his client, dead Billy, who now, he claims, is able to have court standing and perform intervention.]

*(Given the express direction to brief the question, however, the discussion below sets forth the proper gubernatorial powers at play here.)*

C. *The Governor's Powers*

As noted above, the governor is the supreme executive officer of the state. There can be no question that in that capacity Governor Richardson has authority to engage the services of professionals to assist him in accomplishment of those duties. Lawyers are certainly within that group, as is witnessed by Geno Zamora, the Governor's chief legal counsel.

**[AUTHOR'S COMMENT: Robins is here making a false argument based on omission. The governor can engage an attorneys services. But the matter here is not services, but violating the division of executive and judicial powers. The omission is the illegal nature of Robins's appointment.]**

The source of power behind such appointments is likely found in the "inherent general power of appointment in the executive." *Matheson v. Ferry*, 641 P.2d 674, 682 (Ut 1982); *Hadley v. Washburn*, 67 S.W. 592 (Mo. 1902) (appointment of election commissioners is an inherent executive power); *Application of O'Sullivan*, 158 P.2d 306, 309 (Mont. 1945) ("the power of appointment is an executive function which cannot be delegated to the judiciary); *State v. Brill*, 111 N.W. 294, (1907) (legislature prohibited from requiring judges at appoint members to a board of control unrelated to the judiciary on a separation of powers theory grounded in the presumption that the power of appointment is inherently executive).

**[AUTHOR'S COMMENT: Robins, wildly spewing irrelevant legal cases, is omitting something else in his argument here: the U.S. Constitution which guarantees separation of powers!]**

This inherent power must also allow the Governor to appoint attorneys to address his concerns and/or further his interests outside his immediate circle.

**[AUTHOR'S COMMENT: Robins gives dramatic proof that this Billy the Kid Case was Richardson's baby. Then he jumps with a legal *non sequitor*, but to the ulterior motive of the whole publicity-seeking hoax: the Billy the Kid pardon.]**

The governor has the "power to grant reprieves and pardons." N.M. Const. Art. V Sec. 6. Undersigned counsel intends on seeking a pardon for Billy the Kid. Certainly Governor Richardson is within his inherent appointment power to hire counsel to advise him on the merits of such a pardon.

**[AUTHOR'S COMMENT: Tricky Robins omits that pardon advising gives no legal justification to be appointed to this court seeking the exhumation of Catherine Antrim. He is just functioning as an amateur historian.]**

That the power extends to pardons of long-dead individuals is clear because our Constitution extends that power to pardon offences under the Territorial Laws of New Mexico. N.M. Const. Art. XXII Sec 5.

(Footnote: Posthumous pardons are not unusual. In fact, Lenny Bruce was pardoned by Governor Patake in New York just last month.)

**[AUTHOR'S COMMENT: Robins is omitting that Territorial law left pardon to the discretion of the Governor. All Richardson had to do was to pardon Billy if he wanted to. The rest of the hoaxers' exhumation gambit was just a dog and pony show for publicity.]**

That the appointment is consistent with the statutorily granted powers is shown by consideration of two different status. Counsel's appointment here is in the nature of an appointment as a public defender; a portion of their work effort will go towards exposing the merits of a pardon. 1978 NMSA §§31-15-1, *et. seq.* The public defender department is within the executive branch and is headed [sic-by] an appointee of the governor. 1978 NMSA §§31-15-4A. The duty and function of the department is to have attorneys serve as defense counsel "as necessary and appropriate." 1978 NMSA §§31-15-7B(10).

**[AUTHOR'S COMMENT: Robins transcends to the absurd: saying he is in an exhumation court to decide on a pardon; saying he is a public defender of a corpse; saying that all that makes his non-constitutional appointment justified.]**

The Governor has apparently deemed it necessary and appropriate to seek guidance from undersigned counsel on matters related to the Kid and potential pardon.

Similarly, the Governor has authority to request the appointment of prosecutorial attorneys. 1978 NMSA, Section 8-5-2B provides that a governor may request the attorney general to appoint counsel in "all actions civil or criminal" in which the governor believes the state is "interested." The governor's pardon power gives the state an interest [sic-in] legal matters involving a potential candidate for pardon and Governor Richardson could rely on Section 8-5-2B's power at the appropriate time. This should not be read to mean that Governor Richardson is assuming power to appoint attorneys to act on behalf of the State, a power that lies exclusively with the Attorney General. It is referenced here as another example of how the governor is authorized in several instances to procure the assistance of attorneys.

**[AUTHOR'S COMMENT: Though he managed to slip in the raison d'être for the Billy the Kid Case: pardon plus publicity, Robins has not justified his appointment by Governor Richardson for this court – since it cannot be justified, being illegal *ultra vires*.]**

## Point Three
## What Interests Are of Importance Here

A. *The Law of Standing*

As has been established, this is an action in equity. New Mexico's Supreme Court wrote: "The equity right of intervention in proper cases has always been recognized. The equitable test is, 'Does the intervener stand to gain or lose by the judgment.'" *Stovall v. Vesely*, 38 N.M. 415, 34 P.2d 862, 864 (1934)

[AUTHOR'S COMMENT: The actual test here is that Robins has no living or existing client to have an interest.]

Billy the Kid's interest here is his legacy.

[AUTHOR'S COMMENT: The actual test here is also for the level of Judge Quintero's morals. That single sentence says it all: the use of Quintero's court for an illegally appointed attorney, speaking for a dead man, whose "interest" is not a legal one, but a sentimental "legacy" - whatever that means. And Robins and Quintero both failed their credibility tests.]

As noted in previous briefing the very question of his life and death will be impacted by the results of the Petitioners' investigation.

[AUTHOR'S COMMENT: Robins's argument is irrelevant but revealing of hoax motive: the thrust always seemed to establish long-discredited pretender, "Brushy Bill" Roberts as Billy the Kid - and give him the pardon. Robins, throughout the Billy the Kid Case, gave hints of being a "Brushy" believer.]

B. *The Planned Request For Pardon Confers Standing Here*

Undersigned counsel intends to ask Governor Richardson that he pardon Billy the kid for the murder conviction of Sheriff Brady on several known bases including the fact that then Territorial Governor Lew Wallace reneged on his promise to pardon the Kid.

[AUTHOR'S COMMENT: Here it comes, folks. This is the leap that finally cracked the hoax for me. See that Robins seemed to be talking about the pardon for Billy Bonney. He will immediately segue into the pretenders - as if one is really Billy. So the pardon he is discussing is not for the real Billy at all! That switcheroo is followed by his irrelevant and meaningless legal blather.]

There were at least two individuals that laid claim to Billy the Kid's identity years after his alleged shooting by Garrett. **Both of them apparently led long and peaceful and crime-free lives.** [author's boldface]

As was recently recognized by the court in *Mestiza v. DeLeon,* 8 S.W. 3d 770 (Tx. Ct. App. - Corpus Christi - (1999) this interest is sufficient to properly confer standing. There an inmate imprisoned on murder conviction sought the exhumation of the victim's body on the basis that the exhumation could lead to new evidence to support a habeas corpus claim. While not deciding the merits, the Texas court determined that the inmate's interest in showing the improper conviction was sufficient to confer standing. That certainty is an analogous situation here.

The reasons that the exhumation is sought is to disinter the remains of Billy the Kid's mother for the extraction of Mitochondrial DNA.

As such, Ms. Antrim presents the only source of such DNA. Should the exhumation be denied, Billy the Kid will be forever denied the opportunity to make use of modern technology to shed light on his life and death.

> **[AUTHOR'S COMMENT: Do not miss that the issue here is merely an argument for a Billy the Kid pretender: namely that Billy's death is in question. Omitted is that there exists no historical reason for doubt Billy's killing by Pat Garrett.]**

**Should the DNA extracted from Ms. Antrim confirm that one of the potential Kids was in fact Billy the Kid, undersigned counsel will be able to make an even stronger argument for pardon by citing to the long years of law abiding life.** [author's boldface]

> **[AUTHOR'S COMMENT: HERE IS THE SENTENCE THAT CRACKED THE BILLY THE KID CASE HOAX. And here is the almost full-blown hoax plot: prove a pretender by faking DNA, then pardon him: Oliver "Brushy Bill" Roberts – as THE Billy the Kid!]**

*C. A Comparison of Interests*

This Court has allowed the intervention of the Town of Silver City in this matter. The municipal politicians there have apparently authorized the Town's Mayor to oppose the exhumation. Billy the Kid acknowledges the existence of case law that accords standing to the owners of the cemetery concerned in such proceedings.

874

What is of interest here, is that such standing is often given to the cemetery owner because it may be the only entity that can represent the wishes of the deceased, an element typically considered in whether to order an exhumation. *Theodore*, 57 N.M. at 438, *Estate of Conroy*, 530 A2d 212, 530 N.Y. S.2d 668 (N.Y.Super. 1988)

As expected, the Mayor here opposes the exhumation and is positioned to present evidence in support of its objection. Whether or not that truly represents the interests of Ms. Antrim can never be known. Given the identity of the decedent and the time that has passes since her death, the Mayor cannot possibly have any direct evidence of Ms. Antrim's wishes. As such, the evidence that is presented by the Mayor can be viewed as best, supposition, or at worst, utterly unreliable.

One is left to question why such a party with such a remote interest and lack of express knowledge about the decedent's wishes is conferred standing while the interests of Billy the Kid go unheard if this Court denier him standing. Allowing such a party to appear and present evidence while denying the same opportunity to a party that has been appointed to represent the interests of the decedent's son does not seem prudent nor fair.

## Point Four
## The *Telfer* Case and Impact on This Case

The *Telfer* case is of no major consequence here.

[AUTHOR'S COMMENT: This statement is evidence that Robins has nerve as well as nuttiness. The *Telfer* case was fatal to the Catherine Antrim exhumation for two reasons. First, the blocked exhumation attempt on the Billy the kid grave of Lois Telfer from 1961 to 1962, established precedent for that grave being permanently blocked because of uncertain location and risk of disturbing remains. Second, the Catherine Antrim exhumation intended to match remains to that grave. Being blocked, it removed the need to exhume her. And the pretenders did not need to be exhumed to prove that they were not Billy - their non-matching histories and preposterous tales alone undid them. And, in what follows, Robins hides all that.]

First, since neither of the parties here were parties there, the doctrines of res judica and collateral estoppel cannot possibly apply against the current litigants. *Brantley Farms v. Carlsbad Irrigation District*, 124 N.M. 698, 702, 954 p.2d 763 (1998).

Second, the body sought to be exhumed there was the purported body of Billy the Kid and not the subject of this request, his mother. Third, the basis for the request was that the Ft. Sumner burial site had been abandoned and not maintained for years. The petitioner's desire was to re-inter the body in a "decent and respectable burial place" in Lincoln, New Mexico. The factual and legal matters there are thus distinct to those here. That one was denied cannot serve to prohibit the exhumation of the other.

The opponents of exhumation may rely on the *Telfer* court's finding that "it is no longer possible to locate the site of the grave of the said William H. Bonney" as a means to argue that the exhumation of Ms. Antrim for DNA would be futile. Even if such a factual finding was true and correct the technology available now as opposed to 1962 is such that a new factual inquiry would be likely to yield different results.

[AUTHOR'S COMMENT: This argument about "new technology" is misstatement. Technology cannot show where Billy Bonney himself rests in the Fort Sumner cemetery. Technology cannot prevent disturbing overlapping remains of Charles Bowdre or other unknown remains. But more to the point, there is no need for exhumation, since the premise that Billy was not killed by Pat Garrett is false.]

Even if the body buried in Ft., Sumner cannot possibly be exhumed for comparable DNA, a denial here is not called for. As has been mentioned there are at least two other individuals who claim to have been the Kid. Surely *Telfer* would not be a binding precedent to deny exhumations of grave sites in Texas or Arizona.

[AUTHOR'S COMMENT: Robins is back on track to his real goal: getting to the pretender graves. But his argument makes no sense. Why should Catherine Antrim be dug up to compare withy crazy old coots who can easily be debunked historically?]

Point Five
**Exhumation is Proper**

The Sheriffs invoke the jurisdiction of this Court in an attempt to exhume the remains of Catherine Antrim. The Court has express statutory authority to so order. It is a crime in New Mexico to knowingly and willfully disturb or remove remains of any person interred in a cemetery. 1978 NMSA, § 30-12-12. The criminal statute, however, recognizes three exceptions. Disinterment is allowed "pursuant to an order of the district court, the provisions of Section 24-14-23 NMSA 1978 or as otherwise permitted by law." This request falls into the first and last exceptions.

[AUTHOR'S COMMENT: By the time of this Brief, Robins must be aware that the exhumation is being blocked by the Office of the Medical Investigator, and that Attorney Sherry Tippett had lied about getting its permission. He is, thus. attempting to get the court to act independently of the OMI.]

The leading exhumation case in New Mexico is *Theodore*, 57, N.M. 434 and sets forth as follows:

[AUTHOR'S COMMENT: The *Theodore* case, whose description follows, has to do with <u>digging up and relocating</u> a body - absolutely noting to do with the Antrim exhumation at hand.].

> In determining whether authority to disinter a body **and bury it elsewhere** should be granted, controlling consideration seems generally to be given by the courts to the following factors, (1) the interest of the public; (2) wishes of the decedent; (3) rights and feelings of those entitled to be heard by reason of relationship; (4) the rights and principles of religious bodies or other organizations which granted the right to inter the body in the first place of burial, and (5) the question of whether or not consent was given to the burial in the first place of interment by the one claiming the right of removal.

(emphasis added).

The bolded language is important because it shows that *Theodore* is not directly on point.

**[AUTHOR'S COMMENT: More than "not directly on point," it is totally irrelevant - which Robins next blithely admits himself. Apparently, however, Robins needed filler, since he lacks real legal arguments or precedents for representing a corpse as his sole client, digging up someone else for no reason, and having no standing to even be in court for himself or for dead Billy the Kid.]**

The exhumation there was for the purpose of moving remains from one grave site (preferred by the decedent's brother) to another site (preferred by the plaintiff's widow). That is not the case here. Petitioners asking for an exhumation that is of importance in their investigation surrounding the Lincoln County Wars [sic] and the shooting of Billy the Kid.

The distinction renders some of the *Theodore* factors of no consequence and the others of limited precedential value. Since the Ms. Antrim remains will be replaced in the same burial site, the 4th and 5th factor, which involves the decedent's ties to the "first place of burial" sought to be abandoned are of no consequence here. The first three factors remain.

1st Factor Public Interest, Billy the Kid's name is forever tied to New Mexico and to that of another legendary figure of the Old West, Sheriff Pat Garrett. A commonly held version of history paints a picture of an ambush in which Garrett killed the Kid in Ft. Sumner where most believe the Kid still lies at rest. This version has been questioned. It is the investigation into whether Garrett killed the Kid that has prompted these investigators to seek exhumation.

**[AUTHOR'S COMMENT: This is pure hoaxer illogic. The only ones to "question" history are the hoaxers themselves for their stunt. There is no "public interest" - meaning value - there is only the self-serving motives of the hoaxers – and the definite "lack of public interest" by destroying New Mexican's iconic Old West history and its tourist sites.]**

2nd Factor, the Decedents wishes. In spite of Silver City's position to the contrary, we simply do not know what the decedent's wishes would be. Given the present circumstances, however, where her remains could possibly provide critical evidence to be used by modern day advocates to clear her son's name, one might easily surmise that Silver City's dogged attempt to resist exhumation would not be appreciated by Ms. Antrim.

[AUTHOR'S COMMENT: This is Robins at his most slippery. First of all, he is now near-channeling Catherine Antrim to express "her wishes." Secondly he is misstating Silver City's position. The Mayor has standing not to guess "wishes," but to protect the sanctity of her grave from exactly the groundless publicity stunt that the hoax represents. Thirdly, Robins is floating pure hoaxer illogic. The only ones "questioning" history are the hoaxers themselves for their stunt. There is no "public interest" - meaning value - there is only the self-serving motives of the hoaxers. Fourthly, is the most outrageous thrust: that Catherine Antrim would want to be dug up to "prove" that he son was the old and crazy faker "Brushy Bill."]

3rd Factor, Surviving Relatives Wishes. There are no relatives of Ms. Antrim currently before the Court. This Court can take judicial notice from the *Telfer* case, that at least one of her claimed relatives was not adverse to the concept of exhumation since the disinterment of Billy the Kid was sought in 1962 [sic - 1961, denied in 1962]

[AUTHOR'S COMMENT: Robins is omitting that Lois Telfer was never established as kin to Billy the Kid. And no opinion was expressed by her as the exhuming Catherine Antrim anyway – her faked kinship notwithstanding.]

The closest party currently before the Court is in fact Billy the Kid as represented by the undersigned counsel. As is apparent from the arguments set forth in this brief, the kid's [sic] interests would be furthered by the exhumation.

[AUTHOR'S COMMENT: Here it is again folks. Robins is channeling - without shame - dead Billy to say that HE, BILLY THE KID (meaning more bizarrely: he "Brushy Bill" Roberts) wants his mom dug up!]

The "limitation of "currently before the Court" was used above because of undersigned counsel is aware of certain individuals who claim to be related to Ms. Antrim who at worst will likely testify in support of exhumation and may even attempt to intervene in this matter.

[AUTHOR'S COMMENT: Robins is apparently referring to Elbert Garcia (who was included in the list of those receiving a copy of this brief, but was called "Albert), a Santa Rosa, New Mexico, resident who wrote an incoherent book claiming that his grandmother, Abrana Garcia, had an illegitimate child fathered by Billy the Kid. And he believes he is the descendant of that man. But "Bert" Garcia has never done the more obvious exhumation to explore his hopes for a more exciting family tree: exhuming Abrana's actual husband, "Bert's" putative grandfather to see if it is that man, not Billy the Kid, to whom he is related. Bert Garcia adds to his silliness, by having photos in his book of things left to the family by Billy. Among them is a bolo tie; the bolo being invented in 1940!]

Billy the Kid believes that the evidence adduced at the exhumation hearing will certainly support an order of exhumation here.

[AUTHOR'S COMMENT: Oops, Robins has crossed into the "Exorcist" movie's territory. He has "disappeared" as an entity; only dead Billy is talking now. The creepy thought is that Robins not be faking. He may really think he IS "Brushy Bill" incarnate.]

As such, Billy the Kid's mother's name, will forever be tied with other famous names and legendary figures: Czar Nicholas II of Russia and his family, John Paul Jones, President Zachary Taylor, Jesse James, Butch Cassidy and the Sundance Kid. All these individuals were themselves exhumed for various reasons. Other lesser known, or perhaps less colorful figures, have also been exhumed. They include Samuel Mudd (conspirator in the assassination of Abraham Lincoln), Haile Selassie (former emperor of Ethiopia), Czar Lazar (14th century Serbian monarch), Medgar Evers (civil rights leader, Carl A. Weiss (alleged assassin of Huey Long). Those whose exhumation has been proposed at various times in the past include, Meriwether Lewis. John Wilkes Booth, John F. Kennedy, Lee Harvey Oswald and J. Edgar Hoover.

[AUTHOR'S COMMENT: Just because other name-recognition people have been exhumed (some for the same type of frivolous publicity stunt being tried here), is irrelevant to exhuming Catherine Antrim for no reason at all. In fact, one is left with a suspicion that other corpses, here listed, fell victim to the same senseless desecration and selfish profit being attempted by Robins and the other hoaxers. One can also contemplate that for some of the poor bunch of bodies above, no one cared enough about their dignity to protect them from the attacks of shovels.]

Clearly, exhumation as a truth seeking device has been used throughout history. Exhumation has also been the subject of case law and legal discourse. See, 61 U. Colo.L.Rev. 567, Evidentiary Autopsies, 1990; 21 A.L.R.2d. 538, *Annotation*, Power of a Court to Order Disinterment and Autopsy or Exhumation for Evidential Purpose in a Civil Case."

[AUTHOR'S COMMENT: Again Robins is using irrelevant legal precedent. First of all, this is allegedly a criminal murder case, not a civil one. More important, the murder case is a groundless hoax: there is no matter to solve by "truth-seeking; nor are there any sources of DNA for that "truth-seeking." Billy was historically and indubitably killed on July 14, 1881, not an innocent victim to allow Robin's fantasized "Brushy" to live on.]

The current state of knowledge and technology, and its expected refinement and expansion, will likely make it even more of a common occurrence in the future. It is proper to allow such an inquiry here.

## III. CONCLUSION

The foregoing has established that the undersigned counsel may legally and properly appear in these proceedings on behalf of, and to represent the interests of Billy the Kid. They are ready to present testimony and evidence to further support their interests that the exhumation of the Kid's mother, Ms. Catherine Antrim be allowed to proceed.

[AUTHOR'S COMMENT: Only in his fevered and delusional "Brushy Bill" dreams, has Robins established anything at all "legal" to justify being in Court and channeling dead Billy. One is left with the eerily echoing "They are ready ..." Are "they" Robins and his dead buddy Ollie Roberts (creepily as Billy), or just Robins and his co-counsel, David Sandoval - present with his New Mexico law license and signature because Robins had just a Texas one?]

Respectfully submitted this _5th_ day of January, 2004.

Heard, Robins, Cloud, Lubel & Greenwood, L.L.P.

By: _David Sandoval_
Bill Robins III
David Sandoval
Address and Telephone Numbers
**ATTORNEYS FOR BILLY THE KID**

[AUTHOR'S COMMENT: Really, in boldface, Robins and Sandoval are listed as Billy's lawyers! And New Mexico taxpayers footed the district court bills in Grant and De Baca Counties for these hoaxing antics.]

APPENDIX: 61. Attorney Sherry J. Tippett. . "Sixth Judicial District Court, State on New Mexico, County of Grant. Case No. MS-2003-11." "In the Matter of Catherine Antrim. Petitioner's [sic] Brief in Chief in Support of Exhumation." January 5, 2004.

## IN THE MATTER OF CATHERINE ANTRIM
## BILLY THE KID'S PRE-HEARING BRIEF

Comes now Petitioners Tom Sullivan, Sheriff of Lincoln County, Steve Sederwall, Deputy Sheriff of Lincoln County and Mayor of Capitan and Gary Graves, Sheriff of De Baca County (hereinafter "Petitioners") and by and through their Attorney, Sherry J. Tippett, hereby file this Brief in Chief in Support of the Exhumation of Catherine Antrim.

### HISTORY:

Petitioners filed a Petition to Exhume the Remains of Catherine Antrim on October 10, 2003. The Petition was made in conjunction with Investigation No. 2003-274 filed in the Lincoln County Sheriff's Office and Case No. 03-06-135-01 filed in the De Baca County Sheriff's Office. These investigations were filed for the purpose of determining the guilt or innocence of Sheriff Pat Garrett in the death of William H. Bonney aka "Billy the Kid." Probable cause is clearly laid out in the investigation statement. Catherine Antrim is the undisputed mother of William Bonney (hereinafter "Billy the Kid").

Notice of the Petition to Exhume the Remains was published in four consecutive weeks beginning October 16, 2003 in the Silver Coty Daily Press. On October 31, 2003 the Town filed a motion to intervene in this matter, such intervention was opposed by the Petitioners. Hearing on the intervention was initially set for November 21, 2003, however, on November 14, 2003, Judge James Foy recused himself from the matter. On November 25, 2003 the attorneys for Billy the Kid filed an unopposed Motion to Intervene and Request for Expedited Hearing. On December 5, 2003, Joani Amos-Staats filed a Motion to Intervene and Request for Expedited Hearing. Ms. Amos-Staats was also unopposed. On December 8, 2003 a hearing was held on the motions to intervene filed by the Town of Silver City, Billy the Kid and Joani Amos-Staats. On December 9, 2003 an order was entered granting the Town and Ms. Amos-Staats intervention in this case. The question of standing by Petitioners to bring this matter as well as the Intervention of Billy the Kid was reserved by this court until after the hearing set for Tuesday, January 27, 2004. The December 9, 2003 Order also outlined a briefing schedule of which this brief is responsive.

## 1. THEODORE VS. THEODORE

The December 9th Order directed all parties to brief the factors found in Theodore v. Theodore, 57 N.M. 434, 259 P.2d 795 (1953). The case of Theodore v. Theodore is a declaratory judgment case whereby a widow wished to exhume and relocate the remains of her late husband against the wishes of her husband's brother. The Supreme Court of New Mexico in a rather religiously intoned decision, denied the request of the widow to exhume her late husband, noting the "sanctity of eternal rest." The Theodore case is over fifty years old and is based on biblical quotes and Christian religious tenets. The Court ends the opinion by noting that "the accident of death struck not once but twice, if, indeed not thrice in quick succession in the ranks of those disturbing the tomb of Tut-Ankh-Amen." Id. 57, N.M. at 439. A great deal has changed in the intervening years in the area of scientific evidence, in particular the solid evidentiary tool of DNA. Moreover, the courts are no longer likely to rely on religious grounds, biblical quotes or incidents of superstition as a basis for deciding legal issues relating to the exhumation of a body in 2004.

> [AUTHOR'S COMMENT: The Theodore case is misused, since "authority to disinter a body and bury it elsewhere" is irrelevant to Antrim's exhumation, which fails justification because of uncertain location of her remains for DNA matching to the Kid's remains – also in an uncertain location, and with a 1962 precedent case blocking their exhumation. So the Antrim exhumation fails by Tippett's own reasoning: DNA. So everything that follows here is moot.]

In determining whether authority to disinter a body and bury it elsewhere should be granted, the court in Theodore listed the following factors: 1) the interest of the public, 2) wishes of the decedent, 3) rights and feelings of those entitled to be heard by reason of relationship, 4) the rights and principles of religious bodies or other organizations which granted the right to inter the body in the first place of burial, and 5) the question of whether or not consent was given to the burial in the first place of interment by the one claiming the right of removal.

In applying these factors to the case at hand, it is important to note two details that are factually distinguishable from the Theodore case.

1) The petitioners do not wish to have the body of Catherine Antrim relocated to another city, as did the widow in the Theodore case. The exhumation would be performed professionally with expert forensic scientists familiar with DNA analysis and procedure.

2)      Catherine Antrim has already been disturbed from "eternal rest" when the Town of Silver City moved her remains in 1882 [sic – 1881]. To the best of Petitioners knowledge, there was no opposition to the exhumation and reburial of her remains at that time.

*a. Interest of the Public:* Since the early 1990's, DNA testing has been used as a research tool in various high profile cases including the cases involving Thomas Jefferson (where slaves have attempted to establish lineage) as well as the exhumation and DNA testing of Jesse James. See 15 Harv. Blackletter J. 211, DNA and the Slave-Descendant Nexus: A Theoretical Challenge to Traditional Notions of Heirship Jurisprudence. Spring 2000. In the Jesse James case, a Missouri District Judge issued an Order to Exhume the remains of Jesse James. A team of forensic scientists then opened James' grave and obtained DNA samples. Similar to the case at hand, the exhumation was supported by the only known descendant, Jesse James IV. Mitochondrial DNA tests compared two teeth from James with living relatives. George Washington University Professor James Starrs, who has also been consulted on the case at hand, led the James exhumation and found that with better than 99% certainty that the remains were of Jesse James. Id. at 214. See also James E. Starrs, Recent Developments in Federal and State Rules Pertaining to Medical and Scientific Expert Testimony. 34 Duq. L. Rev. 813 (1996). DNA testing in ancestry and paternity cases is a relatively new tool which is extremely useful to society in finding the truth. Finding the truth in any legal proceeding is always in the public interest ...

[AUTHOR'S NOTE: Tippett's arguments are still irrelevant, because in her cited modern cases of Jefferson and James, there are living kin sources of DNA for matchings. Tippett and crew have no verifiable useable DNA on the planet. And there is no "public interest" if she has no way of proving her claims.]

*b. Wishes of the Decedent:* To the best of Petitioners' knowledge, there are no known wishes of Catherine Antrim burial requests, however, Petitioners must again note that Mrs. Antrim has been moved once by the very party that now opposes her exhumation on the grounds that she deserves "eternal rest."

[AUTHOR'S NOTE: Since Tippett lied about OMI giving exhumation permission in her October 10, 2003 brief, one can assume the above is a willful lie, not ignorance: since it is known that Antrim's remains were moved in 1881, without public official scrutiny, by a private citizen, John Miller, who purchased the cemetery land. So the "moving" party had not been Silver City back then.]

*c. Rights and Feelings of those Entitled to be Heard by Reasons of Relationship*: The only known, alleged heirs to Catherine Antrim are Elbert Garcia of Santa Rosa New Mexican Dr. Roman Mireles of Whittier, California. Both Mr. Garcia and Dr. Miriles support of the exhumation [sic] and wish to provide DNA samples to compare with Catherine Antrim's remains to establish lineage ...

**[AUTHOR'S NOTE: Tippett is again lying. Garcia and Morales merely claim a relationship to the Kid – but have no basis; consequently they have no kinship standing for the exhumations. Garcia, in particular, claims the Kid was his grandfather. But he has not exhumed his actual grandfather to check DNA. Even the hoaxers gave up on presenting these fellows soon afterward.]**

*d. The Rights and Principles of Religious Bodies and Other Organizations Which Granted the Right to Inter the Body in the First Place of Burial:* To the best of Petitioners' knowledge, there is no certainty of the religious beliefs of Catherine Antrim, other than the inference that she may have been of Presbyterian faith due to the fact that she was married to William Antrim in the Presbyterian Church in Santa Fe. However, the Presbyterian Church did not inter Mrs. Antrim.

*e. The Question of Whether or not Consent was Given to the Burial in the First Place of Interment by the One Claiming the Right of Removal:* This question is not applicable to the facts in this matter ...

### *Conclusions Regarding Theodore case*:

In summary, three of the five factors laid out in the <u>Theodore</u> to be considered before an Order of Exhumation is granted are not applicable ... Public interest appears to be the moist important factor in the current Petition ... The case law clearly supports exhumation where evidence of probative value will be obtained. The second most important factor are the wishes of known heirs, both of whom, as mentioned above, support exhumation.

**[AUTHOR'S NOTE: Tippett is again lying 100%.]**

## 2. <u>RIGHT OF PETITIONERS TO BRING THIS ACTION</u>:

Two of the three Petitioners are duly elected Sheriffs in the State of New Mexico. One Petitioner is a Deputy Sheriff and also the duly elected Mayor of Capitan, New Mexico. Prior to filing the Petition a Probable Cause statement was prepared in conjunction with Case # 2003-274. The Probable Cause statement was finalized on 12/31/03 and is attached as Exhibit I.

[AUTHOR'S NOTE: I got this Probable Cause Statement Plaintiffs' Exhibit 1 – through the Kennedy Han law firm as a public document. Before that, then-Sheriff Sullivan denied it in my IPRA requests.]

In essence, this investigation was launched because there were too many unanswered questions regarding the alleged murder of Billy the Kid by Sheriff Pat Garrett. Such questions include the lack of knowledge surrounding the gun used by Billy the Kid to kill Deputy Bell and its implication, based on additional facts, that Sheriff Garrett may have had a hand in the escape of Billy the Kid from the Lincoln County Jail. See Exhibit 2, attached, The Sworn Affidavit of Homer D. Overton, next door neighbor of Mrs. Pat Garrett.

[AUTHOR'S NOTE: I got the Homer Overton Affidavit as this Plaintiffs' Exhibit 2 through the Kennedy Han law firm as a public document. Before that, then-Sheriff Sullivan denied all Case 2003-274 records in my IPRA requests. Also, Tippett is lying again. Overton was not a neighbor, only a brief visitor in 1940 when the widow was dead for four years.]

On the day of the purported killing of Billy the Kid, Sheriff Garrett's own deputy expressed his doubt as to whether Garrett had actually shot Billy the kid when he said "Pat, the Kid would not come to this place: you have shot the wrong man." … In addition, there are discrepancies between where the body was found in the official Coroner's Jury Report (the report stated that the body was found on the floor of Maxwell's bedroom) and the eyewitness accounts which state the body was moved immediately following the shooting to the carpenter's shop where it was laid out on a workbench.

[AUTHOR'S NOTE: "Discrepancies" as to "where the body was found" appears to be Tippett's own weird contribution, since the hoaxers do not use it. Also, it makes no sense, since moving a body does not change where it was killed.]

There are other inconsistencies found in the report (second bullet went through the headboard of the bed; however, the Petitioners have located the headboard from Maxwell's bed and there are no bullet holes in it).

[AUTHOR'S NOTE: Tippett is unaware that the alleged headboard – which I also saw – is missing its entire central panel; leaving only a thin outer frame. There is no place for a bullet hole!]

Lastly, two other documents lend credence to the possibility that Garrett did not shoot Billy the Kid on July 14, 1881. A Work Progress Administration (WPA) Federal Writer's Project compiled a book of oral histories from the citizens of Lincoln County. The book, entitled "Early Days in Lincoln County" was compiled by Frances E. Totty and published by the Library of Congress, Folklore-Life History (1938). This book documents the following statement made by Charles Reuark [sic - Remark] a Lincoln resident:

> The people around Lincoln say Garrett didn't kill Billie (sic) the Kid. John Poe was with Garrett the night he was supposed to … said that he didn't see the man that Garrett killed. I can take you to the grave in Hell's High Acre, an old government cemetery, where Billie (sic) was supposed to be buried and show you the grave. The cook at Pete Maxwell's was always putting flowers on the grave and praying at it. This woman thought a lot of Billie (sic), but after Garrett killed the man at Maxwell's home her grandson was never seen again and Billie (sic) was seen by Bill Nicholi an Indian scout. Bill saw him in Mexico.

**[AUTHOR'S NOTE: This information was contributed to the Probable Cause Statement for Case No. 2003-274 by fellow hoaxer U.S. Marshals Service Historian David Turk.]**

In summary, the probable cause statement in this case indicates conflicting statements between Pat F. Garrett and Dept. Poe; blatant inconsistencies between the Coroner's Jury Report and eyewitness accounts as to the location of the body after the murder; evidence that does not match the eyewitness accounts of the shooting, and statements by current citizens that believe Garrett assisted Billy the Kid's escape. Cumulatively, this evidence clearly supports the Petitioners contention that probable cause exists to go forward with the exhumation of Catherine Antrim for the purpose of finding whether or not Billy the Kid was killed by Pat Garrett on July 14, 1881 in Fort Sumner.

**[AUTHOR'S NOTE: Tippett's argument has merely been a restatement of the Probable Cause's hoaxed claims – as already debunked in the above text. Furthermore, her argument is irrelevant, since there exists no valid DNA in Catherine Antrim's gravesite to establish anything. And exhumation would be blocked by the counter-petition of Joani Amos-Staats anyway.]**

Because the probable cause test is met by the Petitioners, it is clear they have standing as law enforcement officials to bring this Petition as a necessary part of their investigation …

[AUTHOR'S NOTE: In the start of the hoax, the hoaxers constantly claimed law enforcement standing. They only did a switcheroo to "hobbyists" for my IPRA request and litigation.]

Other than discovering the truth in this matter, and resolving these questions once and for all, the Petitioners have no stake whatsoever in this lawsuit. Rumor to the contrary notwithstanding, there is no book deal, no movie deal and no plan to sell tickets to the exhumation of Catherine Antrim.

[AUTHOR'S NOTE: Too bad that Tippett is now dead. She would have to eat her words. And the hoaxers' film crew tire marks over Antrim's grave when Tippett was writing this, should have given her pause anyway as the media circus was starting.]

### 3. PUBLIC INTEREST:

In determining whether to grant authority to disinter a body, one factor to be considered is "interest to the public" ... The public interest is always served by discovering the truth ... The history of the Lincoln County Wars [sic - War] is a very rich and important part of the history of New Mexico. No doubt that much more will be learned about this period and the players involved in the two warring factions of the Lincoln County war by going forward with this investigation ... Intense is the interest, both nationally and internationally, in matters involving Billy the Kid, the Lincoln County Wars [sic] and the general history of New Mexico in the 1880's. While it is true that no one will likely be charged with a crime if this investigation is allowed to go forward, this factor alone should not bar the Petitioners from discovering the truth.

### 4. IN RE APPLICATION OF LOIS TELFER, PETITIONER FOR THE REMOVAL OF THE BODY OF WILLIAM H. BONNEY, DECEASED FROM THE FT. SUMNER CEMETERY FOR REINTERMENT IN THE LINCOLN, NEW MEXICO CEMETERY:

In Re Application of Telfer was filed on June 26, 1961 by a New York beautician claiming to be the only surviving heir of Billy the Kid. See Petition No. 3255, De Baca County District Court ... The Telfer Petition requested the court to issue an Order of Exhumation to disinter the remains of Billy the Kid and remove the remains from the Ft. Sumner cemetery to the Village of Lincoln cemetery ... The County of De Baca intervened in the case as well as Louis A. Bowdre, heir of Charlie Bowdre. In denying the Petition the District Court Judge, E.T. Hensely [sic – Kinsley], found that "the remains of William H. Bonney are still buried in the said Fort Sumner Cemetery." De Baca Case No. 3255, Final

Decree April 6, Findings of Fact, Paragraph 4 (1962). However, in Paragraph 2 of the Conclusions of Law, the Judge states that the "Petition herein cannot be granted since the site of the grave of William H. Bonney, deceased, cannot be located." Id. at 3. Paragraph 3 of the Conclusions of Law also states that relief cannot be granted "since a search for the grave of the said William H. Bonney, deceased, in order to disinter said body, will inevitably lead to disturbing the remai8ns of other persons, buried in said cemetery, including the said Charles Bowdre, deceased. Id. aqt 3.

Conclusion No. 3 appears to be inconsistent with Conclusion No. 2. It is unclear how the judge can find that the remains of Bowdre will be disturbed if, as Conclusion 2 indicates, the grave cannot be located. In any event, the entire record of this case has been reviewed by Petitioners counsel and it does not appear that any experts testified on: A) the exact location of Billy the Kid's grave and B) whether the remains could be exhumed without disturbing other human remains.

**[AUTHOR'S NOTE: This argument makes no sense. Since it is impossible to tell exactly where Billy is buried, and his gravesite has three contiguous bodies - one being Bowdre's - other remains would be disturbed. Furthermore, the Bowdre family is still prepared to testify against Billy's exhumation on the same basis as in the Telfer case.]**

The holding in the Telfer Application is over forty years old and again, the tool of DNA and other sophisticated devices used to determine both the exact location of remains and whether those remains can be exhumed without disturbing other bodies was not available ...

**[AUTHOR'S NOTE: Tippett still does not get it that there exists no DNA to distinguish bones as Billy's; and if skeletons were detected at the current grave-site, they could not be disrupted, since one might be protected Bowdre's.]**

## CONCLUSION:

Petitioners Sheriffs' Sullivan, Graves and Deputy Sheriff and Mayor Sederwall have established probable cause for Investigations No. 2003-274. The Petitioners have shown that they have legitimate right to bring this action and have met the standing requirements under New Mexico law. Petitioners have also shown that it is in the public interest to exhume the remains of Catherine Antrim and proceed with this investigation.

Respectfully submitted,
Sherry J. Tippett
Attorney for Petitioners

**APPENDIX: 62. Gale Cooper's Courtroom Display Board of Law Enforcement Nature of Case No. 2003-274, for Evidentiary Hearing of January 21, 2011**

---

# LINCOLN COUNTY SHERIFF'S DEPARTMENT CASE # 2003-274
## "BILLY THE KID CASE INVESTIGATION"

### THE MURDER CASE: FILED - 2003:
AGAINST PAT GARRETT

\*\*\*\*\*\*\*\*\*\*\*\*\*\*\*\*\*\*\*\*\*

PROBABLE CAUSE STATEMENT

Pat Garrett is a murderer in Fort Sumner on July 14, 1881

SUB-INVESTIGATION

Garrett helped Billy the Kid kill deputy guards on April 28, 1881

SHERIFF SULLIVAN
DEPUTY SEDERWALL
UNDERSHERIFF VIRDEN

### FORENSIC INVESTIGATION I - 2003-2004:
TWO EXHUMATION ATTEMPTS

\*\*\*\*\*\*\*\*\*\*\*\*\*\*\*\*\*\*\*\*\*

DIG UP BILLY AND HIS MOTHER FOR DNA

If DNA does not match, an innocent victim is in the Fort Sumner grave and Pat Garrett is a murderer.

FAILED: EXHUMATIONS BLOCKED; NO DNA

### FORENSIC INVESTIGATION II - 2004:
CARPENTER'S BENCH FORENSICS

\*\*\*\*\*\*\*\*\*\*\*\*\*\*\*\*\*\*\*\*\*

GETTING "DNA OF BILLY THE KID"

Dr. Henry Lee gets specimens from carpenter's workbench
Orchid Cellmark Lab extracts DNA

SUCCESS: ALLEGED BILLY THE KID DNA OBTAINED

SHERIFF VIRDEN
DEPUTY SULLIVAN
DEPUTY SEDERWALL

### FORENSIC INVESTIGATION III- May 19, 2005:
ARIZONA EXHUMATIONS OF BILLY THE KID CLAIMANT

\*\*\*\*\*\*\*\*\*\*\*\*\*\*\*\*\*\*\*\*\*

DNA MATCHINGS

Bench DNA matched with John Miller
Bench DNA matched with William Hudspeth

SUCCESS: DNA MATCH IS CLAIMED

### FORENSIC INVESTIGATION IV - 2007:
EXHUMATION OF BILLY THE KID CLAIMANT "BRUSHY BILL"

\*\*\*\*\*\*\*\*\*\*\*\*\*\*\*\*\*\*\*\*\*

FAILED: BLOCKED BY TEXAS OFFICIALS

APPENDIX: 63. Gale Cooper Gale Cooper's Courtroom Display Board of the Dr. Henry Lee and Orchid Cellmark Requested Records, for Evidentiary Hearing of January 21, 2011

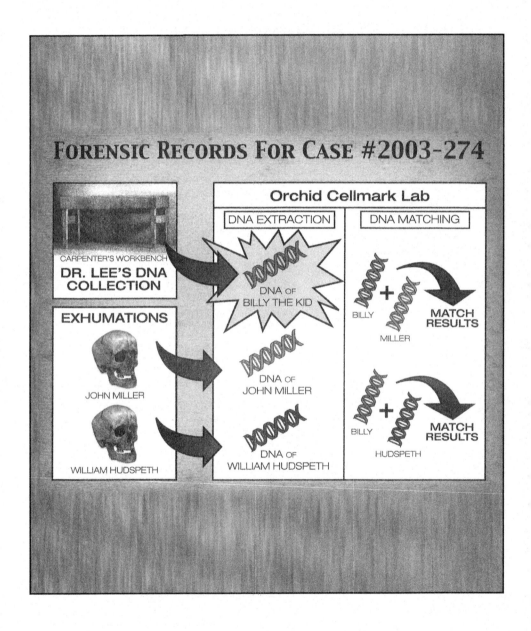

APPENDIX: 64. Gale Cooper termination letter to Attorney Martin E. Threet: "Re: Termination of legal services for Gale Cooper and the *De Baca County News* vs Lincoln County Sheriff Rick Virden et al case." February 21, 2011

Dear Attorney Threet:

After careful consideration and legal consultation, I have decided to terminate your legal services for my Sandoval District Case: Gale Cooper and the *De Baca County News* vs Lincoln County Sheriff Rick Virden et al.

Thus, this letter constitutes my notification of that decision and my ending of any and all future services by you with regard to that case.

**BACKGROUND OF CASE:**

Begun in 2007 with the pro bono services of the Barnett law firm, my Sandoval County District Court open records violation case is against Lincoln County Sheriff Rick Virden and his participating deputies, Messrs. Tom Sullivan and Steve Sederwall, for refusal to turn over their forensic DNA records of Lincoln County Sheriff's Department Case # 2003-274 - named by them the "Billy the Kid Case or Investigation."

That open records violation case was initiated in my capacity as an investigative author exposing the Billy the Kid Case as an historic/forensic hoax: a subject treated in my book *MegaHoax: The Strange Plot to Exhume Billy the Kid.*

The broader purposes of my open records violation case were: 1) protecting Old West history of Pat Garrett and Billy the Kid; 2) sustaining the state's public records act law; and 3) demonstrating an unusual example of corrupt cronyism in New Mexico politics.

In keeping with that broader purpose, was my intent to depose, not only my defendants, but other public official participants in the Billy the Kid Case, including then governor, Bill Richardson, and his major political donor, Attorney Bill Robins III.

My termination of Barnett law firm services occurred in 2008 after Attorney Mickey Barnett's forthright and appreciated communication to me of a conflict of interest (his good friend, State Senator Rod Adair, asked him to "kill the case," allegedly to protect Sheriff Rick Virden).

In 2008, communicating all the above information, I engaged the pro bono services of Attorney Blair Dunn for that open records violation case. As a relatively new lawyer, Attorney Dunn included you, also pro bono, as his associate and mentor, for added expertise. However, after Attorney Dunn moved to South Dakota, your role increased in terms of your performing that open records violation case's Hearings without his presence.

The judge's granting of our Motion for Summary Judgment on November 20, 2009 demonstrated both the merits of my case and the fine legal work performed by yourself and Attorney Dunn.

In 2010, however, the defendants ignored the judge's order and still withheld the demanded forensic records. This response resulted in the judge's scheduling an all-day Evidentiary Hearing bench trial for January 21, 2011.

## CONCERNS:

My concerns, leading to my decision to terminate your services, date to the period leading up to and including that Evidentiary Hearing bench trial of January 21, 2011. The concerns are as follows:

- FAILURE TO ACT ON OUR FILED MOTION TO EXCEED PAGES: Since the November 20, 2009 Motion for Summary Judgment Hearing, we had a motion before the judge to include my massive, arguably necessary, and historically important pieces of evidence into the case (as "Exhibit B: 1-64"). Though on the docket, that motion was not brought up by you or Attorney Dunn at the November 2009 Motion for Summary Judgment Hearing. Subsequently, despite my repeated requests for inclusion of that critical information, that motion was never again raised with the judge.

- DISTURBING ADVICE REGARDING DEFENDANT VIRDEN: On September 14, 2010, you sent me a fax which concerned me (enclosed), in which you encouraged me to dismiss defendant Virden as per one of his attorney's (Henry Narvaez) offer to have him "get the information." Since records recovery was Virden's responsibility, and its lack was the reason for my case, I refused. Furthermore, I was aware that Henry Narvaez, was your close associate of 30 years. But you immediately and appropriately communicated my refusal of the offer. Nevertheless, I felt uneasy by your statement in the fax that "it is a good thing to do [dismiss Virden], it will short circuit all this terrible situation ..." In truth, such an acceptance would have ruined my case, since Virden was the only defendant who was the responsible Records Custodian. And no records were actually being presented. It seemed to me to be only a "sucker offer." But you had never informed me of any conflict of interest with the Narvaez law firm, so I again allayed my concerns.

- LOST DEPOSITION OPPORTUNITIES: From the start of my work with you and Attorney Dunn, I requested depositions of Governor Bill Richardson and Attorney Bill Robins III. And after I learned, on March 9, 2010, that Lincoln County Attorney Alan Morel had gossiped about himself secreting the requested records, I requested his deposition also. But I was informed by you and Attorney Dunn that depositions were legally premature. Then, after the September 9, 2010 Hearing granting the Evidentiary Hearing, I was told that depositions were now appropriate, and that your office would send out the subpoenas for them. And I was never informed of any inhibitory problems like conflict of interest or political discomfort. As months passed, I was told by your staff that there was difficulty serving the subpoenas – especially on Attorney Morel. But when I informed your office that I could easily get him served in a day by a local contact, it was admitted to me that no attempt at service had been made. And it appears that the other subpoenas were likewise delayed. The result was that Attorney Morel evaded deposition, and Attorney Robins was scheduled so late that there was no time to subpoena Attorney David Sandoval, named as important by Attorney Robins. And Governor Richardson, as expected, claimed executive privilege; but you refused to subpoena him again in January, after he was out of office. So lost was valuable pre-trial information. And lost were the weeks upon weeks of my work writing those depositions (up to 70 pages for Morel).

- ISSUE OF PRE-TRIAL WITNESS SUBPOENAS: When I spoke to the judge's court reporter a week before the Evidentiary Hearing trial, she said no witness list had been submitted by our side. When you and I met on Monday, January 17th, you said you would subpoena Virden, Sullivan, Sederwall, and Morel; and even called in your secretary, Pam Eckstrom, to confirm that information for the process server.

2) Concerns pertaining to the pre-trial preparations:

- DRAMATIC IMPORTANCE OF TRIAL: I had made it clear to you and to Attorney Dunn that this trial was my hoped-for, show piece victory – after my 8 years of exposing the Billy the Kid Case hoax, 4 years of fighting to get its incriminating documents, months of writing all its depositions (which could now be used for witness questioning), and laboring to print and label multiple copies of the massive amounts of evidence. In addition, there was the dramatic issue of the defendants' contempt of the judge's records turn-over order, 14 months earlier. Furthermore, with witnesses Virden, Sullivan, Sederwall, and Morel, I felt the perniciousness of their long-term collusion to conceal the documents could be revealed. To that end, and trusting in your own excellent courtroom presentations and moving oratory in past Hearings, I invited interested people from all over New Mexico – including Pat Garrett's grandchildren - as well as hiring a videographer to film the anticipated historic event in Billy the Kid and open records act history. And I felt that the judge, who from the start had said he was interested in the case, had generously given us the luxury of a whole day to show off our evidence.

- OUR MEETING OF MONDAY, JANUARY 17th: I brought to your office the huge amount of work I had done for the trial: Exhibit B folders with 80 labeled pieces of evidence; indexes for those exhibits arranged by topics (like "Existence of Records"); outline for possible trial organization; opening statement; hundreds of pages of deposition questions I wrote, which could be used in witness examinations; and multiple 2' x 3' exhibit boards of key exhibits, as well as 2' x 3' exhibit boards of full-color, illustrated flow charts I had made showing the progression of the DNA records production and the overview of the forensics in the Billy the Kid Case.

- MOTION TO EXCEED PAGES: Once again I emphasized that I wanted Exhibit B: 1-80 presented at the start of the trial; and even wrote in that step in a suggested list of trial issues.

- OUR WHOLE-DAY MEETING WITH ATTORNEY DUNN ON JANUARY 18th: Meeting in your office, you, me, and Attorney Dunn reviewed the trial issues. Since my knowledge of the Billy the Kid Case specifics was great, it was decided to use me as the first witness to provide details and to reference the exhibits; and then to use me later to rebut their witnesses, while again presenting exhibits. At the end of the day I left with the understanding that Attorney Dunn would do the opening argument and you would conduct the trial for the rest of the day. I was confident that as a team of three we would put on a spectacular trial – and any earlier concerns were allayed.

3) Concerns pertaining to the January 21, 2011 trial are as follows:

- CONGREGATING AT YOUR OFFICE: The day of the trial, you, me, and Attorney Dunn met at your office. I was given no indication of anything being changed or amiss with regard to our trial plans; and, of course, felt confident.

- SHOCK JUST BEFORE TRIAL: The shock occurred just before the 9 AM start of the trial. As I was setting up the materials on our table, Attorney Dunn said to me that you had told him that *he alone* would be doing the entire trial! He did not say why you had backed out. And only when I subsequently got legal consultation was I informed that in a circumstance like that – the loss of my lead attorney without prior notice - I should have been given the option of a conference outside the courtroom in which I could decide if I wanted the judge to receive a request by my attorneys for a postponement and continuance.

- WITNESSES' NON-ATTENDANCE: Next it became apparent that you had not subpoenaed my witnesses as promised and as needed. So only Sheriff Rick Virden and his past deputy, Steve Sederwall, came. So I lost my two crucial witnesses: past sheriff and deputy, Tom Sullivan - who had admitted to knowledge of each of the requested documents in his August 18, 2008 deposition - and Lincoln County Attorney Alan Morel – who had boasted privately about possessing the requested documents.

- THE FIASCO TRIAL: Though Attorney Dunn showed himself to be impressively poised when taking over without notice, it was clear that this was his first trial (the court reporter even having to show him how to enter exhibits). In addition, not knowing he would have total responsibility, apparently left him less focused on the big pictures: contempt of the judge's past order, and Virden as the solely responsible Records Custodian. What resulted was the most traumatic experience of my life: a combination of my feeling blindsided by your betrayal of me and my case, and my watching my years of preparation go down the drain for lack of presentation. And, while this fiasco was taking place, you merely alternated your silence with falling asleep! But you did advise Attorney Dunn to give no closing argument. So, the case, already adrift for lack of my massive evidence, ended with no clear closure. The result was that the judge merely weakened his past decision – by inappropriate focus on Sederwall instead of Virden - which put my obtaining the records in jeopardy. And lost was my opportunity to showcase the just defeat of a preposterous hoax and its public officials' audacious violation of open records law.

To make the specifics of my dissatisfaction more clear, the following provides a summary of trial's problems and set-backs: with the big picture being the focus of records production responsibility lessened on Virden and put on Sederwall.

1. NON-PARTICIPATION IMPROPRIETY: Purposefully withheld from the trial were your 50 years of courtroom experience, unquestionable skill in courtroom control, oratorical drama, and even assistance to Attorney Dunn.
2. NOT INFORMING ME OF MY LEGAL OPTIONS: Before the trial began, I was not informed of my legal right to ask that my attorneys request a continuance from the judge - given that one of my attorneys suddenly found himself unable to participate.
3. LOSS OF CRITICAL WITNESSES: Your lack of subpoenaing of my witnesses, allowed Messrs. Sullivan and Morel evade the trial, thus, terribly weakening my case.
4. LOSS OF EXHIBIT B: Despite our having a Motion to Extend Pages, it was not brought up; so most of my evidence never reached the court record.
5. BLOCKING OF NEWSPAPER ARTICLES: When Attorney Dunn did not counter the defense objection to my entering newspaper articles as evidence of the records' existence, you did not, to my knowledge, assist him with the argument that their multiple quotes by the defendants contributed (among other evidence) to my knowledge that the records existed. So all those exhibits were lost to the court.
6. NOT ENTERING PROOFS OF RECORDS EXISTENCE: Available were the August 18, 2008 depositions of Messrs. Sullivan and Sederwall, in which both described knowledge of the records requested.

(I had even separated out and labeled each of their comments to that effect.) When it became clear that Attorney Dunn was omitting that crucial information, you did not direct him to enter it into the record.

7. VIRDEN TESTIMONY: In Attorney Dunn's examination of Sheriff Virden, he never emphasized the central point of the trial: why, as sheriff, had he not taken out a court order and obtained the requested records. And, even though you yourself had mentioned that option in our meeting the day before, you did not come to Attorney Dunn's assistance by reminding him of that line of questioning. In addition, you also apparently did not encourage Attorney Dunn to express outrage at Sheriff Virden's contempt of court by ignoring a judge's order from 14 months past.

8. SEDERWALL TESTIMONY: Though I had warned both of you repeatedly not to permit Mr. Sederwall prolonged testifying because he is such an excellent liar. Yet he was allowed to monopolize most of the afternoon with his rambling gibberish, and without a single objection from us. In addition, I had made clear that he should not be shown the "Lincoln County Sheriff's Department Supplemental Report," since he had concocted, in his 2008 deposition, that it was a "forgery." Nevertheless, it was shown to him, with the predicted response; and with the judge's resulting refusal of it as an exhibit. In addition, Mr. Sederwall's preposterously long and exhausting testimony used up the valuable time that could have been used by putting me back on the stand for rebuttal, or leaving more time for a closing argument. Furthermore, our lack of objections gave him credibility and an appearance of importance in the case which, I feel, ultimately misled the judge in formulating a decision skewed to him. So, in my opinion, Mr. Sederwall's time on the stand did great damage to my case – thought it was entirely preventable by the very same objections used in the morning by Attorney Kevin Brown with me whenever I gave narrative answers during my own examination.

9. SULLIVAN DEPOSITION LOSS: The loss of Mr. Sullivan as a witness was another loss for presenting evidence of the records' existence – and resulted from his not being appropriately subpoenaed.

10. MOREL LOSS: The loss of Attorney Morel as a witness was another loss for presenting evidence of the records' existence – and resulted from his not being appropriately subpoenaed.

11. NO CLOSING ARGUMENT: Your stopping Attorney Dunn from doing a closing argument followed the earlier problem of permitting Mr. Sederwall's endless blather. And, it is my opinion, that with the case so adrift by then, needed were a few sentences returning focus to Virden and to his contempt for the judge's past order. Yet as a seasoned trial lawyer and masterful orator, you <u>halted purposefully</u> that last chance by Attorney Dunn to recover somewhat the badly lost ground.

12. JUDGE'S DECISION: Given the lack of focus on Virden, the missed inclusion of crucial evidence, the lack of oratory about contempt, the

unnecessary focus on Sederwall, it was no wonder that the judge weakened his prior order by naming Sederwall instead of Virden for records turn-over, and never even mentioned contempt. <u>And this situation – as well as the rest of my complaints listed here - is not a criticism of Attorney Dunn, who functioned miraculously in almost untenable circumstances for an unprepared trial novice.</u> The problem rests, in my opinion, squarely on your shoulders for leaving him in that position, and by your producing primarily silence or somnolence, instead of assistance, throughout the trial.

13. MY HUMILIATION: At the end, I was left humiliated: appearing unprepared by evidence to support my claim of records existing, and unprotected by my legal representation – as if you yourself felt my case did not merit your active participation. And the tragedy is that only with the trial conducted as this one was, could that false appearance have been created – since my evidence is impeccable, and our original plan for our three-fold participation would have been unbeatable. And, of course, the "show" that I had hoped to present to the interested spectators from all over New Mexico fell far down from its expected heights.

## SUMMARY:

In summary, the Evidentiary Hearing trial on January 21, 2011 became the most traumatic event of my life because the crisis was both unexpected and unnecessary. Instead, the trial should have been a joyful culmination of thousands of hours and thousands of dollars worth of my work.

I do not know why you made the many deleterious choices you did; and the reasons are now irrelevant. It remains to me to see if I can repair the damage now done. But irreparable is any possibility of my trusting you to participate in any manner at all in the remaining parts of my case.

## RESOLUTION:

As I stated, I am terminating the use of your legal services on my Virden et al case. And, as in the situation with Attorney Mickey Barnett, in any future damages Hearing, all your prior billings will obviously be presented.

And though this letter documents potentially serious professional ethics issues involved in your lead-up to and your conduct in my Evidentiary Hearing trial, at this time, I, nevertheless, choose to take no action against you.

Please confine all future communication with me to writing to insure clear communication.

Sincerely,
Gale Cooper

APPENDIX: 65. Gale Cooper. "Plaintiff Gale Cooper's Pre-Evidentiary Hearing Brief." November 14, 2012. (Copied to Attorneys Patrick Griebel for the De Baca County News, Henry Narvaez for Sheriff Virden, and Kevin Brown for Sullivan and Sederwall)

THIRTEENTH JUDICIAL DISTRICT COURT
COUNTY OF SANDOVAL
STATE OF NEW MEXICO

GALE COOPER and DE BACA COUNTY NEWS,
a New Mexico Corporation,

Plaintiffs,

vs.                              No. D-1329-CV-2007-01364

RICK VIRDEN, LINCOLN COUNTY SHERIFF and CUSTODIANOF THE RECORDS OF THE LINCOLN COUNTY SHERIFF'S OFFICE; and STEVEN M. SEDERWALL, FORMER LINCOLN COUNTYDEPUTYSHERIFF; and THOMAS T. SULLIVAN, FORMER INCOLN COUNTY SHERIFF AND FORMER LINCOLN COUNTY DEPUTY SHERIFF,

Defendants.

## PLAINTIFF GALE COOPER'S PRE-EVIDENTIARY HEARING BRIEF

COMES NOW, Plaintiff Gale Cooper ("Plaintiff Cooper"), as *pro se*, and submits this Brief for the Court-ordered Evidentiary Hearing on new evidence, and prior to the Court-ordered mediation, to support sanctions and Inspection of Public Records Act ("IPRA") damages against the Defendants for discovery abuse and for willful non-compliance with records production. Exhibits will be provided in the Evidentiary Hearing, and not in this Brief.

### I. INTRODUCTION

This enforcement case ("the litigation") arose from Plaintiff Cooper's records requests. The Defendants, without statutory or factual justification, have refused all records, have ignored Court-ordered turn-overs, have shamed recovery attempts, and have given tampered records to the Court as genuine. Plaintiff Cooper contends that these evasions merit stringent punishments.

### II. SUMMARY OF PROCEEDINGS

#### A. IPRA RECORDS REQUESTS

1. RECORDS: Requested records are from Lincoln County Sheriff's Department Case No. 2003-274 ("Case 2003-274"), which alleged that, by DNA, Pat Garrett could be proved to be a murderer of an innocent victim; and that William Bonney a/k/a Billy the Kid had survived as an old-timer. A sub-investigation was the Kid's jailbreak murders of his deputy guards.

2. REQUESTS (April 2007 to June 2007): Plaintiff Cooper, on April 24, 2007, first requested from Virden records of: (a) Dr. Henry Lee's ("Lee") DNA recovery from a carpenter's bench; and (b) Orchid Cellmark Laboratory's ("Orchid Cellmark") DNA from Lee's specimens and (c) DNA from exhumed bones; and (d) DNA matchings of bench's DNA to bones' DNA.

3. ALL RECORDS REFUSED: No denial by 14-2-11(B) was given. No exception by 14-2-1 (A)(1-9) was used. Virden responded merely that his deputies, Sullivan and Sederwall, had records and called them private property in their June 21, 2007 "Memorandum" to him.

## B. COMPLAINT TO ENFORCE IPRA (October 15, 2007, Amended November 2, 2007)

Plaintiff Cooper brought a 14-2-12(A)(2) IPRA enforcement suit against Virden as records custodian, and against his Deputy investigators as his agents. In his March 5, 2008 Motion to Dismiss, Virden denied "possession or control of the records requested." P. 2, ¶ B. 1 At the Motion's Hearing, the Court determined proper venue, and continued the litigation.

## C. DISCOVERY: DEPOSITIONS (August 18, 2008, September 8, 2008)

1. SULLIVAN AND SEDERWALL: In their August 18, 2008 depositions, they called the records trade secrets from a private hobby; and Sederwall said he had a Lee bench report.

3. VIRDEN: On September 8, 2008 - following his September 3, 2008 turn-over of his alleged file of Case 2003-274 - said he possessed no requested records in that file.

## D. SUMMARY JUDGMENT HEARING (November 20, 2009)

1. Plaintiff Cooper argued that Virden "could either file request demands that these two people [Sullivan and Sederwall] deliver records or he could go ahead and write to Henry Lee and he could write to Orchid Cellmark, give me these." TR 11/20/09, p. 16, ln. 18-21.

2. Virden's counsel stated: "We simply cannot produce something that we don't have and never did. ... [H]e doesn't know if this laboratory report [sic] exists." *Id.* p. 20, ln. 6-18. Sullivan's and Sederwall's counsel argued they were not public official deputy employees. *Id.* p. 24, ln. 23-25.

3. Granted was Plaintiffs' Motion for Summary Judgment, with the Court finding: (a) Sullivan and Sederwall acted as Lincoln County Deputies; (b) the investigation was by the Lincoln County Sheriff's Department; and (c) the evidence was public record to be turned over.

## E. SEDERWALL TURN-OVER OF LEE FLOORBOARD REPORT (February 18, 2010)

## F. HEARING ON MOTION FOR PRESENTMENT (March 9, 2010)

Virden produced no records, arguing that: "we not be required to produce documents that we are not in possession of." TR 3/9/10 p. 6, ln. 1-2. Sederwall's counsel falsely presented the unrequested Lee floorboard report as meeting the records request. *Id.* p. 6, ln 15-26.

## G. VIRDEN TURN-OVER OF SAME LEE FLOORBOARD REPORT (April 6, 2010)

## H. HEARING ON MANDATORY ORDER OF PRODUCTION (September 9, 2010)

Plaintiff Cooper argued for sanctions of monetary fine, contempt, and incarceration for ignoring Court-ordered turn-over. TR 9/9/10 p. 11, ln.9-12. An Evidentiary Hearing was ordered.

## I. VIRDEN'S LEE AND ORCHID CELLMARK REQUESTS (October 26, 2010)

1. On November 22, 2010, Plaintiff Cooper was given Virden's October 26, 2010 letter to Lee, and Lee's November 12, 2010 response letter. But the request letter was a sham, without records' identification. And no follow-up letter was sent to Lee to get his report(s).

2. On November 22, 2010, Plaintiff Cooper was also given Virden's October 26, 2010 letter to Orchid Cellmark; and Orchid Cellmark's November 2, 2010 response letter and e-mail to him; and a CD of Virden's November 2, 2010 phone call to Orchid Cellmark. The Orchid Cellmark requests were sham, providing no identifying information to obtain the records.

## J. SEDERWALL TURN-OVER OF LEE WORKBENCH REPORT (November 10 , 2010)

## K. EVIDENTIARY HEARING (January 21, 2011)

1. Virden's counsel argued: "[W]e hope after you hear the evidence in this case, your Honor, you will find that number one, these documents don't exist. And number two, if they do exist, the Sheriff never had them, and couldn't possibly turn over, and he's gone beyond what the public records act requires in this case to try to obtain them." TR 1/21/11, p. 26, ln. 17-22.

2. Sullivan and Sederwall said the case was their private hobby. Their counsel gave the  Court Lee's workbench report as Exhibit E, and gave Lee's floorboard report as Exhibit F.

3. The Court found that the Kid's killing and the deputy killings were a single case by the Lincoln County Sheriff's Department Office, and that its records were public documents. Sederwall was ordered to get the Orchid Cellmark file and provide it to Virden.

## L. SEDERWALL REQUESTS RECORDS FROM DR. RICK STAUB (February 3, 2011)

Sederwall's letter to Orchid Cellmark was sham, lacking records' identification.

## M. HEARING ON MOTION FOR PRESENTMENT (September 23, 2011)

1. Sederwall presented his sham letter to Orchid Cellmark. TR 9/23/11, p. 5, ln. 10-11.

2. Plaintiff Cooper said the Lee floorboard reports had discrepancies. *Id.* p. 6, ln. 12-14.

## N. HEARING ON SUPPLEMENTING THE RECORD AND FOR SANCTIONS; AND CO-PLAINTIFF'S MOTION FOR PAST ATTORNEYS' FEES (January 17, 2012

1. Plaintiff Cooper alleged that the Lee reports were tampered, and requested sanctions.

2. Co-Plaintiff made a motion, without Plaintiff Cooper, for fees for past attorneys.

3. The Court ordered Sederwall to get "original reports;" sanctions were delayed; and past attorneys' fees were awarded.

## O. SEDERWALL TURN OVER OF COMBINED WORKBENCH AND FLOORBOARD LEE REPORT (January 31, 2012)

Sederwall turned over a fourth version of the Lee report. Unlike the others, its header stated Case 2003-274 and the law enforcement titles. But it was a copy, lacking signatures.

## P. CO-PLAINTIFF'S SUBPOENA OF ORCHID CELLMARK RECORDS (April, 2012)

By subpoena, the Co-Plaintiff obtained over a hundred pages of Orchid Cellmark records for Case 2003-274. Copy of these records were given to Plaintiff Cooper's counsel.

## Q. HEARING ON SECOND MOTION TO SUPPLEMENT THE RECORD AND A REQUEST FOR SANCTIONS (May 31, 2012)

1. Plaintiff Cooper presented the fourth Lee report as proving tampering of the past three Lee reports to remove the Case 2003-274 connection. Sanctions were requested.

2. The subpoenaed Orchid Cellmark records were given to the Court as proof that those records existed. Calvin Ostler was identified in them as the Orchid Cellmark client.

3. Virden's counsel argued: "Is my client ... responsible for records that he never created, he never received, he never possessed, maintained or held, or even had knowledge of? That's the question before you, Your Honor," TR 5/31/12, p. 21, ln. 14-24.

4. Defendants' depositions were requested because of the new evidence, and as sanctions.

5. The Court delayed decision on sanctions, but granted the depositions.

## R. SEDERWALL DEPOSITION (July 26, 2012)

Sederwall admitted that Lee reports were rewritten to remove the law enforcement information. He admitted that he knew Calvin Ostler was the Orchid Cellmark client.

## S. VIRDEN DEPOSITION (July 27, 2012)

Virden admitted that his Case 2003-274 file had information that confirmed records' existence and that provided recovery options. He said Sullivan and Sederwall were his deputies. He admitted he could have called Lee or Calvin Ostler, the Orchid Cellmark client, but had not. And he identified the Orchid Cellmark subpoenaed records as part of Case 2003-274.

## II. ARGUMENT

## A. SUMMARY OF ARGUMENT

Public officials, under 14-2-5, must provide records as "an integral part of the routine duties of public officers and employees." "The citizen's right to know is the rule and secrecy is the exception." *State of New Mexico ex. rel. Newsome V. Alarid*, 90 N.M. 790 568 P.2d at 797. Inspection ensures that officials "are honestly, faithfully, and competently performing their function as public servants." *Id.* at 1241. IPRA protects "the public from having to rely solely on the representation of public officials that they have acted appropriately." *City of Farmington v. The Daily Times,* 2009-NMCA-057, ¶ 17, 146 N.M. 349, 210 P.3d 246.

IPRA damages under 14-2-10, 14-2-11(A)-(C), and 14-2-12 apply to this litigation. Without using 14-2-1(A) exceptions, or proper denial under 14-2-11(B)(1)-(3), the Defendants: (a) misstated custodial duty as just possession; (b) called public records trade secrets; and (c) made sham recovery attempts. Also, Defendants' violations fall under NMRA 1-011 for ignoring Court-ordered records presentment, and giving false records as genuine; and fall under NMRA 1-037 for discovery abuse by tampering of records' content, and by willful concealing of records.

Additionally, the Defendants' excuse of records not existing, burdens the requester with proof. This is contrary to the Supreme Court decision in *State of New Mexico ex. rel. Newsome v. Alarid,* 90 N.M. 790 568 P.2d at 1241. "Nowhere in *Newsome* does our Supreme Court place a burden on the party requesting the documents. Instead, Newsome clearly places the burden ... upon the custodian to justify why the records sought to be examined should not be furnished." *City of Farmington v. The Daily Times,* 2009-NMCA-057, ¶ 17, 146 N.M. 349, 210 P.3d 246. In fact, IPRA redress exists because inappropriate records refusal "enables a plaintiff to establish injury." *San Juan Agric. Water Users Ass'n. v. KNME-TV,* 2011-NMSC-011, __ N.M. __, __ P.3d. And Plaintiff Cooper's possession now of Orchid Cellmark records proves their existence.

Demonstrable is that Dr. Lee and Orchid Cellmark, via client, Calvin Ostler, were easily accessible for records requests. So IPRA's time-based damages in 14-2-11(C)(1)-(2) are merited. "IPRA's damage provisions are intended to encourage public entities' prompt compliance with records requests." *Derringer v. State,* 2003-NMCA-073, ¶¶ 11, 15, 133 N. M. 721, 68 P.3d 961. For Defendants like those in this litigation, Rules 11 and 37 also offer punitive remedies.

## B. ARGUMENT AS TO VIRDEN

1. Virden, the admitted custodian, provided no requested records. In the request phase, he gave no proper denial under 14-2-11(B)(1)-(3). In both request and enforcement phases, his refusals were based only on lacking possession, which ignores 14-2-6(A), which establishes responsibility "regardless of whether the records are in that person's actual physical custody or control." And 14-2-6(E) repeats retrieval responsibility by including as "public records" those held "on behalf of any public body." The New Mexico Court of Appeals stated that "public agencies must produce all records, even those held by or created by a private entity 'on behalf of' the public agency." *Toomey v. Truth or Consequences,* NM Ct. Ap. No. 30,795, p. 4, (2012). As to "on behalf of," a Florida Supreme Court's test was: if "the services contracted for are an integral part of the agency's chosen decision-making process." *News & Sun-Sentinel Co. v. Schwab, Twitty & Hanser Architectural Group, Inc.,* 596 So. 2d 1029 (Fla. 1992). Certainly, Case 2003-274's DNA records were "integral" to solving its murder by Pat Garrett.

2. Ignorance of records' existence is no IPRA exception, but Virden used it to refuse recovery, even though his file for Case 2003-274 demonstrated the records and their location; and, in addition, his Deputies, Sullivan and Sederwall, had admitted they had records.

3. And Virden's recovery attempts, three years into litigation, were shams.

## C. ARGUMENT AS TO SULLIVAN AND SEDERWALL

Defendants Sullivan and Sederwall, the law enforcement investigators for Case 2003-274, used only misrepresentations to refuse records production.

1. Contrary to all evidence, Sullivan and Sederwall denied being deputies.

2. They denied being records custodians. But 14-2-11(B)(2) makes any person connected to the records "responsible for the denial [of records]." IPRA Compliance Guide, 2004, p. 31, for 14-2-7 states: "[O]ther employees may, on behalf of the records custodian, furnish public records for inspection." And, as Virden's deputies, they were his agents. "[A] a person may appoint an agent to do the same acts and achieve the same legal consequences by the performance of an act as if he or she had acted personally." 3 Am. Jur. 2d *Agency* § 18, at 422 (2002).

3. Sullivan's and Sederwall's argument of being unsalaried as "reserve deputies" is irrelevant to their records responsibility, since "[a]n agent is a person who, by agreement with another called the principal, represents the principal in dealings with third persons or transacts some other business ... for the principal, with or without compensation." UJI 13-401, NMRA.

4. In their June 21, 2007 "Memorandum," they admitted to having records, but illogically called them private property - at the same time as resigning as Deputies! Other evidence of using public office for private gain was Sederwall's website selling official Case 2003-274 records.

4. Sederwall, under Court order, made a sham records request to Orchid Cellmark, even though he admitted, in his July 26, 2012 deposition, that he knew Calvin Ostler was the client.

5. Sederwall admitted, in his July 26, 2012 deposition, to involvement in altering Lee reports by rewritings to remove the original law enforcement information in Lee's "first" report.

## D. ARGUMENT AS TO SANCTIONS

1. Sanctions are based on a party's misconduct towards the court. *United Nuclear Corp. v. General Atomic Co.* 96 N.M. 155, 241, 629 P.2d 231, 317 (1980). If a party unearths discovery abuses during the trial, the district court may award sanctions under SCRA 1986, Rules 1-037. *Enriquez v. Cochran,* 126 N.M. 196 (1998), 967 P.2d 1136, 1998 –NMCA- 157.

2. January 17, 2012 and May 31, 2012 Hearings requested sanctions for Lee reports' tampering and presenting them as "original." And the plaintiff-subpoenaed Orchid Cellmark records prove they existed. Furthermore, the September 9, 2010 Hearing had requested contempt and incarceration for the Defendants' refusal to follow Court-ordered records production.

## E. ARGUMENT AS TO IPRA DAMAGES

1. "IPRA includes remedies to encourage compliance and facilitate enforcement." *San Juan Agric. Water Users Ass'n. v. KNME-TV,* 2011-NMSC-011, ¶ 12. "The Legislature's punitive intent in imposing a cost for non-disclosure is evident." *Bd. of Comm'rs of Doña Ana County v. Las Cruces Sun-News,* 2003-NMCA-102, 134 N.M. 283, 76 P.3d 36. Those IPRA "Damages" are: (a) 14-2-10 and 14-2-11(B)(C) for improper records denial(s); (b) 14-2-12 for attorney fees and costs following the Court's final judgment; and (c) "IPRA Compliance Guide" for 14-2-12, p. 43, "for unspecified damages awarded to a private person prevailing in enforcement action."

2. At this stage of the litigation, improper denial under 14-2-11(B) applies:

If a writen request has been denied, the custodian shall provide the requester with a writen explanation of the denial. The writen denial shall: (1) describe the records sought; (2) set forth the names and titles or positions of each person responsable for the denial; and (c) be delivered or mailed to the person requesting the records within fifteen days after the request for inspection was received.

3. At this stage of the litigation, non-production without statutory basis - and with records proved to be recoverable – merits monetary damages under 14-2-11(C)(1)-(4) as follows:

> "A custodian who does not deliver or mail a written explanation of denial within fifteen days after a written receipt for inspection is subject to an action to enforce the provisions of the Inspection of Public Records Act and the requester may be awarded damages. Damages shall: (1) be awarded if the failure to provide a timely explanation of denial is determined to be unreasonable; (2) not to exceed one hundred dollars ($100) per day; (3) accrue from the day the public body is in noncompliance until a written denial is issued; and (4) be payable from the funds of the public body."

Calculation of said monetary damages begins fifteen days after Plaintiff Cooper's April 24, 2007 request, to the present. And the records denials are four: (a) Lee's true report of DNA specimen recoveries; (b) Orchid Cellmark's DNA from Lee's specimens; (c) Orchid Cellmark's extractions from exhumed bones; and (d) Orchid Cellmark's matchings of Lee's specimen's DNA to the bones; though these categories each represent a multitude of records.

4. Damages should be maximum under 14-2-11(C)(1)-(4). "[W]hen a company chooses ... not to produce, to destroy and to do everything in its power to make sure that the other side does not get what they have a legitimate right to receive under the rules of discovery, then the court itself feels that it must protect the process of production of documents ... Likewise it is hard to imagine that appellant would not have retrieved this information immediately had it consisted of beneficial rather than damaging material." *Garcia vs. Berkshire Life Ins. Co. of America,* 569 F.3d 1174 (2009).

5. Damages under 14-2-11 do not duplicate future damages under 14-2-12, since IPRA lists them separately, and since their remedies have separate intents.

### III. CONCLUSION

WHEREFORE, after providing ample evidence that the Defendants have violated IPRA law, and also committed sanctionable offences against the Court, Plaintiff Cooper respectfully moves the Court to consider, for the Evidentiary Hearing, the following: (1) sanctions under NMRA 1-011 and 1-1037; (2) award to her as a sanction her costs for the Defendants' depositions of July 26 and 27, 2012; (3) award to her of maximum damages under 14-2-11; (4) future award to her of damages of attorneys' fees and her costs under 14-2-12; and (5) granting her such other relief as the Court deems necessary and just.

Respectfully Submitted,
via personal hand Delivery to Sandoval District Court
*Gale Cooper* 11/14/12
Contact information

**APPENDIX: 66. Gale Cooper. "Addendum to Plaintiff Cooper's Opposition Reply To Virden's Objection to Plaintiff Cooper's Pre-Evidentiary Hearing Brief." November 14, 2012. (Copied to Attorneys Patrick Griebel for the De Baca County News, Henry Narvaez for Sheriff Virden, and Kevin Brown for Sullivan and Sederwall)**

THIRTEENTH JUDICIAL DISTRICT COURT
COUNTY OF SANDOVAL
STATE OF NEW MEXICO

GALE COOPER and DE BACA COUNTY NEWS,
a New Mexico Corporation,

Plaintiffs,

vs.                No. D-1329-CV-2007-1364

RICK VIRDEN, LINCOLN COUNTY SHERIFF and CUSTODIANOF THE RECORDS OF THE LINCOLN COUNTY SHERIFF'S OFFICE; and STEVEN M. SEDERWALL, FORMER LINCOLN COUNTY DEPUTYSHERIFF; and THOMAS T. SULLIVAN, FORMER INCOLN COUNTYSHERIFF AND FORMER LINCOLN COUNTY DEPUTY SHERIFF,

Defendants.

**ADDENDUM TO PLAINTIFF COOPER'S OPPOSITION REPLY TO VIRDEN'S OBJECTION TO PLAINTIFF COOPER'S PRE-EVIDENTIARY HEARING BRIEF**

COMES NOW, Plaintiff Gale Cooper ("Plaintiff Cooper"), as *pro se*, for this addendum to her "Reply in Opposition to Defendant Rick Virden's Objection to Plaintiff Cooper's Pre-Evidentiary Brief" ("the Objection") to debunk specifically Virden's Inspection of Public Records Act ("IPRA") contentions about his custodial duties; i.e, that turn-over applies just to directly possessed records; that retrieving records not in direct possession is not required; that the requester has the burden of proof for records' existence and for writing records request letters; and that his request letters without follow-up constitute records "recovery." Plaintiff Cooper alleges that Virden's IPRA contentions are willful misstatements to mislead the Court in hopes of averting punitive legal consequences of total IPRA non-compliance and of discovery abuse.

**I. BACKGROUND**

A. PLAINTIFF COOPER'S PRE-EVIDENTIARY HEARING BRIEF, NOVEMBER 14, 2012

    1. Plaintiff Cooper's November 14, 2012 Pre-Hearing Brief ("the Brief") (Exhibit 1) was for the Evidentiary Hearing of December 18, 2012, and arose from the Court's ruling in the May 31, 2012 Hearing on "Second Motion to Supplement the Record and for Sanctions" which stated: "Im going going to order the deposition to be taken of all Defendants. The only limit I'm placing on the deposition[s] is that

it be limited to – it's broad, actually – anything having to do with the DNA evidence or evidence that is subject of this case." TR 5/31/12, P. 33, ln. 21-25.

    2. Plaintiff Cooper's Brief argued for sanctions and IPRA damages against Virden based on Virden's total non-production of requested records, though said records had been established to exist and established to be recoverable.

### B. SHERIFF VIRDEN'S OBJECTION TO PLAINTIFF COOPER'S PRE-EVIDENTIARY HEARING BRIEF, DECEMBER 17, 2012 : AS TO ITS IPRA ARGUMENTS

    1.   OVERALL: Virden denied the Brief's allegations of IPRA non-compliance by stating: a) "the Sheriff has never been served with written discovery in this case;" b) [h]e has produced his entire file twice in connection with the two times Plaintiffs deposed him;" c) "there is no evidence that the Sheriff has failed to produce every document in his possession pertaining to this matter;" d) he has "never 'refused' Cooper's IPRA requests; e) "[i]t was impossible for the Sheriff to turn over records to Cooper, let alone *refuse* to do so, when he didn't know such records existed, and which he never had in his possession;" and f) that it was "outrageous" to call Virden's recovery attempts "shamed," and "her [Cooper's] attorney never drafted a [request] letter for the Sheriff to send, so the Sheriff sent his own letters." Pp. 3, ¶ ¶ 2-3; P. 4, ¶¶ 1-2.

    2.   OUT-OF-STATE "PRECEDENT CASES": Argued was that "Cooper also ignores pertinent law" [in her allegations]. Virden stated: "[N]o New Mexico law has addressed whether a duty exists for a records custodian to obtain or produce public records never in possession of the records custodian." Pp. 5, ¶ 2. Virden provided two out-of-state cases as follows:

    a). The Louisiana Court of Appeals *CII Carbon, LLC v. St Blanc*, 764 So.2d 1229 (La.App.2000) was cited with a ruling that "the requested documents were not public records because the defendants never had possession of them, did not prepare them, and never retained them … recognizing that requiring defendants to produce documents they never prepared, retained, or had possession of would [require] a governmental entity to have to make available documents it never prepared, let alone had never seen." P. 5, ¶ 3.

    b). The Tennessee Appeals Court *Kersey v. Bratcher*, 253 S.W.3d 625 (Tenn.App 2007), was quoted as: "the plaintiff requested a court file [from the court clerk] … The court recognized that where it was a physical impossibility for the clerk to furnish the court file because it was in the custody of the judge, the clerk had no duty to do so." P. 5, ¶ 4; P. 6, ¶ 1.

## II. ARGUMENT

### A. SUMMARY OF ARGUMENT

    Virden alleged IPRA justifications for zero records production since Plaintiff Cooper's records request of April 24, 2007 are based on false premises about IPRA: a) that custodial duty applies only to "direct possession;" and b) that "recovery" of outside records is not required. Also false is stating New Mexico has no laws to the contrary, while citing irrelevant Louisiana and Tennessee laws. Apparent is a hope of misleading the Court to believing that Virden met his custodial responsibilities. These false claims, if accepted, would end viability of IPRA law.

B. ARGUMENT

1. OVERALL IPRA: The allegations in I, B, 1, a) to f) above, are dispensed of simply by inserting IPRA law as follows: a) §14-2-8(C) shows that the "Procedure for Requesting Records" was done correctly by Plaintiff Cooper; but Virden wants "written discovery," not part of the request process; b) Virden's turn-over of non-requested records is merely records denial under §14-2-11(A) "Procedure for Denied Requests," in that "inspection of public records ... has not been permitted [to Plaintiff Cooper] within fifteen days of receipt by the ... custodian;" c) turning over "every document in his possession" does not free Virden from §14-2-6(A) custodial responsibility "whether the records are in that person's direct physical custody and control," or from §14-2-6(F) for public records held "on behalf of any public body;" d) Virden "refused" all "Cooper's IPRA requests" by non-IPRA excuses (my deputies took them), and, without statutory justification, produced no records; e) repeating "possession only" for his custodial duty under §14-2-6(A)(F); and f) denying as "sham" his unspecific letters written three years after the request and without follow-up, while requiring that "her [Plaintiff Cooper] attorney" should draft the request letters, ignores IPRA's burden of recovery under §14-2-5 "Purpose of Act, which makes providing records "an integral part of the routine duties of public officers and employees."

2. OUT-OF-STATE LAW: Virden justifies his IPRA non-compliance by using out-of-state precedent case law, omitting that "different and varying Freedom of Information Acts [are] passed by the individual states."[1] Virden justifies use of out-of-state law by claiming that "no New Mexico law" addresses "whether a duty exists for a records custodian to obtain or produce public records never in possession of the records custodian." This ignores *Toomey v. Truth or Consequences*, NM Ct. Ap. No. 30,795, p. 4, (2012) (Exhibit 2) Appeals Court ruling that "public agencies must produce all records, even those held by or created by a private entity 'on behalf of' the public agency." This Toomey case was decided five months before Virden's Objection, and was cited in Plaintiff Cooper's Brief a month before Virden's Objection, making Virden's use of self-serving out-of-state law appear disingenuous. And, certainly, the forensic DNA records created by Dr. Henry Lee and Orchid Cellmark Lab, requested by Plaintiff Cooper, were held by those "private entities," and were intrinsic to solving Virden's Sheriff's Department forensic DNA murder case No. 2003-274. Plaintiff Cooper's Brief, in addition, cites other precedent cases that contradict Virden's misstatement of his responsibilities under IPRA for records retrieval, and also demonstrate Virden's requirement for records retrieval.

3. USE OF LOUISIANA CASE: *CII Carbon, LLC v. St Blanc*, 764 So.2d 1229 (La.App.2000) (Exhibit 3) used by Virden contradicts New Mexico's IPRA law, because Louisiana's "Public Records Law" limits a custodian's responsibility for records never in "custody or control." But New Mexico's IPRA law takes precedence, and states the opposite under §14-2-6(A); i.e., holding the custodian "responsible" for "a public body's public records, regardless of whether the records are in that person's actual custody or control;" and deeming "public records" recoverable under §14-2-6(F) when held "on behalf of any public body."

4. USE OF TENNESSEE CASE: *Kersey v. Bratcher*, 253 S.W.3d 625 (Tenn.App 2007) (Exhibit 4) is misstated as well as irrelevant, but is used by Virden

---

[1] Wikepedia. "Freedom of Information Act (United States)"

for his "possession" argument by aserting that *Kersey v. Bratcher* ruled that a clerk could not turn over a file "in the custody of the judge." But the actual ruling states only that appellant John C. Kersey refused to "sit on the office couch while viewing the File," instead of "standing over her [the clerk]." So the ruling was merely: "[I]i is reasonable  to request persons requesting access to public records to do so in a specific location that will not interfere with the operation of the office."

5. TRUE RECOVERABILITY OF RECORDS: As shown in Plaintiff Cooper's Brief, the requested   records in question were in existence and were recoverable by custodian Virden.

### III. CONCLUSION

WHEREFORE, Plaintiff Cooper, after providing ample evidence that Defendant Virden has misstated IPRA law, has disregarded New Mexico precedent law cases, and has used Louisiana and Tennessee cases merely to mislead the Court as to his custodial duties, repeats with increased adamance her contentions that Virden deserves sanctions for willful attempts to mislead the Court and for discovery abuse; as well as deserves damages enforcement under §14-2-11 and §14-2-12 for IPRA violations; as well as deserving the enforcement of any other relief as the Court deems necessary and just.

Respectfully Submitted,
via personal hand Delivery to Sandoval District Court
*Gale Cooper*   11/14/12
Contact information

## APPENDIX: 67. Judge George P. Eichwald. "Findings of Fact and Conclusions of Law and Order of the Court." May 15, 2014.

THIRTEENTH JUDICIAL DISTRICT COURT
COUNTY OF SANDOVAL
STATE OF NEW MEXICO

GALE COOPER and DE BACA COUNTY NEWS,
a New Mexico Corporation,
                    Plaintiffs,
v.                                                 No. D-1329-CV-2007-1364

RICK VIRDEN, LINCOLN COUNTY SHERIFF and CUSTODIAN OF THE RECORDS OF THE LINCOLN COUNTY SHERIFF'S OFFICE; and STEVEN M. SEDERWALL, FORMER LINCOLN COUNTY DEPUTYSHERIFF; and THOMAS T. SULLIVAN, FORMER INCOLN COUNTYSHERIFF AND FORMER LINCOLN COUNTY DEPUTY SHERIFF,
                    Defendants.

## FINDINGS OF FACT AND CONCLUSIONS OF LAW AND
## ORDER OF THE COURT

All requested Findings of Fact and Conclusions of Law are denied except such as are herein incorporated by the Court.

## FINDINGS OF FACT

1. This Court has jurisdiction over the parties and subject matter of this litigation.

2. Plaintiff De Baca County News is no longer a party to this litigation as it has settled all matters in controversy with Defendants.

3. On January 14, 2014 Plaintiff Gale Cooper (hereinafter Cooper) filed a voluntary dismissal against Defendant Thomas Sullivan as Defendant Sullivan is now deceased.

4. The matter in controversy is for enforcement of the New Mexico Inspection of Public [Records] Act, Section 14-2-1 et seq. NMSA 1978 (IPRA) and concerning the Defendants' refusal to turn over requested DNA records of Lincoln County Sheriff's Department Case No. 2003-274, "Billy the Kid Case," ("Case 2003-274").

5. Case 2003-274 is a murder case, filed in 2003 in the Lincoln County Sheriff's Department by Sheriff Tom Sullivan (hereinafter Sullivan) and his commissioned Deputy Steve Sederwall (hereinafter Sederwall) to be solved by forensic DNA acquisitions and matching, and accusing the suspect Pat Garrett of murdering an innocent victim instead of Billy the Kid; with a sub-investigation of Billy the Kid's double homicide of Deputies James Bell and Robert Olinger.

6. From 2003 to 2004, Case 2003-274's New Mexico exhumation attempts on Billy the Kid and his mother for matching DNA were legally blocked so no DNA was obtained.

7. In 2004 Billy the Kid's DNA was allegedly obtained for Case 2003-274 by Dr. Henry Lee (hereinafter Lee) from an old carpenter's bench on which Billy the Kid [was] laid after being shot. Lee's specimens were sent for DNA processing to Orchid Cellmark Lab (hereinafter Orchid Cellmark) in Texas.

8. In 2005 newly elected Lincoln County Sheriff Rick Virden (hereinafter Virden) deputized Sullivan and Sederwall to continue Case 2003-274 by exhuming Billy the Kid's identity claimants John Miller and "Brushy Bill" Roberts for DNA match[ing] with Lee's bench DNA to solve the Garrett murder.

9. On May 19, 2005, for Case 2003-274, John Miller and William Hudspeth were exhumed in Arizona and their bones were taken to Orchid Cellmark for DNA extractions and for DNA matching to the carpenter's bench DNA.

10. From April 24, 2007 to June 26, 2007 Plaintiff Cooper made IPRA records requests from Sheriff Virden for Case 2003-274 through her then attorney Mickey Barnett ("request phase"). Requested records were for:

   A. Lee's DNA recoveries from the carpenter's bench;
   B. Orchid Cellmark's DNA extractions from Lee's specimens;
   C. Orchid Cellmark's DNA extractions for the two Arizona bodies; and
   D. Orchid Cellmark's DNA matchings for the carpenter's bench [DNA] to the bodies [DNA].

11. In the request phase, no records were given and their denials were improper: without valid IPRA exceptions; with Sullivan and Sederwall after having resigned their deputyship on June 21, 2007 admitting to records possession, but calling them private hobby "trade secrets;" with Virden denying having any Case 2003-274 records; and with Virden not attempting to recover records from Sullivan, Sederwall, Lee, or Orchid Cellmark.

12. The case at hand for enforcement of IPRA was filed on October 15, 2007.

13. In their August 18, 2008 depositions Sullivan and Sederwall admitted knowing that the requested records existed, and admitted that Sederwall possessed Lee's carpenter's bench report.

14. On September 3, 2007 [sic – 2008], by subpoena duces tecum, Virden turned over his Case 2003-274 file of one hundred ninety-three (193) pages; lacking requested records, but with documents confirming the DNA investigation and having contact information for records recovery.

15. In his September 8, 2008 deposition Virden denied knowledge of requested records.

16. On November 20, 2009 Partial Summary Judgment was issued in favor of Plaintiffs and against Defendants declaring the records requested were public, were created in official capacities, and should be turned over.

17. On February 18, 2010 Sederwall turned over to the Plaintiffs an unrequested nine (9) page Lee report on courthouse floorboards. Its header had no link to Case 2003-274. It was signed by Lee and Calvin Ostler. In the March 9, 2010 Presentment Hearing, the Court was told that this floorboard report was the only Lee report in Sederwall's possession.

18. On October 26 2010 Virden first made records requests to Lee and Orchid Cellmark but never followed up to recover the records after Lee responded that he had one report, and Orchid Cellmark responded that it would send the records if released by their client.

19. On November 10, 2010 Sederwall turned over to the Plaintiffs a sixteen (16) page Lee report on the carpenter's bench but [it] was lacking a link to Case 2003-274.

20. An Evidentiary Hearing was held on January 21, 2011 and Virden argued that he could not turn over records that were not in his direct possession and which he did not know existed. Sederwall's Lee courthouse floorboard report was entered as Exhibit "F," and the carpenter's bench report was entered as Exhibit "E." At this hearing the Court reminded the parties that the Partial Summary Judgment previously entered on November 20, 2009 found that the Defendants and the investigation were official and connected to the Lincoln County Sheriff and that all evidence was public record and that all information should be turned over to Plaintiffs.

20. [sic – numbering incorrect] In July, 2011 Cooper recognized that the Lee courthouse floorboard report (entered as Exhibit "F") was a rewrite of the alleged same floorboard report given on November 10, 2010, and that this rewriting also put in doubt the authenticity of the carpenter's bench report (Exhibit "E").

21. At a September 23, 2011 Presentment Hearing Cooper alerted the Court of the discrepancies in the Lee reports.

22. On January 17, 2012 a Hearing on Sanctions was conducted and Plaintiffs stated that there were no records productions and allegations of altered Lee

reports. Production of the original Lee report was ordered. Plaintiff De Baca County News requested attorney's [sic – attorneys'] fees which were granted.

23. On January 31, 2012 Sederwall turned over a twenty-five (25) page "original" Lee report combining the courthouse floorboard and the carpenter's bench. Its header identified Lee's work as for Case 2003-274.

24. On March 20, 2012 Plaintiff De Baca County News subpoenaed the Orchid Cellmark records for Case 2003-274, receiving one hundred thirty-three (133) pages on April 20, 2012. The records included DNA results from Lee's specimens and from the two exhumed Arizona bodies.

25. On May 31, 2012 a Hearing for Sanctions was conducted. The newest Lee report was presented as evidence of altering of the past Lee reports to conceal the law enforcement header, but was also called not original as lacking signatures. The subpoenaed Orchid Cellmark records were entered as evidence to prove records' existence. Sanctions included the ordering of new depositions of the Defendants.

26. In his June 26, 2012 deposition Sederwall admitted to: removing law enforcement information from later Lee reports; called the twenty-five (25) page Lee report he first received from Lee as original; and admitted to knowing that the Orchid Cellmark client was Calvin Ostler.

27. In his June 27, 2012 deposition Virden admitted to: waiting three (3) years into litigation to write record requests to Lee and Orchid Cellmark; not requesting from Lee the report when Lee wrote back that he had one; and not trying to find out the client's name after Orchid Cellmark wrote back that it was required to send Virden the requested records.

28. Cooper challenged De Baca County News standing which the Court denied.

29. At an Evidentiary Hearing conducted on December 21 [sic – 18], 2012 and February 4, 2013 Virden admitted: that the subpoenaed Orchid Cellmark DNA records were from Case 2003-274 but gave no valid explanation for waiting three (3) years to begin records recovery or for not following up on the resulting responses to get the records. Witness Seterwall [sic], still calling Case 2003-274 his private hobby, admitted to altering the first Lee report's header to remove Case 2003-274 information; and admitted to creating the other report versions given to the Court and lacking law enforcement information.

30. Court ordered mediation between Cooper and Defendants was unsuccessful.

## CONCLUSIONS OF LAW

1. Section 14-2-5 NMSA 1978 states, "The intent of the legislature in enacting the Inspection of Public Records Act is to ensure as the policy of the State of New Mexico, that all persons are entitled to the greatest possible information regarding the affairs of government and the official acts of public officers and employees."

2. Section 14-2-8© NMSA 1978 states, "No person requesting records shall be required to state the reason for inspecting records."

3. Cooper's status as an author is irrelevant in requesting records under IPRA and [she] is entitled to receive document[s] which were requested.

4. Without statutory justification, no requested records were produced by the Defendants.

5. The requested records exist, and have been recoverable from the time of the request phase.

6. After De Baca County News' subpoena outside IPRA requirement, the requested Lee report and the Orchid Cellmark DNA matchings remain unrecovered.

7. Section 14-2-5 NMSA 1978 states, "To provide persons with such information is ... an integral part of the routine duties of public officers and employees. Virden produced no requested records and gave no statutory justification for non-recovery, in violation of IPRA.

8. Virden did not comply with Section 14-2-11(B)(1-3) NMSA 1978, "Procedure for Denied Requests: by providing the requester with a written explanation of the "denial" listing: "the records sought", "each person responsible for the denial," and "mailed to the person requesting the records within fifteen days after the request." Improper denial under Section 14-2-11(C) subjects the custodian to monetary [up to $100 per day] damages.

9. In both the request and enforcement phases, Virden's records recovery refusal[s] have been misplaced and ignored IPRA by arguing that recovery pertains only to records in direct physical possession. Section 14-2-6(A) NMSA 1978 states enforcement custodial responsibility "regardless of whether the records are in that person's actual physical custody and control." Section 14-2-6(F) NMSA 1978 repeats that "public records" can be held "on behalf of any public body." *Toomey v. Truth or Consequences,* N.M. Ct. Ap. No. 30,795, P.4. (2012) clearly stated "public agencies must produce all record[s], even those held by or created by a private entity 'on behalf of' the public agency.["] The DNA records of Lee and Orchid Cellmark were held on behalf of Lincoln Sheriff's Office by Lee and Orchid Cellmark, and are intrinsic to solving its Pat Garrett murder Case 2003-274.

10. Virden was obligated to recover records from it [sic- his] deputy agents. *Ronald A. Coco, Inc. v. St Paul's Methodist Church of Las Cruces, N.M., Inc.*, 78, N.M. 97, 99, 428 P.2d 636, 638 (1967), states, in part, "Unquestionably, insofar as an agent's acts are with the agent's authority they are in legal contemplation of the acts of the principal."

11. Ignorance of records existence was argued by Virden to refuse recovery. Ignorance is not an IPRA exception under Section 14-2-1(A) (1-8) NMSA 1978. Virden's lack or [sic - of] knowledge of records is disingenuous, since his deputies admitted to records possession, his Case 2003-274 file showed DNA investigations and recovery options, Lee responded to Virden and Lee had the record, and Orchid Cellmark responded to Virden that it had the records. Virden's questioning the existence of records burdens the requester with proof, contrary to the decision in *State of New Mexico ex Re.* [sic – rel.] *Newsome v. Alarid*, 90 N.M. 790, 568 P.2d 1236 (1977), which held that the burden is placed upon the custodian to justify why the records sought to be examined should not be furnished. See also, *City of Farmington v. The Daily Times*, 2009-NMCA-057, 146, N.M. 349, 210 P.3d 246.

12. Virden ignored Section 14-2-7(E)(5) NMSA 1978, "the responsibility of a public body to make available public records for inspection." Virden waited three (3) years into litigation to seek records, then did not actually try to recover them from Lee and Orchid Cellmark. To prevent stonewalling, IPRA has time based damages in NMSA Section 14-2-11. IPRA damage provisions are intended to encourage public entities' prompt compliance with records requests. *Derringer v. State*, 133 N.M. 721, 68 P.3rd 691 9(Ct. App. 2003).

13. As public officials, under Section 14-2-5 NMSA 1978, Sullivan and Sederwall had to provide records as, "an integral part of the routine duties of public officers and employees."

14. As commissioned deputies, under Section 13[sic - 14]-2-11(B)(2) NMSA 1978, along with Virden, they were "responsible for the denial of records." As Virden's deputies, they were his agents. "A person may appoint an agent to do the same acts and achieve the same legal consequences by performing of an act as if he or she had acted personally." 3 Am. Jur. 2d Agency Section 18, at 422 (2002). Section 4-41-9 NMSA 1978 states, "The said deputies are hereby authorized to discharge all the duties which belong to the office of sheriff, that may be placed under their charge by their principals, with the same effect as though they were executed by the respective sheriffs."

15. Sullivan and Sederwall said they were hobbyists and the records were private property. Sullivan's and Sederwall's argument of being "unsalaried "reserve deputies" is irrelevant to the records responsibility, since "an agent is a person who, by agreement with another called the principal, represents the principal in dealings with third persons or transacts some other business ... for the principal, with or without compensation. UJI 13-401, NMRA.

16. In their June 21, 2007 "Memorandum" to Virden, Sullivan and Sederwall admitted to having Case 2003-274 records, but called them private property, while at the same time resigning their public official positions as deputies. Furthermore, from 2010 to 2012, Sederwall offered Case 2003-274 records for sale on his own billythekidcase.com website.

17. After being court-ordered, Sederwall made a non-specific records request for Orchid Cellmark on February 3 [sic – 5], 2011; later admitting in his June 26, 2012 deposition, that he knew Calvin Ostler was the Orchid Cellmark client contact for getting records released.

18. In his June 26, 2012 deposition, Sederwall admitted to willful involvement in altering Lee reports by rewritings to remove the original law enforcement information in Lee's "first" report sent to him as Lincoln County Deputy Sheriff. Section 14-2-6(F) NMSA 1978 defines "public records" as "all documents, papers, letters, books, maps, tapes, photographs, recordings and other materials, regardless of physical form or characteristics, used, created, received, maintained or held by or on behalf of any pubic body and related to public business, whether or not the records are required by law to be created or maintained." The plain language implication is that the records are to be "originals" of [sic – or] true "duplicates" of the original. Under Rule 11-1001(D) NMRA 1978, "an original of a writing is the writing itself. Rile [sic –Rule] 11-101(E) NMRA 1978 states "a duplicate is a counterpart produced by the same impression as the original ... which accurately reproduces the original." Neither an "original" nor a "duplicate" report was presented, only altered records which do not comply with IPRA law.

19. The Defendants' actions and/or inactions in responding to Plaintiff's IPRA requests are in violation of IPRA law and subject to sanctions.

20. Damages for enforcement of a denied request to inspect records are governed by Section 14-2-12(D) NMSA 1978, not Section 14-2-11(C) NMSA 1978. [NOTE: This is untrue.] The statutory maximum per-day penalty of Section 14-2-11(C) NMSA 1978 does not create any standard for an amount of damages under Section 14-2-12 (D) NMSA 1978. *Faber v. King*, 2013-NMCA-080, 306 P.3d 519, cert. granted, 2013-NMCERT-007.

21. Section 14-2-12(D) provides for damages, "which we hold must be somehow specified as to their true nature by the district court." *Faber v. King*, 2013-NMCA-080 {15}.

22. Punitive damages cannot be recovered in absence of compensatory or nominal damages. *Madrid v. Marquez*, 2001-NMCA-087 pp. 3, 131, N.M. 132, 33 P.3d 683.

23. UJI 13-1832, NMRA reads in part, "Nominal damages are a trivial sum of money ... awarded to a party who has established right to recover, but has not established that she is entitled to compensatory damages."

24. Plaintiff Cooper has established that she has a right to recover but has not established that she is entitled to compensatory damages and is awarded one thousand dollars ($1,000.00) as nominal damages against Defendants.

25. UJI 13-1827, NMRA allows the award of punitive damages if the conduct of the Defendants is malicious, willful, reckless, wanton, or in bad faith.

26. Defendants' conduct in not providing the requested records enumerated in Findings of Fact 10, is willful, wanton, and in bad faith.

27. Defendants' conduct in providing altered records as discussed in Findings of Facts 25, 26, and 29 and Conclusions of Law 18 is wanton, willful, and in bad faith.

28. Based on Defendants' conduct, Plaintiff Cooper is entitled to punitive damages in the amount of one hundred thousand dollars ($100,000.00) against Defendants.

29. Section 14-2-12(D) allows for an award of attorney's fees and costs.

30. Plaintiff Cooper is awarded attorney's [sic – attorneys'] fees which have not been previously paid.

31. Plaintiff Cooper is awarded her costs.

## ORDER

IT IS THEREFORE ORDERED Judgment be entered in favor of Plaintiff Cooper against Defendants as follows:

1. Nominal Damages in the amount of thousand dollars ($1,000.00);

2. Punitive Damage in the amount of one hundred thousand dollars ($100,000.00);

3. Attorney's fees which have not been previously paid;

4. Plaintiff is awarded costs and shall provide the Court with an affidavit supporting her costs within ten (10) days of the filing of these Findings of Fact and Conclusions of Law and Order of the Court;

5. Interest shall accrue at the rate of 8.75 percent per annum commencing from the date of the filing of the Judgment in this matter.

6. Plaintiff shall prepare the Judgment reflecting the Court's decision, approved as to form by counsel for Defendants, within fifteen (15) days of the filing of these Findings of Fact, Conclusion[s] of Law and Order of the Court.

*George P. Eichwald*
GEORGE P. EICHWALD
District Judge

# SOURCES

# ANNOTATED BIBLIOGRAPHY:

## SOURCES FOR BILLY THE KID CASE HOAX AND PRETENDERS EXPOSÉ
### (WITH CASE 2003-274, ITS EXHUMATIONS, ITS PARDON ATTEMPT, ITS 20th CENTURY BILLY THE KID PRETENDERS, ITS INVESTIGATIONS, ITS OPEN RECORDS LITIGATION, AND ITS TAXPAYER COSTS )
### &
## SOURCES FOR 19th CENTURY BILLY THE KID HISTORY

# SOURCES FOR BILLY THE KID CASE HOAX AND PRETENDERS EXPOSÉ

## *BOOKS*

Airy, Helen L. *Whatever Happened to Billy the Kid?* Santa Fe, New Mexico: Sunstone Press. 1993. (**John Miller as Billy the Kid.**)

Althouse, Bill. *Frozen Lightening: Bill Richardson's Strike on the Political Landscape of New Mexico.* Buckman, New Mexico: Thinking Out Loud Press. 2006.

Bugliosi, Vincent. *Outrage: The Five Reasons Why O.J. Simpson Got Away With Murder.* New York and London: W.W. Norton & Company. 1996. (**Exposé of Dr. Henry Lee improprieties, Pages 47-49.**)

Burns, Walter Noble. *The Saga of Billy the Kid.* Stamford, Connecticut: Longmeadow Press. 1992. (**Original printing: 1926, Doubleday.**)

Chamberlain, Kathleen, comp. *Billy the Kid and the Lincoln County War: A Bibliography.* Albuquerque, New Mexico: Center for the American West, University of New Mexico. 1997.

Cooper, Gale. *Billy the Kid's Pretenders: Brushy Bill and John Miller.* Albuquerque, New Mexico: Gelcour Books. 2012.

_____. *Billy the Kid's Writings, Words, and Wit.* Albuquerque, New Mexico: Gelcour Books. 2012.

_____. *MegaHoax: The Strange Plot to Exhume Billy the Kid and Become President.* Albuquerque, New Mexico: Gelcour Books. 2012.

Cline, Donald. *Alias Billy the Kid: The Man Behind the Legend.* Santa Fe: New Mexico: Sunstone Press. 1986. (**The work of an historian cited by the promulgators as backing them.**)

Garcia, Elbert A. *Billy the Kid's Kid 1875-1964, The Hispanic Connection.* Santa Rosa, New Mexico: Los Products Press. 1999. (**Unproven Billy the Kid grandson claimant; active participant in early Billy the Kid Case**)

Garrett, Pat F. *The Authentic Life of Billy the Kid The Noted Desperado of the Southwest, Whose Deeds of Daring and Blood Made His Name a Terror in New Mexico, Arizona, and Northern Mexico.* Santa Fe, New Mexico: New Mexico Printing and Publishing Co. 1882.

Hefner, Bobby E. *The Trial of Billy the Kid.* Hico, Texas: Bosque River Publishing Co. 1991. **(Brushy Bill Roberts as Billy the Kid)**

Jameson, W.C. and Frederic Bean. *The Return of the Outlaw Billy the Kid.* Plano, Texas: Republic of Texas Press. 1997. **("Brushy Bill" Roberts as Billy the Kid.)**

Kaplan, Harold I., M.D. and Benjamin J. Sadock, M.D. *Synopsis of Psychiatry.* Philadelphia: Lippincott Williams & Wilkins. 1994. **(Confabulation, Page 285)**

Klein, Aaron and Brenda J. Elliott. "Impeachable Offences: The Case for Removing Barak Obama From Office." Washington, D.C.: WND Books. 2013. **(Eric Holder criminality)**

Malkin, Michelle. *Culture of Corruption: Obama and His Team of Tax Cheats, Crooks, and Cronies.* Washington, D.C.: Regnery Publishing, Inc. 2009. **(Richardson criminality)**

Metz, Leon C. *Pat Garrett. The Story of a Western Lawman.* Norman: University of Oklahoma Press. 1974.

Miller, Jay. *Billy the Kid Rides Again: Digging for the Truth.* Santa Fe, New Mexico: Sunstone Press. 2005. **(Reprint of his syndicated articles from his column, "Inside the Capitol" - an exposé of the Billy the Kid hoax.)**

Morrison, William V. and C.L. Sonnichsen. *Alias Billy the Kid.* Albuquerque: University of New Mexico Press. 1955. **("Brushy Bill" Roberts as Billy the Kid.)**

Nolan, Frederick. *The Lincoln County War: A Documentary History.* Norman: University of Oklahoma Press. 1992.

_____. *The West of Billy the Kid.* Norman: University of Oklahoma Press. 1998. **(See page 7 for quote on the Eugene Cunningham hoaxed photo of Catherine Antrim.)**

Palast, Greg. *The Best Democracy Money Can Buy.* New York: A Plume Book. 2004. **(Manny Aragon exposé is on page 214.)**

_____. *Armed Madhouse.* New York: Penguin Group USA. 2007. **(Richardson exposé.)**

Pittmon, Geneva. Roberts Family Bible with genealogy. **(Showing "Brushy Bill" Roberts was under 2 years only when Billy the Kid was killed)**

Poe, John W. *The Death of Billy the Kid.* (Introduction by Maurice Garland Fulton). Boston and New York: Houghton Mifflin Company. 1933. **(Pages 22 and 25-26 show Rudolph quote and part omitted from Probable Cause Statement.)**

Richardson, Bill, with Michael Ruby. *Between Worlds: The Making of an American Life.* New York: G.P. Putnam's Sons. 2005

Siringo, Charles. *The History of Billy the Kid.* Santa Fe: New Mexico. Privately Printed. 1920. **(Reproduces the Jim East letter on pages 96-107)**

Sonnichsen, C.L. and William V. Morrison. *Alias Billy the Kid.* Albuquerque, New Mexico: University of New Mexico Press. 1955. **(Brushy Bill Roberts as Billy the Kid)**

Utley, Robert M. *Billy the Kid. A Short and Violent Life.* Lincoln and London: University of Nebraska Press. 1989.

Valdez, Jannay P. and Bobby E. Hefner. *Billy the Kid: "Killed" in New Mexico ... Died in Texas: A biography, a defense of Billy the Kid ... who died in 1950, not 1881 ... a true, suppressed, and hidden story.* Dallas, Texas: Outlaw Publications. 1995. **(Brushy Bill Roberts as Billy the Kid)**

Weddle, Jerry. *Antrim is My Stepfather's Name. The Boyhood of Billy the Kid.* Monograph 9, Globe, Arizona: Arizona Historical Society. 1993.

## GUIDES, PAMPHLETS (CHRONOLOGICAL ORDER)

Turk, David S. Historian U.S. Marshals Service. "Research Report: The U.S. Marshals Service and Billy the Kid. To Be Added in its Present Entirety, with Exhibits, to Lincoln County, New Mexico Case # 2003-274." U.S. Marshals Service Executive Services Division. December, 2003.

## PRESS RELEASES (GOVERNOR BILL RICHARDSON)

Richardson, Bill. "Governor Bill Richardson Announces State Support of Billy the Kid Investigation." June 10, 2003. (**Announcement at State Capitol of state backing of case # 2003-274 and listing of the participants: Tom Sullivan, Steve Sederwall, Gary Graves, Sherry Tippett, and Paul Hutton.**)
_____. "Gov. Bill Richardson Appoints Criminal Defense Lawyer to NM Supreme Court." November 2, 2007. (**Husband of Randi McGinn**)
_____. "Governor Bill Richardson to Consider Billy the Kid Pardon Petition." Press release. December 16, 2010. (**Floating the Randi McGinn petition**)
_____. "Governor Richardson to Announce his decision on Billy the Kid Pardon Request Tomorrow." Press release. December 30, 2010.

## NEWSPAPER, MAGAZINE, AND INTERNET ARTICLES (CHRONOLOGICAL ORDER)

Blythe, Dee. "Billy the Kid Landmarks Fast Vanishing: Historic Spots Hard to Find; Markers Needed." *Clovis, New Mexico Evening News-Journal*. Volume 9. Number 2. Section E. Monday, May 31, 1937. (**Photo and article about Maxwell family furniture**)
Humphreys, Sexson. "Pardon My 6-Shooters: Billy the Kid? Governor to Decide; 'Pardon Me, I'm Alive,' Says Billy the Kid." *The Indianapolis News*. Thursday, November 30, 1950. Indiana Historical Society. Lew Wallace Collection (M292). Box 14. Folder 12.
Smith, Gene. "The National Police Gazette." *American Heritage Magazine*. Volume 23. Issue 6. October, 1972. (**Reference for debunking David Turk's "Report."**)
Hutton, Paul Andrew. "Dreamscape Desperado." *New Mexico Magazine*. Volume 68. Number 6. Pages 44-58. June, 1990.
Reed, Ollie. "Board approves Hubbard license." *Albuquerque Tribune*. Page 1, A1. December 4, 2002.
Benke, Richard. AP. "Billy the Kid's Life and Death May Be Put to the DNA Test: Officials want to exhume the body of the outlaw's mother to test a Texas man's claim that he was Bonney. If so, Pat Garrett didn't kill the kid." *The Nation*. January 18, 2004.
Clark, Guy C., Executive Director of New Mexico Coalition Against Gambling. " 'Dollar Bill' Richardson." *Albuquerque Journal Op-Ed*. December 16, 2002.
Janofsky, Michael. "122 Years Later, the Lawmen Are Still Chasing Billy the Kid." *The New York Times*. Vol. CLII, No. 52,505. Pages 1 and A31. June 5, 2003. (**First national announcement of case.**)
DellaFlora, Anthony. "State Not Kidding Around: Governor won't mind if probe of the notorious 19th century N.M. outlaw boosts tourism." *Albuquerque Journal*. No. 162. Pages 1 and A1. June 11, 2003. (**First major New Mexico announcement of Billy the Kid Case.**)

Bommersbach, Jana. "Digging Up Billy: If Pat Garrett didn't kill the Kid, who's buried in his grave?" *True West*. Volume 50. Issue 7. Pages 42-45. August/September 2003.

_____. "From Shovels to DNA: The inside story of digging up Billy." *True West*. Volume 50. Issue 7. Pages 42-45. October/November, 2003.

No Author. AP. "Authorities call for exhumation of Billy the Kid's mother to solve mystery." *Silver City Sun News*. October 11, 2003.

_____. "Billy the Kid's mother may be exhumed." October 11, 2003.

Jameson, W.C. and Leon Metz. "Was Brushy Bill Really Billy the Kid? Experts face off over new evidence." *True West*. Volume 50. Issue 10. Pages 32-33. November/December, 2003.

Murphy, Mary Alice. "Billy the Kid 'Hires' a Lawyer." *Silver City Daily Press Internet Edition*. http://www.thedailypress.com/NewsFolder/11.17.2.html. November 17, 2003.

Boyle, Alan. "Billy the Kid gets a lawyer: 122 years after shootout, attorney to gather information for a pardon." msnbc.com. November 18, 2003.

Fecteau, Loie. "No Kidding: Governor Taps Lawyer For Billy." *Albuquerque Journal*. Page 1, A6. November 19, 2003.

No Author. AP. "Lawyer Appointed to Represent Dead Outlaw." *Silver City Sun News*. http://www.krqe.com/expanded.asp?RECORD_KEY%5bContent. November 19, 2003.

No Author. "Lawmakers Consider Posthumous Pardon for Billy the Kid." *abqtrib.com News*. November 21, 2003.

Boyle, Alan. "Billy the Kid's DNA Sparks Legal Showdown: Sheriffs and mayors face off over digging up remains from the Old West." *msnbc.com*. November 21, 2003.

Romo, Rene. "Kid's Mom May Stay Buried: Silver City wins round to block exhumation for outlaw's DNA." *Albuquerque Journal*. Section D3. December 9, 2003.

Janna Bommersbach. "Breaking Out More Shovels: Fort Sumner's Sheriff Gary Graves commits to digging up Billy the Kid's Grave." *True West*. Volume 51. Issue 1. Pages 46-47. January/February, 2004. (**Hoax-backing article**)

Benke, Richard. AP. "N.M. Re-Opens Case of Billy the Kid." Yahoo! News. January 13, 2004.

_____. "Billy the Kid's Life and Death May Be Put to DNA Test: Officials want to examine the body of the outlaw's mother to test a Texas man's claim that he was Bonney. If so, Pat Garrett didn't kill the Kid." *The Nation*. January 18, 2004. (**Uses fake Overton Affidavit given by Attorney Sherry Tippett**)

No Author. AP. "Billy the Kid hearing delayed for months: Sheriffs need more time to prepare arguments for exhuming remains of outlaw's mother." January 23, 2004.

Miller, Jay. "Digging Up the Latest on Billy the Kid." *Las Cruces Sun-News*. February 3, 2004.

Gonzales. Carolyn. "Hutton writes wild frontier stories for History Channel." *University of New Mexico Campus News*. Volume 39. No. 12. February 16, 2004.

Miller, Jay. "The Billy the Kid Code." *Las Cruces Sun-News*. March 29, 2004.

Nathanson, Rick. "Grave Doubts: 'Investigating History' series tries to clear up the mysteries surrounding Billy the Kid." *Albuquerque Journal Weekly TV Guide: Entertainer*. Pages 3, 5. April 24, 2004.

Garrett, Wm. F. "Letters to the Editor." *De Baca County News*. Page 4. May 6, 2004.

Murphy, Mary Alice and Melissa St. Aude. "Sederwall, Sullivan uninvited to ball." *Silver City Daily Press Internet Edition*. June 10, 2004.

Hill, Levi. "Billy the Kid Stirring Up Dust in Silver City." *Las Cruces Sun-News*. Section 5A. Page 1, A2. June 12, 2004.

No Author. "Attorney Refuses Judge's statements concerning exhumation." *thedailypress.com*. June 15, 2004. (**Attorney Tippett repeats her OMI misrepresentations.**)

Richardson, Bill. "Verbatim: I have to decide whether to pardon him. But not right away – after the investigation, after the state gets more publicity." *Time*. Vol. 163. No. 25. Page 17. June 21, 2004.

Romo, Rene. "Back off on Billy, Gov. Asked: Silver City says inquiry into death of Kid would harm state tourism. *Albuquerque Journal*. Section B-1, B-5. June 23, 2004.

No Author. "Lincoln county deputy sheriff sends his own letter to governor." *Silver City Daily Press*. Pages 1, 13. . June 25, 2004. **(Letter from Sederwall.)**

No Author. "Editorials: New Racing Schedule Tramples Horseman." *Albuquerque Journal*. June 26, 2004.

Miller, Jay. "Inside the Capitol. Bizarre case of Billy the Kid." *Roswell Daily Record*. Page A4. July 2, 2004.

Romo, Rene. "Forensic Expert on Billy's Case: Questions Remain on Outlaw's Fate." *Albuquerque Journal*. Page 1. August 2, 2004. **(Falsely claims blood on bench; says "trace blood")**

No Author. "Forensic expert joins Billy the Kid inquiry in New Mexico." *AP SignOnSanDiego.com*. August 2, 2004.

Miller, Jay. "Inside the Capitol. Sheriffs slippery on Billy the Kid Case." *Roswell Daily Record*. Page A4. August 9, 2004.

Cherry, Doris. "Forensics 101 for 'Billy'." *Lincoln County News*. Pages 2, 10. August 12, 2004. **(Quotes Sullivan's lie: "a lot" of blood on bench)**

Miller, Jay. "Inside the Capitol. Expert questions Kid probe." *Roswell Daily Record*. Page A4. August 20, 2004.

_____. "Inside the Capitol. Hat dance on probe funding." *Roswell Daily Record*. Page A4. September 1, 2004.

_____. "Inside the Capitol. Three sheriffs push Kid Case." *Roswell Daily Record*. Page A4. September 5, 2004.

_____. "Inside the Capitol. Sheriffs hoax is world-class." *Roswell Daily Record*. Page A4. September 8, 2004.

_____. "Inside the Capitol. Kid gets day in court Sept. 27." *Roswell Daily Record*. Page A4. September 12, 2004.

_____. "Inside the Capitol. Kid probe making us think." *Roswell Daily Record*. Page A4. September 13, 2004.

Stinnett, Scot. "De Baca County Citizens' Committee Files Petition for Recall of Sheriff Gary Graves." *De Baca County News*. September 14, 2004.

Miller, Jay. "Inside the Capitol. Who is Attorney Bill Robins?" *Roswell Daily Record*. Page A4. September 15, 2004.

Green, Keith. "Mountain Asides: Billy's restless bones are stirred up once again. *RuidosoNews.com*. September 16, 2004.

Miller, Jay. "Inside the Capitol. Kid Case: David fights Goliath." *Roswell Daily Record*. Page A4. September 17, 2004.

_____. "Inside the Capitol. Many reasons to dig up Kid." *Roswell Daily Record*. September 19, 2004. Page A4.

_____. "Inside the Capitol. Nothing to worry about." *Roswell Daily Record*. Page A4. September 20, 2004.

Stallings, Dianne. "Showdown in the County Seat." *RuidosoNews.com* September 21, 2004. **(Commissioner Leo Martinez's meeting.)**

Miller, Jay. "Inside the Capitol. Who speaks for Pat Garrett?" *Roswell Daily Record*. September 22, 2004. Page A4.

Stallings, Dianne. "Showdown in the County Seat: shouting match erupts at County Commissioners meeting Tuesday over investigation of Billy the Kid." *Ruidoso News*. September 22, 2004.

Cherry, Doris. "Lincoln County 'War' Heats Up Over 'Billy: Capitan Mayor Tracks His Kind of '---' To County Commission Meeting. Tells Jay Miller where to go: wonders why commissioner has his panties in a wad." *Lincoln County News*. Vol. 99. No. 38. Pages 1-3. September 23, 2004. **(Commissioner Martinez stops the hoaxers' exhumation of Billy the Kid)**

922

Miller, Jay. "Inside the Capitol. Is there a new Santa Fe Ring?" *Roswell Daily Record*. Page A4. September 24, 2004.

Stinnett, Scott. "Rest in Peace, Billy! Exhumation case dismissed." *De Baca County News*. Vol. 104. No. 2. Pages 1, 5, 6. September 30, 2004.

Miller, Jay. "Inside the Capitol. Fort Sumner celebrates win." *Roswell Daily Record*. Page A4. October 1, 2004.

No author. "Fraud Alleged at Cellmark, DNA Testing Firm." TalkLeft: The Politics of Crime. http://www.talkleft.com./new_archives/008809.html. November 18, 2004.

Jana Bommersbach. "Kid Exhumation Nixed: Billy and his mom to rest in peace. *True West*. Volume 52. Issue 1. Pages 68-69. January/February 2005. (**Hoaxbacking article**)

Massey, Barry. "Casinos, contracting lawyers fund Madrid." The New Mexican. http://www.freenewmexican.com/news/13746.html May 14, 2005.

Roosevelt, Margot. "Bill Richardson: The Presidential Contender." *Time*. August 22, 2005. Vol. 166. No. 8. Page 50. August 22, 2005. (**Identifying him as likely leak in Wen Ho Lee case**)

Stinnett, Scott. "Judge rules Graves recall can proceed: Parker finds probable cause after two-day hearing." *De Baca County News*. Vol. 104. No. 49. Pages 1, 4, 10. August 25, 2005. (**The Recall Hearing of Sheriff Gary Graves**)

_____. "Testimony paints Graves as 'above the law': Recall probable cause hearing emotional, contentious." *De Baca County News*. Vol. 104. No. 50. Pages 1, 5, 6, 8, 9, 10. September 1, 2005.

Auslander, Jason. "N.M. state treasurers indicted in kickback scheme, thousands taken." *New Mexican*. September 16, 2005.

Carter, Julie. "Follow the Blood: In the Billy the Kid Case, Miller Exhumed." *RuidosoNews.com*. October 6, 2005. (**Sederwall lies about blood being on bench; ; has Sederwall's "dead men don't bleed" quote; has the Lonnie Lippman photo of Sederwall holding John Miller skull**)

Sullivan, Tom. "Letters: Your Opinion." *RuidosoNews.com*. October 21, 2005. (**Sullivan letter to the editor: "Why are they so afraid of the truth?"**)

Carter, Julie. "Billy the Kid in Prescott? *New Mexico Stockman*. Pages 38, 39, 76. November, 2005.

Romo, Rene. "Billy the Kid Probe May Yield New Twist. *Albuquerque Journal*. *ABQ Journal.com*. November 6, 2005. (**Claims Sullivan and Sederwall have John Miller's DNA**)

No Author. "after a big fundraiser by his pal, casino owner. R.D. Hubbard..." "The Journal Op-ed Page." *Albuquerque Journal*. December 12, 2005.

Struckman, Robert. "Bitterroot man hopes to uncover truth about Billy the Kid." (Misshttp://www.helenair.com/articles/2006/03/13/montana/a05031306_01.txt (Missoulian) March 13, 2006.

Dodder, Joanna. "Officials could face charges for digging up alleged Billy the Kid." *The Daily Courier of Prescott Arizona*. April 12, 2006. (**Sullivan claims DNA in "two months," and fakes Hudspeth skeleton as John Miller's and makes up left scapula bullet wound**)

Banks, Leo W. "The New Billy the Kid? The mad search for the bones of an American outlaw icon has come to Arizona." *Tucson Weekly*. http://www.tucsonweekly.com/gbase/Currents/Content?oid=oid:81013 April 13, 2006. (**Sullivan lies that bench is "saturated with blood; Dr. Rick Staub says DNA extracted from William Hudspeth not John Miller**)

Carter, Julie. "Digging up bones, Arizona may protest Miller exhumation." jcarter@tularosa.net. April 19, 2006.

Carter, Julie. "Culture Shock: The cowboys and the Kid go to France. jcarter@tulerosa.net. May 5, 2006. (**Says Sullivan worked on movie 9 months**)

Shafer, Mark. "N.M. pair may face charges in grave case." May 13, 2006. markshafer @ArizonaRepublic.com. http://www.azcentral.com/arizonarepublic/local/articles/0513billythekid0513.html

Myers, Amanda Lee. "New Mexicans Dig Up Trouble in Arizona." *Albuquerque Journal, New Mexico and the West.* Page B4. May 14, 2006. **(Also in gulfnews.com; confirms "Dallas lab" is doing DNA comparisons)**
_____. "Billy the Kid Still 'Wanted.' " gulfnews.com. http://archive.gulfnews.com/articles/06/05/16/10040234.html. May 16, 2006.

McCarthy, Todd. "Requiem for Billy the Kid." May 20, 2006. Variety.com. http://www.variety.com/review/VE1117930570?categoryid=2220&cs=1&nid=2562.

No author. "Out of Competition/Cannes Classics: Requiem for Billy the Kid. Festival de Cannes May 17-28, 2006." http://www.festival-cannes.fr/films/fiche_film.php?langue=4355535. May 20, 2006. **(Sullivan and Sederwall called two sheriffs)**

McCoy, Dave. "L 'Ouest Américain." MSN Movies. http://movies.msn.com/movies/canneso6/dispatch8. May 25, 2006.

Bennett, Ray. "Requiem for Billy the Kid." TheHollywoodReporter.com. May 26, 2006. **(Best demonstration of the hoax damage to history.)**

Smith, Emily C. "What an honor for two of New Mexico's finest citizens ...." Letter to the Editor. *RuidosoNews.com.* http://ruidosonews.com/apps/pbcs.dll/article?AID=/20060602/OPINION03/6060203 42/101 June 2, 2006. **(Advertising the hoaxers.)**
_____. "The cowboys are back in town, film in six months." jcarter@tulerosa.net. June 9, 2006. **(Describes plans for more programs)**

Valdez, Jannay. "Digging Up the Truth About Billy." *RuidosoNews.com.* http://ruidosonews.com/apps/pbcs.dll./article?AID=/2006069/OPINION03/6060903 51/101... June 9, 2006.

Dodder, Joanna. "Back at Rest: Bones of Billy the Kid return to Prescott." *The Daily Courier. h*ttp://prescottdailycourier.com/print.asp?ArticleID=40353&Section ID=1&SubSectionID=1. July 9, 2006.

Daniels, Bruce. "O Fair New Mexico." ABQNewsSeeker (from ABQjournal.com) http://www.adqjournal.com/abqnews/index.php?option=com_cont ent&task=view d=117... July 14, 2006.

No Author. AP. "PRESCOTT, Ariz. - Prosecutors won't seek charges against two men who exhumed the remains of a man who claimed to be the outlaw Billy the Kid." AOL News. October 23, 2006.
_____. AP. "Billy the Kid Case Dropped." *Albuquerque Journal. Metro.* D3. October 24, 2006.
_____. AP. "Men Who Exhumed Billy the Kid Won't Be Charged." *New York Sun.* http://www.nysun.com/article/42176. October 24, 2006. **(Claims Sullivan and Sederwall did Arizona exhumation, have Miller DNA, and sent to Orchid for matchings to bench DNA)**
_____. AP. "Arizona: No Charges Sought for Exhuming Remains." *New York Times.* A-26. http://www.nytimes.com/2006/10/24/us/24brfs-002.html?r=1&oref=slogin. October 24, 2006.

No Author. Forged Check Article with check photo of Case 2003-274 "Private Donor Fund." *Ruidoso News.* Page 1. November 25, 2006.

Martínez, Tony and Alison. "Better Days Ahead for New Mexico Highlands University?" *The Hispanic Outlook in Higher Education.* December 4, 2006.

Cameron, Carl. "New Mexico Gov. Bill Richardson says He's Running for President in 2008." FoxNews.com. December 7, 2006.

No Author. "AG won't investigate governor's hires." newmexicomatters.com: RichardsonWatch. December 19, 2006.

Goddard, Terry. "Guest Opinion: Public officials not above law. *Arizona Star.* January 5, 2007.

Geissler, Jeff. AP. "Richardson to explore presidential bid. New Mexico Democrat hopes to become nation's first Hispanic president." January 19, 2007.

924

Turk, David S. "Billy the Kid and the U.S. Marshals Service." *Wild West*. Volume 19. Number 5. Pages 34 – 41. February 2007. (**Turk's expurgated "U.S. Marshals Service and Billy the Kid" from Probable Cause Statement.** )

Cole, Thomas J. "Govzilla 24/7: As Governor, Bill Richardson Has Pushed an Aggressive Agenda and is Wildly Popular - But Critics Grumble That He's a Power-hungry, Self-aggrandizing Bully." *The Sunday Journal (Albuquerque Journal)*. No. 42. Pages A1, A10-A14. February 11, 2007.

Crowley, Candy. "Richardson Pitch: Regular guy with extraordinary résumé." CNN Washington Bureau. March 14, 2007.

Jason Strykowski. "A Tale of Two Governors ... And one Kid." *True West*. Vol. 54. Issue 5. Page 64. May, 2007.

No Author. AP. "Billy the Kid Exhumation a Possibility." *Roswell Daily Record.* May 2, 2007. (**From Stephenville, Texas AP on "Brushy Bill" exhumation attempt; Sederwall claims has John Miller's DNA**)

Carter, Julie. "Brushy Bill targeted for DNA testing; Billy the Kid workbench goes on display." *Ruidoso News*. May 3, 2007.

No Author. AP. "Manhunt for Real Billy the Kid Goes On: Deputy hopes DNA will finally reveal outlaw's true identity." *Albuquerque Journal*. May 4, 2007. B3.

Zorosec, Thomas. "DNA could solve mystery of Billy the Kid." Chron.com - Houston Chronicle. May 9, 2007. (**From Hamilton, Texas; "Brushy Bill" exhumation attempt** )

No Author. AP. "Texas town denies request to exhume Billy the Kid claimant." *Houston Chronicle*. May 11, 2007.

_____. "Evidence Hidden in Spector Trial." BBC Internet News. May 24, 2007. (**Dr. Henry Lee alleged as destroying evidence**)

_____. "Famed experts credibility takes a hit at Spector trial." CNN.com LAW CENTER. May 25, 2007. (**Dr. Henry Lee allegedly destroyed evidence**)

Barry, John. "Lax and Lazy at Los Alamos: Officials at nuclear weapons laboratory, already struggling to calm concerns over security lapses, now have two more breaches to explain." newsweek.com. June 25, 2007.

Cole, Thomas J. "Tycoon Backs Gov. All the Way: Hobbs businessman has helped raise millions, but he's had his share of controversy." *Albuquerque Journal*. No. 189. A1, A7, A8. July 8, 2007.

Turk, David S. "Billy the Kid and the U.S. Marshals Service." *Wild West*. Vol. 19. No. 5. pp. 34-39. February, 2007.

Cole, Thomas J. "Cope Makes Most of His Millions in Oil, Gas." *Albuquerque Journal*. July 8, 2007.

Nagourney, Adam and Jeff Zeleny. "First a Tense Talk With Clinton, Then Richardson Backs Obama." NYTIMES.com. March 22, 2008.

Weisman, Jonathan. "A Coveted Endorsement. Richardson Throws Support to Obama." Washingtompost.com. March 22, 2008.

Stallings, Dianne. "Billy the Kid case straps county for insurance." *RuidosoNews.com*. August 13, 2008.

Carter, Julie. "Lincoln County deputies resign commissions for Kid case." *Ruidosonews.com*. August 16, 2007. (**Beginning of ploy to call Case 2003-274 a "hobby"**)

Romo, Rene. "Seeking the Kid, Minus Badges. Deputies Resign to Hunt for Billy." *Albuquerque Journal*. No. 230. pp. 1-2. August 18, 2007.

Brunt, Charles D. "Suit Targets Investigation Into Billy the Kid's Death. *Albuquerque Journal*. August 28, 2008. (**FOG joins as parallel Virden et al IPRA case**)

Haussamen, Heath and Trip Jennings (of the *New Mexico Independent)*. "State is cooperating with federal probe of GRIP bonds." nmploitics.net. August 29, 2008.

Concerned Citizens of Lincoln County. "Should Lincoln County Have Grave Concerns Over A Person Like Steve Sederwall Running for Sheriff? *Lincoln County News*. October 16, 2008. p. 6.

Braun, Martin Z. and William Selway. "Grand Jury Probes Richardson Donor's New Mexico Financing Fee." bloombergnews.com. December 15, 2008.

Dunn, Geoffrey. "Richardson's Lies Have Finally Caught Up With Him." December 15, 2008. huffingtonpost.com. December 15, 2008.

Pickler, Nedra. "Richardson withdraws bid to be commerce secretary." breitbart.com. January 4, 2009.

No Author. "Bill Richardson bows out of commerce secretary job." CNN.com. January 4, 2009.

No Author. "Bill Richardson Withdraws Nomination as Commerce Secretary." FOXNews.com. January 4, 2009.

Ridgeway, James. "Why Did Obama's Transition Team Ignore Bill Richardson's Long History of Dubious Dealings?" motherjones.com. January 4, 2009.

Stephanopolous, George. "George's Bottom Line: Impossible for Obama to Keep Richardson." abcnews.com. January 4, 2009.

Pickler, Nedra. "Richardson withdrawals name. 'Pay-to-play' probe won't be completed by Cabinet hearings." *Albuquerque Journal*. No. 5. Page 3B. January 5, 2008.

Toensing, Gale Courey. "Politically-connected lawyer charged in hit-and-run death of Pueblo man." KRQE-TV.com. January 2, 2009.

Auslander, Jason. "Police work to dispel hit-run rumors." sfnewmexican.com. January 9, 2009. **(Rumor of Richardson fleeing crime scene)**

Sher, Lauren and Susan Aasen. "Whistleblower in Blago Case: Corruption 'Never Ceased to Amaze Me.'" abcNews.go.com. January 9, 2009.

No Author. "Richardson cleared in hit-and-run crash." KRQE News 13. January 10, 2009 . **(Quoted was Santa Fe Police Chief Eric Johnson)**

Haussamen, Heath. "Wonkett skewers gov over weekend boat crash" nmpolitics.net. January 10, 2009. **(Richardson denies boat crash responsibility, says napping)**

Dendahl, John. "Exclusive: Leaving Emperor Bill's Realm - Years of Buyer's Remorse Lie Ahead." familysecuritymatters.org. January 12, 2009. (Also printed as Dendahl, John (Former gubernatorial candidate). "Leaving Emperor Bill's realm - and the corruption of New Mexico." *Ruidosonews.com*. January 15, 2009.)

Lowy, Joan. "69 computers missing from nuclear weapons lab: 69 computers missing from Los Alamos nuclear weapons lab, including 13 stolen last year." newsweek.com. February 11, 2009.

Murdoch, Rupert. "Statement From Rupert Murdoch." *New York Post Online*. February 24, 2009. **(Taking responsibility for racist-like political cartoon)**

Barr, Andy. "Bill Richardson Tarnished by Scandal." Politico.com. February 9, 2009.

No Author. "William M. Tweed." Wikipedia: Wikimedia Foundation, Inc. (Internet). March 9, 2009.

Lloyd, Jonathan. AP. "Phil Spector Convicted of Second-degree Murder." *NBC Los Angeles Internet (Beta LA/News)*. April 13, 2009.

Sullivan, Eileen. Washington AP. "Republicans criticize report on right wing groups." (Appeared under *Drudge Report* as "Big Sis Feels Heat for Homeland Warning on 'Radicals.'" April 16, 2009. **(Janet Napolitano calls vets potential terrorists.)**

Rattman, Peter and Craig Karmin. "Rattnet involved in inquiry on fees." *Wall Street Journal*." April 17, 2009. **(Quadrangle Group investment fund scandal, ultimately involving Richardson)**

Pollack, Andrew. "DNA Evidence Can Be Fabricated, Scientists Show." NYTimes.com (TimesPeople, Science). August 17, 2009.

Eaton, Leslie. "Gov. Richardson Says Feds Won't File Charges in Corruption Probe." The Wall Street Journal Digital Network. August 27, 2009.

McKinley, James C. Jr. and Michael Haederle. "No Charges for Governor After Inquiry Into Contract. NYTimes.com. August 27, 2009.

Gallagher, Mike and Dan Boyd. "In the Clear: Feds Criticize Gov's Office But Skip Indictments. *Albuquerque Journal*. No. 240. Pages 1A – 2A. August 28, 2009.

Newell, Jim. "Bill Richardson & Pals Smash Into Docked Boat, Flee." wonkette.com. September 10, 2009.

Coleman, Michael. "Gov. Blames Journal for '1 of Worst' Label." *Albuquerque Journal.* Section C. Page 1. April 22, 2010. (**Richardson polled as most corrupt and incompetent governor in country.**)

Miller, Jay. "Kid's Pardon a Publicity Stunt." "Inside the Capitol" syndicated column "Inside the Capitol" and blog, insidethecapitol.blogspot.com. June 23, 2010.

Stinnett, Scot. "Billy the Kid historian says pardon all part of the hoax." *De Baca County News.* Pages 3, 9. June 24, 2010. (**Reprint of my Jay Miller article without commentary**)

Romero, Nick Arno. "Forget the Kid; Real Outlaws are in Capital [sic]." *Albuquerque Journal.* Letter to the Editor. July 10, 2010.

No Author. "Billy the Kid 'to be pardoned.' " *Press Trust of India (Hindustan Times)* and Pakistan *Daily Express.* July 11, 2010. (**Richardson's pardon publicity move - with "Brushy" as Billy.**)

Romo, Rene. "Gov. Weighs Pardon for Billy the Kid." *Albuquerque Journal. Saturday,* No. 205. Front page, lead story, cont. A6. July 24, 2010.

Licón, Adriana Gómez. "Pardon form New Mexico governor unlikely for Billy the Kid." *El Paso Times.* July 29, 2010.

Sharpe, Tom. "English kin trace path of 'Billy the Kid's' ex-boss: Tunstall's murder sparked Lincoln County War." *The New Mexican.* July 29, 2010.

Massey, Barry. Associated Press. Santa Fe. "Billy the Kid To Be Pardoned, 130 Years Later? Lawman's Grandchildren Outraged; 'Would You Issue A Pardon For Someone Who Made His Living As A Thief?' National, international, and internet publications. July 30, 2010. (**Introduction of Garrett family opposition. In *The Washington Times* and msnbc.com as "NM governor considers pardon for Billy the Kid," and huffingtonpost.com as "Billy the Kid Pardon: Pat Garrett's Descendants Outraged At Bill Richardson's Suggestion to Pardon Gunslinger."**)

Gardner, David. Los Angeles. "Pat Garrett's family plan showdown over plans to finally pardon Billy the Kid." London's *Daily Mail Online.* July 31, 2010.

Boardman, Mark. "The Lunacy of Billy the Kid." *True West.* Volume 57. Issue 8. Pages 42-47. August 2010. (**Defamatory article about me**)

Massey, Barry. Associated Press. Santa Fe. "NM gov meets with lawman Pat Garrett's descendants." August 4, 2010. www.wthr.com/global/story.asp?s=12926188.

Vaughn, Chris. "Texas Town seeks New Mexico pardon for Billy the Kid." *Fort Worth Star-Telegram.* August 14, 2010. (**Bid for "Brushy Bill" Roberts pardon.**)

Lacey, Marc. "Old West Showdown Is Revived. *New York Times.* August 15, 2010. (**Richardson shape-shifted to "amateur historian."**)

No Author. "A Tale of Two Billys." *New English Review: The Iconoclast.* (Internet). August 15, 2010.

Gordon, Bea. "Examining Legend: The Pardoning of Billy the Kid.. New Mexico Gov. Bill Richardson's talking about exonerating the state's most famous outlaw. But at what cost?" www.newwest.net/topic/article/29850/C37/L37/ August 17, 2010.

Massey, Barry. Associated Press. Santa Fe. " 'Billy the Kid' pardon effort draws Wild West showdown." Wilkes-Barre, Pennsylvania. *The Times Leader.* August 21, 2010. (**Introduction of William N. Wallace and Indiana Historical Society opposition. In starpress.com of east central Indiana as "Should Billy the Kid Be Pardoned?"**)

Miller, Jay. "When is a promise not a promise?" *Inside the Capitol.* August 30, 2010. (**Apparently legitimizing the McGinn-Richardson pardon**)

Sides, Hampton. "Not-So-Charming Billy." *NY Times Opinion Section Op-Ed Contributor.* September 6, 2010.

Richardson, Bill. "Governor Bill Richardson to Consider Billy the Kid Pardon Petition." Press release. December 16, 2010. (**Floating the Randi McGinn petition**)

Martinez, Edecio. "Billy the Kid to be Pardoned 130 Years Later." CBSNEWS.com. December 27, 2010.

Guarino, Mark. "Outgoing New Mexico Gov. Bill Richardson is considering a pardon for celebrated outlaw Billy the Kid. An informal e-mail poll shows support. But time is running out." Associated Press. December 29, 2010.

Levy, Glen. "Will Billy the Kid Be Pardoned? Governor Has Until Friday." TIME NewsFeed.com. December 29, 2010.

Richardson, Bill. "Governor Richardson to Announce his decision on Billy the Kid Pardon Request Tomorrow." Press release. December 30, 2010.

Burke, Kelly David. "Billy the Kid Pardon?" FoxNews.com. December 30, 2010.

Hopper, Jessica. "Gov. Bill Richardson: 'I've Decided Not to Pardon Billy the Kid.' " ABCNEWS.com. December 31, 2010.

Rojas, Rick. "No Pardon for Billy the Kid. New Mexico Gov. Bill Richardson says, 'The Romanticism appealed to me ... but the facts and evidence did not support it." *Los Angeles Times*. December 31, 2010.

Watson, Kathryn. "Alas, no pardon for Billy the Kid: New Mexico's Richardson says close call." washingtontimes.com. December 31, 2010. **(With "waste time" quote by Governor Susana Martinez)**

No Author. "Richardson Declines to Pardon Outlaw Billy the Kid." FoxNews.com. December 31, 2010.

Lacey, Marc. "For 2nd Time in 131 Years, Billy the Kid is Denied Pardon." *New York Times*. Page A10. January 1, 2011.

Todd, Jeff. "Trial seeks truth in Billy the Kid case." KRQE. February 17, 2011.

Nikolewski, Rob. "The shoe finally drops: New Mexico files lawsuits in federal and state courts in 'pay to play' scandal." New Mexico watchdog.org. May 6, 2011.

Milton, Susan. "New Mexico's Richardson buys Cape home." *Cape Cod Times*. December 10, 2011.

Romo, Rene. "Fight Won, Questions Remain: Billy the Kid DNA Report Released." *Albuquerque Journal*. Front Page and Page B1. April 29, 2012.

Terrell, Steve. "Attorney, gun-control activist found dead in Albuquerque home." *The New Mexican*. May 17, 2012. **(Death of Sherry Tippett)**

Gutierrez, Crystal. "Math check lessens Fierro's prison time: Attorney Killed pedestrian and drove away." KRQE.com. June 9, 2012. **(Hit-and-run killer attorney Fierro serves under 4 years)**

Kalvelage, Jim. "Ruidoso in danger: Little Bear Fire burns 10K acres, residents evacuate, Steve Pearce expresses outrage" *Ruidoso News*. June 10, 2012. **(Mention of the 2004 Peppin Fire; in Smokey Bear Capitan Mountains)**

Haussamen, Heath. "Lawyer's tenure on sunshine board needs to end." Heath Haussamen on N.M. politics. nmpolitics.net. July 2, 2012. **(Exposé of insider deal in Governor Martinez administration)**

Massey, Barry. "Court: Records Act Applies to Contractor." Associated Press. July 31, 2012. **(Massey omits Deborah Toomey's name, credits FOG amicus curiae)**

Kreuger, Joline Gutierrez. "UpFront." *Albuquerque Journal*. Page A1. August 3, 2012. **(Murder suspicion in death of Attorney Mary Han)**

Slotnick, Daniel E. "William N. Wallace, Former Times Reporter, Dies at 88." *New York Times*. August 14, 2012.

Farberov, Snejana. " 'This State is Going to hell': GOP leader in trouble after blasting New Mexico governor for dishonoring General Custer by meeting with Native-Americans." Dailymailonline.com. August 25, 2012 **(Pat Rogers and racism)**

Sullivan, John. "Yale football devotee Wallace '45 dies at 88." New Haven, Connecticut: *Yale Daily News*. August 29, 2012.

Drury, Ian and Martin Robinson. " 'I don't want to live in a world where everything I do is recorded,' says America's most wanted man as he comes out of hiding to reveal why he blew the whistle on US online spying." DailyMailOnline.com. June 10, 2013. . **(Snowden whistle blowing NSA's spying on citizens)**

Sandlin, Scott. "Billy the Kid case costs taxpayers nearly $200K: Billy the Kid lives on in battle of public records." *Albuquerque Journal.* Front Page, Page A2, Page A8. No. 162. June 11, 2013. **(Damage control to falsely minimize taxpayer costs and repeat blood on bench hoaxing)**

Cherry, Doris. "Modern Billy the Kid 'Cases' Cost Public Plenty: County Shells Out Bucks for Failing to Release Information." *Lincoln County News.* Volume 109. Number 6. Front Page and Pages 7-8. June 27, 2013. **(Based on my June 18, 2013 letter to the Lincoln County Commissioners)**

No Author. "Revealed: Eric Holder told the Russians that Edward Snowden will NOT face the death penalty or torture if he's returned to the U.S." Dailymailonline.com. July 26, 2013.

No Author. "Is that a joke, Mr. President? Obama tells Jay Leno that America does NOT spy on its citizens – in wake of Edward Snowden saga." DailyMailOnline.com. August 7, 2013.

No Author. "Obama uses TV appearance with Jay Leno to discuss Edward Snowden." Dailymailonline.com. August 7, 2013.

Gardner, Joshua. " 'It cost the public dearly': Snowden says media have failed as government watchdogs in his first interview since NSA leaks." DailyMailOnline.com. August 13, 2013.

Zucco, Erica. "AG questions suicide ruling of civil rights attorney. Eyewitness News KOB.com. August 16, 2013. **(Regarding Mary Han)**

Maloy, Camie. "It's amazing how Governor Martinez, who uses her special needs sister's ..." "MailBag." *People.* Volume 80. Number 8. August 19, 2013.

Goldman, Adam and Kimberly Dozier. "Edward Snowden covered Electronic Tracks." Dailymailonline.com. August 24, 2013.

No Author. "UC to spend up to $6m on crumbling mansion for New President Janet Napolitano despite tuition fees doubling and teacher layoffs due to budget cuts." DailyMailOnline.com. September 18, 2013.

Keneally, Meghan. "NSA employees used phone tapping to spy on their girlfriends and 'cheating' husbands: Investigation into abuses of power at NSA." DailyMailOnline.com. September 27, 2013.

Edmonds, Lizzie. " 'My Nessie picture IS a hoax!': Cruise boat skipper who took 'the most convincing Loch Ness Monster photo ever' admits he faked the image with a fibre-glass hump." Dailymailonline.com. October 4, 2013.

Stallings, Dianne. "Former Lincoln County Sheriff Tom Sullivan Dies in Texas." *Ruidoso News.* October 22, 2013.

No Author. "Former Lincoln Co. Sheriff Tom Sullivan Dies in Texas." *ABQnews online.* October 23, 2013. **(Repeats Dianne Stallings *Ruidoso News* article)**

Villagran, Lauren. "Award Ends Suit Over Billy the Kid Records." *Albuquerque Journal.* May 20, 2014.

Massey, Barry. "Author Awarded $100,000 in 'Billy the Kid' Lawsuit. Associated Press. *Santa Fe New Mexican* and *Washington Times.* May 21, 2014.

Lalire, Greg. "Author Wins 'Kid' Lawsuit." *Wild West* magazine. October, 2014.

# *MISCELLANEOUS SOURCES: LETTERS, E-MAILS, BLOGS, WEBSITE, PERSONAL COMMUNICATIONS (CHRONOLOGICAL ORDER)*

Morrison, William V. "Copy of transcript sent by Wm V. Morrison, El Paso, Texas." Donation letter sent to the Indiana Historical Society: Morrison's typed copy of Lew Wallace Jr.'s [March 13?, 1879] first "pardon deal" letter to Governor Lew Wallace. October, 1950. Indiana Historical Society. Lew Wallace Collection. M292. Folder 9. Box 3.

Pittmon, Geneva. "My uncle was Not Billy the Kid ..." Letter to Joe Bowlin with enclosed copy of the Roberts family Bible's genealogy page. Private collection Frederick Nolan. December 16, 1987. (**Showing Oliver P. Roberts date of birth as August 26, 1879 - less than 2 years old at Billy the Kid's death**)

Andrews, Pat. Chairman GRIEF (Gambling Research Information & Education Foundation). Quotes blog on April 15, 2003 from "Dockside must be watched closely"/ No author given/6.25.02/*Indianapolis Star* and "Casino fined $2.26 million over allegations of prostitution" and Mike Smith/7.30.02/*Las Vegas Sun*. (**On R.D. Hubbard's corruption**)

Valdez, Jannay. "Re: Billy the Kid (Brushy Bill Roberts), E-Mail To: Frederick Nolan "Author." September 12, 2004. (**Potential death threat to Frederick Nolan.**)

Valdez, Jannay. "Perpetuating Pat Garrett's Lie." Amazon.com Customer Review. December 28, 2005. (**Review of Jay Miller's *Billy the Kid Rides Again* from a "Brushy Bill" believer perspective**)

Boze Bell, Bob. "The Wild is back in the West." BBB's Blog. April 24, 2006. (**Announcement of invitation of Sullivan and Sederwall to Cannes Film Festival.**) http://www.truewestmagazine.com/weblog/blogger1.htm

Nolan, Frederick. "Response." May 22, 2006 E-Mail To Gale Cooper. (**Response of D. Ceribelli from the *New York Times* Executive Editor's Desk. Did not take article.**)

Saar, Meghan. To Gale Cooper. "BTK Hoax Article." E-Mail To Gale Cooper. January 31, 2006. (***Wild West* regarding my anti-hoax proposal**)

Cooper, Gale. To New Mexico Congresswoman Heather Wilson and Campaign Manager Enrique Knell. "Re: Information relevant to campaign claims of Attorney General Patricia Madrid's corruption." September 11, 2006.

_____. To New Mexico Congresswoman Heather Wilson and Campaign Manager Enrique Knell. "Re: Additional information relevant to the New Mexico Billy the Kid Case." September 22, 2006.

_____. To Kelly Ward, Campaign Manager for John Dendahl. "Re: For campaign perspective – Enclosed reference copy of Freedom of Information Act (FOIA)/New Mexico Inspection of Public Records Act (IPRA) request to Governor Bill Richardson." September 22, 2006.

_____. To John Dendahl. "RE: Documents Pertinent to Investigation of Billy the Kid Case Legal Improprieties." January 9, 2007.

_____. To Congressman Steve Pearce. "Bring to your attention an ongoing corruption case in Lincoln County ..." March 12, 2007.

_____. To New Mexico GOP Chairman Allen Weh. "RE: RICO Case." March 14, 2007.

_____. To State Senator Rod Adair. "Re: Overview of the Billy the Kid Case and its political scandal." April 3, 2007.

Sederwall, Steve. "To "Loretta. 'Wild Goose Chase.' " http://disc.server.com/discussion.cgi?disc=167540;article=33266;title=Billy%20the%20Kid"http://disc.server.com/discussion.cgi?disc=167540;title=Billy%20the%20Kid May 4, 2007. (**Admitting that John Miller DNA could not match bench DNA since John Miller did not claim bench death scene**)

_____. "Billyondabrain."http://disc.server.com/discussion.cgi?disc=167540; article=33266;title=Billy%20the%20Kid" May 13, 2007.

Nolan, Frederick. "Re: Maxwell Family Questions." E-Mail To: Gale Cooper. May 15, 2007. (**About dates of sale of Maxwell's Fort Sumner buildings**.)

Nolan, Frederick. "Re: Fame at Last!" E-Mail To Gale Cooper and others. February 22, 2010. (**His making TV program with hoaxers**)

Miller, Jay. "Re: Pardon Articles - Questions." E-Mail to Gale Cooper. September 6, 2010. (**Stating: "Steve Sederwall evidently wants to peddle your books ..."**)

Ford, Simon. "Subj. Questions regarding Orchid-Cellmark." E-Mail to Gale Cooper. January 31, 2011. (**Consultation on mixed DNA samples and DNA separation costs**)

Miller, Kenny. Personal communication to author about family history and showing Maxwell family objects - including the carpenter's bench, bedstead, and washstand - and providing photos of them to author. 2011 to 2012. (**Information from Maxwell family descendant**)

Sederwall, Steve. "billythekidcase.com" Website. From October (?) 2010 to 2012(?). (**For $25.00 membership selling Case 2003-274 records**)

Doland, Gwyneth. "Re: Resignation of Pat Rogers." E-Mail to NMFOG members. July 20, 2012. (**Rogers resigns from FOG**)

Rogers, Pat. "[M]y prompt resignation ..." E-Mail of Pat Rogers to FOG Board President Terri Cole and FOG Board. July 20, 2012. (**Resigns before FOG Board can discuss investigative reporter Heath Haussamen's "concerns" about Rogers's FOG membership**)

No Author. "Brushy Bill Roberts and Billy the Kid – The Complete Facts." http://www.angelfire.com/mi2/billythekid/brushy.html. (No date) (**Brushy Bill Roberts as Billy the Kid**)

## *TELEVISION PROGRAMS*

History Channel. "Investigating History: Billy the Kid." Week of April 24, 2004 and May 2, 2004.

David Letterman Show. January 15, 2009. (**Jokes about Richardson's corruption and withdrawal as Commerce Secretary.**)

National Geographic International Discovery ID Channel. "History Mysteries." 2010. (**Sederwall presenting the fake Dr. Lee Deputy James Bell top-of-the-stairs murder "investigation;" with Frederick Nolan participating as "fame at last"** )

# BILLY THE KID CASE HOAX DOCUMENTS (PRE-SANDOVAL COUNTY IPRA LITIGATION) (BY LOCATION AND CHRONOLOGICAL ORDER)

## ALBUQUERQUE, NEW MEXICO

Zumwalt, Ross E. "Response of Office of Medical Investigator to Petition to Exhume Remains of Catherine Antrim. In the Matter of Catherine Antrim. Case No. MS 2003-11." Sixth Judicial Court, County of Grant, State of New Mexico. January 9, 2004. (**Exhumation refused based on invalid DNA. Plot map of Catherine Antrim's grave was an Exhibit. Petitioners and Judge Quintero ignored the OMI.**)

_____. "Affidavit of Ross E. Zumwalt, MD. In the Matter of Catherine Antrim." Case No. MS 2003-11 Sixth Judicial Court, County of Grant, State of New Mexico. January 9, 2004.

Komar, Debra. "Deposition of Debra Komar, Ph.D. In the Matter of Catherine Antrim." Case No. MS 2003-11." Sixth Judicial Court, County of Grant, State of New Mexico. Taken by Attorney for Town of Silver City Adam S. Baker. January 20, 2004.

## CAPITAN, NEW MEXICO

Sederwall, Steve, "Mayor's Report." *Village of Capitan: Capitan Village Hall News.* Capitan, New Mexico. May 5, 2003. (**Announces filed Billy the Kid Case**)

# FORT SUMNER, NEW MEXICO
## (EXHUMATION ATTEMPT ON BILLY THE KID)

Breen, Victor C. and John Humphrey, Jr., Attorneys for Louis A Bowdre. "Motion to Intervene. In Re Application of Lois Telfer, Petitioner for the Removal of the Body of William H. Bonney, Deceased, From the Ft. Sumner Cemetery in Which He is Interred for Reinterment in the Lincoln, New Mexico, Cemetery." Case No. 3255. In the District Court of the Tenth Judicial District, County of De Baca. December 5, 1961. (**Louis Bowdre was the relative of Charles Bowdre whose grave is contiguous to William Bonney's.**)

Kinsley, E.T. District Judge. "Decree. In Re Application of Lois Telfer, Petitioner for the Removal of the Body of William H. Bonney, Deceased, From the Ft. Sumner Cemetery in Which He is Interred for Reinterment in the Lincoln, New Mexico, Cemetery." Case No. 3255." In the District Court of the Tenth Judicial District Within and For the County of De Baca. April 6, 1962. (**Petition for exhumation Billy the Kid denied on basis that his grave could not be located and the search would disturb Bowdre's remains. That precedent was ignored by the current Petitioners and their attorneys.**)

De Baca County Commissioners Special Meeting." Minutes. (Powhatan Carter III, Chairman; Joe Steele; Tommy Roybal; Nancy Sparks, County Clerk. To whom it may concern. "The De Baca County Commissioners are in full support of Village of Fort Sumner's stand against exhuming the body of Billy the Kid." September 25, 2003. (**Voted against exhumation.**)

Robins, Bill III and David Sandoval, Mark Acuña, Attorneys for Co-Petitioner Billy the Kid and Sheriff-Petitioners. "In the Matter of William H. Bonney, aka 'Billy the Kid': Petition for the Exhumation of Billy the Kid's Remains." Case No. CV-04-00005. Tenth Judicial District, County of De Baca, State of New Mexico. February 26, 2004. (**Robins joins Acuña to exhume the Kid**)

Robins, Bill III and David Sandoval, Attorneys for Co-Petitioner Billy the Kid. "In the Matter of William H. Bonney, aka 'Billy the Kid': Notice of Excusal." Case No. CV-2004 [sic]-00005. Tenth Judicial District, County of De Baca, State of New Mexico. March 5, 2004. (**Petitioners' removal of honest Judge Ricky Purcell from hearing the case.**)

Jimenez Maes, Petra, Chief Justice. "In the Matter of William H. Bonney, aka 'Billy the Kid': Order Designating Judge." Case No. CV-2004-00005. Tenth Judicial District, County of De Baca, State of New Mexico. April 1, 2004. (**Richardson appointee Ted Hartley is appointed to case**)

Baker, Adam S. and Herb Marsh, Jr., Attorneys for the Village of Fort Sumner. "In the Matter of William H. Bonney, aka 'Billy the Kid': Village of Fort Sumner's Unopposed Motion to Intervene." Case No. CV-04-00005. Tenth Judicial District, County of De Baca, State of New Mexico. April 12, 2004.

_____. "In the Matter of William H. Bonney, aka 'Billy the Kid': Response in Opposition to the Petitioners for the Exhumation of Billy the Kid's Remains. In the Matter of William H. Bonney, aka 'Billy the Kid.' " Case No. CV-04-00005. Tenth Judicial District, County of De Baca, State of New Mexico. April 12, 2004.

Hartley, Teddy L. "In the Matter of William H. Bonney, aka 'Billy the Kid': Order." Case No. CV-04-00005. Tenth Judicial District, County of De Baca, State of New Mexico. April 20, 2004. (**Intervention of Village of Fort Sumner granted**)

Baker, Adam S. and Herb Marsh, Jr., Attorneys for the Village of Fort Sumner. "In the Matter of William H. Bonney, aka 'Billy the Kid': Response in Opposition to the Petition for the Exhumation of Billy the Kid's Remains." Case No. CV-04-00005. Tenth Judicial District, County of De Baca, State of New Mexico. May 6, 2004.

Baker, Adam S. and Herb Marsh, Jr. "In the Matter of William H. Bonney, aka 'Billy the Kid': Village of Fort Sumner's Motion to Dismiss Against William H. Bonney Under Rule 1-107(A)." Case No. CV-04-00005. Tenth Judicial District, County of De Baca, State of New Mexico. June 24, 2004. **(That dead Billy is not real)**

_____. "In the Matter of William H. Bonney, aka 'Billy the Kid': Village of Fort Sumner's Motion For Proof of Attorneys' Authority To Act On Behalf Of William H. Bonney." Case No. CV-04-00005. Tenth Judicial District, County of De Baca, State of New Mexico. June 24, 2004. **(Confronting that dead Billy cannot have a lawyer)**

_____. "In the Matter of William H. Bonney, aka 'Billy the Kid': Village of Fort Sumner's Motion to Dismiss Against Petitioners Sullivan, Sederwall, and Graves for Lack of Standing." Case No. CV-04-00005. Tenth Judicial District, County of De Baca, State of New Mexico. June 24, 2004. **(Invalid murder case)**

_____. "In the Matter of William H. Bonney, aka 'Billy the Kid': Memorandum in Support Of Village of Fort Sumner's Motion to Dismiss Against Petitioners Sullivan, Sederwall, and Graves for Lack of Standing." Case No. CV-04-00005. Tenth Judicial District, County of De Baca, State of New Mexico. June 24, 2004. **(Invalid murder case)**

Hartley, Teddy L. District Judge. "Notice of Hearing. "In the Matter of William H. Bonney, aka 'Billy the Kid': Notice of Hearing." Case No. CV-04-00005. Tenth Judicial District, County of De Baca, State of New Mexico. July 6, 2004. **(Hearing set for September 27, 2004)**

Acuña, Mark Anthony, Attorney for the Petitioners Sullivan, Sederwall and Graves. "In the Matter of William H. Bonney, aka 'Billy the Kid': Petitioner's Response to the Village of Ft. Sumner's Motion to Dismiss." Case No. CV-04-00005." Tenth Judicial District, State of New Mexico, County of De Baca. July 29, 2004.( **Acuña argues Sheriff-petitioners' standing based on law enforcement)**

Robins, Bill III and David Sandoval; Attorneys for the Billy the Kid; and Adam S. Baker and Herb Marsh, Jr., Attorneys for the Village of Fort Sumner. "In the Matter of William H. Bonney, aka 'Billy the Kid': Stipulation of Dismissal." Case No. CV-04-00005. Tenth Judicial District, County of De Baca, State of New Mexico. August 23, 2004.

Valdez, Jannay. "Re: Billy the Kid (Brushy Bill Roberts), To: Frederick Nolan "Author." September 12, 2004. **(Response to Nolan's exhumation opposition.)**

"In the Matter of De Baca County Sheriff Gary Graves. Petition for Order Allowing Recall Vote." Case No. CV-04-00019. Tenth Judicial District Court, State of New Mexico, County of De Baca. September 13, 2004. **(Recall starts against Sheriff Gary Graves.)**

Acuña, Mark Anthony and Adam S. Baker, Attorneys for Petitioners Graves, Sullivan and Sederwall; and the Village of Fort Sumner. "In the Matter of William H. Bonney, aka 'Billy the Kid': Stipulation of Dismissal With Prejudice." Case No. CV-04-00005. Tenth Judicial District, County of De Baca, State of New Mexico. September 24, 2004. **(Petitioners give up forever at Fort Sumner. Definitive victory against Billy the Kid exhumation.)**

# HAMILTON, TEXAS
## (EXHUMATION ATTEMPT ON "BRUSHY BILL" ROBERTS)

Cooper, Gale. "Billy the Kid Case in a Nutshell." Faxed letter to Hamilton, Texas, Mayor Roy Rumsey. May 3, 2007. **(Background about current attempt to dig up "Brushy Bill.")**

Virden, R.E. Lincoln County Sheriff. To Hamilton, Texas, Mayor Roy Ramsey [sic]. "This letter will inform you that Tom Sullivan and Steve Sederwall are both commissioned deputies ..." No date, but around May 2007. **(Confirms Virden's participation in the attempt to exhume "Brushy Bill" Roberts.)**

Cooper, Gale. "RE: Lincoln County Sheriff's Department's 2007 attempt to exhume Oliver "Brushy Bill" Roberts. Faxed letter to Hamilton, Texas, Mayor Roy Rumsey. September 11, 2008.

Rumsey, Roy. Hamilton Mayor. "RE: Lincoln County Sheriff's Department's 2007 attempt to exhume Oliver Roberts." Faxed letter to Gale Cooper. September 12, 2008. (**Confirmation that the case is closed**)

# LINCOLN COUNTY, NEW MEXICO
## (CASE 2003-274 DOCUMENTS; EXHUMATION ATTEMPTS ON BILLY THE KID AND CATHERINE ANTRIM)

Virden, R.E. Lincoln County Undersheriff report. "I participated in the investigative reconstruction ..." April 28, 2003. (**Participation in Case # 2003-274.**)

Sullivan, Tom. Lincoln County Sheriff. "Lincoln County Sheriff's Department is currently conducting an investigation ..." Letter to Charles Ryan, Director Arizona Department of Corrections. April 30, 2003. (**Describes Garrett as murderer and planned exhumations of John Miller and "Brushy Bill" Roberts**)

_____. "Given the nature of the investigation, we believe it would be appropriate for you to appoint a special counsel ..." Letter to Governor Bill Richardson. May 14, 2003.

_____. "Denial Letter." Pre-printed form to my attorney, Randall M. Harris. October 8, 2003. (**IPRA denial for the Probable Cause Statement using IPRA exception of ongoing law enforcement investigation.**)

Sullivan, Tom. Sheriff, Lincoln County Sheriff's Office, and Steven M. Sederwall. Deputy Sheriff, Lincoln County Sheriff's Office. "Lincoln County Sheriff's Office, Lincoln County, New Mexico, Case: William H. Bonney, a.k.a. William Antrim, a.k.a. The Kid, a.k.a. Billy the Kid: An Investigation into the events of April 28, 1881 through July 14, 1881 – seventy-seven days of doubt." No Date. (**Possible rejected precursor to the Probable Cause Statement for Case # 2003-274. This document was part of the Lincoln County Sheriff's Department case file for 2003-274.**)

_____. "Lincoln County Sheriff's Department Case #2003-274 Probable Cause Statement." Filed in Lincoln County Sheriff's Department. Carrizozo, New Mexico. December 31, 2003. (**Became publicly available as "Plaintiff Exhibit 1 in Petitioner's Attorney Sherry Tippett's Silver City "Brief in Chief in Support of the Exhumation of Catherine Antrim." Case No. MS 03-011." Sixth Judicial Court, County of Grant, State of New Mexico." January 5, 2004**) [See Poe, John William. "The Killing of Billy the Kid." (a personal letter written at Roswell, New Mexico to Mr. Charles Goodnight, Goodnight P.C., Texas) July 10, 1917. Earle Vandale Collection. 1813-946. No. 2H475. Center for American History. University of Texas at Austin. (**Has the Milnor Rudolph quote and the part purposefully omitted from Probable Cause Statement for Case 2003-274.**)]

Overton, Homer D. aka Homer D. Kinsworthy. "Affidavit for Lincoln County Sheriff's Department Case #2003-274 Probable Cause Statement." December 22, 2003. (**Fake swearing Garrett's widow –dead in 1936 - told him in 1940 that Garrett did not kill the Kid. Became publicly available as "Plaintiff Exhibit 1 in Petitioner's Attorney Sherry Tippett's Silver City "Brief in Chief in Support of the Exhumation of Catherine Antrim." Case No. MS 03-011." Sixth Judicial Court, County of Grant, State of New Mexico." January 5, 2004**)

No Author. "Contact List, William H. Bonney Case # 2003-274, Lincoln County Sheriff's Office & Investigators." No Date. (2003 or 2004 because Sullivan is still Sheriff). (**In Lincoln County Sheriff's Department Case 2003-274 file.**)

Virden, Rick, Lincoln County Sheriff. "Deputy Sheriff Commission [Card] to Tom Sullivan." January 1, 2005.

_____. "Deputy Sheriff Commission [Card] to Steven Sederwall." February 25, 2005.

Sederwall, Steven M., Lincoln County Sheriff's Deputy Investigator. "Lincoln County Sheriff's Department Supplemental Report, Case #2003-274. Subject: Exhumation of John Miller. Location: Arizona Pioneers' Cemetery, Prescott, Arizona." May 19, 2005. (**Arizona exhumations John Miller and William Hudspeth**)

Virden, R.E. Lincoln County Sheriff. letter to Jay Miller. "We are interested in the truth surrounding Billy the Kid and are continuing the investigation ..." November 28, 2005. (**Virden confirms continuing Billy the Kid case and deputizing Sullivan and Sederwall for it.**)

Lee, Henry, Dr. Letter to Jay Miller. "In response to your letter dated March 27, 2006 ..." May 1, 2006. (**Lee confirms sending his carpenter's bench and floorboard report to Lincoln County Sheriff's Department.**)

"Jordan, Wilma" aka Gale Cooper. To David Turk, Historian U.S. Marshals Service. "Looking for the truth is good ..." June 15, 2006. (**Attempt to get the Turk's "U.S. Marshal's Service and Billy the Kid " pamphlet.**)

Turk, David. Historian U.S. Marshals Service. To "Wilma Jordan." "Thank you for your thoughtful and thorough letter ..." July 3, 2006. (**Tracked "Wilma's" address; refuses to give his "U.S. Marshal's Service and Billy the Kid "pamphlet.**)

Cooper, Gale. IPRA Request. To Sheriff Virden. September 22, 2006.

Sullivan, Tom and Steve Sederwall. To Lincoln County Attorney Alan Morel. "The Dried Bean. 'You Believin' Us or Them Lyin' Whores.' " September 30, 2006. (**Exhibit 4 in IPRA response to me of October 11, 2006 from Sheriff Rick Virden through Lincoln County Attorney Alan Morel.**)

Cooper, Gale.. To Congressman Steve Pearce. "Bring to your attention an ongoing corruption case in Lincoln County ..." March 12, 2007.

Cooper, Gale. To State Senator Rod Adair. "Re: Overview of the Billy the Kid Case and its political scandal." April 3, 2007. (**For Lincoln and Chavez Counties**)

Virden, R.E. Lincoln County Sheriff. To Hamilton, Texas, Mayor Roy Ramsey [sic]. "This letter will inform you that Tom Sullivan and Steve Sederwall are both commissioned deputies ..." No date, but around May 2007. (**Confirms Virden's participation in the attempt to exhume "Brushy Bill" Roberts, and calls Sullivan and Sederwall commissioned deputies for Case # 2003-274.**)

Kent, Kerry. ML Claims Examiner. "Tom, I'm sending you a letter advising that the IJ $10,000 limit for attorneys fees is gone ..." E-Mail. August 9, 2008. (**Though proving taxpayer costs of my IPRA litigation, they were ignored and the huge plaintiffs' bill was incurred**)

Stewart, Tom. Lincoln County Manager. "Subject: FW: IJ 20282/Billy the Kid File. County Commissioners, For the first time I can recall as county manager, we have run out of insurance coverage on a case." E-Mail. August 9, 2008. (**Though proving taxpayer costs of my IPRA litigation, the defendants ignored the liability and ultimately incurred the huge plaintiffs' bill**)

Virden, Rick. Lincoln County Sheriff's Department Case 2003-274 file turn-over. September 3, 2008. (**By subpoena duces tecum; 193 pages**)

Sederwall, Steve. "billythekidcase.com." Sederwall's pay for view website with Case 2003-274 records. October, 2010 online.

Cooper, Gale. "Re: Open letter to Lincoln County Commissioners about Lincoln County Sheriff's Department **Case No. 2003-274** and Sandoval County District Court **Cause No. D-1329-CV-1364**, Gale Cooper and De Baca County News vs. Rick Virden, Lincoln County Sheriff and Custodian of the Records of the Lincoln County Sheriff's Office; and Steven M. Sederwall, Former Lincoln County Deputy Sheriff; and Thomas T. Sullivan, Former Lincoln County Sheriff and Former Lincoln County Deputy Sheriff." June 18, 2013. (**Summary of Billy the Kid Case hoax, IPRA litigation, and costs**)

# SILVER CITY, NEW MEXICO
## (EXHUMATION ATTEMPT ON CATHERINE ANTRIM)

Tippett, Sherry. Attorney. To Richard Gay, Assistant to the Chief of Staff, Governor Richardson's Office. "Memorandum, RE: Exhumation of Catherine Antrim." July 11, 2003. (**Tippett's secret communication with Richardson about Antrim exhumation, with lie of OMI backing exhumation.**)

_____. To Steve Sederwall and Lincoln County Sheriff. "In the Matter of Catherine Antrim, Order." October 10, 2003 (mailing date). (**This shocking document is an unsigned order in anticipation of the Antrim exhumation and claiming Medical Examiner [sic] participation. From the Lincoln County Sheriff's Department Case file for # 2003-274.**)

Tippett, Sherry. Attorney for Petitioners Sullivan, Sederwall, and Graves. "In the Matter of Catherine Antrim: Petition to Exhume Remains." Case No. MS 03-011. Sixth Judicial Court, County of Grant, State of New Mexico. October 10, 2003. (**Start of exhumation attempts; perjury about permission from OMI**)

Kennedy, Paul J., Adam S. Baker, Thomas F. Stewart, Robert L. Scavron, Attorneys for Mayor Terry Fortenberry on Behalf of the Town of Silver City. "In the Matter of Catherine Antrim: Motion to Intervene." Case No. MS 03-011. Sixth Judicial Court, County of Grant, State of New Mexico. October 31, 2003. (**Start of my exhumation opposition**)

_____. "In the Matter of Catherine Antrim: Response in Opposition to the Petition to Exhume Remains." Case No. MS 03-011. Sixth Judicial Court, County of Grant, State of New Mexico. October 31, 2003.

Baker, Adam S. Attorneys for Mayor Terry Fortenberry on Behalf of the Town of Silver City. "Case No. MS 03-011. Sixth Judicial Court, County of Grant, State of New Mexico. In the Matter of Catherine Antrim: Request for Hearing." November 4, 2003.

Foy, Jim, District Judge. "In the Matter of Catherine Antrim: Notice of Recusal." Case No. MS 03-011. Sixth Judicial Court, County of Grant, State of New Mexico. November 14, 2003. (**Honest Judge Foy removes himself**)

Miranda, Velia C., District Court Clerk. "In the Matter of Catherine Antrim: Notice of Assignment/Designation of District Judge H.R. Quintero." Case No. MS 03-011. Sixth Judicial Court, County of Grant, State of New Mexico. November 14, 2003. (**Entry of Richardson appointee judge**)

Tippett, Sherry J. Attorney for Petitioners Sullivan, Sederwall and Graves. "In the Matter of Catherine Antrim: Petitioner's Response in Opposition to the Town of Silver City's Motion to Intervene." No. MS. 2003-11. State of New Mexico, County of Grant, Sixth Judicial District Court. (Unfiled) No Date.

Robins, Bill III and David Sandoval, Attorneys for Billy the Kid. "In the Matter of Catherine Antrim: Billy the Kid's Unopposed Motion for Intervention and Request for Expedited Disposition." Case No. MS 2003-11. Sixth Judicial Court, County of Grant, State of New Mexico. November 26, 2003. (**First petition with Billy the Kid as Petitioner with Petitioners, Sullivan, Sederwall, and Graves.**)

Amos-Staats, Joani. "In the Matter of Catherine Antrim: Joani Amos-Staats' [sic] Response in Opposition to the Petition to Exhume." Case No. MS 2003-11. Sixth Judicial Court, County of Grant, State of New Mexico. December 5, 2003.

_____. "In the Matter of Catherine Antrim: Joani Amos-Staats' [sic] Motion to Intervene and Request for Expedited Hearing." Case No. MS 2003-11. Sixth Judicial Court, County of Grant, State of New Mexico. December 8, 2003.

_____. "In the Matter of Catherine Antrim: Joani Amos-Staats' [sic] Response in Opposition to the Petition to Exhume Remains." Case No. MS 2003-11. Sixth Judicial Court, County of Grant, State of New Mexico. December 8, 2003.

Kennedy, Paul J., Adam S. Baker, Thomas F. Stewart, Robert L. Scavron, Attorneys for Mayor Terry Fortenberry on Behalf of the Town of Silver City. "In the Matter of Catherine Antrim: Reply in Support of the Town of Silver City's Motion to Intervene." Case No. MS 2003-11. Sixth Judicial Court, County of Grant, State of New Mexico. December 8, 2003. (**Justifying need to protect Antrim grave**)

Tippett, Sherry J. Attorney for Petitioners Sullivan, Sederwall and Graves. "In the Matter of Catherine Antrim: Petitioners Response in Opposition to the Town of Silver City's Motion to Intervene." Case No. MS 2003-11. Sixth Judicial Court, County of Grant, State of New Mexico. December 8, 2003. (**Tippett lies by saying town has no "legal interest" to intervene**)

Quintero, H.R. District Judge. "In the Matter of Catherine Antrim: Order." Case No. MS 03-011. Sixth Judicial Court, County of Grant, State of New Mexico. December 9, 2003. (**Rescheduling hearing from January 6, 2004 to January 27, 2004.**)

Altamirano, Benny. State Senator. "Senate Memorial Number ____." Undated (December 17, 2003?). (**Prepared for Altamirano on December 17, 2003 by Attorney Sherry Tippett.**)

Tippett, Sherry J. Attorney. To Mayor Steve Sederwall, Sheriff Tom Sullivan, Sheriff Gary Graves. "Attached is a copy of Judge Quintero's Order of December 9, 2003, ruling on our Hearing ..." December 17, 2003. (**States surety that they will win on January 27, 2004; urges completing the Probable Cause Statement; encloses her pre-printed senate proposal to back the case from Senator Benny Altamirano.**)

Baker, Adam S. Attorneys for Mayor Terry Fortenberry on Behalf of the Town of Silver City. "In the Matter of Catherine Antrim: Intervenor Town of Silver City's Brief on Petition to Exhume." Case No. MS 03-011. Sixth Judicial Court, County of Grant, State of New Mexico. January 5, 2004. (**Arguing 1962 precedent case of Lois Telfer blocking exhumation**)

Tippett, Sherry J. Attorney. To Mayor Steve Sederwall, Sheriff Tom Sullivan, Sheriff Gary Graves. "In the Matter of Catherine Antrim: Petitioners Brief in Chief in Support of Exhumation." Case No. MS 2003-11. Sixth Judicial Court, County of Grant, State of New Mexico. January 5, 2004. (**Major hoax document with Probable Cause Statement and Homer Overton Affidavit as Plaintiff exhibits**)

Robins, Bill III and David Sandoval. Attorneys for Billy the Kid. "In the Matter of Catherine Antrim: Billy the Kid's Pre-Hearing Brief." Case No. MS 2003-11. Sixth Judicial Court, Grant County. January 5, 2004. (**Major hoax document arguing from pardon and "Brushy Bill" Roberts as Billy – CRACKED THE HOAX**)

Tippett, Sherry. Attorney for law enforcement Petitioners Tom Sullivan, Steve Sederwall, Gary Graves. "In the Matter of Catherine Antrim: Petitioner's [sic] Brief in Chief in Support of Exhumation." Case No. MS 2003-11. Sixth Judicial Court, Grant County. January 5, 2004.

Amos-Staats, Joani. "In the Matter of Catherine Antrim: Intervenor Joani Amos-Staats' [sic] Brief on Petition to Exhume." Case No. MS 2003-11. Sixth Judicial Court, County of Grant, State of New Mexico. January 6, 2004.

Komar, Debra. "In the Matter of Catherine Antrim: Affidavit of Debra Komar, PhD." Case No. MS 2003-11. Sixth Judicial Court, Grant County. January 9, 2004.

Zumwalt, Ross. "In the Matter of Catherine Antrim: Affidavit of Ross E. Zumwalt, M.D." Case No. MS 2003-11. Sixth Judicial Court, Grant County. January 9, 2004. (**With Antrim plot map exhibit of overlapping graves**)

Snead, William E. Attorney for Office of Medical Investigator. "In the Matter of Catherine Antrim: Response of Office of Medical Investigator to Petition to Exhume Remains of Catherine Antrim." Case No. MS 2003-11. Sixth Judicial Court, Grant County. January 13, 2004. (**Opposition of OMI to exhumation**)

Kennedy, Paul J., Adam S. Baker, Thomas F. Stewart, Robert L. Scavron, Attorneys for Mayor Terry Fortenberry on Behalf of the Town of Silver City. "In the Matter of Catherine Antrim: Response in Opposition to Petitioners' Brief in Chief." Case No. MS 2003-11. Sixth Judicial Court, County of Grant, State of New Mexico. January 21, 2004.

_____. "In the Matter of Catherine Antrim: Silver City's Response in Opposition to Petitioners' Motion for Continuance." Case No. MS 2003-11. Sixth Judicial Court, County of Grant, State of New Mexico. January 21, 2004.

Quintero, H.R. District Judge, Division 1. "In the Matter of Catherine Antrim: Order of Continuance." Case No. MS 03-011. Sixth Judicial Court, County of Grant, State of New Mexico. January 23, 2004. (**Court orders Petitioner's attorney, Sherry Tippett, as a sanction, to pay airfare for witness, Frederick Nolan.**)

Robins, Bill III and David Sandoval. Attorneys for Billy the Kid. "In the Matter of Catherine Antrim: Billy the Kid's Brief on the Question of Ripeness." Case No. MS 2003-11. Sixth Judicial Court, Grant County. February 24, 2004. (**Setting up Quintero's sending the exhumation to Fort Sumner**)

Snead, William E. Attorney for Office of Medical Investigator." "In the Matter of Catherine Antrim: Brief of the Office of the Medical Investigator Concerning Ripeness of the Pending Motion to Enter Order of Exhumation for Catherine Antrim." Case No. MS 2003-11. Sixth Judicial Court, Grant County. February 24, 2004.

Acúna, Mark Anthony and Sherry J. Tippett. Attorneys for Petitioners Sullivan, Sederwall and Graves. "In the Matter of Catherine Antrim: Petitioners' Brief on the Question of Ripeness." Case No. MS 2003-11. Sixth Judicial Court, Grant County. February 24, 2004.

Baker, Adam S. and Thomas F. Stewart, Robert L. Scavron, Attorneys for Silver City and Joani Amos-Staats. "In the Matter of Catherine Antrim: Silver City's and Joani Amos-Staats' [sic] Joint Motion to Dismiss on Grounds of Ripeness." Case No. MS 2003-11. Sixth Judicial Court, County of Grant, State of New Mexico. February 24, 2004.

Acúna, Mark Anthony. Attorney for Petitioners Sullivan, Sederwall and Graves. "In the Matter of Catherine Antrim: Entry of Appearance." Case No. MS 03-011. Sixth Judicial Court, County of Grant, State of New Mexico. February 26, 2004. (**Replacing Tippett for law enforcement Petitioners**)

Robins, Bill III and David Sandoval. Attorneys for Billy the Kid. "In the Matter of Catherine Antrim: Response to Motion to Dismiss." Case No. MS 2003-11. Sixth Judicial Court, Grant County. March 10, 2004.

Quintero, Henry R. "In the Matter of Catherine Antrim: Decision and Order." Case No. MS 03-011." Sixth Judicial Court, County of Grant, State of New Mexico. April 2, 2004. (**Judge allows dead Billy the Kid to be a Petitioner; and dismisses the Antrim exhumation without prejudice with stipulation that DNA should be obtained first from the Kid's grave before his mother's.**)

Fortenberry, Terry D, Mayor; Thomas A. Nupp Councilor District 2; Steve May, Councilor District 4; Gary Clauss, Councilor District 3; Judy Ward, Councilor District 1; Alex Brown, Town Manager; Cissy McAndrew, Executive Director Chamber of Commerce; Frank Milan, Director Silver City Mainstreet Project; Susan Berry, Director Silver City Museum. "Open Letter to Governor Bill Richardson." June 21, 2004.

Kemper, Lisa. Kennedy Han, PC. Controller, (via fax). To Gale Cooper. "*In the Matter of Catherine Antrim, 6th Judicial Dist. Ct. Case No. MS 2003-001*, "This is to confirm our receipt of payment ..." Baker, Adam. Confirmation of payment of Attorney Sherry Tippett's Judge Henry Quintero sanction by Attorney Bill Robins III. September 1, 2004. (See "Order of Continuance. In the Matter of Catherine Antrim. Case No. MS 03-011.") Filed January 23, 2004. Sixth Judicial Court, County of Grant, State of New Mexico. Signed: H.R. Quintero, District Judge, Division 1." April 28, 2004, (**Court sanctions Tippett, and Robins pays.**)

# YAVAPAI (PRESCOTT) AND
# MARICOPA COUNTIES, ARIZONA
### (EXHUMATIONS JOHN MILLER AND WILLIAM HUDSPETH)

Tunnell, Dale. To Jeanine Dike. "Subject: RE: Disinterment of Wm Bonney." May 3, 2005.

Dike, Jeanine. To Dale Tunnell. "Subject: Disinterment of Wm Bonney." May 3, 2005.

_____. To Dale Sams. "Subject: FW: Disinterment Wm Bonney." May 3, 2005.

_____. To Dale Sams. "Subject: FW: Disinterment Wm Bonney." May 4, 2005.

Sams, Dale. To George Thompson. "Subject: Disinterment." May 4, 2005. (**Confirms Sams has no idea where the Miller grave is located.**)

Sederwall, Steven M., Lincoln County Sheriff's Deputy Investigator. "Lincoln County Sheriff's Department Supplemental Report, Case #2003-274. Subject: Exhumation of John Miller. Location: Arizona Pioneers' Cemetery, Prescott, Arizona." May 19, 2005. (**Arizona exhumations John Miller and William Hudspeth**)

Fulginiti, Laura C. Ph.D., D-ABFA. Forensic Anthropologist. To Dale L. Tunnell, Ph.D. "RE: Exhumation, Pioneer Home Cemetery, Prescott, Arizona." June 2, 2005. (**Forensic report of the John Miller William Hudspeth exhumations.**)

Sederwall, Steven. To Misty Rodarte. "Subject: Billy the Kid." July 6, 2005.

Winter, Anne. "To: Tim Nelson; Alan Stephens. Subject: Pioneer Home, Grave, Billy the Kid and DNA." August 18, 2005. (**Has attachment of Pioneers' Home Supervisor Gary Olson's cover-up letter to her and implied internal cover-up. Also states that Sullivan paid for the exhumation.**)

_____. "To: Tim Nelson; Alan Stephens. Subject: Billy the Kid." September 8, 2005. (**"80% DNA match ..." The Doomsday Document**)

Olson, Gary. Superintendent Arizona Pioneers' Home. To David Snell. "You recently asked the Arizona Pioneers' Home if a body in its cemetery had been exhumed ..." October 3, 2005. (**Confirms original cover-up of John Miller exhumation.**)

Winter, Anne. "To Gary Olson. Subject: RE: the kid." October 17, 2005 (**Requesting any DNA results yet to him.**)

Olson, Gary. "To Anne Winter. Subject: RE: the kid." October 17, 2005. (**Reporting on no DNA results yet to him.**)

Winter, Anne. "To: Jeanine L'Ecuyer. Subject: FW: the kid." October 17, 2005. (**Reporting on no DNA results yet to Olson.**) JournalABQ@aol.com. "To: Gary Olson. Subject: re. John Miller." October 19, 2005. (**Reporter Rene Romo seeking information.**)

Olson, Gary. "To: Anne Winter. Subject: FW: re. John Miller." October 20, 2005. (**Cover-up `planned for Romo. "I thought you and the Governor may want to know about this request."**)

Winter, Anne. "To: Tim Nelson; Alan Stephens. Subject: FW: re. John Miller. October 20, 2005. (**Cover-up plan for Romo presentation: "Remember there was the legal issue that they dug up two bodies."**)

_____. "To: Jeanine L'Ecuyer. Subject: FW: re. John Miller." October 25, 2005. (**Planning cover-up for media requests.**)

Sederwall, Steven. "To: Barbara J. Miller; Steve McGregor; Rick Staub; Misty Rodarte; Emily Smith; Bob Boze Bell. Subject: in the Albuquerque Journal." November 6, 2005. (**Copy Romo article.**)

Olson, Gary. "To Anne Winter, Mark Wilson. Subject: FW: in the Albuquerque Journal." November 7, 2005. (**Copy Romo article.**)

Winter, Anne. "To: Jeanine L'Ecuyer; Tim Nelson; Alan Stephens. Subject: Billy the Kid. November 7, 2005. (**Reporting Gary Olson's cover-up in KPNX interview.**)

Snell, David. To Shiela Polk. Yavapai County Attorney. "I feel it is my duty to report to you that graverobbers are plying their trade ..." March 11, 2006. (**Arizona citizen initiating criminal investigation of Miller/Hudspeth exhumations.**)

Cahall, Anna, Detective Prescott Police Department. "CASE REPORT 0600012767." April 5, 2006. (**Concerning the John Miller exhumation; interviews with Sullivan, Sederwall, Tunnell**)

Savona, Glenn A. Prescott City Prosecutor. To Shiela Sullivan Polk, Yavapai County Attorney. "Re: Police Department DR# 2006-12767 Arizona Pioneers' Home Cemetery." April 13, 2006. (**Calls exhumations potential felonies, and moves case up to County Attorney.**)

Jacobson, Marcia. "To Anne Winter, Policy Advisor for Health, Office of the Governor, and Chief Randy Oaks, Prescott Police Department. Re: Disinterment of bodies at Arizona Pioneer's [sic] Home Cemetery." March 30, 2006. (**Attempted cover-up of John Miller and William Hudspeth exhumations.**)

Cooper, Gale. To Detective Anna Cahall. Prescott Police Department. "Re: Exhumation of John Miller and adjacent grave for pursuing the New Mexico Billy the Kid Case." April 13, 2006.

_____. To Detective Anna Cahall. Prescott Police Department. "Re: Pertinent articles regarding exhumation of John Miller and remains from adjacent grave for alleged promulgation of the New Mexico Billy the Kid Case, a murder investigation." April 17, 2006.

_____. To Arizona Senate President Ken Bennett. (via fax). "RE: Billy the Kid Case Arizona Exhumations." April 20, 2006.

_____. To Carol Landis. (Office of the Yavapai County Prosecutor). "Re: Billy the Kid Case Arizona Exhumations. As per our telephone conversation, attached are articles regarding the exhumation of John Miller and remains in an adjacent grave for alleged promulgation of the New Mexico Billy the Kid Case, a so-called murder investigation. Attached also is the cover sheet sent to Detective Anna Cahall to provide case overview. The case is entirely a historical, legal, and forensic science hoax." April 21, 2006.

_____. To Arizona Senate President Ken Bennett. (via fax). "RE: Billy the Kid Case Arizona Exhumations. As a Follow-up." April 25, 2006.

_____. To Deputy County Attorney Steve Jaynes and County Attorney Dennis McGrane. (via fax) "Re: Information on the New Mexico Billy the Kid Case pertinent to the Arizona John Miller exhumations." May 2, 2006.

Sederwall, Steve. To confidential recipient. "Well we have the governor reaching out to the Arizona to stop this investigation." May 16, 2006.

Cooper, Gale. To Arizona Senate President Ken Bennett. (via fax). "Re: Follow-up on Prescott, Arizona John Miller exhumation." May 17, 2006.

_____. To Attorney Jonell Lucca (via fax). "Re: Case # CA20006020516. Follow-up to our telephone conversation of June 9, 2006, to address the issue of Permit for the exhumations of John Miller and the remains from an adjacent grave for promulgation of the New Mexico Billy the Kid Case, a murder investigation." June 12, 2006.

_____. To Attorney Jonell Lucca (via fax). "Re: Case # CA20006020516. Follow-up to my fax of June 12, 2006, to address additional issues pertinent to the exhumations of John Miller and William Hudspeth, done for promulgation of the New Mexico Billy the Kid Case, an alleged murder investigation." July 11, 2006.

Sams, Dale. Arizona Pioneers' Home Administrator. To Gale Cooper. Confirming approximate date of John Miller's birth as 1850. August 8, 2006.

Cooper, Gale. To Attorney Jonell Lucca (via fax). "Re: Case # CA20006020516. Follow-up to my fax of July 11, 2006, to address issues pertinent to the promulgators of the New Mexico Billy the Kid Case (which resulted in the exhumations of John Miller and William Hudspeth); with added focus on its alleged forensic experts and co-participants." August 11, 2006.

Cooper, Gale. To Attorney Jonell Lucca. "Re: Enclosed reference copy of Freedom of Information Act (FOIA) to Governor Janet Napolitano regarding her possible participation in the Prescott, Arizona exhumations of John Miller and William Hudspeth, and their legal issues related to Maricopa County Prosecutor's Office Case # CA20006020516." September 22, 2006.

_____. To Len Munsil, Arizona Republican candidate for governor. "Re: Enclosed reference copy of Freedom of Information Act (FOIA) request to Governor Janet Napolitano regarding her possible involvement in the Prescott, Arizona exhumations of John Miller and William Hudspeth, and their legal issues related to Maricopa County Prosecutor's Office Case # CA 2006020516." September 22, 2006. (No response.)

Cooper, Gale. To Attorney Jonell Lucca. "Re: Information pertaining to Case # CA20006020516 (exhumations of John Miller and William Hudspeth) - American Academy of Forensic Science Ethics and Conduct Complaint against Dr. Henry Lee." October 2, 2006.

_____. To Senator John McCain. "New Mexico Billy the Kid Case and Governor Janet Napolitano." October 10, 2006.

_____. To Arizona Senate President Ken Bennett / Nick Simonetta. (via fax). "RE: Follow-up on Maricopa County Prosecutor's Office Case # CA 200602516 considering possible felony indictments ..." October 16, 2006.

Lucca, Jonell L. To Dr. Gale Cooper. "This letter is to inform you that the Maricopa County Attorney's Office has declined to file charges ..." October 17, 2006. (Switching of suspects to Jeanine Dike and Dale Tunnell from Sullivan and Sederwall.)

McCain, John. To Gale Cooper. "Your situation is under the jurisdiction of Governor Janet Napolitano ..." October 27, 2006.

Cooper, Gale. To Attorney Jonell Lucca. "Re: Maricopa County Case # CA20006020516." October 30, 2006. (Confirmation of getting her case termination letter, and asking why she changed suspects. Never answered.)

Sams, Dale. "Re: Statement." November 4, 2006. (Statement in response to a letter using his name and addressed to Mr. Alan Morel, Lincoln County Attorney, and signed by Tom Sullivan and Steve Sederwall.)

Cooper, Gale. "New Mexico Billy the Kid Case and possible involvement of Governor Janet Napolitano ..." . Letter to Senator John McCain. January 9, 2007.

McCain, John. To Gale Cooper. "Members of Congress are precluded from inquiring into matters pending before the courts ..." January 25, 2007. (Refused follow-up on illegal exhumations)

Cooper, Gale. To Arizona Attorney General Terry Goddard. "Presentation of alleged prosecutorial improprieties relating to the exhumation of remains of John Miller and William Hudspeth at the Arizona Pioneers' Home Cemetery." March 21, 2007. (No response.)

_____. To Len Munsil, former Arizona Republican candidate for governor. "Re: Scandalous political cover-up by Governor Napolitano's Office and Maricopa County Prosecutor's Office ..." March 21, 2007. (No response.)

Sederwall, Steve. "To "Loretta. 'Wild Goose Chase.' " http://disc.server.com/discussion.cgi?disc=167540;article=33266;title=Billy%20the %20Kid"http://disc.server.com/discussion.cgi?disc=167540;article=33266;title=Bill y%20the%20Kid May 4, 2007. (Admitting that John Miller DNA could not match bench DNA since John Miller did not claim bench death scene)

_____. "Billyondabrain."http://disc.server.com/discussion.cgi?disc=167540; article=33266;title=Billy%20the%20Kid" May 13, 2007.

Cooper, Gale. To Detective Anna Cahall. Prescott Police Department. "Re: Freedom of Information Act Request for Records of Prescott Police Department Case No. 06-12767. September 11, 2008. (No response)

## MISCELLANEOUS LEGAL DOCUMENTS

### LIONEL LIPPMAN ARRESTS

Texas Department of Public Safety Conviction Records Database. Dates of arrests for Lionel Whitby Lippman: June 11, 1973 (San Antonio, Bexar County, forgery and passing), July 7, 1970 (San Antonio, Bexar County, assault with intent to commit rape), and February 17, 1970 (San Antonio, Bexar County, vehicular theft), **(Photographer of Sederwall with John Miller skull.)**

### STEVE SEDERWALL ARREST

Warrant of Arrest. "State of Oklahoma, County of LeFlore, vs. Steve Sederwall. Filed February 10, 1983. **(Accusation of Steve Sederwall with crime of Assault and Battery on or about February 8, 1983 – Case No. CRM-83-55.)**
Kirkland, Ray. "State of Oklahoma vs A.B. McReynolds, Jr., John (Nick) Moore and Steve Sederwall. Case No. CRM-83-55." February 9, 1983. **(Affidavit accusing Steve Sederwall and others with crime of Assault and Battery upon a Darryl Gene Williams.)**
Order of Dismissal of State of Oklahoma vs. A.B. McReynolds, Jr., John (Nick) Moore and Steve Sederwall. March 17, 1983.

### THEN-STATE SENATOR ROD ADAIR'S
### PAT GARRETT PARK PROPOSAL

Adair, Rod. "Senate Capital Outlay Request 01, State of New Mexico, 48th Legislature - Second Session - 2008: CHAVES CO PAT GARRETT PARK CONST & EQUIP." Page 5.

# MY BILLY THE KID CASE HOAX EXPOSÉ
# INVESTIGATIONS BY OPEN RECORDS
# *(CHRONOLOGICAL ORDER)*

### RECORDS REQUESTS BY JAY MILLER, AS MY AGENT

Miller, Jay. To Steve Sederwall, Mayor of Capitan and Deputy Sheriff of Lincoln County. "FOIA/IPRA." May 13, 2004.
_____. To Village of Capitan Records Custodian. "I would like to inspect and copy the following documents of Steve Sederwall ..." May 13, 2004.
_____. To County Clerk of Lincoln County/Records Custodian, Lincoln County Courthouse. "Re: I would like to inspect the following documents of Tom Sullivan, elected Sheriff of Lincoln County." May 13, 2004.
_____. To County Clerk of DeBaca County/Records Custodian. "Freedom of Information Act Request: Inspect and copy records pertaining to Gary Graves, elected sheriff ..." May 13, 2004.
Morel, Alan P. Lincoln County Attorney. "RE: Freedom of Information Act Request dated May 13, 2004." Letter to Jay Miller. May 19, 2004. **(Calls Sederwall deputy and Case 2003-274 an IPRA exempt criminal investigation)**
Grassie, Anna Gail. (For Village of Capitan and Mayor Steve Sederwall). To Jay Miller. "Reference: Freedom of Information Request from Jay Miller dated May 13, 2004." May 25, 2004.

Miller, Jay. To Michael Cerletti, Secretary, Department Tourism. "RE: FOIA/IPRA on Billy the Kid Case promulgators and Department of Tourism." May, 28, 2004.

_____. To Attorney Alan P. Morel. "Re: Response to your letter dated May 19, 2004 on behalf of the County Clerk of Lincoln County and Lincoln County Sheriff Tom Sullivan." June 1, 2004.

_____. To Mayor Steve Sederwall. "FOIA/IPRA on Steve Sederwall as Mayor of Capitan and Deputy Sheriff of Lincoln County." June 1, 2004.

Morel, Alan P. Lincoln County Attorney. To Jay Miller. "RE: Response to your letter dated May 19, 2004 on behalf of the County Clerk of Lincoln County and Lincoln County Sheriff Tom Sullivan. June 1, 2004.

Sederwall, Steven: Mayor. To Jay Miller. "I am in receipt of your letter dated June 1, 2004." June 3, 2004.

Morel, Alan P. Lincoln County Attorney. To Jay Miller. "RE: Freedom of Information Act Request June 1, 2004." June 4, 2004.

Cerletti, Mike (through Jon Hendry, Director of Marketing). To Jay Miller. "Reply to your freedom of information request." June 7, 2004. (**Denied participation of Tourism Department.**)

Miller, Jay. To Lincoln County Attorney Alan Morel. "Copy all documents relevant to David Turk, historian for the U.S. Marshals Service ..." June 9, 2004.

_____. To Mayor of Capitan and Deputy Sheriff of Lincoln County Steve Sederwall. "Evade response by claiming that you were being addresses solely in your capacity as Mayor ..." June 9, 2004.

_____. To Sheriff Gary Graves and Nancy Sparks, De Baca County Clerk. "Freedom of Information Act Request: I would like to inspect any and all documents relevant to David Turk ..." June 9, 2004.

Sederwall, Steven M. To Jay Miller. "This office has no records ..." June 10, 2004.

Miller, Jay. To Mayor Steve Sederwall. "FOIA/IPRA on Steve Sederwall as Mayor of Capitan and Deputy Sheriff of Lincoln County." June 10, 2004.

_____. To Attorney General Patricia Madrid. "Re: Follow-up on FOIA/IPRA Request to Lincoln County Sheriff Tom Sullivan." June 14, 2004. (**This was stonewalled. No response ever came.**)

Sparks Nancy. County Clerk. (For Sheriff Gary Graves). To Jay Miller. "Re: FOIA/IPRA request for records of De Baca County Sheriff Gary Graves." June 14, 2004.

Miller, Jay. To Mayor of Capitan and Deputy Sheriff of Lincoln County Steve Sederwall. "Thank you for your prompt response to my letter of June 1, 2004 ... " June 21, 2004.

_____. To Attorney General Patricia Madrid. RE: Follow-up on FOIA/IPRA Requests to Steve Sederwall, Mayor of Capitan and Deputy Sheriff of Lincoln County." June 21, 2004.

_____. To Lincoln County Attorney Alan Morel. "I would like to inspect and copy any and all documents relevant to your client Tom Sullivan, Sheriff of Lincoln County with regard to a statement made by his attorney Sherry Tippett ..." June 23, 2004.

_____. To Mayor of Capitan and Deputy Sheriff of Lincoln County Steve Sederwall. "To inspect and copy all records relevant to your attorney, Sherry Tippett's, claims ..." June 23, 2004.

_____. To Michael Cerletti, Secretary Tourism. "Thanks for your response ..." June 23, 2004.

Morel, Alan P. Lincoln County Attorney. To Jay Miller. "RE: Freedom of Information Act Request/Inspection of Public Records Act Request dated June 23, 2004."

Lama, Albert J. Assistant Attorney General. To Jay Miller. "Concerning an alleged violation of the Inspection of Public Records Act by the Lincoln County, De Baca County, and Village of Capitan." June 24, 2004. (**This was sent to Assistant AG Mary Smith, who later covered for Sederwall.**)

Miller, Jay. To Attorney General Patricia Madrid. "Re: Follow-up on FOIA/IPRA Requests to Steve Sederwall, Mayor of Capitan and Deputy Sheriff of Lincoln County." June 21, 2004. **(This was information on the "maturing problem" not a complaint, but was used to close the case.)**

Graves, Gary W. De Baca County Sheriff. To Jay Miller. "I am writing in response to your request ..." June 22, 2004. **(Denies information on David Turk.)**

Miller, Jay. To Sheriff Gary Graves. "Freedom of Information Act Request: Inspect and copy all records relevant to your attorney, Sherry Tippett ..." June 23, 2004.

_____. To Sheriff Gary Graves and Nancy Sparks. "Re: FOIA/IPRA request for records." June 25, 2004.

Graves, Gary W. De Baca County Sheriff. To Jay Miller. "I do not maintain requests for travel reimbursements ..." June 29, 2004. **(His clerk did send the records!)**

_____. To Jay Miller. "As per your FOIA/IPRA Request on June 23, 2004 ..." June 29, 2004. **(Denies records on Attorney Sherry Tippett.)**

_____. To Jay Miller. "I do not maintain or have any records in reference to Sherry Tippett ..." June 29, 2004.

Miller, Jay. To Attorney Alan Morel. "Re: Deputizing of Capitan Mayor Steve Sederwall as referenced in your letter dated June 4, 2004 on behalf of Lincoln County Sheriff Tom Sullivan." July 1, 2004.

Morel, Alan P. Attorney for Lincoln County. To Jay Miller. "Re: Deputizing of Capitan Mayor Steve Sederwall as referenced in your letter dated June 4, 2004 on behalf of Lincoln County Sheriff Tom Sullivan." July 1, 2004.

_____. To Jay Miller. "RE: Freedom of Information Act/Inspection of Public Records Act Request dated June 23, 2004." July 2, 2004.

Sparks, Nancy. De Baca County Clerk. "I have sent you everything I have on Sheriff Graves ..." July 2, 2004.

Prelo, Marc. Attorney for Village of Capitan. To Jay Miller. "RE: Village of Capitan/Freedom of Information Act - Inspection of Public Records Request. July 5, 2004. **(Response for Sederwall to Jay Miller)**

Miller, Jay. To Assistant AG Mary Smith. "Re: Response to your letter of June 24, 2004." July 8, 2004.

_____. To Sheriff Gary Graves. "Re: Follow-up on your responses to my prior FOIA/IPRA requests." July 8, 2004.

Morel, Alan P. Lincoln County Attorney. Letter to Jay Miller. "RE: Freedom of Information Act Request dated July 1, 2004." July 9, 2004. **(Statutes justifying deputizing Sederwall, with statutes)**

Smith, Mary H., Assistant Attorney General. To Jay Miller. "Re: Determination of Inspection of Public Records Act Complaint v Village of Capitan." August 3, 2004. **(Rejection of IPRA complaint.)**

_____. To Jay Miller. "Re: Determination of Inspection of Public Records Act complaint v De Baca County." August 3, 2004. **(Rejection of IPRA complaint.)**

Miller, Jay. To Sheriff Tom Sullivan. "Re: David Turk, Historian for the U.S. Marshals Service." August 5, 2004.

_____. To Office of General Counsel - FOIA REQUEST, Attn. Arleta Cunningham, U.S. Marshal's Service. "Re. David Turk, historian for U.S. Marshal's Service, FOIA on Sederwall/Sullivan/Graves/ Billy the Kid Case." August 5, 2004.

_____. To Assistant AG Mary Smith. "Re. Response to your letter of August 3, 2004 about determination of my IPRA complaint v Mayor of Capitan Steve Sederwall, who also represents himself as Deputy Sheriff of Lincoln County; and the Village of Capitan." August, 10, 2004.

Sullivan, Tom, Lincoln County Sheriff. "In response to your 'Inspection of Public Records Act" request dated August 5, 2004." August 18, 2004. **(Refuses IPRA records on David Turk based on ongoing criminal investigation).**

Morel, Alan P. Lincoln County Attorney. To Jay Miller. "In response to your "Information Act Request dated August 5, 2004." August 18, 2004.

Miller, Jay. To Deputy Attorney General Stuart Bluestone. "Re: Complaint and appeal for assistance with regard to non-compliance with FOIA/IPRA requests made to Capitan Mayor Steve Sederwall, who represents himself as Deputy Sheriff of Lincoln County and the Village Clerk of Capitan." August 28, 2004. **(No response)**

_____. To Deputy Attorney General Stuart Bluestone. "Re: Complaint and appeal for assistance with regard to non-compliance with FOIA/IPRA requests made to Lincoln County Sheriff Tom Sullivan and Lincoln County Clerk." September 4, 2004. **(No response).**

Utley, Robert M. "Billy Again." September 16, 2004. **(Sent to Jay Miller and forwarded to me regarding role of Paul Hutton in Billy the Kid Case.)**

Virden, R.E. Lincoln County Sheriff. Letter to Jay Miller. "We are interested in the truth surrounding Billy the Kid and are continuing the investigation ..." November 28, 2005. **(Key hoax document: Virden confirms continuing Billy the Kid case and deputizing Sullivan and Sederwall for it.)**

Smith Mary. Assistant Attorney General. To Jay Miller. "Re: Inspection of Public Records Act complaint v Steve Sederwall, Mayor of Capitan and Lincoln County Deputy Sheriff." May 17, 2005. **(Nine months later: Rejection of complaint.)**

Bordley, William E. To Jay Miller. "Freedom of Information/Privacy Act Request No. 2004USMS7634, Subject: David Turk, Historian U.S. Marshals Service, FOIA on Sederwall/Sullivan/Graves/Billy the Kid Case." June 22, 2005. **(Note that this response to the Turk FOIA was a year later! It had Turk's taxpayer monies used.)**

Miller, Jay. To William E. Bordley, Associate General Counsel/FOIPA Officer, U.S. Marshal's Service. "Follow-up on your response titled Freedom of Information Act Request No. 2004USMS7634 Subject: David Turk, Historian U.S. Marshal's Service, FOIA on Sederwall/Sullivan/Graves/Billy the Kid Case." July 25, 2005.

DeZulovich, Mavis. FOI/PA Liaison, Office of Public Affairs. To Jay Miller. "This letter is in response to your Freedom of Information/Privacy Act Request No. 2004USMS7634 in reference to David Turk. August 24, 2005. **(States Turk is not Probable Cause Statement author but references his pamphlet..)**

Virden, R.E. Lincoln County Sheriff. To Jay Miller. "We are interested in the truth surrounding Billy the Kid and are continuing the investigation ..." November 28, 2005. **(Confirmation from Virden that continued the Billy the Kid case and deputized Sullivan and Sederwall for it.)**

Miller, Jay. To Paul Hutton. "As a journalist following the Billy the Kid Case ..." February 6, 2006.

_____. To Attorney General Patricia Madrid. "Re: Follow-up on non-response by Attorney General to my September 4, 2004 Complaint and Appeal for assistance with regard to non-compliance by past Lincoln County Sheriff Tom Sullivan with my FOIA/IPRA Requests." March 20, 2006.

_____. To Paul Hutton. "Repeat of one sent to you on February 6, 2006, because I received no response to it." March 20, 2006.

_____. To Sheriff Rick Virden. "Inspection of Public Records Act/Freedom of Information Act request." March 27, 2006.

_____. To Attorney Marc Prelo. "Re: Follow-up on Freedom of Information Request response dated July 5, 2004." March 27, 2006. **(Requests information on his use of taxpayer money for Sederwall's Billy the Kid Case participation.)**

Prelo, Marc Attorney. To Jay Miller. "RE: Village of Capitan/Freedom of Information Act – Inspection of Public Records Request." March 31, 2006. **(Confirms his use of taxpayer money for Sederwall's Billy the Kid Case participation.)**

Morel, Alan P. Lincoln County Attorney. To Jay Miller. "RE: Freedom of Information Act/Inspection of Public Records Act request dated March 27, 2006, to Lincoln County Sheriff Rick Virden. April 3, 2006.

Morel, Alan P. Letter to Jay Miller. "Re: Follow-up on Freedom of Information Act Request Responses Dated May 19, 2004 and June 4, 2004." April 17, 2006. **(Confirms his salary for Billy the Kid Case participation.)**

Miller, Jay. To Attorney General Patricia Madrid. "Re: Follow-up on FOIA/IPRA Request to Lincoln County Sheriff Tom Sullivan." May 6, 2006. **(This repeat of the June 14, 2004 IPRA complaint was stonewalled. No response ever.)**

_____. To Assistant Attorney General Mary Smith. "Re. Response to your letter of May 17, 2005 rejecting my IPRA complaint against then Mayor of Capitan Steve Sederwall, who also represented himself as Deputy Sheriff of Lincoln County." May 6, 2006.**(No response.)**

Sides, John D. Director, Investigative Division of Attorney General. "Re: Impersonating a Peace Officer File 5264." May 18, 2006. **(After 2 year stonewall, merely refers him to D.A. Scot Key.)**

Miller, Jay. To Assistant Attorney General Mary Smith. "Re. Response to your letter of May 17, 2005 rejecting my IPRA complaint against then Mayor of Capitan Steve Sederwall, who also represented himself as Deputy Sheriff of Lincoln County." June 13, 2006. **(Repeat complaint with new information. No response.)**

_____. To Paul Hutton. "Re. Clarification of my letter to you dated March 20, 2006, and reframing of it as a FOIA/IPRA Request." June 13, 2006.

Hutton, Paul "I was never the 'state historian' ...". Letter to Jay Miller. June 20, 2006.

Miller, Jay. To Attorney Mark Acuña. "Re. Follow-up on your legal participation in the New Mexico Billy the Kid Case and participation of the Jaffe Law Firm in the New Mexico Billy the Kid Case." June 22, 2006. **(No response.)**

_____. To Attorney General Patricia Madrid. "Re. FOIA/IPRA Request with regard to your relationship with Attorney Bill Robins III and/or his law firm Heard, Robins, Cloud, Lubel & Greenwood LLP." August 8, 2006.

_____. To Attorney Mark Acuña.. "Re. Follow-up on my unanswered letter of June 22, 2006 with regard to your legal participation in the New Mexico Billy the Kid Case and the participation of your Jaffe Law Firm in the New Mexico Billy the Kid Case." August 8, 2006. **(No response).**

_____. To Mavis DeZulovich. FOIA/PA Liaison U.S. Department of Justice. "Re: Follow-up to your August 24, 2005 response to my Freedom of Information Act request No. 2004USMS7634 in reference to David Turk, Historian for the U.S. Marshals Service." August 8, 2006. **(Requesting copy of David Turk's pamphlet on Billy the Kid and its bibliography.)**

_____. To Dr. Rick Staub, Director Orchid Cellmark Lab. "Re: The participation by you and Orchid Cellmark in the New Mexico Billy the Kid Case." August 8, 2006. **(No response.)**

Kupfer, Elizabeth, Records Custodian. To Jay Miller. "Need additional time ..." August 14, 2006.

Miller, Jay. To Attorney General Patricia Madrid. "RE: FOIA/IPRA request regarding Attorney Bill Robins III and/or his law firm Heard, Robins, Cloud, Lubel, and Greenwood." August 24, 2006.

Cedrick, Nikki. FOIA/PA Liaison U.S. Department of Justice. "Per your FOI request No. 2004USMS7634." August 31, 2006. **(Refuses copy of David Turk's pamphlet on Billy the Kid.)**

Miller, Jay. To Attorney General Patricia Madrid. "Re: Second FOIA/IPRA Request with regard to documentation of financial relationship of Attorney General Patricia Madrid and/or her Office, and Attorney Bill Robins III and/or his law firm Heard, Robins, Cloud, Lubel, and Greenwood LLP." September 1, 2006.

_____. To Assistant Attorney General Mary Smith. "Re. Response to your letter of May 17, 2005 rejecting my IPRA complaint against then Mayor of Capitan Steve Sederwall, who also represented himself as Deputy Sheriff of Lincoln County." September 1, 2006. **(No response.)**

Miller, Jay. To Deputy Attorney General Stuart Bluestone. "Re: Follow-up on your recent telephone call to me about my current, repeated, FOIA/IPRA non-compliance complaints to Attorney General Patricia Madrid with regard to Tom Sullivan's and Steve Sederwall's participation in the Billy the Kid Case in their capacities as public officials." September 1, 2006. **(No response).**

Bordley, William E. Associate General Counsel/FOIPA Officer for U.S. Department of Justice. To Jay Miller. "Re: Freedom of Information/Privacy Act Request No. 2006USMS9782 Subject: Copy of Report Entitled *The U.S. Marshals Service and Billy the Kid*." September 5, 2006. **(Refuses copy of David Turk's pamphlet on Billy the Kid.)**

Kupfer, Elizabeth, Records Custodian. To Jay Miller. "Need additional time ..." September 6, 2006.

Miller, Jay. To Nikki Cedrick, FOIA/PA Liaison U.S. Department of Justice. "Re: Follow-up to your August 31, 2006 response to my Freedom of Information Act request No. 2004USMS7634 in Reference to David Turk, Historian for the U.S. Marshals Service; and request for clarification." September 11, 2006.

Sederwall, Steven. To Jay Miller. "Subject: What is wrong? Can I help?" September 19, 2006. **(Exhibit 3 in IPRA response to me of October 11, 2006 from Sheriff Rick Virden through Lincoln County Attorney Alan Morel.)**

Miller, Jay. To Steven Sederwall. "Response: Subject: What is wrong? Can I help?" September 20, 2006. **(Exhibit 3 in IPRA response to me of October 11, 2006 from Sheriff Rick Virden through Lincoln County Attorney Alan Morel.)**

Smith, Glenn R., Deputy Attorney General and Elizabeth Kupfer, Custodian of Public Records. (For Attorney General Patricia Madrid). To Jay Miller." RE: Inspection of Public Records Request." September 20, 2006.

## RECORDS REQUESTS DIRECTLY BY GALE COOPER

Cooper, Gale. To Governor Bill Richardson and Records Custodian for FOIA/IPRA Requests. "Re: Freedom of Information Act (FOIA)/Inspection of Public Records Act (IPRA) request concerning participation of Governor Bill Richardson in the New Mexico Billy the Kid Case and related issues." September 22, 2006.

_____. To Governor Janet Napolitano. "Re: Freedom of Information Act (FOIA) request pertaining to the Prescott, Arizona exhumations of John Miller and William Hudspeth at the Arizona Pioneers' Home Cemetery on May 19, 2005." September 22, 2006.

_____. To Sheriff Rick Virden. "Re: Freedom of Information Act (FOIA)/New Mexico Inspection of Public Records Act (IPRA) request pertaining to Lincoln County Sheriff's Department Case # 2003-274 ("Billy the Kid Case") and to its May 19, 2005 Prescott Arizona exhumations of John Miller and William Hudspeth." September 22, 2006.

Morel, Alan P. Lincoln County Attorney. To Gale Cooper. "Re: Freedom of Information Act/Inspection of Public Records Act Request dated September 22, 2006, to Lincoln County Sheriff Rick Virden." September 29, 2006. **(Requesting more time to respond based on "excessively burdensome or broad.")**

Maestas, Marcie. Records Custodian for Governor Bill Richardson. To Gale Cooper, M.D. "Received your request to inspect certain records ..." October 3, 2006.

Morel, Alan P. Lincoln County Attorney. To Gale Cooper. "RE: Freedom of Information Act (FOIA)/New Mexico Inspection of Public Records Act (IPRA) to Lincoln County Sheriff Ricky [sic] Virden and the Lincoln County Records Custodian, dated September 22, 2006." October 11, 2006. **(Enclosed intimidating Sullivan-Sederwall document: "The Dried Bean," and Morel participating in reporting me to U.S. Marshals Service.)**

Maestas, Marcie. Records Custodian for Governor Bill Richardson. To Gale Cooper, M.D. "Response to your Inspection of Public Records request received by our office on September 28, 2006 ..." October 13, 2006. **(Denial of each item, but miscellaneous documents provided.)**

Michael R. Haener. Deputy Chief of Staff to Governor Janet Napolitano. "Enclosed records responsive to your request ..." November 13, 2006.

Cooper, Gale. To Governor Janet Napolitano. "Re: Repeated Freedom of Information Act (FOIA) request pertaining to the Prescott, Arizona exhumations of John Miller and William Hudspeth at the Arizona Pioneers' Home Cemetery on May 19, 2005." March 20, 2007. **(Repeated because of no response).**

_____. To Governor Janet Napolitano's Records Custodian. "Re: Repeat submission of incompletely answered Freedom of Information Act request dated September 22, 2006. March 21, 2007.

_____. To January Contreras, Policy Advisor for Health for Governor Janet Napolitano. "Re: Freedom of Information Request." June 29, 2007.

Shilo Mitchell, Deputy Press Secretary for Governor Janet Napolitano. To Gale Cooper, M.D. ""We have no responsive documents ..." August 2, 2007.

Cooper, Gale. To January Contreras, Policy Advisor for Health for Governor Janet Napolitano. "Re: Non- response to my Freedom of Information Act request dated June 29, 2007." August 10, 2007.

_____. "Re: Freedom of Information Act request pertaining to New Mexico Governor Bill Richardson's Grand Jury investigation(s) concerning CDR Financial Products, Inc." To Attorney General Eric Holder. May 25, 2010.

_____. "Re: Freedom of Information Act request pertaining to New Mexico Governor Bill Richardson's Grand Jury investigation(s) concerning CDR Financial Products, Inc." To President Barak Obama. May 25, 2010.

_____. "Re: Freedom of Information Act request pertaining to New Mexico Governor Bill Richardson's Grand Jury investigation(s) concerning CDR Financial Products, Inc." To New Mexico U.S. Attorney Greg Fouratt Obama. May 25, 2010.

Hardy, David M. Section Chief, Record/Information Dissemination Section. "Subject: Bill Richardson, January 2008 – Present, FOIPA Request No.: 1149852-000." To Gale Cooper. U.S. Department of Justice, Federal Bureau of Investigation. June 28, 2010. **(Refused records as being on a "third party")**

Stewart, William G. II. Assistant Director. "Subject of Request: Gov. Bill Richardson (grand jury investigation), Request Number 2010-2058." To Gale Cooper. U.S. Department of Justice. July 14, 2010. **(Refused information based on "personal privacy")**

_____. "Subject of Request: Gov. Bill Richardson (grand jury investigation), Request Number 2010-2045." To Gale Cooper. U.S. Department of Justice. July 28, 2010. **(Refused information based on "personal privacy")**


# GALE COOPER INVESTIGATIONS OF
# DR. HENRY LEE AND ORCHID CELLMARKLAB)
# (CHRONOLOGICAL ORDER)

## BACKGROUND

Bugliosi, Vincent. *Outrage: The Five Reasons Why O.J. Simpson Got Away With Murder.* New York and London: W.W. Norton & Company. 1996. **(Exposé of Dr. Henry Lee improprieties, Pages 47-49.)**

No author. "Fraud Alleged at Cellmark, DNA Testing Firm." TalkLeft: The Politics of Crime. http://www.talkleft.com./new_archives/008809.html. November 18, 2004.

## LETTERS BY AND TO JAY MILLER, AS MY AGENT

Miller, Jay. "Re: Forensic consultation in the New Mexico Billy the Kid Case." Letter to Dr. Henry Lee. March 27, 2006. (**Enclosed Lee's articles with forensic claims.**.)

Lee, Henry, Dr. "In response to your letter dated March 27, 2006 ..." Letter to Jay Miller. May 1, 2006. (**Lee confirms sending his carpenter's bench and floorboard report to Lincoln County Sheriff's Department**.)

Miller, Jay. "Re: Follow-up on your letter of May 1, 2006 responding to my request of March 27, 2006 for information on your forensic consultation in the New Mexico Billy the Kid Case." Letter to Dr. Henry Lee. June 15, 2006.

_____. "Re: Follow-up to my letter of June 15, 2006 with regard to your forensic consultation in the New Mexico Billy the Kid Case." Letter to Dr. Henry Lee. August 8, 2006. (**No response to his role as stated in the multiple enclosed articles.**)

_____. "Re: The participation by you and Orchid Cellmark in the New Mexico Billy the Kid Case." Letter to Dr. Rick Staub. August 8, 2006. (**No response.**)

## LETTERS BY AND TO GALE COOPER

Cooper, Gale. To Haskell Pitluck, AAFS Ethics Committee Chairman and members of the AAFS Ethics Committee. "Re: Formal Ethics Complaint against Dr. Henry Lee for his work as a forensic expert in Lincoln County, New Mexico, Sheriff's Department Case # 2003-274 ('the Billy the Kid Case')." October 2, 2006..

Cooper, Gale. To Haskell Pitluck, AAFS Ethics Committee Chairman. "Re: Follow-up on my October 2, 2006 complaint on Dr. Henry Lee to the Ethics Committee of the American Academy of Forensic Sciences." March 5, 2007.

_____. To Dr. Bruce Goldberger. President AAFS. "Re: Informing of non-action to date on my American Academy of Forensic Sciences Ethics Committee complaint filed October 2, 2006 against Dr. Henry Lee." April 10, 2007.

Goldberger, Bruce. Dr. and President AAFS. Fax letter to Gale Cooper. "I have received the complaint today ..." April 12,, 2007.

_____. To Gale Cooper. (via fax) "You should receive a letter from Mr. Pitluck in the coming week or two ..." May 4, 2007.

Pitluck, Haskell M. AAFS Ethics Committee Chairman. To Gale Cooper, M.D. "Ethics Committee has completed its investigation ..." May 9, 2007. (**Denial of ethical violation by Dr. Lee based solely on his report to Lincoln County Sheriff's Department. Date of report given as February 5, 2005.**)

Cooper, Gale. To Haskell Pitluck, AAFS Ethics Committee Chairman. "Re: Follow-up on the May 9, 2007 AAFS response to my October 2, 2006 Ethics Complaint on Dr. Henry Lee. May 30, 2007. (**Clarification requested for vague answers.**)

_____. To Dr. Bruce Goldberger. President AAFS. "Re: Informing you about the need for clarification in the May 9, 2007 AAFS Ethics Committee response to my AAFS Ethics and Conduct Complaint of October 2, 2006 against Dr. Henry Lee." May 30, 2007.

Pitluck, Haskell M. AAFS Ethics Committee Chairman. To Gale Cooper, M.D. "Ethics Committee has completed its investigation ..." June 2, 2007. (**Denial of any responsibility by Dr. Lee for "actions or statements of others."**)

Cooper, Gale. Letter to Rene Romo. *Albuquerque Journal.* "Re: Attributions made by you in your August 2, 2004 *Albuquerque Journal* article titled 'Forensic Expert on Billy's Case: Questions Remain on Outlaws Fate.' " June 19, 2007.

_____. To Haskell Pitluck, AAFS Ethics Committee Chairman. "Re: Requested clarification of your responses of May 9, 2007 and June 2, 2007 to my October 2, 2006 AAFS Ethics Complaint against Dr. Henry Lee." June 19, 2007.

Cooper, Gale. To Deb Slaney. Albuquerque Museum of Art and History. "Re: Information request for Dreamscape Desperado exhibit." June 29, 2007. (**Documentation for carpenter's bench blood claim requested.**)

Pitluck, Haskell M. AAFS Ethics Committee Chairman. To Gale Cooper, M.D. "Ethics Committee has completed its investigation ..." July 6, 2007. (**Third denial of my Lee ethics complaint, with refusal to explain ignoring the evidence**)

Cooper, Gale. To Albuquerque Museum of Art and History Director Cathy Wright. "Re: Information request concerning past Dreamscape Desperado exhibit." July 30, 2007. (**Concerning their labeling of the carpenter's bench as having blood according to Dr. Henry Lee.**)

Slaney, Deborah. Curator of History at the Albuquerque Museum of Art and History. To Gale Cooper. "Re: Information request concerning past Dreamscape Desperado exhibit." August 6, 2007. (**Claim that Paul Hutton, not Dr. Lee, made the bench blood statement.**)

Walz, Kent. Editor-in-Chief *Albuquerque Journal*. To Gale Cooper. "Response to your letter concerning Rene Romo's story of August 2, 2004." August 13, 2007. (**Denial of Dr. Lee's refuting the forensic claims attributed to him.**)

## *INVESTIGATIONS OF HOAXERS BY RICO CASE TO FBI*

Cooper, Gale. To New Mexico U.S. Attorney David Iglesias. "Re: Enclosed reference copy of Freedom of Information Act (FOIA)/New Mexico Inspection of Public Records Act (IPRA) request concerning participation of Governor Bill Richardson in the New Mexico Billy the Kid Case and related issues." September 22, 2006.

_____. To New Mexico U.S. Attorney David Iglesias. "Re: Enclosed reference copy of Freedom of Information Act (FOIA)/New Mexico Inspection of Public Records Act (IPRA) request to Lincoln County Sheriff Rick Virden regarding his conducting the New Mexico Billy the Kid Case (Lincoln County Sheriff's Department Case # 2003-274) and its issues related to Maricopa County, Arizona Case # CA 2006020516 (pertaining to the Prescott, Arizona exhumations of John Miller and William Hudspeth.) September 22, 2006.

_____. To FBI Squad 5. "Re: RICO Complaint against New Mexico and Arizona public officials promulgating together Lincoln County Sheriff's Department Case # 2003-274 and De Baca County Sheriff's Department Case # 03-06-136-01 ('The Billy the Kid Case'). October 10, 2006.

_____. To FBI Special Agent Mark Humphrey. "RE: Additional evidence for my RICO complaint sent to you on October 10, 2006." October 30, 2006.

_____. To FBI Special Agent Mark Humphrey. "RE: Personal threats from Lincoln County Attorney Alan Morel, Lincoln County Sheriff Ricky Virden, alleged Lincoln County Deputy Tom Sullivan, and alleged Lincoln County Deputy Steve Sederwall.." October 30, 2006.

_____. To FBI Supervisor of White Collar Crime Attorney Mary Higgins. "RE: Copy of documentation of RICO complaint filed with Special Agent Mark Humphrey on October 10, 2006 with addendum of October 30, 2006. October 30, 2006.

Iglesias, David, U.S. Attorney and Mary L. Higgins, Assistant U.S. Attorney. Letter to Gale Cooper, M.D. "Re: Copy of RICO Complaint Concerning the 'Billy the Kid Case.' " November 16, 2006. (**Rejection of complaint.**)

_____. To New Mexico GOP Chairman Allen Weh. "RE: RICO Case." March 14, 2007.

Cooper, Gale. To FBI Special Agent Mark Humphrey. "Re: RICO Complaint against Governor Bill Richardson and other, New Mexico, public officials." January 29, 2008. (**Second complaint.**)

Humphrey, Mark D. To Gale Cooper. "We are in receipt of your complaint ..." February 5, 2008. (**Rejection of second complaint.**)

## INVESTIGATIONS OF CULPABLE ATTORNEYS BY
## STATE BAR ASSOCIATION COMPLAINTS

Cooper, Gale. To State Bar of New Mexico, The Disciplinary Board. "RE: State Bar of New Mexico Disciplinary Board Ref. # 26036: Professional Misconduct Complaint against New Mexico Attorney Alan P. Morel." November 13, 2006.

Long, Christine E., Special Assistant Disciplinary Counsel. To Dr. Gale Cooper. "Re: Complaint filed against Alan P. Morel, Esq." December 11, 2006. (**Rejection of complaint.**)

Cooper, Gale. To State Bar of Arizona A/CAP Division. "RE: Inquiry Complaint to Arizona State Bar Concerning Allegations of Legal Misconduct Against Maricopa County Prosecutor's Office's Deputy Attorney Jonell Lucca." January 5, 2007.

Worth, Ariel I. Staff Bar Counsel, State Bar of Arizona. To Gale Cooper. "Re: File No. 07-0060 Jonell L. Lucca Respondent." Letter to me. February 27, 2006. (**Rejection of complaint.**)

Cooper, Gale. To Worth, Ariel I. Staff Bar Counsel, State Bar of Arizona. "Re: Response to letter titled 'Re: File No. 07-0060 Jonell L. Lucca Respondent.'" March 21, 2007.

Worth, Ariel. Staff Bar Counsel, State Bar of Arizona. To Gale Cooper. "RE: File No: 07-0060. Jonell L. Lucca, Respondent." Letter to me. November 2, 2007. (**Second rejection of my Bar complaint.**)

Cooper, Gale. "Complaint Against Attorney Mickey Barnett, by Client Gale Cooper, to the New Mexico Bar Association Disciplinary Board, an Agency of the New Mexico Supreme County." Letter. January 19, 2013. (**259 pages of my evidence that I was Barnett's only client for records requesting, and Stinnett never made a request**)

Taylor, Anne L., Assistant Disciplinary Counsel. "Re: Complaint against Mickey Barnett, Esq." Letter to me. February 22, 2013. (**"No finding he lied under oath;" complaint denied**)

Cooper, Gale. "Appeal of Disciplinary Board denial, and request for reinstatement of complaint." Letter. March 8, 2013. (**Added Barnett's billings to show I was his only client for records requesting**)

Slease, William D., Chief Disciplinary Counsel. "Re: Your Complaint Against Mickey Barnett, Esq." Letter to me. March 14, 2013. (**My appeal will be reviewed**)

Gurley, Curtis R., Disciplinary Board Member. "Re: Your Complaint Against Mickey Barnett, Esq." Letter to me. April 12, 2013. (**"Disciplinary Counsel conducted appropriate investigation and further investigation is not required"**)


# PARDON THRUST IN BILLY THE KID CASE HOAX
# (INCLUDING ARTICLES) (CHRONOLOGICAL ORDER)

Cooper, Gale. "Re: Referred by Bob McCubbin." E-mail to Susannah Garrett. June 13, 2010.

Miller, Jay. "Kid's Pardon a Publicity Stunt." "Inside the Capitol" syndicated column and blog, insidethecapitol.blogspot.com. June 23, 2010. (**Papers refused to print; on blog only**)

Stinnett, Scot. "Billy the Kid historian says pardon all part of the hoax." *De Baca County News.* Pages 3, 9. June 24, 2010. (**Reprint of my Jay Miller article without commentary**)

Garrett, Jarvis Patrick "JP." "RE: Meeting" "... I would like el pinto." E-mail to Gale Cooper. June 29, 2010. (**Meeting with JP in which he suggested a meeting with Richardson**)

Cooper, Gale. "Lunch with Tourism Secretary." E-mail to JP and Susannah Garrett. July 9, 2010. (**I set up lunch with Mike Cerletti, Jay Miller, and the Garretts at La Fonda**)

———————. "Subj: Listing of Garrett Damages." E-mail to JP Garrett. July 10, 2010.

Romero, Nick Arno. "Forget the Kid; Real Outlaws are in Capital [sic]." *Albuquerque Journal.* Letter to the Editor. July 10, 2010.

No Author. "Billy the Kid 'to be pardoned.' " *Press Trust of India (Hindustan Times)* and Pakistan *Daily Express.* July 11, 2010. (**Richardson's pardon publicity move - with "Brushy" as Billy.**)

Cooper, Gale. "Re: More Thoughts on Pardon Write-Up." "... the key is that Richardson has no other way of justifying a pardon – except by making 'Brushy' a possibility. And ... he'll use as fake evidence his hoaxed murder investigation against Pat Garrett ... Richardson has to be stopped." E-mail to Susannah Garrett. July 15, 2010.

———————. "Re: Friday Meeting." "... I'll meet you at La Plazuela at noon." E-mail to Susannah Garrett. July 15, 2010.

Garrett, Jarvis Patrick "JP." "Petition in Opposition to Pardon of Billy the Kid." July 20, 2010. (**Made for signings at the Ruidoso Wild West Round-up**)

Romo, Rene. "Gov. Weighs Pardon for Billy the Kid." *Albuquerque Journal. Saturday,* No. 205. Front page, lead story, cont. A6. July 24, 2010.

Garrett, Jarvis Patrick "JP," Susan Floyd Garrett, and Pauline Garrett Tillinghast. "Representatives of the Garrett Family. "... As grandchildren of Pat Garrett, we have watched with outrage and sadness ..." Letter to Governor Richardson. July 25, 2010. (**Prepared with my input**)

Licón, Adriana Gómez. "Pardon form New Mexico governor unlikely for Billy the Kid." *El Paso Times.* July 29, 2010.

Sharpe, Tom. "English kin trace path of 'Billy the Kid's' ex-boss: Tunstall's murder sparked Lincoln County War." *The New Mexican.* July 29, 2010.

Massey, Barry. AP. "Billy the Kid To Be Pardoned, 130 Years Later? Lawman's Grandchildren Outraged; 'Would You Issue A Pardon For Someone Who Made His Living As A Thief?' National, international, and internet publications. July 30, 2010. (**Introduction of Garrett family opposition. In *The Washington Times* and msnbc.com as "NM governor considers pardon for Billy the Kid," and huffingtonpost.com as "Billy the Kid Pardon: Pat Garrett's Descendants Outraged At Bill Richardson's Suggestion to Pardon Gunslinger."**)

Cooper, Gale. Re: Old West Royalty." "Don't forget that you are all Old West royalty." E-mail to Garrett family. July 31, 2010.

Gardner, David. Los Angeles. "Pat Garrett's family plan showdown over plans to finally pardon Billy the Kid." London's *Daily Mail Online.* July 31, 2010.

Garrett, Jarvis Patrick "JP," Susan Floyd Garrett, and Pauline Garrett Tillinghast. "Representatives of the Garrett Family. "Re. August 2, 2010 meeting with you concerning your possible pardon of Billy the Kid ..." Letter to Governor Richardson. August 2, 2010. (**Prepared with my input to say they would be bringing an historical expert. When Richardson found out that was me, he refused me entry**)

Cooper, Gale. "Garrett Family Statement to Governor Bill Richardson." August 4, 2010. (**Prepared with input from the Garrett family for their meeting with Richardson**)

Massey, Barry. Associated Press. Santa Fe. "NM gov meets with lawman Pat Garrett's descendants." August 4, 2010. www.wthr.com/global/story.asp?s=12926188.

Cooper, Gale. "Re: Thanks." "I want to thank you and your children for the tremendous effort and grace that went into the Richardson meeting." E-mail to Garrett family. August 5, 2010.

Garrett, Susannah. "Re: Thanks." "Thanks for all your valuable and supportive presence through all this." E-mail to Gale Cooper. August 5, 2010.

Richardson, Bill. "Dear Garrett Family, Thank you for meeting with me ..." Letter to the Garretts. August 9, 2010. (**Follow-up to the August 4, 2010 meeting**)

Cooper, Gale. "Subj: Sample Wallace Family Statement." E-mail to William N. Wallace. August 10, 2010.

Wallace, William N. "Re: Sample Wallace Family Statement." ... "I have sent Governor Richardson by e-mail a modified version of the proposed 'Wallace Family' letter. E-mail to Gale Cooper. August 10, 2010.

Brockman, Paul, Director Indiana Historical Society Manuscript Collections. "... there is no written documentation of any 'pardon promise...' " Letter to Bill Richardson. August 11, 2010.

Cooper, Gale. "Re: Copy of *MegaHoax*." Letter to William N. Wallace. August 11, 2010.

_____. "Re: More on 1900, 1902 Wallace Articles." E-mail to Barry Massey. August 12, 2010.

_____. "Subj: More on Pardon Issue" "... [Y]ou are my best and last hope for ending Governor Bill Richardson's seven year hoaxing of Billy the Kid history ..." E-mail to William N. Wallace. August 13, 2010.

Nolan, Frederick." Re: Pardon Question." "... To the best of my knowledge no contemporary of the Kid's ever mentioned his 'deal' with Wallace ..." E-mail to Gale Cooper. August 13, 2010.

Cooper, Gale. "Re: Talking Points on Pardon Issue." E-mail to William N. Wallace. August 14, 2010.

Brady, Nicole. "Re: More on Past Brady Opposition." "... I don't imagine much of a role for myself ..." E-mail to Gale Cooper. August 30, 2010. (**Refusal of KOB reporter and Sheriff William Brady granddaughter to help**)

Vaughn, Chris. "Texas Town seeks New Mexico pardon for Billy the Kid." *Fort Worth Star-Telegram.* August 14, 2010. (**Bid for "Brushy Bill" Roberts pardon.**)

Lacey, Marc. "Old West Showdown Is Revived. *New York Times.* August 15, 2010. (**Richardson shape-shifted to "amateur historian."**)

No Author. "A Tale of Two Billys." *New English Review: The Iconoclast.* (Internet). August 15, 2010.

Gordon, Bea. "Examining Legend: The Pardoning of Billy the Kid.. New Mexico Gov. Bill Richardson's talking about exonerating the state's most famous outlaw. But at what cost?" www.newwest.net/topic/article/29850/C37/L37/ August 17, 2010.

Massey, Barry. Associated Press. Santa Fe. " 'Billy the Kid' pardon effort draws Wild West showdown." Wilkes-Barre, Pennsylvania. *The Times Leader.* August 21, 2010. (**Introduction of William N. Wallace and Indiana Historical Society opposition. In starpress.com of east central Indiana as "Should Billy the Kid Be Pardoned?"**)

Miller, Jay. "When is a promise not a promise?" *Inside the Capitol.* August 30, 2010. (**Apparently legitimizing the McGinn-Richardson pardon**)

Sides, Hampton. "Not-So-Charming Billy." *NY Times Opinion Section Op-Ed Contributor.* September 6, 2010.

Wallace, William N. . "Re: Reply wnwallace: "Barry Massey of the AP has ready from me a reaction quote should Gov. Richardson go ahead with the pardon. E-mail to Gale Cooper. September 16, 2010.

Cooper, Gale. "Re: Reply wnwallace: 'That powerful stance of yours gives me hope that it can deter Governor Richardson's pardon publicity stunt." E-Mail to William N. Wallace. September 16, 2010.

McGinn, Randi. "RE: Application for Pardon for Henry McCarty, AKA William Bonney or Billy the Kid." Letter to Shammara Henderson, Legal Counsel Governor Richardson. December 14, 2010 (**The McGinn pardon petition; possible Richardson attorney and wife of Attorney Charlie Daniels, appointed in 2007 to Supreme Court by Governor Richardson**)

Richardson, Bill. "Governor Bill Richardson to Consider Billy the Kid Pardon Petition." Press release. December 16, 2010. **(Floating the Randi McGinn petition)**

Garrett, Jarvis Patrick "JP." "No Subject." "... the petitioner for the pardon is Randi McGinn, so what's her link to Richardson ..." E-mail to Gale Cooper. December 16, 2010.

_____. "I'm just an ordinary person ..." Letter to Attorney Randi McGinn. (Unpublished) December 16, 2010. **(Opposition to pardon with legal argument against gubernatorial versus presidential pardon)**

McGinn, Randi. "I too am just an ordinary person ..." E-mailed letter to JP Garrett. (Unpublished) December 16, 2010. **(Repeat of her legalese promise-is-a-promise argument from her petition)**

Garrett, Susannah. "RE; The Pardon Draft to Eric." "... I think a panel of historians should debate ..." E-mail to Eric Witt. December 18, 2010. **(To Richardson's Deputy Chief of Staff)**

Wallace, William N. "Governor Richardson - Your imminent action ..." Letter to Bill Richardson. December 21, 2010. **(Opposition to Billy the Kid pardon)**

_____. "Subject: BtK/WnWallace." ... Ms. Cooper: I have sent the following to governor ..." E-mail to Gale Cooper. December 21, 2010. **(Copy of opposition letter)**

Garrett, Jarvis Patrick, JP. "Subj: Wallace draft." "I'm just sending you my thoughts ..." E-mail to William N. Wallace. December 26, 2010. **(I put the Garretts and Wallace together)**

Martinez, Edecio. "Billy the Kid to be Pardoned 130 Years Later." CBSNEWS.com. December 27, 2010.

Guarino, Mark. "Outgoing New Mexico Gov. Bill Richardson is considering a pardon for celebrated outlaw Billy the Kid. An informal e-mail poll shows support. But time is running out." Associated Press. December 29, 2010.

Levy, Glen. "Will Billy the Kid Be Pardoned? Governor Has Until Friday." TIME NewsFeed com. December 29, 2010.

Garrett, Jarvis Patrick, JP. "RE: CNN Comment ... press letter revised." E-mail to Gale Cooper. December 30, 2010.

Ray, Alarie. "Subj: FW: Governor Bill Richardson to Announce Decision on Billy the Kid Pardon Request Tomorrow." E-mail forwarded to Gale Cooper. December 30, 2013.

Richardson, Bill. "Governor Richardson to Announce his decision on Billy the Kid Pardon Request Tomorrow." Press release. December 30, 2010.

Burke, Kelly David. "Billy the Kid Pardon?" FoxNews.com. December 30, 2010.

Garrett, Jarvis Patrick "JP." "No Subject" "yea!!! no pardon!!! =" E-mail to Gale Cooper. December 31, 2010.

Hopper, Jessica. "Gov. Bill Richardson: 'I've Decided Not to Pardon Billy the Kid.' " ABCNEWS.com. December 31, 2010.

Rojas, Rick. "No Pardon for Billy the Kid. New Mexico Gov. Bill Richardson says, 'The Romanticism appealed to me ... but the facts and evidence did not support it." *Los Angeles Times*. December 31, 2010.

Watson, Kathryn. "Alas, no pardon for Billy the Kid: New Mexico's Richardson says close call." washingtontimes.com. December 31, 2010. **(With "waste time" quote by Governor Susana Martinez)**

No Author. "Richardson Declines to Pardon Outlaw Billy the Kid." FoxNews.com. December 31, 2010.

Wallace, William N. "Your persistence ... enabled common sense." E-mail To Gale Cooper. December 31, 2010.

Lacey, Marc. "For 2nd Time in 131 Years, Billy the Kid is Denied Pardon." *New York Times*. Page A10. January 1, 2011.

# IPRA VIOLATION LITIGATION
# FOR THE BILLY THE KID CASE HOAX:

Sandoval County District Cause No. D-1329-CV-2007-1364, Gale Cooper and De Baca County News, a New Mexico Corporation, PLAINTIFFS, vs. Rick Virden, Lincoln County Sheriff and Custodian of Records; and Steven M. Sederwall, Former Lincoln County Deputy Sheriff; and Thomas T. Sullivan, Former Lincoln County Sheriff and Former Lincoln County Deputy Sheriff, DEFENDANTS. (CHRONOLOGICAL ORDER)

## INSPECTION OF PUBLIC RECORDS ACT STATUTE

Madrid, Patricia A. Attorney General. *Inspection of Public Records Act Compliance Guide. Fourth Edition. The "Inspection of Public Records Act" NMSA 1978, Chapter 14, Article 2: A Compliance Guide for New Mexico Public Officials and Citizens.* Santa Fe: Office of the Attorney General. January 2004.

King, Gary, Attorney General. "IPRA Guide: The Inspection of Public Records Act NMSA 1978, Chapter 14, Article 2; A Compliance Guide for New Mexico Public Officials and Citizens. Seventh Edition. 2012.

## PRECEDENT CASES (CHRONOLOGICAL)

### DEBORAH TOOMEY IPRA LITIGATION

Toomey, Deborah. New Mexico Supreme Court "Emergency Petition for Writ of Mandamus." Case No. 31,952. September 8, 2008. (**For "extraordinary relief" on District Court Case Nos. D-0721-CV2009-98 and -99**)

_____. "I Remember" Public Comment speech to Truth or Consequences City Commissioners. May 26, 2009.

_____. New Mexico Court of Appeals No. 30, 795. "Brief in Chief." Appeal from the Seventh Judicial Court County of Sierra, Case No. D-0721-CV-2009-159. Hon. Matthew Reynolds. July 8, 2011.

_____. Seventh Judicial District Court County of Sierra, "Motion for Summary Judgment." State of New Mexico, ex rel. Deborah Toomey, an individual, Plaintiff vs. City of Truth or Consequences, Mary Penner, Sierra Community Council, and Jay Hopkins, Defendants, No. D-0721-CV2009-98, Hon. William Sanchez. January 13, 2012. (**District court case that led to appeal**)

Vanzi, Hon. Linda M., Chief Judge Celia Foy Castillo, and Judge Cynthia A Fry. Appeal. Court of Appeals of New Mexico. State of New Mexico, ex rel. Deborah Toomey, an individual, Plaintiff-Appellant vs. City of Truth or Consequences, Mary Penner, Sierra Community Council, and Jay Hopkins, Defendants-Appellees, No. 30,795. July 26, 2012. (**Key precedent case for me**)

Massey, Barry. "Court: Records Act Applies to Contractor." Associated Press. July 31, 2012. (**Massey omits Toomey's name, giving credit to FOG amicus curiae**)

### OTHER IPRA PRECEDENT CASES

*Ronald A. Coco, Inc. v. St. Paul's Methodist Church of Las Cruces, N.M., Inc.* 78 NM 97, 99, 428 P.2d 636, 638. 1967.

*State of New Mexico ex rel. Newsome v. Alarid,* 90 NM 790 568 P.2d at 1236, 1241, 1243. 1977.

*Bd. of Comm're of Doña County v. Las Cruces Sun News,* 2003-NMCA-102, ¶ 29, 134 NM 283, 76 P.3d 36. 2003.

*Bd. of Comm're of Doña County v. Las Cruces Sun News,* 2003-NMCA-102, 134 NM 238, 76 P.3d 36. 2003.

*City of Farmington v. The Daily Times,* 2009-NMCA-057, 146 nm, 349, 210 p.3D 246. 2009.

*Foy v. New Mexico Educational Retirement Board,* County of Bernalillo Cause No. D 202-CV-2009-1587. 2009. (ongoing)

*San Juan Agric. Water Users Ass'n. v. KNME-TV,* 2011-NMSC-011, 150 N.M. 64, 257 P.3d 884. 2011.

Kennedy, Roderick T. Chief Judge and Judge Linda M. Vanzi and Judge J. Miles Hanisee. *Faber v. King,* Court of Appeals of New Mexico. No. 31,446. April 25, 2013

# CONSECUTIVE PLAINTIFF ATTORNEYS

## *ATTORNEY MICKEY BARNETT AND FIRM PLUS FOUNDATION FOR OPEN GOVERNMENT (FOG)*

Cheves, Philip W. Barnett Law Firm. To Sheriff Rick Virden. "Re: Request for Inspection of Public Records." April 24, 2007. (**Start of my records requesting for the Dr. Henry Lee and Orchid Cellmark forensic DNA records**)

Morel, Alan P., Lincoln County Attorney. To Barnett Law Firm. "Re: Freedom of Information Act/Inspection of Public Records Act Request Dated April 24, 2007." April 27, 2007. (**Fakes Case 2003-274 as only deputy murder investigation.**)

Cheves, Philip W, Barnett Law Firm. To Sheriff Rick Virden. "Re: Request for Inspection of Public Records." May 9, 2007.

_____. To Alan P. Morel, Esquire. "Re: Request for Inspection of Public Records." May 9, 2007.

Morel, Alan P., Lincoln County Attorney. To Barnett Law Firm. "RE: Freedom of Information Act/Inspection of Public Records Act Request to Sheriff Rick Virden Dated May 9, 2007." May 11, 2007. (**Lies that Lincoln County have no Case 2003-274 records "whatsoever"**))

_____. To Barnett Law Firm. "RE: Freedom of Information Act/Inspection of Public Records Act Request to Alan P. Morel, Esq., Dated May 9, 2007." May 14, 2007. (**Fakes "deputies too records" excuse**)

Cheves, Philip W., Barnett Law Firm. To Alan P. Morel, Esquire. "Re: Request for Inspection of Public Records." June 8, 2007.

Cheves, Philip W., Barnett Law Firm. "Re: Request for Inspection of Public Records" to Tom Sullivan. June 14, 2007.

_____. "Re: Request for Inspection of Public Records" to Steve Sederwall. June 14, 2007.

Morel, Alan P., Lincoln County Attorney. Thomas Stewart, Lincoln County Manager, and Rick Virden, Lincoln County Sheriff. To Tom Sullivan and Steve Sederwall. "Re: Request for Inspection of Public Records." June 21, 2007. (**This is attached Morel's letter of June 22, 2007 as feigned records recovery attempt from Sullivan and Sederwall.**)

Sederwall, Steven M. and Thomas T. Sullivan. To Rick Virden, Lincoln County Sheriff. "Memorandum. Subject: Billy the Kid Investigation." June 21, 2007. (**Key hoax document attached to the Morel letter of 22, 2007, blames Richardson and Robins for case and attaches $6,500 in "bribery" checks to Sullivan**)

Morel, Alan P. Lincoln County Attorney. To Barnett Law Firm. "RE: Freedom of Information Act/Inspection of Public Records Act Request to Alan Morel, Esq., Dated June 8, 2007." June 22, 2007. **(Attached was the Sullivan-Sederwall June 21, 2007 "Memorandum.")**

_____. To Barnett Law Firm. "RE: Freedom of Information Act/Inspection of Public Records Act Request to Alan P. Morel, Esq., dated June 8, 2007." June 26, 2007. **(Last response before litigation – and is not a correct denial under IPRA law; is double-talking the deputies' resignations in the June 21, 2007 "Memorandum")**

Barnett, Mickey. "Verified Complaint for Declaratory Judgment Ordering Production of Certain Records and Information." October 15, 2007. **(Start of litigation for Cause No. D-1329-CV-2007-1364, repeats records in first request)**

_____. "Verified First Amended Complaint for Declaratory Judgment Ordering Production of Certain Records and Information." November 1, 2007. **(Removes Lincoln County as defendant, repeats records in first request)**

Zimitski, Dewayne. Process server for Steve Sederwall and Tom Sullivan. "Affidavit of DeWayne Zimitski for Cause No. D 1329 CV 2007-01364." December 27, 2007.

Cooper, Gale. To Attorney General Gary King. "Re: Informing about an IPRA violation case: Sandoval County Thirteenth Judicial District Cause No. D-1329-CV2007-1364." January 22, 2008.

_____. To Attorney Leonard DeLayo for FOG. "Re: Sandoval County Thirteenth Judicial District Court Cause No. D 1329 CV2007-1364; an IPRA violation case." January 22, 2008.

Werkmeister, Nicole. Attorney for Narvaez law firm. "Motion to Dismiss Based on Improper Venue and Failure to State a Claim." March 5, 2008.

Brown, Kevin M. Attorney for defendants Sullivan and Sederwall. To Barnett Law Firm. "Thomas T. Sullivan's Responses to Request for Production of Documents, No. D-1329-CV-2007-01364." March 17, 2008. **(Claims not public records, and defendant does not have them..)**

_____. To Barnett Law Firm. "Steven M. Sederwall's Responses to Request for Production of Documents." March 17, 2008. **(Claims not public records, and defendant does not have them..)**

Barnett, Mickey. "Plaintiffs' Response to the Motion of Defendant Rick Virden to Dismiss For Improper Venue and Failure to State Claim." March 24, 2008.

Shandler, Zachary. (For Attorney General Gary King). To Gale Cooper M.D. "RE: Gale Cooper and De Baca County News vs. Lincoln County et al., Cause No. D-1329-CV2007-1364." April 3, 2008.

Stinnett, Scot. To Gale Cooper. (via e-mail). "IPRA Case Updates." August 12, 2008. **(About FOG probably joining IPRA case.)**

Sullivan, Thomas T. "Deposition." August 18, 2008. **(Taken by Mickey Barnett)**

Sederwall, Steven M. "Deposition."" August 18, 2008. **(Taken by Mickey Barnett)**

Barnett, Mickey. Attorney. To Gale Cooper. (via e-mail). "FOG is in." August 22, 2008.

Virden, Rick. "Deposition." September 8, 2008. **(Taken by David Garcia)**

Werkmeister, Nicole. "Re" Gale Cooper, et al, v. Rick Virden, et al. Thirteenth Judicial District Court Cause No. D-1329-CV-2007-01364." Attorney. Letter to Attorney Mickey D. Barnett. September 3, 2008. **(Virden turn-over by subpoena duces tecum of Sheriff's Department file for Case # 2003-274 – minus any forensic documents; calls case criminal investigation under IPRA)**

Virden, Rick. Case 2003-274 file Turn-over. September 3, 2003. **(By subpoena duces tecum; 193 pages)**

Rogers, Patrick J. Attorney. "Docs for editing. To: Mickey Barnett; David A. Garcia." (via e-mail). Monday, September 22, 2008. (Forwarded to Gale Cooper on September 25, 2008.) **(Threat FOG to pressure for dismissing Virden)**

Cooper, Gale. From Attorney David Garcia. (via e-mail). "Re: FW: Docs for editing." September 25, 2008.

Cooper, Gale. "Subj. IPRA Case Communication for Review. To Attorneys Barnett and Garcia and Scot Stinnett." (via e-mail). September 28, 2008. **(IPRA case overview, our legal relationship, and responses to the Rogers e-mail.)**
_____. To Attorney Leonard DeLayo. "Fwd: Response regarding IPRA Case." September 29, 2008. **(IPRA case overview for Barnett of September 28, 2008 with responses to the Rogers e-mail.)**

Rogers, Patrick. Forwarded from Scot Stinnett. (via e-mail). "No Subject." September 30, 2008. **(A copy of an e-mail from Attorney Rogers to Attorney DeLayo pushing for Sederwall as Records Custodian.)**
_____. "Re: Second Response To Your FOG Proposal." To Gale Cooper. (via e-mail) October 1, 2008 4:40:27 AM.. **(Attorney Rogers holds to Sederwall as Records Custodian or FOG withdrawal.)**

Barnett, Mickey D. Attorney. "Re: Sullivan Sederwall Depositions. To Gale Cooper." (via e-mail). October 1, 2008. **("Taken the wind out of my sails" communication.)**

Brown, Kevin M. Attorney. "Re: Cooper v. Lincoln County, et al. No. D-1329-CV-07-1364. To Patrick J. Rogers." October 16, 2008.

Cooper, Gale. To Attorney Pat Rogers. "Re: Response documents forwarded to me by e-mail on October 20, 2008 concerning NMFOG's actions in relation to my IPRA case No. D-1329-CV-1364." October 27, 2008.

Rogers, Patrick J. Attorney. Letter of withdrawal as the FOG attorney pertaining to my IPRA case. November 10, 2008.

Cooper, Gale. "Re: My response to your letter of October 16, 2008 to Attorney Pat Rogers, and my dissociation from the referenced Foundation For Open Government communications." Letter to Brown. November 17, 2008.

## *ATTORNEYS MARTIN E. THREET AND BLAIR DUNN*

Threet, Martin E. Attorney and Attorney A. Blair Dunn. "Plaintiffs' Motion for Summary Judgment." July 31, 2009.

Werkmeister, H. Nicole. "Attorney. Defendant Rick Virden's Response to Plaintiff's [sic] Motion for Summary Judgment and Cross-Motion for Summary Judgment." August 29, 2009.

Brown, Kevin. Attorney. "Defendants Sederwall and Sullivan's Response to Motion for Summary Judgment." September 2, 2009.

Threet, Martin E. and A. Blair Dunn, Attorneys for Plaintiffs. "Plaintiffs' Reply and Motion to Exceed Page Limit For Exhibits." September 29, 2009. **(Attempt to enter my extensive evidence into court record)**

Hearing for "Plaintiffs' Motion for Summary Judgment." Transcript. November 20, 2009. **(Plaintiffs' Motion for Summary Judgment Granted.)**

Brown, Kevin. "I am enclosing the document Mr. Sederwall received from Dr. Lee ..." Letter. February 18, 2010. **(Color copy of unrequested Lee floorboard report)**

Lee, Henry and Calvin Ostler. "Forensic Research and Training Center Forensic Examination Report: "Examination of Lincoln County Court House." February 25, 2005. **(Given to Plaintiffs on February 18, 2010 by Brown and on April 6, 2010 by Werkmeister as a requested Lee report – but was the fake Version I (9 pages) of an unrequested floorboard report )**

Threet, Martin E. "I am returning the Lee report ..." Letter to Brown. (Rejecting and returning the Lee floorboard report) February 25, 2010.

"Presentment Hearing." Transcript. March 9, 2010. **(Key testimony: defendants' offering unrequested (tampered) Lee floorboard report as fulfilling records turn-over; lying that it is only record in Sederwall's possession)**

Eichwald, George P., District Judge. "Order Granting Plaintiff's Motion for Summary Judgment and Denying Defendant Virden's Cross Motion for Summary Judgment and Order Granting Leave to File Interlocutory Appeal" March 12, 2010. **(Grants evidentiary hearing.)**

Werkmeister, Nicole. "Attached is the Forensic Examination Report From Dr. Henry Lee ..." Fax cover letter. April 6, 2010. **(Copy faxed of same unrequested (fake) Lee floorboard report from Brown was enclosed)**

Eichwald. George P., District Judge. "Order Granting Plaintiffs' Motion for Summary Judgment and Denying Defendant Virden's Cross-Motion for Summary Judgment and Order Granting Leave to File Interlocutory Appeal." March 12, 2010. **(Major Plaintiff victory)**

_____. "This letter is to follow-up ..." Letter. April 12, 2010. **(Repeat attempt to say unrequested Lee floorboard report met IPRA request)**

Threet, Martin E. "Take a look at this letter ..." Fax cover letter to me. April 13, 2010. **(Werkmeister sending fake floorboard Lee report to us)**

Threet, Martin E. "The time for interlocutory appeal having passed ..." Letter to Werkmeister and Brown. May 3, 2010 **(Documents no defendants' appeal or judge's summary judgment)**

Hearing for "Mandatory Order of Disclosure and Production Hearing." Transcript. September 9, 2010.

Threet, Martin E. "Re: Billy the Kid. "Henry Narvaez has again repeated his assurance to me that if we will agree to dismiss Virden ..." Fax to me. September 14, 2010. **(Threet's unscrupulous attempt to trick me into dismissing Virden)**

_____. "Re: Plaintiff's response to letter from Sheriff Rick Virden. It is the position of my clients ..." Letter. September 27, 2010.

Virden, Rick. "It is my understanding that on May 22, 2004, Steve Sederwall ..." Letter to Henry Lee. October 26, 2010. **(sham recovery attempt to Dr. Henry Lee)**

_____. "It is my understanding that in the spring or summer of 2004, Steve Sederwall sent a blood sample(s) to Orchid Cellmark ..." Letter "To Whom It May Concern." October 26, 2010. **(sham recovery attempt to Orchid Cellmark)**

Narvaez Law Firm. Billing to New Mexico County Insurance Authority. October 31, 2010. **(Listing secret meetings with Attorney Threet to dismiss Virden)**

Gulliksen, Joan., Orchid Cellmark Customer Liaison, Forensics. "Orchid Cellmark is in receipt of your letter requesting DNA documents ..." Letter to Virden. November 2, 2010. **(Orchid Cellmark response requesting client name to release records; confirms records existence; Virden did not get the records)**

_____. "Orchid Cellmark, this is Joan ..." Transcript of telephone call from Virden. November 2, 2010. **(Gulliksen states needs client name to release records; Virden did no follow-up)**

_____. "Orchid Cellmark, this is Joan ..." E-mail to Virden. November 2, 2010. **(Gulliksen states needs client name to release "DNA documents pertaining to Billy the Kid; Virden did no follow-up)**

Brown, Kevin. "Enclosed please find a copy of another report dated February 25, 2005 which deals with the examination of furniture by Dr. Lee." Letter to Threet. November 10, 2010. **(Sending Lee's (tampered) bench report; different font than the (tampered) floorboard report)**

Lee, Henry and Calvin Ostler. "Forensic Research and Training Center Forensic Examination Report: "Examination of furniture from Pete Maxwell's of July 15, 1881." February 25, 2005. **(Given to Plaintiffs on November 10, 2010 as Lee bench report (16 pages) – but was its fake Version I )**

Werkmeister, Nicole. Letter to Threet. November 4, 2010. **(Shaming Virden recovery of Orchid Cellmark records; saying Lee did not respond)**

Lee, Henry. "This letter is in response to your letter ..." Letter to Virden. November 12, 2010. **(response to Virden that Lee has report; Virden never asked for it!)**

Narvaez Law Firm. "Stipulated Order of Dismissal with Prejudice." Fax to Attorney Martin E. Threet. No Date. **(Never submitted; failed attempt to trick me)**

Werkmeister, Nicole. Letter to Threet. November 22, 2010. (**copies of Virden's sham Lee and Orchid Cellmark requests sent to Threet**)

Robins, Bill III. Deposition taken by Attorney Martin E. Threet. January 6, 2011.

"Evidentiary Hearing on Plaintiff's Motion for Mandatory Order of Disclosure and Production." Transcript. January 21, 2011. (**Defendants gave tampered Lee Floorboard report (9 pages) Version II entered as Exhibit F; tampered Lee bench report (16 pages) Version I entered as Exhibit E; Threet slept through hearing leading to my firing of him; almost no evidence was entered by Threet and Dunn**)

Lee, Henry and Calvin Ostler. "Forensic Research and Training Center Forensic Examination Report: "Examination of furniture from Pete Maxwell's of July 15, 1881." February 25, 2005. (**Given to Court on January 21, 2011 as Lee bench report (16 pages), Exhibit E – but was its fake Version I** )

Lee, Henry and Calvin Ostler. "Forensic Research and Training Center Forensic Examination Report: "Examination of Lincoln County Court House." February 25, 2005. (**Given to Court on January 21, 2011 as Lee floorboard report (9 pages), Exhibit F – but was its fake Version II** )

Brown, Kevin. "I represent Steve Sederwall ..." Letter to Dr. Staub. February 3, 2011. (**Sederwall's court-ordered bogus Orchid Cellmark recovery attempt**)

Cooper, Gale. "Re: Termination of legal services for Gale Cooper and the *De Baca County News* vs Lincoln County Sheriff Rick Virden et al case." Letter to Attorney Martin E. Threet. February 12, 2011. (**Termination of Threet**)

_____. "Subj: Change of Legal Representation for Virden et al." E-mail to Attorney Blair Dunn. April 13, 2011. (**Termination of Dunn**)


## *ATTORNEYS JOHN TIWALD AND WILLIAM RIORDAN*

Brown, Kevin. Letter. June 7, 2011. (**Follow-up to Sederwall's court-ordered January 31, 2012 turn-over of false "original" Lee report (25 pages); now giving a CD with its color and unsigned version** )

"Presentment Hearing." Transcript. September 23, 2011. (**Plaintiffs presenting discrepancies in the Lee reports**)

Eichwald, George P., District Judge. "Order on Hearing of January 21, 2011." September 28, 2011. (**Joined the deputy killings and Kid killing investigations; calling them and records public**)


## *ATTORNEYS PATRICK GRIEBEL AND WILLIAM RIORDAN*

Riordan, William and Patrick Griebel. "Plaintiffs' Requested Findings of Fact and Conclusions of Law." November 4, 2011.

Cooper, Gale. "Re: Immediate termination of services for Sandoval District Court Cause No. D-1329-CV-07-1364." Letter to Attorney Griebel. November 21, 2011.

Griebel, Patrick and Jeremy Theoret. "Plaintiff's Motion for Payment of Damages, Costs and Fees." December 12, 2011. (**Co-Plaintiff Scot Stinnett goes rogue and ultimately throws case into appeal by premature filing**)

_____. "Plaintiff's Reply in Support of Motion for Payment of Damages, Costs and Fees." January 13, 2012.

Hearing on "Plaintiffs' Motion to Supplement the Record and a Request for Sanctions, and Co-Plaintiff's Motion For Attorney Fees." January 17, 2012 (**Lee reports presented for sanctions as forged/tampered; and Co-plaintiff Stinnett requests fees for past attorneys. Judge grants 100% fees**)

Brown, Kevin. Court-ordered turn-over of 25 page, "original" Lee report. January 31, 2012.

Eichwald, George P., District Judge. "Order on Plaintiffs Motion to Supplement the Record and Request for Award of Sanctions against Defendants." February 23, 2012. (**Ordered Sederwall to produce original Lee report**)

Lee, Henry and Calvin Ostler. "Forensic Research and Training Center Forensic Examination Report." February 25, 2005. (**Court-ordered turn-over to Plaintiffs on January 31, 2012 as "original" Lee report (25 pages) combining bench, floorboards, and washstand - but had faked Lee signature and no Ostler signature; came with same envelope dated April 15, 2005 and addressed to Sederwall from Lee – that Sederwall had been giving since his August 18, 2008 deposition!**)

Griebel, Patrick J. Attorney for Scot Stinnett. "Subpoena for Production or Inspection to Laboratory Corporation of America." March 29, 2012. (**Non-IPRA subpoena of records from Orchid Cellmark parent company; see below "Orchid Cellmark Records"**)

_____. "Reply in Support of Plaintiff's Motion for Order to Show Cause." April 11, 2012. (**Co-Plaintiff's attempt to get Sullivan and Sederwall "Private Donor Fund" checking account information**))

Narvaez, Henry. Attorney for Virden. Billing Account No. 43-166B to New Mexico Association of Counties Risk Management. April 30, 2012. (**With April 25, 2012 billed to taxpayers for a phone conversation with hoax-backing reporter Rene Romo of the *Albuquerque Journal***)

Hearing on "Plaintiffs' Second Motion to Supplement the Record and a Request for Sanctions." May 31, 2012 (**Lee reports presented for sanctions as forged/tampered. Judge grants depositions**)

Brown, Kevin. Court-ordered turn-over of another 25 page, "original" Lee report. June 7, 2012. (**CD of same report as given on January 31, 2012, but with color photos and no signatures**)

Lee, Henry and Calvin Ostler. "Forensic Research and Training Center Forensic Examination Report." February 25, 2005. (**Given by court order to Plaintiffs on June 7, 2012 as another "original" Lee report – on CD with 25 pages, with color photos, without any signatures**)

Sederwall, Steven. Deposition. June 26, 2012.

Virden, Rick. Deposition. June 27, 2012.

"Status Conference." Transcript. September 21, 2012.

Eichwald, George P., District Judge. "Order." For Status Conference of September 21, 2012. (**Court-ordered mediation and Evidentiary hearing**)

Eichwald, George P., District Judge. "Order." For Settlement Conference of March 26, 2013. (**Court-ordered mediation and Evidentiary hearing**)

# *ORCHID CELLMARK RECORDS SUBPOENAED OUTSIDE IPRA BY CO-PLAINTIFF (RECEIVED APRIL 20, 2012)*

Griebel, Patrick J. Attorney for Scot Stinnett. "Subpoena for Production or Inspection to Laboratory Corporation of America." March 29, 2012. (**Non-IPRA subpoena of records from Orchid Cellmark parent company; got 133 pages of results of Lee's floorboards and bench, and Arizona exhumations; missing DNA matching results of bench to remains**)

## SELECT ORCHID CELLMARK RECORDS

Evidence Bag Photo. Chain of Custody Label: "Case No. 2003-274, Underside Bench 4. Date: 07,31,04." Below is written Orchid Cellmark Case and Specimen No. 4444-002B. July 31, 2004. **(Joining Case 2003-274 to Orchid Cellmark Case No. 4444)**

Ostler, Calvin D. "Dear Mr. Staub, It was a pleasure to speak with you ..." Letter to Dr. Rick Staub. August 3, 2004. **(Asking to keep Lee and Sederwall tests separate)**

_____. FedEx Mailing Envelope and tracking information to "Rick Staub, Orchid Cellmark." August 3, 2004. **(Specimens delivered August 4, 2004)**

"Orchid Cellmark Evidence Evaluation Worksheet Case No. 4444 A and B." August 16, 2004. **(Identifying Calvin Ostler as the Orchid Cellmark client; listing together specimens pertaining to Lee's courthouse and bench specimen-gathering)**

"Orchid Cellmark Forensics E-Gel Load Sheet: E-gel ID Number 124480." March 1, 2005. **(Example of gel separations of the DNA specimens)**

"Orchid Cellmark Evidence Evaluation Worksheet Case No. 4444." April 13, 2006. **(Identifying Calvin Ostler as the Orchid Cellmark client; listing together specimens pertaining to the Arizona John Miller-William Hudspeth exhumations.**

"Orchid Cellmark Chain of Custody for Case No. 4444." May 19, 2005. **(On date of John Miller exhumation and signed by Orchid Cellmark Director Rick Staub with the south and north grave specimens he collected listed)**

"Orchid Cellmark Laboratory Report - Forensic Identity - Mitochondrial Analysis for 4444." January 26, 2009. **(Identifying Calvin Ostler as the Orchid Cellmark client; listing together specimens pertaining to reports requested by me: Lee's from bench and Orchid Cellmark's from the Arizona graves.)**

## DEFENDANTS' NEW MEXICO COURT OF APPEALS CASES AGAINST DISTRICT COURT CAUSE NO. D-1329-CV2007-1364: Nos. 31,926 and 32,060 (RESULTING FROM CO-PLAINTIFF STINNETT'S PREMATURE ATTORNEYS' FEE REQUEST – WHICH I DID NOT JOIN)

Werkmeister, Nicole. Narvaez law firm for Virden. "Defendant-Appellant's Application for Interloculatory Appeal." Case No. 31,926. February 14, 2012.

Griebel, Patrick. Attorney for Plaintiff-Appellant De Baca County News. "Plaintiff-Appellees Response in Opposition to Defendant-Appellants' Application for Interloculatory Appeal." Case No. 31,926. February 29, 2012.

Barnett, Mickey, Blair Dunn, Martin E. Threat, and John Tiwald, Past Plaintiffs' Attorneys. "Response of Plaintiffs' Former Counsel Barnett Law Firm, Blair Dunn, Martin E. Threet, and John Tiwald Filed in Opposition to Defendant Appellants' Application for Interloculatory Appeal." Case No. 31,926. February 29, 2012.

Cooper, Gale, Plaintiff-Appellee. "Gale Cooper's Notice of Pro Se Appearance in New Mexico Court of Appeals." Case No. 31,926. March 5, 2012.

Sutin, Jonathan B. and Michael E. Vigil. New Mexico Court of Appeals Judges. "Order: Application is Denied of Defendant-Appellant Sheriff Rick Virden." Case No. 31,926. March 20, 2012.

Brown, Kevin. Attorney for Sullivan and Sederwall. "Docketing Statement." Case No. 32,060. April 9, 2012. (**Brown appeals fee issue**)

Cooper, Gale, Plaintiff-Appellee. "Gale Cooper's Notice of Pro Se Appearance in New Mexico Court of Appeals." Case No. 32,060. April 24, 2012.

Narvaez, Henry. Attorney for Virden. Defendant-Appellant Sheriff Rick Virden's Brief-in-Chief. Case No. 32,060. "August 8, 2012.

Griebel, Patrick and Jeremy Theoret. Attorneys for De Baca County News. "Plaintiff/Appellee De Baca County News' Motion to Strike Defendant/Appellant Virden's Brief-in-Chief and Entries of Appearance." Case No. 32,060. August 8, 2012.

_____. "Plaintiff-Appellee Gale Cooper's Motion to Dismiss Based on Procedural Irregularities and Fatal Flaws." Case No. 32,060. August 17, 2012.

_____. "Plaintiff-Appellee Gale Cooper's Motion to Delay Response(s) Until Court Ruling on Dismissal or on Completion of Transcript." Case No. 32,060. September 4, 2012.

Werkmeister, Nicole. Werkmeister, Nicole. Narvaez law firm for Virden. "Defendant-Appellant Sheriff Rick Virden's Response in Opposition to Plaintiff's Motion to Dismiss." Case No. 32,060. September 4, 2012.

_____. "Plaintiff-Appellee Gale Cooper's Motion to Petition for Permission to Reply to Defendant-Appellants Thomas T. Sullivan and Steven M. Sederwall's Response to District Court Defendant Virden's Response to Her Motion to Dismiss." Case No. 32,060. September 11, 2012.

Sutin, Jonathan B., New Mexico Court of Appeals Judge. "Order." Case No. 32,060. September 14, 2012.

_____. "Order to Show Cause." September 21, 2012. (**Wants brief on why Virden is not a party to appeal**)

Cooper, Gale. "Plaintiff-Appellee Gale Cooper's Motion to Petition for Permission to Reply to October 2, 2012 Response of Attorney Henry Narvaez for District Court Defendant Virden." Case No. 32,060. October 5. 2012.

Sutin, Jonathan B., New Mexico Court of Appeals Judge. "Order." Case No. 32,060. October 23, 2012. (**Denies my motion to remove Virden as a party**)

Brown, Kevin. Attorney for Sullivan and Sederwall. "Defendants-Appellants Sederwall and Sullivan's Brief in Chief." Case No. 32,060. October 26, 2012.

Cooper, Gale, Plaintiff-Appellant. "Plaintiff-Appellee Gale Cooper's Motion to Stay Proceedings Until District Court Adjudication on the Lack of Standing of Plaintiff-Appellee De Baca County News." Case No. 32,060. November 29, 2012.

Jones, Wendy. Chief Clerk. "Order." Case No. 32,060. December 11, 2012. (**Briefing on De Baca's lack of Standing**)

Griebel, Patrick and Jeremy Theoret. Attorneys for De Baca County News. "Plaintiff/Appellee De Baca County News' Answer To Defendants' Briefs-in-Chief." Case No. 32,060. December 17, 2012.

Fry, Cynthia, New Mexico Court of Appeals Judge. "Order." Case No. 32,060. December 27, 2012. (**Request answer brief from me**)

Cooper, Gale, Plaintiff-Appellant. "Plaintiff-Appellee Gale Cooper's Answer to Defendants' Briefs in Chief." Case No. 32,060. December 27, 2012.

_____. "Plaintiff-Appellee Gale Cooper's Motion to Supplement the Record Proper Regarding Lack of Standing of Plaintiff-Appellee De Baca County News. January 2, 2013.

Fry, Cynthia, New Mexico Court of Appeals Judge. "Stipulated Motion for Dismissal With Prejudice; On Direct Appeal From the Thirteenth Judicial District Court, The Hon. George P. Eichwald, District Judge, No. D-1329-CV-2007-01364." Case No. 32,060. April 24, 2013. (**Outcome of Mediation of March 27, 2013**)

## *GALE COOPER IN DISTRICT COURT AS PRO SE*

Cooper, Gale. "Plaintiff Gale Cooper's Request to Delay Presentation of Her Status Conference Order." October 17, 2012.

_____. "Plaintiff Gale Cooper's Court Ordered Request for Evidentiary Hearing Already Scheduled for December 18, 2012." November 1, 2012

Brown, Kevin. Attorney for Sullivan and Sederwall. "Motion and Consolidated Memorandum to Dismiss the Amended Complaint Filed by Plaintiff De Baca County News for Lack of Standing and Subject Matter Jurisdiction." November 6, 2012. **(Evidence that Brown was unethically forewarned about the standing issue by an attorney I had interviewed for new representation – I did not file on this issue until November 14, 2012)**

Cooper, Gale. "Plaintiff Gale Cooper's Entry of Pro Se Appearance." November 13, 2012

_____. "Plaintiff Gale Cooper's Pre-Evidentiary Hearing Brief." November 14, 2012.

_____. "Plaintiff Gale Cooper's Motion to Dismiss Co-Plaintiff De Baca County News Based on Lack of Standing." November 14, 2012.

_____. "Affidavit of Gale Cooper." November 14, 2012. **(Attesting to Stinnett's lack of standing, and my being only records-requesting client)**

_____. "Plaintiff Gale Cooper's Pre-Evidentiary Hearing Brief." November 14, 2012.

_____. "Plaintiff Gale Cooper's Motion to Dismiss Co-Plaintiff De Baca County News Based on Lack of Standing." November 14, 2012. **(Stinnett did not file records requests)**

Barnett, Mickey. Past Plaintiff Attorney. "Affidavit of Mickey Barnett." November 16, 2012 and filed with Court as an exhibit on November 20, 2012. **(Lies under oath that Stinnett was his records-requesting client (boiler-plated with affidavit for Stinnett)**

Stinnett, Scot. "Affidavit of Scot Stinnett." November 16, 2012 and filed with Court on November 19, 2012. **(Lies under oath that he was Barnett's client in records request phase and that he filed the records requests. Proof for me that he was the most despicable player in Billy the Kid Case hoax: a traitor)**

Cooper, Gale. "Plaintiff Gale Cooper's Response to 'Defendants Sullivan's and Sederwall's Motion and Consolidated Memorandum to Dismiss the Amended Complaint Filed by De Baca County News for Lack of Standing and Subject Matter Jurisdiction." November 20, 2012.

_____. "Plaintiff Gale Cooper's Response to 'Defendant Rick Virden's Notice of Joinder in Defendants Sederwall and Sullivan's Motion of Consolidated Memorandum to Dismiss the Amended Complaint Filed by De Baca County News for Lack of Standing and Subject Matter Jurisdiction and Plaintiff Gale Cooper's Motion to Dismiss Co-Plaintiff De Baca County News Based on Lack of Standing." November 20, 2012.

Griebel, Patrick. Attorney for De Baca County News. "Plaintiff De Baca County News' Response to Defendant [sic] Sederwall and Sullivan's Motion of Consolidated Memorandum to Dismiss the Amended Complaint Filed by De Baca County News for Lack of Standing and Subject Matter Jurisdiction." November 20, 2012.

Narvaez, Henry, Attorney for Virden. "It is our position that those deposition [sic] and exhibits are not relevant to the subject matter of the hearing..." Letter to Gale Cooper. November 20, 2012. **(Trying to keep out depositions of June 26-27, 2012; and refusing to stipulate)**

Cooper, Gale. District Court Pro Se. "Plaintiff Gale Cooper's Motion for Legal Action Against Attorney Mickey Barnett and Scot Stinnett for Production of False Affidavits Claiming Standing of the De Baca County News to Refute Plaintiff Gale Cooper's Motion to Dismiss Co-Plaintiff De Baca County News Based on Lack of Standing." November 27, 2012. (**My response to the Barnett-Stinnett lying affidavits**)

_____. "Plaintiff Gale Cooper's Motion to Compel Alan Morel's Subpoena Compliance and to Include Penalties for Non-Compliance, and Opposition to Defendant Rick Virden's Motion to quash Subpoena of Alan Morel, Esq. and for Protective Order." November 27, 2012.

_____. "Addendum to Plaintiff Gale Cooper's Motion to Compel Alan Morel's Compliance With Subpoena to be a Witness in Evidentiary Hearing of December 18, 2012." November 30, 2012.

_____. "Plaintiff Gale Cooper's Request for Expedited Hearing on Filed Motion to Compel Alan Morel's Subpoenaed Appearance for Evidentiary Hearing on December 18, 2012 and for Contempt." December 3, 2012.

_____. "Plaintiff Gale Cooper's Request for Expedited Hearing Prior to Evidentiary Hearing of December 18, 2012 and for Dismissal of Co-Plaintiff De Baca County News Based on Lack of Standing." December 10, 2012.

_____. "Plaintiff Gale Cooper's Addendum of Evidence for Requested Expedited Hearing on Dismissal of Co-Plaintiff De Baca County News Based on Lack of Standing." December 10, 2012.

_____. "Plaintiff Gale Cooper's Witness List for Evidentiary Hearing on December 18, 2012." December 10, 2012.

_____. "Plaintiff Gale Cooper's Addendum to Witness List for Evidentiary Hearing on December 18, 2012." December 14, 2012.

"Evidentiary Hearing." Transcript. December 18, 2012. (**Judge upholds Stinnett's standing against my motion to dismiss; Virden testifies**)

Cooper, Gale. "Plaintiff Gale Cooper's Opposition Reply to Virden's Objection to Plaintiff Cooper's Pre-Evidentiary Hearing Brief." December 21, 2012.

_____. "Plaintiff Gale Cooper's Request for Continuation of December 18, 2012 Evidentiary Hearing." December 21, 2012.

Eichwald, George P., District Court Judge. "Order Denying Motions to Dismiss De Baca County News on Standing Grounds." December 26, 2012.

Cooper, Gale. "Addendum to Plaintiff Cooper's Opposition Reply to Virden's Objection to Plaintiff Cooper's Pre-Evidentiary Hearing Brief." December 26, 2012.

_____. "Plaintiff Gale Cooper's Motion for Sanctions Against Defendants Virden and Sederwall for Non-Stipulation of Depositions and Exhibits for the December 18, 2012 Evidentiary Hearing." December 26, 2012.

_____. "Plaintiff Gale Cooper's Motion for Reconsideration of Admission of Defendants Virden's and Sederwall's Depositions and Exhibits for the Continued December 18, 2012 Evidentiary Hearing." December 26, 2012.

_____. "Plaintiff Gale Cooper's Motion to Compel Defendants' Production of the Requested Forensic DNA Records of Lincoln County Sheriff's Department Case No. 2003-274." January 3, 2013.

_____. "Plaintiff Gale Cooper's Addendum to Witness List for Evidentiary Hearing on February 4, 2013." January 14, 2013.

_____. "Complaint Against Attorney Mickey Barnett, by Client Gale Cooper, to the New Mexico Bar Association Disciplinary Board, an Agency of the New Mexico Supreme County." Letter. January 19, 2013. (**259 pages of my evidence that I was Barnett's only client for records requesting, and Stinnett never made a request**)

Cooper, Gale. "Plaintiff Gale Cooper's Motion for Expedited Hearing on Her Filed Motions Pertaining to the February 4, 2013 Evidentiary Hearing." January 14, 2013.

Taylor, Anne L., Assistant Disciplinary Counsel. "Re: Complaint against Mickey Barnett, Esq." Letter to me. February 22, 2013. (**"No finding he lied under oath;" complaint denied**)

"Evidentiary Hearing." Transcript. February 4, 2013. (**Sederwall and Morel testify**)

Cooper, Gale. "Notice of Filing of Attached Plaintiff Gale Cooper's Proposed Findings of Fact and Conclusions of Law." February 27, 2013.

_____. "Plaintiff Gale Cooper's Proposed Findings of Fact and Conclusions of Law." February 27, 2013.

_____. "Appeal of Disciplinary Board denial, and request for reinstatement of complaint." Letter. March 8, 2013. (**Added Barnett's billings to show I was his only client for records requesting**)

Slease, William D., Chief Disciplinary Counsel. "Re: Your Complaint Against Mickey Barnett, Esq." Letter to me. March 14, 2013. (**My appeal will be reviewed**)

Gurley, Curtis R., Disciplinary Board Member. "Re: Your Complaint Against Mickey Barnett, Esq." Letter to me. April 12, 2013. (**"Disciplinary Counsel conducted appropriate investigation and further investigation is not required"**)

Cooper, Gale. "Plaintiff Gale Cooper's Motion to Request Award of Her Costs and Damages From Defendants and to Request Award of Sanctions Against Defendants." May 23, 2013.

_____. "Affidavit of Gale Cooper." May 22, 2013. (**Sworn costs**)

_____. "Plaintiff Gale Cooper's Request for Hearing." May 23, 2013. (**For Costs and damages and compelling records production**)

Brown, Kevin and Henry Narvaez. "Joint Response to Plaintiff Gale Cooper's Motion to Request Award of Her Costs and Damages From Defendants and to Request Award of Sanctions Against Defendants." June 7, 2013. (**Legally inadequate response**)

Cooper, Gale. "Re: Open letter to Lincoln County Commissioners about Lincoln County Sheriff's Department **Case No. 2003-274** and Sandoval County District Court **Cause No. D-1329-CV-1364**, Gale Cooper and De Baca County News vs. Rick Virden, Lincoln County Sheriff and Custodian of the Records of the Lincoln County Sheriff's Office; and Steven M. Sederwall, Former Lincoln County Deputy Sheriff; and Thomas T. Sullivan, Former Lincoln County Sheriff and Former Lincoln County Deputy Sheriff." June 18, 2013. (**Summary of Billy the Kid Case hoax, its IPRA litigation, and its costs and damages**)

_____. "Plaintiff Gale Cooper's Notice of Briefing Completion with Repeated Request for Hearing." July 1, 2013.

_____. "Addendum to Plaintiff Gale Cooper's Motion to Request Award of Her Costs and Damages From Defendants and to Request Award of Sanctions Against Defendants." July 1, 2013.

Hearing for Plaintiff Gale Cooper's Motion to Request Award of Her Costs and Damages From Defendants and to Request Award of Sanctions Against Defendants." Transcript. December 18, 2013. (**Judge said ruling in 90 days**)

Cooper, Gale. "Re: Request for NMRA 1.054.1 intervention in Cause No. D-1329-CV-01364." March 25, 2014. (**Complaint to District Court Chief Judge Louis McDonald about Judge George Eichwald's refusal to rule** )

_____. "Re: Refusal of my request for intervention for ruling in Cause No. D-1329-CV-01364." April 2, 2014. (**Repeat request to after he himself refused to make Eichwald rule** )

Romero, Jennifer. "*Cooper v. Virden*, D-1329-CV-2007-1364." April 4, 2014. (**Judge McDonald has staff attorney answer for him to evade making Eichwald rule**)

Cooper, Gale. "Answer to April 4, 2014 response letter about my requests for intervention for a ruling in Cause No. D-1329-CV-2007-01364." April 17, 2014. (**Response to McDonald's refusal to intervene for a ruling**)

_____. "Writ of Mandamus or Superintending Control" to the New Mexico Supreme Court. May 12, 2014.

Eichwald, George P. "Findings of Fact and Conclusions of Law and Order of Court." May 15, 2014.

Cooper, Gale. Withdrawal of Writ of Mandamus or Superintending Control" to the New Mexico Supreme Court. May 22, 2014.

_____. "Plaintiff Gale Cooper's Court-Ordered Submission of Verified Costs. May 22, 2014.

_____. "Judgment." May 22, 2014. (**My court-ordered submission of final judgment for judge's signature.**)

# NEW MEXICO ASSOCIATION OF COUNTIES RISK MANAGEMENT BILLINGS/PAYMENTS (SEPARATE IPRA INVESTIGATION ON DEFENSE ATTORNEYS IN VIRDEN ET AL LITIGATION)

Kent, Kerry. ML Claims Examiner. "Tom, I'm sending you a letter advising that the IJ $10,000 limit for attorneys fees is gone ..." E-Mail. August 9, 2008. (**Though proving taxpayer costs of my IPRA litigation, they were ignored and the huge plaintiffs' bill was incurred**)

Stewart, Tom. Lincoln County Manager. "Subject: FW: IJ 20282/Billy the Kid File. County Commissioners, For the first time I can recall as county manager, we have run out of insurance coverage on a case." E-Mail. August 9, 2008. (**Though proving taxpayer costs of my IPRA litigation, the defendants ignored the liability and ultimately incurred the huge plaintiffs' bill**)

Cooper, Gale. "Re: Inspection of Public Records Act request for financial records ..." Letter sent to Lincoln County Clerk Rhonda Burrows. April 9, 2010

Morel, Alan P. Lincoln County Attorney. "RE: Inspection of Public Records Act request for financial records ..." Letter to me. April 13, 2010. (**Requests more time**)

_____. "RE: IPRA Request dated April 9, 2010. Letter to me. April 22, 2010. (**No requested financial information was provided, but almost 150 pages of irrelevant pending legal cases of Morel's were included; and there were minutes of Commissioner Leo Martinez's meeting condemning the Billy the Kid Case for its liability to the County!**)

Cooper, Gale. "Re: Inspection of Public Records Act records request pertaining to Risk Management's payment ..." Letter to Alex Cuellar, Records Custodian General Services Division, Rick Management. June 18, 2010. (**Beginning of run-around to keep me from getting the records; returned as wrong address – though correct address**)

_____. Faxed my June 18, 2010 IPRA request as he told me by phone. July 12, 2010.

Cuellar, Alex. Records Custodian General Services Division, Rick Management, Public Information Officer/Records Custodian. Requests more time to respond. Letter to me. July 19, 2010.(**Stalling – knows he is not the custodian**)

_____. "Concerning your records request dated June 18, 2010 ..." July 29, 2010. (**Exceeded statutory reply time of 3-15 days; run-around; referred me to Risk Manager Steve Kopelman and Lincoln County Clerk Rhonda Burrows**)

Cooper, Gale. "Re: Inspection of Public Records Act records request ..." Letter to Rhonda Burrows. August 23, 2010.

Cooper, Gale. "Re: Forwarding of Inspection of Public Records Act request ..." Letter to Steve Kopelman. August 23, 2010. (No response)

Werkmeister, Nicole. Attorney for Virden. "Re: IPRA Request dated August 23, 2010." Letter to me. August 27, 2010. (Werkmeister says Lincoln County has no records so denies me records – to throw me off the track)

Cooper, Gale. "Re: No response to Inspection of Public Records Act request ..." Letter to Steve Kopelman. September 28, 2010. (Kopelman telephone call ignoring my requirement for written response)

_____. "Re: Response to your letters." My letter to Werkmeister. September 28, 2010. (Asking her role in my requests)

Werkmeister, Nicole. Attorney for Virden. "Re: Response to September 28, 2010 letter re IPRA Request dated August 23, 2010." Letter to me. August 27, 2010. (Werkmeister says she does not represent Risk Management – but does not direct me to correct records custodian)

Cooper, Gale. "Re: Inspection of Public Records Act records request ..." Letter to Rhonda Burrows. October 12, 2010.

Werkmeister, Nicole. Attorney for Virden. "Re: Response to letter dated October 14, 2010 ..." Letter to me. (Refused billing records as attorney client privilege)

Cooper, Gale. "Re: Confirmation of your telephone call ..." Letter to Steve Kopelman. October 29, 2010. (Repeated writing only)

Stephenson, Cynthia. Risk Management Coordinator. "Enclosed are the documents in response ..." Letter to me. November 18, 2010. (Multiple service blank-outs)

Burrows, Rhonda. Lincoln County Clerk. "Ms. Werkmeister ... is the attorney retained to represent the interest of Lincoln County ..." Letter to me. December 6, 2010. (No requested records provided)

Werkmeister, Nicole. Attorney for Virden. "Re: IPRA Request dated August 23, 2010 and October 12, 2010." Letter to me. December 14, 2010. (She refuses me records because not in Lincoln County "possession")

Stephenson, Cynthia. Risk Management Coordinator. "Enclosed please find two billing statements ..." Letter to me. January 11, 2011. (Had the important, secret, September, 2010 Threet meetings with the Narvaez firm: Narvaez Law Firm. Billing to New Mexico County Insurance Authority. October 31, 2010.)

Cooper, Gale. "Re: Inspection of Public Records Act (IPRA) requests ..." Letter to Steve Kopelman. March 14, 2011. (To retrieve the blanked-out services)

_____. "Re: Non-Compliance with Inspection of Public Records Act request dated March 14, 2011. (No response)

Stephenson, Cynthia. Risk Management Coordinator. "This letter is in request [sic] to your March 14, 2011 Inspection of Public Records Act request ..." Letter to me. April 22, 2011.

Cooper, Gale. "Re: Inspection of Public Records Act request ..." Letter to Steve Kopelman. November 29, 2011. (Trying to find out role of secret attorney in Friedman, Boys, and Hollander )

_____. "Re: Inspection of Public Records Act request ..." December 5, 2011. (Trying to find out role in cover-up of Richardson's lawyer, Peter Kierst)

Stephenson, Cynthia. Risk Management Coordinator. "This letter is in request [sic] to your November 29, 2011 and December 5, 2011 Inspection of Public Record Act request [sic] ..." Letter to me. December 15, 2011.

Cooper, Gale. "Re: Inspection of Public Records Act request ..." January 23, 2012. (Trying to uncover names of secret hoax attorneys)

Stephenson, Cynthia. Risk Management Coordinator. "This is in response to your recent letter dated January 23, 2012 ..." Letter to me. January 31, 2012. **(Denies any information about secret attorneys)**

Kopelman, Steve. Risk Management Director & General Counsel. "This is in response to your recent letter requesting documents ..." Letter to me. June 5, 2010 [sic – 2012].

Cooper, Gale. "Re: Inspection of Public Records Act request ..." Letter to Steve Kopelman. September 24, 2012. **(No response)**

_____. "Re: Resent September 24, 201`2 unanswered Inspection of Public Records Act request ..." Letter to Steve Kopelman. October 17, 2012.

Kopelman, Steve. Risk Management Director & General Counsel. "This is in response to your letter received by this office October 17, 2012." Letter to me. November 1, 2012.

Cooper, Gale. "Re: Inspection of Public Records Act request ..." Letter to Steve Kopelman. February 12, 2013. **(Updating my billing records, and adding appeals case)**

Asghedom, Rahwa, Risk Management Specialist. "Attached please find Public Records Act records you requested ..." Letter to me. February 27, 2013.

Stephenson, Cynthia. Risk Management Coordinator. "This letter is in request to your March 14, 2011 Inspection of Public Records Act request ..." April 22, 2011. **(Filled in the earlier blank-outs that concealed Attorney Threet conspiring with defense to dismiss Virden without my knowledge)**

Cooper, Gale. "Re: Inspection of Public Records Act request ..." Letter to Steve Kopelman. March 30, 2013. **(Updating my billing records)**

_____. "Re: IPRA non-compliance complaint ..." March 30, 2011. **(For blanking-out of services)**

Asghedom, Rahwa, Risk Management Specialist. "This is in response to two March 30, 2013 Inspection of Public Records Act requests ..." Letter to me. April 15, 2013. **(Blanking-out of services continued)**

Cooper, Gale. "Re: Inspection of Public Records Act request for court-ordered settlements ..." Letter to Steve Kopelman. May 6, 2013.

Asghedom, Rahwa, Risk Management Specialist. "This is in response your May 6, 2013 Inspection of Public Records Act request ..." Letter to me. May 14, 2013.

Cooper, Gale. 'Re: Formal complaint and request for intervention ..." Letter to Attorney General Gary King. May 14, 2011. **(Attempt to get 52 blanked-out services on attorney billings)**

Shandler, Zachary A. Assistant Attorney General, Deputy Director, Civil Division. "The Attorney General's Office is in receipt of your May 14, 2013 letter ..." Letter to Gale Cooper. Letter to me. June 3, 2013. **(Calling blank-outs attorney confidentiality of "tactical information)**

Cooper, Gale. "Re: Inspection of Public Records Act request for court-ordered settlements ..." Letter to Steve Kopelman. June 11, 2013. **(Questioning ceiling on defense attorney costs)**

Asghedom, Rahwa, Risk Management Specialist. "This is in response your June 11, 2013 Inspection of Public Records Act request ..." Letter to me. June 24, 2013. **(Denied there was a ceiling to costs officials could accrue)**

# SOURCES 19ᵗʰ CENTURY
# BILLY THE KID HISTORY

## GLOBAL REFERENCES:

## BILLY THE KID AND THE LINCOLN COUNTY WAR PERIOD

Nolan, Frederick. *The Lincoln County War: A Documentary History*. Norman: University of Oklahoma Press. 1992.
_____. *The West of Billy the Kid*. Norman: University of Oklahoma Press. 1998.

\* \* \* \* \* \* \*

## WILLIAM HENRY BONNEY ("BILLY THE KID")

### AUTHORSHIP / TESTIMONY / INTERVIEWS

*BILL OF SALE*

Bonney, W H. "Know all persons by these presents ..." (Hoyt Bill of Sale). Thursday, October 24, 1878. Collection of Panhandle-Plains Historical Museum, Canyon, Texas. (Item No. X1974-98/1)

*LETTERS TO LEW WALLACE*

Bonney, W H. "I have heard you will give one thousand $ dollars for my body which as I see it means alive ..." March 13 (?), 1879. Fray Angélico Chávez Historical Library, Santa Fe, New Mexico. Lincoln County Heritage Trust Collection. (AC481).
_____. "I will keep the keep the appointment ..." March 20, 1879. Indiana Historical Society. M0292.
_____. "... on the Pecos." ("Billie" letter fragment). March 24 (?), 1879. Indiana Historical Society. M0292. **(Authenticated by Gale Cooper)**
_____. "I noticed in the Las Vegas Gazette a piece which stated that 'Billy the Kid' ..." December 12, 1880. Indiana Historical Society. Lew Wallace Collection. M0292.
_____. "I would like to see you ..." January 1, 1881. Indiana Historical Society. Lew Wallace Collection. M0292.
_____. "I wish you would come down to the jail and see me ..." March 2, 1881. Fray Angélico Chávez Historical Library, Santa Fe, New Mexico. Lincoln County Heritage Trust Collection. (AC481).
_____. "I wrote you a little note day before yesterday ..." March 4, 1881. Indiana Historical Society. Lew Wallace Collection. M0292.
_____. "For the last time I ask ..." March 27, 1881. Indiana Historical Society. Lew Wallace Collection. M0292.

*LETTER TO SQUIRE WILSON*

Bonney, W H. "Friend Wilson ..." March 18, 1879. Robert N. Mullin Collection. File RNM, IV, NM, 43. Nita Stewart Haley Memorial Museum. Haley Library. Midland, Texas. (Original in Indiana Historical Society.)

### *LETTER TO EDGAR CAYPLESS*

Bonney, W H. "I would have written before ..." April 15, 1881. Copy in William Kelleher's *Violence in Lincoln County;* originally reproduced in Griggs *History of the Mesilla Valley.* (**Original is lost.**)

### *LETTER (POSSIBLY DICTATED) FOR EDGAR WALZ*

Regulator. "Mr. Walz. Sir ..." Letter to Edgar Walz. July 13, 1878. Adjutant General's Office. File 1405 AGO 1878. (Quoted in Maurice Garland Fulton, *History of the Lincoln County War.* Tucson: University of Arizona Press. 1975. pages 246-247, and Frederick Nolan, *The Lincoln County War: A Documentary History*, page 310.)

### *NEWSPAPER INTERVIEWS (CHRONOLOGICAL)*

Wilcox, Lucius "Lute" M. (city editor, owner, J.H. Koogler). "The Kid. Interview with Billy Bonney The Best Known Man in New Mexico." Las Vegas *Gazette.* December 28, 1880. (**Has quote about "the laugh's on me this time"**)
_____. Interview, at train depot. Las Vegas *Gazette.* December 28, 1880. (**Has "adios" quote.**)
No Author. "At least two hundred men have been killed in Lincoln County during the past three years ..." Santa Fe *Daily New Mexican.* March 28, 1881.
No Author. "Something About the Kid." Santa Fe *Daily New Mexican.* April 3, 1881. (**With quotes "this is the man" and "two hundred men have been killed ... he did not kill all of them."**)
No Author. "I got a rough deal ..." *Mesilla News.* April 15, 1881.
Newman, Simon N. Ed. Interview with "The Kid." *Newman's Semi-Weekly.* April 15, 1881.
_____. Departure from Mesilla. *Newman's Semi-Weekly.* April 15, 1881.
No Author. "Advise persons never to engage in killing." *Mesilla News.* April 16, 1881.

### *TESTIMONY*

Angel, Frank Warner. *In the Matter of the Examination of the Causes and Circumstances of the Death of John H. Tunstall a British Subject.* Report filed October 4, 1878. Angel Report. Microfilm File Case Number 44-4-8-3. Record Group 060. Microfilm No. M750. Roll 1. National Archives and Records Administration. U. S. Department of Justice. Washington, D.C. (**Deposition of William H. Bonney. June 8, 1878. pp. 314-319.**)
No Author. *Dudley Court of Inquiry. (May 2, 1879 - July 5, 1879).* 16W3/16/28/6. Boxes 1923-1923A. File Number QQ1284. National Archives and Records Administration. Old Military and Civil Branch. Records of the Office of the Judge Advocate General. Washington, D.C. (**Testimony of William H. Bonney. May 28 and 29, 1879.**)

## WILLIAM BONNEY BIOGRAPHICAL BOOKS

Abbott, E.C. ("Teddy Blue") and Helena Huntington Smith. *We Pointed Them North: Recollections of a Cowpuncher.* Norman, Oklahoma: University of Oklahoma Press. 1955. (**Billy the Kid's multiculturalism, page 47.**)
Anaya, Paco. *I Buried Billy.* College Station, Texas: Creative Publishing Company. 1991.
Ball, Eve. *Ma'am Jones of the Pecos.* Tucson, Arizona: The University of Arizona Press. 1969.
Bell, Bob Boze. *The Illustrated Life and Times of Billy the Kid.* Cave Creek, Arizona: Boze Books. 1992. (Frank Coe quote about the Kid's cartridge use, page 45.)

Bell, Bob Boze. *The Illustrated Life and Times of Billy the Kid.* Second Edition. Phoenix, Arizona: Tri Star-Boze Publications, Inc. 1996.

Burns, Walter Noble. *The Saga of Billy the Kid.* Stamford, Connecticut: Longmeadow Press. 1992. (Original printing: 1926, Doubleday.) **(About Billy's outlawry: pages 54, 57; about pardon: page 152 )**

_____. *"I also know that the Kid and Paulita were sweethearts."* Unpublished letter to Jim East. June 3, 1926. Robert N. Mullin Collection. File RNM, IV, NM, 116-117. Nita Stewart Haley Memorial Museum, Haley Library. Midland, Texas.

*Coroner's Jury Report for William Bonney. July 15, 1881.* (Copy) Herman Weisner Collection. Lincoln County Papers. New Mexico State University Library at Las Cruces. Rio Grande Historical Society Collection. Box No. 1. Folder Name: Billy the Kid Legal Documents. Folder No. 14C. 26.

Garrett, Pat F. *The Authentic Life of Billy the Kid The Noted Desperado of the Southwest, Whose Deeds of Daring and Blood Made His Name a Terror in New Mexico, Arizona, and Northern Mexico.* Santa Fe, New Mexico: New Mexico Printing and Publishing Co. 1882. (Reprint used: New York: Indian Head Books. 1994.) **(About the kid's devil, page xxvii; about Garrett's possible guilty feelings, pages 218-219.)**

Hendron, J. W. *The Story of Billy the Kid. New Mexico's Number One Desperado.* New York: Indian Head Books. 1994.

Jacobsen, Joel. *Such Men as Billy the Kid. The Lincoln County War Reconsidered.* Lincoln and London: University of Nebraska Press. 1994.

Kadlec, Robert F. *They "Knew" Billy the Kid. Interviews with Old-Time New Mexicans.* Santa Fe, New Mexico: Ancient City Press. 1987.

Keleher, William A. *Violence in Lincoln County 1869-1881.* Albuquerque, New Mexico: University of New Mexico Press. 1957

McFarland, David F. Reverend. *Ledger: Session Records 1867-1874. Marriages in Santa Fe New Mexico. "Mr. William H. Antrim and Mrs. Catherine McCarty." March 1, 1873.* (Unpublished). Santa Fe, New Mexico: First Presbyterian Church of Santa Fe.

Meadows, John P. Ed. John P. Wilson. *Pat Garrett and Billy the Kid as I Knew Them: Reminiscences of John P. Meadows.* Albuquerque: University of New Mexico Press. 2004.

Mullin, Robert N. *The Boyhood of Billy the Kid.* Monograph 17, Southwestern Studies 5(1). El Paso, Texas: Texas Western Press. University of Texas at El Paso. 1967.

Poe, John W. *The Death of Billy the Kid.* (Introduction by Maurice Garland Fulton). Boston and New York: Houghton Mifflin Company. 1933.

_____. "The Killing of Billy the Kid." (a personal letter written at Roswell, New Mexico to Mr. Charles Goodnight, Goodnight P.C., Texas) July 10, 1917. Earle Vandale Collection. 1813-946. No. 2H475. Center for American History. University of Texas at Austin.

Rakocy, Bill. *Billy the Kid.* El Paso, Texas: Bravo Press. 1985.

Rasch, Phillip J. *Trailing Billy the Kid.* Laramie, Wyoming: National Association for Outlaw and Lawman History, Inc. with University of Wyoming. 1995.

Russell, Randy. *Billy the Kid. The Story - The Trial.* Lincoln, New Mexico: The Crystal Press. 1994.

Siringo, Charles A. *The History of Billy the Kid.* Santa Fe: New Mexico. Privately Printed. 1920.

Tuska, Jon. *Billy the Kid. His Life and Legend.* Westport, Connecticut: Greenwood Press. 1983.

Utley, Robert M. *Billy the Kid. A Short and Violent Life.* Lincoln and London: University of Nebraska Press. 1989.

Weddle, Jerry. *Antrim is My Stepfather's Name. The Boyhood of Billy the Kid.* Monograph 9, Globe, Arizona: Arizona Historical Society. 1993. **(Quotes from Mary Richards about Billy on pages 19-20. )**

Wild, Azariah F. "Daily Reports of U. S. Secret Service Agents, Azariah F. Wild." Microfilm T-915. Record Group 87. Rolls 306 (June 15, 1877 - December 31, 1877), 307 (January 1,1878 - June 30, 1879), 308 (July 1, 1879 - June 30, 1881), 309 ( (July 1, 1881 - September 30, 1883), 310 (October 1, 1883 - July 31, 1886). National Archives and Records Department. Department of the Treasury. United States Secret Service. Washington, D. C.

No Author. "The Prisoners Who Saw the Kid Kill Olinger." Herman Weisner Collection. Accession No. MS249. Lincoln County Papers. New Mexico State University Library at Las Cruces. Rio Grande Historical Collections. Box No. 30. Folder Name: The Prisoners who saw the Kid Kill Olinger. Box No. T-8.

## WILLIAM BONNEY BIOGRAPHICAL
## NEWSPAPER ARTICLES (CHRONOLOGICAL)

No Author. Grant County *Herald*. May 10, 1879. Results of the Lincoln County Grand Jury. **(Also published in the Mesilla *Thirty Four*. Confirmation of the William Bonney testimony and James Dolan and Billy Campbell murder indictments, from page 224 of William Keleher, *Violence in Lincoln County*.)**

No Author. Editorial. "Powerful Gang of Outlaws Harassing the Stockman." Las Vegas *Gazette*. December 3, 1880. **(Condemnation of William Bonney as an outlaw leader; and resulting, according to William Keleher, who quotes it in his *Violence in Lincoln County*, on pages 286-288, as motivating Bonney's response letter of December 12, 1880 to Governor Lew Wallace.)**

Wallace, Lew. "Billy the Kid: $500 Reward." December 22, 1880. Las Vegas *Gazette*.

No Author. "A Big Haul! Billy Kid, Dave Rudabaugh, Billy Wilson and Tom Pickett in the Clutches of the Law." *The Las Vegas Daily Optic*. Monday, December 27, 1880. Vol. 2, No. 45. Page 4, Column 2.

No Author. "Outlaws of New Mexico. The Exploits of a Band Headed by a New York Youth. The Mountain Fastness of the Kid and His Followers - War Against a Gang of Cattle Thieves and Murderers - The Frontier Confederates of Brockway, the Counterfeiter." *The Sun*. New York. December 22, 1880. Vol. XLVIII, No. 118, Page 3, Columns 1-2.

No Author. " 'The Kid.' The greatest excitement prevailed yesterday when the news was abroad that Pat Garrett and Frank Stewart had arrived in town bringing with them Billy 'the Kid.' " Las Vegas *Gazette*. December 27, 1880.

Wilcox, Lucius "Lute" M. "Interview With The Kid." *Las Vegas Gazette*. December 28, 1880.(From "Billy the Kid: Las Vegas Newspaper Accounts of His Career, 1880-1881." W.M. Morrison - Books, Waco, Texas. 1958.) **(With "laugh's on me" quote, and mention of the dead horse blocking escape at Stinking Springs.)**

No Author. "A Bay-Mare. Everyone who has heard of Billy 'the kid' has heard of his beautiful bay mare." Las Vegas *Morning Gazette*. Tuesday, January 4, 1881.

No Author. "The Kid. Billy 'the Kid' and Billy Wilson were on Monday taken to Mesilla for Trial." *Las Vegas Morning Gazette*. Tuesday, March 15, 1881.

Newman, Simon. "In the Name of Justice! In the Case of Billy Kid." *Newman's Semi-Weekly*. Saturday, April 2, 1881.

No Author. "Billy the Kid. Seems to be having a stormy journey on his trip Southward." *Las Vegas Morning Gazette*. Tuesday, April 5, 1881.

Koogler, J. H. "Interview with Governor Lew Wallace on 'The Kid.'" *Las Vegas Gazette*. April 28, 1881.

No Author. "The Kid." *Santa Fe Daily New Mexican*. May 1, 1881. Vol. X, No. 32, Page 1, Column 2.

No Author. "Billy Bonney. Advices from Lincoln bring the intelligence of the escape of 'Billy the Kid.' " *Las Vegas Daily Optic*. Monday, May 2, 1881.

No Author. "The Kid's Escape." *Santa Fe Daily New Mexican.* Tuesday Morning, May 3, 1881. Vol. X, No. 33, Page 1, Column 2.

Wallace, Lew. "Billy the Kid. $500 Reward." *Daily New Mexican.* May 3, 1881. Vol. X, No. 33, Page 1, Column 3.

No Author. "Dare Devil Desperado. Pursuit of 'Billy the Kid' has been abandoned." *Las Vegas Daily Optic.* May 4, 1881.

No Author. "More Killing by Kid." Editorial. *Santa Fe Daily New Mexican.* Wednesday Morning, May 4, 1881. Vol. X, No. 34, Page 1, Column 2.

No Author. "Kid was then in Albuquerque ..." *Santa Fe Daily New Mexican.* May 5, 1881. p.4. c. 1.

No Author. "The question if how to deal with desperados who commit murder has but one solution - kill them." *Las Vegas Daily Optic.* Tuesday, May 10, 1881.

No Author. "Billy 'the Kid.' " Las Vegas *Gazette.* Thursday, May 12, 1881.

No Author. "The Kid was in Chloride City ..." *Santa Fe Daily New Mexican.* May 13, 1881. p.4. c. 3.

No Author. "Billy 'the Kid' is in the vicinity of Sumner." Las Vegas *Gazette.* Sunday, May 15, 1881.

No Author. "The Kid is believed to be in the Black Range ..." *Santa Fe Daily New Mexican.* May 19, 1881. p.4. c. 1.

No Author. "Billy the Kid was last seen in Lincoln County ..." *Santa Fe Daily New Mexican.* May 19, 1881. p.4. c. 1.

No Author. " 'Billy the Kid' has been heard from again." *Las Vegas Daily Optic.* Friday, June 10, 1881.

No Author. " 'Billy the Kid.' He is Reported to Have Been Seen on Our Streets Saturday Night." *Las Vegas Daily Optic.* Monday Evening, June 13, 1881. Vol. 2, No. 188, Page 4, Column 2.

Wilcox, Lute, Ed. "Billy the Kid would make an ideal newspaper-man in that he always endeavors to 'get even' with his enemies." *Las Vegas Daily Optic.* Monday Evening, June 13, 1881. Vol. 2, No. 188, Page 4, Column 1.

No Author. "Land of the Petulant Pistol. 'Billy the Kid' as a Killer." *Las Vegas Daily Optic.* Wednesday Evening, June 15, 1881. Vol. 2, No. 190.

No Author. "Barney Mason at Fort Sumner states the 'Kid' is in Local Sheep Camps." *Las Vegas Morning Gazette.* June 16, 1881.

No Author. "The Kid." *Santa Fe Daily New Mexican.* June 16, 1881. Vol. X, No. 90, Page 4, Column 2.

No Author. "Billy the Kid." *Las Vegas Daily Optic.* Thursday, June 28, 1881.

No Author. " 'The Kid' Killed." *Las Vegas Daily Optic.* July 18. 1881.

Wallace, Lew. "Old Incident Recalled," *The* (Crawfordsville) *Weekly News-Review,* December 20, 1901. Lew Wallace Collection. Indiana Historical Society. M0292.

_____. "General Lew Wallace Writes a Romance of 'Billy the Kid' Most Famous Bandit of the Plains: Thrilling Story of the Midnight Meeting Between Gen Wallace, Then Governor of New Mexico, and the Notorious Outlaw, in a Lonesome Hut in Santa Fe." *New York World Magazine.* Sunday, June 8, 1902. Lew Wallace Collection. Indiana Historical Society. M0292.

## LEW WALLACE WRITINGS ABOUT/TO WILLIAM BONNEY

### *LETTERS (CHRONOLOGICAL)*

Wallace, Lew. Letter to W H. Bonney. "Come to the house of Squire Wilson ..." March 15, 1879. Indiana Historical Society. Lew Wallace Collection. M0292. Box 4. Folder 6.

_____. Letter to W. H. Bonney. "The escape makes no difference in arrangements ..." March 20, 1879. Indiana Historical Society. Lew Wallace Collection. M0292. Box 4. Folder 6.

Wallace, Lew. Letter to Carl Schurz. "A precious specimen named 'The Kid,' whom the sheriff is holding ..." March 28, 1879. Letters to Carl Schurz. Herman Weisner Collection. Lincoln County Papers. New Mexico State University Library at Las Cruces. Rio Grande Historical Collections. Box No. 7. Folder Name: Interior Dept. 1851 1914. Folder No. L2. From Department of the Interior, Washington, D. C. Territorial Papers, M-364. Group 48. Roll 8.

_____. Letter to Carl Schurz. "A precious specimen nick-named 'The Kid'." March 31, 1879. Indiana Historical Society. Lew Wallace Collection. M0292. Box 4. Folder 1.

_____. Request for draft of "Billy the Kid" $500 Reward Proclamation. December 13, 1880. Herman Weisner Collection. Lincoln County Papers. New Mexico State University Library at Las Cruces. Rio Grande Historical Collections. Box No. 13. Folder Name: Wallace, Gov. N. M. Box No. W3. From Lew Wallace Papers. New Mexico State Records Center. Santa Fe, New Mexico.

## NOTES

Wallace, Lew. "Statements by Kid, made Sunday night March 23, 1879." March 23, 1879. Indiana Historical Society. Lew Wallace Collection. M0922. Box 4. Folder 7.

## DEATH WARRANT FOR WILLIAM BONNEY

Wallace, Lew. "To the Sheriff of Lincoln County, Greeting ..." April 30, 1881. Indiana Historical Society. Lew Wallace Collection. M0292. Box 9, Folder 11.

## REWARD NOTICES

Wallace, Lew. "Billy the Kid: $500 Reward." Las Vegas *Gazette*. December 22, 1880.
_____. "Billy the Kid. $500 Reward." May 3, 1881. *Daily New Mexican*. Vol. X, No. 33. p. 1, c. 3.

## REWARD POSTERS

Greene, Chas. W. "To the New Mexican Printing and Publishing Company." May 20, 1881. (Bill to Lew Wallace for Reward posters for "Kid"). Indiana Historical Society. Lew Wallace Collection. M0292. Box 4, Folder 18.
_____. "I enclose a bill ..." Letter to Lew Wallace for "Kid" wanted posters. June 2, 1881. Indiana Historical Society. Lew Wallace Collection. M0292. Box 4, Folder 18.
Indiana Historical Society. Lew Wallace Collection. M0292. Box 4, Folder 18.

## ARTICLES (CHRONOLOGICAL)  (All from the Indiana Historical Society. Lew Wallace Collection. No. M0922)

"Wallace's Words ..." (interview with Lew Wallace conducted in Washington, D.C. on January 3, 1881), Chicago *The Daily Inter Ocean*, January 4, 1881, p. 2, c. 4.
(Richard Dunham's May 2, 1881 encounter with Billy the Kid), *Santa Fe Daily New Mexican*, May 5, 1881, p.4, c. 3.
(O.L. Houghton's Conversation with Lew Wallace, before May 26, 1881), *The Las Vegas Daily Optic*, May 26, 1881, p.4, c.4.
"Billy the Kid ..." (Lew Wallace interviewed on June 13, 1881), Crawfordsville (Indiana) *Saturday Evening Journal*, June 18, 1881. Indiana Historical Society. Lew Wallace Collection. M0292.

"Street Pickings," *Crawfordsville* (Weekly) *Review* – *Saturday Edition*, January 6, 1894. Lew Wallace Collection. Indiana Historical Society.

Wallace, Lew. "Old Incident Recalled," *The* (Crawfordsville) *Weekly News-Review*, December 20, 1901. Lew Wallace Collection. Indiana Historical Society.

_____. "General Lew Wallace Writes a Romance of 'Billy the Kid' Most Famous Bandit of the Plains: Thrilling Story of the Midnight Meeting Between Gen Wallace, Then Governor of New Mexico, and the Notorious Outlaw, in a Lonesome Hut in Santa Fe." *New York World Magazine.* Sunday, June 8, 1902. Page 4. Lew Wallace Collection. Indiana Historical Society. M0292.

# HISTORICAL FIGURES (PERIOD)

## ANGEL, FRANK WARNER

### PRESIDENT HAYES MEETING

Mullin, Robert N. Re: Frank Warner Angel Meeting With President Hayes August, 1878. Binder RNM, VI, M. (Unpublished). Midland, Texas: Nita Stewart Haley Memorial Library and J. Evert Haley History Center. (Undated).

### LETTER

Angel, Frank Warner. "I am in receipt of a copy of a letter sent you by one Wm McMullen ..." Letter to Carl Schurz. September 9, 1878. The Papers of Carl Schurz 1842 - 1906 in 165 Volumes. Library of Congress 1935. General Correspondence July 26, 1878 - October 7, 1878. Shelf Accession No. 14,803. Container 45.

### PAPERS

McMullen, William. "In view of the existing troubles in our territory I appeal ..." Letter to Carl Schurz. August 24, 1878. The Papers of Carl Schurz 1842 - 1906 in 165 Volumes. Library of Congress 1935. General Correspondence. July 26, 1878 - October 7, 1878. Shelf Accession No. 14,803. Container 45.

McPherson, Mary E. Letters and Petitions to President Rutherford B. Hayes re: Removal Governor Axtell and the Santa Fe Ring. Frank Warner Angel File. Microfilm File Case Number 44-4-8-3. Record Group 060. Microfilm Roll M750. National Archives and Records Administration. U.S. Department of Justice. Washington, D. C.

### REPORTS

Angel, Frank Warner. Examination of charges against F. C. Godfroy, Indian Agent, Mescalero, N. M. October 2, 1878. (Report 1981, Inspector E. C. Watkins; Cited as Watkins Report). M 319-20 and L147, 44-4-8. Record Group 075. National Archives and Records Administration. U. S. Department of Justice. Washington, D. C.

_____. In the Matter of the Examination of the Causes and Circumstances of the Death of John H. Tunstall a British Subject. Report filed October 4, 1878. Angel Report. Microfilm File Case Number 44-4-8-3. Record Group 060. Microfilm No. M750. Roll 1. National Archives and Records Administration. U. S. Department of Justice. Washington, D.C.

Angel, Frank Warner. *In the Matter of the Investigation of the Charges Against S. B. Axtell Governor of New Mexico.* Report and Testimony. October 3, 1878. Angel Report. Microfilm Case File No. 44-4-8-3. Record Group 060. Microfilm Roll M750. National Archives and Records Administration. U.S. Department of Interior. Washington, D.C.

_____. *In the Matter of the Lincoln County Troubles. To the Honorable Charles Devens, Attorney General.* October 4, 1878. Angel Report. Microfilm Case File No. 44-4-8-3. Record Group 060. Microfilm Roll M750. National Archives and Records Administration. U. S. Department of Justice. Washington, D. C.

## NOTEBOOK

Theisen, Lee Scott. "Frank Warner Angel's Notes on New Mexico Territory, 1878." *Arizona and the West,* 18 (4) (Winter 1976) 333-370.

## AXTELL, SAMUEL BEACH

Angel, Frank Warner. *In the Matter of the Investigation of the Charges Against S. B. Axtell Governor of New Mexico.* Report and Testimony. October 3, 1878. Angel Report. Microfilm Case File No. 44-4-8-3. Record Group 060. Microfilm Roll M750. National Archives and Records Administration. U.S. Department of Interior. Washington, D.C.

_____. "The Honorable C. Schurz ... I enclose copies of letter received by me from Gov. Axtell (marked A) and my reply there to (marked B)." August 24, 1878. Microfilm Roll M750. National Archives and Records Administration Record Group 060. Microfilm Case Number 44-4-8-3. U.S. Department of Interior. Washington D. C.

_____. "The Hon. C. Schurz, Secretary of the Interior, Sir: I have just been favored by a call from W. L. Rynerson Territorial Dist. Attorney 3rd District New Mexico - in the interest of Gov. Axtell." (Letter) September 6, 1878. Microfilm M750. National Archives and Records Administration Record Group 060. Microfilm Case Number 44-4-8-3. U. S. Department of Interior. Washington D. C.

Axtell, Samuel B. "Hon. Carl Schurz. Sir: I have today mailed to you a reply to the charges on file in your Dept against me." (Letter regarding charges in Colfax County). Microfilm Roll M750. National Archives and Records Administration Record Group 060. Microfilm Case Number 44-4-8-3. U.S. Department of Interior. Washington D. C.

_____. "To the President. I am unable to enforce the law ..." (Telegram). March 3, 1878. Microfilm Roll M750. National Archives and Records Administration Record Group 060. Microfilm Case File Number 44-4-8-3. U.S. Department of Interior. Washington D. C.

Bradstreet, George P. "Referring to the nomination of Sam'l B. Axtell of Ohio to be Chief Justice of the Supreme Court of New Mexico ... he is alleged to have been removed by President Hayes ..." (Presentation to the U. S. Senate Chamber). Microfilm Roll M750. National Archives and Records Administration Record Group 060. Microfilm Case Number 44-4-8-3. U.S. Department of Interior. Washington D. C.

Elkins, Stephen B. "To the President. Referring to a conversation had with you last week ... Hon S. Elkins favors appointment Axtell, Ex Gov. as Gov'r of New Mexico". (Letter) March 23, 1881. (Received Executive Mansion April 6, 1881). Microfilm Roll M750. National Archives and Records Administration Record Group 060. Microfilm Case Number 44-4-8-3. U.S. Department of Interior. Washington D. C.

Springer, Frank. "Hon Carl Schurz, Secretary of the Interior. Sir: I endorse herewith, directed to the President charges against S. B. Axtell Governor of New Mexico ..." (Letter) June 10, 1878. Frank Warner Angel File. Microfilm Roll M750. National Archives and Records Administration Record Group 060. Microfilm Case Number 44-4-8-3. U. S. Department of Interior. Washington D. C.

# BRADY, WILLIAM

Brady, William. Affidavit of July 2, 1876 concerning appointment as Administrator for the Emil Fritz Estate. Copied from the original District Court Record. In private collection.

_____. Affidavit of August 22, 1876 documenting business debts to L.G. Murphy and Co. pertaining to the Emil Fritz Estate. Copied from the original District Court Record. In private collection.

_____. Affidavit of July _, 1876 of Resignation as Emil Fritz Estate Administrator. Copied from the original District Court Record. In private collection.

_____. Affidavit of August 22, 1876 confirming giving Alexander McSween the books of the L.G. Murphy Company for the purpose of making business debt collections. Copied from the original District Court Record. In private collection.

_____. "List of Articles Inventoried by Wm Brady sheriff in the suit of Charles Fritz & Emilie Scholand vs A.A. McSween now in the dwelling house belonging to A.A. McSween." (undated) In private collection.

Bristol, Warren. "Action of Assumpsit to command Sheriff Brady of Lincoln County to attach goods of Alexander A. McSween." February 7, 1878. District Court Record. (Private Collection).

_____. Preprinted form for "Writ of Attachment" (Printed and sold at the office of the Mesilla News) filled out to command the Sheriff of Lincoln County to attach goods of Alexander McSween for a suit of damages for ten thousand dollars. February 7, 1878. District Court Record. (Private Collection).

Lavash, Donald R. *Sheriff William Brady. Tragic Hero of the Lincoln County War.* Santa Fe, New Mexico: Sunstone Press. 1986.

# CASEY FAMILY

Klasner, Lilly. Eve Ball. Ed. *My Girlhood Among Outlaws.* Tucson, Arizona: The University of Arizona Press. 1988.

# CATRON, THOMAS BENTON

Cleaveland, Norman, *A Synopsis of the Great New Mexico Cover-up.* Self-printed. 1989.

_____. *The Great Santa Fe Cover-up. Based on a Talk given Before the Santa Fe Historical Society on November 1, 1978.* Self-printed. 1982.

_____. *The Morleys - Young Upstarts on the Southwest Frontier.* Albuquerque, New Mexico: Calvin Horn Publisher, Inc. 1971.

Dunham, Harold H. "New Mexican Land Grants with Special Reference to the Title Papers of the Maxwell Grant." *New Mexico Historical Review.* (January, 1955) Vol. 70. No. 1. pp. 1 - 23.

Hefferan, Vioalle Clark. *Thomas Benton Catron.* Albuquerque, New Mexico: University of New Mexico. Zimmerman Library. Unpublished Thesis for the Degree of Master of Arts. 1940.

Keleher, William A. *The Maxwell Land Grant. A New Mexico Item.* Albuquerque, New Mexico: University of New Mexico Press. 1964.

Lamar, Howard Robert N. *The Far Southwest 1846 - 1912. A Territorial History.* New Haven and London: Yale University Press. 1966.

Montoya, María E. *Translating Property. The Maxwell Land Grant and the Conflict Over Land in the American West, 1840-1900.* Berkeley and Los Angeles: University of California Press. 2002.

Mullin, Robert N. "A Specimen of Catron's Dirty Work. Sworn Affidavit of Samuel Davis." October 1, 1878. Binder RNM IV, EE. (Unpublished). Midland, Texas: Nita Stewart Haley Memorial Library and J. Everts Haley Historical Center.

Mullin, Robert N. "Catron Embarrassed Throughout His Life by an Affliction." (Date Unknown). Binder RNM, IV, M. (Unpublished). Midland, Texas: Nita Stewart Haley Memorial Library and J. Everts Haley Historical Center.

_____. Catron letter to Governor S. B. Axtell to intervene in Lincoln County. May 30, 1878. Binder RNM IV, EE (Unpublished). Midland, Texas: Nita Stewart Haley Memorial Library and J. Everts Haley Historical Center.

_____. "Prior to Lincoln County War Catron Had Defended Colonel Dudley." (No Date). Notes from "Lincoln County War Cast of Characters." Midland, Texas: Nita Stewart Haley Memorial Library and J. Everts Haley Historical Center.

Murphy, Lawrence R. *Lucien Bonaparte Maxwell. Napoleon of the Southwest.* Norman: University of Oklahoma Press. 1983.

Pearson, Jim Berry. *The Maxwell Land Grant.* Norman: University of Oklahoma Press. 1961.

Sluga, Mary Elizabeth. *Political Life of Thomas Benton Catron 1896-1912.* Albuquerque, New Mexico: University of New Mexico. Zimmerman Library. Unpublished Thesis for the Degree of Master of Arts. 1941.

Westphall, Victor. "Fraud and Implications of Fraud in the Land Grants of New Mexico." *New Mexico Historical Review.* 1974. Vol. XLIX, No. 3. 189 - 218.

_____. *Thomas Benton Catron and His Era.* Tucson, Arizona: University of Arizona Press. 1973.

Wooden, John Paul. *Thomas Benton Catron and New Mexico Politics 1866-1921.* Albuquerque, New Mexico: University of New Mexico. Zimmerman Library. Unpublished Thesis for the Degree of Master of Arts. 1959.

No Author. Catron Files Statement Ranch in Tax Dispute Case. Herman of Sole ownership of Carrizozo Weisner Collection. Lincoln County Papers: New Mexico State University Library at Las Cruces. Rio Grande Historical Collections. Box No. 2. Folder Name "T. B. Catron Tax Troubles." Folder No. C-8.

## CHAPMAN, HUSTON

Chapman, Huston. Letter to Governor Lew. Wallace. November 29, 1878. Herman Weisner Collection. Lincoln County Papers: New Mexico State University Library at Las Cruces. Rio Grande Historical Collections. Box No. 2. Folder Name H. J. Chapman. Box No. C-9.

## CHISUM, JOHN SIMPSON

Hinton, Harwood P., Jr. "John Simpson Chisum, 1877-84." *New Mexico Historical Review* 31(3) (July 1956): 177 - 205; 31(4) (October 1956): 310 - 337; 32(1) (January 1957): 53 - 65.

Klasner, Lilly. Eve Ball. Ed. *My Girlhood Among Outlaws.* Tucson, Arizona: The University of Arizona Press. 1988.

## COE FAMILY

Coe, George. Joyce B. Nunis, Jr. Ed. *Frontier Fighter. The Autobiography of George Coe Who Fought and Rode With Billy the Kid.* Chicago: R. R. Donnelley and Sons Company. 1984.

Coe, Wilbur. *Ranch on the Ruidoso. The Story of a Pioneer Family in New Mexico, 1871 - 1968.* New York: Alfred A. Knopf. 1968.

## DEDRICK BROTHERS

No Author. "Arrests of Dedricks. Legal Documents." Herman Weisner Collection. Lincoln County Papers. New Mexico State University Library at Las Cruces. Rio Grande Historical Collections. Box 1. Folder Name Lincoln County Bonds. Folder No. B-8.

Upham, Elizabeth. (Related by marriage to Daniel Dedrick). Personal interviews. 1998.
Upham, Marquita. (Relative by marriage to Daniel Dedrick). Personal interview. 1998.

## DOLAN, JAMES J.

Angel, Frank Warner. *In the Matter of the Examination of the Causes and Circumstances of the Death of John H. Tunstall a British Subject.* Report filed October 4, 1878. Angel Report. Microfilm File Case Number 44-4-8-3. Record Group 060. Microfilm No. M750. Roll 1. National Archives and Records Administration. U. S. Department of Justice. Washington, D.C. (James J. Dolan Deposition. June 20, 1878. pp. 235-247.)

Dolan, James. "Confidential Letter to Lew Wallace." December 31, 1878. Herman Weisner Collection. Lincoln County Papers: New Mexico State University Library at Las Cruces. Rio Grande Historical Collections. Box No. 4. Folder Name. Fulton's File. Folder No. F3.

Murphy, Lawrence G. "Will of Lawrence G. Murphy." Herman Weisner Collection. Lincoln County Papers. Accession No. MS 249. New Mexico State University Library at Las Cruces. Rio Grande Historical Collections. Box No. 11. Folder Name: Murphy, Lawrence G. No. P15.

Nolan, Frederick. Biographical information on James Dolan. Unpublished. Personal communication 2005.

No Author. *Proceedings of a Court of Inquiry in the Case of Col. N.A.M. Dudley (May 2, 1879-July 5, 1879).* File Number QQ1284. (Boxes 3304, 3305, 3305A). Court Martial Case Files 1809-1894. Records of the Office of the Judge Advocate General – Army. Record Group 153. National Archives and Records Administration. Old Military and Civil Branch. Washington, D.C. (James J. Dolan Testimony. June 5, 1879.)

Wild, Azariah F. "Daily Reports of U. S. Secret Service Agents, Azariah F. Wild." Microfilm T-915. Record Group 87. Rolls 307 (January 1,1878 - June 30, 1879) and 308 (July 1, 1879 - June 30, 1881). National Archives and Records Department. Department of the Treasury. United States Secret Service. Washington, D. C.

## DUDLEY, NATHAN AUGUSTUS MONROE

No Author. *Dudley Court of Inquiry. (May 2, 1879 - July 5, 1879).* Record No. 16W3/16/28/6. Boxes 1923 - 1923A. File No. QQ1284. National Archives and Records Administration. Old Military and Civil Branch. Records of the Office of the Judge Advocate General. Washington, D. C.

## ELKINS, STEPHEN BENTON
*BIOGRAPHY*

Cleaveland, Norman, *A Synopsis of the Great New Mexico Cover-up.* Self-printed. 1989.
_____. *The Great Santa Fe Cover-up. Based on a Talk given Before the Santa Fe Historical Society on November 1, 1978.* Self-printed. 1982.
_____. *The Morleys - Young Upstarts on the Southwest Frontier.* Albuquerque, New Mexico: Calvin Horn Publisher, Inc. 1971.

Lambert, Oscar Doane. *Stephen Benton Elkins. American Foursquare.* Pittsburgh, Pennsylvania:
    University of Pittsburg Press. 1955.

Montoya, María E. *Translating Property. The Maxwell Land Grant and the Conflict Over Land in the American West, 1840-1900.* Berkeley and Los Angeles: University of California Press. 2002.

Westphall, Victor. *Thomas Benton Catron and His Era*. Tucson, Arizona: University of Arizona Press. 1973.

*LETTERS*

Devens, Charles. "To honorable S. B. Elkins re. T. B. Catron continuing to act as U. S. Attorney." November 12, 1878. Angel Report. Microfilm File Case No. 44-4-8-3. Record Group 060. National Records and Archives Administration. Microfilm No. M750. Roll 1. U. S. Department of Justice. Washington, D.C.

Elkins, Stephen B. "Asking delay of action upon charges against U. S. Atty. Catron ..." September 24, 1878. Angel Report. Microfilm File Case No. 44-4-8-3. Record Group 060. National Records and Archives Administration. Microfilm No. M750. Roll 1. U. S. Department of Justice. Washington, D.C.

_____. "Regarding Attorney General's decision on T.B. Catron." Letter. September___, 1878. Angel Report. Microfilm File Case No. 44-4-8-3. Record Group 060. National Records and Archives Administration. Microfilm No. M750. Roll 1. U. S. Department of Justice. Washington, D.C.

_____. "Relative to resignation of T. B. Catron U.S. Attorney." Letter. November 10, 1878. Angel Report. Microfilm File Case No. 44-4-8-3. Record Group 060. National Records and Archives Administration. Microfilm No. M750. Roll 1. U. S. Department of Justice. Washington, D.C.

_____. "To the President. Referring to a conversation had with you last week ... Hon. S. B. Elkins favors appointment Axtell, ExGov. as Gov'r of New Mexico." (Letter) March 23, 1881. (Received Executive Mansion April 6, 1881). Microfilm Roll M750. National Archives and Records Administration. Record Group 060. Microfilm Case File Number 44-4-8-3. U.S. Department of Interior. Washington, D. C.

## EVANS, JESSIE

McCright, Grady E. and James H. Powell. *Jessie Evans: Lincoln County Badman*. College Station, Texas: Creative Publishing Company. 1983.

No Author. "Charges against Jessie Evans and John Kinney." Doña Ana County Criminal Docket Book. August 18, 1875 to November 7, 1878. Herman Weisner Collection. Accession No. MS249. Lincoln County Papers: New Mexico State University Library at Las Cruces. Rio Grande Historical Collections. Box No. 13. Folder Name: Venue, Change of. Folder No. V3.

## FOUNTAIN, ALBERT JENNINGS

Gibson, A. M. *The Life and Death of Colonel Albert Jennings Fountain*. Norman: University of Oklahoma Press. 1965.

## FRITZ FAMILY (CHARLES FRITZ AND EMILIE SCHOLAND)

Fritz, Charles. Affidavit of September 18, 1876 claiming that Emil Fritz had a will. Probate Court Record. In private collection.

_____. Affidavit of September 26, 1876 Authorizing Alexander McSween to Receive Payments for the Emil Fritz Estate. Probate Court Record. In private collection.

_____. Affidavit of December 7, 1877 to order Alexander McSween to pay the Emil Fritz insurance policy money. Probate Court Record. In private collection.

_____. Affidavit sworn before John Crouch, Clerk of Doña Ana District Court, for Writ of Attachment issued against property of Alexander A. McSween. Probate Court Record. February 6, 1878. In private collection.

_____ and Emilie Scholand. Attachment Bond sworn before John Crouch, Clerk of Doña Ana District Court, against Alexander A. McSween for indebtedness to them. February 6, 1878. In private collection.

Scholand, Emilie and Charles Fritz. Affidavit of September 26, 1876 appointing McSween to collect debts for the Emil Fritz Estate. Copied from the original District Court Record. In private collection.

Scholand, Emilie. Affidavit of December 21, 1877 Accusing Alexander McSween of Embezzlement. Copied from the original District Court Record. In private collection.

No Author. Diagram showing parcels of land to each of the heirs of Emil Fritz. Herman Weisner Collection. Accession No. MS249. Lincoln County Papers: New Mexico State University
Library at Las Cruces. Rio Grande Historical Collections. Box No. 11. Folder Name Charles Fritz Estate. Box No. P1

## GARRETT, PATRICK FLOYD "PAT"

Garrett, Pat F. *The Authentic Life of Billy the Kid The Noted Desperado of the Southwest, Whose Deeds of Daring and Blood Made His Name a Terror in New Mexico, Arizona, and Northern Mexico.* Santa Fe, New Mexico: New Mexico Printing and Publishing Co. 1882.

Glenn, Skelton. "Pat Garrett as I Knew Him on the Buffalo Ranges." (Unpublished) 1890. Haley Memorial Library and History Center. Midland, Texas. Robert N. Mullin Collection. Binder RNM, II, D. 4. (**Garrett's killing of Joe Briscoe**)

Metz, Leon C. *Pat Garrett. The Story of a Western Lawman.* Norman: University of Oklahoma Press. 1974.

Mullin, Robert N. "Killing of Joe Briscoe." Letter to Eve Ball. (Unpublished). January 31, 1964. Haley Memorial Library and History Center. Midland, Texas. Robert N. Mullin Collection. Binder RNM, VI, H. Midland, Texas:

_____. "Pat Garrett. Two Forgotten Killings." *Password: The El Paso County Historical Society.* Summer, 1965. Volume X, Number 2. Haley Memorial Library and History Center. Midland, Texas. Robert N. Mullin Collection. Binder RNM, III, B. 20. (**Garrett's murders of Joe Briscoe and no first name Reed**)

_____. "Pat Garrett. Two Forgotten Killings. a. Research Notes and Worksheets." (Unpublished) Haley Memorial Library and History Center. Midland, Texas. Robert N. Mullin Collection. Binder RNM, III, B. 20. 1965.

Upson, Ash. Letter from Garrett's Ranch to Upson's Nephew, Frank S. Downs, Esq. re. "His Drawers and pigeon holes of his desk were full of letters, deeds, bills, notes, agreements, & C. I have burned bushels of them and am not through yet." October 20, 1888. (Unpublished). Binder RNM, V1-MM. Midland, Texas: Nita Stewart Haley Memorial Library and J. Everts Haley Historical Center.

Wild, Azariah F. "Daily Reports of U. S. Secret Service Agents, Azariah F. Wild." Microfilm T-915. Record Group 87. Rolls 306 (June 15, 1877 - December 31, 1877), 307 (January 1,1878 - June 30, 1879), 308 (July 1, 1879 - June 30, 1881), 309 (July 1, 1881 - September 30, 1883), 310 (October 1, 1883 - July 31, 1886). National Archives and Records Department. Department of the Treasury. United States Secret Service. Washington, D. C.

ARTICLE (Lew Wallace Collection. Indiana Historical Society) "[Pat F. Garrett] Recommended by Gen. Wallace," *The* (Crawfordsville) *Weekly News-Review*, December 20, 1901. Collection Indiana Historical Society.

## HOYT, HENRY F.

Bonney, William H. Bill of Sale to Henry Hoyt. October 24, 1878. Collection of Panhandle-Plains Historical Museum. Canyon, Texas. (Item No. X1974-98/1)

Hoyt, Henry F. Handwritten note on back of Bill of Sale. 1927. Collection Indiana Historical Society. Lew Wallace Collection. M0292, Box 14, Folder 11.

Hoyt, Henry F. Letter to Lew Wallace Jr. "This time it is <u>me</u> that is apologizing ..." April 27, 1929. (Unpublished). Collection Indiana Historical Society. Lew Wallace Collection. M0292, Box 14, Folder 11.

_____. *A Frontier Doctor*. Boston and New York: Houghton Mifflin Company. 1929. **(Describes Billy's superior abilities, pp. 93-94.)**

## JONES, BARBARA ("MA'AM") AND FAMILY

Ball, Eve. *Ma'am Jones of the Pecos*. Tucson: University of Arizona Press. 1969.

## KINNEY, JOHN

Mullin, Robert N. "Here Lies John Kinney." *Journal of Arizona History*. 14 (Autumn 1973). pp. 223 - 242.

No Author. "Charges against Jessie Evans and John Kinney." Doña Ana County Criminal Docket Book. August 18, 1875 to November 7, 1878. Herman Weisner Collection. Accession No. MS249. Lincoln County Papers: New Mexico State University Library at Las Cruces. Rio Grande Historical Collections. Box 13. Folder Name: File Name. Venue, Change of. Folder No. V-3.

No Author. "Obituary of John Kinney." *Prescott Courier*. August 30, 1919. Obituary Section.

No Author. Obituary. "Over the Range Goes Another Pioneer." *Journal Miner*. Tuesday Morning, August 26, 1919.

## LEONARD, IRA

Nolan, Frederick. Biography and photograph of Ira Leonard. Unpublished. Personal communication 2005.

No Author. *Proceedings of a Court of Inquiry in the Case of Col. N.A.M. Dudley (May 2, 1879 - July 5, 1879)*. File Number QQ1284. (Boxes 3304, 3305, 3305A). Court Martial Case Files 1809-1894. Records of the Office of the Judge Advocate General - Army. Record Group 153. National Archives and Records Administration. Old Military and Civil Branch. Washington, D.C.

See also: WALLACE, LEW for letters

## MATTHEWS, JACOB BASIL

Fleming, Elvis E. *J.B. Matthews. Biography of a Lincoln County Deputy*. Las Cruces, New Mexico: Yucca Tree Press. 1999.

## MAXWELL FAMILY

Cleaveland, Norman. *The Morleys - Young Upstarts on the Southwest Frontier*. Albuquerque, New Mexico: Calvin Horn Publisher, Inc. 1971.

Dunham, Harold H. "New Mexican Land Grants with Special Reference to the Title Papers of the Maxwell Grant." *New Mexico Historical Review*. (January 1955) Vol. 30, No. 1. pp. 1 - 23.

Keleher, William A. *The Maxwell Land Grant. A New Mexico Item*. Albuquerque, New Mexico: University of New Mexico Press. 1964.

Lamar, Howard Roberts. *The Far Southwest 1846 - 1912. A Territorial History*. New Haven and London: Yale University Press. 1966.

Montoya, María E. *Translating Property. The Maxwell Land Grant and the Conflict Over Land in the American West, 1840-1900.* Berkeley and Los Angeles, California: University of California Press. 2002.

Murphy, Lawrence R. *Lucien Bonaparte Maxwell. Napoleon of the Southwest.* Norman: University of Oklahoma Press. 1983.

Pearson, Jim Berry. *The Maxwell Land Grant.* Norman: University of Oklahoma Press. 1961.

Poe, Sophie. *Buckboard Days.* Albuquerque, New Mexico: University of New Mexico Press. 1964.

Taylor, Morris F. *O. P. McMains and the Maxwell Land Grant Conflict.* Tucson, Arizona: The University of Arizona Press. 1979.

No Author. "Mrs. Paula M. Jaramillo, 65 Died Here Tuesday." *The Fort Sumner Leader.* Official Newspaper County of De Baca. December 20, 1929. No. 1158, Page 1, Column 1.

## McSWEEN, ALEXANDER

Angel, Frank Warner. *In the Matter of the Examination of the Causes and Circumstances of the Death of John H. Tunstall a British Subject.* Report filed October 4, 1878. Angel Report. Microfilm File Case Number 44-4-8-3. Record Group 060. Microfilm No. M750. Roll 1. National Archives and Records Administration. U.S. Department of Justice. Washington, D.C. Deposition given June 6, 1878, pp. 5-183.

_____. *In the Matter of the Lincoln County Troubles. To the Honorable Charles Devens, Attorney General.* October 4, 1878. Angel Report. Microfilm File Case Number 44-4-8-3. Record Group 060. Microfilm No. M750. Roll 1. National Archives and Records Administration. U.S. Department of Justice. Washington, D. C.

Bristol, Warren. Action of Assumpsit to command Sheriff of Lincoln County to attach goods of Alexander A. McSween. February 7, 1878. District Court Record. In private collection.

_____. Preprinted form in his name for "Writ of Attachment" (Printed and sold at the office of the Mesilla News) filled out to command the Sheriff of Lincoln County to attach goods of Alexander McSween for a suit of damages for ten thousand dollars. February 7, 1878. In private collection.

Fritz, Charles. Affidavit sworn before John Crouch, Clerk of Doña Ana District Court, for Writ of Attachment issued against property of Alexander A. McSween. Probate Court Record. February 6, 1878. In private collection.

_____ and Emilie Scholand. Attachment Bond sworn before John Crouch, Clerk of Doña Ana District Court, against Alexander A. McSween for indebtedness to them. February 6, 1878. In private collection.

McSween, Alexander, *Will. February 25, 1878.* Herman Weisner Collection. Accession No. MS249. Lincoln County Papers. New Mexico State University Library at Las Cruces. Rio Grande Historical Collections. Box No. 10. Folder Name. Will and Testament A. McSween. Box No. M15.

## POE, JOHN WILLIAM

Poe, John W. "The Killing of Billy the Kid." (a personal letter written at Roswell, New Mexico to Mr. Charles Goodnight, Goodnight P.C., Texas) July 10, 1917. Earle Vandale Collection. 1813-946. No. 2H475. Center for American History. University of Texas at Austin. **(Has the Milnor Rudolph quote and the part purposefully omitted from Probable Cause Statement for Case 2003-274.)**

Poe, Sophie. *Buckboard Days.* Albuquerque, New Mexico: University of New Mexico Press. 1964.

## TULAROSA DITCH WAR FIGHTERS

Rasch, Philip J. "The Tularosa Ditch War," *New Mexico Historical Review* 43(3). (July 1968). pp. 229-235.

## TUNSTALL, JOHN HENRY

Angel, Frank Warner. *In the Matter of the Examination of the Causes and Circumstances of the Death of John H. Tunstall a British Subject.* Report filed October 4, 1878. Angel Report. Microfilm File Case Number 44-4-8-3. Record Group 060. Microfilm Roll No. M750. Roll 1. National Archives and Records Administration. U. S. Department of Justice. Washington, D.C.

_____. *In the Matter of the Lincoln County Troubles. To the Honorable Charles Devens, Attorney General October 4, 1878.* Angel Report. Microfilm Case File No. 44-4-8-3. Record Group 060. Microfilm Roll No. M750. National Archives and Records Administration. U. S. Department of Justice. Washington, D. C.

Nolan, Frederick W. *The Life and Death of John Henry Tunstall.* Albuquerque, New Mexico: The University of New Mexico Press. 1965.

## WALLACE, LEW

*BIOGRAPHICAL BOOKS*

Jones, Oakah L. "Lew Wallace: Hoosier Governor of Territorial New Mexico. 1878-81." *New Mexico Historical Review. 59(1)* (January, l984).

Morsberger, Robert E. and Katherine M. Morsberger. *Lew Wallace: Militant Romantic.* New York: McGraw - Hill Book Company. 1980.

Stephens, Gail. "Shadow of Shiloh: Major General Lew Wallace in the Civil War." Indianapolis: Indiana Historical Society Press. 2010.

Wallace, Lew. *An Autobiography. Vol. I.* New York and London: Harper and Brothers Publishers. 1997.

_____. *An Autobiography. Vol. II.* New York and London: Harper and Brothers Publishers. 1997.

*AUTHORSHIP OF BOOKS*

Wallace, Lew. *An Autobiography. Vol. I.* New York and London: Harper and Brothers Publishers. 1997.

_____. *An Autobiography. Vol. II.* New York and London: Harper and Brothers Publishers. 1997.

_____. *Ben-Hur: A Tale of the Christ.* New York: Harper & Brothers, Franklin Square. 1880.

*COLLECTED PAPERS*

Wallace, Lew. Collected Papers. Microfilm Project Sponsored by the National Historical Publications Commission. Microfilm Roll No. 99. Santa Fe, New Mexico: State of New Mexico Records Center and Archives. 1974.

_____. Collected Papers. Indiana Historical Society. Lew Wallace Collection. M0292.

*AMNESTY PROCLAMATION*

Wallace, Lew. "Proclamation by the Governor." November 13, 1878. Indiana Historical Society. Lew Wallace Collection. M0292. Box 3. Folder 17.

*LETTERS (ALPHABETICAL AND CHRONOLOGICAL LISTING)*

### TO AND FROM WILLIAM BONNEY (See William H. Bonney)

### FROM, TO, AND ABOUT ATTORNEY HUSTON CHAPMAN

Chapman, Huston I. "You will please pardon me for presuming so much upon your kindness ..." October 24, 1878. Indiana Historical Society. Lew Wallace Collection. M0292. Box 3. Folder 16.

Wallace, Lew. "I enclose you a copy of a letter from Las Vegas ..." (Letter to Edward Hatch about Chapman) October 28, 1878. Indiana Historical Society. Lew Wallace Collection. M0292. Box 3. Folder 16.

Chapman, Huston I. "You must pardon me for so often presuming upon your kindness ..." November 29, 1878. Indiana Historical Society. Lew Wallace Collection. M0292. Box 3. Folder 18.

### FROM JAMES J. DOLAN

Dolan, James. "On my arrival at Fort Stanton, I repeated Your Explanation &c to the Comd'g Officer (Gen'l Dudley) ..." Letter to Lew Wallace. December 31, 1878. Indiana Historical Society. Lew Wallace Collection. M0292. Box 3. Folder 19.

### TO AND FROM COMMANDER N.A.M. DUDLEY

Wallace, Lew. "Your favor containing the duplicate accounts of the messenger who posted the President's Proclamation ..." November 30, 1878. Indiana Historical Society. Lew Wallace Collection. M0292. Box 3. Folder 18.

Dudley, Nathan Augustus Monroe Dudley. "This being regular report day, I respectfully state ..." March 1, 1879. Indiana Historical Society. Lew Wallace Collection. M0292. Box 4. Folder 4. **(Blaming Lincoln County problems on rustlers)**

Wallace, Lew. "The public interests with which I am charged make it, in my judgment, exceedingly improper for me to answer publicly your letters in the New Mexican ..." Indiana Historical Society. Lew Wallace Collection. M0292. Box 3. Folder 19.

### TO SECRETARY OF STATE WILLIAM M. EVARTS

Wallace, Lew. "I have the honor to acknowledge receipt by telegram of the President's Proclamation ..." October 9, 1878. Indiana Historical Society. Lew Wallace Collection. M0292. Box 3. Folder 15.

_____. "I take the liberty of sending you a copy of the Democratic organ of New Mexico ..." November 18, 1878. Indiana Historical Society. Lew Wallace Collection. M0292. Box 9. Folder 10.

### FROM PRESIDENT JAMES ABRAM GARFIELD

Garfield, James Abram. "I have this morning finished reading "Ben-Hur" ...." April 19, 1881. Indiana Historical Society. Lew Wallace Collection. M0292. Box 4. Folder 17.

### TO SHERIFF PATRICK F. GARRETT

Wallace, Lew. "To the Sheriff of Lincoln County, New Mexico, Greeting ..." April 30, 1881. Indiana Historical Society. Lew Wallace Collection. M0292. Box 9. Folder 11. **(Death Warrant for William Bonney)**

FROM AND TO GENERAL EDWARD HATCH

McCrary, George W. "This will be presented to you by General Lew Wallace ... " Letter to General Edward Hatch. September 18, 1878. Indiana Historical Society. Lew Wallace Collection. M0292. Box 3, Folder 14. (**Wallace to report as Governor**)

Wallace, Lew. "You will oblige me very much ..." Letter to General Edward Hatch. October 20, 1878. Indiana Historical Society. Lew Wallace Collection. M0292. Box 3. Folder 16.

_____. "I think all that is needed now for pacification of Lincoln County is ..." October 26, 1878. Indiana Historical Society. Lew Wallace Collection. M0292. Box 3. Folder 16.

_____. "I enclose you a copy of a letter from Las Vegas ..." October 28, 1878. Indiana Historical Society. Lew Wallace Collection. M0292. Box 3. Folder 16. (**About Huston Chapman**)

_____. "In a communication ... I requested for reasons stated, a safe-guard for Mrs. McSween ..." November 9, 1878. Indiana Historical Society. Lew Wallace Collection. M0292. Box 3. Folder 17. (**About Susan McSween**)

_____. "I am in receipt of Col. Dudley's reply to the charges against him ..." November 14, 1878. Indiana Historical Society. Lew Wallace Collection. M0292. Box 3. Folder 17. (**Has quote: "the "reply is perfectly satisfactory"**)

Wallace, Lew. "I am constrained to request that Lieut Col. N.A.M. Dudley, Commanding at Fort Stanton, be relieved ..." December 7, 1878. Indiana Historical Society. Lew Wallace Collection. M0292. Box 3. Folder 18.(**Removal of Dudley**)

Hatch, Edward. "The men Scurlock and Bonney at Sumner ..." February 1, 1879. Indiana Historical Society. Lew Wallace Collection. M0292. Box 4, Folder 4.

Wallace, Lew. "I have information that William Campbell, J.B. Matthews, and Jesse Evans were of the party engaged in the killing ..." March 5, 1879. Indiana Historical Society. Lew Wallace Collection. M0292. Box 4, Folder 4.

Hatch, Edward. Letter to Lew Wallace. March 6, 1879. Indiana Historical Society. Lew Wallace Collection. M0292. Box 4, Folder 4.

Wallace, Lew. "In your communication today, speaking of the arrest of Campbell ..." March 6, 1879. Indiana Historical Society. Lew Wallace Collection. M0292. Box 4, Folder 4.

_____. "I have reliable information that J.A. Scurlock and Charles Bowdre are now at a ranch called Taiban ..." March 6, 1879. Indiana Historical Society. Lew Wallace Collection. M0292. Box 4, Folder 4.

_____. "I have just ascertained that 'The Kid' is at a place called Las Tablas ..." March 6, 1879. Indiana Historical Society. Lew Wallace Collection. M0292. Box 9, Folder 10.

_____. "I have the honor to repeat the request made on a former occasion that Lt. Col. N.A.M. Dudley be relieved ..." March 7, 1879. Indiana Historical Society. Lew Wallace Collection. M0292. Box 4, Folder 4.

Hatch, Edward. "Lieutenant Colonel N.A.M. Dudley is hereby relieved ..." (Field Order) March 8, 1879. Indiana Historical Society. Lew Wallace Collection. M0292. Box 4, Folder 4.

Wallace, Lew. "I beg leave to request that you allow Captain Carroll to remain ... in command of Fort Stanton." March 9, 1879. Indiana Historical Society. Lew Wallace Collection. M0292. Box 4, Folder 4.

Hatch, Edward. "Col. Dudley has received his order ..." March 11, 1879. Indiana Historical Society. Lew Wallace Collection. M0292. Box 4, Folder 5.

TO PRESIDENT RUTHERFORD B. HAYES

Wallace, Lew. "I avail myself of your request this morning. It is hardly necessary to give reasons for a preference of the Italian mission ..." March 9, 1877. Indiana Historical Society. Lew Wallace Collection. M0292. Box 3. Folder 13.

_____. "The feuds recently in Lincoln county, New Mexico, left at large many thieves and murderers ..." March 31, 1879. Indiana Historical Society. Lew Wallace Collection. M0292. Box 4. Folder 7. **(Asking for martial law for Lincoln and Doña Ana counties)**

Hayes, Rutherford B. "We are greatly obliged by your kindness." January 9, 1881. Indiana Historical Society. Lew Wallace Collection. M0292. Box 4. Folder 16. **(Gift of *Ben Hur*)**

TO JUDGE ADVOCATE CAPTAIN HENRY H. HUMPHREYS

Wallace, Lew. "Since requesting March 7, 1879 that Lt. Col. N.A.M. Dudley be relieved ..." May 10, 1879. Indiana Historical Society. Lew Wallace Collection. M0292. Box 4. Folder 10.

TO LINCOLN COUNTY SHERIFF GEORGE KIMBRELL

Wallace, Lew. "The duty of keeping the peace in the county and arresting offenders is devolved by the law upon you ..." April 2, 1879. Indiana Historical Society. Lew Wallace Collection. Box 4, Folder 8.

TO AND FROM IRA E. LEONARD:

Leonard, Ira E. "You have undoubtedly learned ere this of the assassination of H.I. Chapman ..." February 24, 1879. Indiana Historical Society. Lew Wallace Collection. M0292. Box 4. Folder 3.

Wallace, Lew. "It is important to take steps to protect the coming court." April 6, 1879. Indiana Historical Society. Lew Wallace Collection. M0292. Box 4. Folder 15.

_____. "Your favors both received. The arrest of Wilson was a blow at the right time ..." April 9, 1879. Indiana Historical Society. Lew Wallace Collection. M0292. Box 4. Folder 9. **(With quote: "To work trying to do a little good, but with the world against you, requires the will of a martyr")**

Leonard, Ira E. "I was disappointed at not seeing you when I went to the Fort." April 12, 1879. Lew Wallace Collection. M0292. Box 4. Folder 9.

Wallace, Lew. "Your favor with the prisoners received." April 13, 1879. Indiana Historical Society. Lew Wallace Collection. M0292. Box 4. Folder 9.

Leonard, Ira.. "He is bent on going for the Kid ..." April 20, 1879. Indiana Historical Society. Lew Wallace Collection. M0292. Box 4. Folder 9.

_____. "When you left here I promised to write you concerning events transpiring here ..." May 20, 1879. Indiana Historical Society. Lew Wallace Collection. M0292. Box 4. Folder 10. **(With quote: "the Santa Fe Ring that has been so long an incubus on the government of this territory")**

_____. "I write to you in pencil because I am laboring for breath ..." May 23, 1879. Indiana Historical Society. Lew Wallace Collection. M0292. Box 4. Folder 11. **(With quote: "we are pouring 'hot shot' into Dudley")**

_____. "Dudley commenced on the defense Tuesday afternoon ..." **(With quote: "I am thoroughly and completely disgusted with their proceedings.")** June 6, 1879. Indiana Historical Society. Lew Wallace Collection. M0292. Box 4. Folder 11.

Wallace, Lew. "To work trying to do a little good, but with the world against you, requires the will of a martyr. Indiana Historical Society. Lew Wallace Collection.

Leonard, Ira. "... the assassination of H. I. Chapman ..." February 24, 1879. Indiana Historical Society. Lew Wallace Collection.

_____. "One Wm Wilson, a saloon keeper ..." April 9, 1879. Indiana Historical Society. Lew Wallace Collection.

Wallace, Lew. "Your favors both received." April 9, 1879. Indiana Historical Society. Lew Wallace Collection.

Leonard, Ira.. "He is bent on going for the Kid ..." April 20, 1879. Indiana Historical Society. Lew Wallace Collection. (**About District Attorney Rynerson.**)

_____. "... the Santa Fe ring that has been so long an incubus on the government of this territory." May 20, 1879. Indiana Historical Society. Lew Wallace Collection.

_____. "... we are pouring 'hot shot' into Dudley ..." May 23, 1879. Indiana Historical Society. Lew Wallace Collection. M0292.

_____. "I am thoroughly and completely disgusted with their proceedings." June 6, 1879. Indiana Historical Society. Lew Wallace Collection.

_____. "... they would not enter our objections ..." "... would not allow us to show the conspiracy formed with Dolan beforehand ..." "I tell you Governor as long as the present incumbent occupies the bench all that Grand Juries may do to bring to justice these men every effort will be thwarted by him and the sympathizers of that side." June 13, 1879. Indiana Historical Society. Lew Wallace Collection. M0292. Box 4. Folder 11.

_____. "Nothing has been accomplished in the least ..." July 5, 1879. Indiana Historical Society. Lew Wallace Collection. M0292. Box 4. Folder 11.

## TO AND FROM SECRETARY OF WAR GEORGE McCRARY

Wallace, Lew. "By the statute now in force ..." October 4, 1878. Indiana Historical Society. Lew Wallace Collection. M0292. Box 3. Folder 15.

McCrary, George. "I have the honor to acknowledge the receipt of your letter..." November 13, 1878. Indiana Historical Society. Lew Wallace Collection. M0292. Box 3. Folder 17.

Wallace, Lew. "I have the honor to acknowledge the receipt of two communications from you..." November 23, 1878. Indiana Historical Society. Lew Wallace Collection. M0292. Box 3. Folder 18.

## TO LINCOLN JAILOR JUAN PATRÓN

Wallace, Lew. "Please select ten of your Rangers ..." March 3, 1879. Indiana Historical Society. Lew Wallace Collection. M0292. Box 4. Folder 4. (**To arrest Josiah Scurlock and William Bonney**)

_____. "Please report to Sheriff Kimbrell ..." March 3, 1879. Indiana Historical Society. Lew Wallace Collection. M0292. Box 4. Folder 4.

_____. "Be good enough to send word to all your men to turn out soon as possible ..." March 19, 1879. Indiana Historical Society. Lew Wallace Collection. M0292. Box 4. Folder 6.

## FROM LIEUTENANT GEORGE PURLINGTON

Purlington, George. "The District Court adjourned on Thursday ..." May 3, 1879. Indiana Historical Society. Lew Wallace Collection. M0292. Box 4. Folder 10. (**Letter to Adjutant General with copy sent to Wallace; about the Court's indictments**)

TO AND FROM CARL SCHURZ

Schurz, Carl. "I transmit herewith an order from the President ..." September 4, 1878. Indiana Historical Society. Lew Wallace Collection. M0292. Box 3. Folder 14. **(Suspension of New Mexico Governor S.B. Axtell)**

Wallace, Lew. "I have the honor to inform you ..." October 1, 1878. Indiana Historical Society. Lew Wallace Collection. M0292. Box 3. Folder 15. **(Informing Schurz that he qualified as Governor)**

_____. "I have the honor to enclose herewith a requisition ..." October 4, 1878. Indiana Historical Society. Lew Wallace Collection. M0292. Box 3. Folder 15.

_____. "As the basis of the request which I have to infer..." October 5, 1878. Indiana Historical Society. Lew Wallace Collection. M0292. Box 3. Folder 15. **(Condition of Lincoln County and requesting President to declare martial law)**

_____. [Telegram] "I received by mail last night a petition signed by the Probate Judge ...".". October 14, 1878. Indiana Historical Society. Lew Wallace Collection. M0292. Box 3. Folder 15. **(Giving situation and asking martial law for Lincoln and Doña Ana Counties)**

_____. "I have the honor to inform you that since the posting of the President's Proclamation ...." October 22, 1878. Indiana Historical Society. Lew Wallace Collection. M0292. Box 3. Folder 16.

_____. "I have appointed Mr. Epifanio Vigil, of this city, Interpreter and Translator ...." October 22, 1878. Indiana Historical Society. Lew Wallace Collection. M0292. Box 3. Folder 16.

_____. "Herewith please find bond ...." October 22, 1878. Indiana Historical Society. Lew Wallace Collection. M0292. Box 3. Folder 16.

No signatures. (In Wallace's handwriting). "Yesterday, at the request of Governor Wallace the undersigned, physicians ...." October 23, 1878. Indiana Historical Society. Lew Wallace Collection. M0292. Box 3. Folder 16. **(Focus on refurbishing Palace of the Governors)**

_____. "Be good enough, at your earliest convenience, to call attention of the President ...." October 24, 1878. Indiana Historical Society. Lew Wallace Collection. M0292. Box 3. Folder 16.

_____. "I enclose a paper, signed by all the leading attorneys ..." November 13, 1878. Indiana Historical Society. Lew Wallace Collection. M0292. Box 3. Folder 17. **(Urging judgeship for Ira Leonard)**

_____. "I have the honor to forward to you the following report." November 13, 1878. Indiana Historical Society. Lew Wallace Collection. M0292. Box 3. Folder 17. **(Announces his Amnesty Proclamation)**

Schurz, Carl. "In reply to your letter ..." November 14, 1878. Indiana Historical Society. Lew Wallace Collection. M0292. Box 3. Folder 17. **(Given bond for arms)**

_____. "Replying to your two telegrams ..." November 15, 1878. Indiana Historical Society. Lew Wallace Collection. M0292. Box 3. Folder 17. **(Ira Leonard's judgeship appointment sent to the Attorney General for consideration)**

_____. "I acknowledge the receipt of your letter ..." November 23, 1878. Indiana Historical Society. Lew Wallace Collection. M0292. Box 3. Folder 18. **(Praise of his Amnesty Proclamation, has approval of President)**

Wallace, Lew. "It has not unexpectedly happened that delay, involving expense ..." November 26, 1878. Indiana Historical Society. Lew Wallace Collection. M0292. Box 3. Folder 18. **(Wants extradition of fugitive criminals)**

Schurz, Carl. "In compliance with the suggestion of the Secretary of State ..." November 30, 1878. Indiana Historical Society. Lew Wallace Collection. M0292. Box 3. Folder 18. **(About extradition of fugitive criminals)**

Schurz, Carl. "I have received your letter ..." December 9, 1878. Indiana Historical Society. Lew Wallace Collection. M0292. Box 3. Folder 19. (**Answering about anyone in Senate trying to defeat his confirmation as Governor**)

Wallace, Lew. "I have the honor to report that affairs of the Territory are moving on quietly ..." December 21, 1878. Indiana Historical Society. Lew Wallace Collection. M0292. Box 3. Folder 19.

Schurz, Carl. "I have received your report ..." December 28, 1878. Indiana Historical Society. Lew Wallace Collection. M0292. Box 3. Folder 19.

Wallace, Lew. "I have the honor to enclose you a copy of a communication ..." January 17, 1879. Indiana Historical Society. Lew Wallace Collection. M0292. Box 4. Folder 1. (**Bad condition of Palace of the Governors**)

_____. "... I have just returned from Trinidad, Col ..." February 5, 1879. Indiana Historical Society. Lew Wallace Collection. M0292. Box 4. Folder 2. (**Bringing his family to Santa Fe**)

_____. "... I beg to call your attention to the condition of the house called the "Palace" ...." February 12, 1879. Indiana Historical Society. Lew Wallace Collection. M0292. Box 4. Folder 2.

_____. "The Hon. A.G. Porter, Comptroller, is kind enough to inform me ..." February 26, 1879. Indiana Historical Society. Lew Wallace Collection. M0292. Box 4. Folder 3. (**Funds requested**)

_____. "I take the liberty of enclosing herewith the accounts in duplicate of Mr. Epifanio Vigil ..." February 26, 1879. Indiana Historical Society. Lew Wallace Collection. M0292. Box 4. Folder 3. (**Funds requested**)

_____. "One H.I. Chapman, lawyer, was assassinated ...." February 27, 1879. Indiana Historical Society. Lew Wallace Collection. M0292. Box 4. Folder 3.

Schurz, Carl. "I have the honor to acknowledge the receipt of your letter of the 1st inst." March 11, 1879. Indiana Historical Society. Lew Wallace Collection. M0292. Box 4. Folder 5.

Wallace, Lew. "My time has been so constantly occupied in getting my work into operation ..." March 21, 1879. Indiana Historical Society. Lew Wallace Collection. M0292. Box 4. Folder 7. (**Lists: 'The Kid – William Bonney**)

_____. "Today I forwarded a telegram to you, with another to the President ..." March 31, 1879. Indiana Historical Society. Lew Wallace Collection. M0292. Box 4. Folder 7. (**"Precious specimen" letter**)

_____. "I have official information that a court of inquiry for Col. Dudley has been ordered ..." April 4, 1879. Indiana Historical Society. Lew Wallace Collection. M0292. Box 4. Folder 8.

_____. "I have the honor to inform you that affairs in Lincoln County are progressing ..." April 18, 1879. Indiana Historical Society. Lew Wallace Collection. M0292. Box 4. Folder 9.

_____. "In a recent letter descriptive of the situation in Lincoln County, I alluded to the necessity of breaking up illicit transactions in cattle." April 25, 1879. Indiana Historical Society. Lew Wallace Collection. M0292. Box 4. Folder 9.

_____. "I enclose account in duplicate for services in overhauling and removing Territorial archives ..." May 1, 1879. Indiana Historical Society. Lew Wallace Collection. M0292. Box 4. Folder 10.

_____. "I have the honor to inform you that all the recent reports, military and otherwise, justify me ..." May 5, 1879. Indiana Historical Society. Lew Wallace Collection. M0292. Box 4. Folder 10.

_____. "I had the honor a few weeks ago of writing you respecting a balance of contingent fund due this Executive Office ..." May 5, 1879. Indiana Historical Society. Lew Wallace Collection. M0292. Box 4. Folder 10.

Wallace, Lew. "Enclosed please find a copy of the report of the commandant at Fort Stanton." June 11, 1879. Indiana Historical Society. Lew Wallace Collection. M0292. Box 4. Folder 11.

Schurz, Carl. "I have received your letter of the 3rd inst. ..." July 10, 1879. Indiana Historical Society. Lew Wallace Collection. M0292. Box 4. Folder 12.

Wallace, Lew. "The accompanying document received from Fort Stanton which will explain itself." July 30, 1879. Indiana Historical Society. Lew Wallace Collection. M0292. Box 4. Folder 12.

Schurz, Carl. "Referring to your letter of the 30th ultimo ..." August 29, 1879. Indiana Historical Society. Lew Wallace Collection. M0292. Box 4. Folder 12.

Wallace, Lew. "In reply to the communication of Acting Secretary Bell ..." September 15, 1879. Indiana Historical Society. Lew Wallace Collection. M0292. Box 4. Folder 13. **(On John Jones killing Jim Beckwith and Bob Olinger killing John Jones)**

_____. "The enclosed communication received yesterday from Mr. Louis Scott, U.S. Consul ..." December 29, 1879. Indiana Historical Society. Lew Wallace Collection. M0292. Box 4. Folder 13.

_____. "I have the honor to inform you that the Legislature of this Territory adjourned ..." February 16, 1880. Indiana Historical Society. Lew Wallace Collection. M0292. Box 4. Folder 14.

Schurz, Carl. "I have received your letter ..." May 24, 1880. Indiana Historical Society. Lew Wallace Collection. M0292. Box 4. Folder 15.

Wallace, Lew. "I have returned from a tour through the counties ..." July 23, 1880. Indiana Historical Society. Lew Wallace Collection. M0292. Box 4. Folder 14. **(Reporting result of time in the south counties and recommends Ira Leonard for judgeship to replace Warren Bristol.)**

_____. "I have the honor to report that I returned to this city ..." November 30, 1880. Indiana Historical Society. Lew Wallace Collection. M0292. Box 4. Folder 14.

_____. "From private advices received from Lincoln county ..." December 7, 1880. Indiana Historical Society. Lew Wallace Collection. M0292. Box 4. Folder 15. **(Pursuit of outlaws by people in Lincoln County)**

_____. "I have private business urgently requiring my presence in New York city ..." December 14, 1880. Indiana Historical Society. Lew Wallace Collection. M0292. Box No. 4. Folder 15. **(Mention's - without giving names - the sheriff [Garrett] tracking the "leader of the outlaws" [Billy] for whom he has set a "$500 reward.")**

_____. "I have the honor to submit the following matter for consideration ..." December 15, 1880. Indiana Historical Society. Lew Wallace Collection. M0292. Box 4. Folder 15.


## TO AND FROM ATTORNEY DAVID SHIELD

Shield, David. "It is rumored that 'Eight long Affidavits' are in your possession ..." February 11, 1879. Indiana Historical Society. Lew Wallace Collection. M0292. Box 4. Folder 2. **(Commander Dudley's defamatory affidavits about Susan McSween)**

Wallace, Lew. "I am in receipt of your letter of this date requesting inspection ..." February 19, 1879. Indiana Historical Society. Lew Wallace Collection. M0292. Box 4. Folder 2. **(Refuses to give copies of Dudley's affidavits about Susan McSween)**

## TO AND FROM JUSTICE OF THE PEACE JOHN B. WILSON

Wallace, Lew. "I hasten to acknowledge receipt of your favor of the 11th Jan. ult. ..." January 18, 1879. Indiana Historical Society. Lew Wallace Collection. M0292. Box 4. Folder 1.

_____. "Your favors are both in hand and place me under renewed obligation. ..." February 6, 1879. Indiana Historical Society. Lew Wallace Collection. M0292. Box 4. Folder 2.

_____. "I understand that affidavits will be filed with you against the prisoners. ..." March 8, 1879. Indiana Historical Society. Lew Wallace Collection. M0292. Box 4. Folder 4.

_____. "I enclose a note for Bonney." March 20, 1879. Indiana Historical Society. Lew Wallace Collection. M0292. Box 4. Folder 6.

## *TESTIMONY*

No Author. *Dudley Court of Inquiry. (May 2, 1879 - July 5, 1879).* Record No. 16W3/16/28/6. Boxes 1923-1923A. File Number QQ1284. National Archives and Records Administration. Old Military and Civil Branch. Records of the Office of the Judge Advocate General. Washington, D.C.

## *ANGEL NOTEBOOK*

Angel, Frank Warner. "To Gov. Lew Wallace, Santa Fe, N. M., 1878." Indiana Historical Society. Lew Wallace Collection. M0292. F372 **(Cover of notebook written for Wallace reads: "Gov. Lew Wallace, Santa Fe, N.M." Microfilm No. F372. From a document now missing from the collection)**

Theisen, Lee Scott. "Frank Warner Angel's Notes on New Mexico Territory, 1878." *Arizona and the West,* 18 (4) (Winter 1976) 333-370.

## *NOTES ON WILLIAM BONNEY INTERVIEW*

Wallace, Lew. "Statements by Kid, made Sunday night March 23, 1879." (Cover sheet reads: "Fort Stanton, March 20, 1879. William Bonney ("Kid") relative to arrangement with him." Indiana Historical Society. Lew Wallace Collection. M0292. Box 4. Folder 6.

## *ARTICLES (CHRONOLOGICAL)*

Wallace, Lew. "Wallace's Words ..." January 3, 1881), Chicago *The Daily Inter Ocean.* January 4, 1881. p. 2, c. 4. Indiana Historical Society. Lew Wallace Collection. M0292. **(Interview with Wallace conducted in Washington, D.C.)**

No Author. "Richard Dunham's May 2, 1881 encounter with Billy the Kid.", *Santa Fe Daily New Mexican,* May 5, 1881, p.4, c. 3. Indiana Historical Society. Lew Wallace Collection. M0292.

No Author. "The Thug's Territory. Stage Robbers and Cut-Throats Have Things Their Own Way in New Mexico. Gen. Lew Wallace Anxious to Punish the Crime That is So Prevalent – A Chapter About "Billy the Kid' - The Governor has a Narrow Escape From Being Spanked." *St. Louis Daily Globe-Democrat.* Monday Morning, May 16, 1881. Page 2, Columns 5 and 6. (Copy in private collection of Mike Pitel)

No Author. (O.L. Houghton's Conversation with Lew Wallace, before May 26, 1881), *The Las Vegas Daily Optic,* May 26, 1881, p.4, c.4. Indiana Historical Society. Lew Wallace Collection. M0292.

No Author. "Billy the Kid ..." (Lew Wallace interviewed on June 13, 1881), Crawfordsville (Indiana) *Saturday Evening Journal,* June 18, 1881. Indiana Historical Society. Lew Wallace Collection. M0292.

No Author. "Lew Wallace's Foe. Threatened by 'Billy the Kid.' The Writing of 'Ben Hur' Interrupted. An Incident of the Soldier-Author's Career in New Mexico. *San Francisco Chronicle.* December 10, 1893. Indiana Historical Society. Lew Wallace Collection. M0292. Box 14. Folder 11.

No Author. "Street Pickings," *Crawfordsville* (Weekly) *Review – Saturday Edition,* January 6, 1894. Indiana Historical Society. Lew Wallace Collection. M0292.

No Author. "An Old Incident Recalled," *The* (Crawfordsville) *Weekly News-Review,* December 20, 1901. Indiana Historical Society. Lew Wallace Collection. M0292.

Lewis, E.I. "Gen. Wallace's Feud with Billy the Kid, When the General Was Governor of New Mexico and Billy Bonne Was the Most Dangerous Western Outlaw. He Was a Waif and Was Reared in Indiana. *The Indianapolis Press.* Saturday, June 23, 1900. Page 7. Indiana Historical Society. Lew Wallace Collection. M0292. Box 14. Folder 11.

Wallace, Lew. "General Lew Wallace Writes a Romance of 'Billy the Kid," Most Famous Bandit of the Plains." June 8, 1902. *New York Sunday World Magazine.* Page 4. Indiana Historical Society. Lew Wallace Collection. M0292. Original in OMB 23. Box 1. Folder 5. Copy in Box 14. Folder 11.

*REWARD NOTICES FOR WILLIAM BONNEY*

Wallace, Lew. "Billy the Kid: $500 Reward." Las Vegas *Gazette.* December 22, 1880.
_____. "Billy the Kid. $500 Reward." May 3, 1881. *Daily New Mexican.* Vol. X, No. 33. p. 1, c. 3.

*REWARD POSTERS FOR WILLIAM BONNEY*

Greene, Chas. W. "To the New Mexican Printing and Publishing Company." May 20, 1881. (Bill to Lew Wallace for Reward posters for "Kid"). Indiana Historical Society. Lew Wallace Collection. M0292. Box 4, Folder 18.
_____. "I enclose a bill ..." Letter to Lew Wallace for "Kid" wanted posters. June 2, 1881. Indiana Historical Society. Lew Wallace Collection. M0292. Box 4, Folder 18.

*DEATH WARRANT FOR WILLIAM BONNEY*

Wallace, Lew. "To the Sheriff of Lincoln County, Greeting ..." April 30, 1881. Indiana Historical Society. Lew Wallace Collection. M0292. Box 9, Folder 11.

## WILD, AZARIAH

Brooks, James J. *1877 Report on Secret Service Operatives.* (September 26, 1877). "On Azariah Wild." p.392. Department of the Treasury. United States Secret Service. Washington, D.C.

Wild, Azariah F. "Daily Reports of U. S. Secret Service Agents, Azariah F. Wild. Microfilm T-915. Record Group 87. Rolls 306 (June 15, 1877 - December 31, 1877), 307 (January 1, 1878 - June 30, 1879), 308 (July 1, 1879 - June 30, 1881), 309 (July 1, 1881 - September 30, 1883), and 310 (October 1, 1883 - July 31, 1886). National Archives and Records Department. Department of Treasury. United States Secret Service. Washington, D. C.

Wild, Azariah. Telegraph on counterfeit bills. January 4, 1881. Herman Weisner Collection. Lincoln County Papers. New Mexico State University Library at Las Cruces. Rio Grande Historical Collections. Box No. 11. Folder Name: Olinger, Robert and James W. Bell. Folder No. O-1.

# LINCOLN COUNTY WAR

Angel, Frank Warner. *Examination of charges against F. C. Godfroy, Indian Agent, Mescalero, N. M. October 2, 1878.* (Report 1981, Inspector E. C. Watkins; Cited as Watkins Report). M 319-20 and L147, 44-4-8. Record Group 075. National Archives and Records Administration. U.S. Department of Justice. Washington, D. C.

—————————. *In the Matter of the Examination of the Causes and Circumstances of the Death of John H. Tunstall a British Subject.* Report filed October 4, 1878. Angel Report. Microfilm File Case Number 44-4-8-3. Record Group 060. Microfilm No. M750. Roll 1. National Archives and Records Administration. U.S. Department of Justice. Washington, D.C.

—————————. *In the Matter of the Investigation of the Charges Against S. B. Axtell Governor of New Mexico. Report and Testimony. October 3, 1878.* Angel Report. Microfilm Case File No. 44-4-8-3. Record Group 060. Microfilm Roll M750. National Archives and Records Administration. U.S. Department of Interior. Washington, D.C.

—————————. *In the Matter of the Lincoln County Troubles. To the Honorable Charles Devens, Attorney General. October 4, 1878.* Angel Report. Microfilm Case File No. 44-4-8-3. Record Group 060. Microfilm Roll M750. National Archives and Records Administration. U. S. Department of Justice. Washington, D. C.

Cramer, T. Dudley. *The Pecos Ranchers in the Lincoln County War.* Orinda, California: Branding Iron Press. 1996.

Fulton, Maurice Garland. Robert N. Mullin. Ed. *History of the Lincoln County War.* Tucson, Arizona: The University of Arizona Press. 1997.

Jacobson, Joel. *Such Men as Billy the Kid. The Lincoln County War Reconsidered.* Lincoln and London: University of Nebraska Press. 1994.

Keleher, William A. *Violence in Lincoln County 1869-1881.* Albuquerque, New Mexico: University of New Mexico Press. 1957.

Mullin, Robert N. Re: Frank Warner Angel Meeting with President Hayes. August, 1878. Binder RNM, VI, M. (Unpublished). Midland, Texas: Nita Stewart Haley Memorial Library and J. Evert Haley History Center. (Undated).

Nolan, Frederick W. *The Life and Death of John Henry Tunstall.* Albuquerque, New Mexico: The University of New Mexico Press. 1965.

—————————. *The Lincoln County War: A Documentary History.* Norman: University of Oklahoma Press. 1992.

—————————. *The West of Billy the Kid.* Norman: University of Oklahoma Press. 1998.

Rasch, Philip J. *Gunsmoke in Lincoln County.* Laramie, Wyoming: National Association for Outlaw and Lawmen History, Inc. with University of Wyoming. 1997.

—————————. Robert K. DeArment. Ed. *Warriors of Lincoln County.* Laramie: National Association for Outlaw and Lawmen History, Inc. with University of Wyoming. 1998.

Utley, Robert M. *High Noon in Lincoln. Violence on the Western Frontier.* Albuquerque, New Mexico: University of New Mexico Press. 1987.

Wilson, John P. *Merchants, Guns, and Money: The Story of Lincoln County and Its Wars.* Santa Fe, New Mexico: Museum of New Mexico Press. 1987.

No Author. "Amnesty for Matthews and Long in the Third Judicial Court April Term 1879." Herman Weisner Collection. Lincoln County Papers. New Mexico State University Library at Las Cruces. Rio Grande Historical Collections. Box No. 1. Folder Name. Amnesty. Folder No. 4.

No Author. "Brady Inventory McSween Property." Herman Weisner Collection. Lincoln County Papers. New Mexico State University Library at Las Cruces. Rio Grande Historical Collections. Box No. 10. Folder Name. Will and Testament A. McSween. Folder No. M15.

No Author. "Charges against Jessie Evans and John Kinney." Doña Ana County Civil and Criminal Docket Book. August 18, 1875 to November 7, 1878. Herman Weisner Collection. Accession No. MS249. Lincoln County Papers. New Mexico State University Library at Las Cruces. Rio Grande Historical Collections. Box No. 13. Folder Name. Venue, Change Of. Folder No. V3.

No Author. "Dismissal of Cases Against Dolan, Matthews, Peppin, October 1879 District Court." Herman Weisner Collection. Lincoln County Papers. New Mexico State University Library at Las Cruces. Rio Grande Historical Collections. Box No. 13. Folder Name. Venue, Change Of. Folder No. V3.

"Disturbances in the Territories, 1878 - 1894. Lawlessness in New Mexico." Senate Documents. 67th Congress. 2nd Session. December 5, 1921 - September 22, 1922. pp. 176 - 187. Washington, D.C.: Government Printing Office. 1922.

No Author. *Dudley Court of Inquiry. (May 2, 1879 - July 5, 1879).* Record No. 16W3/16/28/6. Boxes 1923-1923A. File Number QQ1284. National Archives and Records Administration. Old Military and Civil Branch. Records of the Office of the Judge Advocate General. Washington, D.C.

No Author. "Killers of Tunstall. February 18, 1879." Herman Weisner Collection. Lincoln County Papers. New Mexico State University Library at Las Cruces. Rio Grande Historical Collections. Box No. 12. Folder Name: Tunstall, John H. Folder No. T1.

No Author. "Lincoln County Indictments July 1872 – 1881." Herman Weisner Collections. Lincoln County Papers. New Mexico State University Library at Las Cruces. Rio Grande Historical Collections. Box No.8. Folder Name. Lincoln Co Indictments. Folder No. L11.

# Acknowledgments

My kindest recompense to all the people who generously shared information, but are not named in this book, is to say: "I promised to keep you secret. And I did."

For all the cited expert consultants, your generosity was as great as your reputations. I take responsibility for any mistakes.

Much thanks is owed to Marlyn Bowlin, loving caretaker of Billy Bonney's Fort Sumner cemetery and of his history; and my fellow traveler in opposing the hoax until her untimely demise.

The great achievement of stopping Billy the Kid Case hoaxers' exhumations at gravesites of Billy the Kid and his mother goes to the Kennedy Han Law Firm, Attorney Robert Scavron, Attorney Herb Marsh, past Lincoln County Commissioner Leo Martinez, and brave public officials in Silver City and Fort Sumner.

Special appreciation goes to journalist Jay Miller, who courageously printed my hoax-exposing articles in his New Mexico "Inside the Capitol" syndicated newspaper column; then proxied my early open records requests. He also sent, in his name, my investigative letters to Professor Paul Hutton, Dr. Henry Lee, and U.S. Marshals Service Historian David Turk.

Awe goes to *pro se* litigant, Deborah Toomey, whose bravery and legal brilliance achieved her 2012 New Mexico Court of Appeals victory that strengthened that state's open records law.

And for any who worked independently to stop the Billy the Kid Case hoax, I say, "Each of you is a hero."

For the hoaxers, their enablers, and my betrayers in my litigation: thank you also. Without you all, this story would not have been possible - or even conceivable.

Appreciation is owed to Mario Burgos and his group, Mudhouse Creative, for thinking up the word "shovelgate."

That leaves my mother, Dr. Rose Cooper, whose loving advice about my eleven year fight - "What do you need this misery for?" - was appreciated. Also, her sister, Attorney Ann Kaplan, generously shared her perspective on lawyers and politicians: "What else did you expect?"

# Index

## BARNETT LAW FIRM, P.A.

AMY B. BAILEY
MICKEY D. BARNETT
PHILLIP W. CHEVES
DAVID A. GARCIA, OF COUNSEL

CERTIED MAIL                    April 24, 2007
RETURN RECEIPT REQUESTED
AND FIRST CLASS MAIL
Sheriff Rick Virden
Lincoln County Sheriff's Office
PO Box 278
Carrizozb, NM 88301-0278

Re:    Request for Inspection of Public Records

Dear Sheriff Virden:

This office represents Gale Cooper, M.D.. Pursuant to the
Records Act, Section 14-2-8 et seq. NMSA 1978, this letter is our writ
the public records identified as follows:

1.    Please provide any and all records and reports of
or conclusions provided in any form at all to the Lincoln Cou
Department by Dr. Henry Lee as the stated "forensic expert" u
Lincoln Cou
Sheriff's Dep
findings.
"findings"
from Dr. H
which the
Bonney w
remains
Hudspet
investig
matchin
Hudspe
beach
graph

# IPRA GUIDE

## THE INSPECTION OF PUBLIC RECORDS ACT
NMSA 1978, Chapter 14, Article 2

A Compliance Guide for
Mexico Public Officials and Citizens

## SHELL GAMES WITH 2003-274

DEFINITION: (1) Trick of hiding a pea under walnut shells; (2) Swindle by substitution

| PEA --- TRUTH | SHELL --- COVER-UP |
|---|---|
| CASE IS A FORENSIC/HISTORIC HOAX | DEFINITION 2003-274: GARRETT MURDER |
| SULLIVAN WAS ITS SHERIFF & DEPUTY FROM 2003-JUNE 21, 2007 | DEFINITION 2003-274: KID MURDERS |
| SEDERWALL WAS ITS DEPUTY FROM 2003-JUNE 21, 2007 | MURDER CASE WITH DNA FORENSICS |
| LAW ENFORCEMENT FOR GRANT & DE BACA EXHUMATION PETITIONS, DEPARTMENTAL LETTERS, & PRESS | NOW SAYS WAS ONLY HISTORICAL HOBBYIST |
| BEFORE 2007, RECORD REFUSALS AS IPRA 14-2-1(A)(4) CRIMINAL | NOW SAYS WAS ONLY HISTORICAL HOBBYIST |
|  | HAVE NO 2003-274 DOCUMENTS AS HOBBYISTS |

# Lincoln County "War" Heats Up Over 'Billy'

## Capitan Mayor Tracks His Kind of
Tells Jay Miller where to go: WO

by Doris Cherry

Had words been bullets
there would have been several casualties in the Lin-
County Courthouse
when t

case was filed in the Lincoln
County Sheriff,
April 200

County Commission Meet
ber bes

# Memorandum

To:      Rick Virden, Lincoln County Sheriff
From:    Steven M. Sederwall & Thomas T. Sullivan
Subject: Billy the Kid Investigation
Date:    Thursday, June 21, 2007

On April 28, 2003 we began a quest for the truth, looking into the "escape of W
and the double homicide of James Bell & Robert Olinger."¹ We chose this as a
and did not want to burden the county financially. The idea was to bring mode
police investigative methods to uncover the truth of the escape of the Kid and
deputies. We had planned to file a report with the Sheriff at the end of
which the public could then access if they so desire.

At the beginning of the investigation
investigating a century-
great deal

STATE OF NEW MEXICO
COUNTY OF SANDOVAL
THIRTEENTH JUDICIAL DISTRICT

1
2
3    NO. D 1329 CV 2007-01364
4
5    GALE COOPER and DE BACA COUNTY NEWS
6    a New Mexico Corporation,
7
8    VS.
9    RICK VIRDEN, LINCOLN COUNTY SHERIF
     and CUSTODIAN OF RECORDS OF THE
10   LINCOLN COUNTY SHERIFF; and STEV
     M. SEDERWALL, FORMER LINCOLN COU
11   SHERIFF; and THOMAS T. SULLIVAN,
     FORMER LINCOLN COUNTY SHERIFF D
12   FORMER LINCOLN COUNTY DEPUTY S

13                    Deposition of Stev
14                            1:30
                       August
15                    1096 Med
                  Ruidoso, Ne
              XICO RULES

# MEGA HOAX

### the strange plot to
### exhume Billy the Kid and
### become president

Gale Cooper, M.D
Author of Joy of the Birds

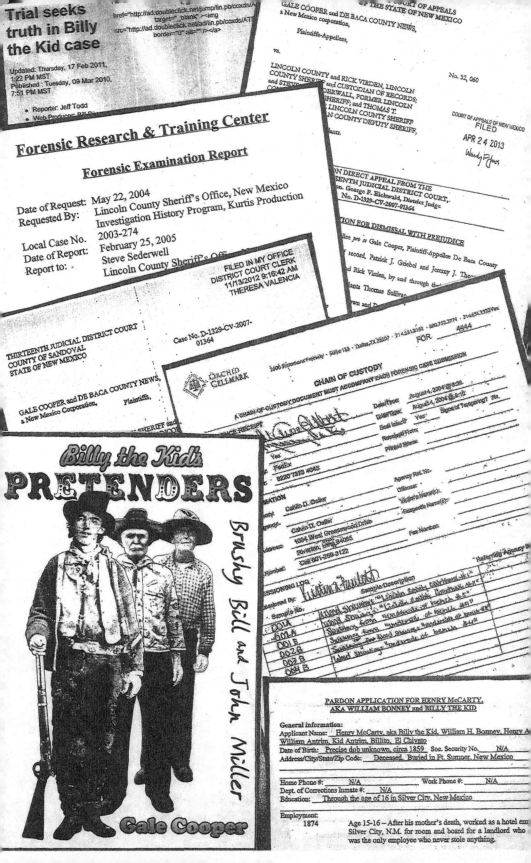

## Forensic Research & Training Center

### Forensic Examination Report

Date of Request: May 22, 2004
Requested By: Lincoln County Sheriff's Office, New Mexico
Investigation History Program, Kurtis Production
Local Case No. 2003-274
Date of Report: February 25, 2005
Report to: Steve Sederwell
Lincoln County Sheriff's Off...

FILED IN MY OFFICE
DISTRICT COURT CLERK
11/13/2012 9:16:42 AM
THERESA VALENCIA

THIRTEENTH JUDICIAL DISTRICT COURT
COUNTY OF SANDOVAL
STATE OF NEW MEXICO

GALE COOPER and DE BACA COUNTY NEWS,
a New Mexico Corporation,    Plaintiffs,

...SHERIFF and...

Case No. D-1329-CV-2007-01364

THE STATE OF NEW MEXICO
GALE COOPER and DE BACA COUNTY NEWS,
a New Mexico corporation,

Plaintiffs-Appellees,

vs.

LINCOLN COUNTY and RICK VIRDEN, LINCOLN
COUNTY SHERIFF and CUSTODIAN OF RECORDS;
and STEVE... ...DERWALL, FORMER LINCOLN
...SHERIFF; and THOMAS T.
...LINCOLN COUNTY SHERIFF
...N COUNTY DEPUTY SHERIFF,

No. 32,060

COURT OF APPEALS OF NEW MEXICO
FILED

APR 24 2013

COURT OF APPEALS OF NEW MEXICO
FILED

...N DIRECT APPEAL FROM THE
...ENTH JUDICIAL DISTRICT COURT,
...on. George P. Eichwald, District Judge
...No. D-1329-CV-2007-01364

...ION FOR DISMISSAL WITH PREJUDICE

...llee pro se Gale Cooper, Plaintiff-Appellee De Baca County

...f record, Patrick J. Griebel and Jeremy J. The...

...d Rick Virden, by and through th...

...ants Thomas Sullivan...

...wn and D...

ORCHID CELLMARK

3600 Signature Freeway · Suite 123 · Dallas, TX 75237 · 214.853.1305 · 800.752.2774 · 214.854.1325 Fax

CHAIN OF CUSTODY

FOR _____ 4444

A CHAIN OF CUSTODY DOCUMENT MUST ACCOMPANY EACH FORENSIC CASE SUBMISSION

Date/Time    August 4, 2004 @ 8:28
...Time    August 4, 2004 @ 8:10
Seal Intact    Yes    Signs of Tampering?    No
Returned From:
Printed Name:

...Yes
FedEx
8220 7273 4043

Agency Ref. No.
Offense:
Victim's Name(s):
Suspect's Name(s):

...CATION    Calvin D. Ostler

Calvin D. Ostler
1094 West Greenwood Drive
Riverton, ... 84065
Cell 801-259-3122    Fax Number:

Referring Agency

...SIONING LOG

| Sample No. | Sample Description |
| --- | --- |
| 001A | Blood Staining... |
| 001A | Blood Staining... |
| 001 B | ...form wrist/cuff of bench... |
| 002 B | ...from wrist/cuff of bench... |
| 003 B | ...Blood Staining wristband of bench... |
| 004 B | Blood Staining wristband of bench... |

PARDON APPLICATION FOR HENRY McCARTY,
AKA WILLIAM BONNEY and BILLY THE KID

**General information:**
Applicant Name: Henry McCarty, aka Billy the Kid, William H. Bonney, Henry A...
William Antrim, Kid Antrim, Billito, El Chivato
Date of Birth: Precise dob unknown, circa 1859    Soc. Security No.    N/A
Address/City/State/Zip Code:    Deceased. Buried in Ft. Sumner, New Mexico

Home Phone #:    N/A    Work Phone #:    N/A
Dept. of Corrections Inmate #:    N/A
Education:    Through the age of 16 in Silver City, New Mexico

Employment:
1874    Age 15-16 – After his mother's death, worked as a hotel em...
Silver City, N.M. for room and board for a landlord who
was the only employee who never stole anything.

**Billy the Kid's PRETENDERS**

Brushy Bill and John Miller

Gale Cooper

CPSIA information can be obtained
at www.ICGtesting.com
Printed in the USA
BVOW06s1420311016
466507BV00015B/185/P